ENGLISH GRAMMAR & COMPOSITION

Very Useful for All Competitive Examinations

ENGLISH GRAMMAR & COMPOSITION

Very Useful for All Competitive Examinations

Approximately

10000 Sentences, 7000 Solved Questions
7000 Words Knowledge, 550 Solved Exercises

by
SC GUPTA

ARIHANT PUBLICATIONS (INDIA) LIMITED

ARIHANT PUBLICATIONS (INDIA) LTD.

卐 Administrative & Production Offices

Corporate Office: 4577/15, Agarwal Road, Darya Ganj, New Delhi -110002
Tele: 011- 47630600, 23280316; Fax: 011- 23280316

Head Office: Kalindi, TP Nagar, Meerut (UP) - 250002
Tele: 0121-2401479, 2512970, 4004199; Fax: 0121-2401648

All disputes subject to Meerut (UP) jurisdiction only.

卐 Sales & Support Offices

Agra, Ahmedabad, Bengaluru, Bhubaneswar, Chennai, Delhi, Guwahati, Haldwani, Hyderabad, Jaipur, Jalandhar, Kolkata, Kota, Lucknow, Nagpur, Meerut & Pune

卐 ISBN **978-93-5176-874-6**

卐 Price : **₹ 375**

PO No. : TXT-59-T070221-4-26

Typeset by Arihant DTP Unit at Meerut

PRINTED & BOUND BY
ARIHANT PUBLICATIONS (I) LTD. (PRESS UNIT)

For further information about the products from Arihant
log on to **www.arihantbooks.com** or email to **info@arihantbooks.com**

Merits of the

यह Book प्रत्येक उस छात्र के लिए महत्त्वपूर्ण है जो किसी भी Competitive Examination में Appear हो रहा है। इस Book में न केवल Grammar Part को बहुत विस्तृत रूप से प्रस्तुत किया गया है, बल्कि Grammar के हर Topic से सम्बन्धित Test Yourself Exercises भी दी गई हैं। Competitive Examinations में आने वाले Grammar से सम्बन्धित प्रश्नों का समाधान बहुत ही सरल तरीके से बताया गया है एवं विभिन्न Competitive Examinations में आये प्रश्नों को Solve किया गया है।

इस Book लगभग 550 Solved Exercises दी गई हैं जिनमें लगभग 7,000 प्रश्नों को Solve किया गया है। इसके अतिरिक्त Grammar के हर rules को समझाते हुए लगभग 10,000 वाक्यों को भी दिया गया है। यह Book Grammar के हर Topic को Comprehensively, Cover करती है। इस Book में दी गई Test Yourself Exercises को Solve करने से छात्रों में प्रश्नों को हल करने का दृढ़ विश्वास जाग्रत होता है।

Specific Exercises for Competitive Examinations

Competitive Examination में बैठने वाले छात्रों हेतु इस Book में Spotting Errors, Cloze Test, Phrase Substitution, Ordering of Sentences, Double Blanks एवं Correct the Sentence से सम्बन्धित Exercises दी गई है। इन Exercises में विभिन्न Competitive Examinations में आये प्रश्नों को भी Solve किया गया है। Spotting Errors में Answers को Justification के साथ बताया गया है।

Word Power Section

इस Book का Word Power का Section बहुत महत्त्वपूर्ण एवं Comprehensive है। इसमें Word Power से सम्बन्धित हर प्रकार के प्रश्नों को हल किया गया है। इस Book में लगभग 7,000 शब्दों की जानकारी किसी न किसी रूप में दी गई है। Competitive Examinations में आने वाले अधिकांश Words आपको इस Book मिलेंगे।

Composition Section

इस Book के Composition Section में Comprehensions, Precis Writing, Letter Writing, Report Writing एवं Paragraph Writing को शामिल किया गया है। Book में न केवल हर प्रकार की Solved Exercises ही दी गई हैं। बल्कि निम्न बिन्दुओं पर छात्रों के लिए मार्गदर्शन भी दिया गया है।

(1) How to attempt the comprehensions?
(2) How to write a good precis?
(3) How to write good letters?
(4) How to write a good report?
(5) How to write a paragraph?

इस Book का उद्देश्य छात्रों को हर प्रकार के Competitive Examination हेतु तैयार करना एवं उन्हें हर प्रकार के प्रश्नों से परिचित कराना है। Book में दी गई विभिन्न Exercises को स्वयं Solve करने से छात्रों में इस तरह के प्रश्नों को Solve करने का आत्मविश्वास जाग्रत होता है। हमें विश्वास है Competitive Examination की तैयारी करने हेतु यह Book आपकी निश्चित ही मददगार होगी।

with good wishes...

SC Gupta
129-South West Block
Near Eid Gah Alwar (Rajasthan)
Ph: 0144-2700438

Contents

CHAPTER

01

SOME BASIC TERMS OF ENGLISH

इस Book में प्रयुक्त विभिन्न Terms की जानकारी संक्षिप्त रूप में इस अध्याय में दी जा रही है।

(1) Alphabet : अंग्रेजी भाषा के Alphabet में 26 letters होते हैं जिन्हें Capital letters एवं Small letters में निम्न दो प्रकार से लिखा जाता है। Small letters एवं Capital letters का उच्चारण समान रहता है, लेकिन आकृति भिन्न होती है। Capital letters का प्रयोग कब किया जाएगा, यह जानना शुद्ध अंग्रेजी लिखने हेतु आवश्यक है, इसकी सम्पूर्ण जानकारी सम्बन्धित अध्याय में दी गई है।

A B C D E F G H I J K L M N O P Q R S T U V W X Y Z — *Capital Letters*

a b c d e f g h i j k l m n o p q r s t u v w x y z — *Small Letters*

(2) Word (शब्द) : Letters को आपस में मिलाकर लिखने से उनका कोई अर्थ निकलता है तो उसे Word (शब्द) कहा जाता है। एक Word बनाने के लिए कम से कम एक स्वर एवं एक व्यंजन का होना आवश्यक है। स्वर न होने पर स्वर की ध्वनि वाला व्यंजन होना आवश्यक है। लेकिन एक ही letters वाले शब्द जैसे : A, I, O इत्यादि इसके अपवाद हैं।

(A= एक, I = मैं, O = ओ)

(3) Sentence (वाक्य) : दो या अधिक Words को पास-पास लिखने से बनने वाले शब्द समूह का कोई अर्थ निकलता है, तो इस शब्द समूह को वाक्य Sentence कहा जाता है।

Sentence के मुख्य रूप से दो भाग होते हैं :

(i) Subject एवं (ii) Predicate

(i) **Subject** : कार्य को करने वाला Subject (कर्ता) कहलाता है।

(ii) **Predicate** : Subject जो कार्य करता है, उसे Predicate कहते हैं।

Sentence मुख्यतया चार प्रकार के होते हैं :

(a) Simple Sentence में एक ही Finite Verb होता है।

(b) Compound Sentence में दो या अधिक Principal Clauses होते हैं, जो एक-दूसरे से Co-ordinating Conjunction द्वारा जुड़े होते हैं।

(c) Complex Sentence में कम से कम एक Principal Clause तथा एक या अधिक Sub-ordinate Clause होता है।

(d) Mixed Sentence ऐसे Sentences हैं जो Simple, Compound या Complex Sentence से अलग हैं, Mixed Sentence कहलाते हैं।

(4) Clause : शब्दों का ऐसा समूह जो एक Sentence का ही एक भाग है जिसमें एक Finite verb एवं एक Subject होता है, Clause कहलाता है।
Clause is such a group of words that forms part of a sentence, and contains a subject and a finite verb.
Clause तीन प्रकार की होती हैं :

(i) **Principal Clause :** ऐसे Clause होती है, जो स्वयं में स्वतन्त्र होती है एवं जिसका स्वयं का पूर्ण अर्थ निकलता है।

(ii) **Co-ordinate Clause :** यह Clause भी एक स्वतन्त्र Clause है, जिसका स्वयं का अर्थ निकलता है। यह Simple Sentence की तरह होती है जो अन्य clause से Coordinating Conjunction *जैसे* and, but, for, or etc. से संयुक्त होती है।

(iii) **Sub-ordinate Clause** : यह Clause एक स्वतन्त्र Clause नहीं है जिसका स्वयं का पूर्ण अर्थ नहीं निकलता है। यह अपने पूर्ण अर्थ के लिए अन्य Clause पर निर्भर होती है। यह Clause अन्य Clause से Sub-ordinating Conjunction जैसे : as, why, because, since, before, unless, though, although, lest, as soon as, provided, etc. से संयुक्त होती है। Sub-ordinate Clause का, इस Clause द्वारा किये जाने वाले कार्य के अनुसार तीन भागों में वर्गीकरण किया जाता है :

(i) Noun Clause (ii) Adjective Clause (iii) Adverb Clause

(5) Phrase : शब्दों का एक ऐसा समूह जिसका कुछ अर्थ तो निकलता है, लेकिन पूर्ण अर्थ नहीं निकलता, Phrase कहलाता है।
'A group of words which make sense, but not complete sense, is called a Phrase' जैसे :
Red Tapism, Ins and outs , Hand in gloves etc.

(6) Parts of Speech : वाक्य (Sentence) में प्रयुक्त विभिन्न प्रकार के शब्दों को आठ भागों में विभाजित किया गया है

(i) Noun (ii) Pronoun (iii) Adjective (iv) Adverb
(v) Preposition (vi) Verb (vii) Conjunction (viii) Interjection.

(7) Affirmative Sentence : ऐसे वाक्य जो negative नहीं हैं, Affirmative Sentence कहलाते हैं।

(8) Assertive Sentence : ऐसे वाक्य जिनमें कुछ कथन किया गया हो, Assertive sentence कहलाते हैं।
I was not present there. I have taken a decision.

(9) Imperative Sentence : ऐसे वाक्य जिनमें आदेश (order) निर्देश (direction, command), प्रार्थना (request), सुझाव (suggestion), सलाह (advice) का भाव निहित रहता है। जैसे :
(a) Shut the door. (b) Consult a good physician.

(10) Optative Sentence : ऐसे वाक्य जिनसे Good wishes प्रार्थना, अभिवादन या इच्छा व्यक्त की जाती है, Optative Sentence कहलाते हैं। जैसे :
(a) God bless you! (b) Long live the queen!

(11) Exclamatory Sentence : ऐसे वाक्य जो अफसोस, घृणा, दु:ख, आश्चर्य, प्रसन्नता, शाबाशी देने का भाव व्यक्त करते हैं, Exclamatory Sentence कहलाते हैं। जैसे :
(a) Hurrah! we have won the match. (b) Oh! she died so young.

(12) Colloquial : इसका अर्थ होता है, conversational , informal जो बातचीत में प्रयोग होता है।

(13) Complement : इसका अर्थ होता है, पूरक। Complement वाक्य का वह भाग है जो वाक्य में Subject या Object को स्पष्ट करता है। जो Subject की पूर्ति करता है, या Subject को स्पष्ट करता है, उसे Subjective Complement तथा जो Object की पूर्ति करता है, या Object को स्पष्ट करता है, उसे Objective Complement कहते हैं। *जैसे* :
(i) Gopesh became a *teacher*. (ii) Nisha is a *girl*.
वाक्य (i) teacher एवं (ii) में girl, subject को स्पष्ट करते हैं। ये Subjective Complements हैं।
(iii) We elected Ram our *monitor*. (iv) Her father named her *Sheela*.
वाक्य (iii) monitor, एवं (iv) में Sheela, Objective Complements हैं।

(14) Cognate Object : जब वाक्य में verb के meaning की similarity में object का प्रयोग होता है तो ऐसा object, Cognate Object कहलाता है। जैसे :

(i) He fought a fierce fight. (ii) Rahim sang a sad song.

उपरोक्त वाक्यों में song, fight, क्रमश: verb; sang एवं fought के cognate objects है।

(15) Syllable : Word (शब्द) का वह भाग जो एक बार में बोला जाता है Syllable कहलाता है। एक Word (शब्द) एक या अधिक Syllable का हो सकता है।

A syllable is a part of a word that contains a single vowel sound and that is pronounced as a unit. So, For example 'book' has one syllable, and 'reading' has two syllables.

(i) **One Syllable** : Word Run, sit, come, go, my, he etc.
(ii) **Two Syllable** : Words Mon-day, four- teen, fa - ther, sun -day etc.
(iii) **Words with more than two syllable :** Won-der-ful, beau-ti-ful , de-mo-cra-cy, im-po-ssi-ble.

(16) Vowels : अंग्रेजी भाषा में A, E, I, O, U को Vowels (स्वर) माना गया है। इनके अतिरिक्त कई व्यंजन (consonants) भी स्वर की ध्वनि हेतु प्रयुक्त होते हैं।

(17) Consonants : A, E, I, O, U के अतिरिक्त शेष सभी Alphabets व्यंजन (Consonants) कहलाते हैं। अंग्रेजी भाषा में 21 व्यंजन एवं 5 स्वर होते हैं।

(18) Prefix : मूल शब्द के साथ पहले जुड़े कुछ अक्षर; जैसे Im, in, un, en, dis, em इत्यादि, Prefix कहलाते हैं। Prefix द्वारा नए शब्द का निर्माण किया जाता है। जैसे : Impossible, impure, incompetent, enroute, encourage, dislike, embark, empower, defame.

(19) Suffix : मूल शब्द के बाद लगे हुए अक्षर जैसे age, ed, ist, ing, em, ish, en, ship इत्यादि Suffix कहलाते हैं। Suffix द्वारा भी नए शब्द का निर्माण किया जाता है। *जैसे* leakage, breakage, gifted, talented, rightist, socialist, friendship, hardship etc.

(20) Premodifier : वह शब्द जो noun से पहले आता है एवं उसके अर्थ में वृद्धि करता है, Premodifier कहलाता है। जैसे :

(i) He misbehaved with an *invited* friend. (ii) They sold the *cursed* house.

उपरोक्त वाक्यों में Invited एवं Cursed, Premodifier है।

(21) Slang : Slang consists of words, expressions and meanings that are informal and are used by the people who know each other very well and quite familiar with one-another. (Generally abusive language) पूर्ण परिचित व्यक्तियों द्वारा प्रयुक्त अनौपचारिक विशेष शब्द, expressions, सामान्य रूप से गाली जैसे शब्द इत्यादि।

(22) Tense : Tense is that form of a verb which shows not only the time of an action, but also the state of an action or event.

(23) Sequence of Tense (काल क्रम) : वे नियम जो यह निर्धारित करते हैं कि किसी वाक्य में Subordinate Clause कि क्रिया (Verb) का Tense क्या होगा अर्थात् यदि Principal Clause में verb का Tense Present, Past या Future है Subordinate Clause में कौन-सा Tense प्रयुक्त होना चाहिए जिससे वाक्य संरचना सही हो। इसका निर्धारण जिन सिद्धान्तों, नियमों के अन्तर्गत किया जाता है उन्हें Sequence of Tense के अन्तर्गत सम्मिलित किया गया है।

(24) Noun : किसी व्यक्ति, वस्तु, स्थान, गुण, कार्य या अवस्था के नाम को Noun (संज्ञा) कहा जाता है।

A noun is a word used as name of a person, place or thing.

'Thing' शब्द बहुत विस्तृत है, इसमें सभी चीजों का समावेश हो जाता है।

Types of Noun

Noun पाँच प्रकार के होते हैं :

(i) **Proper Noun :** (व्यक्तिवाचक) A Proper Noun refers the name of a person, place or thing. जैसे : Ram, Alwar, Table etc.

(ii) **Common Noun :** (जातिवाचक) A Common Noun refers the name given to persons, things or places of the same kind or class. जैसे King, boy, girl, city etc.

(iii) **Collective Noun :** (समूहवाचक) A Collective Noun is the name of a group of persons or things taken together and spoken of as a whole, as unit. जैसे : Team, Committee, Army etc. सामान्यतया Collective noun का प्रयोग singular में होता है यदि इसका प्रयोग Plural में किया जाता है तो वह Common noun बन जाता है।

(iv) **Material Noun :** (पदार्थवाचक) A Material Noun is the name of metal or substance of which things are made of. जैसे Silver, Iron, Wood etc. Material Nouns, Countable नहीं होते हैं अर्थात् इनकी गिनती नहीं की जा सकती है। इन्हें मापा या तौला जा सकता है। इनके साथ सामान्यतया singular verb का प्रयोग किया जाता है एवं इनके पहले Article का प्रयोग नहीं किया जाता है।

(v) **Abstract Noun :** (भाववाचक) Abstract noun in general refers the name of quality, action or state. जैसे : Honesty, Bravery (quality), Hatred, Laughter (action), Poverty, Young (state). Art एवं science जैसे : Physics, Chemistry, Music, Grammar इत्यादि भी Noun में शामिल किए जाते हैं।

(a) Abstract Noun, ऐसे गुण, भाव, क्रिया एवं अवस्था को व्यक्त करता है जिन्हें न तो Physically Touch किया जा सकता है, न ही देखा नहीं जा सकता है, केवल महसूस किया जा सकता है।

(b) Abstract Noun का प्रयोग सामान्यतया Singular में किया जाता है।

(25) The Noun Case : वाक्य में Noun का अन्य शब्दों के साथ सम्बन्ध Noun case द्वारा व्यक्त होता है।

(i) **Nominative Case :** जब noun का प्रयोग वाक्य में subject की तरह होता है तो वह noun-nominative Case में होता है अर्थात् वाक्य में noun जब verb के साथ subject का कार्य करता है तो वह noun-nominative case में प्रयुक्त होता है। When a noun is used as subject of the verb in a sentence it is in nominative case.

(ii) **Possessive Case :** एक वाक्य में एक noun को दूसरे noun पर हक या Relation स्थापित करने के लिए प्रयोग होता है तो noun के साथ apostrophe का प्रयोग किया जाता है। जिस noun के साथ apostrophe के प्रयोग होता है वह noun, possessive case में प्रयुक्त होती है।

(iii) **Objective Case :** जब noun का प्रयोग वाक्य में verb के object की तरह होता है तो वह noun, objective case में प्रयुक्त होता है।

When a noun is used as an object of the verb in a sentence, it is in objective case.

(iv) **Nominative of Address :** जो noun किसी व्यक्ति या वस्तु को सम्बोधित करने के लिए प्रयुक्त हो वह nominative of address की तरह प्रयुक्त होता है।

Read the following sentences

(1) Boys, don't make a noise. (2) Harish, wait for me.

उपरोक्त वाक्यों में Boys, Harish को सम्बोधित (Addressed) किया गया है, Nouns के इस प्रकार के प्रयोग को Nominative of address कहा जाता है।

(v) **Case in Apposition** If two nouns referring to the same person or thing are in apposition, one is placed immediately after the other, with no conjunction joining them, as 'Her father, Naresh Chandra, left home three months ago.'

जब दो nouns एक ही व्यक्ति या वस्तु को बताते हैं अर्थात् दोनों Noun एक ही व्यक्ति के बारे में स्पष्ट करते हैं तो बाद वाला Noun पहले वाले Noun का Case in apposition कहलाता है।

(26) Object and Complement : किसी वाक्य में Verb के बाद आने वाला Noun या Pronoun यदि उसी वाक्य में आये अन्य Noun या Pronoun से कोई समरूपता (Sameness) रखता है, तो वह Verb का complement कहलाता है। जैसे : Ramesh plays football. यहाँ football—Object है क्योंकि इसकी Ramesh से कोई समरूपता नहीं है।

Active voice से *Passive voice* बनाते समय *object*, को ही *subject* बनाया जा सकता है, *complement* को नहीं। इसका अर्थ यह हुआ कि जिस वाक्य में object नहीं है उसका Passive नहीं बन सकता है।
Ramesh writes a letter. यहाँ *letter* एक *object* है इसका *Passive* बन सकता है।
A letter is written by Ramesh.
लेकिन *Ramesh is my friend.* यहाँ *my friend, Complement* है। अतः इसका *Passive* नहीं बन सकता है क्योंकि इस वाक्य में कोई *object* नहीं है।

(27) Determiners & Adjectives : Traditional Grammar में Determiners को Adjective से अलग नहीं किया गया है। Determiners, Adjectives का ही भाग है। Determiners के रूप में परिवर्तन नहीं होता है; जैसे; A, an, the, some, all, much, both, few, whole, etc. इनमें कोई Suffix या Prefix जोड़कर, कोई परिवर्तन नहीं किया जा सकता है जबकि Adjectives के रूप में परिवर्तन सम्भव है; जैसे : Black से Blackish, Blackness; Good से Goodness, Fast को Faster, Fastest बनाया जा सकता है।

(28) Synthesis : यह एक ऐसी प्रक्रिया है जिसके द्वारा बहुत से वाक्यों को जोड़कर एक वाक्य बनाया जाता है अर्थात् दो या अधिक वाक्यों को संयुक्त कर, एक Simple, Compound, Complex या Mixed Sentence बनाने की प्रक्रिया को Synthesis of Sentence कहा जाता है।

(29) Analysis : इसका अर्थ है, वाक्य में विद्यमान clauses की पहचान करना एवं वाक्य किस प्रकार का है, इसकी जाँच करना अर्थात् वाक्य में यह जानना कि कौन-सी clause; principal , coordinate, subordinate clause है? फिर यह जानना कि वाक्य simple/compound/complex /mixed किस प्रकार का है?

(30) Conjunction : यह ऐसा शब्द है जो शब्दों या वाक्यों को आपस में जोड़ता है। इसे Sentence Linker भी कहा जाता है।

Definition A Conjunction is a word that joins words or sentences together.

A conjunction is a joiner, a word that connects (conjoins) parts of a sentence.

(A) **Coordinating Conjunctions :** ये Conjunctions दो समान Rank के Sentences या Words को जोड़ते हैं। इस तरह के मुख्य Conjunctions हैं: For, And , Nor, But, Or, Yet, So.

(B) **Subordinating Conjunctions :** इन Conjunctions द्वारा एक Subordinating Clause को अन्य Clause से जोड़ा जाता है। (Subordinating Clause वह Clause है जो अपने पूर्ण अर्थ के लिए अन्य Clause पर निर्भर होता है।) इस तरह के मुख्य Conjunctions हैं : after, although, as, as if, as long as, as though, because, before, even if, even though, if, if only, in order that, now that, once, rather than, since, so that, than, that, though, till, unless, until, when, whenever, where, whereas, wherever, while, once, rather than.

(C) **Correlative Conjunctions :** जो Conjunctions pairs में प्रयोग किए जाते हैं उन्हें Correlative Conjunctions कहते हैं। जैसे : Either......or, Neither......nor, Both......and, Whether......or, Not only......but also.

Remember Correlative conjunctions are always used in pairs. They join similar elements. When joining singular and plural subjects, the subject closest to the verb determines whether the verb is singular or plural.

(31) Adverb : यह वाक्य में ऐसा शब्द है जो Verb या Adjective या अन्य Adverb या Adverbial phrase को विशेषता प्रदान करता है/संशोधित करता है/उसके अर्थ में कुछ वृद्धि/परिवर्तन करता है।

An adverb is that word in a sentence which modifies the meaning of verb or adjective or another adverb or adverbial phrase.

(32) Pronoun : जो शब्द Noun की जगह प्रयुक्त होता है, उसे Pronoun कहते हैं।

Generally (but not always) pronouns stand for (pro + noun) or refer to a noun, an individual or individuals or thing or things (the pronoun's antecedent) whose identity is made clear earlier in the text.

(33) Preposition : वाक्य में ऐसा शब्द है, जो सामान्यतया noun /pronoun के पूर्व प्रयुक्त होता है एवं noun/pronoun का सम्बन्ध, वाक्य में प्रयुक्त अन्य शब्दों से व्यक्त करता है।

Preposition is a word placed before a Noun or Pronoun, denotes the relation, the person or thing referred by it, has with something else.

A preposition is followed by a noun. It is never followed by a verb.

(34) Subject-Verb Agreement : एक वाक्य में Verb एवं Subject के मध्य एक Agreement होता है। जब Subject singular है तो verb भी singular लगेगी। *'The verb must agree with its subject in number and person'.*

—***Nesfield***

(35) Weak Verbs : Verbs which require - ed, - d or - t to be added to the Present Tense to form the Past indefinite, are called Weak Verbs; as :

Present	***Past***	***Past Participle***
Sell	Sold	Sold
Burn	Burnt	Burnt
Think	Thought	Thought
Lend	Lent	Lent

(36) Strong Verbs : Verbs that form their Past Tense by merely changing the vowel in their Present form, without adding an ending are called Strong Verbs; as :

Present	***Past***	***Past Participle***
Abide	Abode	Abode
Bear	Bore	Borne
Become	Became	Become
Find	Found	Found

Now-a-days, Verbs are being classified as Regular and Irregular Verbs.

(37) Regular Verbs : वे Verbs जिनके मूल रूप में t, d या ed लगाने पर उसका Past Tense बनता है। जैसे

Present	***Past***	***Past Participle***
Talk	Talked	Talked
Live	Lived	Lived

(38) Irregular Verbs : जिन Verbs की Past Form, Verb के मूल रूप में d, ed, t, लगाने से नहीं बनती उन्हें Irregular verbs कहा जाता है। ऐसी Verbs की Past Form बनाने हेतु कोई नियम निर्धारित नहीं है। जैसे:

Present	***Past***	***Past Participle***
See	Saw	Seen
Go	Went	Gone
Come	Came	Come

(39) Stative Verbs : कुछ Verbs का प्रयोग सामान्य स्थिति में Continuous form में नहीं किया जाता है। इस तरह की Verbs को Stative Verbs कहा जाता है। Stative का अर्थ है fixed, अर्थात् स्थायी। इस तरह की Verb एक Permanent कार्य को बिना प्रयास के स्थायी रूप से होने वाले कार्य को व्यक्त करती है। इस तरह की verbs का प्रयोग Continuous form में नहीं किया जाता है। इन verbs को Non-Conclusive Verbs भी कहते हैं जैसे:

See, hear, smell, taste, feel, look, know, have, understand etc.

(40) Dynamic Verbs : Dynamic का अर्थ होता है क्रियाशील, गतिशील। यह Stative का विपरीतार्थक शब्द है। जब कोई Verb; Temporary, Momentary या Dynamic कार्य हेतु प्रयुक्त होती है तो वह Dynamic Verb कहलाती है। जैसे:

(a) He is swimming; (b) She is going;
(c) Ram is coming.

(41) Inchoative Verbs : Verbs जो किसी कार्य से प्रारम्भ होने को व्यक्त करती हैं, Inchoative verbs कहलाती हैं। The term, Inchoative verb is used for a verb that denotes the beginning ,development or final stage, of a change of condition.
—*Guide to patterns and usage in English by AS Hornby*

इस तरह की मुख्य verbs हैं Get, Become, Grow etc.

(a) My father is getting weaker. (b) It is getting dark.

(42) Transitive Verbs (सकर्मक क्रियाएँ) : ऐसी verbs जिनके साथ object प्रयुक्त हो Transitive Verbs कहलाती हैं। Transitive का अर्थ है passing over अर्थात् जिन verbs में action, कर्ता तक ही सीमित नहीं रहकर, Object (किसी अन्य वस्तु) पर pass over होता है।

जैसे: Ramesh hits a ball.

यहाँ hits एक transitive verb की तरह प्रयुक्त हुआ है, जिनमें action, कर्ता तक ही सीमित नहीं रहा है बल्कि Object; ball पर pass over हुआ है।

सामान्यतया verb यदि ***'क्या'*** *या* ***'किसको'*** *प्रश्न करने पर यदि हमें उत्तर प्राप्त होता है तो वह verb, Transitive है। जैसे उपरोक्त वाक्य में verb से 'क्या' प्रश्न करने पर हमें 'a ball' उत्तर मिला। अत: hits एक Transitive Verb है।*

(43) Intransitive Verbs : Intransitive verbs में action object कर्ता तक ही सीमित रहता है, object पर pass over नहीं होता है। *जैसे*

(a) He sleeps in the bed. (b) Shyam speaks loudly.

इन वाक्यों में verb; sleeps एवं speaks, Intransitive Verbs हैं, इनमें action कर्ता तक ही सीमित रह गया है। किसी object पर pass over नहीं हुआ है। इन verbs से 'क्या' 'किसको' प्रश्न करने पर कोई उत्तर प्राप्त नहीं होता है।

Important

अधिकांश verbs का प्रयोग, Transitively एवं Intransitively, दोनों प्रकार हो सकता है।

---

(44) Auxiliary Verbs : इन्हें सहायक क्रियाएँ (Helping Verbs) भी कहा जाता है। Do, does, did, is, am, are, was, were, have, has, had, इत्यादि Primary Auxiliary Verbs तथा will, shall, may, can, should, would, could, might, must, ought, dare, need, used to; Modal Verbs कहलाती हैं।

(45) Linking Verbs or Notional Verbs : जब Auxiliary (helping) Verbs किसी वाक्य में मुख्य verb को support नहीं करती हैं बल्कि मुख्य verb की तरह प्रयुक्त होती हैं तो उस स्थिति में इन्हें Linking Verbs या Notional Verbs कहा जाता है। जैसे:

(a) I have a book and a pencil. (b) She is a beautiful girl.

उपरोक्त वाक्यों में underlined verbs; have तथा is—Linking verbs या Notional Verbs हैं।

(46) Modals : ये भी Auxiliary verbs होते हैं, ये verbs के mood (अवस्था/भाव) को व्यक्त करते हैं। Mood या Modes एक ही बात है। चूँकि ये verbs के भाव, क्रियाविधि को व्यक्त करते हैं। अत: इन्हें Modals कहा जाता है।

(47) Finite Verbs : जिन verbs में subject के Number, Person, एवं Tense के अनुसार परिवर्तन होता है, Finite Verbs कहलाती हैं।

(48) Non-Finites Verbs : ये ऐसी verbs होती हैं, जिन पर वाक्य के tense एवं subject के person एवं number कोई प्रभाव नहीं पड़ता है।

(49) Infinitive : इन्हें सामान्यता 'to + verb' के रूप में जाना एवं पहचाना जाता है। जैसे : to play, to go, to walk etc.लेकिन कभी-कभी 'to' नहीं भी आता है। इस प्रकार की Infinitive को Bare Infinitive (Infinitive without to) कहा जाता है। जैसे: I saw him go, I bade him go etc. यहाँ go, bare infinitive है।

(50) Split Infinitives : Infinitive के बीच में (to एवं infinitive) कोई भी adverb या शब्द लिखना traditional grammar में गलत माना जाता है, लेकिन आजकल बहुत से लेखक Split of Infinitives को सही मानने लगे हैं।

Split of Infinitives को avoid करना ही उचित है।

As per modern grammarians one adverb may be inserted between the infinitive.

I ask you to kindly grant me one day leave only.

Here insertion of adverb 'kindly' is well accepted now-a-days.

(51) Gerund : Verb की एक ऐसी form है, जो verb में 'ing' (Verb + ing) लगाने से बनती है एवं noun का कार्य करती है। Gerund को Verbal Noun भी कहते हैं।

"Gerund is such a form of verb that ends in 'ing' and has the force of a noun and a verb."

(52) Participle : Verb का ऐसा रूप है, जिसमें verb के साथ-साथ Adjective के गुण पाए जाते हैं। Participle को इसीलिए Verbal Adjective भी कहा जाता है।

(53) Unattached or Dangling Participle : Participle वाक्यों में Adjective का कार्य करते हैं। अत: Participle के साथ एक noun या pronoun का सम्बन्धित (related) होना आवश्यक है। यदि Participle के साथ कोई noun या pronoun सम्बन्धित नहीं है तो वह Participle, Unattached or Dangling Participle है। जैसे:

(a) Being a cold morning, I didn't go to office.
(b) Being a rainy day, the school remained closed.

उपरोक्त दोनों वाक्यों में प्रयुक्त Participle 'Being' Unattached Participle है, यहाँ Being के साथ कोई Noun या Pronoun लगाना आवश्यक है। अत: इन वाक्यों को निम्न प्रकार लिखा जाना चाहिए :

(1) It, being a cold morning, I didn't go to office. Or The morning being cold, I didn't go to office.
(2) It, being a rainy day, the school remained closed. Or The day being rainy, the school remained closed.

(54) Inversion : Affirmative वाक्यों का structure सामान्यतया निम्न प्रकार का होता है।

Subject + Verb + ...

Verb का प्रयोग Subject के बाद किया जाता है।

Interrogative वाक्यों में सामान्यता Verb का प्रयोग Subject से पूर्व निम्न प्रकार का होता है

Verb + Subject + ...

Interrogative वाक्यों के अतिरिक्त बहुत से Adverbs एवं Adverbial expressions का प्रयोग जब clause के प्रारम्भ में होता है तो Verb, Subject के पहले आती है। वाक्यों में Verb का Subject के पहले आना Inversion कहलाता है।

Inversion of the Verb : *"Certain adverbs and adverb phrases, most with a restrictive or negative sense, can for emphasis be placed first in a sentence or clause and are then followed by the inverted (i.e. Interrogative) form of the verb."*

–Thomson and Martinet

(55) Synonym : It is a word or expression which means the same as another word or expression. The term 'industrial democracy' is often used as a synonym for worker participation.

(56) Antonym : The antonym of a word is a word which means the opposite. Day and Night are antonyms.

(57) Heteronym : It is a word that has the same spelling as another word but with a different pronunciation and meaning. These words are sometimes also called homographs.

(58) Autogram : A self-referencing sentence is a sentence that describes itself. For example, "This sentence has five words." An autogram is a self-referencing sentence that describes its letter content.

(59) Contronym : The word contronym (also the synonym antagonym) is used to refer to words thatby, some freak of language evolution, are their own antonyms. Both contronym and antagonym are relatively recent neologisms; however, there is no alternative term that is more established in the English language. As :

(a) **fast**—quick, unmoving

(b) **fix**—restore, castrate

(60) Malapropism : It is the use of an incorrect word in place of a similarly sounding correct word. As :

(a) Parents try to 'install' these virtues in their children.

(b) He became 'affluent' in French, Italian, Latin and Greek.

(61) Palindrome : It is a word or sentence that reads the same forward as it does backward. The words a and I are perhaps the simplest and least interesting palindromes; the word 'racecar' and the name 'Hannah' are more interesting and illustrative.

(62) Palingram : It is a sentence in which the letters, syllables, or words read the same backward as they do forward. The sentence, 'He was, was he?' is a word palingram, because the words can be placed in reverse order and still read the same. The sentence, ''I did, did I?'' is not only a word palingram but a letter palingram (palindrome) as well.

(63) Pangram : It is a sentence that contains all letters of the alphabet. Less frequently, such sentences are called holalphabetic sentences. As :

The quick brown fox jumps over a little lazy dog.

In this sentence there are all 26 English alphabets.

(64) Eponym : It is someone or something whose name is or is thought to be the source of something's name (such as a city, country, era, or product); Xerox is a brand of photocopy machine; that word, too, has been since adopted to refer to any brand of photocopy machine and, moreover, also employed as a verb to describe the act of photocopying.

(65) Adjunct : It is a word or group of words which indicates the circumstances of an action, event or situation. An adjunct is usually a prepositional phrase or an adverb group.

(66) Contraction : It is a shortened form of a word or words.

(i) 'It's' (with an apostrophe) should be used only as a contraction for 'it is'.

(ii) can't is the contraction form of cannot.

(67) Positive Degree : The Positive Degree of an Adjective is the Adjective in its general form. It denotes the mere existence of some quality.

(68) Comparative Degree : It denotes a higher degree of the quality than the positive. The comparative is used when two things are compared.

(69) Superlative Degree : It denotes the highest degree of the quality. It is used when more than two things are compared.

Positive	*Comparative*	*Superlative*
Good	Better	Best
Strong	Stronger	Strongest
Tall	Taller	Tallest

(70) Mood : It is the mode or manner in which the action denoted by the verb is presented. There are three types of mood

(a) **Indicative Mood** *"A verb which makes a statement or asks a question or expresses a supposition which is assumed as a fact, is in the Indicative Mood."* **—Wren and Martin**

(i) He goes to college daily.	*Statement*
(ii) She writes legibly.	*Statement*
(iii) Are you fine?	*Question*
(iv) Have you found your pen?	*Question*
(v) If it rains, we shall go for a picnic.	*Supposition*
(vi) If she wants it, I shall give it to her.	*Supposition*

(b) **Imperative Mood** A verb which expresses a command, an exhortation, an entreaty or a prayer, is in Imperative mood.

(i) Open the door.	*Command*
(ii) Wait here.	*Command*
(iii) Take care of your health.	*Exhortation*
(iv) Don't worry, try again.	*Exhortation*
(v) Please help me.	*Entreaty*
(vi) Have mercy upon the poor.	*Entreaty*

(c) **Subjunctive Mood**

(I) **Present Subjunctive :** Where a wish or hope is expressed by the verb, it is in Present subjunctive mood. As :

(i) God bless you.

(ii) May God grant you success

(iii) If the verb expresses desire, intention, resolution etc it is in subjunctive mood. As :

(iv) We recommended that the monthly rent be increased to two thousand rupees.

(v) It is suggested that a subway be built to relieve the congestion.

(vi) I move that Mr Sharma be appointed Executive Director.

(II) **Past Subjunctive :** Past subjunctive is used : (I) After the verb 'wish', to denote an unreal situation or a situation contrary to fact.

KNOW THE ENGLISH FUNDAMENTALS

1. How many words are there in the English language?

Ans About a million, may be more.

It is difficult to calculate the exact number of words. If we calculate all of scientific nomenclature, this could easily double the figure. For example there are apparently some one million insects already described, with several million more awaiting description. The two largest dictionaries—the Oxford English Dictionary and M. Webster's Third New International Dictionary—each includes around half a million words.

2. What is the longest word in the dictionary?

Ans It might be **supercalifragilisticexpialidocious** (which appears in the Oxford English Dictionary), unless we want to count names of diseases (Such as **'pneumonoultramicroscopicsilicovolcanoconiosis'**, defined by the Oxford English Dictionary as **'a fictitious word alleged to mean'** a lung disease caused by the inhalation of very fine silica dust' but occurring chiefly as an instance of a very long word"), places such as air pwllgwyngyll go gery chwyrnd robwlll lantysiliogogogoch', a village in Wales, chemical compounds apparently there is one that is 1,913 letters long, and also a few words found only in Joyce's Finnegans Wake.

Other words famous for being sesquipedalian: antidisestablishmentarianism ("opposition to the disestablishment of the Church of England").

Floccinaucinihilipilificationhonorificabilitudinitatibus (which appears in Shakespeare's Love's Labour's Lost, and which has been cited as [dubious] evidence that Francis Bacon wrote Shakespeare's plays).

3. What does 'floccinaucinihilipilification' mean?

Ans It means 'the estimation of something as worthless.

But it is usually used only as an example of a very long word, sometimes held to be the longest. The Oxford English Dictionary labels it "humorous" and gives the following citations for it: I loved him for nothing so much as his floccinaucinihilipilification of money. ***—William Shenstone, Letters***

They must be taken with an air of contempt, a floccinaucinihilipilification of all that can gratify the outward man. ***—Sir Walter Scott, Journal***

4. What does pneumonoultramicroscopicsil-icovolcanoconiosis mean?

Ans It is defined by the Oxford English Dictionary as "a factitious word alleged to mean 'a lung disease caused by the inhalation of very fine silica dust' but occurring chiefly as an instance of a very long word."

5. How can I figure out what does a Roman numeral stand for?

Ans. **Conversion Table**

1	2	3	4	5	6	7	8	9	10	20	30	40	50	60	70
I	II	III	IV	V	VI	VII	VIII	IX	X	XX	XXX	XL	L	LX	LXX

Conversion Table

80	90	100	500	1000
LXXX	XC	C	D	M

You should add the numbers together if numbers of the same size are placed next to each other or if a smaller number is placed to the right of a larger number. For example

II = 2, III = 3, VI = 6, VIII = 8, XX = 20, XXI = 21, CC = 200

You should subtract the smaller number from the larger if a smaller number is placed to the left of a larger number. For example

IV = 4, IX = 9, XL = 40, CD = 400, CM = 900

Sometimes you are to perform both operations: For example

XIV = 14, XIX = 19, XXIV = 24, XCI = 91, XCIX = 99, MCM = 1900,

MCMXLVII = 1947, MCML = 1950, MCMLXVIII = 1968

6. Does bimonthly mean twice a month or every two months?

Ans Every "two" months (usually). Bi-means 'two', so bimonthly means "happening every two months"—but it also means "happening twice a month". Another word for the latter is 'semimonthly'.

7. What is a thesis statement?

Ans A thesis statement is a one-or two-sentence condensation of the argument or analysis that is to follow in an essay. After you've chosen the question your essay will answer, compose one or two complete sentences answering that question.

8. What is a simile and give some examples of it?

Ans A simile is a word or phrase by which anything is likened to something else. A simile is often introduced by like or as. See the following examples of simile :

(a) Happy as a clam, (b) As easy as piem, (c) Soft as sifted flour.

It differs from a metaphor in that the comparison in a metaphor is a implicit: "Achilles is a lion; "She's a tigress," "He seems gruff but he's really just an old pussy cat." The statement "that man is a fox" is a metaphor; but "that man is like a fox" is a simile.

9. What is a run-on sentence?

Ans Run-on sentence is an ungrammatical construction in which two or more independent clauses are improperly joined without a conjunction or appropriate punctuation. The effect is that the reader loses the main idea of the sentence. As:

Example:

(a) He doesn't need me he just calls to make himself feel better.

Here you could use a semicolon. :

(b) He doesn't need me; he just calls to make himself feel better.

Another example

(b) I went to the store I was out of beer. Here you could either use a semicolon or a conjunction, such as because :

I went to the store because I was out of beer.

10. What is a *linking verb*?

Ans A linking verb is usually a form of be or seem that identifies the predicate of a sentence with the subject. ***Example :*** "Achilles is a lion." 'Is' links Achilles lion, identifies Achilles with a lion. 'Achilles' is the subject of the sentence and 'is a lion' is the predicate. A linking verb is also called a copulas.

11. What is *ambiguity in writing?*

Ans **Ambiguity in writing** : whose meaning cannot be understood by its context.
Ambiguity may be introduced accidentally, confusing the readers and disrupting the flow of reading. If a sentence or paragraph jars upon reading, there is lurking ambiguity. It is particularly difficult to spot one's own ambiguities. It is strongly recommended that one should let another person read one's writing before submission for publication.

12. What is an *annotated bibliography?*

Ans An annotated bibliography is a list of citations to books, etc with notes for each citation.
An annotated bibliography is a list of citations to books, articles, and documents. Each citation is followed by a brief (usually 100-150 words) descriptive and evaluative paragraph, the annotation. The purpose of the annotation is to inform the reader of the relevance, accuracy, and quality of the sources cited.

13. What is *MLA style?*

Ans It is the style recommended by the **Modern Language Association** for preparing scholarly manuscripts and student research papers. It concerns itself with the mechanics of writing, such as punctuation, quotation, and documentation of sources.

14. What is *redundancy in writing?*

Ans The use of language that can be eliminated without incurring a loss of meaning, is called redundancy in writing.
Redundancy in writing usually comes from these sources: Wordy phrases. **Example** : 'In view of the fact that' instead of "since" or "because." Employing obvious qualifiers when a word is implicit in the word it is modifying. **Example** : "Completely finish." If you have incompletely finished something, you haven't finished it at all.
Using two or more synonyms together. **Example** : 'Thoughts and ideas.'

15. What is the difference between *its* and *it's*?

Ans Its is the possessive form of it. It's is a contraction of it is or it has.

Example

It's a common mistake.

The boat has a hole in its hull.

The confusion arises from the dual function of the 's' ending, which can indicate either possession or contraction, as in : John's Pizzas are the best (="The Pizzas which are John's — that is, in that he makes them — are the best"); John's going to have to buy some more files soon (="John is going to have to buy some more files soon"). However, 's' is never used to indicate possession in pronouns. We do not write hi's (instead of his).

16. What is the difference between *i.e.* and *e.g.*?

Ans i.e. means "that is" (to say), e.g. means "for example.
" i.e. is an abbreviation for Latin id est, "that is." e.g. is for exempli gratia, "for the sake of example." So you can say, "I like citrus fruits, e.g., oranges and lemons"; or, "I like citrus fruits, i.e. the juicy, edible fruits with leathery, aromatic rinds of any of numerous tropical, usually thorny shrubs or trees of the genus Citrus."

17. What is the difference in usage for like vs. as?

Ans The rule is: "As, comes before a clause."
If the word is followed by a clause, a group of words with both a subject and a verb, use as: He liked the restaurant, as any gourmet would. If no verb follows, choose like: He walks like a platypus. However, in casual usage, like is gaining steadily as in "He tells it like it is," or "She eats ice-cream like it's going out of style." The informal use of like to introduce a clause is fine in conversation or casual writing, but to be grammatically correct, remember the **"as comes before a clause"** rule.

18. What is the difference between *there* and *their*? *Your* and *you're*? How can I remember these?

Ans 'Their' and 'your' are possessive forms used as modifiers before nouns. They basically mean: 'belonging to them' and 'belonging to you,' respectively: You're is a contraction of 'you are': 'You're doing fine.'

19. What is the difference between *dinner* and *supper*?

Ans Supper is a light evening meal; served in early evening if dinner is at midday or served late in the evening at bedtime. Dinner is the main meal of the day served in the evening or at midday.

20. What is the only word in the English language that has three consecutive sets of double letters?

Ans **Bookkeeper**. Also **bookkeeping** If you are willing to accept a hyphenated word, **sweet-toothed** is another.

21. What is the origin of the word *fuck*?

Ans It is remotely derived from the Latin futuere and Old German ficken/fucken. Originally, this was a quite acceptable word! It was recorded in a dictionary in 1598 (John Florio's A World of Words). It is remotely derived from the Latin future and Old German ficken/fucken meaning 'to strike or penetrate', which had the slang meaning 'to copulate'. Eric Partridge, a famous etymologist, said that the German word was related to the Latin words for pugilist, puncture, and prick. The word, which entered English in the late 15th century, became more rare in print in the 18th century when it came to be regarded as vulgar. It was even banned from the Oxford English Dictionary. In 1960, Grove Press (in the US) won a court case permitting it to print the word legally for the first time in centuries—in D H Lawrence's Lady Chatterley's Lover (Written in 1928). One folk etymology, which is incorrect, is that it derives from "[booked] for unlawful carnal knowledge."

22. What is the rule for determining whether or not to write out a number as a word?

Ans In general, write out the first nine cardinal (1-9) numbers; use figures for 10 and above. In general, write out the first nine cardinal (1-9) numbers (except for address numbers 2-9, dates, decimals, game scores, highways, latitude/longitude, mathematical expressions, measurement/weight, money/financial data, percentages, proportion, scientific expressions, statistics, technical expressions, temperature, time, unit modifiers, votes, and numbers not written out in a proper noun) and any number that begins a sentence; use figures for 10 and above. The first nine ordinal (1st-9th) numbers are usually written out, especially when describing order in time or location.

23. What is the word meaning *'to throw out of a window'*?

Ans Defenestrate : Its roots are Latin de-, 'out of' and fenestra, "window." Defenestration is the noun form of the word. It is also a computing jargon term for "the act of exiting a window system in order to get better response time from a full-screen program" or "the act of discarding something under the assumption that it will improve matters" or "the act of dragging something out of a window (onto the screen)" [source: Jargon File].

24. What is the plural of *virus*?

Ans Viruses.

It is not viri, or (Which is worse) virii. True, the word comes directly from Latin, but not all Latin words ending in -us have -I as their plural. Besides, viri is the Latin word for 'men' (Plural of vir, man, the root the English virile). There is in fact no written attestation of a Latin plural of virus.

25. What is one English word ends in-*mt*?

Ans Dreamt.

Dreamt is the expected answer to this question, but there is at least one other word: amt.

26. Can I use *'and'* (or *'but'*, etc.) at the start of a sentence?

Ans Yes.

The old 'rule' that we should not begin a sentence with a conjunction (and or but) has actually gone by the wayside these days. Occasionally, especially in casual writing, you can begin a sentence with and or but. These words are mainly used to join elements within a sentence, but they have begun sentences since long.

27. What two words make the contraction *'ain't'*? Is it proper?

Ans 'Ain't' is a contraction of 'am not.' It is not considered proper.

'Ain't' is not accepted by many as it suggests illiteracy and the inability to speak properly. It can be used jokingly. The widely used aren't I ?, though illogical (No-one says I are), is used in speech, but in writing there is no acceptable substitute for the stilted am I not?

28. What word *rhymes* with *orange*?

Ans No word rhymes with orange.

In an episode of the old children's TV show H R Pufnstuf, the character Witchiepoo sang a song that went :

Oranges poranges, who says, oranges poranges,
who says, oranges poranges,
who says– there ain't no rhyme for oranges!

29. What's the difference between *main and helping verbs*?

Ans A helping verb accompanies the main verb in a clause and helps to make distinctions in mood, voice, aspect and tense.

A helping or auxiliary verb such as have, can, or will accompanies the main verb in a clause and helps to make distinctions in mood, voice, aspect, and tense. The main verb represents the chief action in the sentence.

30. When do you use *lie* and *lay*?

Ans To **lay** is to place something; to **lie** is to recline. To **lay** is to place something. It is always followed by an object, the thing being placed. To **lie** is to recline, **For example** : He lays the book down to eat. She lies quietly on the chaise.

Part of the source of the confusion is the past tense of lie, which is lays: She lays on the chaise all day. The past participle of lie is lain, as in - She has lain there since yesterday, as a matter of fact. The past tense of lay is laid, as is the past participle.

31. What should be the spacing between sentences?

Ans Traditionally, students in typing classes have been taught to put two spaces between sentences. In typewritten texts, one space between words was fine, but two spaces seemed necessary to make the break apparent. To be strictly accurate, only one standard word space should be inserted between the end of one sentence and the start of the next. However, strict application of this rule in the world of automated composing systems can cause readability problems, because several factors affect how the spaces appear in the composed text.

The issue of spacing between sentences should be decided for individual typing jobs, not applied across all projects as a standard. If readability won't suffer, only one space should appear between sentences; if readability is an issue, two spaces can be used. Whichever choice you make, ensure that it is implemented uniformly throughout the text.

32. When do you *capitalize* words like mother, father, grandmother and grandfather when writing about them?

Ans When they are used as proper nouns .You should capitalise these when referring to your own relatives: "Hello, Mother." A good rule to follow is to capitalise them if they are used as proper nouns. If used as common nouns, don't capitalise: 'We honour all mothers in May.'

33. When do you use *well or good*?

Ans In general, use well to describe an activity, **good** to describe a thing. When it is an activity being described, use well, as in 'He did well in the spelling bee.' Well is an adverb here, describing the verb. When it is a condition or a passive state being described, use good, as in 'You're looking good tonight!'. Good is an adjective here, describing the noun.

With feel good/ feel well, it is more complicated. In this case, the word well is being used an adjective meaning 'healthy' — so it is OK to say, 'I feel well.' You can say 'I feel good' also, but it is more informal.

34. Where does the phrase *"The whole nine yards"* originate?

Ans It is said to have originated among construction workers.The 'nine yards' is said to refer to the maximum capacity a cement-mixer truck can carry—nine cubic yards of cement. This is disputed, however.

35. When was the first dictionary made?

Ans The western tradition of dictionary-making began with the Greeks when changes in the language made many words in the literature unintelligible to readers. During the Middle Ages, when Latin was the language of learning, dictionaries of Latin words were compiled.

The first dictionary of English appeared in 1604—Robert Cawdry's 'A Table Alphabetical'. This work contained about 3,000 words, but was so dependent upon three sources that it can rightly be called a plagiarism. Early dictionaries were generally small and defined "hard" words and were made by men in their leisure time as a hobby. John Kersey the Younger is regarded as the first professional Lexicographer whose introductory work, A New English Dictionary, appeared in 1702. Kersey's accomplishments were superseded in the 1720s by Nathan Bailey's innovative work, An Universal Etymological English Dictionary. For the rest of that century, it was actually more popular than Dr Samuel Johnson's Dictionary!

36. When do you use *'whom'* instead of *'who'* ?

Ans Use **who** when a nominative pronoun is appropriate, and whom when an objective pronoun is appropriate.Who is a nominative pronoun (meaning it acts as a subject) and is used :

As the subject of a verb, as in— It was Raj who rescued the cat. As the complement of a linking verb, as in—They know who you are.

Whom is an objective pronoun (meaning it serves as an object) and is used:

As the object of a verb, as in—Whom did you see there?

As the object of a preposition, as in—That is the group to whom the credit belongs.

Who and whom seem to cause more difficulty than other pronouns. Thus, when in doubt, substitute him and see if that sounds right. If him is OK, then whom is OK. **For example** : "You talked to whom? You talked to him." It would be incorrect to say 'You talked to he'.

37. Which is right: *"I wish it were..."* or *"I wish it was..."* ?

Ans 'I wish it were...'

There is often confusion about were (a past subjunctive) and was (a past indicative). In conditional sentences where the condition is unreal or not yet real and in that clauses after to wish, use were : "I wish it were true that he loved me" or "If anyone were to ask me to stay, I would refuse." Were is also used following 'as if' and 'as though': "The toddler wore the towel proudly, as though it were a Superman cape." Were is also part of these fixed expressions: as it were, if I were you.

38. When do we use *that* and *which*?

Ans Generally, use **that** for persons or things, **which** only for things.

In current usage, **that** refers to persons or things and **which** is used mainly for things. The standard rule says **that** one uses that only to introduce a restrictive or defining relative clause — one that identifies the person or thing being talked about. An example is—The fort that Akbar built has to be taken down, and the clause that Akbar built describes which fort has to be taken down, *i.e.* it is restrictive. In contrast, which is used only with non-restrictive or non-defining clauses. This type of clause gives additional information about something that has already been identified in the context. An example —The students have been complaining about the assigned book, which is hard to understand. The clause which is hard to understand is nonrestrictive as it does not indicate the specific book being complained about. In a sentence including a nonrestrictive clause, the sentence would still be clear even if the clause were omitted. One will find that **which** sounds more natural than **that** in such a sentence, which is a great double-check of the grammar.

Some people very strictly use **that** only in restrictive clauses and **which** is nonrestrictive clauses. However, even in good prose one will find the use of which in restrictive clauses is very common and considered grammatically acceptable.

39. What are William Safire's *Rules for writers*?

Ans

- Remember to never split an infinitive.
- The passive voice should never be used.
- Do not put statements in the negative form.
- Verbs have to agree with their subjects.
- Proofread carefully to see if you words out.
- If you reread your work, you can find on rereading a great deal of repetition can be by rereading and editing.
- A writer must not shift your point of view.
- And don't start a sentence with a conjunction. (Remember, too, a preposition is a terrible word to end a sentence with.)
- Don't overuse exclamation marks(!).
- Place pronouns as close as possible, especially in long sentences, as of 10 or more words, to their antecedents.
- Writing carefully, dangling participles must be avoided.
- If any word is improper at the end of a sentence, a linking verb is.
- Take the bull by the hand and avoid mixing metaphors.
- Avoid trendy locutions that sound flaky.
- Everyone should be careful to use a singular pronoun with singular nouns in their writing. Always pick on the correct idiom.
- The adverb always follows the verb.
- Last but not least, avoid cliches like the plague; seek viable alternatives.

40. Do adverbs always end with-*ly*?

Ans No.

Though many adverbs are formed by the addition of -ly to an adjective (sad/sadly), there are many other formations, like : apart, downstairs, underfoot, always, backwards — and also ever, now, often, once, soon etc.

41. How do I use the words *might* and *may*?

Ans **May** expresses likelihood while **might** expresses a stronger sense of doubt or a contrary to fact hypothetical.

The difference in degree between "You may be right" and "You might be right" is slight, but not insignificant: If I say you may be right about something, there is a higher degree of probability that you are right about it than if I say you might be right about something. "You think Einstein is the most brilliant physicist, who ever lived? "You may be right." versus "You think it's going to rain this afternoon even though the sun is shining this morning? Well, you might be right." May expresses likelihood while might expresses a stronger sense of doubt or a contrary to fact hypothetical: "We might have been able to go if Kyle hadn't been so slow."

42. A misogynist hates women. What do you call *a person who hates men*?

Ans A misandrist.

The word misandrist comes from Greek, mis-, a prefix meaning 'hate' + andr-, 'man' + -ist.

43. Does any word use the vowels a, e, i, o and u in it?

Ans Yes.

Here are some, with their distinctions : Longest word with each vowel used once: subcontinental, countermanding.

Longest word with each vowel used once, including 'y' : uncomplimentary.

Shortest word with each vowel used once: sequoia.

Shortest word with each vowel used once, including 'y' : eukaryotic.

Word with each vowel used once in order: facetious.

Word with each vowel used once in order, including 'y' : facetiously.

Word with each vowel used once in reverse order : subcontinental.

44. Does a comma go after *i.e.* or *e.g.*?

Ans By nature, they are preceded by a mark of punctuation, usually a comma. Generally both are followed by a comma in American English, though not in British English, *e.g.*, may also be followed by a colon, depending on the construction. In British English, it is often written as *eg* with the periods omitted.

45. Do you hyphenate numbers?

Ans "Sometimes. Whole numbers twenty-one through ninety-nine are hyphenated, whether used alone or as part of a larger number. A whole number followed by hundred, thousand etc, would be written as, For example "one hundred," and not hyphenated. In a phrase like "one hundred and ten years," no hyphenation should be added.

46. Are philharmonic and symphony the same?

Ans Yes.

A **philharmonic** is a **symphony** orchestra or the group that supports it. A **symphony** is a large orchestra. An orchestra is a large group of musicians who play together on various instruments, usually including strings, woodwinds, brass instruments, and percussion instruments. So, the answer is 'yes' that philharmonic and symphony orchestra are synonymous.

47. Do I put a comma before and?

Ans Sometimes ... "The use of a "serial comma" (in a series such as "bread, butter and beer") is a matter of taste. You can either leave it in or take it out ("bread, butter and beer" works just as well). But its absence can sometimes change the meaning, so read your sentence carefully. The Alt. Usage. English FAQ cites the example of an author who dedicated his novel thus: "To my parents, Ayn Rand and God." Clearly the author should not have omitted the serial comma in this case. Use commas in a compound sentence to clarify meaning or add emphasis. You do want to use a comma to separate clauses of a sentence which have and between them. If there's no and, use a semicolon instead: She hadn't left the computer all week; by Friday she was climbing the walls.

48. Are there any English words that do not have vowels?

Ans It depends what you mean by "vowel" and "word." There are two things we mean by the word "vowel" : a speech sound made with the vocal tract open a letter of the alphabet standing for a spoken vowel (Look up vowel for a more detailed definition.) Cwm and crwth do not contain the letters a, e, i, o, u, or y the usual vowels (that is, the usual symbols that stand for vowel sounds) in English. But in those words the letter 'w' simply serves instead, standing for the same sound that 'oo' stands for in the words boom and booth. Dr, nth (as in 'to the nth degree'), and TV also do not contain any vowel symbols, but they, like cwm and crwth, do contain vowel sounds.

Shh, psst, and mm-hmm do not have vowels, either vowel symbols or vowel sounds. There is some controversy whether they are in fact "words", however. But if a word is "the smallest unit of grammar that can stand alone as a complete utterance, separated by spaces in written language and potentially by pauses in speech" (as it is according to The Cambridge Encyclopaedia of Language), then those do qualify. Psst, though, is the only one that appears in the Oxford English Dictionary.

49. What is the difference between *idiom* and *slang*?

Ans **Idiom** is yesterday's slang and **slang** is tomorrow's idiom.

In other words, idiom is slang that has, through use and over time, become acceptable to use in informal language.

English has countless interesting and amusing examples of idiom and slang.

From time to time, we will look at some so that you can add the ones that appeal to you to your repertoire.

50. What are *sentence fragments*?

Ans Sentence fragments are incomplete sentences. They can be phrases or clauses that have been punctuated as if they were sentences. Sentence fragments can also be called English minor sentences. Sometimes it is quite acceptable to use them, but the secret is to know when.

51. When can you use sentence fragments?

Ans When you write conversations, because you are writing how people speak, and people very seldom speak in complete sentences.

(a) What's going to happen to Boyde, now that Bill is dead?
(b) Don't know.
(c) Do you care?
(d) Nope. Don't know and don't care!

Sometimes when you write stories or personal accounts, you might intentionally use sentence fragments for special effect:

It stopped, turning its head this way, that way.
Listening.
Listening to the silence.
Listening and waiting.

52. What is the difference, if any, between using '*once in a while*' and '*once and a while*'?

Ans These two idioms mean the same thing—occasionally. The latter, might well have grown up as a misunderstanding of "once in a while" or a confusion of that phrase and "once and for all". Use "once in a while."

53. What is the difference between the word "*into*" and the words "*in to*?" Which is most appropriate when?

Ans Whenever the 'to' is a particle of the infinitive, be sure to keep them separate:

See the following sentences :

(a) We dropped in to visit my friend.
(b) He just stepped in to pay the bill.
(c) You wouldn't want people walking into your dinner.

We use **"into"** to express motion or direction as per following :

(a) He stared into her eyes.
(b) She walked into the store to say hello.
(c) She drove into the side of the garage.

ARTICLES

'A', 'An', 'The', Articles कहलाते हैं। Modern Grammar के अनुसार Articles एक प्रकार के Determiners हैं। A/An को Indefinite तथा The को Definite Articles कहते हैं।

Articles

(A)	**(B)**
1. Indefinite–A/An	**2. Definite–The**

क्या आप जानते हैं कि हम हिन्दी के निम्न प्रकार के वाक्यों का अंग्रेजी अनुवाद करते समय A/An का प्रयोग क्यों करते हैं?

(a) यह कुर्सी है।	This is a chair.
(b) सीता ने गाना गाया।	Sita sang a song.
(c) यह छतरी है।	This is an umbrella.

इन हिन्दी वाक्यों में 'एक' नहीं होते हुए भी, इनका अंग्रेजी अनुवाद करते समय हमने A/An का प्रयोग किया है।

वाक्यों में Singular Countable Noun से पूर्व, यदि वह अनिश्चित है, तो Article, A/An का प्रयोग अवश्य किया जाता है। इन वाक्यों का यह अनुवाद गलत है :

(a) This is chair.	*(Incorrect)*
(b) Sita sang song.	*(Incorrect)*
(c) This is umbrella.	*(Incorrect)*

'A'/'An'—Indefinite Article- कहाँ A, कहाँ An लगेगा?

(1) A/An का प्रयोग अनिश्चित (Indefinite) Singular Noun से पूर्व किया जाता है। (निश्चित होने पर Noun के पूर्व 'The' का प्रयोग किया जाता है) इसी कारण से A/An को Indefinite articles कहा जाता है। जैसे:

(a) I have a purse.	(b) He sang a song.
(c) This is an inkpot.	(d) Ram is a boy.

(2) जिस शब्द से पूर्व A/An का प्रयोग करना है, यदि उस शब्द के उच्चारण की प्रथम ध्वनि (First sound of pronunciation) स्वर है तो An का प्रयोग होगा, अन्यथा A का प्रयोग होगा।

(a) अंग्रेजी भाषा में A, E, I, O, U, का स्वर (Vowels) माना गया है। कई शब्द इन Vowels से शुरू तो हो सकते हैं, लेकिन मुख्य बात है, उस शब्द के उच्चारण की। यदि यह ध्वनि व्यंजन है, तो A का प्रयोग होगा। यदि यह ध्वनि स्वर है तो an का प्रयोग करना होता है। जिस शब्द के पूर्व हमें a या an लगाना है, यदि उसके उच्चारण की प्रथम ध्वनि, हिन्दी वर्णमाला के स्वर से उच्चारित है तो, an लगाएँ अन्यथा a का प्रयोग करें।

हिन्दी वर्णमाला में अ, आ, इ, ई, उ, ऊ, ए, ऐ .... स्वर माने जाते हैं। हिन्दी भाषा में 16 स्वर होते हैं जबकि अंग्रेजी में मात्र 5 स्वर माने गए हैं।

An umbrella	*अम्ब्रेला*	*A union*	*यूनियन*
A one rupee note	*वन*	*A universtiy*	*यूनिवर्सिटी*
A ewe .	*यू*	An honest	ऑनेस्ट

शब्द का प्रथम letter क्या है? यह महत्त्वपूर्ण नही है, महत्त्वपूर्ण है, उसके उच्चारण की प्रथम ध्वनि (First sound of pronunciation)।

*(b) अंग्रेजी भाषा में एक अक्षर, कई प्रकार की ध्वनि हेतु प्रयुक्त होता है। जिन अक्षरों को **स्वर (A, E, I, O, U) माना गया है, उनका प्रयोग बहुत बार व्यंजनों (Consonants) की तरह होता है।** बहुत से व्यंजन स्वर का कार्य करते हैं। **हो सकता है शब्द का प्रथम अक्षर M, F, N, X, S, L, H हो, लेकिन उच्चारण की प्रथम ध्वनि (First sound of pronunciation) स्वर हो तो ऐसे शब्दों के पूर्व an का प्रयोग होगा। जैसे:***

*(a) He is an **MLA / M***	*(एमएलए/एमपी)*
*(b) He lodged an **FIR**.*	*(एफ आई आर)*
*(c) Shashi is an **NCC** officer.*	*(एनसीसी)*
*(d) He is an **SDO**.*	*(एसडीओ)*
*(e) I have an **x-ray** machine.*	*(एक्स-रे)*
*(f) She in an **LLB**.*	*(एलएलबी)*
*(g) I have been waiting for an **hour**.*	*(ऑवर)*
*(h) He is an **heir** to the throne.*	*(ऐअर)*
*(i) Ram is an **honest** person.*	*(ऑनेस्ट)*

Correct use of A/An

(1) A house	(11) A historical fair	(21) A humble person	(31) A husband
(2) A heinous crime	(12) A young man	(22) A ewe	(32) A university
(3) A unity	(13) A union	(23) A eulogy	(33) A one rupee note
(4) A one eyed man	(14) A uniform	(24) A useful book	(34) A useful feature
(5) A unique decision	(15) A united front	(25) A unified plan	(35) A year
(6) A USA ally	(16) A forest officer	(26) A Member of Parliament	(36) A UK ship/European
(7) An hour	(17) An hourly meeting	(27) An hour's daybreak	(37) An honour
(8) An honorary post	(18) An honourable person	(28) An honest man	(38) An heir
(9) An honorarium	(19) An F.O.	(29) An MP/MLC	(39) An IAS/IPS/ILO
(10) An SP/SDO	(20) An M.A/M.Sc/M Com	(30) An RTS/RTC/RO	(40) An RC worker

Specific use of A/An

(1) **Singular Countable noun से पूर्व A/An का प्रयोग किया जाता है। Countable का अर्थ है, जिसकी गिनती की जा सकती है। जैसे:**

(a) I have a pen.
(b) She has a car.
(c) Ram has an umbrella.
(d) She is a girl.

यदि noun से पूर्व कोई Adjective आता है तो A/An को उस Adjective के पहले लगाते हैं। यदि कोई Adverb पूर्व में आया हो तो a/an को उस Adverb से पूर्व लगाते हैं।

(a) Sita is a beautiful girl. *(Adjective)*
(b) She is an intelligent lady. *(Adjective)*
(c) Sakshi is an extremely beautiful girl. *(Adverb)*

(2) **सामान्य रूप से Proper Noun से पूर्व A/ An का प्रयोग नहीं होता है। लेकिन निम्न स्थिति में Proper Noun से पूर्व A/ An का प्रयोग किया जा सकता है। जैसे:**

(a) This novel is written by a Maneesh.
(b) This book is written by a Suresh.

Maneesh एवं Suresh, proper noun हैं, जब ये वक्ता के लिए अनजान हैं तो इनसे पूर्व 'a' के प्रयोग का अर्थ किसी (कोई) मनीष या सुरेश हो जाता है। यह किताब किसी सुरेश, मनीश नाम के व्यक्ति ने लिखी है जो वक्ता के लिए अनजान है।

(3) **Exclamatory वाक्यों में What के बाद Singular, Countable nouns से पूर्व A/An का प्रयोग किया जाता है। जैसे:**

(a) What a grand building!
(b) What a pretty girl !

(4) **'प्रति माह' या 'प्रति वस्तु कीमत' के सन्दर्भ में प्रयोग करने पर A/An का प्रयोग किया जाता है। जैसे :**

(a) She can run twelve kilometres an hour.
(b) Rice sells fifty rupees a kilo.
(c) I earn ₹ twenty thousands a month.
(d) This train runs seventy kms an hour.

(5) **कुछ गिनती बताने वाले शब्द जैसे** A hundred, A thousand, A million, A dozen, A couple से पूर्व 'a' लगता है। Half से पूर्व a का प्रयोग निम्न प्रकार किया जाता है; जैसे : 3½ kilo—Three and a half kilo. 2¼ metre—Two and a quarter metre.

(a) I have a hundred pens.
(b) He has a thousand rupees.
(c) She has to walk two and a quarter kilometres daily.
(d) I have purchased a dozen eggs.

(6) **Profession (व्यवसाय) से पूर्व, A /An का प्रयोग किया जाता है।** *जैसे :*

(a) He is an MP/ MLA/ MLC/ SDO/ FO.
(b) She is a nurse/ teacher/ dentist.
(c) He is a manager/carpenter/cobbler.
(d) Mr. Sharma is an engineer/architect.

(7) **किसी विशिष्ट व्यक्ति की विशेषताओं के सम्बन्ध में किसी अन्य व्यक्ति को पहचान दी जाए तो A/An का प्रयोग किया जाता है। जैसे:**

(a) He is a Hitler. (A despot like Hitler)
(b) He is a Gandhi. (As great as Gandhi)
(c) He is a second Dara Singh. (A wrestler as great as Dara Singh)

(8) **किसी जाति विशेष को व्यक्त करने के लिए Singular countable noun से पूर्व A /An का प्रयोग किया जाता है। जैसे:**

(a) A dog is an animal.
(b) A peacock is a bird.

(9) **जब वाक्य में Verb (क्रिया) का प्रयोग Noun की तरह किया जाता है, उससे पहले A/An लगाया जाता है। जैसे:**

(a) He goes for a walk daily. (Walk (verb) used as noun)
(b) He has gone for a ride. (Ride is a verb used as noun)
(c) Last Sunday, I had a long talk with them. (Talk is a verb used here as noun)
(d) I want to have a rest /a drink / a bath. (Rest/drink/bath are verbs used as noun)

(10) **Many/rather/quite/such के बाद यदि singular noun आता है तो उससे पूर्व A/An का प्रयोग किया जाता है। जैसे:**

(a) Many a woman would welcome such a chance.
(b) It is rather a pity, I say.
(c) It was quite an impossible task.
(d) It was a foolish argument.

(11) **यदि Adjective से पहले so, as, too, how, quite का प्रयोग होता है तो उसके बाद A/An (Indefinite Article) का प्रयोग किया जाता है। जैसे:**

(a) It is too heavy a parcel for me to carry.
(b) She is as beautiful a girl as you are ever likely to meet.
(c) Ram is not so big a fool as you think.
(d) How serious a crime had been committed was not realised by him.

(12) **कुछ विशेष Phrases में A/An का प्रयोग होता है। जैसे:**

In a fix, in a hurry, in a nutshell, make a noise, make a foot, keep a secret, as a rule, at a discount, at a stone's throw, a short while ago, at a loss, take a fancy to, take an interest in, to have a drink, go for a walk, have a good education, make a foot, tell a lie, take a bath, half a kilo, a matter of chance.

(a) He has a good knowledge of Sanskrit. (b) It is a pity.
(c) Never tell a lie. (d) Do not make a noise.
(e) I am going to take a bath. (f) Twelve inches make a foot.

A/An का प्रयोग निम्न स्थिति में नहीं करना चाहिए

(a) किसी भी Plural noun से पूर्व A/An का प्रयोग नहीं किया जाता है।

(b) Proper noun से पूर्व A/An का प्रयोग नहीं किया जाता है। किसी देश, राज्य, शहर, दिन, माह, व्यक्ति, वस्तु के नाम को Proper noun कहा जाता है।

Note *(अपवाद-वक्ता के लिए व्यक्ति अनजान है या किसी विशिष्ट व्यक्ति की विशेषता के सन्दर्भ में प्रयोग किया जा सकता है)*

(c) Uncountable nouns से पूर्व A/An का प्रयोग सामान्यतया नहीं किया जाता है। जैसे :
Advice, Accommodation, Bagg-age, Luck, Luggage, News, Permission, Progress, Scenery, Weather, Traffic, Knowledge, Music, Milk, Homework, Stone, Brick, Wine, Beauty etc.

(a) She has gone to purchase some bread.
(b) Enjoy your vacations! I hope you have good weather.
(c) No news is good news. (d) India has made good progress in the field of IT.
(e) He brought his furniture by train. (f) The wall is made of stone and brick.

(d) Uncountable nouns के पूर्व जब A/An का प्रयोग किया जाता है तो इन्हें कुछ शब्दों का प्रयोग करके, Countable बनाया जाता है या इनके प्रयोग से ही Noun के Countable होने का पता चलता है। *जैसे :*

(a) I have a good news for you. (b) I have a piece of bread.
(c) I have a milk bar. (d) He gave me a piece of information.
(e) She is a beauty. (a beautiful girl) (f) He threw a stone. (a piece of stone)

(e) Inchoate Verb, turn का प्रयोग जब noun के साथ किया जाता है तो noun से पूर्व Indefinite Article A/An का प्रयोग नहीं किया जाएगा। *जैसे:*

(a) I hope you will never turn traitor. (b) Is it wise for a great general to turn politician?
(c) When her husband left she had to turn cook.

यहाँ nouns; traitor, politician, cook के पूर्व A/An नहीं लगाया गया है।

Articles : A/An and One–Difference

(1) A/An Articles हैं, जबकि One एक Adjective है।

(2) Hundred, Thousand, Million, Billion etc के पूर्व 'a' का प्रयोग 'one' से ज्यादा उचित माना गया है।
100 = a hundred, 1000 = a thousand ,100000 = A hundred thousand.
हम A hundred one से a hundred and ninety nine तथा A thousand one से a thousand and ninety nine तक में 'a' का प्रयोग कर सकते हैं लेकिन 1160 = One thousand one hundred sixty में 'one' का प्रयोग ही किया जाएगा।

(3) प्रतिदिन, प्रति सप्ताह, प्रति किलो कीमत या दर के लिए 'a' का प्रयोग ही किया जाएगा 'one' का नहीं।
Sixty rupees a kilo, ₹ five thousands a week, four times a day, Sixty kilometres an hour, Ten rupees a dozen. **उक्त में A/An की जगह one का प्रयोग नहीं किया जा सकता है।**

(4) 'A' एवं 'one' का noun के साथ प्रयोग करने पर भिन्न-भिन्न अर्थ निकलता है। A/an का अर्थ any या every से भी होता है। जैसे:

(a) One screw driver is not enough. *(We need two or more screw drivers.)*
(b) A screw driver is a useful tool. *(Screw drivers are useful tools.)*

(5) 'One' का प्रयोग another/other के साथ किया जा सकता है, 'a' का प्रयोग नहीं। जैसे:
(a) One student wants to read, another wants to play.
(b) One day he came early, another day he was very late.

(6) 'One' का प्रयोग day/week/month/year/summer/winter etc या महीनों/दिनों के नाम के पूर्व किया जा सकता है, जो उस दिन/समय होने वाली घटना के सन्दर्भ में प्रयुक्त होता है। जैसे:
(a) One night there was a terrible storm. (b) One day a tiger entered our house.
(c) One winter the snow fell early.

(7) One day का प्रयोग किसी दिन के अर्थ में किया जाता है। जैसे:
(a) One day you'll realise your mistake. (b) One day you will be sorry, you treated her so badly.

(8) 'One' का प्रयोग a/an के pronoun के समरूप भी किया जाता है। जैसे:
(a) Did you get a ticket? Yes, I managed to get one.
'One' का बहुवचन (plural) उक्त प्रयोग में some होगा। जैसे:
Did you get tickets? Yes, I managed to get some.

'The'-Definite Article

'The', definite article है। इसका प्रयोग छात्रों द्वारा बिना सोचे-समझे बहुतायत में किया जाता है। 'The' का उचित प्रयोग English grammar का महत्त्वपूर्ण अंग है। छात्रों को 'The' के प्रयोग को सावाधानीपूर्वक समझना चाहिए।

Use of 'The': इसका प्रयोग उस noun से पूर्व किया जाता है, जो निश्चित है, विशेष है या जिसकी चर्चा पूर्व में की जा चुकी है। 'The' को इसीलिए Definite article कहा जाता है।

Rules :

***Rule* 1** **जब किसी पूर्व निर्धारित वस्तु के बारे में कहा जाता है। जैसे**

(a) I found a bag. The bag contained a coin. The coin was made of gold.
(b) She brought a silk saree. The saree is very costly.

वाक्य (a) में bag से पूर्व सर्वप्रथम 'a' का प्रयोग किया गया है, बाद में 'the' का प्रयोग किया गया है, क्योंकि यह bag पूर्व निर्धारित, निश्चित हो गया है। इसी तरह coin से पहले 'a' का प्रयोग किया गया है, बाद में 'the' का, क्योंकि अब coin पूर्व निर्धारित, निश्चित हो चुका है। इसी तरह वाक्य (b) में पहले saree से पूर्व 'a' तथा बाद में 'the' का प्रयोग किया गया है। अन्य उदाहरण देखें

(a) This is the hotel where she lives. (b) The man in blue dress is my brother.
(c) The tall man standing near your father is a minister.

यहाँ The का प्रयोग, एक निश्चित, निर्धारित Noun को व्यक्त करता है।

Exception: IMPORTANT

First and subsequent reference When we first refer to something in written text, we often use an indefinite article to modify it. Read the following example :
(a) "I'd like a glass of orange juice, please", John said.
(b) "I put the glass of juice on the counter already", Shilpa replied.

Exception:

When a modifier (Adjective) appears between the article and the noun, the subsequent article will continue to be indefinite.
(a) "I'd like a big glass of orange juice, please", John said.
(b) "I put a big glass of juice on the counter already", Sheila replied.

Rule 2 **Comparative degree से पूर्व, जब इसका प्रयोग Adverb की तरह किया जाए। जैसे:**

(a) The more she gets, the more she demands.
(b) The sooner he completes, the better it is.
(c) The more you work, the more you get.

Rule 3 **जब Comparative degree से पूर्व कोई Selection करना व्यक्त हो या Comparison व्यक्त हो तो 'The' का प्रयोग होता है। जैसे:**

(a) He is the stronger of the two. (b) This is the better of the two novels.

Rule 4 **शरीर के अंगों (Parts of the body) के पूर्व 'The' का प्रयोग होता है। जैसे:**

(a) He was wounded in the arm. (b) Ram hit him in the head.

Rule 5 **Superlative degree से पूर्व 'The' का प्रयोग किया जाता है। जैसे:**

(a) He is the best student of our class. (b) She is the most beautiful girl in this school.

लेकिन यदि Superlative degree 'most' का प्रयोग very के अर्थ में हो तो उससे पहले 'The' नहीं लगता है। *जैसे*:

(a) She is a most beautiful girl. (b) This is a most useful reference book.

Rule 6 **Singular noun के पूर्व जब 'The' का प्रयोग किया जाता है तो वह उस जाति विशेष की विशेषता बताता है। जैसे**

(a) The tiger is a fierce animal. (b) The dog is a faithful animal.

Rule 7 **धार्मिक समुदायों के नाम, साम्राज्यों के नाम, इतिहास की घटनाओं, वंशजों के नाम, राजनैतिक दलों के नाम, ट्रेन, जहाज, अखबार के नाम, महत्त्वपूर्ण भवनों के नाम, नदियों के नाम, नहरों के नाम, समुद्र के नाम आदि के पूर्व 'The' का प्रयोग किया जाता है। जैसे:**

(a) The Ganga, The Godawari, The Sutlej. (b) The Pacific, The Red Sea, The Indian Ocean.
(c) The Hindus, The Muslims, The Sikhs (d) The Intercity, The Rajdhani Express.
(e) The B J P, The Congress, The Communist Party.
(f) The Boeing, The Vikrant. (g) The bay of Bengal, The gulf of Mexico.
(h) The Taj Mahal, The Char Minar. (i) The French Revolution, The Quit India Movement.
(j) The Hindustan Times, The Indian Express.

Rule 8 **जो वस्तुएँ unique हैं, उससे पूर्व 'The' का प्रयोग होता है। जैसे:**

The sun, The earth, The world, The universe etc लेकिन Heaven, Hell, Goc, Parliament के पूर्व 'The' का प्रयोग नहीं होता है। जैसे:

(a) The sun sets in the west. (b) The earth revolves round the sun.
(c) Go to hell. (No 'the') (d) Gods reside in heaven. (No 'the')
(e) He will raise this issue in Parliament. (No 'the')

Rule 9 **धार्मिक ग्रन्थों के नाम के पूर्व 'The' का प्रयोग किया जाता है। जैसे :**

The Ramayan, The Quran, The Bible etc.

(a) The Ramayan is a sacred book. (b) The Quran s also a sacred book.

लेकिन Valmiki's Ramayan, Banabhatta's Kadambari, जैसी स्थिति में, इनके पूर्व 'The' नहीं लगता है।

Rule 10 **व्यक्ति के पद के पूर्व 'The' का प्रयोग किया जाता है। जैसे:**

(a) The Chairman will decide the matter.
(b) The meeting was presided over by the Executive Director.
(c) This decision is taken by the Prime Minister.

Rule 11 Nationality (राष्ट्रीयता) व्यक्त करने वाले शब्दों से पूर्व 'The' का प्रयोग किया जाता है। जैसे:

(a) The English defeated the French. (b)The Indian Cricket team has won the match.

Rule 12 जब Adjective का प्रयोग Noun की तरह किया जाता है, उससे पहले 'The' लगाने पर वह पूरे समुदाय को दर्शाता है। जैसे:

(a) The young and the old, the poor and the rich, the male and the female all supported Gandhi ji.

(b) Three per cent posts are reserved for the disabled.

(c) The poor are generally trustworthy.

(d) The rich should help the poor.

Rule 13 जब कोई वस्तु Understood होती है, तो उससे पूर्व 'The' का प्रयोग किया जाता है। जैसे:

(a) Kindly return the book. (That I gave you)

(b) Can you turn off the light? (The light in the room.)

(c) He has gone to the railway station. (The railway station of the town)

(d) I want to meet the manager. (The manager of the Bank)

(e) Did you like the story? (That I told you yesterday)

Rule 14 Job एवं Profession से पूर्व The का प्रयोग होता है। जैसे:

(a) He likes the banking profession. (b) Do you like the teaching job?

Rule 15 किसी Proper noun के बाद जब कोई Adjective उसी Noun को qualify करते हुए लगाया जाता है। जैसे:

Ashoka, the great : Napoleon, the warrior.

Rule 16 Ordinals से पूर्व 'The' का प्रयोग किया जाता है। first, second, third .....ordinals तथा one, two, three... cardinals कहलाते हैं। जैसे:

(a) The second lesson of this book is very difficult.

(b) He is the first to arrive in the meeting.

Rule 17 Musical instrument, किसी आविष्कार (Invention) के नाम के पूर्व, 'The' का प्रयोग किया जाता है। जैसे:

(a) She can play the Tabla / Violin / Trumpet. (b) Who invented the Telephone / Telescope?

Rule 18 Go to the cinema, Go to the theatre में Cinema एवं Theatre से पूर्व 'The' लगता है। जैसे:

(a) He went to the cinema yesterday. (b) She is going to the theatre.

Rule 19 Committee, club, foundation तथा Trust के नाम के पूर्व 'The' लगता है। जैसे:

The Lions Club, The Rotary Club, The United Nation, The WHO, The Ford Foundation, The Rajiv Gandhi Trust etc.

Rule 20 कुछ Phrases में 'The' का प्रयोग स्वत: ही होता है। जैसे:

(a) What is the matter? (b) Come to the point.

(c) She came to the rescue. (d) Keep to the left.

(e) The market is hot with the rumour. (f) He is in the wrong.

Rule 21 Plural nouns से पहले 'The' का प्रयोग किया जाता है, यदि वाक्य के reference के अनुसार Plural noun, particular/definite हो गया हो। जैसे:

(a) The boys of this college are very intelligent.

(b) The girls of this hostel are very beautiful.

(c) The books, we saw in the market, were duplicate.

Rule 22 **जब कोई Noun, किसी गुण या भाव को व्यक्त करे, तो उससे पूर्व भी 'The' का प्रयोग होता है। जैसे:**

(a) The judge (moral of judge) in him, prevailed upon the husband *(Love of husband) and he sentenced his wife to death.*

(b) The moralist (spirit of moralist) in Gandhi ji revolted against the tyranny of the British.

Rule 23 **Same से पूर्व 'The' का प्रयोग comparison हेतु होता है। जैसे:**

(a) These books are the same as we saw in that shop. (b) Your pen is the same as mine.

Rule 24 **यदि दो या अधिक noun एक ही व्यक्ति या वस्तु के लिए प्रयुक्त हुए हों तो 'The' का प्रयोग पहले Noun के पूर्व किया जाता है। जैसे:**

(a) The secretary and treasurer was present there.

(b) The counsellor and faculty was working in the office.

यहाँ secretary and treasurer तथा counsellor and faculty एक ही व्यक्ति है।

Rule 25 **'The' का प्रयोग Country के नाम से पूर्व नहीं होता है लेकिन यदि Country के नाम के साथ Republic, Kingdom, States जुड़े हुए हों तो 'The' का प्रयोग इनसे पूर्व किया जाता है। जैसे: The Republic of Ireland, The Dominion Republic, The United States, The United Kingdom etc.**

(a) He visited India and the United States. (b) They went to Canara and the United Kingdom.

Rule 26 **'The' का प्रयोग Plural names of Countries/ Islands/ Mountains/ Person के साथ होता है। जैसे:**

The Netherlands, The Lakshadweep islands, The Philippines, The Andes, The Alps, The Himalayas, The Johnsons, The Raymonds, The Ambanis etc.

Sicily island, Bermuda island, Java island; Everest, Etna, Abu (Name of Mountain) इत्यादि के साथ 'The' का प्रयोग नहीं होगा।

Rule 27 **East, West, North, South के साथ 'The' का प्रयोग होता है लेकिन यदि इनके साथ किसी Place का नाम जोड़ा गया हो तो 'The' का प्रयोग नहीं होगा। इसी तरह Northern, Southern , Eastern, Western से पूर्व 'The' का प्रयोग नहीं होगा।**

(a) The sun rises in the east. (b) He is going to North America.

(c) Rajasthan is in Western India. (d) Sweden is in Northern Europe.

Rule 28 **बहुत सी महत्त्वपूर्ण Buildings एवं Institutions के नाम शब्दों से मिलकर बने होते हैं। जिनमें से एक शब्द किसी व्यक्ति या स्थान का नाम होता है, ऐसे नाम के साथ 'The' कर प्रयोग नहीं किया जाता है।**

जैसे : Delhi Airport, Victoria Station, London Zoo, Jaisingh Palace, Indira Gandhi Airport, Edinburgh Castle, Jaipur Place इत्यादि, लेकिन अन्य नामों जैसे–The Royal Palace, The Char Minar, The White House, The Red Square, The Taj Mahal इनके साथ 'The का प्रयोग होता है।

This is a generally accepted rule, there are several exceptions.

Rule 29 **Sky, Moon, World, Sea, Country, Environment से पूर्व 'The' का प्रयोग किया जाता है। जैसे:**

(a)The sky is dark and the Moon is shinning. (b) The sea seems calm today.

(c) Do you live in a town or in the country? (d) We must do something to protect the environment.

Space से पूर्व 'The' नहीं लगता है, जब space का अर्थ 'अन्तरिक्ष' से होता है, लेकिन यदि space जगह के अर्थ में प्रयुक्त हुआ हो तो 'The' प्रयोग होता है। जैसे:

(a) There are lacs of stars in space. (b) He tried to park his car there, but the space was too small.

'Sea' के साथ 'The' का प्रयोग नहीं होगा। जैसे:

(a) We go to sea as sailors. (b) He is at sea now-a-days (on a voyage).

***Rule* 30** **इस प्रकार के Sentence Structure : The + Name + of +.... में 'The' का प्रयोग किया जाता है। जैसे:**

(a) The Bank of America is a big bank.
(b) The tower of London is a great tower.
(c) The Great Wall of China is a historical monument.

***Rule* 31** **यदि दो या अधिक Unmarried Sister को संयुक्त रूप से पत्र लिखा जाए तो 'The' का प्रयोग होगा। जैसे:**

The Misses + Surname The misses Smith.

***Rule* 32** **'Office' का प्रयोग जब place of work के सनदर्भ में हो तो The का प्रयोग होगा। जैसे:**

(a) He is at the office. (b) He is in the office.

He is in office means to hold an official (usually political) position. To be out of office to be no longer in power. ***A Practical English Grammar—Thomson and Martinet.***

CAUTION

Even after you learn all the principles behind the use of these articles, you will find an abundance of situations where choosing the correct article or choosing whether to use one or not will prove chancy.

Icy highways are dangerous.
The icy highways are dangerous.
And both are correct.

No Article–Zero Article

Articles का प्रयोग छात्रों को बहुत सावधानी से करना चाहिए। नीचे दी गई स्थितियों में Articles का प्रयोग नहीं किया जाता है।

(1) School, College, University, Bed, Church, Court, Hospital, Prison, Market से पूर्व Article 'The' का प्रयोग उस स्थिति में नहीं किया जाता जब वहाँ जाने का उद्देश्य, वही हो, जिस हेतु इनका निर्माण किया गया है। जैसे:

(a) I go to college at 10 am. (For the purpose of study)
(b) He went to Church on Sunday. (For making prayer)
(c) He went to market to purchase a TV. (To purchase)
(d) We went to bed at 10 pm yesterday. (To sleep)

लेकिन यदि इन स्थानों पर जाने का उद्देश्य अन्यथा हो तो इनसे पहले 'The' लगता है। जैसे

(a) The school is near to Ram's house.
(b) I will meet you near the court.
(c) I found her near the church.
(d) I will take tram from the church.
(e) I sat on the bed.
(f) We went to the prison to meet the superintendent.
(g) He went to the college to meet the class teacher.

(2) Appoint, made, nominate, elect, declare के बाद यदि कोई Noun आता है तो उससे पूर्व Articles का प्रयोग नहीं होता है। जैसे:

(a) He was elected MLA.
(b) He was appointed supervisor.
(c) He was nominated secretary.
(d) We made him monitor.
(e) He was declared captain of our team.

(3) खाने के नाम (Lunch, dinner, supper, breakfast) के पूर्व Articles का प्रयोग सामान्य स्थिति में नहीं किया जाता है। जैसे:

(a) I couldn't have breakfast this morning. (b) He was invited to dinner.
(c) I had lunch at 1 pm.

लेकिन यदि खाने के नाम के साथ कोई adjective लगा हो या खाना particular हो गया हो तो Articles का प्रयोग किया जाता है। जैसे:

(a) He arranged a nice dinner. (b) The dinner hosted by the queen was superb.

(4) बीमारियों (Disease) के नाम से पूर्व सामान्यतया कोई Article नहीं लगता है। जैसे:

(a) She is suffering from fever. (b) He died of Cholera.

लेकिन यदि diseases का नाम Plural में हो जैसे: Mumps, Measles तो इनके पूर्व The का प्रयोग किया जाता है। *जैसे:* The measles is a contagious disease.

(5) भाषा में नाम, रंग के नाम के पहले Article का प्रयोग नहीं होता है। जैसे:

(a) I can speak Hindi, but I can't speak English (b) He likes blue and white colour.

लेकिन यदि colour का नाम एक adjective की तरह किसी Countable noun के साथ प्रयुक्त हुआ है तो Article का प्रयोग किया जाता है। जैसे:

(a) She has a blue saree. (b) I have a red pen.

(6) कुछ Titles जैसे : Emperor Ashoka, President Kalam, Queen Victoria, Captain Cook के साथ भी Article 'The' का प्रयोग नहीं होता है। The Emperor Ashoka गलत है। लेकिन 'The' का प्रयोग Title 'The Duke of York' के साथ होता है। जैसे :

(7) यदि दो अलग-अलग adjective एक ही Countable Noun के लिए प्रयुक्त हों तो Article का प्रयोग पहले वाले adjective के साथ ही होगा। जैसे:

(a) This is a Hindi and English learning book. (b) This is an English and Hindi dictionary.

(8) Plural noun से पूर्व Article को प्रयोग तब नहीं किया जाता, जब Plural noun किसी वर्ग को व्यक्त करता है। जैसे:

(a) Lawyers are generally witty. (b) Bankers are generally honest.
(c) Doctor are paid more than teachers. (d) Teachers are generally hard workers.

(9) 'The' का प्रयोग noun + number के साथ नहीं होता है। *जैसे:*

(a) Our train arrives at platform 6. (b) I need shoes in size 18.

(10) सामान्यतया watch television में television से पूर्व 'The' का प्रयोग नहीं होता है। लेकिन listen to the radio में radio से पूर्व 'The' लगता है। जैसे:

(a) I often listen to the radio. (b) I heard the news on the radio.
(c) I watched the news on television. (d) I don't watch television at night.

(11) कई Shops, Restaurants, Hotels, Banks के साथ उन व्यक्तियों के नाम जुड़े रहते हैं जिन्होंने इन्हें शुरू किया है। इनके साथ 'The' का प्रयोग नहीं किया जाता है। जैसे:

Lloyds Bank, Mcdonalds, Jack's Guest House, Harrods (Shop), Raymonds (Shop).

(12) Church के नाम के साथ Saints के नाम जुड़े रहते हैं, इसके साथ भी 'The' का प्रयोग नहीं किया जाता है। जैसे:

St John's Church, St Paul's Cathedral.

(13) कम्पनियों के नाम, Airlines के नाम के साथ भी 'The' का प्रयोग नहीं होता है। जैसे:

Fiat (not the fiat), Sony, Kodak, British, Airways, IBM, Reliance etc.

(14) विषयों (Subjects) के नाम के पूर्व सामान्यतया Articles का प्रयोग नहीं करते हैं। जैसे:

(a) I am student of Political Science. (b) He is learning French.
(c) I secured 88% marks in English. (d) He is good at Physics.

(15) 'Kind of ' के बाद 'The' का प्रयोग नहीं किया जाता है। जैसे:

(a) What kind of bird it was! (b) What kind of girl she is!

(16) कुछ ऐसे Phrases जिनमें Preposition के बाद object आता है इनमें Articles का प्रयोग नहीं होता है। जैसे:

at hand, by name, by bus, by train, by plane, in jail, at dinner, underground, in jest, by water, on horseback, at sunset, in debt, in hand, all day, all night, at noon, at night, by post etc.

(17) कुछ ऐसे Phrases जिनमें Transitive verb के बाद object आता है इनमें Articles का प्रयोग नहीं होता है। जैसे:

to catch fire, to leave school / college, to give ear, to bring word, to lay size, to lose heart, to set sail, to send word, to cast anchor etc.

(18) जब किसी abstract noun द्वारा feelings या emotions को कथन की तरह व्यक्ति किया जाए तो Articles का प्रयोग नहीं किया जाता है। जैसे:

(a) Honesty is the best policy. (b) Virtue has its own reward.

लेकिन यदि Abstract noun द्वारा किसी व्यक्ति/जीव या वस्तु की qualities से सम्बन्ध स्थापित किया जाए तो उसके पूर्व article, the, लगता है। जैसे:

(a) He possesses the swiftness of a tiger. (b) He has the cunningness of crow.

(19) जब Common Noun का प्रयोग विस्तृत अर्थ में किया जाता है तो उससे पूर्व Articles नहीं लगता है। जैसे:

(a) Man is an intelligent animal. (b) Birds fly.
(c) Fish live in water. (d) Cows eat grass.

(20) सामान्यतया Proper noun से पूर्व Articles का प्रयोग नहीं किया जाता है, लेकिन यदि Proper noun का प्रयोग एक Common noun की तरह होता है तो उससे पहले Articles का प्रयोग किया जाता है। जैसे:

(a) Akbar was a great king. (b) Agra is a beautiful city.

यहाँ Akbar, Agra, proper noun है

(a) Jaipur is the Paris of India. (b) Kashmir is the Switzerland of Asia.
(c) Ramesh is the Sachin of our college. (d) Mumbai is the Manchester of India.

यहाँ Paris, Switzerland, एवं Sachin का प्रयोग common noun की तरह हुआ है।

(21) यदि Superlative degree से पूर्व My, His, Her जैसे Possessive Pronoun का प्रयोग हो तो 'The' नहीं लगता है। जैसे:

(a) He is my best friend. (b) Ram is his best friend.

(22) बहुत सी महत्त्वपूर्ण Buildings एवं Institutions के नाम दो शब्दों से मिलकर बने होते हैं। जिनमें से एक शब्द किसी व्यक्ति या स्थान का नाम होता है, ऐसे नाम के साथ 'The' का प्रयोग नहीं किया जाता है। जैसे:

Delhi Airport, Victoria Station, London Zoo, Jaisingh Palace, Indira Gandhi Airport, Edinburgh Castle, Jaipur Place इत्यादि इनके साथ 'The' का प्रयोग नहीं किया जाता है

(23) 'The' का प्रयोग Country के नाम के पूर्व नहीं होता है लेकिन यदि Country के नाम के साथ Republic, Kingdom, States जुड़े हुए हों तो 'The' का प्रयोग इनसे पूर्व किया जाता है। जैसे The Republic of Ireland, the Dominioan Republic, the United States, the United Kingdom etc. जैसे:

(a) He visited Mexico and the United States. (b) They went to Canara and then the United Kingdom.

(24) Work के साथ सामान्यतया 'The' का प्रयोग नहीं किया जाता है। जैसे:

(a) He is on his way to work (b) She is at work.
(c) They haven't back from work yet.

(25) **'Office' का प्रयोग जब position के सन्दर्भ में हो तो The का प्रयोग नहीं किया जाता है। जैसे:**
He is in office—means to hold an official usually political) position.
To be out of office—to be no longer in power.

A Practical English Grammar—Thomson and Martinet.

(26) **Town का प्रयोग जब subject के Town या speaker के Town के अर्थ में हो तो Town से पहले 'The' नहीं लगता है। जैसे:**
(a) We go to town sometimes to meet our mother.
(b) We went to town last year and remained there for a week.

(27) **'Nature' का प्रयोग जब प्रकृति के अर्थ में हो तो इसके पूर्व 'The' का प्रयोग नहीं होगा। जैसे:**
If you interfere with nature you will suffer for it.

(28) **'Games' के नाम के पूर्व 'The' का प्रयोग नहीं होता। जैसे:**
(a) I play golf. (b) He plays cricket.

(29) **'Seasons ' के नाम के पूर्व 'The' का प्रयोग नहीं होता है। जैसे:**
(a) In Spring we like to clean the house. (b) She is planning to visit her parents in winter.

(30) **'Time of day ' के नाम के पूर्व 'The' का प्रयोग नहीं होता है। जैसे:**
(a) We travelled mostly by night. (b) We'll be there around midnight.

TEST YOURSELF *Exercises*

01

(A) ***Put appropriate articles in the blanks:*** **[RAS 1991]**

...... businessman of ..... colony was shot dead by...... armed intruder on Sunday night . ... dead man's wife also received .... gunshot, but she is said to be progressing in ..... Civil Hospital . ..... murder is said to be ...... result of .... old dispute over some agricultural land between ...... killer and his victim.

(B) ***Put appropriate articles in the blanks:*** **[RAS 1992]**

India is one of .... very big countries in the world. If a man takes ..... quickest train, he will take nearly.......week to go from one end of India to the other. One who leaves Ramnad in ...... South on .... first day of .... month will perhaps get to Srinagar in .... North only about .... sixth of .... same month.

(C) ***In the following sentences, fill in the blanks with appropriate articles:*** **[RAS 1994]**

Number..... hundred and two .... house next door to us, is for sale. It's quite .... nice house with .... big rooms........ back windows look out on ....park. I don't know what......... price ..... owners are asking . You could give them .... and make them .... offer.

02

Rewrite the sentences after filling the blanks with articles wherever necessary.

(1) (A) Who are .... men that are standing there in .... lane?

(B) ....tallest gentlemen is .... teacher, ...man who has ....stick in his hand is .... teacher's uncle. He lives in Chennai. He has come here to attend .... wedding. I don't know who .... third man is. I know ...... person sitting beside .... teacher.

(C) I'm sorry to have detained you. Are you going to ....bank ?

(2) Once .... man had......... strange goose. It laid......... golden egg every day .... man was very lucky to possess such .... precious creature. One day he thought, "One golden egg .... day is not sufficient. I shall kill ....goose and get hold of all ....gold contained in it." He then killed .... goose, but find not ...... single egg.

03

Rewrite the following sentences after filling up the blanks with suitable articles, wherever necessary :

I know Ram's brother. He is ....officer in............... Ministry of Foreign Affairs. He is posted in .... States. He is .... youngest officer there. He enjoys .... work and plays .... game of tennis in evenings. For his breakfast he takes .... apple, ... egg and ....cup of coffee only. He is ..... good fellow.

04

Rewrite the following sentences after filling up the blanks with suitable articles wherever necessary:

Once ....old saint saw .... kite catch.......... little mouse. He felt sorry for .... mouse. He took .... orange and aimed at ....kite, which dropped ....mouse and by his holy power turned it into ....young maiden.

05

Insert suitable articles wherever necessary:

(1) Shyam plays .... Piano.

(2) ....Iron is .... hard metal.

(3) Who invented .... Microscope?

(4) .... Delhi is .... beautiful city.

(5) This man is .... second Hitler.

(6) I met him at .... church.

(7) He is .... student of mathematics.

(8) I went to .... hospital to meet my friend.

(9) .... bed is broken.

(10) Please give me .... five-rupee note.

(11) .... Sun rises in .... East.

(12) He wrote his name at .... top of .... page.

(13) I'll go there in .... morning.

(14) It is .... very useful book.

(15) Do not make .... noise.

06

Fill in the blanks with articles wherever necessary:

(1) He went to .... college to meet .... class teacher.

(2) I will take .... tram from ....Church.

(3) He came and sat on .... bed.

(4) He has already gone to .... bed.

(5) Ram was appointed .... clerk.

(6) Suresh was declared .... captain of our team.

(7) Ramesh invited Sarla for .... dinner yesterday.

(8) He organised .... nice lunch in honour of .... President.

(9) .... dinner hosted by Ram was superb.

(10) .... measles is .... contagious disease.

(11) He died of .... cholera.

(12) She has been suffering from .... fever for three days.

(13) He can speak .... Hindi, but I can't speak .... English.

(14) I like .... blue colour.

(15) When I went to .... home, Raja was watching .... TV.
(16) I heard .... news on .... radio.
(17) He is .... rich man, he always go by .... car.
(18) Three per cent posts are reserved for .... disabled and two per cent for...........ex-servicemen.
(19) He went first to .... Mexico and then to .... USA.
(20) Ram took .... action with ....swiftness of .... tiger.

07

Rewrite the following sentences after filling up the blanks with suitable articles wherever necessary:

During .... first two years .... village project had .... awful time. .... Mission had accepted .... use of .... farm from .... affluent landowner and ....natives believed .... story that this land would be returned to ....owner after ten years. .... project never started.

08

Insert suitable articles wherever they are missing:

(1) Pt Jawahar Lal Nehru was.......... first Prime Minister of free India.
(2) Indian Government wants to build......... strong India.
(3) She has never touched.......... onion.
(4) After discussing this matter for..........hour or two we are sure to arrive at ....decision.
(5) Pt Nehru was...............great man. He struggled hard to attain ....freedom from..... Britishers.

09

Insert suitable articles wherever necessary:

(1) Ram is .... good boy.
(2) .... European woman came to America.
(3) Mohan is .... NDA Officer.
(4) I want to buy .... book.
(5) Sita is .... teacher.
(6) He comes here once .... week.
(7) He is .... honourable leader.
(8) He is ....honest person.
(9) Twelve inches makes .... foot.
(10) He has .... good knowledge of Mathematics.
(11) This is .... house I live in .
(12) .... bag I found yesterday contained .... key chain.
(13) It is .... matter of chance.
(14) .... poor can be trusted.
(15) Have you found .... purse you lost yesterday?

10

Insert suitable articles wherever necessary:

(1) The teacher asked .... easy question.
(2) Give me .... book to read please.
(3) Ram secured .... second position in .... school.
(4) He is .... MLA.
(5) Cat is not .... faithful animal.
(6) I am looking for .... remunerative job.
(7) .... honesty is .... best policy.
(8) I found .... purse last night.
(9) I'll go there in .... evening.
(10) Always speak .... truth.
(11) Never tell .... lie.
(12) He likes .... black pent.
(13) Did Mohan get .... job he applied for?
(14) Will you close .... windows, please?
(15) He was invited for .... dinner.

11

Rewrite the following sentences after filling up the blanks with suitable articles wherever necessary:

Once there were elections . ... entire polling station seemed to be .... huge mass of humanity. Men and women all seemed to be quite conscious of their votes. I had seen .... old man insisting on the polling officer and he would not even return .... identity slip. Women had come in groups and were putting on colourful clothes. .... polling stations assumed .... shape of .... fair and .... crowd also behaved likewise. It was really .... pleasure to see them in such .... jolly mood. It was ..... nice scene.

12

Insert suitable articles wherever necessary:

(1) Will you like to have .... cup of tea?
(2) .... room is airy.
(3) .... dog is a faithful animal.
(4) Will you go to .... hospital to see your friend?
(5) There are sixty seconds in .... minute.
(6) Take ....umbrella with you.
(7) I have made................. mistake.
(8) I saw .... old man yesterday.
(9) This poem is written by .... foreign writer.
(10) I found .... book last night........book is very useful.
(11) He is .... able man.
(12) He has applied for .... post of an officer.
(13) .... camel is ....ship of ... desert.
(14) ....Earth revolves round ....Sun.
(15) Kalidas is .... Shakespeare of .... India.

13

Rewrite the following sentences after filling up the blanks with suitable articles wherever necessary:

Once .... businessman of ....colony was shot dead by ....armed intruder on Sunday night. .... dead man's wife also received .... gunshot, but she is said to be progressing in .... Civil Hospital . ... murder is said to be .... result of .... old dispute over financial matters between killer and his victim.After three days .... killer surrendered before ....police.

14

Fill in the blanks with a, an or the:

(1) Ram gave me .... one-rupee note.
(2) She bought .... ink-pot,............ bag and...........umbrella yesterday.
(3) Has .... postman brought any letter for me today?
(4) .... camel can go .... long distance without water.
(5) This is one of .... most interesting books I have ever read.
(6) ......Kashmir is .... Switzerland of India.
(7) ...... teachers of this school are very liberal and intelligent.
(8) Let us discuss .... matter seriously.
(9) He is .... honour to his profession.

(10) .... scheme failed for want of sufficient funds.
(11) I ordered .... servant to leave .... room.
(12) Italy is .... European country.
(13) There is .... hourly tram service on this route.
(14) God made .... country and man made................. town.
(15) Kalidas is .... Shakespeare of India.
(16) Do you know ....way to .... railway station ?
(17) You cannot doubt .... honesty of these men.
(18) .... friend in need is ....friend indeed.
(19) May we have .... pleasure of your company for lunch?
(20) We should always follow .... good and love.................. beautiful.

Spotting Errors (Articles)

15

Find the errors in the following sentences:

(1) Of the two (a)/ solutions the second was (b)/ definitely better. (c)/ No error (d)
(2) I have been (a)/ informed that (b)/ Mr Clinton visits Rajasthan (c)/ following month. (d)/ No error (e)
(3) In the field of invention (a)/ the credit goes to a man (b)/ who convinces the world (c)/ with his arguments (d)/ not to the man who simply thinks. (e)/ No error (F)
(4) He claims to be a scientist (a)/ but in reality he (b)/ does not know even (c)/ A B C of science. (d)/ No error (e)
(5) Her father (a)/forbade her to go (b)/to cinema (c)/with Mohan. (d)/ No error (e)
(6) It is an impossible-task (a)/to calculate number (b) / of creatures living (c)/ on Earth. (d)/ No error (e)
(7) The man (a)/ is the only living creature (b)/ that can speak (c)/ and smile. (d)/ No error (e)
(8) He is an atheist (a)/ but today he is going (b)/ to the church (c)/ for offering prayer. (d)/ No error (e)
(9) You should not spend (a)/ good part of the day (b)/ in marketing only. (c)/ No error (d)
(10) Whatever little (a)/ milk left in the bottle (b)/ was drunk by your cat. (c)/ No error (d)

16

Find the errors in the following sentences:

(1) She leads (a)/ a luxurious life (b)/ so she visits everywhere (c)/ by a car. (d)/ No error (e)
(2) The principal instructed (a)/ the girls to return (b)/ to the college (c)/ before the sunset. (d)/ No error (e)
(3) You must (a)/ be true to your words (b)/ in order to enjoy (c)/the real reputation in the life. (d)/ No error (e)
(4) She is the (a)/most beautiful girl. (b)/ No error (c)
(5) It was an insight (a)/ and perseverance of the lady doctor (b)/ that many women were (c)/ able to lead normal life. (d)/ No error (e)
(6) It is a pity (a)/ that the daughter of millionaire (b)/ is involved in (c)/ the bank robbery. (d)/ No error (e)
(7) He was in a trouble (a)/ when he saw (b)/ a truck running (c)/ towards his car. (d)/ No error (e)
(8) The fruits of (a)/all the modern luxuries (b)/ lie in the science. (c)/ No error (d)
(9) I advised him (a)/ to take the heart (b)/ in all odd circumstances. (c)/ No error (d)
(10) Little knowledge (a)/ of computers that she possessed (b)/ proved a boon for her (c)/ in getting job. (d)/ No error (e)

17

Find the errors in the following sentences:

(1) We (a)/ saw (b)/ a elephant (c)/ in the zoo. (d)/ No error (e)

(2) It is (a)/ a most (b)/ beautiful (c)/ painting of the gallery. (d)/ No error (e)

(3) Mr Gaurav Sharma (a)/ is (b)/ coming to (c)/ dinner. (d)/ No error (e)

(4) I (a)/ go (b)/ to cinema (c)/ every sunday. (d)/ No error (e)

(5) He (a)/ went there (b)/ a hour (c)/ ago. (d)/ No error (e)

(6) He (a)/ always speaks (b)/ truth. (c)/ No error (d)

(7) Kashmiri (a)/shawls (b)/ are made of (c)/ the hair of sheep. (d)/ No error (e)

(8) The Taj mahal (a)/is (b)/ situated (c)/ at the Agra. (d)/ No error (e)

(9) Bible (a)/ said that (b)/ the sun (c)/ goes round the Earth. (d)/ No error (e)

(10) An horse (a)/ is (b)/ running (c)/ in the ground. (d)/ No error (e)

18

Find the errors in the following sentences:

(1) An European (a)/ dish (b)/ is (c)/ very famous. (d)/ No error (e)

(2) Rome (a)/ was (b)/ not built (c)/ in a day. (d)/ No error (e)

(3) Ritika (a)/ helps (b)/ poor and (c)/ the sick people. (d)/ No error (e)

(4) The Sapna (a)/ is a very (b)/ beautiful (c)/ girl. (d)/ No error (e)

(5) I (a)/ saw (b)/ an one rupee note (c)/ on the road. (d)/ No error (e)

(6) The boy (a)/is (b)/ swimming (c)/ in the pool. (d)/ No error (e)

(7) Here is a red (a)/ shirt (b)/ which Sapna gave me (c)/yesterday. (d)/ No error (e)

(8) Shatabdi Express (a)/ runs (b)/ very (c)/ fast. (d)/ No error (e)

(9) Parul (a)/ was also invited (b)/ to the lunch hosted by the queen, (c)/ at her cottage yesterday. (d)/No error (e).

(10) My uncle (a)/is (b)/ a (c)/ SP. (d)/ No error (e)

19

Find the errors in the following sentences:

(1) Gold (a)/ is (b)/ an useful (c)/ metal. (d)/ No error (e)

(2) This is (a)/ a good dress (b)/ but (c)/ that's a better one. (d)/ No error (e)

(3) Rupam (a)/ presented me (b)/ a ring (c)/. The ring is lost. (d)/ No error (e)

(4) The Punjabi (a)/ is (b)/a sweet language (c)/ of Punjab. (d)/ No error (e)

(5) Adnan Sami (a)/ is the (b)/ most popular (c)/ singer in Indian film industry. (d)/ No error (e)

(6) The Sun (a)/ rises (b)/ in (c)/ East. (d)/ No error (e)

(7) The teaching (a)/ profession (b)/ is (c)/ good for women. (d)/No error (e)

(8) The milk (a)/ is (b)/ good (c)/for health. (d)/ No error (e)

(9) I (a)/ think (b)/ a baby (c)/ is crying. (d)/ No error (e)

(10) Kunal (a)/ was (b)/ sent to (c)/ a prison. (d)/ No error (e)

20

Find the errors in the following sentences:

(1) I (a)/ will go (b)/ there (c)/ by train or bus. (d)/ No error (e)

(2) My parents (a)/ sometimes (b)/ come to school (c)/ to see the principal. (d)/No error (e)

(3) Riya (a)/ went home (b)/ very late (c)/ last Monday. (d)/ No error (e)

(4) The winters (a)/ are (b)/ generally very (c)/ cold here. (d)/ No error (e)

(5) The monkeys (a)/ jumps (b)/ on (c)/ the trees. (d)/ No error (e)

(6) The dog (a)/ is (b)/ a (c)/ faithful animal. (d)/ No error (e)

(7) Chief Minister (a)/ will (b)/ decide (c)/ the matter. (d)/ No error (e)

(8) Kshitiz (a)/ is (b)/ a (c)/ honest boy. (d)/ No error (e)

(9) The Sun (a)/ rises in (b)/ the East (c)/ is an universal truth. (d)/ No error (e)

(10) Times of India (a)/ is a most popular (b)/ newspaper (c)/of these days. (d)/No error (e)

21

Find the errors in the following sentences:

(1) Three children (a)/ died (b)/ in a (c)/ bus accident yesterday. (d) /No error (e)

(2) The Mahatma Gandhi (a)/ was (b)/ also called (c)/ 'Bapu'. (d)/ No error (e)

(3) Chinese (a)/ are (b)/ fond of (c)/ chowmin. (d)/ No error (e)

(4) Taj Mahal (a)/ is a (b)/ beautiful (c)/ building in Agra. (d)/ No error (e)

(5) The capital (a)/ of (b)/ UK is (c)/ London. (d)/ No error (e)

(6) My mother (a)/ is cooking (b)/ in a (c)/ kitchen. (d)/ No error (e)

(7) The teacher (a)/ called a (b)/ last boy (c)/ standing in the queue. (d)/ No error (e)

(8) The apple (a)/ a day (b)/ keeps (c)/ the doctors away. (d)/ No error (e)

(9) The more (a)/ I learn history (b)/ the more (c)/ I get bored. (d)/ No error (e).

(10) The intelligent (a)/ should (b)/ help (c)/ the duffer. (d)/ No error (e)

(11) Shreya (a)/ gave (b)/ me (c)/ the watch. (d)/ No error (e)

22

Find the errors in the following sentences:

(1) In the conclusion it (a)/may be said (b)/ that the writer has surpassed/(c) the ethical norms. (d)/ No error (e)

(2) It is the most/(a) important point that (b)/ you have to/(c) understand well.(d)/ No error (e)

(3) He said to me, (a)/ "I think you (b)/ will never/ (c)turn a traitor." (d)/ No error (e)

(4) Ramesh told me (a)/ that he first went (b)/ to the Mexico and/(c) then to the Netherlands. (d)/ No error (e)

(5) My mother forbade/(a) my sister to/(b) go to theatre at night. (c)/ No error (d)

(6) One should be true/(a) to one's words in/(b)order to earn good name/(c) and fame in the life. (d)/ No error (e)

(7) I have been waiting/(a) for her/(b) for more than/(c) half a hour. (d)/ No error (e)

(8) You should not spend (a)/ good port of the day (b)/ in gossiping ans wandering (c)/ here and there. (d) /No error (e)

(9) Will you please (a)/ give me (b)/ Little milk (c)/ for my cat. (d)/ No error (e)

(10) He informed me (a)/ that he had gone (b)/ to the church (c)/ to offer prayers. (d)/ No error (e)

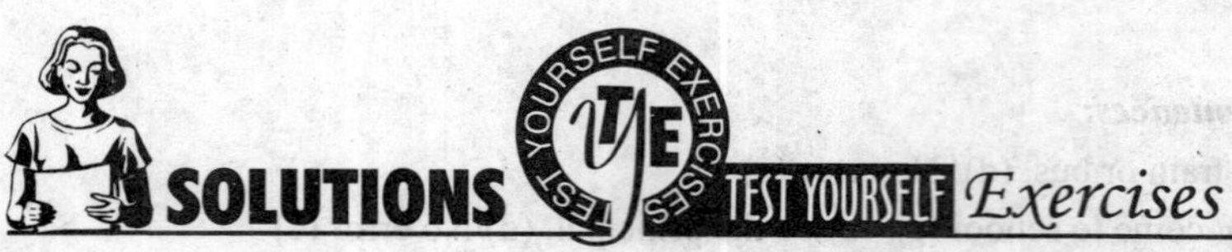

Solution TYE : 01

(A) A, the, an, The, a, The, the, the, an, the. **(B)** the, the, a, the, the, a, the, the, the.
(C) ×, the, a, ×, the, the/a, ×, the, a, an.

Solution TYE : 02

(1) (A) Who are the men that are standing there in the lane?

(B) The tallest gentlemen is a teacher, the man who has a stick in his hand is the teacher's uncle. He lives in Chennai. He has come here to attend a wedding . I don't know who the third man is. I know the person sitting beside the teacher.

(C) I'm sorry to have detained you. Are you going to the bank ?

(2) Once a man had a strange goose. It laid a golden egg every day. The man was very lucky to possess such a precious creature. One day he thought, "One golden egg a day is not sufficient. I shall kill the goose and get hold of all the gold contained in it." He then killed the goose, but find not a single egg.

Solution TYE : 03

I know Ram's brother. He is an officer in the Ministry of Foreign Affairs. He is posted in the states. He is the youngest officer there. He enjoys the work and plays the game of tennis in evenings. For his breakfast he takes an apple, an egg and a cup of coffee only. He is a good fellow.

Solution TYE : 04

Once an old saint saw a kite catch a little mouse. He felt sorry for the mouse. He took àn orange and aimed at the kite which dropped the mouse and by his holy power turned it into a young maiden.

Solution TYE : 05

(1) the, (2) x, a, (3) the, (4) ×, a, (5) a, (6) the,
(7) a, (9) The, (10) a, (11) The, the, (12) the, a, (13) the,
(14) a, (15) a.

Solution TYE : 06

(1) the, the, (2) a, the, (3) the, (4) ×, (5) ×, (6) ×,
(7) ×, (8) a, the, (9) The, (10) The, a, (11) ×, (12) ×,
(13) ×, ×, (14) ×, ×, (15) ×, ×, (16) the, the, (17) a, ×, (18) the, the,
(19) ×, the, (20) the, the, a.

Solution TYE : 07

During the first two years the village project had an awful time.The Mission had accepted the use of a farm from an affluent landowner and the natives believed the story that this land would be returned to the owner after ten years.The project never started.

Solution TYE : 08

(1) Pt Jawaharlal Nehru was the first Prime Minister of free India.
(2) Indian Government wants to build a strong India.
(3) She has never touched an onion.
(4) After discussing this matter for an hour or two we are sure to arrive at a decision.
(5) Pt Nehru was a great man. He struggled hard to attain freedom from the Britishers.

Solution TYE : 09

(1) a, (2) A, (3) an, (4) a, (5) a, (6) a,
(7) an, (8) an, (9) a, (10) a, (11) the,
(12) The, a, (13) a, (14) The, (15) the.

Solution TYE : 10

(1) an, (2) a, (3) the, the, (4) an, (5) a, (6) a,
(7) ×, the, (8) a, (9) the, (10) the, (11) a, (12) the,
(13) the, (14) the, (15) ×.

Solution TYE : 11

Once there were elections. The entire polling station seemed to be a huge mass of humanity. Men and women all seemed to be quite conscious of their votes. I had seen an old man insisting on the polling officer and he would not even return the identity slip. Women had come in groups and were putting on colourful clothes. The polling stations assumed the shape of a fair and the crowd also behaved likewise. It was really a pleasure to see them in such a jolly mood. It was a nice scene.

Solution TYE : 12

(1) a, (2) The, (3) The, 4. the, 5. a, 6. an,
(7) a, (8) an, (9) a, 10. a, the, 11. an, 12. the,
(13) The, the, the, (14)The, the, (15) the, x.

Solution TYE : 13

Once a businessman of the colony was shot dead by an armed intruder on Sunday night . The dead man's wife also received a gunshot, but she is said to be progressing in the Civil Hospital. The murder is said to be the result of an old dispute over financial matters between the killer and his victim. After three days the killer surrendered before the police.

Solution TYE : 14

(1) a, (2) an, a, an, (3) the, (4) A, a (5) the, (6) ×, the
(7) The, (8) the, (9) an, (10) The, (11) the, the, (12) a,
(13) an, (14) the, the, (15) the, (16) the, the, (17) the, (18) A, a,
(19) the, (20) the, the.

Solution TYE : 15

(1) (c) better से पहले 'the' का प्रयोग करें। Comparative degree के adjective द्वारा जब किसी choice का निर्धारण होता है तो उससे पहले 'the' का प्रयोग किया जाता है। जैसे: He is the stronger of the two wrestlers.

(2) (d) following से पूर्व 'the' लगाएँ। यहाँ following month, particular हो गया है।

(3) (b) a man, की जगह the man का प्रयोग करें। यहाँ man, particular हो गवा है।

(4) (d) ABC के पूर्व 'the' लगाएँ। to emphasise, 'the' is necessary.

(5) (c) cinema से पूर्व 'the' लगता है। go to the cinema, go to the theatre जैसी pharases में 'the' का प्रयोग होता है।

(6) (b) number से पहले 'the' लगाएँ the number का अर्थ निश्चित संख्या होता है। the number of वैसे भी phrase की तरह प्रयुक्त होता है।

(7) (a) man से पहले 'the' को Delete करें। man का प्रयोग जब मानव-जाति (in broader sense) के लिये होता है तो उससे पहले 'the' का प्रयोग नहीं किया जाता है।
Man is a social animal.
Man is mortal.

(8) (c) Church के पहले 'the' का प्रयोग उस स्थिति में गलत है जबकि वहाँ जाने का उद्देश्य, prayer हेतु है। यदि church जाने का उद्देश्य अन्य कोई कार्य हो तो 'the' लगेगा।

(9) (b) good part से पहले 'a' लगाएँ। a good part of the day, phrase की तरह प्रयुक्त होता है।

(10) (a) Little से पहले 'the' लगेगा। यहाँ the little का अर्थ-जो भी थोड़ा-सा से है।

Solution TYE : 16

(1) (d) by a car, नहीं होगा, by car होगा by car, by bus, by train के बीच में article नहीं लगता है।

(2) (d) Before sunset होगा ('the' को delete करें।) before sunset, before noon, after day break में 'the' का प्रयोग नहीं होता है। निम्न वाक्यों में अन्तर समझने का प्रयास करें:

He returned home after sunset.

He returned home after the sun had set.

(3) (d) life से पहले the नहीं लगेगा। जब life का प्रयोग व्यापक अर्थ में हो तो the का प्रयोग नहीं होता है, लेकिन life का प्रयोग यदि particular अर्थ में है तो article का प्रयोग करना होता है।

He is leading a happy life.

The life of this patient has spoiled by the doctor.

(4) (a) 'the' की जगह 'a' का प्रयोग करें। यहाँ a most का अर्थ a very beautiful से है। जब most का अर्थ comparison के लिए न होकर, 'very' के अर्थ में होता है तो 'a' का प्रयोग किया जाता है।

(5) (a) 'an' की जगह 'the' का प्रयोग होगा। किसी भी चीज को महत्त्व देने हेतु 'the' का प्रयोग किया जाता है।

(6) (b) Millionaire से पहले 'a' लगेगा। यह एक countable noun है अत: article लगाना होगा।

(7) (a) trouble से पहले 'a' नहीं लगेगा। in danger, in trouble, in detail, in debt, in comparison, in fact जैसे: phrases में बीच में article का प्रयोग नहीं होता है।

(8) (c) Science से पहले 'the' का प्रयोग नहीं होगा। science, life, का प्रयोग जब व्यापक अर्थ में होता है, तो इनसे पहले 'the' का प्रयोग नहीं होता है।

(9) (b) take heart होगा। take heart, take care जैसे: phrases में बीच में Article का प्रयोग नहीं होता है।

(10) (a) Little से पहले 'the' का प्रयोग होगा। 'the little' का अर्थ-जो भी थोड़ा से है।

Solution TYE : 17

(1) (c) Here ''a'' is used with elephant instead of ''an''. An elephant is correct.

(2) (b) It is a most beautiful painting. Use the before most , being Superlative.

(3) (e) No error

(4) (c) I go to the cinema every Sunday. When ''club'', ''cinema'', ''pictures'', ''theatres'', are used for their primary purpose of entertainment. ''The'' is used before them.

(5) (c) Replace 'a' by 'an'. Here ''an'' will be used instead of ''a'' because ''h'' is silent .

(6) (c) He always speaks the truth.

(7) (a) The Kashmiri shawls, 'The' is used before nouns which name the inhabitants of a country or city collectively.

(8) (d) Delete 'The' before Agra, being proper noun.

(9) (a) The Bible said . 'The' is used before the names of renowned books of religion or literature.

(10) (a) A horse is running in the ground. 'A' is used with the singular countable nouns which is pronounced with the consonant sound.

Solution TYE : 18

(1) (a) ''A'' European dish is very famous. Here 'European' begins with vowel ''E'' even then its sounds ''yoo'' or ''u''.

(2) (e) ''A'' is used with certain numerical terms to give the sense of ''one''.

(3) (c) Ritika helps the poor and the sick people.

(4) (a) Sapna is a very beautiful girl. " The" is not used before proper noun.

(5) (c) I saw a one rupee note on the road. ''A'' is used with nouns pronounced with consonant sound.

(6) (a) A boy is swimming in the pool. ''A'' is used with the singular countable nouns.

(7) (a) Here is the red shirt which Sapna gave me yesterday. Red shirt has become particularised.

(8) (a) The Shatabdi Express . ''The'' is used before the names of well-known trains.

(9) (e) No error. 'The' is used before particular meals.

(10) (c) My uncle is an SP Here, 'An' is used before a consonant which sounds like a vowel.

Solution TYE : 19

(1) (c) Gold is a useful metal. Before useful we should put 'a' instead of 'an'.

(2) (e) 'A' is used with positive and comparatives but not with superlatives.

(3) (e) 'The' is used before a noun which is repeated after it has been introduced once.

(4) (a) Punjabi 'The' is not used before name of the language.

(5) (e) No error. 'The' is used with the superlative degree of adjective.

(6) (d) in the east. 'The' is used with the name of 'directions' like east, west, north, wouth.

(7) (e) 'The' is used with the professions like the nursing, the medical profession.

(8) (a) Milk is good for health. 'The' article are omitted before proper nouns, material nouns, uncountables etc in general.

(9) (c) the baby.

(10) (d) Kunal was sent to prison. The article is omitted before church, prison, hospital, college , school and bed, when the visit to these place is for the purpose they are primarily built.

Solution TYE : 20

(1) (e) The Article is omitted before modes of transportation or travel. Always use by bus,by car, by train, etc.

(2) (c) Insert 'the' before school .When the visit to places : school, Church, hospital , prison are for the purpose other than they are primarily built , always use 'the' before these nouns.

(3) (e) No error ''The'' is not used before name.

(4) (a) Remove the before 'Winters'. Do not use article before name of the seasons.

(5) (a) Monkeys jumps on the trees. The article is omitted before plural countable nouns when they tell about class or cast etc.

(6) (e) ''The'' is used before a singular countable noun meant to represent a whole class or kind.

(7) (a) Insert 'The' before Chief Minister . Use the before designation.

(8) (c) Kshitiz is an honest boy. Here 'an' is used before a word beginning with silent ''H''. (Honest)

(9) (d) The sun rises in the east is a universal truth. 'A' is used before a word beginning with the sound 'u' pronounced as 'yoo'or 'u').

(10) (a) The 'Times of India' .... 'The' is used before the name of the newspapers and magazines.

Solution TYE : 21

(1) (e) No Error

(2) (a) Delete ''the'' before Mahatma Gandhi. Article is not used before a name proper noun).

(3) (a) The chinese............ ''The'' is used before nationality.

(4) (a) The Taj Mahal .... 'The' is used such name of Monuments.

(5) (c) 'The' is used before name of country like UK , USA etc.

(6) (c) My mother is working in the kitchen . Here 'The' is used before the noun which can be understood easily.

(7) (b) The teacher called the last boy........... 'The' is used before the ordinals.

(8) (a) An apple...... ''An'' is used here before a word beginning with a vowel a,e,i,o,u,) sound.

(9) (e) ''The'' is here used twice, with comparative to show that two things increase or decrease in the same proportion.

(10) (e) Here ''the intelligent'' means intelligent person and the ''duffers'' means duffer persons.

(11) (d) Shreya gave me a watch. "A" is used before a word beginning with a consonant.

Solution TYE : 22

(1) (a) Conclusion के पहले 'the' नहीं लगेगा। कुछ Phrases जैसे: In detail, in fear, in hope, in problem, in condusion का ध्यान दें, इनमें बीच में 'the' का प्रयोग नहीं होगा।

(2) (a) most के पहले 'the' की जगह 'a' लिखना होगा।। जब Superlative degree, most का प्रयोग Comparison हेतु किया जाता है तो 'the' लगाना होगा। यहाँ most का प्रयोग 'very' के अर्थ में हुआ है अत: 'a' लगेगा।

जैसे:

Sarla is the most beautiful girl in the college.

Sarla is a most beautiful girl.

(3) (d) Inchoative Verb, Turn के साथ noun के पूर्व 'a' का प्रयोग किया जाएगा।

(4) (c) Mexico से पूर्व 'the' का प्रयोग नहीं होगा। Plural name of countries या जिन Countries के नाम के साथ States or Republic जुड़ा हो, उनके पूर्व ही 'the' का प्रयोग किया जाता है।

(5) (c) theatre से पूर्व the लगायें। go to the cinema/go to the theatre आदि phrases का इसी तरह प्रयोग किया जाता है।

(6) (d) life से पहले 'the' नहीं लगेगा। Life का प्रयोग जब विस्तृत अर्थ में हो तो life से पूर्व 'the' नहीं लगता है। विशेष अर्थ में life से पूर्व article लगता है। जैसे:

She leads a happy life.

The life of villagers is paralysed due to earthquake.

(7) (d) hour से पूर्व 'a' की जगह 'an' लगेगा।

(8) (b) a good part of the day. good part से पहले 'a' लगेगा।

(9) (c) little से पूर्व 'a' लगेगा। a little का अर्थ होता है 'थोड़ा-सा'।

(10) (c) Church से पूर्व Church, Hospital, School, Prison इत्यादि जाने का उद्देश्य इसलिए हो जिसके लिए इनका निर्माण हुआ है तो इनसे पूर्व 'the' नहीं लगेगा।

TRANSLATION AND TENSE

Translation अर्थात् अनुवाद करना एक कला (Art) है। एक भाषा के वाक्य का दूसरी भाषा में रूपान्तरण करना, **Translation** (अनुवाद) कहलाता है। अधिकांश हिन्दी भाषी छात्रों को हिन्दी वाक्यों का अंग्रेजी में अनुवाद करना बहुत कठिन कार्य प्रतीत होता है। **अंग्रेजी भाषा एक विदेशी भाषा है**। अधिकांश छात्रों द्वारा अंग्रेजी का अध्ययन मात्र परीक्षा पास करने हेतु किया जाता है। रटकर अंग्रेजी की परीक्षा पास तो कर ली, लेकिन अंग्रेजी से हमेशा भय बना रहा।

आइए हम आपको हिन्दी वाक्यों का अंग्रेजी में अनुवाद करने के कुछ सरल तरीकों से अवगत कराते हैं।

(A) अनुवाद हेतु सर्वप्रथम आवश्यकता है कि आपको वाक्य में प्रयुक्त विभिन्न भागों (Parts of speech) जैसे : Subject, Verb, Object, Adverb, Preposition etc. की पहचान करना आना चाहिए।

(B) वाक्य जिस Tense का है, उस Tense में अंग्रेजी वाक्य का विन्यास (Structure of sentence) क्या है? इसके लिए Tenses का ज्ञान आवश्यक है। बिना Tenses की पूर्ण जानकारी हुए, शुद्ध अंग्रेजी लिखना सम्भव नहीं है।

(C) **विभिन्न नियमों का ज्ञान :** सही अनुवाद हेतु, हमें Tenses के ज्ञान के बाद, विभिन्न नियमों का ज्ञान होना चाहिए। जैसे:

(a) Subject Verb agreement का ज्ञान।
(b) Sequence of Tenses का ज्ञान।

(c) Rules regarding, Determiners, Articles, Adverbs, Adjectives, Prepositions, Noun, Pronoun, Conjunctions, Interjections, Modals इत्यादि का ज्ञान।

(d) Reported Speech एवं Voices के नियमों का ज्ञान।

(D) विभिन्न प्रकार के Sentences; Simple, Compound, Complex etc. का ज्ञान।

Translation Made Easy

सर्वप्रथम आपको यह जानना आवश्यक है कि वाक्य (sentence) में प्रयुक्त विभिन्न भागों (यथा Subject, Verb, Object, Preposition, etc.) की पहचान कैसे की जाए? इन भागों की अंग्रेजी बनाकर इन्हें किस प्रकार वाक्यों में सुव्यवस्थित रखा जाए?

(1) Subject (कर्ता) की पहचान एवं स्थिति

किसी भी वाक्य में Subject कर्म को करने वाला होता है। वाक्य में जो भी कार्य करने वाला है, वह **Subject (कर्त्ता)** है। साधारण हिन्दी वाक्य में अन्तिम शब्द (यदि वाक्य के अन्त में है, हूँ, हो इत्यादि आता है तो इससे पहले वाला शब्द) जो वास्तव में वाक्य की क्रिया (Verb) है, से **कौन**, **किसने** अथवा **किन्होंने** जैसे प्रश्न करने पर जो उत्तर आता है, वह ही उस वाक्य का **Subject (कर्ता)** है।

निम्न वाक्य को देखें:

(i) राम फुटबॉल खेलता है।
इस वाक्य के अन्तिम शब्द 'है' से पूर्व वाले शब्द **'खेलता'** (जो वास्तव में verb है) से **कौन** प्रश्न करने पर उत्तर मिलता है—**राम**। अत: **राम** इस वाक्य का **Subject** है। उपरोक्त वाक्य में खेलता verb है।

अन्य वाक्य देखें :

(ii) राजेश शाम को पाँच बजे गोमती नदी में तैरता है।

यहाँ वाक्य के अन्तिम शब्द 'है' से; पूर्व वाले शब्द **'तैरता'** से प्रश्न किया गया, **कौन तैरता है?** उत्तर मिला, **राजेश**-तो इस वाक्य का Subject हुआ **राजेश**।

(2) Verb (क्रिया) की पहचान एवं स्थिति

Verb एक वाक्य का विशेष महत्त्वपूर्ण भाग है।

हिन्दी वाक्य के अन्तिम शब्द (यदि वाक्य के अन्त में हैं, हूँ, इत्यादि हैं तो उससे पहले का शब्द) को **Verb (क्रिया)** कहते हैं। उपरोक्त वाक्य (i) में **'खेलता'** verb है, वाक्य (ii) में **'तैरता'** Verb है।

(3) Object (कर्म) की पहचान एवं स्थिति

(A) हिन्दी वाक्य में Subject एवं Verb की पहचान करने के बाद आपको Verb से **कहाँ, किसको, किनको** जैसे : प्रश्न करने पर जो उत्तर मिलता है, वह वाक्य का कर्म **(Object)** है।

उपरोक्त वाक्य में, वाक्य (i) की verb-**खेलता** से **क्या** प्रश्न करने पर उत्तर मिलता है—**फुटबॉल**। अत: वाक्य का object **फुटबॉल** है।

वाक्य (ii) में Verb **'तैरता'** से **'कहाँ'** प्रश्न करने पर, उत्तर मिलता है **'गोमती नदी में'**। अत: वाक्य का Object **गोमती नदी** है।

(B) **Tense की पहचान एवं Structure of Sentence:** हिन्दी वाक्य को अंग्रेजी में translate करने हेतु हमें वाक्य के Tense को पहचान कर,उसके वाक्य विन्यास के अनुसार वाक्य के विभिन्न भागों (Parts of Sentence) के अंग्रेजी शब्दों को लिखना चाहिए। जैसे :

राम फुटबॉल खेल रहा है।

यह Present continuous का वाक्य है। इसका Sentence Structure निम्न होता है; (आगे Present continuous के अध्याय में स्पष्ट किया गया है)

Subject + is/am/are + V-IV + object. **[V-IV=V + I + ing]**

इस structure के अनुसार part of speech लिखने पर ; Ram + is + playing + football

Ram is playing football. इस वाक्य का अनुवाद हो गया।

इसी प्रकार-**रमेश ने एक किताब लिखी।**

यह Past Indefinite का वाक्य है। Past Indefinite के वाक्यों का Sentence Structure निम्न होता है :

Subject + V-II + object. इस तरह से इस वाक्य का अनुवाद निम्न होगा :

Ramesh wrote a book.

इस तरह से सरल वाक्यों का अंग्रेजी में अनुवाद उक्त प्रकार से किया जा सकता है। अन्य प्रकार के वाक्यों का अनुवाद करने हेतु हमें अंग्रेजी भाषा के सभी Aspects, Rules का ज्ञान होना चाहिए।

पुन: लेख है कि अंग्रेजी भाषा में प्रवीणता हेतु **अंग्रेजी रटें नहीं, बल्कि अभ्यास करें**।

NOTE

(a) यदि हिन्दी वाक्य में 'हमेशा, कभी नहीं, अक्सर' जैसे शब्द, आएँ तो इनका अनुवाद Verb से पहले लिखना होता है। जैसे

वह हमेशा सच बोलता है।	*He always speaks the truth.*
राम अक्सर यहाँ आता है।	*Ram often comes here.*

*(b) **Prepositions (विभक्तियाँ) एवं स्थिति** : वाक्य में आने वाली विभक्तियाँ (जैसे; से, में, को, पर, के, etc. prepositions हैं। सामान्यतया prepositions को हिन्दी वाक्य में जिस शब्द के बाद इनका प्रयोग हुआ है। अंग्रेजी अनुवाद करते समय, उस शब्द के अनुवाद के पहले लगाया जाता है।*

उपरोक्त तरीके, आपको अनुवाद करने में सरलता एवं सुविधा हेतु सुझाए गए हैं। अंग्रेजी अनुवाद हेतु बार-बार practice की आवश्यकता है। पूर्णतया नियमों में कैद होकर, अनुवाद के तरीके बताना सम्भव नहीं है। आपको छोटे वाक्यों के अनुवाद करने की practice करनी है। फिर बड़े वाक्यों का अनुवाद करना है।

निम्न वाक्यों से practice करें :

ये Present Indefinite Tense के वाक्य हैं। इनका Sentence Structure निम्न होता है

Subject + Verb I form ('s' or 'es' with singular number third person) + Object

(1) मैं (Subject) खेलता (Verb) हूँ। — I play.

(2) मैं फुटबॉल (Object) खेलता हूँ। — I play football.

(3) मैं प्रतिदिन फुटबॉल खेलता हूँ। — I play football daily.

(4) मैं प्रतिदिन शाम को फुटबॉल खेलता हूँ। — I play football in the evening daily.

(5) मैं प्रतिदिन शाम को 5 बजे फुटबॉल खेलता हूँ। — I play football at 5 O'clock in the evening daily.

(6) मैं प्रतिदिन कॉलेज के मैदान पर शाम को 5 बजे फुटबॉल खेलता हूँ।
I play football at the college ground at 5 o'clock in the evening daily.

इस तरह से छोटे-छोटे वाक्यों से अनुवाद करने की practice करके, बड़े वाक्यों का अनुवाद सरलता से किया जा सकता है। इसी तरह अन्य वाक्य देखें :

(1) वह लिखता है। — He writes.

(2) वह एक पत्र लिखता है। — He writes a letter.

(3) वह प्रतिदिन एक पत्र लिखता है। — He writes a letter daily.

(4) वह अपने पिता को प्रतिदिन एक पत्र लिखता है। — He writes a letter to his father daily.

शुद्ध अनुवाद हेतु आपको अंग्रेजी भाषा से सम्बन्धित सभी Rules एवं Exceptions का ज्ञान होना आवश्यक है।

Tense

Tense शब्द का उद्‌भव Latin शब्द tempus means, time से हुआ है।

Concept of Tense and Time

Tense एवं Time : Tense एवं Time अलग-अलग Concept हैं। Time एक Natural Concept है, जबकि Tense अंग्रेजी अध्ययन हेतु Grammatical Concept है। Tense का सम्बन्ध English Grammar से है। Tense एवं Time समान Concept नहीं है। ऐसे बहुत से वाक्य हो सकते हैं जो Future Time में कार्य के सम्पन्न होने को प्रदर्शित करते हैं, लेकिन English Grammar के नियमानुसार, उन पर Present Tense के नियम लागू होते हैं। उनका अनुवाद Present Tense के नियमानुसार किया जाएगा। जैसे :

(1) She is coming tomorrow. (2) Sita is going to Delhi tomorrow.

(3) Mr. Sharma retires in the month of December.

ये वाक्य future time/action को बताते हैं, लेकिन उनका अनुवाद Present Tense के नियमानुसार किया जाता है। अत: Tense एवं Time दो अलग-अलग Concept हैं। अब आपको tense एवं time का concept भली-भाँति समझ में आ गया होगा।

Tense तीन प्रकार के होते हैं :

(1) Present Tense (2) Past Tense (3) Future Tense

What is Tense?

Tense is that form of a verb which shows not only the time of an actions, but also the state of an action or event.

Forms of Verbs

Modern Grammar में Verbs को Regular एवं Irregular Verbs में वर्गीकृत किया गया है। Regular Verb वे Verbs हैं जिनके मूल रूप में t, d या ed लगाने पर उसका Past Tense बनता है। जैसे :

Talk	Talked	Talked
Live	Lived	Lived

जिन verbs की Past Forms, Verb के मूल रूप में d, ed, t लगाने से नहीं बनती, उन्हें Irregular verbs कहा जाता है। ऐसी Verbs की Past Forms बनाने हेतु कोई नियम निर्धारित नहीं है। जैसे :

See	Saw	Seen
Go	Went	Gone
Come	Came	Come

Verbs : Singular या Plural, Present Tense में ही होती हैं। सभी Verbs को Plural एवं Present Tense में माना जाता है। Verbs के साथ Present Tense में s या es लगाने से वह Singular बनती है।

Five Forms of Verbs

I Present	II Past	III Past Participle	IV Present Participle	V Infinitive
Arise	arose	arisen	arising	to arise
Arrive	arrived	arrived	arriving	to arrive
Abide	abode	abode	abiding	to abide
Abuse	abused	abused	abusing	to abuse
Awake	awoke	awaken	awaking	to awake
Be	was/were	been	being	to be
Bear	bore	borne	bearing	to bear
Bear	bore	born	bearing	to bear
Become	became	become	becoming	to become
Blow	blew	blown	blowing	to blow
Break	broke	broken	breaking	to break
Bring	brought	brought	bringing	to bring
Behold	beheld	beheld	beholding	to behold
Buy	bought	bought	buying	to buy
Catch	caught	caught	catching	to catch
Climb	climbed	climbed	climbing	to climb
Come	came	come	coming	to come
Choose	chose	chosen	choosing	to choose
Dig	dug	dug	digging	to dig
Do	did	done	doing	to do
Draw	drew	drawn	drawing	to draw
Drink	drank	drunk	drinking	to drink
Deal	dealt	dealt	dealing	to deal

I Present	II Past	III Past Participle	IV Present Participle	V Infinitive
Dream	dreamt	dreamt	dreaming	to dream
Dwell	dwelt	dwelt	dwelling	to dwell
Eat	ate	eaten	eating	to eat
Earn	earned	earned	earning	to earn
Elect	elected	elected	electing	to elect
Electrify	electrified	electrified	electrifying	to electrify
Enjoy	enjoyed	enjoyed	enjoying	to enjoy
Enrol	enrolled	enrolled	enrolling	to enrol
Enter	entered	entered	entering	to enter
Err	erred	erred	erring	to err
Excite	excited	excited	exciting	to excite
Excuse	excused	excused	excusing	to excuse
Feel	fed	fed	feeding	to feed
Fall	fell	fallen	falling	to fall
Fight	fought	fought	fighting	to fight
Find	found	found	finding	to find
Flow	flowed	flowed	flowing	to flow
Fly	flew	flown	flying	to fly
Forget	forgot	forgotten	forgetting	to forget
Forbid	forbade	forbidden	forbidding	to forbid
Freeze	froze	frozen	freezing	to freeze
Forsake	forsook	forsaken	forsaking	to forsake
Get	got	got	getting	to get
Give	gave	given	giving	to give
Grow	grew	grown	growing	to grow
Gain	gained	gained	gaining	to gain
Gamble	gambled	gambled	gambling	to gamble
Govern	governed	governed	governing	to govern
Graze	grazed	grazed	grazing	to graze
Greet	greeted	greeted	greeting	to greet
Guide	guided	guided	guiding	to guide
Hide	hid	hidden	hiding	to hide
Hang	hung	hung	hanging	to hang
Hold	held	held	holding	to hold
Have	had	had	having	to have
Hurt	hurt	hurt	hurting	to hurting
Ignore	ignored	ignored	ignoring	to ignore
Imagine	imagined	imagined	imagining	to imagine
Injure	injured	injured	injuring	to injure
Insult	insulted	insulted	insulting	to insult
Intend	intended	intended	intending	to intend
Invade	invaded	invaded	invading	to invade

I Present	II Past	III Past Participle	IV Present Participle	V Infinitive
Invent	invented	invented	inventing	to invent
Join	joined	joined	joining	to join
Joke	joked	joked	joking	to joke
Judge	judged	judged	judging	to judge
Jump	jumped	jumped	jumping	to jump
Kneel	knelt	knelt	kneeling	to kneel
Kill	killed	killed	killing	to kill
Kick	kicked	kicked	kicking	to kick
Lie	lay	lain	lying	to lie
Lend	lent	lent	lending	to lend
Borrow	borrowed	borrowed	borrowing	to borrow
Light	lighted	lighted	lighting	to light
Lose	lost	lost	losing	to lose
Let	let	let	letting	to let
Leak	leaked	leaked	leaking	to leak
Lead	led	led	leading	to lead
Lick	licked	licked	licking	to lick
Like	liked	liked	liking	to like
Listen	listened	listened	listening	to listen
Look	looked	looked	looking	to look
Love	loved	loved	loving	to love
Make	made	made	making	to make
Mean	meant	meant	meaning	to mean
Mar	marred	marred	marring	to mar
March	marched	marched	marching	to march
Marry	married	married	marrying	to marry
Mind	minded	minded	minding	to mind
Miss	missed	missed	missing	to miss
Mix	mixed	mixed	mixing	to mix
Mortgage	mortgaged	mortgaged	mortgaging	to mortgage
Nap	napped	napped	napping	to nap
Neglect	neglected	neglected	neglecting	to neglect
Nurse	nursed	nursed	nursing	to nurse
Obey	obeyed	obeyed	obeying	to obey
Object	objected	objected	objecting	to object
Offend	offended	offended	offending	to offend
Open	opened	opened	opening	to open
Oppose	opposed	opposed	opposing	to oppose
Oppress	oppressed	oppressed	oppressing	to oppress
Order	ordered	ordered	ordering	to order
Prove	proved	proved	proving	to prove
Purchase	purchased	purchased	purchasing	to purchase
Pay	paid	paid	paying	to pay

I Present	II Past	III Past Participle	IV Present Participle	V Infinitive
Pardon	pardoned	pardoned	pardoning	to pardon
Persist	persisted	persisted	persisting	to persist
Polish	polished	polished	polishing	to polish
Ponder	pondered	pondered	pondering	to ponder
Post	posted	posted	posting	to post
Practise	practised	practised	practising	to practise
Pray	prayed	prayed	praying	to pray
Prepare	prepared	prepared	preparing	to prepare
Press	pressed	pressed	pressing	to press
Pretend	pretended	pretended	pretending	to pretend
Progress	progressed	progressed	progressing	to progress
Quit	quit	quit	quitting	to quit
Quarrel	quarrelled	quarrelled	quarrelling	to quarrel
Question	questioned	questioned	questioning	to question
Quench	quenched	quenched	quenching	to quenched
Ride	rode	ridden	riding	to ride
Read	read	read	reading	to read
Ring	rang	rung	ringing	to ring
Sell	sold	sold	selling	to sell
Send	sent	sent	sending	to send
Sow	sowed	sown	sowing	to sow
Spend	spent	spent	spending	to spend
Sit	sat	sat	sitting	to sit
Speak	spoke	spoken	speaking	to speak
Spell	spelt	spelt	spelling	to spell
Sweep	swept	swept	sweeping	to sweep
See	saw	seen	seeing	to see
Shake	shook	shaken	shaking	to shake
Shine	shone	shone	shining	to shine
Sink	sank	sunk	s nking	to shine
Swear	swore	sworn	swearing	to swear
Swim	swam	swum	swimming	to swim
Shoot	shot	shot	shooting	to shoot
Sling	slung	slung	slinging	to sling
Saw	sawed	sawn	sawing	to saw
Shear	sheared	sheared	shearing	to shear
Spoil	spoiled	spoilt	spoiling	to spoil
Strive	strove	striven	striving	to strive
Swell	swelled	swelled	swelling	to swell
Set	set	set	setting	to set
Shut	shut	shut	shutting	to shut
Take	took	taken	taking	to take
Teach	taught	taught	teaching	to teach

I Present	II Past	III Past Participle	IV Present Participle	V Infinitive
Think	thought	thought	thinking	to think
Thrust	thrust	thrust	thrusting	to thrust
Tread	trod	trodden	treading	to tread
Undergo	underwent	undergone	undergoing	to undergo
Undo	undid	undone	undoing	to undo
Unify	unified	unified	unifying	to unify
Vacate	vacated	vacated	vacating	to vacate
Value	valued	valued	valuing	to value
Vanish	vanished	vanished	vanishing	to vanish
Violate	violated	violated	violating	to violate
Vomit	vomited	vomited	vomiting	to vomit
Win	won	won	winning	to win
Weep	wept	wept	weeping	to weep
Wake	woke	waked	waking	to wake
Wear	wore	worn	wearing	to wear
Weave	wove	woven	weaving	to weave
Wash	washed	washed	washing	to wash
Wed	wedded	wedded	wedding	to wed
Wound	wounded	wounded	wounding	to wound
Water	watered	watered	watering	to water
Want	wanted	wanted	wanting	to want
Waste	wasted	wasted	wasting	to waste
Wave	waved	waved	waving	to wave
Weaken	weakened	weakened	wakening	to weaken
Weigh	weighed	weighed	weighing	to weigh
Wink	winked	winked	winking	to wink
Wipe	wiped	wiped	wiping	to wipe
Wire	wired	wired	wiring	to wire
Yawn	yawned	yawned	yawning	to yawn
Yield	yielded	yielded	yielding	to yield

(A) *Verb की I, II, III form के बारे में हम पूर्ण परिचित हैं। Verb की IV form (Present Participle Form) I form में ing लगाने से बनती है। Verb की V form (Infinitive) I form से पहले to लगाने से बनती है।*

(B) *यदि Verb के अन्त में ie आता है तो ie, y में बदल जाता है तथा फिर ing लगाने से उसकी IV Form बन जाती है। जैसे Die-Dying, Lie-Lying, और यदि Verb के अन्त में e आता है तो ing लगाते समय e हट जाता है जैसे Wire-Wiring, Shine-Shining.*

(C) *यदि Verb के अन्त में कोई व्यंजन (consonant) आए और उस consonant से पूर्व कोई short vowel भी हो तो ऐसी Verb की IV form बनाते समय वह consonant दो बार आता है; जैसे :*

Quarrel	*Quarrelling*	*Quit*	*Quitting*
Swim	*Swimming*	*Begin*	*Beginning*
Stop	*Stopping*	*Run*	*Running*
Occur	*Occurring*	*Vomit*	*Vomitting*

Present Tense

कार्य सम्पन्न होने की स्थिति; State of an action के अनुसार Present Tense को चार भागों में विभाजित किया गया है :

(1) Present Indefinite
(2) Present Continuous
(3) Present Perfect
(4) Present Perfect Continuous

Read the following sentences :

(1) वह खेलता है।	He plays.
(2) वह खेल रहा है।	He is playing.
(3) वह खेल चुका है।	He has played.
(4) वह तीन घण्टे से खेल रहा है।	He has been playing for three hours.

Sentence (1) Simple Present or Present Indefinite का वाक्य है।

Sentence (2) Present Continuous का वाक्य है।

Sentence (3) Present Perfect का वाक्य है।

Sentence (4) Present Perfect Continuous का वाक्य है।

Note : उपरोक्त वाक्यों में प्रयुक्त verbs: plays, playing, has played, has been playing कार्य की स्थिति (state of an action) को स्पष्ट करती हैं।

Present Indefinite Tense

Read the following sentences

(1) मैं खेलता हूँ।	I play.
(2) वह लिखता है।	He writes.
(3) सूरज पूरब में उगता है।	The Sun rises in the East.
(4) ट्रेन यहाँ आती है।	Here comes the train.
(5) वह सदा सच बोलता है।	He always speaks the truth.
(6) मैं रोता हूँ।	I weep.
(7) रमेश सुबह 6 बजे घूमने जाता है।	Ramesh goes for a walk at 6 A.M
(8) मेरे पिताजी सायं 7 बजे घर आते हैं।	My father comes home at 7 P.M
(9) हमारा कॉलेज जुलाई के महीनें में खुलता है।	Our college opens in the month of July.
(10) हम हर वर्ष शिमला जाते हैं।	We go to Shimla every year.

उपरोक्त सभी वाक्य Present Indefinite Tense के हैं। Present Indefinite Tense के वाक्यों का अंग्रेजी अनुवाद करते समय निम्न Sentence Structure प्रयुक्त होता है

Subject + V-I (s or es) + Object

वाक्य संख्या 2, 3, 4, 5, 7, 8, एवं 9 में verb के साथ s या es का प्रयोग हुआ है, क्योंकि इन वाक्यों में कर्ता (subject) ***Singular number, third person*** *है।*

Singular number का अर्थ है एकवचन अर्थात् जो एक से अधिक नहीं है। (जो plural नहीं है)

Third person का अर्थ है जिसके बारे में हम बात करते हैं। (I, we, you के अतिरिक्त)

Persons

I Person	II Person	III Person
I	You	He, She, It, Name
We		They, My friends etc.

Numbers

Singular Number	Plural Number	Singular Number	Plural Number
I	We	It	It
You	You	Brother	Brothers
She, He	They	Applicant	Applicants

I, Singular number है, लेकिन Third person नहीं है। इसी तरह They, Third person है लेकिन Singular number नहीं है। अत: इनके साथ verb में 's' या 'es' नहीं लगाया जाएगा।

Singular number, third person:

He, She, It, Name, My friend, My brother, His sister, his brother, My father etc.

कुछ महत्त्वपूर्ण बिन्दू

(1) Simple Present में सबसे महत्त्वपूर्ण बिन्दु है, जब Subject, singular number, third person है तो verb के साथ s या es जोड़ दिया जाता है।

Verb के साथ 'es' का प्रयोग कब किया जाएगा?

यदि Verb का अन्तिम अक्षर ss,o, z, x, ch, sh है तो Subject, singular number, third person के साथ 'es' जोड़ा जाता है। अन्य स्थिति में verb के साथ 's' जोड़ा जाता है:

(1) I go. — He goes.
(2) I kiss. — She kisses.
(3) We search.— He searches.
(4) They fetch. — She fetches.
(5) We clash. — He clashes.
(6) I quiz. — He quizzes.

अन्य सभी verb के साथ केवल 's' लगता है; जैसे:

(1) We play.— He plays.
(2) I pray.— He prays.
(3) You say.— He says.
(4) I pay.— He pays.

(2) जब Verb का अन्तिम अक्षर y है एवं इससे पूर्व का अक्षर व्यंजन (Consonant) है तो subject, singular number, third person के साथ Simple Present में y को ies में बदला जाता है। जैसे:

(1) They fly kites. — He flies kites.
(2) I try. — Sita tries.
(3) Girls cry. — Suman cries.
(4) I verify.— She verifies.

Negative and Interrogative Sentences

Present Indefinite के Negative एवं Interrogative Sentences का Structure निम्न होता है:

Negative **Subject + do/does not + V-I + Object**

Interrogative **Do/Does + Subject + V-I + Object ?**

1. *Negative व Interrogative वाक्यों में V-I के साथ 's' या 'es' नहीं लगाना चाहिए।*
2. *Does का प्रयोग Singular Number, third person, subject के साथ होता है।*

	Affirmative		Negative		Interrogative
(1)	I play chess.	—	I do not play chess.	—	Do I play chess?
(2)	He goes to office.	—	He does not go to office.	—	Does he go to office?
(3)	They write a lesson.	—	They do not write a lesson.	—	Do they write a lesson?
(4)	It rains.	—	It does not rain.	—	Does it rain?
(5)	We sing a song.	—	We do not sing a song.	—	Do we sing a song?

Interrogative-Negative Sentences

इस तरह के वाक्य, जिनमें प्रश्न के साथ-साथ नकारात्मकता भी हो, Interrogative Negative वाक्य कहलाते हैं। इस प्रकार के वाक्यों का Structure निम्न होता है :

Do/Does + Subject + Not + V-I + Object? ... (I)

Or **Don't/Doesn't + Subject + V-I + Object?** ... (II)

I-Structure लिखते समय उपयुक्त होता है एवं II-Structure बोलते समय उपयुक्त होता है, दोनों ही सही हैं।

Changing Affirmative to Interrogative Negative :

(a) He goes to market.	*Affirmative*
Does he not go to market?	*Interrogative Negative*
Doesn't he go to market?	*Interrogative Negative*
(b) I play football.	*Affirmative*
Do I not play football ?	*Interrogative Negative*
Don't I play football?	*Interrogative Negative*

(1) इस तरह के वाक्यों में भी V-I के साथ 's' या 'es' नहीं लगाना चाहिए।

(2) Doesn't or Does का प्रयोग जैसा पूर्व में भी बताया गया है, Singular number, third person- Subject के साथ किया जाता है।

Do not use 's' or 'es' with the verb in Negative and Interrogative sentences in Present Indefinite.

Use of Present Indefinite in Various Situations

(1) सर्वकालिक सत्य (Eternal Truths) एवं घटनाओं हेतु :

(a) The Sun rises in the East. (b) Birds fly.
(c) The Earth revolves round the Sun. (d) The Sun sets in the West.

(2) प्रतिदिन सामान्य रूप से किए जाने वाले कार्यों के लिए :

(a) I get up early in the morning. (b) My mother goes to temple everyday.
(c) My father goes to office at 10 A.M. (d) He plays football daily.

(3) Direct Narration में जब Reporting Verb, Simple Present Tense में हो तो, Reported Speech में कोई भी Tense होने पर, उसमें कोई परिवर्तन नहीं होता है। जैसे :

(a) Ram tells that Shyam was playing cricket. (b) He says that it will rain tomorrow.

(4) कुछ Verb का प्रयोग सामान्यतः Present Indefinite में ही करना उचित रहता है। इस सम्बन्ध में Present Continuous में विस्तृत रूप से बताया गया है। इस तरह की Verb हैं : see, hear, think, have, look, appear, seem, belong etc.

(a) I hear, they are going to USA next year. (b) I see her enjoying the picnic.

(5) TV एवं Radio पर Commentaries में Simple Present Tense का प्रयोग किया जाता है। जैसे :
Raju passes the ball to Saluja, Saluja passes it to Sonu, who heads it passes the goalkeeper and scores!

(6) Here एवं There से शुरू होने वाले exclamatory वाक्यों में भी Simple Present Tense का प्रयोग किया जाता है। जैसे :

(a) There she lives! (b) There goes the bell!
(c) Here comes the train! (d) Here she comes!

(7) Newspapers की Headlines में भी Simple Present का ही प्रयोग, सामान्यतया किया जाता है। जैसे :
Thief Escapes, Cricket Match Draws, Peace Talks Fail.

(8) किसी Planned Future Action हेतु भी Present Indefinite का प्रयोग किया जाता है। जैसे :

(a) Our college opens in the month of July.
(b) He reaches here tomorrow.
(c) We leave America at 10:30 next Monday.
(d) Mr. Sharma retires on 31st December.

(9) Simple Present Tense का प्रयोग always, never, occasionally, sometimes, often, usually, every week, on Sundays, twice a year, every year etc. के साथ किया जाता है। जैसे :

(a) She always speaks the truth.
(b) He sometimes goes for a walk.
(c) He never tells a lie.
(d) Rahim often comes late.
(e) He occasionally visits church.
(f) They go to church on Sundays.

(10) Whenever एवं When के साथ Simple Present Tense का प्रयोग किया जाता है। जैसे :

(a) Whenever it rains, the roof leaks.
(b) When you open the window, a light goes on.
(c) Whenever he comes, he stays here for a day.
(d) When he comes here, he brings fruits.

(11) जब main verb, future में हो तो Conditional sentences में if, till, as soon as, when, unless, before, until, even if, in case, as के बाद Present Indefinite का प्रयोग किया जाता है। जैसे :

(a) We shall wait till she arrives.
(b) I shall not go there even if it rains.
(c) I shall go to market, if it rains.
(d) I shall go to Jaipur in case she asks me.
(e) We shall move as soon as the taxi arrives.
(f) I shall start my work as he comes.
(g) Unless he works hard, he will not pass.
(h) I shall wait until it strikes seven.
(i) When he comes, I shall give him a gift.
(j) Before he comes, I shall finish my work.

This is very important point. Students should learn it properly.

(12) Quotations एवं किसी के कथन को Simple Present में लिखा जाता है। जैसे :

(a) Our teacher says, "The sun rises in the east."
(b) Shakespeare says, "Neither a borrower nor a lender be."
(c) Ram says, "Birds fly and fish swim."

Present Continuous Tense

Present Continuous को Present Progressive or Present Imperfect भी कहा जाता है।

Read the following sentences :

(1) मैं पढ़ा रहा हूँ।	I am teaching.
(2) वह पढ़ रहा है।	He is reading.
(3) हम बाजार जा रहे हैं।	We are going to market.
(4) राम खेल रहा है।	Ram is playing.
(5) सरला गा रही है।	Sarla is singing.
(6) तुम लिख रहे हो।	You are writing.
(7) हम गा रहे हैं।	We are singing.
(8) वर्षा हो रही है।	It is raining.
(9) छात्र लड़ रहे हैं।	The students are fighting.
(10) बच्चे शोर मचा रहे हैं।	The children are making a noise.

इस तरह के वाक्य Present Continuous के अन्तर्गत आते हैं। सामान्यतया इस तरह के वाक्यों के अन्त में रहा, रहे, रही है, जैसे शब्द आते हैं। जब कोई कार्य वर्तमान में जारी या लगातार Regular process में सम्पन्न हो रहा होता है, तो ऐसे वाक्य Present Continuous Tense के वाक्य माने जाते हैं। इस तरह के वाक्यों का अंग्रेजी अनुवाद करने हेतु निम्न Sentence Structure प्रयुक्त होता है।

Subject + is / am / are + V-I + ing + object

सामान्य नियम : Present Continuous के वाक्यों में Subject के साथ helping verb, is/am/are का प्रयोग करते हैं तथा verb की I form के साथ ing (IV form/V-4) लगाते हैं।

He, She, It, Name, (Singular number, third person) के साथ 'is' तथा I के साथ 'am' एवं We, You, They, (plural) के साथ 'are' helping verb का प्रयोग किया जाता है।

Negative and Interrogative Sentences

Present Continuous एवं Negative एवं Interrogative Sentences का Structure निम्न होता है :

Negative **Subject + is/are/am + not + V-IV + Object.**

Interrogative **Is/are/am + Subject + V-IV + Object?**

Affirmative	Negative	Interrogative
(1) I am writing.	I am not writing.	Am I writing?
(2) They are playing.	They are not playing.	Are they playing?
(3) He is watching T.V.	He is not watching T.V.	Is he watching T.V?
(4) She is singing a song.	She is not singing a song.	Is she singing a song?
(5) I am reading.	I am not reading.	Am I reading?

Interrogative-Negative Sentences

Interrogative-Negative Sentences का structure निम्न होता है :

Is/are/am + Subject + not + V-IV + Object ?

Or **Isn't/Aren't + Subject + V-IV + Object ?**

Note : Am I not की जगह Interrogative Negative में Aren't I लिखा जाता है।

Changing Affirmative to Interrogative Negative :

Affirmative	Interrogative Negative
(1) I am going to hospital.	Am I not going to hospital? Aren't I going to hospital?
(2) It is raining.	Is it not raining? Isn't it raining?

Use of Present Continuous Tense in various situations

(1) ऐसे कार्य जो वर्तमान में जारी हैं (at the time of speaking) के लिए :

(a) He is writing a letter.
(b) He is playing football.
(c) Ramesh is teaching in the class.
(d) Kuku is reading a book.

(2) ऐसे कार्यों हेतु भी Present Continuous का प्रयोग किया जाता है जो at the time of speaking नहीं हो रहे होते हैं, लेकिन Regular Process में लगातार हो रहे हैं। जैसे :

(a) He is writing a novel now-a-days.
(b) Sita is learning English Grammar now-a-days.
(c) I am serving in this office.
(d) Harish is reading in class XII.

(3) Near future में सम्पन्न होने वाले planned or arranged action हेतु भी Present Continuous का प्रयोग किया जाता है। जैसे :

(a) They are going to Delhi tomorrow.
(b) He is coming tomorrow.
(c) We are meeting today in the evening.
(d) She is coming by 7 A.M. train on Monday.

ये सभी वाक्य, कार्य का होना future time में व्यक्त करते हैं, लेकिन English Grammar के नियमानुसार, इनको Present Continuous में माना जाता है।

(4) Always, continually, constantly, forever के साथ Present Continuous का प्रयोग ऐसे कार्य हेतु किया जाता है जो व्यक्ति आदतन, दूसरों की इच्छा के विपरीत frequently करता है। जैसे :

(a) She is always complaining.
(b) You are forever finding faults with others.
(c) His wife is continually crying these days.
(d) They are constantly disturbing us.

(5) Stative and Dynamic Verbs—कुछ verbs का प्रयोग सामान्य स्थिति में Continuous form में नहीं किया जाता है। इस तरह की Verbs को Stative Verbs कहा जाता है। Stative का अर्थ है fixed, अर्थात् स्थायी। इस तरह की Verb एक Permanent कार्य को, लगातार बिना प्रयास, के स्थायी रूप में होने वाले कार्य को व्यक्त करती है। इस तरह की Verbs का प्रयोग Continuous form में नहीं किया जाता है। इन Verbs को Non-Conclusive Verbs भी कहते हैं।

Stative या Nonconclusive Verbs को पाँच भागों में वर्गीकृत किया जा सकता है :

(a) **Verbs of Perception :** See, hear, smell, taste, feel etc. जब इन Verbs का प्रयोग, बिना किसी विशेष प्रयास के, सामान्य स्थिति में होता है तो इन्हें Present Simple में ही प्रयोग किया जाना उचित है। खुली आँख से स्वत: ही देखने (see) का कार्य होता है, उसी तरह नाक, कान, जीभ (smell, hear, taste हेतु) का उपयोग व्यक्ति स्वत: ही करता है। स्पर्श (feel) भी एक स्वत: होने वाला कार्य है। लेकिन अगर इन verbs का प्रयोग किसी विशेष उद्देश्य हेतु किया जाता है तो इनको continuous में प्रयोग किया जा सकता है। इन verbs में notice, recognise भी शामिल कर लिए गए हैं।

(b) **Verbs of Appearance :** Look, resemble, seem, appear etc.

(c) **Verbs of Emotions :** Want, desire, wish, hate, hope, like, refuse, believe, doubt, loathe, mind, care, detest, adore, appreciate, admire, fear, expect etc.

(d) **Verbs of Thinking :** Think, suppose, agree, consider, trust, remember, forget, know, understand, perceive, realise, recollect etc.

(e) **Verbs of Possession :** Belong, owe, own, possess, contain, have etc.

ये verbs, stative verbs या Non-conclusive verbs भी कहलाती हैं। इनका प्रयोग सामान्य अर्थ में Present Continuous में करना गलत है। इनका प्रयोग सामान्यतया Simple Present में किया जाता है। *निम्न वाक्यों को देखे :*

Incorrect	**Correct**
(1) We are seeing with our eyes.	(1) We see with our eyes.
(2) Are you hearing a strange noise?	(2) Do you hear a strange noise?
(3) We are smelling with our nose.	(3) We smell with our nose.
(4) I am feeling you are wrong.	(4) I feel you are wrong.
(5) The water is feeling cold.	(5) The water feels cold.
(6) The coffee is tasting bitter.	(6) The coffee tastes bitter.
(7) How much am I owing you?	(7) How much do I owe you?
(8) I am hating it.	(8) I hate it.
(9) I am having a car.	(9) I have a car.
(10) I am thinking.	(10) I think.
(11) I am understanding.	(11) I understand.
(12) The book belonging to me.	(12) The book belongs to me.
(13) He is resembling his brother.	(13) He resembles his brother.
(14) I am believing in God.	(14) I believe in God.
(15) I am loving her.	(15) I love her.
(16) I am remembering him.	(16) I remember him.
(17) Are you smelling some thing burning?	(17) Do you smell something burning?

(18) The milk is tasting sour.	(18) The milk taste sour.
(19) This is feeling like silk.	(19) This feels like silk.
(20) I am differing from you on this point.	(20) I differ from you on this point.

लेकिन निम्न स्थितियों में इन Verb का प्रयोग Continuous में करना सही है :

(1) The Session Judge is hearing our case. (2) We are thinking of going to USA next year.
(3) He is minding (looking after) the children, while his wife is away.
(4) I am seeing my lawyer today.
(5) I am having some difficulties with this puzzle.
(6) Are you forgetting your manners? (A reminder)
(7) The dog is smelling the packet of food.
(8) She is tasting the sauce to find out whether it is tasteful or not.
(9) The doctor is feeling the pulse of the patient.
(10) He is looking for his glasses.

Dynamic Verbs : Dynamic का अर्थ होता है क्रियाशील, गतिशील। यह Stative का विपरीतार्थक शब्द है। जब कोई Verb; Temporary, Momentary या Dynamic कार्य हेतु प्रयुक्त होती है तो वह Dynamic Verb कहलाती है। जैसे: He is swimming., She is going., Ram is coming.

Important

Stative Verbs का प्रयोग, किन्हीं अवस्था में जब Continuous form में होता है, तो ये Dynamic Verb बन जाती है। जब इनका प्रयोग Temporary / Dynamic कार्य हेतु होता है। जैसे :

(1) We see with our eyes.	(Permanent-Stative verb see)
(2) I am seeing the teacher tomorrow.	(Temporary-Dynamic verb)
(3) I have a maruti car.	(Permanent-Stative verb have)
(4) I am having a nice time.	(Temporary-Dynamic verb)
(5) This apple tastes sweet.	(Permanent-Stative verb taste)
(6) She is tasting an apple.	(Temporary-Dynamic verb)
(7) We smell with our nose.	(Permanent-Stative verb smell)
(8) He is smelling flower.	(Temporary-Dynamic verb)
(9) I forget what she said.	(Permanent-Stative verb forget)
(10) I am forgetting her name.	(Temporary-Dynamic verb)

Present Perfect Tense

सामान्यतया ऐसे वाक्य, जो वर्तमान में कार्य का पूर्ण रूप होना व्यक्त करते हैं, में Present Perfect का प्रयोग किया जाता है।

Read the following sentences :

(1) वह जा चुका है।	He has gone.
(2) ट्रेन आ चुकी है।	The train has arrived.
(3) मैं नहा चुका हूँ	I have taken bath.
(4) वह सो चुकी है।	She has slept.
(5) सुरेश अभी-अभी आया है।	Suresh has just arrived.
(6) अभी-अभी 7 बजे हैं।	It has just struck seven.
(7) मैंने अपना प्रोजेक्ट पूर्ण कर लिया है।	I have completed my project.
(8) महेश ने अपना कार्य पूर्ण कर लिया है।	Mahesh has completed his work.
(9) अध्यापक ने खाना खा लिया है।	The teacher has taken food.
(10) महेश अभी-अभी आया है।	Mahesh has just arrived.

इस तरह के वाक्य, जिनमें कार्य का पूर्ण होना वर्तमान समय में व्यक्त होता है, में Present Perfect का प्रयोग किया जाता है।

Present Perfect : वर्तमान + पूर्ण अर्थात् कार्य का वर्तमान में पूर्ण होना।

इस तरह के वाक्यों का अंग्रेजी अनुवाद करने के लिए निम्न Structure का प्रयोग किया जाता है :

Subject + has / have + V-III + Object.

Helping Verb, 'has' का प्रयोग, Singular number third person के साथ होता है, जैसे : He, she, it, name, my brother, my mother etc. जबकि 'have' का प्रयोग सभी *जैसे* I, You, We, They, or any plural subject के साथ किया जाता है। इसमें Verb की III form का प्रयोग किया जाता है।

Negative and Interrogative Sentences

Present Perfect के Negative एवं Interrogative Sentences का Structure निम्न होता है :

Negative — **Subject + has/have + not + V-III + Object.**

Interrogative — **Has/have + Subject + V-III + Object ?**

Affirmative	**Negative**	**Interrogative**
(1) I have taken lunch.	I have not taken lunch.	Have I taken lunch?
(2) They have gone.	They have not gone.	Have they gone?
(3) Sita has arrived.	Sita has not arrived.	Has Sita arrived?
(4) We have played.	We have not played.	Have we played?
(5) He has gone.	He has not gone.	Has he gone?

सामान्य नियम:

(i) Negative वाक्यों में Helping verb, has/have के बाद not लगाया जाता है। शेष वाक्य के structure में कोई अन्तर नहीं आता है।

(ii) Interrogative वाक्यों में Helping verb, have/has का प्रयोग subject से पहले किया जाता है। शेष वाक्य के structure में कोई परिवर्तन नहीं होता है।

Interrogative-Negative Sentences

Interrogative-Negative sentences का Structure निम्न होता है:

Has/have + Subject + not + V-III + Object ? ***Or***

Hasn't/haven't + Subject + V-III + Object ?

Interrogative-Negative वाक्यों में have/has को Subject से पूर्व रखकर, not को Subject के बाद रखकर वाक्य बनाए जाते हैं या दूसरे Structure के अनुसार Haven't/hasn't को Subject से पहले रखकर संकुचित किया जा सकता है। जैसे:

Affirmative	**Interrogative Negative**
(1) He has taken food.	Has he not taken food? Hasn't he taken food?
(2) I have done my work.	Have I not done my work? Haven't I done my work?

Important

Present Perfect Tense की विशेषता यह है कि इसमें कार्य तो पूर्ण हो चुका होता है लेकिन हम कार्य का प्रभाव वर्तमान में महसूस करते हैं। यह एक तरह से Past एवं Present tense का मिश्रित रूप है। इस Tense से ऐसे कार्य का बोध होता है जो भूतकाल में सम्पन्न हो चुका है, लेकिन वर्तमान परिस्थितियों में भूतकाल में पूर्ण हुए कार्य के सम्बन्ध में कुछ कहते है।

निम्न वाक्यों को ध्यानपूर्वक देखें:

(1) I have completed my work. (now I am ready to accompany you.)
(2) He has lost his pen. (so he is sad.)
(3) He has eaten all the apples. (so no more is available for you.)

Use of Present Perfect Tense in various situations

(1) जब कोई कार्य भूतकाल में शुरू हुआ हो एवं अब भी जारी हो तो Present Perfect का प्रयोग किया जा सकता है। ऐसी स्थिति में Present Perfect के साथ since/for का प्रयोग किया जाता है। जैसे :

(a) He has lived in this house for five years. (He is still living.)
(b) He has taught in this college for three years. (He is still teaching.)
(c) I have known him for three years. (I know him today also.)
(d) She has been ill since Monday. (She is still ill.)

उपरोक्त सभी वाक्य यह प्रदर्शित करते हैं कि कार्य भूतकाल में शुरू हुआ एवं अभी भी जारी है।

Important

जो कार्य Past में शुरू हुआ एवं अभी भी चल रहा है, उसके लिए दो Tenses प्रयोग किए जा सकते हैं।

Present Perfect Continuous एवं (B) Present Perfect कुछ Verb जिनका प्रयोग Continuous form में नहीं किया जा सकता है, उनके लिए Present Perfect का प्रयोग करना उचित रहता है। ऐसी Verb के बारे में पूर्व में Present Continuous के अन्तर्गत बताया गया है।

I have been knowing her for three years. *Incorrect*
I have known her for three years. *Correct*

---

(2) Present Perfect का प्रयोग ऐसी स्थिति में भी किया जाता है जिनमें कार्य के पूर्ण होने का समय नहीं दिया गया हो एवं कार्य पूर्ण हुआ है या नहीं, इसका पता नहीं चलता है। जैसे :

(a) Have you read 'Hamlet'?
(b) Have you ever been to America?
(c) He has been to America.
(d) He has gone to America.
(e) Have you ever been up in a balloon ?
(f) I've never known him to accept bribe.

(See the difference between sentence (c) and (d) : He has been to America, indicates that he once visited America, but he is not in America now. He has gone to America, means that he is in America at the moment or on his way to America.)

(3) Present Perfect का प्रयोग ऐसी स्थिति हेतु भी किया जाता है जिनमें कार्य अभी-अभी (वर्तमान में) पूर्ण होता है। जैसे :

(a) It has just struck seven.
(b) The bus has just arrived.
(c) He has just gone out.
(d) She has just completed her work.
(e) Tom has just rung up.
(f) The cat has just had kittens.

(4) Present Perfect का प्रयोग ऐसे कार्यों हेतु भी किया जाता है जो Past में पूर्ण हो चुके हैं लेकिन हमें उन कार्यों का प्रभाव वर्तमान में महसूस हो रहा है। जैसे :

(a) The lift has broken down. (So we have to use the stairs.)
(b) I have completed my work. (Now I am free.)
(c) He hasn't arrived yet. (So we are still waiting for him.)
(d) He has eaten all the fruits. (Now no more available for you.)

(5) Yet, always, never, already, upto now, today, often, several times, lately, recently, so far, ever का प्रयोग Present Perfect में किया जाता है। जैसे :

(a) Have the children gone to school yet?
(b) Has Ramesh left yet?
(c) I have already visited Agra.
(d) I have already seen this film.
(e) Have you ever been to Russia?
(f) I have never been down a mine.

(g) I have often been there.
(h) I have read this novel several times.
(i) Have you done much work this week?
(j) I haven't seen her today.
(k) Hari hasn't come to college this morning
(l) She hasn't been well lately.
(m) He has been here recently. (lately/recently means at any time during the last week/month etc. When recently used with Past tense it means a short time ago.)
(n) Upto the present every thing has been straight forward.
(o) We have no trouble so far.
(p) Have you ever fallen off horse?
(q) They have always answered my letters.
(r) I have never been late for work.

(6) निम्न प्रकार के Sentences Structure में भी Present Perfect का प्रयोग किया जाता है। जैसे :

This/It/That is the first/second/third/only/best/worst etc.

(a) This is the best whisky, I have ever drunk.
(b) This is the easiest job, I have ever had.
(c) This is the worst novel, I have ever read.
(d) This is the only book he has written.
(e) This is the first time that I have heard her song.
(f) This is the third time you have asked me the same question.
(g) That is the fifth banana you have eaten so far.

(7) 'It is' के साथ Present Perfect का प्रयोग Sentences Structure में किया जा सकता है। जैसे :

(a) It is three years since I have seen her.
(b) It is two months since I have smoked a cigarette.

(8) Present Perfect का प्रयोग सामान्यतया पत्र-लेखन में किया जाता है। जैसे :

(a) We have carefully considered your request and have decided to take the action as per following.
(b) I am sorry I haven't written you before as I have been very busy lately as my father has been away.

(9) किसी Past Action हेतु वार्तालाप, सामान्यतया Present Perfect में शुरू किया जाता है। जैसे :

(a) Where have you been? — I've been to the cinema.
(b) What have you bought? — I have bought one saree only.

(10) वाक्य में Conditional Clause के साथ Present Perfect Tense का प्रयोग Future Time को व्यक्त करता है। जैसे:

(a) I can't decide until I've discussed the matter with my wife.
(b) I will come as soon as I've finished writing this letter.

The Present and Present Perfect Tenses may indicate future time in temporal and conditional clauses. **Guide to patterns and usage in English page 98 - A. S. Hornby.**

Important

यद्यपि Present Perfect Tense, Past एवं Present का मिश्रण है, तथापि यह ध्यान रखें कि Present Perfect Tense में Past time के adverbs जैसे last night/ last year/month/week, ago, short while ago, yesterday, day before yesterday इत्यादि का प्रयोग नहीं किया जाता है।

(a) He has gone to Jaipur last night. *Incorrect*
He went to Jaipur last night. *Correct*
(b) Ram has arrived shortwhile ago. *Incorrect*
Ram arrived shortwhile ago. *Correct*
Past time के adverbs के साथ Simple Past का प्रयोग किया जाता है।

Present Perfect Continuous Tense

ऐसे कार्यों हेतु जो कुछ समय पूर्व से लगातार जारी हैं एवं अभी तक पूर्ण नहीं हुए हैं, के लिए Present Perfect Continuous का प्रयोग किया जाता है।

Read the following sentences :

(1) वह दो घण्टे से खेल रहा है।	He has been playing for two hours.
(2) वह दो बजे से खेल रहा है।	He has been playing since 2 O'clock.
(3) सीता सुबह से तुम्हारा इन्तजार कर रही है।	Sita has been waiting for you since morning.
(4) राम एक माह से किताब लिख रहा है।	Ram has been writing a book for a month.
(5) रमेश 1997 से यहाँ रह रहा है।	Ramesh has been living here since 1997.
(6) सरला जून से इस कॉलेज में पढ़ा रही है।	Sarla has been teaching in this college since June.
(7) वर्षा बहुत देर से हो रही है।	It has been raining for a long time.
(8) वे सुबह से टीवी देख रहे हैं।	They have been watching TV since morning.
(9) मैं दो घण्टे से पढ़ रहा हूँ।	I have been studying for two hours.
(10) हेमा 3 घण्टे से नाच रही है।	Hema has been dancing for three hours.

इस तरह के वाक्यों का अंग्रेजी में अनुवाद करने के लिए निम्न Sentence Structure का प्रयोग किया जाता है :

Subject + has/have been + V-IV + Object + since/for + ...

इस Structure के अनुसार उपरोक्त वाक्यों का अंग्रेजी में अनुवाद करने से पूर्व निम्न बिन्दूओं पर ध्यान दें :

(A) **For/Since :** Present Perfect Continuous में समय हेतु for, since का प्रयोग किया जाता है। for का प्रयोग Period of time जैसे : for two hours, for 15 days, for 10 days, for a long time, for a long period, for some time, हेतु किया जाता है, for अवधि को बताता है। जबकि Since का प्रयोग Point of time जैसे since 2 O' clock, since morning, since Monday, since January, since 1997, since last night etc. हेतु किया जाता है।

(B) Has been का प्रयोग singular number, third person, (He, She, It, Name, My brother, My friend etc.) के साथ तथा Have been का प्रयोग I एवं II person तथा Plural Subject के साथ किया जाता है।

Negative and Interrogative Sentences

Present Perfect Continuous के Negative एवं Interrogative Sentences का Structure निम्न होता है-

Negative —Subject + has/have + not + been + V-IV + Object + since/for + ...

Interrogative — Has/have + subject + been + V-IV + Object + since/for + ... ?

Read the following sentences :

(1) I have been swimming for two hours.	*Affirmative*
I have not been swimming for two hours.	*Negative*
Have I been swimming for two hours?	*Interrogative*
(2) He has been playing since morning.	*Affirmative*
He has not been playing since morning.	*Negative*
Has he been playing since morning ?	*Interrogative*
(3) It has been raining since morning.	*Affirmative*
It has not been raining since morning.	*Negative*
Has it been raining since morning?	*Interrogative*
(4) They have been singing since 2 O'clock.	*Affirmative*
They have not been singing since two O'clock.	*Negative*
Have they been singing since 2 O'clock?	*Interrogative*

(5) She has been cooking for two hours. *Affirmative*
She has not been cooking for two hours. *Negative*
Has she been cooking for two hours? *Interrogative*

Interrogative-Negative Sentences

Interrogative Negative Sentences का Structure निम्न होता है :

Has/have + Subject + not + been + V-IV + Object + since/for + ...?

Or

Hasn't/haven't + Subject + been +V-IV + Object + since/for + ...?

Affirmative Sentences	**Interrogative-Negative**
(1) He has been playing for two hours.	Has he not been playing for two hours? Hasn't he been playing for two hours?
(2) They have been making a noise since morning.	Have they not been making a noise since morning? Haven't they been making a noise since morning?

Use of Present Perfect Continuous Tense in various situations

(1) जब कोई कार्य भूतकाल से लगातार होता रहा है एवं अभी भी जारी है तो ऐसी स्थिति में Present perfect Continuous का प्रयोग किया जाता है। जैसे :

(a) वह दो घण्टे से पढ़ाई कर रहा है। He has been studying for two hours.
(b) वह दो माह से राम के साथ रहता है/रह रहा है। He has been living with Ram for two months.
(c) वह दो दिन से सो रहा है। He has been sleeping for two days.
(d) सीता सोमवार से उसका इन्तजार कर रही है। Sita has been waiting for him since Monday.

Difference between Present Continuous and Present Perfect Continuous

Read the following sentences :

	Present Continuous	**Present Perfect Continuous**
(a)	वह खेल रहा है।	वह दो बजे से खेल रहा है।
(b)	रमेश पढ़ रहा है।	रमेश दो घण्टे से पढ़ रहा है।
(c)	वर्षा हो रही है।	वर्षा सुबह से हो रही है।

Present Continuous में कार्य लगातार जारी है लेकिन वाक्य से यह पता नहीं चलता कि कार्य कब से जारी है या कितनी अवधि से जारी है। जबकि Present Perfect Continuous में यह स्पष्ट हो जाता है कि कार्य कब से जारी है या कुछ अवधि से जारी है। छात्रों को इस अन्तर को स्पष्ट रूप से समझ लेना चाहिए। अधिकांश छात्र Present Perfect Continuous के वाक्यों की अंग्रेजी निम्न प्रकार से बनाते हैं :

He is playing for two hours. *Incorrect*
He has been playing for two hours. *Correct*

Comparison of the Present Perfect and Present Perfect Continuous

यदि कोई कार्य Past में शुरू हुआ एवं अभी भी जारी है (पूर्ण नहीं हुआ है) तो उसके लिए Present Perfect या Present Perfect Continuous का प्रयोग किया जा सकता है। जैसे :

(a) How long have you learnt Hindi? How long have you been learning Hindi?
(b) She has slept for three hours. She has been sleeping for three hours.
(c) It has rained for a long time. It has been raining for a long time.

लेकिन कुछ Verbs (जैसा Present Continuous के अध्याय में स्पष्ट किया गया है) का प्रयोग Continuous form में नहीं किया जा सकता है, ऐसी Verbs के साथ Present Perfect का ही प्रयोग किया जा सकता है। जैसे :

(a) How long have you known her?

(b) He has been in hospital since Monday.

(2) Present Perfect Tense द्वारा व्यक्त किए गए repeated actions को Present Perfect Continuous form में भी बताया जा सकता है। जैसे :

(a) I have written ten letters since morning.
I have been writing letters since morning.

(b) I have knocked several times. I don't think anyone's in.
I have been knocking, I don't think anyone's in.

(In general, Present Perfect Continuous expresses an action which is apparently uninterrupted.)

See the difference :

(a) I have polished the car. (Means that this job has been completed)

(b) I have been polishing the car. (Means this is how I have spent the last hour. It does not necessarily means that the job is completed.

See more sentences :

(1) She has been taking tuitions this year.
(इसका अर्थ है कि वह लगातार वर्ष के शुरू से tuitions कर रही है, वर्तमान में भी जारी है।)

(2) I have been reading this novel all the day.
(इसका अर्थ हुआ कि मैं सारे दिन इस novel को पढ़ता रहा हूँ, कार्य पूर्ण नहीं हुआ है।)

(3) He has been working late every evening this week.
(It implies that he has been working late this week and will perhaps do so for the rest of the week.)

(4) Please excuse my dirty clothes. I have been cleaning the car.
(I have cleaned the car. Now it is fit to use.)

There is no clear line of division between the use of the Present Perfect and the Present Perfect Progressive, but the examples and the notes to them may give some guidelines.

Past Tense

कार्य की अवस्था के अनुसार Past Tense को चार भागों में वर्गीकृत किया गया है :

(1) **Past Indefinite** सीता ने गाना गाया। (Sita sang a song)

(2) **Past Continuous** सीता गाना गा रही थी। (Sita was singing a song.)

(3) **Past Perfect** सीता गाना गा चुकी थी। (Sita had sung a song.)

(4) **Past Perfect Continuous** स्शीता 9 बजे से गाना गा रही थी। (Sita had been singing a song since 9 O'clock.)

उपरोक्त चारों वाक्य Past Tense के हैं, लेकिन कार्य की अवस्था के अनुसार ये Past Tense की अलग-अलग श्रेणियों को स्पष्ट करते हैं।

Past Indefinite Tense

Past Indefinite or Past Simple का प्रयोग ऐसे वाक्यों में होता है, जिनमें भूतकाल में कार्य का पूर्ण होना अथवा सम्पन्न होना बताया गया हो।

Read the following sentences :

(1) सीता ने राम को पत्र लिखा	Sita wrote a letter to Ram.
(2) वे फुटबॉल खेले।	They played football.
(3) रविशंकर ने एक T.V. खरीदा।	Ravi Shankar purchased a T.V.
(4) कल वर्षा हुई थी।	It rained yesterday.
(5) कल वह जयपुर गया।	He went to Jaipur yesterday.
(6) साक्षी ने अपने कपड़े धोए।	Sakshi washed her clothes.
(7) मैंने एक किताब लिखी।	I wrote a book.
(8) वह कल यहाँ आया।	He came here yesterday.
(9) रहीम ने ₹100 दान दिए।	Rahim donated one hundred rupees.
(10) मैंने उसकी सहायता की।	I helped her.

इस तरह के वाक्यों का अंग्रेजी में अनुवाद करने के लिए निम्न Sentence Structure का प्रयोग किया जाता है :

Subject + V-II + Object

Negative and Interrogative Sentences

Past Indefinite के Negative एवं Interrogative Sentences का Structure निम्न होता है:

Negative — Subject + did not + V-I + Object.
Interrogative — Did + Subject + V-I + Object?

	Affirmative	Negative	Interrogative
(1)	He wrote.	He did not write.	Did he write?
(2)	She went.	She did not go.	Did she go?
(3)	They played.	They did not play.	Did they play?
(4)	Ram abused.	Ram did not abuse.	Did Ram abuse?
(5)	Radha made a mistake.	Radha did not make a mistake.	Did Radha make a mistake?

Interrogative-Negative Sentences

Interrogative-Negative Sentences का Structure निम्न होता है

Did + Subject + not + V-I + Object ? ***Or***

Didn't + Subject + V-I + Object ?

	Affirmative	Interrogative-Negative
(1)	He watched T.V.	Did he not watch T.V.?
		Didn't he watch T.V.?
(2)	He went to market.	Did he not go to market?
		Didn't he go to market?

Past Indefinite के वाक्यों को जब Negative या Interrogative या Interrogative Negative में बदलते हैं तो Verb की first form का प्रयोग होता है।

Use of Past Indefinite Tense in various situations

(1) ऐसे कार्य जो भूतकाल (Past time) में पूर्ण हो गए हों, उनमें सामान्यतया कार्य पूर्ण होने का एक definite time (yesterday, last year etc.) का पता चलता है। जैसे :

(a) An accident took place yesterday.
(b) I wrote a letter day before yesterday.
(c) He came last night.
(d) She telephoned me last night.

(2) ऐसे कार्य (जिनमें कार्य पूर्ण होने का समय नहीं दिया गया हो) जो भूतकाल में सम्पन्न/पूर्ण हो गए। जैसे :

(a) He went to market.
(b) I donated five thousand rupees.
(c) She washed her clothes.
(d) Ramesh bought a pen.

(3) भूतकाल की आदत को व्यक्त करने हेतु भी Simple Past का प्रयोग किया जाता है। जैसे :

(a) He always carried this bag.
(b) She never went to church.
(c) She always asked for a cup of tea.
(d) He never missed the train.

Past की आदत बताने के लिए 'used to' का भी प्रयोग किया जाता है। इसको विस्तृत रूप से, 'Modals' के अध्याय में स्पष्ट किया गया है।

(a) He used to smoke ten cigarettes daily. (He does not smoke now.)
(b) He used to walk in the morning. (He does not walk now.)

(4) Direct Narration में यदि Reporting Verb, Past Tense में हो तथा Reported Speech में Present Indefinite हो तो ऐसे वाक्यों को Indirect में परिवर्तित करते समय, Present Indefinite को Past Indefinite में बदला जाता है। जैसे:

(a) He said, "I go to market." He said that he went to market.
(b) Ram said to Sita, "Laxman goes into the forest". Ram told Sita that Laxman went into the forest.

(5) Conditional sentences में भी if के साथ Past Indefinite का प्रयोग किया जाता है। जैसे :

(a) If I had a map I would give it to her. (But I haven't a map. The meaning is 'Present.')
(b) If he tried to blackmail me, I would inform you.
(But I don't expect that he will try to blackmail me. The meaning here is 'Future'.)

Grammar के अनुसार उपरोक्त वाक्यों में Verb की Second Form का प्रयोग किया जाता है। अत: ये Past के वाक्य दिखाई देते हैं। वास्तविकता में पहला वाक्य वर्तमान (Present) को तथा दूसरा वाक्य भविष्य (Future) को व्यक्त करता है।

(6) जब दो कार्य sequence में एक के बाद दूसरा तुरन्त समाप्त हो जाता है तो Past Indefinite का प्रयोग किया जाता है। ऐसे वाक्यों में सामान्यतया before, conjunction का प्रयोग होता है। जैसे :

(a) He switched on the light before he opened the door.
(b) The train started just before I reached the station.
(c) He changed his dress before he went to bed.
(d) She switched off the light before he locked the door.

(7) जब दो घटना साथ-साथ घटित होती हैं तब भी Past Indefinite का प्रयोग किया जाता है। जैसे :

(a) When the queen entered the hall, the orchestra played the National Anthem.
(b) When the P.M. entered the meeting room, all congratulated him.

(8) Wish एवं If only के साथ Simple Past का प्रयोग एक Unreal past को व्यक्त करता है एवं Present स्थिति को स्पष्ट करता है। जैसे :

(a) I wish I were a millionaire. (I am not a millionaire.)
(b) I wish I knew her. (I don't know her.)
(c) If only I knew her. (I don't know her.)
(d) If only he allowed me to deliver a lecture. (He doesn't allow me.)

(9) निम्न Structure में भी Simple Past का प्रयोग एक Unreal Past को व्यक्त करता है तथा Present स्थिति (Present Time Situation) को स्पष्ट करता है। जैसे :

(a) It is time we went home. (It is time for us to go home.)
(b) It is time you finished. (It is time for you to finish.)
(c) It is high time we left. (It is proper time for us to leave.)
(d) 11 O'clock ! it is time you went home. (It is time for you to go home.)

(10) Would rather का प्रयोग निम्न Structure में Past Tense के साथ Preference व्यक्त करता है

Subject + would rather+Subject + Past Tense

We can use 'would rather' to say that one person would prefer another or others to do something.
"Practical English Usage - page 484 Michael Swan'

अर्थात् would rather का इस Sentence Structure में प्रयोग अन्य व्यक्ति/व्यक्तियों द्वारा कोई कार्य कराने के लिए Preference को व्यक्त करता है। जैसे :

(a) I'd rather you went office now.
(b) Tomorrow's is difficult I'd rather you came next Sunday.
(c) Shall I open the door? I'd rather you didn't.
(d) Would you like him to paint it ? I'd rather he didn't (paint it.)

Had rather का प्रयोग भी Would rather के समान ही किया जा सकता है।
Would rather का प्रयोग अधिक किया जाता है।

Past Continuous Tense

ऐसे कार्य हेतु जो भूतकाल (Past) में जारी (Continue) थे, Past Continuous का प्रयोग किया जाता है। जैसे :

Read the following sentences :

(1) वह बाजार जा रहा था। He was going to market.
(2) रमेश पत्र लिख रहा था। Ramesh was writing a letter.
(3) वह गाना गा रही थी। She was singing a song.
(4) वह सो रही थी She was sleeping.
(5) वे फुटबॉल खेल रहे थे। They were playing football.
(6) रहीम पढ़ रहा था। Rahim was studying.
(7) वर्षा हो रही थी। It was raining.
(8) मैं खेल रहा था। I was playing.
(9) तुम कपड़े धो रही थीं। You were washing clothes.
(10) हम ऑफिस जा रहे थे। We were going to office.

Past Continuous के वाक्यों में कार्य का जारी रहना भूतकाल में व्यक्त होता है। इस तरह के वाक्यों का अंग्रेजी अनुवाद करने हेतु निम्न Sentence Structure प्रयुक्त होता है।

Subject + was/were + V-IV + Object

Verb की IV form, Verb की first form में ing लगाने से बनती है। 'Was' का प्रयोग Singular Subject के साथ किया जाता है जबकि 'were' का प्रयोग Plural Subject के साथ किया जाता है। You को Plural माना गया है।

Negative and Interrogative Sentences

Past Continuous के Negative एवं Interrogative Sentences का Structure निम्न होता है :

Negative — Subject + was/were + not + V-IV − Object
Interrogative — Was/were + Subject + V-IV + Object ?

	Affirmative	Negative	Interrogative
(1)	He was playing.	He was not playing.	was he playing ?
(2)	They were smoking.	They were not smoking.	Were they smoking ?
(3)	I was reading.	I was not reading.	Was I reading ?
(4)	Sita was cooking.	Sita was not cooking.	Was Sita cooking ?
(5)	We were dancing.	We were not dancing.	Were we dancing ?

Interrogative-Negative Sentences

Interrogative negative Sentences का Structure निम्न होता है :

Was/Were + Subject + not + V-IV + Object ?

Or **Wasn't/weren't + Subject + V-IV + Object ?**

	Affirmative	Interrogative-Negative
(1)	He was going to market.	Was he not going to market? Wasn't he going to market?
(2)	They were playing cards.	Were they not playing cards? Weren't they playing cards?

Use of Past Continuous Tense in various situations

(1) **ऐसे कार्य जो भूतकाल (Past time) में लगातार जारी रहे थे। जैसे :**
- (a) He was playing cricket.
- (b) They were watching T.V
- (c) She was swimming in the river.
- (d) Rahim was repairing the car.

(2) **ऐसे कार्य जो व्यक्ति past में आदतन एवं frequently करता रहा था। ऐसे वाक्यों में always, continually, constantly जैसे adverbs का प्रयोग किया जाता है। जैसे :**
- (a) He was always abusing others.
- (b) She was constantly crying those days.
- (c) They were continually threatening us.
- (d) She was always grumbling.

(3) **ऐसी स्थिति में भी Past Continuous का प्रयोग किया जाता है, जब कोई दूसरी घटना घटित हुई हो, एवं अन्य कोई कार्य भी जारी रहा हो। जैसे :**
- (a) When he arrived, his wife was washing her clothes.
- (b) The boy was knocked down by a car, while he was crossing the road.
- (c) Where were you living, when the war broke out?
- (d) The sun was just setting as they reached the hill.

(4) **एक साथ दो कार्य होते रहने की स्थिति में भी Past Continuous का प्रयोग दोनों कार्यों हेतु किया जाता है। जैसे :**

(a) While she was cooking, I was washing the clothes.
(b) While I was singing, Ramesh was reading.
(c) While they were playing, I was watching T.V
(d) While he was reading, Sita was playing.

Past Perfect Tense

Past Perfect Tense का प्रयोग ऐसे कार्यों हेतु किया जाता है जो भूतकाल में पूर्ण हो गए थे। सामान्यतया भूतकाल में जब दो कार्य एक के बाद दूसरा पूर्ण हो गया था, तो पहले पूर्ण हुए कार्य हेतु, Past Perfect तथा दूसरे पूर्ण हुए कार्य हेतु Past Indefinite का प्रयोग किया जाता है। जैसे :

Read the following sentences :

(1) मेरे स्टेशन पहुँचने से पूर्व ट्रेन जा चुकी थी।	The train had departed before I reached the station.
(2) तुम्हारे सो जाने के बाद सीता यहाँ आई थी।	Sita came here after you had slept.
(3) गाड़ी आने के बाद, वह स्टेशन पहुँचा था।	He reached the station, after the train had arrived.
(4) डॉक्टर के आने से पूर्व मरीज मर चुका था।	The patient had died before the doctor came.
(5) उसके कॉलेज पहुँचने से पूर्व छात्र कक्षा से जा चुके थे।	The students had left the class before he reached college.

इस तरह के वाक्यों का अंग्रेजी अनुवाद करने हेतु निम्न Sentence Structure प्रयुक्त होता है :

Subject + had + V-III + (before/after)+.... (Past Indefinite) +....

Past Perfect Tense का प्रयोग दो भूतकाल की घटनाओं में ही हो, ऐसा नहीं है। यह Past Perfect का सामान्य प्रयोग है। Past Perfect का use अन्य स्थितियों में आगे बताया गया है।

(1) *Past perfect में had के साथ V-III (Verb की III form) लगाई जाती है।*
(2) *यह दो भूतकाल की घटनाओं के सन्दर्भ में वाक्य है तो पहले पूर्ण होने वाले कार्य हेतु Past Perfect Tense का प्रयोग तथा बाद में पूर्ण होने वाले कार्य हेतु Past Indefinite का प्रयोग किया जाता है।*
(3) *After/before/when इत्यादि conjunctions का प्रयोग वाक्य के सन्दर्भ को देखकर किया जाता है।*

Negative and Interrogative Sentences

Past Perfect के Negative एवं Interrogative Sentences का Structure निम्न होता है :

Negative — **Subject + had + not + V-III+ Object.**
Interrogative — **Had + Subject + V-III + Object ?**

	Affirmative	Negative	Interrogative
(1)	She had written a novel.	She had not written a novel.	Had she written a novel?
(2)	Ram had gone to Agra.	Ram had not gone to Agra.	Had Ram gone to Agra?
(3)	I had played a match.	I had not played a match.	Had I played a match?
(4)	She had advised Sita.	She had not advised Sita.	Had she advised Sita?
(5)	She had warned you.	She had not warned you.	Had she warned you?

Interrogative-Negative Sentences

Interrogative-Negative Sentences का structure निम्न होता है :

Had + Subject + not + V-III + Object ?

Or **Hadn't + Subject + V-III + Object ?**

	Affirmative	**Interrogative-Negative**
(1)	I had already visited Agra.	Had I not already visited Agra? Hadn't I already visited Agra?
(2)	The train had departed before I reached there.	Had the train not departed before I reached there? Hadn't the train departed before I reached there?

Use of Past Perfect Tense in Various Situations

(1) Past Perfect का प्रयोग निम्न प्रकार के वाक्यों में भी किया जाता है। ऐसे वाक्यों के दो भाग नहीं होते, लेकिन वाक्यों को देखने से स्पष्ट होता है कि कार्य, वर्तमान से पूर्व ही पूर्ण हो चुका है। जैसे :

(a)	उसने मुझे पहले ही सूचित कर दिया था।	He had already informed me.
(b)	मैंने उसे पहले ही चेतावनी दे दी थी।	I had already warned him.
(c)	वह बहुत पहले ही वहाँ पहुँच चुकी थी।	She had reached there much earlier.
(d)	मैं इससे पूर्व जयपुर नहीं गया था।	I had never been to Jaipur before.

(2) जैसा पूर्व में बताया गया है, दो ऐसी घटनाओं या कार्यों हेतु जो एक निश्चित समय या घटना के बाद, दूसरी घटना या कार्य पूर्ण हुआ है। जैसे :

(a) I had reached college before the Principal came.
(b) She had completed her work before I reached there.
(c) The chief guest had arrived before we reached there.
(d) Ram had slept before it struck seven.
(e) When I reached the station, the train had already left.
(f) They ran out to play after they had completed their class work.
(g) As soon as they had finished their class work they ran out to play.

(a) Conjunction; when, before, after, as soon as इत्यादि का प्रयोग वाक्य के सन्दर्भ के अनुसार किया जाता है।
(b) यदि दो कार्य एक के बाद दूसरा एक sequence में पूर्ण हुए हों तो दोनों वाक्यों में Past indefinite का प्रयोग किया जाता है। Past Indefinite की विवेचना में इसे समझाया गया है।

(3) Past Perfect का प्रयोग Verbs; hope, expect, think, intend, want, suppose के साथ ऐसी Past आशाओं, इच्छाओं, कल्पनाओं के सन्दर्भ में किया जाता है जो पूर्ण नहीं हुईं। जैसे :

(a) We had hoped that you would cooperate us. (but you didn't cooperate.)
(b) I had intended to go to USA last year. (but I couldn't go.)
(c) She had thought of paying us a visit. (but due to some reasons she couldn't visit.)
(d) We had expected that she would attend the party. (but she didn't attend.)
(e) They had wanted to donate some money, but none was present there. (so they couldn't donate any money.)

(4) Direct से Indirect Narration में परिवर्तित करते समय Past Indefinite एवं Present Perfect को Past Perfect में बदला जाता है। (When Reporting verb is in the Past) जैसे :

(a) She said to me, "I have already read that novel."
She told me that she had already read that novel.

(b) He said to me, "Tony died two days ago."
He told me that Tony had died two days before.

(5) Past Perfect का प्रयोग ऐसे action हेतु since/for/always के साथ किया जा सकता है जो at the time of speaking (वक्ता के बोलते समय) से पूर्व भूतकाल में शुरू हो चुके थे। जैसे :

(a) Ram had been a soldier for ten years.
(b) Ram had been a soldier since he was seventeen.
(c) Jackob had waited for an hour, was very angry with his wife, when she eventually turned up.
(d) Jackob had waited since five O'clock, was very angry with his wife, when he eventually turned up.

(6) Conditional Sentences में भी Past Perfect का प्रयोग किया जाता है। जैसे :

(a) यदि वह मुझसे मिलता तो मैं उसकी मदद करता। If he had met me, I would have helped him.
(b) यदि वह मुझे सूचित करता तो मैं वहाँ अवश्य जाता। If he had informed me, I would have gone there positively.
(c) यदि वह मेरे पास आती तो मैं उसे एक उपहार देता। If she had come to me, I would have given her a gift.

इस तरह के वाक्य यह स्पष्ट करते हैं कि कार्य नहीं हुआ। यह एक महत्त्वपूर्ण Structure है, छात्रों को ध्यान से समझना चाहिए।

If + Subject + had + V-III +....+ would have +V-III +...

इस तरह के वाक्यों के पहले भाग में had + V-III दूसरे भाग में would have के साथ Verb की III form का प्रयोग किया जाता है।

If he had come to me, I would have helped him. Or
Had he come to me, I would have helped him.
इन दोनों वाक्यों का अर्थ समान है, कोई अन्तर नहीं है।

Important

The Past Perfect is also the past equivalent of the Simple Past Tense, and is used when the narrator or subject looks back on earlier action from a certain time in the past.

-A Practical English Grammar Thomson and Martinet page 176

Tom was 23 when our story begins. His father had died five years before and since then Tom had lived alone. His father had advised him not to get married till he was 35 and Tom intended to follow this.

Note the Difference of Meaning in the Following Sentences

(1) She heard voices and realised that there were three people in the next room.
(They were still there.)

(2) She saw empty glasses and cups and realised that three people had been in the room.
(They were no longer there.)

(3) He arrived at 2.30 and was told to wait in the VIP lounge.
(He received instructions after his arrival.)

(4) He arrived at 2.30. He had been told to wait in the VIP lounge.
(He received instructions before arrival or possibly before the journey started.)

Past Perfect Continuous Tense

Past Perfect Continuous Tense का प्रयोग ऐसे कार्य हेतु किया जाता है जो at the time of speaking से पूर्व भूतकाल से लगातार जारी थे।

Read the following sentences :

(1) राम दो घण्टे से टी०वी० देख रहा था।	Ram had been watching T.V. for two hours.
(2) राम दो बजे से टी०वी० देख रहा था।	Ram had been watching T.V. since 2 O' clock.
(3) जैकब वर्ष 1997 से इस कॉटेज में रह रहा था।	Jackab had been living in this cottage since 1997.
(4) वर्षा सुबह से हो रही थी।	It had been raining since morning.
(5) निशा प्रात: 11 बजे से मेरा इन्तजार कर रही थी।	Nisha had been waiting for me since 11 O'clock in the morning.

इस तरह के वाक्यों का अंग्रेजी अनुवाद करने हेतु निम्न Sentence Structure प्रयुक्त होता है

Subject + had been + V-IV +.......+since/for + ...

Subject के साथ had been तथा Verb की IV form लगती है। Since का प्रयोग Point of time *जैसे* 2 O'clock, Monday, January, 2001, Morning, Evening के साथ तथा for का प्रयोग Period of time (अवधि) *जैसे* long time, some time, two hours, fifteen years इत्यादि हेतु किया जाता है।

Negative and Interrogative Sentences

Past Perfect Continuous के Negative एवं Interrogative Sentences का Structure निम्न होता है :

Negative **Subject + had + not + been + V-IV + Object ?**

Interrogative **Had + Subject + been + V-IV + Object ?**

(1)	He had been waiting for her since morning.	*Affirmative*
	He had not been waiting for her since morning.	*Negative*
	Had he been waiting for her since morning?	*Interrogative*
(2)	She had been writing letters for two hours.	*Affirmative*
	She had not been writing letters for two hours.	*Negative*
	Had she been writing letters for two hours?	*Interrogative*
(3)	Ram had been playing since 2 O'clock.	*Affirmative*
	Ram had not been playing since 2 O'clock.	*Negative*
	Had Ram been playing since 2 O'clock?	*Interrogative*
(4)	I had been trying to contact her for two hours.	*Affirmative*
	I had not been trying to contact her for two hours.	*Negative*
	Had I been trying to contact her for two hours?	*Interrogative*
(5)	Sita had been crying since morning.	*Affirmative*
	Sita had not been crying since morning.	*Negative*
	Had Sita been crying since morning?	*Interrogative*

Interrogative-Negative Sentences

Interrogative Negative Sentences का Structure निम्न होता है :

Had + Subject + not + been + V-IV+ Object + since/ for + time ?

Or **Hadn't + subject + been + V-IV + Object + since / for + time ?**

Affirmative	**Interrogative-Negative**
(1) I had been flying kites since morning.	Had I not been flying kites since morning? Hadn't I been flying kites since morning?
(2) She had been waiting for me for an hour.	Had she not been waiting for me for an hour? Hadn't she been waiting for me for an hour?

Use of Past Perfect Continuous Tense in Various Situations

(1) **Past Perfect Continuous का प्रयोग ऐसे action हेतु किया जाता है जो Past में किसी समय बिन्दु (Point of time) या अवधि (Period of time) से लगातार जारी थे। जैसे :**

(a) He had been working since dawn.
(b) She had been waiting for him for two hours.
(c) I had been flying kites since morning
(d) We had been playing cricket for three hours.

(2) **Past Perfect के repeated action को भी Past Perfect Continuous में व्यक्त किया जा सकता है। जैसे :**

(a) He had tried five times to contact her.	*Past Perfect*
He had been trying to contact her.	*Past Perfect Continuous*
(b) He had tried many times to get the job there.	*Past Perfect*
He had been trying to get the job there.	*Past Perfect Continuous*

An action in the Past Perfect can sometimes be expressed as a continuous action in the Past Perfect Continuous. **- A Practical English Grammar : A.J. Thomson, A.V. Martin**

Future Tense

कार्य की अवस्था के अनुसार Future Tense को चार भागों में वर्गीकृत किया गया है :

(1) Future Indefinite :	वह एक पत्र लिखेगा। He will write a letter.
(2) Future Continuous :	वह एक पत्र लिख रहा होगा। He will be writing a letter.
(3) Future Perfect :	वह एक पत्र लिख चुका होगा। He will have written a letter.
(4) Future Perfect Continuous :	वह एक घण्टे से पत्र लिख रहा होगा। He will have been writing a letter for an hour.

उपरोक्त चारों वाक्य Future Tense के हैं, लेकिन कार्य की अवस्था के अनुसार ये Future Tense की अलग-अलग श्रेणियों को स्पष्ट करते हैं।

Future Indefinite Tense

भविष्य में सामान्यतया सम्पन्न होने वाले कार्यों हेतु Future Indefinite का प्रयोग होता है।

Read the following sentences :

(1) वह जयपुर जाएगा।	He will go to Jaipur.
(2) सीता गाना गाएगी।	Sita will sing a song.
(3) वे फुटबॉल खेलेंगे।	They will play football.

(4)	हम घर की सफाई करेंगे।	We shall clean the house.
(5)	मैं पढ़ाई करूँगा।	I shall study.
(6)	वह कार्य कर सकता है।	He can do this work.
(7)	शायद आज वर्षा होगी।	It may rain today.
(8)	वर्षा अवश्य होगी।	It must rain.
(9)	उसे जाने दो।	Let him go.
(10)	आओ हम बाजार चलें।	Let us go to market.

उक्त सभी वाक्य Future Indefinite के हैं। इनसे कार्य का भविष्य में सम्पन्न होना व्यक्त होता है।

याद रखें जो Present अथवा Past नहीं है, वह Future है। उक्त वाक्यों में may, can, must के प्रयोग को समझने का प्रयास करें। इन Verbs के प्रयोग से यह पता चलता है कि जो भी कार्य होगा, वह भविष्य में होगा। Let का प्रयोग भी यह स्पष्ट करता है कि कार्य भविष्य में ही होगा। अत: ये सभी वाक्य Future Indefinite के हैं। इस प्रकार के वाक्यों का अंग्रेजी अनुवाद करने के लिए निम्न Sentence Structure प्रयुक्त होता है

Subject + will / shall /can /may etc. + V-I

(1) Shall का प्रयोग I एवं We (I Person) के साथ, will का प्रयोग अन्य सभी जैसे He, She, They, It, You etc. (Second and Third Person) के साथ होता है।

(2) जब Shall का प्रयोग II एवं III person के साथ किया जाता है तो यह Promise, Threat या कार्य करने की determination को व्यक्त करता है। Modals का प्रयोग, कर्ता की Intention जाहिर करता है।

(3) Can, May के प्रयोग के सम्बन्ध में Modals का अध्याय देखें।

(4) Let वाक्य के प्रारम्भ में आता है एवं इसके साथ Objective Case में Pronoun का प्रयोग किया जाता है। जैसे Let him, Let us, Let them, Let her, (him, us, them, her, objective case pronouns हैं) कभी भी Let I, Let he, Let she नहीं लिखा जाता है।

(5) I shall, को I'll एवं He will को He'll लिखा जा सकता है। जब कभी भी shall/Will के प्रयोग की उलझन से बचना हो तो Abbreviated form : I'll, He'll का प्रयोग कर लेना चाहिए।

Negative and Interrogative Sentences

Future Indefinite के Negative एवं Interrogative Sentences का Structure निम्न होता है :

Negative — Subject + Will / shall + not + V-I + Object

Interrogative — Will / shall + Subject + V-I + Object ?

	Affirmative	Negative	Interrogative
(1)	He will write.	He will not write.	Will he write?
(2)	I shall buy a T.V.	I shall not buy a T.V.	Shall I buy a T.V.?
(3)	He will go to Agra.	He will not go to Agra.	Will he go to Agra?
(4)	They will come tomorrow.	They will not come tomorrow.	Will they come tomorrow?
(5)	Ram will play.	Ram will not play.	Will Ram play?
(6)	We will attend the party.	We will not attend the party.	Will we attend the party?

Will not को Won't तथा Shall not को Shan't के रूप में भी लिखा जा सकता है।

Interrogative-Negative Sentences

Interrogative-Negative Sentences का Structure निम्न होता है :

Will / Shall + Subject + not + V-I + Object ?

Or **Won't / Shan't + Subject + V-I + Object ?**

(a) I shall buy a T.V. — *Affirmative*
Shall I not buy a T.V.? or Shan't I buy a T.V.? — *Interrogative-Negative*

(b) He will go to market. — *Affirmative*
Will he not go to market? or Won't he go to market? — *Interrogative-Negative*

Use of Future Indefinite Tense in Various Situations

(1) सामान्यतया भविष्य में सम्पन्न होने वाले कार्यों के लिए Simple Future का प्रयोग किया जाता है। First person के साथ Shall तथा Second person and Third person के साथ will का प्रयोग करते हैं। जैसे :

(a) I shall write a letter.
(b) He will go to Delhi on next Monday.
(c) We may play a match.
(d) She will buy a pen.

(2) Clause of condition एवं clause of time वाले वाक्यों में Future Indefinite का प्रयोग किया जाता है। इस सम्बन्ध में विस्तार से Present Indefinite के अध्याय में बताया गया है। जैसे :

(a) I shall go to market, if it rains.
(b) I shall go to Jaipur in case she asks me.
(c) We shall move as soon as the taxi arrives.
(d) I shall start my work as he comes.

(3) Will be/Shall be का प्रयोग निम्न प्रकार किया जाता है

(a) Tomorrow will be Monday.
(b) He will be twenty five in January.
(c) I shall be fifty on next birthday.
(d) He will be happy to meet you.

(4) Simple Future का प्रयोग ऐसी भविष्य की घटनाओं हेतु भी किया जाता है जो हम समझते हैं कि सामान्य रूप से घटित होंगी। जैसे :

(a) Winter will come again.
(b) Birds will build their nests.
(c) People will make plans.
(d) We shall eat and enjoy.

Some Important Structures to Denote Future Actions

(5) Use of going to form : for future actions : Verb की 'going to' form का प्रयोग सामान्यतया ऐसी स्थिति में किया जाता है जब वक्ता की intention (इरादा) भविष्य में होने वाले किसी कार्य के शीघ्र सम्पन्न होने के सन्दर्भ में जाहिर करना होता है। जैसे :

Future Indefinite	**Use of 'going to' form**
(a) I shall buy a T.V.	I am going to buy a T.V.
(b) He will write a letter.	He is going to write a letter.
(c) She will inform him.	She is going to inform him.
(d) We shall do this work.	We are going to do this work.

'going to' का प्रयोग, कार्य के शीघ्र सम्पन्न होने को व्यक्त करता है जबकि Simple Future कार्य के भविष्य में सम्पन्न होने को व्यक्त करता है।

(6) **Future actions हेतु 'about to' का प्रयोग निम्न प्रकार से किया जा सकता है :**

(a) The train is about to start. — ट्रेन जाने वाली है।
(b) The shop is about to close. — दुकान बन्द होने वाली है।
(c) The Chief Guest is about to arrive. — मुख्य अतिथि आने वाले हैं।

इस तरह के वाक्यों में is/am/are + about to का प्रयोग किया जाता है।

(7) **Present Indefinite के वाक्यों द्वारा भी Future action को बताया जा सकता है। जैसे :**

(a) Mr. Sharma retires on 31st December. (b) The President visits Gujarat tomorrow.

(8) **Present Continuous के वाक्यों द्वारा भी Future actions को बताया जा सकता है। जैसे :**

(a) We are meeting today in the evening. (b) The wedding is on Sunday next.

(9) **Is/am/are + to + V-I द्वारा भी Future actions को व्यक्त किया जा सकता है। जैसे :**

(a) I am to go there. — मुझे वहाँ जाना है।
(b) He is to complete his work. — उसे अपना कार्य पूर्ण करना है।
(c) They are to come here tomorrow. — उन्हें यहाँ आना है।
(d) She is to sing a song. — उसे एक गाना गाना है।

जिन वाक्यों में जाना, करना इत्यादि आएँ उनके लिए is/am/are + to + V-I का प्रयोग किया जाता है। It is very important structure.

Future Continuous Tense

Future Continuous का प्रयोग सामान्यतया ऐसे कार्यों हेतु किया जाता है जो भविष्य में जारी रहेंगे।

Read the following sentences :

(1) मैं शाम को थीसिस लिख रहा हूँगा। — I shall be writing the thesis in the evening.
(2) वे शाम को क्रिकेट खेल रहे होंगे। — They will be playing cricket in the evening.
(3) कुकु कॉलेज में पढ़ रही होगी। — Kuku will be reading in the college.
(4) हम रात को टीवी देख रहे होंगे। — We shall be watching T.V. in the night.
(5) वह कपड़े धो रही होगी। — She will be washing the clothes.
(6) वह आज आ रहा होगा। — He will be coming today in the evening.
(7) वह सोमवार को सविता के साथ शादी कर रहा होगा। — He will be marrying with Savita on Monday.
(8) मैं कल जयपुर जा रहा हूँगा। — I shall be going to Jaipur tomorrow.
(9) राम कल इस समय खेल रहा होगा। — Ram will be playing at this time tomorrow.
(10) अगले माह मोहन यहाँ रुक रहा होगा। — Mohan will be staying here next month.

इस तरह के वाक्य में future continuous का प्रयोग भविष्य में जारी रहने वाले कार्य को व्यक्त करता है। इस तरह के वाक्यों का अंग्रेजी अनुवाद करने हेतु निम्न Sentence Structure प्रयुक्त होता है :

Subject + will/shall be + V-IV + Object

इस तरह के वाक्यों में will/shall be के बाद Verb की IV form (Verb की first from + ing) लगाई जाती है।

Difference between Present Continuous and Future Continuous

(showing some future time event)

(a) I am seeing the Principal tomorrow. — *Present Continuous*
(b) I'll be seeing the Principal tomorrow. — *Future Continuous*

वाक्य (a) एक Planned action या arrangement (पहले से तय) को बताता है जबकि दूसरा वाक्य normal course में कार्य होने को बताता है, हो सकता है वह उसी office में कार्य करता हो।

Negative and Interrogative Sentences

Future Continuous के Negative एवं Interrogative Sentences का Structure निम्न होता है :

Negative — **Subject + will/shall + not + be + V-IV + Object.**

Interrogative — **Will/Shall + Subject + be + V-IV + Object ?**

Affirmative	**Negative**	**Interrogative**
(1) I shall be going to market.	I shall not be going to market.	Shall I be going to market?
(2) She will be washing the car.	She will not be washing the car.	Will she be washing the car?
(3) Ram will be playing chess.	Ram will not be playing chess.	Will Ram be playing chess?
(4) We shall be watching T.V.	We shall not be watching T.V.	Shall we be watching T.V.?
(5) They will be playing.	They will not be playing.	Will they be playing?

(1) *Negative sentences, not को Will/Shall के बाद 'be' से पूर्व लगाते हैं।*
(2) *Interrogative sentences में Will/Shall को Subject से पूर्व लगाया जाता है, शेष Structure वही रहता है। अन्त में (?) लगाया जाता है।*

Interrogative-Negative Sentences

Interrogative Negative Sentences का Structure निम्न होता है

Will / Shall + Subject +not + be + V-IV + Object ?

Or **Won't /Shan't + Subject + be + V-IV + Object ?**

Affirmative	**Interrogative-Negative**
(1) I shall be playing cricket tomorrow.	Shall I not be playing cricket tomorrow? Shan't I be playing cricket tomorrow?
(2) They will be washing their clothes.	Will they not be washing their clothes? Won't they be washing their clothes?

Future Perfect Tense

Future Perfect का प्रयोग ऐसे कार्यों को व्यक्त करने हेतु किया जाता है जो भविष्य में किसी निश्चित समय या किसी अन्य कार्य के होने तक पूर्ण हो जायेंगे।

Read the following sentences :

(1) वह अगले वर्ष तक इस योजना को पूर्ण कर चुकेगा।
He will have completed this project by next year.

(2) सरिता अगले माह घर वापस आ चुकेगी। (आ जाएगी)।
Sarita will have returned home by next month.

(3) डॉक्टर के यहाँ पहुँचने से पूर्व मरीज मर चुकेगा।
The patient will have died before the doctor reaches here.

(4) घण्टी बजने से पूर्व मैं स्कूल पहुँच जाऊँगा (चुकूँगा)।
I shall have reached school before the bell rings.

(5) वर्ष 2005 तक वह अपनी पढ़ाई पूरी कर लेगा (चुकेगा)।
He will have completed his studies by the year 2005.

इस तरह के वाक्यों का अंग्रेजी अनुवाद करने हेतु निम्न Structure प्रयुक्त होता है :

Subject + will / shall + have + V-III + Object.

(1) यदि वाक्य में एक अन्य वाक्य जुड़ा है, जो कार्य पहले पूर्ण होगा, उसमें Future Perfect का प्रयोग होता है एवं जो कार्य बाद में पूर्ण होगा उसमें Present Indefinite का प्रयोग होता है। यह एक महत्त्वपूर्ण बिन्दु है। जैसे:
मेरे स्टेशन पहुँचने से पूर्व गाड़ी जा चुकेगी। इस वाक्य में 'गाड़ी जा चुकेगी' पहले पूर्ण होने वाला कार्य है। अत: इसके लिए Future Perfect का प्रयोग किया जाता है, जबकि 'मेरे स्टेशन पहुँचने' यह बाद में पूर्ण होने वाला कार्य है, इसके लिए Present Indefinite का प्रयोग किया जाता है।
The train will have departed before I reach the station.
(2) Future Perfect में has का प्रयोग नहीं होता है केवल have का ही प्रयोग होता है।
(3) Use 'by', instead of 'in' in Future Perfect tense for time reference.

Negative and Interrogative Sentences

Future Perfect के Negative एवं Interrogative Sentences का Structure निम्नलिखित होता है :

Negative — **Subject + shall/will + not + have + V-III + Object.**
Interrogative — **Shall/Will + Subject + have + V-III + Object ?**

(1) He will have completed his work by tomorrow. *Affirmative*
He will not have completed his work by tomorrow. *Negative*
Will he have completed his work by tomorrow? *Interrogative*

(2) They will have reached here by 7 P.M. *Affirmative*
They will not have reached here by 7 P.M. *Negative*
Will they have reached here by 7 P.M. ? *Interrogative*

(3) She will have washed her clothes by 3 P.M. *Affirmative*
She will not have washed her clothes by 3 P.M. *Negative*
Will she have washed her clothes by 3 P.M.? *Interrogative*

(4) I shall have written a book by next month. *Affirmative*
I shall not have written a book by next month. *Negative*
Shall I have written a book by next month? *Interrogative*

(5) Ram will have completed that work by 2005. *Affirmative*
Ram will not have completed that work by 2005. *Negative*
Will Ram have completed that work by 2005 ? *Interrogative*

(1) Negative sentences में not का प्रयोग Shall/Will के बाद एवं Have से पूर्व होता है।
(2) Interrogative sentences में Shall/Will को Subject से पूर्व लगाते हैं तथा (?) वाक्य के अन्त में लगाते हैं।

Interrogative-Negative Sentences

Interrogative, Negative वाक्यों का Structure निम्न होता है:

Shall/Will + subject + have + not + V-III + object?

Or **Won't /Shan't + Subject + have + V-III + Object?**

	Affirmative	Interrogative-Negative
(1)	He will have repaired the car by 5 P.M..	Will he not have repaired the car by 5 P.M.? Won't he have repaired the car by 5 P.M.?
(2)	I shall have informed her by tomorrow.	Shall I not have informed her by tomorrow? Shan't I have informed her by tomorrow?

Use of Future Perfect Tense in Various Situations

(1) भविष्य में किसी समय पर पूर्ण हो चुकने वाले कार्यों हेतु Future Perfect का प्रयोग किया जाता है। जैसे :

(a) I shall have passed my graduation by next year.
(b) He will have completed his work by tomorrow.
(c) The mechanic will have repaired the car by 7 P.M.
(d) By the end of this year I shall have saved ₹ 1 lac.

(2) जब कोई एक कार्य दूसरे कार्य के पूर्ण होने के बाद पूर्ण हो तो इस तरह के वाक्यों में पहले पूर्ण होने वाले कार्य के लिए Future Perfect एवं जो कार्य बाद में पूर्ण होगा उसमें Present Indefinite का प्रयोग होता है। जैसे :

(a) The student will have left the class before the teacher comes.
(b) The Principal will have started before I reach there.
(c) The function will have started before we reach there.
(d) The mechanic will have repaired the TV before it strikes eight.

(3) ऐसे कार्यों हेतु जिनके बारे में हम यह समझते हैं कि उसका ज्ञान उसे पहले से ही होगा। जैसे :

(a) You will have heard about Mother Teressa.
(b) You will have heard about our plans of investment.
(c) He will have read the newspaper so far.
(d) They will have heard about the accident by this time.

इस तरह के वाक्य, जो वस्तुत: किसी future action को व्यक्त नहीं करते हैं, बल्कि वक्त की assumptions के अनुसार, अन्य की जानकारी हो चुकने की सम्भावना बताते हैं।

Future Perfect Continuous

Future Perfect Continuous का प्रयोग ऐसे वाक्यों हेतु होता है जो भविष्य में किसी समय तक जारी रहेंगे। ऐसे वाक्यों में समय का सन्दर्भ आवश्यक है। जैसे :

(1) सात बजे वे दो घण्टे से खेल रहे होंगे।
They will have been playing for two hours by 7 O'clock.

(2) वह अगले माह में इस कार्यालय में चार वर्ष से कार्य कर रही होगी।
She will have been working in this office for four years by the next month.

(3) वर्ष 25 में रमेश इस मकान में 5 वर्ष से रह रहा होगा।
Ramesh will have been living in this house for five years by the year 2005.

(4) अगले सोमवार को हम सुबह से पतंग उड़ा रहे होंगे।
We shall have been flying kites since morning on next Monday.

(5) 15 अगस्त, 2006 को राहुल इस कॉलेज में तीन वर्ष से पढ़ा रहा होगा।
Rahul will have been teaching in this college for three years on 15th August, 2006.

इस तरह के वाक्यों का अंग्रेजी अनुवाद करने हेतु निम्न Sentence Structure प्रयुक्त होता है

Subject + will / shall + have been + V-IV + Object + Since/For + ...

(1) इस तरह के वाक्यों में Will / Shall के साथ have been (has been का नहीं) का प्रयोग होता है।

(2) *Since का प्रयोग Point of time के लिए (जैसे : since January, since 2 O'clock, since morning, since 2005 इत्यादि) तथा For का प्रयोग Period of time (जैसे : for two hours, for 15 years, for sometime etc) के लिए होता है।*

(3) *समय हेतु सामान्यतया by का प्रयोग किया जाता है, लेकिन on का भी प्रयोग वाक्य के सन्दर्भ को ध्यान में रखकर किया जा सकता है।*

Negative and Interrogative Sentences

Future Perfect Continuous के Negative एवं Interrogative Sentences का Structure निम्न होता है

Negative — **Subject + shall /will +not + have been + V-IV + ...**

Interrogative — **Shall / Will + Subject + have been + V-IV...?**

Changing Affirmative to Negative and Interrogative :

(1)	I shall have been playing football.	*Affirmative*
	I shall not have been playing football.	*Negative*
	Shall I have been playing football?	*Interrogative*
(2)	They will have been working ...	*Affirmative*
	They will not have been working ..	*Negative*
	Will they have been working...?	*Interrogative*
(3)	Ram will have been writing a book...	*Affirmative*
	Ram will not have been writing a book....	*Negative*
	Will Ram have been writing a book...?	*Interrogative*
(4)	She will have been washing her clothes...	*Affirmative*
	She will not have been washing her clothes...	*Negative*
	Will she have been washing her clothes...?	*Interrogative*
(5)	Ganesh will have been watching T.V	*Affirmative*
	Ganesh will not have been watching T.V ...	*Negative*
	Will Ganesh have been watching T.V ..?	*Interrogative*

Interrogative-Negative Sentences

Interrogative Negative Sentences का Structure निम्न होता है :

Will/Shall + Subject + not + have been + V-IV + Object?

Or **Won't/Shan't + Subject + have been + V-IV + Object?**

(1)	I shall have been playing match since morning.	*Affirmative*
	Shall I not have been playing match since morning? *Or*	*Interrogative-Negative*
	Shan't I have been playing match since morning?	*Interrogative-Negative*
(2)	He will have been watching T.V for two hours.	*Affirmative*
	Will he not have been watching T.V for two hours? *Or*	*Interrogative-Negative*
	Won't he have been watching T.V for two hours?	*Interrogative-Negative*

Future Perfect Continuous में Will/Shall के साथ have been का प्रयोग होता है, has been का प्रयोग नहीं होगा।

01

Translate the following sentences into English :

(1) मैं आम खाता हूँ।
(2) हम रोज पढ़ते हैं।
(3) वर्षा होती है।
(4) वह यहाँ काम करती है।
(5) वह राम से मिलना चाहती है।
(6) तुम बाजार जाते हो।
(7) वह चाय नहीं पीता है।
(8) मैं बहुत तेज भागता हूँ।
(9) वह गाना गाती है।
(10) राम अपना पाठ याद करता है।
(11) वह प्रतिदिन सुबह कॉलेज जाता है।
(12) वे सुबह 5 बजे मैदान में खेलने जाते हैं।
(13) सीता हमेशा गरीबों की सहायता करती है।
(14) रमेश कभी भी झूठ नहीं बोलता है।
(15) सूरज पूरब में उगता है एवं पश्चिम में छिपता है।
(16) क्या आप मेरा नाम जानते हैं।
(17) पृथ्वी चन्द्रमा के चारों ओर नहीं घूमती है।
(18) सीता प्रतिदिन एक पाठ याद करती है।
(19) रमेश पतंग उड़ाता है।
(20) वह कपड़े नहीं धोती है।

02

Correct the following sentences.

(1) I writes a letter.
(2) He go to temple daily
(3) Sita crys.
(4) He fly kites.
(5) He do not play.
(6) Does I write a letter?
(7) Do she swims?
(8) Does she goes to school?
(9) Ram does not tells a lie.
(10) He never verifys the bills.

(1) जब Subject, Singular Number, Third Person है तो verb के साथ s या es लगता है।
(2) जब Verb का अन्तिम अक्षर o, z, ss, x., ch, sh है es लगता है।
(3) यदि Verb का अन्तिम अक्षर y एवं उससे पूर्व कोई व्यंजन (Consonant) आया है, तो Subject, Singular Number, Third Person की स्थिति में y -ies में बदल जाता है।

03

Translate the following sentences into English :

(1) मैं आम खा रहा हूँ।
(2) वह सच बोल रही है।
(3) रमेश फुटबॉल खेल रहा है।
(4) राम झूठ बोल रहा है।
(5) वह पढ़ रही है।
(6) वह अपना काम कर रही है।
(7) वह जयपुर जा रहा है।
(8) पक्षी उड़ रहे हैं।
(9) क्या तुम खेल रहे हो?
(10) ठण्डी हवा बह रही है।
(11) बूँदा-बाँदी हो रही है।
(12) वह अपने मित्र को पत्र लिख रहा है।
(13) सीता गाय का दूध निकाल रही है।
(14) राम मेरा इन्तजार नहीं कर रहा है।
(15) क्या वह बाजार नहीं जा रही है?
(16) वह आजकल एक किताब लिख रहा है।
(17) वह तुम्हें गाली दे रहा है।
(18) मैं सुन रहा हूँ।
(19) मैं देख रहा हूँ।
(20) वह कॉलेज में पढ़ा रहा है।

04

Correct the following sentences :

(1) You is playing.
(2) I is reading.
(3) They are read.
(4) She does not swimming.
(5) Is it rains?
(6) Are she cooking?
(7) Am he playing?
(8) Is you coming?
(9) I is going to play.
(10) She are speaking.
(11) I am seeing.
(12) I am having a car.
(13) I am understanding.
(14) He is knowing me.
(15) He is resembling his brother.

(1) Present Continuous में helping verb का प्रयोग निम्न प्रकार से किया जाता है :
I के साथ am, you, we, they, any plural के साथ are तथा He, she, it, name, any singular के साथ is लगता है तथा verb की IV form (1st form + ing) लगती है।

(2) कुछ verb जैसे see, hear, have, own, understand; इत्यादि का प्रयोग सामान्य स्थिति में continuous form में नहीं किया जाता है।

05

Translate the following sentences into English :

(1) मैं आम खा चुका हूँ।
(2) वे जा चुके है।
(3) वर्षा हो चुकी है।
(4) ट्रेन अभी आई है।
(5) अभी सात बजे हैं।
(6) मैं पत्र लिख चुका हूँ।
(7) हम अपना काम समाप्त कर चुके हैं।
(8) बच्चे सो चुके हैं।
(9) वह बहुत खेल चुका है।
(10) उन्होंने यह प्रश्न हल कर लिया है।
(11) वह पिछले रविवार से बीमार है।
(12) वह मुझे पाँच वर्ष से जानता है।
(13) वे यहाँ पाँच साल रह चुके हैं।
(14) क्या वह अभी आया है?
(15) उसने अपना पाठ याद नहीं किया है।
(16) वह अमेरिका में रह चुका है।
(17) क्या वह देहली जा चुका है?
(18) क्या सीता कपड़े नहीं धो चुकी है?
(19) मैंने अपना पाठ याद कर लिया है।
(20) ट्रेन अभी-अभी आयी है।

06

Translate the following sentences into English :

(1) हम सुबह से खेल रहे हैं।
(2) मैं दो वर्षों से यहाँ रह रहा हूँ।
(3) वह चार बजे से पढ़ रहा है।
(4) वह सुबह से सो रहा है।
(5) मैं चार वर्षों से प्रथम आ रहा हूँ।
(6) मैं कई दिनों से खाना नहीं खा रही हूँ।
(7) वह कई घण्टों से हँस रहा है।
(8) वह सन् 2000 से यहाँ पढ़ रहा है।
(9) वह दो घण्टे से वही प्रश्न हल कर रहा है।
(10) वह सुबह से भाग रहा है।
(11) मैं सुबह से तुम्हारा इन्तजार कर रहा हूँ।
(12) वर्षा कल शाम से लगातार हो रही है।
(13) वर्षा चार दिन से हो रही है।
(14) क्या आप सीता का कल से इन्तजार नहीं कर रहे हैं?
(15) वह दो दिन से नहीं पढ़ रहा है।
(16) क्या वह चार वर्षों से इस परीक्षा की तैयारी नहीं कर रहा है?
(17) रमेश दो बजे से फुटबॉल खेल रहा है।
(18) माताजी एक घण्टे से कपड़े धो रही है।
(19) पापा सुबह 7 बजे से अखबार पढ़ रहे हैं।
(20) मैं सायं से टीवी देख रहा हूँ

7.

Correct the following sentences :

(1) He have gone to Jaipur.
(2) I has played.
(3) They have arrived yesterday.
(4) Have he played a match?
(5) Ram has gone two minutes ago.
(6) He not has taken food.
(7) He was ill since Monday.
(8) I have been playing since two hours.
(9) He has been swimming for 2'O clock.
(10) Has she cooking for two hours?
(11) Have I been not playing for one hour?
(12) She have just arrive.
(13) Raju is playing for three hours.
(14) I known him.
(15) They have been not reading since an hour.

(1) Present Perfect में I, You, We, They एवं any plural subject के साथ have तथा He, She, It, Name, any singular के साथ has का प्रयोग किया जाता है।
(2) Verb की III form का प्रयोग किया जाता है।
(3) Present Perfect में, Past time के adverbs जैसे : yesterday, ago इत्यादि का प्रयोग कभी नहीं होता है।
(4) Present Perfect Continuous में since का प्रयोग, Point of time जैसे : morning, evening, 2 O'clock, January, February etc, के साथ होता है। For का प्रयोग अवधि जैसे : 2 hours, 15 days etc के साथ होता है। Verb की IV form लगती है।

08

Translate the following sentences into English :

(1) मैंने एक पत्र लिखा।
(2) मैं बाजार गया।
(3) अध्यापक ने मुझे कल पढ़ाया था।
(4) राम ने एक कविता लिखी थी।
(5) सीता ने गाना नहीं गाया।
(6) क्या वह कल जयपुर गया?
(7) क्या अध्यापक ने तुम्हें सजा दी थी?
(8) वह तुम पर हँसा था।
(9) वह जयपुर में एक सप्ताह ठहरा।
(10) क्या तुम कल वहाँ गए थे?
(11) मैंने कल एक पत्र लिखा।
(12) सीता ने कपड़े धोए।
(13) उसने कल ऑफिस को साफ किया।
(14) वह कल 5 बजे उठा एवं दो घण्टे तक पढ़ा।
(15) उसने मुझे टेलीफोन किया।
(16) राम ने श्याम को गाली दी।
(17) क्या उसने टी.वी. सीरियल देखा?
(18) क्या राम कल यहाँ नहीं आया था?
(19) राम ने कल सुबह 7 बजे से 8 बजे तक टी.वी. देखा।
(20) हमने कल एक फिल्म देखी।

09

Translate the following sentences into English :

(1) राम सुबह फुटबॉल खेल रहा था।
(2) तुम कल बाजार जा रहे थे।
(3) रमा आज सुबह गाना गा रही थी।
(4) माँ हमारा खाना तैयार कर रही थी।
(5) वह किताब पढ़ रहा था।
(6) वह झूठ बोल रहा था।
(7) पक्षी आकाश में उड़ रहे थे।
(8) वर्षा हो रही थी।
(9) राम और मोहन लड़ रहे थे।
(10) माँ दोपहर को सो रही थी।
(11) जब मैं घर पहुँचा तो वह कपड़े धो रही थी।
(12) जब मैं पढ़ रहा था तो मेरा भाई टी.वी. देख रहा था।
(13) जब वर्षा हो रही थी तो मैं सो रही थी।
(14) सुरेश मेरा इन्तजार कर रहा था।
(15) रमेश झूठ नहीं बोल रहा था।
(16) क्या सीता नदी में तैर नहीं रही थी?
(17) क्या कल 5 बजे वर्षा नहीं हो रही थी?
(18) क्या गीता सुबह गाना नहीं गा रही थी?
(19) रमेश फुटबॉल खेल रहा था जबकि मैं काम कर रहा था।
(20) मेरे पिताजी कल 5 बजे ऑफिस में काम कर रहे थे।

10

Correct the following sentences :

(1) He gone to Jaipur.
(2) He just went to Jaipur.
(3) He did not went to Jaipur.
(4) Did he came yesterday?
(5) He did not opened the door.
(6) He were not going.
(7) I were not doing that.
(8) You was making a noise.
(9) She did not asked me.
(10) Did he not reminded you?
(11) Was you not playing?
(12) Were not you writing?
(13) Was not I watching movie?
(14) Were she not cooking?
(15) Were they playing not football?

11

Translate the following sentences into English :

(1) मेरे स्टेशन पहुँचने से पहले गाड़ी रवाना हो चुकी थी।
(2) डॉक्टर के आने से पहले मरीज मर चुका था।
(3) मेरे वहाँ पहुँचने से पहले वह जा चुका था।
(4) घण्टी बजने से पहले मैं स्कूल पहुँच गया था।
(5) जब मैं उसके घर पहुँचा तो वह भोजन कर चुका था।
(6) मैच पहले ही आरम्भ हो चुका था।
(7) वह इन खिलौनों से पहले ही खेल चुका था।
(8) पुलिस के आने से पहले ही चोर भाग चुके थे।
(9) मैं इस खेल को पहले ही देख चुका था।
(10) वह तीन दिन से बीमार था।
(11) सीता ने उसे पहले ही चेतावनी दी थी।
(12) मेरे ऑफिस पहुँचने से पूर्व, चपरासी घर जा चुका था।
(13) राम के बस स्टैण्ड पर पहुँचने के पूर्व बस जा चुकी थी।
(14) सात बजने से पूर्व मैं अपनी पढ़ाई पूरी कर चुका था।
(15) राम के घर पहुँचने से पूर्व सीता खाना बना चुकी थी।
(16) उसने मुझे पहले से सूचित नहीं किया था।
(17) क्या उसने तुम्हें पहले चेतावनी नहीं दी थी?
(18) क्या वह पाँच दिन से बीमार था?
(19) मेरे घर पहुँचने से पूर्व कुकु खाना नहीं बना चुकी थी।
(20) क्या वह तुम्हारे यहाँ पहुँचने से पूर्व मर चुका था?

12

Translate the following sentences into English :

(1) मोहन सुबह से पढ़ रहा था।
(2) वह सुबह से भोजन बना रही थी।
(3) क्या राम काफी लम्बे समय से खेल रहा था?
(4) वह दो महीने से कविता लिख रहा था।
(5) विमला दो घण्टे से पढ़ रही थी।
(6) कमला मई से इस काम को कर रही थी।
(7) तुम्हारी माँ सुबह से कपड़े धो रही थी।
(8) लड़के दो घण्टे से शोर कर रहे थे।
(9) तुम सन् 2001 से जयपुर में रह रहे थे।
(10) वह सुबह से रो रहा था।

13

Correct the following sentences :

(1) I had knew her for five years.
(2) If he has come to me, I would have helped him.
(3) If I had a pen, I will give you
(4) She had not play.
(5) Ram told Sita that I have seen your photos.
(6) The train had departed before I reach the station.
(7) Had she warn you before?
(8) Ram had been waiting for me since two hours.
(9) Had Sita been not cooking since morning?
(10) Suresh had been writing a book since three months.

(11) It had been raining for last evening.
(12) He told that he has been writing a letter for the last one hour.
(13) Had not he waiting for you for two hours?
(14) Maya had already inform me.
(15) Gita not had been waiting for you since January.

(1) Past Perfect में had के साथ verb की III form लगती है।
(2) Conditional Sentences में had + V-III के साथ would have + V-III का प्रयोग होता है।
(3) Conditional Sentences में had + noun के साथ will का प्रयोग नहीं होगा, would का प्रयोग होगा।
(4) Past Perfect Continuous में had been के साथ Verb की IV form का प्रयोग होता है।
(5) Since का प्रयोग, Point of time के साथ होता है तथा For का प्रयोग अवधि Period of time के साथ होता है।
(6) Indirect narration में यदि reporting verb past में है तो, reporting speech में have been की जगह had been का प्रयोग होगा।

14

Translate the following sentences into English :

(1) मैं कल बाजार जाऊँगा।
(2) विमला भोजन पकाएगी।
(3) वह यह काम आज नहीं करेगा।
(4) हम आज आम खाएँगे।
(5) वह जयपुर जाएगा।
(6) वह पत्र लिखेगा।
(7) तुम कल स्कूल जाओगे।
(8) मैं फुटबॉल खेलूँगा।
(9) हम रात को सोएँगे।
(10) वह आज शाम को घूमने जाएगा।
(11) वह कल आ सकता है।
(12) वर्षा हो सकती है।
(13) राम कल अवश्य आएगा।
(14) मैं बाजार नहीं जाऊँगा।
(15) क्या वह चाय नहीं लेगा?
(16) क्या सीता तुम्हें पत्र नहीं लिखेगी?
(17) वह कल मैच नहीं खेलेगा।
(18) क्या हर्ष पढ़ाई नहीं करेगा?
(19) क्या तुम यह कार ठीक नहीं करोगे?
(20) क्या सीता खाना नहीं बनाएगी?

15

Translate the following sentences into English :

(1) मैं कल इस समय पत्र लिख रहा हूँगा।
(2) मेरा भाई पढ़ रहा होगा।
(3) हम गाना गा रहे होंगे।
(4) वह अपना पाठ याद कर रहा होगा।
(5) राम फुटबॉल खेल रहा होगा।
(6) माँ खाना बना रही होगी।
(7) सीता रो रही होगी।
(8) क्या विमला नाच रही होगी?
(9) हम रात को सो रहे होंगे।
(10) क्या अध्यापक इस समय पढ़ा रहा होगा ?
(11) राम ऑफिस जा रहा होगा।
(12) इस समय वर्षा हो रही होगी।
(13) क्या सीता खाना बना रही होगी?
(14) क्या कल इस समय वर्षा नहीं हो रही होगी?
(15) हर्ष अखबार पढ़ रहा होगा।
(16) मनीष देहली जा रहा होगा।
(17) क्या मनीष इस समय टीवी देख रहा होगा?
(18) क्या सीता मेरा इन्तजार कर रही होगी?
(19) कल हम इस समय जयपुर में क्रिकेट मैच देख रहे होंगे।
(20) क्या वह खेल रहा होगा?

16

Correct the following sentences :

(1) Let I go there.
(2) We will play a match.
(3) Will he not played?
(4) If he will come, I shall go.
(5) He will be play tomorrow.
(6) He will be staying here yesterday.
(7) Ram shall not be playing football.
(8) Will not he be going to market?
(9) Suchi will about to come.
(10) Will not you play?

(1) Future Indefinite में I, We के साथ Shall एवं II तथा III Person के साथ Will का प्रयोग होता है।
(2) Let के साथ I, we, he, she नहीं लगाते हैं बल्कि us, him, her लगाते हैं।
(3) Will not से प्रश्न शुरू करने पर Won't लिखा जाएगा।

17

Translate the following sentences into English :

(1) मैं मंगलवार तक यह काम समाप्त कर चुकूँगा।
(2) राम सन् 2001 तक अपनी पढ़ाई कर चुकेगा।
(3) सूरज ढलने से पहले पक्षी सो चुकेंगे।
(4) मेरे वहाँ पहुँचने से पहले वह जा चुकेगा।
(5) तुम्हारे जाने से पहले माँ खाना बना चुकी होगी।
(6) पुलिस के आने से पहले चोर भाग चुके होंगे।
(7) तुम आठ बजे तक अपने घर पहुँच चुके होगे।
(8) मेरे पहुँचने से पहले गाड़ी जा चुकी होगी।
(9) तुम्हारे वहाँ पहुंचने से पहले लड़के अपना मैच समाप्त कर चुके होंगे।
(10) मैं 7 बजे तक स्कूल पहुँच चुका हूँगा।
(11) राम कल इस समय तक दो घण्टे पढ़ चुका होगा।
(12) रमेश कल 5 बजे तक अपना प्रोजेक्ट पूरा नहीं कर चुकेगा।
(13) क्या वह 5 बजे तक टी.वी. ठीक कर चुकेगा।
(14) रमेश तीन बजे तक अपनी पढ़ाई पूरी कर चुकेगा।
(15) मेरे घर पहुँचने से पूर्व वर्षा रुक चुकेगी।
(16) उसके अस्पताल पहुँचने से पूर्व डॉक्टर जा चुकेंगे।
(17) वह सायं तक अपना कार्य पूरा नहीं कर चुकेगा।
(18) क्या वह सायं तक अपना कार्य पूरा नहीं कर चुकेगा?
(19) क्या रमेश तीन बजे तक अपनी पढ़ाई पूरी नहीं कर चुकेगा?
(20) मैं 7 बजे तक ऑफिस नहीं पहुँच चुकूँगा।

18

Translate the following sentences into English :

(1) वे सुबह से खेल रहे होंगे।
(2) लड़के चार बजे से मैदान में खेल रहे होंगे।
(3) माली सुबह से पौधों को सींच रहा होगा।
(4) राम दो घण्टे से अपना पाठ याद कर रहा होगा।
(5) मोहन कल शाम से सो रहा होगा।
(6) लड़के दोपहर से शोर मचाते रहे होंगे।
(7) तुम चार दिन से पढ़ते रहे होंगे।
(8) वे चार बजे से अपना समय नष्ट कर रहे होंगे।
(9) लड़के दो बजे से क्रिकेट खेल रहे होंगे।
(10) लड़कियाँ चार घण्टे से भोजन पका रही होंगी।
(11) क्या वह सुबह से पतंग उड़ा रहा होगा?
(12) वह दो घण्टे से घर की सफाई कर रहा होगा।
(13) सीता कल इस समय से मेरा दो घण्टे से इन्तजार कर रही होगी।
(14) क्या वह दो घण्टे से प्रार्थना नहीं कर रही होगी?
(15) रमेश कम-से-कम दो घण्टे से कार साफ कर रहा होगा।
(16) वह दो बजे से टीवी नहीं देख रही होगी।
(17) राजेश वर्ष 2009 में 15 वर्ष से इस मकान में रह रहा होगा।
(18) सुरेश वर्ष 2008 में चार वर्ष से इस कॉलेज में पढ़ा रहा होगा।
(19) सीता वर्ष 2007 में तीन वर्ष से इस स्कूल में पढ़ रही होगी।
(20) रमेश कल 5 बजे दो घण्टे से पढ़ रहा होगा।

19

Correct the following sentences :

(1) The students will have left the school before the Principal came.
(2) The train will have arrived before I reaches the station.
(3) He would have reached here before the sunset.
(4) Will he has completed his work by tomorrow?
(5) Will he have not repaired the car by 7 P.M.?
(6) He will has been waiting for you for three days.
(7) Will not he have been waiting for you since morning?
(8) Ram will have not been playing at this time tomorrow.
(9) Will the girls have played the game at 7 P.M.?
(10) He will have finish the work by 8 P.M.

(1) जब दो कार्य के सन्दर्भ में Future Perfect का प्रयोग किया जाता है तब एक भाग में will/shall have + V-III का प्रयोग होता है तथा दूसरे भाग में Present Indefinite Tense प्रयुक्त होता है।
(2) Future Tense के वाक्यों में Will/Shall के साथ has का प्रयोग नहीं किया जाता है। हमेशा have का ही प्रयोग किया जाता है।
(3) Will not/Shall not से यदि प्रश्न शुरू किया जाता है तो Won't/Shan't से शुरू किया जाएगा।
(4) Negative वाक्यों में not का प्रयोग Will के बाद होगा। Will have के बाद not लिखना गलत है।
(5) Future में समय के सन्दर्भ हेतु सामान्यतया by का प्रयोग किया जाता है।

NOTE

(1) If you want to inquire about a person's actions in the future, avoid the Simple Future, as it will make it sound like a request.
Compare : (X) and (Y)
(X) Will you be visiting him tomorrow ? (= I just wonder.)
(Y) Will you visit him tomorrow ? (= a request or an inquiry about his intentions).

(2) If you want to make it clear that the subject won't be doing something in the future, not because he does not want to, but due to circumstances, avoid the Simple Future.
Compare : (X) and (Y)
(X) He won't come to my party. (= he refuses to come.)
(Y) He won't be coming to my party. (= he can't.)

(3) If you want to use a future activity as an excuse, avoid to be going to, as that would make it sound like a personal preference at the moment. Use the Present Continuous instead, to make it clear that it is something you had already arranged, that you are engaged elsewhere.
I'm sorry, I'd love to have a game of chess with you, but I'm taking Mary out for dinner tonight. (I'm going to take ...would make it sound as if you prefer Mary's company to your friend's.)

(4) It is safe to use WILL for the three persons, except in questions asking for instructions or advice, where we use SHALL:
Shall I take your luggage upstairs? / What shall I do if John is late (= what do you want /expect me to do?)

More Exercises (Tense)

20

Write the letter* a, b, c, *or* d *of the correct answer in the brackets :

(1) When the Principal entered the class, a student .... on the blackboard.
(a) wrote (b) was writing (c) writes (d) is writing ( )

(2) She .... TV when her husband came.
(a) watch (b) was watching (c) is watching (d) watched ( )

(3) He always........ to prove that the earth revolves round the sun.
(a) tried (b) tries (c) was trying (d) is trying ( )

(4) He saw me by chance and .... the car.
(a) stop (b) stopped (c) stops (d) was stopping ( )

(5) How many pegs of wine .... yesterday?
(a) you have drank (b) were you drinking
(c) did you drink (d) do you drink ( )

(6) I was watching TV when she .... in.
(a) comes (a) came (c) come (d) was coming ( )

(7) She cut her finger while she .... vegetables.
(a) cutting (b) was cutting (c) cut (d) had cut ( )

(8) She still remembers the day when she first .... to church.
(a) went (b) was going (c) gone (d) going ( )

(9) The train had left before I .... the station.
(a) reach (b) was reaching
(c) reached (d) reaches ( )

(10) Had you worked hard, you ....passed?
(a) would (b) will (c) would have (d) will have ( )

21

Write the letter* a, b, c, *or* d *of the correct answer in brackets :

(1) We hope that Papa .... soon.
(a) come (b) is coming
(c) will come (d) shall come ( )

(2) Neelam is learning how ....
(a) to type (b) to typing
(c) typing (d) type ( )

(3) Someone .... away my bike within an hour.
(a) takes (b) took
(c) has taken (d) had taken ( )

(4) There are no taxies available because taxi drivers .... on strike.
(a) went (b) go
(c) have gone (d) will go ( )

(5) He .... suffering from fever since the last week.
(a) is (b) was
(c) has been (d) has ( )

(6) She has been suffering from malaria since she .... her job.
(a) leaves (b) had left
(c) left (d) has been leaving ( )

(7) They .... the students on educational tour on next Monday.
(a) were taking (b) have taken
(c) are taking (d) have been taking ( )

(8) I have just hired a typewriter and I .... type now-a-days.
(a) am learning (b) have learnt
(c) learnt (d) will learn ( )

(9) By July 2005, she .... in this firm for eleven years.
(a) will work (b) will have been working
(c) will be working (d) has been working ( )

(10) The train .... before we reach the station.
(a) will have departed (b) has departed
(c) is departing (d) was departing ( )

22

Write the letter* a, b, c, *or* d *of the correct answer in brackets :

(1) India .... freedom in 1947.
(a) attains (b) attained
(c) has attained (d) was attained ( )

(2) He .... out for an evening walk after he had taken my dinner.
(a) go (b) went
(c) have gone (d) will go ( )

(3) My sister was in the bathroom when she ...... the call-bell.
(a) rang (b) have rung
(c) ring (d) am ringing ( )

(4) She .... a better job next month.
(a) will get (b) have got
(c) got (d) get ( )

(5) He .... when the phone rang.
(a) cook (b) is cooking
(c) was cooking (d) has cooked ( )

(6) I went into the hostel to see what students ....
(a) are doing (b) did
(c) were doing (d) doing ( )

(7) While she .... in the garden it began to drizzle.
(a) watered (b) has watered
(c) was watering (d) had watered ( )

(8) When I reached the station, I found Shashi .... for me.
(a) was waiting (b) waits
(c) waited (d) waiting ( )

(9) I opened the door and saw that it ....
(a) rained (b) has rained
(c) was raining (d) were raining ( )

(10) .... you like milk or tea?
(a) Are (b) Have
(c) Does (d) Do ( )

(11) Columbus .... America.
(a) discovers (b) discovered
(c) has discovered (d) had discovered ( )

(12) He .... born in 1984.
(a) is (b) has
(c) was (d) had ()

(13) No, she is not here,she .... just .... out.
(a) has, gone (b) is, going
(c) was, going (d) will have, gone ()

(14) We .... a friendly cricket match in the evening.
(a) were playing (b) have played
(c) played (d) are playing ()

(15) What .... you going to do with this briefcase ?
(a) will (b) shall
(c) are (d) were ()

(16) An honest man always .... the truth.
(a) speak (b) speaks
(c) spoke (d) speaking ()

23

Translate the following sentences into English :

(1) मनीष चार बजे से खेल रहा है।
(2) वह रोजाना सुबह 6 बजे घूमने जाता है।
(3) मेरे पिताजी सायं 5 बजे ऑफिस से घर वापस आते हैं।
(4) मैं सुबह 5 बजे उठकर एक घण्टे अवश्य पढ़ता हूँ।
(5) वह रोजाना छः बजे स्टेशन जाता है।
(6) वह एक घण्टे से अखबार पढ़ रहा है।
(7) राजेश कॉलेज से आ चुका है।
(8) मोहन जयपुर जा चुका है।
(9) रमेश बाजार जा चुका है।
(10) पूजा ट्रेन से कोलकाता जा रही है।
(11) मैं आधा घण्टे घूमने जाता हूँ।
(12) वह दो घण्टे से पढ़ रहा है।
(13) मैं पढ़ रहा हूँ।
(14) मैं खाना खा रहा हूँ।
(15) मैं स्कूल जा रहा हूँ।
(16) मैं खेल रहा हूँ।
(17) मैं सोने जा रहा हूँ।
(18) मैं पढ़ चुका हूँ।
(19) वह स्कूल से आ चुका है।
(20) वह सो चुका है।
(21) वह 10 बजे रात को सोता है।
(22) वर्षा सुबह से हो रही है।
(23) वर्षा 2 घण्टे से हो रही है।
(24) पूजा खाना बना रही है।
(25) रमेश गाना गा रहा है।
(26) सीता कॉलेज जा रही है।

24

Correct the following sentences :

(1) Sarita go to office at 10 A.M. daily.
(2) She has been cooking meal from 7 A.M.
(3) Nisha is playing Tabla for two hours.
(4) Rani have just come from college.
(5) They have been residing here since four years.
(6) They goes to field at five A.M.
(7) Ram do his work in time.
(8) He drink coffee in the morning.
(9) Mr Sharma teachs us English grammar.
(10) Sakshi catchs the train at 8 O'clock.
(11) He flys kite on Sunday.
(12) We takes bath together in the river .
(13) We have been playing for 12 O'clock.
(14) Raheja has been singing since one hour.
(15) He pass all the tests without fail.

25

Translate the following sentences into English :

(1) वह कल दुर्घटनाग्रस्त हो गया।
(2) हमने अपना काम शुरू किया।
(3) मैं पिछले महीने मुम्बई गयी थी।
(4) हमने कई फल खाए।
(5) डाकिया ने कॉलोनी में पत्र बाँटे।
(6) रानी ने मधुर गीत गाया।
(7) वह जयपुर में पढ़ती थी।
(8) वह मुझे गाली देती थी।
(9) हम वहाँ जाया करते थे।
(10) तुम उस बगीचे में खेलते थे।
(11) वे मेरे घर में आया करते थे।
(12) हम क्रिकेट खेला करते थे।
(13) तुम हमेशा मुझे डाँटते थे।
(14) उसने कुएँ से पानी खींचा।
(15) वह मेरा नाम भूल गया।
(16) हम स्कूल में जाया करते थे।
(17) चूहा शेर पर उछला।
(18) हम नदी में स्नान किया करते थे।
(19) पत्ता पेड़ से गिरा।
(20) मैं रात में बहुत देर से सोता था।
(21) राहुल रोता था।
(22) तुम घूमने जाया करते थे।
(23) तुम कसरत किया करते थे।
(24) वह मुझसे लड़ाई किया करता था।
(25) मैंने झाड़ियों में एक चूहा देखा।
(26) तुमने तेज गति से गाड़ी चलाई थी।
(27) उसने अपना गृह कार्य किया।
(28) बकरी भाग सकी।
(29) तुम यहाँ आ सके।
(30) उसने मुझे एक गिफ़्ट दिया।
(31) सियाराम ने सुन्दर पुष्प तोड़े।
(32) मैंने उसे एक पेन दिया।
(33) तुमने अपने सेवक को बुलाया।
(34) सीमा ने कल एक परीक्षा दी।
(35) राम ने कल एक कविता लिखी।
(36) निशा कल अपने घर गयी।
(37) मैंने बालकों को ईनाम बाँटे।
(38) तुमने भरपेट भोजन किया।

26

Translate the following sentences into English :

(1) विद्यार्थी कठिन परिश्रम कर रहे थे।
(2) वह भोजन पका रही थी।
(3) माली पेड़ों को पानी दे रहा था।
(4) सीता कल एक बहुत अच्छा गाना गा रही थी।
(5) वह बर्तन साफ कर रही थी।
(6) हम शोर मचा रहे थे।
(7) मेरे पापा पत्र लिख रहे थे।
(8) हम स्टेडियम में दौड़ रहे थे।
(9) लड़कियाँ निबन्ध लिख रही थीं।
(10) पक्षी आकाश में उड़ रहे थे।
(11) गाय खेत में चर रही थी।
(12) तुम मेज साफ कर रहे थे।
(13) तुम चोर को पकड़ रहे थे।
(14) लड़के चाय पी रहे थे।
(15) डाकिया पत्र ला रहा था।
(16) वे दरवाजा बन्द कर रहे थे।
(17) मैं स्कूल जा रहा था।
(18) मैं तुम्हें गालियाँ दे रहा था।
(19) वे फूल तोड़ रहे थे।
(20) हम आइस-क्रीम खा रहे थे।

27

Translate the following sentences into English :

(1) अध्यापक के आने से पहले विद्यार्थी चले गए थे।
(2) तुम्हारे आने से पहले मैंने अपना कार्य समाप्त कर लिया था।
(3) पुलिस के आने से पहले चोर घर से भाग चुका था।
(4) चोर के जाने के पश्चात् पुलिस वहाँ पहुँची थी।
(5) सोने से पहले तुमने दरवाजा क्यों नहीं बन्द किया था?
(6) बच्चे के रोने के बाद माँ ने उसे दूध कब दिया था?
(7) मेरे सोने से पहले तुम यहाँ क्यों नहीं आए थे?
(8) मेरे सोने के पश्चात् तुम यहाँ से क्यों चले गए थे?
(9) क्या डॉक्टर के आने से पहले रोगी मर गया था?
(10) क्या डॉक्टर के जाने के बाद रोगी मर गया था?

28

Correct the following sentences :

(1) Tejpal and his friends were playing chess for two hours.
(2) Sita had been cooking for 2 O'clock.
(3) Rahim gone to market.
(4) The teacher was taught us Hindi at that time.
(5) Ramesh had took your purse.
(6) The girl had been crying since an hour.
(7) We had been playing chess since two hours.
(8) The train arrived before we reached there.
(9) The patient had fainted than the doctor came.
(10) My friends was coming by bus.

29

Translate the following sentences into English :

(1) मनीष कल कानपुर आएगा।
(2) मनीष शायद कल कॉलेज आएगा।
(3) शायद वह ट्रेन से या बस से आ रहा होगा।
(4) मैं आज यह पुस्तक पढ़ूँगा।
(5) मैं कल यहाँ आऊँगा।
(6) हम तुम्हारे साथ आगरा चलेंगे।
(7) हम तुम्हारी सहायता करेंगे।
(8) वह कल कॉलेज अवश्य जाएगा।
(9) वे कल तुम्हारी सहायता करेंगे।
(10) चपरासी घण्टी बजाएगा।
(11) आज बारिश होगी।
(12) मैं अंग्रेजी लिख, पढ़ सकता हूँ
(13) वह इस समय अपने मित्रों के साथ क्रिकेट खेल रहा होगा।
(14) मेरा मित्र दोपहर दो बजे तक कानपुर से वापस आ जाएगा।
(15) राम इस समय अवश्य पढ़ रहा होगा।

30

Translate the following sentences into English :

(1) वह सुबह से खेल रही होगी।
(2) वह एक वर्ष से कम्प्यूटर सीख रहा होगा।
(3) वह इस समय नहीं पढ़ रहा होगा।
(4) वह इस समय खाना बना रही होगी।
(5) वे घर पर तुम्हारी प्रतीक्षा कर रहे होंगे।
(6) हमारे मित्र शाम की गाड़ी से आ रहे होंगे।
(7) शायद वह इस समय खाना बना रही होगी।
(8) वह ट्रेन से अवश्य आ रहा होगा।
(9) वह इस समय खेल रहा होगा।
(10) शायद वह अस्पताल गया होगा।
(11) मैं 7 बजे से पहले अलवर पहुँच जाऊँगा।
(12) चपरासी घण्टी बजा रहा होगा।
(13) वे लड़कियाँ नदी में स्नान कर रही होंगी।
(14) मोर छत पर नाच रहे होंगे।
(15) बच्ची फिर से रो रही होगी।
(16) मेरे अस्पताल पहुँचने से पूर्व डॉक्टर जा चुका होगा।
(17) डॉक्टर के आने से पूर्व मरीज मर चुका होगा।
(18) मैं सन् 2011 में रिटायर्ड हो चुकूँगा।
(19) मेरे पिताजी के आने से पूर्व ट्रेन चल चुकेगी।
(20) मुझे इस काम को तुरन्त पूर्ण करना चाहिए।

31

Correct the following sentences (Future Tense) :

(1) They will be playing cricket for two hours.
(2) Let I play tabla.
(3) We should obeyed our elders.
(4) She will be gone to market at this time .
(5) The patient will die before the doctor reaches here.
(6) I shall be living in Alwar for 8 years by the year 2010.
(7) He will waiting for you.
(8) Let the students played.
(9) He must be coming by Rajdhani Express.
(10) He should be completed his work by next Monday.

32

Fill in the blanks with correct form of the verbs (Present and Past) given in brackets in the space given :

(1) It is already 4 P.M. They..........(not arrive) yet.
(2) Rashmi is not in the hostel. She.....(go) out.
(3) Sita........(hurt) her leg. She can't walk fast.
(4) Suresh has no more books to sell. He .... (sell) all the books.
(5) They ....(play) the second match in the morning.
(6) Shilpa.......(reach) home last evening.
(7) They ....(complete) their project just now.
(8) Ramesh.........(finish) his work before Rakhi came.
(9) The girl ....(fall) from the roof while......(fly) a kite.
(10) It..........(rain) heavily since Monday.
(11) Raksha ....(fall) down while she..........(walk) in the gallery.
(12) Ranu.........(slip) while she.........(climb) up the roof.
(13) The light.........(go) out while we..........(have) drinks in the hotel.
(14) Swami ......(ring) the bell at 4 P.M. daily.
(15) We ....(live) in this country since India attained freedom.
(16) We..........(wait) for the train for last three hours.
(17) Ankita.........(read) the 'Ramayana' daily in the morning.
(18) A dog...........(bite) him, while she.......(pass) through the forest last week.
(19) Smrita..........(write) an story when Rahul......... (enter) the room.
(20) They.............(climb) up the ladder when they ....(hear) a loud sound.
(21) When Seema arrived, they ....(take) them lunch.
(22) They ....(play) football for half an hours when it started to rain.
(23) We.............(try) hard for ten weeks when we succeeded in solving the puzzle.
(24) He............(put) hard to secure first Rank for three years. He finally achieved the success.
(25) She...........(suffer) from fever for more than five days when she received the appointment letter.

33

Fill in the blanks with the future continuous /perfect/perfect continuous form of the verbs given in the brackets :

(1) ....she..........(go) home after Holi ?
(2) The students ....(work) on their project next year.
(3) The gardener ....(water) the plants at 7 P.M. in the evening tomorrow.
(4) Ramesh ....(repair) his bicycle all the day tomorrow.
(5) Her brother..........(study) in this college next year positively.
(6) You........(complete) your work by the end of this month.
(7) By the end of next year I..........(finish) my project positively.
(8) The farmers...........(plough) all their fields before the monsoon reaches.
(9) We.............(manufacture) remote controlled planes by the end of the next year.
(10) By next month, you............(visit) all the famous lake of Udaipur.
(11) Rahul ....(practise) it for two months by January next.
(12) Sangita.......(teach) English for two years by March, 2006.
(13) Mr Prassana.....(work) in this hospital for three years by December 2006.
(14) We.........(serve) in this firm for three years by January 2007.
(15) I........(live) here for twenty years by November 2003.

34

Write the letter a, b, c, or d of the correct answer in brackets :

(1) My wife always .... in the evening.
(a) cooks (b) cook
(c) has cooked (d) is cooking ( )

(2) I .... a coat because it is very cold today.
(a) wears (b) wear
(c) am wearing (d) have worn ( )

(3) The sun rises in the east and......in the west.
(a) is setting (b) sets
(c) set (d) setting ( )

(4) Look there, he .... after the thief.
(a) running (b) runs
(c) run (d) is running ( )

(5) An iron ball .... on water.
(a) not float (b) does not float
(c) not floats (d) do not float ( )

(6) Misha .... in class X.
(a) is studying (b) studies
(c) study (d) studying ( )

(7) Where are you? I .... in the drawing room.
(a) work (b) working
(c) am working (d) works ( )

(8) I .... depressed when I go for the interview.
(a) felt (b) am feeling
(c) feels (d) feel ( )

(9) The wind .... very speedily tonight.
(a) is blowing (b) blowing
(c) are blowing (d) blow ( )

(10) Are you .... an exercise on Present Tense now?
(a) do (b) does
(c) doing (d) did ( )

(11) She will go out only when the rain ....
(a) stops (b) stop
(c) is stopping (d) stopped ( )

35

Read the following sentences to find whether there is any error in any part :

(1) I have come to (a) know that (b) his father has died (c) three days ago (d).

(2) When you will find (a) out a solution (b) to this problem (c) you will be awarded a prize (d).

(3) Before the alarm had stopped (a) ringing (b) Nisha had telephoned (c) the police (d).

(4) This is the first time that I see such an interesting movie.
a b c d

(5) Whenever he is coming here, he brings many gifts for me.
a b c d

(6) Now-a-days he teaches English because the teacher of English has gone for a month's leave.
a b c d

(7) "It is high time you are starting this business" said Ram to Mahesh.
a b c d

(8) I will let you know as soon as I will get any news in this regard.
a b c d

(9) When I will cross fifty, my wife will cross forty five.
a b c d

(10) The secret of his good health lies in the fact that he is getting up early and goes to bed early.
a b c d

36

Read the following sentences to find whether there is any error in any part :

(1) The students sitting on the dais studied here for three years but they have never created any problem.
a b c d

(2) A philogynist is a person who loves woman but a misogynist is a person who is hating woman.
a b c d

(3) It is appearing to me that you are trying to destabilise the present committee.
a b c d

(4) I have been knowing her for many years but I don't know where she works.
a b c d

(5) If he would have done this he would have done wrong and would have deceived many of his relatives.
a b c d

(6) The victim tried to tell us what has happened but his words were not audible.
a b c d

(7) I want you to pick up the box of eggs gently and kept it in the corner carefully.
a b c d

(8) She came to the party much later than I expect. **[Bank Baroda PO]**
a b c d

(9) I lived here for five years so I know about the problems of this colony.
a b c d

(10) The chairman had not taken any decision until he had studied the case thoroughly.
a b c d

(11) They got everything ready for the visitors long before they reached there.
a b c d

(12) He switched on the light before he entered the room. No error
a b c d e

(13) I have been admiring her for the voice with which she is gifted.
a b c d

(14) He was with me till now so don't punish him for the delay.
a b c d

(15) Several survey reports indicate that the number of drug addicts is grown gradually.
a b c d

(16) "Here is coming up Bachchan!", said he when he was waiting for him.
a b c d

(17) I could not recall when she has told me about her affair with Gopal.
a b c d

(18) Four and four always made eight cannot be questioned by anyone.
a b c d

(19) She hopes to become an engineer after she will complete her education.
a b c d

37

Read the following sentences to find whether there is any error in any part :

(1) When you will find (a)/ a solution to this problem (b)/ you will be able (c)/ to get this project. (d)
(2) The teacher told us (a)/ that we should remain (b)/ in the hostel (c)/ if it rains. (d)
(3) I could not recall (a)/ what she has advised me (b)/ in this matter. (c)
(4) By this time tomorrow (a)/ she has had reached (b)/ there positively. (c)
(5) I will inform (a)/ you as soon as (b)/ I will get any news (c)/ about his health. (d)
(6) A recent survey (a)/ indicates (b)/ that the number of drug addicts (c)/ grew day by day. (d)
(7) Before the alarm (a)/ had stopped ringing (b)/ Reena had pulled up the shade. (c)
(8) If I was you (a)/ I would have told (b)/ the principal (c)/ to keep his mouth shut. (d)
(9) I want you (a)/ to pick up the box (b)/ of glasses gently (c)/ and kept it on the table carefully. (d)
(10) The victim tried (a)/ to tell us what has happened (b)/ but his words (c)/ were not audible. (d)

38

Read the following sentences to find whether there is any error in any part :

(1) It is appearing to me (a)/ that you are working against (b)/ your friends. (c)
(2) A misogynist is (a)/ a person who is hating woman (b)/ but a philogynist is a person (c)/ who loves woman. (d)
(3) The secret of his (a)/ good health lies (b)/ in the fact (c)/ that he is getting up before sunrise. (d)
(4) He said to me, (a)/ "It is high time (b)/ you are starting (c)/ this new business." (d)
(5) I came to know (a)/ that your father (b)/ has died (c)/ last month. (d)
(6) If we had Ramesh (a)/ in our team, we (b)/ would have won the match. (c)
(7) My friend said to me, (a)/"When have (b)/ you come here?" (c)
(8) I have been knowing (a)/ him for the last five years (b)/ but now I don't know (c)/ where he lives. (d)
(9) He lived here (a)/ since 1998, (b)/ so he knows everything (c)/ about this town. (d)
(10) I have been working (a)/ in this firm (b)/ for the last twenty years. (c)/No error (d)

39

(A) *Supply the correct tense forms of the verbs given in the brackets :* **[RAS 1998]**

(i) When we (take) our exams, we'll have a holiday.
(ii) I (leave) these flowers at the hospital for you. I (go) there anyway to visit my cousin.
(iii) When I reached the school, the first bell (already go).
(iv) Only the wearer (know) where the shoe (pinch).

(v) He (play) the guitar outside her house when someone opened the window and (throw) out a bucket of water.

(vi) I wish you (tell) me you already (buy) the book.

(B) ***Supply the correct tense forms of the verbs given in the brackets.*** **[RAS 1997]**

(i) I (not like) the dance last night.

(ii) Please sit here until my husband (come).

(iii) She (play) tennis since 4 O'clock.

(iv) My friend (not see) me for many years when I met him last week.

(C) ***Supply the correct tense forms of the verbs given in the brackets :*** **[RAS 1994]**

(i) They (build) that bridge when I (be) here last year. They (not finish) it yet.

(ii) Lend me your rubber. I (make) a mistake and (wish) to rub it out.

(iii) I wish I (know) his name.

(iv) When the aeroplane landed, the pilot (find) that one of the wings (be damaged) by a shell.

(v) Look, a man (run) after the bus. He (want) to catch it.

(D) ***Supply the correct tense forms of the verbs given in the brackets :*** **[RAS 1992]**

(i) If (be) a ghost. I (try) to frighten all the people I dislike.

(ii) He (know) her a long time before he finally (get) married to her.

(iii) What you (do) just now while I (wash) the dishes ?

(iv) I always (tell) you to comb your hair, but you never (do) what I say.

(v) I hope it (not rain) when the bride (leave) the church.

40

Fill in the blanks:

(A) ***Supply the correct tense form of the verbs given in the brackets :*** **[RAS 1996]**

The city of Katagum .... (build) in the form of an oblong with the chief's house in the centre .... (look) like an old English castle. There .... (be) a high clay tower, with a wall around it about twenty feet high; inside the courtyard ....(be) small houses for women and servants. The chief himself and his soldiers .... (occupy) the upper part of the three storied tower in times of alarm and danger. All round the tower walls small holes .... (cut), through which archers could fire their arrows at an attacking enemy.

(B) ***Supply the correct tense form of the verbs given in the brackets :*** **[RAS 1989]**

"The fire..... (look) very serious",....... (say) a young soldier, "But I wonder why they .... (not order) everyone to leave the building till the fire .... (to be extinguished)." Suddenly a great tongue of flame .... (shoot) out of a window on the fourth floor and the broken glass.....(begin) to fall. I ....(look) at the soldier and he (look) at me. "Come on", he said "We......(go) to see what ....(happen) there".

(C) ***Fill in the blanks :*** **[RAS 1989]**

When I .... home yesterday, I .... the noise of a fire engine and when I......... up, I......... that smoke was .... out of the fourth floor of a high rise building. I .... over to the place and .... a small group of people who all were ...... at the smoke and .... together in serious tones as if something really serious .... happened.

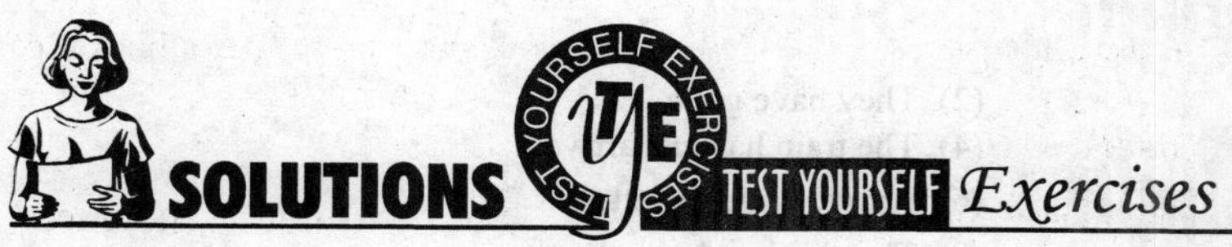

Solution TYE 01

(1) I eat a mango.
(2) We read daily.
(3) It rains.
(4) She works here.
(5) She wants to meet Ram.
(6) You go to the market.
(7) He does not take tea.
(8) I run very fast.
(9) She sings a song.
(10) Ram learns his lesson.
(11) He goes to college at 10 A.M. daily.
(12) They go to play at the field at 5 A.M. daily.
(13) Sita always helps the poor.
(14) Ramesh never tells a lie.
(15) The sun rises in the east and sets in the west.
(16) Do you know my name?
(17) The earth does not revolve round the moon.
(18) Sita learns a lesson daily.
(19) Ramesh flies kites.
(20) She does not wash clothes.

Solution TYE 02

(1) I write a letter.
(2) He goes to temple daily.
(3) Sita cries.
(4) He flies kites.
(5) He does not play.
(6) Do I write a letter?
(7) Does she swim?
(8) Does she go to school?
(9) Ram does not tell a lie.
(10) He never verifies the bills.

Solution TYE 03

(1) I am eating a mango.
(2) She is speaking the truth.
(3) Ramesh is playing football.
(4) Ram is telling a lie.
(5) She is reading.
(6) She is doing her work.
(7) He is going to Jaipur.
(8) Birds are flying.
(9) Are you playing ?
(10) The cool wind is blowing.
(11) It is drizzling.
(12) He is writing a letter to his friend .
(13) Sita is milking the cow.
(14) Ram is not waiting for me.
(15) Is she not going to market?
(16) He is writing a book now-a-days.
(17) He is abusing you.
(18) I am hearing.
(19) I see.
(20) He is teaching in the college.

Solution TYE 04

(1) You are playing.
(2) I am reading.
(3) They are reading.
(4) She is not swimming.
(5) Is it raining?
(6) Is she cooking?
(7) Is he playing?
(8) Are you coming?
(9) I am going to play.
(10) She is speaking.
(11) I see.
(12) I have a car.
(13) I understand.
(14) He knows me.
(15) He resembles his brother.

Solution TYE 05

(1) I have eaten a mango.
(2) They have gone.
(3) It has rained.
(4) The train has just arrived.
(5) It has just struck seven.
(6) I have written a letter.
(7) We have finished our work.
(8) The children have slept.
(9) He has played a lot.
(10) They have solved this problem.
(11) He has been ill since last Sunday.
(12) He has known me for five years.
(13) They have lived here for five years.
(14) Has he just come?
(15) He has not learnt his lesson.
(16) He has been to America.
(17) Has he gone to Delhi?
(18) Has Sita not washed clothes?
(19) I have learnt my lesson.
(20) The train has just arrived.

Solution TYE 06

(1) We have been playing since morning.
(2) I have been residing here for two years.
(3) He has been studying since 4 O'clock.
(4) He has been sleeping since morning.
(5) I have been securing first position for four years.
(6) I have not been taking food for many days.
(7) He has been laughing for many hours.
(8) He has been studying here since the year 2000.
(9) He has been solving the same question for two hours.
(10) He has been running since morning.
(11) I have been waiting for you since morning.
(12) It has been raining regularly since yesterday evening.
(13) It has been raining for four days.
(14) Have you not been waiting for Sita since yesterday?
(15) He has not been studying for two days.
(16) Has he not been preparing for this examination for four years?
(17) Ramesh has been playing football since 2 O'clock.
(18) My mother has been washing clothes for an hour.
(19) My father has been reading newspaper since 7 O'clock in the morning.
(20) I have been watching T.V. since evening.

Solution TYE 07

(1) He has gone to Jaipur.
(2) I have played.
(3) They arrived yesterday.
(4) Has he played a match?
(5) Ram has just gone.
(6) He has not taken food.
(7) He has been ill since Monday.
(8) I have been playing for two hours.
(9) He has been swimming since 2 O'clock.
(10) Has she been cooking for two hours?
(11) Have I not been playing for an hour?
(12) She has just arrived.
(13) Raju has been playing for three hours.
(14) I know him.
(15) They have not been reading for an hour.

Solution TYE 08

(1) I wrote a letter.
(2) I went to market.
(3) The teacher taught me yesterday.
(4) Ram wrote a poem.
(5) Sita did not sing a song.
(6) Did he go to Jaipur yesterday?
(7) Did the teacher punish you?
(8) He laughed at you.
(9) He stayed at Jaipur for a week.
(10) Did you go there yesterday?
(11) I wrote a letter yesterday.
(12) Sita washed the clothes.

(13) He cleaned the office yesterday.
(14) He woke up at 5 A.M. yesterday and studied for two hours.
(15) He telephoned me.
(16) Ram abused Shyam.
(17) Did he watch TV serial?
(18) Did Ram not come here yesterday? or Didn't Ram come here yesterday?
(19) Ram watched TV from 7 to 8 A.M. yesterday.
(20) We saw a movie yesterday.

Solution TYE 09

(1) Ram was playing football in the morning.
(2) You were going to the market yesterday.
(3) Rama was singing a song in the morning.
(4) Mummy was preparing our food.
(5) He was reading a book.
(6) He was telling a lie.
(7) The birds were flying in the sky.
(8) It was raining.
(9) Ram and Mohan were fighting.
(10) Mummy was sleeping at noon.
(11) When I reached there she was washing the clothes.
(12) While I was reading, my brother was watching TV.
(13) While it was raining, I was sleeping.
(14) Suresh was waiting for me.
(15) Ramesh was not telling a lie.
(16) Was Sita not swimming in the river?
(17) Was it not raining at 5 O'clock yesterday?
(18) Was Geeta not singing in the morning? or Wasn't Geeta singing in the morning?
(19) Ramesh was playing football, while I was working.
(20) My father was working in office at 5 O'clock yesterday.

Solution TYE 10

(1) He went to Jaipur.
(2) He went to Jaipur a short while ago.
(3) He did not go to Jaipur.
(4) Did he come yesterday?
(5) He did not open the door.
(6) He was not going.
(7) I was not doing that.
(8) You were making a noise.
(9) She did not ask me.
(10) Did he not remind you?
(11) Were you not playing?
(12) Weren't you writing?
(13) Wasn't I watching movie?
(14) Was she not cooking?
(15) Were they not playing football?

Solution TYE 11

(1) The train had departed before I reached the station.
(2) The patient had died before the doctor came.
(3) He had left before I reached there.
(4) I had reached the school before the bell rang.
(5) When I reached his house he had taken his food.
(6) The match had already started.
(7) He had already played with these toys.
(8) The thieves had fled before the police came.
(9) I had already seen this game.
(10) He had been ill for three days.
(11) Sita had already warned him.
(12) The peon had gone to his house before I reached the office.
(13) The bus had departed before Ram reached the bus stand.
(14) I had completed my studies before it struck seven.
(15) Sita had cooked before Ram reached home.

(16) He had not informed me before.
(17) Had he not warned you before?
(18) Had he been ill for five days?
(19) Kuku had not cooked food before I reached home.
(20) Had he died before you reached here?

Solution TYE 12

(1) Mohan had been studying since morning.
(2) She had been cooking the food since morning.
(3) Had Ram been playing for a long time?
(4) He had been writing a poem for two months.
(5) Vimla had been studying for two hours.
(6) Kamla had been doing this work since May.
(7) Your mother had been washing the clothes since morning.
(8) The boys had been making noise for two hours.
(9) You had been living in Jaipur since 2001.
(10) He had been weeping since morning.

Solution TYE 13

(1) I had known her for five years.
(2) If he had come to me, I would have helped him.
(3) If I had a pen, I would give you.
(4) She had not played.
(5) Ram told Sita that he had seen her photos.
(6) The train had departed before I reached the station.
(7) Had she warned you before?
(8) Ram had been waiting for me for two hours.
(9) Had Sita not been cooking since morning?
(10) Suresh had been writing a book for three months.
(11) It had been raining since last evening.
(12) He told that he had been writing a letter for the last one hour.
(13) Hadn't he been waiting for you for two hours?
(14) Maya had already informed me.
(15) Gita had not been waiting for you since January.

Solution TYE 14

(1) I shall go to market tomorrow.
(2) Vimla will cook the food.
(3) He will not do this work today.
(4) We shall eat mangoes today.
(5) He will go to Jaipur.
(6) He will write a letter.
(7) You will go to school tomorrow.
(8) I shall play football.
(9) We shall sleep at night.
(10) He will go for a walk today in the evening.
(11) He may come tomorrow.
(12) It may rain.
(13) Ram must come tomorrow.
(14) I shall not go to the market.
(15) Will he not take tea?
(16) Will Sita not write you letters?
(17) He will not play the match tomorrow.
(18) Will Harsh not study?
(19) Will you not repair this car?
(20) Will Sita not cook food?

Solution TYE 15

(1) I shall be writing a letter tomorrow at this time.
(2) My brother will be studying.
(3) We will be singing a song.
(4) He will be learning his lesson.
(5) Ram will be playing football.
(6) Mother will be cooking the food.
(7) Sita will be weeping.
(8) Will Vimla be dancing?
(9) We will be sleeping at night.
(10) Will the teacher be teaching at this time?
(11) Ram will be going to office.
(12) It will be raining at this time.
(13) We will be watching cricket match at Jaipur at this time tomorrow.

(14) Will he be playing?
(15) Will Sita be cooking the food?
(16) Will it not be raining at this time tomorrow?
(17) Harsh will be reading the newspaper.
(18) Maneesh will be going to Delhi.
(19) Will Maneesh be watching TV at this time?
(20) Will Sita be waiting for me?

Solution TYE 16

(1) Let me go there.
(2) We shall play a match.
(3) Will he not play?
(4) If he comes, I shall go.
(5) He will be playing tomorrow.
(6) He will be staying here tomorrow.
(7) Ram will not be playing football.
(8) Won't he be going to market?
(9) Suchi is about to come.
(10) Won't you play?

Solution TYE 17

(1) I shall have finished this work by Tuesday.
(2) Ram will have finished his studies by 2006.
(3) The birds will have slept before the sun sets.
(4) He will have gone before I reach there.
(5) Mother will have cooked food before you go.
(6) The thieves will have fled before the police come.
(7) You will have reached your home by 8 O'clock.
(8) The train will have departed before I reach.
(9) The boys will have finished their match before you reach there.
(10) I shall have reached school by 7 O'clock.
(11) Ram will have studied for two hours by this time tomorrow.
(12) Ramesh will not have completed his project by 5 O' clock tomorrow.
(13) Will he have repaired TV by 5 O'clock?
(14) Ramesh will have completed his studies by 3 O'clock.
(15) The rain will have stopped before I reach home.
(16) The doctors will have gone before he reaches the hospital.
(17) He will not have completed his work by evening.
(18) Will he not have completed his work by evening?
(19) Will Ramesh not have completed his studies by 3 O'clock?
(20) I shall not have reached the office by 7 O'clock.

Solution TYE 18

(1) They will have been playing since morning.
(2) The boys will have been playing at the ground since 4 O'clock.
(3) The gardener will have been watering the plants since morning.
(4) Ram will have been learning his lesson for two hours.
(5) Mohan will have been sleeping since yesterday evening.
(6) The boys will have been making a noise since noon.
(7) You will have been studying for four days.
(8) They will have been wasting their time since 4 O'clock.
(9) The boys will have been playing cricket since 1 O'clock.

(10) The girls will have been cooking food for four hours.
(11) Will he have been flying kites since morning?
(12) He will have been cleaning the house for two hours.
(13) Sita will have been waiting for me for two hours by this time.
(14) Will she not have been praying for two hours?
(15) Ramesh will have been cleaning the car at least for two hours.
(16) She will not have been watching TV since 2 O'clock.
(17) Rajesh will have been living in this house for 15 years by the year 2009.
(18) Suresh will have been teaching in this college for four years by the year 2008.
(19) Sita will have been reading in this school for three years by the year 2007.
(20) Ramesh will have been studying for two hours at 5 O'clock tomorrow.

Solution TYE 19

(1) The students will have left the school before the Principal comes.
(2) The train will have arrived before I reach the station.
(3) He will have reached here before the sunsets.
(4) Will he have completed his work by tomorrow?
(5) Will he not have repaired the car by 7 P.M.?
(6) He will have been waiting for you for three days.
(7) Won't he have been waiting for you since morning?
(8) Ram will not have been playing at this time tomorrow.
(9) Will the girls have played the game by 7 P.M.?
(10) He will have finished the work by 8 P.M.

Solution TYE 20

(1) (b)	(2) (b)	(3) (a)	(4) (b)	(5) (c)	(6) (b)
(7) (a)	(8) (a)	(9) (c)	(10) (c)		

Solution TYE 21

(1) (c)	(2) (a)	(3) (c)	(4) (c)	(5) (c)	(6) (c)
(7) (c)	(8) (a)	(9) (b)	(10) (a)		

Solution TYE 22

(1) (b)	(2) (b)	(3) (a)	(4) (a)	(5) (c)	(6) (c)
(7) (c)	(8) (d)	(9) (c)	(10) (d)	(11) (b)	(12) (c)
(13) (a)	(14) (c)	(15) (c)	(16) (b)		

Solution TYE 23 (Present Tense)

(1) Manish has been playing since 4 O'clock.
(2) He goes for a walk at 6 O'clock daily in the morning.
(3) My father returns home from his office at 5 P.M.
(4) I study for an hour after getting up at 5 A.M.
(5) He goes to station daily at 6 O'clock.
(6) He has been reading the newspaper for an hour.
(7) Rajesh has returned from college.
(8) Mohan has gone to Jaipur.

(9) Ramesh has gone to market.
(10) Pooja is going to Kolkata by train.
(11) I go for a walk for half an hour.
(12) He has been reading for two hours.
(13) I am reading.
(14) I am taking food.
(15) I am going to school.
(16) I am playing.
(17) I am going to bed.
(18) I have read.
(19) He has returned from school.
(20) He has slept.
(21) He goes to bed at 10 P.M.
(22) It has been raining since morning.
(23) It has been raining for two hours.
(24) Pooja is cooking.
(25) Ramesh is singing a song.
(26) Sita is going to college.

Solution TYE 24 (Present Tense)

(1) change 'go' to 'goes'
(2) change 'from' to 'since'
(3) change 'is' to 'has been'
(4) change 'have' to 'has'
(5) change 'since' to 'for'
(6) change 'goes' to 'go'
(7) change 'do' to 'does'
(8) change 'drink' to 'drinks'
(9) change 'teachs' to 'teaches'
(10) change 'catchs' to 'catches'
(11) change 'flys' to 'flies'
(12) change 'takes' to 'take'
(13) change 'for' to 'since'
(14) change 'since' to 'for'
(15) change 'pass' to 'passes'

Solution TYE 25

(1) He met with an accident yesterday.
(2) We began our work.
(3) I went to Mumbai last month.
(4) We ate many fruits.
(5) The postman delivered letters in the colony.
(6) Rani sang a sweet song.
(7) She read in Jaipur.
(8) She abused me.
(9) We used to go there.
(10) You played in that garden.
(11) They used to come to my home.
(12) We used to play cricket.
(13) You always scolded me.
(14) He drew water from the well.
(15) He forgot my name.
(16) We used to go to school.
(17) The mouse jumped on the lion.
(18) We used to bath in the river.
(19) The leaf fell from the tree.
(20) I slept very late at night.
(21) Rahul wept.
(22) You used to walk.
(23) You used to take exercise.
(24) He used to fight with me.
(25) I saw a mouse in the bushes.
(26) You drove the car very fast.
(27) He did his homework.
(28) The goat could run.
(29) You could come here.
(30) He gave me a gift.
(31) Siyaram plucked beautiful flowers.
(32) I gave him a pen.
(33) You called your servant.
(34) Seema took a test yesterday.
(35) Ram wrote a poem yesterday.
(36) Nisha went her home yesterday.
(37) I gave away prizes to the children.
(38) You ate to your hearts content.

Solution TYE 26

(1) The students were working hard.
(2) She was cooking.
(3) The gardener was watering the plants.
(4) Sita was singing a very good song yesterday.
(5) She was cleaning the utensils.
(6) We were making a noise.
(7) My father was writing a letter.
(8) We were running in stadium.
(9) The girls were writing the essay.
(10) The birds were flying in the sky.
(11) The cow was grazing in the field.
(12) You were cleaning the table.
(13) You were catching the thief.
(14) Boys were taking tea.
(15) The postman was bringing the letters.
(16) They were closing the gate.
(17) I was going to school.
(18) I was abusing you.
(19) They were plucking flowers.
(20) We were eating ice-cream.

Solution TYE 27

(1) The students had gone before the teacher came.
(2) I had finished my work before you came.
(3) The thief had gone out of the house before the police came.
(4) The police reached there after the thief had gone.
(5) Why had you not closed the door before you slept?
(6) When did the mother give milk to the baby after it had wept ?
(7) Why did you not come here before I had slept?
(8) Why had you not gone from here after I slept?
(9) Had the patient died before the doctor came ?
(10) Did the patient die after the doctor had gone?

Solution TYE 28 (Past Tense)

(1) change 'were' to 'have been'
(2) change 'for' to 'since'
(3) change 'gone' to 'went'
(4) change 'taught' to 'teaching'
(5) change 'took' to 'taken'
(6) change 'since' to 'for'
(7) change 'since' to 'for'
(8) insert 'had' after 'train'
(9) change 'than' to 'before'
(10) change 'was' to 'were'

Solution TYE 29

(1) Maneesh will come to Kanpur tomorrow.
(2) Maneesh may come to college tomorrow.
(3) He may be coming by train or by bus.
(4) I shall read this book today.
(5) I shall come here tomorrow.
(6) We shall go to Agra with you.
(7) We shall help you.
(8) He must go to college tomorrow.
(9) They will help you tomorrow.
(10) The peon will ring the bell.
(11) It will rain today.
(12) I can read and write English.
(13) He will be playing cricket with his friends at this time.
(14) My friend will have returned from Kanpur by 2 O'clock in the noon.
(15) Ram must be studying at this time.

Solution TYE 30

(1) She will have been playing since morning.
(2) He will have been learning computer for an year.
(3) He will not be reading at this time.
(4) She will be cooking at this time.
(5) They will be waiting for you at home.
(6) Our friends will be coming by evening train.
(7) She may be cooking at this time.
(8) He must be coming by train.
(9) He must be playing at this time.
(10) He may have gone to hospital.
(11) I shall have reached Alwar before seven.
(12) The peon will be ringing the bell.
(13) Those girls will be bathing in the river.
(14) Peacocks will be dancing on the roof.
(15) The baby will be crying again.
(16) The doctor will have left before I reach the hospital.
(17) The patient will have died before the doctor comes.
(18) I shall have retired in the year 2011.
(19) The train will have started before my father comes.
(20) I should complete this work immediately.

Solution TYE 31

(1) change 'will be' to 'will have been'
(2) change 'I' to 'us'
(3) change 'obeyed' to 'obey'
(4) change 'gone' to 'going'
(5) change 'will die' to 'will have died'
(6) change 'shall be' to 'shall have been'
(7) insert 'be' to after 'will'
(8) change 'played' to 'play'
(9) no change
(10) change 'should be' to 'will have'

Solution TYE 32

(1) have not arrived
(2) has gone
(3) has hurt
(4) has sold
(5) have played
(6) reached
(7) have completed
(8) have finished
(9) fell, flying
(10) has been raining
(11) fell, was walking
(12) slipped, was climbing
(13) went, were having
(14) rings
(15) have been living
(16) have been waiting
(17) reads
(18) bit, was passing
(19) was writing, entered
(20) climbed, heard
(21) had been taking
(22) had been playing
(23) had been trying
(24) had been putting
(25) had been suffering

Solution TYE 33

(1) will be going
(2) will be working
(3) will be watering
(4) will be repairing
(5) will be studying
(6) will have completed
(7) will have finished
(8) will have ploughed
(9) will have manufactured
(10) shall have visited
(11) will have been practising
(12) will have been teaching
(13) will have been working
(14) shall have been serving
(15) shall have been living

Solution TYE 34

(1) a, (2) c, (3) b, (4) d, (5) b, (6) a,
(7) c, (8) d, (9) a, (10) c, (11) a.

Solution TYE 35

(1) (c) has died की जगह केवल died लिखा जाएगा। Present Perfect के साथ Past time के Adverb (यहाँ three days ago) का प्रयोग नहीं किया जाता है।

(2) (a) When के बाद will का प्रयोग नहीं किया जाएगा, जब main clause में भी will का प्रयोग किया गया हो। When you find out a solution .... लिखें।

(3) (a) Had stopped की अपेक्षा stopped ही लिखा जाएगा। Past Perfect में जो कार्य पहले होता है, उसके लिए Past Perfect एवं बाद में पूर्ण होने वाले कार्य के लिए Past Indefinite का प्रयोग किया जाता है।

(4) (c) I see की जगह I have seen लिखा जाएगा। ध्यान रखें निम्न expressions के साथ Present Perfect Tense प्रयोग किया जाता है।

(a) This/that/ it is the first/second/third .... time/chance.

(b) That/this/ it is the only ....

(c) This/that/it is the best/worst/ finest/most interesting. जैसे :

This is the first timethat I have heard her song/singing in public.

(5) (a) Whenever he comes here लिखा जाएगा। यह आदतन किया जाने वाला act है, जिसके लिए Present Indefinite का प्रयोग होगा।

(6) (b) he teaches की जगह he is teaching लिखा जाएगा। Temporary कार्य हेतु Present Continuous का प्रयोग होता है।

(7) (b) You started लिखा जाएगा। ध्यान रखें It is high time / It is time / I wish / If /As if इत्यादि के साथ सामान्यतया Past Indefinite का प्रयोग किया जाता है।

(8) (c) Will get की जगह 'get' ही आएगा। जब main clause में will का प्रयोग किया गया हो तो if/as soon as/when/before/as/in case etc के साथ Present Indefinite का प्रयोग होता है।

(9) (a) I will cross की जगह I cross ही आएगा। प्रश्न (8) का explanation देखें।

(10) (c) he is getting up की जगह he gets up होगा। आदतन किए जाने वाले कार्यों हेतु Present Indefinite का प्रयोग होता है।

Solution TYE 36

(1) (b) studied की जगह have studied होगा। sitting on the dais एवं have never created का प्रयोग यह व्यक्त करता है कि वाक्य को Present Tense में माना गया है।

(2) (d) Who is hating की जगह who hates लिखा जाएगा। Universal truth/eternal truth के लिए Present Indefinite का प्रयोग होता है।

(3) (a) It is appearing की जगह It appears लिखा जाएगा। यहाँ appear का प्रयोग seem के अर्थ में हुआ है अत: Present Continuous का प्रयोग नहीं किया जाएगा। Present Indefinite का प्रयोग किया जाएगा। Appear का प्रयोग यदि 'जनता' के सामने आने या प्रकाशित होने के सन्दर्भ में हो तो Continuous में इसका प्रयोग किया जा सकता है; जैसे:

(a) His next novel is appearing this month.

(b) Now an eminent author is appearing on the stage.

(4) (a) I have been knowing की जगह I have known लिखा जाएगा। know, verb का प्रयोग Continuous में नहीं किया जाता है!

(5) (a) If he had done this लिखा जाएगा। इस तरह के conditional वाक्यों का Structure निम्न होगा :

It + subject + had + V-III ....would have + V-III

(6) (b) has happened की जगह had happened लिखा जाएगा। जब वाक्य में सब जगह Past Tense है, तो Present Perfect का प्रयोग गलत है।

(7) (c) Kept it की जगह keep it होगा। वाक्य में Past Tense का प्रयोग अनावश्यक किया गया है।

(8) (d) I expect की जगह I had expected आएगा। कार्य Past में हुआ है, अत: expect के साथ had expected (past to past) का प्रयोग होगा।

(9) (a) I lived की जगह I have lived होगा। सारा वाक्य Present Tense में है। एवं वाक्य का सन्दर्भ बताता है कि वह आज भी वहाँ रहता है।

(10) (a) The chairman did not take लिखा जाना चाहिए। जब वाक्य में एक clause had + V-3 का प्रयोग होता है तो दूसरे clause में Past Indefinite का प्रयोग होता है।

(11) (a) They got की जगह They had got लिखा जाएगा जब वाक्य में दो कार्य एक के बाद दूसरा पूर्ण होता है तो पहले पूर्ण होने वाले कार्य के लिए Past Perfect का प्रयोग किया जाता है।

(12) (e) No Error

(13) (a) I have been admiring की जगह I admire लिखा जाना चाहिए, क्योंकि know, admire, adore, trust, believe, rely, hope etc. का प्रयोग सामान्यतया Continuous में नहीं किया जाता है।

(14) (a) He was की जगह He has been लिखा जाएगा, क्योंकि till now, के साथ past का प्रयोग नहीं होता है।

(15) (d) Is grown की जगह is growing आएगा।

(16) (a) Here is coming की जगह Here comes लिखा जाएगा। Exclamatory वाक्यों में Present Indefinite का निम्न प्रकार से प्रयोग होता है :

Here comes the tram! There works Sita!

(17) (b) She has told की जगह she had told लिखा जाना चाहिए। जब वाक्य में Past tense का प्रयोग हो तो Present Perfect का प्रयोग नहीं होगा।

(18) (b) made की जगह makes लिखें। Universal truth / mathematical calculations/historical facts हेतु Present Indefinite का प्रयोग किया जाता है।

(19) (C) She will complete की जगह she has completed लिखा जाना चाहिए। She hopes का प्रयोग Future अर्थ के लिए किया गया है चूँकि engineer बनने से पूर्व education पूर्ण करनी है अत: Present Perfect का प्रयोग होगा।

निम्न वाक्यों को देखें :

I'll come as soon as I have finished writing this letter.
I can't decide until I have discussed the matter with my wife.
I'll buy it for you when I have the money.

The Present and Present Perfect tense may indicate future time in temporal and conditional clause.

A.S Hornby (*Guide to Pattern and Usage in English page 98.*)

Solution TYE 37

(1) (a) 'will' को delete करें। When के बाद वाक्य में will का प्रयोग नहीं करते हैं। When, it, before, after, until के बाद will का प्रयोग नहीं किया जाता है।

(2) (d) if it rains की जगह if it rained होना चाहिए। जब Reporting verb, Past Tense में है, तो reported speech भी Past Tense में होगा।

(3) (b) she has की जगह she had होना चाहिए। Principal clause में Past की घटना है, तो subordinate clause में भी Past Tense ही आएगा।

(4) (b) has had reached की जगह will have reached होगा। यह Future Perfect का वाक्य है।

(5) (c) 'will' को delete करें। Conditional clauses में as soon as, when, after, before if, के बाद Future Tense का प्रयोग नहीं होता है।

(6) (d) grew की जगह is growing होगा। The sentence is in Present tense.

(7) (b) had stopped की जगह केवल stopped होगा; जैसे:
He had died before the doctor came. Conditional sentences में जो कार्य बाद में होता है, उसमें Past Indefinite Tense का प्रयोग होता है।

(8) (a) If I was की जगह If I were होगा इस तरह के conditional वाक्यों में 'were' का प्रयोग किया जाता है।

(9) (d) kept की keep होगा। जब सारा वाक्य Present Tense में है तो 'kept' लगाना गलत है।

(10) (b) What has happened की जगह What had happened होगा। जब वाक्य Past में है तो यहाँ Present Perfect का use करना गलत है।

Solution TYE 38

(1) (a) It is appearing की जगह It appears होना चाहिए। Appear एक verb of perception है, इसका प्रयोग Present Indefinite में होता है। अन्य verb of perceptions है; smell, see, hate etc.

(2) (b) is hating की जगह hates होगा। hate भी verb of emotion है, जिसका Continuous में प्रयोग नहीं किया जाता है।

(3) (d) he is getting up की जगह he gets up होगा। Present habit को बताने हेतु Present Indefinite का प्रयोग किया जाता है।

(4) (c) You are starting की जगह You started होना चाहिए।
It is high time, It is time, I wish, if , As if के साथ Past Indefinite का प्रयोग किया जाता है।

(5) (c) has died की जगह died आएगा। Past time के Adverbs (यहाँ last month, ago, last year) Present Perfect का प्रयोग नहीं होता है।

(6) (a) We had की जगह we had had होना चाहिए; जैसे
If he had come to me, I would have helped him.
If he had had in our group, we would have won the shield.

(7) (b) When have की जगह when did लिखा जाएगा। Past में किसी question हेतु when did का प्रयोग होता है।

(8) (a) I have been knowing की जगह I have known होगा। Know ,see, appear, believe आदि verbs का प्रयोग Continuous Tense में करना अनुचित है।

(9) (a) lived की जगह has been living होगा। वाक्य की संरचना से अभी भी उसका रहना जाहिर होता है।

(10) (d) वाक्य सही है।

Solution TYE : 39

(a) (i) have taken (ii) left, had gone (iii) had already gone (iv) knows, pinches (v) was playing, threw (vi) told, had already bought

(b) (i) did not like (ii) comes (iii) has been playing (iv) had not seen.

(c) (i) were building, was have not finished (ii) have made, wish (iii) knew (iv) found, had been damaged (v) is running, wants.

(d) (i) were, would try (ii) had known, got (iii) were you doing, was washing (iv) tell, do (v) won't rain, leaves.

Solution TYE 40

(a) was built, looking, was, were, occupied, (would occupy), were cut.

(b) is looking, said, are not ordering, is extinguished, shot, began, looked, looked, shall go, has happened (is happening).

(c) reached, heard, went, saw, coming, went, saw, grazing, talking, had.

SEQUENCE OF TENSE

वह नियम जो यह निर्धारित करते हैं कि किसी वाक्य में subordinate Clause की क्रिया (Verb) का Tense क्या होगा? अर्थात् यदि Principal Clause में verb का Tense : Present, Past या Future है, तो Subordinate Clause में कौन-सा Tense प्रयुक्त होना चाहिए, जिससे वाक्य संरचना सही हो। इसका निर्धारण, जिन सिद्धान्तों, नियमों के तहत क्रिया जाता है, उन्हें Sequence of Tense के अन्तर्गत सम्मिलित किया गया है।

Rules

(1) यदि Principal Clause में क्रिया Past Tense में है, तो Subordinate Clause में भी क्रिया साधारणतया Past Tense में होती है।

Read the following sentences :

(a) My father assured me that he would buy a bike for me.
(b) He failed because he didn't work hard.
(c) He asked me what she was reading.
(d) I thought that I could win the race.
(e) Ram said that he would come on Monday.

Exceptions

(i) यदि Subordinate Clause में कोई Universal Truth, Mathematical Calculation, Historical Facts, Moral Guidelines हो, तो Subordinate Clause सामान्यतया Present Tense में आती है। जैसे :

(a) He said that the earth revolves round the sun.
(b) We learnt at school that the truth always triumphs.
(c) He said that two and two is four.
(d) Krishna told in 'Geeta' that life is not victory but battle.
(e) Ram said that man is mortal.
(f) I was happy to note that India is progressing.
(g) Newton discovered that the apple falls because of gravitational force of earth.

(ii) यदि Subordinate Clause किसी तुलना करने वाले Conjunction यथा than से शुरू हो, तो Subordinate Clause में verb किसी भी tense में हो सकती है। जैसे :

(a) He loved me more than he loved you.
(b) He loved me more than he loves you.
(c) He loved me more than he will love you.

(iii) लेकिन यदि Subordinate Clause एक adjective clause है, तो भी Subordinate Clause में verb किसी भी tense में हो सकती है। जैसे:

(a) I visited the place where accident took place.
(b) I visited the village where he lives.
(c) I visited the hotel where she will stay.

(2) यदि Principal Clause में verb, Present या Future Tense में है, तो Subordinate Clause में verb किसी भी Tense में हो सकती है। जैसे:

(a) He says that she passed the examination.
(b) He says that she will come tomorrow.
(c) Ram says that he likes that girl.
(d) Ram will say that Sita is a beautiful girl.
(e) Ram will say that he didn't like that girl.
(f) He will say that he will pass the examination positively.

Exceptions

(i) यदि Subordinate Clause if, till, as soon as, when, unless, before, until, even if, as इत्यादि से शुरू हो एवं Principal Clause में verb, Future में हो, तो Subordinate Clause में verb; Present Indefinite में आती है। जैसे:

(a) We shall not go to market if it rains.
(b) He will wait till she comes.
(c) We will start as soon as the taxi arrives.
(d) I shall ask him, when he meets me.
(e) I shall not go before he comes.
(f) I shall not help him unless he asks me.
(g) I shall help him even if he doesn't ask me.
(h) He will start as the taxi arrives.

(ii) यदि वाक्य if, when, unless, till, as etc. से शुरू हो, तो इनके साथ Present Indefinite का प्रयोग होगा तथा Principal Clause में Future का प्रयोग होगा। जैसे :

(a) If he comes, I shall accompany him.
(b) When he comes, I shall start.
(c) As the taxi arrives, we will start.
(d) Till he comes, we will wait here.
(e) Unless he requests me, I shall not help him.
(f) Until he comes, you should wait here.
(g) As he telephones, you should/must inform the police.

CHAPTER

06

NOUN

किसी व्यक्ति, वस्तु, स्थान,गुण, कार्य या अवस्था के नाम को Noun (संज्ञा) कहा जाता है।

A noun is a word used as name of a person, place or thing. 'Thing' शब्द बहुत विस्तृत है, इसमें सभी चीजों का समावेश हो जाता है।

Types of Noun

Noun पाँच प्रकार के होते हैं :

1. **Proper Noun** (व्यक्तिवाचक): A proper noun refers to the name of a person, place or thing.
   जैसे: Ram, Alwar, Tom etc.
   In each of the following sentences, the proper nouns are highlighted:
   (a) **Ram** is my friend. (b) I live at **Alwar**.
   (c) He is **Tom**.

2. **Common Noun** (जातिवाचक): A common noun is a noun referring to a person, place or thing in a general sense–usually, you should write it with a capital letter only when it begins a sentence.

   जैसे: King, boy, girl, city etc.
   In each of the following sentences, the common nouns are highlighted:
   (a) According to the **sign,** the nearest **town** is 80 km away from here.
   (b) All the **gardens** in the **neighbourhood** were invaded by **beetles** this **summer.**
   (c) The road **crew** was startled by the **sight** of three large **cats** crossing the **road.**

3. **Collective Noun** (समूहवाचक): A collective noun is the name of a group of persons or things taken together and spoken of as a whole, as unit. जैसे: Team, Committee, Army etc. सामान्यतया Collective Noun का प्रयोग Singular में होता है यदि इसका प्रयोग Plural में किया जाता है तो वह Common Noun बन जाता है।

   In each of the following sentences, the highlighted word is a collective noun:
   (a) The **flock** of geese spends most of its time in the pasture.
   The collective noun ''geese'' takes the singular verb ''spends.''
   (b) The **jury** is dining on take-out chicken tonight.
   In this example the collective noun ''jury'' is the subject of the singular compound verb ''is dining.''
   (c) The steering **committee** meets every Wednesday afternoon.
   Here the collective noun ''committee'' takes a singular verb, ''meets.''

4. **Material Noun** (पदार्थवाचक): A material noun is the name of metal or substance, of which thing are made of. जैसे: Silver, Iron, Wood etc.

The highlighted words in the following sentences are all material nouns

(a) The necklace is made of **gold.**
(b) She has purchased a tea set of **silver.**
(c) He got his furniture made of teak **wood.**

Material Nouns, Countable नहीं होते हैं अर्थात् इनकी गिनती नहीं की जा सकती है। इन्हें मापा या तौला जा सकता है इनके साथ सामान्यतया *singular verb* का प्रयोग किया जाता है एवं इनके पहले *Article* का प्रयोग नहीं किया जाता है।

5. **Abstract Noun** (भाववाचक): Abstract noun in general refers, the name of quality, action or state. जैसे: Honesty, Bravery (quality), Hatred, Laughter (action), Poverty, Young (state). Art एवं Science जैसे: Physics, Chemistry, Music, Grammar इत्यादि भी Noun में शामिल किए जाते हैं।

(a) *Abstract Noun,* ऐसे गुण, भाव, क्रिया एवं अवस्था को व्यक्त करता है जिन्हें *Physically Touch* नहीं किया जा सकता है, देखा नहीं जा सकता है, केवल महसूस किया जा सकता है।
(b) *Abstract Noun* का प्रयोग सामान्यतया *Singular* में किया जाता है।

The highlighted words in the following sentences are all abstract nouns

(a) Buying the emergency lights was an **afterthought.**
(b) **Justice** often seems to slip out of our grasp.
(c) It is believed that **schizophrenia** is transmitted genetically.

Other Kinds of Noun

1. ***Countable Nouns :*** A countable noun is a noun with both a singular and a plural form, and it names anything (or anyone) that one can count.

In each of the following sentences, the highlighted words are countable nouns:

(a) We painted the **tables** red and the **chairs** blue.
(b) She found six silver **dollars** in the **toe** of a **sock.**
(c) The oak **tree** lost three **branches** in the **hurricane.**

2. ***Non-Countable Nouns :*** A non-countable noun is a noun which does not have a plural form, and which refers to something that one cannot usually count. A non-countable noun always takes a singular verb in a sentence. Non-countable nouns are similar to collective nouns, and are the opposite of countable nouns.

The highlighted words in the following sentences are non-countable nouns:

(a) J Priestly discovered **oxygen.**
The word ''oxygen'' cannot normally be made plural.
Since ''oxygen'' is a non-countable noun, it takes the singular verb ''is'' rather than the plural verb ''are.''

(b) They decided to sell the **furniture.**
We cannot make the noun''furniture'' plural.

(c) The **furniture** is heaped in the middle of the room.
Since ''furniture'' is a non-countable noun, it takes a singular verb, ''is heaped.''

Some nouns are both non-countable and countable.

Sometimes a word that means one thing as a noncountable noun has a slightly different meaning as a countable noun. Remember, then, that the classifications count and noncount are not absolute.

Time is a good example.

1. Time is money.
2. One should not waste the time on trifles.
Here use of **Time** is non-countable.

See the following examples:

(a) On his last visit to Disney world , he climbed Space mountain seven times.
(b) I have called her five times.
(c) Here time is used as countables.

Important Rules of Nouns

Rule 1

कुछ Nouns का प्रयोग हमेशा Plural form में ही रहता है। इन Nouns के अन्त में लगे 's' को हटाकर, इन्हें Singular नहीं बनाया जा सकता है। ये दिखनें में भी Plural लगते हैं, एवं इनका प्रयोग भी Plural की तरह होता है। ऐसे Nouns निम्न हैं:

Alms, amends, annals, archives, ashes, arrears, athletics, auspices, caves, species, scissors, trousers, pants, clippers, bellows, gallows, fangs, eyeglasses, goggles, belongings, breeches, bowels, braces, binoculars, customs, congratulations, dregs, earnings, entrails, embers, fetters, fireworks, lodgings, lees, odds, outskirts, particulars, proceeds, proceedings, regards, riches, remains, savings, shambles, shears, spectacles, surroundings, tidings, troops, tactics, thanks, tongs, vegetables, valuables, wages etc.

(a) Where are my pants?
(b) Where are the tongs?
(c) The proceeds were deposited in the court.
(d) All his assets were seised.
(e) He sees dissidents as the dregs of society.
(f) Alms were given to the beggars.
(g) The embers of the fire were still burning.
(h) He hated always to be the bearer of bad tidings.

'Means'-Singular यदि इसके साथ a या every का प्रयोग हो, या इसका प्रयोग 'way to an end' तरीका/रास्ता के अर्थ में किया जाए।

'Means'-Plural यदि इसका प्रयोग Income के अर्थ में किया जाए। जैसे :

(a) My means were reduced substantially.

(b) Every means is good if the end is good.

Rule 2

कुछ Nouns दिखने में Plural लगतें हैं लेकिन अर्थ में Singular होते हैं। इनका प्रयोग हमेशा Singular में ही होता है। जैसे: News, Innings, Politics, Summons, Physics, Economics, Ethics, Mechanics, Mathematics, Mumps, Rickets, Billiards, Draughts, etc.

(a) No news is good news.
(b) Economics is a good subject.
(c) Draughts is a good game.
(d) Ethics demands honesty in working.

Rule 3

कुछ Nouns दिखने में Singular लगते हैं। लेकिन इनका प्रयोग हमेशा Plural में होता है। जैसे: cattle clergy, cavalry, infantry, poultry, peasantry, children, gentry, police etc. इनके साथ कभी भी 's' नहीं लगाया जाता, जैसे: cattles, childrens लिखना गलत है। क्योंकि ये Noun स्वयं में ही Plural हैं।

(a) Cattle are grazing in the field.
(b) Our infantry have marched forward.
(c) There are no gentry in the colony.
(d) Police have arrested the thieves.

Rule 4

कुछ Nouns का प्रयोग, केवल Singular form में ही किया जाता है। ये Uncountable Nouns हैं। इनके साथ Article A/An का प्रयोग भी नहीं किया जाता है। जैसे: Scenery, Poetry, Furniture, Advice, Information, Hair, Language, Business, Mischief, Bread, Stationery, Crockery, Luggage, Baggage, Postage, Knowledge, Wastage, Money, Jewellery, Breakage.

(a) The scenery of Darzeeling is very charming.
(b) I have no information about her residence.
(c) He transported his furniture by train.
(d) The mischief committed by him is unpardonable.
(e) His hair is black.
(f) He has no knowledge of grammar.

(i) उक्त nouns को कभी भी s लगाकर pluralise नहीं किया जाता है। जैसे: Sceneries, informations, furnitures, hairs इत्यादि लिखना गलत है।

(ii) यदि उक्त Noun को Singular या Plural forms में बनाना आवश्यक हो तो, इनके साथ कुछ शब्द जोड़कर किया जा सकता है। जैसे:

(a) He gave me a piece of information.
(b) All pieces of information given by her were reliable.
(c) Many kinds of furniture are available in that shop.
(d) I want a few articles of jewellery.
(e) He purchased some packets of bread.
(f) Please show me some items of office stationery.

(iii) यदि Hair का प्रयोग Countable की तरह हो तो Hairs हो सकता है। जैसे: one hair, two hairs. I need your two grey hairs.

Rule 5

कुछ Nouns, Plural एवं Singular दोनों में एक ही रूप में रहते हैं। जैसे: deer, fish, crew, family, team, jury, carp, pike, trout, aircraft, counsel etc.

(a) Our team is the best.
(b) Our team are wearing their new uniform.
(c) The jury is considering its judgement.
(d) The jury are considering their verdict.
(e) One fish is there in the pond.
(f) There are many fish in the pond.

Rule 6

कुछ Nouns जो अर्थ में तो Plural होते हैं, लेकिन यदि इनके पूर्व कोई निश्चित संख्यात्मक विशेषण (Definite numeral adjective) का प्रयोग किया जाता है, तो इन Nouns को Pluralise नहीं किया जाता है। जैसे: Pair, score, gross, stone, hundred, dozen, thousand, million, Billion etc.

(a) I have two pair of shoes.
(b) I have two hundred rupees only.
(c) She purchased three dozen pencils.
(d) He has already donated five thousand rupees.
(e) It is a three feet wall.
(f) It is five feet in width.

लेकिन यदि इनके साथ Indefinite countable का प्रयोग हो तो इन्हें Pluralise किया जाता है। जैसे: dozens of women, hundreds of people, millions of dollars, scores of shops, many pairs of shoes, thousands millions etc.

Rule 7

यदि किसी Noun के बाद Preposition आता है एवं फिर वही Noun आता है तो वह Noun Singular रहता है। जैसे:

(a) Town after town was devastated.
(b) Row upon row of pick marble looks beautiful.
(c) He enquired from door to door.
(d) Ship after ship is arriving.

इस तरह के वाक्यों में Towns after Towns, Rows upon Rows, doors to doors या ships after ships लिखना गलत है।

Rule 8

किसी वाक्य में Numeral Adjective के बाद a half, या a quarter आता है तो Noun को Numeral Adjective के बाद रखा जाता है। एवं फिर a half या a quarter लिखा जाता है। *जैसे:*

(a) He gave me one rupee and a half.
(b) She gave me two rupees and a quarter.

इन वाक्यों को निम्न प्रकार लिखा जाना गलत होगा। ध्यान दें

(a) He gave me one and a half rupees. *(Incorrect)*
(b) She gave me two and a quarter rupees. *(Incorrect)*

यदि numeral adjective एवं fraction को and से जोड़ा गया हो एवं वाक्य में multiply के अर्थ में प्रयुक्त हो तो noun का प्रयोग Plural number में a half/ a quarter के बाद होगा। जैसे :

(a) Two and a quarter times.
(b) One and a half times

यहाँ वाक्य में multiply किया गया है। अतः Noun 'times' Plural में a quarter / a half के बाद प्रयुक्त हुआ है।

Rule 9

Common Gender Nouns जैसे: Teacher, student, child, clerk, advocate, worker, writer, author, leader, musician etc. ऐसे Nouns हैं जिनका प्रयोग male एवं female दोनों के लिए किया जाता है। इन्हें Dual Gender भी कहा जाता है। जब इस तरह के Noun का प्रयोग Singular में किया जाता है तो Third person, Singular Pronoun का एवं Masculine Gender (he/his/him) का प्रयोग सामान्य रूप से किया जाता है। जैसे:

(1) Every candidate should write his (her) name.
(2) Every person should perform his (her) duty.
(3) No one should abuse h1is (her) neighbour.

यहाँ विवाद का विषय यह है कि हम 'his' Masculine Gender का प्रयोग करें? 'her' का भी प्रयोग किया जाता है। इस सम्बंध में यदि legal matter हो तो his या her जो भी आवश्यक हो उसे स्पष्ट कर देना चाहिये। कुछ विद्वान यहाँ their का प्रयोग करके, इस विवाद का समाधान करना चाहते हैं जो कि उचित नहीं लगता है। अधिकांश विद्वानों ने यहाँ 'his' Masculine Gender का प्रयोग सही माना है।, अत: हमें Masculine Gencer का प्रयोग करना चाहिए।

Rule 10

Common Gender के Nouns के पूर्व Lady का प्रयोग किया जाए या Woman का, यह भी एक रोचक बिन्दु है। सामान्य बोल-चाल में हम Lady Teacher, Lady Doctor कहते हैं। हिन्दी में महिला शिक्षक, महिला डॉक्टर शब्दों का ही प्रयोग किया जाता है न कि औरत शिक्षक,औरत डॉक्टर। भारत में हमने हिन्दी से अंग्रेजी बनाना सीखा है। अत: हम Woman की जगह Lady का प्रयोग करते हैं। विद्वानों के अनुसार Woman Teacher या Woman Doctor कहना Lady Teacher/ Lady Doctor से ज्यादा उपयुक्त एवं उचित है।

Rule 11

कुछ Nouns हमेशा Feminine Gender हेतु ही उपर्युक्त होते हैं। जैसे: blonde, maid, mid wife, coquette, virgin etc. सामान्यतया Virgin का प्रयोग feminine gender में तथा bachelor का प्रयोग masculine gender में किया जाता है, लेकिन आजकल इनका प्रयोग दोनों genders में किया जा रहा है। जैसे:

(a) Ram is a bachelor. (b) Sita is a bachelor.
(c) Rahim is a virgin. (d) Rehana is a virgin.

Noun–Gender

Gender को चार भागों में विभाजित किया गया है:

1. **Masculine Gender (पुल्लिंग)**: ऐसे Noun जो male sex को व्यक्त करते हैं, Masculine gender कहलाते हैं। जैसे: Tiger, Power, Violence, Father, Sun, Summer, Time, Thunder etc.
2. **Feminine Gender (स्त्रीलिंग)**: ऐसे Noun जो Female sex को व्यक्त करते हैं, Feminine Gender कहलाते हैं। जैसे: Tigress, Woman, Lioness, Mother, Sister, Peace, Nature, arth, Goddess etc.
3. **Common Gender (उभयलिंग)**: ऐसे Noun जो स्त्री एवं पुरुष दोनों के लिए प्रयुक्त होते हैं, Common Gender कहलाते हैं। जैसे: Child, Baby, Teacher, Servant, Student, Cousin, Infant, Thief, Neighbour etc.
4. **Neuter Gender (नपुंसकलिंग)**: ऐसे Noun जो उन निर्जीव वस्तु को व्यक्त करते है, जो न male हैं और न ही female हैं, Neuter Gender कहलाते हैं, जैसे: Copy, Book, Room, Paper, TV, Box, etc.

Rules for Changing Masculine Noun to Feminine Noun

Rule 1

कुछ cases में Masculine Noun के बाद 'ess' लगाने से Feminine Noun बनाया जा सकता है। जैसे:

Masculine	Feminine	Masculine	Feminine
Author	Authoress	Baron	Baroness
Count	Countess	Giant	Giantess
Host	Hostess	Heir	Heiress
Jew	Jewess	Lion	Lioness
Mayor	Mayoress	Manager	Manageress
Peer	Peeress	Patron	Patroness
Poet	Poetess	Priest	Priestess
Prophet	Prophetess	Tailor	Tailoress
Tutor	Tutoress	Steward	Stewardess
Shepherd	Shepherdess	Postmaster	Postmistress

Rule 2

कुछ cases में Masculine Noun के अन्तिम vowel एवं उसके पहले आने वाले consonant को हटाकर 'ess' जोड़ने में भी Feminine Noun बन जाता है। जैसे:

Masculine	Feminine	Masculine	Feminine
Actor	Actress	Ambassador	Ambassadress
Benefactor	Benefactress	Director	Directress
Hunter	Huntress	Negro	Negress
Prince	Princess	Tiger	Tigress
Waiter	Waitress	Viscount	Viscountess

Rule 3

कुछ cases में Masculine Noun के शब्दों में कुछ change किया जाता है एवं अन्त में 'ess' लगाने पर भी Feminine Noun बन जाता है। जैसे:

Masculine	Feminine	Masculine	Feminine
Abbot	Abbess	Duke	Duchess
Emperor	Empress	God	Goddess
Governor	Governess	Master	Mistress
Marquis	Marchioness	Sorcer	Sorceress

Rule 4

कुछ cases में Compound Masculine Noun के first or second शब्द में कुछ change किया जाता है। जैसे:

Masculine	Feminine	Masculine	Feminine
Man-servant	Maid-servant	Milkman	Milkmaid
Doctor	Lady-Doctor	Peacock	Peahen
Washerman	Washerwoman	Landlord	Landlady
Buck-Rabbit	Doe-Rabbit	Father-in-law	Mother-in-law
Brother-in-law	Sister-in-law	Step-Father	Step-Mother
He-bear	She-bear	He-goat	She-goat
Bull-calf	Cow-calf	Cock-sparrow	Hen-sparrow
Jack-ass	Jenny-ass	Dog-wolf	Bitch-wolf
Tomcat	She-cat	Stepbrother	Stepsister
Headmaster	Headmistress	Grandson	Granddaughter

Rule 5

Foreign words एवं अन्य विविध शब्दों के Masculine एवं Feminine Gender नीचे दिए गए हैं। There is no rule for such words. As:

Masculine	Feminine	Masculine	Feminine
Administrator	Administratrix	Shepherd	Shepherdess
Beau	Belle	Czar	Czarina
Executor	Executrix	Hero	Heroine
Lad	Lass	Monsieur	Madam
Prosecutor	Prosecutrix	Signor	Signora
Sultan	Sultana	Testator	Testatrix
Viceroy	Vicereine	Bachelor	Maid
Boar	Sow	Boy	Girl
Brother	Sister	Cock	Hen
Colt	Filly	Drake	Duck
Dog	Bitch	Drone	Bee
Buck	Doe	Bull	Cow
Earl	Countess	Father	Mother
Friar	Nun	Bridegroom	Bride
Gander	Goose	Gentleman	Lady
Hart	Roe	He	She
Horse	Mare	Husband	Wife
King	Queen	Lord	Lady
Man	Woman	Male	Female

Mr	Miss	Nephew	Niece
Sheep	Ewe	Sir	Madam
Son	Daughter	Sire	Dame
Uncle	Aunt	Widower	Widow
Fox	Vixen	Wizard	Witch
Ox	Cow		

Noun–Number (Singular-Plural)

Singular Noun: इससे एक व्यक्ति, एक स्थान या एक वस्तु का बोध होता है, जैसे: Boy, Girl, Table.

Plural Noun: इससे एक से अधिक व्यक्ति, स्थान या वस्तुओं का बोध होता है, जैसे: Cities, Boys, Girls.

Changing Singular to Plural : Some Rules

Rule 1

कुछ Noun के अन्त में s लगाने से वह Plural बन जाता हैं, जैसे: Boy, Girl, Kite, Telephone etc.

Rule 2

जिन Noun के अन्त में s, ss, ch, sh, z या x आता है उनका plural बनाने के लिए अन्त में es जोड़ दिया जाता है। जैसे:

Singular	Plural	Singular	Plural
Bus	Buses	Class	Classes
Fox	Foxes	Church	Churches
Watch	Watches	Quiz	Quizzes
Switch	Switches	Tax	Taxes
Ass	Asses	Dish	Dishes
Canvas	Canvases	Box	Boxes
Fix	Fixes	Coach	Coaches

इसके कुछ Exceptions भी हैं। जैसे:

Singular	Plural	Singular	Plural
Stomach	Stomachs	Locus	Loci
Radius	Radii	Ox	Oxen

Rule 3

कुछ Noun के अन्त में 'o' आता है एवं उससे पूर्व कोई व्यंजन (consonant) हो तो, उसका Plural बनाने के लिए Noun के अन्त में es लगाते हैं। जैसे:

Singular	Plural	Singular	Plural
Hero	Heroes	Mango	Mangoes
Potato	Potatoes	Cargo	Cargoes
Mosquito	Mosquitoes	Echo	Echoes

इसके कुछ Exceptions भी हैं। जैसे:

Singular	Plural	Singular	Plural
Canto	Cantos	Piano	Pianos
Dynamo	Dynamos	Solo	Solos
Memento	Mememtos	Photo	Photos
Ratio	Ratios	Quarto	Quartos

Rule 4

यदि किसी Noun के अन्त में double vowel लगे हुए हों तो उसका Plural बनाने के लिए उसके अन्त मे s लगा दिया जाता है। जैसे:

Singular	Plural	Singular	Plural
Bee	Bees	Radio	Radios
Tree	Trees	Woe	Woes
Zoo	Zoos	Portfolio	Portfolios

Rule 5

यदि Noun के अन्त में y आए एवं y से पूर्व कोई व्यंजन आता है, तो y की जगह ies लगाने से उसका Plural बन जाता है। जैसे:

Singular	Plural	Singular	Plural
Cry	Cries	City	Cities
Doll	Dolls	Bomb	Bombs
Country	Countries	Dictionary	Dictionaries
Family	Families	Lorry	Lorries
Pony	Ponies	Reply	Replies

Rule 6

यदि Noun के अन्त में y आए एवं y से पूर्व कोई Vowel आता है, तो s लगाने से उसका Plural बन जाता है। जैसे:

Singular	Plural	Singular	Plural
Key	Keys	Way	Ways
Donkey	Donkeys	Valley	Valleys
Ray	Rays	Toy	Toys
Monkey	Monkeys	Storey	Storeys

Rule 7

यदि Noun के अन्त में f या fe आए तो Plural बनाने के लिए f या fe को हटाकर ves लगाते है। जैसे:

Singular	Plural	Singular	Plural
Calf	Calves	Life	Lives
Half	Halves	Leaf	Leaves
Wife	Wives	Elf	Elves
Thief	Thieves	Knife	Knives
Wolf	Wolves	Shelf	Shelves

इसमें कुछ Exceptions भी हैं। जैसे:

Singular	Plural	Singular	Plural
Belief	Beliefs	Proof	Proofs
Chief	Chiefs	Roof	Roofs
Cliff	Cliffs	Safe	Safes
Dwarf	Dwarfs	Scarf	Scarfs
Grief	Griefs	Strife	Strifes
Gulf	Gulfs	Turf	Turfs

Rule 8

Compound Noun में मुख्य शब्द के साथ 's' लगाने पर उसका Plural बन जाता है। जैसे:

Singular	Plural	Singular	Plural
Brother-in-law	Brothers-in-law	Bed-room	Bed-rooms
Commander-in-chief	Commanders-in-chief	Step-daughter	Step-daughters
Maid-servant	Maid-servants	Pea-hen	Pea-hens
Peacock	Peacocks	Mother-in-law	Mothers-in-law
Sister-in-law	Sisters-in-law	Member of Parliament	Members of Parliament
**Man servant	Men servants	**Woman conductor	Women conductors
**Man nurse	Men nurses	**Woman engineer	Women engineers
*Man hater	Man haters	*Woman lover	Woman lovers
*Man lover	Man lovers		

Note the difference among the plurals of nouns with single star (*) and with double star (**)

Rule 9

निम्न आठ Nouns ऐसे हैं जिनका Plural बनाने के लिए Inside Vowels में परिवर्तन करते हैं। जैसे:

Singular	Plural	Singular	Plural
Man	Men	Mouse	Mice
Woman	Women	Louse	Lice
Foot	Feet	Goose	Geese
Tooth	Teeth	Dormouse	Dormice

Rule 10.

निम्नलिखित चार Nouns ऐसे हैं जिनका Plural बनाने के लिए en या ne जोड़ते हैं। जैसे:

Singular	Plural	Singular	Plural
Child	Children	Cow	Kine (Cows)
Ox	Oxen	Brother	Brethren

Rule 11.

कुछ Nouns के दो तरह के Plural बनते हैं जिनका अर्थ भी अलग होता है। जैसे:

(1) Brother
Brothers—Sons of the same parent.
Brethren—Members of a society or community.

(2) Cloth
Cloths—Unstitched cloth.
Clothes—Stitched clothes (Garments)

(3) Die
Dies—Stamps used for printing and coining.
Dice—Small cubes used in games.

(4) Index
Indexes—Tables of contents in a book.
Indices—Signs used in algebra.

Some Typical Plural Nouns (Number)

(A) Latin words: Latin के कुछ शब्द, जिनके अन्त में um आता है, एकवचन होते हैं। इनको Plural बनाने के लिए um हटाकर 'a' लगाया जाता है। जैसे:

Singular	Plural	Singular	Plural
Addendum	Addenda	Agendum	Agenda
Datum	Data	Dictum	Dicta
Ovum	Ova	Memorandum	Memoranda
Erratum	Errata	Stratum	Strata

आजकल Agenda एवं Data का प्रयोग Singular एवं Plural दोनों में किया जाने लगा है। जैसे:

(a) The agenda has been finalised.

(b) The agenda of the meeting are drawn today.

(c) The data is incomplete.

(d) More data are required.

Important

Latin के निम्न शब्दों पर ध्यान दें: इन शब्दों के पीछे भी 'um' आता है, लेकिन इनके Plural बनाने हेतु पीछे 's' लगाया जाता है। जैसे:

Singular	Plural	Singular	Plural
Asylum	Asylums	Forum	Forums
Museum	Museums	Pendulum	Pendulums
Premium	Permiums	Quorum	Quorums
Petroleum	Petroleums	Formula	Formulae/Formulas

Medium का प्रयोग जब means या agency के रूप में किया जाता है, तो इसका Plural-media होता है, लेकिन जब medium का प्रयोग Spiritual sense में किया गया हो तो इसका Plural, mediums होगा।

(B) कुछ Latin words के अन्त में us आता है। इनका plural 'us' को 'i' में बदलकर बनाया जाता है। जैसे:

Singular	Plural	Singular	Plural
Radius	Radii	Locus	Loci
Syllabus	Syllabi	Genius	Genii

(C) कुछ Greek शब्दों के अन्त मे 'is' आता है। इनका Plural, 'is' को es में बदलकर बनाया जाता है। जैसे:

Singular	Plural	Singular	Plural
Analysis	Analyses	Basis	Bases
Crisis	Crises	Thesis	Theses
Hypothesis	Hypotheses	Parenthesis	Parentheses

(D) कुछ Greek शब्दों के अन्त में 'on' आता है। इनका Plural 'on' को 'a' में बदलने से वनता है। जैसे:

Singular	Plural	Singular	Plural
Phenomenon	Phenomena	Criterion	Criteria

(E) अन्य कई प्रकार के Nouns के Plural निम्न प्रकार बनते हैं:

Singular	Plural	Singular	Plural
If	Ifs	But	Buts
I	I's	T	T's
5	5s	10	10s
P	P's	MP	MPs
BA	BAs	MA	MAs
ATM	ATMs	UPC	UPCs

(F) कुछ Nouns का Singular में अर्थ, Plural form के साथ पूर्णतया अलग होता है, अत: इनका प्रयोग सावधानीपूर्वक करना चाहिए। जैसे:

Singular	Plural	Singular	Plural
Air (हवा)	Airs (दिखावटी)	Alphabet (वर्णमाला)	Alphabets (भाषाएं)
Compass (सीमा)	Compasses (एक यन्त्र)	Manner (तरीका)	Manners (व्यवहार)
Number (संख्या)	Numbers (मात्राएँ)	Pain (तकलीफ)	Pains (प्रयत्न)
Physic (दवा)	Physics (भौतिकी)	Premise (प्रस्तावना)	Premises (भवन)
Quarter (चौथाई भाग)	Quarters (छोटे मकान)	Iron (लोहा)	Irons (जंजीरें)
Return (वापसी)	Returns (हिसाब, आय)	Effect (प्रभाव)	Effects (सामान)
Force (शक्ति)	Forces (सेना)	Good (अच्छा)	Goods (सामान)
Sand (बालू)	Sands (रेगिस्तान)	Water (पानी)	Waters (समुद्र)
Wood (लकड़ी)	Woods (जंगल)	Ground (जमीन)	Grounds (कारण)
Abuse (दुरुपयोग)	Abuses (कुरीतियाँ)	Advice (सलाह)	Advices (सूचनाएँ)

Use of Apostrophe with's

(A) Apostrophe का उपयोग Possessive case के लिए निम्न स्थिति में करना ही उचित है। जैसे:

(1) Living things
- (a) Mohan's book
- (b) a cow's horn
- (c) a woman's purse

(2) Thing personified as
- (a) week's holiday
- (b) earth's surface

(3) Space time or weight as
- (a) a day's leave
- (b) well's water
- (c) a pound's weight

(4) Certain dignified objects as
- (a) the court's orders
- (b) at duty's call
- (c) a razor's edge
- (d) a needle's point

(5) Familiar phrases as
- (a) at his wit's end
- (b) at a stone's throw

अन्य cases में apostrophe को avoid करना उचित होगा।

(B) यदि Plural शब्द का अन्तिम शब्द 's' है तो apostrophe का प्रयोग करते समय 's' नहीं लगाते हैं, केवल (') apostrophe का ही प्रयोग करते हैं। जैसे:

(1) Horses' tail.
(2) Boys' college.
(3) Girls' school.
(4) Working girls' hostel.

Words with hissing sound of s में भी s नहीं लगता है।

for peace' sake, for conscience' sake, for goodness' sake, for Jesus' sake

(C) कुछ शब्द his, hers, yours, mine, ours, its, theirs के साथ apostrophe नहीं लगाते हैं, जैसे : Yours faithfully, Yours truly, Ours garden , his pen, hers purse, theirs room.

(D) निम्न titles के साथ apostrophe अन्तिम शब्द के साथ ही लगाते हैं। जैसे:

(a) Governor-general's instructions.
(b) Commander-in-chief's orders.
(c) My son-in-law's sister.
(d) Ram and Sons's shop.

(E) **Do not use 'Double apostrophe':** We should try to avoid double apostrophe in a sentence:

(a) My wife's secretary's mother has expired.
इसकी जगह हमें लिखना चाहिए।
The mother of my wife's secretary has expired.

(b) Mrs Kuwrani's now chairperson of society's proposal was rejected . *Incorrect*
The proposal of Mrs Kuwrani, now chairperson of society was rejected. *Correct*

(F) Anybody/Nobody/Everybody/Somebody/Anyone/Someone/No one/Everyone के साथ Apostrophe 's' का प्रयोग किया ज़ाता है। जैसे:

(a) Everyone's concern is no one's concern.
(b) Everybody's business is nobody's business.

यदि इनके बाद else प्रयोग हो तो apostrophe को else के साथ लगाते हैं। जैसे:
(a) I can rely on your words, not somebody else's.
(b) I obey your orders and nobody else's.
(यहाँ Somebody's else या Nodody's else लिखना गलत होगा।)

Functions of Noun - Case

Noun द्वारा वाक्य में किए गए कार्यों को हम छ: भागों में विभाजित कर सकते है:

(1) Subject of the verb
(2) Object of the verb
(3) Complement of the verb
(4) Possessivity
(5) Apposition to a noun
(6) Nominative of address

Noun द्वारा वाक्य में किए गए कार्यों के आधार पर noun के cases को define किया गया है। ये cases हैं:

1. Nominative case
2. Objective case
3. Possessive case
4. Complement of the verb
5. Case in apposition
6. Nominative of address
7. Nominative absolute

(1) Nominative Case: जब noun का प्रयोग वाक्य में subject की तरह होता है, तो वह noun, nominative case में होता है अर्थात् वाक्य में noun जब verb के साथ subject का कार्य करता है, तो वह noun, nominative case में प्रयुक्त होता है। When a noun is used as subject of the verb in a sentence, it is in nominative case.

Read the following sentences:

(a) Ram writes an essay.
(b) Sarla reads a novel.
(c) Rahim is playing chess.
(d) The thief has ran away.

वाक्य 1, 2, 3, 4 में Ram, Sarla, Rahim, एवं Thief (Nouns) क्रमश: verbs; writes, reads, playing, ran के subject की तरह प्रयुक्त हुए हैं। अत: यह सभी nominative case में हैं।

(2) Objective Case: जब noun का प्रयोग वाक्य में verb के object की तरह होता है, तो वह noun, objective case में प्रयुक्त हुए है।

When a noun is used as an object of the verb in a sentence it is in objective case.

Read the following sentences:

(a) He eats an apple.
(b) She plays football.
(c) I write a letter.
(d) Shyam cooks food.

उपरोक्त वाक्यों में सभी underlined words (noun), verbs के object की तरह प्रयुक्त हुए हैं अत: इन्हें (nouns) objective case में प्रयुक्त होना कहा जाता है।

Two objects in a sentence (Direct and Indirect objects)

कई वाक्यों में दो object होते हैं:

(a) He gave me an umbrella. (b) She gave you a pen. (c) Rahim brought a cream for her.

उपरोक्त वाक्यों में दो object हैं। Living noun, indirect object तथा non-living noun, direct object कहलाते हैं। In above sentences; me, you, her are indirect objects and umbrella, pen and cream are direct (non-living) objects.

Direct Object की जानकारी के लिए verb से what प्रश्न करने पर जो उत्तर प्राप्त होता है वह direct object तथा Indirect object की जानकारी के लिए verb से whom प्रश्न करने पर जो उत्तर आता है वह indirect object है।

(3) Possessive Case : एक वाक्य में एक noun का दूसरे noun पर हक या Relation स्थापित करने के लिए प्रयोग होता है, तो noun के साथ apostrophe का प्रयोग किया जाता है। जिस noun, के साथ apostrophe का प्रयोग होता है, वह noun, possessive case में प्रयुक्त होती है। जैसे:

(a) Ramesh's wife.
(b) Rahim's seat.
(c) Sarla's mother.
(d) Mira's saree.

उपरोक्त वाक्यों में nouns का प्रयोग अन्य सम्बन्धित nouns के साथ possessive case में हुआ है।

यदि उक्त वाक्यों में से underlined words (nouns) teachers, engineer, sad doctor को हटा दिया जाए तो सभी वाक्य, 'अर्थहीन' (meaningless) हो जाएँगे। शेष वाक्य का कोई अर्थ ही नहीं निकलेगा। चूँकि teacher, engineer, sad, doctor से वाक्य पूर्ण (complete) होगा, इन वाक्यों को पूर्णता मिलेगी अत: इन noun को complement of the verb कहा जाता है। complements साधारणतया is, am, are, was, were, appear, look, seem, become, choose, grow, make, taste आदि क्रियाओं के बाद प्रयुक्त होते हैं।

(4) Complement of the Verb : निम्न वाक्यों पर ध्यान दें:

(a) She is a teacher.
(b) You are an engineer.
(c) He is sad.
(d) She became a doctor.

Subjective Complements and Objective Complements

Subjective Complements

Read the following sentences:

(a) Shyam became a doctor.
(b) Ram became an engineer.
(c) Jairam appears happy.
(d) She seems sad.

उपरोक्त वाक्यों में doctor, engineer, happy, sad सभी complements हैं, जो वाक्य के कर्ता (subject) को पूर्णता प्रदान करते हैं अत: ये subjective complements कहलाते हैं।

Objective Complements:

Read the following sentences:

(a) We made Ramesh monitor.
(b) I consider him trustworthy.
(c) Her parents called her 'Chinkoo'.
(d) He was elected M. P.

उपरोक्त वाक्यों में monitor, trustworthy, Chinkoo, M.P. सभी complements हैं, जो कि सम्बन्धित verbs के Object की तरह प्रयुक्त हुए हैं। इन्हें objective complements कहा जाता है।

(5) Case in Apposition: Apposition का अर्थ होता है having near अर्थात् पास-पास रखना।

Read the following sentences:

(a) Ram, his brother, is an honest man.
(b) Harish, his son, is a naughty boy.
(c) Sita, her daughter, is a beautiful girl.

जब दो nouns एक ही व्यक्ति या वस्तु को बताते हैं अर्थात् दोनों noun एक ही व्यक्ति के बारे में स्पष्ट करते हैं। बाद वाला noun पहले वाले noun का case in apposition कहलाता है। उक्त वाक्यों में his brother, his son, her daughter सभी मुख्य कर्ता [Ram, Harish, Sita (main subject)] को स्पष्ट करते हैं।
अत: ये सम्बन्धित noun (Ram, Harish, Sita) के case in apposition हैं।

Apposition: If two nouns referring to the same person or thing are in apposition, one is placed immediately after the other, with no conjunction joining them, as in 'Her father, Naresh Chandra, left home three months ago.'

(6) Nominative of address:

Read the following sentences:

(a) Boys, don't make a noise.
(b) Harish, wait for me.
(c) Suresh, go to Jaipur.
(d) Rahul, come here.

उपरोक्त वाक्यों में Boys, Harish, Suresh, Rahul को सम्बोधित (Addressed) किया गया है। Nouns के इस प्रकार के प्रयोग को nominative of address कहा जाता है अर्थात् जो noun किसी व्यक्ति या वस्तु को सम्बोधित करने के लिए प्रयुक्त हो वह nominative of address की तरह प्रयुक्त होता है।

(7) Nominative Absolute:

Read the following sentences:

(a) God willing, we shall have good harvest this time.
(b) The sea being smooth, we went for a sail.
(c) Weather premitting, we shall go to Simla.

उक्त वाक्यों में God, weather; Nouns का प्रयोग nominative case में हुआ है। ये शब्द मुख्य वाक्य से present participle द्वारा जोड़े गए हैं। Nouns के इस तरह के कार्य को nominative absolute कहा जाता है।

Exercises

01.

Correct the following sentences :

1. Her hairs are curly.
2. Our elders gave us many advices.
3. I have many work to do.
4. Sita has sold all her furnitures.
5. She gave me informations about this bank.
6. The sceneries of Himachal Pradesh are very charming.
7. The peoples are hard working.
8. The cattles are grazing in the field.
9. I want a paper.
10. I bring fruits and vegetables from the market.
11. You must continue your study.
12. These news are false.
13. They go to Agra during the summer vacations.
14. Her spectacle is very nice.
15. She has a twenty rupees note.

02.

Correct the following sentences :

1. He got only passing marks.
2. Ram was true to his words
3. Ten miles are a long distance.
4. They want two dozens apple
5. I want two pairs of white shoes.
6. Rahul has finished two third of his work.
7. The chair's legs are broken.
8. Good night, I am so glad to meet you.
9. There is no space in the car.
10. We should help the poors.
11. She left for Delhi by 8:30 O'clock bus.
12. One of his son is a teacher.
13. Amazing stories are an interesting book.
14. This is my son's in law house.

03.

Correct the following sentences :

1. I brought my furnitures by goods train.
2. I saw two beautiful fishes in the pond.
3. Thomson's poetries are very charming.
4. Is your scissors dull?
5. Light travel faster than sound.
6. All the furnitures of my house have been stolen.
7. A poet and writer are dead.
8. The committee was divided on this issue.
9. Mathematics are not a difficult subject.
10. My sympathies are always with the poor.
11. The mother both carried her son and daughter from the burning house .
12. My sister serves in boy's school.
13. Rohan's and Mohan's house is very far from here.
14. There are many news published in local paper.
15. The teacher has taught the alphabets.

04.

Correct the following sentences :

1. Please reply your's faithfully.
2. I go for a two miles walk daily.
3. She loves either you or I.
4. There are four breads in the kitchen.
5. One should not hate the poors.
6. The magistrate passed order of his release.
7. She has committed not one but many mischiefs.
8. The first inning is going to over now.
9. There is no place in this compartment.
10. He bought some stationeries.
11. My mother's brother's son has come.
12. There are a few peoples who are really honest.
13. Give me ten pices.
14. There were no gentries in that function.

05.

Correct the following sentences :

1. He is a sixty years old man.
2. A five men committee had a three hours meeting yesterday.
3. An all parties meeting was called to consider the drought situation in the country.
4. There is two ways traffic here, so no problem of traffic blockage.
5. How can our country accept the two nations theory?
6. He has gone to market to purchase vegetable.
7. He said, "Riches has wings".
8. I asked him where was his spectacles.
9. She said that she was suffering from measle.
10. She said, "Please give him an alm".

06.

Correct the following sentences :

1. Shelly's poetries are great.
2. I saw beautiful sceneries in Kashmir last year.
3. He has purchased new machineries.
4. He said, "He has purchased very costly crockeries".
5. There were very heavy traffics on the road.
6. She has bought very beautiful furnitures.
7. He gave me many informations.
8. I am going to purchase some stationeries.
9. Ram said, "The hair of Sita are black".
10. This house is made of bricks and stones.

07.

Correct the following sentences :

1. Cities after cities were destroyed by the army.
2. Hours after hours were passed, but she didn't turn up.
3. Ram said, "I beg from doors to doors daily."
4. Ships after ships were sailing by those days.
5. Rows upon rows of pink marble are soothing to the eyes.
6. I gave her three and a half apples.
7. The meeting was held for three and a quarter hours.
8. The length of this hall is three times and a half to that hall.
9. His salary is two times and a half to that of mine.
10. I have two and a half rupees only.

08.

Correct the following sentences :

1. What the peoples think, I can't say?
2. Who owns these poultries?
3. He is my cousin brother.
4. How many 3s are there in 31313?
5. How many cattles you have?
6. I have only ten five rupees's notes.
7. He has written a nice poetry.
8. Today I have received two month's wages.
9. What is this book's price?
10. There are only two females in the garden.

Spotting Errors (Noun)

09.

Read the following sentences to find whether there is any error in any part :

1. He acted not (a)/ as per my advice (b)/ but somebody else. (c)
2. Pakistan's problems (a)/are also as (b)/serious as (c)/that of India. (d)
3. When I reached (a)/at the gate of his (b)/house I found his (c)/locking up the gate. (d)
4. Many of the question (a)/appeared in this question paper (b)/are too difficult (c)/to solve. (d)
5. I visited (a)/Ram's and Sita's house (b)/and found the couple missing. (c)
6. All the girls students (a)/are advised to (b)/ attend the meeting positively. (c)
7. She gave me (a)/two important informations (b)/I had been waiting for (c)/the last two months. (d)
8. The English teacher (a)/gave him a home work (b)/to complete that (c)/by night positively. (d)
9. She could not complete (a)/even the two third (b)/of the book (c)/owing to her busy schedule. (d)
10. All the woman teachers (a)/are agitating (b)/against the haughty attitude (c)/of the Principal. (d)
11. He informed that (a)/he had lost a packet (b)/of the hundred (c)/rupees notes. (d)
12. He has ordered (a)/bricks for the proposed (b)/shopping complex. (c)
13. She has ordered (a)/two dozens of copies (b)/of English Book by Mr Gupta. (c)
14. She uses a good (a)/quality of shampoo (b)/so her hairs are (c)/black. (d)
15. I known nothing (a)/about her (b)/ whereabout. (c)

Solution TYE 01

1. Her hair is curly.
2. Our elders gave us many pieces of advice.
3. I have much work to do.
4. Sita has sold all her furniture.
5. She gave me information about this bank.
6. The scenery of Himachal Pradesh is very charming.
7. The people are hard working.
8. The cattle are grazing in the field.
9. I want a piece of paper.
10. I bring fruit and vegetables from the market.
11. You must continue your studies.
12. This news is false.
13. They go to Agra during the summer vacation.
14. Her spectacles are very nice.
15. She has a twenty rupee note.

Solution TYE 02

1. He got only pass marks .
2. Ram was true to his word.
3. Ten miles is long distance.
4. They want two dozen apples.
5. I want two pair of white shoes.
6. Rahul has finished two thirds of his work.
7. The legs of the chair are broken.
8. Good evening, I am so glad to meet you.
9. There is no room in the car.
10. We should help the poor.
11. She left for Delhi by 8 : 30 bus.
12. One of his sons is a teacher.
13. Amazing stories is an interesting book.
14. This is my son -in-law's house.

Solution TYE 03

1. I brought my furniture by goods train.
2. I saw two beautiful fish in the pond.
3. Thomson's poetry is very charming.
4. Are your scissors dull?
5. Light travels faster than sound.
6. All the furniture of my house have been stolen.
7. A poet and writer is dead.
8. The committee were divided on this issue.
9. Mathematics is not a difficult subject.
10. My sympathy is always with the poor.
11. The mother carried both her son and daughter from the burning house.
12. My sister serves in boys' school.
13. Rohan and Mohan's house is very far from here.
14. There are many items of news published in the local paper.
15. The teacher has taught the letters of alphabet.

Solution TYE 04

1. Please reply, yours faithfully.
2. I go for a two mile walk daily.
3. She loves either you or me.
4. There are four pieces of bread in the kitchen.
5. One should not hate the poor.
6. The magistrate passed orders of his release.
7. She has committed not one but many acts of mischief.
8. The first inning is going to be over now.
9. There is no room in this compartment.
10. He bought some stationery.
11. The son of my mother's brother has come.
12. There are few people, who are really honest.
13. Give me ten pice.
14. There were no gentry in that function.

Solution TYE 05

1. He is a sixty year old man.
2. A five man committee had a three hour meeting yesterday.
3. An all party meeting was called to consider the drought situation in the country.
4. There is two way traffic here so no problem of traffic blockage.
5. How can our country accept the two nation theory.
6. He has gone to market to purchase vegetables.
7. He said, "Riches have wings."
8. I asked him where were his spectacles.
9. She said that she was suffering from measles.
10. She said, "Please give him alms."

(A) वाक्य संख्या (1) से (5) तक में compound word मे noun, adjective की तरह कार्य कर रहा है। अत: noun, singular ही रहेगा noun का pluralise करना गलत है।

(B) वाक्य संख्या (6) से (10) में प्रयुक्त noun हमेशा plural में ही प्रयुक्त होते हैं एवं इनके साथ plural verb का ही प्रयोग होता है। इनके साथ लगा 's' हटाना गलत है।

Such nouns are: annals, ashes, arrears, athletics, auspices, bellows, breeches, belongings bowels, braces, binoculars, billiards,brains, customs, scissors, stairs, surrounding, trousers, tongs, tactics, thanks, cards, congratulations, caves, earnings, mumps, measles, proceeds, proceedings, glasses, greens, lodgings, wages, valuables etc.

Solution TYE 06

1. Shelly's poetry is great.
2. I saw beautiful scenery in Kashmir last year.
3. He has purchased new machinery.
4. He said, "He has purchased very costly crockery."
5. There was very heavy traffic on the road.
6. She has bought very beautiful furniture.
7. He gave me a lot of information.
8. I am going to purchase some stationery.
9. Ram said, "The hair of Sita is black."
10. This house is made of brick and stone.

उक्त वाक्यों में प्रयुक्त noun हमेशा singular ही रहते हैं। इनको pluralise नहीं किया जाता है। इस तरह के nouns हैं: Peotry, scenery, machinery, drapery, stationery, jewellery, sultery, crockery, luggage, baggage, knowledge, postatge, breakage, haltage, wastage, percentage, polish, foolish, dust, furniture, traffic, coffee, money, music rabbish, dirt, information etc.

Solution TYE 07

1. City after city was destroyed by the army.
2. Hour after hour was passed but she didn't turn up.
3. Ram said , "I beg from door to door daily."
4. Ship after ship was sailing by those days.
5. Row upon row of pink marble is soothing to the eyes.
6. I gave her three apples and a half.
7. The meeting was held for a three hours and a quarter.
8. The length of this hall is three and a half times to that hall.
9. His salary is two and a half times to that of mine.
10. I have two rupees and a half only.

(A) वाक्य 1 से 5 तक में upon/after के पहले एवं बाद में आने वाले noun को pluralise करने की गलती की गई है। ध्यान रखें upon/after के पहले एवं बाद में repeated noun सदा singular में आते हैं।

(B) जब Numeral adjective के साथ fraction को जोड़कर, गुणा (Multiply) करने के सन्दर्भ में प्रयोग होता है तो वह noun, plural number में a half या a quarter के बाद लगता है। जैसा वाक्य 8 एवं 9 से स्पष्ट है। लेकिन अन्य स्थिति में noun, numeral adjective के साथ लगाया जाता है न कि half एवं a quarter के साथ जैसा अन्य वाक्य 6, 7, 10 से स्पष्ट है।

Solution TYE 08

1. What the people think I can't say?
2. Who owns these poultry?
3. He is my cousin.
4. How many 3's are there in 31313?
5. How many cattle you have?
6. I have only ten five rupee notes.
7. He has written a nice poem. or He has written nice poetry.
8. Today I have received two months wages.
9. What is the price of this book?
10. There are only two women in the garden.

Solution TYE 09

1. (c) else की जगह else's लिखना होगा । यहाँ somebody else's का अर्थ किसी अन्य की advice से है न कि किसी अन्य व्यक्ति से। अत: apostrophe का use करना होगा।
2. (d) India की जगह India's होगा। यहाँ Pakistan की problems की तुलना India की problem से की जा रही है न कि India से।
3. (c) 'his' की जगह 'him' का प्रयोग होगा। यहाँ locking एक participle की जगह प्रयुक्त हुआ है। अत: इससे पहले objective case (him) का प्रयोग होगा न कि possessive case (his) का। जैसे :

   Swimming is a good exercise.

   I found him swimming in the pool.

   Swimming/walking का प्रयोग जब gerund के रूप में होता है तो इसका अर्थ है, तैरना, टहलना। लेकिन जब इनका प्रयोग participle के रूप में होता है, तो इसका अर्थ होता है, तैरते हुए, टहलते हुए।

4. (a) question की जगह questions आएगा। After phrases : 'of the' like 'one of the', 'many of the', plural noun is used .

5. (b) Ram's and Sita's की जगह Ram and Sita's होना चाहिए। जब दो noun एक ही वस्तु के possession को बता रहे हों तो एक ही apostrophe का प्रयोग होगा।

6. (a) girls students की जगह girl students होना चाहिए। एक compound noun में मुख्य शब्द को ही plural किया जाता है। जैसे:

1. boy friend	—	boy friends
2. maid servant	—	maid servants

7. (b) two important informations की जगह two important pieces of information होगा। Information एक uncountable noun है। अत: इसके साथ a, two, three etc नहीं लगता है।

8. (b) gave him a home work की जगह gave him home work होगा। Home work, uncountable noun है, इससे पहले article (a/an) का प्रयोग गलत है। ध्यान रखें कि home work, class work, urgent work से पहले a या an का प्रयोग नहीं होता है। यदि work का प्रयोग किसी author की किसी रचना के सन्दर्भ मे हुआ हो तो article का प्रयोग कर सकते हैं। जैसे:

(1) Hamlet is a popular work by Shakespeare.
(2) All the works of Bernard Shaw are worth reading.
(3) 'An easy approach to English' is a good work by Mr S.C. Gupta.

9. (b) two-third की जगह two-thirds होगा। यहाँ Book के एक part के बारे में बात हो रही है। अत: thirds लिखा जाएगा।

10. (a) Woman teachers की जगह women teachers होगा। man, woman के साथ plural noun आता है, तो men, women हो जाता है। जैसे:

Man supervisor	—	Men supervisors
Woman cleaner	—	Women cleaners

11. (d) rupees की जगह rupee लिखें। साधारणतया हम one hundred rupees कहते हैं। यहाँ one hundred rupees केवल adjective की तरह कार्य कर रहा है, अत: rupee singular ही रहेगा।

12. (b) Bricks की जगह pieces of brick होगा क्योंकि brick, stone, iron chalk, uncountable, material noun हैं।

13. (b) two dozen copies होगा। Q. No. 11 का Explanation देखें।

14. (c) hairs are की जगह 'hair is' होगा।

15. (c) Whereabout की जगह Whereabouts (पता) होगा।

CHAPTER

07

PRONOUN

Pronoun : जो शब्द Noun की जगह प्रयुक्त होता है, उसे Pronoun कहते हैं।

Generally (but not always) pronouns stand for (pro + noun) or refer to a noun, an Indiividual or individuals or thing or things (the pronoun's antecedent) whose identity is made clear earlier in the text. For example

(A) Ramesh found a purse. He picked it up and gave it to Sarla. She threw it into a river.
इस वाक्य में He, Ramesh (noun) के लिए it, purse (noun) के लिए तथा she, Sarla (noun) के लिए प्रयुक्त हुए हैं। अत: He, it एवं She, Pronouns हैं।

Sloppy use of pronouns is unfair

(1) They say that eating beef is bad for you.

(2) They is a pronoun referring to someone, but who are they? Caws? Whom do they represent?

It is not necessary that all pronouns will refer to an antecedent.
Everyone here earns over a thousand dollars a day.
The word 'everyone' (Pronoun) has no antecedent.

Kinds of Pronoun

Pronoun को निम्न प्रकार से वर्गीकृत किया गया है:

(1) Personal Pronoun (पुरुषवाचक)
(2) Reflexive Pronoun (निजवाचक)
(3) Emphatic Pronoun (दृढतावाचक)
(4) Reciprocal Pronoun (परस्परतावाचक)
(5) Demonstrative Pronoun (संकेतवाचक)
(6) Indefinite Pronoun (अनिश्चितवाचक)
(7) Interrogative Pronoun (प्रश्नवाचक)
(8) Distributive Pronoun (विभाजकवाचक)
(9) Relative Pronoun (सम्बन्धवाचक)
(10) Exclamatory Pronoun (विस्मयवाचक)

1. Personal Pronoun

निम्न वाक्यों पर ध्यान दें:

(a) **I** am a boy. — **We** are boys.
(b) **You** are a girl. — **You** are girls.
(c) **He** is a man. — **They** are men.
(d) **It** is a child. — **They** are children.

इन वाक्यों में I, We, जो first person को You, Second Persons को He, She, It, They, third person को व्यक्त करते हैं। ये सभी Personal Pronouns हैं।

वे Pronoun जो वाक्य में व्यक्ति का बोध कराते हैं, Personal Pronouns कहलाते हैं। उक्त वाक्यों में I, We—First Person, You—Second Person Pronoun तथा He, She, It, They—Third Person Pronoun कहलाते हैं।

इन वाक्यों में Pronoun का प्रयोग Nominative Case (कर्ता कारक), Objective Case (कर्म कारक) एवं Possessive Case (सम्बन्ध) (सम्बन्ध कारक) की तरह किया जा सकता है। Pronoun का सही प्रयोग, शुद्ध अंग्रेजी लिखने के लिए आवश्यक है।

Forms of Personal Pronoun

Look at the following table:

Pronoun	Nominative Case	Objective Case	Possessive Case
I	I	Me	My, Mine
We	We	Us	Our, Ours
You	You	You	Your, Yours
He	He	Him	His
She	She	Her	Her, Hers
It	It	It	Its
They	They	Them	Their, Theirs

उक्त तालिका से यह स्पष्ट है कि I के साथ Objective Case में me तथा Possessive Case में my, mine का प्रयोग होता है एवं She के साथ Objective Case में her तथा Possessive Case में her, hers का प्रयोग किया जाता है। Its का प्रयोग जब Pronoun की तरह Possessive Case में किया जाता है तो apostrophe का प्रयोग नहीं किया जाता है। (It's का अर्थ It is जबकि Its का अर्थ है, इसका या उसका)।

(1) अधिकांश Personal pronoun के Possessive case में दो रूप हैं। My, our, your, her, their, Possessive adjective कहलाते हैं, क्योंकि ये वाक्य में एक Adjective की तरह Noun को विशेषता प्रदान करते हैं। जैसे:

(a) He is my friend.
(b) This is your pen.
(c) That is our house.
(d) That is her book.

(2) His का प्रयोग adjective की तरह भी होता है। एवं Pronoun की तरह भी होता है:

(a) This is his pen. (Adjective—Possessive)
(b) This pen is his. (Pronoun—Possessive)

(3) निम्न वाक्य Possessive case में Pronoun के प्रयोग को व्यक्त करते हैं:

(a) That house is ours.
(b) This pen is mine.
(c) Those books are yours.
(d) That book is hers.
(e) These shoes are theirs.
(f) Every country has its peculiar traditions.

Singular-Plural

निम्न Table में Personal Pronoun के Singular एवं Plural दिये गये हैं:

I Person		II Person		III Person	
Singular	**Plural**	**Singular**	**Plural**	**Singular**	**Plural**
I	We	You	You	He, She, It	They
My	Our	Your	Your	His, Her	Their
Mine	Ours	Yours	Yours	Hers, Its	Theirs
Me	Us	You	You	Him, Her, It	Them

Personal Pronoun: Use and Rules

(1) यदि एक वाक्य में भिन्न-भिन्न Persons के Pronoun एक ही Verb के साथ प्रयुक्त होते हैं तो उनको लिखने का क्रम (Order) निम्न प्रकार होता है:

(A) **Singular** सबसे पहले You (Second Person), उसके बाद He (Third Person) एवं उसके बाद I (First Person), Good Manners की दृष्टि से लिखा जाता है। इसको याद रखने का तरीका है 2 + 3 + 1(Second + Third + First + Person Pronoun) जैसे:

(a) You, he and I are partners.
(b) He and I are good friends.
(c) You and he are working in the same office.
(d) You and I can do this work.

(B) **Plural** में यह क्रम 1 + 2 + 3 होता है। जैसे:

(a) We and you cannot live together.
(b) We, you and they can purchase that complex.

(C) यदि वाक्य में कोई गलती का सन्दर्भ आए या कोई भूल या अपराध का जिक्र हो या वाक्य का भाव सकारात्मक नहीं हो तो Pronouns का क्रम 1 + 2 + 3 की तरह होना चाहिए। जैसे:

(a) I and you are responsible for the loss.
(b) You and he spoiled the party.
(c) I and he will beg sorry for the misconduct.

(2) यदि वाक्य में एक से अधिक भिन्न-भिन्न Persons के Pronoun का प्रयोग होता है एवं उनके लिए एक ही Plural Pronoun का प्रयोग किया जाए तो Third एवं First Person के साथ First Person Plural; Second एवं Third Person के साथ Second Person Plural एवं Second एवं First के लिए First Person Plural Pronoun का प्रयोग होगा। यदि तीनों Persons का प्रयोग हुआ है तो Pronoun—First Person Plural होगा।

III + I	–	I Person Plural
II + III	–	II Person Plural
II + I	–	I Person Plural

जैसे: (a) You and I have done <u>our</u> job.
(b) You and he have completed <u>your</u> job.
(c) He and I have done <u>our</u> duty.
(d) You he and I have completed <u>our</u> duty.

(3) Collective Noun के साथ, Pronoun का प्रयोग उस स्थिति में Singular (and Neuter Gender) में होता है जब Collective Noun का प्रयोग एक Unit के रूप में हो, यदि Collective Noun का प्रयोग Unit की तरह न होकर, बिखरा (Divided or Separate) हुआ होता है तो Plural Pronoun का प्रयोग किया जाता है। जैसे:

(a) The crew revolted and murdered <u>its</u> captain.
(b) After three days the jury gave <u>its</u> verdict.
(c) The fleet will reach <u>its</u> destination in a month.

- *Collective noun, एक unit की तरह प्रयुक्त है एवं Pronoun, its, Singular एवं Neuter Gender में प्रयुक्त है। Look at the following sentences :*
  - *(a) The jury were divided in their opinions.*
  - *(b) The society took the decision without leaving their seats.*
  - *(c) The government decided to revise their plans outlays.*
- *यहाँ Collective Noun; Jury, Society, Government के साथ pronoun का प्रयोग एक Unit नहीं व्यक्त करके, separateness, division, individuality व्यक्त करता है।*

(4) जब दो या अधिक Nouns and, से संयुक्त होते हैं तो Pronoun, Plural होगा। जैसे:

(a) Ram and Mohan went to their school.
(b) Suresh and his family members have completed their work.

(5) जब दो Singular Nouns, and से संयुक्त हों एवं दोनों के पूर्व Each या Every का प्रयोग हुआ हो तो Pronoun भी Singular होगा। जैसे:

(a) Every soldier and every sailor was in his place.
(b) Each officer and each clerk has joined his duty.

(6) Each, Either एवं Neither के साथ हमेशा Singular Pronoun एवं Singular Verb का प्रयोग किया जाता है। जैसे:

(a) Each of the students is ready to do his duty.
(b) Either of the two students gets his gift.
(c) Neither of them gets his turn.

(7) जब दो या अधिक Singular Nouns 'or', 'Either.....or', 'Neither.....nor' से संयुक्त किए जाते हैं तो Pronoun, Singular प्रयोग किया जाता है। जैसे:

(a) Ram or Shyam should deposit his dues.
(b) Either Ramesh or Ganesh lost his purse.
(c) Neither Ram nor Shyam has completed his work.

(8) जब एक Plural एवं एक Singular Noun, 'or' या 'nor' से संयुक्त किए जाते हैं तो Pronoun-Plural लगता है। जैसे:

(a) Either the Principal or the teachers failed in their duty.
(b) Neither the teacher nor the students have done their work.

(9) तुलनात्मक (Comparative) वाक्यों में than या as के बाद Pronoun की Nominative Form का प्रयोग होगा या Objective Form का। यह इस पर निर्भर है कि वाक्य का अर्थ क्या है। जैसे:

(a) I love you more than he (loves you).
(b) I love you more than (I love) him.
(c) I shall give you as many pens as (I shall give) him.
(d) I am as intelligent as he (is).

इस तरह के वाक्यों में वाक्य को अर्थ के अनुसार पूरा करके देख लेने पर यह समझ में आ जाता है कि वाक्य में Pronoun की Nominative Form का प्रयोग होगा या Objective Form का।

आजकल कुछ Verb (Verbs of incomplete predication जिनका अर्थ being or becoming के सन्दर्भ में होता है) के साथ than/as के बाद Nominative Form की जगह Objective Form में भी Pronoun का प्रयोग किया जाने लगा है। परीक्षा के दृष्टिकोण से आप पूर्व में बताये नियम का ही ध्यान रखें। जैसे: He is taller than me. इसे भी सही माना जाता है।

(10) 'to be' Form Verb के बाद आने वाला Pronoun उसी Case में होना चाहिए, जिस Case में Verb 'to be' के पहले आने वाला Noun या Pronoun प्रयुक्त हुआ है। जैसे:

(A) (a) It is I. (b) It is he. (c) This is she.

उपरोक्त वाक्यों में It एवं This का प्रयोग Nominative Case में हुआ है। अत: Pronoun, I, He एवं She, Nominative Case में प्रयुक्त हुआ है। लेकिन कई विद्वान आजकल

(B) (a) It is me. (b) This is me. (c) This is her. (d) This is him.

इन वाक्यों को सही मानते हैं। अत: (A) एवं (B) दोनों ही सही हैं। दोनों ही प्रकार के वाक्य प्रचलन में हैं।

यदि इस तरह के वाक्यों में who/which के साथ जब Clause का प्रयोग होता है। Verb 'to be' के बाद आने वाला Pronoun हमेशा Nominative case में प्रयोग किया जाता है। जैसे :

(a) It is he who is responsible. *(b) It is she who refused the offer.*
(c) It is I who saw her yesterday. *(d) It is he who will pay you.*

(C) यहाँ Who के साथ Clause का प्रयोग हुआ है। अत: Verb to be 'is' के साथ आने वाला Pronoun, Nominative Case में (he, she) लगाना उचित है।

ध्यान दें

Verb 'to be' के पहले आने वाला Noun/Pronoun यदि Objective Case मे है तो इसके बाद आने वाला Noun या Pronoun भी Objective Case में ही आता है।

(a) I know the girl to be her. (b) I recognised the student to be him.

यहाँ to be मे पहले में girl एवं student, Verb; know एवं recognised के Object हैं। अत: यहाँ Pronoun her एवं him, Objective Case में हैं।

Pronoun 'It'

'It' का प्रयोग निम्न के लिये होता है :

(1) For thing without life (निर्जीव वस्तुओं के लिए) :
   (a) Here is your pen. Please take it.

(2) For Animals (पशुओं के लिए) :
   (a) He has a cat. It is very beautiful. (b) I have a dog. It is very faithful.

(3) For young child (यदि उनमें male-female का अन्तर न करना हो) :
   (a) When he saw the child, it was playing. (b) The baby has spoiled its dress.

(4) किसी Noun या Pronoun को महत्त्व देने हेतु 'It' का प्रयोग निम्न प्रकार किया जाता है :
   (a) It is you, who can solve this problem.
   (b) It was I, who called you.
   (c) It was at Simla where the agreement was signed.
   (d) It is the place where he was murdered.

(5) एक अनिश्चित कर्त्ता (Indefinite Nominative) के रूप में 'It' का प्रयोग निम्न प्रकार होता है :
   (a) It rains. (b) It snows.
   (c) It thunders. (d) It blows.

(6) समय, मौसम के सन्दर्भ में 'It' का प्रयोग निम्न प्रकार होता है:
   (a) It is 7 O'clock. (b) It is fine
   (c) It is winter. (d) It is summer.

(7) Exclamatory वाक्य में It का प्रयोग निम्न प्रकार किया जाता है:
   (a) What a beautiful bird it is! (b) What a large building it is!

(8) It का प्रयोग निम्न प्रकार के वाक्यों में भी किया जाता है:
   (a) It is easy to find faults with others. (b) It is confirm that he is wrong.
   (c) It is doubtful whether she will join here. (d) It is uncertain that she will come.
   (e) He is telling what is not true : as he knows it.
   (f) He deserved the award, as we knew it.
   (g) I think it is wrong to travel without proper ticket.
   (h) I consider that it is pity to waste time.

   It को Impersonal Pronoun भी कहा जाता है।

'It' and 'This'

'This' वाक्य के कर्त्ता के रूप में कार्य करता है। इसका प्रयोग किसी वस्तु/व्यक्ति के नाम बताने, पहचान कराने एवं प्रगाढ़ता प्रकट करने हेतु किया जाता है। जैसे:

(a) This is my friend.
(b) This is a cat.
(c) This is All India Radio.
(d) This is my brother.
(e) This is 2345714.
(f) This is BBC/Voice of America.

जबकि It का प्रयोग समय, मौसम आदि हेतु किया जाता है या विशेष structures में जैसा ऊपर बताया गया है वहाँ किया जाता है। जैसे :

(a) It is 7 o'clock.
(b) It is very cold today.
(c) It is morning.
(d) It is winter.
(e) It is raining.
(f) It is 7:30 by my watch.

2. Reflexive Pronoun

My, your, him, her, it में self जोड़ने पर एवं our, your, them में selves जोड़ने पर Reflexive Pronoun बनाए जाते हैं। ये वाक्य में Object की तरह प्रयुक्त होते हैं एवं वाक्य के Subject को ही व्यक्त करते हैं।

"These are called Reflexive because the action done by the subject turns back (reflects) upon the subject."

—Wren & Martin

Look at the following sentences:

(a) He hurt himself.
(b) We ruined ourselves.
(c) You ruined yourself.
(d) I hurt myself.
(e) She ruined herself.
(f) They ruined themselves.

Rules

Rule 1

कुछ Transitive Verbs के साथ Reflexive Pronoun का प्रयोग किया जाता है। Transitive Verb के साथ Object का आना आवश्यक है, जब इन verb के साथ कोई Object नहीं होता है, तो Reflexive Pronoun लगाकर object की पूर्ति करनी होती है। ऐसी verbs हैं : avail, absent, enjoy, resign, apply, revenge, exert etc. जैसे:

(a) I absented myself from the office.
(b) I revenged myself upon her.
(c) He availed himself the opportunity.
(d) They enjoyed themselves the pleasure of weather.

Rule 2

कुछ Verbs जब इनका प्रयोग intransitively किया जाता है तो इनके साथ Reflexive Pronoun का प्रयोग नहीं किया जाता है। ऐसी Verbs हैं : Keep, break, set, bathe, make, stop, steal, qualify, move, open, draw, rest, roll, burst, hide, feed, gather etc. सामान्यतया इन verbs का प्रयोग intransitively ही होता है। जैसे:

(a) He kept away from the function. *Correct*
He kept himself away from the function. *Incorrect*
(b) Let us rest at the bed. *Correct*
Let us ourselves rest at the bed. *Incorrect*
(c) She hid in the room. *Correct*
She hid herself in the room. *Incorrect*

Rule 3

Reflexive Pronoun का निम्न प्रकार से प्रयोग किया जाना गलत है:

(a) Myself is R.C. Gupta.
(b) Himself will do it.
(c) Myself will go there.
(d) Herself can solve it.

3. Emphatic Pronoun

Reflexive Pronoun एवं Emphatic Pronoun बनावट व देखने में एक समान होते हैं। Emphatic Pronoun का प्रयोग किसी Noun/Pronoun का emphasis (महत्व बढ़ाने) करने हेतु किया जाता है। जैसे:

(a) I myself solved this question.
(b) She herself found the solution.
(c) He himself came to see the patient.
(d) You yourself admitted your fault.

Emphatic Pronoun का प्रयोग subject के तुरन्त बाद किया जाता है।

4. Reciprocal Pronoun

ये (each other, one another) ऐसे Pronouns हैं जो दो Pronouns से मिलकर बनते हैं एवं परस्पर सम्बन्ध को व्यक्त करते हैं। जैसे:

(a) The two friends quarrelled with each other.
(b) They all gave gifts to one another.
(c) These two students love each other.
(d) They saved themselves by helping one another.

सामान्यतया (पुरानी धारणा के अनुसार) each other का प्रयोग दो के लिए एवं one another का प्रयोग दो से अधिक के लिए किया जाता है। आजकल, विभिन्न विद्वान लेखकों द्वारा यह अन्तर समाप्त-सा कर दिया है एवं each other का प्रयोग भी दो से अधिक के लिए तथा one another का प्रयोग दो के लिए किया जाने लगा है।

For you and I are foreigners to one another. **—Aldous Huxley**

The artistic result of Volpone is not due to any effect that Volpone, Mosca, Corvino, Corbaccio, and Voltore have upon each other. **—T.S. Eliot**

'Each other' and 'One another are only two Reciprocal Pronouns. These are always used objectively.'

5. Demonstrative Pronoun

This, That, These, Demonstrative Pronouns हैं। इनके तुरन्त बाद verb का प्रयोग किया जाता है।

Demonstrative Pronoun is used to point out the object to which it refers. As:

(a) This is the gift from my mother.
(b) That is the Tajmahal.
(c) These are the books, I found in the bag.
(d) That is my house.

यदि किसी वाक्य में Demonstrative Pronoun के बाद verb का प्रयोग न करके Noun का प्रयोग किया गया हो तो ये Adjective की तरह प्रयुक्त होते हैं न कि Pronoun की तरह। जैसे:

(a) This pen is mine. *(b) That book is hers.* *(c) These books are his.*

इन वाक्यों में This, That, These का प्रयोग Adjective की तरह हुआ है।

6. Indefinite Pronoun

ये Pronouns किसी निश्चित वस्तु या व्यक्ति को प्रकट नहीं करते हैं। ऐसे Pronouns हैं—Some, One, Someone, All, A few, Others, No one, Nobody, Anyone etc.

A pronoun that refers to person or thing in a general way (not in a definite way) is called Indefinite Pronoun.

(a) Some have joined the party.
(b) All went to Jaipur.
(c) A strict diet is appropriate for only a few.
(d) Do good to others.
(e) Someone has stolen my watch.
(f) One should mind one's own business.
(g) One must avail oneself of every good opportunity.
(h) Some passengers were injured.

One का प्रयोग Nominative, Reflexive एवं Possessive तीनों cases में अपने रूप one, oneself, one's में ही प्रयुक्त होता है। One के साथ his का प्रयोग करना या अन्य किसी Pronoun का प्रयोग करना गलत है।

One should do his duty. — *Incorrect*
One should do one's duty. — *Correct*

7. Interrogative Pronoun

Who, Whom, Whose, Which, What; Interrogative Pronouns हैं। इनका प्रयोग प्रश्न पूछने हेतु किया जाता है। Interrogative pronouns are used for making querries or asking questions.

Look at the following sentences :

(a) What is that?
(b) Who is he?
(c) Which is your pen?
(d) Whose bag is this?
(e) Whom do you want to talk?
(f) What is your name?

(1) उपरोक्त वाक्यों में प्रयोग किए गए सभी underlined words, Interrogative Pronouns हैं।

(2) What का प्रयोग सामान्यतया वस्तुओं या कार्यों के लिए होता है। जैसे :

(a) What is your father? (Father का क्या व्यवसाय है?)
(b) What is your name?
(c) What is this?

(3) Who, Whose, Whom का प्रयोग व्यक्तियों के लिए किया जाता है। Who का प्रयोग Nominative Case में, Whose का प्रयोग Possessive Case में एवं Whom का प्रयोग Objective Case में किया जाता है। जैसे :

(a) Who is he?
(b) Whom did you see today?
(c) Whose bag is this?

आजकल कई विद्वान Whom की जगह Who का ही प्रयोग करने लगे हैं। जैसे:

(a) Who have you called?
(b) Who do you want to meet?
(c) Who are you talking to?

(4) Which का प्रयोग व्यक्तियों एवं वस्तु के लिए selection/choice के लिए सामान्यतया किया जाता है जैसे:

(a) Which is your umbrella?
(b) Which book is yours?
(c) Which school do you like most?

(5) कभी-कभी What एवं Which के साथ Preposition का प्रयोंग निम्न प्रकार से होता है :

(a) What is this table made of?
(b) What train will you go by?
(c) Which year were you born in?
(d) Which colony do you live in?
(e) Which magazine are you searching for?
(f) Which class do you read in?

8. Distributive Pronoun

Each, Everyone, Either एवं Neither; Distributive Pronouns हैं। ये Pronouns एक व्यक्ति/वस्तु (one at a time) को व्यक्त करते हैं, अतः ये singular होते हैं एवं इनके साथ हमेशा Singular verb का प्रयोग होता है।

Look at the following sentences :

(a) Each of the students gets a prize.
(b) Each got his turn.
(c) Either of the two will win the race.
(d) Neither of those two students can secure first position.
(e) Everyone of the students was happy.
(f) Each of the two students received a medal.

(1) Everyone का प्रयोग हमेशा दो से अधिक के सन्दर्भ में होता है, जबकि Each का प्रयोग दो या दो से अधिक के लिए, हो सकता है। दो के लिए everyone का प्रयोग कभी नहीं किया जाता है।

(2) Either एवं Neither का प्रयोग सामान्यतया दो के सन्दर्भ में किया जाता है। दो से अधिक के लिए Any, No one, None का प्रयोग करना चाहिए।

(3) Distributive pronouns के साथ Third person, Singular pronoun, Masculine Gender (he, his, him) का प्रयोग किया जाता है। जैसे:

(a) Everyone should obey his parents. *(b) Neither of these two students has received his prize.*

(4) यदि वाक्य में Distributive pronouns के बाद Feminine Gender के Noun का प्रयोग हुआ है तो 'her' pronoun का प्रयोग करना आवश्यक है। ध्यान रखें इस Case में he, him, his का प्रयोग गलत होगा। जैसे:

(a) Neither of these two girls has deposited her fees.
(b) Either of the two girls has received her gift.
(c) Each of the girls has donated her pocket money.
(d) Everyone of the women has a choice of her own.

यदि Feminine noun की जगह Plural pronouns (us/them/you) का प्रयोग हुआ हो तो Singular Masculine Gender Pronoun का प्रयोग किया जाएगा। जैसे :

(a) Neither of them has done his duty. *(b) Each of them has forgot his purse.*

Position of Pronoun 'Each'

एक वाक्य में Pronoun 'Each' को कहाँ लिखा जाना चाहिए, यह एक महत्त्वपूर्ण बिन्दु है। इन वाक्यों पर *ध्यान दें* :

(a) I bought each of these books for rupees fifty. *Incorrect*
I bought these books each for rupees fifty. *Incorrect*
I bought these books for rupees fifty each. *Correct*
Each का प्रयोग numeral के बाद में किया जाना ही उचित है।

अन्य वाक्यों को देखें :

(b) These tables cost each two hundred rupees. *Incorrect*
These tables cost two hundred rupees each. *Correct*
जब वाक्य में numeral नहीं हो तो देखें :
These men received each a prize. *Incorrect*
These men received a prize each. *Incorrect*
Each of the men received a prize. *Correct*
वाक्य के शुरू में ऐसे Case में Each का प्रयोग ही सही प्रयोग होगा।

9. Relative Pronoun

Relative Pronoun refers to some noun going before, which is called its antecedent.

Relative Pronouns (who/which/that/what/whose/whom) ऐसे Pronouns हैं जो इससे पूर्व आए Nouns को इंगित करते हैं एवं इस Noun को उस Relative Pronoun का antecedent (which comes before) कहा जाता है। जैसे:

(a) I know Sarla who has just gone out.
(b) I have found the bag which I lost yesterday.
(c) This is the magazine that she gave me.

उक्त वाक्यों में who, which, that, Relative Pronouns एवं Sarla, bag, magazine इनके antecedents हैं।

Rules

Rule 1

Relative Pronouns का वाक्य में subject या object की तरह प्रयोग किया जाता है। ये Conjunction का भी कार्य करते हैं। जैसे:

(a) The bag that is there is yours. *Subject*
(b) The bag that I found yesterday is hers. *Object*

Rule 2

Relative Pronouns, who एवं whom का प्रयोग निर्जीव वस्तु के लिए नहीं किया जाता है। इनका प्रयोग व्यक्ति एवं living nouns हेतु किया जाता है। Who का प्रयोग Nominative case में तथा whom का प्रयोग Objective Case में किया जाता है। people एवं those के साथ who का ही प्रयोग किया जाता है। जैसे:

(a) I like the boy who helps the poor. *Nominative case*
(b) This is the girl whom all admire. *Objective case*
(c) I know all those who were involved in the case.
(d) All the people who took the membership are happy.

Rule 3

Whose का Possessive Case में प्रयोग सामान्यतया व्यक्ति एवं जानवर के लिए किया जाता है। कई स्थितियों में whose का प्रयोग non- living nouns हेतु भी किया जाता है। जैसे:

(a) This is the boy whose parents have died.
(b) A girl whose hair is curly looks beautiful.
(c) The sun whose rays give us light is adored like God.
(d) The dog whose colour is white has become mad.

Rule 4

Which का प्रयोग non-living nouns एवं animals हेतु किया जाता है। जैसे:

(a) The book which I purchased yesterday is useless.
(b) The dog which was caught by the municipality has died.
(c) The house which has green gate is hers.

(1) Relative Pronoun की तरह which का प्रयोग करते समय Preposition हमेशा उससे पहले लगाई जाती है। जैसे:
(a) This is the magazine about which Ramesh told you.
(b) I don't remember the date on which you were married.
(c) The post for which you want to apply is on adhoc basis.
(d) The brief case of which clock was damaged has been stolen.
(2) कई वाक्यों में which पूरे clause के लिए ही प्रयुक्त होता है। इस तरह 'that' का प्रयोग नहीं होता है। जैसे:
(a) He killed all the animals which was a cruel act.
(b) She says that she is honest which is not true.

Rule 5

What का प्रयोग वस्तुओं के लिए किया जाता है एवं इससे पूर्व कोई antecedent नहीं आता है। वाक्यों में Antecedent का प्रयोग होने पर what की जगह that का प्रयोग होगा। जैसे:

(a) What can't be cured must be endured.
(b) What he told you is not correct.
(c) I know what you want to say.
(d) What I told you yesterday, is a secret.

Rule 6

'But' का प्रयोग कई वाक्यों में Relative Pronoun की तरह भी होता है। जैसे:

(a) There is none but abuses him. (but means who does not abuse him.)
(b) There is no problem but has a solution. (but has = which does not have.)

इस तरह के वाक्यों में but clause एक objective clause की तरह प्रयुक्त होता है।

Rule 7

(A) That का प्रयोग living एवं non-living, nouns के लिए, singular एवं plural दोनों nouns के साथ होता है। जैसे:

(a) I have lost the book that you gave me.
(b) I haven't read the magazine that the teacher suggested to me.
(c) He that is content is happy.
(d) Uneasy lies the head that wears a crown.

(B) That से पूर्व कोई preposition नहीं लगाया जाता है। यदि preposition लगाने की आवश्यकता हो तो वह वाक्य के अन्त में लगता है। जैसे:

(a) We know the hotel that she lives in.
(b) This is the lady that I told you about.
(c) I understand the point that you are hinting at.
(d) This is the house that I told you about.

Superlative degree के बाद that का प्रयोग who या which की अपेक्षा अधिक उचित माना जाता है। जैसे:

(a) He is the most eloquent speaker that I have ever heard.
(b) Patel was the greatest man that India produced.

(C) निम्न शब्दों के साथ 'that' का प्रयोग किया जाता है:

All, any, anybody, anything, much, nothing, little, somebody, no one, none,
the same + noun, the only + noun etc.

(a) All that glitters is not gold.
(b) There was none that didn't support the cause.
(c) It is for nothing that I have been trying to find.
(d) There is much that he needs.

(e) There was not any that could be followed.
(f) There was somebody that raised the matter.
(g) This is the same girl that we met yesterday.
(h) This is the only girl that secured more than 90% marks.

(D) **Interrogative Pronoun** 'who', एवं 'what' के बाद 'that' का ही प्रयोग किया जाता है। जैसे:
(a) What is it that you can't solve. (b) What is there that I can't see.
(c) Who am I that you should care for. (d) Who was there that you were talking with ?

(E) जब दो Antecedents जिनमें एक व्यक्ति को एवं दूसरा जानवर या वस्तु को व्यक्त करे तो Relative Pronoun 'that' का प्रयोग किया जाता है। जैसे:
(a) The boy and his dog that entered the temple were caught by the people.
(b) The lady and her cat that created the nuisance were arrested by the police.

(F) Same एवं such के बाद as या that का ही प्रयोग होता है, who या which का प्रयोग नहीं करना चाहिए। जैसे
(a) This is the same fellow that came yesterday also.
(b) My books are same as yours.
(c) His reply was such as we never expected from him.

Rule 8

Relative Pronoun—Importance of comma—जब वाक्य में who/which/Relative Pronoun का प्रयोग हो एवं उससे पहले comma लगाया हो तो ऐसी clause को Principal Clause कहा जाता है। जैसे:
(a) My friend,(comma) who lives in America has sent me a camera.
(b) The book, (comma) which I purchased yesterday is useless.
लेकिन यदि who/which के पहले comma नहीं लगा हो तो वह Adjective Clause होती है। जैसे:
(c) My friend who lives in America has sent me a camera.
(d) The book which I purchased yesterday is useless.

उपरोक्त वाक्य (a) एवं (b) में underlined clause; Principal Clause है तथा वाक्य (c) एवं (d) में underlined clause, Adjective Clause है।

Rule 9

वाक्य में Relative Pronoun का antecedent, possessive case में नहीं होना चाहिए। यह एक गलत structure है। जैसे:
(a) These are chairman's instructions that must be followed.
(b) I went to Sarla's house, who is my class fellow.

इन दोनों वाक्यों में Relative Pronoun 'that' एवं 'who' के antecedents, chairman एवं Sarla हैं जो Possessive Case में है, यह गलत structure है। अत: इन वाक्यों को निम्न प्रकार से लिखा जाना चाहिए:
(a) These are the instructions of the chairman that must be followed.
(b) I went to the house of Sarla who is my class fellow.

Rule 10

Relative Pronoun Who/Which के पहले and या but का प्रयोग करने से यदि वे अपने antecedent से दूर होते हैं तो यह एक गलत प्रयोग होगा। जैसे:
(a) Suresh is a good player and who is my class fellow.
(b) This is a good magazine and which should be read by everyone.
(c) This is a good car but which is very costly.

उपरोक्त वाक्यों में who/which के बाद and या but का प्रयोग सही नहीं है। वाक्य से and/but को हटाना होगा।

Relative pronoun के पूर्व and/but का प्रयोग तब ही किया जा सकता है, जब वाक्य में एक से अधिक Relative Pronouns का प्रयोग किया जाता है। जैसे:
This is a magazine which is really good and which should be read by everycne.

Compound Relative Pronouns

Whoever, whosoever, whomsoever, whatever, whichever, whatsoever, इत्यादि Compound Relative Pronouns हैं। इनका प्रयोग वाक्य में बिना antecedent के होता है। इनका antecedent इन्हीं में सम्मिलित (included) रहता है। जैसे:

Whatever	*anything which.*
Whichever	*anything which.*
Whoever/whosoever	*any person who.*
Whomsoever	*any person whom.*

(a) You can eat whatever you like.
(b) You can take whichever you like.
(c) Whoever/Whosoever joins our party is welcome.
(d) I shall employ whomsoever you recommend.

Omission of Relative Pronoun

कुछ वाक्यों में Relative Pronoun, Verb या Preposition के Object के रूप में प्रयोग किये जाते हैं। ऐसे वाक्यों में कई विद्वान/लेखक Relative Pronoun को omit करके भी वाक्य रचना को सही मानते हैं। जैसे:

(a) This is the bag that I bought yesterday.
This is the bag I bought yesterday.

(b) The man whom I met yesterday is very intelligent.
The man I met yesterday is very intelligent.

Grammar rules के अनुसार objective case में whom का प्रयोग होता है। लेकिन आजकल whom का प्रयोग काफी अप्रचलित हो गया है, who का प्रयोग किया जाने लगा है। जैसे:

(a) The man whom I invited is his friend.
The man who I invited is his friend.

(b) The man whom I spoke to is his friend.
The man who I spoke to is his friend.

इन वाक्यों में whom की जगह who का प्रयोग Grammar के दृष्टिकोण से सही नहीं है, लेकिन आजकल यह प्रयोग किया जा रहा है।

10. Exclamatory Pronoun

A pronoun used as an exclamation is called an Exclamatory Pronoun.

(a) **What** ! You don't know Sonia Gandhi ?
(b) **What** ! You lost the chain ?

उपरोक्त वाक्यों में What, Exclamatory Pronoun है।

Who/Whom

(1) Who and whom for persons : who and whom are normally reserved for persons, but they may be used for animals when they are thought of in a semi-personal way (My dog, **who** is getting old now, and of countries, when the people rather than the territory are referred to : India, **who** feels very strongly on this matter.)

(2) Who and whom as relative Pronouns : As relative pronouns, who and whom are preceded by a comma when they introduce a non-defining clause, but the comma must not be used when the clause is a defining one.

(3) Who as subject, whom as object

Who is used for the subject and the complement of a verb:

(i) My father, **who** works in a bank, is retiring soon.

(ii) My father, **who** is sixty next year, works in a bank.

Whom is used for the object and when governed by a Preposition:

(i) The man **whom** you rescued from the sea has recovered.

(ii) The newspaper editor, to **whom** we all owe so much, is leaving the company.

But in questions introduced by an interrogative pronoun which is governed by a preposition which comes at the end of the sentence it is more usual to use who:

(i) <u>Who</u> is that letter from? (ii) <u>Who</u> was this poem written by?

In spoken English or colloquial written style, **who** is now almost universally used. But even here, **whom** must always be used after a preposition at the beginning of a sentence:

(i) To **whom do I** send it?

(4) Who/whom in relative clauses : A frequent source of trouble is sentences of this type:

(i) The person who (or whom?) we thought was guilty proved to be innocent.

(ii) The man who (or whom?) we feared we had injured proved to be unharmed.

The temptation is always to use whom, presumably because it is felt that the word is the object of thought and feared (or whatever verb takes their place in other sentences); but it is not. In the first sentence, it is the subject of was guilty, hence **who** is correct and in the second, the object of had injured hence **whom** is required. We thought and we feared have the force of parentheses, and could be moved to another part of the sentence:

The person who was guilty we thought.... ;

The man whom we had injured we feared...Even the Times Literary Supplement had this sentence:

(i) The German people, **whom** Hitler had determined should not survive defeat, did in fact survive.

Obviously who should have been used, since it is the subject of should not survive. And The Sunday Times made the same mistake in this headline:

(i) The entire Magazine, except Lifespan, is devoted this week to 100 men and women **whom** Sunday Times writers and expert consultants believe will be making headlines in the Britain of the 1980s.

Again, **who** should have been used as it is the subject of will be making when it goes with an infinitive, however, **whom** is always required:

(i) The person **whom** we thought to be guilty.

If there is any doubt, a useful test is to substitute the personal pronoun he or him; if he would be used, the correct relative is who; if him, it is whom:

(i) We thought he was guilty. (therefore **who**)

(ii) We feared we had injured him. (therefore **whom**)

(iii) We thought him to be guilty. (therefore **whom**)

(5) Questions: A similar difficulty may arise with questions :

(i) **Who** (not **whom**) do you think we saw? because it is the object of saw.

(6) Whom is never indirect object : Whom is not used as an indirect object. We do not say the boy *whom* I gave the book, or ask *whom* did you give the book ? It must be to *whom* (or the preposition may be placed at the end).

(7) The verb after who: Who is the same number and person as its antececent, and takes its verb accordingly:

(i) It is I *who* am to blame.

The rules regarding the use of the co-ordinating conjunctions 'and' and 'but' before 'who' are the same as those for which. ***—Current English Usage by F.T. Wood***

Whose and Who's

Care chould be taken not to confuse **whose** with **who's (meaning 'who is ,'who has')**, a mistake that is easily made as, like its and it's, they are pronounced the same. Even the journalists of The Times Educational Supplement are not always so careful as they should be, as this headline shows :

(i) **Whose** Afraid of the Big Bad Comprehensive?

And here is the mistake the other way round from ***The* Observer**

(i) I relished the anticipation of clever people, cleverly swapping anecdotes, cleverly punning, cleverly imitating others, indiscreetly prognosticating who'd get who's job.

—Current English Usage by F.T. Wood

Points to Remember

(A) REFER CLEARLY to a specific noun : Don't be vague or ambiguous.

(a) Although the motorcycle hit the tree, it was not damaged. (Is "it" the motorcycle or the tree?)

(b) I don't think they should show violence on TV. (Who are "they"?)

(c) Vacation is coming soon, which is nice.
(What is nice, the vacation or the fact that it is coming soon?)

(d) Jack worked in a national forest last summer. This may be his life's work.
(What word does "this" refer to?)

(e) If you put this sheet in your notebook, you can refer to it.
(What does "it" refer to, the sheet or your notebook?)

Such type of ambiguity must be avoided.

(B) *The indefinite pronouns anyone, anybody, everyone, everybody, someone, somebody, no one, and nobody are always singular. This is sometimes perplexing to writers who feel that everyone and everybody (especially) are referring to more than one person. The same is true of either and neither, which are always singular even though they seem to be referring to two things.*

01

Correct the following sentences:

(1) Let you and I go to play.
(2) There is close relation between he and I.
(3) You, he and I have done their job.
(4) You and he could not complete his work.
(5) He and I have fastened his belts.
(6) I, you and he were present in the function.
(7) I and you are strangers.
(8) You and I are responsible for this loss.
(9) He and I were the main accused.
(10) You, he and I must beg sorry for the misconduct.

02

Correct the following sentences:

(1) Neither of these four vehicles will do.
(2) Anyone of the two girls can solve this puzzle.
(3) Either of the three students is responsible for the loss.
(4) None of the two girls could complete the job.
(5) One should obey his elders.
(6) One should respect not only his own parents but also others.'
(7) One should take care not to make himself obnoxious to others.
(8) Each girl and every madam tried their best to finish the work before 7 P.M.
(9) Every man and every woman have their own fascination.
(10) Every leader and every citizen have a duty towards their country.

03

Correct the following sentences:

(1) Each of the employees have to arrange their own vehicle.
(2) Every one of them were given their table and chair.
(3) Either Ramesh or Sita have left their tiffin box.
(4) Either the teacher or the students have left his classroom unlocked .
(5) Please take the buffalo to her shed.
(6) The cow has hurt her legs.
(7) This is easy to get her agreed.
(8) This was he who arrived first in the meeting.
(9) It is to certify that Mr. A is our employee.
(10) This is 8 O'Clock by my watch.

04

Correct the following sentences :

(1) All which she said was incorrect.
(2) Who was the girl which came to meet you?
(3) What is his opinion about the work which you have completed?
(4) I always purchase the item which is best in the market.
(5) This is the same shirt which I saw in the shop.
(6) Who is she? Who can abuse me like this?
(7) Only those employees should be promoted whom are sincere.
(8) The leaders which do not love their country are not respected.
(9) Those whose live in glass houses should not throw stones at others.
(10) What was the reply, which she submitted?

05

Correct the following sentences:

(1) It was me who telephoned you yesterday.
(2) The girl whom you spoke to in the office is my friend.
(3) My brother and myself are glad to get your greetings.
(4) I am not one of those who cannot keep his promise.
(5) It is not us who are responsible for the delay.
(6) They admired his wife and he.
(7) What place are you going?
(8) Which house do you live?
(9) She has absented from duty today again.
(10) I could not avail of the opportunity I got last year.
(11) The treatment received by me was such, which I never expected.
(12) His expectation is the same which is hers.
(13) One cannot bear his insult like this.
(14) My house is bigger than their.
(15) This is a secret between you and I.

06

Fill in the blanks with Interrogative Pronouns:

(1) We went to Ranjana's party .... we enjoyed very much.
(2) Anajali went to the doctor .... told her to rest for seven days atleast.
(3) .... does your sister live?
(4) .... book do you like?
(5) .... did you finish the game?
(6) The woman .... I met yesterday lent me her umbrella.
(7) The horse .... I selected won the race yesterday .
(8) He did not know .... to say then.
(9) Shakespeare, ... is the world's greatest dramatist, was born in a cottage .
(10) The Superintendent of Police, ... work is very precarious, takes care of public safety and law and order .

07

Fill in the blanks with Interrogative Pronouns :

(1) What is the name of the man .... car you borrowed?
(2) I don't know the name of the woman to .... I spoke on the phone.
(3) .... teaches you Sanskrit?
(4) .... is your problem?
(5) I gave him all the money .... I had.
(6) Ashish is the man .... son won the scholarship.
(7) Our flight was delayed .... meant we had to wait for hours at the airport.
(8) Jitu is one of my friends .... I have known for a very long time.
(9) The book .... you gave me is very useful for the pregnant ladies.
(10) Swimming , ... is a good sport also , makes people healthy and bold.

08

Add the Relative Pronouns to the following sentences:

(1) Gypsum is a mineral .... is extracted from the Earth.
(2) There is nothing .... I can do for you.
(3) This is the house .... I was born.
(4) My parents had left for college .... I reached home.
(5) He is a famous scientist about ....many books have been written.
(6) Madam Curie, ... discovered radium, was one of the greatest women of her age.
(7) The book ,............ you gave me is not so useful for learning English speaking.
(8) Where is the man .... sold me the detergent powder ?
(9) That is the lady .... golden chain was snatched yesterday.
(10) The girl .... you see at the desk is the receptionist.

09

Correct the following sentences:

(1) Everyone should obey their parents.
(2) Sita must do their duties.
(3) Each girl and every student was busy in her their work.
(4) Either Pramod or Narendra has learnt their lesson.
(5) Nisha or Sushma was teaching their son.
(6) Either Rohan or his friends forgot his books.
(7) You, he and I am friends.
(8) He I and you went to Nehru garden yesterday.
(9) Manish and I should learn my lesson.
(10) You and Sushma should read her book.
(11) He, you and I must do my work.
(12) Ram and Shyam help one another.
(13) Three children love each other.
(14) Two friends love one another.
(15) It is I who is your friend.

10.

Correct the following sentences:

(1) That is one of the girls who has stolen eggs.
(2) It is me who am speaking on this topic.
(3) That is one of the interesting books that has appeared this year.
(4) This is the only one of his stories that are worth reading.
(5) It is I who is answering the question.
(6) The boy which is sitting in the corner reads in my class.
(7) She who walk in the evening gets energy.
(8) The sun whom rays give life to earth is a source of energy.
(9) This is the same toy which I gave you.
(10) Uneasy lies the head which wears the crown.
(11) All which glitters is not silver.
(12) Man is the only animal which can use his intelligence.
(13) That is the best which you can do.
(14) The girl and her cat who had entered my house were locked.
(15) I have read Milton's poems who was a romantic poet.

11

Correct the following sentences:

(1) You self did this work.
(2) Who do you want?
(3) Neither Sushma nor Indu were wanted.
(4) The girls absented from the class.
(5) One should do his duty.
(6) I was not so rich as him.
(7) This is the boy whose all admire.
(8) This is the girl whom marks are highest.
(9) Either of these roads lead to the hospital.
(10) Yourself admitted the guilt.
(11) You, he and I are in the wrong.
(12) You are stronger than me.
(13) It is me.
(14) Only you and him can do that work.
(15) If I were him, I should help you.

12

Correct the following sentences:

(1) This is mine pen.
(2) Between you and I, Mohan is a thief.
(3) Let me take your leave .
(4) He cannot bearing separation from me.
(5) Good girls like you and she should not abuse others.
(6) This pen is superior to your.
(7) Every men and every women should obey their elders.
(8) He availed of the chance.
(9) He will not object to me going there.
(10) He is a good player is not it ?

Spotting Errors (Pronoun)

13.

Read the following sentences to find where, there is any error in any part:

(1) The board of directors (a)/want the facilities (b)/of car and accommodation (c)/or itself. (d)

(2) Every teacher (a)/and every student (b)/of this school is determined to do their best (c)/for the benefit of all. (d)

(3) The officer (a)/as well as the (b)/clerks absented themselves (c)/from the office. (d)

(4) There were (a)/five active workers (b)/and three lazy one (c)/in the factory. (d)

(5) There is none (a)/who can support you (b)/in this crucial period. (c)

(6) Any of the (a)/two photos which reflect (b)/the natural beauty of Kashmir (c)/is worthseeing. (d)

(7) The guests (a)/whom we were talking (b)/about have arrived (c)/are my relatives. (d)

(8) He introduced (a)/to the chairman as (b)/the president of the (c)/workers association. (d)

(9) As a student (a)/of arts (b)/you are much better (c)/than him. (d)

(10) He hates everybody (a)/and everything who (b)/reminds him (c)/of his blunder. (d)

14

Read the following sentences to find where, there is any error in any part:

(1) Whomever (a)/does not come in time (b)/will not be allowed (c)/to mark his presence. (d)

(2) The six partners (a)/are at daggers drawn (b)/so they do not talk (c)/ to each other. (d)

(3) If some one has (a)/completed the work (b)/he may leave (c)/No error.(d)

(4) She lent me (a)/some money with the condition (b)/that I should return (c)/the same within a month. (d)

(5) The teacher instructed (a)/ the peon to let (b)/ the students and I (c)/ go into the office of Principal. (d)

(6) The candidate (a)/ being a commerce graduate (b)/she is eligible (c)/for the post of accountant. (d)

(7) In all circumstances (a)/I have helped him (b)/and he knows. (c)

(8) I don't appreciate (a)/him who laugh (b)/at of thers without (c)/ any reason. (d)

(9) You and myself (a)/ will enjoy the function (b)/being arranged in honour of (c)/ the new Principal. (d)

(10) He asked for (a)/ permission to go to the cinema (b)/ but his mother(c)/did not give. (d)

Solution TYE 01

(1) Let you and me go to play.

(2) There is close relation between him and me.

(3) You, he and I have done our job.

(4) You and he could not complete your work.

(5) He and I have fastened our belts.

(6) You, he and I were present in the function.

(7) You and I are strangers.

(8) I and you are responsible for this loss.

(9) I and he were the main accused.

(10) I, you and he must beg sorry for the misconduct.

Solution TYE 02

(1) None of these four vehicles will do.
(2) Either of the two girls can solve this puzzle.
(3) Anyone of the three students is responsible for the loss.
(4) Neither of the two girls could complete the job.
(5) One should obey one's elders.
(6) One should respect not only one's own parents but also others.'
(7) One should take care not to make oneself obnoxious to others.
(8) Each girl and every madam tried her best to finish the work before 7 P.M.
(9) Every man and every woman has his own fascinations.
(10) Every leader and every citizen has a duty towards his country.

(a) वाक्य संख्या (1) से (4) : Neither/ Either/ Both का प्रयोग दो के लिए एवं None/No one/Any one/All का प्रयोग दो से अधिक के लिए किया जाता है।
(b) वाक्य संख्या (5) से (7) : One's या Oneself का प्रयोग होगा। His या Himself का प्रयोग करना गलत है।
(c) वाक्य संख्या (8) से (10) : यदि दो Nouns आपस में and से जोड़े गए है एवं उनसे पूर्व Each/Every लगता है तो Singular Verb एवं Singular Pronoun (his/her) का प्रयोग किया जाता है।

Solution TYE 03

(1) Each of the employees has to arrange his own vehicle.
(2) Every one of them was given his table and chair.
(3) Either Ramesh or Sita has left his/her (or this) tiffin box.
(4) Either the teacher or the students have left their classroom unlocked.
(5) Please take the buffalo to its shed.
(6) The cow has hurt its legs.
(7) It is easy to get her agree.
(8) It was he who arrived first in the meeting.
(9) This is to certify that Mr. A is our employee.
(10) It is 8 O'Clock by my watch.

Solution TYE 04

(1) All that she said was incorrect.
(2) Who was the girl that came to meet you?
(3) What is his opinion about the work that you have completed?
(4) I always purchase the item that is the best in the market.
(5) This is the same shirt that I saw in the shop.
(6) Who is she that can abuse me like this?
(7) Only those employees should be promoted who are sincere.
(8) The leaders who do not love their country are not respected.
(9) Those who live in glass houses should not throw stones at others.
(10) What was the reply that she submitted?

Solution TYE 05

(1) It was I who telephoned you yesterday.
(2) The girl who you spoke to in the office, is my friend.
(3) My brother and I are glad to get your greetings.
(4) I am not one of them who cannot keep their promise.
(5) It is not we who are responsible for the delay.

(6) They admired his wife and him.
(7) What place are you going to?
(8) Which house do you live in?
(9) She has absented herself from duty today again.
(10) I could not avail myself of the opportunity I got last year.
(11) The treatment received by me was such as I never expected.
(12) His expectation is the same as is hers.
(13) One cannot bear one's insult like this.
(14) My house is bigger than theirs.
(15) This is a secret between you and me.

Solution TYE 06

(1) which,	(2) who,	(3) Where,	(4) Which,	(5) When,
(6) whom,	(7) which,	(8) what,	(9) who,	(10) whose.

Solution TYE 07

(1) whose,	(2) whom,	(3) Who,	(4) What,	(5) that,
(6) whose,	(7) that,	(8) whom,	(9) which,	(10) which.

Solution TYE 08

(1) which,	(2) that,	(3) where,	(4) when,	(5) whom,
(6) who,	(7) which,	(8) who,	(9) whose,	(10) whom.

Solution TYE 09

(1) Everyone should obey his parents.
(2) Sita must do her duties.
(3) Each girl and every student was busy in work.
(4) Either Pramod or Narendra has learnt his lesson.
(5) Nisha or Sushma was teaching her son.
(6) Either Rohan or his friends forgot their books.
(7) You, he and I are friends.
(8) You, he and I went to Nehru garden yesterday.
(9) Manish and I should learn our lessons.
(10) You and Sushma should read your book.
(11) You, he and I must do our work.
(12) Ram and Shyam help each other.
(13) Three children love one another.
(14) Two friends love each other.
(15) It is I who am your friend.

Solution TYE 10

(1) That is one of the girls who have stolen eggs.
(2) It is I who am speaking on this topic.
(3) That is one of the interesting books that have appeared this year.
(4) This is the only one of his stories that is worth reading.
(5) It is I who am answering the question.
(6) The boy who is sitting is the corner reads in my class.
(7) She who walks in the evening gets.
(8) The sun whose rays give life to earth is a source of energy.
(9) This is the same toy that I gave you.
(10) Uneasy lies the head that wears the crown.
(11) All that glitters is not silver.
(12) Man is the only animal that can use his intelligence.
(13) That is the best that you can do.
(14) The girl and her cat that had entered my house were locked.
(15) I have read poems of Milton who was a romantic poet.

Solution TYE 11

(1) You yourself did this work.
(2) Whom do you want?
(3) Neither Sushma nor Indu was wanted.
(4) The girls absented themselves from the class.
(5) One should do one's duty.
(6) I was not so rich as he.
(7) This is the boy whom all admire.
(8) This is the girl whose marks are highest.
(9) Either of these roads leads to the hospital.
(10) You yourself admitted the guilt.
(11) I, he and you are in the wrong.
(12) You are stronger than I.
(13) It is I.
(14) Only you and he can do that work.
(15) If I were he I should help you.

Solution TYE 12

(1) This is my pen.
(2) Between you and me, Mohan is a thief.
(3) Let me take leave of you.
(4) He cannot bear separation from me.
(5) Good girls like you and her should not abuse others.
(6) This pen is superior to yours.
(7) Every man and every woman should obey his their elders.
(8) He availed himself of the chance.
(9) He will not object to my going there.
(10) He is a good player, isn't it?

Solution TYE 13

(1) (d) 'itself' की जगह 'themselves' आएगा। यहाँ Board of Directors का प्रयोग as Collective Noun की तरह नहीं हुआ है।

(2) (c) 'their' की जगह 'his' आएगा। जब दो Singular Noun, Each एवं Every से जुड़े होते हैं, तो Singular Verb एवं Possessive Pronoun भी Singular (यहाँ his) प्रयोग होता है।

(3) (c) 'themselves' की जगह 'his' आएगा। यहाँ Subject 'officer' है जब दो Nouns: as well as, besides, in addition etc. से संयुक्त होते हैं तो Verb एवं Pronoun पहले वाले Noun के अनुसार प्रयोग होते हैं।

(4) (c) 'lazy one' की जगह 'lazy ones' होना चाहिए। One का प्रयोग Singular के लिए एवं ones का प्रयोग plural हेतु किया जाता है।

(5) (b) 'Who' की जगह 'that' का प्रयोग करें। याद रखें, All/none/same/only/ के साथ सामान्यतया Relative Pronoun 'that' का प्रयोग होता है। जैसे:
All that glitter is not gold. He is the same man that supported me.
Same के साथ Relative Pronoun 'as' का प्रयोग किया जाएगा, यदि इसके बाद Verb का प्रयोग नहीं हुआ है। This is the same house as mine.

(6) (a) 'Any' की जगह 'Either' का प्रयोग होगा। Either का प्रयोग दो के लिए होता है।

(7) (b) 'Whom' की जगह 'who' का प्रयोग किया जाएगा। **Whom**—Objective Case है, **Who**—subject Case है।

जब किसी वाक्य में Who एवं Whom के प्रयोग के मध्य कोई confusion है तो आप, वाक्य में subject एवं verb की संख्या गिन लें। यदि verb की संख्या, subject से अधिक है तो 'who' का प्रयोग करें। यहाँ वह भी ध्यान रखना होगा कि 'and' से संयुक्त verbs एक ही subject के लिए प्रयुक्त होते हैं। जैसे:
She came and spoke to me. यहाँ verb came एवं spoke, 'and' से संयुक्त है। अतः एक ही subject के लिए प्रयुक्त है। वाक्य सं (7) को देखें :
The guests whom we were talking about have arrived, are my relatives.
s-1 s-2 v-2 v-3 v-1
यहाँ दो subject हैं, guests एवं we जो क्रमशः are एवं were, verbs को लेते हैं। तीसरी verb है have arrived इसके लिए कोई subject नहीं है। अतः इस वाक्य में whom की जगह who आएगा, जो subject का कार्य करता है।
Other example
The candidates whom we have chosen are sincere and energetic.
s-1 s-2 v-2 v-1
यहाँ whom का प्रयोग सही है। Here are two verbs and two subjects so the use of whom is justified.

कुछ verbs, जैसे absent, present, enjoy, introduce, confine, devote, sacrifice, prostrate etc, transitive verbs हैं जिनके बाद या तो कोई Object आता है या Reflexive Pronoun का प्रयोग किया जाता है। जैसे :
She enjoyed the picnic. She enjoyed herself in the picnic. अन्य उदाहरण ;
He prostrated before the king who has returned after two years.
यहाँ prostrated एक transitive verb है।
अत: इसके बाद himself लगाना होगा।
He prostrated himself before the king who has returned after two years.

---

(8) (a) introduced के बाद Reflexive Pronoun himself भी लगाना होगा।

(9) (d) 'him' की जगह 'he' ही आएगा। 'than' के बाद यदि दो Subjects के मध्य तुलना की जाए तो nominative case का प्रयोग होगा न कि object case का। 'he' nominative case एवं 'him' object case है। देखें :
She was more surprised than me to see the circus girl coming towards us.
यहाँ भी 'me' की जगह I का प्रयोग होगा क्योंकि तुलना दो Subjects, 'she' एवं I में है।

(10) (b) 'Who' की जगह 'Which' या 'That' का प्रयोग करना होगा।
जब किसी Pronoun के पहले आए दो Noun, and से संयुक्त होते हैं तो Pronoun अपने पास आए Noun से govern होता है।
यहाँ पास वाला Noun, everything है अत: यहाँ 'Which' या 'That' का प्रयोग होगा।

Solution TYE 14

(1) (a) 'Whomever' की जगह 'Whoever' होगा। Whomever, Objective case है जबकि, Whoever Nominative case है जो अपने साथ Verb, does not come ले रहा है। Also see the explanation to question no. 7.

(2) (d) 'Each other' की जगह 'one another' होगा। each other का सामान्यतया प्रयोग दो के लिए किया जाता है।

(3) (d) वाक्य सही है।

(4) (d) 'the same' की जगह 'it' आयेगा। 'the same' का प्रयोग हमेशा एक Adjective की तरह होता है। 'the same' का प्रयोग Pronoun की तरह करना गलत है। जैसे :
(1) This is the same pen as mine. (2) It is the same chair as yours.

(5) (c) 'I' की जगह 'me' होगा। Let के साथ Pronoun हमेशा Objective case में आता है। जैसे :
(1) Let you and me go there. (2) Let you and him prepare a proposal.

(6) (c) She को delete करें क्योंकि यहाँ She लगाने की आवश्यकता नहीं है। This is the pen, which I lost it yesterday. यहाँ भी it का प्रयोग अनावश्यक है।

(7) (c) Knows के बाद it लगाना आवश्यक है।

(8) (b) 'Laugh' की जगह 'laughs' होगा Laugh, him के लिए प्रयुक्त हुआ है जो Singular Pronoun है।

(9) (a) 'myself' के बदले 'I' होगा। ध्यान दें, Reflexive pronoun, कभी भी वाक्य में Subject की तरह प्रयुक्त नहीं हो सकता है। साधारण बोलचाल में हम myself को subject की तरह प्रयोग करते हैं। जैसे:

Myself is Suresh.	*Incorrect*
I am Suresh.	*Correct*
Yourself is responsible.	*Incorrect*
You are responsible.	*Correct*

(10) (d) give के बाद 'it' लगेगा। Give एक transitive verb है, इसके साथ Object लगाना आवश्यक है।

CHAPTER

08

DETERMINERS/ ADJECTIVES

Traditional Grammar में Determiners को Adjective से अलग नहीं किया गया है। Determiners, Adjectives का ही भाग है जिनमें निम्न विशेषताएँ पाई जाती हैं:

(1) Determiners के रूप में परिवर्तन नहीं होता है। जैसे: A, an, the, some, all, much, both, few, whole, etc. इनमें कोई Suffix या Prefix जोड़कर कोई परिवर्तन नहीं किया जा सकता है। जबकि Adjectives के रूप में परिवर्तन सम्भव है, जैसे: Black से Blackish, Blackness; Good से Goodness, Fast को Faster, Fastest बनाया जा सकता है।

(2) Determiners का प्रयोग हमेशा Noun से पहले होता है। जबकि Adjectives का प्रयोग Noun के पहले भी हो सकता है एवं बाद में भी। Determiner का प्रयोग होने पर यह निश्चित हो जाता है कि इसके बाद Noun अवश्य आयेगा।

(3) वाक्य में Determiner एवं Adjective दोनों का प्रयोग हो तो पहले Determiner, फिर Adjective एवं फिर Noun आता है। Adjective का प्रयोग Determiner के पहले नहीं किया जा सकता है। जैसे:
(a) He is a boy. (b) He is a good boy. (c) I have some pencils. (d) I have some coloured pencils.

उपरोक्त वाक्यों में a, some; Determiners हैं तथा good एवं coloured, adjectives हैं। वाक्य (a) एवं (c) में Determiners का प्रयोग Noun से पहले हुआ है। (b) एवं (d) वाक्यों में Determiner + Adjective + Noun का प्रयोग हुआ है।

Adjectives

Adjective वह शब्द है जो एक वाक्य में प्रयुक्त Noun या Pronoun को विशेषता प्रदान करता है।

An Adjective is a word, when used with a noun or pronoun adds something to the meaning of noun or pronoun.

Look at the following sentences:

(a) She is a <u>good</u> girl. (b) Alwar is a <u>small</u> city.
(c) He gave me <u>five</u> pencils. (d) This is <u>my</u> pen.

उपरोक्त वाक्यों में Underlined words, Adjectives हैं।

Kinds of Adjectives

(1) Proper Adjective (2) Adjective of Quality (3) Adjective of Quantity
(4) Adjective of Number (5) Demonstrative Adjective (6) Interrogative Adjective
(7) Emphasising Adjective (8) Exclamatory Adjective (9) Possessive Adjective

(1) Proper Adjective : Proper noun से बनने वाले Adjectives, Proper Adjectives कहलाते हैं। जैसे: Indian, African, American, European etc. India से Indian, Africa से African बने हैं। India एवं Africa Proper Nouns हैं।

(2) Adjective of Quality : ये किसी व्यक्ति, वस्तु या स्थान की quality (विशेषता) बताते हैं जैसे: Honest man, beautiful lady, big city, large building, beautiful palace, black dog, white tiger etc. These are also called defining adjectives.
सभी underlined words, Adjective of Quality हैं जो सम्बन्धित noun की विशेषता बता रहे हैं।

(3) Adjective of Quantity : यह Noun की quantity (परिमाण, मात्रा) को व्यक्त करता है। जैसे: Whole, Some, Enough, Sufficient, No, Full, Entire etc.

(4) Adjective of Number : यह व्यक्तियों, वस्तुओं की संख्या व्यक्त करता है, या यह उनके क्रम (Order) को व्यक्त करता है। जैसे: One, Two....., Many, Few, All, Some, First, Second,....... Last, next etc.

Adjective of Number को तीन भागो में विभाजित किया गया है:

(a) Definite Number Adjectives : जो exact number or order (निश्चित संख्या या क्रम) की जानकारी देता है जैसे: One, Two, Three ..... ये cardinals कहलाते हैं।
First, Second, Third .... ये ordinals कहलाते हैं।

(b) Indefinite Number Adjectives : ये exact number (निश्चित संख्या या क्रम) व्यक्त नहीं करते हैं। जैसे: Any, All, Few, Some, Several, Many, Certain etc.

(c) Distributive Adjectives : Either, Each, Every, Neither etc, distributive adjectives हैं जो Distribution को व्यक्त करते हैं।

(5) Demonstrative Adjectives : It points out which person or thing. इस तरह के Adjectives हैं: This, That, These, Such, Those etc. ये विशेषण Particular व्यक्ति या स्थान को व्यक्त करते हैं।

(6) Interrogative Adjectives : What, Whose, Which, Where जैसे शब्द जो प्रश्न करते हुए Adjective का कार्य करते हैं, Interrogative Adjectives कहलाते हैं।

(7) Emphasising Adjectives : Own, Very, Quite जैसे शब्द जो noun को Emphasise (Impress upon) करने हेतु प्रयुक्त होते हैं, Emphasising adjectives कहलाते हैं।

(8) Exclamatory Adjectives : What का प्रयोग वाक्य में exclamation हेतु प्रयुक्त होता है। जैसे:
What a beautiful girl !, What an idea !

(9) Possessive Adjectives : My, His, Her, Your, Their इत्यादि Possessive Adjectives है जो Noun का अधिकार (हक) व्यक्त करते हैं।

Correct Use of Some 'Adjectives'

(1) Each/Every/Either/Neither

Each/Every/Either/Neither के साथ हमेशा Singular Noun का प्रयोग होता है एवं Verb भी Singular ही लगती है। जैसे:

(a) Each student gets a prize.
(b) Every seat was occupied.
(c) Either book is useful.
(d) Neither book is useful.

यदि वाक्य में *Every* के बाद कोई plural adjective of number (two, three, four etc) का प्रयोग हो तो उसके बाद आने वाला Noun, plural होगा। जैसे:

(a) She takes medicine every three hours.
(b) He visits here every two months.

(2) Each/Every

(A) Each एवं Every दोनों का अर्थ समान है। Each का प्रयोग दो से अधिक के लिए भी होता है, जबकि Every का प्रयोग दो से अधिक के लिए ही होता है। जैसे :

(a) Each of the two girls gets a prize.
(b) Each of the ten students gets a prize.
(c) Every student gets a prize.
(d) Every candidate was given a certificate.

Each — *Two and more than two.*
Every — *More than two.*

(B) Each का प्रयोग निश्चित संख्या हेतु, तथा Every का प्रयोग अनिश्चित संख्या हेतु किया जाता है। जैसा वाक्य (b), (c) एवं (d) से स्पष्ट है।

(C) Each का प्रयोग उस समय किया जाता है जब, वस्तु या व्यक्ति को Individuality, या Separate Action व्यक्त करना हो। Every का प्रयोग Group में Action को व्यक्त करता है। जैसे :

(a) Each student was given a certificate by the Chief Guest one by one.
(b) Each student went to meet the Chairman in line.
(c) Every student has a book.
(d) Every student was happy.

(D) Each एक Pronoun भी है एवं एक Adjective भी है। अत: Each के बाद 'of' का प्रयोग किया जा सकता है। लेकिन Every केवल Adjective है। अत: Every के बाद 'of' का प्रयोग करना गलत होगा। जैसे :

Each of the teachers is doing his work. — *Correct*
Every of the teachers is doing his work. — *Incorrect*

(E) Each and every दोनों का इस तरह का प्रयोग दो से अधिक हेतु ही किया जा सकता है, दो के लिए केवल each का ही प्रयोग करना होता है। जैसे :

Each and every student received a prize.

(3) Either/Both

Either का अर्थ है : दोनों में से एक या दोनों।
Both का अर्थ है : दोनों
Either का अर्थ 'या तो' उस स्थिति में होता है जब एक भाग, दूसरे भाग का ही Complement होता है। जैसे :
Either side of the road, Either hand.
Both का प्रयोग तब किया जाता है, जब वस्तु के इस प्रकार दो भाग नहीं होते हैं।
Look at the following sentences:

(a) There was water on either side of the highway.
(b) His either son went to America.

वाक्य (b) में Either की जगह Both का प्रयोग होगा एवं Son की जगह Plural Noun, Sons का प्रयोग होगा। (Either के साथ singular noun का प्रयोग होता है) His Both sons went to America.

(4) Little/A little/The little

Little का प्रयोग uncountable के साथ किया जाता है। Little का अर्थ नकारात्मक (नगण्य या कुछ नहीं) होता है। A little का अर्थ 'कुछ', 'थोड़ा सा' होता है। जबकि The little का अर्थ 'जो सब कुछ थोड़ा सा' (not much but all that is) होता है।

Use of little—नगण्य या कुछ नहीं :

(a) He takes little interest in parental business. (He has hardly any or no interest.)
(b) We have little hope of his recovery. (उसके ठीक होने की आशा नगण्य, न के बराबर है।)
(c) He has little knowledge of computers. (उसकी जानकारी न के बराबर है।)

A little : Not much but some—'कुछ' ,'थोड़ा सा':

(a) We have a little hope of his recovery. (उसके ठीक होने की कुछ आशा है।)
(b) A little knowledge is always dangerous. (थोड़ी जानकारी खतरनाक होती है।)
(c) He takes a little interest in parental business. (वह थोड़ा ध्यान देता है।)

The little : Not much but all there is—'जो सब कुछ थोड़ा सा':

(a) The little money she had, was also spent on medicines.
(जो कुछ थोड़ा सा धन था, अब कुछ नहीं बचा है)
(b) Use the little time you have in a proper way now. (जो कुछ थोड़ा सा समय बचा है)
(c) He has wasted the little money he had in gambling.
(जो कुछ थोड़ा सा धन वह सब, अब कुछ नहीं बचा है।)

(5) Few/A Few/The Few

Few का प्रयोग Countables के लिए किया जाता है। Few का अर्थ नकारात्मक (नगण्य, न के बराबर) होता है। A few का अर्थ, 'कुछ' होता है, जबकि The few का अर्थ 'जो भी थोड़ा सा सब'।

(A) Use of 'Few': Means 'Hardly any'–नगण्य, न के बराबर

(a) Few people are fully happy. (नगण्य व्यक्ति)
(b) Few men are free from any disease. (न के बराबर या कोई नहीं)
(c) Few women can avoid talking. (न के बराबर)
(d) Few women can keep secrets. (न के बराबर, कोई नहीं)

(B) Use of 'A few' — means 'थोड़े से' (not many)

(a) A few person can write correct English. (कुछ व्यक्ति)
(b) He asked me a few questions. (कुछ प्रश्न)
(c) He died only a few months ago. (कुछ माह पूर्व)
(d) A few students secured more than 80% marks in Physics.

(C) Use of 'The Few' — means 'not many but all there are'—'जो भी थोड़ा सा सब':

(a) The few utensils she had, were taken by the thief. (थोड़े से सारे अब और बर्तन नहीं बचे हैं।)
(b) The few clothes he had, all burnt in fire. (थोड़े से कपड़े, सारे, अब और कपड़े नहीं।)
(c) The few members of the committee all took part in the demonstration. (सभी सदस्य थोड़े से)
(d) The few books he had, were taken by the thief. (थोड़ी सी सारी किताबें)

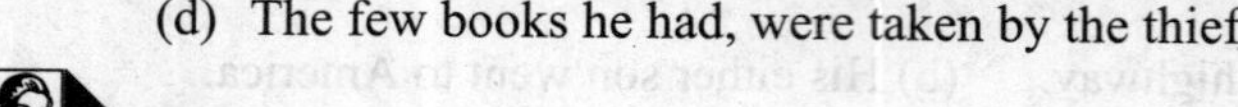

Few का अर्थ Negative (नगण्य) में होता है एवं A few तथा The few का अर्थ Positive में होता है। इनका सही प्रयोग करना महत्त्वपूर्ण है।

(6) Fewer/Less/Lesser

(A) Fewer का प्रयोग countables में 'कम संख्या' हेतु किया जाता है।
(B) Less का प्रयोग Uncountables हेतु 'थोड़ी मात्रा' हेतु किया जाता है। Price एवं number के साथ less का प्रयोग नहीं करना चाहिए।
(C) Lesser का अर्थ होता है कम महत्त्वपूर्ण। जैसे :
(a) Fewer persons were present in the meeting.
(b) No fewer than ten persons were killed in the accident.

(c) I have less time for my preparations.
(d) He has less money to buy a T.V.
(e) Many lesser speakers also came to speak.
(f) Many lesser leaders were present in the function.
(g) She had fewer chores, but she also had less energy.
(h) We spent less than forty dollars on our trip.

Generally, when we're talking about countable things, we use the word fewer; when we're talking about measurable quantities that we cannot count, we use the word less.

(7) Later/Latest/Latter/Last

Later एवं Latest का प्रयोग सामान्य रूप से समय के सन्दर्भ में किया जाता है। Latter एवं Last का प्रयोग स्थिति (क्रम) के सन्दर्भ में किया जाता है। जब दो के लिए स्थिति/क्रम के सन्दर्भ में प्रयोग किया जाना हो तो Latter का, एवं दो से अधिक के सन्दर्भ में Last का प्रयोग (बांद वाले को बताने के लिए) किया जाता है। Latest का अर्थ होता है: Last up to now only, अर्थात् अब तक जो अन्तिम है जबकि Last का अर्थ होता है अन्तिम, उसके बाद कोई नहीं (Finally last).

Look at the following sentences:

(a) I will come later. (बाद में)
(b) He came later than I. (मेरे बाद, समय के अनुसार)
(c) Between Ram and Shyam, the latter is more intelligent. (क्रम के बाद में अर्थात् Shyam)
(d) Of iron and silver, the latter is known as white metal. (क्रम में बाद वाला अर्थात् Silver)
(e) This is the latest fashion. (अब तक का सबसे अन्तिम, नया)
(f) This is the latest technology. (अब तक की सबसे अन्तिम, नई)
(g) At last the chairman distributed the prizes. (अन्त में, उसके बाद कुछ नहीं हुआ)
(h) Lord Mountbatten was the last Governor General of India. (अन्तिम, उसके बाद कोई नहीं)

(8) Elder/Eldest/Older/Oldest

Elder एवं Eldest का प्रयोग एक ही परिवार के सदस्यों हेतु किया जाता है। Older/Oldest का प्रयोग व्यक्तियो एवं वस्तुओं दोनों के लिए किया जा सकता है। Elder के साथ हमेशा 'to' Preposition प्रयुक्त होता है, जबकि Older के साथ 'than' Preposition प्रयुक्त होता है। जैसे :

(a) Ram is my elder brother.
(b) Ram is older than Shyam.
(c) This is the oldest college in our city.
(d) The older people should be respected.
(e) My mother is the eldest member of our family.
(f) Sunder and Purinder are real brothers. Sunder is elder to Purinder.

(9) Farther/Further/Farthest

Farther का अर्थ होता है तुलनात्मक रूप से अधिक दूर (Far— Farther—Farthest) यह Far की Comparative degree है तथा Farthest, Far की Superlative degree है, जिसका अर्थ है सबसे अधिक दूर। Further का अर्थ होता है Additional (अतिरिक्त) Farther एवं Farthest का प्रयोग दूरी के सन्दर्भ में तथा Further का प्रयोग Action या सूचना आदि के सन्दर्भ में सामान्यतया किया जाता है। जैसे:

(a) Mumbai is farther from Alwar than from Jaipur.
(b) No further action is required.
(c) Please don't make further delay.
(d) It is the farthest place from the railway station.

(10) Some/Any

Some का प्रयोग सामान्यतया Affirmative वाक्यों में Countables एवं Uncountables दोनों के साथ किया जा सकता है। Interrogative Aentence में Some का प्रयोग Request या Commands के रूप में किया जाता है। Some के साथ Request का अर्थ सामान्य रूप से मान ली जाने वाली Request के लिए होता है। जैसे :

(a) I shall buy some books. *Countables*
(b) They have purchased some fruit. *Uncountables*
(c) Will you give me some milk? *Request*
(d) Can you lend me some rupees? *Request*

Any का प्रयोग सामान्यतया Negative एवं Interrogative वाक्यों में Countables एवं Uncountables दोनों के लिए किया जा सकता है। जैसे :

(a) I don't have any pen.
(b) Have you any novel?
(c) He hasn't purchased any fruits.
(d) Did anyone come here?
(e) They do not have any chair.
(f) I haven't watched any serial today.

(11) No any

'No any' कोई phrase नहीं है। अत: इसका प्रयोग गलत है। जैसे :

निम्न में वाक्य (a) अशुद्ध है :

(a) I have no any book.
(b) I have no any pencil.

चूँकि No एवं any दोनों adjective हैं। अत: दोनों एक noun का गुण नहीं बता सकते। अत: दोनों का एक साथ प्रयोग गलत है।

(12) Near/Next

Near का प्रयोग दूरी के सन्दर्भ में किया जाता है। जबकि Next का प्रयोग क्रम (Order) के सन्दर्भ में किया जाता है। जैसे :

(a) Ram lives near to my school.
(b) My house is near to the station.
(c) She is sitting next to her father.
(d) I will meet you at the next crossing.

(13) Much/Many

Much—परिमाण (quantity) के लिए प्रयुक्त होता है।

Many—संख्या (Number) को व्यक्त करता है।

Much एवं many का प्रयोग सामान्यतया Negative एवं Interrogative वाक्यों में किया जाता है। जैसे :

(a) I haven't much patience.
(b) She hasn't much money.
(c) Have you much money?
(d) I haven't many chairs.
(e) He hasn't many cars.
(f) Have you many friends?

---

(1) Affirmative वाक्यों में Much/Many का प्रयोग Subject के साथ हो सकता है लेकिन Object के साथ नही होता है। जैसे:
(a) Many people came to see the temple. (b) Much milk was required.
यहाँ people एवं milk, Subjects हैं, अत: इनके साथ Many/Much का प्रयोग उचित है। लेकिन यदि इनका प्रयोग Object की तरह निम्न प्रकार किया जाये तो गलत होगा। जैसे:
(a) I know many persons. (b) I learned many poems.
(c) He bought much sugar. (d) She put much water.
यहाँ Many/Much का प्रयोग एक Object की तरह Affirmative Sentences में किया गया है जो गलत है।
Affirmative Sentences में ध्यान रखें:

(2) Affirmative Sentences में Object की तरह much/many की अपेक्षा निम्न phrases का प्रयोग करना चाहिए :
a lot of, lots of, a plenty of a large quantity of, a large number of etc.

(3) *Much/Many* के साथ *as, how, too* का प्रयोग करने पर, इनका *(Much/Many)* प्रयोग *Subject* एवं *Object* के साथ भी किया जा सकता है। जैसे:

(a) She has too many friends.
(b) I don't have too much milk.
(c) I don't remember how many persons came here.
(d) You can purchase as many books as you like.
(e) You can take as much water as you need.
(f) I don't know how much sugar is needed.

(14) Whole/All

(A) Whole का प्रयोग जब एक Adjective की तरह किया जाता है, तो इससे पहले 'the' का प्रयोग करना चाहिए। जैसे:

(a) He wasted the whole day. (b) I worked the whole day.

(B) Whole का प्रयोग जब Proper Noun के पहले किया जाता है, तो इससे पहले 'the' तथा बाद में of का प्रयोग किया जाता है। जैसे:

(a) The whole of India mourned the death of Rajeev Gandhi.
(b) The whole of Rajas than was in the grip of drought.

(C) All का प्रयोग जब Plural Noun के साथ किया जाता है, तो All के बाद 'The' का प्रयोग करना होता है। Possessive Noun या Pronoun के साथ All हमेशा उससे पहले लगता है। जैसे:

(a) All the students were happy. (b) All the girls were present.
(c) All my friends went to party. (d) He spent all his money.

(15) Both

(A) Both का प्रयोग जब वाक्य में एक Adjective की तरह किया जाता है, तो इसके बाद 'the' का प्रयोग किया जाता है।

'The' का प्रयोग कभी भी Both के पहले नहीं होता है। जैसे:
(a) I know both the women. *(b) She knows both the boys.*

(B) Personal Pronouns के साथ Both of का प्रयोग किया जाता है। जैसे :

(a) Both of them can come tomorrow. (b) She invited both of us.

(C) Both का प्रयोग Pronouns के बाद Object की तरह भी किया जाता है। जैसे :

(a) She invited us both. (b) She sends you both her love.

(D) Both .....not के प्रयोग की जगह Neither of them का प्रयोग करना चाहिए। जैसे :

(a) Both of them are not here. *Incorrect*
(b) Neither of them is here. *Correct*

(16) As ..... as/So ..... as

As.........as का प्रयोग तुलनात्मक वाक्यों में Similarity/Likeliness व्यक्त करने हेतु किया जाता है।

So..........as का प्रयोग ऐसे वाक्यों में Unlikeliness, dissimilarity, (negative वाक्यों) व्यक्त करने हेतु किया जाता है। जैसे:

(a) He is as intelligent as his sister. (b) This shirt is as good as mine.
(c) He is not so intelligent as his sister. (d) This shirt is not so good as mine.

(17) Another/Other/Any other

Another का प्रयोग Singular Noun के साथ, तथा Other का प्रयोग Plural Noun के साथ किया जाता है। Any other का प्रयोग सामान्यतया Negative वाक्यों में Singular एवं Plural दोनों तरह के Nouns के साथ हो सकता है। जैसे :

(a) He has purchased another book.
(b) She has visited other places.
(c) I haven't seen any other place.
(d) They haven't visited any other places.

(18) First/Foremost

First का प्रयोग क्रम में, 'प्रथम' के लिए होता है; जबकि Foremost का अर्थ 'महत्त्वपूर्ण' होता है। जैसे :

(a) Ram was the first to arrive here.
(b) Indira Gandhi was the foremost politician of her time.

(19) Verbal/Oral

Verbal एवं Oral को समान अर्थ में आजकल प्रयुक्त किया जाने लगा है। Oral का अर्थ होता है 'जबानी'। जबकि Verbal का अर्थ होता है शाब्दिक। A verbal picture, an oral message.

(a) There is verbal similarity in these two essays.
(b) He informed me orally about his absence.

(20) Due to/Owing to

(a) Due to का अर्थ 'result of' (कारण से) जबकि Owing to का अर्थ 'Because of' (इस कारण) Due to का में 'to' का प्रयोग एक Preposition की तरह हुआ है।

(b) Due to का प्रयोग Subject + Verb के बाद किया जाता है। 'Owing to' का सामान्यतया प्रयोग वाक्य के शुरू में होता है।

Look at the following sentences:

(a) He failed due to his negligency.
(b) Owing to his negligency he failed.
(c) The accident was due to carelessness.
(d) Owing to carelessness, there was an accident.

(21) Good versus Well

In both casual speech and formal writing, we frequently have to choose between the adjective good and the adverb well. With most verbs, there is no contest : when modifying a verb, use the adverb.

(a) He swims well.
(b) He knows only too well who the murderer is.

However, when using a linking verb or a verb that has to do with the five human senses, you want to use the adjective instead.

(c) How are you? I'm feeling good, thank you.
(d) After a bath, the baby smells so good.
(e) Even after my careful paint job, this room doesn't look good.

Many writers, however, will use well after linking verbs relating to health, and this is all right. In fact, to say that you are good or that you feel good implies not only that you're ok physically but also that your spirits are high.

How are you?
I am well, thank you.

(22) Bad versus Badly

When your puppy died (assuming you loved your puppy), did you feel bad or badly? Applying the same rule that applies to good versus well, use the adjective form after verbs that have to do with human feelings. You felt bad. If you said you felt badly, it would mean that something was wrong with your faculties for feeling.

Rules : Adjectives

Rule 1

जब किसी वस्तु का Comparison किया जाता है तो Compare करते समय उस वस्तु को Exclude करना चाहिए। जैसे :

(a) Iron is harder than any metal.

इस वाक्य का अर्थ है कि Iron किसी भी metal से अधिक hard है। किसी भी metal में Iron भी सम्मिलित है। अत: इस वाक्य को निम्न प्रकार लिखा जाना चाहिए :

Iron is harder than any other metal.

(b) This building is larger than any building in the town. *Incorrect*
This building is larger than any other building in the town. *Correct*

(c) He is more intelligent than any student of his class. *Incorrect*
He is more intelligent than any other student of his class. *Correct*

(d) Ram is stronger than all students. *Incorrect*
Ram is stronger than any other student. *Correct*

Rule 2

एक वाक्य में दो Comparative Adjectives का एक साथ प्रयोग करना गलत है। जैसे :

(a) He is more wiser than you. *Incorrect*
He is wiser than you. *Correct*

(b) I am comparatively better today. *Incorrect*
I am better today. *Correct*
I am comparatively well today. *Correct*

(c) I didn't find more costlier gift. *Incorrect*
I didn't find more costly gift. *Correct*

यदि एक Adjective Comparative Degree में है तो उसके साथ Positive Degree का प्रयोग किया जाता है। 'Comparatively' शब्द के साथ भी Comparative Degree के Adjective का प्रयोग नहीं करना चाहिए।

Comparative से पहले Rather का प्रयोग किया जा सकता है:
She is rather better today.
लेकिन ऐसे वाक्यों में fairly का प्रयोग नहीं करना चाहिए।
She is fairly better toda. यह गलत है।

Rule 3

कुछ Adjectives जैसे: Senior, Junior, Posterior, Superior, Inferior, Anterior, इत्यादि के साथ Preposition 'to' का प्रयोग किया जाता है। इनके साथ More या Less का प्रयोग नहीं होता है। ये सभी Adjectives, Latin भाषा से ग्रहण किए गए हैं। Elder, prefer एवं preferable के साथ भी 'to' का ही प्रयोग होता है। जैसे :

(a) He is superior to me.
(b) She is junior to me.
(c) Ram is senior to Shyam.
(d) He came prior to me.

Major, Minor, Exterior, Interior, Outer, Lower, Ulterior, Upper, Former, Inner इत्यादि शब्द दिखने में Comparative Degree Adjectives लगते हैं। ये Comparative degree नहीं हैं। इनका प्रयोग Comparison हेतु नहीं किया जा सकता।

Rule 4

जब एक ही व्यक्ति या वस्तु की दो Qualities की तुलना की जाती है तो 'er' से बने Comparative Adjective का प्रयोग नहीं करना चाहिए बल्कि More का प्रयोग करना चाहिए। जैसे :

(a) Ram is more strong than intelligent. *(यहाँ stronger का प्रयोग गलत होगा)*
(b) She is more clever than intelligent. *(यहाँ cleverer का प्रयोग गलत होगा)*

Rule 5

Superlative Adjective से पूर्व 'the' का प्रयोग होता है। लेकिन Superlative Adjective से पूर्व कोई Possessive pronoun का प्रयोग हुआ हो तो इससे पहले 'the' का प्रयोग नहीं होता है। जैसे :

(a) She is the best student in our college.
(b) She is the most beautiful girl in our college.
(c) She is my best friend.
(d) This is his best dress.

Rule 6

जब दो वस्तुओं का Comparison किया जाता है तो वाक्य से उन वस्तुओं का ही Comparison स्पष्ट होना चाहिए। कई बार Comparison करते समय निम्न प्रकार की गलती की जाती है :

(a) The climate of Alwar is hotter than Jaipur. *Incorrect*
The climate of Alwar is hotter than that of Jaipur. *Correct*
(b) My shoes are better than you. *Incorrect*
My shoes are better than yours or your shoes. *Correct*

Rule 7

Comparative Degree का प्रयोग, दो वस्तुओं या व्यक्तियों हेतु किया जाता है। दो से अधिक के लिए Comparative Degree का प्रयोग नहीं करना चाहिए। जैसे :

(a) Which is better ; Tea, coffee or milk? *Incorrect*
(b) Which is easier, Physics, Chemistry or Maths? *Incorrect*

Rule 8

दो वस्तुओं की तुलना हेतु Superlative Degree का प्रयोग नहीं किया जाता है। जैसे :

(a) He is the best of the two students.
(b) Which is the cheapest ; silver or gold?

Rule 9

वाक्य में दो Superlative का प्रयोग एक साथ किया जाना गलत है। जैसे :

(a) He is the most strongest of all. *Incorrect*
He is the strongest of all. *Correct*
(b) The river is the most longest of all. *Incorrect*
The river is the longest of all. *Correct*

Rule 10

Superlative के साथ other or else का प्रयोग करना भी गलत है। जैसे :

(a) She is the most beautiful of all girls. *(not all other girls)*
(b) He is the strongest of all students. *(not all other students)*

Rule 11

Superlative के साथ सामान्यतया 'of' का प्रयोग किया जाता है, लेकिन जब स्थान (place) कर सन्दर्भ हो तो 'in' का प्रयोग किया जाता है। जैसे :

(a) Kolkata is the dirtiest city in India.

(b) Udaipur is the most beautiful city in Rajasthan.

Rule 12

कई वाक्यों में 'a most' का प्रयोग Very के अर्थ में किया जाता है। जैसे :

(a) This is a most interesting book. *(in the library)*

(b) She is a most beautiful girl. *(in the school)*

ऐसे वाक्यों में Superlative की तरह in the library, or in the school का प्रयोग नहीं होगा।

Rule 13

Superlative Degree, Best एवं Most के साथ कई बार Like का प्रयोग निम्न तरह से किया जाता है। यह सही प्रयोग है, इसमें Superlative से पहले 'the' का प्रयोग नहीं किया जाता है। जैसे :

(a) Which of the story do you like most?

(b) Which of the magazine do you like best?

Rule 14

जब एक से अधिक Adjectives को and से जोड़ा जाता है तो सभी Adjectives एक ही Degree में होने चाहिए। या तो सब Comparative में हों या सब Superlative में होने चाहिए। जैसे :

(a) Ram is wiser and stronger than Shyam. *Correct*

(b) Ram is wise and stronger than Shyam. *Incorrect*

Rule 15

कई Adjectives अपने Meaning के कारण न तो comparative की तरह प्रयोग किये जा सकते हैं न ही Superlative की अन्य Degree के साथ। इनके साथ Very या अन्य कोई Adverb, इनको Emphasise करने के लिए प्रयुक्त नहीं किया जा सकता है। ऐसे Adjectives निम्न हैं :

Absolute, Perfect, Full, Complete, Entire, Whole, Chief, Extreme, Unique, Universal, Circular, Square, Round , Ideal, Flat, Impossible etc.

यद्यपि आजकल कुछ लेखक Full, Fuller, Fullest एवं Perfect, More Perfect एवं Most Perfect तथा Most Impossible एवं Most Universal का प्रयोग करने लगे हैं। शेष Adjective का इस तरह प्रयोग नहीं किया गया है।

Rule 16

Kind एवं Sort, Singular Number होते हैं। इनके साथ This या That का प्रयोग होता है। इनके साथ These या Those का प्रयोग करना गलत है। जैसे:

(a) I don't like this kind of dresses. (b) He doesn't like that kind of shirts.

(c) I don't like these kinds of shirts. *Incorrect*

(d) I don't like those kind of shirts. *Incorrect*

Rule 17

One of ....If not .... Superlative कुछ वाक्यों का Structure इस तरह का होता है। जैसे :

(a) He is one of the greatest writers, if not the greatest writer.

(b) This is one of the largest buildings, if not the largest in the world.

(c) This is one of the longest rivers, if not the longest in the world.

इस तरह के वाक्यों में one of the superlative के बाद plural noun प्रयुक्त होती है तथा if not the superlative के बाद singular noun प्रयुक्त होती है। साधारणतया ऐसे वाक्यों में if not the superlative के बाद noun को नहीं लिखा जाता है।

Rule 18

One of the superlative .... among :

निम्न वाक्यों पर ध्यान दें :

(a) He is one of the best students in our school. (b) He is one of the best sportsmen of all.

यहाँ One of the + superlative के बाद आने वाला Noun Plural में होगा। यह एक महत्त्वपूर्ण तथ्य है।

Rule 19

कुछ वाक्य ऐसे होते हैं जिनमें Adjective की Comparative Degree का प्रयोग दोनों भागों में निम्न प्रकार से होता है:

(a) The more she gets, the more she demands.
(b) The richer a man is, the larger house he owns.
(c) The more I try to please her the more angry she becomes.

इस प्रकार के वाक्यों में दोनों **Comparative Degrees** से पहले 'the' का प्रयोग होता है।

Rule 20

कुछ वाक्यों का structure इस तरह का होता है ....Comparative + and + comparative.

(a) He is getting richer and richer.
(b) The weather is getting cooler and cooler.

ऐसे वाक्यों में comparative से पूर्व 'the' का प्रयोग नहीं होता है।

Rule 21

कुछ वाक्यों का structure निम्न प्रकार का होता है:

(a) She runs as fast as, if not faster than Shyam.
(b) He is as good as if not better than you.
(c) The house is as large as if not larger than that.

ऐसे वाक्यों में *as..............as* (दोनों बार *as*) का प्रयोग होता है तथा दूसरे भाग में *Comparative degree* का प्रयोग होता है।

Rule 22

Comparative को ओर महत्त्व (Emphatic) देने हेतु Much / Far / By For / Far And Away / Still का प्रयोग निम्न प्रकार किया जाता है

(a) Ram is much wiser than Shyam. (b) This magazine is far better than that.
(c) The book is better by far. (d) This magazine is still better.

All the का प्रयोग करने से भी *Comparative* को *Emphatic* महत्त्वपूर्ण बनाया जाता है।

(a) It is all the better. *(b) That was all the more interesting.*

Position of Adjectives

(1) सामान्यतया Adjective का प्रयोग उस Noun के पहले किया जाता है जिसे वह विशेषता प्रदान करता है। जैसे :

(a) He is a good boy. (b) She is a beautiful girl.

(2) जब कई Adjectives एक Noun के साथ प्रयुक्त होते हैं, तो इन Adjectives को Noun के बाद लगाया जाता है। जैसे :

(a) The soldier, fearless and determined attacked the enemy quickly.

(b) A girl, intelligent and beautiful won the race.

(3) यदि वाक्य में Indefinite Pronoun का प्रयोग हो तो Adjective का सामान्यतय प्रयोग इसके बाद करते हैं जैसे :

(a) It is something important. (b) Is there anything interesting?

(c) I have nothing new to say. (d) He is someone powerful.

(4) कई बार निम्न स्थिति में Adjective का प्रयोग (मुख्यतया पदवी हेतु) Noun के बाद किया जाता है। जैसे :

Akbar the great, Louis the III, Alexander the great.

(5) कुछ निम्न Phrases में Adjective, Noun के बाद आता है। जैसे :

Notary public, Time immemorial, Body politic, God Almighty, Heir Apparent, Sum total, God Incarnate, Governor-General, etc.

कुछ Adjectives जैसे: Asleep, Alone, Ashamed, Alike का प्रयोग वाक्य में Predicatively होता है जैसे :

(a) The child is asleep. (b) The baby is awake.

(c) I am alone. (d) They look alike.

(6) जब Adjective के साथ कोई Phrase या Words उसे स्पष्ट करने हेतु प्रयुक्त होते हैं तो Adjective को Noun के बाद लगाते हैं। जैसे :

(a) A man, wiser than his fellows solved the question within a minute.

(b) She is a girl, benevolent in nature.

(7) Poetry में Adjective का प्रयोग कई बार Noun के बाद किया जात है। जैसे :

'O man with friends dear! Children dear was if yesterday.

Also Remember The Following Tips For Placing Adjectives Correctly :

(1) Adjectives (only, even, almost, nearly, just) should be placed in front of the words they modify.

You will only need to plant one package of seeds. *Incorrect*

You will need to plant only one package of seeds. *Correct*

(''Only'' modifies ''one,'' not ''need.'')

(2) Place modifying phrases and clauses so that readers can see at a glance what they modify.

The robber was described as a tall man with a black moustache weighing 150 pounds. *Incorrect*

The robber was described as a six-feet-tall man weighing 150 pounds with a black moustache.(''150 pounds'' describes the man, not the moustache.) *Correct*

(3) Sentences should flow from subject to verb to object without lengthy detours along the way. When adverbs separate subject from verb, verb from object or helping-verb from main-verb, the result can be awkward.

John, after trying to reach the ball, decided to get a ladder. *Incorrect*

After trying to reach the ball, John decided to get a ladder. *Correct*

(Subject and Verb are no longer separated.)

(4) Adjectives indicating colour-Adjectives indicating colour usually precede adjectives indicating materials, proper adjectives, and defining adjectives, but follow other types of attributive adjective. In the following examples, the adjectives indicating colour are underlined.
e.g. 'threatening black clouds' ; 'her new red leather jacket'; 'a square brown mahogany table.'

(5) Adjectives indicating materials–Attributive adjectives indicating the materials from which objects are made usually follow any adjectives indicating colour and precede any proper or defining adjectives. In the following examples, adjectives indicating materials are underlined.
e.g. 'a beautiful blue silk saree' ; 'five red iron coat hangers'; 'the clean marble floor',

(6) The position of proper adjectives– Proper adjectives usually follow all other types of attributive adjective except defining adjectives.
Proper adjectives are usually derived from proper nouns referring to places or persons. In the following examples, the proper adjectives are underlined.e.g. 'sparkling British wine' ; 'three black brick Georgian manor houses'.
In the first example, the proper adjective British is derived from the place name Britain, and indicates the place of origin of the wine. In the second example, the proper adjective Georgian is derived from George, the name of an English king, and indicates that the houses are built in a style developed during the reign of that king.
It should be noted that proper adjectives may sometimes precede adjectives indicating materials, as in the following examples. This occurs when the adjective indicating a material is used as a type of defining adjective, to help identify what type of object is being described.
e.g. 'African straw hats' ; 'An Indian pearl necklace.'

The-ed ending adjectives are often accompanied by prepositions.

Read the following examples:

(1) We were tired of all the lights after a while.
(2) We were annoyed by the elephants.
(3) We were bored by the ringmaster.
(4) We were confused by the noise.
(5) We were disappointed by the motorcycle daredevils.
(6) We were disappointed in their performance.
(7) We were embarrassed by my brother.
(8) We were exhausted from all the excitement.
(9) We were excited by the lion-tamer.
(10) We were excited about the high-wire act, too.
(11) We were frightened by the lions.
(12) We were introduced to the ringmaster.
(13) We were interested in the tent.
(14) We were irritated by the heat.
(15) We were opposed to leaving early.
(16) We were satisfied with the circus.
(17) We were shocked at the level of noise under the big tent.
(18) We were surprised by the fan's response.
(19) We were surprised at their indifference.
(20) We were worried about the traffic leaving the parking lot.

Formation of Adjectives

(1) कुछ Adjectives, Noun में कुछ शब्द जोड़ने से बनते हैं। जैसे :

Noun	Adjective	Noun	Adjective
Sick	Sicken	Glory	Glorious
Gold	Golden	Boy	Boyish
Fool	Foolish	Laugh	Laughable
Play	Playful	Courage	Courageous
Care	Careful	Envy	Envious
Trouble	Troublesome	Man	Manly
Shame	Shameless	King	Kingly
Sense	Senseless	Woman	Womanish

(2) कुछ Adjectives, verb में कुछ शब्द जोड़ने से बनते हैं। जैसे :

Verb	Adjective	Verb	Adjective
Tire	Tiring	Move	Movable
Talk	Talkative	Eat	Edible

(3) कुछ Adjectives, अन्य Adjectives में ही कुछ शब्द जोड़ने से बनाये हैं। जैसे :

Adjective	Adjective	Adjective	Adjective
Colour	Colourful	Black	Blackish
Green	Greenish	Whole	Wholesome
Yellow	Yellowish	Three	Threesome

Formation of Comparative and Superlative Adjective

(1) कुछ Comparative/Superlative Adjective, Verb की Positive Form (I form) के साथ er एवं est लगाने से बनते हैं। जैसे :

Positive	Comparative	Superlative
Sweet	Sweeter	Sweetest
Young	Younger	Youngest
High	Higher	Highest
Old	Older	Oldest

(2) जब Positive के अन्त में e आता हो तो Comparative बनाने के लिए केवल r तथा Superlative बनाने के लिए केवल st ही जोड़ना होता है। जैसे :

Positive	Comparative	Superlative
White	Whiter	Whitest
Noble	Nobler	Noblest
Wise	Wiser	Wisest
Large	Larger	Largest
Safe	Safer	Safest
Fine	Finer	Finest

(3) जब Positive के अन्त में Y आता है एवं उससे पूर्व एक व्यंजन आता है तो y का परिवर्तन i में हो जाता है तथा er तथा est लगाने से Comparative एवं Superlative Adjective बनते हैं जैसे :

Positive	**Comparative**	**Superlative**
Easy	Easier	Easiest
Lovely	Lovelier	Loveliest
Happy	Happier	Happiest
Heavy	Heavier	Heaviest
Healthy	Healthier	Healthiest
Pretty	Prettier	Prettiest
Merry	Merrier	Merriest

(4) जब Positive के अन्त में कोई Single Consonant आता हो, उससे पहले Vowel आता हो तो Comparative एवं Superlative बनाते समय यह Consonant दो बार आता है (Double हो जाता है)। जैसे :

Positive	**Comparative**	**Superlative**
Wet	Wetter	Wettest
Big	Bigger	Biggest
Hot	Hotter	Hottest
Fat	Fatter	Fattest

(5) कुछ Cases में Comparative एवं Superlative Adjective बनाने के लिए Adverb, More एवं Most का प्रयोग करते हैं। जैसे :

Positive	**Comparative**	**Superlative**
Difficult	More Difficult	Most Difficult
Important	More Important	Most Important
Careless	More Careless	Most Careless
Beautiful	More Beautiful	Most Beautiful
Courageous	More Courageous	Most Courageous
Useful	More Useful	Most Useful

(6) कुछ Adjective अपने positive form से बिल्कुल अलग बनते हैं, इसके लिए कोई नियम नहीं है । जैसे :

Positive	**Comparative**	**Superlative**
Ill, Bad	Worse	Worst
Much	More	Most
Fore	Former	Foremost, First
Late	Later	Latest
Good, Well	Better	Best

Exercises

01.

Fill in the blanks with suitable determiners : **[RAS 1996]**

(1) Small cars are more economical than big..... .
(2) I bought .... mangoes.
(3) Have you .... sugar ?
(4) .... knowledge of English is essential for all of us.
(5) Clean .... floor properly.
(6) .... room is airy.

02.

Fill in the blanks with suitable determiners : **[RAS 1997]**

(1) Will you have .... cake ?
(2) There isn't .... sugar in the bowl.
(3) I'll have a cigarette; will you have .... too ?

03.

Fill in the blanks with suitable determiners : **[RAS 1998]**

(1) Uneasy lies ...... head that wears .... crown.
(2) .... women of India are as beautiful as .... of Europe.
(3) He got admission in .... University in........ USA.
(4) He started learning .... piano at .... age of ten.

04.

Fill in the blanks with appropriate determiners :

(1) .... people have car. *(A few/ A little)*
(2) Give me .... time to decided the matter. *(a few/ a little)*
(3) He drank .... the water. *(all/whole)*
(4) Delhi is .... from Alwar than Jaipur. *(further/farther)*
(5) He is senior .... me . *(than/to)*
(6) There are .... children outside the room. *(some/any)*
(7) Have you .... question? *(some/any)*
(8) Please give me .... water. *(some/any)*
(9) Has he bought .... dress? *(some/any)*
(10) He can't find .... banana tree? *(some/any)*
(11) She has .... flowers of rose. *(some/any)*
(12) I could not get .... note book there. *(some/any)*
(13) Nisha did not eat .... mango. *(some/any)*
(14) Will you please lend me .... money? *(some/any)*
(15) She must give me .... time to finish this work. *(some/any)*
(16) Is there .... money in your pocket? *(some/any)*
(17) .... dreams are very romantic. *(Some/Any)*
(18) Sorry, I am stranger here, I have .... knowledge about this place. *(few/little)*
(19) She has .... clothes. *(some/any)*
(20) He has not .... car. *(some/any)*

05.

Fill in the blanks with few/a few/the few :

(1) It is a work of .... month.
(2) He will come back in .... days.
(3) I have read all .... novels, I had.
(4) .... people can speak English correctly.
(5) I have invited all .... friends, I have.
(6) .... day's rest is necessary for the patient.

06.

Fill in the blanks with little/a little/the little :

(1) I have .... influence in the political field now.
(2) There is .... hope of his recovery, he is very serious.
(3) She had donated .... property, she had.
(4) He slept .... and felt better.
(5) .... knowledge is a dangerous thing.
(6) Please wait .... I am just coming.
(7) I have no milk left with me. I have already given to cat .... milk, I had.

07.

Fill in the blanks with near/next :

(1) Mr. Sharma lives .... to Ram's house.
(2) Radhika will speak .... to Sarla.
(3) The railway station is .... to my school.
(4) I will meet you at the .... crossing.
(5) This matter will be discussed again in the .... meeting.

08.

Fill in the blanks with much/many :

(1) How .... students are there in the hostel?
(2) .... people comes to see this temple daily.
(3) He doesn't have .... money to donate.
(4) I love you very ....
(5) There are .... balls in the store room.
(6) I am .... obliged to you for your timely help.
(7) .... girls were absent yesterday.

09.

Fill in the blanks with suitable determiners :

(1) I haven't .... time.
(2) There are not .... boys in the class.
(3) There is .... food left, so you will not go hungry.
(4) .... good comes of impoliteness.
(5) We must find an excuse; .... excuse will do.
(6) Can I have .... coffee?
(7) Don't eat .... more of ice-cream. Leave .... of it for your brother.
(8) Neither man could come .... men were ill.
(9) .... trains are slow, others are fast.
(10) Has he money .... to buy a car?
(11) She went to market to buy .... things.
(12) .... men here are expected to do their duty.
(13) She gave .... child .... ice-cream.
(14) There was .... snow last winter.
(15) Few people like cold weather, ... people like warm weather.
(16) There were shady trees on .... side of the road.
(17) .... man should do his best.
(18) These flowers are pink, ... are yellow ones.
(19) .... team could score a goal. So it was a drawn match.
(20) .... children play in the park everyday.

10.

Fill in the blanks in the following sentences with elder/eldest/older/oldest :

(1) Ram is .... than me.
(2) My father is the .... member of our family.
(3) My father is .... than your father.
(4) My brother is .... to me.
(5) This is the .... building in our village.
(6) How .... are you ?
(7) My .... brother is an IAS officer.
(8) This building is .... than that.
(9) We should respect to our ....
(10) The .... he grew, the more demands he made.

11.

Fill in the blanks with last/later/latest/latter :

(1) At .... the President gave thanks to the audience.
(2) Ram came .... than Shyam.
(3) This is the .... technology in the field of computer science.
(4) Between Ram and Shyam, the .... is more intelligent.
(5) The .... half of the century saw many revolutions.
(6) Ram was promoted as officer at a .... date.
(7) The .... chapter of this book is very interesting.

12.

Correct the following sentences :

(1) Whole girls were present in the function.
(2) All the third books are in our course.
(3) This is mine bed, which is your ?
(4) None of these two books is useful.
(5) A good deal of persons were present at the railway station.
(6) All the sides of the coin are shining.
(7) He alone lives in such a large house.
(8) The both girls have arrived.
(9) She is among the four first merit holders.
(10) Lord Ram was an incarnate God.

13.

Correct the following sentences :

(1) Our all members are very co-operative.
(2) His all books have been burnt in fire.
(3) I bought tickets three for Delhi.
(4) The Great Ashoka was a brave king.
(5) This custom has been observed since immemorial time.
(6) Have you new anything to tell me about the incident?
(7) Ram is as taller as his brother.
(8) Sita is not more beautiful as Rita.
(9) Gold is more precious than any metal.
(10) She is not that all reliable.

14.

Correct the following sentences :

(1) To drive is as difficult as fishing.
(2) It is as difficult to swim as driving.
(3) It is not as easy to write as reading.
(4) They had better died than surrender before the enemy.
(5) I had rather read than wasting my time here.
(6) He is junior than me.
(7) According to Ram, milk is preferable than tea.
(8) She is more wiser than her brother.
(9) My house is better than Ram.
(10) The climate of Udaipur is better than Jaipur.

15.

Correct the following sentences :

(1) There are lesser rooms in this hotel than that .
(2) Take this tablet with a few milk.
(3) Your problem is comparatively easier than that of mine.
(4) The quality of this detergent powder is comparatively better .
(5) He runs as faster, if not fast than you.
(6) Sita is as beautiful as if not beautiful than her sister.
(7) The more you hide something, the most you expose yourself.
(8) This is all the more better.
(9) The valley goes deep and deep after this point.
(10) Ram said, "I am very better now."

16.

Correct the following sentences :

(1) The cloth of this suit is very inferior.
(2) This is longest river in the world.
(3) He is the richest of all man in the city.
(4) He is the strongest of all other students in the college.
(5) Ramesh is one of the best student in the college.
(6) He is my the best friend.
(7) Ramesh is one of the strongest persons, if not the strongest in the town.
(8) I shall purchase the bigger of all these houses.
(9) Mr. Sharma is the most ideal teacher.
(10) This is more the best college in the city.

17.

Correct the following sentences :

(1) I have the best and a cheaper magazine.
(2) This is out and in the best hospital.
(3) Which of these books do you like the most ?
(4) I don't like these kind of apples.
(5) I don't like these sort of men.
(6) The poors should be helped.
(7) That was a most excellent opportunity to earn good money.
(8) She reached here the earliest of both girls.
(9) This is the much best school.
(10) She is getting weak and weaker.
(11) He is braver than stronger.
(12) The quality of this shirt is superior than yours.
(13) Ram came prior than me .
(14) The Ghee of Haryana is better than Rajasthan.
(15) He is more intelligent than any student of his class.

18.

Read the following sentences to find whether there is any error in any part :

(1) Kolkata is further (a)/from Alwar (b)/than Jaipur (c)/the capital of Rajasthan. (d)
(2) Ramesh is smarter (a)/enough to get (b)/selected for this (c)/post, without any recommendations. (d)
(3) He said, "Priyanka (a)/is the most unique (b) /singer of (c)/our college. (d)"
(4) This shirt is (a)/comparatively better (b)/than that (c)/we saw in corner shop yesterday. (d)
(5) Everyone was surprised to note (a)/that Rahim married a girl (b)/who was more beautiful and more tall (c)/than he. (d)
(6) A lots of books (a)/on English grammar are (b)/available with me but (c)/this one is the best. (d)
(7) I told her (a)/that it would be all (b)/the more better (c)/if she herself talked to the groom. (d)
(8) She does not have (a)/some money to buy (b)/a new refrigerator (c)/so she is worried. (d)
(9) Now-a-days (a)/the weather (b)/is getting more cold (c)/and colder. (d)
(10) All the books (a)/were indeed interesting (b)/but that one was (c)/the more interesting. (d)
(11) There were only two (a)/warriors but each and every (b)/warrior was equal (c)/to six persons. (d)

(12) Whole the chapter (a)/of this grammar book is full of errors (b)/that shows the (c)/carelessness of the proof reader. (d)
(13) Can we rely (a)/on this agency (b)/for the last news (c)/of the day. (d)
(14) Ram is junior than (a)/Shyam and (b)/Ram is older (c)/than Ganesh. (d)
(15) The militants (a)/entered the palace (b)/from the utmost gate (c)/with guns hidden in their clothes. (d)
(16) "She can't sing (a)/much than (b)/four songs at (c)/a stretch", he informed. (d)
(17) It is well know (a)/that Mrs. Indira Gandhi (b)/was the first statesman (c)/of her time. (d)

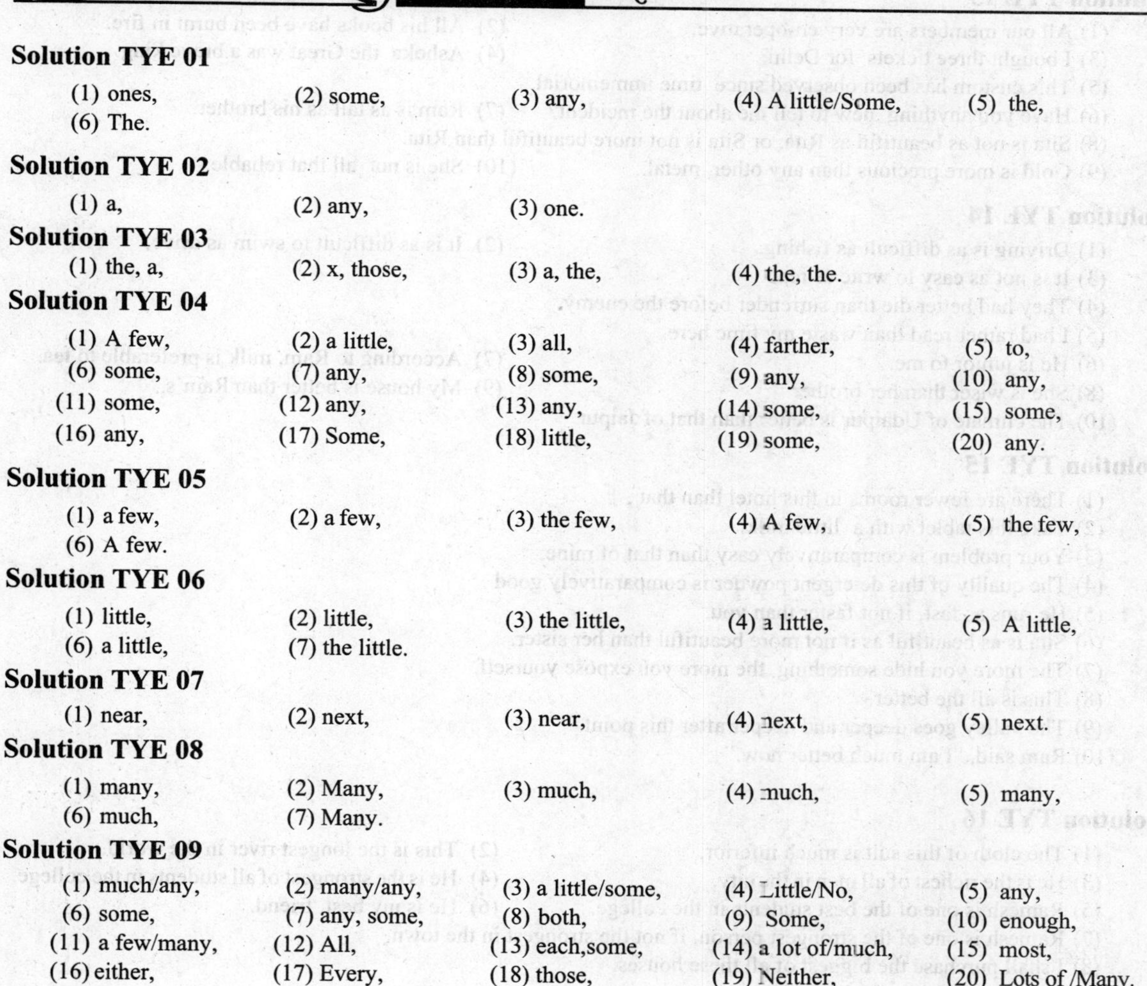

Solution TYE 01

(1) ones, (2) some, (3) any, (4) A little/Some, (5) the,
(6) The.

Solution TYE 02

(1) a, (2) any, (3) one.

Solution TYE 03

(1) the, a, (2) x, those, (3) a, the, (4) the, the.

Solution TYE 04

(1) A few, (2) a little, (3) all, (4) farther, (5) to,
(6) some, (7) any, (8) some, (9) any, (10) any,
(11) some, (12) any, (13) any, (14) some, (15) some,
(16) any, (17) Some, (18) little, (19) some, (20) any.

Solution TYE 05

(1) a few, (2) a few, (3) the few, (4) A few, (5) the few,
(6) A few.

Solution TYE 06

(1) little, (2) little, (3) the little, (4) a little, (5) A little,
(6) a little, (7) the little.

Solution TYE 07

(1) near, (2) next, (3) near, (4) next, (5) next.

Solution TYE 08

(1) many, (2) Many, (3) much, (4) much, (5) many,
(6) much, (7) Many.

Solution TYE 09

(1) much/any, (2) many/any, (3) a little/some, (4) Little/No, (5) any,
(6) some, (7) any, some, (8) both, (9) Some, (10) enough,
(11) a few/many, (12) All, (13) each,some, (14) a lot of/much, (15) most,
(16) either, (17) Every, (18) those, (19) Neither, (20) Lots of /Many.

Solution TYE 10

(1) older, (2) eldest, (3) older, (4) elder, (5) oldest,
(6) old, (7) elder, (8) older, (9) elders, (10) older.

Solution TYE 11

(1) last, (2) later, (3) latest, (4) latter, (5) latter,
(6) later, (7) last.

Solution TYE 12

(1) All the girls were present in the function.
(2) All the three books are in our course.
(3) This is my bed, which is yours ?
(4) Neither of these two books is useful.
(5) A number of persons were present at the railway station.
(6) Both the sides of the coin are shining.
(7) He lives alone in such a large house.
(8) Both the girls have arrived.
(9) She is among the first four merit holders.
(10) Lord Ram was God incarnate.

Solution TYE 13

(1) All our members are very co-operative.
(2) All his books have been burnt in fire.
(3) I bought three tickets for Delhi.
(4) Ashoka the Great was a brave king.
(5) This custom has been observed since time immemorial.
(6) Have you anything new to tell me about the incident?
(7) Ram is as tall as his brother.
(8) Sita is not as beautiful as Rita. or Sita is not more beautiful than Rita.
(9) Gold is more precious than any other metal.
(10) She is not all that reliable.

Solution TYE 14

(1) Driving is as difficult as fishing.
(2) It is as difficult to swim as drive.
(3) It is not as easy to write as read.
(4) They had better die than surrender before the enemy.
(5) I had rather read than waste my time here.
(6) He is junior to me.
(7) According to Ram, milk is preferable to tea.
(8) She is wiser than her brother.
(9) My house is better than Ram's.
(10) The climate of Udaipur is better than that of Jaipur.

Solution TYE 15

(1) There are fewer rooms in this hotel than that .
(2) Take this tablet with a little milk.
(3) Your problem is comparatively easy than that of mine.
(4) The quality of this detergent powder is comparatively good .
(5) He runs as fast, if not faster than you.
(6) Sita is as beautiful as if not more beautiful than her sister.
(7) The more you hide something, the more you expose yourself.
(8) This is all the better.
(9) The valley goes deeper and deeper after this point.
(10) Ram said, "I am much better now."

Solution TYE 16

(1) The cloth of this suit is much inferior.
(2) This is the longest river in the world.
(3) He is the richest of all men in the city.
(4) He is the strongest of all students in the college.
(5) Ramesh is one of the best students in the college.
(6) He is my best friend.
(7) Ramesh is one of the strongest person, if not the strongest in the town.
(8) I shall purchase the biggest of all these houses.
(9) Mr. Sharma is an ideal teacher.
(10) This is much the best college in the city.

Solution TYE 17

(1) I have the best and the cheapest magazine.
(2) This is out and out the best hospital.
(3) Which of these books do you like the most?
(4) I don't like this kind of apples.
(5) I don't like this sort of men.
(6) The poor should be helped.
(7) That was an excellent opportunity to earn good money.
(8) She reached here the earliest, of all girls.
(9) This is the best school.
(10) She is getting weaker and weaker.
(11) He is more brave than strong.
(12) The quality of this shirt is superior to yours.
(13) Ram came prior to me.
(14) The Ghee of Haryana is better than that of Rajasthan.
(15) He is more intelligent than any other student of his class.

Solution TYE 18

(1) (a) Change further to farther. Farther का अर्थ अधिक दूर तथा further का अर्थ आगे होता है। Farther 'far' की comparative degree है।

(2) (a) 'Smarter' की जगह 'smart' लिखा जायेगा। ध्यान रखें: enough के पूर्व, positive degree का प्रयोग होता है।

(3) (b) Unique के पूर्व, the most को delete करें। ध्यान रखें : कुछ adjectives unique, full, whole, square universal etc. अपने अर्थ के कारण superlative degree की तरह प्रयुक्त होते हैं। इनको compare नहीं किया जा सकता है। more unique, more complete या more square लिखना एवं most unique, most complete या most square लिखना गलत है।

(4) (b) Comparatively के साथ positive degree के Adjective का प्रयोग होता है। अत: या तो comparatively good लिखा जायेगा या केवल better लिखा जायेगा।

(5) (c) 'more tall' की जगह 'taller' होगा। सामान्यतया one syllable adjective का comparative उसमें 'er' या 'r' जोड़कर बनाया जाता है।

(6) (a) 'A lots of' की जगह या तो 'lots of' लिखें या 'A lot of' लिखें।

(7) (c) 'more better' लिखना गलत है। avoid double comparative. 'more' को delete करें।

(8) (b) 'Some money' की जगह 'any money' लिखा जायेगा। इस तरह के negative वाक्यों में 'some' की जगह 'Any' का प्रयोग होता है।

(9) (c) 'More cold' की जगह 'colder' लिखा जायेगा। इस तरह के वाक्यों में comparative degree of adjective का प्रयोग निम्न प्रकार से होता है। जैसे:
(a) He is becoming stronger and stronger.
(b) The weather is getting hotter and hotter.

(10) (d) 'more' की जगह 'most' का प्रयोग किया जायेगा। जब दो से अधिक वस्तुओं के साथ तुलना हो तो superlative degree of adjective का प्रयोग किया जाता है। दो वस्तुओं हेतु comparative degree का प्रयोग होता है।

(11) (b) change each and every to 'each'. ध्यान रखें : each का प्रयोग दो हेतु, किन्तु 'each and every' या 'every' का प्रयोग हमेशा दो से अधिक के लिए होता है।

(12) (a) 'whole the' की जगह 'the whole' लिखा जायेगा। Whole के पूर्व The लगता है।

(13) (c) 'last' की अपेक्षा 'latest' लिखा जायेगा। समय के सन्दर्भ late की comparative एवं superlative degree later, latest है।

(14) (a) 'than' की जगह 'to' का प्रयोग होगा। Junior, senior, prior etc. के साथ to का प्रयोग किया जाता है।

(15) (c) 'utmost' की जगह 'outermost' लिखा जायेगा। out का comparative, outer एवं superlative; outermost होता है। utmost का अर्थ complete (पूर्णतया) होता है। यहाँ utmost का गलत प्रयोग हुआ है।

(16) (b) much' की जगह 'more' का प्रयोग होगा। much-positive degree का adjective है जिसका comparative more है।

(17) (c) यहाँ 'first' की जगह 'foremost' का प्रयोग किया जायेगा first का अर्थ प्रथम होता है जबकि foremost का अर्थ most notable (सर्वाधिक चर्चित) होता है। वाक्य के सन्दर्भ के अनुसार foremost का प्रयोग ही उचित है।

ADVERBS

Adverb : यह वाक्य में ऐसा शब्द है जो verb या अन्य Adjective अन्य Adverb या Adverbial phrase को विशेषता प्रदान करता है/ संशोधित करता है/उसके अर्थ में कुछ वृद्धि/परिवर्तन करता है।

An adverb is that word in a sentence which modifies the meaning of verb or adjective or another adverb or adverbial phrase.

Look at the following sentences :

(a) He ran fast. —Verb ran को संशोधित करता है।

(b) These are very sweet mangoes. —Adjective, sweet को संशोधित करता है।

(c) He speaks very loudly. —Adverb, loudly को संशोधित करता है।

(d) He was sitting close beside her. —Adverbial phrase, beside her को संशोधित करता है।

सभी underlined शब्द Adverbs हैं। जब Adverb का प्रयोग वाक्य के शुरू में होता है तो वह सारे वाक्य को संशोधित करता है; जैसे :

(a) Certainly she is right. (b) Fortunately we escaped unhurt.

Kinds of Adverb

Adverbs को सामान्यतया तीन भागों में वर्गीकृत किया गया है:

Adverb

Simple | Relative | Interrogative

(A) Simple Adverbs : ये वाक्य में प्रयुक्त कुछ शब्दों (Verb, Adverb, Adjective, Adverbial phrase) को संशोधित करते हैं।

(B) Relative Adverbs : ये शब्दों को भी संशोधित करते हैं एवं सम्पन्न कार्यों के मध्य Relation भी व्यक्त करते हैं।

(C) Interrogative Adverbs : ये प्रश्न भी करते हैं एवं शब्दों को भी संशोधित करते हैं। इनका अलग-अलग विवेचन आगे दिया गया है।

(A) Simple Adverbs

Simple Adverbs को उनके द्वारा सम्पन्न कार्यों के अनुसार निम्न प्रकार वर्गीकृत किया गया है :

(1) **Adverb of Time :** Daily, since, yesterday, soon, tomorrow etc.
ये कार्य के सम्पन्न होने के समय को व्यक्त करते हैं।

(2) **Adverb of Place :** Here, there, everywhere, in, away, up etc.
ये कार्य के स्थान को व्यक्त करते हैं।

(3) **Adverb of Frequency or Number :** Frequently, again, often, seldom, once, twice, etc. यह कार्य कितनी बार हुआ, को व्यक्त करते हैं।

(4) **Adverb of Manner :** Fast, swiftly, quickly, easily, slowly, loudly, so, bravely etc. ये कार्य किस प्रकार (in what manner) सम्पन्न हुआ, को व्यक्त करते हैं।

(5) **Adverb of Degree or Quantity :** fully, very, rather, perfectly, pretty, almost. ये adverbs, degree, quantity को व्यक्त करते हैं।

(6) **Adverb of Affirmation and Negation :** certainly, surely, seldom, never, always, definitely etc.

ये सकारात्मकता या नकारात्मकता को व्यक्त करते हैं जो Adverb (certainly, surely, definitely etc.) सकारात्मकता (affirmation) को व्यक्त करते हैं उन्हें Adverb of affirmation कहते हैं एवं जो नकारात्मकता (never, don't etc.) को व्यक्त करते हैं उन्हें Adverb of Negation कहते हैं।

(7) **Adverb of Reasons :** therefore, hence, on account of etc. ये कार्य के कारण को व्यक्त करते हैं।

(8) **Adverb of Contrast :** However, though etc. ये वाक्य में विरोधाभास (contrast) को व्यक्त करते हैं।

(9) **Adverb of Condition :** Had, if etc. ये वाक्य में शर्त की उपस्थिति को व्यक्त करते हैं।

(10) **Adverb of Extent :** So far, till now etc. ये वाक्य में कार्य की हद (extent of work) को व्यक्त करते हैं।

कौन-सा Adverb, वाक्य में किस तरह का कार्य सम्पन्न करता है, उसी के अनुसार उसका नामकरण किया जाता है। अर्थात् कार्य के रूप एवं कार्य की स्थिति के अनुसार यह बताया जा सकता है कि यह Adverb कौन-सा है।

(B) Relative Adverbs

इस तरह के Adverbs हैं : What, When, Where, Why, How, Whatever, Whither, Wherever, Whence etc. यह Adverb antecedent को refer करते हैं। यह Antecedent के साथ सम्बन्ध व्यक्त करते हैं। यदि वाक्य में Antecedent नहीं है तो Adverb एक Relative Adverb नहीं है, यह Interrogative adverb हो सकता है। जैसे:

(a) I know where she lives.
(b) I understand the point what you say.
(c) I remember the house, where he lived.
(d) I forgot the time, when Puja Express arrives.

उपरोक्त वाक्यों में Where, What, Where, When, Relative Adverbs हैं जो antecedents के साथ सम्बन्ध को व्यक्त करते हैं। Antecedent means which comes before.

(C) Interrogative Adverbs

ये Adverbs, प्रश्न करने हेतु प्रयुक्त होते हैं। जैसे: When, how, what, where, how much, how long, how many, etc.

(a) What is your name?
(b) Where are you going?
(c) When did he come?
(d) How are you?

सभी underlined शब्द Interrogative Adverbs हैं जो प्रश्न करने हेतु प्रयुक्त हुए हैं।

Yes and No Adverbs : जो Adverbs, Yes या No के रूप में पूरे वाक्य को ही स्पष्ट करते हैं Yes or No Adverbs कहलाते हैं। जैसे:

(a) Do you know me? Yes. (Yes, I know you.)
(b) Have you played? No. (No, I haven't played.)

यहाँ Yes एवं No द्वारा दिया गया Answer पूरे वाक्य को व्यक्त करता है। ये Yes And No Adverbs कहलाते हैं।

Simple/Relative/Interrogative Adverbs

Simple Adverb वाले वाक्य Simple sentence होते हैं जबकि Relative Adverb वाले वाक्य Complex sentence होते हैं। Simple Adverb का प्रयोग वाक्य के शुरू में, मध्य में, अन्त में, कहीं भी हो सकता है, जबकि Relative Adverb वाक्य के मध्य में (Antecedent के बाद) आते हैं। Interrogative Adverb वाक्य के शुरू में प्रयुक्त होते हैं।

What is your name? — Underlined शब्द Interrogative Adverb है।

I know where she lives. — 'Where' Relative Adverb है जो antecedent के साथ सम्बन्ध को व्यक्त करता है।

Adverb/Adjective

कुछ शब्द, Adverb एवं Adjective दोनों तरह प्रयुक्त हो सकते हैं। जैसे:

Adverb	Adjective
(a) He ran fast.	He is a fast runner.
(b) She has only two books.	She is the only daughter of her parents.
(c) Come back.	He entered from the back door.
(d) They work hard.	He is a hard worker.

वाक्य में शब्द के प्रयोग के आधार पर ही यह कहा जा सकता है कि यह Adverb है या Adjective है।

Remember *Most is an adjective, but **almost** is an adverb.*
*Easy is an adjective, but **easily** is an adverb.*
***Good** is an adjective, but **well** is an adverb.*

Position and Rules of Adverbs

Adverbs का प्रयोग वाक्य में किस जगह किया जाए, यह एक महत्वपूर्ण बिन्दु है। Adverb को गलत जगह पर लगाने पर, वाक्य का अर्थ ही परिवर्तित हो सकता है। नीचे लिखे वाक्यों से यह स्पष्ट हो जाता है।

(a) Only she can speak. (केवल वह बोल सकती है)

(b) She can only speak. (वह केवल बोल सकती है, लिख नहीं सकती)

(c) She can speak only. (वह केवल बोल सकती है, अन्य कोई कार्य, जैसे घर का कोई कार्य, बाजार का कोई कार्य नहीं कर सकती है)

इस तरह Adverb, only की वाक्य में स्थिति में परिवर्तन होने से वाक्य का अर्थ बदल जाता है। अत: Adverb को वाक्य में कहाँ पर लगाना है (Position of Adverb) एक महत्वपूर्ण बिन्दु है।

(1) Adverb of Manner : जैसे : slowly, quickly, carefully, easily, calmly, fast etc वाक्य में verb के बाद लगाए जाते हैं, लेकिन यदि वाक्य में verb का object भी है तो object के बाद इन्हें लगाना चाहिए।

Correct use	Incorrect use
(a) He talks well.	He well talks.
(b) He speaks English fluently.	He speaks fluently English.
(c) It is raining regularly.	It is regularly raining.
(d) I read my book carefully.	I carefully read my book.

सभी underlined शब्द Adverbs of manner हैं।

(2) Adverb of Time एवं Adverb of Place :

Adverb of Time : (जैसे Now, then, soon, today, next day, yet etc) एवं Adverb of Place : (जैसे: Here, there, on etc) भी verb के बाद लगते हैं लेकिन verb का कोई object भी है तो ये object के बाद प्रयुक्त होते हैं।

Correct use	Incorrect use
(a) She will come soon.	She soon will come.
(b) He will go to Jaipur the next day.	He will next day go to Jaipur.
(c) He has not arrived yet.	He has yet not arrived.
(d) He lives here.	He here lives.
(e) Ram works there.	Ram there works.
(f) There are books everywhere.	There are everywhere books.

Note : सभी underlined words adverbs हैं।

(3) Adverb of Frequency : जैसे: Always, often, daily, generally, never, rarely एवं अन्य कुछ Adverbs जैसे almost, just, hardly, nearly, already का प्रयोग सामान्यतया subject एवं verb के बीच किया जाता है।

यदि verb में एक से अधिक शब्द हैं जैसे: has advised, have seen तो इन adverbs का प्रयोग have/has, Auxiliary verb के बाद किया जाता है।

Correct use	Incorrect use
(a) His mother never cooks food.	His mother cooks food never.
(b) He always speaks the truth.	He speaks the truth always.
(c) He often comes late.	He comes late often.
(d) He has never advised me.	He never has advised me.
(e) We have never seen an aeroplane.	We never have seen an aeroplane.
(f) I have just arrived.	I just have arrived.

(A) यदि वाक्य में is/am/are/was/were जैसी Auxiliary verbs का प्रयोग हुआ हो तो ये Adverbs इनके बाद लगते हैं। जैसे:

(a) He is always ready. *(b) She is often late.*

(c) They are generally late. *(d) We are always happy.*

(B) यदि वाक्य में verb को Importance देनी हो, जोर देना हो या short answer देना हो तो इन adverbs को Auxiliary verb या verb के पहले प्रयोग किया जाता है। जैसे :

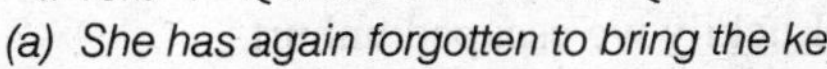

(a) She has again forgotten to bring the keys.
Yes, she always does forget to bring the keys. or Yes, she always does.

(b) Do you go by car?
Yes, I usually do.

(C) Auxiliary; have to/used to के साथ उक्त Adverbs का प्रयोग उनसे पूर्व किया जाता है। जैसे :

(a) I often have to go on foot. *(b) He always used to take umbrella.*

(c) She never has to walk alone.

(D) Adverb, not का प्रयोग हमेशा Auxiliary के बाद एवं Principal verb के पहले किया जाता है। जैसे :

(a) I have not done my work. *(b) He did not go to Jaipur.*

(c) She will not write an application. *(d) I do not go to school.*

(4) Adverb : Enough का प्रयोग उस शब्द के बाद किया जाता है, जिसे वह qualify करता है। enough से पहले हमेशा positive degree का adjective या Adverb रहेगा। Comparative degree के बाद enough का प्रयोग नहीं होता है। जैसे:

(a) I have money enough to buy a shirt.
(b) The building is large enough for the guest house.
(c) I have time enough to have lunch.
(d) They have clothes enough to wear for a weak.

जब enough का प्रयोग adjective की तरह होता है तो यह noun की विशेषता बताता है तब यह noun के पहले या बाद में आ सकता है लेकिन जब यह adverb की तरह प्रयुक्त होता है तो हमेशा बाद में लगता है।

(5) Adverb: only एवं even को हमेशा उस word से पहले लगाना चाहिए, जिसके लिए इनका प्रयोग किया जाता है।

(a) I cannot write even correct Hindi.
(b) He has only one car. (उसके पास एक कार है)
(c) Only he has a car. (केवल उसके पास कार है)
(d) He cannot do even this work.

(6) Order of Adverbs यदि एक वाक्य में कई तरह के Adverbs का प्रयोग हुआ हो तो सबसे पहले Adverb of manner, फिर Adverb of place एवं फिर Adverb of time आता है।

(a) She spoke loudly at the meeting yesterday.
1 2 3
(b) He is crying loudly at the field now.
1 2 3
(c) He was going to Jaipur yesterday.
2 3
(d) She comes regularly at the ground daily.
1 2 3

उक्त वाक्यों में
1. Adverb of Manner — M
2. Adverb of Place — P
3. Adverb of Time — T. को व्यक्त करते हैं।

M	P	T
1	2	3

NOTE

यदि वाक्य में कई Adverbs of time का प्रयोग हो तो सबसे पहले, सबसे छोटा Time फिर उससे बड़ा, फिर सबसे बड़े Time को रखा जाना चाहिए। जैसे:

(a) He came here at 7 O' clock in the morning on Monday.
(b) She was born at 6 O' clock in the evening on Sunday in 1987.

(7) यदि कोई Adverb किसी adverb / adjective या adverbial phrase को modify करता है तो उस adverb को पहले लगाते हैं। जैसे :

(a) His speech was very funny .
(b) She is very intelligent.
(c) He likes very sweet mangoes.
(d) They were standing close beside the canteen.

(8) जब Adverb सारे वाक्यों को ही संशोधित करता है तो उसे वाक्य के शुरू में प्रयोग करते हैं। जैसे:

(a) Certainly she will meet us there.
(b) Luckily we escaped unhurt.
(c) Always help the poor.

(9) जब किसी वाक्य में not का प्रयोग किया गया हो तो negative adverb का प्रयोग नहीं करना चाहिए। वाक्य में Double negative होना गलत है। जैसे:

(a) I will not find her nowhere. *Incorrect*
I will not find her anywhere. *Correct*
(b) No one scarcely visits here. *Incorrect*
No one visits here. *Correct*

(10) Else के साथ हमेशा 'but' Adverb का प्रयोग किया जाता है। 'than' का प्रयोग करना गलत है। जैसे:

(a) Go anywhere else than Pakistan. *Incorrect*
Go anywhere else but Pakistan. *Correct*
(b) Call her any thing else than bitch. *Incorrect*
Call her any thing else but bitch. *Correct*

(11) Intransitive verbs के साथ Adverb का प्रयोग verb के तुरन्त बाद ही किया जाता है। जैसे:

(a) He died calmly.
(b) She spoke softly.
(c) He disappeared immediately.

Comparatives of Adverbs

(a) जिस प्रकार Adjective की तीन Degrees of comparison होती हैं उसी प्रकार कुछ Adverb की भी तीन तुलनात्मक अवस्थाएँ होती हैं: (1) Positive degree (2) Comparative degree (3) Superlative degree.

Positive	Comparative	Superlative
(1) Short	Shorter	Shortest
(2) Late	Later	Latest /Last
(3) Hard	Harder	Hardest
(4) Fast	Faster	Fastest
She ran fast.	She ran faster.	She ran the fastest of all girls.

इस तरह के Adverbs में comparative degree बनाने हेतु er तथा superlative degree बनाने हेतु est लगाते हैं।

(b) कुछ Adverb के अन्त में ly आता है, उनकी Comparative degree बनाने के लिए more तथा Superlative degree बनाने के लिए most का प्रयोग किया जाता है। जैसे:

Positive	Comparative	Superlative
Slowly	More slowly	Most slowly
Wisely	More wisely	Most wisely
Swiftly	More swiftly	Most swiftly
Skilfully	More skilfully	Most skilfully

(1) He ran *swiftly*.

(2) He *ran more swiftly* than Ramesh.

(3) He *ran most swiftly* among all students.

लेकिन early, more early, most early गलत है।

क्योंकि early—earlier—earliest होता है।

नीचे कुछ adverb की Comparative एवं Superlative degree बताई गई है

Positive	Comparative	Superlative
badly, ill	worse	worst
well	better	best
little	less	least
much	more	most
far	father	farthest
forth	further	furthest
near	nearer	nearest

Adverb of Manner, Adverb of Degree एवं Adverb of Time के अतिरिक्त अन्य प्रकार के Adverbs की Comparative या Superlative degree नहीं बनाई जा सकती है। When, then, where, there, once इत्यादि की भी Comparative या Superlative degree नहीं बनाई जा सकती है।

Some Important Adverbs

Too, Much/Very, Very much/much, Too much/Much too/ only too, Since/Ever Since, Presently/Just now, Late/Lately, Hard/Hardly, Most/Mostly, Before/Ago, No/Not/So, Still/Yet/Already, There, Fairly/ Rather, Just, Early/Soon/Quickly, Sseldom or never/Seldom if ever.

(1) 'Too': इसका अर्थ होता है, More than enough अर्थात् excess (अतिशय)। Too का प्रयोग very के अर्थ में करना गलत है। Very का अर्थ होता है बहुत, जबकि 'Too' का अर्थ होता है excess (अतिशय)। यदि हम किसी मित्र को देखकर यह कहें I am too glad to meet you. तो इसका अर्थ होगा कि "मैं आपसे मिलकर इतना खुश हूँ जितना नहीं होना चाहिए।"

(A) **Too + infinitive:** Too के बाद 'to'infinitive का प्रयोग एक negativity व्यक्त करता है। जैसे:

(a) He is too weak to walk. वह इतना अधिक कमजोर है कि चल नहीं सकता।

(b) She is too poor to pay her fee. वह इतनी गरीब है कि अपनी फीस जमा नहीं करा सकती।

(B) 'Too' का प्रयोग भी के लिए किया जाता है; जैसे:

(a) He too went to America.

(b) He lost his bag and books too.

(C) 'Too' का निम्न प्रयोग करना भी उचित है। यहाँ too का अर्थ अत्यधिक से है; जैसे:

(a) You are too weak in English.
(b) He is too poor.
(c) She is too ugly.
(d) Ram is too dull.

(2) Much / Very :

(A) Much का प्रयोग Comparative degree के Adverb या Adjective के पहले किया जाता है। जबकि very का प्रयोग Positive degree है। जैसे:

(a) Ram is much stronger than Rahim.
(b) She is much more beautiful than Sarla.
(c) Ram is a very strong man.
(d) Sarla is a very intelligent girl.

(B) Very much का प्रयोग Comparative degree से पूर्व किया जाता है। जैसे:

(a) He is very much stronger than Sonu.

(b) Suresh is very much cleverer than Shalu.

(C) जब Superlative degree के साथ much का प्रयोग किया जाता है। तो यह 'the' के पहले आता है, जबकि very का प्रयोग 'the' के साथ तथा superlative के पहले होगा। जैसे:

(a) Nisha is much the best girl in the college.

(b) Rahul is much the best sportsman in the town.

(c) Nisha is the very best girl in the college.

(d) Rahul is the very best sportsman in the town.

(D) Much 'एवं very में एक महत्वपूर्ण अन्तर यह है कि much का प्रयोग past participle या verb के साथ होता है, जबकि very का प्रयोग present participle के साथ किया जाता है। जैसे:

(a) He was much shocked. *Past Participle*

(b) She was much surprised. *Past Participle*

(c) The news is very interesting. *Present Participle*

(d) The situation was very distressing. *Present Participle*

(e) She talks much. (He talks very—यह गलत है)

(f) He boasts much. (He boasts very—यह गलत है)

(E) कुछ phrases में past participle के साथ very का स्वत: ही प्रयोग होता है। जैसे: very pleased, very tired, very dejected etc.

(3) Very much / much : सकारात्मक वाक्यों (Affirmative sentences) में very much का प्रयोग किया जाता है, जबकि negative sentences में much का ही प्रयोग होता है। जैसे:

(a) I like her very much.
(b) I don't like her much.
(c) She works very much.
(d) She doesn't work much.

(4) Too much / much too / only too : Too much या much too दोनों का अर्थ समान है। Too much के प्रयोग के बाद noun का प्रयोग होता है एवं much too के प्रयोग के बाद Adjective या Participle का प्रयोग किया जाता है। दोनों का अर्थ है: excess, more than limits, इतना ज्यादा जितना नहीं होना चाहिए। जैसे:

(a) His behaviour gave me too much pain. *Noun*
(b) His behaviour was much too painful. *Adjective*

Only too : Only too का अर्थ होता है बहुत (very) इसका प्रयोग very के अर्थ में किया जा सकता है

He will be only too happy to meet you.

Means = He will be very happy to meet you.

Only too का अर्थ too से पूर्णतया अलग है।

(5) Since/Ever since : Since का प्रयोग perfect tense में किया जाता है इसका अर्थ होता है: जब से, तब से I have been playing football since 7 O'clock.

कभी-कभी वाक्य में since का प्रयोग अन्त में किया जाता है एवं इससे पूर्व ever का प्रयोग किया जाता है। Ever since का अर्थ होता है, **तब** से जैसे:

(a) I first met her three years ago and have remembered her face ever since.
(b) I saw her five years ago and had been trying to meet her ever since.

(6) Presently / Just now : Persently का अर्थ at present (इस समय) के लिए एवं शीघ्र (soon) ही future में होने वाले कार्य के लिए किया जाता है। Just now का प्रयोग वर्तमान मे पूर्ण होने वाले कार्य (Present Perfect) हेतु किया जाता है। जैसे:

(a) I am presently busy. (b) I shall discuss the matter presently.
(c) I shall go presently. (d) He has arrived just now.
(e) I have completed my work just now. (f) She has gone out just now.

Just now का अर्थ a moment ago भी होता है। इस अर्थ में इसका प्रयोग Past Tense में किया जाता है। जैसे:

(a) Did you hear a noise just now? (b) She rang up just now.

(7) Late / Lately : Late का अर्थ है देरी से, जबकि Lately का अर्थ होता है: 'अभी' (Recently). जैसे:

(a) He came late today. (b) He has come lately. *Recently*
(c) She has finished her work lately. (d) You are late.

Lately का प्रयोग present perfect में होता है, क्योंकि यह वर्तमान में पूर्ण होने वाले कार्य को व्यक्त करता है।

(8) Hard/Hardly : Hard का अर्थ होता है कठिन, जबकि Hardly का अर्थ Negative में नहीं से लिया जाता है। जैसे:

(a) He works hard. वह कड़ी मेहनत करता है।
(b) He hardly works. वह लगभग कार्य नहीं करता है।

(9) Most / Mostly : Most का अर्थ है सबसे अधिक, जबकि Mostly का अर्थ है, अधिकांश भाग। जैसे:

(a) He is the most intelligent student of all.

(b) The candidates were mostly from rural area.

(c) The audience consisted mostly of girls.

(10) Before/Ago दोनों का अर्थ है पहले। Before का प्रयोग Past या Present Perfect के साथ हो सकता है, जबकि Ago का प्रयोग Present Perfect के साथ नहीं हो सकता है। जैसे:

(a) I never before seen such a beautiful lady. (b) I have visited this place before.

(c) I came here two days ago. (d) He died three days ago.

He has arrived ten minutes ago. *Incorrect*

(Present perfect के साथ Ago का प्रयोग नहीं किया जा सकता है।)

(11) No/Not/So : Not का प्रयोग Auxiliary के बाद किया जाता है जबकि No का प्रयोग Noun से पूर्व किया जाता है। जैसे:

(a) I have no pen. (b) I haven't any pen.

(c) He has no idea. (d) He does not have any idea.

(A) *कुछ verbs जैसे: believe, think expect, suppose, afraid के साथ not का प्रयोग निम्न प्रकार भी हो सकता है :*

(a) Will she cooperate you? I believe not. *(b) Can you help me? I'm afraid not.*

(c) Does she like you? I think not.

(B) *इस तरह की verb (believe, think expect, suppose, afraid) के साथ so का प्रयोग noun clause के एवज में निम्न प्रकार से किया जाता है:*

(a) Is he alright? Yes, I think so. *(b) Wil he cooperate you? Yes I hope so.*

(C) *Not का प्रयोग यदि infinitive या gerund के साथ हो तो 'not' हमेशा infinitive एवं gerund के पहले लगाया जाएगा :*

(a) I advised him not to smoke. *(b) You are right in not helping her.*

---

(12) Still/Yet/Already :

(A) Still का प्रयोग वर्तमान में हो रहे कार्य के लिए किया जाता है। भूतकाल (Past) के लिए इसका सामान्यतया प्रयोग नहीं होता है। जैसेः

(a) He is still asleep. (b) It is still raining.

(B) Not yet का प्रयोग भविष्य में पूर्ण होने की आशा वाले कार्यों के लिए किया जाता है। जैसे:

(a) Has she come? not yet. (b) The jeep hasn't arrived yet.

(C) प्रश्न के साथ yet का प्रयोग ऐसे कार्य हेतु किया जाता है जिनके पूर्ण होने की आशा थी, वे पूर्ण हुए या नहीं? जैसेः

(a) Is lunch ready yet? (b) Has the jeep arrived yet?

सामान्यतया yet वाक्य के अन्त में आता है।

Yet का प्रयोग अधिकांशतया Negative एवं Interrogative वाक्यों में किया जाता है। Affirmative वाक्यों में yet का प्रयोग 'still' के समान ही किया जाता है।

We have yet to hear from the government.

(We are still waiting to hear from the government.)

Already : इसका अर्थ है पहले से, जब कोई कार्य आशा से पहले पूर्ण हुआ होता है तो सामान्यतया Already का प्रयोग किया जाता है। जैसेः

(a) When is she coming? She is already here (b) You must visit Agra. I have already visited.

तीनों words (still, yet, already) का प्रयोग past moment बताने के लिए भी हो सकता है। जैसे :

I went to see if she had woke up yet. But she was still asleep.

This was irritating as her friends had already arrived.

Position in a sentence : Still एवं already का प्रयोग सामान्यतया वाक्य के मध्य में किया जाता है। कुछ स्थिति में already का प्रयोग वाक्य के अन्त में भी हो सकता है। जैसे :

Are you here already? You must have come by some fast mode.

Yet सामान्यतया वाक्य के अन्त में आता है। Not के साथ yet उसके तुरन्त बाद लगता है। जैसे:

(a) Don't eat the apples, they aren't yet ripe. (b) The apples are not yet ripe.

(13) There: इसका प्रयोग जब वाक्य के शुरू में किसी चीज के होने को बताता है, तो वाक्य में subject अनिश्चित रहता है। ऐसे वाक्यों का Structure निम्न प्रकार का होता है

There + to be form of verb + ...

(a) There is a glass on the table. (b) There are two books under the bed.

(14) Fairly/Rather: Fairly का प्रयोग good sense में तथा Rather का प्रयोग bad sense में होता है। दोनों का अर्थ 'मात्रा' को व्यक्त करता है। जैसे:

(a) The weather is rather hot. *Correct*
The weather is fairly hot. *Incorrect*

(b) Coffee is fairly hot. *Correct*
(इसका अर्थ है; कॉफी अच्छी गर्म है)
Coffee is rather hot. *Incorrect*
(इसका अर्थ है; कॉफी न पसन्द आने योग्य गर्म है)

(c) I like her as she is rather beautiful. *Incorrect*
I like as she is fairly beautiful. *Correct*

(15) Just: इसका अर्थ है 'सभी'। Just का प्रयोग सामान्यतया Present Perfect में किया जाता है :

(a) He has just arrived. (b) They have just gone out.

Just का अर्थ एकदम सही समय हेतु भी किया जाता है। तब इसका प्रयोग Simple Past में भी किया जा सकता है। जैसे:

(a) They just caught the train. (b) She just managed to leave.

Just का प्रयोग समय हेतु निम्न प्रकार किया जाता है :

(a) It has just struck seven. अभी-अभी 7 बजे हैं।
(b) It has just struck three. अभी-अभी 3 बजे हैं।

(16) Early/Soon/Quickly : Early का प्रयोग Adjective एवं Adverb दोनों तरह से किया जाता है। जैसे :

(a) He came in early morning. (b) Roses blossomed early this spring.

early का यहाँ अर्थ है, सुबह शुरू होने के तुरन्त बाद या बसंत शुरू होने के तुरन्त बाद। Early का प्रयोग निर्धारित समय से पूर्व के लिए भी होता है। जैसे:

(a) She came early in the meeting. (b) The Chief guest came early.

जबकि, soon का प्रयोग after a point of time, के अर्थ में किया जाता है। जैसे:

(a) She came to meet me soon after Ram arrived.
(b) Get well soon.
(c) The work was hard, but she soon used to it.
'Soon' means a short time after a point of time.

Quickly : इसका अर्थ, कार्य करने की गति से लिया जाता है।

Come and see us quickly. (Means make the arrangement fast)
Come and see us soon. (Means come and see us before long)

He did the repair quickly but not very well.

I hope you can do the repair soon. I need the car.

(Michael Swan. Practical English Usage.)

(17) Seldom or never/ Seldom if ever : Seldom के साथ या तो or never या if ever आता है। (Seldom or ever लिखना गलत है) जैसे:

(a) She seldom or never tells lies.

(b) She seldom if ever asks the boys the reason of their absence.

Adverb *vs* Preposition

ध्यान रखें Adverb से पूर्व Preposition का प्रयोग करना गलत है। Adverb से पूर्व Prepostion का प्रयोग नहीं किया जाता है। जैसे:

(a) With most humbly I beg to draw. *Incorrect*

(b) You should speak with patiently and with confidently. *Incorrect*

इन वाक्यों में with का प्रयोग सर्वथा गलत है। ध्यान रखें।

(1) *वाक्य में जब this/last/next/all के बाद समय बताने वाले शब्दों जैसे: Morning, Evening, Noon, Night, Day, Week, Month, Year etc का प्रयोग होता है इनके साथ Preposition का प्रयोग नहीं किया है, क्योंकि ऐसी स्थिति में ये 'Adverb of time' की तरह प्रयुक्त होते हैं। जैसा हमने बताया है Adverb के साथ Preposition का प्रयोग नहीं किया जाता है। जैसे:*

(a) They reached here this morning. *(b) She will go to Jaipur next Monday.*

(c) She worked all morning/ evening. *(d) Ram will come next year.*

(e) Sita was married last year. *(f) We came here last week.*

(2) *जब समय बताने वाले शब्दों से पूर्व this/last/next/all जैसे शब्द नहीं आते हैं तो Preposition का प्रयोग किया जाता है। जैसे:*

(a) He will go in the morning. *(b) We will meet you in the evening.*

(3) *इसी तरह 'Home' जो एक noun है, यदि इससे पूर्व कोई adjective नहीं लगा है तो यह वाक्य में adverb of place की तरह प्रयुक्त होता है। ऐसी स्थिति में इसके पूर्व कोई adverb (जैसे 'to') नहीं लगाते हैं। जैसे:*

(a) She goes home everyday. *(b) I go home in the evening.*

Adverb *vs* Infinitive (Split Infinitive)

Traditional Grammar में Infinitive (to+Verb) के मध्य adverb का आना गलत माना जाता है। जैसे:

I request you to kindly pay my salary today.

ऐसा माना जा रहा है कि To pay (Infinitive) के बीच Kindly (Adverb) का आना गलत है। इसे Split Infinitive कहा जाता है। लेकिन Modern English में एक Adverb तक Infinitive के मध्य आना प्रचलन में आ गया है एवं विभिन्न विद्वानों ने इसे उचित ठहराया है।

Split Infinitive with a single adverb may be allowed **—G.H. Vallins**

I request you to kindly grant me one day leave.

एक से अधिक Adverb को लिखना आज भी गलत नहीं माना जाता है।

Infinitive के बीच 'not' का प्रयोग पूर्णतया गलत है। जैसे :

I asked him to not go there. *Incorrect*

I asked him not to go there. *Correct*

01

Correct the following sentences:

(1) She takes generally her breakfast at 8 A.M.
(2) Ram only came here last Saturday.
(3) Ramesh was too tired when he came here.
(4) Sita came quicker than I expected.
(5) We wanted a better and efficient Office Assistant.
(6) It was much cold last night.
(7) I visited her frequently while in New York.
(8) He will be quite sorry to know that.
(9) The water of this tank is too cold.
(10) He ran very fastly.

02

Correct the following sentences:

(1) Hari was fortunately not available in the hostel.
(2) It was nothing else than her arrogance.
(3) He feels comparatively better today.
(4) Come at 7 O'clock to my office.
(5) I seldom or ever refused the leave.
(6) He quickly ran away from the site.
(7) Firstly you think over the words and then speak.
(8) I go often to the Durga Temple.
(9) No one hardly goes to church daily.
(10) I care a straw for it.

03

Correct the following sentences:

(1) We were very delighted to get the news.
(2) Call me anything else than a fraud.
(3) They could not find her nowhere.
(4) I only solved two sums.
(5) She peacefully died yesterday.
(6) Do you know to drive?
(7) I went directly to Meerut.
(8) It is very cold to go for a walk today.
(9) Parul runs fastly than Nalini.
(10) If you run fast, you would have won the race.

04

Correct the following sentences:

(1) Hari speaks clear.
(2) Sita writes neat.
(3) Sarla hit the thief hardly on the head.
(4) He is perfectly quite right.
(5) The speaker spoke enough loud to be heard easily.
(6) Ram is much old.
(7) The story is much interesting.
(8) Ram comes here seldom.
(9) I am very satisfied with her conduct.
(10) The train will arrive just now.
(11) The film was mostly over when you entered.
(12) He fared bad in the second innings.
(13) Repeat again what you have said.
(14) Breathe deeply when you walk.

05

Correct the following sentences:

(1) He cautiously drives.
(2) She heartily loves Ram.
(3) There were everywhere flowers in the garden.
(4) Ram comes at the field regularly everyday.
(5) She has been absenting herself frequently from the office.
(6) Ram already has finished his work.
(7) I see her frequently in the market.
(8) She has often to go by tram.
(9) He is intelligent wonderfully.
(10) Sita regularly visits her friend Sarla.

06

Correct the following sentences:

(1) I drive seldom after sunset.
(2) He explained clearly the method of transplantation the heart.
(3) The parents heartily love their children.
(4) Three passengers were unfortunately injured.
(5) You are forbidden not to write on the table.
(6) The day is hot too.
(7) I was too tired after the swimming.
(8) Sita loves her only daughter too much.
(9) The new medicines have given her too much relief.
(10) I met none else than your real brother.

07

Correct the following sentences:

(1) She quickly writes.
(2) Unless you do not work hard, you can't succeed.
(3) The news is much interesting.
(4) He seldom or ever refuses a genuine request.
(5) You seldom or ever find a grammatical error in this book.
(6) Ram ran very fastly.
(7) They last evening went to Jaipur.
(8) I only solved two sums in an hour.
(9) The matter has been very discussed.
(10) I do not know to swim.

08

Correct the following sentences:

(1) They have gone to Jaipur yesterday.
(2) He has left this place five minutes ago.
(3) Do you know him? Yes, I donot.
(4) Do you know him? No, I do.
(5) The teacher asked him to not sleep in the class.
(6) Could you lend me your umbrella? Oh, no, I can.
(7) She will today go to Mumbai.
(8) With most humbly and respectfully, I beg to apprise.....
(9) I have not pen with me.
(10) There was no an intelligent student to solve that question.

Spotting the Errors (Adverbs)

09

Read the following sentences to find whether there is any error in any part:

(1) "Under no circumstances (a)/ we can help you (b)/ in this immoral project." (c)/said the Chairman. (d)/No error (e)

(2) Somebody informed (a)/ the contractor that his (b)/ brother had only died (c)/ five days before. (d)/No error (e)

(3) She is very senior (a)/ to me, so I (b)/cannot defy her orders. (c)/ No error (d)

(4) Who can believe (a)/ that she was not (b)/ hardly hit (c)/ by the death of her son. (d)/No error (e)

(5) Hardly she likes (a)/ to hear my name (b)/ after the dispute which occurred (c) / between us last year. (d)/No error (e)

(6) Only by discussing with (a)/ the officer concerned (b)/ they found out (c)/ the person behind the fraud. (d)/No error (e)

(7) The house is very good (a)/ but too much small (b)/ to accommodate (c)/ the full family. (d)/No error (e)

(8) He does not (a)/ know to make (b)/ friends so he is leading (c)/ a lonely life. (d)/No error (e)

(9) Every member of the family (a)/ is addicted to drinking (b)/ and so Asha is. (c)/ No error (d)

(10) He was very tired (a)/ of work so he said (b)/ that he would (c)/ not accompany us. (d)/No error (e)

10

Read the following sentences to find whether there is any error in any part:

(1) Shakshi was exorbitantly paid (a)/ for how skilful she (b)/ welcomed the visitors. (c)/ No error (d)

(2) She is almost quite competent (a)/for the post of Marketing Executive (b)/so if given a chance (c)/ she can show the results. (d)/No error (e)

(3) The student requested (a)/ the principal to be enough kind (b)/ to grant him seven days leave. (c)/No error (d)

(4) He has been trying (a)/ to persuade her for several months (b)/ but he has (c)/ not still succeeded. (d)/No error (e)

(5) Before the game he felt surely (a)/ of wining, but within five minutes (b)/ he realised that he was wrong. (c)/ No error (d)

(6) The amount which the company (a)/ paid to the dependents of (b)/ the deceased was (c)/ fairly unjustified. (d)/No error (e)

(7) Although he only earns (a)/ sixteen hundred rupees per month (b)/ yet he manages his (c)/ family well. (d)/No error (e)

(8) I liked that opportune moment (a)/ where the workers proved themselves (b)/ and came out victorious. (c)/ No error (d)

(9) Where else (a)/ did you go besides (b)/ the bank? (c)/ No error (d)

(10) I hardly ever (a)/ see him (b)/ because in my opinion (c)/he is not a reliable man. (d)/No error (e)

(11) He is a linguist (a)/ and always tries to (b)/ make his students (c)/ pronounce the words correctly. (d)/No error (e)

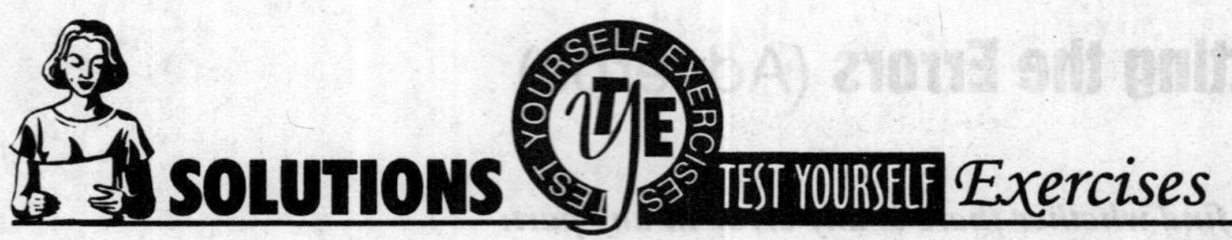

Solution TYE : 01

(1) Generally she takes her breakfast at 8 A.M.

(2) Ram came here only last Saturday.

(3) Ramesh was much tired when he came here.

(4) Sita came quickly than I expected.

(5) We wanted a better and more efficient Office Assistant.

(6) It was very cold last night.

(7) I frequently visited her while in New York.

(8) He will be very sorry to know that.

(9) The water of this tank is very cold.

(10) He ran very fast.

Solution TYE : 02

(1) Fortunately Hari was not available in the hostel.

(2) It was nothing else but her arrogance.

(3) He feels better today.

(4) Come to my office at 7 O'clock.

(5) I seldom or never refused the leave.

(6) He ran away quickly from the site.

(7) First you think over the words and then speak.

(8) I often go to the Durga Temple.

(9) Hardly any one goes to church daily.

(10) I do not care a straw for it.

Solution TYE : 03

(1) We were much delighted to get the news.

(2) Call me anything else but a fraud.

(3) They could not find her anywhere.

(4) I solved only two sums.

(5) She died peacefully yesterday.

(6) Do you know how to drive?

(7) I went direct to Meerut.

(8) It is too cold to go for a walk today.

(9) Parul runs faster than Nalini.

(10) Had you run fast you would have won the race.

Solution TYE : 04

(1) Hari speaks clearly.
(2) Sita writes neatly.
(3) Sarla hit the thief hard on the head.
(4) He is perfectly right.
(5) The speaker spoke loud enough to be heard easily.
(6) Ram is very old.
(7) The story is very interesting.
(8) Ram seldom comes here.
(9) I am much satisfied with her conduct.
(10) The train will arrive shortly.
(11) The film was almost over when you entered.
(12) He fared badly in the second innings.
(13) Repeat what you have said.
(14) Breathe deep when you walk.

Solution TYE : 05

(1) He drives cautiously .
(2) She loves Ram heartily.
(3) There were flowers everywhere in the garden.
(4) Ram comes regularly at the field everyday.
(5) She has been frequently absenting herself from the office.
(6) Ram has already finished his work.
(7) I frequently see her in the market.
(8) She often has to go by tram.
(9) He is wonderfully intelligent .
(10) Sita visits her friend Sarla regularly.

Solution TYE : 06

(1) I seldom drive after sunset.
(2) He clearly explained the method of transplantation the heart.
(3) The parents love their children heartily.
(4) Unfortunately three passengers were injured.
(5) You are forbidden to write on the table.
(6) The day is too hot.
(7) I was very tired after the swimming.
(8) Sita loves her only daughter very much.
(9) The new medicines have given her much relief.
(10) I met none else but your real brother.

Solution TYE : 07

(1) She writes quickly.
(2) Unless you work hard, you can't succeed.
(3) The news is very interesting.
(4) He seldom or never refuses a genuine request.
(5) You seldom or never find a grammatical error in this book.
(6) Ram ran very fast.
(7) They went to Jaipur last evening.
(8) I solved only two sums in an hour.
(9) The matter has been much discussed.
(10) I do not know how to swim.

Solution TYE : 08

(1) They went to Jaipur yesterday.

(2) He left this place five minutes ago.

(3) Do you know him? Yes, I do .

(4) Do you know him? No, I don't.

(5) The teacher asked him not to sleep in the class.

(6) Could you lend me your umbrella? Oh, no, I can't.

(7) She will go to Mumbai today.

(8) Most humbly and respectfully, I beg to apprise.....

(9) I have no pen with me.

(10) There was not an intelligent student to solve that question.

Solution TYE : 09

(1) (b) "We can" की जगह can we आएगा। जब वाक्य Under no circumstances से शुरू होता है तो Verb, Subject से पहले (Inversion is applied) आती है।

(2) (c) Only का प्रयोग died के बाद होगा। brother had died only five days before. He only died का अर्थ है 'केवल वह मेरा' He died only three days ago. का अर्थ है 'वह केवल तीन दिन पहले मरा'।

(3) (a) Very senior की जगह much senior लिखें।

Very का प्रयोग Positive degree के adjective के पूर्व किया जाता है। much का प्रयोग comparative degree के adjective के पूर्व किया जाता है। जैसे:

He is a very strong boy.

He is much stronger than you.

(4) (c) Hardly hit की जगह hit hard लिखें। hardly का अर्थ 'न के बराबर' (negative) होता है, जबकि hard का अर्थ 'कठिन'/'कड़ा' होता है।

(5) (a) Hardly does she like लिखें। जब वाक्य Hardly, Seldom से शुरू होते हैं तो Auxiliary verb, Subject से पहले (Inversion is applied) आती है।

(6) (a) Only को 'with' से पहले लिखें। By discussing only with. Only का प्रयोग सामान्यतया उस word से पहले किया जाता है जिसे महत्व दिया जा रहा है।

(7) (b) Too much की जगह much too small होना चाहिए।

सामान्यतया too much का प्रयोग noun से पूर्व होता है, much too का प्रयोग adjective से पूर्व होता है।

जैसे:

It gives me too much pleasure.

It is much too pleasure some.

(8) (b) Know to make की जगह know how to make होगा। जैसे:

I know how to swim.

He knows how to cook .

(9) (c) So Asha is की जगह so is Asha होगा। इस तरह के वाक्यों में सहायक क्रिया Subject से पहले आती है।

जैसे: (Inversion is applied) :

I don't like such cheap things nor does she.

(10) (e) वाक्य सही है।

Solution TYE : 10

(1) (b) How skilfully होगा skilful एक adjective है जबकि यहाँ skilfully (Adverb), verb received को qualify कर रहा है।

(2) (a) Almost का प्रयोग गलत है। quite से पहले किसी adverb का प्रयोग किया जाता है।

(3) (b) to be kind enough होगा। enough (as adverb) का प्रयोग उस शब्द के बाद आता है। जिसे वह qualify कर रहा है। जैसे :

He is intelligent enough to solve this problem .

लेकिन enough का प्रयोग adjective के रूप में noun से पूर्व एवं बाद में दोनों तरह हो सकता है जैसे:

I have enough money.

I have money enough to ......

(4) (d) Still की जगह yet आएगा। not succeeded yet. Still का प्रयोग affirmative वाक्यों में होता है, जबकि yet का प्रयोग सामान्यतया negative वाक्यों में किया जाता है।

(5) (a) Surely की जगह sure लिखें। verbs of perception जैसे: feel, small, appear, look, seem आदि अपने बाद Adjective लेते हैं, न कि Adverb.

(6) (d) Fairly की जगह rather या quite का प्रयोग करें। Fairly का प्रयोग सामान्यतया good sense में होता है।

(7) (a) He earns only होगा only, almost, even etc. का प्रयोग हमेशा उस Phrase या शब्द से पहले किया जाता है जिसे वह qualify करता है। जैसे:

(1) Only she visited the temple.

(2) She gave him only three rupees.

(8) (b) Where की जगह when का प्रयोग होगा। 'Where'—adverb of place है तथा time के लिए Adverb of time, 'when' का प्रयोग किया जाता है।

(9) (a) Else delete करें यहाँ else लगाने की आवश्यकता नहीं है, क्योकि besides का प्रयोग किया गया है। Besides एवं else का यहाँ एक ही अर्थ है।

(10) (e) वाक्य सही हैं। Hardly ever का अर्थ 'बहुत कम' होता है।

(11) (b) And so he always tries to होना चाहिए। जैसे: She is intelligent, so she can solve it.

CHAPTER

10

THE VERBS

Verb (क्रिया) Latin भाषा में शब्द Verbum से निकलता है। इसका अर्थ है a word (एक शब्द)। verb से कार्य का करना या होना स्पष्ट होता है। **कोई भी वाक्य बिना Verb के अपूर्ण है, अधूरा है। Verb वाक्य का एक महत्त्वपूर्ण part** है। Verb को निम्न प्रकार से वर्गीकृत किया जा सकता है :

VERB
- **Main Verbs**
  - **Transitive**
  - **Intransitive**
- **Auxiliary Verbs**
  - **Primary**
  - **Modal**

नीचे लिखे वाक्यों को देखें :

(a) I am playing —am (auxiliary verb), play (main verb)
(b) He is writing—is (auxiliary verb), write (main verb)
(c) They are reading—are (auxiliary verb), read (main verb)

Main Verbs

(1) Transitive Verbs (सकर्मक क्रियाएँ)

ऐसी verbs जिनके साथ object प्रयुक्त हो, Transitive verbs कहलाती हैं। Transitive का अर्थ है passing over अर्थात् जिन verbs में action कर्ता तक ही सीमित नहीं रहकर Object (किसी अन्य वस्तु) पर pass over होता है। जैसे :

(a) Ramesh hits a ball.
(b) He rings the bell.

यहाँ hits एवं rings, transitive verb की तरह प्रयुक्त हुई हैं जिनमें action कर्ता तक ही सीमित नहीं रहा है बल्कि Object; ball एवं bell पर pass over हुआ है।

सामान्यतया verbs से **'क्या'** या **'किसको'** प्रश्न करने पर **यदि** हमें उत्तर प्राप्त होता है तो वह verb, Transitive है। जैसे उपरोक्त वाक्य (a) से 'क्या' प्रश्न करने पर हमें 'a ball' उत्तर मिला। अत: hits एक Transitive verb है।

(2) Intransitive Verbs (असकर्मक क्रियाएँ)

Intransitive verbs में action कर्ता तक ही सीमित रहता है, object पर pass over नहीं होता है। जैसे :

(a) He sleeps in the bed.
(b) Shyam speaks loudly.

इन वाक्यों में verb; sleeps एवं speaks, intransitive verbs हैं, इनमें action कर्ता एक ही सीमित रह गया है। किसी object पर pass over नहीं हुआ है। इन verbs से 'क्या' 'किसको' प्रश्न करने पर कोई उत्तर प्राप्त नहीं होता है।

Important : अधिकांश verbs का प्रयोग Transitively एवं Intransitively दोनों प्रकार से हो सकता है।

Read the following sentences :

Verbs used Transitively
(a) He **speaks** the truth.
(b) The students **rang** the ball.
(c) He **flies** kites.

Verbs used Intransitively
(a) Sita **speaks** slowly.
(b) The bell **rang** loudly.
(c) A bird **flies.**

(a) जब verb का प्रयोग transitively होता है तो इसके साथ object अवश्य आता है लेकिन जब **verb** का प्रयोग Intransitively होता है तो इसके साथ कोई object नहीं आता है।

(b) किसी भी **verb** के लिए यह कहना कि यह transitive verb है या Intransitive verb है गलत है। इसकी बजाय हमें यह कहना चाहिए कि **verb** का प्रयोग Transitively या Intransitively हुआ है।

Auxiliary Verbs

Auxiliary Verbs को हम Primary Verbs एवं Modal Auxiliary Verbs में वर्गीकृत कर सकते हैं।

(1) Primary Auxiliary Verbs

Primary Auxiliary Verbs को तीन भागों में वर्गीकृत किया गया है :

(1) **Verbs 'to be'** : Is, am, are, was, were
(2) **Verbs 'to have'** : have, has, had
(3) **Verbs 'to do'** : do, does, did

(2) Modal Auxiliary Verbs

Primary Auxiliary Verbs

'to be' form of Verbs

Auxiliary Verb 'To be' (Is/ Am/ Are/ Was/ Were) : Is /Am/ Are, तीनों verbs का प्रयोग Present Tense में तथा was/were का प्रयोग Past Tense में होता है। Is का प्रयोग Present Tense में singular number, third person 'Subject' के साथ होता है। Am का प्रयोग केवल 'I' के साथ होता है। Are/were का प्रयोग Plural Subject के साथ होता है। Was का प्रयोग Past Tense में Singular Subject के साथ होता है।

इन Auxiliaries का प्रयोग present/past continuous के Affirmative/ Negative /Interrogative वाक्यों में होता है। इसके लिये Tense का अध्याय देखें। इनका प्रयोग Active/Passive, Direct/Indirect Structures में भी होता है। इसके आगे सम्बन्धित अध्याय में बताया जायेगा।

Use of 'to be' form of Verbs in Various Sentence Structures

(1) Subject +is /am/are/was/were +noun/pronoun:

(a) He is a boy.
(b) She is a girl.
(c) They are students.
(d) We were friends.
(e) I am a man.
(f) You are a sportsman
(g) It was me.
(h) It is mine.
(i) These shirts are not of my size.
(j) They were partners.

उपरोक्त वाक्यों में Auxiliary verbs के साथ noun /pronoun का प्रयोग हुआ है।

(2) Wh word + is/am/are + subject :

(a) What is that?
(b) Who is that ?
(c) What age is he?
(d) What are apples today?
(What are apples 'means' what price are apples?)
(e) What is your father?
(f) Who is he?

इस तरह के वाक्यों मे Wh words से प्रश्न किया गया है।

(3) Subject + is/am/are/was/were + adjective :

(a) She is asleep.
(b) He is ready.
(c) It was dark.
(d) Sita is a beauty.
(e) The students were exhausted.
(f) I was happy.

इस तरह के वाक्यों में Auxiliary verbs (to be) के साथ adjective का प्रयोग होता है।

(4) Subject+ is/am/are/was/were + preposition + adjective/possessive pronoun : Auxiliary 'to be' का प्रयोग निम्न प्रकार के वाक्य बनाने में भी किया जाता है।

(a) Sita is in good health now.
(b) We are all fully tired.
(c) They were out of breath (breathless).
(d) At last he was at liberty (free).
(e) This gift is for you.
(f) I am quite well.
(g) Everything is in proper place.
(h) The car was in good condition.

(5) Auxiliary 'to be ' के बाद to infinitive का प्रयोग निम्न प्रकार किया जाता है। ऐसे वाक्यों का structure निम्न होता है :

Subject + to be form verb + to infinitive :

(a) He is to come on Sunday. उसे रविवार को आना है।
(b) I am to complete this work. मुझे यह कार्य पूरा करना है।
(c) They are to assemble in the hall. उन्हें हाल में एकत्र होना है।
(d) They were to attend the party. उन्हें पार्टी में उपस्थित होना था।
(e) He was to go to Jaipur. उसे जयपुर जाना था।
(f) Sita was to come here. सीता को यहाँ आना था।
(g) Who is to blame? किसे दोष देना है?
(h) That house is to let. वह मकान किराये पर देना है।

It is a very important structure used in daily routine.

(6) There के साथ Auxiliary 'to be ' का प्रयोग एक महत्वपूर्ण वाक्य संरचना है। जैसे :
There + is /am/are/was/were + subject *Or*
There + is/am/are/was/were + subject + adverbial adjective

ये दोनों sentence structure का English writing एवं speaking में काफी प्रयोग होता है। जैसे :

(a) There is a cow. वहाँ एक गाय है।
(b) There was a large crowd . वहाँ बहुत भीड़ थी।
(c) There are three tables in the room. कमरे में तीन मेज है।
(d) There were three persons. वहाँ तीन आदमी थे।
(e) There is a girl waiting for you. वहाँ एक लड़की तुम्हारा इन्तजार कर रही है।
(f) There are several hotels in this town. इस कस्बे में कई होटल हैं।

(7) जब वाक्य का Subject एक Infinitive (+to) के रूप में होता है, तो निम्न Sentence structure का प्रयोग उचित लगता है। To meet you is nice की जगह It is nice to meet you लिखना एवं बोलना ज्यादा उचित है। जैसे :

It + be + adjective/noun + to infinitive :

(a) It is so nice to walk here with you.
(b) It was a pleasant surprise to talk with her.
(c) It is a mistake to ignore their advice.
(d) It is so wonderful to swim here with you.

(8) जब उक्त वाक्यों को How/what का प्रयोग करके exclamatory वाक्यों में परिवर्तन किया जाता है तो ऐसे वाक्यों का structure निम्न होता है :

How/What + adjective/noun + (it +be) + to infinitive

(a) How nice to walk here with you!
(b) What a pleasant surprise to talk with her!
(c) What a mistake to ignore their advice!
(d) How wonderful to swim here with you!

(9) जब वाक्य का Subject एक gerund या gerundial phrase होता है तो It का प्रयोग करते हुए निम्न Structure प्रयुक्त होता है :

It+(to be form) + adjective/noun + gerund

(a) It is so nice walking here with you.
(b) It is wonderful lying on the beach all day.
(c) It was worthwhile running that lady club last year.
(d) It's no good crying over spilt milk.

(10)जब वाक्य में Clause , Subject के complement के रूप में प्रयुक्त हो , (अर्थात् बिना clause के subject को पूर्णता नहीं मिले), ऐसे वाक्यों का structure निम्न होता है :

Subject + to be form of verb+ clause (subject complement):

(a) The trouble is (that) all hotels are shut.
(b) Is this what your are searching for?
(c) This is where she works.
(d) Everything was as we had left it.

Underline part, का subject complement, clause है।

(11)जब वाक्य में clause एक subject की तरह प्रयुक्त हो तो सामान्यतया 'that' को omit किया जाता है एवं वाक्य का structure निम्न होता है :

It + to be form of verb + noun/adjective + clause (as subject)

(a) It is time you started.
(b) It is doubtful whether he would be able to attend the function.
(c) It was a mystery how the thieves entered into the house.
(d) It is a good news you have found a job.

(12)Auxiliary verb 'to be' का प्रयोग निम्न प्रकार के वाक्य बनाने में भी किया जाता है :

Subject+is/am/are/was/were + adverbial adjunct :

(a) He is here in the room.
(b) The magazine you are looking for is here on the table.
(c) It's there is the library.
(d) My house is near the post office.
(e) Was anything up there in the hall?
(f) The index is on page 6.

Here/there को सामान्यतया वाक्य के अन्त में लिखते हैं लेकिन exclamatory वाक्यों में इन्हें वाक्य के शुरु में लिखा जाता है। जैसे :

(a) Here is your friend! *(b) Here comes the bus!* *(c) There she goes!* *(d) There he lives!*

सभी underlined phrases, adverbial adjunct को व्यक्त करते हैं। adverbial adjunct का अर्थ adverb के साथ जुड़ा part of sentence है।

(13) जब वाक्य का subject ; for + noun /pronoun + to infinitive होता है तो ऐसे वाक्यों में auxiliary 'to be' का प्रयोग It के साथ निम्न structure में होता है :

It + to be + for + noun/pronoun + to infinitive :

(a) It was very difficult for him to live in this cold region.
(b) It was the rule for male and female to sit apart.
(c) It is very easy for anyone to talk to her.
(d) Is it easy for a rich girl to find a smart husband?

(14) Auxiliary 'were' का प्रयोग एक महत्वपूर्ण sentence structure निम्नलिखित है :

If + subject + were + complement :

(a) If I were a king ! — यदि मैं राजा होता! (काश मैं राजा होता।)
(b) If I were young again! — यदि मैं पुन: जवान हो सकता! (काश मै पुन: जवान हो पाता।)
(c) If she were a bird! — यदि वह पक्षी होती! (काश वह पक्षी होती।)

इस तरह के वाक्यों को निम्न structure द्वारा भी समान अर्थ में लिखा जा सकता है:

Were + subject + complement :

(a) Were I a king!
(b) Were I young again!
(c) Were she a bird!
(d) Were we ministers!

उपरोक्त sentence structures के अतिरिक्त to be form of verbs, is/am/are/was/were का प्रयोग present एवं Past Tense में continuous form में Affirmative, Negative एवं Interrogaive structure किया जाता है। Tense के अध्याय को ध्यानपूर्वक पढ़ें, इनका प्रयोग कहाँ एवं किस तरह किया जाता है समझ में आ जायेगा।

Auxiliary Verb 'to have' (Have/ Has/ Had)

Have / Has/ Had का प्रयोग Present, Past एवं Perfect Continuous Tenses में विभिन्न स्थितियों में किया जाता है। इसे आपको Tense के अध्याय में विस्तृत रूप से हर प्रकार के sentence structure (Affirmative, Negative, Interrogative एवं Interrogative Negative) में स्पष्ट किया गया है। Have/Has/Had के Tense में प्रयोग के अतिरिक्त अन्य use निम्न हैं :

(1) **Have/Has/Had का प्रयोग, किसी वस्तु पर मालिकाना हक, स्वामित्व (Possession, ownership) व्यक्त करने हेतु निम्न प्रकार किया जाता है वाक्य का structure निम्न होता है :**

Subject + have/has/had + noun ***Or*** **Subject + have/has/had + got + noun**

Have के साथ got का प्रयोग करने से वाक्य में उस वस्तु का महत्त्व बढ़ जाता है:

(a) I have a car.
(b) I have got a car.
(c) He has a book.
(d) He has got a book.
(e) He had a beautiful house.
(f) He had got several good opportunities.

(A) इस sentence structure का प्रयोग Relationship (सम्बन्ध) को व्यक्त करने हेतु भी किया जाता है। जैसे :

(a) I have two sisters.
(b) She has two sons.
(c) I have five friends.
(d) They have two brothers.
(e) I had two sons.
(f) He had a daughter.

(B) इस sentence structure द्वारा किसी व्यक्ति या वस्तु के पास उसके अनेक भागों के होने को भी व्यक्त किया जा सकता है।जैसे:

(a) A man has two legs.
(b) A cow has four legs.
(c) The room has four walls.
(d) A chair has four legs.
(e) Ramesh has six fingers in his right hand.
(f) This table has only three legs.

(C) Have/ had का प्रयोग take /receive /experience के अर्थ में भी निम्न प्रकार किया जाता है

(a) I have my dinner at 9 P.M. *(take)*
(b) I have my bath in the morning. *(take)*
(c) I had no problem in searching his house. *(experience)*
(d) I had many messages from my past employer. *(receive)*

(2) **Have/Has/Had का प्रयोग कार्य की अनिवार्यता (Urgency), करने की बाध्यता (force or compulsion of doing) को भी व्यक्त करता है। ऐसे वाक्यों का structure निम्न होता है :**

Subject + have/has/had+ infinitive:

(a) He has to complete this work today. — उसे यह कार्य आज ही पूरा करना है। (अनिवार्यता)
(b) I have to go to Jaipur tomorrow. — मुझे कल जयपुर जाना है। (अनिवार्यता)
(c) I had to sell my house. — मुझे मकान बेचना पड़ा था। (बाध्यता)
(d) He had to suffer the loss. — उसे नुकसान उठाना पड़ा था। (बाध्यता)
(e) He will have to come here. — उसे यहाँ अना पड़ेगा। (बाध्यता)
(f) They will have to obey me. — उन्हें मेरी आज्ञा माननी पड़ेगी। (बाध्यता)

इस तरह के वाक्य, अनिवार्यता, बाध्यता को स्पष्ट करते हैं। इस तरह के वाक्य दैनिक जीवन में बहुत प्रयोग में आते हैं। छात्रों को इस structure को अच्छी तरह समझ लेना चाहिए।

(3) **Have/Has/Had का causative verb की तरह प्रयोग निम्न प्रकार होता है। Causative verb की तरह प्रयोग का अर्थ है, कर्ता स्वयं कार्य नहीं करता है। बल्कि वह कार्य होने का कारण (cause) है। अर्थात् वह दूसरों से कार्य करवाता है।**

(a) I had him punished for his negligence.
(b) I have a house built by her.
(c) Suresh has his thesis written by somebody.
(d) I had my book published.

इस तरह के वाक्यों में get/made का भी प्रयोग किया जाता है। आगे 'causative verb' में यह बताया गया है।

(4) **Have been/has been का निम्न प्रकार के structure में प्रयोग देखें :**

Subject + have/has been + noun (noun with preposition) :

(a) I have been a professor.
(b) He has been a banker.
(c) I have been to USA.

उपरोक्त वाक्य यह स्पष्ट करते हैं कि भूतकाल में वह व्यक्ति एक Professor, Banker रह चुका है लेकिन अब नहीं है।

I have been to USA.

इस वाक्य का अर्थ है कि मैं अमेरिका रह चुका हूँ लेकिन अब वहाँ नहीं हूँ।

See the difference between the following sentences :

(a) He has been to USA.
(b) He has gone to USA.

दूसरे वाक्य का अर्थ है कि वह अमेरिका जा चुका है या तो वहाँ पहुँच चुका है या रास्ते में है।

(5) **Verbs; expect, hope, wish, want etc. के साथ had का प्रयोग past perfect में, ऐसी past इच्छाओं को व्यक्त करता है जो पूर्ण नहीं हुई। जैसे:**

(a) I had expected to pass IAS. (but I didn't pass)
(b) I had hoped to meet her in the party. (but I didn't meet her)

(6) **Have/had के साथ had का प्रयोग देखने को मिलता है।**

(a) I have had my lunch.
(b) He has had her breakfast.
(c) She had had her breakfast early in the morning.
(d) He will have had his lunch by now.

उपरोक्त वाक्यों में पहले have या had का प्रयोग present perfect या past perfect के अनुसार होता है तथा दूसरा had का प्रयोग verb की III form (जो present /past perfect में लगानी आवश्यक है) की तरह (have = take के लिये) हुआ है।

7. **Have /has/had के साथ negative एवं Interrogative वाक्य निम्न प्रकार से बनाये जा सकते हैं :**

Affirmative	Negative	Interrogative
(a) I have a pen.	I have no pen. I don't have a pen.	Have I a pen? Do I have a pen?
(b) She has a car.	She has no car. She doesn't have a car.	Has she a car? Does she have a car ?
(c) He had a house.	He hadn't a house. He did not have a house.	Had he a house? Did he have a house?

(8) **Have का प्रयोग सामान्यतया continuous form में नहीं किया जाता है। लेकिन यदि have का अर्थ, experience या enjoy या take से हो तो इसका प्रयोग निम्न प्रकार किया जाता है :**

(a) They are having a party.
(b) I am having a difficult time now a days.
(c) She is having a nice time with her husband.

(9) **Use of had better :**
निम्न वाक्यों को देखें :

(a) I had better talk him at once.
(This would be a good thing to do or the best thing to do.)
(b) You had better not miss the train.
(It would be unwise to miss the train.)

'not का प्रयोग यहाँ better के बाद हुआ है।

(c) You had better go.
(It would be best for you to go. *Or* I advise you to go.)

Auxiliary Verb 'to do' (Do/Does/Did)

(1) **Do/does/did का प्रयोग negative एवं interrogative वाक्यों में present एवं past tense में सामान्यतया किया जाता है। इस तरह का प्रयोग tense के अध्याय में विस्तार रूप से बताया गया है।**

(2) **Do, Does, Did, का प्रयोग affirmative वाक्यों में निम्न स्थितियों को व्यक्त करता है :**

(1) I do go to her.	मैं उसके पास जाता तो हूँ।
(2) She does come here.	वह यहाँ आती तो है।
(3) He did come yesterday.	वह यहाँ कल आया तो था।
(4) He does read.	वह पढ़ता तो है।
(5) He does learn his lessons well.	वह अपने पाठ याद करता तो है।
(6) She does take medicines daily.	वह रोजाना दवाएँ लेती तो है।
(7) She did take medicines daily.	वह रोजाना दवाएँ लेती तो थी।

(3) **निम्न वाक्यों में do, does, did का प्रयोग emphasis हेतु किया जाता है। देखें :**

Have a cup of tea.	Do have a cup of tea.
Have a seat, please.	Do have a seat, please.
Write to me.	Do write to me.

उपरोक्त वाक्यों में Do का प्रयोग वाक्यों को Interrogative नहीं बनाता है बल्कि यह वक्ता की अधिक विनम्रता, आग्रहयुक्त विनम्रता प्रदर्शित करता है।

The so-called emphatic do has many used in English :

(1) To add emphasis to an entire sentence :
He does like eggs. He really does!
(2) To add emphasis to an imperative :
Do come in. (actually softens the command)

(3) *To add emphasis to a frequency adverb :*
(a) He never did understand his mother.
(b) She always does manage to hurt her mother's feelings.
(4) *To contradict a negative statement :*
(a) You didn't do your homework, did you? Oh, but I did finish it.
(5) *To ask a clarifying question about a previous negative statement*
Raju didn't take the purse. Then who did take the purse?
(6) *To indicate a strong concession :*
Although the Jack denied any wrong-doing, they did return some of the presents.

---

(4) Do का प्रयोग adequacy, suitability बताने हेतु भी निम्न प्रकार किया जाता है :

(a) I haven't got a torch.
Will a matchbox do? — क्या माचिस उपयुक्त रहेगी?
No a matchbox won't do. — I am trying to find out the gas leak.
(A match box will be unsuitable.)
(b) Would ₹ 100/- do? (= be adequate) — No it wouldn't. I need ₹ 1000.

(5) To do with का प्रयोग concern के अर्थ में भी किया जा सकता है :

It has nothing to do with you. — (It doesn't concern you.)
It was nothing to do with me. — (It didn't concern me.)

(6) Forms of do are useful in expressing similarity in conjunction with 'so' and 'neither' :

(a) My wife hates eggs and so does my son.
(b) My wife doesn't like eggs ; neither do I.

(7) 'Do' is also used to avoid the repetition of the verb :

(a) Shalini excelled in language studies; **so did** his brother.
(b) Rahul studies as hard as his sister **does.**

One Principal Verb + Two Auxiliaries

कई वाक्यों में एक Principal Verb के साथ दो Auxiliaries का प्रयोग किया जाता है। जैसे :

(a) She neither can nor will help him.
(b) He did not and should not talk to him.
(c) He neither will nor can solve it.
(d) They did not and will not help you.

उपरोक्त वाक्यों में principal verb (help, talk, solve, help) एक ही है लेकिन auxiliaries दो हैं। यहाँ दोनों auxiliary verbs के साथ principal verb की एक ही अवस्था का ही प्रयोग किया गया है। जो दोनों auxiliaries के साथ अलग-अलग रूप से भी प्रयोग करें तो भी सही प्रयोग होगा। लेकिन निम्न वाक्यों को देखें :

(a) He neither has talked nor will talk to me.
(b) They have not helped and will not help you.

उपरोक्त वाक्यों में Principal verb का रूप दोनों auxiliaries के साथ बदला हुआ दिखाई दे रहा है। Has के साथ talked तथा will के साथ talk का ही प्रयोग होगा। इसी तरह दूसरे वाक्य में have के साथ helped तथा will के साथ help का ही प्रयोग सही है। यदि इन वाक्यों को निम्न प्रकार लिखा जाये तो गलत होगा।

(a) He neither has nor will talk to me. — *Incorrect*
(b) They have not and will not help you. — *Incorrect*

छात्रों को इस प्रकार की गलती से बचना चाहिए। यह एक महत्त्वपूर्ण बिन्दु है।

Causative Verbs

Causative verbs show that somebody/something is indirectly responsible for an action. The subject doesn't perform the action itself, but causes someone/something else to do it instead. For example :

Yesterday I had my hair cut.

1. I didn't cut my own hair, but I made someone else do it for me instead—I ''caused'' them to cut my hair.
   Read the following sentences
   (a) I made her sing a song.
   (b) I made him polish my shoes.
   (c) I got my clothes washed by him.
   (d) I got my thesis written by him.
2. इन वाक्यों में कर्ता स्वयं कार्य नहीं करता है। बल्कि वह अन्य से कार्य करवाता है। कार्य अन्य से करवाने हेतु जो verbs प्रयुक्त होती हैं वे causative verbs कहलाती है। इस तरह की verbs, get, make, have, keep etc हैं। जैसे :
   (a) I made him laugh.
   (b) I made him write a letter.
   (c) He made me polish his shoes.
   (d) I kept her waiting.
   (e) He keeps me away from the office.
   (f) I shall make him complete the project today.
3. Active voice में सामान्य रूप से make, keep का प्रयोग किया जाता है तथा Passive voice में have, get का प्रयोग किया जाता है। जैसे :
   (a) I got my shoes polished by him.
   (b) I got my car repaired by the mechanic.
   (c) I got my clothes washed by her.
   (d) I had a song sung by her.
   (e) I had the thesis written by him.
   (f) I had my clothes washed by her.
   (g) I shall get the project completed by him today.

सामान्यतया get का प्रयोग विनम्रता, अनुरोध को व्यक्त करता है एवं make, have का प्रयोग बाध्यता, दबाव, विवशता के सन्दर्भ में होता है।

LET

Let can be used as a causative verb.

Let means a person gives permission for another person to do it.

See the following examples :

(a) I can let this car cool.

(b) Would you let me join your party?

Help

Help can also be used as a causative.

It means a person assists another person to do it.

See the following examples :

(a) I helped her to pack the luggage.

(b) Would you help me deliver this box?

The most common error with causatives is using 'to' unnecessarily. For example :

(a) We made Jack to finish his supper. *Incorrect*
We made Jack finish his supper. *Correct*

(b) I let Jim to clean up the mess. *Incorrect*
I let Jim clean up the mess. *Correct*

Linking Verbs or Notional Verbs

जब Auxiliary (helping) verbs किसी वाक्य में मुख्य verb को support नहीं करते है बल्कि मुख्य verb की तरह प्रयुक्त होते हैं तो उस स्थिति में इन्हें linking verb या Notional verbs कहा जाता है। जैसे :

(1) I <u>have</u> a book and a pencil.
(2) She <u>is</u> a beautiful girl.
(3) He <u>has</u> a table made of wood.
(4) You <u>do</u> your work now .
(5) She <u>was</u> sad.
(6) You <u>were</u> happy.
(7) He <u>is</u> my elder brother.
(8) He <u>is</u> a poor fellow.

उपरोक्त वाक्यों में underlined verbs, Linking verbs या Notional Verbs हैं।

A linking verb connects a subject and its complement. Linking verbs sometimes called copulas. Linking verbs are often forms of the verb 'to be' as above. But are sometimes verbs related to the five senses (look, sound,smell, feel, taste) and sometimes verbs that somehow reflect a state of being (appear, seem, become, grow, turn, prove, remain). What follows the linking verb will be either a noun complement or an adjective complement : ***See the following examples :***

(a) This room smells bad. *(b) I feel great.* *(c) A victory today seems unlikely.*

A handful of verbs that reflect a change in state of being are sometimes called resulting copulas. ***They, too, link a subject to predicate adjective.***

See the following sentences :

(a) His face turned purple.
(b) She became older.
(c) The dogs ran wild.
(d) The milk has gone sour.

Inchoative Verbs

Inchoative Verbs जो किसी कार्य के प्रारम्भ होने को व्यक्त करती है, Inchoative verbs कहलाती हैं।

The term inchoative verb is used for a verb that denotes the beginning, development or final stage, of a change of condition. **—Guide to patterns and usage in English by AS Hornby**

इस तरह की मुख्य Verbs हैं Get, Become, Grow etc.

My father is getting weaker.
He has become the richest man in the town.
It is growing dark.
It is getting dark.

इस तरह की अन्य verbs है : come, go, turn, fall, run, wear.

(a) The paper of the book turn yellow.
(b) Will his dream come true?
(c) Ram soon fell asleep.
(d) The carpet is wearing thin.
(e) The supply of water is running low now-a-days.

(A) Get : Inchoative verb—get का प्रयोग सर्वाधिक किया जाता है। Get का प्रयोग अधिकांश Continuous form में होता है। Get का प्रयोग निम्न structure में Adjective की Positive एवं Comparative degree के साथ तथा Participles के साथ किया जाता है। जैसे :

(a) Sugar is getting scarcer.
(b) It is getting dark.
(c) He is getting weaker.
(d) She is getting older.
(e) Ramesh often gets quarrelsome when he's been drinking.

Get का प्रयोग Continuous form में become के अर्थ में होता है। Past tense में (get का past got) यह किसी action की final stage को व्यक्त करता है।

(f) He is getting to be (= becoming) a good pianist. (g) He got to be (become) my best friend.
(h) They got to words and then to blows (*i.e.,* began) arguing and then fighting.

Get का प्रयोग कई phrases जैसे : get rid of, get clear of, get out of में सामान्यतया प्रचलन मे है।

(B) Become : Get की भाँति become का प्रयोग काफी प्रचलित है। Become का प्रयोग Adjective की Positive एवं Comparative degree के साथ तथा Participle के साथ निम्न sentence structure में किया जाता है :

(a) How did you become acquainted with her?
(b) He became suspicious.
(c) The leaves became red in autumn.
(d) The child became pale and thin.

'Become' का प्रयोग Noun के साथ भी होता है :

(a) On leaving school she became an actress.
(b) He soon became the richest man in the town.
(c) Are you likely ever to become a principal.

(C) Grow : Grow का प्रयोग भी get एवं become की तरह Adjective की positive एवं comparative degree के साथ तथा participle के साथ निम्न sentence structure में किया जाता है। जैसे :

(a) Time is growing short. (Time is getting short.)
(b) It is growing dark. (or It is getting dark or It is becoming dark.)
(c) The sea is growing calm.
(d) The child is growing thinner. (The child is getting thinner.)
(e) He is growing more and more like his father.

(D) Come : Come का प्रयोग adjective की positive एवं comparative degree के साथ तथा past participle की 'un' form (undone, unstitched, untied etc) के साथ किया जाता है। Past participle के साथ come का प्रयोग unsatisfactory or undesirable position को बताता है। जैसे :

(a) My dreams have come true.
(b) The hinge has come loose.
(c) The knot came untied.
(d) My shoe laces have come undone.
(e) The seam came unstitched.

Come का प्रयोग infinitive 'to' के साथ निम्न प्रकार होता है :

(a) How did she come to hear the news.
(b) When I came to know them better....
(c) Now-a-days the streets have come to be used as parking places for cars.
(d) She came to believe that......

(E) Go : Go का प्रयोग adjective के साथ एक निश्चित परिवर्तन को व्यक्त करता है जैसे :

(a) His hair has gone white.
(b) He went mad.
(c) She is going bald.
(d) Her cheeks went a very pretty pink.
(e) My telephone has gone dead.
(f) The milk went sour.

'Go' का प्रयोग कुछ prepositional phrases जैसे : go to bed, go to pieces में सामान्यतया प्रचलन में है।

(a) They started to go off the idea. (Go off—not like)
(b) He went to sleep. (fell asleep)
(c) She nearly went to pieces when her father died. (Fell to pieces—lost her control)

(F) Turn : Turn का प्रयोग adjective की positive एवं comparative degree के साथ निम्न structure में होता है :

(a) The weather has turned much colder.
(b) The oranges are turning red.
(c) The ink turns black when it dries.

Turn का प्रयोग nouns के साथ किया जाता है। ऐसी स्थिति में noun के साथ indefinite article का प्रयोग किया जाता है। जैसे :

(a) I believe you'll never turn traitor.
(b) Is it wise for a great general to turn politician?
(c) When her servant left, she had to turn cook. (become cook for the household)

(G) Run : Run का प्रयोग Adjectives, dry, low एवं short के साथ किया जाता है जो कि परिवर्तन को व्यक्त करता है। जैसे :

(a) The well has run dry. (No water)
(b) The cows are running dry. (not giving milk)
(c) Supplies are running short/low.

(H) Fall : का प्रयोग adjective की positive degree के साथ ही होता है। Comparative degree के साथ नहीं होता है। जैसे :

(a) He fell sick / ill.
(b) When do the taxes fall due ?
(c) The post of manager fell vacant.
(d) She soon fell asleep.

Fall का प्रयोग prepositional phrases जैसे : fall out of favour, fall behind the time, fall to pieces में भी प्रचलन में है।

Modals

Modals, Auxiliary verbs होती हैं, ये verb की mood (अवस्था/भाव) को व्यक्त करती हैं। Mood या modes एक ही बात है। चूँकि ये verbs के भाव, क्रियाविधि को व्यक्त करते हैं अत: इन्हें Modals कहा जाता है।

Modals की विशेषताएँ :

(1) इनका प्रयोग एक helping verb की तरह मुख्य क्रिया के साथ होता है।

(2) Modals पर कर्ता के Number; singular या plural होने, या कर्ता के person (I, II, III, person) का कोई प्रभाव नहीं पड़ता है। जैसे :

(a) I can do it.
(b) They can do it.
(c) He can do it.
(d) You can do it.

कर्ता चाहे Singular है या plural, first person है या second or third person, modal 'can' का रूप अपरिवर्तित रहता है जबकि अन्य helping verb (is, am, are etc.) कर्ता number एवं person के अनुसार अलग-अलग लगती है।

(3) Modals के साथ हमेशा verb की first form लगती है।

(4) Ought एवं used के बाद 'to' का प्रयोग आवश्यक है।

(5) कुछ modals जैसे need, dare, used का प्रयोग main verbs की तरह भी हो सकता है। अत: उन्हें marginal modals या semi-modals कहा जाता है।

Use of Modals

May/Might

May : इसका प्रयोग निम्न अवस्था हेतु किया जा सकता है :

(1) अनुमति (permission) माँगने एवं अनुमति देने के लिए। जैसे :

(a) May I go now? — *Permission* माँगना
Yes you may. — *Permission* देना
(b) May I borrow two books from the library? — *Permission* माँगना
You may borrow one book at a time. — *Permission* देना
(c) May I come in? — *Permission* माँगना
Yes you may. — *Permission* देना

(2) May का प्रयोग informal request हेतु किया जाता है। जैसे :

(a) May I have the salt, please?
(b) May I borrow your pen?

(3) May का प्रयोग किसी घटना के घटित होने की अनिश्चितता, सम्भावना के साथ व्यक्त करता है एवं Might प्रयोग एक Remote possibility को व्यक्त करता है। जैसे :

(a) The sky is cloudy, it may rain today. — *Possibility*
(b) The sky is not cloudy but a change in weather is always possible it might rain today. — *Remote possibility*
(c) He has purchased hundred tickets of lottery, he may win a prize. — *Possibility*
(d) He might win the first prize. — *Remote possibility*

इस तरह may का प्रयोग सम्भावना तथा might का प्रयोग दूरस्थ सम्भावना (Remote possibility) व्यक्त करता है।

(4) May का प्रयोग good wishes, desires हेतु किया जात है। जैसे :

(a) May God bless you ! (b) May you live long !

(5) Purpose व्यक्त करने के लिए भी may/might का प्रयोग किया जा सकता है। जैसे :

(a) We eat so that we may live.
(b) He works hard so that he may earn good livelihood.
(c) I play so that I may have good health. (d) They died so that we might live.

(6) आश्चर्य व्यक्त करने एवं जानकारी हेतु भी may का प्रयोग निम्न प्रकार होता है :

(a) Who may be my friend here? (आश्चर्य)
(b) How old she may be? (जानकारी)
(c) When may we expect you? (जानकारी हेतु किया जाता है।)

Might

(1) Might का request हेतु प्रयोग more politeness व्यक्त करता है। यह वक्ता की hesitation, आत्मविश्वास की कमी एवं request के स्वीकार न होने की स्थिति को व्यक्त करता है। जैसे :

(a) Might I borrow your golden necklace? (b) Might I talk to the P.M.?
(c) Might I borrow your car?

(2) Might, may का past tense भी है। Might का प्रयोग present tense में भी हो सकता है। Direct से Indirect narration में परिवर्तन करते समय may को might में बदला जाता है।

(a) He asked if he might come in. (b) He said that it might rain that day.
(b) Might I borrow your sofa set ?

(3) May एवं might का perfect tense में प्रयोग :

(a) He may have been wounded. (We do not know so far, but he is perhaps injured, possibility exists)
(b) He has not arrived so far. He may have taken a wrong way. (We don't know the actual position, but as he has not arrived so far, so the possibility is that he may have taken a wrong way.)
(c) He might have been wounded. [that was a possibility in the past. (but he was not wounded)] इसका अर्थ है कि वह घायल हो सकता था।
(d) You might have invited me to your wedding. (but you didn't invite.)
(e) She might have come, if we asked her. (but we didn't ask her.)

Perfect tense में may का प्रयोग, वर्तमान में एक सम्भावना को व्यक्त करता है। जबकि might का प्रयोग past में किसी घटना के घटित होने की संभावना (जो वास्तव में घटित नहीं हुई) को बताता है।

Can

(1) Can का प्रश्न में प्रयोग, वक्ता का आश्चर्य (Astonishment), अधीरता (Impatience) क्रोध (Anger) को दर्शाता है जैसे :

(a) What can he do? (b) What can she say, I wonder?
(c) Where can he go? (d) How can she resign?

(2) Can का प्रयोग परिस्थितिजन्य सम्भावना (Circumstantial possibility) को व्यक्त करता है। जैसे :

(a) You can ski on the hills now-a-days. (As there is enough snow.)
(b) You can go there by road now. (As the road is ok now.)

(3) Can का प्रयोग शारीरिक क्षमता (Physical capacity), योग्यता (Capability) मानसिक एवं ज्ञान के कारण योग्यता (Mental ability) को व्यक्त करता है। जैसे :

(a) I can solve this puzzle. (b) Can you lift this suitcase?
(c) He can read without glasses. (d) Can you speak French?

(4) Can का प्रयोग परिस्थितिजन्य योग्यता या दूसरे व्यक्ति की योग्यता (Capacity, capability) हेतु भी किया जाता है। जैसे :

(a) Can you lend me ten lac rupees?
(Are you in a position to do so ? Are you having this much amount surplus?)

(b) Can you attend the meeting tomorrow?
(Are you free tomorrow?)

May and Can

(1) Permission हेतु may एवं Can का प्रयोग First person के साथ निम्न प्रकार होता है :
I/We के साथ can का बहुत common प्रयोग है।

(a) I can meet the chairman whenever I want. (It means I have already been granted permission.)

(b) I can purchase stationery items whenever I need. (It means I have already been given authority.)

यद्यपि इस तरह के वाक्यों में may का भी प्रयोग किया जा सकता है। जैसे :
I may purchase stationery items whenever I need.
I may meet the chairman whenever I want.
लकिन ऐसे वाक्यों में may की अपेक्षा can का प्रयोग अधिक प्रचलित है।

(2) Second Person के साथ may का प्रयोग तब किया जाता है जब वक्ता (speaker) द्वारा अनुमति दी गई हो। जैसे :
You may park your vehicle here.
(इसका अर्थ हुआ कि I give you permission to park your vehicle here. It does not mean that you have authority to park your vehicle here.)

Can का प्रयोग II person के साथ उसकी authority को व्यक्त करता है। जैसे :
You can park your vehicle here.
(You have authority to park your vehicle here.)

Can का इस तरह प्रयोग, I allow you / the police allow you / you have an authority or a right to park your vehicle here के अर्थ में होता है। इसी तरह You can take rest in library room.
इसका अर्थ हुआ You have an authority/A competent authority has allowed you.

(3) Third Person के साथ may का प्रयोग Speaker द्वारा दी गई permission को व्यक्त करता है। जैसे :
He may take my umbrella. He may take my scooter.
इस तरह के वाक्यों का अर्थ हुआ कि I give him permission.......
ऐसे वाक्यों में Can का प्रयोग भी किया जा सकता है।
He can take my car. He can use my phone.
यहाँ Can का अर्थ subject की authority व्यक्त करता है अर्थात उसे car या phone हेतु कोई Formal Permission की आवश्यकता नहीं है। Relation इतने informal एवं close हैं।

Difference Between 'May' and 'Can'

(a) In certain circumstances an officer may ask a driver to take a vision test.

(b) An officer can ask a driver to take a vision test.

(c) If allowed, an accused person may appeal against the judgement of High court.

(d) An accused person can appeal against the judgement of High court in criminal cases.

'May' shows the authority given by someone else. 'Can' shows authority lying with the subject.

Difference Between 'May NOT' and 'CAN NOT'

May not का प्रयोग Improbability (सम्भावना नहीं लेकिन है भी) को व्यक्त करता है। जबकि cannot का प्रयोग असम्भावना (Impossibility) को व्यक्त करता है। जैसे :

(a) The news may not be true. (may or may not be true.)
(b) The news cannot be true. (There is no possibility of its coming out to be true.)
(c) You may go from A to B, by changing train at C or you may go by way of D, but you cannot go direct. (As there is no direct route from A to B.)
(d) You cannot go there by water. (As there is no water route.)

Can/Could

(1) Can एवं Could दोनों का प्रयोग Request हेतु किया जा सकता है। Could से more politeness जाहिर होती है। जैसे :
(a) Can you give me your umbrella?
(b) Could you lend me your sofa set?
(c) Could you please send me an application form? (Could you is a very good way of introducing a request. It is an alternative to would you ? And a little more polite.

A Practical English Grammar —Thomson and Martin

(2) Could का प्रयोग past ability को व्यक्त करता है। जैसे :
(a) When I was young, I could climb any tree.
(b) When Ram was young, he could swim across this river.

(3) Could का प्रयोग वर्तमान में आवश्यकता (Necessity), क्षमता (ability) के सन्दर्भ में निम्न प्रकार किया जाता है :
(a) Could you run the business by yourself ? (If it becomes necessary.)
(b) Could you get another job? (If you are terminated from here.)

(4) Could का प्रयोग present perfect में एक ऐसी past possibility को व्यक्त करता है जो पूर्ण नहीं हुई। जैसे :
(a) He could have caught the train, if he had hurried. (But he didn't catch the train.)
(b) He could have done it without much problem. (But he didn't do it.)
(c) He could have sent a message. (But he didn't send.)

(5) Can के past tense के रूप में could का प्रयोग होता है। जैसे :
(a) Ramesh told me that he could lend me his umbrella.
(b) I did all that I could.

(6) काल्पनिक (Unreal) conditions में could का प्रयोग निम्न प्रकार होता है :
(a) If I had more money, I could build a temple.
(b) If I had wings, I could fly to Himalayas.

Shall /Will

(1) Traditional Grammar के अनुसार I/we (I person) के साथ Shall तथा II, III person के साथ will का प्रयोग मान्य है।

(2) I person (I/we) के साथ जब will का प्रयोग तथा II and III person के साथ जब shall का प्रयोग किया जाता है तो वह determination, threat, warning, promise को व्यक्त करता है।

आजकल will/shall के प्रयोग मे उक्त अन्तर लगभग समाप्त हो गया है। लेकिन हमें Modals के संदर्भ में Traditional Grammar के अनुसार ही चलना है।

Shall

(1) Shall का प्रयोग I person के साथ एक सामान्य future action को व्यक्त करता है। II एवं III person के साथ shall का प्रयोग Promise, Determination, threat, warning को व्यक्त करता है। जैसे :

(a) I shall go to market tommorrow. — *Future action*
(b) He shall pay you on Monday. — *Promise*
(c) He shall work hard to achieve success. — *Determination*
(d) Anyone find involved shall be punished. — *Warning, threat*
(e) You shall be transferred if you don't work properly. — *Warning, threat*
(f) We shall play hockey. — *Future action*

(2) II एवं III person के साथ shall का प्रयोग Determination, Compulsion, Bindings, एक force व्यक्त करता है। जैसे :

(a) You shall go to meet him tomorrow. (You are instructed to go and meet him.)
(b) She shall complete her work by tomorrow. (She has to complete her work by tomorrow.)

(3) 'Shall not' का II एवं III person के साथ प्रयोग prohibition (निषेध) को व्यक्त करता है। जैसे :

(a) You shall not meet him.
(b) Nobody shall write on the table.
(c) She shall not attend the night party.

(4) Shall का I person के साथ एक प्रश्न के रूप में प्रयोग, दूसरे की इच्छा जानने हेतु या अपनी सेवाएँ देने हेतु किया जाता है। जैसे :

(a) Shall I open the door?
(b) Shall I carry this box into the room for you?
(c) Shall I thread the needle for you?
(d) Shall I assist you?

(5) Shall का III person के साथ प्रयोग या एक noun के साथ प्रयोग दूसरे की इच्छनुसार कार्य करने को व्यक्त करता है। जैसे :

(a) Shall Rahim wait for you? (Do you want him to wait for you?)
(b) Shall the messenger wait outside? (Do you want the messenger to wait outside?)

Will

(1) Will का प्रयोग II and III person के साथ सामान्य future action को बताता है, जबकि I person के साथ will का प्रयोग Threat, warning, promise, determination को व्यक्त करता है। जैसे :

(a) He will go tomorrow.
(b) You will work here.
(c) I will see you. — *Threat, warning*
(d) I will pay you on Monday. — *Promise*
(e) I will achieve my goal. — *Determination*
(f) I will never speak to him. — *Determination*

(2) Will का प्रयोग प्रश्न के रूप में formal request को व्यक्त करता है। जैसे :

(a) Will you close the door?
(b) Will you bring me a glass of water?

(3) 'Will' का प्रयोग सभी persons के साथ सम्भावना (probability) व्यक्त करता है। Will not (won't) का प्रयोग refusal (इन्कार) को व्यक्त करता है। जैसे :

(a) I won't go there.
(b) He will not sanction your leave.
(c) He will be in the park.
(d) Today is 15th August schools will be closed.

(4) Won't (will not) का प्रयोग जब प्रश्न के रूप में किया जाता है तो यह Invitation को व्यक्त करता है। जैसे :

(a) Won't you have a cup of tea?
(b) Won't you meet her?
(c) Won't you stay for a day?

(5) Will का प्रयोग Instructions, command को भी व्यक्त करता है। जैसे :

(a) All the cadets will attend the parade. *Instructions, command*
(b) The girls will not wear the shorts. *Instructions, command*
(c) You will deliver the welcome speech. *Instructions, command*

(6) 'Will' का प्रयोग III person के साथ सामान्य आदत को व्यक्त करता है। जैसे :

(a) The women will not keep mum. *Habit*
(b) The girls will talk. *Habit*
(c) He will smoke. *Habit*
(d) The minister will come late. *Habit*

Should/Would

Should

(1) Should का प्रयोग Duty (कर्त्तव्य), Responsibility (जिम्मेदारी), Advice (सलाह) Probability (सम्भावना) Expectation (आशा) Presumption (पूर्व अनुमान) Moral obligation (नैतिक दायित्व) Mild command (नम्र आदेश) व्यक्त करता है। जैसे :

(a) One should obey one's elders. *Duty*
(b) You should obey your parents. *Moral obligation*
(c) The rich should help the poor. *Expectation*
(d) You should work hard. *Advice*
(e) You should find her in the play-ground. *Probability*
(f) You should take care of your health. *Advice*
(g) You should take care of your brief case. *Responsibilily*
(h) You should complete your work everyday. *Mild command*
(i) He should be reading now. *Probability*
(j) He should be worried about me. *Presumption*
(k) They should be anxious about us. *Presumption*

(2) Conditional sentences में lest के साथ हमेशा should का प्रयोग किया जाता है। यह एक Important use है। जैसे :

(a) Move fast lest you should miss the bus. जल्दी चलो कहीं तुम्हारी बस न छूट जाये।
(b) Work hard lest you should fail. मेहनत, करो, कहीं ऐसा न हो कि तुम फेल हो जाओ।

Lest का अर्थ कहीं ऐसा न हो कि होता है।

(3) Should का प्रयोग purpose व्यक्त करने हेतु किया जाता है, तब वह may व्यक्त करते हुए किया जाता है, तब वह एवं might के अर्थ को समान रखता है। जैसे :

(a) I taught her so that she should pass. (She might pass.)
(b) I scolded him so that he should work hard. (He might work hard.)

(4) Should का Perfect Tense में प्रयोग इस तथ्य को स्पष्ट करता है कि जो कार्य जिस रूप में किया जाना चाहिये था, वह नहीं किया गया। जैसे :

(a) He should have gone by morning bus. (but he didn't go.)
(b) She should have informed me about the incident. (but she didn't inform me.)
(c) Ramesh should have submitted the bills. (but he didn't submit.)

Would

(1) Would का प्रयोग will की अपेक्षा अधिक polite request को बताता है। Request हेतु will को अपेक्षा would का प्रयोग अधिक मान्य है। Would का प्रयोग दूसरे की इच्छा (Willingness) जानने हेतु भी किया जाता है। जैसे :

(a) Would you accompany me to the railway station? *Polite request*
(b) Would you send me an application form? *Polite request*
(c) Would you sing at the concert tomorrow? *Willingness query*

(2) Would का प्रयोग likelihood, presumption ,एवं probability को भी व्यक्त करता है। जैसे :

(a) He would be in the field. *Likelihood*
(b) She would be in the club at this time. *Probability*
(c) She would be cooking now. *Likelihood*
(d) She would be about 80 now. *Presumption*

(3) Rather के साथ would का प्रयोग preference (प्राथमिकता) को व्यक्त करता है। जैसे :

(a) I would rather rest now.
(b) I would rather study than see a movie.
(c) I would rather play than rest now.

(4) 'Wish' के साथ 'will' का प्रयोग नहीं किया जाता है। wish के साथ would का प्रयोग strong desire /willingness स्पष्ट करता है। जैसे :

(a) I wish you would fight this election.
(b) I wish you would support her fully.
(c) I wish they would agree to this proprosal.

(5) Unreal (काल्पनिक) परिस्थितियों को व्यक्त करने हेतु भी would का प्रयोग conditional sentences में किया जाता है। जैसे :

(a) If I had one crore rupees, I would donate fifty lacs to the trust
(b) If I had wings I would fly to Europe.
(c) If I were the king, I would make you any chief adviser.
(d) If a tiger came into the room, what would you do?

(6) Conditional sentences में past perfect के sentences में would का प्रयोग किसी कार्य के past में न होने को व्यक्त करता है। जैसे :

(a) If he had come to me, I would have given him a job. (He didn't come.)
यदि वह मेरे पास आता तो मैं उसे नौकरी दे देता।
(b) If she had asked me, I would have helped her. (But she didn't ask me.)
यदि वह मुझे कहती तो मैं उसकी सहायता करता।

(7) Would —'will' का past है, Direct से Indirect narration में परिवर्तन करते समय reporting verb past में होने पर will को would में बदलते हैं। जैसे :

(a) He told me that he would go to Jaipur the next day.
(b) He told me that she would not agree to the proposal.

Important

Should, could,would, might का प्रयोग past tense SJeb present tense दोनों में किया जाता है लेकिन shall, will, may ,can का प्रयोग past tense में नहीं किया जाता है। कई बार परीक्षाओं में प्रश्न will/would, shall/should, may/might, can/ could,के reference में आते हैं। इस बिन्दु का ध्यान रखकर answer लिखें।

Must

Must का प्रयोग present time एवं future time दोनों प्रकार के Actions हेतु किया जा सकता है। Must का कोई past tense नहीं होता है। Reported speech में direct से indirect में परिवर्तन करते समय कई स्थितियों में इसे 'had to' में भी परिवर्तित किया जाता है। जैसे :

(1) Must का प्रयोग command, compulsion, order (निर्देश, दबाव, आदेश) का भाव दर्शाता हैं जैसे :
- (a) Soldiers must obey orders without any question.
- (b) All the girls must attend the function.
- (c) You must do as you are told.

(2) Must से moral duty/obligation भी व्यक्त होता है। जैसे :
- (a) We must respect our elders.
- (b) You must help your friends in need.

(3) Must से necessity, urgency, circumstantial compulsion (जरूरत, आवश्यकता, परिस्थिति दबाव) भी व्यक्त होता है। जैसे :
- (a) I must leave now otherwise I may miss the train.
- (b) The electricity will be cut off at 9 A.M. so I must complete my work before.

(4) 'Must not' का प्रयोग prohibition, Emphatic advice (निषेध एवं दबाव मुक्त सलाह) हेतु भी किया जाता है जैसे :
- (a) Students must not resort to copying. *Prohibition*
- (b) You must not miss the classes. *Emphatic advice*
- (c) You must not talk to that fellow. *Prohibition*
- (d) Visitors must not feed the animals. *Prohibition*

(5) Must से strong probability/likelihood भी व्यक्त किया जाता है। जैसे :
- (a) She must be eighty now.
- (b) They have not arrived so far. They must have taken a wrong turning.

(6) जब प्रश्न must से शुरू किया जाता हैं एवं उसका Answer यदि affirmative में हो तो must का प्रयोग किया जाता है, लेकिन यदि Answer, Negative में दिया जाये तो Needn't का प्रयोग करना चाहिए। जैसे :

(a) Must I attend the meeting ?
Yes, you must .
No, you needn't.

(b) Must I raise the issue in the board meeting?
Yes, you must.
No, you need not.

(7) Must का perfect tense में प्रयोग भूतकाल में किसी कार्य के होने की प्रबल सम्भावना को व्यक्त करता है।
- (a) He must have passed the test in first attempt.
- (b) They must have reached there in time.

Need

Need का प्रयोग Ordinary verb एवं Modal Auxiliary verb दोनों की तरह किया जा सकता हैं। इसीलिए इसे **Semi-Modal** या **Marginal Modal** कहा जाता है। जैसे :

(1) Modal के रूप में need का प्रयोग सामान्यतया Interrogative एवं Negative वाक्यों में किया जाता है।
- (a) He need not talk to her.
- (b) Need he talk to her?
- (c) You needn't wear a tie.
- (d) Need I wear a tie?

(2) Perfect tense में needn't का प्रयोग ऐसे कार्य को व्यक्त करता है जो वास्तव में नहीं किया जाना ही उचित था। Needn't का अर्थ होता है। आवश्यक नहीं होना या जरूरत नहीं होना । जैसे :
- (a) He needn't have written such a detailed essay. (The essay was to be written in 300 words only.)
- (b) You needn't have bought such a costly gift. (waste of money)
- (c) You needn't have written to him, as he phoned me shortly. (but you had written, thus wasting of time.)
- (d) They needn't have left home at 8.00, the train doesn't arrive till 10.00 (So they will have two hours to wait.)

(3) जब need से कोई प्रश्न किया जाता है एवं उसका Answer यदि affirmative में है तो must प्रयोग किया जाना चाहिए। Negative में Answer हेतु needn't का प्रयोग होता है। जैसे :

Need I go there?
Yes, you must.
No, you needn't.

(4) Principal verb की तरह need का प्रयोग निम्न प्रकार से होता है :

(a) He needs my assistance.
(b) I need your help.
(c) He needed my help.
(d) He does not need my help.
(e) I do not need your advice is the matter.
(f) He did nct need my assistance.
(g) Does he need my help?
(h) Do you need my help?

जब need का प्रयोग principal verb की तरह होता है तो सामान्यतया इसके Affirmative sentences में जरूरत या आवश्यकता (meaning) के सन्दर्भ में होता है। Need का principal verb की तरह प्रयोग जब Negative में या Interrogative में किया जाता है तो Do, Does, Did का प्रयोग Ordinary verb की तरह करते हैं।

Used to

इसका उच्चारण यूज्ड टू होता है। यह भी एक Marginal or Semi-Modal है। Used to का Negative form used not to होता है। Used to के negative हेतु didn't use to का भी प्रयोग किया जाता है। इसी तरह used to को Interrogative में प्रयोग करते समय used को Did + subject + use to + verb की तरह भी प्रयोग किया जा सकता है।

(1) Used to का प्रयोग यह व्यक्त करता है कि भूतकाल में कोई कार्य आदतन किया जाता था लेकिन अब नहीं किया जाता है। जैसे:

(a) He used to drink daily. (Now he does not drink.)
(b) I used to smoke one packet of cigarettes. (Now I do not smoke.)
(c) He used to go for a walk. (Now he does not go for a walk.)

(2) Used to का वर्तमान से अभ्यस्त (accustomed) के सन्दर्भ में प्रयोग निम्न प्रकार किया जाता है :

(a) I am used to take tea in the morning .
मैं सुबह चाय पीने का अभ्यस्त हूँ।
(b) He is used to read the newspaper with morning tea.
वह सुबह चाय के साथ अखबार पढ़ने का आदी है।
(c) He would soon used to live at Mumbai.
(d) I am used to cooler's noise.

(3) Used to का Negative एवं Interrogative में प्रयोग निम्न प्रकार किया जा सकता है :

(a) I used not to smoke daily. *Negative*
Or I did not use to smoke earlier. *Negative*
(b) He used to play chess at college. *Affirmative*
He didn't use to play chess at college. *Negative*
Used he to play chess at college ? *Interrogative*
Did he use to play chess at college? *Interrogative*

For making negative of such sentences we can use either 'used not to' or 'did not use to'. In interrogative sentences we can use either 'Used + subject + to' or 'Did + subject + use + to' structure as shown above.

Dare

Dare का प्रयोग Principal Verb एवं Modal verb दोनों प्रकार से होता है इसलिए dare को भी **Marginal modal or Semi modal** कहा जाता है।

Use of Dare as Modal

(1) Dare का modal की तरह प्रयोग सामान्यतया Negative एवं Interrogative sentences में होता हैं जब इसका Modal की तरह प्रयोग होता है। तो इसके साथ 'to' का प्रयोग नहीं होता है। dare का अर्थ होता है, दु:साहस करना, चुनौती देना। जैसे :

(a) He dare not say like this.
(b) I dare not talk to the chairman.
(c) Dare he not say like this ?
(d) Dare I talk to the chairman?
(e) He dare not oppose you.
(f) Dare he oppose you?
(g) Dare she complain against you?
(h) She dare not complain against you.

(2) How के साथ dare का प्रयोग वक्ता का आश्चर्य, गुस्सा एवं सदमा (surprise, anger or shock) व्यक्त करता है। जैसे :

(a) How dare you speak like this ?
(b) How dare my wife leave without my permission?
(c) How dare you act in this manner?
(d) How dare he say so ?

(3) Nobody, anybody, एवं somebody etc. के साथ जब dare का प्रयोग modal की तरह किया जाता है, तो इसके साथ 'to' का प्रयोग भी किया जा सकता है एवं नहीं भी किया जा सकता है। जैसे :

(a) Nobody dare to comment like that.
(b) Nobody dare comment like that.
(c) Somebody dare complain in the matter.
(d) Somebody dare to complain in the matter.

(4) Daresay का अर्थ होता है शायद, सम्भवतया (perhaps, it is expected, I expect) Daresay का प्रयोग I के साथ ही किया जाता हैं जैसे :

(a) I daresay he will come.
(b) I daresay she may agree.
(c) I dare say it will rain
(d) I daresay they will be happy to get this news.

Daresay को साथ-साथ एवं अलग-अलग (dare say) दोनों प्रकार से लिखा जा सकता है।

(5) Dare का प्रयोग जब Principal Verb की तरह किया जाता है तो इसके साथ 'to' का प्रयोग किया जाता है। Singular number, third person: subject के साथ 's' लगाया जाता है एवं Do, Does का प्रयोग Negative एवं Interrogative वाक्यों में किया जाता है। जैसे :

(a) He dares to oppose you.
(b) He does not dare to oppose you.
(c) Does he dare to oppose you?
(d) Do you dare to speak against him?
(e) You do not dare to speak against him.
(f) We do not dare to talk to the president.

Ought to

Ought के साथ हमेशा 'to' लगता हैं। **Ought to** एवं **should** का प्रयोग एवं अर्थ लगभग समान हैं।

(1) Ought to का प्रयोग Advice (सलाह) moral obligation (नैतिक दायित्व), Duty (कर्त्तव्य) को व्यक्त करता है। जैसे :

(a) You ought to consult a physician. *Advice*
(b) We ought to respect our parents. *Moral duty*
(c) We ought to help our friends. *Moral obligation*
(d) You ought to follow the advice of the doctor. *Advice*

(2) Ought के साथ not का प्रयोग किसी दायित्व को पूर्ण न करने के सन्दर्भ में किया जाता है या Advice के रूप में किया जाता हैं जैसे :

(a) You ought not to treat your friends like this.
(b) Children ought not to watch T.V. so long.
(c) You ought not to talk to the elders in this manner.
(d) You ought not to smoke so much.

(3) Ought to का perfect tense में प्रयोग व्यक्त करता है कि जो कार्य सम्पन्न होना चाहिए था वह कार्य नहीं किया गया। जैसे :

(a) She ought to have invited him in the function. (But she didn't invite him.)
(b) He ought to have helped him in that matter. (But he didn't help him.)
(c) He ought to have opposed the move. (But he didn't oppose.)
(d) They ought to have come in time. (But they didn't come in time.)
(e) You ought to have stopped at the traffic light. (But you didn't stop.)

(4) सामान्यतया ought to एवं should को समान अर्थ एवं समान प्रयोग के सन्दर्भ में एक जैसा माना जाता है लेकिन formal notices या अन्य कोई सूचना के लिए 'should' का प्रयोग किया जाता है, 'ought' का हीं जैसे :

(a) Students should be prepared to donate the blood.
(b) Travellers should be in possession of the following documents.
(c) On hearing the alarm bell, the students should leave their rooms immediately.

उपरोक्त वाक्यों में 'Ought to' **का प्रयोग ही होगा।**

(5) Ought to का प्रयोग Present, Past, Future tense में समान रूप से हो सकता है। जैसे :

(a) I ought to talk to him today.
(b) I ought to talk to him tomorrow.
(c) I know I ought to talk to him.
(d) I know I ought to have talked to him.

Sentences Expressing Commands, Requests, Invitations, Advice, Suggestions and Wishes

(निर्देश, आदेश, प्रार्थना, निमंत्रण, सलाह, सुझाव एवं इच्छा व्यक्त करने वाले वाक्य)

Commands

Commands व्यक्त करने हेतु विभिन्न Sentence Structures का प्रयोग किया जा सकता है। जैसे :

(1) Imperative Sentence :

(A) निम्न प्रकार के imperative वाक्य, निर्देश/आदेश व्यक्त करने हेतु प्रयुक्त होते हैं। जैसे :

(a) Do your work.
(b) Do hurry.
(c) Don't make a noise.
(d) Complete your work.
(e) Eat your dinner, boys.
(f) Be quite, Ritu.

(B) Let से शुरू होने वाले Imperative Sentence भी Command को व्यक्त करते है। जैसे :

(a) Let us go there.
(b) Let us not be alarmed by rumours.
(c) Let us work together in this emergency.
(d) Let them go by Jeep.

(C) Third Person के साथ subject + Shall का मुख्य रूप से Written regulations में Command हेतु प्रयुक्त होता है। जैसे :

(a) Girls shall enter the names of their guests in the register. *Hostel Rules*
(b) The account of the society shall be operated jointly by the President and the treasurer. *Regulations of society*
(c) The President and the Secretary shall be elected every year. *Regulations of society*

(D) Subject + will का प्रयोग Third person के साथ Command हेतु निम्न प्रकार किया जाता है।'will' का प्रयोग सामान्यतया तब होता है जब Command देने वाले व्यक्ति को यह विश्वास होता हैं कि उसकी आज्ञा का पालन होगा। अधिकांशतया 'will' का प्रयोग Written Instructions हेतु एक authority द्वारा किया जाता है। जैसे :

(a) The captain will report the arrival of his team to the Sports officer. *Principal*

(b) The officers will attend the Republic Day function positively. *Secretary*

आपस की बातचीत में II person के साथ भी will का प्रयोग command हेतु प्रयुक्त होता है।

(c) You will not mention my name to anybody.
(d) You will not disclose your identity to her.

(E) 'Must का प्रयोग भी command हेतु किया जाता है। जैसे :

(a) You must not smoke at the public place.
(b) The police must assist the passengers in getting out of the drowned coaches.
(c) Dogs must be kept on leads in this area.

(F) Command हेतु 'to be' form of verb का प्रयोग निम्न प्रकार किया जा सकता है :

(a) You are to report for further duties to the C.O.
(b) This railway crossing is to be manned at all times.
(c) You are to deposit entry fees first.

Requests

Requests हेतु may/might/can/could आदि का प्रयोग I/We (Ist person) के साथ निम्न प्रकार किया जाता है:

(A) **May/Might** :

(a) May I have a photocopy of this page?
(b) May I have your pen, please ?
(c) Might I use / borrow your sofa set, please?
(d) Might I talk to the Chairman ?

Might का प्रयोग more politeness व्यक्त करता हैं यह वक्ता की hesitation एव आत्मविश्वास की कमी तथा Request को स्वीकार न होने जैसी स्थिति को व्यक्त करता है।

(B) **Can/Could** :

Can का प्रयोग Informal way में किया जा सकता है। जैसे :

(a) "Can I have an apple?" said the little boy.
(b) "Can I take one more chocolate ?" asked the baby.

Could का प्रयोग more politeness व्यक्त करता है।

(a) Could I have a cup of tea?
(b) Could I use your phone?
(c) Could I see Mr. Ram?

(C) Could का प्रयोग II person के साथ Request हेतु किया जा सकता है। जैसे :

(a) Could you please show me the way to the hospital?
(b) Could you lend me ₹ 500/- ?

"Could you is a very good way of introducing a request. It is an alternative to would you and a little more polite."

–A Practical English Grammar—Thomson and Martin.

(D) **Will/Would**

Will का प्रयोग formal request हेतु निम्न प्रकार किया जाता है :

(a) Will you shut the door? (b) Will you bring a glass?

Would का प्रयोग 'will' की अपेक्षा अधिक Politeness को व्यक्त करता है। Request हेतु will की जगह would का प्रयोग अधिक उपयुक्त है। जैसे :

(a) Would you deposit my application at the bank? (b) Would you accompany me to the hospital?
(c) Would you be kind enough to keep me informed? (d) Would you please count your amount ?

Invitations

Will/would : Will/would का प्रयोग Invitations हेतु निम्न प्रकार किया जाता है। जैसे :

(a) Will you have a cup of tea? (b) Would you like a cup of hot coffee?
(c) Won't you come in ? (d) Won't you have a cup of tea?
(e) Won't you have a coffee?

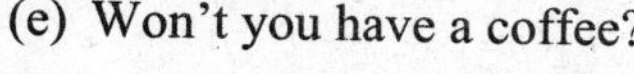

उक्त वाक्य प्रश्न की तरह प्रयुक्त नहीं हो रहे हैं बल्कि एक Invitation को व्यक्त करते हैं जबकि Do you want a cup of tea? एक Invitation नहीं है। इसी तरह निम्न वाक्य भी प्रश्न की तरह लगाते हैं लेकिन Invitation को व्यक्त करते हैं।

Advices

(A) Should, Ought to एवं Must का प्रयोग Advices हेतु निम्न प्रकार किया जाता है :

(a) You should improve your vocabulary. (b) You ought to clean your car.
(c) You must learn this lesson, it is important.

Should एवं Ought to का प्रयोग समान अर्थ में होता है जबकि Must का प्रयोग Emphatic advice या आवश्यकता को व्यक्त करता है।

(B) 'Had better' का प्रयोग भी सलाह हेतु निम्न प्रकार किया जाता हैं :

(a) You had better change your dress. (b) You had better not wait any longer.
(c) He had better stop gambling now. (d) He had better stop taking drugs.

(C) If I were का प्रयोग should/would के साथ निम्न Structure में सलाह हेतु किया जाता है :

(a) If I were you I would buy this house.
इसका अर्थ हुआ कि He advised me to buy that house.

(b) If I were you I would/should lodge an FIR against her.
इस वाक्य का अर्थ हुआ कि : He advised me to lodge an FIR against her.

(D) Why don't you .... का प्रयोग भी सलाह या सुझाव हेतु प्रयुक्त किया जा सकता है :

(a) Why don't you meet the Chairman?
(b) Why don't you take a leave?

इस तरह वाक्य वक्ता ही सलाह/सुझाव को व्यक्त करते है।

(E) It is time you + Past tense का प्रयोग भी सलाह/सुझाव हेतु प्रयुक्त किया जाता है :

It is time you bought a new shirt. It is time you bought a new car.

इन वाक्यों का अर्थ हुआ कि
He said it was time I bought a new shirt/car.
ये वाक्य सलाह/सुझाव के रूप में व्यक्त हैं।

Suggestions

(A) Suggestions सुझाव हेतु let का प्रयोग काफी प्रचलन में है :

(a) Let us clean the house.
(b) Let us play football.
(c) Let us go to temple.
(d) Let's not watch TV now.
(e) Let's not sleep so early.

(B) Why not एवं Why don't का प्रयोग भी Suggestion हेतु निम्न प्रकार किया जाता है :

(a) Why don't we discuss this point again?
(b) Why don't we meet tomorrow and settle the things?
(c) Why not meet and finalise the things?
(d) Why not inform everything to the parents?

(C) What about का प्रयोग भी Suggestion हेतु किया जा सकता है :

(a) What about having a drink?
(b) What about meeting the chairman?

ये वाक्य सुझाव को व्यक्त करते हैं।

Wishes

(A) 'Wishes' हेतु 'May' का प्रयोग निम्न प्रकार किया जाता है :

(a) May God grant you success !
(b) May God bless you !
(c) May you have a pleasant journey!

(B) इसी प्रकार निम्न Sentences द्वारा भी Wishes को व्यक्त किया जाता है :

(a) God save the queen!
(b) Long live the king!
(c) God bless you!

(C) साधारणतया निम्न वाक्यों द्वारा भी 'wishes' को व्यक्त किया जाता है :

(a) Well, have a pleasant stay !
(b) Enjoy yourself !
(c) Good Night, have a sound sleep !

(D) Verb, 'wish का प्रयोग निम्न प्रकार के Sentence Structure में किया जाता हैं। यदि 'Wish', present or future time के सन्दर्भ में की गई हैं तो 'wish' के साथ clause में Past tense का प्रयोग होगा। जैसे :

I wish I knew how to operate it. (but I don't know.)
I wish I knew her address. (but I don't know her address.)
I wish I were rich. (I am not rich.)

'Wish' के साथ Clause में Past perfect tense का प्रयोग, अपूरित (Unfulfilled) इच्छा को व्यक्त करता है। जैसे :

I wish I had known how to operate it. (I didn't know.)
I wish I could help you. (I didn't help you.)
I wish I could pay your dues. (I didn't pay your dues.)

(E) Exclamatory वाक्यों में If only का प्रयोग भी 'wish' को व्यक्त करता है। ध्यान करें 'that' का प्रयोग If only के बाद कभी नहीं किया जाता है। जैसे :

If only the rain would stop! (I wish the rain would stop!)
If only I knew her address!
If only I had known her address!

(F) 'Wish' का प्रयोग infinitive 'to' के साथ सामान्यतया निम्न Structure में होता है। जैसे :

(a) Where do you wish me to stay?
(b) What do they wish me to cook?
(c) What do they wish/want me to do?

(G) Wish का प्रयोग preposition 'for' के साथ निम्न प्रकार किया जाता है। यहाँ 'wish for' का प्रयोग "feel or express a desire for" के अर्थ में होता है। जैसे :

(a) What do you wish for? said the Jenie.
(b) I have everything that man can wish for.
(c) He had everything that a man could wish for.

(H) वाक्यों में if clause के साथ 'will' का प्रयोग नहीं किया जाता है। जैसे :

If he will come, I will accompany him. *Incorrect*
If he comes, I will accompany him. *Correct*

Important Use of Will

लेकिन if clause के साथ will का प्रयोग दूसरे की willingness को जानने हेतु request हेतु या आग्रह (insistence) हेतु *निम्न प्रकार किया जा सकता है*:

If you will help me,we can finish by six. (If you will be so kind as to help me.)
If you'd help me (if you'd be so kind as to help me), we could finish by six.

यहाँ will एक auxiliary की तरह प्रयुक्त नहीं हुआ है बल्कि यह एक verb की तरह, दूसरे की willingness को जानने के लिए प्रयुक्त है।

"When will is not an auxiliary for the future tense but a verb indicating or asking about willingness, it may occur in an if clause. **Guide to Patterns and Usage in English by A.S Horndy. Page 232**

इसी तरह Will एवं would का प्रयोग जब insist के अर्थ में होता है तब भी ये if clause के साथ प्रयुक्त हो सकते हैं जैसे :

(a) If you will bet (If you insist on betting) on horse races, you mustn't complain if you lose your money.
(b) If he would bet (If he insisted on betting) on horse races in spite of your warning, he deserved to lose his money.

(I) Shall के साथ I/We का प्रयोग एक प्रश्न की तरह दूसरे व्यक्ति की इच्छा (wishes) जानने हेतु निम्न प्रकार किया जाता है। यह अपनी सेवाएँ देने हेतु एक offer की तरह भी प्रयुक्त होता है :

Shall I thread the needle for you?
Shall I iron your trousers?
Shall we put the box into the train for you?

Shall का प्रयोग third person के साथ जिस व्यक्ति से प्रश्न किया गया, उसकी इच्छा जानने हेतु निम्न प्रकार से किया जाता है :

(a) Shall he carry your luggage up stairs? (Do you want him to do this?)
(b) Shall the messenger wait? (Do you want him to wait?)

(J) Shall की जगह be + to infinitive का प्रयोग भी 'wish' हेतु निम्न प्रकार किया जा सकता है :

Is the messenger to stay?
What is he to do next?
He asked me whether the taxi should wait. (Whether I wanted the taxi to wait.)

(K) I should/would like की अपेक्षा I'd like का प्रयोग इच्छा व्यक्त करने हेतु अधिक किया जाता है :

(a) I'd like to be present in the party. (I wish I were present in the party.)
(b) I'd have liked to be present in the party. (I wish I had been in the party.)

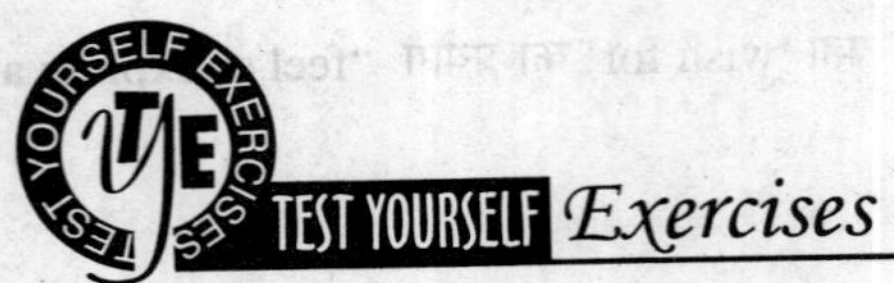

01

Translate the following sentences into English :

(1) मेरे पास एक कैमरा है।
(2) मेरे एक भाई एवं दो बहिन हैं।
(3) मै रात को 9 बजे खाना खाता हूँ।
(4) मुझे आज ही जयपुर जाना है। *(अनिवार्यता)*
(5) उसे यह कार्य आज ही पूरा करना है। *(अनिवार्यता)*
(6) सीता को ऑफिस जाना होगा।
(7) तुम्हें मेरी आज्ञा का पालन करना पड़ेगा।
(8) राम ने अपना पत्र किसी अन्य से लिखवाया।
(9) वह एक प्रोफेसर रह चुका है।
(10) वह अमेरिका में रह चुका है।

02

Translate the following sentences into English :

(1) मैंने अपना नाश्ता ले लिया है।
(2) वह यहाँ आती तो है।
(3) वह दवाएँ लेता तो है।
(4) सीता गाना गाती तो है।
(5) इस कमरे में पाँच दीवारें है।
(6) हाथी के चार पाँव होते है।
(7) मेरे पास किताबें नहीं हैं।
(8) मैने उसे हँसाया।
(9) उसने मुझसे अपने जूतों पर पॉलिश करवाई।
(10) राम कल जयपुर गया तो था।
(11) सुरेश रोजाना पढ़ाता तो था।
(12) कृपया एक कप चाय पीजिएगा।
(13) कृपया मुझे पत्र अवश्य लिखें।
(14) मैं उससे यह काम कराऊँगा।
(15) मैंने उससे घर की सफाई करवाई।

03

Correct the following sentences :

(1) I possess two brothers.
(2) She possesses three sisters.
(3) I have not books.
(4) He has his book write by Ramesh.
(5) He was a earlier banker.
(6) She have been to London.
(7) I have have my lunch.
(8) I had have my work completed by him.
(9) Do has a cup of coffee?
(10) I do went to meet her.
(11) She does learns his lessons well.
(12) He did came here yesterday.
(13) I received a song sung by her.
(14) I found my clothes washed by him.
(15) She neither talked nor will speak to him.

Modals

04

Fill in the blanks with can, could, may, might :

(1) .... you live long!

(2) .... you read when you were five?

(3) My father .... speak and write five languages.

(4) You .... write on both sides of the paper.

(5) We thought it .... rain.

(6) He said he .... always come when called.

(7) .... you ride your bicycle up to that hill?

(8) I ran fast so that I .... catch the train.

(9) He tried to solve the sum but he .... not.

(10) Do not put off till tomorrow what you .... do today.

05

Fill in the blanks with shall, will, should, would :

(1) .... you do me a favour?

(2) When......... I see you again?

(3) .... we go to the pictures today ?

(4) His daughter .... be sixteen next month.

(5) The wound .... not heal in spite of all the treatment he had.

(6) .... that I were rich!

(7) Had you worked hard, you......... have passed the examination.

(8) As you sow, so .... you reap.

(9) Those who live in glass houses .... not throw stones at others.

(10) If you .... see him, give him my regards.

06

Fill in the blanks with appropriate forms of 'must, need, dare, ought to, used to' :

(1) The door .... painting.

(2) I .... smoking but I gave it up last year.

(3) You .... come and have dinner with me.

(4) He has lost your book and he .... not tell you.

(5) You .... have written to him yesterday.

(6) .... he wait any longer ?

(7) He .... pay you the loan he owes you.

(8) .... you speak rudely to your father?

(9) I .... be a clerk, but now I am an officer.

(10) What cannot be cured .... be endured.

07

Use appropriate modal to fill in the blanks :

(1) .... you, please, stop talking?

(2) You .... go only when you have finished your work.

(3) .... you rather have tea or coffee?

(4) I .... try again if you wish.

(5) You .... not hurry, there is plenty of time.

(6) I .... like you to do as I tell you.

(7) If only they .... keep quiet for a moment.

(8) .... God bless you!

(9) You .... be mad to do this.

(10) I .... learn English, and none shall stop me.

(11) I .... prefer not to give any explanation.

08

Use appropriate modal to fill in the blanks :

(1) One ……… obey one's parents.
(2) You ……… go home whenever you like.
(3) I ……… like you to answer my question properly.
(4) My father says we ……… buy some sweets.
(5) ……… God give you courage to face it!
(6) ……… you like to have lunch now?
(7) ……… you please tell me where the Cinema House is?
(8) It ……… rain, it is so sultry.
(9) The doctor said that the patient ……… recover.
(The doctor was not very sure about it.)
(10) You ……… insist on being given your share. (Note the stress on the word 'insist'.)
(11) ………God bless you!

09

Use appropriate modal to fill in the blank :

(1) You ……… have given me a helping hand. It was your moral duty.
(2) I ……… try to get you a job. I promise.
(3) Arun is not a weak student. He is also not a very good student. He ……… however, pass.
(4) The student politely said to the teacher, "……… I have a word with you?"
(5) You ……… go now. (Permission)
(6) ……… you please close the door ? (A polite request in the form of a question)
(7) It ……… rain soon. (It is likely to happen)
(8) You ……… see a doctor at once. (It is an advice)
(9) We ……… hurry. We are very late.
(10) I'm afraid I ……… tell you that. It is a secret.

Question Appeared in Rajasthan Administrative Services Examinations in Previous Years

10

Identify the notion/concept expressed by each of the following sentences by choosing one of the three alternatives mentioned against each sentence :

(1) No smoking ! (Advice/prohibition/threat)
(2) I wish you'd be quiet. (Request /wish/suggestion)
(3) I'm seeing the Principal this afternoon. (Likelihood/ determination/ arrangement)
(4) You needn't have hurried. (Absence of necessity/ prohibition/ suggestion of hesitation)
(5) It might rain before evening. (Possibility/ strong possibility/ remote possibility)

11

Restructure the following sentences using may, might, must, ought to, wish, only :

(1) Candidates are required to answer at least five out of ten questions.
(2) He was not careful enough.
(3) Perhaps he was hurt.
(4) Please make a little less noise. (You can make it less if you wish to.)
(5) Please be quiet. (Request)

12

Fill in the blanks by supplying the appropriate modal :

(1) You ……… have watered the flowers, for it is going to rain.
(2) If we had taken the other road we ……… have arrived earlier.
(3) The bank closes at two but the manager.... allow you to get in. (Remote possibility)
(4) ……… you please send me an application form ? (Request)
(5) As John was the only person who visited us yesterday. It ……… be he who left the main gate open. (Probability)
(6) You ……… read his latest book.
(7) She ……… speak three languages when she was twelve.
(8) I ……… see quite clearly what the children are doing in the garden.
(9) He ……… be at least sixty.
(10) Your job ……… be very demanding but at least it isn't boring.

13

Fill in the blanks by supplying the appropriate modals :

(1) Usha ……… run a hundred yard in ten seconds.
(2) ……… his soul rest in peace !
(3) The baby is crying, he ……… be hungry.
(4) ……… you tell me the way to the post-office, please ?
(5) You ……… keep your scooter locked.
(6) ……… I bring you a cup of coffee ?
(7) When I was a boy. I ……… walk forty miles in a day.
(8) I have come to ask if Ram ……… use your bicycle tomorrow.
(9) ……… you have another cup of tea ?
(10) All of us ……… die.
(11) Drivers know that they ……… stop when they come to the main road. (Obligation)
(12) If you have a bad throat, you ……… smoke. (Prohibition)

Solution TYE 01

(1) I have a camera. *Or* I have got a camera.
(2) I have one brother and two sisters.
(3) I have my dinner at 9 pm.
(4) I have to go to Jaipur today.
(5) He has to complete this work today.
(6) Sita will have to go to office.
(7) You will have to obey my orders.
(8) Ram got his letter written by some one else.
(9) He has been a professor.
(10) He has been to America.

Solution TYE 02

(1) I have had my breakfast.
(2) She does come here.
(3) He does take medicines.
(4) Sita does sing a song.
(5) The room has five walls.
(6) The elephant has four legs.
(7) I have no books.
(8) I made him laugh.
(9) He made me polish his shoes. *Or* He got his shoes polished by me.
(10) Ram did go to Jaipur yesterday.
(11) Suresh did study daily.
(12) Do have a cup of tea.
(13) Do write me a letter.
(14) I shall get this work done by him.
(15) I made him clean the house. *Or* I got the house cleaned by him.

Solution TYE 03

(1) I have two brothers.
(2) She has three sisters.
(3) I have no books.
(4) He has his book written by Ramesh.
(5) He has been a banker.
(6) She has been to London.
(7) I have had my lunch.
(8) I had had my work completed by him.
(9) Do have a cup of coffee
(10) I did go to meet her.
(11) She does learn her lessons well.
(12) He did come here yesterday.
(13) I had a song sung by her.
(14) I had my clothes washed by him.
(15) She neither has talked nor will speak to him.

Solution TYE 04

(1) May, (2) Could, (3) can, (4) may, (5) might
(6) could, (7) Can, (8) might (9) could, (10) can.

Solution TYE 05

(1) Will, (2) shall, (3) Shall, (4) will, (5) would,
(6) Would, (7) would, (8) shall, (9) should, (10) should.

Solution TYE 06

(1) needs, (2) used to, (3) must, (4) dare, (5) ought to,
(6) need, (7) ought to, (8) dare, (9) used to, (10) must.

Solution TYE 07

(1) Will you, please, stop talking?
(2) You can (or should) go only when you have finished your work.
(3) Would you rather have tea or coffee?
(4) I will try again if you wish.
(5) You need not hurry, there is plenty of time.
(6) I should like you to do as I tell you.
(7) If only they would keep quiet for a moment.
(8) May God bless you!
(9) You should be mad to do this.
(10) I will learn English and none shall stop me.
(11) I should prefer not to give any explanation.

Solution TYE 08

(1) One should obey one's parents.
(2) You may go home whenever you like.
(3) I should like you to answer my question properly.
(4) My father says we shall buy some sweets.
(5) May God give you courage to face it!
(6) Would you like to have lunch now?
(7) Will you please tell me where the Cinema House is?
(8) It may rain, it is so sultry.
(9) The doctor said that the patient might recover.
(10) You must insist on being given your share.
(11) May God bless you!

Solution TYE 09

(1) You should have given me a helping hand. It was your moral duty.
(2) I will try to get you a job. I promise.
(3) Arun is not a weak student. He is also not a very good student. He can however pass.
(4) The student politely said to the teacher, "Could I have a word with you?"
(5) You can go now.
(6) Would you please close the door ?
(7) It may rain soon.
(8) You should see a doctor at once.
(9) We must hurry. We are very late.
(10) I'm afraid I cannot tell you that. It is a secret.

Solution TYE 10

(1) Prohibition,
(2) Request
(3) Arrangement,
(4) Absence of necessity,
(5) Remote possibility.

Solution TYE 11

(1) Candidates must answer at least five out of the ten questions.
(2) He ought to have been more careful.
(3) He may have been hurt.
(4) You might make a little less noise.
(5) I wish you would be quiet.

Solution TYE 12

(1) need not, (2) would, (3) might (4) Would, (5) might
(6) should (7) could, (8) can, (9) must, (10) may.

Solution TYE 13

(1) can, (2) May, (3) must (4) Will, (5) should/must,
(6) Shall (7) could, (8) may, (9) Will, (10) will,
(11) must, (12) must not.

SYNTAX : SUBJECT-VERB AGREEMENT

Syntax का अर्थ होता है, Sentence Structure. अंग्रेजी में वाक्य संरचना के नियमों को जानना, शुद्ध अंग्रेजी लिखने हेतु आवश्यक है। Syntax के दो प्रमुख अंग है:

(1) Concord or Agreement : By concord is meant formal agreement in person, number, gender or tenses between various parts of a sentence. अर्थात् वाक्य के विभिन्न भागों में सामंजस्य, Person, Number एवं Gender तथा Tense के अनुसार किन नियमों के अनुसार होता है, इसका अध्ययन Agreement or concord के अन्तर्गत किया जाता है।

(2) Order (Position) : वाक्य के विभिन्न भागों को किस क्रम में रखा जाना है? Word Order (Position in a sentence) की चर्चा हम Preposition, Adverb, Conjunction etc में अलग-अलग विस्तृत रूप से करेंगे।

Subject-Verb Agreement

एक वाक्य में Verb एवं Subject के मध्य एक Agreement होता है जब Subject singular है तो verb भी singular लगेगी।

"The verb must agree with its subject in number and person."

—Nesfield

(a) I am playing.
(b) They are playing.
(c) He is playing.
(d) We are playing.

वाक्य संख्या (a) एवं (c) में Subject singular हैं अत: verb 'am', 'is' singular हैं तथा वाक्य संख्या (b) एवं (d) में subject plural हैं अत: verb 'are' plural है।

(1) *Verbs—Singular या Plural, Present Tense में ही होती है। सभी Verbs को Plural एवं Present Tense में माना जाता है। Verbs के साथ Present Tense में s या es लगाने से वह Singular बनती है।*

(2) *To be form of Verbs; (is, am, are, was, were) ये Verbs, Singular में अलग-अलग Persons के साथ अलग-अलग Verb काम आती हैं, जैसे : I के साथ am, You के साथ are, He के साथ is जबकि Plural में इनका रूप एक ही रहता है। Present Tense में are तथा Past tense में were जैसे : We are, You are, They are एवं We were, You were, They were.*

(3) *Shall, Will, Should एवं Would के साथ हमेशा Have का प्रयोग किया जाता है, इनके साथ कभी भी Has लगाने की गलती न करें।*

Subject-Verb Agreement v/s Rules of Correct Use of Verbs

Exceptions to the Rule: The verb must agree with its subject in number and person.

Rule 1

कुछ वाक्य ऐसे होते हैं जिनमें Singular subject होते हुए भी Plural verb का प्रयोग किया जाता है।

(A) जब वाक्य में 'कल्पना' का भाव या असम्भव प्राय: शर्त का भाव प्रदर्शित होता है। जैसे:

(1) I wish I were the Prime Minister.
(2) I wish I were a bird.
(3) Were he a king !
(4) Were she an eagle, she would fly to me.
(5) She ordered as if she were my mother.
(6) If I were you, I would kill him.

इन सब वाक्यों में एक कल्पना का भाव, एक असम्भव प्राय: शर्त का भाव प्रदर्शित हो रहा है। इस प्रकार के वाक्यों में 'were' का प्रयोग Singular subject के साथ होता है।

(B) जब वाक्यों में verbs; bless, save, help, live का प्रयोग इच्छा, अभिलाषा; (desire, wish) या आशीर्वाद का भाव प्रकट करता है तो singular subject के साथ भी bless, save, help, live, की plural form का प्रयोग करता है (अर्थात् blesses, saves, helps या lives की तरह इनका प्रयोग नहीं किया जा सकता है। जैसे:

(1) God save the queen.
(2) God help you.
(3) Long live the king.
(4) God bless you with a son.

(C) जबकि वाक्य में Dare एवं Need का प्रयोग Modals की तरह किया जाता है, तो Subject, Singular होने पर भी Dare एवं Need रहते हैं।(Dares या Needs नहीं होते हैं। इसके बारे में विस्तार से Modal verbs में बताया गया है।

नीचे लिखे वाक्यों पर ध्यान दें :

(1) He need not to go there. (Needs नहीं होगा)
(2) She dare not oppose your proposal. (Dares नहीं होगा)
(3) Need he go there?
(4) One need not write anything to him.
(5) Dare she oppose you?
(6) He dare not speak like this.

उपरोक्त वाक्यों में 'Dare' एवं 'Need' का प्रयोग Modal Auxiliary verb की तरह हुआ है। Generally in negative and interrogative sentences 'Dare' and 'Need' are used as Modals.

Rule 2

यदि दो अलग-अलग Noun, एक ही व्यक्ति या वस्तु के लिए प्रयुक्त हो तो Verb-Singular लगती है। जैसे:

(a) The poet and painter has died.
(b) The Project Director and Additional Collector is on tour.
(c) The clerk and counsellor was present in the meeting.

यहाँ poet, painter, Project, Director, Additional Collector एवं clerk, counsellor एक ही व्यक्ति के लिए प्रयुक्त हुए है। यह भी ध्यान रखे कि ऐसे वाक्यों में Article का प्रयोग Noun के साथ ही होता है।

Rule 3

जब दो Noun, जो लगभग एक-सा भाव या अर्थ रखते हैं, का प्रयोग एक-दूसरे का महत्त्व बढ़ाने हेतु किया जाता है, तो भी Verb singular लगती है। जैसे:

(a) The scheme and plan of my life differs from that of yours.
(b) His authority and command is indeed great.
(c) The benefit and advantage from this business is enormous.

Rule 4

दो Noun जो यद्यपि समानार्थक नहीं हैं, लेकिन एक Phrase की तरह प्रयुक्त होते हैं तो भी Verb-Singular लगती है। Actually ये दो Noun एक ही idea को व्यक्त करते हैं। जैसे:

(a) Bread and butter is a good breakfast. (b) Slow and steady wins the race.

(c) "Early to bed, early to rise" is a good habit. (d) Pen and ink is needed by me.

Rule 5

जब दो या अधिक singular nouns; or, either...or, neither ...nor से जोड़े गए हों तो Verb, singular लगती है। जैसे:

(a) No man or woman was present there. (b) Either Sita or Ram was present in the party.

(c) Neither he nor she is responsible for this loss.

Rule 6

जब दो या अधिक nouns अलग-अलग Number के हों (अर्थात् कोई Plural हो, कोई Singular हो) तो Plural number वाला Noun ही Verb के साथ लगाना चाहिए एवं Verb भी Plural ही लगती है। जैसे:

(a) Neither the Principal nor the teachers were present in the function.

(b) Either Ramesh or his friends have stolen the watch.

(c) Ramesh or his friends are abusing him.

Rule 7

यदि दो या अधिक Subjects; Either ...or, Neither...nor, or से जुड़े हुए हों तथा different persons के हों तो Verb अपने पास वाले Person के अनुसार ही लगती है। जैसे:

(a) Either you or I am to go there. (b) Neither he nor you are to attend them.

(c) You or Ramesh is responsible for the loss. (d) He or I am to go there .

Rule 8

जब एक Collective noun जैसे : Committee, Army, Crowd, Mob, Society, Assembly, Parliament, Council, Crew, Staff, Jury, Fleet, Majority इस तरह से प्रयुक्त होती है, जैसे एक Unit (इकाई) हो तो Verb Singular लगती है। जैसे:

(a) The Parliament has passed the bill. (b) Army was deployed at the border.

(c) The fleet has reached the port. (d) The Assembly is in session now-a-days.

(e) The mob moves towards Parliament. (f) The jury has taken a unanimous decision.

लेकिन यदि collective noun एक Unit की तरह action नहीं लेती है, बल्कि वाक्य में divided प्रतीत होती हो या विभिन्न सदस्यों में एकमत नहीं हो तो plural verb लगाई जाती है।

(a) The committee are divided over the proposal. (b) The jury are divided in opinion.

(c) The audience were getting bored.

Rule 9

यदि एक Plural noun एक निश्चित quantity या amount को एक Unit की तरह व्यक्त करता है, तो Verb singular लगती है। जैसे:

(a) Five kilograms is not a heavy weight. (b) Hundred rupees is a big amount for him.

(c) Six miles is not a long distance.

लेकिन यदि इनसे Plurality का बोध होता है तो Verb plural लगेगी। जैसे:

(a) Five years have passed. (b) Two thousand rupees were charged by him.

Rule 10

कुछ Nouns जो देखने में Plural लगते हैं, लेकिन अर्थ में Singular होते हैं ऐसे Noun के साथ Verb singular लगती है। ऐसे Nouns निम्नलिखित हैं:

Physics, Mathematics, Economics, News, Gallows, Billiards, Innings, Wages, Alms etc.

(a) No news is good news.
(b) Physics/Economics/Maths is a good subject.
(c) Billiards is a game.
(d) First innings was spoiled due to rain.

Rule 11

Each एवं Every के साथ जुड़े हुए singular noun (each एवं every के साथ हमेशा Singular noun ही आता है) के साथ Verb singular लगती है। जैसे:

(a) Each boy and girl has to attend the function.
(b) Every man, woman and child was happy to meet with the President.
(c) Each minute and each second is precious.
(d) Each male and every female was protesting against that law.

Rule 12

कुछ Noun जो दिखने में singular होते हैं, लेकिन अर्थ में Plural होते हैं, के साथ Plural verb ही प्रयोग में आती है, जैसे: Dozen, Hundred, Million, Cattle, People, Score, Thousand, Gentry, Police, Peasantry, Company, Alphabet, Progeny, Offspring, Clergy, Infantry etc.

(a) The cattle are grazing in the field.
(b) A score were saved by him.
(c) Not less than a dozen were injured.
(d) The people were fully satisfied.

Rule 13

जब दो Subjects, Not only....but also से जुड़े हों तो Verb अपने पास वाले subject के अनुसार लगाई जाती है। जैसे:

(a) Not only the Principal but also the teachers were playing the match.
(b) Not only the students but also the class teacher was also involved in the discussion.

Rule 14

जब एक Subject के साथ beside, as well as, and not, in addition to, like, with, together with जैसे जोड़ने वाले conjunctions से अन्य subject या कोई शब्द जुड़े हुए हों तो Verb वाक्य में पहले आने वाले subject के अनुसार लगती है। जैसे:

(a) Ram and not his friends was present there.
(b) The house with all its belongings was sold.
(c) The President as well as the members has come.
(d) The pigeon like other birds has wings.
(e) Four questions in addition to the first question have to be answered.

Rule 15

जब किसी वाक्य में Other या another के बाद कोई Noun आए तो ध्यान रखें other के बाद Plural Noun एवं Plural Verb लगती है तथा another के बाद Singular Noun एवं Singular Verb का प्रयोग किया जाता है। जैसे:

(a) There are so many other hotels better than this.
(b) There is another hotel near the Railway Station.

Rule 16

The poor, The rich, The disabled, The young, The old, The English, The French इत्यादि पूरी Class को व्यक्त करते हैं (The poor का अर्थ है सभी गरीब लोग, The rich का अर्थ होता है सभी धनी लोग) इनके साथ Plural verb का प्रयोग किया जाता है एवं The poors, The riches लिखना गलत है। जैसे:

(a) The poor are trustworthy.
(b) The rich are generally unkind to the poor.

Rule 17

जब दो Singular Subjects को and से जोड़ा जाता है, तो Verb Plural लगती है। जैसे:

(a) He and she were present in the function.

(b) Ram and Rahim are friends.

Rule 18

Hair (बाल) का प्रयोग singular में किया जाता है एवं Singular verb लगती है, लेकिन यदि बालों की Counting के हिसाब से इसका प्रयोग हो तो Verb plural लगेगा। जैसे:

(a) His hair is black.

(b) Five hairs of the horse are needed by him.

Rule 19

सामान्यत: All एवं Some के साथ यदि Countable noun आता है तो वह Noun भी Plural होगा एवं verb भी Plural लगाई जाएगी, लेकिन यदि All के साथ कोई Uncountable noun आता है तो Verb-Singular लगाई जाती है। जैसे :

(a) All the tigers are wild animals.

(b) All the money was taken away by the thief.

(c) Some animals are faithful.

(d) Some milk in needed.

लेकिन यदि all का प्रयोग वाक्य में एक Unit की तरह हो रहा है तो इसके साथ singular Verb लगाई जाएगी। जैसे:

(a) He informed the police all that happened last night.

(b) I would inform you all that was discussed in the meeting.

(उपरोक्त वाक्यों में all का प्रयोग एक Unit की तरह हो रहा है।)

Rule 20

यदि एक वाक्य में Most of के बाद Countable noun आता है तो ध्यान रखें वह Plural ही आएगा तथा उसके बाद Verb भी Plural ही लगेगी लेकिन Noun यदि Uncountable आता है तो Verb-Singular लगती है। जैसे:

(a) Most of the persons are dishonest.

(b) Most of apples are rotten.

(c) Most of the milk was impure.

(d) Most of the sugar was wet with water.

Rule 21

यदि वाक्य में Half of का प्रयोग किया जाता है तो ध्यान रखें Half of के बाद यदि Countable noun आता है, तो वह भी Plural ही होगी एवं verb भी Plural ही होगी। यदि Noun uncountable हो तो Verb-singular लगती है। जैसे:

(a)About half of the students were present there.

(b) He said that half of the hostlers were absent.

(c) Half of the milk was spoiled.

(d) Half of the land was cultivated and half was uncultivable.

Rule 22

There के बाद आने वाली Verb Plural या Singular होगी, इस तथ्य पर निर्भर होगी कि वाक्य का Subject Plural है या Singular । जैसे:

(a) There is a girl in the room.

(b) There are ten students in the class.

(c) There was a queen.

(d) There were several ministers in the party.

Rule 23

कुछ nouns, जैसे furniture, luggage, information, advice, work, knowledge, equipment, behaviour, scenery, traffic, fruit, electricity, music, progress, weather, nonsense, sense, etc. uncountable noun हैं इनको Pluralise नहीं किया जा सकता है अर्थात् furniture को furnitures लिखना या information को informations लिखना पूर्णतया गलत है। इनसे पहले article - a/an का प्रयोग भी नहीं किया जा सकता है एवं इनके साथ हमेशा Singular verb का प्रयोग होता है। जैसे:

(a) Work is worship.

(b) Knowledge is power.

(c) His behaviour was not proper.

(d) His advice in the matter is trustworthy.

(e) The scene of Kashmir is indeed beautiful.

इस तरह की Nc ns को Countable बनाने के लिए इनके साथ कुछ शब्द, जैसे: a piece of information, a piece of advice, a packet of urniture लगाया जा सकता है।

Rule 24

As follows (एक phrase) की जगह as follow लिखना गलत है। अंग्रेजी में as follows ही लिखा जाता है। जैसे:

(a) The main points are as follows. (not as follow)
(b) The details are as follows. (not as follow)

Rule 25

The following एवं the undersigned का प्रयोग यदि singular subject के लिए हुआ तो Verb-singular अन्यथा Verb plural लगेगा। जैसे:

(a) The following are the new prices of the items.
(b) Undersigned has taken a decision. S.K. Jain
(c) We, the undersigned request the pleasure of your company. S.K. Jain and P.K. Jain
(d) The following is the summary of the discussions held in the meeting.

Rule 26

कई वाक्यों में Singular noun का Repetition, preposition के बाद होता है ऐसे वाक्यों में Singular Verb लगती है। जैसे:

(a) Man after man was coming there.
(b) One month after another has passed.
(c) Ship after ship is arriving regularly.
(d) He begs from door to door.

Rule 27

कुछ Noun जो दिखने में भी Plural लगते हैं, दो भागों में बने होते हैं जैसे : Scissors, pants, trousers, binoculars, tongs, spectacles, shorts, breeches, shoes, scales, glasses, googles etc. इनके साथ Plural verb का ही प्रयोग किया जाता है। जैसे:

(a) My shoes are new.
(b) The scissors are blunt.
(c) His pants are tight.
(d) Her spectacles are beautiful.

लेकिन यदि इनके साथ चम्पत का प्रयोग किया जाए तो verb-singular लगती है। जैसे:

(a) Only a pair of shoes is required.
(b) A pair of scissors was purchased by me.

Rule 28

कुछ nouns ऐसे हैं, जो Singular एवं Plural दोनों forms में एक ही रूप में रहते हैं। इनके साथ Verb वाक्य के सन्दर्भ के अनुसार लगती है। ऐसे Noun हैं। जैसे: Sheep, fish, deer, pice etc.

(a) A sheep is a beautiful animal.
(b) Many sheep are grazing there.
(c) I found a pice.
(d) I found five pice.
(e) There are many fishes in the pond. Incorrect
There are many fish in the pond. Correct

Rule 29

यदि किसी वाक्य में infinitive, gerund, phrase या कोई clause, subject का कार्य करता है, या subject की तरह प्रयोग में आता है, तो singular verb का प्रयोग किया जाता है। जैसे:

(1) Swimming is a good exercise. *Gerund*
(2) To swim is good for you. *Infinitive*
(3) How to start it is a big question. *Phrase*
(4) That she is poor is known to me. *Clause*

Rule 30

More than one के साथ किसी noun का प्रयोग किया जाए तो Verb-singular लगेगी। जैसे:

(a) More than one worker was absent. (b) More than one student was killed.

More than one यद्यपि एक Plural संख्या को व्यक्त करता है, लेकिन उसके साथ singular verb का ही प्रयोग किया जाता है। इस सम्बन्ध में Mr. Fowler ने Modern English usage में लिखा है।

More than one, though its sense is necessarily plural, is treated as a sort of compound of 'one', following its constructions and agrees with a singular noun and takes a singular noun and takes a singular verb-More than one workman was killed, not 'workmen' or 'were'.

– Fowler

Rule 31

कई वाक्यों में more का प्रयोग निम्न प्रकार होता है :

(1) More books than one have been purchased by her.
(2) More girls than one were present in the party.
(3) More students than one have attended the class.
(4) More workmen than one are not traceable .

इस तरह के वाक्यों में Plural verb का प्रयोग किया जाता है।

Rule 32

कुछ वाक्यों में noun के बाद Preposition एवं फिर noun आता है। जैसे:

(1) The quality of these goods is well known.
(2) Financial help from all the countries was received.
(3) The colour of this shirt is liked by all.
(4) Your views on this matter are supported by all.
(5) The details of the accident were not received by us so far.
(6) The cost of production of steel goods is increasing.
(7) Economic cooperation between India and Pakistan is increasing.
(8) The smell of these flowers is liked by all.

उपरोक्त वाक्यों का Structure: noun + preposition + noun की तरह का है। ऐसे वाक्यों में verb, preposition से पहले आने वाले noun के अनुसार लगती है। वाक्य संख्या 5 एवं 5 के अतिरिक्त सभी वाक्यों में preposition से पहले आने वाला noun singular है। अत: verb singular लगाई गई है।

यदि वाक्य में एक से अधिक noun, preposition के साथ आए तो भी verb, सबसे पहले आने वाले preposition के पहले आने वाले noun के अनुसार लगाई जाती है। जैसे:

(1) The manager's remarks in a newspaper about the conduct of the player were not appreciated by any one.........(1)

(2) The cost of production of steel items is increasing everywhere.

Rule 33

जब वाक्य में इन phrases का प्रयोग होता है: a number of, lots of, a lot of, plenty of, a quarter of, part of, percent of, proportion of, none of, remainder of, two-third of, most of, some of, majority of, much of, many of, a good deal of, a great deal of, heaps of तो verb, of के बाद आने वाले noun के अनुसार लगाई जाती है। यदि of के बाद आने वाला noun plural है तो verb भी plural लगेगी। जैसे:

(1) Plenty of sugar is required. (2) Plenty of chairs have been purchased.
(3) A lot of books were destroyed in fire. (4) A lot of milk was sent there.

यदि of के बाद कोई Countable noun है तो वह Plural होगा एवं यदि unccuntable noun है तो वह singular होगा। जैसे:

(a) A number of boys, Plenty of books. *(Boys and books are countables.)*

(b) Plenty of milk, a lot of sugar. *(Milk and sugar are uncountables.)*

इस तरह के अन्य वाक्य निम्न हैं :

(1) *A large proportion of the* northern army was British. – **H.G. Wells**

(2) *The rest of* the prose *of the age is too voluminous* – **I. Evans**

(3) *Most of* those *who use it* are probably unaware that assets is itself a s ngular. – **Fowler**

(4) *There* were a number of such little reasons. – **A. Huxley**

(5) *The majority of* writers never pass that stage. – **E. Pound**

(6) *Much of* time is lost.

(7) *Much of the sugar is impure.* (Much of के बाद uncountable noun आता है।)

Rule 34

यदि वाक्य में A number या The number का प्रयोग हुआ है, तो ध्यान रखें the number के साथ हमेशा singular verb लगती है तथा A number के साथ हमेशा Plural verb लगती है।

The number का अर्थ होता है एक निश्चित संख्या, यह collective noun की तरह प्रयुक्त होता है एवं singular verb का प्रयोग किया जाता है।

A number का अर्थ होता है 'बहुत' (many) तो इसके साथ Plural verb ही प्रयोग में लाई जाएगी। जैसे:

(1) The number of students opted English in Administrative Services is generally small.

(2) The number of candidates appeared in SSC this year was very large.

(3) A number of English books are available in library.

(4) There were a number of students waiting for their turn.

Rule 35

None के साथ सामान्य रूप से Singular verb का प्रयोग सही माना जाता है, लेकिन Modern English में none के साथ Plural verb का भी प्रयोग किया जाने लगा है। इस सम्बन्ध में grammarians में काफी मतभेद हैं। जैसे:

(1) It is mistake to suppose that the pronoun 'none' is singular only and must at all costs be followed by singular verb.—***Fowler***

(2) 'None' was originally used only as singular but it has also acquired a plural meaning. —***Nesfield***

(3) 'None' is an abbreviated form of not one or no one and would therefore seem to be singular, but in its context it usually has a plural sense. —***Vallins***

इस तरह none का प्रयोग singular एवं plural दोनों ही स्थिति में किया जा सकता है।

नीचे लिखें वाक्यों पर ध्यान दें :

(1) None but the brave deserves the reward. *Singular*

(2) None were injured. *Plural*

(3) None of the minor characters were present on the day of rehersal. *Plural*

(4) None of his works shows his capabilities and his calibre. *Singular*

Rule 36

(A) यदि किसी वाक्य का Subject, कोई Relative pronoun जैसे : who, which, that है, तो verb, इस Relative Pronoun के Antecedent के अनुसार लगती है। (Antecedent का अर्थ होता है पहले आने वाला) अत: Relative Pronoun के पहले आने वाला noun या pronoun यदि Singular है तो Verb भी Singular, यदि Plural हो तो Verb plural लगेगी या यह कहें कि Relative Pronoun से पूर्व आने वाला noun या pronoun ही verb को अनुशासित करता है।

जैसे:

(1) It is I who have telephoned you.
(2) It is he who is responsible for this loss.
(3) The book that is here is mine.
(4) The books that are here are mine.
(5) The woman, who is in black saree, is my wife.
(6) The women, who are standing there, are my sisters.

(B) **कुछ वाक्य ऐसे होते हैं जिनमें one of के साथ Relative Pronoun भी आता है। जैसे:**

(1) He is one of those who do not attend the meeting.
(2) It is one of the problems that hamper the work.

ऐसे वाक्यों में one of के बाद आने वाले Noun या Pronoun के अनुसार Verb लगाई जाती है। उपरोक्त दोनों वाक्यों में one of के बाद (noun/pronoun) Those एवं problems आए हैं अत: verb; do एवं hamper भी Plural है।

Rule 37

जब वाक्यों में 'Nothing but' आता है तो Verb हमेशा Singular ही लगेगी चाहे Nothing but के बाद आने वाला noun; singular हो या plural. जैसे:

(1)Nothing but hill is seen.
(2) Nothing but birds is seen.
(3)Nothing but girls is there.
(4) Nothing but a student is there.

Rule 38

यदि दो Singular nouns के पहले 'no' का प्रयोग हो तो verb-singular लगती है। जैसे:

(1) No boy and no girl was present in the party.
(2) No man and no woman was swimming at that time.

Rule 39

जब अंकगणितीय figures, and से जोड़े जाते हैं, तो verb-singular भी हो सकती है और plural भी। जैसे:

(1) Four and four is eight
(2) Four and four are eight.

जब Singular verb का प्रयोग होता है तो इसका अर्थ है कि and से संयुक्त अंको को एक Unitary Concept माना गया है। जब Plural Verb का प्रयोग होता है, तो इन्हें अलग-अलग माना गया है, इस सम्बन्ध में Norman Lewis के निम्न कथन पर ध्यान दें:

Five and Five is ten : Right—But don't jump to the conclusion that 'five and five are ten' is wrong both verbs are equally accepted

—Norman Lewis

साधारणतया Singular verb का प्रयोग उचित रहता है।

Rule 40

कई वाक्य ऐसे होते हैं जिनमें 'as' का प्रयोग करते समय as के बाद subject का प्रयोग नहीं करते हैं (या subject understood होता है।) ऐसे वाक्यों में verb का प्रयोग वाक्य के अर्थ के अनुसार ही करना चाहिए अर्थात् यदि अर्थ के अनुसार subject-singular है तो verb-singular एवं यदि अर्थ के अनुसार subject-plural है तो verb-plural लगेगी। जैसे:

(1) There were not so many workers as were required.
(2) There were not so many workers as was expected.

पहले वाक्य में As के बाद 'they' subject understood है। अत: 'were' Plural verb का प्रयोग हुआ है। दूसरे वाक्य में as के बाद subject 'it' understood है। अत: 'was' singular verb का प्रयोग किया गया है।

Rule 41

कई वाक्यों में 'as' के समान ही than के बाद Subject, understood होता है। यदि यह subject-singular है तो verb, singular एवं यदि यह subject, plural है तो plural verb का प्रयोग किया जाता है। जैसे:

(1) There were more casualties than was reported.

(2) There were more books than were required.

पहले वाक्यों में than के बाद 'it' understood होता है एवं दूसरे वाक्य में than के बाद 'they' understood है। अतः पहले वाक्य में 'was' तथा दूसरे वाक्य में 'were' का प्रयोग किया गया है।

Rule 42

Everyone, Everybody, Nobody, Somebody, No one, Each one, Someone के साथ Singular Verb लगती है। जैसे

(1) Everyone was happy to get this news.

(2) Somebody is coming here.

(3) Each one was given a gift.

(4) Someone is there in the hall.

Rule 43

Either of, Each of, Neither of के साथ भी singular verb का प्रयोग होता है। ध्यान रखें, Either of, Each of एवं Neither of के बाद Subject (noun) plural आता है। जैसे:

(a) Each of the students was given a gift.

(b) Either of the magazines is useful.

(c) Neither of the books is cheap.

(d) Neither of the girls was beautiful.

Rule 44

किसी वाक्य में Verb उसके Subject के अनुसार लगती है न कि Complement के अनुसार। नीचे के वाक्यों से यह बात स्पष्ट हो जाती है। जैसे:

(1) Our only guide were the stars. *Incorrect*

Our only guide was the stars. *Correct*

(2) The stars was our only guide. *Incorrect*

The stars were our only guide. *Correct*

Rule 45

कुछ verbs के बाद 'as' अवश्य लगता है। ये verbs है : regard, describe, represent, portray, depict, mention, define, treat. जैसे:

(a) You ought to have regarded him as your brother.

(b) He was described by his wife as the most harmless man.

(c) He portrayed him as a typical country farmer.

(d) Someone has defined genius as an infinite capacity for learning.

(e) You should have treated him as your brother.

Rule 46

कुछ Verbs के बाद 'as' नहीं लगता है। ये verbs है: name, call, term, think, consider, nominate, appoint.

(a) The Chairman nominated Hari secretary of the society.

(b) Ram called him a fool, a rogue and a crook.

(c) Ram calls his wife 'Situ'.

(d) I think him an intelligent man.

(e) I consider it a badly managed organisation.

***Note :** Verb 'act' एवं 'pass' के साथ 'as' का प्रयोग निम्न प्रकार के sentences में होता है*

(f) He acted as Principal. *(g) He passed as a gentleman.*

Inversion

What is 'Inversion'?

Affirmative वाक्यों का Structure सामान्यतया निम्न प्रकार का होता है

Subject + Verb + ...

Verb का प्रयोग Subject के बाद किया जाता है।

Interrogative वाक्यों में सामान्यतया Verb का प्रयोग Subject से पूर्व निम्न प्रकार होता है

Verb + Subject + ...?

Interrogative वाक्यों के अतिरिक्त बहुत से Adverbs एवं Adverbial expressions का प्रयोग जब clause के प्रारम्भ में होता है तो Verb, Subject के पहले आती है। वाक्यों में Verb का Subject के पहले आना Inversion कहलाता है।

Inversion of the Verb : *"Certain adverbs and adverb phrases, most with a restrictive or negative sense, can for emphasis be placed first in a sentence or clause and are then followed by the inverted (i.e. interrogative) form of the verb."*

—Thomson and Martinet.

Inversion दो प्रकार का होता है:

(1) **जब Auxiliary Verb का प्रयोग तो Subject के पहले किया जाता है, लेकिन मुख्य Verb (Main Verb) का प्रयोग Subject के बाद ही होता है। जैसे:**

Never does he go to temple. Hardly does he come here.

उक्त वाक्यों में Auxiliary 'does' का प्रयोग Subject से पूर्व तथा Main Verbs—go एवं come का प्रयोग Subject के बाद किया गया है।

(2) **जब मुख्य Verb या Auxiliary + मुख्य Verb का प्रयोग Subject के पहले किया जाता है। जैसे:**

(a) Round the corner went *Jacob*. — *Main verb + Subject*

(b) Under a tree was sitting an old *lady*. — *Auxiliary+ Main Verb + Subject*

Examples of Inversion

(1) Hardly, rarely, scarcely, seldom, never का प्रयोग जब वाक्य को शुरू करने के लिए होता है। जैसे:

(a) Hardly does she go to church.
(b) Seldom had I seen such a healthy baby.
(c) Never does she go to temple.
(d) Scarcely ever did they manage to meet the deadline.
(e) Rarely is she absent from duty.

(2) Not only .... but also का प्रयोग जब Verbs के पूर्व किया जाता है। जैसे:

(a) Not only did she watch TV but she also cooked meal.
(b) Not only does he rob her but he also smashes everything.

(3) No sooner का प्रयोग जब वाक्य को शुरू करने हेतु किया जाता है। जैसे:

(a) No sooner had she seen her husband than she hugged him.
(b) No sooner did he see the dead body of his wife than he burst into tears.

(4) No........ से बने expressions जैसे: Under no circumstances, In no way, On no account, On no condition, At no time के साथ Inversion का प्रयोग किया जाता है। जैसे:

(a) Under no circumstances shall I accept this proposal.
(b) On no condition will she sell the house.
(c) In no way will I forgive her.
(d) On no account must this button be pushed.

(5) Only के साथ प्रयुक्त Adverbial expressions जैसे : Only yesterday, only the day before yesterday, Only last month, Only last fornight, Only after a month/ year, Only then, Only in this way, Only when, Only by doing this thing, Only in a few schools/colleges/countries/continents etc. के साथ Inversion का प्रयोग किया जाता है।

जैसे:

(a) Only yesterday did he buy that car.
(b) Only by taking risk did he save the life of the minister.
(c) Only by accepting the condition, did he join this job.
(d) Only by shouting was she able to make herself heard.

(6) Adverbial expressions showing place (स्थान) के साथ Inversion लगता है। ऐसे Expression : Outside the gate, under the table, In the valley, Along the border, Round the corner, On a hill etc. हैं: जैसे:

(a) In the valley did I see a strange man. (b) On a hill did he find a new revolver.
(c) Outside the gate did he notice something moving.

इसी तरह के अन्य Adverbial expression निम्न हैं, जिनके साथ Inversion लगता है, लेकिन do/did का प्रयोग नहीं किया जाता है। Under a tree, On the bed, ten/five miles beyond the school/college/city, Nowhere else etc.

(a) Under a tree was sleeping an old lady. (b) On the bed was sitting her friend.
(c) Five miles beyond the city was a mysterious palace.

(7) Here/There/Away/Out/Up/Indoor/Outdoors/In/Down/ इत्यादि से शुरू होने वाले वाक्यों में Inversion का प्रयोग है। जैसे:

(a) Down fell a dozen apples. (b) In came the child weeping.
(c) Here comes the train. (d) There goes Sita.
(e) Away went Ram.

जब इस तरह के वाक्यों में Subject के रूप में pronoun आए तो Verb, उस Subject के बाद प्रयोग किया जाता है। जैसे:
(a) There she goes. (b) Away he went.
(c) Here she comes.

(8) So के साथ Adverb of manner का प्रयोग वाक्य के शुरू में होने पर भी Inversion लगता है। जैसे:

(a) So well did he organise the function that everyone started praising him.
(b) So absurdly did he speak that everyone was offended.
(c) So suspicious did he become that he couldn't talk to her properly.

(9) To such a degree/To such an extent/ To such a point/To such a length से जब वाक्य शुरू होता है, तो Inversion का प्रयोग होता है। जैसे:

(a) To such an extent he made the investment that people started trusting him.
(b) To such a degree they made a noise that Principal had to call the police.

(10) निम्न प्रकार के वाक्यों में भी Inversion का प्रयोग होता है। जैसे:

(a) Were I a bird! (If I were a bird एवं were I a bird का एक ही अर्थ है)
(b) Had he come to me, I would have helped him.
(It he had come to me, I would have helped him
वाक्य (b) को इस तरह भी लिखा जा सकता है)
(c) Soniya went to church, so did I.
(यहाँ so did I का अर्थ है I went there too)
(d) She did not visit the Agra, neither did I. (e) He did not go there, nor did I.

ध्यान रखें so, Neither, Nor के साथ Inversion का प्रयोग सामान्यतया उस स्थिति में होता है जब इनके साथ Subject उसी कार्य को करता है जैसा दूसरे ने किया है। (To show the similarity in action) जैसा उक्त वाक्यों (c),(d),(e) से स्पष्ट है।

(f) "Let us play cricket", proposed Ram.
"Let us go to market", said Sita.
"Do it for me", said Krishna.
"Go there", instructed Rahim.

जब Direct Narration में Reported Speech के बाद Reporting Verb का प्रयोग होता है तो Inversion का प्रयोग होता है, लेकिन जब Reporting Verb के साथ Pronoun का प्रयोग होता है तो Inversion का प्रयोग नहीं होता है। जैसे:
"Do it for me", she said
"Go there", he instructed.
She एवं he, pronoun हैं।

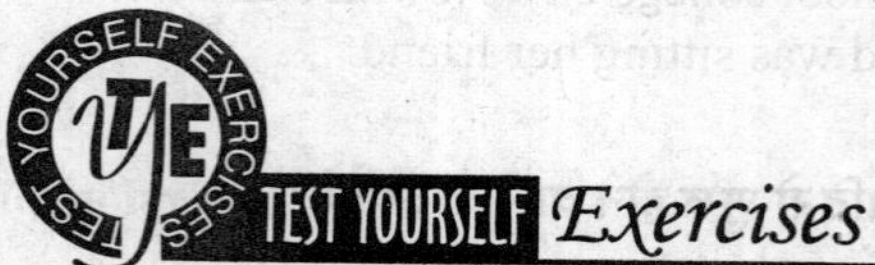

01

Read the following sentences to find whether there is any error in any part:

(1) "Under no circumstances (a) I can help you (b) in this venture" (c) said Sita. (d)

(2) "I don't like (a) such a bright colour (b) nor she does", (c) he said to Ram. (d)

(3) "Every member of (a) his family is (b) addicted to gambling (c) and so John is. (d)

(4) Never before (a) I had been asked (b) to go there (c) by bus. (d)

(5) On no account (a) this switch must (b) be touched. (c)

(6) "Seldom I had seen (a) such a (b) beautiful girl", (c) said Mohanti. (d)

(7) Under a tree (a) was sleeping an (b) old lady (c) with her young child. (d) No error (e)

(8) To such a degree (a) he created (b) the problems that (c) people thrashed him. (d)

(9) Not only she watched (a) the news (b) but she also (c) cooked food. (d)

(10) No sooner the plane landed at the (a) airport than (b) a group of armed (c) commandos surrounded it. (d)

Verbs

02

Fill in the blanks with suitable forms of verbs given in the brackets:

(1) He (live) in Kolkata for five years.
(2) At the moment he (play) in the park.
(3) I (wish) I knew the girl's name.
(4) She (take) a bath when the telephone rang.

(5) I already (tell) you that you should work hard.
(6) Ram always (remember) that honesty is the best policy.
(7) Ramesh (leave) his house before I called on him.
(8) They always (believe) that love is stronger than hate.
(9) She told me that her mother (go) to the doctor half an hour before.
(10) I (wash) my hands when he came.
(11) I already (tell) you what to do under these circumstances.
(12) It is high time you (start) working with full zeal.

03

Fill in the blanks with suitable forms of verbs given in the brackets:

(1) Ramesh (pass) the post-office on his way to office every day.
(2) He (watch) television when Ramesh came in.
(3) He (tell) me that she had never met you.
(4) He (read) since 2 O'clock.
(5) If you promise to work hard I (allow) you to go on leave.
(6) The doctor (arrive) just before Sita went away.
(7) The sun (shine) by day and the moon by night.
(8) She (attend) college since May last.
(9) You (receive) your award tomorrow.
(10) I (have) dinner last night at 9 O'clock.
(11) I (write) a letter before I went to play.
(12) He (read) the newspaper when Ram came in.

04

Fill in the blanks with suitable forms of verbs given in the brackets:

(a) A farmer was very fond of the two animals. When he (come) out for a stroll, these two creatures (amuse) him. One day as the farmer (walk) in the garden, these pets (run) away from him. He (search) for them but of no avail.
(b) He (be) a black man. One winter morning he (look) out of his window as he (dress). He (not hate) the winter now, for he (know) that it (be) merely the spring asleep and that the flowers (rest).

05

Fill in the blanks with suitable forms of verbs given in the brackets.

(1) When they left this morning, the sun................ (shine)
(2) The Chairman cannot see anybody as he .... some letters. (dictate)
(3) If it is possible, we ....to Chennai tomorrow. (go)
(4) Ram .... from fever since yesterday night. (suffer)
(5) We .... nothing to eat for three days. (have)
(6) He said that he .... for a walk today in the evening. (go)
(7) If I were you I .... to accept the bribe! (refuse)
(8) We .... at the news of his defeat. (surprise)
(9) He.................. while stealing the jewels. (catch)
(10) The children .... at the prospect of going for a picnic. (please)
(11) She .... of herself. (ashamed)
(12) Ravi Shankar .... by the Music Society. (honour)
(13) .... you .... playing cricket? (like)
(14) .... the doctor .... to see you yesterday? (come)
(15) .... it .... all the year round here? (rain)

06

Fill in the blanks with suitable forms of verbs given in the brackets:

(1) She saw that the clock.............. (to stop)
(2) He replied that he .... better. (to feel)
(3) Ramesh .... so hard that he is certain to succeed. (to work)
(4) He speaks as one who .... (to know)
(5) So long as the rain ... I stayed in office. (to continue)
(6) If I go to market I .... a pen for you. (to bring)
(7) A child always.... magazines about ghosts. (to enjoy)
(8) He .... to Delhi last week. (to go)
(9) They .... in Jaipur for three years. (to stay)
(10) They............. here for the last two hours. (to wait)
(11) I .... to her day before yesterday. (to write)
(12) These students .... cricket next Sunday. (to play)
(13) It .... when they went out. (to rain)
(14) Cow .... grass. (to eat)
(15) We .... to the pictures yesterday. (go)

07

Fill in the blanks with suitable forms of verbs given in the brackets:

(1) She .... letters yesterday. (write)
(2) The construction of new hotel .... stopped. (be)
(3) I .... English for three years now. (study)
(4) I .... her for a very long time. (know)
(5) He................ away last week. (go)
(6) We.................. tennis together last June. (play)
(7) I enjoy .... a good social film. (watch)
(8) The little boy admitted that he .... the glass. (break)
(9) She forgot .... the door when she went to market. (lock)
(10) As she .... there, someone bumped into her. (wait)
(11) He will unlock the door when he .... here. (get)
(12) He would have done it if you .... him so. (tell)
(13) He is used to .... on a hard bed so he does not mind. (sleep)
(14) He managed to avoid ....hit by the bat. (be)

08

Rewrite the following with the correct forms of the verbs given within the brackets:

(1) I (sleep) soundly and (dream) that a dog (enter) the room. I (spring) off the bed.
(2) The shot (wound) the elephant. It (rush) back into the forest.
(3) We (plan) to go to a hill station. Last year we (go) to Shimla. We (decide) to go somewhere else this time.
(4) Railways (connect) almost all the big cities and towns. In olden days people (use) to travel on horse-back or bullock carts. Travelling (become) easy now. We can imagine the difficulty the people (face) in the past.

09

Fill in the blanks with suitable forms of verbs given in the brackets:

(a) Yesterday I (go) to the market to buy a pen. I ought to have (purchase) a good one but I (choose) a cheap one with the result that it (do) not write smoothly now.
(b) I (wake) up early in the morning. I (go) out for a walk. Suddenly the wind (blow) violently. Many trees were (bring) down.
(c) The next morning his landlord (bring) him two pieces of news with his breakfast. One was that someone had (plant) a most beautiful climbing rose in the lane, the other was that Mr. Ramesh couldn't be (find) anywhere in the village. Everyone was (worry) about him.
(d) A walk through a garden (be) good for health and mind.We (go) for stroll in the Company Garden last Sunday. The flowers (present) a scene of colourfulness and we (feel) very happy.

10

Fill in the blanks with suitable forms of verbs given in the brackets:

(1) His mother (die) three months ago.
(2) We were taught at school that water (boil) at 212°F.
(3) He knew that I had (pass). (4) I should be pleased if he (not come).
(5) When Sahni (be) on his way to the railway station it (begin) to rain.
(6) Bakani (collect) stamps since childhood.
(7) Now tests (carry) on to find out the reaction of the new medicines on animals.
(8) I (go) for a walk daily in the evening. Last evening I (come) back from office rather late. Even though it (be) 7 P.M., I still (go), for my walk as usual. On (return) home I (find) that my little son (injure) his arm seriously. I (rush) to the nearby doctor for first aid.

11

Fill in the blanks with suitable verbs in agreement with the subjects. Select one from those given in the brackets:

(a) Either the mother or the daughter .... made this pudding. (have, has)
(b) A sum of fifty thousand rupees .... paid to him for this piece of land. (were, was)
(c) A variety of subjects .... taught in this school. (is, are)
(d) The father and his daughter .... coming to us today. (is, are)

12

Fill in the blanks with the correct forms of the verbs:

(a) I love nature.The spring season (be) the best of all seasons.There (be) freshness all around. Nature (breath) a new life and (look) colourful like a bride. Beautiful flowers (dance) merrily.
(b) The Taj Mahal (be) beautiful building.The Taj (stand) on the bank of the river Yamuna. It is (make) of white marble. It (have) four marble minarets on which the great dome (stand). Shah Jahan (build) it in memory of his beloved queen, Mumtaz, and it (cost), over three crore of rupees.

13

Fill in the blanks with the correct forms of the verbs.

(a) Sound sleep (be) necessary for good health. Every body (dream) during sleep. Sometimes the dreams (be) pleasant and at others, unpleasant. Last week I (have) a very bad dream.
I (dream) that my class, accompanied by our teachers,(go) to Shimla for the weekend.
(b) Last Sunday (be) a bad day for me as I (spend) the whole of it in bed. When I (get) up at 7 O'clock, I (have) a severe headache and (perspire). My mother (take) my temperature
I (consult) a doctor. He (check) me thoroughly.

14

Fill in the blanks choosing correct forms of the verbs from those given in the brackets:

(1) A flock of sheep........grazing in the ground. (is/are)
(2) Time and tide........for none. (wait/waits)
(3) More than five persons........signed the complaint. (have/has)
(4) One third of the work........lift incomplete. (was/were)
(5) Neither he nor his sister........invited. (was/were)
(6) Sachin is one of the players who........been selected for the match. (have/has)
(7) One of the students of our class........selected. (was/were)
(8) Age and experience........a man wise. (make/makes)
(9) Ten times fifty........five hundred. (is/are)
(10) It is I who........to answer him. (is/am)
(11) The sun........in the east. (rise)
(12) I........her last week at her residence. (meet)

15

Fill in the blanks with correct forms of the verbs given in the brackets:

(1) What........the latest news? (is/are)
(2) Fifty rupees........not a big amount. (is/are)
(3) The United States........a powerful nation. (is/are)
(4) Economics........an interesting subject. (is/are)
(5) Cattle........grazing in the field. (is/are)
(6) Neither of us........ready to go there. (is/are)
(7) Billiards........my favourite game. (is/are)
(8) What I say and what I think........my personal matters. (are/is)
(9) Both of them........good friends. (is/are)
(10) What........the news? (is/are)
(11) Honesty........the best policy. (be)
(12) She........a letter now. (write)

16

Fill in the blanks with suitable forms of verbs given in the brackets:

(1) Half of the apples........ripe. (is/are)
(2) Half of the land........uncultivated. (is /are)
(3) Barking dogs never........ (bite/bites)
(4) A lot of food........still lying on the table. (is/are)
(5) Fifty rupees........not a big sum for him. (is/are)
(6) The Himalayas........a range of mountains. (is/are)
(7) Neither she nor her son........arrived so far. (has/have)
(8) It is I who........to bear the loss. (is/am)
(9) I wish I........a writer. (was/were)
(10) Your trousers........very tight. (is/are)
(11) She........a letter to me last month. (write)
(12) I wish I........a queen. (be)

17

Fill in the blanks with correct forms of the verbs given in the brackets:

(1) Suraj, rather than his friends........guilty. (is/are)
(2) Quarters of this type........three bed rooms. (has/have)
(3) Oil and water........not mix fully. (do/does)
(4) A bunch of keys........found by her. (was/were)
(5) His trousers........not clean. (is/are)
(6) A flock of sheep........grazing in the field. (is/are)
(7) Everyone of the students........present in function. (was/were)
(8) I wish I........a beautiful girl. (was/were)
(9) A set of combs........been lost. (has/have)
(10) I........cricket, when she came. (play)
(11) We........that she would visit the college soon. (expect)

18

Fill in the blanks with suitable forms of the verb given in the brackets:

(1) I........Sita for a long time. (not see)
(2) Who........the Taj Mahal? (build)
(3) Did you........the poem ? (learn)
(4) Ram........here at 5 P.M. daily. (come)
(5) I........here for three years. (live)
(6) She will come here if you........him. (invite)
(7) I........her letter two days ago. (receive)
(8) Sita will assist you if you........her. (ask)
(9) She........come till now. (not)
(10) He........here for the last five years. (work)
(11) Had she worked hard she........ . (pass)
(12) He said earth........round the sun. (move)

19

Correct the following sentences:

(1) Rahul as well as his sisters were present in the party.
(2) Suresh and not his relatives were arrested.
(3) The Principal and the Warden was against the proposal.
(4) Either Ram or his friends was guilty.
(5) Neither Ram nor his friend Shyam were present in the party.
(6) The horse and carriage are at the gate.
(7) His kindness and benevolence are well known to everyone.
(8) His friend and benefactor were present there to protect him.
(9) The jury was divided in their opinion in that case.
(10) The wages of sin are death.
(11) Three parts of the house were left for me to live.
(12) Rahul together with his elder brother were present in the meeting.
(13) Neither of these questions are right.
(14) He qualified himself as an engineer.
(15) She has enlisted herself in the nursing college.

20

Correct the following sentences:

(1) Either he or I is to represent the school.
(2) Neither you nor he are to go now.
(3) The mob move towards the collectorate.
(4) The second innings were spoiled due to fire.
(5) Each hour and each minute are to be utilised by you.
(6) Every young and every old were happy to receive a gift.
(7) Not only the Tajmahal but also other monuments is worth seeing.
(8) The house with all its furniture were auctioned at a very low bid.
(9) The peacock like other birds have wings to fly.
(10) There is another schools better than this.
(11) The poors are never reliable.
(12) All the milk were used in the preparation of sweets.
(13) All the animals were given the proper diet.
(14) She apprised the inspector all that have happened tonight.
(15) Most of the person are reliable.

21

Correct the following sentences:

(1) About half of the girls was present in the hall.
(2) Half of the sugar were spoiled due to heavy rains.
(3) The apparatus purchased by the Nagar Parishad were very old.
(4) The advice of his friend are indeed valuable.
(5) Men after men were coming to visit the art gallery.
(6) One month after another have passed.
(7) His shoes is shining.
(8) Approximately ten sheeps were grazing in the college ground.
(9) A pair of shoes are purchased by her for her husband.
(10) There are many fishes in the aquarium.
(11) Each of the sports women were given a certificate.
(12) I wish I will be the minister!
(13) She ordered as if she is my elder sister.
(14) God saves our queen!
(15) He needs not go to market.

22

Correct the following sentences:

(1) More than one girl were killed in the accident.
(2) God blesses you with success!
(3) Financial help from all the quarters were received.
(4) The quality of these items are appreciated by everyone.
(5) The fragrance of these beautiful flowers are liked by all.
(6) More workman than one are not traceable.
(7) He said, "Plenty of milk are required for the party."
(8) A lot of books and magazines was destroyed by the fire.
(9) The number of students opted Hindi in RAS are generally large.
(10) A number of English magazines is available in the college library.

23

Correct the following sentences:

(1) It is I who is responsible for the loss in the business.
(2) The women who is standing there are my sisters.
(3) He is one of those who does not know anything about the incident.
(4) It is one of the problems that was taken care of by the civil administration.
(5) Nothing but monkeys are seen.
(6) No man and no woman were allowed to enter without payment.

(7) Much of the time were wasted by the students.
(8) More than one man were killed there.
(9) Economic cooperation between India and China are decreasing day by day.
(10) More students than one has participated in the annual function.

Spotting Errors (Verbs)

24

Rewrite the following sentences to find whether there is any error in any part:

(1) He ordered (a)/ as if he (b)/ was my master. (c)
(2) God saves (a)/ the queen Victoria. (b)
(3) If it was so (a)/ poetry (b)/ would cease to matter. (c)
(4) The merit (a)/ of these books (b)/ are known to everyone. (c)
(5) The condition of (a)/ people living in (b)/ rural area (c)/ are very bad. (d)
(6) The smell (a)/of these rose (b)/ flowers are (c)/ very sweet. (d)
(7) The condolence messages (a)/ received on the (b)/ death of Mrs. Gandhi (c)/ speaks highly of her greatness. (d)
(8) Economic cooperation (a)/ between the two countries (b)/ have increased substantially. (c)
(9) A band of musicians (a)/ have been engaged (b)/ for the inaugural function. (c)
(10) The number (a)/ of persons interested (b)/in psychology are (c)/generally small. (d)

25

Rewrite the following sentences to find whether there is any error in any part:

(1) The manager's comments (a)/on the preparation of the test matches (b)/ for this tour (c)/ has been generally praised. (d)
(2) The details (a)/of the incident (b)/was not known (c)/to me. (d)
(3) The majority of (a)/writers never (b)/passes this stage. (c)
(4) A large part of (a)/the distinctive features (b)/of the mind is due to its being (c)/ an instrument of communication. (d)
(5) A part of (a)/the mango (b)/are rotten. (c)
(6) A part of (a)/the mangoes (b)/are rather. (c)/ No error (d)
(7) The governing body at (a)/its first meeting (b)/ have decided (c)/to conduct the test again. (d)
(8) The banker's association (a)/has submitted a memorandum (b)/for the fulfilment of (c)/their demands. (d)
(9) Five quintals of wooden coal (a)/are (b)/his annual requirement (c)/for the unit. (d)
(10) Dickens have criticised (a)/the philosophy (b)/in'Hard Times'. (c)

26

Rewrite the following sentences to find whether there is any error in any part:

(1) All his money (a)/is spent (b) /and all his (c)/hopes ruined. (d)
(2) This rule may (a)/and ought to be (b)/disregarded for the time being. (c)
(3) He is one of the (a)/richest man (b)/if not the richest man (c)/in the world. (d)
(4) We can almost get (a)/everything in (b)/this market. (c)
(5) Every (a)/Tom, Dick and Harry (b)/drink wine these days. (c)
(6) He and I (a)/is partners in (b)/this firm. (c)
(7) He is one of the (a)/great man (b)/that have ever lived. (c)
(8) The magistrate and collector (a)/were (b)/present there (c)/on the spot. (d)
(9) Horse and Carriage (a)/are (b)/waiting there (c)/for the couple. (d)
(10) Rice and fish (a)/are (b)/my favourite dish. (c)

27

Rewrite the following sentences to find whether there is any error in any part:

(1) He is one of the (a)/tallest man (b)/if not the tallest man (c)/in the city. (d)
(2) He made a blunder (a)/and worse than (b)/that a crime. (c)
(3) The wheat (a)/on this farm (b)/is finer than (c)/last year. (d)
(4) I scarcely have (a)/enough silk (b)/for my saree. (c)
(5) Every day (a)/and every night (b)/bring its (c)/own pleasures for every one. (d)
(6) He more than (a)/his parents (b)/are responsible (c)/for his bad habits. (d)
(7) Bread and butter (a)/are (b)/a rich and nourishing food. (c)
(8) Not only she (a)/but all her sisters (b)/has been married (c)/since long. (d)
(9) There are (a)/nothing but (b)/miseries in her life. (c)
(10) Either he (a)/or I is (b)/responsible for the loss. (c)

Solution TYE 01

(1) (b) I can help you की जगह can I help you होगा। under no circumstances के साथ Inversion का प्रयोग होता है
(2) (c) nor she does की जगह nor does she आएगा। इस तरह के वाक्यों में nor के साथ Inversion का प्रयोग होता है।
(3) (d) so John is की जगह so is John लिखा जाएगा। इस तरह के वाक्यों में so के साथ Inversion का प्रयोग होता है।
(4) (a) Never के साथ Inversion लगता है। अत: never had I been लिखा जाएगा।
(5) (b) On no account के साथ Inversion लगता है। अत: must this switch लिखा जाएगा।
(6) (a) Seldom had I seen लिखा जाएगा। seldom/Hardly/ Rarely/Scarcely/Never के वाक्य शुरू होने पर Inversion लगता है।
(7) (e) वाक्य सही है।
(8) (b) To such a degree के बाद Inversion लगता है। अत: he created की जगह did he create आएगा।
(9) (a) A Not only से वाक्य शुरू होने पर Inversion लगता है। Not only did he watch लिखा जाना चाहिए।
(10) (a) No sooner से वाक्य शुरू होने पर Inversion लगता है। अत: No sooner did the plane land होना चाहिए।

Solution TYE 02

(1) He has been living in Kolkata for five years .
(2) At the moment he is playing in the park.
(3) I wish I knew the girl's name.
(4) She was taking a bath when the telephone rang.
(5) I have already told you that you should work hard.
(6) Ram always remembers that honesty is the best policy.
(7) Ramesh had left his house before I called on him.
(8) They always believe that love is stronger than hate.
(9) She told me that her mother had gone to the doctor half an hour before.
(10) I was washing my hands when he came.
(11) I have already told you what to do under these circumstances.
(12) It is high time you started working with full zeal.

Solution TYE 03

(1) Ramesh passes the post-office on his way to office everyday.
(2) He was watching television when Ramesh came in.
(3) He told me that she had never met you.
(4) He has been reading since 2 O'clock.
(5) If you promise to work hard I shall allow you to go on leave.
(6) The doctor arrived just before Sita went away.
(7) The sun shines by day and the moon by night.
(8) She has been attending college since May last.
(9) You will receive your prize tomorrow.
(10) I had dinner last night at 9 O'clock.
(11) I had written a letter before I went to play.
(12) He was reading the newspaper when Ram came in.

Solution TYE 04

(a) A farmer was very fond of the two animals.When he came out for a stroll, these two creatures amused him. One day as the farmer was walking in the garden, these pets ran away from him. He searched for them but of no avail.
(b) He was a black man. One winter morning he looked out of his window as he was dressing. He did not hate the asleep that the flowers were resting.

Solution TYE 05

(1) When they left this morning, the sun was shining.
(2) The Chairman cannot see anybody as he is dictating some letters.
(3) If it is possible we shall go to Chennai tomorrow.
(4) Ram has been suffering from fever since yesterday night.
(5) We have nothing to eat for three days.
(6) He said that he would go for a walk today in the evening.
(7) If I were you I would refuse to accept the bribe.
(8) We were surprised at the news of his defeat.
(9) He was caught while stealing the jewels.
(10) The children were pleased at the prospect of going for a picnic.
(11) She was ashamed of herself.
(12) Ravi Shankar was honoured by the Music Society.
(13) Do you like playing cricket?
(14) Did the doctor come to see you yesterday?
(15) Does it rain all the year round here?

Solution TYE 06

(1) She saw that the clock had stopped.
(2) He replied that he was feeling better.
(3) Ramesh is working so hard that he is certain to succeed.
(4) He speaks as one who knows.
(5) So long as the rain continued I stayed in office.
(6) If I go to market I shall bring a pen for you.
(7) A child always enjoys magazines about ghosts.
(8) He went to Delhi last week.
(9) They have been staying in Jaipur for three years.
(10) They have been waiting here for the last two hours.
(11) I wrote to her day before yesterday.
(12) These students will play cricket next Sunday.
(13) It was raining when they went out.
(14) Cow eats grass.
(15) We went to the pictures yesterday.

Solution TYE 07

(1) She wrote letters yesterday.
(2) The construction of new hotel was stopped.
(3) I have studied English for three years now.
(4) I have known her for a very long time.
(5) He went away last week.
(6) We played tennis together last June.
(7) I enjoy watching a good social film.
(8) The little boy admitted that he had broken the glass.
(9) She forgot to lock the door when she went to market.
(10) As she was waiting there, someone bumped into her.
(11) He will unlock the door when he gets here.
(12) He would have done it if you had told him to so.
(13) He is used to sleeping on a hard bed so he does not mind.
(14) He managed to avoid being hit by the bat.

Solution TYE 08

(1) I was sleeping soundly and dreamt that a dog had entered the room. I sprang off the bed.
(2) The shot wounded the elephant. It rushed back into the forest.
(3) We are planning to go to a hill station. Last year we went to Shimla. We have decided to go somewhere else this time.
(4) Railways connect almost all the big cities and towns. In olden days people used to travel on horse-back or bullock carts. Travelling has become easy now. We can imagine the difficulty the people faced in the past.

Solution TYE 09

(a) Yesterday I went to market to buy a pen. I ought to have purchased a good one but I chose a cheap one with the result that it does not write smoothly now.
(b) I woke up early in the morning. I went out for a walk. Suddenly the wind blew violently. Many trees were brought down.
(c) The next morning his landlord brought him two pieces of news with his breakfast. One was that someone had planted a most beautiful climbing rose in the lane, the other was that Mr. Ramesh couldn't be found anywhere in the village. Everyone was worried about him.
(d) A walk through a garden is good for health and mind.We went for stroll in the Company Garden last Sunday. The flowers presented a scene of colourfulness and we felt very happy.

Solution TYE 10

(1) His mother died three months ago.
(2) We were taught at school that water boils at 212° F.
(3) He knew that I had passed.
(4) I should be pleased if he does not come.
(5) When Sahni was on his way to the railway station it began to rain.
(6) Bakani has been collecting stamps since childhood.
(7) Now tests are being carried on to find out the reaction of the new medicines on animals.
(8) I go for a walk daily in the evening. Last evening I came back from office rather late. Even though it was 7 P.M. I still went for my walk as usual. On returning home I found that my little son injured his arm seriously. I rushed to the nearby doctor for first aid

Solution TYE 11

(a) Either the mother or the daughter has made this pudding.
(b) A sum of fifty thousand rupees was paid to him for this piece of land.
(c) A variety of subjects is taught in this school.
(d) The father and his daughter are coming to us today.

Solution TYE 12

(a) is, is, breathes, looks, dance
(b) is, stands, made, has, stands , built, cost

Solution TYE 13

(a) is, dreams, are, had, dreamed, had gone
(b) was, spent, got, had, was perspiring, took, consulted, checked.

Solution TYE 14

(1) is, (2) wait, (3) have, (4) was, (5) was, (6) have,
(7) was, (8) makes, (9) is, (10) am, (11) rises, (12) met.

Solution TYE 15

(1) is, (2) is, (3) is, (4) is, (5) are, (6) is,
(7) is, (8) are, (9) are, (10) is, (11) is, (12) is writing.

Solution TYE 16

(1) are, (2) is, (3) bite, (4) is, (5) is, (6) are,
(7) has, (8) am, (9) were, (10) are, (11) wrote, (12) were.

Solution TYE 17

(1) is, (2) have, (3) do, (4) is, (5) are, (6) is,
(7) was, (8) were, (9) has, (10) was playing,
(11) had expected.

Solution TYE 18

(1) have not seen, (2) built, (3) learn, (4) comes, (5) have been living,
(6) invite, (7) received, (8) ask, (9) has not, (10) has been working,
(11) would have been passed, (12) moves.

Solution TYE 19

(1) Rahul as well as his sisters was present in the party.
(2) Suresh and not his relatives was arrested.
(3) The Principal and the Warden were against the proposal.
(4) Either Ram or his friends were guilty.
(5) Neither Ram nor his friend Shyam was present in the party.
(6) The horse and carriage is at the gate.
(7) His kindness and benevolence is well known to everyone.
(8) His friend and benefactor was present there to protect him.
(9) The jury were divided in their opinion in that case.
(10) The wages of sin is death.
(11) Three parts of the house was left for me to live.
(12) Rahul together with his elder brother was present in the meeting.
(13) Neither of these questions is right.
(14) He qualified as an engineer.
(15) She has enlisted in the nursing college.

Solution TYPE 20

(1) Either he or I am to represent the school.
(2) Neither you nor he is to go now.
(3) The mob moves towards the collectorate.
(4) The second innings was spoiled due to fire.
(5) Each hour and each minute is to be utilised by you.
(6) Every young and every old was happy to receive a gift.
(7) Not only the Tajmahal but also other monuments are worth seeing.
(8) The house with all its furniture was auctioned at a very low bid.
(9) The peacock like other birds has wings to fly.
(10) There is another school better than this.
(11) The poor are never reliable.
(12) All the milk was used in the preparation of sweets.
(13) All the animals were given the proper diet.
(14) She apprises the inspector all that has happened tonight.
(15) Most of the persons are reliable.

Solution TYE 21

(1) About half of the girls were present in the hall.
(2) Half of the sugar was spoiled due to heavy rains.
(3) The apparatus purchased by the Nagar Parishad was very old.
(4) The advice of his friend is indeed valuable.
(5) Man after man was coming to visit the art gallery.
(6) One month after another has passed.
(7) His shoes are shining.
(8) Approximately ten sheep were grazing in the college ground.
(9) A pair of shoes is purchased by her for her husband.
(10) There are many fish in the aquarium.
(11) Each of the sportswoman given a certificate.
(12) I wish I were the minister.
(13) She ordered as if she were my elder sister.
(14) God save our queen!
(15) He need not go to market.

Solution TYE 22

(1) More than one girl was killed in the accident.
(2) God bless you with success!
(3) Financial help from all the quarters was received.
(4) The quality of these items is appreciated by everyone.
(5) The fragrance of these beautiful flowers is liked by all.
(6) More workman than one is not traceable.
(7) He said, "Plenty of milk is required for the party."
(8) A lot of books and magazines were destroyed by the fire.
(9) The number of students opted Hindi in RAS is generally large.
(10) A number of English magazines are available in the college library.

Solution TYE 23

(1) It is I who am responsible for the loss in the business.
(2) The women who are standing there are my sisters.
(3) He is one of those who do not know anything about the incident.

(4) It is one of the problems that were taken care of by the civil administration.
(5) Nothing but monkeys is seen.
(6) No man and no woman was allowed to enter without payment.
(7) Much of the time was wasted by the students.
(8) More than one man was killed there.
(9) Economic cooperation between India and China is decreasing day by day.
(10) More students than one have participated in the annual function.

Solution TYE 24

(1) (c) was की जगह 'were' आएगा। जब वाक्य में कल्पना (Imaginations) का भाव हो, तो singular subject के साथ 'were' का प्रयोग होता है। जैसे:
I wish I were a king. I wish it were possible.

(2) (a) saves की जगह save आएगा। ऐसे वाक्य जिनमें कोई इच्छा (desire), अभिलाषा (wish) या आशीर्वाद (blessing) का भाव हो तो verbs; bless, live, save एवं help हमेशा plural में आती है अर्थात् इनके साथ s नहीं लगता है। जैसे: May Lord help you! Long live our friendship!

(3) (a) was की जगह 'were' आएगा। Question (1) का explanation देखें। 'If it was so' reflects imaginations.

(4) (c) 'are' की जगह 'is' आएगा। यहाँ subject 'merit' है, जो singular है अत: verb singular होगी।

(5) (d) 'are' की जगह 'is' आएगा। यहाँ subject of the verb, condition है जो singular है। अत: verb भी singular होगी।

(6) (c) 'are' की जगह 'is' लिखें। यहाँ subject of the verb is 'small 'which is singular अत: verb (is) भी singular ही लगेगा।

(7) (d) speaks की जगह speak आएगा verb (speak) का subject, condolence messages है, जो plural है अत: verb, plural होगी।

(8) (c) 'have' की जगह 'has' आएगा subject economic cooperation singular है। अत: verb भी singular होगा।

(9) (b) have been की जगह has been आएगा। A 'band' collective noun है जिसके साथ singular verb का प्रयोग होगा।

(10) (c) 'are' की जगह 'is' आएगा। 'The number' एक निश्चित संख्या को बताता है, collective noun की जगह प्रयुक्त होती है। अत: हमेशा singular verb का प्रयोग किया जाता है।

Solution TYPE 25

(1) (d) 'has been' की जगह 'have been' आएगा। verb का subject, manager's comments है जो कि plural है अत: verb भी plural होगी।

(2) (c) 'was' की जगह were आएगा। subject of the verb—details, plural है। अत: verb भी plural (were) होगी।

(3) (c) passes की जगह pass आएगा। The majority of ए यहाँ 'of' के बाद जो noun आया है, वह plural (writers) है, अत: verb भी plural ही रहेगी।

(4) (c) 'mind is due' की जगह mind are due आएगा। of के बाद (A large part of the distinctive features) आने वाला noun यहाँ plural (features) है। अत: verb भी plural लगेगी।

(5) (c) 'are' की जगह 'is' लिखें। of के बाद (A part of the mango) आने वाला noun (mango) singular है, अत: verb भी singular लगेगी।

(6) (d) No error. of के बाद आने वाला noun (mangoes) plural है, अत: verb भी plural लगेगी।

(7) (c) have की जगह has लिखें governing body, collective noun है अत: verb singular लगेगी।

(8) (d) 'their' की जगह 'its' लगेगा। The banker's association एक collective noun है। अत: यहाँ pronoun, its आएगा।

(9) (b) 'are' की जगह 'is' लिखें 'five quintals एक निश्चित weight को व्यक्त करता है जो collective noun की तरह singular noun का बोध कराता है, अत: verb singular (is) ही लगेगी।

(10) (a) have की जगह has लगेगा Dickens एक व्यक्ति का नाम है।

Solution TYE 26

(1) (d) hopes के बाद 'are' insert करें। जब वाक्य में पहले आने वाली verb (यहाँ 'is') दूसरे noun के number एवं person से मेल नहीं खाती है, तो दूसरे noun के अनुसार अलग से verb का प्रयोग होता है। Hopes, plural है अत: यहाँ plural verb लगेगा।

(2) (a) may के बाद 'be' का प्रयोग करें। प्रश्न (1) का Explanation देखें।

(3) (b) richest man की जगह richest men आएगा। one of के बाद आने वाले adjective के साथ plural noun आता है।

(4) (a) We can almost get की जगह we can get almost लिखना चाहिए। adverb के गलत जगह लिखने से वाक्य का अर्थ ही बदल जाता है।

(5) (c) drink की जगह drinks आएगा। Every, Each के साथ इस तरह के वाक्यों में singular verb लगती है।

6. (b) 'is' की जगह 'are' आएगा। जब दो nouns को and से जोड़ा जाता है तो verb, plural आती है।

(7) (b) one of the के बाद adjective के बाद plural noun आता है 'man' की जगह 'men' लिखें।

(8) (b) were की जगह 'was' लिखे। यहाँ magistrate एवं collector एक ही व्यक्ति को refer करते हैं।

(9) (b) 'are' की जगह 'is' लिखें। Horse and carriage जोड़े की तरह एक ही वस्तु का ज्ञान कराते हैं। अत: verb singular लगेगी।

(10) (b) are की जगह 'is' लिखें Rice and fish एक pair की तरह, एक चीज का ही संकेत करते हैं। अत: verb, singular लगेगी।

Solution TYE 27

(1) (b) tallest man की जगह tallest men लिखें। one of the के बाद आने वाले adjective के साथ plural noun आता है।

(2) (c) That a crime की जगह That committed a crime होगा। वाक्य में भाग (a) में आने वाली verb made के साथ crime का मेल नहीं बैठता है।

(3) (d) Last year की जगह than it was last year लिखें। वाक्य में wheat की quality का comparison, year से हो रहा है, अत: गलत है।

(4) (a) I scarcely have की जगह I have scarcely लिखा जाना चाहिए। Misplacement of adverb can change the meaning of a sentence.

(5) (c) bring की जगह brings आएगा। इस तरह के वाक्यों में singular noun का प्रयोग every /each के साथ होता है।

(6) (c) 'are' की जगह 'is' लिखें। जब दो nouns; as well as, more than, besides etc से संयुक्त हों तो verb से पहले noun के अनुसार लगती है। यहाँ verb 'He' के अनुसार 'is' ही लगेगी।

(7) (b) 'are' की जगह 'is' आएगा। bread and butter, pair की तरह एक ही वस्तु का ज्ञान कराते हैं।

(8) (c) 'has' की जगह 'have' लिखें। जब वाक्य में not only, but also का प्रयोग हो तो verb पास वाले noun के अनुसार लगती है, यहाँ पास वाला noun, her sisters है, अत: verb plural लगेगी।

(9) (a) 'There are' की जगह 'There is' लिखें। Nothing but के साथ singular verb का प्रयोग होता है।

(10) (b) 'is' की जगह 'am' आएगा। ऐसे वाक्यों में verb अपने नजदीक वाले noun या pronoun के अनुसार लगती है यहाँ I है, अत: 'am' लगेगा।

CHAPTER 12

NON-FINITES

Verb को Finite verb, एवं Non-finite verbs में भी वर्गीकृत किया जाता है।

Verb

Finites — Non-Finites

Finite Verb

जिन verbs में subject के Number, Person एवं Tense के अनुसार परिवर्तन होता है, finite verbs कहलाती हैं।

Look at the following sentences :

(a) I like to play. (b) He likes to play. (c) They like to play.
(d) He liked to play. (e) She liked to play. (f) They liked to play.

उक्त वाक्यों में like, finite verb हैं जो first person singular (I) एवं third person plural (they) के साथ तो like ही है, लेकिन third person singular (he) के साथ likes के रूप में है। इसी प्रकार past tense में इसका रूप liked हो गया है। अत: like एक finite verb है।

Non-Finites

उपरोक्त वाक्यों में to play; non-finite verb है जिसका रूप subject के number, person एवं वाक्य के tense से अप्रभावित है। अत: non-finite verbs ऐसी verbs होती हैं, जिन पर वाक्य के tense के subject के person एवं number का कोई प्रभाव नहीं पड़ता है। एक और महत्वपूर्ण बिन्दू है, कि Finite verb का एक subject अवश्य होता है लेकिन Non-finite verb का स्वयं का कोई subject (कर्ता) नहीं होता, बल्कि यह एक object की तरह वाक्य में दिखाई पड़ती है, जैसे : उक्त वाक्यों में like (Finite verb) का subject, I, He, They इत्यादि हैं। जबकि Non-finite verb; to play एक object की तरह प्रयुक्त हुई है।

Non-Finites

Infinitive (With or without to) — Gerund (Verb + ing Verbal noun) — Participle (Verb + ing Verbal adjective)

(1) Infinitive

इसको सामान्यतया 'to + verb' के रूप में जाना एवं पहचाना जाता है। जैसे : to play, to go, to walk etc. लेकिन कभी-कभी 'to' नहीं भी आता है। इस प्रकार की Infinitive को Bare Infinitive (Infinitive without to) कहा जाता है। जैसे :

I saw him go, I bade him go etc. यहाँ go, bare infinitive है।

Forms of Infinitive

Tense एवं voice के अनुसार Infinitive की निम्न forms होती हैं :

(a) Present infinitive simple – (To + infinitive) 'to do, to go.
(b) Present infinitive negative – (Not to + infinitive) not to do, not to go.
(c) Present continuous – (To be + …ing) to be doing, to be going.
(d) Perfect infinitive – (To have + past participle) to have gone, to have done.
(e) Perfect infinitive passive – (To have been + past participle) to have been done.
(f) Present infinitive passive – (To be + past participle) to be done, to be gone.
(g) Perfect continuous infinitive – (To have been + …ing) to have been doing.

Kinds of Infinitive

Infinitive को इनके प्रयोग के आधार पर दो भागों में वर्गीकृत किया जाता है

(1) Simple Infinitive or Noun Infinitive : इनका प्रयोग वाक्य में noun की तरह होता है। जब हिन्दी वाक्य के अन्त में 'ना' या 'नी' लगा हो तो सामान्यता ये simple infinitive को व्यक्त करते हैं। जैसें :

I am to go. मुझे जाना है।
He is about to go. वह जाने को है।

(2) Gerundial Infinitive : जब Infinitive का प्रयोग वाक्य में Adjective या Adverb की तरह होता है तो उसे gerundial infinitive कहा जाता है। जैसे :

(a) The sweet is good to eat. (b) This is the house to let.

Use of Simple Infinitive

Simple Infinitive / Noun Infinitive का प्रयोग निम्न प्रकार से किया जाता हैं :

(1) As subject (कर्ता के रूप में) :

(a) To abuse is wrong. (b) To live peacefully is not easy.
(c) To find fault is very easy.

उपरोक्त वाक्यों में Infinitive (underlined) का प्रयोग कर्ता के रूप में हुआ है। इस तरह के वाक्यों को निम्न प्रकार भी लिखा जा सकता है :

(a) To live peacefully is not easy. It is not easy to live peacefully.
(b) To abuse is wrong. It is wrong to abuse.
(c) To find faults is easy. It is easy to find faults.

(2) As object of a verb (क्रिया के verb के रूप में) :

(a) I love to play. (b) I want to write. (c) I wish to wait there.

यहाँ Infinitive, 'to play', 'to write', 'to wait' का प्रयोग verb के object के रूप में हुआ है।

(3) As object of a preposition (Preposition के object के रुप में) :

(a) The bus is about to start. (b) I have no choice but to go.
(c) The match is yet to finish.

इन वाक्यों में Infinitive 'to start', 'to go', 'to finish' का प्रयोग preposition, about, but एवं yet के object के रूप में किया गया है।

(4) As complement of a verb (क्रिया के पूरक के रूप में) :

(a) He only wishes to be an IAS Officer. (b) His ambition is to build a temple.
(c) Her dream is to purchase the whole city.

उपरोक्त वाक्यों में Infinitive; to be, to build, to purchase का प्रयोग verbs के complements के रूप में किया गया है। बिना इनका प्रयोग किये verb का अर्थ पूरा नहीं होता है। अत: ये verb के पूरक (complementary) कहलाते हैं।

(5) As an objective complement (Object के पूरक के रूप में) :

(a) I saw her go. (b) I bade him go.

(c) I shall have you realise your mistake.

उपरोक्त वाक्यों में Infinitive का प्रयोग objective complement के रूप में हुआ है ध्यान दें : उक्त वाक्यों में object, क्रमश: her, him, you हैं तथा Infinitive इन objects के पूरक के रूप में प्रयुक्त हुए है। यह भी नोट करें कि ये सभी Bare Infinitive हैं।

Use of Gerundial Infinitive

जैसा पूर्व में बताया गया है कि Gerundial Infinitives का प्रयोग वाक्य में Adjective या Adverb की तरह किया जाता है। Gerundial Infinitives का प्रयोग निम्न स्थितियों में किया जाता हैं :

(1) To modify a verb (क्रिया को संशोधित करने हेतु) :

सामान्यतया Infinitives का इस तरह का प्रयोग एक उददेश्य (purpose) को व्यक्त करता है।

(a) He came to meet her. (b) We earn to live happily.

(c) We went there to learn.

उपरोक्त वाक्यों में Infinitive एक purpose को व्यक्त करते है।

(2) To modify a noun (noun को संशोधित करने हेतु) :

(a) There is no chair to sit. (b) I have no money to waste.

(c) I have no magazine to read.

यहाँ Infinitive, noun को विशेषता प्रदान करते हैं।

(3) To modify an adjective (adjective को संशोधित करने हेतु) :

(a) I am happy to meet you. (b) These fruit are delicious to eat.

(c) I was worried to know it.

उपरोक्त वाक्यों में Infinitive, adjectives, happy delicious, worried को quality / modify करते हैं।

(4) To modify the whole sentence (पूरे वाक्य को ही संशोधित करने हेतु) :

(a) To tell the truth, I forgot what I said. (b) To be honest, I indeed didn't recognise her.

(c) To swim in sea water is very easy.

यहाँ Infinitive वाक्य के शुरू में आये हैं एवं पूरे वाक्य को ही संशोधित कर रहे हैं।

Bare Infinitive or Infinitive Without 'to'

जैसा पूर्व में बताया गया है, बहुत सी स्थितियों में Infinitive के साथ 'to' का प्रयोग नहीं किया जाता है।

Use of Bare Infinitive

(1) निम्न Auxiliary verbs के साथ आने वाले Infinitives के साथ 'to' नहीं लगाया जाता है। shall, will, should, do, did, may, might, must, can, could, need.

(a) I shall play. (b) He will come. (c) I should write.

(d) He would write. (e) I may go. (f) He might come.

(g) They must play. (h) He can say. (i) I could talk.

(j) He need not come here.

ought एवं used (ये सभी Modal auxiliaries हैं।) के साथ to का प्रयोग किया जाता हैं। जैसे :
(a) He ought to come here. *(b) He used to smoke.*
(c) I am used to the vehicular noise.

Dare, Need का प्रयोग जब modals की तरह किया जाता है। (सामान्यताया Negative एवं Interrogative वाक्यों में) तो इनके साथ 'to' नहीं लगता है। लेकिन जब इनका प्रयोग principal verbs की तरह किया जाता है तो इनके साथ 'to' का प्रयोग होता है। जैसे :

(a) He dare not speak so.	*As modal*
(b) Dare she complain against you ?	*As modal*
(c) He dares to speak so.	*As principal verb*
(d) She dares to talk like that.	*Principal verb*
(e) He need not go there.	*As modal*
(f) He needs my help.	*As principal verb*

Need के साथ कई स्थितियों में Principal verb की तरह प्रयोग करने पर 'to' लगता है, कई स्थितियों में नहीं भी लगता है।

(2) निम्न verb के बाद आने वाले Infinitive के साथ 'to' का प्रयोग Active voice में नहीं होता है। Bid, let, make, feel, watch, behold, hear, overhear, notice, observe, see, etc.

(a) She bade me go. (b) Let her sing.
(c) I made him sing (d) I didn't notice him go.
(e) I feel her touch. (f) I observed him play.

लेकिन यदि उक्त verb का प्रयोग passive voice में किया जायेगा तो Infinitive के साथ 'to' का प्रयोग होता है। जैसे :

(a) He was made to sing. (b) I was bidden to go.

लेकिन let के साथ passive में भी 'to' नहीं लगेगा : She was let sing.

(3) निम्न शब्दों के साथ Bare Infinitive का ही प्रयोग किया जाता है। had better, would rather, would sooner, sooner than, rather than, had sooner etc.

(a) He had better withdraw.
(b) You had better resign.
(c) He would sooner resign than fight with the boss.
(d) I would go rather than waste my time here.

उक्त वाक्यों के structure का ध्यान रखे। इस तरह के वाक्यों में verb की First form (Infinitive without to) का प्रयोग होता है। इस तरह के वाक्य परीक्षा में कई रूप में पूछे जाते हैं।

(4) वाक्य में यदि conjunction, than का प्रयोग हुआ है तो उसके बाद Bare infinitive का प्रयोग ही होगा। जैसे :

(a) She is better able to speak than write.
(b) He is stronger than I.

(5) Have / has /had के बाद यदि noun या pronoun आता है एवं उसके बाद कोई Infinitive का प्रयोग होता है। तो वह Bare infinitive (Infinitive without to) होगा। जैसे :

(a) I will have him realise his mistake. (b) I had him know his mistakes.
(c) They will have you accept your fault.

(6) निम्न प्रकार के वाक्यों में except to / but to नहीं लगता है।

(a) I can do nothing but protest.
(b) He did nothing but cry.
(c) They did nothing but weep.
(d) The dog does nothing except bark.

(7) Why + Bare infinitive का प्रयोग इस तरह के प्रश्न पूछने के लिए किया जाता है। जिनसे यह जाहिर होता है कि इस तरह का मूर्खतापूर्ण कार्य क्यों किया गया है? जैसे :

(a) Why hire a taxi? (When we have sufficient room to accommodate you.)
(b) Why talk to him? (When he has openly criticized you.)

जबकि Why not + infinitive से सुझाव/सलाह दी जाती है।

(a) Why not consult a doctor?
(b) Why not write to your father?
(c) Why not inform your parents?

Specific Use of Infinitives Rules

(1) निम्न Verbs के बाद सीधे ही Infinitive (With to) का प्रयोग किया जा सकता है

agree appear aim arrange target attempt ask guarantee
bother claim
happen care decide learn choose
demand pretend condescend determine promise
consent resolve prove decline to be determined
seem fail swear hesitate threaten
hope undertake long manage neglect
offer plan prepare be prepared proceed
refuse tend trouble (negative) volunteer vow

(a) He agreed to pay ₹ 250 only.
(b) They are preparing to evacuate the colony.
(c) He refused to surrender.
(d) I volunteered to help with bread and money.
(e) They can't afford to live in this posh area.
(f) I don't bother to answer any question.
(g) We failed to contact her in time.

(2) निम्न Verbs का प्रयोग Verb+Object+Infinitive या Verb+Infinitive किसी भी प्रकार किया जा सकता है : ask, beg, expect, would hate, help, intend, like, would like, would love, mean, prefer, want, wish. जैसे :

(a) He likes to drink well.
(b) He likes his friends to drink well.
(c) I want to go.
(d) I want you to go.
(e) I asked him to come here.
(f) I asked him to speak to Mrs. James.
(g) I begged to go (Please let me go).
(h) I begged him to go (Please go).
(i) I expect her to arrive tomorrow.
(j) I expect to arrive tomorrow.

Care, hate, like, love एवं *prefer* के बाद *Gerund* का प्रयोग किया जा सकता है।

(3) कुछ Verbs का प्रयोग निम्न structure में किया जाता है :

Verb + Object + Infinitive :

advise	forbid	entitle	allow
oblige	teach	bribe	order
tell command	implore	permit	
tempt	compels	induce	persuade
instruct	remind	urge	encourage
invite	request	train	enable
warn	force	make*	hear*
let* see*	watch*	feel*	
help*	notice*	observe*	look at*

(*) लगी हुई Verbs के साथ Infinitive 'without to' (Bare infinitive) का प्रयोग होता है। जैसे :

(a) He persuaded me to go with her.
(b) I have trained these dogs to sniff out drugs.
(c) He encouraged me to try again.
(d) They forbade us to pluck the flowers.
(e) These goggles will enable you to see in dim light.
(f) We watched him clear the table.
(g) They heard the thief crash through the door.
(h) She made me do it.
(i) We helped her finish the homework.

Verbs, show, teach, tell के साथ उक्त Structure में Infinitive का प्रयोग करते समय how का प्रयोग करना आवश्यक है। जैसे :

(a) He showed me how to operate the machine.
(b) He told me how to replace a fuse.
(c) He taught me how to light a cigarette without a match box.

जब कभी 'Skill' बहुत common हो तो how का प्रयोग नहीं भी किया जाता है।

(a) He taught me to ride. *(b) He taught me to write my name.*

(4) Verb + How/what/when/where/which/why + infinitive :

उक्त structure में सामान्यतया verbs; ask, decide, discover, find out, forget, know, learn, remember, see (= understand, perceive), think,understand, want to know, wonder etc का प्रयोग किया जाता है। उसके अतिरिक्त उक्त structure में show+ object + wh-word + infinitive का भी प्रयोग होता है। जैसे :

(a) He knows how to swim.
(b) He discovered how to operate the machine.
(c) I asked him, where to buy fruits at reasonable rate.
(d) I remember when to switch off the machine.
(e) Tell me what to do.
(f) He wants to know how to write a good letter.
(g) I learned how to write a good precis.
(h) I showed him which button to press.
(i) I remembered to get a ticket.
(j) I decided to do it.

Verbs; ask, decide, forget, learn, remember के बाद सीधे ही Infinitive का प्रयोग किया जा सकता है। जैसे :
(a) She learnt to drive a car. *(b) She decide to go to Jaipur.*
(c) She asked to bring a copy. *(d) I remembered to get a ticket.*

(5) Whether + infinitive का प्रयोग verbs, want to know एवं wonder के साथ निम्न प्रकार किया जाता हैं :
(a) I wonder whether to write or not.
(b) I wanted to know whether to protest or keep silence.

(6) Infinitive का the first, the second,............ the last, the only के बाद प्रयोग एवं superlative degree of adjectives के साथ प्रयोग निम्न प्रकार होता है :
(a) Sita loves parties, she is always the first to arrive and the last to leave.
(the first who comes and the last who leaves).
(b) He was the only one to survive the accident.
(the only one who survived).
(c) It was the best play to be performed that year.
(means the best play that was performed that year).

(7) Verbs; assume, believe, feel, suppose, consider, understand का प्रयोग निम्न structure में किया जाता है :
Verb +object + to be :
(a) I assume him to be the best athlete.
(b) I consider him to be an honest person.
(c) I thought her to be a dedicated teacher.
(d) He is supposed to be washing the car.

(8) निम्न nouns के बाद infinitive का प्रयोग सीधे ही किया जा सकता है। ये nouns हैं :

ability	decision effort	promise	willingness
ambition	demand failure	refusal	wish
anxiety	determination	offer	request desire
attempt	eagerness	plan	scheme

(a) He made an attempt to walk without support .
(b) His ability to get the work done is his main assets.
(c) Failure to find the fault may result in termination.
(d) Their offer/plan/promise to rebuild the house was not taken seriously.
(e) His unwillingness to do his work may result in his dismissal.
(f) She made an effort to solve the problem.

(9) Infinitive after 'too',
(I) **too + adjective + infinitive :**
(a) He is too weak to walk. (He is so weak that he cannot walk).
(b) He is too young to get married . (He is so young that he cannot get married).
(c) The box was too heavy to be carried by me.
(d) The grass was too wet to sit on.
(e) The light is too dim to read by.

उपरोक्त वाक्यों में too के बाद adjective प्रयोग होने के बाद infinitive का प्रयोग हुआ है।

(II) कई वाक्यों में too के साथ infinitive का प्रयोग निम्न structure में होता है :

too + adjective +a + noun + infinitive
(a) He is too shrewd a man to rely on anybody.
(b) He is too experienced a driver to mind what anybody say.

(III) too + adverb + infinitive :

(a) It is too soon to say whether the plan will run or not.
(b) He cried too loudly to be understood by any one.
(c) He works too slowly to be much use to her.

too के साथ infinitive का प्रयोग negativity show करता है। इस तरह के वाक्य दैनिक जीवन में बहुत प्रयोग में आते हैं।

(10) Infinitive after enough :

(I) Adjective + enough + infinitive :

(a) He is matured enough to take decisions. (b) She is bold enough to travel by herself.
(c) He is intelligent enough to solve the question. (d) The ice was thick enough to walk on.

उपरोक्त वाक्यों में adjective के बाद enough का प्रयोग हुआ है एवं फिर infinitive का प्रयोग हुआ है।

(II) Adverb + enough + infinitive :

(a) He jumped high enough to win the first prize.
(b) He spoke loudly enough to understand by all.
(c) He walked quickly enough to catch the train.
(d) She ran fast enough to catch the bus.

उपरोक्त वाक्यों में high, loudly, quickly, fast ; adverbs हैं।

(11) So.......... as + infinitive :

(a) He was so foolish as to leave his car unlocked.
(b) He was so intelligent as to argue without any difficult.
(c) Would you be so kind as to forward my request?

So.........as के साथ infinitiveका प्रयोग सामान्यतया (c) की तरह requestहेतु किया जाता है।

(12) Repetition को avoid करने के लिए 'to' का प्रयोग निम्न स्थिति में किया जाता है :

(a) Would you like to accompany me? Yes, I love to.
(b) Did you get a book ? No, I tried to, but there weren't left any.
(c) Why did you hire a taxi? I had to, I was very late.
(d) Does he swim? Not now, but he used to.

उपरोक्त वाक्यों 'to' 'to + infinitive' का कार्य करता दिखाई देता है। Repetition को avoid करने हेतु 'to' का यह महत्त्वपूर्ण प्रयोग है।

(13) Infinitive के बाद में only का प्रयोग कर्ता की निराशा (disappointment), हताशा (frustration) को व्यक्त करता है। जैसे:

(a) He hurried to his house only to find his wife dead.
(b) He survived the crash only to die in the hills.
(c) He hurried to the house only to find that it was looted by the thieves.

उपरोक्त वाक्यों में infinitive का only के बाद प्रयोग कर्ता की निराशा को व्यक्त करता है।

The Split Infinitives

(14) Infinitive के बीच में (to ,एवं infinitive) कोई भी adverb या शब्द लिखना traditional grammar में गलत माना है। लेकिन आजकल बहुत लेखक split of Infinitives को सही मानने लगे है। जैसे :

(a) I. He likes to completely cover the floor. II. He likes to cover the floor completely.
(b) I. He tried to unduly alarm people. II. He tried to alarm people unduly.
(c) I. The patient should try to, if possible, avoid going up and down stairs.
II. If possible, the patient should try to avoid going up and down stairs.

उपरोक्त वाक्यों में वाक्य II, वांक्य I से ज्यादा सही एवं सुन्दर लगता है। Split of Infinitives को avoid करना ही उचित है।

As per modern grammarians one adverb may be inserted between the infinitive.

I ask you to kindly grant me one day leave only.

Here insertion of adverb 'kindly' is well accepted now-a-days.

Continuous Infinitive

जैसा कि पूर्व में बताया गया है Continuous Infinitive की form—**to be + Present Participle** होती है।

Ram may be watching TV at this time.

Use of Continuous Infinitive

(A) Auxiliary Verbs के बाद will/shall/may/might/can/could/must/would/should के साथ Continuous Infinitive का प्रयोग निम्न प्रकार होता है :

(a) They'll be playing now.
(b) He might/may be watching T.V.
(c) He can't /could't be playing.
(d) He can't /couldn't be watching T.V.
(The field is occupied by the election team.)
(Because the cable operators are on strike.)
(e) She must be coming by morning train.
(f) She shouldn't be reading a magazine.
(g) She should be reading her text books.
(h) They would be waiting for us.

(B) Verbs, appear, happen, pretend, seem के साथ सामान्यतया continuous infinitive का प्रयोग होता है। जैसे :

(a) I happened to be looking towards the road when the car stopped.
(b) She seems to be following us.
(c) He appears to be living in that area.
(d) He pretended to be looking for a magazine.

Continuous infinitive का प्रयोग verb, agree, arrange, decide determine, hope, manage, plan के साथ भी किया जा सकता है। जैसे :

(a) I hope to be earning my living in a year's time.

(b) I determined to be waiting at the door. *(c) I agreed to be standing near the tree.*

Perfect Infinitive

जैसा कि पूर्व में बताया गया है Perfect Infinitive की form—**to have+ Past Participle** जैसे : to have gone, to have completed होती है।

Use of Perfect Infinitive

(1) Auxiliary Verbs के साथ Perfect Infinitive का प्रयोग : was/were के साथ Perfect Infinitive का प्रयोग एक unfulfilled Plan या arrangement को व्यक्त करता है। जैसे :

(a) The house was to have been ready so far. (But it is not ready.)
(b) She was to have gone. (But she has not gone.)

(2) Should/would/might/could के साथ Perfect Infinitive का प्रयोग Conditional sentence में किया जाता है। जैसे :

(a) If I had seen him, I would have invited him.
(b) If he had come to me, I might have helped him.
(c) If she had informed, I could have helped her.

ये सभी वाक्य, कार्य पूर्ण न होने को व्यक्त करते हैं।

(3) may/ might के साथ Perfect Infinitive का प्रयोग किया जाता है। जैसे :
He may/might have heard the news so far.
(It is possible that he has heard the news by now.)
यह कार्य पूर्ण होने की Probability को व्यक्त करता है।

(4) Must के साथ Perfect Infinitive का प्रयोग एक निश्चितता (Certainity) को व्यक्त करता है। जैसे :
The thief must have entered through this gate. (Here are his footprints.)

(5) Needn't के साथ Perfect Infinitive का प्रयोग एक ऐसे Past action को व्यक्त करता है जिसकी आवश्यकता नहीं थी। जैसे :

(a) He needn't have watered the plants.
(As it rained a day before.)
(b) You needn't have written him.
(As I had telephonic discussions with him yesterday.)

verbs; appear, hope, pretend, seem का प्रयोग perfect infinitives के साथ निम्न प्रकार होता है :

(a) He pretended to have learned the lesson.
(b) He seemed to have been a great sportsman.
(c) I happened to have driven that kind of jeep before.
(d) He hopes that he will have finished his project by January.

निम्न Verbs के साथ perfect Infinitive का प्रयोग Passive Voice में किया जाता है।
ये Verbs हैं acknowledge, believe, consider, find, how, know, report, say, suppose, think, understand.

(a) They are understood to have left the village.
(b) He was believed to have a great artist.
(c) She is thought to have information which will be useful to the police.
(d) She is known to have been a great leader.

Perfect Continuous Infinitive

Perfect Continuous Infinitive की form—**to have been + Present Participle** होती है।

Use of Perfect Continuous Infinitive

The perfect continuous infinitive का प्रयोग verbs; appear, seem, happen, pretend के बाद किया जा सकता है। जैसे :

(a) He seems to have been standing there since morning.
(b) She appears to have been waiting for a long time.
(c) He pretended to have been studying.

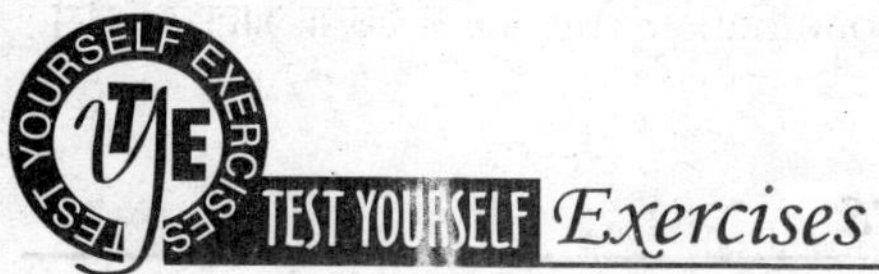

01

Correct the following sentences :

(1) English is difficult to be learnt.
(2) Do you dare refuse me?
(3) I watched her to cross the road.
(4) The act is easy to be performed.
(5) He is better able to act than to sing.
(6) She can do nothing but to abuse him.
(7) Stop to write.
(8) I had sooner run than to walk.
(9) I have decided helping her.
(10) Better to reign in hell than to serve in heaven.
(11) I made him to polish my shoes.
(12) She avoids to do her duties seriously.
(13) I am looking forward to meet you soon.
(14) I got a mechanic repairing my car.
(15) A brave man does not fear dying.
(16) The river is very deep to be crossed by the army.

02

Correct the following sentences :

(1) Please tell me to close it.
(2) I know swim.
(3) I can't decide to get out of this trouble.
(4) I chanced meeting her in the art gallery.
(5) She appears recognising me.
(6) Could you tell me to explain the situation?
(7) There was no board to write.
(8) She hopes of passing with distinction.
(9) She is eager to meeting me.
(10) He went to Jaipur seeing the Jantar Mantar.
(11) She failed winning the prize.
(12) I shall be glad meeting you.

03

Correct the following sentences :

(1) I have no pen to write.
(2) She has a house for furnishing.
(3) I have no house to live.
(4) He requested me going to Jaipur.
(5) He did nothing but to talk and to laugh.
(6) I will have you to remember me.
(7) She was known having hidden the jewellery box.
(8) I would study rather than to waste my time.
(9) They bade me to go.
(10) Let I sing a song.
(11) I observed him to play.
(12) We had him to know his mistakes.

04

Correct the following sentences :

(1) He learned to operate the machine.
(2) I asked him from where to buy shirts at reasonable rates.
(3) I wonder whether go or not.
(4) She pretended to look for some eatables.
(5) Ramesh seems to follow us in his car.
(6) He seemed to be a great musician.
(7) His plan of rebuild the building was not approved by the municipality.
(8) He made an effort to getting pass without copying.
(9) She is too weak that she cannot walk.
(10) She is enough matured to go alone.
(11) She ran enough fast to catch the train.
(12) He was so foolish as left his car unlocked.
(13) Will you be so kind as sanction my leave?
(14) She is the only one secure 95% marks.
(15) She likes to completely change the colour.

SOLUTIONS TYE TEST YOURSELF *Exercises*

Solution TYE 01

(1) English is difficult to learn.
(2) Do you dare to refuse me?
(3) I watched her cross the road.
(4) The act is easy to perform.
(5) He is better able to act than sing.
(6) She can do nothing but abuse him.
(7) Stop writing.
(8) I had sooner run than walk.
(9) I have decided to help her.
(10) Better reign in hell than serve in heaven.
(11) I made him polish my shoes.
(12) She avoids doing her duties seriously.
(13) I am looking forward meeting you soon.
(14) I got a mechanic to repair my car.
(15) A brave man does not fear to die.
(16) The river is very deep to cross by the army.

Solution TYE 02

(1) Please tell me how to close it.
(2) I know how to swim.
(3) I can't decide how to get out of this trouble.
(4) I chanced to meet her in the art gallery.
(5) She appears to recognise me.
(6) Could you tell me how to explain the situation?
(7) There was no board to write on.
(8) She hopes to pass with distinction.
(9) She is eager to meet me.
(10) He went to Jaipur to see the Jantar Mantar.
(11) She failed to win the prize.
(12) I shall be glad to meet you.

Solution TYE 03

(1) I have no pen to write with.
(2) She has a house to furnish.
(3) I have no house to live in.
(4) He requested me to go to Jaipur.
(5) He did nothing but talk and laugh.
(6) I will have you remember me.
(7) She was known to have hidden the jewellery box.
(8) I would study rather than waste my time.
(9) They bade me go.
(10) Let me sing a song.
(11) I observed him playing.
(12) We had him know his mistakes.

Solution TYE 04

(1) He learned how to operate the machine.
(2) I asked him where to buy shirts at reasonable rates.
(3) I wonder whether to go or not.
(4) She pretended to be looking for some eatables.
(5) Ramesh seems to be following us in his car.
(6) He seemed to have been a great musician.
(7) His plan to rebuild the building was not approved by the municipality.
(8) He made an effort to get pass without copying.
(9) She is too weak to walk.
(10) She is matured enough to go alone.
(11) She ran fast enough to catch the train.
(12) He was so foolish as to leave his car unlocked.
(13) Will you be so kind as to sanction my leave?
(14) She is the only one to secure 95% marks.
(15) She likes to change the colour completely.

CHAPTER

13

PARTICIPLE

Participle, verb का ऐसा रूप है जिसमें verb के साथ-साथ Adjective के गुण भी पाए जाते हैं, Participle को इसीलिए Verbal adjective भी कहा जाता है।

Participle तीन प्रकार के होते है :

Participle		
Present Participle **(Verb + ing)** **(Running, singing, walking)**	Past Participle **(verb + d/ed/t)** **(talked, burnt, hurt)**	Perfect Participle **(having + Past Perfect)** **(having done, having seen, having spent)**

Forms of Participle				
Active Voice		**Passive Voice**		
Present (playing)	Perfect (having played)	Present (being played)	Past **(played)**	Perfect **(having been played)**

(1) **Present Participle:** Verb की I form के साथ ing जोड़ने से Present Participle बनता है। जैसे :

(a) It is an interesting novel.

(b) He jumped from a running train.

(c) It was a tiring journey.

(2) **Past Participle:** इसके द्वारा कार्य का Past में पूरा होना व्यक्त किया जाता है। जैसे: burnt, selected, striken etc.

(a) The owner gave a written notice to the tenant.

(b) A burnt child dreads the fire.

(c) Driven by hunger, he begged for food.

(3) **Perfect Participle** के द्वारा एक कार्य के समाप्त होने के बाद दूसरे कार्य के शुरू होने या पूर्ण होने को व्यक्त किया जाता है। सामान्यतया एक वाक्य मे दो घटनाओं के मध्य सम्बन्ध (Relation) Perfect Participle द्वारा स्पष्ट किया जाता है। जैसे :

Having finished, Having written, Having done, Having seen

(Having + Past Participle = Perfect Participle)

Passive Voice में Perfect Participle = having been + Past Participle द्वारा बनता है। जैसे :

having been failed, having been completed.

(a) Having finished my project, I went to play.

(b) Having been failed in BA, he joined the parental business.

Present Participle : Use

(A) इसका प्रयोग Continuous Tense में निम्न प्रकार किया जाता है:

(i) He is playing football.
(ii) They have been reading for an hour.
(iii) Sita was watching T.V.

(B) इसका प्रयोग एक Adjective की तरह भी किया जाता है। जैसे:

(i) It was a tiring journey.
(ii) I read an interesting novel.

(C) Have + Object के साथ Present Participle का प्रयोग निम्न प्रकार होता है:

(i) I will have you swimming within a week.
(As a result of my efforts you will be swimming within a week).

(ii) We had them all dancing.
(We persuaded them to dance).

(iii) I have them both speaking to one another.
(I persuaded or encouraged them to speak to one another).

(iv) If you give such cocktail parties, you will have the neighbours complaining.

(v) If celebrities put their numbers in telephone directories, they'd have everyone ringing them up.

(D) I won't + have + Object + Present Participle का प्रयोग 'I won't / don't allow this के अर्थ में किया जाता है। जैसे :

(a) I won't have them playing cricket in my garden.

(b) I won't have him cleaning his vehicles in the corridor.
(I won't / don't allow him to clean his vehicles in the corridor).

(E) Present Participle का प्रयोग Relative Pronoun + Verb के ऐवज मे निम्न प्रकार किया जा सकता है:

(a) There are many people who wish to visit the temple.
There are many people wishing to visit the temple.

(b) Please segregate the children who need immediate medical assistance.
Please segregate the children needing immediate medical assistance.

(F) Verbs of perception जैसे, see, hear, feel, smell, notice, watch, listen (to) इत्यादि के बाद object + present participle का प्रयोग किया जाता है। जैसे :

(a) I see her passing through the street daily.
(b) I can hear the clock striking.
(c) I felt the car skidding.
(d) I smelt something burning.
(e) I watched them breaking the wall.
(f) Didn't you hear the clock striking?

(1) Verbs, See, Hear, Fell एवं कभी-कभी notice एवं Watch के साथ Object + Bare infinitive का भी प्रयोग प्रचलन में है। सामान्यतया, Infinitive का प्रयोग तब किया जाता है जब action पूर्ण हो जाता है। जैसे :

(a) I saw her leave the college. *(b) I saw him repair the car.*

The use of infinitive implies that the action is complete.

जबकि Participle का प्रयोग कार्य के पूर्ण होने एवं पूर्ण न होने दोनों स्थिति को व्यक्त करता है। जैसे :

I saw her repairing the car.

It could mean that I watched the whole action or that I saw only part of it.

The use of infinitive implies that the action is complete.

(2) Infinitive का प्रयोग एक के बाद दूसरे action की स्थिति में किया जाता है। जैसे :

I saw him enter the office, unlock the almirah, take out a file, photographed it, put it back and left in a hurry.

(G) Catch/find/leave के Present Participle का प्रयोग निम्न Structure में होता है। जैसे :

Catch/find/leave + Object + Present participle:

(i) Catch के साथ Present Participle का प्रयोग एक unfavourable/displeasing स्थिति को व्यक्त करता है। जैसे :

(a) I caught him stealing the purse.

(b) If he catches you using his computer, he will be furious.

(ii) Find के साथ Present Participle का प्रयोग सामान्य स्थिति को व्यक्त करता है। जैसे :

(a) I found her waiting for me.

(b) I found him standing at the gate.

(c) We found a man lying on the road.

(iii) Leave का प्रयोग निम्न प्रकार होता है:

(a) I left her working in the office.
(She was working in the office when I left.)

(b) I left him talking on phone.
(He was talking on phone when I left.)

(H) Present Participle का प्रयोग come / go / spend / waste / be busy के साथ निम्न प्रकार होता है:

(a) We are going shopping today afternoon.
(b) They are going sailing.
(c) Come dancing.
(d) They are going skiing.
(e) He spent a huge amount modernizing his old house.
(f) They wasted five hours trying to find the solution to this problem.
(g) I spend four hours a day travelling.
(h) She doesn't spend much time cooking her meal.
(i) She was busy writing lessons.
(j) She was busy packing.

(I) Other Uses of Present Participle

(a) जब एक ही कर्ता (Subject Same) द्वारा दो कार्य एक साथ (Simultaneously) किये जाते हैं तो एक कार्य हेतु Present Participle का प्रयोग निम्न प्रकार किया जा सकता है :

(i) She went away.

(ii) She cried as she went.
She went away crying.

(iii) She holds the rope with one hand and stretches out the other to the man in the water.
इस वाक्य को Present participle का प्रयोग करते हुए निम्न प्रकार लिखा जा सकता है
Holding the rope with one hand she stretches out the other to the man in the water.

(b) जब एक ही कर्ता द्वारा एक कार्य के पूर्ण होने के साथ ही दूसरा कार्य शुरू किया जाता है तो प्रथम कार्य हेतु Present Participle का प्रयोग किया जा सकता है। जैसे :

(i) He opened the almirah. He took out a file.
Opening the almirah he took out a file.

(ii) He takes off his clothes and creeps cautiously into the water.
Taking off his clothes he creeps cautiously into the water.

(c) यदि दूसरा कार्य, पहले कार्य का ही एक भाग है या इसका परिणाम है तो दूसरे कार्य को Present Participle द्वारा व्यक्त किया जा सकता है। जैसे :

(i) He went out slamming the gate.
(ii) He fired, wounding several persons in the crowd.
(iii) I fell, striking my head against the wall and cutting it.

(यहाँ तीन actions में से, पीछे वाले दो actions, Present participle द्वारा व्यक्त किए गए हैं।)

(D) Present Participle का प्रयोग As/since/because से शुरू होने वाली clause (Subordinate clause) के स्थान पर निम्न प्रकार किया जा सकता है:

(i) As he was a student he was interested in books.
Being a student he was interested in books.
(ii) Because he was ill he didn't go to Jaipur.
Being ill he didn't go to Jaipur.
(iii) Since, he knew that he wouldn't be able to recognize her, he used an addressed plate.
Knowing that he wouldn't be able to recognize her he used an addressed plate.

(E) एक ही वाक्य में एक से अधिक Participles का प्रयोग निम्न प्रकार से किया जा सकता है:

(i) Realizing that he hadn't enough money and not wanting to borrow from his friends, he decided to sell his chain.
(ii) Not knowing the language and having no friends in the city, he found it hard to get a room on rent.

We should not use a Present participle to express an action which is not consistent with the action of the principal clause.
He sailed for Srilanka on Tuesday and arriving their on Saturday. — *Incorrect*
He sailed for Srilanka on Tuesday and arrived their on Saturday. — *Correct*
Here 'sailed' is used in principal clause, so we cannot use 'arriving' in subordinating clause. We should use 'arrived'.

Past Participle—Use

(1) As Adjective: Past Participle का प्रयोग Adjective की तरह किया जाता है। जैसे :

(a) This is a fried fish.
(b) A burnt child dreads the fire.
(c) I need a boiled egg.
(d) Police wanted a written statement.

कुछ Past participles का प्रयोग adjectives की तरह ही होता है, verb की past form की तरह नहीं होता है। ऐसे, Past participles हैं : drunken, bounden, stricken, shrunken, sunken, molten, shorn, cloven, graven. ऐसे past participles, noun को quality करते हैं। जैसे:
A drunken driven, cloven hoof, graven image, stricken heart, sunken ship,shorn sheep, bounden duty.
इन verb की past form, past participle से भिन्न होती है। जैसे:
Drunken-Drunk, Molten-Melted, bounden-bound, shorn-sheared, cloven-clove, graven- graved, stricken-struck, sunken-sunk.

(2) Past Participle का प्रयोग Perfect Tense में किया जाता है। जैसे :

(a) Ram has arrived.
(b) They have completed the work.
(c) I have finished my work.
(d) He had gone to Jaipur.

(3) Past participles का प्रयोग अधिकांशतया passive voice में करते हैं। Past participle का प्रयोग Noun के बाद होता है। जैसे :

(a) This is the book written by me.
(b) Learn the lessons taught by her.
(c) He can't forget the favour shown to him.

लेकिन कुछ past participles जैसे: born, broken, fallen, given, spoken, stolen, torn, written का प्रयोग verb एवं adjective दोनों प्रकार से किया जा सकता है।

(a) This is the broken glass.
(b) That is the window broken by the thief.
(c) Police wanted a written statement.
(d) Where is the letter written by her?

(4) Past Participle का प्रयोग निम्न प्रकार के Passive वाक्यों के स्थान पर भी किया जा सकता है। जैसे :

(a) She was aroused by the noise and leapt to her feet.
Aroused by the noise she leapt to her feet.
(b) The railway bridge had been weakened by successive storms and was no longer safe.
Weakened by successive storms, the railway bridge was no longer safe.

Perfect Participle—Use

(A) जब एक ही कर्ता द्वारा एक कार्य के तुरन्त बाद दूसरा कार्य किया जाता है। तो Present Participle की जगह Perfect Participle का भी प्रयोग किया जा सकता है। जैसे :

(i) Tying one end of the rope to the grill of the door, she threw the other end out of the window.
Having tied one end of the rope to the grill of the door, she threw the other end out of the window.
(ii) Opening the almirah, he took out a file.
Having opened the almirah, he took out a file.

जब Present Participle के प्रयोग से वाक्य का आशय स्पष्ट न हो तो Perfect Participle का प्रयोग करना उचित रहता है।

(B) जब दोनों कार्यों के बीच समय का अन्तराल हो तो Perfect Participle का ही प्रयोग किया जाता है। जैसे :

(a) Having failed thrice, she didn't want to apply again.
(b) Having passed his M.A, he enrolled for Ph. D.

(C) Perfect Participle का प्रयोग उस स्थिति में किया जाता है जब प्रथम कार्य एक समयावधि को व्यक्त करता है। जैसे :
Having been his own boss for many years, he found it unusual to accept orders from another.

Perfect Participle Passive (Having been + Past Participle) का प्रयोग तब किया जाता है, जब Participle द्वारा व्यक्त कार्य, दूसरे Verb द्वारा व्यक्त कार्य के पूर्व पूर्ण होता है।

(a) Having been failed thrice, she didn't try again.
(b) Having been warned about the bandits they deposited the valuables in the lockers.
(c) Having been bitten twice, the courier man refused to deliver the goods unless the dog is chained up.

Errors in the Use of Participles

छात्रों द्वारा Participles के प्रयोग में बहुत गलतियाँ की जाती हैं। परीक्षा में Participles से सम्बन्धित प्रश्न अधिकांशतया निम्न से सम्बन्धित होते हैं :

(I) Unattached or Dangling Participle : Participle वाक्यों में Adjective का कार्य करते हैं। अत: Participle के साथ एक noun या pronoun का सम्बन्धित (related) होना आवश्यक है। यदि Participle के साथ कोई noun या pronoun सम्बन्धित नहीं है तो वह Participle, Unattached or Dangling Participle है। जैसे :

(1) Being a cold morning I didn't go to office. (2) Being a rainy day, the school remained closed.

उपरोक्त दोनों वाक्यों में प्रयुक्त Participle—'Being' Unattached Participle है, यहाँ Being के साथ कोई noun या Pronoun लगाना आवश्यक है। अत: इन वाक्यों को निम्न प्रकार लिखा जाना चाहिए।

(1) It being a cold morning I didn't go to office. *Or*
The morning being cold, I didn't go to office.

(2) It being a rainy day, the school remained closed. *Or*
The day being rainy, the school remained closed.

(II) Misrelated Participle : कई Participle वाले वाक्यों के दो भाग होते हैं। एक भाग में Participle होता है। जब Participle वाले भाग में कोई Subject नहीं है, तो दूसरे भाग के Subject को ही participle का Subject माना जाता है। यहाँ यह ध्यान रखना आवश्यक है कि यदि वाक्य के दोनों भागो का Subject एक ही है तो वाक्य सही होगा। यदि वाक्य के दोनों भागों में अलग-अलग Subject की आवश्यकता है एवं Participle वाले भाग में Subject नहीं दिया गया है तो यह वाक्य एक गलत (Incorrect) वाक्य होगा। यह misrelated Participle का उदाहरण है। जैसे:

Standing near the gate, a dog caught her.

इस वाक्य के दो भाग हैं, पहला Standing near the gate इसका कोई Subject नहीं है। एक भाग दूसरे a dog caught her, इसका Subject-dog है। यदि dog को ही पहले भाग का Subject माना जाये तो इसका अर्थ होगा कि Dog was standing near the gate जो कि गलत होगा। अत: यहाँ Standing एक Misrelated Participle है। सही वाक्य होगा:

While she was standing near the gate, a dog caught her.

See more such sentences:

(a) Waiting for the train, a brick fell on my feet. *Incorrect*
While I was waiting for the train, a brick fell on my feet. *Correct*

(b) When using this machine it must be remembered to unlock it first. *Incorrect*
When using this machine, you must remember to unlock it first. *Correct*

(c) Deciding to join the navy, the recruiter happily pumped Jack's hand. *Incorrect*
(The recruiter is not deciding to join the navy;Jack is).
The recruiter happily pumped Jack's hand after learning that Jack had decided to join the navy. *Correct*

(d) When watching films, commercials are especially irritating. *Incorrect*

(a) *One option would be to change the subject so that it names the actor that the modifier implies :*
(i) When watching films, I find commercials especially irritating.

(b) *Another option would be to turn the modifier into a word group that includes the actor :*
(ii) When I am watching films, commercials are especially irritating.
Both (i) and (ii) are correct.

Important : लेकिन कुछ participles—Considering, regarding, concerning, taking, speaking, touching इत्यादि का प्रयोग बिना Noun/pronoun से सम्बन्धित (related) हुए भी किया जा सकता है। जैसे :

(a) Considering the price, the quality of the cloth is good.
(b) Speaking roughly, the distance between Delhi and Alwar is 150 kms.
(c) Taking every point into consideration, the proposal is very attractive.

Participles का इस तरह से प्रयोग एक preposition की भाँति होता है।

How to Detect Errors?

(A) ध्यान रखें कि Participle के साथ एक Subject का attached/related (सम्बन्धित) होना आवश्यक है। जब किसी वाक्य में एक Clause से Participle का प्रयोग किया हुआ हो तो इस Participle से पूर्व दूसरे Clause में उपलब्ध Subject को लगाकर देखें। यदि उस Subject के साथ यह Participle सही अर्थ देता है, तो Participle का सही प्रयोग किया गया है, अन्यथा वाक्य में गलती है। निम्न उदाहरण देखें :

Walking through the jungle, he saw a white tiger.

इस वाक्य मे Walking एक Participle है इसके साथ कोई Subject नहीं है। वाक्य के दूसरे Clause में 'he' Subject है। इसे Participle से पूर्व लगाने पर 'he' walking (while he was walking) बनता है। जिसका अर्थ सही निकलता है। अत: Participle का सही प्रयोग किया गया है।

Walking towards the gate, a plate slipped from his hand.

इस वाक्य में 'Walking' Participle है। इसके साथ कोई Subject नहीं है। अत: दूसरे Clause के Subject 'plate' को इसके पूर्व लगाने पर a plate walking towards the gate (While a plate walking towards the gate.) बनता है, जिसका कोई सही अर्थ नही निकलता है। अत: Participle के प्रयोग में गलती है। यहाँ Participle का Subject, plate नहीं हो सकता है। वाक्य के दूसरे Clause को भी देखने से पता चलता है कि वाक्य को निम्न अर्थ देने का प्रयास किया गया है:
''जब वह दरवाजे की तरफ चल रहा था तो एक प्लेट उसके हाथ से छूट गई।''

इस अर्थ को पूर्णता देने हेतु, अर्थ स्पष्ट करने हेतु, वाक्य को निम्न प्रकार लिखा जाना चाहिए:

While he was walking towards the gate, a plate slipped from his hand.

अब यह वाक्य सही है।

Being a rainy day, he didn't go to the office.

यहाँ Being (Participle) के साथ प का प्रयोग करें, तो He being a rainy day, एक अर्थहीन वाक्य बनता है। चूँकि rain, day, weather, time इत्यादि हेतु 'it' (Introductory Subject) का प्रयोग किया जाता है अत: Being से पूर्व it लगाने से वाक्य सही बन जाता है एवं उसका सही अर्थ निकलता है। जैसे :

It being a rainy day, he didn't go to the office.

(B) कई बार परीक्षा में Active एवं Passive के साथ Participle के प्रयोग के सन्दर्भ में प्रश्न पूछे जाते हैं। जहाँ Active का प्रयोग किया जाना चाहिए वहाँ Passive का प्रयोग करके प्रश्न हल किया जाता है। निम्न उदाहरण देखें:

Having been taken lunch, he went to office.

यहाँ been का प्रयोग अनावश्यक/गलत किया गया है। यह Passive Structure में है। इसका अर्थ यह हुआ 'लंच खिलाये जाने के बाद, वह ऑफिस गया' जबकि वाक्य का आशय है 'लंच लेने के बाद वह ऑफिस गया।' अत: इसे निम्न प्रकार लिखा जाना चाहिए

Having taken lunch, he went to office.

Having deserted by his wife, he became a hermit.

इस वाक्य में Having के बाद been का प्रयोग करना आवश्यक है। इस वाक्य में 'Having' का प्रयोग Participle की तरह हुआ है जिसके साथ Subject 'he' का प्रयोग करने पर 'he having deserted by his wife' बनता है जिसका कोई सही अर्थ नहीं निकलता है। यहाँ Participle का प्रयोग Passive में होना आवश्यक है। अत: यहाँ Having been का प्रयोग करने पर:

Having been deserted by his wife, he became a hermit.

(अर्थात् पत्नी द्वारा छोड़ देने पर वह संन्यासी बन गया) यह Participle का सही प्रयोग है।

Likewise : The sun having been risen, the fog dispersed. *Incorrect*

The sun having risen, the fog dispersed. *Correct*

Exercises

01

Correct the following sentences :

(1) Being Sunday, I am thinking to go to a movie.
(2) Remember the lessons teach by the teacher.
(3) Where is the book wrote by Mr. Gupta?
(4) Ploughing his fields some old statues were found.
(5) I want a wrote complaint.
(6) There is no drink water in the office.
(7) Having satisfied with his reply, I didn't take any action.
(8) Tired, I couldn't work any more.
(9) Left from hand to mouth, he yet maintains his standard of living.
(10) Having referred to your application, I beg to write........

02

Correct the following sentences :

(1) In regard to my qualification, I beg to submit.
(2) Sleeping in the house, a thief entered their house.
(3) Having injured he went to hospital.
(4) Turn to the left you can see the palace.
(5) Walking in the forest a lion was seen.
(6) Don't get off a ran bus.
(7) The ship has sunken.
(8) Having been worked hard he got tired.
(9) Having opened the drawer she took out a knife.
(10) We must provide good education to grow children.

03

Fill in the blanks with correct form of non- finite verbs : (Infinitive/Gerund/ Participle) :

(1) His speech left me .... (to think/thought/thinking)
(2) Some boys like .... the T.V. (to watch/watch)
(3) Sita is good at .... (swim/swimming/to swim)
(4) I had an aversion .... meet. (to eat/ to eating)
(5) It is wrong .... a lie before the judge at least. (to tell/telling/have told)
(6) He had rather .... than beg. (to starve/starve/starved)
(7) My greatest pleasure is .... while alone. (singing/to sing/sung)
(8) He wears a .... look today. (worrying/worried/to worry)
(9) You had better .... nothing. (to say/saying/say/said)
(10) .... is a good exercise for the young. (to swim/swimming)

04

Fill in the blanks with correct form of non- finite verbs (Infinitive/Gerund/Participle)

(1) I watched her .... and come often. (going/go /to go)
(2) .... is easier than reading. (to play/having played/playing)
(3) I found his daughter .... (to cry/crying/have cried)
(4) She denied .... any force to get him accept his fault. (used/to use/using)
(5) I hate .... and cheating. (to lie/lying)
(6) He said, "He has given up ...." (to smoke/smoking/have smoked)

(7) I remember .... her in the park. (seeing/to see)
(8) She stopped .... others. (to advise/advising/had advised)
(9) They want us .... for the girls to arrive. (waiting/to wait)
(10) .... many times, he doesn't want to try again now. (Failing/Failed/Having failed)
(11) .... that she was early, she went to meet her friends. (To know/Having know/Knowing)
(12) The book .... on the chair is mine. (lye/lying)
(13) Please excuse my .... early today. (leave/left/leaving)
(14) She disliked my .... on Sunday. (work/working).
(15) .... out of the window, she saw a strange creature. (Looked/Looking/Having looked)

05

Read the following sentences to find whether there is any error in any part :

(1) Being often ill (a)/ and frequently absent (b)/ she had no opportunity to complete his work (c)/ or do much of it toto. (d)
(2) Taking breakfast (a)/ he went to the office (b)/ and ordered the staff (c)/ to complete the work without any further delay. (d)
(3) Without taking proper care (a)/ the doctors would (b)/ not have been saved (c)/ the life of this patient. (d)
(4) Going towards the gate (a)/ with a cup of tea (b)/ somebody switched off (c)/ the light. (d)
(5) He does nothing (a)/ nothing but to find faults (b)/ with others (c)/ and laugh at them. (d)
(6) The Chief Minister (a) should not let (b)/ the terrorist activities (c)/ to grow in our state. (d)
(7) Many persons are coming (a)/ to his concert (b)/ to hear him to sing (c)/ the religious songs. (d)
(8) Having had reached (a)/ the station, you (b)/ may make a telephone (c)/ to your boss. (d)
(9) It is better to stay (a)/ at home than to go to market (b)/ when it is raining. (c)
(10) When he entered the home (a)/ he found the child sleeping (b)/ and the fan moves slowly. (c)
(11) He asked me to (a)/ completely forget her (b)/ but only I know it is not possible. (c)

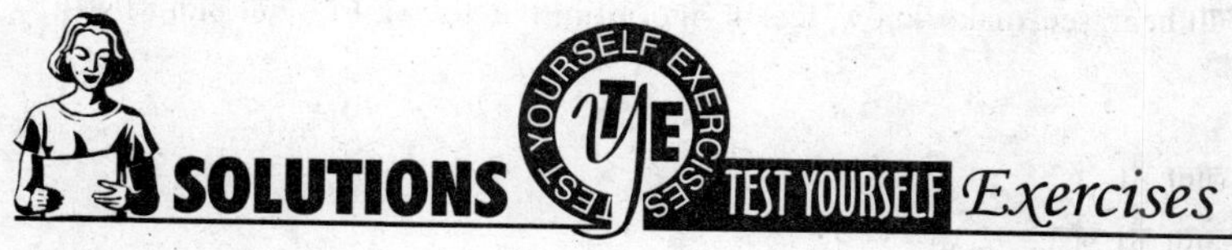

Solution TYE 01

(1) It being Sunday, I am thinking to go to a movie.
(2) Remember the lessons taught by the teacher.
(3) Where is the book written by Mr. Gupta?
(4) While ploughing his fields he found some old statues.
(5) I want a written complaint.
(6) There is no drinking water in the office.
(7) Having been satisfied with his reply, I didn't take any action.
(8) Being tired, I couldn't work any more.
(9) Living from hand to month, he yet maintains his standard of living.
(10) Referring to your application, I beg to write....

Solution TYE 02

(1) Regarding my qualification I beg to submit.
(2) While they were sleeping in the house, a thief entered their house.
(3) Having been injured he went to hospital.
(4) Turning to the left you can see the palace.
(5) While, I was walking in the forest I saw a lion.
(6) Don't get off a running bus.
(7) The ship has sunk.
(8) Having worked hard he got tired.
(9) Opening the drawer she took out a knife.
(10) We must provide good education to growing children.

Solution TYE 03

(1) thinking, (2) to watch, (3) swimming, (4) to eating, (5) to tell,
(6) starve, (7) to sing, (8) worried, (9) say, (10) Swimming.

Solution TYE 04

(1) go, (2) Playing, (3) crying, (4) using, (5) lying,
(6) smoking, (7) seeing, (8) advising, (9) to wait, (10) Having failed,
(11) Knowing, (12) lying, (13) leaving, (14) working, (15) Looking.

Solution TYE 05

(1) (D) do' से पहले to का प्रयोग होगा। Or से पहले to complete है तो or के बाद भी 'to do' आयेगा।
(2) (A) After taking breakfast या Having taken breakfast लिखा जायेगा।
(3) (C) been का प्रयोग गलत है।
(4) (A) While he was going towards the gate होगा।
(5) (B) Nothing but के बाद to का प्रयोग गलत है। जैसे :
He does nothing, but watch TV.
(6) (D)'to' हटाना होगा। let के बाद infinitive 'to' का प्रयोग नहीं होता है।
(7) (C) to sing की जगह केवल sing आयेगा। hear, see, make, know, feel के बाद infinitive 'to' का प्रयोग नहीं होता है। जैसे:
I see her walk.
I feel her presence.
(8) (A)'Had' का अनावश्यक प्रयोग किया जाता है।
(9) (B) than के बाद 'to' का प्रयोग नहीं होता है। जैसे:
It is better to study than wander here and there.
(10) (C) fan moving slowly होना चाहिए।
(11) (B) Completely forget her की जगह forget her completely होगा। यहाँ infinitive को गलत split किया गया है।

CHAPTER

14

GERUND

Gerund, verb की एक ऐसी form है जो verb में 'ing' (Verb + ing) लगाने से बनती है एवं noun का कार्य करती है। Gerund को verbal Noun भी कहते हैं।

"Gerund is such a form of verb, that ends in 'ing' and has the force of a noun and a verb"

–Wren and Martin

अर्थात् Gerund verb में ing जोड़ने से बनता है एवं वाक्य में noun का कार्य भी करता है। जैसे : Walking, Running, Reading, Writing etc.

Present Participle V/s Gerund

Present Participle एवं Gerund का रूप एक जैसा होता है, लेकिन जहाँ Gerund वाक्य में एक Verb + noun का कार्य करता है। वहाँ Participle; verb + adjective का कार्य करता है। Gerund को Verbal Noun तथा Participle को Verbal Adjective कहते हैं।

Gerund V/s Simple Infinitive

Gerund वाक्यों में Verb + Noun (Verbal Noun) की तरह function करता है, इसो प्रकार Simple Infinitive जिसे Noun Infinitive भी कहते हैं, वह भी वाक्य में verb + noun का कार्य करता है। इसी कारण से बहुत से वाक्यों में (With certain verbs) Gerund या Simple Infinitive किसी का भी प्रयोग किया जा सकता है। ऐसा करने से वाक्य के अर्थ में कोई अन्तर नहीं आता है। निम्न verb के साथ Gerund या Infinitive किसी का भी प्रयोग किया जा सकता है:

advise	hate	propose	used to
agree	intend	recommend	want
allow	like	regret	ashamed
	love	remember	afraid
can/could bear	mean	require	sorry
cease	need	start	go
continue	permit	stop	prefer
forget	try		

Gerund	**Infinitive**
(a) They began playing.	(a) They began to play.
(b) We prefer taking tea.	(b) We prefer to take tea.
(c) He never ceased complaining about the quality.	(c) He never ceased to complain about quality.
(d) I can't bear waiting so long.	(d) I can't bear to wait so long.
(e) I intend buying it.	(e) I intend to buy it.
(f) He advised me writing today.	(f) He advised me to write today.
(g) He doesn't allow parking here.	(g) He doesn't allow us to park here.

Some Specific Uses of Gerund/Infinitive

(A) Be afraid of : Be afraid of + Gerund + Noun / pronoun :

(a) She never swam far out. She is afraid of getting caught.

(b) I didn't tell her because I was afraid of upsetting her.

Be afraid के साथ Gerund का प्रयोग कर्त्ता के भय को व्यक्त करता है।

Be afraid + Infinitive

(a) I was afraid to jump (so I didn't jump). (b) He was afraid to complain (so he didn't complain.)

इस तरह का प्रयोग (Be afraid + Infinitive) कर्ता के भयाक्रांत होने को व्यक्त करता है, जिसके कारण उसने वह कार्य ही नहीं किया (Too frightened to perform an action.)

(B) Be sorry for + gerund :

I am sorry for making such a noise in the morning.

Gerund का प्रयोग सामान्यतया पिछले action के साथ किया जाता है। यद्यपि Immediate action हेतु भी Gerund का प्रयोग हो सकता है। जैसे :

I am sorry for disturbing you.

लेकिन यहाँ Infinitive का प्रयोग अधिक उपयुक्त माना जाता है।

I am sorry to disturb you.

I am sorry that ....का प्रयोग वास्तविक खेद (Regret) या दु:ख (Sadness) व्यक्त करता है।

जैसे : I am sorry that you failed this time again.

जबकि : I am sorry to say that he has not arrived yet.

इस तरह के वाक्य औपचारिकता के रूप में खेद व्यक्त करते हैं।

(C) Be ashamed of + Gerund : You must be ashamed of lying to me. Ashamed of के साथ Gerund का प्रयोग past action हेतु किया जाता है। जैसे :

I am ashamed to tell you what this table cost.

Would be के साथ ashamed + Infinitive का प्रयोग कर्ता को भविष्य में किसी कार्य को करने से रोकता है। जैसे :

I would be ashamed to refuse her.

I would be ashamed to ask for help.

(D) Go on का अर्थ होता है continue करना। इसका प्रयोग सामान्यतया Gerund के साथ किया जाता है। लेकिन verbs; explain, talk, tell इत्यादि के साथ Go on का प्रयोग Infinitive के साथ होता है। जैसे :

He went on to talk about his accident.

He went on to tell us about the present situation of unemployment.

(E) Regret, Remember, Forget : इन verbs के साथ Gerund का प्रयोग सामान्यतया तब किया जाता है जब Gerund द्वारा किसी Earlier action के बारे में बताया गया हो। जैसे :

(a) I regret abusing you last night. (Abusing the first action, regret is the second.)

(b) I remember reading about this invention in a magazine.
(reading is the first action and remember is the second.)

Forget के साथ Gerund का प्रयोग सामान्यतया Negative होता है। जैसे :

(a) I will never forget waiting for her so long.

(b) We will never forget waiting for the robbers to come.

लेकिन जब Regret, Remember एवं Forget द्वारा Earlier action के बारे में बताया जाये तो Infinitive का प्रयोग किया जाता है।

(a) I regret to inform you that you have again failed this time.
(यहाँ regret प्रथम (earlier) action तथा Inform करना द्वितीय action है)

(b) I will remember to post the letter.

(यहाँ भी remember प्रथम (earlier) action तथा letter post करना द्वितीय (subsequent) action है।)

(c) I often forget to write my address.

(यहाँ भी Forget, earlier action तथा write, subsequent action है)

(F) Advise, Allow, Permit, Recommend : उक्त verbs के साथ वाक्य में जब सम्बन्धित व्यक्ति का जिक्र किया जाता है तो Infinitive का प्रयोग होता है। लेकिन यदि सम्बन्धित व्यक्ति का सन्दर्भ वाक्य में नहीं हो तो Gerund का प्रयोग होगा। जैसे :

(a) He advised me to leave at once. He advised leaving at once.

(b) She recommends us to buy this soap. She recommends buying this soap.

Allow एवं permit के साथ Gerund का प्रयोग करते समय object नहीं लगता है। अत: यदि object लगता है तो Infinitive का प्रयोग किया जाता है। जैसे :

(a) He allowed me to use the scooter.
(b) They allowed us to play there.
(c) He doesn't allow swimming there.
(d) They do not permit playing there.

(G) Agree, Agree to :

Agree के साथ Infinitive का प्रयोग होता है। जैसे :

(a) He agreed to wait a month. (b) They agreed to accommodate us.

Agree to (preposition) के साथ Gerund का प्रयोग निम्न प्रकार से होता है :

(a) She agreed to my leaving early. (b) He agreed to my coming late for a weak.

Use of Gerund

(1) As subject (कर्त्ता के रुप में) :

(a) Swimming is good for health. (b) Seeing is believing .

(c) Fishing is a good profession.

उपरोक्त वाक्यों में Swimming, Seeing एवं Fishing (Gerunds) का प्रयोग वाक्य के Subject के रुप में हुआ है।

(2) As object of a verb (क्रिया के कर्म के रुप में) :

(a) I love fishing. (b) He loves telling stories.

(c) Stop shouting.

यहाँ Gerunds fishing, telling एवं shouting verbs के objects हैं।

(3) As object of a preposition (Preposition के object के रुप में) :

(a) He is fond of writing letters. (b) We are tired of waiting.

(c) I am against speaking ill of others.

इन वाक्यों में Gerunds: writing, preposition, of का object है तथा waiting एवं Speaking क्रमश: preposition; of एवं against के objects हैं।

(4) As complement of a verb (verb के पूरक के रुप में) :

(a) What I love is making friends ! (b) His weakness is writing slowly.

(c) What I hate is abusing others !

यहाँ Gerund के बिना verb अपूर्ण है। अत: Gerund, verb के पूरक की तरह प्रयुक्त हुए हैं।

(5) As an objective complement (object के पूरक के रुप में) :

(a) It was foolish of him crying now. (b) It is worthless requesting to him.

(c) It is no use running after her.

यहाँ Gerund का प्रयोग objective complement की तरह किया है।

Specific Use of Gerund Rules

Rule 1

जब वाक्यों में verb, preposition के तुरन्त बाद आती है, तो Gerund का प्रयोग किया जाता है। जैसे:

(a) He is fond of fishing.
(b) She is good at swimming.
(c) He is too afraid of losing.
(d) I am tired of arguing.
(e) I felt cold after swimming.
(f) I am sorry for telling you all this.
(g) There is no point in arguing now.
(h) Are you not interested in making money?

Rule 2

कुछ verbs + preposition / adverb combination के बाद Gerund का ही प्रयोग किया जाता है। ऐसी verbs है। care for, give up, keep on, look forward to, put off, see about, take to etc.

(a) We do not care for standing in queues.
(b) We are looking forward to meeting you in the party.
(c) He has given up smoking since long.

Rule 3

'to' का प्रयोग जब preposition की तरह होता है तो उसके बाद gerund का प्रयोग किया जायेगा। 'to' का प्रयोग preposition की तरह हुआ है या नहीं इसको जानने के लिए उसके बाद noun या pronoun लगाकर देखें, यदि उसके बाद noun या pronoun लगाया जा सकता है तो 'to' का प्रयोग preposition की तरह हुआ है अन्यथा as part of Infinitive.

(a) I am looking forward to meeting you. ('To' used as preposition)
(b) I am accustomed to smoking. ('To' used as preposition)
(c) I want to go there. ('To' used as part of Infinitive)
(d) Will you like to come in? ('To' used as part of Infinitive)

Rule 4

निम्न verbs के बाद Gerund का ही सामान्यतया प्रयोग किया जाता है :

admit	keep (= continues)	anticipate	loathe
appreciate	mean (= involve)	consider	miss
avoid	mind (= object)	defer	pardon
dislike	propose (= suggest)	delay	postpone
enjoy	remember (= recollect)	deny	practise
detest	prevent	dread	recollect
escape	resent	excuse	resist
risk	fancy (= imagine)	imagine	suggest
finish	save	involve	understand
forgive	stop (= cease)		

(a) He admitted taking the bribe.
(b) You should avoid overeating.
(c) He detests waiting.
(d) I dislike standing here.
(e) We dreads getting old.
(f) I do not enjoy teaching.
(g) He kept crying.
(h) I do not want to risk getting wet.
(i) We couldn't help laughing.
(j) I don't find there anything worth buying.
(k) She is determined to get a seat even if it means standing is all the night.

Rule 5

यदि Verb के साथ possessive adjective या pronoun object आता है, तो उसके बाद Gerund का ही प्रयोग किया जाता है। जैसे:

He insisted on my reading the letter.
He resented on my refusing the entry.

(a) Please forgive my / me calling you so early.
(b) We can't prevent him wasting his own money.
(c) I indeed appreciate your giving me so much of your time.

Rule 6

Possessive case का प्रयोग Gerund के case में निम्न प्रकार किया जाता है :
We do not remember our mother's protesting against this proposal.
Apostrophe's को omit करके भी Gerund का निम्न प्रकार प्रयोग किया जाता है। यह अधिक उचित प्रयोग है।
We do not remember our mother protesting against this proposal.

Rule 7

Perfect Gerund जैसे: having worked, having spoken etc. का प्रयोग एक past action हेतु निम्न प्रकार किया जाता है:

(a) He was accused of having deserted his ship.
(b) He denied having been involved in the murder.

Rule 8

Verb : mind—special case

(a) Infinitive के साथ कभी भी verb, mind का प्रयोग नहीं होता है।
(b) 'mind' का प्रयोग मुख्यतया Interrogative एवं negative वाक्यों में किया जाता है। जैसे :
    (a) I don't mind waiting here.
    (b) Would you mind waiting for some time?
    (c) 'Mind' के बाद सामान्यतया Gerund या noun/pronoun/possessive adjective के बाद Gerund का प्रयोग किया जाता है। जैसे:
        (a) I don't mind working here.
        (b) I don't mind his sitting there.
        (c) I didn't mind her living there.

Rule 9

Gerundial form के साथ कई noun संयुक्त होकर Compound noun की तरह प्रयुक्त होते हैं, इन्हें Gerund ही माना जाता है।

ऐसे Compound noun है

Sleeping child, freezing point, blotting paper, walking stick, a dancing master, dining room, retiring age etc.

Using Possessives with Gerunds : A note

Do we say "I can't stand him singing in the shower", or do we say "I can't stand his singing in the shower"? Well, you have to decide what you find objectionable: is it him, the fact that he is singing in the shower, or is it the singing that is being done by him that you can't stand? Chances are, it's the latter, it's the singing that belongs to him that bugs you. So, we would say, "I can't stand his singing in the shower."

On the other hand, do we say "I noticed your standing in the alley last night"? Probably not, because it's not the action that we noticed; it's the person. So, we'd say and write, instead, "I noticed you standing in the alley last night." Usually, however, when a noun or pronoun precedes a gerund, that noun or pronoun takes a possessive form. This is especially true of formal, academic writing.

Exceptions

(a) When the noun preceding the gerund is modified by other words, use the common form of that noun, not the possessive.
Federico was pleased by Carlos's making the Dean's List for the first time. ***but***
Federico was pleased by Carlos, his oldest son, making the Dean's List for the first time.

(b) When the noun preceding the gerund is plural, collective, or abstract, use the common form of that noun, not the possessive.
Professor Villa was amazed by her students working as hard as they did.
The class working collaboratively was somebody else's idea.
It was a case of old age getting the better of them.

(c) There are certain situations, in which the possessive and the gerund create an awkward combination. This seems to be particularly true when indefinite pronouns are involved.
I was shocked by somebody's making that remark.
This would be greatly improved by saying, instead. I was shocked that somebody would make that remark.

(d) This is also true when the ''owner'' of the gerund comes wrapped in a noun phrase:
I was thankful for the guy next door shoveling snow from my drive way.
It has been adopted from *Grammar Dimensions: Form Meaning, and Use. Jan Frodesen and Janet Eyring.*

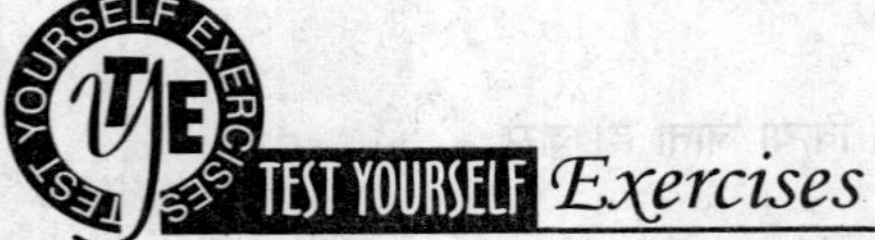

Exercises

01

Correct the following sentences :

(1) She is good at write.
(2) He is afraid to lose the game.
(3) I cannot forget you for you helping me.
(4) It is totally useless to cry over the past misdeeds.
(5) He said, "Don't give up to try again."
(6) Would you mind to work with me?
(7) She is fond of being admire.
(8) I am sorry for me getting late.
(9) I am happy at your arrival at schedule time.
(10) To drink being his habit, we didn't go with him.

02

Correct the following sentences :

(1) I enjoy to travel.
(2) Check the air before to start the generator.
(3) It is no good to work with him.
(4) Some people prefer to spend money to earn it.
(5) I am thinking to leave my job and going back to my native place.
(6) She said to me, "Don't forget to lock the door before go to bed."
(7) I heard someone crying but I failed seeing anyone.
(8) She has finished to wash the clothes.
(9) I prefer to play football to reading my course books.
(10) A novice can't learnt to spelling without being help.

03

Fill in the blanks with appropriate words:

(1) Try .... being late for office. (to avoid/avoiding)
(2) We have nothing to do but .... for her. (waiting/to wait/wait)
(3) Does your wife object .... on holidays? (to work/to working/have worked)
(4) Sita was charged and fined for .... without lights.(driving/have driven/drove)
(5) When he spoke, it was very difficult for me .... (to understood/to understand/ understanding)
(6) .... an aim, the hunter shot the lion. (Took/ To Take/ Taking)
(7) .... his work, he went to market. (Completing/Having completed/After complete)
(8) .... inside a bus is prohibited. (To smoke/Smoking/Have smoking)
(9) The students refused .... the hostel. (leaving/to leave/lefting)
(10) I had sooner .... than walk. (ran/run/to run/running)
(11) Tell me .... this typical machine. (operation/how to operate/operating system)
(12) Most of the students like .... cricket. (to play/playing/have playing)
(13) He is too young .... this movie. (watching/watch/to watch)
(14) He advised me, "You had better .... now." (leaving/leave/left)
(15) The office needs proper .... (cleanliness/cleaning/to clean)

Solution TYE 1

(1) She is good at writing.
(2) He is afraid of losing the game.
(3) I cannot forget you for your helping me.
(4) It is totally useless crying over the past misdeeds.
(5) He said, "Don't give up trying again."
(6) Would you mind working with me?
(7) She is fond of being admired.
(8) I am sorry for my getting late.
(9) I am happy at your arriving at schedule time.
(10) Drinking being his habit, we didn't go with him.

Solution TYE 2

(1) I enjoy travelling.
(2) Check the air before starting the generator.
(3) It is no good working with him.
(4) Some people prefer spending money to earning it.
(5) I am thinking of leaving my job and going back to my native place.
(6) She said to me, "Don't forget to lock the door before going to bed."
(7) I heard someone cry, but I failed to see anyone.
(8) She has finished washing the clothes.
(9) I prefer playing football to reading my course books.
(10) A novice can't learn to spell without being helped.

Solution TYE 3

(1) to avoid, (2) wait, (3) to working, (4) driving,
(5) to understand, (6) Taking, (7) Having completed, (8) Smoking,
(9) to leave, (10) run, (11) how to operate, (12) playing,
(13) to watch, (14) leave, (15) cleaning.

CHAPTER

15

REPORTED SPEECH
(Direct-Indirect Narrations)

वक्ता के कथन को Narration या Speech कहा जाता है।

किसी भी कथन को दो तरह से व्यक्त किया जा सकता है :

(i) Direct Speech (ii) Indirect Speech

(i) Direct Speech or Direct Narration : जब वक्ता के कथन को 'ज्यों का त्यों' (हू-ब-हू) व्यक्त किया जाता है, तो उसे Direct Narration कहा जाता है। Direct Narration को Inverted Commas में बन्द किया जाता है।

(ii) Indirect Speech or Indirect Narration : जब वक्ता के कथन को अपने शब्दों में व्यक्त किया जाये तो उसे Indirect Narration कहा जाता है।

Indirect Narration में वक्ता के कथन का आशय नहीं बदलता है केवल कथन का तरीका बदल जाता है।

Reporter/Reporting Verb/Reported Speech/Verb of Reported Speech

Reporter : वक्ता को Reporter कहा जाता है।

Reporting Verb : वक्ता द्वारा जिस verb का प्रयोग किया जाता है उसे Reporting verb कहा जाता है।

Reported Speech : Inverted Commas ("....") के भीतर जो वाक्य रहता है उसे Reported speech कहा जाता है।

Verb of Reported Speech : Reported Speech (Inverted commas के अन्दर के वाक्य) की verb को Verb of Reported Speech कहा जाता है।

She said to me, "I am going to Jaipur."

इस वाक्य में She—Reporter है, said—Reporting verb है।

"I am going to Jaipur."—Reported speech है तथा am going — Reported Speech की verb है।

(a) Reported Speech हमेशा Capital letter से शुरू होता है एवं Inverted commas में बन्द रहता है।

(b) Direct से Indirect में बदलने पर Inverted commas हटा दिये जाते हैं।

Rules of Changing Direct Speech into Indirect Speech

Direct speech को Indirect Speech में परिवर्तन के नियमों के दो भागों में विभाजित किया जा सकता है :

(1) सामान्य नियम : वे नियम सभी प्रकार के वाक्यों पर साधारणतया लागू होते हैं।

(2) विशेष नियम : ये नियम अलग-अलग प्रकार के वाक्यों के लिए अलग-अलग हैं।

General Rules

Rule 1

Direct speech से Indirect Speech में परिवर्तन होने पर Inverted commas हट जाते हैं।

Rule 2

सबसे पहले Reporting verb का Tense देखें।

(a) यदि Direct narration में Reporting verb, Present या Future tense में है तो Indirect में परिवर्तन करते समय Reported speech के tense में कोई परिवर्तन नहीं किया जाता है।

(b) Reporting verb के Past, में होने की स्थिति में Rules आगे दिए गये हैं।

Rule 3

Indirect Speech में परिवर्तन होने पर Reported Speech के Persons का परिवर्तन निम्न प्रकार होता है :

(a) First person : Reporting verb के Subject के अनुसार बदलता है।

(b) Second person : Reporting verb के Object के अनुसार बदलता है।

(c) Third person : इसमें कोई परिवर्तन सामान्यतया नहीं होता है।

(d) Person : का परिवर्तन करते समय यह ध्यान रखें कि यदि person बहुवचन है तो परिवर्तन बहुवचन के अनुसार होगा। यदि person, possessive case में है तो परिवर्तन उसी अनुसार होगा। person का परिवर्तन Direct से Indirect में परिवर्तन का एक महत्त्वपूर्ण भाग है। ध्यान रखें: person का number एवं case नहीं बदला जाता है। Pronouns का परिवर्तन निम्न Table के अनुसार होता है।

निम्न Table को ध्यान से पढ़े एवं समझें :

Forms of Personal Pronouns

Person	Nominative Case	Objective Case	Possessive Case	
			Possessive Adjective	Possessive Pronoun
I Person	I	me	my	mine
	we	us	our	ours
II Person	you	you	your	yours
III Person	he	him	his	his
	she	her	her	hers
	it	it	its	X
	they	them	their	theirs

Rule 4

यदि Reporting verb say, says,will say या said रहे तो Indirect speech में भी say, says, will say या said ही रहेगी लेकिन यदि Reporting verb के साथ 'to' लगा हो तो परिवर्तन निम्न प्रकार होता है :

say to — tell   says to — tells   said to — told

tell या told के बाद object आना आवश्यक है। जैसे

He tells,"Ram is playing". *Incorrect*

He told, " I am going". *Incorrect*

He told that he was going. *Incorrect*

ये वाक्य गलत हैं, क्योंकि यहाँ Tells/ told के साथ कोई object नहीं है।

यहाँ tells की जगह says एवं told की जगह said का प्रयोग किया जाना चाहिए था।

Rule 5

Indirect Speech में बदलने पर reporting verb के बाद सामान्य वाक्यों में that का प्रयोग किया जाता है।

उक्त नियमों को ध्यान में रखते हुए निम्न वाक्यों का Direct से Indirect में परिवर्तन पर ध्यान दें

(a) He says, "I am going to Jaipur". *Direct*
He says that he is going to Jaipur. *Indirect*

(b) She says to me, " You are writing a letter to him." *Direct*
She tells me that I am writing a letter to him. *Indirect*

(c) They say to Ram, " We will go to Jaipur." *Direct*
They tell Ram that they will go to Jaipur. *Indirect*

वाक्य (a) :

(i) सबसे पहले देखें कि Reporting verb का Tense क्या है। यह Present tense है। अत: Reporting Speech के Tense में कोई परिवर्तन नहीं होगा।

(ii) Reporting verb, says है। अत: Indirect में भी says ही रहेगी।

(iii) Reported Speech में I, First person pronoun है जो कि Subject (he) के अनुसार बदलकर I का He हो जायेगा और am, verb बदलकर is हो जायेगी।

वाक्य (b) :

(i) सबसे पहले देखें कि Reporting verb का Tense क्या है। वाक्य की Reporting verb का tense, present है। अत: Reported Speech के tense में कोई परिवर्तन नहीं होगा।

(ii) Reporting verb, says to बदलकर tells हो जायेगी।

(iii) Reported Speech में you एवं him, II एवं III person pronouns हैं। II person pronoun (you)—object के अनुसार बदलता है। अत: object 'me' के अनुसार I हो जायेगा। III person pronoun—him में कोई परिवर्तन नहीं होगा। इस प्रकार के वाक्यों को Direct से Indirect में बदला जा सकता है। इस प्रकार के अन्य वाक्य देखें :

(a) Ramesh says to me, "I am your fast friend." *Direct*
Ramesh tells me that he is my fast friend. *Indirect*

(b) I say to her, "I will not talk to you." *Direct*
I tell her that I will not talk to her. *Indirect*

(c) He says to me, "I can teach you." *Direct*
He tells me that he can teach me. *Indirect*

(d) Hari says to Shalu, "I am your brother and you are my sister." *Direct*
Hari tells Shalu that he is her brother and she is his sister. *Indirect*

(e) He will say to Shalu , "I love you." *Direct*
He will tell Shalu that he loves her. *Indirect*

(f) I say to Shyam, "I will help you". *Direct*
I tell Shyam that I will help him. *Indirect*

यद्यपि Reported Speech का Tense नहीं बदलता है लेकिन Indirect Speech में pronoun या subject में परिवर्तन होने पर Reported Speech की verb का रूप बदल जाता है। वाक्य (a) में am का is, वाक्य (d) में am का is एवं वाक्य (e) में love का loves में परिवर्तन हुआ है।

Reporting Verb in the Past

Rule 6

यदि Reporting verb, Past tense में है तो Reported Speech में जो भी Tense होता है। इसका past हो जाता है। Reported Speech में Tense में परिवर्तन निम्न प्रकार होगा :

Tense of Reported Speech

Direct Narration	Indirect Narration
(1) Present Indefinite	Past Indefinite
(2) Present Continuous	Past Continuous
(3) Present Perfect	Past Perfect
(4) Persent Perfect Continuous	Past Perfect Continuous
(5) Past Indefinite	Past Perfect
(6) Past Continuous	Past Perfect Continuous
(7) Past Perfect	No change of tense
(8) Past Perfect Continuous	No change of tense

Change in Future Sentences (Reported Speech)

(1) Will / shall	Would / should
(2) Can	Could
(3) May	Might
(4) Could /should /would /might	No change

Rule 7

जब Reporting verb, Past tense में है तो Reported Speech में आये कुछ शब्दों में परिवर्तन होता है। जैसे :

Direct Narration	Indirect Narration
(1) This	That
(2) These	Those
(3) Here	There
(4) Hence	Thence
(5) Hither	Thither
(6) Now	Then
(7) Ago	Before
(8) Thus	So
(9) Today	That day
(10) Tomorrow	The next day / the following day
(11) Yesterday	The previous day
(12) Last week / month / year	The previous week / month / year
(13) The last fort night	The previous fort night
(14) The day before yesterday	The day before the previous day

Look at the Following Solved Examples : TENSEWISE

Present Indefinite

(1) He said to me, "I never eat sweets." *Direct*
He told me that he never ate sweets. *Indirect*

(2) He said to Hina, "I love you". *Direct*
He told Hina that he loved her. *Indirect*

Present Continuous

(1) Ram said to Shyam, "I am watching T.V". *Direct*
Ram told Shyam that he was watching T.V. *Indirect*

(2) They said to Rahim, "We are playing football." *Direct*
They told Rahim that they were playing football. *Indirect*

Present Perfect

(1) Sita said, "I have already cooked". *Direct*
Sita said that she had already cooked. *Indirect*

(2) Ram said to Shyam, " I have seen her today". *Direct*
Ram told Shyam that he had seen her that day. *Indirect*

Present Perfect Continuous

(1) Sonu said to me, "I have been reading for an hour". *Direct*
Sonu told me that he had been reading for an hour. *Indirect*

(2) Shyam said to Ram, "Sita has been playing since morning." *Direct*
Shyam told Ram that Sita had been playing since morning. *Indirect*

Past Indefinite

(1) She said to Ram, "I went to Jaipur last week." *Direct*
She told Ram that she had gone to Jaipur the previous week. *Indirect*

(2) Ramesh said to me, "I telephoned you yesterday." *Direct*
Ramesh told me that he had telephoned me the previous day. *Indirect*

Past Continuous

(1) She said to me, "I was waiting for you." *Direct*
She told me that she had been waiting for me. *Indirect*

(2) Shyam said to Sita , "You were playing tennis." *Direct*
Shyam told Sita that she had been playing tennis. *Indirect*

Past Perfect

(1) He said to me, "I had completed my project". *Direct*
He told me that he had completed his project. *Indirect*

(2) She said to Meena, "Ram had already visited Agra". *Direct*
She told Meena that Ram had already visited Agra. *Indirect*

Past Perfect Continuous

(1) He said , "I had been playing chess for two hours." *Direct*
He said that he had been playing chess for two hours. *Indirect*

(2) I said to you, "Ram had been waiting for you since 2 O'clock." *Direct*
I told you that Ram had been waiting for you since 2 O'clock. *Indirect*

Future Indefinite

(1) Ram said to Meena, "I shall write a letter." *Direct*
Ram told Meena that he would write a letter. *Indirect*

(2) Sita said to Kuku , "You will attend the party tomorrow." *Direct*
Sita told Kuku that she would attend the party the next day. *Indirect*

Future Continuous

(1) Rahim said to Ram, "Sita will be waiting for you." *Direct*
Rahim told Ram that Sita would be waiting for him (Ram). *Indirect*

(2) I said to her, "I shall be writing an essay". *Direct*
I told her that I should be writing an essay. *Indirect*

Future Perfect

(1) Sita said to Ram, "I will have completed my work". *Direct*
Sita told Ram that she would have completed her work. *Indirect*

(2) She said to me, "Ram will have vacated the room". *Direct*
She told me that Ram would have vacated the room. *Indirect*

Future Perfect Continuous

(1) Nisha said to me, "I shall have been reading the book." *Direct*
Nisha told me that she would have been reading the book. *Indirect*

(2) Chanchal said to Ekta, "We shall have been visiting the fair tomorrow". *Direct*
Chanchal told Ekta that they would have been visiting the fair the next day. *Indirect*

उपरोक्त वाक्यों में हमने सभी 12 Tenses के उदाहरण दिये हैं। आपने देखा कि Past Perfect, Past Perfect Continuous के वाक्यों के Tense में कोई परिवर्तन नहीं हुआ है।

उक्त नियम के अनुसार यदि Reporting verb, Past tense में है तो Reported speech के वाक्य का Tense, नियमानुसार परिवर्तित किया जाता है। इस नियम के निम्न अपवाद हैं। यह Important बिन्दु है।

Rule 8

यदि Reported Speech में कोई Universal Truth (सर्वकालिक सत्य), Proverb (कहावत), Mathematical fact (गणितीय तथ्य), Historical fact (ऐतिहासिक तथ्य), Habitual Act (आदतन क्रिया) या कोई Morality (नैतिकता) का सन्दर्भ हो तो ऐसे वाक्यों को जब Indirect में परिवर्तित करते हैं तो Reporting verb के Past Tenses में होने पर भी इनका Tense नहीं बदलता है। Look at the following sentences :

(1) He said, "The sun sets in the west." *Direct*
He said that the sun sets in the west. *Indirect*

(2) He said, "Man is Mortal." *Direct*
He said that the man is mortal. *Indirect*

(3) The teacher said, "India became Republic on 26th January 1950". *Direct*
The teacher said that India became Republic on 26th January, 1950. *Indirect*

(4) She said to me, "Honesty is the best policy." *Direct*
She told me that honesty is the best policy. *Indirect*

(5) She said, "Two and two is four." *Direct*
She said that two and two is four. *Indirect*

(6) He said, "London is the capital of U.K." *Direct*
He said that London is the capital of U.K. *Indirect*

(7) He said, "Mr. Narendra Modi is the P.M. of India." *Direct*
He said that Mr. Narendra Modi is the P.M. of India. *Indirect*

(8) He said, "Kashmir is in the north of India". *Direct*
He said that Kashmir is in the north of India. *Indirect*

(9) He said to me, " I go for a walk daily." *Direct*
He told me that he goes for a walk daily.(Habit) *Indirect*

(10) Ram said to me, "I get up early in the morning daily." *Direct*
Ram told me that he gets up early in the morning daily.(Habit) *Indirect*

(11) Radha said to her, " I go to office at 10 O'clock." *Direct*
Radha told her that she goes to office at 10 O' clock. *Indirect*

(12) The saint said, ''Man proposes and God disposes.'' *Direct*
The saint said that man proposes and God disposes. *Indirect*

(13) The teacher said, ''Something is better than nothing.'' *Direct*
The teacher said that something is better than nothing. *Indirect*

(14) The teacher said, "A stitch in time saves nine." *Direct*
The teacher said that a stitch in time saves nine. *Indirect*

वाक्य संख्या (6 एवं 7) में बताये गए तथ्य में यदि कोई परिवर्तन नहीं हुआ है, तो हम Reported Speech के Tense में कोई परिवर्तन नहीं करते हैं। यदि परिवर्तन हो गया हो तो हमें Tense में परिवर्तन करना होगा।

Specific Rules

Interrogative Sentences

Interrogative Sentences को सामान्य रूप से दो भागों में विभाजित किया जाता है :

(1) ऐसे प्रश्न जिनका Answer—Yes या No में दिया जा सकता है। जैसे :
(a) Are you happy? Yes or No
(b) Do you know me? Yes or No
(c) Will you accompany me? Yes or No

(2) ऐसे प्रश्न जिनका Answer—Yes या No में नहीं दिया जा सकता है। These are also called 'Wh questions'. ऐसे Interrogative sentences ऐसे प्रश्न होते हैं जिनका Answer, Yes या No में नहीं दिया जा सकता है। ऐसे प्रश्नों में कुछ जानकारी दी गई होती है। जैसे :
(a) Where do you live? (b) What is your name? (c) How are you?

इस तरह के प्रश्न Wh-words, जैसे : What, Where, Which, Who, How, etc. से शुरू होते हैं।

Rule 1

प्रथम प्रकार के Interrogative Sentence जो Auxiliary verb से शुरू होते हैं जिनका Answer, Yes/No में दिया जा सकता है उनको Indirect में परिवर्तित करते समय 'that' की जगह if या whether का प्रयोग किया जाता है।

Rule 2

Indirect Speech में Interrogative Sentences को Assertive Sentence में बदला जाता है अर्थात् Indirect Speech में परिवर्तन होने के बाद, वाक्य एक प्रश्न के रूप में नहीं रहता है तथा वाक्य के अन्त में लगा Question Mark (?) भी हट जाता है। वाक्य का Tense एवं Pronoun पूर्व में बताए नियमानुसार बदले जाते हैं।

Rule 3

Reporting verb ; say, says, said की जगह ask, asks, asked प्रयोग किया जाता है। कई बार ask की जगह Inquire या enquire of का प्रयोग किया जाता है। enquire of का प्रयोग तब किया जाता है जबकि इसके बाद object (जैसे He enquired of me) लगता है।

Look at the following solved examples :

(1) She said to me , "Are you going to college?" *Direct*
She asked me whether I was going to college. *Indirect*

(2) She said to Shyam, "Have you an extra copy?'' *Direct*
She asked Shyam if he had an extra copy. *Indirect*

(3) He said , "Am I looking smart?" *Direct*
He asked if he was looking smart. *Indirect*

(4) He said to me , " Can you write a letter?" *Direct*
He asked me if I could write a letter. *Indirect*

(5) She said to me, "Will you help me?" *Direct*
She asked me if I would help her. *Indirect*

Important

Interrogative वाक्य को Direct से Indirect में बदलते समय इसे Assertive बनाना आवश्यक है। छात्रों को यह कठिन कार्य लगता है। देखें: एक Interrogative वाक्य में verb हमेशा Subject के पहले आती है। जैसा कि वाक्य संख्या 1, 2, 3 से स्पष्ट होता है

(a) Are you going? (b) Have you an extra copy? (c) Am I looking smart?

इन वाक्यों को Assertive बनाने के लिए verb को subject (नये pronoun) के बाद रखना होता है एवं वाक्य का Tense Reporting verb यदि Past Tense में हो तो पीछे बताये नियमानुसार बदलना होता है। अतः Are you going को I was going में बदलना होगा। इसी प्रकार से Have you an extra copy को He had an extra copy तथा Am I looking smart को He was looking smart में बदलना होगा। Pronoun का परिवर्तन पूर्व में बताए गए नियमानुसार होगा तथा Tense में भी परिवर्तन बताए नियमानुसार किया जाएगा।

Rule 4

यदि Interrogative Sentence के साथ वाक्य में उसका उत्तर भी जुड़ा हुआ है तो ध्यान रखें, Yes में Answer देते समय assertive में देना होगा एवं No में Answer देते समय Negative में Answer देना होगा। जैसे :

(1) She said to me, "Can you solve this question?" "No", I said.
She asked me if I could solve that question, I said, I couldn't or I replied in negative.

(2) He said to me, " Do you know me ? "I said, "Yes".
He asked me if I knew him, I said, I did or I replied in affirmative.

Rule 5

ऐसे Interrogative Sentences जो Wh-Words से शुरू होते हैं। (जिनका Answer Yes/No में नहीं दिया जा सकता) ऐसे वाक्यों को जब Indirect में परिवर्तित करते हैं तो Conjunction; that/ if / whether नहीं लगता है बल्कि Wh-Words ही Conjunction का कार्य करते हैं जैसे हमने पूर्व में बताया है। Indirect Speech में वाक्य Interrogative में नहीं रहता है उसे Assertive बनाना आवश्यक है। वाक्य में आये Pronoun एवं Tense में परिवर्तन पूर्व में बताए गए नियमानुसार ही होता है।

Look at the following solved examples :

(1) He said to her, "What do you want?" *Direct*
He asked her what she wanted. *Indirect*

(2) He said to me, "Why are you happy?" *Direct*
He asked me why I was happy. *Indirect*

(3) Ram said to Hari, "Where do you live?" *Direct*
Ram asked Hari where he lived. *Indirect*

(4) She said to Hari, "When will you come?" *Direct*
She asked Hari when he would come. *Indirect*

(5) Ram said to Sita, " Who are you?" *Direct*
Ram asked Sita who she was. *Indirect*

(6) Sita said to Mohan, "How many cars have you?" *Direct*
Sita asked Mohan how many cars he had. *Indirect*

(7) I said to Shyam, "Which class do you read in?" *Direct*
I asked Shyam which class he read in. *Indirect*

(8) I said to the teacher, "How many students are there in the school?" *Direct*
I asked the teacher how many students there were in the school. *Indirect*

(9) He said to me, "Which team won the match?" *Direct*
He asked me which team had won the match. *Indirect*

(10) He said to me, "What is your planning ?" *Direct*
He asked me what my planning was. *Indirect*

Rule 6

Shall I/Weसे शुरू होने वाले प्रश्न

(A) इस तरह के प्रश्नों से जब कोई सूचना (information) हो या कोई Speculation हो। जैसे :

(i) **Direct** : "Shall I ever see her again ?", he said . *Speculation*

Indirect : He wondered if he would ever see her again.

(ii) **Direct** : "When shall I know the result of the election?" Ram asked.

Indirect : Ram asked when he would know the result of the election.

इस तरह के वाक्यों में shall को would में परिवर्तित किया जाता है।

(B) जब कोई सलाह या प्रार्थना की गई हो। जैसे :

(i) **Direct** : He said to the customer, "Shall we despatch these letters?"

Indirect : He asked the customer if they should despatch those letters.

(ii) **Direct** : "What shall I say father ?" he said.

Indirect : He asked his father what he should say.

इस तरह के वाक्यों में सलाह या प्रार्थना का भाव रहता है। यहाँ Indirect speech में shall को should में परिवर्तित किया जाता है। जब इस तरह के वाक्यों में choice पूछी जाती है। जैसे :

(i) **Direct** : "Shall I lock the room or leave it unlocked ?" Rajesh said.

Indirect : Rajesh asked whether he should lock the room or leave it unlocked.

इस तरह के वाक्यों में whether का प्रयोग किया जाता है।

(C) जब Shall का प्रयोग वाक्य में 'offer' (प्रस्ताव) के सन्दर्भ में किया जाता है। जैसे :

(i) **Direct** : "Shall I bring you something to eat?" she said.

Indirect : She offered to bring me something to eat.

(D) जब Shall का प्रयोग एक सुझाव के अर्थ में हो। जैसे :

(i) **Direct** : "Shall we meet again tomorrow?" he said.

Indirect : He suggested to meet again the next day.

इस तरह के वाक्यों में suggested का प्रयोग करके Indirect speech में परिवर्तित किया जाता है।

Rule 7

Will you / would you / could you से शुरू होने वाले प्रश्नों को Indirect speech में परिवर्तित करते समय, वाक्य का भाव देखकर Reporting verb में परिवर्तित किया जाता है। जैसे :

(i) **Direct** : He said, "Will you be there on Monday''? (Ordinary question)

Indirect : He asked if he would be there on Monday.

(ii) **Direct** : He shouted, "Will you keep silence?"

Indirect : He shouted at me to keep silence. *Or* He ordered me to keep silence.

(iii) **Direct :** He asked, "Would you like to do job in USA?"

Indirect : He asked if I would like to do job in USA.

(iv) **Direct** : He said, "Would you like a lift?"

Indirect : He offered me a lift.

(v) **Direct** : He said, "Would you like to have a drink?"

Indirect : He invited me for a drink. *Or* He offered me a drink.

Imperative Sentences

Imperative Sentence ऐसे वाक्य हैं जिनमें आदेश (Order), निर्देश (Direction, Command) प्रार्थना (Request), सुझाव (Suggestion), सलाह (Advice) का भाव निहित रहता है। ऐसे वाक्यों को Indirect Narration में परिवर्तित करते समय निम्न नियमों का ध्यान रखें :

Rule 1

Reporting verb को वाक्य के भाव के अनुसार Order, Command, Advice, Suggest, Request, Warn etc. में परिवर्तित करें।

Rule 2

Conjunction 'that' की जगह 'to' का प्रयोग करें। यदि वाक्य Negative है तो 'not to' का प्रयोग करें।

Rule 3

वाक्य में यदि Please, Kindly जैसे शब्द हैं तो इनको Indirect Speech में न्हीं रखें। वाक्य के भावार्थ के अनुसार Request का प्रयोग किया जाने से ये स्वत: ही वाक्य के भाव में आ जाते हैं।

Look at the following solved examples :

(1) She said to Ramu, "Please bring my book." *Direct*
She requested Ramu to bring her book. *Indirect*

(2) She said to me, "Have a glass of milk". *Direct*
She asked me to have a glass of milk. *Indirect*

(3) Ram said to Sita, "Take medicines regularly." *Direct*
Ram advised Sita to take medicines regularly. *Indirect*

(4) I said to Hari, "Don't pluck the flowers". *Direct*
I ordered Hari not to pluck the flowers. *Indirect*

(5) The SP said to the SHO, "Shoot the robber". *Direct*
The SP ordered the SHO to shoot the robber. *Indirect*

(6) The Principal said to the students, "Get out from office." *Direct*
The Principal ordered the students to get out from office. *Indirect*

(7) He said , "Follow my instructions". *Direct*
He ordered me to follow his instructions. *Indirect*

(8) He said to Sarla , "Lend me your Physics book". *Direct*
He requested Sarla to lend him her Physics book. *Indirect*

Negative Imperative वाक्यों में जो Do not या Don't जैसे शब्दों से शुरू होते हैं उनमें जैसा हमने पहले बताया है, 'not to' का प्रयोग करते हैं। 'not to' की जगह forbade का प्रयोग भी किया जाता है, लेकिन forbade के साथ वाक्य में not का प्रयोग नहीं करना है, क्योंकि forbade स्वयं ही Negative है, इसका अर्थ है मना करना। जैसे :

(1) *The teacher said to Hari, "Don't write on the table."* *Direct*
The teacher forbade Hari to write on the table. *Indirect*
Or
The teacher instructed Hari not to write on the table. *Indirect*

(2) *The Principal said, "Don't make a noise students."* *Direct*
The Principal forbade the students to make a noise. *Indirect*
Or
The Principal instructed the students not to make a noise. *Indirect*

(3) *She said to me, "Don't part your car here."* *Direct*
She forbade me to park my car there. *Indirect*
Or
She asked me not to park my car there. *Indirect*

Emphatic Imperative (Use of 'Do')

कई बार Imperative वाक्यों को आग्रहपूर्ण (Emphatic) बनाने के लिए 'Do' का प्रयोग किया जाता है, यह 'Do' का प्रयोग मात्र अधिक आग्रह या विनम्रता को प्रदर्शित करने हेतु प्रयुक्त होता है। तो ऐसे वाक्यों को Indirect में बदलते समय 'Do' को हटा दिया जाता है एवं ऊपर बताए गए नियमानुसार वाक्य को Indirect में बदला जाता है। जैसे :

(1) He said to me, "Do have a cup of coffee, please". *Direct*
He requested me to have a cup of coffee. *Indirect*

(2) She said to me , "Do come again." *Direct*
She requested me to come again. *Indirect*

(3) Rahim said to her, "Do have a seat, please." *Direct*
Rahim requested her to have a seat. *Indirect*

Imperative and Tag Question

कई बार Imperative Sentence के साथ एक Tag Question लगा रहता है, Tag Question का प्रयोग अपनी बात का महत्त्व बढ़ाने के लिए अथवा ध्यान आकर्षित कर, उत्तर पाने की आकांक्षा के लिए किया जाता है। इस प्रकार के वाक्यों को Indirect में बदलते समय, Tag Question को महत्त्व नहीं दिया जाता है। शेष वाक्य को पहले बताये नियमानुसार Indirect में बदलते हैं। जैसे :

(1) He said to me, "Open the door, will you ?" *Direct*
He asked me to open the door. *Indirect*

(2) She Said to Ram, "Bring me a glass of water, won't you?" *Direct*
She asked Ram to bring her a glass of water. *Indirect*

(3) The leader said to us, "Caste your votes, will you?" *Direct*
The leader advised us to caste our votes. *Indirect*

Sentences with 'Let'

(A) **Let से शुरू होने वाले वाक्य भी एक प्रकार के Imperative वाक्य ही होते हैं। Let से कई अर्थ निकलते हैं। सुझाव (Suggestion), प्रस्ताव (Proposal) हेतु Let का प्रयोग निम्न प्रकार होता है :**

(1) She said to me, "Let us go to market".
She suggested to me to go to market.
Or
She suggested to me that we should go to market.

(2) He said to me, "Let us purchase this house".
He proposed to me to purchase that house.
Or
He proposed to me that we should purchase that house.

(a) Let से शुरू होने वाले वाक्यों में Imperative वाक्य की तरह 'to' का प्रयोग भी उपरोक्तानुसार कर सकते हैं। जब should का प्रयोग किया जाता हैं तो Conjunction 'that' का प्रयोग suggested/proposed के बाद करना होगा।

(b) यदि Reporting verb–said है तो केवल Suggested या Proposed का प्रयोग होता है एवं Reporting verb, said to होने पर suggested to या proposed to का प्रयोग होगा।

(1) *She said,"Let him complete his work first."*
She suggested that he should complete his work first.

(2) *He said, "Let me solve this problem first."*
He suggested that he should solve that problem first.

(B) **Let से व्यक्ति की इच्छा (Wish) भी व्यक्त की जाती है। ऐसे वाक्यों में Reporting verb, wish का प्रयोग करना चाहिए। जैसे :**

(1) The student said, "Let me take food".
The student wished that he should take food.

(2) The lady said, "Let me have an ice cream pack".
The lady wished that she should have an ice cream pack.

(3) She said, "Let him be my friend".
She wished that he should be her friend.

(C) **Let से Order/Request का भाव भी व्यक्त किया जाता है। ऐसे वाक्यों में Reporting verb, order या request का प्रयोग करते हैं। ऐसे वाक्यों में जब अनुमति माँगी या दी जाती है तो to allow का प्रयोग conjunction की तरह किया जाता है। जैसे :**

(1) The boy said to the teacher, "Let me go home now."
The boy requested the teacher to allow him to go home then.

(2) The Principal said to the peon, " Let the students come in".
The Principal ordered the peon to allow the students come in.

Let से शुरू होने वाले वाक्यों में कभी-कभी Let को to let में बदलकर Indirect Speech में परिवर्तन किया जाता है। जैसे :

(1) I said to her, "Let me go to market" — *I requested her to let me go to market.*

(2) She said to Shyam, "Let him go to Jaipur." — *She requested Shyam to let him go to Jaipur.*

Optative Sentences

(A) ऐसे वाक्य जिनमें Good wishes, प्रार्थना, अभिवादन या इच्छा व्यक्त की जाती है, Optative Sentences कहलाते हैं।

(a) यदि वाक्य में कोई Good wish की गई हो तो Reporting verb को Wished या Prayed में बदला जाता है तथा that, conjunction का प्रयोग किया जाता है तथा वाक्य को Assertive sentence में बदलते हैं। जैसे :

(1) My mother said to my friend, "May you live long !"
My mother wished my friend that he might live long.

(2) She said to Sita, "May God bless you with a son!"
She prayed that God might bless Sita with a son.

(3) She said, "God grant you success !"
She prayed that God might grant me success.

(a) *यहाँ might के साथ verb की I form लगती है।*

(b) *वाक्य (3) में May का प्रयोग नहीं हुआ है तब भी Indirect में might का प्रयोग किया गया है। May की existence ऐसे वाक्यों में मानी जाती है।*

(B) यदि वाक्य में Good morning, good evening, good day इत्यादि का प्रयोग अभिवादनस्वरूप किया गया है तो Reporting verb की जगह Wished का प्रयोग किया जाता है। यदि 'sir' को या जिससे अभिवादन किया गया है, वह भी Inverted commas में है तो उसे बाहर निकाल लिया जाता है। जैसे :

(1) He said to the teacher, "Good morning." — He wished the teacher good morning.

(2) She said, "Good morning, sir !" — She wished the sir good morning.

(3) I said, "Good afternoon, father !" — I wished my father good afternoon.

(C) यदि वाक्य में farewell (विदाई) सूचक शब्द जैसे : Good bye, farewell इत्यादि का प्रयोग किया गया हो तो Reporting verb—bade का प्रयोग किया जाता है। जैसे :

(1) She said to me, " Good bye". — She bade me good bye.

(2) The leader said, "Farewell my friends." — The leader bade his friends farewell.

Exclamatory Sentences

ऐसे वाक्य जो अफसोस, घृणा, दुख, आश्चर्य, प्रसन्नता, शाबाशी देने का भाव व्यक्त करते हैं, Exclamatory sentences कहलाते हैं।

(a) इस तरह के वाक्यों को Indirect में बदलते समय, वाक्य के भावार्थ के अनुसार exclaimed with joy, exclaimed with sorrow, exclaimed with surprise, exclaimed with applause, exclaimed with anger, exclaimed with contempt जैसी Reporting verb का प्रयोग किया जाता है।

(b) Conjunction 'that' का प्रयोग किया जाता है।

(c) Alas, Bravo, Oh, Wow, Wah, Hurrah जैसे शब्दों को Indirect बनाते समय हटा दिया जाता है।

(d) Exclamatory वाक्यों को Assertive वाक्य में बदल दिया जाता है।

(e) यदि वाक्य में कोई इच्छा (जैसे : If I were a bird, If I were the P.M.) प्रकट की गई हो तो Reporting verb, wished का प्रयोग किया जाता है।

Look at the following solved examples :

(1) She said, "If I were a bird !"
She wished that she would be a bird.

(2) He said, "If I were young again !"
He wished that he would be young again.

(3) Ram said, "Alas ! I have been ruined."
Ram exclaimed with sorrow that he had been ruined.

(4) The lady said, "Oh ! my dog is dead."
The lady exclaimed with sorrow that her dog was dead.

(5) He said, "What a beautiful girl Sita is !"
He exclaimed with praise that Sita was a beautiful girl.

(6) We said, "What a nice place it is !"
We exclaimed with surprise that it was a nice place.

(7) They said, "What a great fall!"
They exclaimed with applause that it was a great fall.

(8) The captain said, "Well done! my friends."
The captain exclaimed with applause that his friends had done well.

(9) The player said, "Hurrah ! we have won".
The played exclaimed with joy that they had won.

(10) He said, "Wow ! what a pleasant weather it is!"
He exclaimed with joy that it was a very pleasant weather.

(a) जिन वाक्यों में I were, He were जैसे वाक्य एक इच्छा प्रकट करते हैं, उन्हें Indirect Speech में बदलते समय would be का प्रयोग किया जाता है।

(b) Exclamatory वाक्यों को Assertive वाक्यों में बदलते हैं। निम्न वाक्यों पर ध्यान देने से यह समझ में आ जायेगा।

	Exclamatory	***Assertive***
(1)	*What a beautiful girl she is!*	*She is beautiful girl.*
(2)	*What a nice place it is!*	*It is a very nice place.*
(3)	*What a great fall!*	*It is a great fall.*
(4)	*What an idea!*	*It is a great idea.*
(5)	*What a fool you are!*	*You are a great fool.*
(6)	*How dark the night is!*	*It is a very dark night.*

कुछ अन्य Exclamatory वाक्य देखें जो अधूरे से लगते हैं :

(1) *He said to me, "Congratulations!"*	*He congratulated me.*
(2) *The teacher said to the student, "Stupid!*	*The teacher called the student, stupid.*
(3) *She said," Thank you!"*	*She thanked me.*
(4) *They said to us,"Welcome!"*	*They welcomed us.*
(5) *I said to her,"Happy Christmas!"*	*I wished her happy Christmas.*

Miscellaneous Sentences

(A) जब वाक्यों में व्यक्ति का नाम Inverted commas के अन्दर Reported Speech में सम्मिलित होता है। जैसे :

(1) He said, "Rajeev, I am waiting for you."
He told Rajeev that he was waiting for him (Rajeev).

(2) She said, "Take your purse, Tony."
She asked Tony to take his purse.

(3) Sheela said, "Brother, please help me."
Sheela requested her brother to help her.

(4) He said, "Kuku, what are you doing?"
He asked Kuku what she was doing.

ऐसे वाक्यों में व्यक्ति के नाम को Reporting verb के साथ लगाकर शेष वाक्य को पूर्व वताए गए नियमों के अनुसार Indirect Speech में बदला जाता है।

(B) जब वाक्यों में 'Sir', 'Madam' का प्रयोग Inverted commas के अन्दर Reported Speech के साथ किया गया हो। जैसे :

(1) He said, "May I leave now, Madam ?"
He asked the Madam if he might leave then.

(2) She said, "May I attend the class, Sir ?"
She asked respectfully if she might attend the class.

(C) कुछ वाक्यों में Well, Okay, You, See, You know का प्रयोग किया गया होता है। जैसे :

(1) The receptionist said, "Well, what can I do for you ? "
The receptionist asked politely what she could do for me.

(2) 'Okay', she said, "I will consider your proposal."
She said that she would consider my proposal.

(D) वाक्यों में Must का प्रयोग एक future action या Present action में मजबूरी को प्रकट करता है, तो ऐसे वाक्यों को Indirect Speech में बदलते समय Must को had to में बदलते हैं। जैसे :

(1) She said, "I must leave at once."
She said that she had to leave at once.

(2) Ramesh said, "He must go to Jaipur tomorrow."
Ramesh said that he had to go to Jaipur the next day.

(E) Must not एवं Need not वाले वाक्य में इन शब्दों में कोई परिवर्तन नहीं होता है। जैसे :

(1) He said, "You must not speak to anyone".
He said that I must not speak to anyone.

(2) She said, "You need not purchase this book".
She said that I need not purchase that book.

(F) Would, Should, Could, Might वाले वाक्यों में इन शब्दों में कोई परिवर्तन नहीं होता है। जैसे :

He said, "She would/ should/ could/ might attend the party".
He said that she would/ should /could /might attend the party.

(G) **वाक्य में यदि 'had to' का प्रयोग है तो वह had had to में परिवर्तित हो जाता है।** यहाँ had to एक urgency को बताता है। जैसे :

The poet said, "After the function, I had to rush to my house."
The poet said that after the function he had to rush to his house.

यहाँ had to का प्रयोग Past Prefect Tense की तरह नहीं किया गया है।

(H) **Joint Sentences : जब कई वाक्य एक साथ होते हैं। जैसे :**

(1) She said, "I am a girl. I cannot stay here in night".
She said that she was a girl and added that she could not stay there in night.

(2) Ramesh said, "Sita is going to Jaipur tomorrow. I can also go with her."
Ramesh said that Sita was going to Jaipur next day and he could also go with her.

(3) Payal said, "I will not marry this year. I am preparing for IAS examinations".
Payal said that she would not marry that year and further added that she was preparing for IAS examinations.

(I) **इस प्रकार के वाक्यों को दूसरे वाक्य के लिए added, further added या and शब्द का प्रयोग कर, पूर्व में बताये गए नियमानुसार Indirect Speech में बदला जाता है। जैसे :**

(1) He said, "Do you know who is he ?"
He asked me if I knew who he was.

(2) She said, "Can you find, where are the keys?"
She asked me if I could find where the keys were.
ऐसे वाक्यों में दोनों वाक्यों को ही Reporting verb को Tense के अनुसार बदला जाता है। जैसे :

(3) He said, "Sarla is coming, wait here."
He said that Sarla was coming and asked me to wait there.

(4) He said, "Where is your purse, I have lost mine."
He asked me where my purse was and added that he had lost his.

(5) My father said, "I am going to office, where are you going."
My father said that he was going to office and wanted to know where I was going.
इस प्रकार के वाक्यों को अलग-अलग हमने पूर्व Indirect Speech में आसानी से परिवर्तित किया है। जब इस तरह के वाक्य एक साथ आए तो पूर्व में बताए गए नियमानुसार ही परिवर्तित करें एवं बीच में added, wanted to know etc का प्रयोग करें। जैसे :

(6) The leader said, "Friends, my country men, lend me your support. I will take care of your problems."
The leader addressed the people as friends, my countrymen and requested them to lend him their support. He further added that he would take care of their problems.

(7) "Where are you going Sheela ? Come here and we will talk about our marriage", said he.
He asked Sheela where she was going and added that they would talk about their marriage.

(8) Sita said to Ram, "No, No, I can't play with you. My father has forbidden me to play with you."
Sita told Ram that she could not play with him as her father had forbidden her to play with him.

(J) **Indirect Commands : कई वाक्य ऐसे होते हैं जो देखने में Negative या Interrogative लगते हैं लेकिन उनका अर्थ, आशय एक सलाह (advice), निमंत्रण (Invitation) या प्रार्थना (request) का होता है। इस तरह के वाक्य Indirect Commands कहलाते हैं।** *Look at the following sentences :*

(1) She said, "If I were you, I'd stop smoking."
She advised me to stop smoking.

(2) He said, "Why don't you change your clothes ?"
He advised me to change my clothes.

(3) "Would / could you show me your ticket, please ?" the TC said.
The TC asked me to show him my ticket.

(4) The receptionist said, "If you'd just sign the application form".
The receptionist asked him to sign the application form.

(5) His wife said, "Please, please don't take risk".
His wife begged / implored him not to take risk.

(6) Mrs Jacob said, "Don't forget to order the whisky".
Mrs Jacob reminded him to order the whisky.

Direct से Indirect में परिवर्तित करते समय जैसा पूर्व में भी बताया गया है, वाक्य का आशय नहीं बदलता है। अतः इस प्रकार के वाक्यों को उनके आशय के अनुसार Indirect में परिवर्तित करें। These are very important sentences from examination point of view.

(K) **कई वाक्यों में Reporting verb के बाद कोई Object नहीं आता है। ऐसे वाक्यों को जब Indirect में परिवर्तन करना हो, तो Reported Speech में प्रयुक्त Second person के Pronoun/adjectives को बदलने में छात्रों को परेशानी महसूस होती है। ऐसी स्थिति में वाक्य के आशय को ध्यान में रखते हुए आप अपनी इच्छा से कोई भी उपयुक्त Object चुन सकते हैं एवं उसे Reporting verb के बाद लगा दें। जैसे :**

(i) **Direct** : Sita said, "I am waiting for you."
Indirect : Sita told me that she was waiting for me. *Or*
: Sita told him that she was waiting for him.

(ii) **Direct** : My mother said, "You should take proper diet."
Indirect : My mother told me that I should take proper diet.

(iii) **Direct** : He said, "I do not like to talk to any of you."
Indirect : He told us that he did not like to talk any of us. *Or*
He told them that he did not like to talk to any of them.

(iv) **Direct** : The teacher said, "You should learn the lessons well."
Indirect : The teacher told the students/me/him/her that they / I / he / she should learn the lessons well.

वाक्य के भाव/आशय के अनुसार Object का चयन करना चाहिए।

Some Specific Points of about Reported Speech

(A) **यदि Past Continuous द्वारा कोई Completed Action नहीं बताया जाता है, तो यह Indirect Speech में उसका Tense अपरिवर्तित रहता है। जैसे :**

(1) He said, "When I saw her, she was playing football."
He said that when he saw her, she was playing football.

(2) She said, "When I saw them, they were swimming in the river."
She said that when she saw them, they were swimming in the river.

(3) He said, "When we were living in London we often saw Mr. James.
He said that when they were living in London they often saw/had often seen Mr. James.
इस तरह के वाक्यों में main verb को change किया भी जा सकता है एवं नहीं भी किया जा सकता है।

(B) यदि Past के वाक्य में कोई इस तरह का तथ्य है जो परिवर्तित नहीं हुआ है तो उसका Tense भी अपरिवर्तित रहता है। जैसे :

(1) He said, "I decided not to purchase the house, because it was near the railway track."
He said that he had decided not to purchase the house because it was near the railway track.

(2) They said, "We decided not to buy the house as it was on the main road."
They said that they had decided not to buy the house as it was on the main road.

वाक्य (1) एवं (2) में जो 'fact' अपरिवर्तित है (it was near the railway track; it was on the main road) उनके Tense में Indirect speech में भी कोई परिवर्तन नहीं हुआ है।

(C) Wish एवं It is time के बाद प्रयुक्त Unreal Past Tense के वाक्यों के Tense में Indirect speech में Change करते समय परिवर्तन नहीं होता है। जैसे :

(1) He said, "I wish I didn't have to take examination."
He said he wished he didn't have to take examination.

(2) "It is time we began planning for our examinations", he said.
He said that it was time they began planning for their examinations.

(D) ऐसे वाक्य जिनमें I/he/she/we/they/ had better जैसा Structure मिलता है, उसमें Indirect Speech में परिवर्तित करते समय Tense में कोई परिवर्तन नहीं होता है। लेकिन You had better वाले वाक्यों में Advised + Object का प्रयोग किया जाता है। (यदि Advised का प्रयोग नहीं किया जाये तो इसमें भी कोई परिवर्तन नहीं होगा।) जैसे :

(1) "The children had better go to bed early", said Ram.
Ram said that the children had better go to bed early.

(2) Sita said, "You had better given up smoking."
Sita said that I had better given up smoking.
Sita advised me to give up smoking.

(3) She said, "The old had better go for a walk daily.
She said that the old had better go for a walk daily.

(4) He said, "You had better not drink the tea."
He advised me not to drink the tea.
He said that I had better not drink the tea.

(E) निम्न प्रकार के Conditional Sentences को Indirect में परिवर्तित करते समय If, When इत्यादि शब्दों से पूर्व that का प्रयोग किया जाता है।

(1) He said, "If I had a permit I could get this job."
He said that if he had a permit he could get that job.

(2) He said, "If she had come to me, I would have helped her."
He said that if she had come to him, he would have helped her.

(3) He said, "If I had the tools I could mend the car."
He said that if he had the tools he could mend the car.

(4) She boasted, "I could read when I was there."
She boasted that she could read when she was there.

(5) He said, "When I was a boy, I could stay up as long as I liked."
He said that when he was a boy he could stay up as long as he liked.

01

Change the following sentences into Indirect Narration :

(1) He says, "Ram is a good player."
(2) Rita says, "Kishore sang a song."
(3) You will say, "Ganesh works hard."
(4) Kali will say, "Mira will swim in the river."
(5) He said, "Kalu reads well."
(6) He said, "The birds are flying."
(7) The servant said, "The guest has arrived."
(8) The washerman said, "It has been raining since morning".
(9) The boys said, "The teacher did not come."
(10) I said, "Ganesh was playing."
(11) You said, "Kalu can lift the box."
(12) The teacher said, "Mala may go."
(13) I said, "I shall work hard."
(14) He said, "The boys will write lessons."

02

Change the following sentences into Indirect Narration :

(1) Sheela said, "The earth moves round the sun."
(2) The saint said, "Man is mortal."
(3) The teacher said, "India became free in 1947."
(4) Mohan said, "Babar won the first battle of Panipat."
(5) Mohan said, "Two and two make four."
(6) Sheela said, "Truth always triumphs".
(7) He said, "Mohan could solve the sum."
(8) She said, "It might happen."

03

Change the following sentences into Indirect Narration :

(1) I said, "I am happy."
(2) You said, "We are learning our lesson."
(3) He said, "I am not to blame."
(4) She said, "I do not care for him."
(5) They said, "We trust in God."
(6) I said to him, "You are always late."
(7) You said to me, "You may go."
(8) Sheela said to us, "You must work hard."
(9) Ram said to me, "Sita does not like meat."
(10) I said to him, "He must not tell lies."
(11) He said to me, "Let us go for a walk."
(12) You said to me, "Let us play now."
(13) She said, "I am going now."
(14) I said, "I know this man."
(15) They said, "We are leaving tonight."
(16) He said to me, "I shall see you tomorrow."
(17) She said, "My uncle came yesterday."
(18) I said, "I bought the book last week."
(19) The mother said, "It will rain next month."
(20) She said, "I went to Jaipur a week ago."

04

Change the following sentences into Indirect Narration :

(1) He said to me, "You have made a mistake."
(2) The students said, "We shall play a match tomorrow."
(3) Harish said, "I am going now, mother."
(4) The teacher said, "Honesty is the best policy."
(5) He said to his parents, "I have done my best and can do no more."
(6) The dying man said, "My sons, I am leaving you a treasure buried in my fields."
(7) The Principal said, "Harish is very intelligent."
(8) The Principal said, "Tomorrow will be a holiday."
(9) The Prime Minister said, "National integrity will be preserved at all costs."
(10) The Minister said, "The prices have started falling."
(11) He said to me, "My father went to Mumbai last week."
(12) I said to her, "I may come tomorrow."
(13) The officer said to him, "You will be dismissed if you do not attend the office in time."
(14) The doctor said to him, "You have fallen ill because you over-ate yesterday."

05

Change the following sentences into Indirect Narration :

(1) He said to me, "Do you play hockey ?"
(2) I said to her, "Are you leaving tonight ?"
(3) He said to his friend, "Will you lend me fifty rupees?"
(4) He said to his son, "Have you seen the Tajmahal?"
(5) "Haven't you got a television set ?" he asked me.
(6) The servant said, "Shall I lay the table now?"
(7) "Shall I ever get married?" she said.
(8) Ram said to me, "What are you doing?"
(9) She said to the stranger, "Who are you?"
(10) The teacher said to me, "Which is your pen?"

06

Change the following sentences into Indirect Narration :

(1) His father said to him, "Why did you misbehave?"
(2) I said to Sita, "Where are you going?"
(3) Ram's mother said to him, "How have you failed in the examination?"
(4) The madam said to the boys, "Whose book is this?"
(5) She said to me, "How many boys are there in your school?"
(6) My father said to me, "Are you feeling well?"
(7) He said to her, "Can you lend me your umbrella?"
(8) I said to Harish, "Do you want to settle at Kanpur?"
(9) I said to the servant, "Where is my camera?"
(10) The teacher said to Ganesh, "Why are you not taking the examination?"

07

Change the following sentences into Indirect Narration :

(1) The teacher said, "Never make mischief again."
(2) I said to Sita, "Can you keep it for me till tomorrow?"
(3) She told Ram. "Leave it with me ,but don't come back."
(4) The retailer said, "Where can you find such variety of clothes?"
(5) "My advice," said our madam, "is that you should go home now."
(6) The girl shouted, "What a funny man you are !"
(7) The old man said to his son, "What have you learnt at school?"
(8) The assistant said, "Sir, give me the list of the dealers."
(9) Sohni said, "Rajesh, who has taken away my bike?"
(10) The child said to his mother,"Are you going to office today?"

08

Change the following sentences into Indirect Narration :

(1) "Good morning, sir", said Shyam to his teacher.
(2) "Thank you child, for showing me the way to the hospital," said the old lady.
(3) "Wish you a happy journey," said my wife.
(4) "Hello, Ramesh, how are you doing these days?" said Ashok.
(5) "Alas!," she said, "We have lost badly in the match."
(6) "May you live long, my son !" said my mother.
(7) "This book is full of errors," shouted Mr. Janardhan.
(8) The thief said to the judge, "Please pardon me, sir."
(9) The priest said to her, "May God help you!"
(10) The stranger said, "Good Heavens! What do I see before me !"

09

Change the following sentences into Indirect Narration :

(1) He said, " Two and two make four."
(2) She said, " I saw a tiger here."
(3) Maneesh said, "I may go to Delhi tomorrow."
(4) He asked me, " Where has he gone?"
(5) Sita said to me, "Is it still raining".
(6) He said to me, "When will she come?"
(7) She said to me, "Is Raju your friend?"
(8) She said to me, "Have you a car?"
(9) She said, "Do they play chess?"
(10) Rahim said, "Who are they?"

10

Change the following sentences into Indirect Narration :

(1) Kanika said to Suresh, "Is the tea ready?"
(2) She said to me, " Is it my book?"
(3) Tarmesh said to me, "Will you keep shut?."
(4) Chinkoo said to him, "Get out?"
(5) The teacher said, "Hurry up, students ."
(6) He said to the President, "Please give me one chance."
(7) She said to him, "Please cooperate me."
(8) The teacher said to the girls, "Keep away from the wall!"
(9) She said, "What a pitiful scene?"
(10) He said, "Hurrah! I am the first."

11

Change the following sentences into Indirect Narration :

(1) The queen said, "O, I were young again !"
(2) The Principal said, "Well done! my boys."
(3) He said, "God save the King."
(4) The mother said, "Long live my son!"
(5) She said to me, "Do have some drinks."
(6) Rahul said to him, "Will you go to Jaipur?"
(7) The boy said, "Sir, may I come in?"
(8) Hari said to Rahim, "You must obey your parents."
(9) He said, "I must go to Jaipur next week."
(10) She said, "You need not talk to me."

12

Change the following sentences into Indirect Narration :

(1) He said to me, "Let us go to hospital."
(2) She said, "Let them play."
(3) Ramesh said, "Sarla will not dance."
(4) The professor said, "Alas! I am undone."
(5) He said to me, "Do you know who is there?"
(6) He said, "Thanks for reminding me."
(7) He said, "Hello, what are you doing?"
(8) She said, "Congratulations."
(9) She said, "Farewell my dear friends ."
(10) He said to her, "Good morning !"

13

Change the following sentences into Indirect Narration :

(1) He says, "Mohan will write a letter."
(2) He says to me, "I will go to Mumbai tomorrow."
(3) He said to me, "I am reading a book."
(4) Ram said to me, "I can teach you."
(5) He said, "Mohan has been living here since 2000."
(6) He said, "The sun rises in the east."
(7) He said, "The moon revolves round the earth".
(8) I said to her, "I wrote a letter".
(9) I said to her, "Have you learnt your lesson?"
(10) Ram says to me, "You are smart."
(11) He said to me, "Are you going to Jaipur?"
(12) I said to him, "Who teaches you English?"
(13) I said to Harsh, "Please help me."
(14) Mohan said to me, " Do not tell a lie."
(15) She said, "Good bye, Ramesh."

14

Change the following sentences into Indirect Narration :

(1) My mother said to me, "May you live long!"
(2) I said to Ram, "Let me go there."
(3) He said, "If I were the King!"
(4) He said, "How intelligent Ravi is!"
(5) She said, "Keep this room open."
(6) The captain said, "Well done! my boys."
(7) Ram said, "You need not talk to me."
(8) He said, "What a beautiful picture?"
(9) He said, "I must go to Jaipur next month."
(10) The teacher said, "Hurry up."
(11) She said to me, "Is it still drizzling?"
(12) She said, "I saw a lion here."
(13) He said to me, "What is your father's name?"
(14) Ram said to the servant, "Clean up the house."
(15) She said, "How old are you?"

15

Change the following sentences into Indirect Narration :

(1) He says, "I am ill."
(2) Mohan said to me, "I am doing my work."
(3) I said to him, "I went there on Tuesday."
(4) The teacher said to us, "The earth is round."
(5) The boy said, "I saw him while I was running."
(6) She said, "You need not wail."
(7) I said to him, "Your brother has passed."
(8) I said to him, "Where do you live?"
(9) He said to me, 'Work hard if you want to pass."
(10) He said to me, "Do not go there?"
(11) He said, "What a pitiful scene?"
(12) She said, "Where is the hospital."
(13) The big man said, "Quite right."
(14) "We'll wait for you if you're late", they said.
(15) Ram asked Mohan, "What is the time?"
(16) The saint said to her, "May God help you!"
(17) "Wish you a happy journey", said Harsh.
(18) The boy said, " Hurrah! we have won the match."
(19) Sarla said, "Alas! I have failed."
(20) My mother said to me, "Don't jump on my bed."

16

Change the following sentences into Indirect Narration :

(1) Sumit said, "Father, I want to go abroad after I finish my studies here." **[RAS]**
(2) I said to Sumit,"Why do you want to go abroad? Where actually do you want to go?"
(3) "Don't go home yet," I told my colleague, " Remember you promised to finish your work before leaving." **[RAS]**
(4) "Please listen to me," he answered, "I must go now because my son is very ill." **[RAS]**
(5) "What a relief to know that the girl has passed !" I exclaimed, "now she can get a job."
(6) The station master said to me, "You are very late; it is one full hour since the train left." **[Inspectors of Income-tax]**
(7) Nitin said to me, "Why don't you come with us? Why do you want to be so unsocial"
(8) The gang leader shouted, "Keep together and run, the police are after us."
(9) I said to my companions, "Let them not come with us if they don't want to, let's not wait for them any longer". **[RAS]**
(10) "What a pleasant surprise !" I exclaimed on seeing John in the room, "I never expected to find you here."
(11) I said to Harish, "The man who came to meet you asked if we could see his boss tomorrow."
(12) He said to his Secretary, "Why don't you carry out orders exactly ? Remember if you don't, you will be punished."
(13) I said to the boy, "You have no ticket, get out before you are driven out."
(14) The lecturer paused and said, "Those who are tired of listening to me can go. I shall not mind it."
(15) They said, "How very awkward ! What shall we say to him? **[RAS]**

17

Change the following sentences into Indirect Narration :

(1) Madhur said to his sister, "Before I go to Delhi, I shall meet Sushila." **[Assistants Grade]**
(2) Govind said to Mohit, "Do not come here again or you will get a beating."
(3) John said to James, "Have you come here just to see me or are there some other reasons?"
(4) Abdul said, "What a lovely morning for tennis!" **[Assistants Grade]**
(5) The teacher said to the boy, "Since it is so warm let us go swimming." **[Assistants Grade]**
(6) They said, "Mother, we are not hungry; we shall eat later." **[Assistants Grade]**
(7) He said angrily to his brother, "Why don't you do as you are told"
(8) I said to the visitor, "Don't sit on that chair, it is broken."
(9) My little brother said, "I wish it rains hard, so I don't have to go to school."

(10) "How steep the path is !" they said, "we are quite tired." **[Income-tax Inspectors]**

(11) "Neither a borrower, nor a lender be," said the father to son. **[Income-tax Inspectors]**

(12) "And remember always that true education means the training of the mind," said the V.C. addressing students. **[Income-tax Inspectors]**

(13) The teacher said to his students, "Even in your life and conversation prove worthy of your glorious Alma Mater." **[Income-tax Inspectors]**

(14) The son said to his father reverently, "Do you expect me to have even done this sort of a mean thing." **[Income-tax Inspectors]**

(15) "Don't hang upon me, young man, I do not like flatterers", said the officer to his secretary.

18

Choose the best alternative to complete the sentences given below :

(1) Please tell me :
(a) where is the bus stop
(b) where the bus stop be
(c) where stops the bus
(d) where the bus stop is

(2) I told him :
(a) what the homework was
(b) what was the homework
(c) what was to be the homework
(d) what is the homework

(3) I think :
(a) will be the plane on time
(b) the plane will be on time
(c) the plane to be on time
(d) it will be on time the plane

(4) I didn't know :
(a) what he mean
(b) what did he mean
(c) what did he meant
(d) what he meant

(5) He said :
(a) that the weather colder than usual
(b) the weather be colder than usual
(c) the weather was colder than usual
(d) the weather it is colder than usual

(6) I think :
(a) today it is Wednesday
(b) that is today Wednesday
(c) today is Wednesday
(d) today be Wednesday

(7) He said :
(a) that yesterday he gone downtown
(b) he goes downtown yesterday
(c) he go downtown yesterday
(d) he went downtown yesterday

(8) I believe :
(a) him he is right
(b) he is right
(c) he be right
(d) that he right

(9) She said :
(a) that she was hungry
(b) she hungry
(c) she be hungry
(d) her was hungry

(10) He told us :
(a) that he enjoy the movie
(b) he enjoyed the movie
(c) he be enjoying the movie
(d) that enjoyed the movie

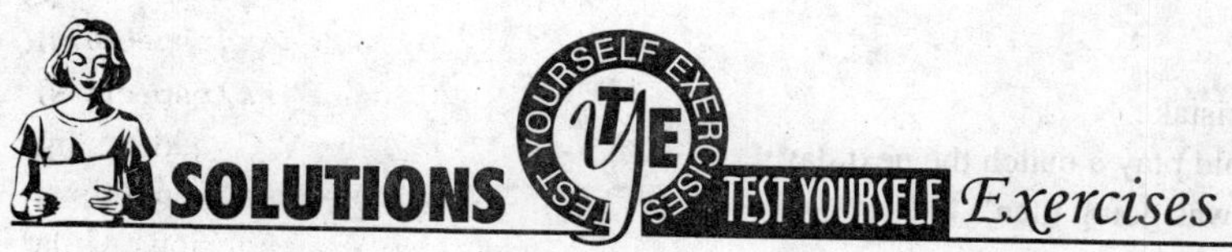

Solution TYE 01

(1) He says that Ram is a good player.
(2) Rita says that Kishore sang a song.
(3) You will say that Ganesh works hard.
(4) Kali will say that Mira will swim in the river.
(5) He said that Kalu read well.
(6) He said that the birds were flying.
(7) The servant said that the guest had arrived.
(8) The washerman said that it had been raining since morning.
(9) The boys said that the teacher had not come.
(10) I said that Ganesh had been playing.
(11) You said that Kalu could lift the box.
(12) The teacher said that Mala might go.
(13) I said that I should work hard.
(14) He said that the boys would write lessons.

Solution TYE 02

(1) Sheela said that the earth moves round the sun.
(2) The saint said that man is mortal.
(3) The teacher said that India became free in 1947.
(4) Mohan said that Babar won the first battle of Panipat.
(5) Mohan said that two and two make four.
(6) Sheela said that truth always triumphs.
(7) He said that Mohan could solve the sum.
(8) She said that it might happen.

Solution TYE 03

(1) I said that I was happy.
(2) You said that you were learning your lesson.
(3) He said that he was not to blame.
(4) She said that she did not care for him.
(5) They said that they trusted in God.
(6) I told him that he was always late.
(7) You told me that I might go.
(8) Sheela told us that we must work hard.
(9) Ram told me that Sita did not like meat.
(10) I told him that he must not tell lies.
(11) He proposed to me that we should go for a walk.
(12) You proposed to me that we should play now.
(13) She said that she was going then.
(14) I said that I knew that man.
(15) They said that they were leaving that night.
(16) He told me that he would see me the next day.
(17) She said that her uncle had come the previous day
(18) I said that I had bought the book the previous week.
(19) The mother said that it would rain the following month.
(20) She said that she had gone to Jaipur a week before.

Solution TYE 04

(1) He told me that I had made a mistake.
(2) The students said that they would play a match the next day.
(3) Harish told his mother that he was going then.
(4) The teacher said that honesty is the best policy.
(5) He told his parents that he had done his best and could do no more.
(6) The dying man told his sons that he was leaving them a treasure buried in his fields.
(7) The Principal remarked that Harish was very intelligent.
(8) The Principal announced that the next day would be a holiday.
(9) The Prime Minister declared that national integrity would be preserved at all costs.
(10) The Minister informed that the prices had started falling.
(11) He told me that his father had gone to Mumbai the previous week.
(12) I told her that I might come the next day.
(13) The officer warned him that he would be dismissed if he did not attend the office in time.
(14) The doctor apprised him that he had fallen ill because he had over-eaten the previous day.

Solution TYE 05

(1) He asked me if I played hockey.
(2) I asked her if she was leaving that night.
(3) He asked his friend if he would lend him fifty rupees.
(4) He asked his son if he had seen the Tajmahal.
(5) He asked me if I hadn't got a television set.
(6) The servant wanted to know if he should lay the table then.
(7) She wondered if she would ever get married.
(8) Ram asked me what I was doing.
(9) She asked the stranger who he was.
(10) The teacher asked me which my pen was.

Solution TYE 06

(1) His father asked him why he had misbehaved.
(2) I asked Sita where she was going.
(3) Ram's mother asked him how he had fared in the examination.
(4) The madam asked the boys whose book that was.
(5) She asked me how many boys there were in my school.
(6) My father asked me whether I was feeling well.
(7) He enquired of her if she could lend him her umbrella.
(8) I enquire of Harish whether he wanted to settle at Kanpur.
(9) I asked the servant where my camera was.
(10) The teacher asked Ganesh why he was not taking the examination.

Solution TYE 07

(1) The teacher warned me never to make mischief again.
(2) I asked Sita if she could keep it for me till the next day.
(3) She asked Ram to leave it with her, but not to come back.
(4) The retailer asked me where I could find such variety of clothes.
(5) Our madam advised us to go home then.
(6) The girl exclaimed that I was a very funny man.
(7) The old man asked his son what he (the son) had learnt at school.
(8) The assistant requested him to give the list of the dealers.
(9) Sohni asked Rajesh who had taken away her (Sohni's) bike.
(10) The child asked his mother whether she was going to office that day.

Solution TYE 08

(1) Shyam respectfully wished his teacher good morning.
(2) The old lady thanked the child for showing her the way to the hospital.
(3) My wife wished me a happy journey.
(4) Ashok greeted Ramesh and asked how he was doing those days.
(5) She exclaimed with sorrow that they had lost badly in the match.
(6) My mother wished me that I might live long.
(7) Mr. Janardhan shouted that, that book was full of errors.
(8) The thief respectfully requested the judge to pardon him.
(9) The priest blessed her that God might help her.
(10) The stranger exclaimed with surprise what he saw before him.

Solution TYE 09

(1) He said that two and two make four.
(2) She said that she had seen a tiger there.
(3) Maneesh said that he might go to Delhi the next day.
(4) He asked me where he had gone.
(5) Sita asked me if it was raining till then.
(6) He asked me when she would come.
(7) She asked me if Raju was my friend.
(8) She asked me if I had a car.
(9) She asked me if they played chess.
(10) Rahim asked who they were.

Solution TYE 10

(1) Kanika asked Suresh if the tea was ready.
(2) She asked me whether it was her book.
(3) Tarmesh asked me if I would keep shut.
(4) Chinkoo ordered him to get out.
(5) The teacher asked the students to hurry up.
(6) He requested the President to give him one chance.
(7) She requested him to cooperate her.
(8) The teacher instructed the girls to keep away from the wall.
(9) She exclaimed that it was a pitiful scene.
(10) He exclaimed with joy that he was the first.

Solution TYE 11

(1) The queen eagerly wished that she were young again.
(2) The Principal exclaimed with applause that the boys had done well.
(3) He prayed that God might save the king.
(4) The mother wished that his son should live long.
(5) She requested me to have some drinks.
(6) Rahul asked him if he would go to Jaipur .
(7) The boy respectfully asked whether he could come in.
(8) Hari told Rahim that he must obey his parents.
(9) He said that he had to go to Jaipur the following week.
(10) She said that I need not talk to her.

Solution TYE 12

(1) He suggested to me that we should go to the hospital.
(2) She advised that they should be allowed to play.
(3) Ramesh said that Sarla would not dance.
(4) The professor exclaimed with sorrow that he was undone.
(5) He asked me if I knew who was there.
(6) He thanked me for reminding him.
(7) He greeted and asked me what I was doing.
(8) She congratulated me.
(9) She bade farewell to his friends.
(10) He wished her good morning.

Solution TYE 13

(1) He says that Mohan will write a letter.
(2) He tells me that he will go to Mumbai tomorrow.
(3) He told me that he was reading a book.
(4) Ram told me that he could teach me.
(5) He said that Mohan had been living there since 2000.
(6) He said that the sun rises in the east.
(7) He said that the moon revolves round the earth.
(8) I told her that I had written a letter.
(9) I asked her whether she had learnt her lesson.
(10) Ram tells me that I am smart.
(11) He asked me if I was going to Jaipur.
(12) I asked him who taught him English.
(13) I requested Harsh to help me.
(14) Mohan advised me not to tell a lie.
(15) She bade Ramesh good bye.

Solution TYE 14

(1) My mother prayed that I might live long.
(2) I requested Ram to let me go there.
(3) He wished that he would be the king.
(4) He exclaimed that Ravi was very intelligent.
(5) She ordered to keep that room open.
(6) The captain shouted with applause that his boys had done well.
(7) Ram said that I need not talk to him.
(8) He exclaimed that it was a beautiful picture.
(9) He said that he would have to go to Jaipur the following month.
(10) The teacher asked to hurry up.
(11) She asked me if it was drizzling till then.
(12) She said that she had seen a lion there.
(13) He asked me what my father's name is.
(14) Ram ordered the servant to clean up the house.
(15) She asked me how old I was.

Solution TYE 15

(1) He says that he is ill.
(2) Mohan told me that he was doing his work.
(3) I told him that I had gone there on Tuesday.
(4) The teacher told us that the earth is round.
(5) The boy said that he had seen him while he (the boy) was running.
(6) She said that I need not wait.
(7) I told him that his brother had passed.
(8) I asked him where he lived.
(9) He advised me to work hard if I wanted to pass.
(10) He forbade me to go there.
(11) He exclaimed that it was a pitiful scene.
(12) She asked where the hospital was.
(13) The big man said that it was quite right.
(14) They told me that they would wait for me if I was late.
(15) Ram asked Mohan what the time was.
(16) The saint wished that God might help her.
(17) Harsh wished me a happy journey.
(18) The boy exclaimed with joy that they had won the match.
(19) Sarla exclaimed with sorrow that she had failed.
(20) My mother asked me not to jump on her bed.

Solution TYE 16

(1) Sumit told his father that he wanted to go abroad after he finished his studies here.
(2) I asked Sumit why he wanted to go abroad and where he actually wanted to go.
(3) I requested my colleague not to go home yet and to remember that he promised to finish his work before leaving.
(4) He answered politely to listen to him and that he must go then because his son was very ill.
(5) I exclaimed with joy that it was a great relief to know that the girl had passed and then she would get a job.
(6) The station master told me that I was very late and it was one full hour since the train had left.
(7) Nitin asked me why I did not come with them. He further asked why I wanted to be so unsocial.
(8) The gang leader shouted to his followers to keep together and run because the police were after them.
(9) I told the companions that they need not come with them if they didn't want to. I suggested that they (the companions) should not wait for them any longer.
(10) I exclaimed on seeing John in the room that it was a very pleasanst surprise, and I had never accepted to find him there.
(11) I told Harish that the man who had come to meet him, had asked if we would see his boss the following day.
(12) He asked his secretary why he did not carry out orders exactly, he warned him that if he did not (carry out orders) he would be punished.
(13) I ordered the boy to get out (as he had no ticket) before he was driven out.
(14) The lecturer paused and said that those who were tired of listening to him could go and that he would not mind that.
(15) They cried out with contempt what they would tell him (by way of explanation), exclaimed that it was very awkward.

Solution TYE 17

(1) Madhur told his sister that before going to Delhi, he would meet Sushila.
(2) Govind told Mohit not to come there again or he would get a beating.
(3) John asked James if he had come there just to see him or there were some other reasons.
(4) Abdul exclaimed that was a lovely morning for tennis.
(5) The teacher suggested the boys that they should go swimming since it was so warm.
(6) They told their mother that they were not hungry, they would eat later.
(7) He angrily asked his brother why he did not do as he was told.
(8) I cautioned the visitor against sitting on that chair, (as) it was broken.
(9) My little brother earnestly wished that it (should) rain so hard that he would not have to go to school.
(10) They exclaimed that the path was very steep and they were quite tired.
(11) The father advised his son neither to be a borrower, nor to be a lender.
(12) Addressing the new graduates the Vice-Chancellor exhorted them to remember always that true education means the training of the mind.
(13) The teacher exhorted his students, ever in their life and conversation, to prove worthy of their glorious Alma Mater.
(14) The son asked his father respectfully if he expected him to have even done that sort of a mean thing.
(15) Addressing the Secretary as young man, the officer advised him not to hang upon him as he (the officer) didn't like flatterers.

Solution TYE 18

(1) (d),	(2) (a),	(3) (b),	(4) (d),
(5) (c),	(6) (c),	(7) (d),	(8) (b),
(9) (a),	(10) (b).		

CHAPTER

16

ACTIVE VOICE PASSIVE VOICE

अभी तक आपने जिन वाक्यों का अध्ययन किया है उनमें कर्ता द्वारा कार्य किया जाता है। कर्ता Active होता है। जैसे:

(a) वह कार ठीक कर रहा है। He is repairing the car.
(b) वे घर की सफाई कर रहे हैं। They are cleaning the house.

ये वाक्य Active voice के हैं, इनमें (कर्ता) (Subject) 'वह', 'वे' हैं जो कार्य करते हैं, Active हैं लेकिन ध्यान दें यदि हमें निम्न प्रकार के वाक्य बनाने हैं। जैसे:

(a) कार ठीक की जा रही है या कार उसके द्वारा ठीक की जा रही है।
(b) घर की सफाई की जा रही है। या घर की सफाई मजदूरों द्वारा की जा रही है।

ऐसे वाक्य जिनमें कर्ता दिखाई नहीं देता है या कर्ता (Subject) की जगह कर्म (Object) प्रमुखता पाता है, ऐसे वाक्यों को समझने एवं ऐसे वाक्यों को अंग्रेजी में अनुवादित करने हेतु हमें Passive Voice के नियमों का अध्ययन करना होगा।

Active Voice *vs* Passive Voice

Voice: The voice of a verb tells whether the subject of the sentence performs or receives the action. In English there are two voices : passive and active.

Active Voice: Active voice वाक्यों में कर्ता (Subject) की प्रमुखता होती है। कर्ता Active होता है। Verb, Active voice में होती है।

In active voice , the subject performs the action expressed by the verb.

Passive Voice: Passive voice में कर्ता (subject) की प्रमुखता नहीं होती बल्कि Object की प्रमुखता होती है, वाक्य Object से शुरू होता है एवं Verb, Passive में होती है।
In passive voice, the subject receives the action expressed by the verb.
निम्न वाक्य को देखें:

(1) He sings a song. *Active voice*

यहाँ He (subject), sings (verb) a song (object) को व्यक्त करता है।

यह वाक्य (1) Active voice में है। वाक्य का Subject He, Active है, कार्य करता है। Verb, sings Active voice में है।

(2) A song is sung by him. *Passive voice*

यह वाक्य (1) का Passive है। इस वाक्य में A song, subject [Object of Sentence (1)] है तथा Verb, sung, [वाक्य 1 की verb की III form] है तथा him, object [वाक्य (1) के Subject He का objective form है।

इस वाक्य में Object [वाक्य (1)] प्रमुख है तथा Verb Passive में है एवं Subject [वाक्य (1)] को प्रमुखता नहीं दी गई है एवं यह Object की तरह वाक्य में प्रयुक्त हुआ है।

(a) कोई वाक्य Active है या Passive यह Verb की form पर निर्भर करता है। यदि Verb, Active है तो वाक्य Active voice में है यदि Verb, Passive है तो वाक्य Passive voice में है।

*(b) **Active Verb:** A verb is in Active voice when its form shows (as in sentence 1) that the subject does some work or subject is Active.*

*(c) **Passive Verb** : A verb is in Passive voice when its form shows (as in sentence 2) that something is done to the subject (of sentence 1) or subject is not Active, but Passive.*

Why and When to Use Passive Structure?

(1) जब Subject का पता नहीं हो या यह बताने की आवश्यकता नहीं हो कि कार्य किसने किया। जैसे:

(a) This mosque was built years ago.
(b) The mirror was broken yesterday.
(c) The shop was looted and three persons were arrested.
(d) A bomb was exploded.

(2) जब Object को महत्व दिया जाना आवश्यक हो। जैसे:

(a) The letter was written by Mr. Ganesh.
(b) The white tiger was killed by the hunter.

(3) Scientific and technical writings में Passive voice का प्रयोग किया जाता है क्योंकि वहाँ कर्ता का महत्व नहीं होता या महत्व invention को दिया जाना हो।

(a) Hydro Chloric Acid is produced when Hydrogen and Chlorine are mixed.
(b) Telephone was invented by Grahambell.

General Rules to Change the Voice

Rule 1 Active Voice से Passive में परिवर्तन करने पर Active का Object, Passive का Subject बन जाता है तथा Active का Subject, Passive में Objective form में बदलकर Object बनता है। जैसे:

I write a letter.	*Active Voice*
A letter is written by me.	*Passive Voice*

Rule 2 Passive Voice में Verb III form में प्रयुक्त होती है तथा उससे पहले is / am / are / was / were / been / being का प्रयोग वाक्य के Tense के अनुसार किया जाता है।

Rule 3 Passive के Subject (नए Subject) के अनुसार Verb, Singular या Plural लगानी होती है। यदि Subject— Singular है तो verb—singular एवं यदि नया subject— plural है तो verb भी plural लगती है। जैसे:

She is helping the students.	*Active*
The students are being helped by her.	*Passive*

यहाँ plural verb—are —subject—students के अनुसार प्रयुक्त हुई है।

Rule 4 Passive Voice में by का प्रयोग उन वाक्यों में Agent हेतु किया जाता है जहाँ कार्य किसी के द्वारा कराया जाता है। 'by' का प्रयोग verb के बाद एवं agent (object) से पूर्व किया जाता है। कुछ स्थितियों में by , एवं agent का प्रयोग नहीं किया जाता है। इसको आगे समझाया गया है।

Rule 5 Passive Voice में Active Voice का कर्ता निम्न प्रकार से Objective form में बदलता है :

Active Voice	Passive Voice	Active Voice	Passive Voice
I	me	She	her
He	him	They	them
You	you	It	it
We	us	Who	whom

Rule 6 सामान्य रूप से Transitive verb (ऐसी verb जो अपने साथ object लेती है) का ही Passive बनता है। जैसे: Sleep, sit, stand, go, come, laugh etc. का Passive नही बनता है लेकिन Intransitive verbs के साथ कोई Preposition लगाया गया हो तो उस स्थिति में इनको भी Passive बनाया जा सकता है।

Active	Passive
(a) They laughed.	No Passive.
(b) They laughed at the teacher.	The teacher was laughed at by them.
(c) None had slept.	No Passive.
(d) None had slept in the bed.	The bed had not been slept in.

Rule 7 Present Perfect Continuous, Past Perfect Continuous एवं Future Perfect Continuous एवं Future Continuous का Passive नहीं बनता है। 12 में से इस प्रकार 8 Tenses का Passive बनता है। Passive बनाते समय Verb का Tense के अनुसार परिवर्तन निम्न प्रकार से होता है :

Tense	Verb (Active)	Verb (Passive)
(1) Simple Present	write / writes	am / is / are written
(2) Simple Past	wrote	was / were written
(3) Simple Future	shall / will write	shall / will be written
(4) Present Continuous	is / am / are writing	is / am / are being written
(5) Past Continuous	was / were writing	was / were being written
(6) Present Perfect	has / have written	has / have been written
(7) Past Perfect	had written	had been written
(8) Future Perfect	will / shall have written	will / shall have been written

उक्त नियमों का ध्यानपूर्वक अध्ययन करें एवं देखे कि किस तरह से Tensewise वाक्यों को Passive में बदला जाता है।

Various Tenses and Change of Voice

Present Tense

(1) **Present Indefinite:** Active Voice में Present Indefinite के वाक्य का structure निम्न प्रकार का होता है :

Subject + Verb-I + Object

He writes a letter.

इसको Passive Voice में बदलने पर :

A letter		*is*		*written*		*by*		*him.*
Subject	+	***is***	+	***V-III***	+	***by***	+	***Object***

इस तरह Passive voice में वाक्य का Structure निम्न होगा:

Subject + is / am / are + V-III + by + Agent (object)

जैसे :

Active	Passive
(a) I love you.	You are loved by me.
(b) She washes the clothes in the evening.	The clothes are washed by her in the evening.

(2) Present Continuous: Present Continuous में Active वाक्य का Structure निम्न प्रकार का होता है

He is writing a letter. **Subject + is / am / are + verb + ing + Object**

इसको Passive में बदलने पर :

A letter	*is*	*being*	*written*	*by*	*him.*	
Subject +	***is*** +	***being*** +	***V-III*** +	***by***	***Object.***	***(Subject of Active)***

इस तरह Passive में वाक्य का structure होगा।

Subject + is / am / are + being + V-III + by + Agent (Object)

जैसे:

Active	**Passive**
(a) We are playing football.	Football is being played by us.
(b) She is making tea.	Tea is being made by her.

(3) Present Perfect: Active Voice में Present Perfect में वाक्य का structure निम्न होता है

Subject + have / has +V-III + Object

I have written a letter.

इसको Passive में बदलने पर :

A letter	*has been*	*written*	*by*	*me.*
Subject +	***has been*** +	***V-III*** +	***by*** +	***Object.***

इस तरह Passive में वाक्य Structure होगा :

Subject + have / has been + V-III + by + Agent (Object)

जैसे:

Active	**Passive**
(a) He has bought a scooter.	A scooter has been bought by him.
(b) He has repaired the car.	The car has been repaired by him.

Past Tense

(1) Past Indefinite: Active voice में Past Indefinite वाक्य का structure निम्न होता है:

I wrote a letter. **Subject + V-II + Object.**

Passive में बदलने पर

A letter	*was*	*written*	*by*	*him.*	
Subject +	***was*** +	***V-II*** +	***by*** +	***Object.***	***(Subject of Active)***

इस तरह Passive वाक्य का Structure होगा

Subject + was / were + V-III + by + Agent (Object)

जैसे:

Active	**Passive**
(a) We won the match.	The match was won by us.
(b) I purchased a pen.	A pen was purchased by me.

(2) Past Continuous: Active Voice में Past Continuous वाक्य का structure निम्न होता है :

Subject + was / were + (verb + ing) + Object

He was writing a letter.

इसे Passive में बदलने पर:

A letter	*was*	*being*	*written*	*by*	*him.*
Subject +	***was*** +	***being*** +	***V-III*** +	***by*** +	***Object***

इस तरह Passive का structure होगा।

Subject + was / were + being + V- III + by + Agent (Object)

जैसे: **Active** | **Passive**

(a) Ram was driving a car. — A car was being driven by Ram.

(b) They were flying the kites. — The kites were being flown by them.

(3) Past Perfect: Active voice में Past Perfect वाक्य का structure निम्न होता है

Subject + had + V-III + Object

He had written a letter.

इसे Passive में बदलने पर:

A letter had been written by him.

इस तरह Passive में वाक्य का structure होगा

Subject + had been + V-III + by + (Agent) Object

जैसे: **Active** | **Passive**

(a) He had killed a dog. — A dog had been killed by him.

(b) They had completed the project. — The project had been completed by them.

Future Tense

(1) Future Indefinite: Active Voice में Future Indefinite में वाक्य का structure निम्न होता है :

Subject + shall / will + V-I + Object

I shall write a letter.

इसे Passive में बदलने पर:

A letter will be written by me.

Subject +will be+ V-III + by + Object (Subject of Active)

इस तरह Passive में वाक्य का structure होगा

Subject + will / shall be + V-III + by + (Agent) Object

जैसे: **Active** | **Passive**

(a) He will give you a gift. — A gift will be given tc you by him.

(b) He will phone you. — You will be phoned by him.

(2) Future Perfect: Active Voice में Future Perfect में वाक्य का structure निम्न होता है:

Subject+ will / shall have+V-III + Object.

I shall have bought a pen.

इसे Passive में बदलने पर :

A pen will have been bought by me.

Subject + will have been + V-III + by + Agent

इस तरह Passive में वाक्य का structure होगा।

Subject + will / shall have been + V-III + by + Agent (Object)

जैसे : **Active** | **Passive**

(a) She will have written a thesis. — A thesis will have been written by her.

(b) Ramesh will have completed the project. — The project will have been completed by Ramesh.

इस प्रकार आपने सभी 8 Tenes के Active से Passive में बदलने के नियम एवं Passive Structure की जानकारी कर ली है। अब आप देखें कि Interrogative वाक्यों को Passive में कैसे बदला जाता है?

Passive of Interrogative Sentences

Interrogative Sentences मुख्यतया दो प्रकार के होते हैं:

(1) Yes / No questions. (2) Wh-questions.

(1) Yes / No questions: को निम्न भागों में विभाजित किया जा सकता है:

(a) Is/am/are से शुरू होने वाले questions: इस तरह के प्रश्नों में Passive वाक्यों का Structure निम्न होगा :

Is / am / are / + subject + being + V-III + by + agent ?

जैसे:

Active	Passive
(1) Is he writing a letter ?	Is a letter being written by him?
(2) Are they ploughing the field?	Is the field being ploughed by them?
(3) Am I catching the thief ?	Is the thief being caught by me?

(b) Do / does से शुरू होने वाले questions: इस तरह के प्रश्नों में Passive वाक्यों का structure निम्न होगा:

Is / am / are / + subject + V-III + by + agent ?

जैसे:

Active	Passive
(1) Does he need a pen ?	Is a pen needed by him ?
(2) Do you like the rooms ?	Are the rooms liked by you ?
(3) Do you write a lesson ?	Is a lesson written by you ?

(c) Did से शुरू होने वाले questions: इस तरह के प्रश्नों में Passive वाक्यों का structure निम्न होगा:

Was / Were + subject + V-III + by + agent ?

जैसे:

Active	Passive
(1) Did he write a letter?	Was a letter written by him?
(2) Did she help you?	Were you helped by him?
(3) Did he phone you?	Were you phoned by him?

(d) Was/were से शुरू होने वाले questions: इस तरह के प्रश्नों में Passive वाक्यों का structure निम्न होगा :

Was/Were + subject + being + V-III + by + agent ?

जैसे:

Active	Passive
(1) Was she cooking food?	Was food being cooked by her?
(2) Were they playing chess?	Was the chess being played by them?
(3) Was he washing the clothes?	Were the clothes being washed by him?
(4) Were you serving your parents?	Were your parents being served by you?

(e) Have / has / had से शुरू होने वाले questions: इस तरह के प्रश्नों में Passive वाक्यों का structure निम्न होगा:

Has/Have/Had + subject + been+ V-III + by + agent ?

जैसे:

Active	Passive
(1) Has he written a book?	Has a book been written by him?
(2) Have they played a match?	Has a match been played by them?
(3) Had she written a letter?	Had a letter been written by her?

(f) Modal Auxiliary verbs से शुरू होने वाले questions : इस तरह के प्रश्नों में Passive वाक्यों का structure निम्न होगा:

Modal Auxiliary + Subject + be + V-III + by + agent ?

जैसे:

Active	Passive
(1) Can she control the situation ?	Can the situation be controlled by her ?
(2) May he cross the river?	May the river be crossed by him?
(3) Should he cut the wood ?	Should the wood be cut by him?
(4) Will you steal the book ?	Will the book be stolen by you?
(5) Will they win the match?	Will the match be won by them?
(6) Would you repair the car?	Would the car be repaired by you?

Important : An Easy Way

ऐसे Interrogative sentences जिनका Answer Yes / No में दिया जा सकता है, helping verb से शुरू होते हैं। ऐसे वाक्यों को Passive में बदलने हेतु हमने ऊपर structure भी बताया है एवं solved example भी दिए हैं। इसका बहुत सरल तरीका है कि (1) Interrogative वाक्यों को Assertive में बदलें। (2) अब उस वाक्य का Passive बनाएँ (3) इस Passive वाक्य में प्रयुक्त helping verb को subject पहले लगाएँ एवं प्रश्नवाचक चिन्ह वाक्य के अन्त में लगाएँ। यह Interrogative वाक्य का Passive होगा।

जैसे : Does he write a letter? —(A)

Assertive — He writes a letter.

Passive — A letter is written by him.

इसकी helping verb को subject से पहले लगाएँ एवं प्रश्नवाचक चिन्ह वाक्य के अन्त में लगायें।

Is a letter written by him?

यह (A) वाक्य का Passive हैं। इसी तरह Has he written a letter?

Assertive — He has written a letter.

Passive — A letter has been written by him. अब Has a letter been written by him?

(2) 'Wh' Words: 'Wh' words जैसे: What, Why, When, Where etc. से शुरू होने वाले प्रश्न। ऐसे प्रश्नों का उत्तर Yes / No में नहीं दिया जा सकता है ऐसे प्रश्नों का Passive निम्न प्रकार से बनाया जा सकता है:

सामान्यतया Wh-words, Active वाक्य के शुरू में आते हैं। उसके बाद helping verb आती है। यदि वाक्य से 'Wh' word हटाकर देखें तो जो वाक्य बचता है उसका जवाब Yes / No में दिया जा सकता है। इस वाक्य को पूर्व में बताए नियमानुसार Passive में बदलें एवं 'Wh'word को इस वाक्य के पहले लगाने से Passive वाक्य बन जाता है। जैसे:

(1) Why have you broken the mirror? इस वाक्य में से Wh word हटाने पर शेष वाक्य रहता है: **Have you broken the mirror?** इस वाक्य का Passive बनाना हमने सीख लिया है। यह एक Yes/No question sentence है। इसका Passive बनेगा: **Has the mirror been broken by you?**

अब इस वाक्य के शुरू में 'Wh' लगाने से यह वाक्य (1) का Passive Voice बन जाएगा।

Why has the mirror been broken by you?

Active	Passive
(1) Why have you broken the mirror?	Why has the mirror been broken by you?
(2) Why do you write a letter?	Why is a letter written by you?
(3) When will you return my pen?	When will my pen be returned by you?
(4) Why are you laughing at her?	Why is she being laughed at by you?
(5) Where did he put the things?	Where were the things put by him?
(6) What did he break?	What was broken by him?
(7) When do you write the lesson?	When is the lesson written by you?
(8) Why does he kick the ball ?	Why is the ball kicked by him?
(9) When do they send the parcel?	When is the parcel sent by them?
(10) Where did she buy the books?	Where were the books bought by her?

Who से प्रारम्भ होने वाले Interrogative sentences: इस तरह के वाक्यों में By whom का प्रयोग सामान्यतया वाक्य के शुरू में करके Passive बनाया जाता है। **जैसे:**

Active	Passive
(1) Who broke this beautiful glass?	By whom was this beautiful glass broken?
(2) Who solved that problem?	By whom was that problem solved?
(3) Who can break this stick?	By whom can this stick be broken?
(4) Who will help her in difficulty?	By whom will she be helped in difficulty?
(5) Who wrote the Ramayana?	By whom was the Ramayana written?
(6) Who has deceived you?	By whom have you been deceived?

Whom से शुरू होने वाले Interrogative sentence: इसमें 'Who' का प्रयोग करके Passive बनाया जाता है। **जैसे:**

Active	Passive
(1) Whom have you invited?	Who has been invited by you?
(2) Whom has he abused?	Who has been abused by him?
(3) Whom has she reported?	Who has been reported by her?

Passive Without Agent

Passive बनाते समय वाक्य के अन्त में किन्हीं परिस्थितियों में by + Agent का प्रयोग नहीं किया जाता है। जैसे जब कर्ता नहीं है या कर्ता का बिना प्रयोग करे भी कार्य चल सकता है या कर्ता understood है। जैसे : यदि Active वाक्य में someone, somebody, nobody, people, इत्यादि कर्ता है।

Active	Passive
(1) People speak English all over the world.	English is spoken all over the world.
(2) Police arrested the thieves.	The thieves were arrested.
(3) Someone has stolen my watch.	My watch has been stolen.
(4) We execute all instructions without delay.	All instructions are executed without delay.
(5) Robbers looted the shop.	The shop was looted.

"In all passive voice exercises the use of 'by' with an agent must be rigorously suppressed, except in those examples where our interest in the predicate has led us to use the passive voice—we should omit the agent where the agent is vague or unknown." **—W.S. Allen (Living English structure)**

Sentences with Modals

(1) यदि किसी वाक्य में कोई Modal Auxiliary verb का प्रयोग किया गया है तो Helping verb हमेशा be ही लगता है।

(2) Modal की स्थिति में कोई परिवर्तन नहीं होता है। शेष वाक्य का Passive पूर्व निर्धारित नियमानुसार बनाएँ।

Active	Passive
(1) Sita could help him.	He could be helped by Sita.
(2) I will write a letter.	A letter will be written by me.
(3) You must write a book.	A book must be written by you.
(4) She should obey your parents.	Your parents should be obeyed by her.
(5) I may purchase a pen.	A pen may be purchased by me.

Imperative Sentences

Imperative Sentences ऐसे वाक्य होते हैं जिनमें आदेश (Order), प्रार्थना (Request) या सलाह (Advice, Suggestion) आदि का भाव व्यक्त होता है। ऐसे वाक्य सामान्यतया मुख्य क्रिया (Principal verb) से शुरू होते हैं।

(A) Sentences with 'Order/Command':

Active	Passive
(1) Shut the window.	Let the window be shut.
(2) Bring a glass of water.	Let a glass of water be brought.
(3) Finish this work.	Let this work be finished.
(4) Switch off the light.	Let the light be switched off.
(5) Inform the police.	Let the police be informed.
(6) Search the brief case.	Let the brief case be searched.
(7) Turn him out.	Let him be turned out.

Order / Command वाले Imperative वाक्यों में साधारणतया passive sentences का structure निम्न प्रकार का होता है :

Let + Subject + be + V-III Active Passive

- *कुछ वाक्यों में 'You are ordered' से भी वाक्यों को शुरू किया जाता है। जैसे :*

(1) *Get out of this office.* — *Active*
You are ordered to get out of this office. — *Passive*

(2) *Bring some glassees of water for them.* — *Active*
You are ordered to bring some glasses of water for them. — *Passive*

इस प्रकार से Passive का structure निम्न होता है: ***You are ordered to +V-I+ object***

(B) Sentences containing Request:

Active	Passive
(1) Please open the door.	You are requested to open the door.
(2) Please help that old lady.	You are requested to help that old lady.
(3) Take this seat, please.	You are requested to take this seat.
(4) Please give me a book.	You are requested to give me a book.
(5) Do it for me please.	You are requested to do it for me.
(6) Please don't disturb me.	You are requested not to disturb me.

इस प्रकार के वाक्यों में Passive का structure निम्न प्रकार का होता है:

You are requested to + V-I + object.

(C) Sentences with Suggestion: Suggestion वाले Imperative sentences को passive में बदलते समय should be का प्रयोग निम्न प्रकार होता है :

Active	Passive
(1) Help the disabled.	The disabled should be helped.
(2) Listen to me.	I should be listened to.
(3) Help the needy and poor.	The needy and poor should be helped.
(4) Always speak the truth.	The truth should always be spoken.
(5) Love the kids.	The kids should be loved.
(6) Hear him now.	He should be heard now.
(7) Help your dear and near.	Your dear and near should be helped.
(8) Love your country .	Your country should be loved.

इस तरह के वाक्यों का passive में structure निम्न प्रकार होता है :

Subject + should be + V-III

(D) Sentences with Advice: जिन वाक्यों में सलाह का भाव होता है उनको Passive में बदलते समय You are advised to का प्रयोग निम्न प्रकार होता है :

Active	Passive
(1) Work hard.	You are advised to work hard.
(2) Get up early .	You are advised to get up early.
(3) Do not smoke.	You are advised not to smoke.
(4) Be careful.	You are advised to be careful.
(5) Think before you speak.	You are advised to think before you speak.

Passive of Infinitive

Active Voice में Infinitive वाले वाक्यों का सामान्यतया Structure निम्न प्रकार होता है :

Subject + is / am / are / was / were/ have / has / had + to + V-I + object

ऐसे वाक्यों का Passive structure निम्न प्रकार होगा :

Subject + is / am / are / was / were / have / has / had + to be + V-III + by + Agent.

Look at the following solved examples:

Active	Passive
(1) I am to finish this work.	This work is to be finished by me.
(2) You are to write an essay.	An essay is to be written by you.
(3) They are to buy a TV.	A TV is to be bought by them.
(4) He was to sell this freeze.	This freeze was to be sold by him.
(5) We were to buy a car.	A car was to be bought by us.
(6) I am to assist him.	He is to be assisted by me.
(7) She has to help him.	He has to be helped by her.
(8) You were to bring him here.	He was to be brought here by you.
(9) The students have to write notes.	Notes have to be written by the students.
(10) Harish had to complete this work.	This work had to be completed by Harish.
(11) Ramesh has to repair this car.	This car has to be repaired by Ramesh.
(12) I have to purchase a pen.	A pen has to be purchased by me.
(13) You have to choose a house.	A house has to be chosen by you.

Miscellaneous Structures

(A) It is time to + V-I + noun से शुरू होने वाले वाक्य :

इस तरह के वाक्यों का passive structure होगा

It is time + for + noun + to be + Verb-I Form

Active	Passive
(1) It is time to close the office.	It is time for the office to be closed.
(2) It is time to supply food.	It is time for food to be supplied.
(3) It is time to stop writing.	It time for the writing to be stopped.
(4) It is time to give the final warning.	It is time for the final warning to be given.

(B) There से शुरू होने वाले वाक्य :

There + be form of verb + noun + infinitive — *Active structure*

इस तरह के वाक्यों का Passive structure निम्न होता है :

There + be form of verb + noun + to be + V-III. — *Passive structure*

Active	Passive
(1) There is a lot of work to complete.	There is a lot of work to be completed.
(2) There are six letters to write.	There are six letters to be written.
(3) There is no time to lose.	There is no time to be lost.
(4) There is no money to donate.	There is no money to be donated.
(5) There is no milk to waste.	There is no milk to be wasted.
(6) There is no work to do.	There is no work to be done.

(C) Passive of Verbs Showing, State of Mind or Feelings: कुछ Verbs ऐसी होती हैं जो कोई action व्यक्त नहीं करती है बल्कि मानसिक स्थिति या भाव को व्यक्त करती है। इस प्रकार की Verbs के passive form में by का प्रयोग नहीं किया जाता है बल्कि उपयुक्त Preposition का प्रयोग किया जाता है। **जैसे:**

Active	Passive	
(1) I know her.	She is known to me.	(Prep.—'to')
(2) He annoyed me.	I was annoyed with him.	(Prep.—'with')
(3) Her behaviour annoyed him.	He was annoyed at her behaviour.	(Prep.—'at')
(4) The news surprised all.	All were surprised at the news.	(Prep.—'at')
(5) The result amazed me.	I was amazed at the result.	(Prep.—'at')
(6) She vexed me.	I was vexed at her.	(Prep.—'at')
(7) Her conduct shocked me.	I was shocked at her conduct.	(Prep.—'at')
(8) He satisfied everybody.	Everybody was satisfied with him.	(Prep.—'with')
(9) This magazine has greatly interested me.	I have been greatly interested in this magazine.	(Prep.—'in')
(10) The news pleased her.	She was pleased with the news.	(Prep.—'with')

इस तरह की कुछ verbs एवं उनके साथ आने वाले preposition निम्न हैं :
Known to, amazed at, annoyed with (some person), annoyed at (something), startled at, vexed at, decorated with, filled with, surprised at, embodied in etc.

(D) Passive of Verbs with Appropriate Prepositions: कुछ verb अपने बाद Prepositions के साथ ही object लेती है। ऐसी verbs के साथ passive form में भी preposition उसी तरह से लगा रहता है।

Active	Passive
(1) He laughed at me.	I was laughed at by him.
(2) The police is enquiring into the matter.	The matter is being enquired into by the police.
(3) Sita smiled at Ram.	Ram was smiled at by Sita.
(4) He looks after his parents.	His parents are looked after by him.
(5) Rahim mocked at our class teacher.	Our class teacher was mocked at by Rahim.

इस तरह की Verbs जो अपने साथ preposition के बाद object लेती हैं निम्न है :
Look at, look after, laugh at, smile at, deride at, mock at etc.

(E) कुछ Sentences की Active Voice में बनावट निम्न प्रकार की होती है :
Subject + ask + object + if / whether + clause
इस तरह के वाक्यों में प्रथम भाग को ही passive में बदला जाता है। शेष वाक्य में कोई परिवर्तन नहीं होता है। जैसे :

Active	Passive
(1) I asked Rani if she went to Jaipur.	Rani was asked if she went to Jaipur.
(2) He asked me when I would complete my work.	I was asked when I would complete my work.
(3) They asked me if I knew his address.	I was asked if I knew his address.
(4) Rajesh asked me when I would return.	I was asked by Rajesh when I would return.

इस तरह के वाक्य में प्रथम भाग को ही Passive में बदला जाता है। शेष वाक्य में कोई परिवर्तन नहीं किया जाता है।

(F) Causative Verbs: जब एक वाक्य में Causative verb का प्रयोग किया जाता है तो इस तरह के वाक्य में subject के बाद Causative verb आता है। जैसे:

Active	Passive
(1) I made him polish my shoes.	He was made to polish my shoes.
(2) He made me sing a song.	I was made to sing a song.
(3) I saw her go.	She was seen to go.
(4) I let him go.	He was let go.

Let के साथ Passive में भी to का प्रयोग नहीं होता है।

(5) They made him king.	He was made king.
(6) We elected him monitor.	He was elected monitor by us.
(7) I found her crossing the road.	She was found crossing the road.
(8) We saw her sing a song.	She was seen to sing a song.

(G) कुछ वाक्य में They believed, People think, People say, We know, Everyone knows जैसे शब्दों से वाक्य शुरू करके that he is ..... से वाक्य पूर्ण होता है। इस प्रकार के वाक्यों का Passive निम्न प्रकार से बन सकता है:

(1) It was/is believed that.............. . (2) He is known / said / believed to be......... .

Look at the following examples:

Active	Passive
(1) They believed that Mr. Shukla was very rich.	It was believed that Mr. Shukla was very rich. Mr. Shukla was believed to be very rich.
(2) We know that some children go wise early.	It is known that some children go wise early. Some children are known to go wise early.
(3) People consider that she is intelligent.	She is considered to be intelligent. It is considered that she is intelligent.
(4) People say that he is a thief.	It is said that he is a thief. He is said to be a thief.
(5) Everyone knows that he is a gangster.	It is known that he is a gangster. He is known to be a gangster.

(H) Double Passive:

(1) They looted the shop and took away the money. *Active*
The shop was looted and the money was taken away. *Passive*

(2) She wrote the book and got published. *Active*
The book was written and got published by her. *Passive*

(3) The police arrested the thieves and sent them to jail. *Active*
The thieves were arrested and sent to jail. *Passive*

(I) Verbs with two objects: जब वाक्य में दो object होते हैं हम जिस object को प्रमुखता देना चाहते हैं उसे subject बनाया जाता है। सामान्यतया व्यक्तियों (Indirect object) को प्रमुखता दी जाती है।

Look at the following examples :

Active	Passive
(1) He gave me a purse.	I was given a purse by him. A purse was given to me by him.
(2) Rahim teaches us English.	English is taught us by Rahim. We are taught English by Rahim.

(3) The Principal asked him a question. — A question was asked him by the Principal. / He was asked a question by the Principal.

(4) Rani gave him a letter. — A letter was given to him by Rani. / He was given a letter by Rani.

Miscellaneous Sentences

(1) He likes people to call him, 'Don'. *Active*
He likes to be called 'Don'. *Passive*

(2) Someone will serve lunch. *Active*
Lunch will be served. *Passive*

(3) None must leave bicycles and scooters unlocked. *Active*
Bicycles and scooters must not be left unlocked. *Passive*

(4) Students may keep the library books for two weeks only. After that they must return them, otherwise they have to pay fine. *Active*
The library books may be kept for two weeks only. After that they must be returned otherwise fine has to be paid. *Passive*

(5) No one can do any thing unless someone gives us accurate information. *Active*
Nothing can be done unless we are given accurate information. *Passive*

(6) They threw him out. *Active*
He was thrown out (by them). *Passive*

(7) One must do one's duty. *Active*
Duty must be done. *Passive*

(8) The officer wants his subordinates to obey him. *Active*
The officer wants to be obeyed by his subordinates. *Passive*

(9) He wants that he should be treated as king. *Active*
He wants to be treated as king. *Passive*

(10) Ram desires his wife to respect his parents. *Active*
Ram desires his parents to be respected by his wife. *Passive*

(11) He wants someone to take photographs. *Active*
He wants photographs to be taken. *Passive*

(12) He recommended using the bullet proof car. *Active*
He recommended that the bullet proof car should be used. *Passive*

(13) I remember them taking me to library. *Active*
I remember being taken to library. *Passive*

(14) We saw them go out. *Active*
They were seen go out. *Passive*

(15) They let us go. *Active*
We were let go. *Passive*

(16) When he arrived home, Police arrested him. *Active*
When he arrived home he was arrested by police. *Passive*

(17) I saw her sing a song. *Active*
She was seen to sing a song. *Passive*

(18) Brutus accused Caesar of ambition. *Active*
Caesar was accused of ambition by Brutus. *Passive*

(19) We elected him secretary of the society. *Active*
He was elected secretary of the society. *Passive*

(20) Her reply shocked me. *Active*
I was shocked at her reply. *Passive*

01

Change the Voice of the following sentences:

Active : Present Indefinite

(1) The movie fascinates me.
(2) The movie bores Jack.
(3) The movie surprises them.

Active : Past Indefinite

(4) The movie bored me.
(5) The movie fascinated Janu.
(6) The movie surprised them.

Active: Present Continuous

(7) I am helping Shanu.
(8) Jane is helping Suresh and Lily.
(9) I am cleaning the bathroom.

Active : Past Continuous

(10) They were cleaning the bedroom.
(11) Surabhi was cleaning the kitchen and gallery.

Present Perfect

(12) I have mailed the gift.
(13) Janu has mailed the gifts.

Past Perfect

(14) Jack had directed the movie.
(15) Prem had directed those movies.

Future Perfect

(16) Johni will have finished the project next month.
(17) They will have finished the projects before then.

Future Indefinite

(18) I will mail the gift.
(19) Janu will mail the gifts.

Future Continuous

(20) I am going to make the cake.
(21) Surbhi is going to make two cakes.

Active : Will/Won't (Will Not)

(22) Shanu will invite Toni to the party.
(23) Shanu won't invite Jack to the party.
(Shanu will not invite Jack to the party).

Active : Can / Can't

(24) Mala can foretell the future.
(25) Toni can't foretell the future.
(Toni can not foretell the future.)

May / May not

(26) Her company may give Kashyap a new office.
(27) The lazy students may not do the homework.

Might/ Might not

(28) Her company might give Kashyap new office.
(29) The lazy students might not do the homework.

Should / Should not

(30) Students should memorise English verbs.
(31) Children shouldn't smoke cigarettes.

Ought to

(32) Students ought to learn English verbs.
(Negative ought to is rarely used.)

Had better / Had better not

(33) Students had better practise English everyday.
(34) Children had better not drink whisky.

Must / Must not

(35) Tourists must apply for a passport to travel abroad.
(36) Customers must not use that door.

Has to / Have to

(37) She has to practise English everyday.
(38) Sarla and Mira have to wash the dishes everyday.

Doesn't have to / Don't have to

(39) Mira doesn't have to clean her bedroom everyday.
(40) The children don't have to clean their bedrooms everyday.

Be supposed to / Not supposed to

(41) I am supposed to type the composition.
(42) I am not supposed to copy the stories in the book.
(43) Jackie is supposed to clean the living room.
(44) She isn't supposed to eat candy and gum.
(45) They are supposed to make dinner for the family.
(46) They aren't supposed to make dessert.

Should / Shouldn't have

(47) The students should have learnt the verbs.
(48) The children shouldn't have broken the window.

Ought to have

(49) Students ought to have learnt the verbs. (Negative ought to is rarely used.)

Supposed to (Past)

(50) I was supposed to type the composition.
(51) I wasn't supposed to copy the story in the book.
(52) Jackie was supposed to clean the living room.
(53) She wasn't supposed to eat candy and gum.
(54) Frank and Jane were supposed to make dinner.
(55) They weren't supposed to make dessert.

May have / May not have

(56) That firm may have offered Kakitana a new job.
(57) The students may not have written the paper.

Might have / Might not have

(58) That firm might have offered Kakitana a new job.
(59) The students might not have written the paper.

02

Change the following sentences into Passive Voice: **[BERU 1999]**

(1) The Government is spending too much money on Operation Pink.
(2) They have built six new helipads at Naila.
(3) She always gives me calendars and diaries at new year.
(4) You will have to amuse him with riddles and bed-time stories.
(5) They discovered a new pill to stimulate the appetite.
(6) It fascinated me.
(7) A duke of the sixteenth century had killed his wife in this room.
(8) He performed his symphony for the first time last week
(9) The owner himself showed them the house.
(10) Have they carried out his instructions?
(11) We have to pick the fruit very early in the morning.
(12) They allowed Harry to go but they did not allow Dick.
(13) Fear of death oppresses some old people.
(14) The judge advised me to the settle the matter out of court.
(15) Rajeev chose his words with care.
(16) If in the sixteenth century they could make history by building monuments, in the twentieth century they can make it by selling and reselling them.
(17) The promised Mary a new doll for her birthday.
(18) No one ever taught me the rudiments of music.
(29) They have proved all his calculations wrong.
(20) No one has climbed this mountain before.
(21) Did you grow these vegetables in your own garden ?
(22) They answered me most rudely in the shop.
(23) You should switch off the electricity when changing a fuse.

03

(A) *Rewrite the following sentences into Passive Voice:* **[RPSC Ajmer]**

(1) They rejected his proposal and laughed at him.
(2) Who is bothering you ?
(3) One must do one's duty.

(B) *Rewrite the following sentences into the Passive Voice:* **[RPSC Ajmer 1989]**

4. Two oxen pull them plough.
5. The murderer hid the knife in the grass.
6. Anyone will rob you if you are not careful.

(C) *Rewrite the following sentences into Passive Voice.* **[RPSC Ajmer 1989]**

7. He asked me to wait.
8. She is running a school these days.
9. Let them do it now.
10. Everyone knows that Mr. A is gang leader.
11. Has someone told you about your result?

(D) *Put the following sentences into Passive Voice:* **[RPSC Ajmer 1989]**

(12) Please sit here and wait till I return.
(13) Has someone made all the necessary arrangements ?
(14) It was clear that the parents had brought the child up well.
(15) They can't put you in prison if they haven't tried you.
(16) People say that tortoises live longer than elephants.

(E) *Put the following sentences into Passive Voice:* **[RPSC Ajmer 1989]**

(17) They did not tell me the truth about the situation.
(18) They will look after you well.
(19) Did they not tell you to he here by six O'clock?
(20) It surprised me to hear someone had robbed you.

(F) *Change the voice of the following sentences:* **[RPSC Ajmer 1989]**

(21) Did you paint these pictures in your own studio?
(22) They have decided to increase the school fees this year.
(23) Anger provokes many people to take hasty decisions which they later regret very much.
(24) You must understand clearly that this is the last time I shall allow it.
(25) You cannot expect the children to understand these problems.

04

Change the following sentences into Passive Voice:

(1) He will have closed his shop by 8 O'clock.
(2) They will have finished the paper by 11 O'clock.
(3) I shall have saved enough money to buy a house by 1990.
(4) He will have advised me.
(5) He can help you.
(6) The child could not climb the tree.
(7) You may return the book next week.
(8) They might win the match.
(9) We should obey our parents.
(10) He would make no promise.
(11) We ought to respect our teachers.
(12) You must do your duty.
(13) You could have solved the sum.
(14) He should have helped his friend.
(15) I would have attended the meeting but for the rain.
(16) Father must have taken away the purse.

05

Change the following sentences into Passive Voice:

(1) Post this letter.
(2) Never tell a lie.
(3) Tell him to go.
(4) Do not pluck flowers.
(5) Cut your coat according to your cloth.
(6) Let him sing a song.
(7) Please shut the door.
(8) Kindly grant me leave.
(9) Hurry up, please.
(10) Work hard.
(11) Do not smoke.
(12) Stand up on the bench.

06

Change the following sentences into Passive Voice:

(1) Do they like their teachers?
(2) Does this shopkeeper sell grocery?
(3) Did they win the match?
(4) Did you grow vegetables?
(5) Is he running a race?
(6) Were they singing songs?
(7) What does this word mean?
(8) Why do you blame us?
(9) Who teaches you English?
(10) Can you solve this sum?

07

Change the following sentences into Passive Voice:

(1) This bottle contains milk.
(2) I know his father.
(3) The report alarmed us.
(4) My progress satisfied my teachers.
(5) You cannot please everybody.
(6) Satish married Kanika.
(7) Her failure surprised us.
(8) Stamp collection interested the boy.
(9) His death shocked us.
(10) His servant has offended him.
(11) I want to buy a house.
(12) Women like men to flatter them.
(13) It is time to take tea.
(14) It is now time to close the shop.
(15) He ran fast to win the race.

08

Change the following sentences into Passive Voice:

(1) Honey tastes sweet.
(2) The rose smells sweet.
(3) He hopes to win a prize.
(4) Thank God.
(5) May you live long!
(6) People take rice all over the world.
(7) One should keep one's promise.
(8) One must endure what one cannot cure.
(9) God helps those who help themselves.
(10) Those who live in glass houses should not throw stones at others.

09

Change the following sentences into Active voice from the Passive:

(1) The plants are being watered by the gardener.
(2) He is not hated by me.
(3) Were you consulted by him?
(4) Your kindness will never be forgotten by me.
(5) The room is being swept by the sweeper.
(6) Good news was being expected by us.
(7) We have been insulted by her.
(8) The clerk had been bribed by them.
(9) Will the lesson have been taught by the teacher?

(10) The poor must be helped by the rich.
(11) Let the poor not be teased.
(12) He was offered a good job by the management.
(13) The matter is being looked into by the judge.
(14) The minister was being waited for by the people.
(15) We were shocked at the news of his death.
(16) By whom were you insulted?

10

Change the following sentences into Passive Voice:

(1) She has invited me.
(2) He has insulted you.
(3) We have painted the doors.
(4) They have won the match.
(5) The peon has posted the letter.
(6) The servant had already cooked food.
(7) He had not seen the Taj before.
(8) I had sold the old newspapers.
(9) They had prepared many plans.
(10) I had never seen such a lovely sight before.

11

Change the following sentences into Passive Voice:

(1) Should we not obey our parents?
(2) Must I help him?
(3) How can I serve my country?
(4) Could you have done it?
(5) Have you finished the assignment?
(6) Has he returned the books?
(7) Had he obtained leave?
(8) Will you have read the book by tomorrow?
(9) What have you drawn?
(10) Who has broken the bottle?

12

Change the following sentences into Passive Voice:

(1) My friends helped me.
(2) She did not like the sari.
(3) They wrote letters.
(4) The teacher corrected our notebooks.
(5) A large crowd cheered the players.
(6) The teacher will teach a new lesson today.
(7) The labourers will repair the road.
(8) We shall serve our country.
(9) She will help us.
(10) They will not disobey me.

13

Change the following sentences into Passive Voice:

(1) It is time to say prayers.
(2) It is necessary to write this essay.
(3) She told me a wonderful story.
(4) Somebody gave her a box of chocolates on her birthday.
(5) They laughed at the blind man.
(6) A car ran over a child.
(7) I am listening to you.
(8) We must obey the laws of the land.
(9) They are watching the sports.
(10) Did you make a noise ?
(11) Shalini threw the ball.
(12) Shall I ever forget those happy days?

14

Change the following sentences into Passive Voice:

(1) The farmer will not have watered the fiels.
(2) Get out of my sight.
(3) We shall no more hear his voice .
(4) People will remember him.
(5) A child cannot lift it .
(6) He might solve it.
(7) We can buy gold, but we cannot buy sympathy.
(8) You might have heard the name of Gandhiji.
(9) There is no money to waste.
(10) The policeman shot down the criminal with a revolver.
(11) You must write your answer on both sides.
(12) They don't allow smoking here.

15

Change the following sentences into Passive Voice:

(1) The fruit-seller sells fruit.
(2) The teacher calls the roll.
(3) My friends help me.
(4) The doctor treats the patients.
(5) Children like sweets.
(6) He writes poems.
(7) Everybody worships the rising Sun.
(8) I do not understand this question.
(9) He does not obey his parents.
(10) He sang a song.

16

Change the following sentences into Passive Voice:

(1) The boy is flying a kite.
(2) You are reading this lesson.
(3) We are not wasting our time.
(4) The farmers are reaping the crops.
(5) The girls are drawing the pictures.
(6) He is deceiving me.
(7) The grandmother was telling a story.
(8) We were expecting good news.
(9) The magician was showing tricks.
(10) The students were solving the sums.

SOLUTIONS TEST YOURSELF *Exercises*

Solution TYE : 01

(1) I am fascinated by the movie.
(2) Jack is bored by the movie.
(3) They are surprised by the movie.
(4) I was bored by the movie.
(5) Janu was fascinated by the movie.
(6) They were surprised by the movie.
(7) Shanu is being helped by me.
(8) Suresh and Lily are being helped by Jane.
(9) The bathroom is being cleaned by me.
(10) The bedroom was being cleaned by them.
(11) The kitchen and gallery were being cleaned by Surbhi.
(12) The gift has been mailed by me.
(13) The gifts have been mailed by Janu.
(14) Those movie had been directed by Jack.

(15) The movies had been directed by Prem.
(16) The project will have been finished by next month by Johny.
(17) The projects will have been finished before ten.
(18) The gift will be mailed by me.
(19) The gifts will be mailed by Janu.
(20) The cake is going to be made by me.
(21) Two cakes are going to be made by Surbhi.
(22) Toni will be invited to the party by Shanu.
(23) Jack won't be invited to the party by Shanu.
(Jack will not be invited to the party by Shanu.)
(24) The future can be foretold by Mala.
(25) The future can't be foretold by Toni.
(The future cannot be foretold by Toni.)
(26) Kashyap may be given a new office by her company.
(27) The homework may not be done by the lazy students.
(28) Kashyap might be given a new office by her company.
(29) The homework might not be done by the lazy students.
(30) English verbs should be memorised by the students.
(31) Cigarettes should not be smoked by children.
(32) English verbs ought to be learnt by students.
(33) English had better be practised by students everyday.
(34) Whisky had better not be drunk by children.
(35) A passport must be applied for by tourists to travel abroad.
(36) That door must not be used by customers.
(37) English has to be practiced by her everyday.
(38) The dishes have to be washed by Sarla and Mira everyday.
(39) Her bedroom doesn't have to be cleaned by Mira everyday.
(40) Their bedrooms don't have to be cleaned by the children everyday.
(41) The composition is supposed to be typed by me.
(42) The stories in the book are not supposed to be copied by me.
(43) The living room is supposed to be cleaned by Jackie.
(44) Candy and gum aren't supposed to be eaten by her.
(45) Dinner for the family is supposed to be made by them.
(46) Dessert isn't supposed to be made by them.
(47) The verbs should have been learnt by the students.
(48) The window shouldn't have been broken by the children.
(49) The verbs ought to have been learnt by the students.
(50) The composition was supposed to be typed by me.
(51) The story in the book wasn't supposed to be copied.
(52) The living room was supposed to be cleaned by Jackie.
(53) Candy and gum weren't supposed to be eaten by her.
(54) Dinner was supposed to be made by them.
(55) Dessert wasn't supposed to be made by them.
(56) Kakitana may have been offered a new job by that firm.
(57) The paper may not have been written by the students.
(58) Kakitana might have been offered a new job by that firm.
(59) The paper might not have been written by the students.

Solution TYE 02

(1) Too much money is being spent on Operation Pink.
(2) Six new helepads have been built at Naila.
(3) I am always given calendars and diaries at new year by her.
(4) He will have to be amused with riddles and bed times stories.
(5) A new pill to stimulate the appetite was discovered.
(6) I was fascinated by it.
(7) The wife of a duke of the sixteenth century was killed by him in this room.
(8) His symphony was performed for the first time last week.
(9) They were shown the house by the owner himself.
(10) Have his instructions been carried out by them ?
(11) The fruit have to be picked very early in the morning.
(12) Harry was allowed to go but Dick was not (allowed to go).
(13) Some old people are oppressed with the fear of death.
(14) I was advised to settle the matter out of court by the judge.
(15) Words were chosen with care by Rajiv.
(16) If history could be made by building monuments in the 16th century it can be made by selling and reselling them in the twentieth century.
(17) Mary was promised a new doll on her birthday.
(18) I was never taught the rudiments of music.
(19) All his calculations have been proved wrong.
(20) This mountain hasn't been climbed before.
(21) Were these vegetables grown in your own garden?
(22) I was most rudely answered in the shop.
(23) The electricity should be switched off when changing a fuse.

Solution TYE 03

(A) (1) His proposal was rejected and he was laughed at.
(2) By whom are you being bothered?
(3) Duty must be done.
(B) (4) The plough is pulled by two oxen.
(5) The knife was hidden in the grass by the murderer.
(6) You will be robbed if you are not careful.
(C) (7) I was asked to wait.
(8) A school is being run by her these days.
(9) Let it be done by them now.
(10) Mr. A is known to be a gang leader.
(11) Have you been told about your result ?
(D) (12) You are requested to sit here and wait here till I return.
(13) Have all the necessary arrangements been made ?
(14) It was clear that the child had been well brought up.
(15) You can't be put in prison if you haven't been tried.
(16) Tortoises are said to live longer than elephants.
(E) (17) I was not told the truth about the situation.
(18) You will be well looked after be them.
(19) Were you not told to be here by six O'clock?
(20) I was surprised to hear you had been robbed.

(F) (21) Were these pictures painted by you in your own studio?
(22) It has been decided to increase the school fees this year.
(23) Many people are provoked by anger to take hasty decisions which are very much regretted later.
(24) It must be understood clearly by you that this is the last time it will be allowed by me.
(25) The children cannot be expected to understand these problems.

Solution TYE 04

(1) His shop will have been closed by him by 8 O'clock.
(2) The paper will have been finished by them by 11 O'clock.
(3) Enough money will have been saved by me to buy a house by 1990.
(4) I shall have been advised by him.
(5) You can be helped by him.
(6) The tree could not be climbed by the child.
(7) The book may be returned by you next week.
(8) The match might be won by them.
(9) Our parents should be obeyed by us.
(10) No promise would be made by him.
(11) Our teachers ought to be respected by us.
(12) Your duty must be done by you.
(13) The sum could have been solved by you.
(14) His friend should have been helped by him.
(15) The meeting would have been attended by me, but for the rain.
(16) The purse must have been taken away by father.

Solution TYE 05

(1) Let this letter be posted.
(2) Let a lie never be told.
(3) Let him be told to go.
(4) Let flowers not be plucked.
(5) Let your coat be cut according to your cloth.
(6) Let a song be sung by him.
(7) You are requested to shut the door.
(8) You are requested to grant me leave.
(9) You are requested to hurry up.
(10) You are advised to work hard.
(11) You are advised not to smoke.
(12) You are ordered to stand up on the bench.

Solution TYE 06

(1) Are their teachers liked by them?
(2) Is grocery sold by this shopkeeper?
(3) Was the match won by them?
(4) Were vegetables grown by you?
(5) Is a race being run by him?
(6) Were songs being sung by them?
(7) What is meant by this word?
(8) Why are we blamed by you?
(9) By whom are you taught English?
(10) Can this sum be solved by you?

Solution TYE 07

(1) Milk is contained in this bottle.
(2) His father is known to me.
(3) We were alarmed at the report.
(4) My teachers were satisfied with my progress.
(5) Everybody cannot be pleased with you.
(6) Kanika was married to Satish.
(7) We were surprised at her failure.
(8) The boy was interested in stamp collection.
(9) We were shocked at his death.
(10) He has been offended with his servant.
(11) I want a house to be bought.
(12) Women like to be flattered by men.
(13) It is time for tea to be taken.
(14) It is now time for the shop to be closed.
(15) He ran fast for the race to be won.

Solution TYE 08

(1) Honey is sweet when (it is) tasted.
(2) The rose is sweet when (it is) smelt.
(3) It is hoped that he will win a prize.
(4) God be thanked.
(5) It is prayed that you may live long.
(6) Rice is taken all over the world.
(7) Promise should be kept.
(8) What cannot be cured must be endured.
(9) Those who help themselves are helped by God.
(10) Stones should not be thrown at others by those who live in glass houses.

Solution TYE 09

(1) The gardener is watering the plants.
(2) I do not hate him.
(3) Did he consult you?
(4) I shall never forget your kindness.
(5) The sweeper is sweeping the room.
(6) We were expecting good news.
(7) She has insulted us.
(8) They had bribed the clerk.
(9) Will the teacher have taught the lesson.
(10) The rich must help the poor.
(11) Do not tease the poor.
(12) The management offered him a good job.
(13) The judge is looking into the matter.
(14) The people were waiting for the minister.
(15) The news of his death shocked us.
(16) Who insulted you?

Solution TYE 10

(1) I have been invited by her.
(2) You have been insulted by him.
(3 The doors have been painted by us.
(4) The match has been won by them.
(5) The letter has been posted by the peon.
(6) Food had already been cooked by the servant.
(7) The Taj had not been seen by him before.
(8) The old newspapers had been sold by me.
(9) Many plans had been prepared by them.
(10) Such a lovely sight had never been seen by me before.

Solution TYE 11

(1) Should our parents not be obeyed by us?
(2) Must he be helped by me?
(3) How can my country be served by me?
(4) Could it have been done by you?
(5) Has the assignment been finished by you?
(6) Have the books been returned by him?
(7) Has leave been obtained by him?
(8) Will the book have been read by you by tomorrow?
(9) What has been drawn by you?
(10) By whom has the bottle been broken?

Solution TYE 12

(1) I was helped by my friends.
(2) The sari was not liked by her.
(3) Letters were written by them.
(4) Our notebooks were corrected by the teacher.
(5) The players were cheered by a large crowd.
(6) A new lesson will be taught by the teacher today.
(7) The road will be repaired by the labourers.
(8) Our country will be served by us.
(9) We shall be helped by her.
(10) I shall not be disobeyed by them.

Solution TYE 13

(1) It is time for prayers to be said.
(2) It is necessary for this essay to be written.
(3) A wonderful story was told to me. *Or*
I was told a wonderful story by her.
(4) A box of chocolates was given to her on her birthday. *Or*
She was given a box of chocolates on her birthday.
(5) The blind man was laughed at by them.
(6) A child was run over by a car.
(7) You are being listened to by me.
(8) The laws of the land must be obeyed.
(9) The sports are being watched by them.
(10) Was a noise made by you ?
(11) The ball was thrown by Shalini.
(12) Will those happy days ever be forgotten by me ?

Solution TYE 14

(1) The fields will not have been watered by the farmers.
(2) You are ordered to get out of my sight.
(3) His voice will be heared no more.
(4) He will be remembered .
(5) It cannot be lifted by a child.
(6) It might be solved by him.
(7) Gold can be bought but sympathy cannot be bought.
(8) The name of Gandhiji might have been heard by you.
(9) There is no money to be wasted.
(10) The criminal was shot down by the policeman with a revolver.
(11) Your answer must be written on both sides.
(12) Smoking is not allowed here.

Solution TYE 15

(1) Fruit is sold by the fruit-seller.
(2) The rolls is called by the teacher.
(3) I am helped by my friends.
(4) The patients are treated by the doctor.
(5) Sweets are liked by children.
(6) Poems are written by him.
(7) The rising Sun is worshipped by every body.
(8) This question is not understood by me.
(9) His parents are not obeyed by him.
(10) A song was sung by him.

Solution TYE 16

(1) A kite is being flown by the boy.
(2) This lesson is being read by you.
(3) Our time is not being wasted by us.
(4) The crops are being reaped by the farmers.
(5) The pictures are being drawn by the girls.
(6) I am being deceived by him.
(7) A story was being told by the grandmother.
(8) Good news was being expected by us.
(9) Tricks were being shown by the magician.
(10) The sums were being solved by the students.

CHAPTER 17

PREPOSITION

Preposition वाक्य में ऐसा शब्द है जो सामान्यतया Noun/Pronoun के पूर्व प्रयुक्त होता है एवं Noun /Pronoun का सम्बन्ध, वाक्य में प्रयुक्त अन्य शब्दों से व्यक्त करता है।

Definition : Preposition is a word placed before a Noun or Pronoun, denotes the relation, the person or thing referred by it, has with something else.

इस परिभाषा से Preposition के सम्बन्ध में निम्नलिखित दो बातें स्पष्ट होती हैं :

(1) Preposition का प्रयोग Noun या Pronoun से पूर्व होता है।

(2) यह Noun या Pronoun का सम्बन्ध, वाक्य में अन्य वस्तु से व्यक्त करता है।

Preposition - Pre (पहले) + Position (स्थिति) अर्थात् जो noun या pronoun के पहले प्रयुक्त होता है।

Rule

There is one very simple rule about prepositions. And unlike most rules, this rule has no exception. A Preposition is followed by a 'Noun'. It is never followed by a Verb.

By 'noun' we include :

(a) noun (cat, money, love)

(b) proper noun (name like India, Mira)

(c) pronoun (him, you, her, us)

(d) noun group (my first job)

(e) gerund (swimming, playing)

A Preposition cannot be followed by a verb. If we want to follow a Preposition by a verb, we must use the '-ing' form which is really a gerund or verb in noun form.

In the following sentences, why is 'to' followed by a verb? That should be impossible, according to the above rule :

Read the following sentences :

(a) I would like to move now.

(b) He used to smoke.

In these sentences, 'to' is not a preposition. It is part of the infinitive ('to move', 'to smoke').

Read the following examples :

(1) The food is <u>on</u> the table.

(2) She lives <u>in</u> China.

(3) Mira is looking <u>for</u> you.

(4) The letter is <u>under</u> your black book.

(5) I ate <u>before</u> coming.

(6) He is swimming <u>in</u> the river.

उपर्युक्त वाक्यों में underlined words, जो Noun या Pronoun का सम्बन्ध अन्य शब्दों से व्यक्त करते हैं, Prepositions हैं।

Important

(1) जिस Noun/Pronoun से पूर्व Preposition प्रयुक्त हुआ है, वह Noun/Pronoun, उस Preposition का Object कहलाता है।

(2) सामान्यतया Preposition का प्रयोग Noun/Pronoun (Object) के पूर्व ही किया जाता है।

निम्न स्थितियों (Positions) में preposition इनके बाद या वाक्य के शुरू में भी प्रयुक्त हो सकते हैं।

Typical Position of Preposition

(1) जब Object-Interrogative Pronoun; जैसे: What, Who, Whom, Which, Where etc; होता है, तो Preposition को वाक्य के अन्त में लगाया जाता है। जैसे:

(a) What are you thinking of ? (b) What is he crying for?
(c) What are you starting at? (d) Which of these chairs did you sit on?

यहाँ What, Who, Which आदि Interrogative Pronouns है, जो underlined words Preposition के Objects हैं।

(2) जब Object-Relative Pronoun, 'that' होता है, तो भी Preposition को वाक्य के अन्त में लगाया जाता है। जैसे:

(a) Here is the magazine that you asked for. (b) This is the dish that she is fond of.
(c) This is the girl that I told you of . (d) I know the colony that he lives in.

(3) जब Object-Infinitive हो तो Preposition को Infinitive के बाद लगाया जाता है। जैसे:

(a) This is a good hotel to stay at. (b) I need a pencil to write with .
(c) It is a beautiful house to live in. (d) This is ball to play with.

(4) कई वाक्यों में Relative Pronoun, Hidden किया हुआ रहता है। इनमें Preposition अन्त में आता है। जैसे:

(a) This is the house (where) I lived in. (b) This is the girl (that) I told you of.

(5) कुछ विविध प्रकार के वाक्यों के अन्त में Preposition लगता है। जैसे:

(a) I hate being laughed at. (b) This I insist on.
(c) He likes being looked at. (d) He is known all the world over.

(6) कुछ वाक्यों में Preposition का प्रयोग शुरू में ही किया जाता है। सामान्यतया ऐसे वाक्य Interrogative होते हैं। जैसे:

(a) By which train did you come ? (b) For whom was instructions given?

Kinds of Preposition

Preposition को मुख्यतया चार भागों में वर्गीकृत किया गया है।

(1) **Simple Prepositions :** जैसे: At, in, for, from, of, off, on, out, till, to, up, with, through, down, by etc. ये एक शब्द के एवं सामान्यतया काम में आने वाले Prepositions हैं।

(2) **Compound Prepositions :** ये Prepositions; a या be अन्य Preposition के साथ मिलकर बनते हैं। जैसे:

about, along, amidst, among, aloud
beside, below, beneath, between, beyond
inside, outside, within, without, underneath

(3) **Phrasal Prepositions :** दो या अधिक शब्दों को जोड़कर बनने वाले Prepositions, Phrasal Preposition कहलाते हैं जैसे:

along with, because of, by means of, for the sake of, in favour of with, in accordance with
in addition to, in case of, in course of, with reference to, with regard to, in respect to
in place of, in spite of, owing to, in comparison to, instead of, according to

(4) **Participle Prepositions :** जब वाक्य में Present Participle का प्रयोग बिना Noun/Pronoun के होता है, तो Present Participle एक Preposition की तरह function करता है। जैसे:
Concerning, Pending, Regarding, Considering, Touching etc.

(a) Pending enquiry into the matter, he was transferred from the office.
(b) Considering the quality, the prices are reasonable.

Some Important Prepositions

(1) At/In/On : These are very commonly used Prepositions :

Note *the use of these prepositions in reference of 'Time' :*

(i) 'At' is used for a Precise Time.

(ii) 'In' is used for Months, Years, Centuries and Long Periods.

(iii) 'On' is used for Days and Dates.

AT Precise Time	IN Months, Years, Centuries and Long Periods	ON Days and Dates
at 3 O'clock	in May	on Sunday
at 10:30 am	in summer	on Tuesday
at noon	in the summer	on 6th March
at dinner time	in 1990	on 25th January, 2007
at bed time	in the 1990s	on Christmas Day
at sunrise	in the next century	on Independence Day
at sunset	in the Ice Age	on my birthday
at the moment	in the past/future	on New Year's Eve

Look at the following examples :

(a) I have a meeting at 10 am. (b) That shop closes at midnight.

(c) Richa went home at lunch time.

(d) Do you think we will go to Saturn in the future?

(e) There should be a lot of progress in the next century.

(f) Where will you be on Independence Day ?

(g) Do you work on Sundays ?

(h) Her birthday is on 26th April.

Note the use of the Preposition of time 'at' in the following expressions :

Expression	Example
at night	The stars shine *at night.*
at the weekend	I don't usually work *at the weekend.*
at Christmas/Easter	I stay with my family *at Christmas.*
at the same time	We finished the test *at the same time.*
at present	He's not home *at present.* Try later.

Note the use of the Preposition of time 'in' and 'on' in these common expressions :

In	On
in the morning	*on Tuesday morning*
in the mornings	*on Saturday mornings*
in the afternoon(s)	*on Sunday afternoons*
in the evening(s)	*on Monday evening*

Impotant

लेकिन last, next, every के साथ At, In या On का प्रयोग नहीं किया जाता है। जैसे:

(i) I went to Mexico last May. (not in last May)

(ii) He's coming back next Sunday. (not on next Sunday)

(iii) I go home every Easter. (not at every Easter)

(iv) We'll call you this evening. (not in this evening)

Note *the use of these Prepositions in reference of 'Place'* :

(i) At is used for a POINT. (ii) In is used for an Enclosed SPACE.

(iii) On is used for a SURFACE.

At Point	In Enclosed Space	On Surface
at the corner	in the garden	on the wall
at the bus stop	in Delhi	on the ceiling
at the door	in India	on the door
at the top of the page	in a box	on the cover
at the end of the road	in my pocket	on the floor
at the entrance	in my wallet	on the carpet
at the crossroads	in a building	on the menu
	in a car	on a page

Look at the following examples :

(a) Ruma is waiting for you at the bus stop.
(b) The shop is at the end of the lane.
(c) When will you arrive at the school?
(d) I live on the 4th floor at 21 Diamond Street in Kolkata.
(e) Do you work in a company?
(f) I have a meeting in Delhi.
(g) Do you live in India?
(h) Saturn is in the Solar System.
(i) The author's name is on the cover of the book.
(j) There are no prices on this menu.
(k) You are standing on my foot.
(l) There was a 'no smoking' sign on the wall.

Please note that these three Prepositions are most commonly used in writing and speaking, so the students must learn the use of these Prepositions very well.

(2) At/In/To/Into :

(A) 'At' स्थिर अवस्था के लिए तथा 'In' गतिशील स्थिति हेतु प्रयोग होता है। जैसे:

(a) She is at home. (b) The train is in motion.

(B) 'At' छोटे स्थान हेतु तथा 'In' बड़े स्थान हेतु प्रयुक्त होता है। जैसे:

(a) He lives at Alwar in Rajasthan.
(b) A temple is situated at Madurai in Tamil Nadu.

(C) 'At' Point of time हेतु तथा 'In' का प्रयोग Period of time हेतु किया जाता है। जैसे:

(a) The train will arrive at 6 am in the morning.
(b) He will meet you in the morning.

(D) In/Into : 'In' का प्रयोग पूर्व में ही जब कोई वस्तु अन्दर होती है, उसके लिए, जबकि 'Into' का प्रयोग गति (movement) के लिए किया गया है। जैसे:

(a) There are three students in the class.
(b) He jumped into the river.

(E) To/Into : दोनों का प्रयोग गतिशीलता प्रदर्शित करता है। इनका प्रयोग वाक्य के अर्थ के अनुसार किया जाता है। To का अर्थ 'का' तथा Into का अर्थ 'अन्दर होता' है। जैसे:

(a) He went to market.
(b) He jumped into the well.

(3) On/To/Onto :

On का समय हेतु प्रयोग

(a) He will come on Monday. (b) Ram will go on 4th June.

To का स्थान हेतु प्रयोग

(a) He will go to Delhi. (b) Ram will go to market tomorrow.

On/Onto : On का प्रयोग स्थिरता एवं गतिशीलता दोनों हेतु किया जा सकता है। जैसे:

(a) Snow fell on the hills. (b) He is sitting on his suitcase.

Onto का प्रयोग मुख्य रूप से गतिशीलता (movement) हेतु तब होता है जब level (तल) change व्यक्त होता है। जैसे:

(a) People climbed onto their roofs. (b) He lifted her onto the table.

(4) With/By : With का प्रयोग Instrument हेतु और By का प्रयोग Agent (कर्ता) हेतु किया जा सकता है। जैसे:

(a) The snake was killed by him with a stick.

(b) The letter was written by Suresh with a pencil.

(5) Since/For/From : Since का प्रयोग Perfect Tense में होता है। For का प्रयोग Perfect Tense में भी एवं अन्य Tense में भी 'समय की अवधि' के लिए होता है। Since का प्रयोग Point of time हेतु जैसे:

Since 6 o'clock/Last night/Last Monday/Since Morning/Evening/Monday/January/2004 etc.

For का प्रयोग अवधि हेतु ; जैसे : for two hours/two days/two years/a long time/some time etc.

From का प्रयोग 'समय से' कार्य होने के सन्दर्भ में होता है। From का प्रयोग Perfect Tense में नहीं होता, अन्य Tense में होता है। जैसे:

(a) He will go to college from next Monday. (b) It has been raining for two hours.

(c) It has been raining since 2 o'clock. (d) He worked for three hours.

From का प्रयोग स्थान के लिए भी होता है। जैसे:

(a) He is from Mumbai. (b) Where do you come from ?

(6) For/During : For का प्रयोग सामान्यतया 'अवधि' हेतु तथा During का प्रयोग 'दौरान' के अर्थ में किया जाता है। जैसे:

(a) He has been ill for three days.

(b) It rained all Sunday, but stopped during the night.

जैसे: During childhood, during middle ages, during holidays, during summer vacations; for a month, for three days, for 15 years etc.

For का अर्थ भी 'के लिए' भी होता है अत: अर्थ के अनुसार for का प्रयोग निम्न प्रकार से भी किया जा सकता है:

(a) I went there for summer vacations. (b) I rented my car for the summer only.

(7) Below/Under : दोनों का अर्थ 'नीचे' होता है। सामान्यतया Under द्वारा वस्तु से Physical contact व्यक्त होता है। एवं Below से Contact व्यक्त नहीं होता है। जैसे:

(a) He placed the lamp below the almirah. (b) He put the books under the pillow.

Under का अर्थ Junior भी होता है।

(a) He is working under me. *Or* He is under me.

Below का प्रयोग dignity के Reference में भी किया जाता है। जैसे:

(a) It is below his dignity to beg for mercy.

(8) In/Within : In कर अर्थ होता है 'में'। यह दिये गए समय के अन्तिम बिन्दु को व्यक्त करने में प्रयुक्त होता है। इसका तात्पर्य कार्य में लगने वाले समय को व्यक्त करना है।

Within का अर्थ होता है 'अन्दर-अन्दर'। यह दी गई 'समय सीमा' को व्यक्त करता है। Within का प्रयोग तब किया जाता है जब कार्य के उससे पहले ही पूर्ण होने की सम्भावना होती है। जैसे:

(a) I will complete the work in a month. (b) I can repair the car within two hours.
(c) He will write a book in three months. (d) He can solve this question within an hour.

(9) Ago/Before : Ago का प्रयोग Past की घटनाओं हेतु तथा Before का प्रयोग घटनाओं/कार्यों के सन्दर्भ में किया जाता है। जैसे :

(a) He came three days ago. (b) The train had left before he reached the station .

(10) Beside/Besides : Beside का अर्थ 'साथ में/बगल में' होता है। जबकि Besides का अर्थ 'अतिरिक्त' (in addition to) होता है। जैसे :

(a) He was sitting beside Sarla. (b) He has a car besides a motor cycle.

(11) Between/Among : Between का प्रयोग सामान्यतया, दो के मध्य के लिए किया जाता है। Among का प्रयोग, दो से अधिक, के मध्य के सन्दर्भ में किया जाता है।

(a) He distributed his property between his two sons.
(b) He distributed his property among the poor.

Between का प्रयोग दो से अधिक के लिए तब किया जा सकता है जब वे परस्पर आबद्ध (closely associated) हों, जैसे :

(a) A treaty was signed between three parties.
(b) He inserted a needle between the close petals of a flower.

(12) Among/Amongst : दोनों का प्रयोग दो से अधिक के सन्दर्भ में होता है। यदि इनके बाद वाक्य में 'the' आता है तो किसी (Among/Amongst) का भी प्रयोग किया जाता है, लेकिन इनके बाद स्वर से प्रारम्भ होने वाले शब्द हैं तो Amongst का प्रयोग किया जाता है। Amongst का प्रयोग कम प्रचलित है। जैसे :

(a) He distributed the toffees among/amongst the poor.
(b) He distributed the toffees amongst us.

(13) Of/Off : Of सम्बन्ध स्थापित करने वाला Preposition जबकि Off से दूर हटने का भाव व्यक्त होता है। जैसे :

(a) He is a member of our family. (b) She is a member of our society.
(c) He is off duty now. (d) He jumped off the tower.

(14) Above/Over : दोनों का अर्थ higher than (ऊँचा) होता है। कई स्थितियों में दोनों में से किसी का भी प्रयोग किया जा सकता है। जैसे:

(a) The helicopter is hovering above/over us. (b) Flags were waved above/over our heads.

Over कई अर्थों; जैसे: Covering (ढकना), on the other side of (दूसरी तरफ), across (आर-पार); में प्रयोग किया जाता है। जैसे:

(a) I put a cloth over her. (b) He lives over this mountain.
(c) There is a bridge over the railway line.
(d) He put a blanket over the dead body.

Over का प्रयोग meal/tea/lunch/drink आदि के सन्दर्भ में निम्न प्रकार किया जा सकता है :

(a) We had a chat over a cup of tea. (b) The matter was decided over the lunch.

लेकिन Above का प्रयोग उक्त अर्थों में नहीं किया जाता है।

above का अर्थ 'earlier' या 'previously' (पूर्व) भी होता है। जैसे:

(a) He lives at the above address. (Previously mentioned)
(b) For details please see (P-1) above (Previously mentioned)

(15) Make of/Make from : दोनों से material (सामग्री) का बोध होता है।

Make of का प्रयोग तब होता है जब वस्तु (सामग्री) की अवस्था में कोई परिवर्तन नहीं होता है। जैसे:

(a) A note book is made of papers. (b) A house is made of bricks.

Make from का प्रयोग तब होता है जब सामग्री की अवस्था बदल जाती है। जैसे:

(a) Butter is made from milk. (b) Paper is made from grass.

(16) In/With :

(a) He is writing in ink. (b) He writes with a pen.

जब Countable noun होता है, तो Instrument हेतु With का प्रयोग होता है। जब Uncountable noun होता है तो in का प्रयोग होता है।

With का प्रयोग कई अर्थों में होता है।

(1) साथ-साथ He is playing with his sister.

(2) कारण He is trembling with fear.

(3) सम्बन्ध I have no relation with her.

(4) तरीका (Manner) He fought with determination.

(5) सहमति I agree with you.

(17) Opposite/In front of : Opposite का प्रयोग विपरीत एवं सामने दोनों अर्थों में होता है। In front of का अर्थ सामने ही होता है।

Ram and Shyam are having a meal. Ram is sitting at one side of the table and Shyam at the other side. तो हम कहेंगे:

Ram is sitting opposite Shyam.

हम यह नहीं कहेंगे कि Ram is sitting in front of Shyam.

Road के दोनों तरफ के मकानों के लिए भी Opposite का प्रयोग होगा।

His house is opposite to ours.

In front of का प्रयोग निम्न प्रकार किया जाता है:

(a) He parked the car in front of the hotel.

(b) He put the plates on the table in front of us.

Preposition + Gerund : कुछ verbs एवं adjectives इस प्रकार के होते हैं जिनके साथ Preposition के बाद हमेशा gerund का प्रयोग होगा। इस तरह की verbs निम्नलिखित हैं :

abstain from	desirous of	pride in
afraid of	angry about/at	bad at
debar from	proud of	succeed in
good at	clever at	crazy about
desist from	repent of	successful in
disqualified from	think of	bent on
dissuade (one) from	hopeful of	insist on
prevent from	fortunate in	meditate on
refrain from	assist in	aim at
hinder (one) from	excel in	passion for
prohibit (one) from	negligent in	excuse for
despair of	perceive in	tired of
confident of	persist in	worried about
fond of	famous for	excited about
glad about	keen on	interested in
disappointed about/ at	fed up with	sick of
sorry about/ for	happy about/ at	

इस सूची के अनुसार जो Preposition प्रयुक्त हुआ है, उसे याद करें क्योंकि यह महत्त्वपूर्ण है

(a) He *prevented* me *from* drinking cold water. (b) He *insisted on* trying again.

(c) He was *debarred from* taking examination. (d) He *succeeded in* achieving his goal.

(e) They are *afraid of* loosing the match. (f) Ram is *angry about* walking in the rain.

(g) Prakash is *good at* working in the garden. (h) I'm *worried about* making mistakes.

(i) This girl is *crazy about* playing tennis.
(j) He is *disappointed about* seeing such a bad report.
(k) We are *excited about* making our own film.
(l) Sunder is *famous for* singing songs.
(m) I'm *fed up with* being treated as a child.
(n) Hina is *fond of* going to parties.
(o) She is *glad about* getting married again.
(p) The children are not *happy about* seeing a doctor.
(q) Are you *interested in* writing poems?
(r) Joe is *keen on* drawing.
(s) She is *proud of* riding a snowboard.
(t) We're *sick of* sitting around like this.
(u) He's *sorry for* eating in the class.
(v) I'm *tired of* waiting for you.
(w) She is *used to* smoking.
(x) He is *clever at* skate boarding.

Ellipsis in Preposition

कई बार वाक्यों में दो या अधिक nouns/pronouns हेतु एक ही Preposition का प्रयोग कर दिया जाता है। ध्यान रखें यदि एक ही Preposition दोनों nouns/pronouns हेतु उपयुक्त है तो यह एक शुद्ध/सही प्रयोग होगा, अन्यथा दोनों nouns/pronouns के साथ अलग-अलग Preposition लगाना होगा। (Ellipsis का अर्थ Omission अर्थात् एक को हटाना)

(a) We should prevent damage and theft of public property. *Incorrect*
यहाँ damage एवं theft के लिए एक ही Preposition 'of ' का प्रयोग किया गया है, जो उचित नहीं है, क्योंकि damage के साथ to एवं theft के साथ of का प्रयोग किया जाना चाहिए। अत: उपयुक्त वाक्य को निम्न प्रकार से लिखा जाना चाहिए :
We should prevent *damage* to and *theft of* public property. *Correct*

(b) He is neither ashamed nor sorry for his misdeeds. *Incorrect*
He is neither *ashamed* of nor *sorry* for his misdeeds. *Correct*

(c) The design of this house is different and inferior to that of other house. *Incorrect*
The design of this house is *different* from and *inferior* to that of other house. *Correct*

Preposition Omitted

निम्न स्थितियों में Preposition का प्रयोग नहीं किया जाता है :

(1) सामान्यतया Transitive verbs के साथ Preposition का प्रयोग नहीं किया जाता है। इस तरह की verbs हैं : Reach, resist, resemble, afford, accompany, attack, assist, pick, pervade, precede, obey, order, combat, benefit, inform, violate etc.

(a) He ordered for a cup of tea. *Incorrect*
He ordered a cup of tea. *Correct*
(b) India attacked on Pakistan. *Incorrect*
India attacked Pakistan. *Correct*
(c) He informed to me yesterday. *Incorrect*
He informed me yesterday. *Correct*

(2) कुछ समय व्यक्त करने वाले शब्दों; जैसे : Morning, evening, day, night, month, week, year इत्यादि; से पूर्व यदि किसी Objective; जैसे : This, that, next, every, last इत्यादि; का प्रयोग हो, तो उस समय व्यक्त करने वाले शब्दों से पूर्व कोई Preposition नहीं लगाना चाहिए। जैसे:

(a) She is going to Jaipur next morning.
(b) I met her last evening.
(c) Ram is coming here next month.

(3) (A) अन्यथा समय व्यक्त करने वाले उक्त शब्दों के पूर्व Preposition आता है। जैसे:

(a) She went in the morning.
(b) I met her in the evening.
(c) Ram is coming here on Sunday.

(B) Yesterday, today, tomorrow के पूर्व भी कोई Preposition नहीं आता है। जैसे:
(a) Please meet me tomorrow. (b) He is arriving today.
(c) He went yesterday.

(4) Home : Home के साथ जब गति (motion) व्यक्त करने वाली verbs; जैसे : go, get इत्यादि; का प्रयोग किया गया हो तो Home के साथ Preposition का प्रयोग नहीं किया जाता है जैसे:
(a) It took them three hours to get home. (b) I went home by bus.
लेकिन यदि home के तुरन्त पूर्व किसी phrase/word का प्रयोग हो, तो Preposition लगता है। जैसे:
(a) She returned to her husband's home. (b) I went to his home.
Home के साथ at का प्रयोग भी किया जाता है। जैसे:
(a) You can do this work at home. (b) We can stay at home.
लेकिन in के तुरन्त बाद home का प्रयोग नहीं किया जाता है। जैसे:
(a) You can do this job in your own home. (b) We can live in our home.

(5) स्थान एवं समय व्यक्त करने वाले शब्दों; जैसे: Last week, last month, abroad, minute, bit, inside, outside इत्यादि के साथ भी सामान्यतया Preposition नहीं लगता है। जैसे:
(a) He came here last month (b) Sita is going abroad next week.
(c) Please wait a minute/bit. (d) Please come inside.
(e) Why are you standing outside?

Some Important Prepositions

Prepositions के नीचे दिए गए प्रयोग से ज्ञात होगा कि वाक्य के सन्दर्भ के अनुसार एक ही शब्द के साथ अलग-अलग Prepositions का प्रयोग किया जाता है। Prepositions का सही प्रयोग रटकर नहीं किया जा सकता है छात्रों को इस हेतु अभ्यास (Practice) करना चाहिए। वाक्य के अर्थ के अनुसार Prepositions का भी प्रयोग करना चाहिए।

A

(1) **Abide at (place) :** I will *abide at* the railway station till the train arrives.
Abide in (house) : She has been *abiding in* my house for the last three months.
Abide by (decision) : She will *abide by* my decision positively.
Abide with (person) : He will *abide with* his friend Suresh in all circumstances.

(2) **Angry at (thing) :** He is *angry at* your way of questioning.
Angry with (person) : Sita is *angry with* Ram.
Angry for (action) : He is *angry for* your laughing at her wife.

(3) **Arrive at (place) :** The train is going to *arrive at* the station within ten minutes.
Arrive in (country) : He is scheduled to *arrive in* India on next Monday.

(4) **Alight on (ground, thing) :** A large number of birds *alight on* the roof of my house.
Alight at (a place) : The groom *alighted* from the elephant *at* her gate.

(5) **Appeal to (person) :** I earnestly *appealed to* the principal to consider the matter again.
Appeal against (decision) : He *appealed against* the decision of the lower court.

(6) **Amuse at (thing) :** He is greatly *amused at* the indifferent attitude of his father.
Amused with (action) : The boys *amused* themselves *with* throwing flowers at the girls.

(7) **Ask for (a thing) :** He *asked* me *for* some help.
Ask from (person) : He *asked* some help *from* me.

(8) **Affiliated to : (University, Board)** Our college is *affiliated to* the University of Punjab.

Affiliated with (a party) : Bajrang Dal is *affiliated with* BJP indirectly.

(9) **Annoyed at (thing) :** He became *annoyed at* my laughing.
Annoyed with (person) : He is *annoyed with* you.

(10) **Antipathy to (thing) :** He has a great *antipathy to* wine.
Antipathy against (person) : You should not have any *antipathy against* your friend Jack.

(11) **Answer to (person) :** You have to *answer to* me for your conduct.
Answer for (action) : He was asked to *answer for* the misbehaviour.

(12) **Arm against (danger) :** We must *arm* ourselves *against* the danger of chemical weapons.
Arm with (weapon) : He *armed* himself *with* a revolver and a knife.

(13) **Atone to (person) :** I tried to *atone to* him by offering market price of the land.
Atone for (action) : He tried to *atone for* the mischief he had committed.

(14) **Award for (action) :** He was *awarded* a gold medal *for* winning 1000 Ft. race.
Awarded to (person) : A silver medal will be *awarded to* the best sports girl.

(15) **Antidote to (medicine) :** Diamond is regarded as an *antidote to* the venom of the snake.
Antidote against (inflection) : Quinine is an *antidote against* Malaria.

(16) **Argue against or about (a matter) :** He went to *argue against* the topic of debate.
He *argued* well *about* the newly introduced bill.
Argue with (person) : Don't *argue with* me unnecessarily.

(17) **Agree in (opinion) :** Ganesh *agrees* with Ram *in* opinion expressed by him.
Agree to (proposal) : I cannot *agree to* his proposal of dividing the property.
Agree with (person) : I fully *agree with* you on this issue.
Agree on (subject) : After a lot of discussion all *agreed on* the terms of agreement.

(18) **Accomplice with (person) :** Her wife was an *accomplice with* the murderer.
Accomplice in (act) : His wife was an *accomplice in* the murder.

(19) **Authority for (action) :** You have no *authority for* instructing me as such.
Authority on (subject) : She is indeed an unquestionable *authority on* Physics.
Authority over (person) : He has no *authority over* me officially.

(20) **Accused of (a crime) :** He is an *accused of* murder.

(21) **Accused by (a person) :** He was *accused by* his wife.

(1) **Blush for (fault) :** She *blushed for* the misbehaviour of her husband.
Blush at (praise) : She *blushed at* the comments of her husband.

(2) **Blind to (deeds, action) :** He should not be *blind to* the misdeeds of his son Rakesh.
Blind in (one eye) : His husband is *blind in* the right eye.

(3) **Born of (parents) :** He was *born of* an orthodox mother.
Born at, in (place) : He was *born at* general hospital at Alwar in Rajasthan.

(4) **Buy from (shop) :** You can *buy* this item *from* any grocery shop.
Buy for (person) : I *bought* this ball pen *for* my son.

(5) **Beg of, from (person) :** I *begged of* him to give me some time to payback.
I *begged* some rice *from* him.
Beg for (person) : I begged him *for* some rice.

C

(1) **Close to (adjective) :** His house is very *close to* the railway station.
Close with (shut) : She *closed* the door *with* a bang.
Close down (to terminate the operation) : He *closed down* his shop within six months.
Close out (to reduce the price) : He *closed out* the price of sugar to increase sales.

(2) **Confer about (consult on a matter) :** Ram and Rahim *confer* together *about* nominating the secretary.
Confer with (consult with a person) : I will *confer with* my father in this matter.

(3) **Contend for (thing) :** Mr. S.S. Shekhawat will *contend for* a seat in Legislative Assembly.
Contend with (person) : You should not *contend with* a person like Lalu Singh.

(4) **Consist in (remain) :** The beauty of this building *consist in* its style and grandeur.
Consist of (composed of) : Our body *consist of* flesh, bone and blood.

(5) **Condemn to (punishment) :** He was *condemned to* death by the judge.
Condemn for (crime) : He was *condemned for* murder by the court.

(6) **Compare to (comparing two different kinds of things) :** Don't *compare* water *to* milk.
Compare with (comparing two things of same class) : Kalidas was *compared with* Shakespeare by several renowned scholars.

(7) **Care for (like) :** I do not *care for* drinks.
Care about (thing) : She takes full *care about* her sarees and make up.

(8) **Consult on (matter) :** We were not *consulted on* the new issue of debentures.
Consult with (person) : You should *consult with* some expert before taking a final decision.

(9) **Controversy on (matter) :** A lot of *controversy* was raised *on* this issue.
Controversy with (person) : I do not have any *controversy with* any of the members on this matter.

(10) **Confide to (to tell) :** You should not *confide* your secrets *to* any body.
Confide in (to pose confidence) : I *confided in* him, but he deceived me.

(11) **Complain of (a thing)** I *complained of* his misconduct to the boss.
Complain to (person) : I *complained* of his misbehaviour *to* his father.

(12) **Compete with (person) :** Can you *compete with* him ?
Compete for *(job)* : I will try my best to *compete for* this job.

(13) **Cause of (problem) :** He is the main *cause of* all this trouble.
Cause for (anxiety) : I do not have any *cause for* anxiety.

(14) **Clothed in (dressing) :** She was *clothed in* a silken dress.
Clothed with (some quality) : She was *clothed with* modesty.

(15) **Connect to (join) :** *Connect* the end of this rod *to* the other.
Connect with (relation) : I have no *connection with* her for the last three years.

D

(1)	**Displeased at (thing) :**	She is not *displeased at* such humourous jokes.
	Displeased with (person) :	Ram is greatly *displeased with* Sita.
(2)	**Disqualified for (post) :**	She was declared *disqualified for* the election.
	Disqualified from (competing) :	He was *disqualified from* taking part in the competition.
(3)	**Dwell upon (to speak) :**	The Chairman *dwelt upon* the importance of truth and honesty.
	Dwell in (country) :	The French *dwell in* France.
	Dwell at (place) :	These days Ram is *dwelling at* his friend's hotel.
	Dwell among (people) :	He is *dwelling among* the tribal.
(4)	**Disgusted at (thing) :**	She became *disgusted at* your silly joke.
	Disgusted with (person or life) :	I am very much *disgusted with* him.
(5)	**Deal with (to do with the matter) :**	This book *deals with* the population problem in India .
	Deal in (trade) :	He *deals in* iron scrap.
	Deal out (distribute) :	The principal should *deal out* equal treatment to all the teachers.
(6)	**Differ on (point) :**	I totally *differ on* this point.
	Differ with (person) :	I *differ with* you on this point.
	Differ from (thing) :	Your views entirely *differ from* that of mine.
(7)	**Die of (a disease) :**	He *died of* hunger.
	Die from (some cause) :	He *died from* hard labour.
(8)	**Destined for (created for) :**	God had *destined* him *for* the post of President of India.
	Destined to (subject) :	He is *destined to* such a pitiable condition.
(9)	**Dine with (person) :**	I am scheduled to *dine with* him tonight.
	Dine on (thing) :	I can't *dine on* same kind of menu daily.
(10)	**Dispense with (do without) :**	Jack can't easily *dispense with* her .
	Dispense to (distribute) :	A judge must *dispense* equal justice *to* all.
(11)	**Dispose of (to sell) :**	She wants to *dispose of* all the goods at the earliest.
	Dispose to (state of things) :	The news of his father's death *disposed* him *to* a deep sorrow.
(12)	**Dispute with (person) :**	Why are you *disputing with* your friends on such a trifle matter.
	Dispute about (thing) :	There was a great *dispute about* the nomination of chairman.

E

(1)	**Embark on (a vessel) :**	She *embarked on* the ship for Srilanka.
	Embark in (new business) :	He has *embarked in* the new business with full fervour.
(2)	**Enter into (thing) :**	They have *entered into* an agreement with Ramesh.
	Enter upon (new course) :	After marriage I *entered upon* a new way of life.
(3)	**Exchange for (thing) :**	She *exchanged* a book *for* a piece of art.
	Exchange with (person) :	I want to *exchange* my views *with* you.
(4)	**Exult at (success) :**	She was *exulted at* her brilliant success.
	Exult over (an enemy) :	Our army *exulted over* the enemy's force.
	Exult in (misery) :	One should not be *exulted in* the misery of others.

(5)	**Eager for (fame) :**	She is very much *eager for* making a name in society.
	Eager in (to find) :	He has involved himself *eagerly in* pursuit of finding the cause of miseries in life.
(6)	**Equivalent for (word) :**	Write a word *equivalent for* 'fear'.
	Equivalent to (money, : thing)	One million is *equivalent to* ten lacs.
(7)	**Exact from (person) :**	Heavy fines were *exacted from* the unruly students.
	Exact in (adjective) :	He is not *exact in* repayment.
(8)	**Expert in (doing) :**	He is *expert in* repairing automobiles.
	Expert at (thing) :	He is *expert at* English Grammar.
(9)	**Enquire of (person) :**	I *enquired of* him the secret of his happiness.
	Enquire into (a matter) :	The police *enquired into* the case of bank robbery.
(10)	**Entrust with (a thing) :**	I *entrusted* him *with* my camera.
	Entrust to (person) :	I *entrusted* my camera *to* him.

F

(1)	**Fit out (equip) :**	The ship was *fitted out* for Srilanka.
	Fit up (furnishing) :	He *fitted up* his house with all necessary furniture.
(2)	**Fascinated with (person) :**	I was *fascinated with* Rekha.
	Fascinated by (thing) :	I was *fascinated by* her manners and looks.
(3)	**False to (person) :**	One should not be *false to* one's friends.
	False of (thing, heart) :	He is not *false of* heart.
(4)	**Fight for (defending) :**	Our army is ready to *fight for* the country.
	Fight with (together) :	We must not *fight with* our friends.
	Fight against (thing) :	We must *fight against* the evil of illiteracy.
(5)	**Familiar to (thing) :**	Your looks are quite *familiar to* that of Sachin.
	Familiar with (person) :	I am *familiar with* him.

G

(1)	**Gaze at (look attentively) :**	Don't *gaze at* these girls, they are the cops.
	Gaze on (look strangely) :	He stood *gazing on* the pathetic scene of accident.
(2)	**Grieve for (person) :**	She was extremely *grieved for* him.
	Grieve at (event) :	Everyone was *grieved at* the death of Rajeev Gandhi.
	Grieve over (thing) :	She *grieved over* my unfortunate loss.
(3)	**Good for (nothing) :**	He is a *good for* nothing fellow.
	Good at (something) :	She is *good at* swimming.

H

(1)	**Held by (person) :**	A condolence meeting was *held by* the staff yesterday.
	Held in (esteem or contempt) :	In the heart of every Indian,Gandhiji is *held in* great respect.
	Held at (place) :	A meeting was *held at* Hope Circus yesterday.

(2)	**Hear of (something) :**	I *heard of* this robbery from Sarla.
	Hear from (person) :	I *heard* this robbery *from* Sarla.
	Hear by (post) :	I *hear by* this letter about your promotion.
(3)	**Happen to (person) :**	Please tell me what *happened to* you in New York.
	Happen at (place) :	This event *happened at* Red Square.
	Happen on (come across) :	While returning from market I *happened on* a gang of thieves.
(4)	**Hidden from (view) :**	The Neem tree has *hidden* your house *from* direct view.
	Hidden by (person, thing) :	My shoes were *hidden by* his sister.

I

(1)	**Introduce to (person) :**	Let me first *introduce* my friend *to* you.
	Introduce into (make modifications) :	The UPSC has *introduced* many changes *into* the syllabus of IAS examination.
(2)	**Invest with (authority) :**	The President *invested* him *with* the honour of Bharat Ratna.
	Invest in (business) :	I am ready to *invest* ₹ 50 lacs *in* this business.
(3)	**Inquire for (a thing) :**	I went there to *inquire for* my lost brief case.
	Inquire into (matter) :	The police will *inquire into* the cause of death.
	Inquire about (concern) :	She came here to *inquire about* the health of her son.
	Inquire of (asking) :	First *inquire of* the way, then move.
(4)	**Involve in (thing) :**	She seems to be *involved in* some serious trouble.
	Involve with (person) :	Don't *involve* yourself *with* such unruly persons.
(5)	**Irritated at (thing) :**	I was greatly *irritated at* his unruly behaviour.
	Irritated against (person) :	She was extremely *irritated against* her husband.
(6)	**Impatient at : (unexpected thing)**	He became *impatient at* the unexpected delay.
	Impatient for (expected thing) :	She is very much *impatient for* the arrival of her husband.
(7)	**Indebted for (thing) :**	I am *indebted for* your timely help.
	Indebted to (person) :	He is greatly *indebted to* Rani for her timely help.

J

(1)	**Jest at (person) :**	I don't like to *jest at* a lunatic person.
	Jest with (thing) :	We should not *jest with* the communal thing.
(2)	**Judge of (giving opinion) :**	Without going in details, how can you *judge of* this matter.
	Judge by (observing) :	*Judging by* her qualifications, I think she is not fit for this job.

K

(1)	**Know by (recognise) :**	A man is *known by* his actions.
	Know for (quality) :	He is *known for* his foolish decisions.

L

(1)	**Live at (a small town) :**	He *lives at* Alwar in Rajasthan.
	Live in (in country, big place) :	He is *living* at Alwar *in* Rajasthan.
	Live on (food) :	He *lives* entirely *on* breads.
	Live for (devote) :	We must *live* and die *for* the cause of truth.
	Live with (a person) :	I *live* here *with* my parents.
(2)	**Liable for (crime) :**	You are *liable for* the death of your wife.
	Liable to (punishment) :	He was held *liable to* imprisonment for three years.
(3)	**Listen for (sound) :**	I am *listening for* the voice of Lata Mangeshkar.
	Listen to (hear attentively) :	We should *listen to* the advice of our elders.
(4)	**Laugh at (make fun) :**	We must not *laugh at* our friends.
	Laugh with (indulge with) :	Better to *laugh with* disabled than to laugh at disabled.

M

(1)	**Married to (a woman) :**	Ramesh was *married to* Sarla.
	Married with (a man) :	Sarla was *married with* Ramesh.
(2)	**Moved with (sorrow) :**	He was actually *moved with* a feeling of sorrow.
	Moved to (tears) :	On hearing the news of sudden death of his wife, all *moved to* tears.
	Moved from (one's determination) :	You can't *move* me *from* my decision with your logics.
	Moved at (a scene) :	He was greatly *moved at* the sight of her mother's dead body.

O

(1)	**Obliged to (person) :**	I am very much *obliged to* you.
	Obliged at (thing) :	I am *obliged at* your timely help.
(2)	**Occupied in (doing a job) :**	He is fully *occupied in* writing a book.
	Occupied by (thing) :	That house is *occupied by* a marriage party.
(3)	**Originate with (person) :**	All the plannings were *originated with* him.
	Originate in (place, cause) :	A fierce fire was *originated in* Connaught Place yesterday.

P

(1)	**Part from (person) :**	I *parted from* my wife in Kumbh.
	Part with (thing) :	He is not ready to *part with* his furniture at any cost.
(2)	**Prepare for (be ready) :**	I am *preparing for* the IAS examination this year.
	Prepare against (danger) :	We must *prepare* ourselves *against* the danger of water pollution.
(3)	**Pray for (thing) :**	My wife *prayed for* my success.
	Pray to (make prayer) :	I *prayed to* God to help me in facing the unwarranted problems.
(4)	**Perish by (famine) :**	Our district was *perished by* the drought last year.
	Perish with (hunger) :	During drought the cattle *perished with* starvation.

(5)	**Plead with (person) :**	He *pleaded with* the Principal for mercy.
	Plead for (thing) :	He *pleaded for* the king for mercy.
(6)	**Play at (cards) :**	They were *playing at* cards.
	Play upon (musical instrument) :	Harish *played upon* the violin in the party.

Q

(1)	**Quick in (doing) :**	He is *quick in* solving questions.
	Quick of (understanding) :	Ramesh is *quick of* understanding the questions.
(2)	**Quarrel over (thing) :**	You must not *quarrel over* the parental property.
	Quarrel with (person) :	We must not *quarrel with* our friends.

R

(1)	**Responsible to (person) :**	An MLA is *responsible to* the Legislative Assembly.
	Responsible for (action) :	She is *responsible for* the loss caused due to her neglience.
(2)	**Reason with (person) :**	I *reasoned with* him on each and every point in this matter.
	Reason about (thing) :	You can't *reason about* the importance of self-respect .
(3)	**Ready for (action) :**	I am *ready for* the match.
	Ready with (something) :	I was totally *ready with* my arguments on that day.
	Ready in (replying) :	I always found her *ready in* her reply.
(4)	**Revenge on (person) :**	He *revenged* himself *on* his enemy.
	Revenge for (action) :	I will positively *revenge for* the insult inflicted on me by her.
(5)	**Reduce to (to decrease) :**	His salary was *reduced to* Rs four thousands only.
	Reduce by (decrease by an amount) :	His salary was *reduced by* three hundred rupees per month.

S

(1)	**Share of (thing) :**	I must be paid my *share of* profit.
	Share with (person) :	I do not *share* my lunch *with* anybody.
(2)	**Skilful at (thing) :**	He is *skilful at* numbers.
	Skilful in (doing a thing) :	He is *skilful in* mathematical calculations.
(3)	**Succeed to (property) :**	He *succeeded to* his uncle's empire.
	Succeed in (doing) :	This time she *succeeded in* IAS examination.
(4)	**Start at (time) :**	I *started at* 10 o'clock in the morning.
	Start from (place) :	I *started* at 10 o'clock in the morning *from* Delhi.
	Started for (place) :	I *started* at 7 o'clock in the morning *for* Delhi.
(5)	**Struggle for (thing) :**	We have to *struggle* hard *for* keeping peace in the country.
	Struggle with (person) :	We should not *struggle with* our neighbours.
(6)	**Serve out (distribute) :**	Sweets were *served out* to the audience.
	Serve up (to give food) :	A nice lunch was *served up* there in the function.
(7)	**Speak for (person) :**	You go there, I have already *spoken for* you to the secretary.
	Speak about (thing) :	He is *speaking about* 'Unemployment Problem'.

(8) **Starved to (death) :** She was *starved to* death by her husband.
Starved with (hunger) : He *starved with* hunger.

(9) **Suited for (action) :** She is not *suited for* the role of vamp.
Suited to (occasion) : Sad song does not *suit to* such an occasion.

(10) **Supply to (person) :** The Municipality is *supplying* water *to* all the colonies in the city.
Supply with (thing) : Government must *supply* poor *with* food and clothing.

T

(1) **Thankful for (thing) :** I am really *thankful for* your timely help.
Thankful to (person) : I am very much *thankful to* you for your kind favour.

(2) **Think over (to consider) :** The society agreed to *think over* the case in the next meeting.
Think on (meditate) : I have been *thinking on* this matter for the last many days.

(3) **Trust in (person) :** *Trust in* God and work hard.
Trust to (thing) : I *trusted to* his words, and he was right.

(4) **Tired of (disgusted) :** I am *tired of* your daily excuses.
Tired with (exhausted) : You seems to be *tired with* the long run.

(5) **Talk with (person) :** I will *talk with* my father on this matter.
Talk about (thing) : I will *talk about* this matter with my parents.
Talk over (discuss) : All the members of the society *talked over* the issue for many hours.

U

(1) **Useful for (thing) :** The bag is very much *useful for* carrying goods.

(2) **Useful to (person) :** I found that these directives are *useful to* me for success in exam.

V

(1) **Vote for (person) :** *Vote for* me please.
Vote on (a resolution) : After having cast *votes on* the resolution, all took lunch.

(2) **Vexed with (person) :** Why are you *vexed with* your wife ?
Vexed at (thing) : He is *vexed at* my jokes.

W

(1) **Wait at (place) :** I will *wait at* church near the hospital.
Wait for (person) : I will *wait for* you upto tomorrow.

(2) **Wake up (to get up) :** She *wakes up* at 6 a.m. daily.
Wake from (to be awaken) : She *waked from* slumber and decided to take action.

(3) **Warn against (an action) :** I have already *warned* you, *against* your such negligence.
Warn of (danger) : I have already *warned* you *of* the risk involved .

Z

(1) **Zealous for (a thing) :** A dedicated worker is always *zealous for* achieving the target.

(2) **Zealous in (a cause) :** We must be *zealous in* the cause of humanity.

Appropriate Prepositions

कुछ शब्दों के साथ सामान्यतया एक निश्चित Preposition का प्रयोग होता है। यद्यपि यहाँ भी वाक्य के अर्थ को समझना आवश्यक है, तथापि नीचे दिए गए शब्द एवं उनके साथ प्रयुक्त Prepositions को बार-बार Revise करने से Prepositions का सही प्रयोग समझ में आ जाता है। परीक्षाओं में Prepositions सम्बन्धी Questions अधिकतर निम्न पर आधारित होते हैं :

1. Abundance of (wealth)
2. Assent to (a proposal)
3. Accustomed to (work)
4. Avail ourselves of (an opportunity)
5. Attain to (a position)
6. Addicted to (drinking, wine etc.)
7. Accede to (a request)
8. Abstain from (food, indulgence etc).
9. Absolved from (a promise, a sin)
10. Acquiesce (an opinion, in proposal)
11. Adhere to (principles)
12. Afraid of (a ghost)
13. Abhorrent to (good nature)
14. Accession to (throne)
15. Assure of (a thing)
16. Absorbed in (study)
17. Acquit (someone) of a charge
18. Acquaintance with (a person)
19. Beware of (cheating)
20. Comply with (one's wishes)
21. Condemn to (death)
22. Cured of (a disease)
23. Comply with (wishes)
24. Coducive to (health)
25. Despair of (success)
26. Desirous of (doing something)
27. Deprive of (something)
28. Devoid of (quality)
29. Duty of (the country)
30. Eligible for (a post)
31. Exception to (a rule)
32. Excuse for (a fault)
33. Envious of (a person or a thing)
34. Exchange a thing with a person
35. Elder to (some family member)
36. Fatal to (one's cause)
37. Fearful of (death)
38. Furnish with (clothes)
39. Greedy of (money)
40. Heir to (ancestral property)
41. Healed of (a disease)
42. Hopeful of (success)
43. Hostile to (a person)
44. Hunger after (fame)
45. Innocent of (a crime)
46. Intimate with (a person)
47. Invite to (dinner)
48. Insist on a (thing)
49. Intimate with (person)
50. Impertinent to (elders)
51. Invite to (dinner)
52. Insight into (a matter or thing)
53. Jealous of (a person)
54. Keep to (the left, the point)
55. Knock at (the door)
56. Key to (success)
57. Mourn for (the dead)
58. Match for (a person)
59. Mad with (anger)
60. Motive for (an action)
61. Need for (help)
62. Need of (a thing)
63. Notorious for (drinking, thing)
64. Occur to (mind)
65. Overwhelmed with (sorrow, grief)
66. Pay for (one's mistakes)
67. Passion for (study)
68. Peculiar to (a person or a thing)
69. Persist in (doing)
70. Pity for (poor, downtrodden)
71. Pleased with (a person)
72. Preface to (a book)
73. Proud of (a thing)
74. Pride on (a thing)
75. Prefer to (a thing)
76. Refrain from (doing some wrong)
77. Repent of (a mistake)
78. Respectful to (a person)

79. Rob (A person) of (a thing)
80. Sentence to (punishment)
81. Short of (money)
82. Side with (a person)
83. Shocked at (a loss)
84. Superior to (a thing)
85. Sure of (some fact)
86. Search for (a thing)
87. Sacred to (a cause)
88. Triumph over (difficulties)
89. Trouble to (person)
90. Vain of (beauty)
91. Want of (money)
92. Wanting in (wisdom)
93. Worthy of (a reward)
94. Yield to (an enemy)
95. Search for (a thing)
96. Sacred to (a cause)
97. Work at (subject)
98. Surrender to (enemy)
99. Stick to (point)
100. Suspect of (something)
101. Translate into (language)
102. Touch upon (subject)
103. Slur on (character)

High Frequency Prepositions

Preposition 'FOR' :

(A) The following nouns take the preposition 'for' after them : apology, appetite, aptitude, affection, ambition, blame, candidate, contempt, craving, capacity, compassion, compensation, desire, esteem, fitness, fondness, guarantee, leisure, liking, match, motive, need, opportunity, partiality, pretext, passion, pity, predilection, remorse, relish.

(B) The following verbs take the preposition 'for' after them : Atone, canvass, care, clamour, feel, hope, mourn, pine, start, stipulate, sue wish, yearn.

(C) The following adjectives and participles take the preposition 'for' after them : anxious, celebrated, conspicuous, customary, designed, destined, eager, eligible, eminent, fit, good, grateful, notorious, prepared, proper, penitent, qualified, ready, sorry, sufficient, useful, zealous.

Preposition 'OF' :

(A) The following nouns take the preposition 'of ' after them : assurance, abhorrence, charge, distrust, doubt, experience, failure, observance, proof, result, want.

(B) The following adjectives and participles take the preposition 'of ' after them : accused, acquitted, afraid, apprehensive, apprised, assured, aware, bereft, bought, cautious, certain, characteristic, composed, confident, conscious, convicted, convinced, covetous, defrauded, deprived, desirous, destitute, devoid, diffident, distrustful, dull, easy, envious, fearful, fond, greedy, guilty, heedless, ignorant, informed, innocent, irrespective, lame, lavish, negligent, productive, proud, regardless, sanguine, sensible, sick, sow, subversive, sure, suspicious, tolerant, vain, void, weary, worthy.

(C) The following verbs take the preposition 'of ' after them : acquit, beware, boast, complain, despair, die, disapprove, dispose, divest, dream, heal, judge, repent, taste.

Preposition 'TO' :

(A) The following nouns take the preposition 'to' after them : allegiance, approach, assent, alternative, access, accession, antidote, antipathy, exception, incentive, indifference, invitation, key, leniency, likeness, limit, menace, obedience, opposition, objection, obstruction, postscript, preface, reference, resemblance, repugnance, sequel, submission, supplement, succession, traitor, temptation.

(B) The following adjectives and participles take the preposition 'to' after them

(i) acceptable, accessible, accustomed, abhorrent, addicted, adequate, adjacent, affectionate, agreeable, akin, alien, alive, amenable, analogous, applicable, appropriate, beneficial, callous, common, comparable, condemned.

(ii) conducive, conformable, congenial, consecrated, contrary, creditable, deaf, derogatory, detrimental, devoted, disastrous, due, entitled, equal, essential, exposed, faithful, fatal, foreign, hostile, impertinent, incidental, inclined.

(iii) Indebted, indifferent, indispensable, indulgent, inimical, insensible, injured, irrelevant, favourable, hurtful, immaterial, impervious, indigenous, liable, limited, lost, loyal, material, natural, necessary.

(iv) offensive, opposite, obedient, obliged, painful, partial, peculiar, pertinent, pledged, preferable, prejudicial, prior, profitable, prone, relevant, repugnant, reduced, related, responsible, restricted, sacred, subject, suitable, sensitive, serviceable, suited, supplementary, true, tantamount.

(C) The following verbs take the preposition 'to' after them : accede, adhere, allot, aspire, assent, attain, allude, apologize, adapt, appoint, ascribe, attend, attribute, belong, consent, contribute, conduce, conform, lead, listen, object, occur, prefer, pretend, refer, revert, stoop, succumb, surrender, testify, yield.

Preposition 'FROM' :

(A) The following nouns take the preposition 'from' after them : abstinence, cessation, deliverance, descent, digression, escape, exemption, inference.

(B) The following verbs take the preposition 'from' after them : abstain, alight, cease, debar, derive, derogate, desist, detract, deviate, differ, dissent, elicit, emerge, escape, exclude, preserve, prevent, prohibit, protect, recoil, recover, refrain.

Preposition 'IN' :

(A) The following adjectives and participles take the preposition 'in' after them : accomplished, accurate, assiduous, absorbed, abstemious, backward, bigot, correct, defective, diligent, deficient, experienced, enveloped, fertile, foiled, honest, implicated, interested, involved, lax, proficient, remiss, versed.

(B) The following verbs take the preposition 'in' after them : acquiesce, delight, employ, enlist, excel, fall, glory, increase, indulge, involve, persevere, persist.

Preposition 'WITH' :

(A) The following adjectives and participles take the preposition 'with' after them : acquainted, affected, beset, busy, compatible, complaint, consistent, contemporary, contented, contrasted, conversant, convulsed, delighted, deluged, disgusted, drenched, endowed, fatigued, fired, gifted, infatuated, infected, infested, inspired, intimated, invested, overcome, popular, replete, satisfied, touched.

(B) The following verbs take the preposition 'with' after them : associate, bear, clash, coincide, comply, condole, cope, correspond, credit, deluge, disagree, dispense, expostulate, fill, grapple, intrigue, meddle, quarrel, remonstrate, side, sympathize, trifle, vie.

Preposition 'ON' :

The following verbs take the preposition 'on' after them : comment, deliberate, decide, depend, determine, dwell, enlarge, embark, encroach, impose, insist, intrude, subsist, trample.

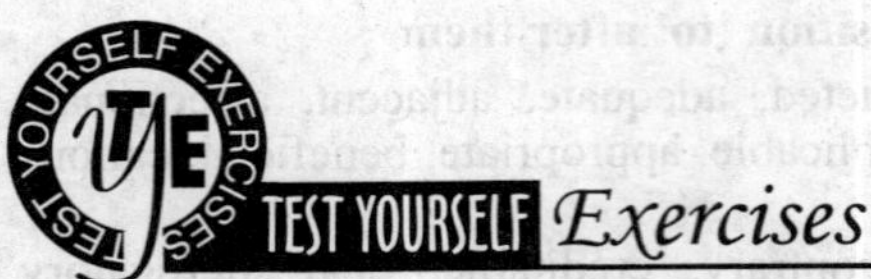

01

Fill in the blanks with appropriate prepositions **:**

(1) Ram killed the snake .... a stick.
(2) He lives .... Alwar.
(3) Rice is selling .... five rupees a kilo.
(4) His car ran .... a dog.
(5) He assured to stand .... me in all circumstances.
(6) I will stand .... for my rights.
(7) He put .... a coat of red colour.
(8) He is proud .... his riches.
(9) He lives .... Mumbai.
(10) In general, acids act .... metals.
(11) Ram was beaten .... by Mohan for no reason.
(12) He sat .... the ground.
(13) He fell the tree .... an axe.
(14) An epidemic broke .... in the town last year.
(15) I called .... her from a distant place.

02

Fill in the blanks with appropriate prepositions **:**

(1) He finished the work .... four hours.
(2) I took him .... a thief.
(3) Mahesh is now rid .... all his troubles.
(4) He sat .... me.
(5) He agreed .... my plan.
(6) The cat ran .... the mouse.
(7) He died .... heart failure.
(8) He fell .... the bed.
(9) They were walking .... the road.
(10) He rushed .... the pathway.
(11) He acted according .... my desire.
(12) We did it ....you.
(13) Anil goes to office .... car.
(14) Look .... the picture.
(15) He ran .... the room and sat .... his father.

03

Correct the following sentences **:**

(1) You cannot prevent me to go to the market.
(2) She refrains to do this work.
(3) I insisted him to attend the class.
(4) He has a passion to learn English grammar.
(5) She is negligent to attend the meetings.
(6) She persisted to write again.
(7) He is bent to fight again.
(8) I am confident to win the match.
(9) He succeeded to pass the examination this time.
(10) I am proud to have a friend like Ram.
(11) I cannot hinder her to enter the temple.
(12) She is desirous to leave the place.
(13) Ram was disqualified to compete in this tournament.
(14) I cannot think to oppose him.
(15) He was prohibited to enter the temple.
(16) You should abstain to drink now.
(17) He intends to go to Jaipur.
(18) It is very difficult to dissuade him to go there.
(19) He is fortunate to get a ticket.
(20) I am hopeful to achieve success.

04

Correct the following sentences **:**

(1) She was neither ashamed nor sorry for her misbehaviour.
(2) She neither objected nor approved of it.
(3) Ram has no interest and passion for cricket.
(4) We must prevent damage and theft of public property.
(5) Please listen and reflect on this topic afterwards.
(6) He asked from her a silly question.
(7) The police investigated into the case.
(8) Ram resembles to his father.
(9) She resigned from her post.
(10) Ram signed to the agreement.
(11) The poet described about the nature.
(12) She must love to her children.
(13) We have discussed on the merits of the issue.
(14) In this article the author has described about poverty.
(15) She criticised upon my action without logic.

05

Fill in the blanks with appropriate prepositions **:**

(1) Morning walk is beneficial .... health.
(2) You are not eligible .... this post.
(3) I find no exception .... this rule of grammar.
(4) She has a great passion .... natural beauty.
(5) You are very much weak .... mathematics.
(6) Suitable reward is an important incentive .... hard work.
(7) I am sick .... the whole episode.
(8) He insisted .... complaining against the officer.
(9) You are to conform .... the rules of the institute.
(10) Your views don't accord .... mine.
(11) She comes .... a very noble family.
(12) His path is beset .... many difficulties.
(13) You are addicted .... gambling.
(14) Your scheme is adverse .... my career.
(15) The court has restored the property .... its true owner.

06

Fill in the blanks with appropriate prepositions :

(1) This is subsequent .... my application dated 5th July.
(2) This is consequent .... your application dated 10th August.
(3) I am fond .... reading newspaper.
(4) You have made all preparations .... the marriage.
(5) I am proud .... my heritage.
(6) He is a descendant .... king.
(7) I have no trust .... him.
(8) She has distrust .... you.
(9) I feel shame .... her conduct.
(10) I am much ashamed .... my son.
(11) We must provide .... the bad days.
(12) God will provide .... our necessities.
(13) It is expected .... you to find the solution.
(14) Such rude behaviour was not expected .... you.
(15) I am disappointed .... you.

07

Fill in the blanks with appropriate prepositions :

(1) She jumped .... the well.
(2) There was no student .... the class.
(3) She agreed .... my scheme.
(4) Ram is sitting .... the kitchen.
(5) He lives .... Delhi.
(6) Please close your office .... 9.30 pm positively.
(7) She goes for a walk .... the morning daily.
(8) He is .... the top.
(9) Please sit .... the green chair.
(10) The dog jumped .... the cat.
(11) She is sitting .... the roof.
(12) The letter was written .... Shyam.
(13) He wrote a letter .... a pen.
(14) A Banyan tree stands .... the Yamuna river.
(15) He has a car .... a scooter.
(16) I will go to school .... next Monday.
(17) I know Hindi, ... Punjabi.
(18) I haven't seen her .... the last three days.
(19) I haven't seen her .... January.
(20) She turned pale .... fear.

08

Insert 'for', 'during' or 'while' in the blanks :

(1) What did Ram say about me .... I was out of the room ?
(2) Rahim read a number of books and magazines .... he was ill.
(3) I went out for dinner last night. Unfortunately, I began to feel ill .... the meal and had to go home.
(4) Please don't interrupt me .... I am speaking.
(5) There were many interruptions .... the Chairman's speech.
(6) Can you lay the table .... I get the dinner ready?
(7) They hadn't had anything to eat..................... they were travelling.
(8) Manisha was very angry with me. She didn't speak to me .... a week.
(9) We usually go out at weekend, but we don't often go out .... the week.
(10) Kamlesh started a new job a few weeks ago. Before that he was out of work .... six month.
(11) I need a change. I think I'll go away .... a few days.
(12) The Chairman delivered a long speech. He spoke .... three hours.
(13) We were hungry when we came. We hadn't had anything to eat .... the journey.
(14) We were hungry when we came. We hadn't had anything to eat .... eight hours.
(15) We met a lot of people .... we were on holiday.
(16) We met a lot of people .... our holiday.
(17) I met Manisha .... I was shopping.
(18) .... we were in Agra, we stayed at a very comfortable hotel.
(19) .... our stay in Agra, we visited a lot of museums and galleries.
(20) The phone rang three times .... they were having dinner.
(21) The phone rang many times .... the night.
(22) I had been away for many years. .... that period, many things had changed.

09

Put 'by' or 'until' in the following sentences :

(1) I'm moving into my new house next month. I'm staying with a friend .... then.
(2) Sorry, but I must go. I have to be at home latest .... 9 o'clock.
(3) I've been offered a lucrative job ...... my friend. I haven't decided yet whether to accept it or not. I have to decided .... next Monday.

(4) I think I'll wait .... Sunday before making a final decision.

(5) It's too late to go shopping. The shops are only open .... 9:30 pm. They'll be closed .... now.

(6) I'd better pay the electricity bill. It has to be paid .... tomorrow positively.

(7) Don't pay the bill today, wait .... next Monday, you can get some relief.

(8) A : Have you finished redecorating your house?
B : Not yet. We hope to finish .... the end of this fortnight.

(9) A : I'm going out now. I'll be back at 7.30 pm. Will you still be there?
B : I don't think so. I'll probably have gone out .... then.

(10) Suresh has gone away. He'll be away .... Saturday.

10

Put 'at', 'on' or 'in' in the following sentences :

(1) The telephone and the doorbell rang .... the same time.

(2) Harish and Sarla always go out for a meal .... their wedding anniversary.

(3) Ramu is 58. He'll be retiring from his job .... two years' time.

(4) I've been invited to a wedding .... 15th August.

(5) Hurry up! We've got to go .... five minutes.

(6) I'm busy just now, but I'll be with you .... a moment.

(7) Ram's brother is a banker, but he's out of work .... the moment.

(8) There are usually a lot of parties .... New Year's Eve.

(9) I hope the weather will be nice .... the weekend.

(10) We travelled overnight to London and arrived .... 5o'clock .... the morning.

(11) The course begins .... 27th June and ends sometime .... August.

(12) It was quite a short novel and easy to read. I read it .... a day.

(13) He might not be at home ..... Tuesday morning but he'll probably be there ...... the afternoon.

(14) My jeep is being repaired at the garage. It will be ready .... two hours.

11.

Choose the appropriate option and write it in the brackets.

(1) The poor have to work .... morning to evening.
(a) in (b) to (c) from (d) before ( )

(2) I go .... swimming every morning.
(a) to (b) for (c) at (d) in ( )

(3) Never laugh .... the disabled.
(a) on (b) from (c) to (d) at ( )

(4) Please wait .... me, I am coming within five minutes.
(a) for (b) by (c) from (d) to ( )

(5) He fell .... love with Sakshi.
(a) by (b) for (c) in (d) with ( )

(6) I got your parcel .... Tuesday.
(a) since (b) for (c) to (d) on ( )

(7) She was married .... an early age.
(a) for (b) of (c) at (d) in ( )

(8) His father died .... the age of sixty three.
(a) at (b) in (c) for (d) of ( )

(9) They will go to Bengalore .... plane.
(a) on (b) in (c) by (d) from ( )

(10). The man .... a beard is my brother.
(a) in (b) of (c) for (d) with ( )

(11) I am grateful .... my friends for their moral support.
(a) for (b) to (c) of (d) with ( )

(12) Gandhiji fought .... the freedom of our country.
(a) by (b) in (c) of (d) for ( )

(13) This watch is a gift .... my uncle.
(a) by (b) from (c) of (d) in ( )

(14) He spoke .... the subject for two hours regularly.
(a) in (b) on (c) of (d) with ( )

(15) They will leave the place ....10 pm
(a) on (b) since (c) for (d) at ( )

12.

Choose appropriate option and write it in the brackets :

(1) She was punished .... stealing a saree.
(a) for (b) by (c) with (d) from ( )

(2) The box belonged .... the landlord.
(a) of (b) with (c) to (d) for ( )

(3) You must finish your project .... 5 o'clock positively.
(a) in (b) for (c) till (d) to ( )

(4) Children are fond .... chocolates and computer games.
(a) for (b) of (c) with (d) in ( )

(5) We get rains .... July every year.
(a) for (b) to (c) on (d) in ( )

(6) His father died .... cancer.
(a) in (b) of (c) by (d) for ( )

(7) He is not popular .... the students.
(a) by (b) among (c) with (d) at ( )

(8) She has great love .... her children.
(a) for (b) of (c) by (d) with ( )

(9) He was prevented .... going to college.
(a) to (b) of (c) by (d) from ( )

(10) Listen .... what your teachers say.
(a) at (b) in (c) to (d) for ( )

(11) Please beware .... the dog.
(a) of (b) with (c) to (d) for ( )

(12) This book is a collection .... Shakespeare's poem.
(a) for (b) of (c) with (d) by ( )

(13) They have quarrelled .... a piece of land.
(a) at (b) on (c) for (d) over ( )

13.

Choose appropriate option and write it in the brackets :

(1) She wants to get rid .... the brown fox.
(a) for (b) to (c) with (d) of ( )

(2) I was invited .... tea by his mother.
(a) for (b) to (c) with (d) in ( )

(3) You cannot see germs .... naked eyes.
(a) by (b) with (c) for (d) in ( )

(4) He is not interested .... playing and skiing.
(a) in (b) for (c) by (d) of ( )

(5) He was fast asleep .... his bed.
(a) into (b) in (c) by (d) for ( )

(6) We have a very good news .... him.
(a) for (b) of (c) to (d) with ( )

(7) They have been reading .... 7 o'clock.
(a) for (b) in (c) since (d) at ( )

(8) Never quarrel .... your friends.
(a) to (b) with (c) by (d) over ( )

(9) The four brothers always quarrelled .... themselves.
(a) to (b) between (c) for (d) among ( )

(10) There were several policemen .... duty on Republic Day.
(a) to (b) on (c) for (d) at ( )

(11) These boys go to college .... college bus.
(a) by (b) on (c) to (d) for ( )

(12) He is not an honest man. You cannot rely .... him.
(a) to (b) for (c) at (d) on ( )

(13) He was fined .... driving negligently.
(a) to (b) of (c) by (d) for ( )

(14) He is often late .... his dinner.
(a) for (b) at (c) to (d) in ( )

(15) Try to reach the village .... the sunset.
(a) before (b) by (c) from (d) of ( )

14.

Choose appropriate option and write it in the brackets :

(1) In the month of December the temperature falls .... 4ºC.
(a) from (b) below (c) at (d) into ( )

(2) A jeep hit him while he was going .... the main road.
(a) on (b) across (c) behind (d) through ( )

(3) She is .... a noble family of Rajputs.
(a) from (b) of (c) among (d) at ( )

(4) The case was put .... the judge and the judge decided it within an year.
(a) at (b) from (c) before (d) of ( )

(5) The bridge .... this river was built in the year 1995.
(a) at (b) over (c) above (d) on ( )

(6) She is suffering .... fever.
(a) with (b) of (c) through (d) from ( )

(7) We saw wounded tiger while passing .... the forest.
(a) from (b) through (c) along (d) among ( )

(8) Chairs are made .... wood.
(a) of (b) from (c) on (d) through ( )

(9) There are tall beautiful coconut trees .... the river.
(a) along (b) at (c) into (d) over ( )

(10) We are proud .... our children.
(a) on (b) at (c) after (d) of ( )

(11) Mt Abu is about five thousand feet .... the sea-level.
(a) above (b) along (c) after (d) behind ( )

(12) His birthday is .... next Sunday.
(a) in (b) at (c) on (d) for ( )

(13) Ramesh fell down while he was running .... a bus.
(a) into (b) after (c) over (d) through ( )

(14) Ramesh is the best .... all the other players.
(a) into (b) among (c) above (d) between ( )

15

Fill in the blanks with appropriate prepositions :

(1) The meeting took place .... the company's corporate office. (at/to/on/by)
(2) It was a very long voyage. We were .... sea for 50 days. (in/at/on/by/to)
(3) I was .... reached last night. (in/on/at/by/for)
(4) The train reached .... Kolkata main station. (in/on/to/at/by)
(5) I lost my passport .... the way to India. (in/at/by/to/on)
(6) He is a genius. He is .... the black lists of many casinos. (on/in/with/by/at)
(7) We reached late at the cinema so we had to sit .... the back row. (on/in/at/to/by)
(8) Is there anything interesting .... the paper today ? (on/by/in/at/from)
(9) Have you ever been .... Mexico ? (in/on/by/to)
(10) These books are .... ₹150/- each. (in/on/with/at)
(11) Some people are .... prison for crimes they have not committed. (in/on/at/by/to)
(12) I am really sorry, but you are standing .... my way. (on/in/at/with/behind)
(13) There was a very serious accident .... the roundabout. (in/at/to/from)
(14) In many countries people drive .... the left. (in/at/by/on/to)
(15) I forgot my umbrella .... the bus. (in/into/by/onto/on)
(16) I am .... love with her. (in/on/with/from)
(17) We are offering solutions .... a price almost anyone can afford. (in/at/on/by/through)
(18) He behaves just like his father. He really takes .... him. (to/from/after/by/at)
(19) That old house is being offered .... sale. (in/at/on/for/by)
(20) It is very difficult to enter .... partnership with a person you do not know very well. (to/on/by/with/into)

Spotting Errors (Prepositions)

16.

Read each sentence to find out whether there is an error in any part :

(1) He was sleeping (a)/in his room when a thief (b)/entered into his house (c)/and took away a lot of things. (d)
(2) In her concluding speech (a)/she said almost nothing (b)/worth listening to. (c)
(3) It was apparent for (a)/everyone present (b)/that if the patient did not receive (c)/immediate medical aid (d)/he would die. (e)
(4) He proposed me (a)/that we should go to the Disco (b)/and then have (c)/dinner at a restra. (d)
(5) There appears (a)/to be a little liaison (b)/among the (c)/two groups of the society. (d)
(6) The team (a)/complained to the manager (b)/against the captain (c)/and the poor facilities provided in the hotel. (d)
(7) Yesterday I met (a)/a man (b)/who was blind with the right eye. (c)
(8) The principal distributed (a)/the sweet among our friends (b)/who bade him forewell. (c)
(9) As per the invitation care (a)/Rahim marries with Sayra (b)/on 13th December Monday. (c)
(10) The debacle of the Congress party (a)/admit no other explanation (b)/than its (c)/poor performance during the last five years. (d)

17.

Read each sentence to find out whether there is an error in any part **:**

(1) The society does not (a)/hold itself responsible (b)/for the loss or damage to (c)/ any item. (d)
(2) In spite of being (a)/very busy at project work (b)/he saves time (c)/to the relatives. (d)
(3) Some persons (a)/get promotions (b)/even if they are not (c)/worthy for them. (d)
(4) While he was returning (a)/from the office (b)/a man attacked on (c)/him with a dagger. (d)
(5) The decline of her moral (a)/was caused by a lot of (b)/factors that were once (c)/fascinating to her. (d)
(6) He took me to a restra (a)/and ordered for two cups (b)/of cold coffee (c)/which the waiter brought in an hour. (d)
(7) There are some animals (a)/than can live both in water and land (b)/without any difficulty. (c)
(8) During his tour (a)/to the south (b)/he visited not only to Chennai (c)/but also Karnataka. (d)
(9) The President Mr Kalam (a)/is much sought after (b)/by school students and (c)/is invited for many functions. (d)
(10) His mother is not well (a)/but he (b)/ does not look for her (c)/properly. (d)

18.

Read each sentence to find out whether there is an error in any part **:**

(1) We may have to await for (a)/a new political revival (b)/to eradicate the (c)/corruption from our economy.(d)
(2) When she was (a)/in jail (b)/she was debarred to send (c)/a letter even to her son. (d)
(3) Despite of the best efforts (a)/put by the doctors (b)/the condition of the patient (c)/is detereorating from bad to worse. (d)
(4) The militant yielded for (a)/the temptation and fell (b)/into the trap (c)/of police.(d)
(5) Many people in India (a)/are dying from hunger (b)/but government seems (c)/to be ignorant of such crude fact. (d)
(6) In difficult times (a)/she prefers keeping her counsel (b)/rather than wandering (c)/here and there for relief. (d)
(7) The persons who are (a)/suffering from diabetes are (b)/advised to substitute (c)/saccharine by sugar. (d)
(8) He always says (a)/that he prefers to go (b)/home to stay in (c)/a hotel at night. (d)
(9) Hardly had we settled down (a)/for the rest (b)/when we were started by the (c)/strange sound of trumpets. (d)
(10) He was able to (a)/free himself with (b)/the debts by (c)/working day and night. (d)

19.

Choose the correct alternative with the correct choice given below each **: [Income-tax Inspectors]**

(1) The shopkeeper does not have the toys, I was looking ....
(a) by *(b)* about *(c)* for *(d)* to
(2) Books are very often compared .... a granary.
(a) with *(b)* to *(c)* by *(d)* at
(3) Divide twelve mangoes .... three boys.
(a) to *(b)* for *(c)* between *(d)* among
(4) To reach their village, they have to change .... a small train at the junction.
(a) on *(b)* to (c) over *(d)* into
(5) Mohan will never pass his SSC examination .... he works hard.
(a) if *(b)* unless *(c)* since *(d)* because

(6) If you live in a corrupt society, you cannot easily rise ..... the prevailing corruption.
(a) upon *(b)* over *(c)* above *(d)* beyond

(7) It was the first time he had eaten a square meal .... he had left the village.
(a) since *(b)* for *(c)* before *(d)* although

(8) They are very grateful .... your kindness.
(a) for *(b)* to *(c)* with *(d)* towards

(9) His mother was 45, when she ......
(a) had died *(b)* died *(c)* was dying *(d)* has died

(10) There was nothing he could do .... wait.
(a) and *(b)* except *(c)* otherwise *(d)* than

20.

Insert the prepositions where they are required : **[I.F.S.]**

David felt sorry (1)..........Mrs Micowber because he was always (2)...........debt. David took books (3)............... the invitation of Mrs Micowber (4).............. the bookstall and sold them (5).......... whatever he could get. The wife (6).............. the booksellers usually paid (7)............... the books (8)........... shillings which David suspected she stole (9)............ her husband's pocket when he was lying (10)................ bed.

21.

Fill in the blanks in each of the following sentences with the appropriate prepositions :

(1) Professor Krishna will take .... as the new Principal tomorrow. **[IIT]**
(2) We all have to adjust ourselves .... new circumstances. **[IIT]**
(3) Young fans clustered .... the film star. **[IIT]**
(4) My son is apprenticed .... Mr Lal, Chartered Accountant. **[IIT]**
(5) You will always be short of money if you live .... your means. **[IIT]**
(6) He accused me .... selling secret information .... the enemy. **[IIT]**
(7) Please write .... ink and put your name .... the top of the page. **[IIT]**
(8) The man .... pipe and long hairs is the brother .... the girl. **[IIT]**
(9) If you do not comply .... the traffic regulations you will get .... the trouble.............. the police. **[IIT]**
(10) She is now married .... a rich merchant. **[IFS]**
(11) I correspond .... her regularly. **[IFS]**
(12) The patient died .... fever. **[IFS]**
(13) This election is different .... mine. **[IFS]**

SOLUTIONS TYE TEST YOURSELF EXERCISES **TEST YOURSELF** *Exercises*

Solution TYE 01

(1) with,	(2) at,	(3) at,	(4) over,	(5) by,
(6) up,	(7) on,	(8) of,	(9) in,	(10) on,
(11) up,	(12) on,	(13) with,	(14) out,	(15) out.

Solution TYE 02

(1) in, (2) for, (3) of, (4) beside, (5) to,
(6) after, (7) of, (8) upon, (9) along, (10) into,
(11) to, (12) for, (13) by, (14) at, (15) into, beside.

Solution TYE 03

(1) You cannot prevent me from going to the market.
(2) She refrains from doing this work.
(3) I insisted him on attending the class.
(4) He has a passion for learning English grammar.
(5) She is negligent in attending the meeting.
(6) She persisted in writing again.
(7) He is bent on fighting again.
(8) I am confident of winning the match.
(9) He succeeded in passing the examination this time.
(10) I am proud of having a friend like Ram.
(11) I cannot hinder her from entering the temple.
(12) She is desirous of leaving the place.
(13) Ram was disqualified from competing in this tournament.
(14) I cannot think of opposing him.
(15) He was prohibited from entering the temple.
(16) You should abstain from drinking now.
(17) He intends going to Jaipur.
(18) It is very difficult to dissuade him from going there.
(19) He is fortunate in getting a ticket.
(20) I am hopeful of achieving success.

Exercise 03 में ऐसे Verbs एवं Adjectives का प्रयोग किया गया है जिसके बाद Infinitive का प्रयोग नही किया जा सकता है। इन Verbs के बाद हमेशा Gerund (Verb + ing) का प्रयोग होता है।

Solution TYE 04

(1) She was neither ashamed of nor sorry for her misbehaviour.
(2) She neither objected to nor approved of it.
(3) Ram has no interest in and passion for cricket.
(4) We must prevent damage to and theft of public property.
(5) Please listen to and reflect on this topic afterwards.
(6) He asked her a silly question.
(7) The police investigated the case.
(8) Ram resembles his father.
(9) She resigned from her post.
(10) Ram signed the agreement.
(11) The poet described the nature.
(12) She must love her children.
(13) We have discussed the merits of the issue.
(14) In this article the author has described poverty.
(15) She criticized my action without logic.

वाक्य (1) से (5) तक Ellipsis in Preposition के अन्तर्गत दो शब्दों के साथ एक ही Preposition लगाकर गलती की गई है। वाक्य (6) से (15) तक में Transitive verb के साथ Preposition लगाने की गलती की गई है।

Solution TYE 05

(1) to, (2) for, (3) to, (4) for, (5) in,
(6) to, (7) of, (8) on, (9) to, (10) with,
(11) from, (12) with, (13) to, (14) to, (15) to.

Solution TYE 06

(1) to, (2) upon, (3) of, (4) for, (5) of,
(6) of, (7) in, (8) of, (9) at, (10) of,
(11) against, (12) for, (13) from (14) from, (15) in.

Solution TYE 07

(1) into, (2) in, (3) on, (4) in, (5) in
(6) at, (7) in, (8) at, (9) on, (10) upon,
(11) on, (12) by, (13) with, (14) beside, (15) besides,
(16) from, (17) besides, (18) for, (19) since, (20) with.

Solution TYE 08

(1) while, (2) while, (3) during, (4) while, (5) during,
(6) while, (7) while, (8) for, (9) during, (10) for,
(11) for, (12) for, (13) during, (14) for, (15) while,
(16) during, (17) while, (18) While, (19) During, (20) while,
(21) during, (22) During.

Solution TYE 09

(1) until, (2) by, (3) by, by (4) until, (5) until, by,
(6) by, (7) until, (8) by, (9) by, (10) until.

Solution TYE 10

(1) at, (2) on, (3) in, (4) on, (5) in,
(6) in, (7) at, (8) on, (9) at, (10) at, in,
(11) on, in, (12) in, (13) on, in, (14) in.

Solution TYE 11

(1) (c), (2) (b), (3) (d), (4) (a), (5) (c),
(6) (d), (7) (c), (8) (a), (9) (c), (10) (d),
(11) (b), (12) (d), (13) (b), (14) (b), (15) (d).

Solution TYE 12

(1) (a), (2) (c), (3) (c), (4) (b), (5) (d),
(6) (b), (7) (b), (8) (a), (9) (d), (10) (c),
(11) (a), (12) (b), (13) (d).

Solution TYE 13

(1) (d), (2) (b), (3) (b), (4) (a), (5) (b),
(6) (a), (7) (c), (8) (b), (9) (d), (10) (b),
(11) (b), (12) (d), (13) (d), (14) (a), (15) (a).

Solution TYE 14

(1) (b), (2) (b), (3) (a), (4) (c), (5) (b),
(6) (d), (7) (b), (8) (a), (9) (a), (10) (d),
(11) (a), (12) (c), (13) (b), (14) (b).

Solution TYE 15

(1) at, (2) at, (3) at, (4) at, (5) on,
(6) on, (7) in, (8) in, (9) to, (10) No preposition,
(11) in, (12) in, (13) at, (14) on, (15) on,
(16) in, (17) at, (18) after, (19) for, (20) into.

Solution TYE 16

(1) (c) entered into की जगह entered his ही आयेगा। go into, jump into हो सकता है। ध्यान रखें : entered upon a career, enter into a conversation, enter into a project/business आदि हो सकता है।

(2) (c) listening to की जगह केवल listening ही होगा। यदि listen के बाद कोई object न हो, तो 'to' का प्रयोग नहीं होता है। जैसे:
Please listen to me. (object)
I was listening but heard nothing.

(3) (a) apparent to होगा।

(4) (a) proposed to होगा। suggested to, proposed to होता है।

(5) (c) among की जगह between आयेगा। सामान्यत: between का प्रयोग दो के लिए तथा among का प्रयोग more than two के लिए किया जाता है।

(6) (d) and about the poor ......होगा।
(I) complained to somebody (II) complained against somebody
(III) complained about/of something होता है।

(7) (c) blind in होगा।
blind in left or right eye या blind of an eye या blind with both eyes आदि होता है।

(8) (b) among की जगह amongst होगा।

यदि among के बाद वाला शब्द किसी vowel sound से उच्चरित (Pronounced) है तो amongst आयेगा। यदि consonant sound से उच्चरित (Pronounced) है तो among ही आयेगा। among एवं amongst दोनों का प्रयोग दो से अधिक के लिए किया जाता है। 'the' से पूर्व among या amongst में से किसी का प्रयोग हो सकता है। जैसे:

among the girls	*Correct*	*amongst the girls*	*Correct*
among out members	*Incorrect*	*amongst our member*	*Correct*
amongst them	*Incorrect*	*among them*	*Correct*

(9) (b) with का प्रयोग नहीं होगा। जब marry का प्रयोग मुख्य verb के रूप में होता है, तो इसके साथ कोई preposition नहीं लगता है। जैसे:
Hari is married to Hina. Hari marries Hina on next Monday.

(10) (b) admits of होगा। 'of' का प्रयोग admits के बाद होगा।

Solution TYE 17

(1) (c) loss of होगा।

यदि दो words, or या and संयुक्त हों एवं अलग-अलग Prepositions लेते हों तो अलग - अलग prepositions लगाने आवश्यक हैं।

(2) (d) to की जगह for का प्रयोग होगा। Save के साथ Preposition निम्न प्रकार से लगते हैं : Save for something, Save somebody from something.
(i) He has saved some money for medicines. (ii) She saved me from drowning.

(3) (d) worthy of होगा। क्योंकि worthy के बाद of, preposition लगता है।

(4) (c) On का प्रयोग अनुचित है। यदि attack का प्रयोग verb के रूप में किया जाये, तो इसके बाद object आता है। लेकिन यदि make के साथ attack का प्रयोग होता है,तो Preposition 'on' लगता है। China made an attack on India.

(5) (a) decline in होगा। Decline of empire/decline of a man सही है। Decline in moral/Decline in prices में decline के साथ in आता है।

(6) (b) order के बाद for का प्रयोग नहीं होगा, क्योंकि order एक transitive verb है, जिसके तुरन्त बाद object आता है।
(i) He ordered a glass of wine. (ii) He ordered him to go to market.

(7) (b) on land आयेगा।

यदि दो words 'and' या 'or' से संयुक्त हों एवं दोनों के साथ अलग-अलग Preposition लगता हो, तो अलग-अलग Prepositions लगने चाहिए।

(8) (c) to का प्रयोग गलत है। visited का प्रयोग जब एक verb के रूप में किया जाता है, तो इसके बाद object आता है लेकिन make के साथ जब visit का प्रयोग किया जाता है, तो 'to' का प्रयोग होता है।
He made a visit to Agra last year.

(9) (d) invited के साथ to का प्रयोग होगा for की जगह to लगायें।
(i) I was invited to a party. (ii) He was invited to lunch.

(10) (c) look after होगा। look after का अर्थ है देखभाल करना।

Solution TYE 18

(1) (a) await के साथ for नहीं लगेगा।
wait for होता है await for गलत है। जैसे :
(i) We are waiting for his arrival. (ii) We are awaiting his arrival.

(2) (c) debarred from sending होगा।
debar/abstain/refrain के साथ from का प्रयोग + verb + ing का प्रयोग होता है।
He abstained from drinking wine.

(3) (a) Despite के साथ of नहीं लगता है। Despite का अर्थ होता है In spite of.

(4) (a) yielded to होगा। yield to का अर्थ होता है। समर्पण (yield to somebody, yield to something) करना।
(i) She yielded to her lover's wish. (ii) He yielded to his enemy.

(5) (b) dying of hunger होगा। die of hunger/die of a disease होता है। die from over working/die from over drinking/die from food poisoning आदि होता है।

(6) (c) rather than का अनुचित प्रयोग किया गया है। इसकी जगह 'to' का प्रयोग होगा। prefer, senior, junior, prior इत्यादि के साथ Preposition 'to' लगता है।

(7) (d) by की जगह for का प्रयोग कीजिए। ध्यान दीजिए : substitute something for something होता है।

(8) (c) to stay in की जगह rather than stay in होगा। जब prefer द्वारा दो verbs की तुलना की जाती है, तो prefer के साथ rather than का प्रयोग होता है। जैसे :
She prefers to write rather than to speak on telephone.

(9) (c) startled at होगा। surprised/startled/amazed/ astonished के साथ Preposition 'at' लगता है।

(10) (b) free himself from होगा। free somebody from something या free from something होता है।

Solution TYE 19

(1) (c),	(2) (b),	(3) (d),	(4) (d),	(5) (b),
(6) (c),	(7) (a),	(8)\ (a),	(9) (b),	(10) (b).

Solution TYE 20

(1) for,	(2) in,	(3) at,	(4) from,	(5) for,
(6) and,	(7) for,	(8) some,	(9) from,	(10) in.

Solution TYE 21

(1) over,	(2) with,	(3) round,	(4) to,	(5) on,
(6) of, to	(7) in, at	(8) with, of	(9) with, in, with,	(10) to,
(11) to,	(12) of,	(13) from.		

CHAPTER

18

Conjunctions

Conjunctions क्या है?

Conjunction ऐसा शब्द है, जो शब्दों या वाक्यों को आपस में जोड़ता है। इसे Sentence Linker भी कहा जाता है।

Definition : A Conjunction is a word that joins words or sentences together.

A Conjunction is a joiner, a word that connects (conjoins) parts of a sentence.

Look at the following sentences :

(a) He is honest and she is intelligent.

(b) I shall either read or write a book.

(c) Three and three make six.

(d) Suresh and Ganesh are friends.

वाक्य (a) एवं वाक्य (b) में Conjunction 'and' एवं 'or' दो वाक्यों को जोड़ने का कार्य कर रहे हैं, जबकि वाक्य (c) एवं (d) में Conjunction 'and' दो शब्दों को जोड़ने का कार्य कर रहा हैं।

Conjunctions are words that join clauses together to make sentences, and show how the meanings of the clauses relate to each other.

Kinds of Conjunction

Conjunctions को निम्नलिखित तीन भागों में वर्गीकृत किया गया है :

(A) Coordinating Conjunction

(B) Subordinating Conjunction

(C) Correlative Conjunction

(A) Coordinating Conjunction : ये Conjunctions दो समान Rank के Sentences या Words को जोड़ते हैं। इस तरह के मुख्य Conjunctions हैं: For, and, nor, but, or, yet, so. An easy way to remember these six conjunctions is to think of the word **F A N B O Y S**. Each of the letters in this somewhat unlikely word is the first letter of one of the Coordinating Conjunctions.

(B) Subordinating Conjunction : इन Conjunctions द्वारा एक Sub ordinating Clause को अन्य Clause से जोड़ा जाता है। (Subordinating Clause वह है जो अपने पूर्ण अर्थ के लिए अन्य Clause पर निर्भर होती है) इस तरह के मुख्य Conjunctions हैं : after, although, as, as if, as long as, as though, because, before, even if, even though, if, if only, in order that, now that, once, rather than, since, so that, than, that, though, till, unless, until, when, whenever, where, whereas, wherever, while.

Note that some of the Subordinating Conjuctions in the above examples like: after, before, since—are also prepositions, but as Subordinate Conjunctions they are being used to introduce a clause and to subordinate the following clause to the independent element in the sentence.

Examples :

After : (a) We are going out to eat after we finish our work.
(b) After the rain stopped, the dog ran into the mud to play.

Since : Since we have lived in Mexico, we have gone to every exhibit at the Royal Hall.

While : (a) While I was waiting in line for my turn, I ate my lunch.
(b) Shalini steamed the corn while Jack fried the steaks.

Although : Although the line was long and the wait over at least three hours, the exhibit was indeed worth it.

Even if : Even if you have already bought your ticket, you will still need to wait in queue.

Because : (a) I love her works because she uses color so brilliantly.
(b) The snowman melted because the sun came out.

Even though : Even though Jack fell asleep, the mobile salesman kept talking.

(C) Correlative Conjunction : जो Conjunctions जोड़े (pairs) में प्रयोग किए जाते हैं, उन्हें Correlative Conjunction कहते हैं। जैसे: Either.......or, Neither...........nor, Both........and, Whether... or, Not only........but also.

Remember

Correlative Conjunctions are always used in pairs. They join similar elements. When joining singular and plural subjects, the subject closest to the verb determines whether the verb is singular or plural.

Important

Coordinating Conjunctions are the simplest kind, and they denote equality of relationship between the ideas they join. Their relatives, Correlative Conjunctions, not only denote equality, but they also make the joining tighter and more emphatic.

Coordinating and Correlative Conjunctions are great when two ideas are of the same importance, but many times one idea is more important than another. Subordinating Conjunctions are used to show which idea is more and which is less important. The idea in the main clause is the more important, while the idea in the subordinate clause (made subordinate by the Subordinating conjunction) is less important. The subordinate clause supplies a time, reason, condition, and so on for the main clause.

Conjunctive Adverbs

Conjunctive Adverbs make up an even stronger category of Conjunctions. They show logical relationships between two independent sentences, between sections of paragraphs, or between entire paragraphs. Conjunctive Adverbs are so emphatic that they should be used sparingly; however, when used appropriately, they can be quite effective.

Such Conjunctive Adverbs are : Also, hence, however, still, likewise, otherwise, therefore, conversely, rather, consequently, furthermore, nevertheless, instead, moreover, then, thus, meanwhile, accordingly.

Examples :

(a) If the salmon is grilled, I will have that; otherwise, I might have the chicken.

(b) James has a garage full of wood working tools. He might, however, have some metric wrenches, too.

(c) I do not recommend that you play with a stick of dynamite lit at both ends. Rather, a ham sandwich would be better for you.

Expletives

Expletives are closely related to conjunctive adverbs. Expletives convey no meaning of their own, but instead serve only to emphasize the statement to which they are attached. As such, then, they technically do not show a logical relationship like time or cause between ideas, and that fact prevents them from being treated as conjunctive adverbs.

Such Expletives are : Of course, indeed, naturally, after all, in short, I hope, at least, remarkably, in fact, on the whole, I suppose, it seems, in brief, I think, clearly, assuredly, definitely to be sure, without doubt, for all that, in any event, importantly, certainly.

Conjunction/Relative Pronoun/Relative Adverb/Preposition

Conjunctions का कार्य मात्र वाक्यों या शब्दों को जोड़ना है, जबकि Relative Pronoun/Relative Adverb/Preposition न केवल Pronoun या Adverb या Preposition का भी कार्य करते हैं, बल्कि वाक्यों को जोड़ते भी हैं।

Look at the following sentences

(a) This is the pen that she gifted me.	*Relative Pronoun*
(b) This the place where I was born.	*Relative Adverb*
(c) He sat beside Shyam.	*Preposition*
(d) He came and he worked.	*Conjunction*

वाक्य (a) में 'that' Noun, pen को भी Refer कर रहा है एवं दो वाक्यों को जोड़ भी रहा है। इसी तरह वाक्य (b) एवं (c) में Underlined words, Adverb एवं Preposition का कार्य कर रहे हैं एवं दो वाक्यों को जोड़ भी रहे हैं, जबकि वाक्य (d) में Conjunction मात्र दो वाक्यों को जोड़ने का कार्य कर रहा है।

Use of Coordinating Conjunction

जैसा पूर्व में बताया गया है Coordinating Conjunctions समान Rank के दो वाक्यों को संयुक्त करते हैं।

AND

(a) To suggest that one work is sequential to another :
Kamini sent in her applications and waited by the phone for a response.

(b) To suggest that one work is the result of another :
Ramesh heard the weather report and promptly went to his house.

(c) To suggest that one idea is in contrast to another (frequently replaced by but in this usage) :
Naresh is brilliant and Shalini has a pleasant smile.

(d) To reflect an element of surprise (sometimes replaced by yet in this usage) :
Mumbai is a rich city and suffers from many elements of urban blight.

(e) To reflect that one clause is conditionally dependent upon another (usually the first clause is an imperative) :

(a) Use your credit cards without care and you'll soon find yourself deep in debt.

(b) Waste your time carelessly and you will soon find yourself out of time to prepare for the examinations.

(f) To suggest a kind of 'comment' on the first clause :
Rajesh became addicted to gambling— and that surprised no one who knew him.

BUT

(a) To reflect a contrast that is unexpected in light of the first clause :
Johny lost a fortune in the stock market, but he still seems able to live quite comfortably.

(b) To reflect in an affirmative sense what the first part of the sentence implied in a negative way (sometimes replaced by on the contrary) :
The club never invested foolishly, but used the services of some intelligent counsellors.

(c) To connect two ideas with the meaning of 'with the exception of, (and then the second word takes over as subject) :
Everybody but Jai Kishan is trying out for the team.

OR

(a) To suggest that only one possibility can be realized, excluding one or the other :
You study hard for this exam or you will not get good marks

(b) To suggest the inclusive combination of alternatives :
We can cook dinner tonight, or we can just eat leftovers.

(c) To suggest a refinement of the first clause :
Saraswati College is the premier all-girls, college in the state, or so it seems to most Saraswati College alumnae.

(d) To suggest a 'restatement' or 'correction' of the first part of the sentence :
There are no tigers in this sanctuary, or so our guide tells us.

(e) To suggest a negative condition :
The sayings of one of the freedom fighters was very important 'Do or die'.

(f) To suggest a negative alternative without the use of an imperative (see use of and above) :
They must approve his political style or they wouldn't keep electing him Chairman.

NOR

The Conjunction NOR is not used as often as the other Conjunctions, so it might feel a bit odd when nor does come up in conversation or writing. It is commonly used in the correlative pair, neither-nor (see below) :

(a) He is neither sane nor intelligent.

(b) That is neither what I said nor what I wanted to say.
'Nor' can also be used with other negative expressions :

(c) That is not what I wanted to say, nor should you interpret my statement as an admission of guilt.

YET

The word YET functions sometimes as an adverb. It can be used reflecting several meanings : (i)in addition ('yet another cause of trouble' or 'a simple yet noble woman'), (ii) even ('yet more expensive'), (iii) still ('he is yet a novice'), (iv) eventually ('they may yet win'), (v) and so soon as now ('he's not here yet'). 'Yet' also functions as a Coordinating Conjunction meaning something like 'nevertheless' or 'but'.

(a) Jack plays basketball well, yet his favourite sport is cricket.

(b) The visitors complained a lot about the heat, yet they continued to play golf here every day.

FOR

The word 'FOR' is most often used as a preposition. It is also used, as a Coordinating Conjunction. Beginning a sentence with the Conjunction 'for' should be avoided. Its function is to introduce the reason for the preceding clause

(a) Ramesh thought he had a good chance to get the job, for his uncle was on the company's board of directors.

(b) Most of the visitors were happy just relaxing under the shade, for it had been a long, dusty journey on the cart.

SO

So, sometimes connects two independent clauses along with a comma, but sometimes it doesn't. For instance, in this sentence :

(a) He is not the only Olympic athlete in his family, so are his brother, sister, and his niece Chetna.
Here the word so means 'as well' or 'in addition'.
In the following sentence, 'So' means 'therefore', the Conjunction and the comma are adequate to the task :

(b) She has always been nervous in large gatherings, so it is no surprise that she avoids crowds of her fans.
When 'So' is used at the beginning of a sentence, it will act as a kind of summing up word, in that case comma is used after it (So) as following :

(c) So, the Judge peremptorily removed the child from the custody of the claimants.

Subordinating Conjunctions

जैसा पूर्व में बताया गया है Subordinating Conjunctions, एक Subordinate Clause को दूसरी Clause से जोड़ते हैं। I purchased a pen, because I had no pen.

'because I had no pen' एक Subordinate Clause है जो अपने पूर्ण अर्थ के लिए अन्य Clause पर निर्भर है। 'because' एक Subordinating Conjunction है।

इस तरह के मुख्य Conjunctions हैं : after, because, that, though, although, till, before, unless, as, when, where, while etc.

Subordinating Conjunction को इनके द्वारा व्यक्त कार्य/अर्थ के अनुसार निम्न भागों में वर्गीकृत किया गया है :

(1) Time : ये Conjunction, समय के सन्दर्भ में प्रयुक्त होते हैं। इस तरह के Conjunctions हैं : when, whenever, till, until, before, after, as soon as, as, since, while etc.

Read the following sentences :

(a) When I went to office, the peon was going to his house.
(b) I have been searching her since I met her.
(c) Ramesh went to his home, after he completed his work.
(d) You should complete the work, before you go to market.
(e) Make hay while the sun shines.
(f) I will start the business, as soon as I get the licence.
(g) He will stay in office until you reach there.

यहाँ Subordinating Conjunction, समय के सन्दर्भ में प्रयुक्त हुए हैं।

(2) Cause or Reason : ये Conjunction, वाक्य में कार्य के Cause या Reason के सन्दर्भ में प्रयुक्त होते हैं। इस तरह के मुख्य Conjunctions हैं : as, because, since etc.

Read the following sentences :

(a) I telephoned to her father as she was not available in office.
(b) He is allowed to enter as he is invited by us.
(c) I can't buy this car, since it is very costly.
(d) She is crying because someone has stolen her purse.

यहाँ Subordinating Conjunction कार्य के कारण के सन्दर्भ में प्रयुक्त हुए हैं।

(3) Purpose : वाक्य में Purpose को व्यक्त करने वाले Conjunctions मुख्यतया ये हैं : that, so that, in order that, lest etc.

Read the following sentences :

(a) We eat that we may live.
(b) He came here, so that he can discuss the plan.
(c) Run fast lest you should miss the train.
(d) He is working hard in order that he can succeed.

यहाँ Subordinating Conjunctions, purpose के सन्दर्भ में प्रयुक्त हुए हैं।

(4) Result or Consequences : परिणाम (Result) के सन्दर्भ में प्रयुक्त होने वाले Conjunctions इस श्रेणी में आते हैं। इस तरह के Conjunctions है : so that, such that, that etc.

Read the following sentences :

(a) The coffee is so hot that I can't drink it.
(b) He spoke in such a loud voice that everyone could hear him well.
(c) She is such a nasty girl that you can't rely on her .

(5) Condition : शर्त के सन्दर्भ में प्रयुक्त होने वाले Conjunctions; जैसे : If, unless, provided, that, supposing etc.; इस श्रेणी में आते हैं।

Read the following sentences :

(a) You cannot succeed unless you work hard.
(b) He will help you if you ask him.
(c) I will pay your dues provided you allow proper discount.
(d) He will be penalised provided that the charges are proved.
(e) Supposing you won a lottery, what would you do?

(6) Place : इन Conjunctions का प्रयोग स्थान के सन्दर्भ में किया जाता है। इस तरह के मुख्य Conjunctions हैं : where, wherever, whither (to what place), whence (from what place) etc.

Read the following sentences :

(a) I found my purse where I left it.
(b) Let her go wherever she likes to go.
(c) Can you inform me whither she has gone?
(d) He went back whence he came.

Whence का अर्थ from what place होता है, अत whence के साथ from का प्रयोग नहीं किया जाता है।

(7) Comparison : इन Conjunctions का प्रयोग तुलना के सन्दर्भ में किया जाता है।

Read the following sentences :

(a) He is as strong as your brother.
(b) She is an intelligent as her brother.
(c) He is not so intelligent as her brother.
(d) He is not so strong as your brother.

As ..... as का प्रयोग likeliness समानता हेतु जबकि so .... as का प्रयोग Negative वाक्यों में unlikeliness हेतु किया जाता है।

(8) Concession : इन Conjunctions का प्रयोग रियायत (Concession) के सन्दर्भ में होता है। इस तरह के Conjunctions हैं : Though, although, yet, notwithstanding, however etc.

Read the following sentences :

(a) She is poor yet she is trustworthy.
(b) I shall not meet her though she comes.
(c) Although he is intelligent, he is simple.
(d) I didn't support him, however I didn't oppose him.
(e) He passed the examination notwithstanding he was not fully prepared.

इस तरह के Subordinating Conjunctions एक प्रकार की रियायत के सन्दर्भ में प्रयुक्त होते हैं।

(9) Manner : ये Conjunctions कार्य विधि को स्पष्ट करते हैं। इस तरह के Conjunctions हैं : as, as though, so far as etc.

Read the following sentences :

(a) He spoke as if he was drunk. (b) She was speaking the truth so far I could judge.
(c) He acted upon as he was instructed. (d) He protested as though he were in opposition.

इन वाक्यों में Subordinating Conjunctions of Manner का प्रयोग हुआ है।

Copulative Conjunctions

Copulative Conjunctions का कार्य मात्र दो वाक्यों को आपस में संयुक्त करना है। इस तरह के Conjunctions हैं : and, and .... also, as well as, Both ... and, well, now etc.

Read the following sentences :

(a) He came and wrote an application. (b) Suresh is a hard worker and his son also.
(c) Both Ram and Shyam will attend the party. (d) Ram has arrived now you can take rest.
(e) Ram as well as his brother was present in the meeting.
(f) You have finished your work, well you can go.

जैसा उक्त वाक्यों से स्पष्ट होता है, वाक्य (a) में दो वाक्य, (i) He came, (ii) He wrote an application को 'and' Conjection की सहायता से जोड़ा गया है।

Alternative Conjunctions

इस तरह के Conjunction द्वारा ऐसे वाक्यों को जोड़ा जाता है जिनमें कोई विकल्प (Alternate) व्यक्त किया जाता है। इस तरह के Conjunctions हैं : or, else, otherwise, either .... or, Neither .... nor etc.

Look at the following sentences :

(a) He should join or he will be terminated. (b) Ram, move fast else you will be late.
(c) Ram, move fast otherwise you will miss the train.
(d) Either obey the orders or leave the job. (e) Neither he nor she was present in the party.

उपरोक्त वाक्यों में विकल्प व्यक्त हो रहा है, अत: Alternative Conjunctions का प्रयोग किया गया है।

Adversative Conjunction

ये Conjunctions दो विरोधात्मक वाक्यों को संयुक्त करने हेतु प्रयोग मे आते हैं। इस तरह के Conjunctions हैं : however, but, still, yet, only, nevertheless, while etc.

Look at the following sentences :

(a) He was not sincere however he got promotion. (b) He is poor, but he is trustworthy.
(c) He is rich yet he is not honest. (d) He is poor yet he has self respect.
(e) He is rich nevertheless he refused to help him.

जब दो वाक्यों में विरोधात्मक तथ्यों अथवा कथनों को व्यक्त किया जाता है, तो ऐसे वाक्यों को Adversative Conjunctions द्वारा संयुक्त किया जा सकता है।

Illative (Inferential) Conjunctions

इस तरह के Conjunction द्वारा ऐसे वाक्यों को संयुक्त किया जाता है जिनमें एक वाक्य दूसरे वाक्य का Inference है, परिणाम है। इस तरह के Conjunctions हैं : for, so, therefore etc.

Read the following sentences :

(a) Something has broken, for I have heard a splash. (b) You are in power, so you are respected.

(c) You worked hard therefore you secured good marks.
(d) He secured good marks, for he worked hard.

उक्त वाक्यों से स्पष्ट है कि एक वाक्य दूसरे वाक्य का परिणाम है।

Some Important Conjunctions

(1) Not only .... but also : इससे जोड़े जाने योग्य वाक्य निम्नलिखित दो प्रकार के हो सकते हैं :

(A) जब दोनों वाक्यों में कर्ता एक हो। (Same Subject)
(B) जब दोनों वाक्यों में कर्ता अलग हो। (Different Subjects)

(A) **जब कर्ता एक हो (When subject is same) :**

Look at the following sentences

(i) (a) Sita is playing chess. (b) Sita is watching T.V.
Sita is not only playing chess but also watching T.V.

(ii) (a) Nisha eats an orange. (b) Nisha cooks food.
Nisha not only eats an orange but also cooks food.

(iii) (a) Girls are watching T.V. (b) Girls are making a noise.
Girls are not only watching T.V. but also making a noise.

ऐसे वाक्यों को Not only..................but also से संयुक्त करने हेतु निम्न नियमों का पालन करें :

(1) दोनों वाक्यों का जो Common part (समान हिस्सा) है पहले उसे लिखें, फिर not only लिखें। उसके बाद पहले वाक्य का शेष भाग वैसा का वैसा ही दें।

(2) इसके बाद but also लिखकर, दूसरे वाक्य का (Common वाले part को छोड़कर) शेष भाग लिख दें।

वाक्य (i) को उपरोक्त नियमों के आधार पर जोड़ने पर सबसे पहले दोनों वाक्यों का Common Part - Sita is लिखा फिर हमने not only लिखा।

Sita is not only playing chess ....
इसके बाद but also लिखा।
Sita is not only playing chess but also ....
अब दूसरे भाग का शेष भाग watching T.V. लिखा।
Sita is not only playing chess but also watching T.V.
इस प्रकार हमारा वाक्य पूरा हो जाता है।

(B) **जब कर्ता अलग-अलग हों (When subjects are different)** :

Look at the following sentences :

(i) (a) Hina is watching T.V. (b) Sheela is watching T.V.
Not only Hina, but also Sheela is watching T.V.

(ii) (a) Ram will play football. (b) Shyam will play football.
Not only Ram but also Shyam will play football.

(iii) (a) The teacher is talking. (b) The girls are talking.
Not only the teacher but also the girls are talking.

(1) जब Subject अलग है तो सबसे पहले Not only लिखकर वाक्य शुरू करे फिर पहले वाक्य का Subject लिखें उसके बाद but also लिखे एवं दूसरे वाक्य का Subject लिखें।

(2) उसके बाद दोनों वाक्यों का Common part लिखें।

(3) but also के बाद जो verb लगेगी वह उसके पास वाले Subject के अनुसार लगेगी, यदि not only के पास वाला Subject plural है तो verb, plural लगेगी एवं यदि Subject singular है तो verb भी singular ही लगेगी। जैसा कि वाक्य (iii) से स्पष्ट है।

Very Important Point

(1) Not only .... but also एक Correlative Conjunction है। इसमें मुख्य बिन्दु यह है कि यदि not only का प्रयोग noun से पूर्व हुआ है तो but also का प्रयोग भी noun से पूर्व ही होना चाहिए। यदि not only का प्रयोग verb से पूर्व हुआ है तो but also का प्रयोग भी verb से पूर्व होना आवश्यक है।

Look at the following sentences :

(a) Ram is watching not only T.V. but also playing football. *Incorrect*
Ram is not only watching T.V. but also playing football. *Correct*

वाक्य (a) में not only का प्रयोग noun (T.V.) के पूर्व हुआ है, जबकि but also का प्रयोग verb (playing) के पूर्व हुआ है। अत: गलत है।

(b) Not only Ram gave me five coins, but also thanked me. *Incorrect*
Ram not only gave me five coins, but also thanked me. *Correct*

यह नियम सभी Correlative Conjunctions; जैसे : Either ...... or, Neither .... nor, Both ..... and, Though .... yet, Whether ...... or इत्यादि; में समान रूप से लागू होता है। यह एक महत्त्वपूर्ण बिन्दु है।

(2) Neither .... nor : इसके लिए दोनों वाक्यों का negative होना आवश्यक है।

(A) जब कर्ता एक ही हो (When subject same) :

Look at the following sentences :

(i) (a) Mohan is not a student. (b) Mohan is not a player.
Mohan is neither a student nor a player.

(ii) (a) She is not cooking. (b) She is not watching T.V.
She is neither cooking nor watching T.V.

(iii) (a) Suresh does not play. (b) Suresh does not read.
Suresh neither plays nor reads

(1) जब Subject एक ही है तो इस तरह वाक्यों के common भाग को सबसे पहले लिखें, फिर neither लिखें। उसके बाद पहले वाक्य का शेष भाग लिख दें। उसके बाद nor लिखें।
ध्यान रखें यदि Article a/an का प्रयोग हुआ है तो वह दोनों बार अलग-अलग लिखा जायेगा।
(2) उसके बाद दूसरे वाक्य के common भाग को छोड़कर शेष भाग लिख दें।
(3) ध्यान रखें दोनों वाक्यों में आया 'not' नहीं लिखना है। Subject singular है तो verb भी singular लगती है।
(4) यह भी ध्यान रखें कि neither एवं nor दोनों का प्रयोग दोनों भागों में noun/object/verb के सामने समान होगा। यदि neither के बाद noun आया है तो nor के बाद भी noun ही आयेगा।

(iv) (a) He does not play football. (b) He does not play hockey.
He neither plays football nor hockey. *Incorrect*
He plays neither football nor hockey. *Correct*

(B) जब कर्ता अलग-अलग हों (When subjects are different) :

Look at the following sentences :

(i) (a) Suresh is not going to Delhi. (b) Ramesh is not going to Delhi.
Neither Suresh nor Ramesh is going to Delhi.

(ii) (a) Kali does not read. (b) Nisha does not read.
Neither Kali nor Nisha reads.

(iii) (a) Kukku will not take tea. (b) Harsh will not take tea.
Neither Kukku nor Harsh will take tea.

(1) सबसे पहले Neither लिखें, फिर वाक्य को लिखें, फिर पहले वाक्य का subject लिखें। इसके बाद nor लिखकर दूसरे वाक्य का subject लिखें, फिर common भाग लिखें।

(2) Nor के बाद लगने वाली verb, nor के साथ लगने वाले subject के अनुसार लगती है। वाक्य (ii) में verb reads लगी है। verb का ध्यान रखें। ऐसे अन्य वाक्य देखें।

(iv) (a) They do not play cricket. (b) He does not play cricket.
Neither they nor he plays cricket.

(v) (a) He does not write a letter. (b) They do not write a letter.
Neither he nor they write a letter.
(Verb should agree with the nearest subject.)

(3) Either ..... or : जब दोनों वाक्य affirmative में हों, तो इन्हें conjunction द्वारा जोड़ा जा सकता है। Neither ..... nor एवं either .... or हेतु दो वाक्यों को जोड़ने के नियम समान हैं।

(A) **जब कर्ता एक हो (When subject is same) :**

Look at the following sentences :

(i) (a) Rajesh plays chess. (b) Rajesh watches T.V.
Rajesh either plays chess or watches T.V.

(ii) (a) She writes a lesson. (b) She reads a book.
She either writes a lesson or reads a book.

(iii) (a) Sita plays chess. (b) Sita plays cricket.
Sita plays either chess or cricket.

(B) **जब कर्ता अलग-अलग हों (When subjects are different) :**

Look at the following sentences :

(i) (a) She plays cricket. (b) I play cricket.
Either she or I play cricket.

(ii) (a) Mahesh is playing. (b) They are playing.
Either Mahesh or they are playing.

(iii) (a) She will go to Mumbai. (b) They will go to Mumbai.
Either she or they will go to Mumbai.

(4) Both .... and

(A) **जब कर्ता एक हो (When subject is same)**

Look at the following sentences :

(i) (a) I am a teacher. (b) I am an author.
I am both a teacher and an author.

(ii) (a) He will buy a car. (b) He will buy a book.
He will buy both a car and a book.

(iii) (a) Ram can write. (b) Ram can teach.
Ram can both write and teach.

Conjunction Both.......... and पर भी वही नियम लागू होते हैं जो Neither......... or, Not only ....but also, Either...........or पर लागू होते हैं।

(B) जब कर्ता अलग-अलग हों **(When subjects are different) :**

Look at the following sentences :

(i) (a) He is my friend. (b) She is my friend.
Both he and she are my friends.

(ii) (a) He is going to market. (b) She is going to market.
Both he and she are going to market.

(iii) (a) Ram will go to Jaipur. (b) Shyam will go to Jaipur.
Both Ram and Shyam will go to Jaipur.

(a) जैसा पूर्व में स्पष्ट किया है, Both ..... and, Conjunction द्वारा दो वाक्यों को जोड़ने पर सामान्यतया वे ही नियम लागू होते हैं जो Not only ...... but also, Neither ...... nor, Either ...... or पर लागू होते हैं।

(b) Both .... and का प्रयोग दो Individual subjects के लिए ही किया जाता है। यदि एक कर्ता He एवं दूसरा कर्ता they है तो conjunction का प्रयोग नहीं किया जाता है।

(c) दोनों कर्ता singular होने की स्थिति में Conjunction Both...and का प्रयोग करने पर verb plural हो जाती है। [देखे वाक्य संख्या (i) और (ii)]

(5) So ..... that : Conjunction so ... that का प्रयोग सामान्यतया too ... to के प्रयुक्त वाक्य के transformation में किया जाता है।

Read the following sentences :

(a) He is too weak to walk. He is so weak that he cannot walk.

(b) She is too old to climb up the hill. She is so old that she cannot climb up the hill.

(c) He was too tired to do any work. He was so tired that he couldn't do any work.

(d) Rahul was too puzzled to speak anything properly.
Rahul was so puzzled that he could not speak anything properly.

(a) 'too......to' का प्रयोग करने वाले वाक्यों में जब so ....that का प्रयोग किया जाता है, तो ध्यान रखें कि too की जगह so का प्रयोग करें, फिर too के बाद प्रयुक्त शब्द को लिखें।

(b) फिर that लिखकर subject को लिखें। इसके बाद cannot लिखकर वाक्य में प्रयुक्त verb एवं object को लिख दें।

(c) यदि वाक्य Past tense में है तो cannot की जगह could not का प्रयोग किया जायेगा। so .... that का प्रयोग negative वाक्यों में किया जाता है।

(6) No sooner .... than :

Look at the following sentences :

(i) (a) She arrives. (b) She begins to clean the house.
No sooner does she arrives than she begins to clean the house.

(ii) (a) The bell rang. (b) The students came out of their classes.
No sooner did the bell ring than the students came out of their classes.

(iii) (a) I had reached the station. (b) The train departed.
No sooner had I reached the station than the train departed.

(1) No sooner के बाद (वाक्यों के Tense के अनुसार) helping verb; do/does/ did/had,had का प्रयोग होता है तथा फिर than का प्रयोग उक्त अनुसार होता है।

(2) Than की Spelling का ध्यान रखें यह 'Then' नही है।

(7) Hardly had ...... when :

Look at the following sentences :

(i) (a) She reached the station. (b) The train arrived.
Hardly had she reached the station when the train arrived.

(ii) (a) He reached here. (b) She went to market.
Hardly had he reached here when she went to market.

(1) Hardly के साथ when का प्रयोग होता है, than या अन्य Conjuction का नहीं।
(2) Hardly had लिखकर, पहला वाक्य पूरा लिख दें, फिर when लिखकर दूसरा वाक्य लिख दें।
(3) Hardly had के बाद verb की third form लगेगी, यह एक महत्त्वपूर्ण बिन्दु है, इसका ध्यान रखें।

(8) As soon as :

Look at the following sentences

(i) (a) She reached the station. (b) The train arrived.
As soon as she reached the station, the train arrived.

(ii) (a) He reached here. (b) She went to market.
As soon as he reached here, she went to market.

As soon as शुरू में लिखकर पहला वाक्य पूरा लिख दें। उसके बाद comma लगाकर दूसरा वाक्य पूरा लिख दें।

Conjunctions : Who, Whom, Whose, Which, When, Where

ये Conjunctions, प्रश्न बनाने हेतु भी प्रयोग में आते हैं एवं दो वाक्यों को संयुक्त करने में भी प्रयुक्त होते हैं। इनका अर्थ प्रश्न करते समय एवं दो वाक्यों को संयुक्त करते समय अलग-अलग होता है।

(1) Who :

Type I –*Look at the following sentences :*

(i) (a) I saw a woman. (b) She wore a red saree.
I saw a woman, who wore a red saree.

(ii) (a) Police arrested a thief. (b) The thief was running.
Police arrested a thief, who was running.

'Who' का Conjunction की तरह जब प्रयोग किया जाता है, तो अर्थ होता है : 'जो' या 'जिसने'

(1) इस तरह के वाक्यों में, पहले वाक्य को पूरा लिखें। उसके बाद, दूसरे वाक्य के subject हेतु 'who' का प्रयोग करके वाक्य को भी पूरा लिख दें।
(2) यहाँ 'who' एक subject की तरह कार्य कर रहा है।

Type II–*Look at the following sentences :*

(i) (a) Sheela secured first position. (b) She belonged to Assam.
Sheela, who belonged to Assam, secured first position.

Or

Sheela, who secured first position, belonged to Assam.

(ii) (a) Ramesh failed again. (b) He did not work hard.
Ramesh, who didn't work hard, failed again.

Or

Ramesh, who failed again, didn't work hard.

(1) इस तरह के वाक्यों को दो प्रकार से 'who' से जोड़ा जा सकता है, प्रथम प्रकार में पहले sentence का subject लिखकर, उसके बाद 'who' लिखें फिर दूसरे sentence के subject को छोड़कर पूरा वाक्य लिख दें। फिर comma लगाकर पहले वाक्य के शेष भाग को लिख दें। यहाँ देखे कि दूसरे वाक्य के subject की जगह हमने 'who' का प्रयोग किया है।

(2) दूसरे तरीके में प्रथम वाक्य का subject लिखकर 'who' लिखें एवं पहले वाक्य का शेष भाग लिख दें, उसके बाद comma लगाकर, दूसरे वाक्य के subject को छोड़कर शेष वाक्य लिख दें।

See more examples :

(i) (a) Ramesh is a good sportsman. (b) He was awarded a prize.
Ramesh, who was awarded a prize, is a good sportsman.

(ii) (a) Sita is a poor girl. (b) She stole my purse.
Sita, who stole my purse, is a poor girl.

(iii) (a) My brother is a banker. (b) He wrote a book.
My brother, who is a banker, wrote a book.

(2) Whom :

Look at the following sentences :

(i) (a) He is the manager. (b) I met him yesterday.
He is the manager whom I met yesterday.

(ii) (a) This is the girl. (b) The teacher punished her today.
This is the girl whom the teacher punished today.

Conjunction के रूप में 'whom' का अर्थ होता है 'जिसे' और 'जिसको'।

(1) 'Whom' एक objective form pronoun है, यह Objective के रूप में वाक्य में प्रयुक्त किया जाता है। अतः वाक्य में जो pronoun, objective form में आया है उसके लिए 'whom' का प्रयोग होगा।

(2) सर्वप्रथम पहला वाक्य लिख दें फिर 'whom' लिखें। 'whom' का प्रयोग उस शब्द के बाद होता है जिसके लिए यह प्रयुक्त हुआ है। जैसे- वाक्य (i) में 'whom' का प्रयोग 'manager' के लिए होता है। अतः 'whom' को manager के बाद लिखना होगा।

(3) इसके बाद दूसरे वाक्य को Pronoun हटाकर लिख दें।

See more examples :

(i) (a) I know the girl. (b) He loves her.
I know the girl whom he loves.

(ii) (a) This is the man. (b) The police arrested him.
This is the man whom the police arrested.

(iii) (a) The clerk has just left out. (b) You want to meet him.
The clerk has just left out whom you want to meet.

(3) Whose :

Look at the following sentences :

(i) (a) I know Suresh. (b) His son passed GATE.
I know Suresh whose son passed GATE.

(ii) (a) This is the girl. (b) Her purse was stolen.
This is the girl whose purse was stolen.

Conjunction के रूप में 'whose' का अर्थ होता है 'जिसका'।

(1) 'Whose' एक Possessive case pronoun है। इसका प्रयोग वाक्य में आये Possessive case pronoun हेतु किया जाता है।
(2) सर्वप्रथम पहला वाक्य लिख दें, फिर 'whose' लिखें एवं उसके बाद दूसरे वाक्य के Possessive case pronoun को छोड़कर, शेष वाक्य को लिख दें।
(3) ध्यान रखें 'whose' का प्रयोग उस शब्द के साथ होगा जिसके लिए वह प्रयुक्त हुआ है। 'whose' के बाद noun अवश्य लगता है।

See more examples :

(i) (a) She is the girl. (b) Her purse was taken by a student.
She is the girl whose purse was taken by a student.

(ii) (a) He is the boy. (b) A student took his umbrella yesterday.
He is the boy whose umbrella a student took yesterday.

(iii) (a) Rani is a good girl. (b) Her father will give her a gift.
Rani, whose father will give her a gift, is a good girl.

(4) Which :

Look at the following sentences :

(i) (a) I gave you a pen. (b) You have lost it.
I gave you a pen which you have lost.

(ii) (a) He lives at Jaipur. (b) Jaipur is a beautiful city.
He lives at Jaipur which is a beautiful city.

'Which' का Conjunction की तरह जब प्रयोग किया जाता है, तो अर्थ होता है: 'जिसे' या 'जो कि'।

(1) 'Which' का प्रयोग निर्जीव वस्तुओं के लिए किया जाता है।
(2) यदि दूसरे वाक्य में It, that या वहीं noun वापस में repeat हुआ हो, तो उसके लिए 'which' का प्रयोग किया जायेगा।
(3) 'Which' का प्रयोग उस शब्द के साथ किया जाता है, जिसके लिए इसका प्रयोग हुआ है। सर्वप्रथम पहला वाक्य लिखें, उसके बाद 'which' लिखें एवं दूसरे वाक्य में आये It, that या repeated noun को छोड़कर शेष वाक्य लिखें।

See more examples :

(i) (a) I had a bat. (b) I gave it to my brother.
I had a bat which I gave to my brother.

(ii) (a) This is the house. (b) I purchased it last year.
This is the house which I purchased last year.

(iii) (a) Ritesh purchased a car. (b) It is very costly.
Ritesh purchased a car which is very costly.

(5) When :

Look at the following sentences :

(i) (a) I was taking bath. (b) He came to my house.
I was taking bath when he came to my house.

(ii) (a) He went to market. (b) She returned from office.
He went to market when she returned from office.

'When' का Conjunction के रूप में अर्थ होता है 'जब'।

'When' का प्रयोग तब किया जाता है, जब एक कार्य पूर्ण हो जाता है।

(1) पहला वाक्य पूरा लिख दें, फिर 'When' लिखकर दूसरा वाक्य लिख दें। यदि किसी noun पुनरावृत्ति (repeat) हुई है तो उसकी जगह he, she, they, it का प्रयोग करें।

See more examples :

(i) (a) My father gifted me a bike. (b) I passed my B.A.
My father gifted me a bike when I passed my B.A.

(ii) (a) He could swim across this river. (b) He was young.
He could swim across this river when he was young.

(iii) (a) The madam rebuked the students. (b) The students made a noise.
The madam rebuked the students when they made a noise.

(6) Where :

Look at the following sentences :

(i) (a) This is the house. (b) I lived here for three years.
This is the house where I lived for three years.

(ii) (a) This is the hospital. (b) She was born here.
This is the hospital where she was born.

'Where' का Conjunction के रूप में अर्थ होता है 'जहाँ'।

जब 'where' से दो वाक्यों को संयुक्त किया जाना होता है तो एक वाक्य में 'स्थान' को व्यक्त करने वाला शब्द (House, Hospital etc.) अवश्य प्रयुक्त होता है। सर्वप्रथम पहला वाक्य लिखें फिर इस स्थान सूचक शब्द के बाद में 'where' लिख दें, फिर दूसरे वाक्य को लिख दें। दूसरे वाक्य में प्रयुक्त शब्द here, there आदि को नहीं लिखें, इन्हें छोड़ दें। वास्तव में इनकी जगह ही 'where' प्रयुक्त होता है।

See more examples :

(i) (a) This is the house. (b) My friend lives here.
This is the house where my friend lives.

(ii) (a) She will go to Shimla. (b) Her parents live.
She will go to Shimla where her parents live.

(iii) (a) This is the hotel 'Taj'. (b) I stayed here last year.
This is the hotel 'Taj' where I stayed last year.

Important Points about Specific Conjunctions

(1) Neither .... nor .... nor .... nor एवं Either .... or .... or .... or : कुछ विद्वानों का मत है कि Neither .... nor .... nor .... nor एवं Either .... or .... or .... or का प्रयोग करना इनके मतानुसार उचित नहीं है। इस सन्दर्भ में Mr. Vallins ने लिखा है कि "The correct correlatives are 'either ..... or'and 'neither ..... nor'." Strictly speaking, we should not add another 'or'or 'nor'since either and neither imply two and two only. लेकिन अन्य विद्वानों; जैसे: Mr T.S. Eliot, Jefferson, Fowler, H Walker के अनुसार Neither ...... nor, Either ..... or के साथ 'nor' एवं 'or' add किए जा सकते हैं।

Look at the following sentences :

(a) *Either from the moralist's point of view, or from the theologian's point of view or from the psychologist's point of view or from that of the political philosopher, or judging by the ordinary standards of likeableness in human beings, Milton is unsatisfactory.* **T.S. Eliot.**

(b) *Neither the brilliancy of Haglitt, nor the harmony of De Quincey, nor the vigour of Macaulay, nor the eloquence of Ruskin, nor the purity of Goldsmith could for a moment be thought capable of expressing the meaning of lamb.* **H. Walker.**

अत: 'Neither ...... nor .... nor .... nor ...' एवं 'Either ...... or .... cr .... or' का नियम सही एवं मान्य है।

(2) No/Not/Never .... or : यदि किसी वाक्य में no/not/never आए या उसके बाद कोई Alternative conjunction लगाना हो तो 'or' का प्रयोग होगा, nor का नहीं।

Look at the following sentences :

(a) I have no chair or stool.
(b) I have never read about her or heard of her.
(c) She does not speak or weep.
(d) He did not say or write anything.

(3) The use of 'That' :

(A) 'That का प्रयोग Direct narration में नहीं किया जाता है। हमेशा Indirect narration में इसका प्रयोग होता है।

(a) He said to me, "That I will go there." *Incorrect*
He told me that he would go there. *Correct*

(B) Indirect narration में 'that' के बाद आने वाले वाक्य का tense, reporting verb यदि past में है तो, Past में ही होगा। वाक्य में आए pronoun भी आवश्यकतानुसार बदले जाते हैं। इस सम्बन्ध में Reported speech के अध्याय में विस्तार से बताया गया है।

(C) Imperative/Optative/Interrogative/Exclamatory वाक्यों में that का प्रयोग Conjunction के रूप में नहीं किया जाता है। इस सम्बन्ध में भी Reported speech के अध्याय में विस्तृत रूप से बताया गया है।

He said that close the door. *Incorrect*
He said that may grant you success. *Incorrect*
He said that how beautiful the girl was. *Incorrect*
He said that where were you going. *Incorrect*

(इस सम्बन्ध में Reported speech के अध्याय को ध्यानपूर्वक पढ़ें।)

(D) कुछ verbs के साथ 'that' का प्रयोग करना आवश्यक है। (that का लोप कर देना गलत माना गया है।) ऐसी verbs हैं : Agree, assert, avert, assume, hold, calculate, conceive, learn, maintain, state, reckon, suggest, understand.

(a) I agree your proposal is very good. *Incorrect*
I agree that your proposal is very good. *Correct*

(b) He asserted he could do that. *Incorrect*
He asserted that he could do that. *Correct*

(c) He suggested we should go there. *Incorrect*
He suggested that we should go there. *Correct*

(E) कुछ verbs जैसे : Believe, hope, suppose, think, presume, afraid of के बाद 'that' को छिपाना, अच्छी अंग्रेजी लिखने हेतु आजकल उचित माना जाने लगा है।

(a) I hope, he is right.
(b) We presume you are innocent.
(c) I suppose you have a good dictionary.
(d) I think he will come.

(F) 'That'v/s 'Whether' : Whether का प्रयोग Choice वाले वाक्यों में किया जाता है। 'Whether' के प्रयोग वाले वाक्यों में 'or not' का प्रयोग, Choice को व्यक्त करता है।

(a) I don't know whether she will go there or not.
(b) He doesn't know whether he will pass or not.

इस तरह के वाक्यों में *whether* की जगह *that* का प्रयोग नहीं किया जा सकता है।

Omitting 'That'

The word **THAT** is used as a Conjunction to connect a subordinate clause to a preceding verb. In this construction that is sometimes called the 'expletive that'. Indeed, the word is often omitted to good effect, but the very fact of easy omission causes some editors to take out the red pen and strike out the conjunction **THAT** wherever it appears. In the following sentences, we can happily omit the 'that' (or keep it, depending on how the sentence sounds to us) :

(a) Isabel knew [that] she was about to be fired.
(b) She definitely felt [that] her fellow employees hadn't supported her.
(c) I hope [that] she doesn't blame me.

Sometimes omitting the **THAT** creates a break in the flow of a sentence, a break that can be adequately bridged with the use of a comma :

(i) The problem is, that production in her department has dropped.
(ii) Remember, that we didn't have these problems before she started working here.

As a general rule, if the sentence feels just as good without the **THAT**, if no ambiguity results from its omission, if the sentence is more efficient or elegant without it, then we can safely omit the that.

Theodore Bernstein lists three conditions in which we should maintain the conjunction THAT :

(A) When a time element intervenes between the verb and the clause : "The boss said yesterday that production in this department was down fifty percent." (Notice the position of 'yesterday'.)

(B) When the verb of the clause is long delayed : "Our annual report revealed that some losses sustained by this department in the third quarter of last year were worse than previously thought." (Notice the distance between the subject 'losses' and its verb, 'were'.)

(C) When a second that can clear up who said or did what : "The CEO said that Isabel's department was slacking off and that production dropped precipitously in the fourth quarter." (Did the CEO say that production dropped or was the drop a result of what he said about Isabel's department? The second that makes the sentence clear.) .... **'Do's, Don'ts and May bes of English Usage' by Theodore Bernstein.**

(D) 'Doubt' एवं 'doubtful' के साथ सकारात्मक (affirmative) वाक्यों में whether का प्रयोग किया जाता है, लेकिन Negative एवं Interrogative वाक्यों में doubt या doubtful के साथ 'that' का प्रयोग किया जा सकता है।

Look at the following sentences :

(a) I doubt whether she will attend the function or not.
(b) It is doubtful whether she will agree or not.
(c) I don't know that she will agree.
(d) Is there any doubt that she will agree?
(e) Is it doubtful that she will agree?

कई बार whether के साथ 'as to' का प्रयोग करके वाक्य बनाए जाते हैं जो कि गलत हैं।

(a) I doubt as to whether she will agree or not. *Incorrect*
I doubt whether she will agree or not. *Correct*
(b) I can't guess as to whether she has gone or not. *Incorrect*
I can't guess whether she has gone or not. *Correct*

(4) **However/But :** However के साथ कभी भी but का प्रयोग नहीं किया जाता है या तो वाक्य में but का प्रयोग होगा या however का।

Read the following sentences :

(a) But his behaviour, however has not changed. *Incorrect*
His behaviour however has not changed. *Correct*

(b) But that, however is not repairable. *Incorrect*
But that is not repairable. *Correct*

(5) Though, although and even though : Though/although के साथ कभी भी but का प्रयोग नहीं किया जाता है या तो yet का प्रयोग किया जाता है या नहीं किया जाता है।

Though, although and even though are used to show a contrast between two clauses :

Our new neighbours are quite nice (this is good) though their two dogs bark all day long. (this isn't good)

We can use though or although with no difference in meaning. But, some differences are :

Though is more common than although in conversation or writing.

Though (but not although) can come at the end of a sentence :

My new bike is really fast. I don't like the colour, though.

Though (but not although) can also be used as an adverb :

I'm not good at reasoning but I can help you with your Geography, though, if you want.

The meaning of though is similar to however, but though is much more common than however in conversation.

Even though can be used to make the contrast between two clauses stronger :

My father got back from work really late, even though he had promised to take mum to the cinema.

(a) Although he is poor, yet he is honest.

(b) Though he is poor, he is honest.

(6) Until/Unless : Until का प्रयोग समय के सन्दर्भ में होता है, जबकि Unless का प्रयोग condition (शर्त) के सन्दर्भ में।

Read the following sentences :

(a) I will stay here until you return.
(b) He will wait until the train arrives.
(c) He can't succeed unless he works hard.
(d) You cannot achieve your goal unless you try for that.

वाक्य (a) एवं (b) में Unless का प्रयोग एवं वाक्य (c) एवं (d) में Until का प्रयोग गलत होगा।

(7) When and while : When का अर्थ होता है 'जब'। While का अर्थ होता है 'जबकि'। When का प्रयोग उस स्थिति में किया जाता है जब एक कार्य पूर्ण हो जाता है।

While का प्रयोग उस स्थिति में किया जाता है जब दो कार्य साथ-साथ हो रहे होते हैं। छात्रों को इस अन्तर को अच्छी तरह समझना चाहिए। प्राय: छात्र When/While का गलत प्रयोग करते हैं।

Look at the following sentences :

(a) When he came here, she was going to market.
(b) I saw a monkey, when I woke up.
(c) He was reading while I was playing.
(d) She was watching T.V. while I was cooking.

(8) As if/As though : As if एवं As though का अर्थ होता है, suppose अर्थात् 'मान लीजिए/मानो'। इनका प्रयोग करते समय इस बिन्दु का ध्यान रखें कि इनके बाद Past conditional का ही प्रयोग होगा, Present form का नहीं। Would/could/did/ was/were/had gone/knew का प्रयोग हो सकता है, लेकिन will/can/do/does/is/have gone/know का प्रयोग नहीं हो सकता।

Look at the following sentences :

(a) He behaves as if he were a king. (b) She orders as though she were the boss.

(c) They asked us for arranging tea and breakfast as if they were our invitees.

(9) Because, as and since : 'Because', 'As' and 'Since' are used to answer the question : 'Why?'

(i) They join two clauses in the same sentence :

(a) I lost my job because I was often late.

(b) Ram resigned because he wanted to spend more time with his family.

(ii) 'Because', 'As' and 'Since' show the relationship between the two clauses

(a) Why did you resign from such a well-paid job, Ram ?

(b) Because I wanted to spend more time with my family.

'Because' is more common than 'As' and 'Since' when the 'reason' is the most important thing. The because-clause usually placed after the main clause :

I went to **Chennai** for a holiday last October because I knew it would be warm and sunny every day I was there.

'As' and 'Since ' are used when the reason is already well-known and/or less important. The 'As' or 'Since' clause often comes at the beginning of the sentence and is separated from the main clause by a comma :

(a) As my family had finished dinner when I got home, I went to this really good beer bar. (I'm telling you about the beer bar. It's not so important 'why' I went there.)

(b) Since it's your birthday, I'll make you breakfast in bed. (I'm going to make you breakfast) (I know, and you know, it's your birthday.)

Since I have no money, I can't go to the movie.

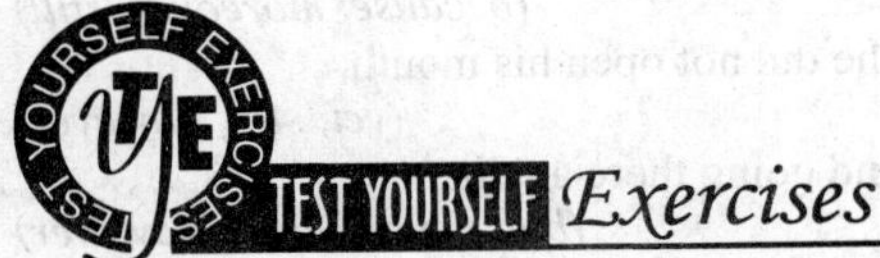

Exercises

01

Join the following pairs of sentences using the connectors given in brackets :

(1) My father is ill. My wife is ill. *(both............ and)*

(2) The teacher was not in the class. The monitor was not in the class. *(neither .... nor)*

(3) He is poor. He is honest. *(though .... yet)*

(4) The book may be in the bag. It may be in the cupboard. *(either .... or)*

(5) There was a violent storm. Many trees were uprooted. *(such .... that)*

(6) The doctor reached. The patient died. *(hardly .... when)*

(7) He is strong. He is brave. *(not only .... but also)*

(8) Do not be a borrower. Do not be a lender. *(neither .... nor)*

(9) It was very dark. We could see nothing. *(so .... that)*

(10) The thief saw the policeman. He ran away at once. *(no sooner .... than)*

02

***Combine each pair of sentences below into one sentence choosing the right conjunction from the following list** since, besides, lest, never, the, less, before, after, otherwise :*

(1) Walk carefully.You may fall.
(2) It's raining.We won't play the match today.
(3) Don't write.The bell has gone.
(4) He was busy. He attended to me.
(5) He is a rich man. He is an M.P.

03

Fill in the blanks by choosing the correct connectors given in brackets :

(1) A student will fail .... he does not work hard. *(because, if, until, though, unless)*
(2) He was late .... it was raining heavily. *(while, after, so, that, when, because)*
(3) .... you have any doubt, please ask me. *(In case, Because, Unless, Until, Though)*
(4) She is more intelligent .... her sister. *(as, than, before, because, that)*
(5) She has changed a lot .... I saw her last. *(when, before, while, as, since)*
(6) She could not get the prize, ... she tried hard for it. *(yet, though, but, when, and)*
(7) We must leave now .... it is getting dark. *(as long as, as soon as, when, since)*
(8) I was taking a bath .... somebody rang the bell. *(as, while, when, as soon as, than)*
(9) He failed in the examination; ...., he didn't lose heart. *(moreover, then, while, nevertheless, until)*
(10) She tried her best; ...., she couldn't succeed. *(besides, in case, however, instead, as long as)*

04

Fill in the blanks with suitable connectors chosen from the ones given in brackets :

(1) We want to respect others feelings................, we should respect the feelings of others. *(nevertheless, similarly, on the other hand)*
(2) We lost the key.We had .... to break the lock open. *(still, for, therefore)*
(3) His parents were transferred to Agra .... he was five years old. *(when, since, while)*
(4) A mechanic was sent for .... our car broke down. *(since, as soon as, because)*
(5) The rent being very high he will not take that house; .... it is very far away from his office. *(because, moreover, still)*
(6) The police asked the suspect question after question, ... he did not open his mouth. *(yet, still, however)*
(7) I have been to the hanging garden four times, ... I won't mind going there again. *(but, nevertheless, however)*
(8) .... much I tried, I could not help him. *(Though, However, As)*
(9) My uncle left for Mexico .... I was six years old. *(when, since, while)*
(10) She was late .... it was raining continuously. *(after, because, while)*

05

Correct the following sentences :

(1) I could neither contact Lila nor Sarla.
(2) Neither he plays nor reads.
(3) She both accused me and my friend Shyam.
(4) Ram not only built a temple but also a mosque.
(5) He has visited both to New York and Mexico.
(6) English is not only difficult to speak but also to write.
(7) She is as much noted for her beauty as for her wisdom.
(8) I have both visited America and Russia.
(9) He neither knows me nor my wife.
(10) Ramesh neither went to Jaipur nor Delhi.

06

Correct the following sentences :

(1) No sooner had he reached the station when the train arrived.
(2) Though he is poor but he is trustworthy.
(3) Hardly had she left the hospital, than it began to rain.
(4) He had neither a car or a scooter.
(5) There was much disturbance both in Jammu as well as in Pahalgaon.
(6) One cannot be both present at New Delhi as well as at Jaipur.
(7) He cannot either read nor write English.
(8) She cannot run nor walk.
(9) He has not any book nor any copy.
(10) I have never seen her nor heard of her.

07

Correct the following sentences :

(1) I do not know that when she will go.
(2) I cannot say that where he is working now-a-days.
(3) I understand she will attend the function.
(4) I hope that you are well now.
(5) I can assert it is right.
(6) I cannot explain that why I like her so much.
(7) I asked my assistant that bring a chair and my mobile.
(8) I agree it is a good oportunity to invest the money.
(9) As she started late, she will miss the train.
(10) Since Ram is a poor fellow, he couldn't buy a new dress.
(11) The reason is because he is not well.

08

Correct the following sentences :

(1) It was generally doubted that India would permit the use of her soil.
(2) It is not doubtful whether she will attend the party.
(3) Is there any doubt whether she will come ?
(4) Keep your body fit like I do.
(5) You are as dear to me as her.
(6) Until he works hard, he can't pass.
(7) Take an umbrella in case it may rain.
(8) You wait here unless the train arrives.
(9) You will succeed, if you will work hard.
(10) If I had wings, I will fly to London.
(11) If I won a lottery, I will buy a big house
(12) If he had worked hard, he would pass.

09

Correct the following sentences :

(1) It is a year since I have met her.
(2) It is a month since she has left for U.S.A.
(3) He speaks as if he was the master.
(4) Ram orders as though he would be a millionaire.
(5) Five years have passed since I had seen her.
(6) A year passed since his wife died.
(7) I was playing when he was watching T.V.
(8) I will go when he will come.
(9) I went there while he awoke.
(10) I will meet you before I shall leave for home.

Spotting Errors (Conjunctions)

10

***Read each sentence to find out whether there is an error in any part* :**

(1) She was not (a)/ so well versed in English (b)/ that they (c)/ had expected. (d)

(2) He not only comes (a)/ here for having lunch (b)/ but also for having a glimpse of (c)/ the beautiful sales girls. (d)

(3) I cannot permit you (a)/ to leave the class (b)/ unless the teacher comes (c)/ and instructs me in the matter. (d)

(4) The patient would not (a)/ have died (b)/ when the doctor had (c)/ come in time. (d)

(5) Three years have passed (a)/ that I returned from (b)/ USA and settled here. (c)

(6) The captain asked (a)/ the players to go (b)/ to market and buy some fruits (c)/ as apples, oranges, bananas etc. (d)

(7) Both the rich (a)/ along with the poor (b)/ are responsible for a great many vices (c)/ with which our country is inflicted. (d)

(8) Since the festival of Diwali is approaching (a)/ so my son has bought (b)/ many fireworks (c)/ as rockets, crackers etc. (d)

(9) The thief had (a)/ hardly put the cash (b)/ in his pocket (c)/ than the owner woke up. (d)

(10) No sooner did we (a)/ find out a solution (b)/ to the problem (c)/ when another problem cropped up. (d)

11.

***Read each sentence to find out whether there is an error in any part* :**

(1) She has lots of money (a)/ and she dare not (b)/ purchase a new car. (c)

(2) She is not only (a)/ sympathetic to the rich patients (b)/ but also to the poor ones. (c)

(3) Because she is intelligent (a)/ therefore she secures highest marks (b)/ in her class. (c)

(4) It was almost five months ago (a)/ since she wrote a letter (b)/ to me (c)/ to remind me of my promise. (d)

(5) The inspector was doubtful (a)/ that the man who had been run over (b)/ by the truck had (c)/ lain there for more than a day. (d)

(6) He instructed me (a)/ that I should do (b)/ all the work as quickly (c)/ like him. (d)

(7) Seldom or (a)/ ever have I sent (b)/ a beggar away without (c)/ giving him something. (d)

(8) Seldom or ever (a)/ have I tried my (b)/ best to help my friends (c)/ who are in need. (d)

(9) The teacher advised (a)/ the students to (b)/ go through the notes as many times as possible (c)/ lest they would fail. (d)

(10) He asked me (a)/ that why I was not appearing (b)/in the examination. (c)

(11) Most of the founding fathers (a)/ of our constitution are (b)/ so reverend as Ambedkar (c)/ if not more. (d)

(12) I don't know (a)/ if any of the members (b)/ of the society is conspiring (c)/ against the chairman or not. (d)

(13) This is the same dog (a)/ which bit her (b)/ while she was going (c)/ to the hospital. (d)

(14) This is not (a)/ such a big problem (b)/ which cannot be solved (c)/ with some efforts. (d)

(15) As he is (a)/ a perfectionist (b)/ so he always insists (c)/ on regular practice. (d)

Solution TYE 01

(1) Both my father and my wife are ill.
(2) Neither the teacher nor the monitor was in the class.
(3) Though he is poor, yet he is honest.
(4) The book may be either in the bag or in the cupboard.
(5) There was such a violent storm that many trees were uprooted.
(6) The doctor had hardly reached when the patient died.
(7) He is not only strong but also brave.
(8) Neither be a borrower nor be a lender.
(9) It was so dark that we could see nothing.
(10) No sooner did the policeman see the thief than he ran away.

Solution TYE 02

(1) Walk carefully lest you should fall.
(2) Since it's raining,we won't play the match today.
(3) Don't write after the bell has gone.
(4) He was busy, nevertheless, he attended to me.
(5) He is a rich man, besides, he is an M.P.

Solution TYE 03

(1) if, (2) because, (3) In case, (4) than, (5) since,
(6) though, (7) since, (8) when, (9) nevertheless, (10) however.

Solution TYE 04

(1) similarly, (2) therefore, (3) when, (4) because, (5) moreover,
(6) still, (7) but, (8) However, (9) when, (10) because.

Solution TYE 05

(1) I could contact neither Lila nor Sarla.
(2) He neither plays nor reads.
(3) She accused both me and my friend Shyam.
(4) Ram built not only a temple but also a mosque.
(5) He has visited both to New York and to Mexico.

Or

He has visited to both New York and Mexico.

(6) English is difficult not only to speak but also to write.
(7) She is noted as much for her beauty as for her wisdom.
(8) I have visited both America and Russia.
(9) He knows neither me nor my wife.
(10) Ramesh went neither to Jaipur nor to Delhi.

Solution TYE 06

(1) No sooner had he reached the station than the train arrived.
(2) Though he is poor yet he is trustwortly.
(3) Hardly had she left the hospital, when it began to rain.
(4) He had neither a car nor a scooter.
(5) There was much disturbance both in Jammu and in Pahalgaon.
(6) One cannot be present both at New Delhi and at Jaipur.
(7) He cannot either read or write English.
(8) She cannot run or walk.
(9) He has not any book or copy.
(10) I have never seen her or heard of her.

Solution TYE 07

(1) I do not know when she will go.
(2) I cannot say where he is working now-a-days.
(3) I understand that she will attend the function.
(4) I hope you are well now.
(5) I can assert that it is right.
(6) I cannot explain why I like her so much.
(7) I asked my assistant to bring a chair and my mobile.
(8) I agree that it is a good oportunity to invest the money.
(9) As she started late, she missed the train.
(10) Since Ram is a poor fellow he can't buy a new dress.
(11) The reason is that he is not well.

Solution TYE 08

(1) It was generally doubted whether India would permit the use of her soil.
(2) It is not doubtful that she will attend the party.
(3) Is there any doubt that she will come ?
(4) Keep your body fit like me . *Or* Keep your body fit as I do.
(5) You are as dear to me as she.
(6) Unless he works hard, he can't pass.
(7) Take an umbrella in case it rains.
(8) You wait here until the train arrives.
(9) You will succeed, if you work hard.
(10) If I had wings, I would fly to London.
(11) If I won a lottery, I would buy a big house.
(12) If he had worked hard, he would have passed.

Solution TYE 09

(1) It is a year since I met her.
(2) It is a month since she left for U.S.A.
(3) He speaks as if he were the master.
(4) Ram orders as though he were a millionaire.
(5) Five years have passed since I saw her.
(6) A year has passed since his wife died.
(7) I was playing while he was watching TV.
(8) I will go when he comes.
(9) I went there when he awoke.
(10) I will meet you before I leave for home.

Solution TYE 10

(1) (c) that की जगह as का प्रयोग होगा, क्योंकि यहाँ वाक्य का structure, so .... as का है।

(2) (a) not only का प्रयोग here not only for having lunch के साथ होगा।
Not only ...... but also से दो subjects/objects/ verbs/gerunds को जोड़ा जाता है। जैसे:
(a) Not only Hari but also Krishna is playing. (Subject)
(b) I have invited not only Hari but also Krishna. (Object)
(c) He not only reads but also plays. (Verbs)
(d) She likes not only swimming but also singing. (Gerunds)

(3) (c) Unless की जगह until का प्रयोग होगा। समय के सन्दर्भ में until का तथा condition के सन्दर्भ में unless का प्रयोग किया जाता है।

(4) (c) when की जगह if का प्रयोग करें। Conditional sentence का structure निम्नवत होता है
If he had come to me, I would have helped him.

(5) (b) that की जगह since का प्रयोग होगा। In perfect tense 'since' is used for point of time and 'for' is used for period of time.

(6) (d) as की जगह like का प्रयोग होगा।
as का प्रयोग nominative के साथ होता है, जबकि like का प्रयोग objective के साथ होता है। जैसे :
(a) He supports a man like me.
(b) He supports a man as I (support).

(7) (b) along with the की जगह 'and' का प्रयोग होगा। Both के साथ and conjunction आता है।

(8) (d) as की जगह like का प्रयोग होगा। as का प्रयोग Nominative case के साथ होता है और like का प्रयोग Objective case के साथ।

(9) (d) than की जगह when का प्रयोग होगा। hardly के साथ conjunction when आता है।

(10) (d) when की जगह than का प्रयोग होगा।
No sooner के साथ than तथा Hardly, scarcely के साथ when का प्रयोग होता है।

Solution TYE 11

(1) (b) and की जगह but का प्रयोग होगा। वाक्य में contrast है।

(2) (a) not only का प्रयोग to the rich से पहले होगा। वाक्य में but also का प्रयोग to the poor के पहले हुआ है अत: वाक्य में balance बनाने हेतु not only का प्रयोग to the rich के पहले करना होगा।

(3) (b) therefore का प्रयोग अनुचित है। because, as, since, for आदि conjunctions के साथ so/therefore आदि का प्रयोग नहीं किया जाता है।

(4) (b) since की जगह that का प्रयोग होगा। साधारणतया since, for का प्रयोग Perfect tense में किया जाता है। वैसे भी ago के बाद that का प्रयोग होता है। The sentence is of Past indefinite.

(5) (b) that की जगह whether का प्रयोग होगा।

(6) (d) like him की जगह as he होगा।
यहाँ comparison दो nominative, I एवं he मे है। अत: as he लिखना होगा।

(7) (b) ever की जगह never का प्रयोग होगा। वाक्य का अर्थ कभी नहीं या अधिकांशतया नहीं है।

(8) (a) or की जगह if का प्रयोग होगा। seldom के साथ या तो seldom if ever या seldom or never आता है। वाक्य के सन्दर्भ के अनुसार इनका प्रयोग किया जाता है।

(9) (d) would की जगह should का प्रयोग होगा। lest के साथ हमेशा should का प्रयोग होगा।

(10) (b) that को हटा दें। Indirect narration में 'wh' questions में कोई conjunction नहीं लगता है।

(11) (c) so की जगह as का प्रयोग होगा। so .... as का प्रयोग negative वाक्यों में होता है। जबकि as .... as का प्रयोग affirmative वाक्यों में जैसे :
(a) Rahim is not so intelligent as Shyam.
(b) Rahim is as intelligent as Shyam.

(12) (b) if की जगह whether का प्रयोग होगा। वाक्य की संरचना whether . . . or पर आधारित है।

(13) (b) which की जगह that का प्रयोग होगा। verb स्पष्ट होती है तो same के साथ that का प्रयोग किया जाता है। जैसे :
This is the same chair that was missing.
जब verb स्पष्ट नहीं होती तो same .... as का प्रयोग सामान्यत: किया जाता है। जैसे :
This is the same chair as mine.

(14) (c) which की जगह as का प्रयोग होगा। ध्यान रखें : Such is followed by as or that.
See the following examples :
(a) Such + noun + as
He is not such a person as I thought .
(b) Such + that
His behaviour was such that I felt hurt.
(c) Such + as + infinitive
Her ailment is not such as to cause worries.

(15) (c) so का प्रयोग नहीं होगा।
As, because, for के साथ so, therefore का प्रयोग नहीं होता है।

CHAPTER

19

The Interjections (!)

Definition : The interjection is always a spoken word that expresses an emotion.

Or

An interjection is a word, used to express some sudden feeling of mind.

अर्थात् Interjection एक ऐसा शब्द है जो हृदय में उठने वाली आकस्मिक भावना, उद्गार को प्रकट करता है। Interjection के अन्त में Sign of exclamation चिन्ह (!) लगाया जाता है।

The word 'interjection' literally means 'something thrown in between' from the Latin inter ('between') and jacer ('throw').

An Interjection, sometimes called a filled pause, is a part of speech that usually has no grammatical connection to the rest of the sentence and simply expresses emotion on the part of the speaker, although most interjections have clear definitions.

Interjection का सम्बन्ध वाक्य की संरचना की grammar इत्यादि से नहीं होता है।

Interjections can be phrases or even sentences as well as words :

As I entered the room—Oh, my God! What I saw! — he was still standing there.

Read the following sentences:

(i) Hurrah ! Our team has won.

(ii) Alas ! He lost his son.

(iii) Bravo ! Well played my boys.

(iv) Ah ! She has gone.

(v) Fie ! She did such thing.

(vi) Oh ! You are here.

(vii) What ! She failed?

(viii) Shh ! Don't make a noise.

(ix) Hush ! Don't talk here.

(x) Hello ! How do you do ?

उपरोक्त सभी वाक्यों में जिस शब्द के साथ चिन्ह (!) लगा है वह शब्द Interjection ही है। उस चिन्ह (!) को Mark of Exclamation कहा जाता है। 'Hello' and 'Goodbye' are also interjections, as are exclamations like Cheers! and Hurray! In fact, very often they are characterized by exclamation marks depending on the stress of the attitude or the force of the emotion they are expressing. 'Well' can also be used as an interjection, for example when put at the beginning of a sentence.

हृदय की आकस्मिक भावनाओं को निम्न Interjections से व्यक्त किया जा सकता है :

(1) Joy (खुशी)—Hurrah, Ha ! Ha !

(2) Sorrow (दु:ख)—Alas !, Ah !, Ha !

(3) Surprise (आश्चर्य)—Oh !, What !

(4) Contempt (घृणा)— Fie !, Bosh!, Shame ! Shame !

(5) Greetings (बधाई)—Bravo !, Well done !

(6) Calling (सम्बोधन)—Hello !, Hey !

(7) Attention (ध्यान)—Listen !, Lo !, Hush !, Shh !, Behold !

उक्त Interjections का प्रयोग भावनाओं के अनुसार किया जाता है।

Interjections are uninflected function words that express the attitude or emotion of the speaker. They are used when the speaker encounters events that cause these emotions — unexpectedly, painfully, surprisingly or in many other sudden ways.

CHAPTER

20

TRANSFORMATION OF SENTENCES

Transformation से आशय है एक Grammatical form से वाक्यों को दूसरी Grammatical form में इस प्रकार बदलना कि उनके अर्थ में कोई परिवर्तन न हो।

'Change' एवं 'Transformation' : Change में वाक्य का अर्थ परिवर्तित हो जाता है, जबकि Transformation में अर्थ समान रहता है।

Ways of Transformation

I. Interchanging degree of Adjective :

एक वाक्य में Positive/Comparative के Adjective को Superlative degree में बदलने पर भी वाक्य के अर्थ में कोई परिवर्तन नहीं आए, इसे निम्न प्रकार से किया जा सकता है :

Degrees : Adjective की निम्नलिखित तीन श्रेणियाँ (Degrees) होती हैं :

(1) Positive degree : यह अपने मूल रूप में रहती है, साधारण कथन में प्रयुक्त होती है।

(2) Comparative degree : यह तुलना हेतु प्रयुक्त होती है। Comparative degree के पश्चात् साधारणतया 'than' का प्रयोग किया जाता है। कुछ Comparative degree; जैसे : Junior, senior; इत्यादि; के साथ to का प्रयोग होता है।

(3) Superlative degree : यह व्यक्ति/वस्तु की सर्वोच्चता व्यक्त करने हेतु प्रयोग की जाती है। जब किसी वस्तु या व्यक्ति को अन्य की तुलना में सर्वश्रेष्ठ बताना होता है, तो Superlative degree का प्रयोग किया जाता है।

(A) Conversion of Positive into Comparative

वाक्य में Positive degree leerve प्रकार से प्रयोग की जा सकती है।

Type I : As ...... as, Type II : So ...... as, Type III : No other .... as ...... as ...... :

Type I – As .... as :

Read the following sentences :

(a) Hira is as tall as Ram. — Ram is not taller than Hira.

(b) Shalu is as intelligent as Ram. — Ram is not more intelligent than Shalu.

(1) As...... as का अर्थ 'समानता' से होता है। Hira is as tall as Ram, इसका अर्थ हुआ कि हीरा, राम के समान लम्बा है। इसको जब Comparative degree में लिखेंगे तो हमें लिखना होगा, राम, हीरा से ज्यादा लम्बा नहीं है अर्थात् Ram is not taller than Hira. (अर्थात् अब वाक्य Negative बनेगा।)

(2) सबसे पहले दोनों subjects की जगह को बदल दें अर्थात् पहले वाले subject को अन्त में रखें एवं दूसरे वाले subject को वाक्य के प्रारम्भ में लिखें।

(3) अब वाक्य में आए helping verb + not + comparative degree + than को लिख दें। इसके बाद subject हम पहले ही लिख चुके हैं।

See more examples :

(i) She is as beautiful as her sister. — Her sister is not more beautiful than she.
(ii) Ramesh is as wise as his father. — His father is not wiser than Ramesh.
(iii) Savita is as religious as her mother. — Her mother is not more religious than Savita.

Type II So .... as : So .... as वाले वाक्य में negative (not) जुड़ा रहता है, अत: transformation के बाद Affirmative वाक्य बनाता है। *Look at the following sentences :*

(a) Ram is not so strong as Shyam. — Shyam is stronger than Ram.
(b) Sita is not so beautiful as Rani. — Rani is more beautiful than Sita.

(1) Not so........ as का प्रयोग 'उतना नहीं' के सन्दर्भ में किया जाता है।
Ram is not so strong as Shyam इसका अर्थ है कि राम, श्याम जितना बलवान नहीं है। इसको Comparative में बदलने के लिए हमें लिखना होगा: श्याम, राम से ज्यादा बलवान है। अर्थात् Shyam is stronger than Ram.

(2) दोनों subjects का परस्पर स्थान बदल दें। उसके बाद helping verb + comparative degree + than लिख दें। इसके बाद subject आएगा जिसके बारे में हम पहले ही बता चुके हैं।

See more examples :

(i) She is not so intelligent as her brother. — Her brother is more intelligent than she.
(ii) Raju is not so wise as Rahim. — Rahim is wiser than Raju.
(iii) Shanu is not so cruel as his friend Chhota. — His friend Chhota is more cruel than Shanu.

Type III—No other .... as .... as :

Look at the following sentences :

(a) No other city in Rajasthan is as beautiful as Jaipur.
Jaipur is more beautiful than any other city in Rajasthan.
(b) No other student in college is as strong as Rahim.
Rahim is stronger than any other student in college.

(1) No other...... as......as का प्रयोग 'अन्य कोई उतना नहीं' के अर्थ में किया जाता है।
No other city in Rajasthan is as beautiful as Jaipur.
इसका अर्थ हुआ कि राजस्थान में अन्य कोई शहर उतना सुन्दर नहीं है जितना कि जयपुर है। जब इसे Comparative में बदलेंगे तो हमें लिखना होगा—जयपुर राजस्थान में अन्य शहरों से अधिक सुन्दर है। अर्थात्
Jaipur is more beautiful than any other city in Rajasthan.

(2) वाक्य के अन्त में आए subject से वाक्य प्रारम्भ करें। उसके बाद helping verb + comparative degree + than + any other लिखें।

(3) उसके बाद No other के बाद वाला वाक्यांश लिख देखें।

See more examples :

(i) No other book in the market is as good as this.
This is better than any other book in the market.
(ii) No other girl in the college is as beautiful as Sita.
Sita is more beautiful than any other girl in the college.
(iii) No other teacher in the school is as dedicated as Mr. Sharma.
Mr. Sharma is more dedicated than any other teacher in the school.

(B) Interchange of Positive, Comparative *and* Superlative :

Positive degree वाले वाक्य को Comparative degree में बदलना हम सीख चुके हैं। अब हम देखेंगे Positive degree के वाक्यों को Superlative degree का प्रयोग करके एवं Superlative degree के वाक्यों को Positive एवं Comparative degree के वाक्यों में किस तरह Transform किया जाए।

Superlative degree के वाक्य मोहन हमारे कॉलेज का सर्वश्रेष्ठ छात्र है अर्थात्
Mohan is the best student in our college.
इसे हम निम्न प्रकार से भी लिख सकते हैं :
मोहन हमारे कॉलेज के अन्य सभी छात्रों से अच्छा है।
Mohan is better than any other student in our colllege. अर्थात्
Comparative degree (better) में हम इसे इस प्रकार से भी लिख सकते हैं :
हमारे कॉलेज का अन्य कोई छात्र, मोहन जितना अच्छा नहीं है अर्थात्
No other student of our college is as good as Mohan. यह positive degree का वाक्य है।
उपर्युक्त वाक्यों का आशय समान है।
See more examples:

(i)	*This is the most beautiful building in our town.*	*Superlative*
	This is the more beautiful than any other building in our town.	*Comparative*
	No other building in our town is so beautiful as this.	*Positive*
(ii)	*Ramesh is the strongest man in the village.*	*Superlative*
	Ramesh is stronger than any other man in the village.	*Comparative*
	No other man in the village is so strong as Ramesh.	*Positive*
(iii)	*Kolkata is the largest city in India.*	*Superlative*
	Kolkata is larger than any other city in India.	*Comparative*
	No other city in India is as large as Kolkata.	*Positive*

Superlative को Comparative में बदलने के लिए than any other का प्रयोग किया जाता है एवं Positive में बदलने के लिए No other + noun +.......as,.........as, or No other + noun +......so.....as का प्रयोग किया जाता है।

कुछ वाक्यों का Structure निम्न प्रकार का होता है। इनमें One of the + Superlative का प्रयोग किया जाता है। इस प्रकार के वाक्यों को Comparative में बदलने हेतु 'most other' का प्रयोग किया जाता है तथा Positive में बदलने हेतु Very few other का प्रयोग निम्न प्रकार से किया जाता है :

(a)	Kalidas was one of the greatest poets.	*Superlative*
	Kalidas was greater than most other poets.	*Comparative*
	Very few other poets were as great as Kalidas.	*Positive*
(b)	Mumbai is one of the most beautiful cities in India.	*Superlative*
	Mumbai is more beautiful than most other cities in India.	*Comparative*
	Very few other cities in India are as beautiful as Mumbai.	*Positive*

Removal of 'Too'

'Too' का प्रयोग वाक्यों में निम्न छह प्रकार से किया जाता है

(1) He is too weak to run. वह इतना अधिक कमजोर है कि दौड़ नहीं सकता है।
(2) The weather is too cold to go out at this time.
मौसम इतना अधिक ठण्डा है कि इस समय बाहर नहीं जाया जा सकता है।
(3) He is too lazy for a sportsman. वह इतना अधिक आलसी है कि एक खिलाड़ी नहीं हो सकता है।
(4) The milk is too hot. दूध आवश्यकता से अधिक गर्न है।

(5) He is too strong for me.
वह इतना अधिक ताकतवर है कि मैं उसकी बराबरी नहीं कर सकता हूँ। (मैं उसके मुकाबले में कुछ नहीं हूँ।)

(6) He is too kind hearted not to forgive me.
वह इतना अधिक दयालु है कि मुझे माफ कर सकता है।

'Too' का अर्थ, excess 'उचित से अधिक' होता है। 'Too' के साथ जब 'to' का प्रयोग किया जाता है, तो यह एक negativity व्यक्त करता है। ऐसे वाक्यों से 'Too' को हटाकर अग्र प्रकार Transform किया जा सकता है :

See the following examples :

Type I :

(a) He is	too	weak	to run.
He is	so	weak	that he cannot run.
(b) She is	too	old	to climb up the tree.
She is	so	old	that she cannot climb up the tree.
(c) He was	too	tired	to do anything.
He was	so	tired	that he could not do anything.

(1) 'Too' की जगह 'so' का प्रयोग करें एवं to + ... की जगह that + subject + cannot + ... का प्रयोग करें।
(2) यदि वाक्य Past tense में है तो cannot की जगह couldnot का प्रयोग होगा।
See more examples:
(1) He is too weak to play cricket. — *He is so weak that he cannot play cricket.*
(2) Ram was too old to lift that weight. — *Ram was so old that he couldn't lift that weight.*

Type II :

Read the following examples

(a) The mountain is	too	high	to climb it up.
The mountain is	so	high	that one cannot climb it up.
(b) The wall is	too	hot	to touch.
The wall is	so	hot	that one cannot touch it.
(c) The scene was	too	pathetic	to see.
The scene was	so	pathetic	that one couldn't see that.

इस तरह के वाक्यों में subject स्पष्ट नहीं होता है, अत: one को subject बनाकर उसका प्रयोग किया जाता है।

See more examples :

(d) This item is too costly to purchase. — This item is so costly that one cannot purchase it.
(e) The road is too slippery to walk. — The road is so slippery that one cannot walk on it.

Type III :

Read the following examples :

(a) He is	too	slow	for a racer.
He is	so	slow	that he cannot be a racer.
(b) He is	too	weak	for a wrestler.
He is	so	weak	that he cannot be a wrestler.
(c) She was	too	dull	for a wrangler.
She was	so	dull	that she could not be a wrangler.

इस तरह के वाक्यों में for a...... के लिए that + subject + cannot + be + ... का प्रयोग किया जाता है। यदि वाक्य Past tense में हो तो cannot की जगह could not का प्रयोग किया जाएगा।

Type IV :

Read the following examples :

(a) The tea is too cold. The tea is colder than it should be.
The tea is colder than it is proper.

(b) He is too clever. He is cleverer than he should be.
He is cleverer than it is proper.

(c) He is too lazy. He is lazier than he should be.
He is lazier than it is proper.

इस तरह के वाक्य जिनमें केवल 'too' का ही प्रयोग होता है, इनमे 'too' का अर्थ 'उचित से अधिक' या 'जितना होना चाहिए, उससे अधिक' होता है। इसमें Adjective की Comparative degree लगाकर than he should be or that it is proper का प्रयोग किया जाता है।

Type V :

Read the following examples :

(a) He is too intelligent for me. He is so intelligent that I am no match for him.
(b) He is too old for the task. He is so old that he is not fit for the task.
(c) The work is too large for me. The work is so large that I cannot handle it.
(d) His position is too bad for solution. His position is so bad that it has no solution.
(e) My heart is too full for words.
My heart is so full that I cannot express it in words.

इस तरह के वाक्यों मे too की जगह so का प्रयोग किया जाता है एवं for ...... को जगह वाक्य के सारांश के अनुसार that it or that I cannot का प्रयोग किया जाता है।

Type VI :

Read the following examples :

(a) He was too intelligent, not to find solution. He was so intelligent that he could find solution.
(b) He is too clever not to understand it. He is so clever that he can understand it.
(c) The hotel is too large not to accommodate all of you.
The hotel is so large that it can accommodate all of you.
(d) She is too generous not to help the poor.
She is so generous that she can help the poor.
(e) His personality is too powerful not to impress every body.
His personality is so powerful that it impresses every body or that it can impress every body.

इस तरह के वाक्यों में 'not to' का प्रयोग होता है तथा transformation के बाद cannot की जगह can या Simple future का प्रयोग किया जाता है। यदि वाक्य Past में हो तो could not का प्रयोग किया जाएगा।

II. Interchange of Affirmative *and* Negative Sentences :

Affirmative वाक्य, एक सकारात्मक statement की तरह होते हैं, जिनमें किसी negative शब्द; जैसे : not, hardly, without, neither, none, no इत्यादि का प्रयोग नहीं होता है।

Affirmative sentence को Negative sentence में transform करते समय यह ध्यान रखना है कि negative वाक्य में प्रयुक्त negative शब्द हटाया जाए तथा वाक्य का सारांश/अर्थ समान रहे।

इस तरह का transformation निम्न प्रकार से किया जाता है :

(1) Using Antonyms : वाक्य में आए शब्दों के Antonyms (विपरीतार्थक शब्द) का प्रयोग करके निम्न प्रकार से Affirmative sentence को Negative sentence में तथा Negative sentence को Affirmative sentence में बदला जा सकता है :

Affirmative	Negative
(a) He is a rich man.	He is not a poor man.
(b) I am innocent.	I am not guilty.
(c) The boss is always right.	The boss is never wrong.
(d) Man is mortal.	Man is not immortal.
(e) This knife is sharp.	This knife is not blunt.
(f) Ram dislikes you.	Ram does not like you.

Negative	Affirmative
(a) He is not an honest person.	He is a dishonest person.
(b) You do not trust him.	You distrust him.
(c) He is not a wise fellow.	He is a foolish fellow.
(d) His habits are not good.	His habits are bad.
(e) She is not a dull girl.	She is an intelligent girl.
(f) You should not deny it.	You should accept it.

(2) Using double negatives : वाक्यों में Negative अर्थ रखने वाले दो शब्दों का प्रयोग करके भी Affirmative को Negative एवं Negative को Affirmative में Transform किया जाता है। जैसे :

Affirmative	Negative
(a) I love her.	I am not without love for her.
(b) I have a car.	I am not without a car.
(c) Every rose has thorns.	There is no rose without thorns.
(d) She is wise.	She is not without wisdom.

Negative	Affirmative
(a) There is no smoke without fire.	Where there is fire there is smoke.
(b) I am not without money.	I have money.
(c) He left no plan untried.	He tried every plan.
(d) No gains without pains.	For gains one has to take pains.

(3) 'To fail' का प्रयोग करने या हटाने से भी transformation किया जाता है। जैसे :

Affirmative	Negative
(a) He played the match.	He did not fail to play the match.
(b) He delivered his speech.	He didn't fail to deliver his speech.
(c) I saw the Taj Mahal.	I did not fail to see the Taj Mahal.
(d) Consult the doctor.	Do not fail to consult the doctor.

Negative	Affirmative
(a) He couldn't catch the train.	He failed to catch the train.
(b) She didn't fail to help the needy.	She helped the needy.
(c) He couldn't see me.	He failed to see me.
(d) He couldn't meet the chairman.	He failed to meet the chairman.

(4) जब Affirmative वाक्यों में only/alone, as soon as, when/whenever का प्रयोग हो तो इनको negative वाक्यों में transform करने के लिए none but, no sooner .... than, never but का प्रयोग किया जाता है। जैसे :

Affirmative	Negative
Only/alone	None but
As soon as	No sooner ..... than
When/whenever	Never but

Look at the following examples :

Affirmative	**Negative**
(a) Only the poor can beg like this.	None but the poor can beg like this.
(b) Only a fool can say like this.	None but a fool can say like this.
(c) The brave alone deserves the award.	None but the brave deserves the award.
(d) Only Ram was present there.	None but Ram was present there.
(e) As soon as I reached there, it started raining.	No sooner did I reach there than it started raining.
(f) As soon as he saw the police, he ran away.	No sooner did he see the police than he ran away.
(g) It always pours when it rains.	It never rains but pours.

Negative	**Affirmative**
(a) None but a girl can talk like this.	Only a girl can talk like this.
(b) None but Nisha can solve it.	Only Nisha can solve it.
(c) No sooner did the thief see the police.	As soon as the thief saw the police, he ran away.
(d) No sooner did I hear the noise, than I came out.	As soon as I heard the noise I came out.
(e) It never rains but pours.	It always pours, when it rains.
(f) There is nobody who dislikes mangoes.	Everybody likes mangoes.

Miscellaneous sentences :

Affirmative	**Negative**
(a) It is a unique item.	There is no item like this.
(b) All the people wept.	There was none but wept.
(c) She seldom comes here.	She does not come here very often.
(d) He goes to office daily.	He never absents himself from office.
(e) We won all the matches.	We didn't lose any match.
(f) His position became worse gradually.	His position didn't improve.
(g) Smoking is prohibited here.	Don't smoke here.
(h) Have patience please.	Don't be impatient.
(i) Keep silence.	Don't make a noise.
(j) A few persons were present there.	Not many persons were present there.
(k) Work hard lest you should fail.	Work hard so that you may not fail.
(l) Run fast lest you should miss the train.	Run fast so that you may not miss the train.

III. Interchange of Assertive *and* Interrogative Sentences :

कई Interrogative sentences, व्याकरणात्मक (Grammatical) structure के अनुसार तो देखने में Interrogative लगते हैं, लेकिन उनका आशय प्रश्न पूछना/प्रश्न करना नहीं होता है। ऐसे Interrogative sentences को बिना अर्थ/आशय को परिवर्तित किए हुए Assertive Sentence में बदला जा सकता है।

इस तरह के Interrogative sentences निम्नलिखित दो प्रकार के होते हैं :

(1) Helping verb (Auxiliary verb) से शुरू होने वाले Interrogative sentences.

(2) Wh-words से शुरू होने वाले Interrogative sentences.

(1) Helping Verbs (Auxiliaries) से शुरू होने वाले Interrogative sentences :

(1) Interrogative sentence का Structure - verb +Subject + ...का होता है।
इसे बदलकर Subject + verb + ... के Structure में वाक्य को लिखें।

(2) यदि Interrogative sentence में no/not या अन्य कोई negative word है तो Assertive sentence बनाते समय, उसे हटा दें। यदि Interrogative sentence में कोई negative word नहीं है तो Assertive sentence में ऐसा word लगाना होगा।

Look at the following examples :

Interrogative	Assertive
(a) Am I not your friend?	I am your friend.
(b) Isn't she beautiful?	She is beautiful.
(c) Didn't I study?	I did study.
(d) Can a blind see?	A blind can't see.
(e) Don't I love her?	I love her.
(f) Shall we ever forget you?	We shall never forget you.
(g) Haven't I a car?	I have a car.
(h) Did I tell a lie?	I told a lie.
(i) Don't I know you?	I know you.
(j) Does not the Earth revolve round the sun?	The earth revolves round the sun.
(k) Won't you have a cup of tea?	Have a cup of tea.

(2) Wh-words से शुरू होने वाले **Interrogative sentences** : इस तरह के Interrogative वाक्यों में यदि कोई Negative word हो, तो Assertive sentence में everyone का प्रयोग किया जाता है। यदि Interrogative sentence में Negative word न हो, तो इसे Assertive sentence में transform करने पर No one/None/No body इत्यादि का प्रयोग किया जाता है। *See the following examples :*

Interrogative	Assertive
(a) Who does not know Amitabh?	Everyone knows Amitabh.
(b) Who does not love his mother?	Everyone loves his mother.
(c) Who will tolerate such an insult?	No one will tolerate such an insult.
(d) Who can live more than 100 years?	No one can live more than 100 year.
(e) Who is more powerful than God?	No one is more powerful than God.
(f) Who does not love his country?	Everyone loves his country.
(g) Who can surpass him in intelligence?	No one can surpass him in intelligence.
(h) What more can I do?	I can't do any more.
(i) Why waste money here?	It is useless wasting money here.
(j) When will you have sense?	You will never have sense.
(k) Why cry over spilt milk?	It is no use crying over spilt milk.
(l) What if you are more intelligent than I?	It does not matter much, even though you are more intelligent than I.
(m) Where will I have peace of mind?	I will nowhere have peace of mind.
(n) How can I forget you?	I can't forget you?
(o) How can I repay you?	I can't repay you.
(p) How does it matter, if you lose?	It does not matter much even if you lose.

IV. Interchange of Exclamatory *and* Assertive Sentences :

Exclamatory sentences ऐसे sentences होते हैं, जो बेहद आश्चर्य, दु:ख, खुशी, क्रोध, नफरत, प्रशंसा इत्यादि को व्यक्त करते हैं। ऐसे वाक्यों को Assertive में बदला जा सकता है एवं Assertive वाक्यों को भी Exclamatory में बदला जा सकता है। इस तरह के वाक्यों में व्यक्त भावना के अनुसार, Assertive में बदलते समय कुछ शब्दों का प्रयोग किया जाता है। Exclamatory वाक्यों को Assertive में बदलने हेतु निम्न प्रक्रिया/नियमों को ध्यानपूर्वक पढ़ें

(1) What/How से शुरू होने वाले वाक्य—सबसे पहले यह समझें कि Assertive वाक्य का structure क्या है। Assertive वाक्यों का structure होता है—Subject + verb + ...

यदि Exclamatory वाक्य में What/How के बाद Adjective/Adverb आता है, तो What/How की जगह very का प्रयोग करें। यदि What के बाद noun आया हो, तो वाक्य के भावार्थ के अनुसार, what की जगह great/nice/fine/ wonderful/ strange/marvellous/peculiar/terrible शब्दों को लगाने से Assertive में बदला जाता है।

Look at the following examples :

Exclamatory	Assertive
(a) What a bird it was !	It was a beautiful bird.
(b) How fast she moves!	She moves very fast.
(c) How hot it is !	It is very hot.
(d) What a nice weather it was!	It was a very nice weather
(e) How odd it looks!	It looks very odd.
(f) What a busy life she leads!	She leads a very busy life.

कई Exclamatory वाक्यों में subject एवं verb व्यक्त नहीं होते हैं, अत: it या किसी subject का प्रयोग करके वाक्यों को Assertive में अग्र प्रकार से transform किया जाता है।

Exclamatory	Assertive
(a) What a scene!	It is a beautiful scene.
(b) What an art!	It is a great work of art.
(c) What a hotel!	It is a grand hotel.
(d) What a fall!	It is a great fall.

(2) कुछ Exclamatory sentences Oh that/would that/Alas इत्यादि से शुरू होते हैं। जैसा हमने पहले बताया कि Assertive वाक्यों का Structure — Subject + verb+ .... होता है, अत: ऐसे वाक्यों नें verb की जगह 'wish' का प्रयोग किया जाता है। कई वाक्यों में wish के बाद 'that' का प्रयोग भी किया जाता है। कुछ में 'It' का प्रयोग भी किया जाता है।

Look at the following examples :

Exclamatory	Assertive
(a) Would that I had not wasted my money!	I wish I had not wasted my money.
(b) O that she were young again!	I wish that she were young again.
(c) Alas! she died so young.	It is sad that she died so young.
(d) O that I were a king!	I wish that I were a king.

(3) कुछ Exclamatory वाक्य Hurrah/ Bravo/ Well-done इत्यादि से शुरू होते हैं एवं खुशी/प्रशंसा का भाव व्यक्त करते हैं। ऐसे वाक्यों को Assertive में बदलते समय It is a matter of ....+ that का प्रयोग किया जाता है।

Look at the following sentences :

Exclamatory	Assertive
(a) Bravo! you secured highest marks.	It is a matter of praise that you secured highest marks.
(b) Hurrah! we have won the match.	It is a matter of joy that we have won the match.
(c) Well done! you get selected.	It is matter of praise that you get selected.
(d) Hurrah! he scored a goal.	It is matter of joy that he scored a goal.

कुछ वाक्यों में ***fie, fie*** *का प्रयोग घृणा/तिरस्कार व्यक्त करने हेतु किया जाता है। ऐसे वाक्यों में It is a matter of contempt that का प्रयोग निम्न प्रकार से किया जायेगा :*

(i) Fie, fie! he is a thief.	*It is a matter of contempt that he is a thief.*
(ii) Fie, fie! she is a prostitute.	*It is a matter of contempt that she is a prostitute.*

(4) कुछ Exclamatory वाक्य if only से शुरू होते हैं, ये वक्त की इच्छा (wish) को व्यक्त करते हैं। इस तरह के वाक्यों हेतु भी I wish का प्रयोग करके इन्हें Assertive में बदला जाता है।

Look at the following sentences :

(a) If only I could meet her once. *Exclamatory*
I wish to meet her once. *Assertive*

(b) If only I could once get selected. *Exclamatory*
I wish to get once selected. *Assertive*

Miscellaneous sentences :

(a) How kind of you to help me! *Exclamatory*
You were kind enough to help me. *Assertive*
It was kind of you to help me. *Assertive*

(b) How foolish of him to abuse the chairman! *Exclamatory*
He was foolish enough to abuse the chairman. *Assertive*
It was foolish of him to abuse the chairman. *Assertive*

(c) A navyman ! afraid of water. *Exclamatory*
It is strange that a navyman should be afraid of water. *Assertive*

(d) An army man and such a coward! *Exclamatory*
It is shocking that an army man should be such a coward. *Assertive*

(e) To think of our getting married ! *Exclamatory*
It is strange that we should get married. *Assertive*

(f) To think of my seeing you in this foreign land! *Exclamatory*
It is strange that I should see you in this foreign land. *Assertive*

Interchange Parts of Speech

वाक्य में प्रयुक्त Part of speech; जैसे : noun, verb, adverb, adjective; को दूसरे में परिवर्तित करने से भी वाक्यों का transformation किया जा सकता है। *See the following examples :*

(1) Changing into Verb :

(a) Smoking is injurious to health. *Adjective*
Smoking injures health. *Verb*

(b) You should give assistance to him. *Noun*
You should assist him. *Verb*

(c) Grahmbell made the invention of telephone. *Noun*
Grahmbell invented the telephone. *Verb*

(d) Her action caused disgrace to the country. *Noun*
Her action disgraced the country. *Verb*

(e) You must render help to her. *Noun*
You must help her. *Verb*

(2) Changing into Noun :

(a) Who discovered India? *Verb*
Who made the discovery of India? *Noun*

(b) Who invented Computer? *Verb*
Who made the invention of Computer? *Noun*

(c) Listen to him attentively. *Adverb*
Listen to him with attention. *Noun*

(d) She is <u>healthy.</u> — *Adjective*
She enjoys good <u>health.</u> — *Noun*

(e) Walk <u>carefully.</u> — *Adverb*
Walk with <u>care.</u> — *Noun*

(f) He fought <u>courageously.</u> — *Adverb*
He fought with <u>courage.</u> — *Noun*

(3) Changing into Adjective :

(a) He confessed his <u>guilt.</u> — *Noun*
He confessed that he was <u>guilty.</u> — *Adjective*

(b) Wine <u>injures</u> liver. — *Verb*
Wine is <u>injurious</u> to liver. — *Adjective*

(c) <u>Fortunately</u> she escaped unhurt. — *Adverb*
She was <u>fortunate</u> to escape unhurt. — *Adjective*

(d) He solved the puzzle <u>easily.</u> — *Adverb*
It was <u>easy</u> for him to solve the puzzle. — *Adjective*

(4) Changing into Adverb :

(a) His success is <u>sure.</u> — *Adjective*
He will <u>surely</u> succeed. — *Adverb*

(b) He does not <u>intend</u> to speak. — *Verb*
He does not speak <u>intentionally.</u> — *Adverb*

(c) Sita sang a <u>sweet</u> song. — *Adjective*
Sita sang a song <u>sweetly.</u> — *Adverb*

(d) He fought with <u>courage</u> — *Noun*
She fought <u>courageously.</u> — *Adverb*

One part of speech से another part of speech में बदलना, एक सरल कार्य है लेकिन छात्रों को विभिन्न parts of speech का ज्ञान होना चाहिए। छात्रों को Noun, Verb, Adverb, Adjective आदि की विशेषताओं को अच्छी तरह समझना चाहिए।

Transformation of Conditional Sentences

सामान्यतया Conditional sentences के दो भाग होते हैं, एक भाग में कुछ शर्त दी गई होती है एवं दूसरे भाग में उस शर्त का परिणाम (Result) व्यक्त होता है। ऐसे वाक्यों को वाक्य के भावार्थ के अनुसार, transform किया जाता है।

See the following examples :

(a) If you work hard, you will pass. | Unless you work hard you will not pass.
Work hard and you will pass. | Work hard in case you want to pass.
Should you work hard you would pass.

(b) Had he come to me, I would have helped him. | If he had come to me, I would have helped him.

(c) In case you support me, I will make a protest. | If you support me, I will make a protest.
Provided you support me, I will make a protest.

(d) One more try and you will achieve it. | If you make one more try, you will achieve it.

(e) If she does not turn up, you will get the job. | In case she doesn't turn up you will get the job.
Supposing she does not turn up, you will get the job.

इस तरह Conditional वाक्यों को Unless/Should/In case/If/Supposing etc. का प्रयोग करके बदला जा सकता है।

Conversion of Simple/Compound/ Complex Sentences

(A) Conversion of Simple Sentence into Compound :

आप जानते हैं कि Simple sentence में एक ही Principal clause होती है (एक ही finite verb होती है), जबकि Compound sentence में दो Principal clauses होती हैं, जो एक-दूसरे से Coordinating conjunction द्वारा जुड़ी रहती हैं। अत: Simple sentence को दो Principal clauses में विभक्त करके, उन्हें Coordinating conjunction द्वारा जोड़ने से Compound sentence बन जाता है। जैसे :

Look at the following examples :

(a) In spite of his poverty he is trustworthy. *Simple*
He is poor yet he is trustworthy. *Compound*

(b) The sun having risen the fog disappeared. *Simple*
The sun rose and the fog disappeared. *Compound*

(c) Besides being beautiful she is intelligent. *Simple*
She is beautiful as well as she is intelligent. *Compound*

(d) The chief rewarded the officer for his excellent work. *Simple*
The clerk did excellent work and so the chief rewarded him. *Compound*

(e) Seeing a lion he fled away. *Simple*
He saw a lion and he fled away. *Compound*

(f) Notwithstanding his problems he is trying again. *Simple*
He has problems yet he is trying again. *Compound*

(g) You should work hard to achieve your goal. *Simple*
You should work hard or you can't achieve your goal. *Compound*

(h) The officer punished the boy for his misbehaviour. *Simple*
The boy misbehaved so the officer punished him. *Compound*

(B) Conversion of Compound Sentence into Complex :

Complex sentence में एक Principal clause होती है एवं एक या अधिक Subordinate clause होती है। Complex sentence बनाते समय Compound sentence (दो Principal clause होती हैं) की एक clause को Subordinating conjunction द्वारा दूसरी clause के साथ जोड़ देना होता है। Subordinating conjunction से जिस clause को जोड़ा जाता है। वह एक Subordinate clause बन जाती है। Subordinate clause तीन प्रकार की होती है :

(1) Noun clause (2) Adjective clause
(3) Adverb clause.

अत: Compound sentence की एक clause को इनमें से कोई भी clause बनाकर, एक Complex sentence बनाया जाता है। वाक्य की स्थिति देखकर ही यह निर्णय लिया जा सकता है कि Subordinate clause किस तरह (Noun/Adjective/Adverb) की बनाई जाती है।

इस हेतु निम्न Subordinating conjunction मुख्यतया प्रयुक्त किए जाते हैं : When, why, where, how, who, which, if that, than, so that, as soon as, else, till, until, unless, because, though, although etc.

Look at the following examples :

(a) Run fast or you will miss the train. *Compound*
Unless you run fast you will miss the train. *Complex*

(b) I am not well so I shall not come to the office. *Compound*
I shall not come to the office as I am not well. *Complex*

(c) She was ill so I helped her. *Compound*
I helped her because she was ill. *Complex*

(d) Check his room and you will find the money. *Compound*
If you check his room you will find the money. *Complex*

(e) He is innocent and I know it. *Compound*
I know that he is innocent. *Complex*

(f) She lost her child and she found it. *Compound*
She found her child that she lost. *Complex*

(c) Conversion of Simple Sentence into Complex :

Simple sentence की एक Principal clause को दो clauses में विभक्त कर, एक clause को Principal clause एवं दूसरी clause को Subordinate clause बनानी होती है। Subordinate clause, Principal clause के साथ Subordinating conjunction द्वारा संयुक्त की जाती है।

Look at the following examples :

(a) I know his address. *Simple*
I know what his address is. *Complex*

(b) She accepted her guilt. *Simple*
She accepted that she was guilty. *Complex*

(c) You should work hard to achieve your goal. *Simple*
You should work hard so that you can achieve your goal. *Complex*

(d) I drink to enjoy. *Simple*
I drink so that I can enjoy. *Complex*

(e) He is too poor to pay his fees. *Simple*
He is so poor that he can't pay his fees. *Complex*

(f) This is my office. *Simple*
This is the office where I work. *Complex*

इसी तरह हम Complex sentence को Simple में तथा Complex sentence को Compound में एवं Compound sentence को Simple में बदल सकते हैं। मुख्य बात है, हमें Simple, Compound एवं Complex sentences की विशेषताओं का ज्ञान होना चाहिए एवं Coordinating/subordinating conjunction की जानकारी होनी चाहिए। हमें Principal clause एवं Subordinating clause (Noun/Adjective/Adverb clause) की जानकारी एवं इनका कहाँ, किस तरह उपयोग किया जाता है यह भी पता होना चाहिए। यदि हमें यह सब कुछ अच्छी तरह से ज्ञात है तो हम conversion बहुत सरलता से कर सकते हैं।

01.

Convert the following Simple sentences into Compound sentences: **[RAS]**

(1) The teacher punished the boy for disobedience.
(2) Running at top speed, he got out of breath.
(3) By his pleasant manners he gained many friends.
(4) Raleigh, taking off his cloak politely, placed it in the muddy street.
(5) In this tower sat the poet gazing on the sea.

Transform the following sentences according to the directions given: **[RPSC (RAS) Ajmer]**

(6) If you do not take exercise, you will be ill. (Convert into a Compound sentence.)
(7) The moment which is lost, is lost forever. (Convert into a Simple sentence.)
(8) Self-made men are always respected. (Turn into a Complex sentence.)
(9) He will not pay unless he is compelled. (Turn into a Simple sentence.)
(10) In the absence of the cat the mice will play. (Turn into a Complex sentence.)
(11) The everyone's surprise, the enterprise completely failed. (Convert into a Compound sentence.)
(12) You must work hard to win the first prize. (Convert into a Compound sentence.)
(13) He was very tired but he kept on working. (Turn into a Simple sentence.)
(14) His silence proves his guilt. (Turn into a Complex sentence.)
(15) Consult the dictionary and you will find the meaning of this word. (Convert into a Complex sentence.)

02.

Join the following pairs into single sentence: **[RPSC (RAS) Ajmer]**

(1) Storms may come. They may destroy the dam.
(2) The girl has gone away. I wanted to marry her.
(3) The king talked to a woman. The woman's four sons had been killed in the war.
(4) He is very clever. He cannot be deceived.
(5) Hiroshima was once a prosperous town. It is now a heap of ruins.
(6) The moon rose. Their journey was not ended.

03.

Rewrite the following sentences using 'than' (Superlative to Comparative Degree):

(1) Switzerland is the most beautiful country in the world. (use 'more beautiful')
(2) Delhi is the biggest city of India. (use 'bigger')
(3) Mahima is the most beautiful girl in the class. (use 'beautiful')
(4) Morning walk is the best exercise for us. (use 'better')
(5) Premji Azim is the richest man in India. (use 'richer')

04.

Rewrite the following sentences using 'as .... as' (Comparative to Positive Degree):

(1) Nikita is taller than Babita. (use'tall')
(2) Reeta is more intelligent than Nita. (use 'intelligent')
(3) America is richer than India. (use 'rich')
(4) Kavita's hair is more beautiful than Vimla's hair. (use 'beautiful')
(5) Alwar is bigger than Tonk. (use 'big')

(6) She is taller than any other girl in the school. (use 'tall')
(7) Mohan is poorer than any other man in the village. (use 'poor')
(8) My mother is more beautiful than any other today in our colony. (use 'beautiful')
(9) Ganga is more famous river than any other river in India. (use 'as famous as')
(10) Jodhpur is hotter than Shimla. (use 'hot')

05.

Change the following sentences from Comparative to Superlative :

(1) Subhash Chandra Bose was greater than any other leader of India (use 'the greatest')
(2) Kolkata is bigger than any other city of India. (use 'the biggest')
(3) Iron is heavier than any other metal. (use 'the heaviest')
(4) Everest is higher mountain in the world. (use 'the highest')
(5) Sonu is fatter than any other boy in the house. (use 'the fattest')
(6) Rani is better than any other girl. (use 'the best')

06.

Interchange of Exclamatory sentences to Assertive sentences :

(1) How cute she is !
(2) What a beautiful sight it is!
(3) What a stupid she is!
(4) What a big building it is!
(5) Oh that, I were the queen of Britain !
(6) O that, I were a bird !
(7) Alas! she died in an accident.
(8) Bravo! you have done well.
(9) Hurrah ! I won the game.
(10) What an attractive person he is !
(11) What a good book it is!
(12) How fast she reads !
(13) What a fine weather it is!
(14) What a sight it is!
(15) How funny!
(16) What a hut!
(17) What a style!
(18) Oh that, I had the wings of bird!
(19) Oh, what a beautiful car to drive !
(20) If I were Miss India !

07.

Interchange of Exclamatory sentences to Assertive sentences :

(1) Such a woman and my wife!
(2) How kind of her to help me!
(3) Fie!fie! you are a murderer.
(4) How sweetly she sings!
(5) How sad was the sight of that deserted place!
(6) What a girl she is!
(7) What a lovely flower!
(8) How strange!
(9) Would that I had never left my village!
(10) Would that my son were alive!
(11) O for a cup of tea!
(12) If only I could find my lost love!
(13) A child and so brave!
(14) How clever of him to cheat her!
(15) How cool the moonlit night is!
(16) Would that I were an I.P.S. officer!
(17) If I could only see her!

08.

Transform the following sentences into Assertive :

(1) Is this the kind of dress to wear in marriage party?
(2) Won't you come in?
(3) Can the dumb speak?
(4) Didn't I tell her to stay here?
(5) Is it not a wise step?
(6) Why wait for him?
(7) Do you like to lose money?
(8) Haven't I warned you against the danger?
(9) Why to accuse him?
(10) How can one change one's nature?

09.

Use the following words as Noun and as Verb :

(1) Close (2) Court (3) Back (4) Head (5) Light

10.

Use the following words as Noun and as Adjective :

(1) Fast (2) Less (3) Like (4) Down (5) Master

11.

Use the following words as Adverb and as Adjective :

(1) Round (2) Next (3) Near (4) Well (5) Slow

12.

Transform the following Simple sentences into Compound sentences :

(1) He should work hard to pass the examination.
(2) Besides making a promise, she keeps it.
(3) For all the problems, he is happy.
(4) The principal rusticated the boy for misbehaviour.
(5) The sun having risen, the fog dispersed.
(6) He died a brilliant death, leaving an example to the world.
(7) Having finished his work, he went to market.
(8) Owing to ill health, she could not prepare the breakfast.

13.

Transform the following Simple sentences into Complex :

(1) She owed her success to my support.
(2) Wise persons do not talk nonsense.
(3) His silence proves his guilt.
(4) Non-vegetarians are not allowed to enter into the temple.
(5) Listen to the elders.
(6) We are sure to win the match.
(7) Intelligent students always succeed.
(8) His ambition is to become an engineer.
(9) Tell me your address.
(10) I have no money to spend.

14.

Transform the following Compound sentences into Complex sentences :

(1) He is a poor man, but he is honest man.
(2) My brother gave me a watch and I have lost it.
(3) She was very tired and so she didn't cook food.
(4) She is still in teens, but she has the wisdom of a matured woman.
(5) I have lost the purse but I have found it now.
(6) She is very affable and so I love her.
(7) He is doing his best and I am sure of it.
(8) Be sincere and you will be respected by everyone.
(9) Send the money in advance or you will not get the magazine.
(10) You are a teetotaller and I know it.

15.

Transform the following Affirmative sentences into Negative sentences :

(1) My sister is wise.
(2) That is impossible.
(3) I shall always remember your kindness.
(4) He is always careful.
(5) A true man is always right.
(6) Sita's voice is Harsh.
(7) We like him.
(8) This student is dull.
(9) We are innocent.
(10) She is always present .
(11) They won the game.
(12) I always treat her fairly.
(13) This knife is blunt.
(14) Everyone was hopeful.

16.

Transform the following sentences into Negative sentences :

(1) She is a bad teacher.
(2) They were doubtful whether it was her.
(3) Ram is a dishonest man.
(4) He is sometimes foolish.
(5) My uncle is a poor man.
(6) Always speak the truth.
(7) I am always happy.
(8) Everyone hates you.
(9) Everyone hides his sorrow.
(10) Everyone praised her dance.
(11) I love him.
(12) She had clothes.
(13) Every rose has thorn.

17.

Transform the following sentences into Question form :

(1) Only the rich can buy that house.
(2) Only Ram can solve this problem.
(3) Only Manish came to see you.
(4) As soon as the thief saw the police, he ran away.
(5) As soon as he saw the monkey, he fled.
(6) As soon as I went inside, it began to rain.
(7) Only seniors need apply.
(8) He disbelieves me.
(9) He failed to catch the thief.
(10) It is wrong to do this work.
(11) Nisha is always sure.
(12) Ram will stay here.
(13) She dislikes you.

18.

Rewrite the following sentences :

(1) Sachin is the best cricket player in India. (use 'better')
(2) Mr. Ganguli is the richest man of our city. (use 'richer')
(3) Neetu is the cleverest girl of our college. (use 'cleverer')
(4) Hockey is the most popular game in India. (use 'more popular')
(5) Akbar was the greatest muslim ruler in India. (use 'greater')
(6) Morning walk is the best exercise for young people. (use 'better')
(7) Pt Nehru was one of the greatest leader of India. (use 'greater')
(8) Rahul Dravid is one of the best batsman of our country. (use 'better')
(9) Indira Gandhi was the most impressive Prime Minister of India. (use 'more impressive')
(10) Nisha is the most intelligent student in the school. (use 'more intelligent')

19.

Rewrite the following sentences using Positive Degree :

(1) Mumbai is the best part of our country. (use 'good')
(2) My brother is the wisest man in the office. (use 'wise')
(3) Naresh is the poorest man in our village. (use 'poor')
(4) Mr. Rohan is the most popular member in our office. (use 'popular')
(5) Iron is the most useful metal. (use 'useful')
(6) Bikaner is the hottest city in Rajasthan. (use 'hot')
(7) Shatabdi Express is the fastest train. (use 'fast')
(8) Nisha is the tallest girl of our school. (use 'tall')
(9) Rajasthan is the most desert state of India. (use 'desert')
(10) America is the richest country in the world. (use 'rich')
(11) A lion is the strongest animal in the forest. (use 'strong')

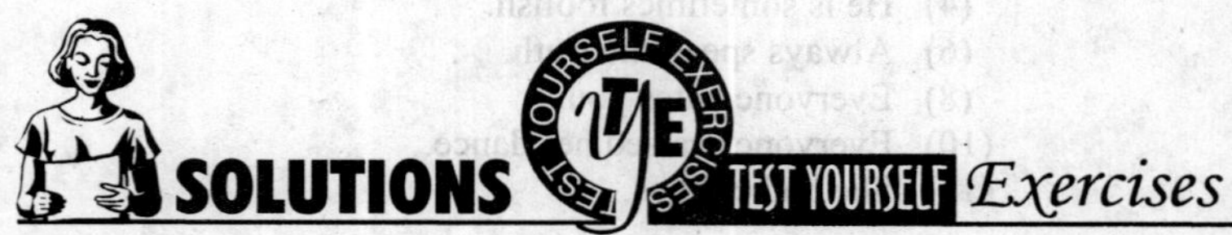

Solution TYE 01

(1) The boy was disobedient and so the teacher punished him.
(2) He ran at top speed so he got out of breath.
(3) He has pleasant manners and therefore he gained many friends.
(4) Raleigh took off his cloak politely and placed it in the muddy street.
(5) The poet sat in this tower and gazed on the sea.
(6) Take exercise otherwise you will be ill.
(7) The moment once lost is lost forever.
(8) The men who are self-made are always respected.
(9) He will pay only under compulsion.
(10) The mice will play when the cat is absent.
(11) The enterprise completely failed and it surprised everyone.
(12) You must work hard so that you may win the first prize.
(13) In spite of being very tired he kept on working.
(14) The fact that he is silent proves his guilt. *Or*
His silence proves that he is guilty.
(15) If you consult the dictionary you will find the meaning of this word.

Solution TYE 02

(1) Storms may come and destroy the dam.
(2) I wanted to marry the girl who had gone away.
(3) The king talked to the woman whose four sons had been killed in the war.
(4) He is too clever to be deceived. *Or*
He is so clever that he cannot be deceived.
(5) Hiroshima, which was once a prosperous town, is now a heap of ruins.
(6) The moon rose before the end of their journey.

Solution TYE 03

(1) Switzerland is more beautiful than any other country in the world.
(2) Delhi is bigger than any other city in the world.
(3) Mahima is more beautiful than any other girl in the class.
(4) Morning walk is better than any other exercise for us.
(5) Premji Azim is richer than any other man in India.

Solution TYE 04

(1) Babita is not as tall as Nikita.
(2) Nita is not as intelligent as Reeta.
(3) India is not so rich as America.
(4) Vimla's hair is not as beautiful as Kavita's hair.
(5) Tonk is not as big as Alwar.
(6) No other girl in the school is as tall as she.
(7) No other man in the village is as poor as Mohan.
(8) No other lady in our colony is as beautiful as my mother.
(9) No other river in India is as famous as Ganga.
(10) Shimla is not as hot as Jodhpur.

Solution TYE 05

(1) Subhash Chandra Bose was the greatest leader of India.
(2) Kolkata is the biggest city of India.
(3) Iron is the heaviest metal.
(4) Everest is the highest mountain in the world.
(5) Sonu is the fattest boy in the house.
(6) Rani is the best girl.

Solution TYE 06

(1) She is very cute.
(2) It is a very beautiful sight.
(3) She is a great stupid.
(4) It is a very big building.
(5) I wish that I were the queen of Britain.
(6) I wish I were a bird.
(7) It is sad that she died in an accident.
(8) It is a matter of praise that you have done well.
(9) It is joyful that I won the game.
(10) He is a very attractive person.
(11) It is a very good book.
(12) She reads very fast.
(13) It is very fine weather.
(14) It is a lovely sight.
(15) It is very funny.
(16) It is a beautiful hut.
(17) It is a good style.
(18) I wish that I had the wings of bird.
(19) I wish that I had a beautiful car to drive.
(20) I wish that I were Miss India.

Solution TYE 07

(1) It is shocking that such a woman should be my wife.
(2) She was kind enough to help me.
(3) It is a matter of contempt that you are a murderer.
(4) She sings very sweetly.
(5) That deserted place presented very sad sight.
(6) She is a peculiar girl.
(7) This is a very lovely flower.
(8) It is very strange.
(9) I wish I had never left my village.
(10) I wish my son were alive.
(11) I wish I had a cup of tea.
(12) I wish I could find my lost love.
(13) It is strange that a child should be so brave.
(14) He was clever enough to cheat her.
(15) The moonlit night is very cool.
(16) I wish I were an I.P.S. officer.
(17) I earnestly desire to see her.

Solution TYE 08

(1) This is not the kind of dress to wear in marriage party.
(2) You come in please.
(3) The dumb can't speak.
(4) I told her to stay here.
(5) It is a wise step.
(6) It is useless to wait for him.
(7) You do not like to lose money.
(8) I have warned you against the danger.
(9) It is wrong to accuse him.
(10) One can't change one's nature.

Solution TYE 09

(1) **Close**	:	The meeting came to a close at 6 p.m.	*Noun*
		Please close the shop now.	*Verb*
(2) **Court**	:	I am going to attend the court of law tomorrow.	*Noun*
		She is regularly courting her boss.	*Verb*
(3) **Back**	:	He carried the load on his back.	*Noun*
		I am not going to back your arguments.	*Verb*
(4) **Head**	:	He has a big head full of white hair.	*Noun*
		She headed the list of investors.	*Verb*
(5) **Light**	:	There is no light in the corridor.	*Noun*
		Light the candle in the room.	*Verb*

Solution TYE 10

(1) **Fast**	:	She keeps fast on every Tuesday.	*Noun*
		He is a fast runner.	*Adjective*
(2) **Less**	:	I won't be contended with less.	*Noun*
		She paid less attention to sports.	*Adjective*
(3) **Like**	:	You cannot see her like again.	*Noun*
		They are man of like physique and stature.	*Adjective*
(4) **Down**	:	I have seen the ups and downs of business.	*Noun*
		The down train was very late yesterday.	*Adjective*
(5) **Master**	:	She is my master.	*Noun*
		He conceived a master strategy.	*Adjective*

Solution TYE 11

(1) **Round**	:	He brought her round to my point of view.	*Adverb*
		It is a round floor.	*Adjective*
(2) **Next**	:	What next are you planning?	*Adverb*
		I shall meet you at the next crossing.	*Adjective*
(3) **Near**	:	Come near and sit here.	*Adverb*
		She is my near relative.	*Adjective*
(4) **Well**	:	Well begun is half done.	*Adverb*
		You are well now.	*Adjective*
(5) **Slow**	:	She is working in a slow manner.	*Adverb*
		She is a slow worker.	*Adjective*

Solution TYE 12

(1) He should work hard or he will not pass the examination.
(2) She not only makes a promise but also keeps it.
(3) Though he is in great problems, yet he is happy.
(4) The boy misbehaved so the principal rusticated him.
(5) The sun rose and the fog dispersed.
(6) He died a brilliant death and left an example to the world.
(7) He finished his work and he went to market.
(8) She was in ill health and so she could not prepare the breakfast.

Solution TYE 13

(1) It was due to my support that she succeeded.
(2) The persons who are wise do not talk nonsense.
(3) The fact that he is silent proves his guilt.
(4) If you are a non-vegetarian, you can't be allowed to enter into the temple.
(5) Listen to what the elders say.
(6) We are sure that we shall win the match.
(7) The students who are intelligent always succeed.
(8) His ambition is that he wants to become an engineer.
(9) Tell me where you live.
(10) I have no money that I can spend.

Solution TYE 14

(1) He is a honest man although he is poor.
(2) I have lost the watch which my brother gave me.
(3) As she was very tired, she didn't cook food.
(4) She has the wisdom of a matured woman, although she is still in teens.
(5) I have found the purse that I had lost.
(6) I love her because she is very affable.
(7) I am sure that he is doing his best.
(8) If you are sincere, you will be respected by everyone.
(9) You will not get the magazine unless you send the money in advance.
(10) I know that you are a teetotaller.

Solution TYE 15

(1) My sister is not a fool.
(2) That is not possible.
(3) I shall not forget your kindness.
(4) He is never careless.
(5) A true man is never wrong.
(6) Sita's voice is not sweet.
(7) We do not dislike him.
(8) This student is not intelligent.
(9) We are not guilty.
(10) She is never absent.
(11) They did not lose the game.
(12) I never treat her badly.
(13) This knife is not sharp.
(14) No one was without hope.

Solution TYE 16

(1) She is not a good teacher.
(2) They were not sure whether it was her.
(3) Ram is not an honest man.
(4) He is not always foolish.
(5) My uncle is not a rich man.
(6) Never tell a lie.
(7) I am never unhappy.
(8) There is no one who does not hate you.
(9) There is no one who does not hide his sorrow.
(10) There was none who did not praise her dance.
(11) I am not without love for him.
(12) She is not without clothes.
(13) There is no rose without thorn.

Solution TYE 17

(1) None but the rich can buy that house.
(2) None but Ram can solve this problem.
(3) None but Manish came to see you.
(4) No sooner did the thief see the police than he ran away.
(5) No sooner did he see the monkey than he fled.
(6) No sooner did I go inside than it began to rain.
(7) None but seniors need apply.
(8) He did not believe me.
(9) He could not catch the thief.
(10) It is not right to do this work.
(11) Nisha is never in doubt.
(12) Ram will not go anywhere.
(13) She does not like you.

Solution TYE 18

(1) Sachin is better than any other cricket player in India.
(2) Mr. Ganguli is richer than any other man of our city.
(3) Neetu is cleverer than any other girl of our college.
(4) Hockey is more popular than any other game in India.
(5) Akbar was greater than any other Muslim ruler in India.
(6) Morning walk is better than any other exercise for young people.
(7) Pt. Nehru was greater than most other leaders of India.
(8) Rahul Dravid is better than most other batsman of our country.
(9) Indira Gandhi was more impressive than any other Prime Minister of India.
(10) Nisha is more intelligent than any other student in the school.

Solution TYE 19

(1) No other part of our country is so good as Mumbai.
(2) No other man in the office is as wise as my brother.
(3) No other man in our village is as poor as Naresh.
(4) No other member in our office is so popular as Mr. Rohan.
(5) No other metal is so useful as Iron.
(6) No other city in Rajasthan is so hot as Bikaner.
(7) No other train is so fast as Shatabdi Express.
(8) No other girl is as tall as Nisha.
(9) No other state of India is so desert as Rajasthan.
(10) No other country in the world is so rich as America.
(11) No other animal in the forest is as strong as lion.

CHAPTER

21

CONDITIONAL SENTENCES

सामान्यतया Conditional sentences में दो clauses होती हैं :

(1) If clause, (2) Main clause

If clause, condition को बताती है, एवं Main clause कार्य के पूर्ण होने या न होने को व्यक्त करती है।

Conditional sentences को मुख्य रूप से निम्नलिखित तीन भागों में वर्गीकृत किया जा सकता है :

(A) जब If clause Present tense में हो।

(B) जब If clause Past tense में हो।

(C) जब If clause Past Perfect tense में हो।

(A) Conditional Sentences : If Clause in Present Tense :

(1) जब If clause, Present tense में होती है, तो Main clause में Future tense निम्न प्रकार से प्रयोग में आ सकता है :

(a) If it rains, he will not come in time.
(b) If he runs fast, he will reach in time.
(c) If the fog gets thicker, the plane may be late.
(d) If it stops snowing, we can reach safely.
(e) If you want to lose weight, you should eat less bread.
(f) If you want to lose weight eat less bread.
(g) If you meet Sita in the party, could you tell her to ring me?

इस तरह के वाक्यों में जिनमें If clause Present में है तथा Main clause में Future का प्रयोग होता है, वह कार्य के पूर्ण होने की probability/ability को व्यक्त करते हैं। ध्यान रखिए जब Main clause में Future का प्रयोग किया है तो If clause में will/shall etc. का प्रयोग नहीं होगा।

(2) जब If clause Present में है एवं Main clause भी Present में है तो ऐसे वाक्य स्वत: (automatic) ही कार्य के होने को व्यक्त करते हैं। जैसे :

(a) If you heat ice it turns to water.
(b) If you boil water it turns to vapours.
(c) If there is shortage of a commodity, its price goes up

(3) If + Present continuous का प्रयोग वर्तमान में होने वाले कार्य या Future arrangement को व्यक्त करते हैं। जैसे :
(a) If you are waiting for a taxi, you should better go there.
(b) If you are looking for Raju, you may find him in the park.
(c) If you are staying for another day, I'll ask the manager to charge you at concessionary rate.
(d) If you are going to purchase a car, I will ask my assistant to show you the dealer's shop.

(4) If + Present Perfect Conditional sentence
(a) If you have finished dinner, I will ask the waiter for ice cream.
(b) If she has written the thesis, I will send it to the professor.
(c) If you haven't seen the Victoria Palace we would better go there today.

(B) Conditional Sentences : If Clause in Past Tense

(1) If clause Past tense में है एवं Main clause में would का प्रयोग होता है। जैसे :
(a) If I had an umbrella I would lend it to you.
(But I haven't an umbrella.)
यदि मेरे पास छतरी होती तो मैं तुम्हें दे देता। (लेकिन मेरे पास छतरी नहीं है।)
(b) If I had a briefcase, I would give it to her.
(But I haven't a briefcase.)
यदि मेरे पास ब्रीफकेस होता तो मैं उसे दे देता। (लेकिन मेरे पास ब्रीफकेस नहीं है।)
ये वाक्य वर्तमान स्थिति को व्यक्त करते हैं। वस्तुत: If clause में Past tense का प्रयोग Past action को व्यक्त करता ही नहीं है।

had के बाद noun का प्रयोग है एवं Main clause में would के बाद Verb-I का प्रयोग हुआ है।
If + subject + had + noun + ... would + V-I

(2) If clause में verb की II form का प्रयोग। जैसे :
(a) If he tried to threaten me I would inform his father.
(But I don't expect that he will try to threaten me.)
यदि उसने मुझे धमकाने का प्रयास किया होता तो मैंने उसके पिता को सूचित कर दिया होता।
(b) If a thief came into my room I would call you.
(But I don't expect a thief to come into my room.
यदि चोर मेरे कमरे में आया होता तो मैंने तुम्हें बुला लिया होता।
(c) If she dyed her hair green everyone would laugh at her.
(But I don't expect that she will dye her hair green.)
यदि उसने बाल हरे रंग में रँगे होते तो प्रत्येक उस पर हँसा होता।
इस तरह के वाक्यों में भी If clause में Past tense का प्रयोग, वास्तविक Past नहीं है, न कोई Past action सूचित करते हैं।
इस तरह के वाक्यों में If clause में verb की II form का तथा Main clause में would + V-I का प्रयोग होता है।

If + subject + V-II + ...would + V-I

Main clause में would की जगह might/could इत्यादि का भी प्रयोग किया जा सकता है। would का प्रयोग certainty को व्यक्त करता है जबकि might का प्रयोग possibility तथा could का प्रयोग ability को व्यक्त करता है। जैसे :

(a) If he tried again he would pass. (certain result)

(b) If he tried again he could pass. (ability)

(c) If he tried again he might pass: (possibility)

(3) यदि If clause में भी Past Indefinite हो एवं Main clause में भी Past Indefinite हो तो ऐसे वाक्य एक के बाद तुरन्त दूसरा कार्य habitually/automatically होने को व्यक्त करते हैं। जैसे :

(a) If anyone abused him he became angry.
यदि किसी ने उसे गाली दी तो वह गुस्सा हो गया।

(b) If she interrupted him he got angry.
यदि उसने उसे टोका तो वह गुस्सा हुआ।

(c) If there was a scarcity of milk, its prices went up.
यदि कभी दूध की कमी हुई तो उसकी कीमतें बढ़ीं।

(d) If there was a short supply of any commodity, prices of that commodity increased.
यदि कभी किसी चीज की कमी हुई तो उसकी कीमतें बढ़ीं।
इस तरह के वाक्य habitual or automatic action को व्यक्त करते हैं। वाक्यों में Past tense, Past time के actions को ही व्यक्त करते हैं।

(C) Conditional Sentences : If Clause in Past Perfect Tense :

इस तरह के वाक्यों का structure निम्न प्रकार का होता है :

If + subject + had + V-III + ... would have + V-III

(a) If he had come to me I would have helped him.
(But he didn't come to me.)
यदि वह मेरे पास आता तो मैं उसकी सहायता करता। (लेकिन वह मेरे पास नहीं आया।)

(b) If she had invited me I would have attended the function.
(But she did not invite me.)
यदि वह मुझे बुलाती तो मैं कार्यक्रम में उपस्थित होता। (लेकिन उसने मुझे नहीं बुलाया।)

(c) If he had tried to cheat me I would have dismissed him.
(But he didn't try to cheat me.)
यदि उसने मुझे ठगने का प्रयास किया होता तो मैं उसे बर्खास्त कर देता।
(लेकिन उसने मुझे ठगने का प्रयास नहीं किया।)

(1) *इस तरह के वाक्यों में Main clause में would की जगह could या might का भी प्रयोग किया जा सकता है। could का प्रयोग ability को तथा might का प्रयोग possibility को व्यक्त करता है। जैसे :*
(a) If we had found her earlier we could have saved her life. (ability)
यदि हम उसे पहले ढूँढ लेते तो उसकी जान बचा सकते थे।
(b) If we had found her earlier we might have saved her life. (possibility)
यदि हम उसे पहले ढूँढ लेते तो सम्भवतया उसकी जान बचा सकते थे।

(2) *Had का प्रयोग Subject से पहले करने पर if को omit किया जा सकता है। निम्न दोनों वाक्यों का अर्थ समान होता है।*
(a) If he had come to me I would have helped him.
(b) Had he come to me I would have helped him.

(3) *If clause में Past perfect continuous का भी प्रयोग निम्न प्रकार किया जा सकता है :*
I was wearing helmet. If hadn't been wearing the helmet I would have been seriously injured.

Other Types of Conditional Sentences

(A) **If clause के साथ would का प्रयोग करके निम्न प्रकार से Conditional sentences बनाए जा सकते हैं :**

(a) If you would like to come I will arrange a party for you.
(b) If you would care to see the photos I will bring them for you.
(c) If he would like to leave his scooter here he can do so.

जब if clause में would का प्रयोग होता है तो Main clause में Simple future का प्रयोग होता है।

(B) **If + should का प्रयोग करके निम्न Conditional sentences बनते हैं :**

(a) If you should have any difficulty in getting newspaper, ring at this number.
(b) If these packets should arrive in a damaged condition, please inform the company at once.

इस तरह के वाक्यों को निम्न प्रकार से भी लिखा जा सकता है :
Should these packets arrive in a damaged condition, please inform the company at once.
Should का प्रयोग यहाँ possibility को व्यक्त करता है, लेकिन ऐसी possibility जो मुश्किल (unlikely) है।

(C) **If + were के प्रयोग से भी Conditional sentences बनते हैं। जैसे :**

(a) If I were you, I would forgive him.
(b) If I were you, I would punish him.
यदि मैं If I were you का यहाँ अर्थ यदि मैं तुम्हारी जगह होता से है।

(D) **Use of 'Until & Unless' in Conditional sentences :**

Until : का अर्थ होता है : जब तक। यह समय के सन्दर्भ में प्रयुक्त होता है। Until के साथ सामान्यतया वाक्य में Not का प्रयोग नहीं किया जाता है। जैसे :

(a) Until he comes back you will wait for him.
जब तक वह वापस न आ जाए तुम उसकी प्रतीक्षा करोगे।
(b) I will stay here until you complete your work.
जब तक तुम अपना कार्य पूर्ण न कर लोगे मैं यहीं रुकूँगा।

Unless : Unless का अर्थ होता है : अगर नहीं। यह भी एक नकारात्मक शब्द है। सामान्यतया Unless के साथ भी not का प्रयोग नहीं किया जाता है। Unless का प्रयोग किसी अन्य शर्त के पूरी होने के सन्दर्भ में किया जाता है। जैसे :

(a) You cannot pass unless you attend the college.
अगर तुम कॉलेज में उपस्थित नहीं रहोगे तो पास नहीं हो सकते।

(b) I cannot go to America unless I have a visa.
अगर मेरे पास वीसा नहीं होगा तो मैं अमेरिका नहीं जा सकता।

See the difference :

(a) You will wait here unless the train arrives. *Incorrect*
You will wait here until the train arrives. *Correct*

(b) You cannot achieve your goal until you work hard *Incorrect*
You cannot achieve your goal unless you work hard. *Correct*

Unless की जगह Until एवं Until की जगह Unless का प्रयोग न करें। Until का प्रयोग समय के सन्दर्भ में तथा Unless का प्रयोग किसी शर्त (condition) के सन्दर्भ मे किया जाता है।

(E) **Use of 'In case' in Conditional sentences : 'In case' का प्रयोग Conditional sentences में भविष्य में किसी घटना के होने की सम्भावना को व्यक्त करता है 'In case' का अर्थ होता है 'यदि ऐसा हो'।**

Look at the following examples :

(a) Inform me in case you need more money.
यदि तुम्हें और धन की आवश्यकता हो (यदि ऐसा हो) तो मुझे सूचित करें।

(b) Turn on the light in case you need my help.
यदि मेरी सहायता की आवश्यकता हो (यदि ऐसा हो) तो लाइट जला देना।

(c) Ring my doorbell in case he comes here.
यदि वह यहाँ आता है तो मेरे दरवाजे की घण्टी बजा देना।

(F) **Use of 'So long' in Conditional sentences : 'So long' (जब तक) का प्रयोग Conditional sentences में निम्न प्रकार होता है :**

(a) I shall support him so long he is here.
जब तक वह यहाँ है मैं उसका समर्थन करूँगा।

(b) You can stay here so long the owner is out of station.
जब तक मालिक बाहर है, तुम यहाँ रुक सकते हो।

(c) So long I am here I will assist in your work.
जब तक मैं यहाँ हूँ मैं तुम्हारे कार्य में मदद करूँगा।

(G) **Use of 'Provided' in Conditional sentences : Provided का अर्थ होता है : शर्त है कि। Provided का प्रयोग Conditional Sentences में निम्न प्रकार होता है :**

(a) I shall attend the meeting provided he also attends.
मैं बैठक में उपस्थित होऊँगा, शर्त है कि वह भी बैठक में उपस्थित रहे।

(b) We shall support you provided you favour us.
हम तुम्हें समर्थन देंगे, शर्त है कि तुम हमारे पक्ष में कार्य करो।

(c) I can pay you rent provided you get the roof repaired.
मैं तुम्हें किराया दे सकता हूँ, शर्त है कि तुम छत की मरम्मत कराओ।

(H) **Use of 'Suppose' in Conditional sentences : 'Suppose' का प्रयोग Conditional sentences में निम्न प्रकार होता है। 'Suppose' का अर्थ होता है मान लीजिए या मान लो। जैसे :**

(a) Suppose a monkey comes here what will you do?
मान लो एक बन्दर यहाँ आ जाता है तो आप क्या करेंगे?

(b) Suppose she doesn't agree what can you do?
मान लीजिए वह सहमत नहीं होती है तो आप क्या कर सकते हैं?

(c) Suppose he didn't turn up, what would you do?
मान लो वह नहीं आया तो आप क्या करेंगे?

(I) **Use of 'But for' in Conditional sentences : 'But for' का अर्थ है : 'यदि ऐसा न हुआ होता' 'But for' का प्रयोग 'if it hadn't happened' के अर्थ में होता है। जैसे :**

(a) But for his help Ramesh would have been ruined.
यदि वह सहायता नहीं करता तो रमेश बर्बाद हो गया होता।

(b) But for the flood, I would have been arrived here yesterday.
यदि बाढ़ नहीं आई होती तो मैं यहाँ कल ही आ गया होता।

(c) But for your company I would have been bored.
यदि तुम्हारा साथ न होता तो मैं बोर हो गया होता।

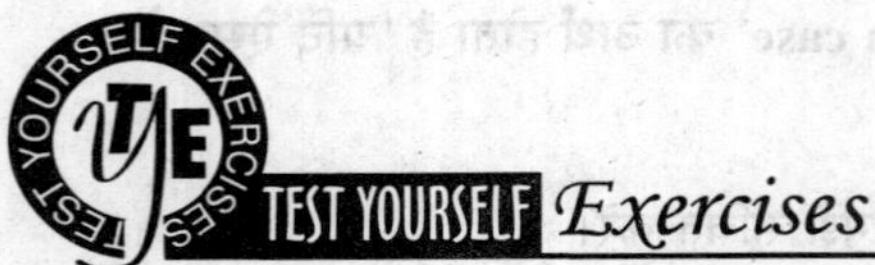

Exercises

01

Correct the following sentences :

(1) If he came to me, I would have given him a pen.
(2) Had he invited me, I would attend the function.
(3) If he had telephoned me, I would have gave him the address.
(4) If a monkey came here, what you will do?
(5) If I had an umbrella, I would have given it to her.

02

Correct the following sentences :

(1) If he will work hard, he will get promotion.
(2) Unless he will ask me, I shall not help him.
(3) If I had a briefcase, I will have lend it to her.
(4) If you will heat ice, it may turn to water.
(5) If you are looking for Sita, you would find her with Ram.

03

Correct the following sentences :

(1) If I was you, I would dismiss him.
(2) Unless he comes back, wait for him.
(3) Until you work hard, you can't beat him.
(4) Suppose she does not agree, what could you do?
(5) If he tried again, he can pass.

04

Fill in the blanks choosing the appropriate word from the brackets :

(1) I will stay here .... you come. *(until/unless)*

(2) .... you work hard, you can't secure first position. *(Until/Unless)*

(3) If I ...... you, I would forgive him. *(was/were)*

(4) If I were him, I .... dismiss you. *(will/would)*

(5) If it rains, he .... not come. *(will/would)*

(6) If you boil water it .... to vapours *(truns/will turn)*

(7) If you are waiting for a taxi, you .... better go there. *(should/would have)*

(8) If he had come here I .... given him a room to stay. *(would/would have)*

(9) If she .... me, I would have attended the function. *(had invited/invited)*

(10) If he tried again he .... pass. *(will/would)*

Solution TYE 01

(1) If he came to me I would give him a pen.

Or

If he had come to me, I would have given him a pen.

(2) Had he invited me, I would have attended the function.

(3) If he had telephoned me, I would have given him the address.

(4) If a monkey came here what would you do?

(5) If I had an umbrella I would give it to her.

Solution TYE 02

(1) If he works hard, he will get promotion.

(2) Unless he asks me I shall not help him.

(3) If I had a briefcase, I would lend it to her.

(4) If you heat ice, it turns to water.

(5) If you are looking for Sita, you will find her with Ram.

Solution TYE 03

(1) If I were you, I would dismiss him.

(2) Until he comes back, wait for him.

(3) Unless you work hard, you can't beat him.

(4) Suppose she does not agree, what can you do?

(5) If he tried again, he could pass.

Solution TYE 04

(1) until, (2) Unless, (3) were, (4) would, (5) will, (6) turns,

(7) should, (8) would have, (9) had invited, (10) would.

CHAPTER

22

UNENGLISH & SUPERFLUOUS EXPRESSIONS

इस chapter में ऐसे English expressions/phrases को बताया जा रहा है जिनका प्रयोग काफी प्रचलित है और अंग्रेज़ी भाषा का हिन्दीकरण किया गया प्रतीत होता है। ऐसे phrases/expressions का प्रयोग किया जाना गलत है, छात्रों को ऐसे phrases/expressions का प्रयोग नहीं करना चाहिए।

(1) Females : Females का प्रयोग women के लिए किया जाना गलत है। Females से sex का ज्ञान होता है।
Male sex or Female sex.
The Females of my house do not agree to this proposal. *Incorrect*
The women of my house do not agree to this proposal. *Correct*

(2) Family Man : Family Man का प्रयोग छात्रों द्वारा A man with a Family के सन्दर्भ में किया जाता है। यह गलत है, पूर्णतया Unenglish है।

(3) Family Members/Parliament Members : इनकी जगह हमें Members of Family or Members of Parliament का प्रयोग करना चाहिए।

(4) To Give Key to the Watch : घड़ी में चाबी भरने हेतु उक्त phrase का प्रयोग करना अंग्रेज़ी का हिन्दीकरण है। इसकी जगह 'To wind the watch' का प्रयोग करना चाहिए।

(5) To Eat Food : यह पूर्णतया Unenglish है। 'I have eaten my food'. इस तरह का प्रयोग पूर्णतया एक Unenglish प्रयोग है। English में अधिकांशत: खाने का नाम प्रयुक्त होता है। जैसे :
Have you had your lunch? Have you had your dinner?
Breakfast हेतु take की जगह have का प्रयोग करना चाहिए।
I have taken my breakfast की जगह हमें लिखना चाहिए। I have had my breakfast.

(6) Sick/Ill : Sick का अर्थ शारीरिक बीमारियों हेतु नहीं करना चाहिए। Sick का अर्थ मानसिक थकान, परेशानियों से होता है।
I am sick *Or* He fell sick की जगह I am ill *Or* He fell ill लिखना चाहिए।
Sick का प्रयोग निम्न अर्थ में सही है:
I am sick of this life means. I am tired of this life.

(7) Pulling on Well : इसका अर्थ ठीक ठाक खींच रहे हैं के अर्थ में करना गलत है। Pulling well ,एक सही English Idiom है जिसका अर्थ है Working in Harmony.
अत: यह लिखना कि We are pulling on well गलत होगा। इसकी जगह We are pulling well together कहना सही है।

(8) Etc : etc. (ecetera) की abbreviated form है। इसका अर्थ है : and others. इसका प्रयोग such as या and के साथ नहीं करना चाहिए। जैसे :
There were many kinds of fruits in his shop, such as apples, mangoes, plums, pears etc.
Or There were many kinds of fruits in his shop such as apples, mangoes, plums and pears etc.

इन दोनों ही वाक्यों में etc. का गलत प्रयोग किया गया है। इनकी जगह हमें लिखना चाहिए था।

There were many kinds of fruits in his shop, such as apples, mangoes, plums so on.

Or

There were many kinds of fruits in his shop like apples, mangoes, plums, pears etc.

(9) Rather Very : Rather का अर्थ होता है: not very, a little. अत: Rather के साथ very का प्रयोग अनुचित है, गलत है। जैसे :

She was rather very happy. *Incorrect*

She was rather happy. *Correct*

Or

She was very happy. *Correct*

(10) Comparative Better : Comparative के साथ better या Adjective comparative degree का प्रयोग नहीं करना चाहिए। जैसे :

She is comparatively better. *Incorrect*

She is comparatively good. *Correct*

She is better. *Correct*

(11) Or Keeping good health : इसका प्रयोग अच्छी अंग्रेजी में मान्य नहीं है। जैसे :

I think now she is keeping good health.

इसकी अपेक्षा यह कहना चाहिए।

I think now she is well.

(12) No mention/No matter : Thanks के प्रत्युत्तर में इन शब्दों का काफ़ी प्रयोग प्रचलित है। इनकी अपेक्षा All right *or* It's all right कहना अधिक उपयुक्त है।

(13) Generally/Always : एक ही वाक्य में Generally एवं Always दोनों का प्रयोग करना गलत है। Generally का अर्थ Always को contradict करता है।

Generally he is always late की जगह हमें मात्र यही कहना चाहिए कि Generally he is late.

(14) Tomorrow morning/Next morning : यदि Present tense का वाक्य है, तो हमें Tomorrow morning का प्रयोग करना चाहिए एवं Past tense के वाक्य के लिए next morning का प्रयोग करना चाहिए। जैसे :

I will go to Jaipur tomorrow morning.

I went to Jaipur the next morning.

(15) As best as he can : इस phrase की जगह as well as he can का प्रयोग करना चाहिए। as well का प्रयोग एक comparison को व्यक्त करता है। best का प्रयोग करने पर Superlative degree of adjective होने के कारण इसका comparative प्रयोग गलत है।

(16) Because/In order that/So that : कारण (cause) को express करने हेतु because का प्रयोग किया जाता है, जबकि Purpose को express करने हेतु in order that या so that का प्रयोग किया जाता है। निम्न वाक्यों को देखें :

We eat because we may live. *Incorrect*

We eat so that we may live. *Correct*

I took medicine because I might get well. *Incorrect*

I took medicine in order that I might get well. *Correct*

(17) In respect of/With respect to : ये दोनों Phrase अलग-अलग अर्थ में प्रयुक्त होते हैं। In respect of, से पूर्व adjective का प्रयोग होता है। इसका अर्थ है In point of some quality. देखें :

He is senior to her in respect of service.

With respect to का प्रयोग किसी subject (noun) के सन्दर्भ में किया जाता है जैसे :

We must have a discussion with respect to the proposal given by him.

(18) Both .... and/as well as/Not only .... but also : उक्त Conjunction का प्रयोग करते समय यह ध्यान में रखें कि जो fact ज़्यादा महत्त्वपूर्ण है, उसे बाद में लिखें। जैसे :

He was both expelled from the school and degraded from his class.

इसकी अपेक्षा हमें लिखना चाहिए :

He was both degraded from his class and expelled from the school.

इसी तरह :

Others as well as I declare this to be justified.

इसे हमें लिखना चाहिए :

I as well as others declare this to be justified.

इसी तरह :

Rahim was not only convicted of the crime, but also accused of it.

इसे निम्न प्रकार से लिखना चाहिए :

Rahim was not only accused of the crime, but also convicted of it.

(19) Another/Other/Any other : Another का प्रयोग singular nouns के साथ और other का प्रयोग plurals के साथ किया जाता है। दोनों का प्रयोग Affirmative sentences में किया जाता है। जबकि Another का प्रयोग Negative statements में करते हैं।

(20) Fair sex : Fair sex का प्रयोग women हेतु किया जाता है। Strictly speaking गलत है। In good English, Fair sex का प्रयोग women हेतु करने को avoid करना चाहिए।

(21) Lately/Latterly : Lately एवं Latterly दोनों का अर्थ recently से लिया जाता है, लेकिन Latterly का प्रयोग comparison हेतु Change of condition हेतु किया जाता है। Lately means recent past. Latterly means most recent.

His wife has left him latterly. *Incorrect*
His wife has left him lately. *Correct*
She has shown a different behaviour lately. *Incorrect*
She has shown a different behaviour latterly. *Correct*

यहाँ Change of condition बताई गई है।

The old man was in a coma latterly towards the end, at the end, finally.
Dad's health has not been good lately.

(22) Pass off : समय (Time) के सन्दर्भ में pass off का प्रयोग प्रचलित है। जैसे :

The time passes off happily *Or* The days pass off happily. उपर्युक्त दोनों वाक्यों में off का प्रयोग गलत है।

Pass off का प्रयोग तब किया जाता है जब कुछ गुजरने के बाद, अन्य कुछ घटना शेष नहीं रहता है। जैसे :

The event passes off peacefully and we resume our routine.

Time के सन्दर्भ में केवल pass का ही प्रयोग करना चाहिए। जैसे :

The time passes happily. The days pass happily.

(23) With a view to : With a view के बाद हमेशा Gerund का प्रयोग होता है। Infinitive (to) का प्रयोग करना गलत है। जैसे :

I journeyed through the different countries of the world with a view to find out the source of true happiness.

इसकी जगह लिखना चाहिए :

I journeyed through the different countries of the world with a view to finding out the source of true happiness.

(24) What to speak of : इसका प्रयोग सामान्यतया not to speak of/not to mention के सन्दर्भ में किया जाता है। जैसे :

What to speak of lunch or dinner, there was no arrangement of breakfast even.

इसकी अपेक्षा यह कहना चाहिए :

There was no arrangement of breakfast even, not to mention lunch or dinner.

इसी तरह :

He can hardly rise from the bed, what to speak of walking.

इसकी अपेक्षा यह कहना चाहिए :

He can hardly rise from the bed, not to speak of walking.

(25) What to do? : यह एक Unenglish expression है। इसकी अपेक्षा यह कहना चाहिए What am I to do ?

(26) To do the needful : इस phrase का उपयोग, अच्छी अंग्रेज़ी में मान्य नहीं है। इसकी अपेक्षा हमें निम्न phrase प्रयोग में लाने चाहिए :

Give the necessary instructions. *Or*
Make the necessary arrangements. *Or*
Give the necessary orders.

(27) Yes/No : Yes एवं No में Answer देते समय निम्न गलतियाँ की जाती है:

Did you find your purse ?
Yes, I did not find it yet.

इसकी जगह हमें लिखना चाहिए

No, I did not find it yet.

यदि प्रश्न का उत्तर Affirmative में हो तो Yes का प्रयोग करें, यदि उत्तर Negative में है तो No से शुरू करें।

(28) Good or bad success : Success के साथ good या bad का प्रयोग करना गलत है। Success may be great or small, important or trivial, but never good or bad.

(29) Splitting of Words : निम्न शब्दों को दो भागों में लिखना गलत है :

Incorrect	Correct	Incorrect	Correct
any body	anybody	can not	cannot
more over	moreover	some times	sometimes
else where	elsewhere	in as much	inasmuch
other wise	otherwise	in stead of	instead of
foot ball	football	head master	headmaster
work man	workman	post man	postman
arm chair	armchair	back-bite	backbite
tea spoon	teaspoon	half penny	halfpenny
not with standing	notwithstanding	mad man	madman

उपरोक्त शब्दों को लिखते समय ध्यान रखें।

(30) Combination of Words : निम्न शब्दों को मिलाकर लिखना गलत है:

Incorrect	Correct	Incorrect	Correct
everyone	every one	someone	some one
alright	all right	inspite of	in spite of
youngman	young man	underage	under age

Superfluous Expressions & Unnecessary Wordiness

Unnecessary Wordiness : कई बार वाक्यों में अनावश्यक शब्दों का प्रयोग किया जाता है। इसे unnecessary wordiness कहा जाता है। जैसे :

(1) **For a long period of time :** यहाँ of time लिखना अनावश्यक है, क्योंकि period के अर्थ में of time का अर्थ समाहित है।

(2) **Return back :** यहाँ back लिखना अनावश्यक है, क्योंकि Return के अर्थ में back का अर्थ समाहित है।

(3) **Cousin brother/Cousin sister :** इसमें brother/sister लिखना अनावश्यक है, क्योंकि Cousin के अर्थ में brother/ sister का अर्थ स्वत: ही समाहित है।

(4) **Retreat back/Recall back/Reimburse back/Recast back/Recede back :** इनके साथ back लिखना अनावश्यक है, क्योंकि Retreat /Recall/Reimburse /Recede/Recast में back का अर्थ समाहित है।

(5) **Restate/Repeat/Reborn/Rewrite/Reiterate/Rearrange/Rebuild :** इनके साथ again का प्रयोग गलत है, क्योंकि इन शब्दों के अर्थ में again का अर्थ समाहित है।

(6) **Supposing /Suppose** के साथ if का प्रयोग गलत है।

(7) **Kindly requested** के साथ kindly का प्रयोग गलत है, क्योंकि request हमेशा kindly ही होती है।

(8) **Await** के साथ for का प्रयोग गलत है, क्योंकि await का अर्थ wait for होता है।

(9) **Comprise/despite** के साथ of का प्रयोग गलत है, क्योंकि :

Comprise means Consist of; Despite means In spite of

(10) **Until/Unless/Forbid/Prohibit/Prevent/Dissuade/Deny/Refuse/Lest** के साथ not का प्रयोग अनुचित है, क्योंकि इनमें Not का meaning समाहित है।

(11) **Flee** के साथ away का प्रयोग गलत है, क्योंकि flee का अर्थ run away होता है।

(12) **Coward** के साथ man का प्रयोग गलत है, क्योंकि coward का अर्थ ही कायर आदमी होता है। इसमें man का अर्थ स्वत: ही समाहित होता है।

(13) **Mutual Agreement** में mutual का प्रयोग अनावश्यक है, क्योंकि agreement तब ही होगा, जब दोनों पार्टियाँ (mutually) स्वीकार करेंगी। इसी तरह Mutual dislike of each other में each other का प्रयोग अनावश्यक है।

(14) **Two twins** में two का प्रयोग गलत है।

(15) **Bifurcated *Or* divided into four quarters** में four का प्रयोग अनावश्यक है।

(16) **Reason because** का एक साथ प्रयोग अनुचित है, या तो Reason का प्रयोग करें या because का।

(17) **Because** के साथ therefore, as का प्रयोग गलत है।

(18) **Equally** और **as good as** दोनों का साथ-साथ प्रयोग कदापि न करें। वाक्य में equally का प्रयोग करें या as good as का।

(19) **Consensus opinion** में opinion लिखना अनावश्यक है। Consensus में opinion का अर्थ समाहित है।

(20) **Final conclusion** में final लिखना अनावश्यक है, क्योंकि conclusion का अर्थ ही final होता है।

(21) **Spouse wife/husband wife/husband** का प्रयोग अनावश्यक है, क्योंकि Spouse के अर्थ में wife/husband का अर्थ समाहित है।

(22) **Consort husband/wife** में husband/wife का प्रयोग करना अनावश्यक है, क्योंकि consort का अर्थ होता है husband or wife of a ruler.

(23) **Funeral service** में service का प्रयोग अनावश्यक है, क्योंकि Funeral एक service ही है।

(24) **Over ride/Over take/Over turn/Over shoot** आदि के साथ पुन: over का प्रयोग करना गलत है।

(25) **With bag and baggage** में with का प्रयोग अनावश्यक है, क्योंकि bag and baggage का अर्थ with all belongings होता है।

He returned bag and baggage.

(26) Mutual friend एक Unenglish expression है, इसका प्रयोग करना गलत है। इसकी जगह Common friend का प्रयोग किया जाता है।

(27) Free ship या **Lecturership** की जगह free studentship या lectureship का प्रयोग सही है।

(28) An English teacher का अर्थ होता है A teacher who is an English (Citizen of England) अत: An English teacher की जगह A teacher of English लिखना सही है।

(29) Passing marks की जगह pass marks लिखना सही है।

(30) Linking road / Linking language की जगह link road/link language लिखना शुद्ध है।

The time passes happily. The days pass happily.

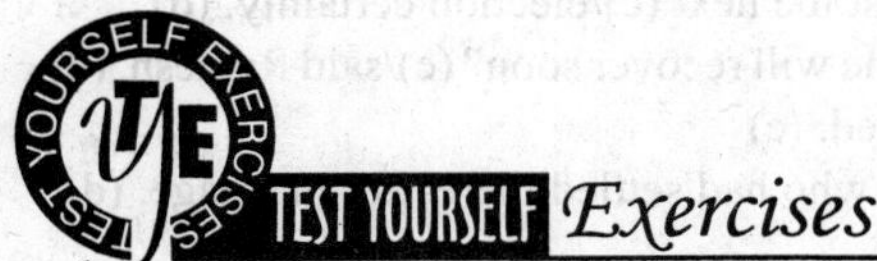

Exercises

01

Correct the following sentences :.

(1) He has been sick since Monday.
(2) I eat my food at 8 pm.
(3) There were many kinds of bag in the shop, such as paper, leather, cloth and canvas etc.
(4) Ramesh said to me, "Sita was rather very happy on that day".
(5) All his family members are planning to visit Jammu and Kashmir.
(6) I give key to my wrist watch at 8 p.m. daily.
(7) I eat my breakfast at 7 a.m. daily.
(8) He said, "Today I am feeling comparatively better".
(9) Sunita always wears blue saree on such functions generally.
(10) She went to Delhi the tomorrow morning.

02

Correct the following sentences :

(1) We eat because we may live.
(2) She didn't attend the meeting so that she was ill.
(3) I took medicine, because I might get well soon.
(4) Both he is a philosopher and a teacher.
(5) Either he is a stupid or a rogue.
(6) Others as well as Ram declares this an unethical act.
(7) The females are not allowed to participate in the competition.
(8) The days pass off happily.
(9) With a view to study the urgent publications he joined the library.
(10) Did you find your pen ? Yes, I didn't find it so far.

03

Correct the following sentences :

(1) I can not play football today.
(2) He achieved good success in B.A. examination.
(3) He sometimes comes to visit his parents.
(4) Everyone will be given a certificate.
(5) Have you found your lost purse?
No, I have found.
(6) It is not the men, but the fair sex, responsible for the present trend in fashion.
(7) Not with standing the present degradation in the society, he believes in fair means even today.
(8) Inspite of increase in turn over, the profit remains the same.
(9) Ram discussed the matter with so many another fellows.
(10) Ram and his other friend Shyam went to Jaipur yesterday.

Problems of Superfluous Expressions

04

Read the following sentences to find whether there is any error in any part :

(1) All the members (a)/of the club are (b)/kindly requested (c)/to attend the meeting. (d)
(2) This is the wristwatch (a)/which my uncle (b)/brought it (c)/for you. (d)
(3) She asked me (a)/where I was going to (b)/and what I had done (c)/the previous day. (d)
(4) He will leave (a)/for Mexico (b)/on Monday (c)/with bag and baggage. (d)
(5) This idea of the (a)/Home Minister's (b)/has put everyone (c)/in serious thoughts. (d)
(6) The teacher forbade (a)/the students not to (b)/make a noise. (c)
(7) Rita, cousin sister of the (a)/MP said that she would (b)/contest the next (c)/election certainly. (d)
(8) "Harish is comparatively better (a)/today and we hope that (b)/he will recover soon" (c)/said Ramesh. (d)
(9) Yesterday in the night (a)/he came by bus (b)/and was disturbed. (c)
(10) In Jaipur she (a)/came across with many (b)/of her friends (c)/who had settled thereafter marriage. (d)

05

Read the following sentences to find whether there is any error in any part :

(1) Pakistan's support (a)/to the terrorists in India (b)/is universally condemned (c)/by all. (d)
(2) Within two hours (a)/we will approach (b)/near Agra (c)/by car. (d)
(3) Suppose if (a)/all problems are solved (b)/what would you do then? (c)
(4) When he lent me (a)/some money, he asked (b)/to return it back (c)/within a week. (d)
(5) Through out the whole year (a)/there was (b)/not a single day (c)/without any incidence of violence. (d)
(6) The recent incidents of corruption (a)/amply illustrate about (b)/ the characters of (c)/our political leaders. (d)
(7) The thing what (a)/ you like is (b)/available in (c)/that departmental store. (d)
(8) He denied that(a)/he was not present(b)/there at the time(c)/the accident took place. (d)
(9) The PM said (a)/that it was his decision (b)/and that nobody (c)/could get it changed. (d)
(10) The students (a)/requested the teacher (b)/to repeat the question (c)/again. (d)

06

Read the following sentences to find whether there is any error in any part:

(1) The reason why (a)/most of the people commit crime (b)/is because they are unware (c)/of the legal complications. (d)
(2) He doesn't hardly know (a)/about the real factors (b)/that have created (c)/so many problems. (d)
(3) My mother asked me (a)/if I have sufficient enough money (b)/to buy the books. (c)
(4) They were quite all right (a)/when they went to the police station (b)/to lodge an FIR. (c)
(5) He stayed in Jammu (a)/for a very short period of time (b)/and then went to (c)/Kolkata. (d)
(6) He reimbursed back (a)/the money which I spent (b)/on his medical treatment. (c)
(7) I have to attend (a)/the funeral service (b)/of my dear departed friend (c)/today. (d)
(8) Unless you do not (a)/pass this examination (b)/you cannot get the job. (c)
(9) I want to know (a)/whether it is (b)/the right and proper time (c)/to start this business. (d)
(10) The second project (a)/of this company was equally as (b)/successful (c)/the first project. (d)

07

Read the following sentences to find whether there is any error in any part :

(1) He was (a)/very friendly enough (b)/to help me (c)/when I was in trouble. (d)
(2) My friend asked (a)/me if there was any place (b)/in the (c)/compartment for him. (d)
(3) I know (a)/that more than hundred (b)/students have applied (c)/for freeship. (d)

(4) Each competitor (a)/tried his best (b)/to defeat one another (c)/in the wrestling match. (d)
(5) He put his sign (a)/at the foot of the (b)/letter and posted it (c)/immediately. (d)
(6) She ran as (a)/fastly as she could (b)/to catch the train. (c)
(7) The officer advised me (a)/to talk to the concerned clerk (b)/in case I feel any (c)/problem in the matter. (d)
(8) Many pupils of this college (a)/are working as teachers (b)/in different (c)/public schools. (d)
(9) He was (a)/awarded cent percent (b)/marks in (c)/mathematics. (d)
(10) All his family members (a)/are social (b)/and cooperative. (c)

08

Read the following sentences to find whether there is any error in any part :

(1) To what has (a)/always puzzled me (b)/is your insincerity (c)/and carelessness. (d)
(2) According to me (a)/every student should (b)/go through the (c)/notes given by the professors. (d)
(3) One of my friends (a) /is in the teaching line (b)/and presently settled (c)/abroad. (d)
(4) Now-a-days she (a)/is living in foreign (b)/but her husband (c)/is in India. (d)
(5) Our English teacher said (a)/that we should practice (b)/regularly if we wanted to improve (c)/our English. (d)
(6) I want to join (a)/lecturership (b)/because I think it is a (c)/peaceful profession. (d)
(7) As my neighbours (a)/are very cooperative (b)/so I do not have (c)/any problem here. (d)
(8) The passing marks (a)/are thirty there (b)/but you have secured (c)/only thirty two marks. (d)
(9) Both of them. (a)/have not (b)/turned up in (c)/the court today(d) No error. (e)
(10) We must wait (a)/for quieter time before (b)/the claims of civilisation (c)/can over ride over the claims of the party spirit. (d)

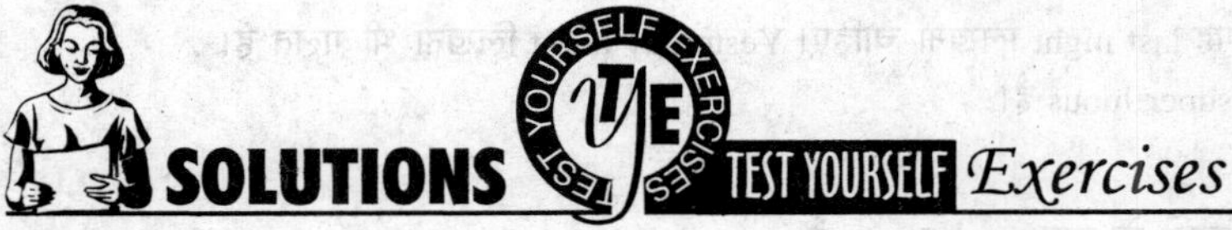

SOLUTIONS TEST YOURSELF *Exercises*

Solution TYE 01

(1) He has been ill since Monday.
(2) I take my dinner at 8 pm.
(3) There were many kinds of bag in the shop, such as paper, leather, cloth and canvas.
(4) Ramesh said to me, "Sita was rather happy on that day."
(5) All the members of his family are planning to visit Jammu and Kashmir.
(6) I wind my wrist watch at 8 pm daily.
(7) I have my breakfast at 7 a.m. daily.
(8) He said, "Today I am feeling better."
(9) Sunita always wears blue saree on such functions.
(10) She went to Delhi the next morning.

Solution TYE 02

(1) We eat so that we may live.
(2) She didn't attend the meeting because she was ill.
(3) I took medicine, in order that I might get well soon.
(4) He is both a philosopher and a teacher.
(5) Either he is a stupid or a rogue.
(6) Ram as well as others declares this an unethical act.
(7) The women are not allowed to participate in the competition.
(8) The days pass happily.
(9) With a view to studying the current publications he joined the library.
(10) Did you find your pen ? No, I didn't find it so far.

Solution TYE 03

(1) I cannot play football today.
(2) He achieved great success in BA examination.
(3) He sometimes comes to visit his parents.
(4) Everyone will be given a certificate.
(5) Have you found your lost purse?
Yes, I have found it.
(6) It is not the men, but the women, responsible for the present trend in fashion.
(7) Notwithstanding the present degradation in the society, he believes in fair means even today.
(8) In spite of increase in turn over, the profit remains the same.
(9) Ram discussed the matter with so many other fellows.
(10) Ram and his another friend Shyam went to Jaipur yesterday.

Solution TYE 04

(1) (c) kindly को Delete करें। Kindly का प्रयोग superfluous है, use either kindly or requested
(2) (c) It का प्रयोग superfluous है।
(3) (b) to का प्रयोग superfluous है।
(4) (d) with का प्रयोग superfluous है, The phrase 'bag and baggage' includes 'with'
(5) (b) Home Minister के साथ apostrophe ('s) का प्रयोग superfluous है।
(6) (b) not का प्रयोग forbade के साथ superfluous है। forbade का अर्थ स्वत: ही negative होता है।
(7) (a) sister या brother का cousin के साथ प्रयोग superfluous है।
(8) (a) Comparatively better दोनों का प्रयोग एक साथ गलत है। या तो लिखना चाहिए
Harish is comparatively good या फिर Harish is better.
(9) (a) Yesterday in the night की जगह last night लिखना चाहिए। Yesterday night लिखना भी गलत है।
(10) (b) across के साथ with का प्रयोग superfluous है।

Solution TYE 05

(1) (d) by all का प्रयोग universally लिखने के बाद superfluous है।
(2) (c) near का प्रयोग approach के साथ superfluous है।
(3) (a) Suppose के साथ if का प्रयोग superfluous है।
(4) (c) back का प्रयोग return के साथ superfluous है।
(5) (a) whole का प्रयोग superfluous है।
(6) (b) Illustrate/describe/discuss के बाद object आता है। यहाँ about का प्रयोग superflous है।
(7) (a) what की जगह which का प्रयोग या The thing को हटाना होगा। what के साथ किसी antecedent का होना आवश्यक है। जैसे
What you like most is this pen.
The thing which you like most is this pen.
(8) (b) not का प्रयोग deny के साथ गलत है। deny/refuse/ prevent/forbid/until/unless सभी negative हैं। इनके साथ not का प्रयोग नहीं होता है।
(9) (c) यहाँ that का प्रयोग superfluous है।
(10) (d) repeat के साथ again का प्रयोग superfluous है। Repeat/Recast/Rewrite के साथ again का प्रयोग नहीं होता है।

Solution TYE 06

(1) (c) जिस वाक्य में reason का प्रयोग होता है उसी में because का प्रयोग superfluous है।
(2) (a) hardly/scarcely स्वयं negative है इनके साथ not या doesn't का प्रयोग गलत है।
(3) (b) sufficient एवं enough का प्रयोग एक साथ नहीं होता है।
(4) (a) quite के साथ all का प्रयोग गलत है। या तो quite को हटाएँ या all को हटाएँ।
(5) (b) of time का प्रयोग superfluous है। या तो for a short period या for a short time का प्रयोग करें।
(6) (a) reimburse/return के साथ back का प्रयोग superfluous है।
(7) (b) funeral के साथ service का प्रयोग superfluous है। funeral स्वयं में ही service है।
(8) (a) Unless/until/forbid/refuse/deny/hardly/ scarcely के साथ not का प्रयोग करें ये सब स्वतः ही negative है।
(9) (c) right या proper में से या तो right का प्रयोग होगा या proper का। दोनों का प्रयोग एक साथ नहीं होता है।
(10) (b) equally का प्रयोग superfluous है। इन वाक्यों को देखें :
Ram and Rahim are equally successful.
Ram is as successful as Rahim.

Solution TYE 07

(1) (b) very का प्रयोग superfluous है।
(2) (b) place की जगह room शब्द का प्रयोग होगा, room in car/compartment/train/bus होता है।
(3) (d) freeship एक Unenglish expression है। free studentship होगा।
(4) (c) one another की जगह the other का प्रयोग होगा। each के साथ other का प्रयोग होता है।
(5) (a) sign की जगह signature होगा। sign एक verb है, जबकि signature एक noun है।
(6) (b) fastly की जगह fast ही होगा। fast एक adjective भी है एवं adverb भी। अतः इसे adverb की तरह प्रयोग करते समय ly लगाने की आवश्यकता नहीं होती है।
He is a fast runner. *Adjective*
He ran fast. *Adverb*
(7) (b) concerned clerk का अर्थ होता है चिन्तित क्लर्क। यहाँ concerned clerk की जगह clerk concerned होगा। जिसका अर्थ होता है सम्बन्धित क्लर्क।
(8) (a) pupils की जगह students होगा। pupils का अर्थ होता है शिष्य। यहाँ वाक्य में pupils शब्द का प्रयोग अनुचित है।
(9) (b) cent percent एक Unenglish expression है। इसकी जगह hundred per cent होगा।
(10) (a) All the members of his family होगा। Standard English में family member या family members का प्रयोग गलत है।

Solution TYE 08

(1) (a) To का प्रयोग superfluous है।
(2) (a) According to me की जगह In my opinion होना चाहिए। First person के साथ According to me का प्रयोग Standard english में मान्य नहीं है। According to us, According to him सही है।
(3) (b) teaching line की जगह teaching profession लिखना चाहिए।
(4) (b) in foreign की जगह abroad होगा या in foreign country लिखना सही होगा।
(5) (a) English Teacher की जगह teacher of English लिखना सही है। English teacher का अर्थ अंग्रेज अध्यापक होता है। न कि अंग्रेजी का अध्यापक।
(6) (b) lectureship होगा। lecturership, Unenglish expression है।
(7) (a) neighbourers कोई English word नहीं है। सही English word neighbours है।
(8) (a) passing marks की जगह pass marks होगा।
(9) (e) वाक्य सही है।
(10) (d) over ride के बाद over का प्रयोग superfluous है।

CHAPTER

23

QUESTION FRAMING

Questions को सामान्यतया निम्नलिखित तीन भागों में वर्गीकृत किया जा सकता है:

(A) Yes/No Questions
(B) Wh Questions
(C) Tag Questions
(D) Alternate Questions
(E) Short Questions
(F) Rhetorical Questions

(A) Yes/No Questions : ऐसे प्रश्न जिनका उत्तर Yes या No में दिया जा सकता है, Yes/No questions कहलाते हैं। इस तरह के प्रश्न, Helping verbs से शुरू होते हैं। जैसे:

(a) Do you know me?
(b) Does she live here?
(c) Is he going ?
(d) Are you not well?
(e) Did he come here?
(f) Was he playing?
(g) Has he come?
(h) Have you a pen?
(i) Had he completed his work?
(j) Will you go to market?
(k) Shall you apply for this job?
(l) Can you do this work?
(m) May I came in?
(n) Would you go there?

उपरोक्त सभी प्रश्न Helping verbs (Auxiliaries) से शुरू हैं एवं इनका उत्तर Yes/No में दिया जा सकता है।

(B) Wh-Questions : ऐसे प्रश्न हैं जो Wh-words; Why, Who, Where, When, Whose, Whom, How, What etc.; से शुरू होते हैं। ऐसे प्रश्नों में कुछ जानकारी चाही गई होती है। इनका उत्तर Yes/No में देना सम्भव नहीं होता है। ऐसे प्रश्नों को Wh-questions के नाम से जाना जाता है। जैसे:

(a) What is your name?
(b) Where do you live?
(c) Who is he?
(d) When did you come?
(e) How are you ?
(f) Whose pen is this?
(g) Whom do you like to meet?
(h) Why did he come?

(C) Tag Questions : इन्हें Question tag या Tag questions के नाम से जाना जाता है। इस तरह के Questions, वाक्य के अन्त में एक पुछल्ले की तरह attach होते हैं। इनका उद्देश्य, अपने कथन को प्रभावशाली बनाना या कथन की ओर श्रोता का ध्यान आकर्षित करना होता है, या अपने कथन की पुष्टि चाहना होता है। इस तरह के questions निम्न प्रकार के होते हैं :

(a) He is going to market, isn't he?
(b) She will help you, won't she?
(c) You are a gentleman, aren't you?
(d) Sugar is sweet, isn't it?

कुछ अन्य प्रकार के प्रश्न भी होते हैं। जैसे:

(D) Alternate Questions :

(a) Are you playing or not?
(b) Will you go or not?
(c) Has she arrived or not?
(d) Did he agree or not?

इस तरह के प्रश्नों में or not लगाकर, एक choice/ alternate व्यक्त किया जाता है। जैसे:

(E) Short Questions :

(a) I am going to buy a car. When/Why/Where/Which car?

(b) He is going to America. When/Why/by which flight?

(c) He has resigned from the service? When/Why/What for?

इस तरह के एक साथ किए गए कई प्रश्न, प्रश्न पूछने वाले की अति उत्सुकता को व्यक्त करते हैं। ऐसे प्रश्नों को Short questions कहा जाता है।

(F) Rhetorical Questions :

(a) Who is not without faults? (Everybody has some faults.)

(b) Who can speak against the chairman? (Nobody can speak.)

(c) Who will live forever? (None can live forever, man is mortal.)

(d) Who can bell the cat? (None can.)

इस तरह के प्रश्न, जिनका Answer सभी को पता होता है, केवल अपनी बात को प्रश्न के रूप ने कहकर, Impress upon करने हेतु प्रयुक्त होते हैं। इस तरह के प्रश्न Rhetorical questions कहलाते हैं।

Framing of Questions

(1) Yes/No Questions : Yes/No questions के बारे में आपने tense के अध्याय में विस्तृत रूप से पढ़ लिया है। अत: हम इसे यहाँ नहीं बता रहे हैं। ध्यान रखें इस तरह के questions का structure निम्न होता है :

Helping verb + subject + verb + object.

Verb की कौन-सी form प्रयुक्त होगी, यह वाक्य के tense पर निर्भर होता है। कई वाक्यों में helping verb मुख्य verb का कार्य करती है। वहाँ verb नहीं लगती है। जैसे:

Affirmative	Interrogative
(a) He is a student.	Is he a student?
(b) She is a girl.	Is she a girl?
(c) He has a pen.	Has he a pen?
(d) They have a car.	Have they a car?

(2) Wh-Questions : पूर्व में बताया गया है, Wh-questions, Wh-words; जैसे: What, Why, Which, When, Where, Who, Whose, Whom, How आदि; से शुरू होते हैं।

(1) यदि वाक्य में कोई भी helping verb नहीं है, तो Do/does/did को Wh-word के बाद लगाकर, प्रश्न शुरू करें। ध्यान रखें, यदि does का प्रयोग किया गया है तो verb के साथ s या es नहीं लगाया जाएगा। यदि 'did' का प्रयोग किया गया है, तो verb की I form लगानी होगी। जैसे:

(a) What does/did he like? *(b) Where does he go?*

(c) Why did he go? *(d) Where did he go?*

(e) When does he come? *(f) When did he come?*

Does वाले Questions के Affirmative sentences में verb के साथ s या es लगता है। इसी प्रकार did वाले questions के Affirmative sentence में verb की II form लगती है।

(2) यदि वाक्य में helping verb (is/am/are/was/were/will/shall/have/has/had etc.) है, तो इन्हें Wh-word के बाद लगाकर प्रश्न बनाया जाता है।

(3) Pronouns (I, you, we, my, our, your, his, her, hers etc.) का प्रयोग answer को समझते हुए या प्रश्न किससे करना है, यह देखकर करना होता है।

अब हम प्रत्येक Wh-word से question बनाने हेतु क्या करना चाहिए, यह देखेंगे।

(A) 'What' से शुरू होने वाले प्रश्न:

Read the following examples:

Answer	Question
(a) His name is Ramesh.	What is his name?
(b) I am playing football.	What are you doing/playing?
(c) I want to play.	What do you want?
(d) He likes this book.	What does he like?
(e) This is calculator.	What is this?
(f) He wrote a letter.	What did he write?
(g) She bought a book.	What did she buy?
(h) He can solve this question.	What can he do ?

What को वाक्य के शुरु में लिखें। उसके बाद यदि कोई helping verb है तो helping verb लिखें। यदि नहीं है तो tense के अनुसार Do/does/did इत्यादि लिखकर उसके बाद subject लिखें, फिर verb + object लिखें। verb के साथ s या es नहीं लगता है (यदि प्रश्न Simple present का है तो) इसी प्रकार Past tense के प्रश्न में verb की I form लगती है।

(B) 'Who' से शुरू करने वाले प्रश्न:

Read the following Examples:

Answer	Question
(a) Ram came here.	Who came here?
(b) He killed the lion.	Who killed the lion?
(c) Sita teaches us English.	Who teaches you English?
(d) Ramesh won the match.	Who won the match?
(e) I am Suresh from Alwar.	Who are you?
(f) Hari has joined the college.	Who has joined the college?
(g) Ram is going to Jaipur.	Who is going to Jaipur?
(h) Ramesh is swimming in the river.	Who is swimming in the river?

वाक्यों में subject की जगह 'Who' लिखें। उसके बाद यदि कोई helping verb है तो helping verb लिखें, नहीं है तो वाक्य में प्रयुक्त verb लिखें। अब pronoun में आवश्यकतानुसार परिवर्तन करने से 'Who' से शुरु होने वाले प्रश्न बन जाते हैं।

(C) 'Whose' से शुरू होने वाले प्रश्न : Whose का अर्थ होता है 'किसका'। अत: whose से प्रश्न तब ही बनाया जा सकता है जब Answer में my, your, his, her, our, their etc का प्रयोग किया गया होता।

See the following examples:

Answer	Question
(a) This is his pen.	Whose pen is this ?
(b) She sold her car.	Whose car did she sell?
(c) Ramesh purchased her house.	Whose house did Ramesh purchase?
(d) I visited his company.	Whose company did you visit?
(e) I saw her bungalow.	Whose bungalow did you see?
(f) I respect your parents.	Whose parents do you respect?
(g) I had found his purse.	Whose purse had you found?
(h) I shall purchase his car.	Whose car will you purchase?

(1) सबसे पहले whose लगायें, उसके बाद noun लिखें। फिर helping verb लिखकर, subject + verb + object लिखें।
(2) Present Indefinite के वाक्यों में does का प्रयोग (as helping verb) होता है, तो verb के साथ लगा s या es हट जाता है।
(3) Past Indefinite के वाक्यों में whose के साथ did का प्रयोग होता है. उस स्थिति में verb की I form लगाई जाती है।

(D) 'Whom' से शुरू होने वाले प्रश्न : Whom का अर्थ होता है 'किसको'। अत: Answer में यदि कोई noun (किसी का नाम) या pronoun होगा तभी who से प्रश्न बनाया जा सकता है।

Read the following examples:

Answer	Question
(a) I know Sita.	Whom do you know?
(b) I like her.	Whom do you like?
(c) The collector rewarded his brother.	Whom did the collector reward?
(d) Your sister was wandering with Sunny.	Whom was my sister wandering with?
(e) I saw his sister in the club.	Whom did you see in the club.
(f) I met Sita in the garden.	Whom did you meet in the garden?

(1) सबसे पहले 'Whom' लिखें, फिर आवश्यकतानुसार helping verb लिखें।
(2) उसके बाद subject लिखकर, शेष वाक्य को लिख दें।
(3) ध्यान रखें did (helping verb) का प्रयोग होने पर प्रश्न में verb की I form लगेगी एवं does का प्रयोग होने पर, verb के साथ लगा s या es हट जाता है।

(E) 'When' से शुरू होने वाले प्रश्न : When से समय का पता चलता है। When का प्रयोग तब ही हो सकता है जब Answer में 'समय' का सन्दर्भ हो।

Read the following examples :

Answer	Question
(a) He came at 8 p.m.	When did he come?
(b) He goes at 10 a.m.	When does he go?
(c) I met her yesterday.	When did you meet her?
(d) I will go to Jaipur next Monday.	When will you go to Jaipur?
(e) Our examination will start on 24th Jan.	When will your examination start?
(f) The train arrived at 5 p.m.	When did the train arrive?

सबसे पहले When लिखें। उसके बाद यदि कोई helping verb है तो helping verb लिखें। यदि नहीं है तो tense के अनुसार Do/does/did इत्यादि लिखकर उसके बाद subject लिखकर, शेष वाक्य को लिखें।
ध्यान रखें, helping verb, does आने पर verb में लगा s या es हट जाता है एवं Past tense में did का प्रयोग होने पर verb की I form लगती है।

(F) 'Where' से शुरू होने वाले प्रश्न : Where से स्थान का बोध होता है। अत: where से प्रश्न तब बनाया जाता है, जब Answer में स्थान का सन्दर्भ आता है।

Read the following examples :

Answer	Question
(a) I am going to market.	Where are you going?
(b) He lives in this room.	Where does he live?
(c) She works here.	Where does she work?
(d) You can find her in the park.	Where can I find her?
(e) He stayed at Alwar.	Where did he stay?
(f) She will go to Delhi.	Where will she go?

(1) सबसे पहले Where लिखें, उसके बाद यदि कोई helping verb है, तो helping verb लिखें। यदि नहीं है तो tense के अनुसार Do/does/did इत्यादि लिखकर उसके बाद subject लिखकर, शेष वाक्य को लिखें।

(2) ध्यान रखें, helping verb, does या did का प्रयोग हो तो पूर्व में बताए अनुसार verb में परिवर्तन करें।

(G) 'Why' से शुरू होने वाले प्रश्न: Why का अर्थ होता है 'क्यों'

Read the following examples:

Answer	Question
(a) I go to school to read.	Why do you go to school?
(b) He came here to meet me.	Why did he come here?
(c) He goes to Jaipur to attend the meeting.	Why does he go to Jaipur?
(d) I am sad because I have failed.	Why are you sad ?
(e) The teacher punished Sita because she was talking.	Why did the teacher punish Sita?
(f) We eat to live.	Why do we eat ?

(1) सबसे पहले Why लिखें, उसके बाद helping verb लिखें। उसके बाद subject + verb + ... लिखना है।

(2) वाक्य में आए because, therefore इत्यादि को छोड़ दें।

(3) Helping verb does/did जब लगायें तो verb में पूर्व में बताए नियमानुसार संशोधन करें।

(H) 'Which' से शुरू होने वाले प्रश्न : Which का अर्थ है कौन-सा। जब question, which से बनाना हो, तो answer में selection, choice या preference का समावेश होता है। जैसे : *Read the following examples:*

Answer	Question
(a) I like green shirt.	Which shirt do you like?
(b) This is the best book on Mathematics.	Which is the best book on Mathematics ?
(c) This is Sarla's bag.	Which is Sarla's bag ?
(d) I do not like the green dress.	Which dress do you not like?
(e) He prefers black tie.	Which tie does he prefer ?

(1) Question के प्रारम्भ में Which लगाते हैं, यदि answer में helping verb है तो which के बाद helping verb लगाते हैं। यदि नहीं है, तो noun लगाकर फिर do, does, did आदि लगाते हैं।

(2) Pronoun में आवश्यकतानुसार परिवर्तन किया जाता है।

(I) 'How' से शुरू होने वाले प्रश्न: How का अर्थ होता है 'कैसे'।

Read the following examples:

Answer	Question
(a) I am fine.	How are you ?
(b) He looks smart.	How does he look?
(c) She is well now.	How is she now?
(d) They are enjoying nicely there.	How are they enjoying there?
(e) He performed well.	How did he perform?

(1) सर्वप्रथम How लिखकर, प्रश्न शुरू करें। उसके बाद helping verb लगायें फिर subject लगायें एवं verb एवं object को लिखें।

(2) जैसा does/did helping verb के सम्बन्ध में पूर्व में बताया गया है, main verb में संशोधन करें।

(J) 'How many' से शुरू होने वाले प्रश्न : How many का अर्थ होता है 'कितने'। Many से संख्या का ज्ञान होता है यह Countables के लिए प्रयुक्त होता है। Many से प्रश्न तब ही बनता है, जब Answer में किसी noun की संख्या व्यक्त की जाती है।

Read the following examples:

Answer	Question
(a) I have three vehicles.	How many vehicles have you?
(b) My father gave me five copies.	How many copies did your father give you?
(c) He bought five books.	How many books did he buy?
(d) They sold three cycles.	How many cycles did they sell?
(e) He has four cars.	How many cars has he?

(1) सबसे पहले How many से वाक्य शुरू करें, फिर noun + helping verb का प्रयोग करें एवं फिर subject लिखकर main verb/object लिखें।

(2) यदि Present Indefinite का वाक्य है एवं helping verb 'does' का प्रयोग किया गया है तो verb के साथ लगा 's or es' हट जाता है, इसी प्रकार Past tense के वाक्यों में helping 'did' का प्रयोग होने की स्थिति में verb की I form ही लगती है।

(K) 'How long' से शुरू होने वाले प्रश्न : How long का अर्थ होता है 'कितनी देर' या 'कितना लम्बा'। अत: Answer में इनका उत्तर है तो ही How long का प्रयोग प्रश्न हेतु किया जा सकता है।

Read the following examples:

Answer	Question
(a) This hall is forty feet long.	How long is this hall?
(b) I have been waiting for you for two hours.	How long have you been waiting for me?
(c) He was there for two hours only.	How long was he there?
(d) He delivered speech for fifty minutes.	How long did he deliver the speech?

(1) How long से प्रश्न शुरू करें, उसके बाद Helping verb + subject लिखें। उसके बाद verb/adverb/object वाक्य की संरचना के अनुसार लिखें।

(2) does/did का प्रयोग होने की स्थिति में verb में संशोधन पूर्व में बताए नियमानुसार करें।

(L) 'How much' से शुरू होने वाले प्रश्न : How much का अर्थ होता है 'कितना'। इसका प्रयोग quantity (मात्रा) के सन्दर्भ में किया जाता है। जब Answer में मात्रा का सन्दर्भ हो तब ही How much से प्रश्न बनता है।

Read the following examples :

Answer	**Question**
(a) He drinks one kg. milk daily.	How much milk does he drink daily?
(b) I spent two hundred rupees today.	How much money did you spend today?
(c) I have two kg sugar.	How much sugar have you?
(d) He purchased five kilo milk.	How much tea did he purchase?

How much से प्रश्न शुरू करें। उसके बाद noun + helping verb लिखकर subject + verb (main) लिख दें, यदि object भी है तो अन्त में लिख दें।

Tensewise Structure of Questions with Wh-words

Present Indefinite

1. Present Indefinite Tense में Affirmative एवं Interrogative sentences का structure निम्न होता है:

Subject + V-I (s or es) + Object. *Affirmative*
Do/Does + Subject + V-I + Object *Interrogative*

तथा Wh-words से शुरू होने वाले Interrogative sentences का प्रयोग structure होता है:

Wh-word + do/does + Subject +V - I +Object ?

(a) What does he do? (b) Where do you play?
(c) Why do you cry? (d) How do you do?

ध्यान से देखने पर ज्ञात होगा कि Wh-word को Interrogative (Auxiliary do/does से शुरू होने वाला) Sentence के पूर्व लगाने से ही इस तरह के प्रश्न बन जाते हैं। जैसे:

He plays.	*Affirmative*
Does he play?	*Interrogative (Auxiliary)*
What does he play?	*Interrogative (Wh-word)*
Where/when/does he play?	*Interrogative (Wh-word)*

See more examples :

(e) I write.	*Affirmative*	
Do I write?	*Interrogative*	*(Auxiliary)*
What do I write?	*Interrogative*	*(Wh-word)*
(f) He writes a letter.	*Affirmative*	
Does he write a letter?	*Interrrogative*	*(Auxiliary)*
What does he do?	*Interrogative*	*(Wh-word)*
(g) She washes clothes at 10 a.m.	*Affirmative*	
Does she wash clothes at 10 a.m.	*Interrogative*	*(Auxiliary)*
When does she wash clothes?	*Interrogative*	*(Wh-word)*
What does she do at 10 a.m?		

'Who' के case में निम्न प्रकार के structure में do/does का प्रयोग नहीं होगा।
(a) Who teaches you English? *(b) Who comes here?*
(c) Who knows you?
लेकिन Interrogative-negative वाक्यों में does not का प्रयोग किया जाता है।
(a) Who does not teach you English? *(b) Who does not come here?*
(c) Who does not know you?

2. Wh-words से शुरू Interrogative negative sentences का structure निम्न होता है:

Wh + do/does + Subject + not + V- I + Object ?

(a) What does he not do?
(b) When do you not read?
(c) What do you not like?
(d) Why do you not protest?
(e) Where does he not stay?

Present Continuous

Present Continuous में Affirmative एवं Interrogative sentences का structure निम्न होता है:

Subject + is/am/are + Verb (ing form) + Object. *Affirmative*
Is/Am/Are + Subject + Verb (ing form) + Object? *Interrogative*

Wh-words से शुरू होने वाले Interrogative sentences का structure निम्न होता है:

Wh-word + is/am/are + Subject + Verb (ing form) + Object?

(a) What am I doing ?
(b) Where are you going?
(c) When is he coming ?
(d) Why is she crying?

Auxiliary verb के पूर्व Wh-word लगाने पर इस तरह के question बनाये जा सकते हैं। अन्य Examples देखें

(I)	*He is going to market.*	*Affirmative*
	Is he going to market?	*Interrogative (Auxiliary)*
	Where is he going?	*Interrogative (Wh-word)*
(II)	*Nisha is reading a book.*	*Affirmative*
	Is Nisha reading a book?	*Interrogative (Auxiliary)*
	What is Nisha reading?	*Interrogative (Wh-word)*
	What is Nisha doing?	*Interrogative (Wh-word)*

Wh-words से शुरू होने वाले Interrogative-negative sentences का structure निम्न होता है:

Wh-word + is/am/are + Subject +Verb (ing form) + object?

(a) Why are you not writing ?
(b) Why is she not speaking ?
(c) What is she not eating ?

Present Perfect

Present Perfect में Affirmative एवं Interrogative sentences का structure निम्न होता है:

Subject + have/has + V- III + object. *Affirmative*
Have/has + subject + V- III + object ? *Interrogative*

Wh-words से शुरू होने वाले Interrogative sentences का structure निम्न होता है:

Wh-word + have/has + subject + V- III + object?

(a) What has he written to his father?
(b) Why has she written to her father?
(c) Where have they gone?
(d) Where have you been?
(e) How has he passed his time ?

इस तरह के प्रश्न बनाते समय Wh-word के बाद Auxiliary, have/has लगाई जाती है।

Interrogative-negative वाक्यों में not, subject के बाद निम्न structure में लगता है:

Wh-word + have /has + Subject +not+ V-III + object?

(a) Why has he not played?
(b) What have they not done?
(c) Where has he not going?

Present Perfect Continuous

Present Perfect Continuous में Affirmative एवं Interrogative sentences का structure निम्न होता है:

Subject + have/has + been + V (ing form) + since/for + ... *Affirmative*
Have/has + subject + been + V (ing form) + Since/for + ...? *Interrogative*

Wh-words से शुरू होने वाले Interrogative sentences का structure निम्न होता है:

Wh-word + have/has+Subject + been + Verb (ing form) + ... ?

(a) What has he been doing since morning?
(b) Why have they been making a noise?
(c) Where have you been playing?
(d) What have you been doing for two hours?
(e) How long have you been waiting for me?

Wh-words से शुरू होने वाले Interrogative-negative sentences का structure निम्न होता है:

Wh-word + have/has + subject + not + been + Verb (ing form) +......... ?

(a) Why have you not been writing ?
(b) Why have they not been keeping silence ?
(c) Why has she not been going with you ?

Past Indefinite

Past Indefinite में Affirmative एवं Interrogative sentences के structure निम्न होते हैं:

Subject + V-II + Object *Affirmative*
Did + subject + V- I + object + ? *Interrogative*

Wh-words से शुरू होने वाले Interrogative sentences का structure निम्न होता है:

Wh-word + did + subject + V-I ?

(a) What did he do?
(b) Where did she go?
(c) Why did you cry?
(d) When did Ram come?
(e) How did he reply?

Wh-word को Auxiliary Verb से पूर्व लगाया जाता है तथा Verb की Ist form का प्रयोग होता है।
Wh-word से शुरु होने वाले Interrogative-negative sentences में not को Subject के बाद निम्न structure में लगाते हैं:
Wh-word+did+sub+not+V-I ?
(a) Why did she not speak to me? (b) Why did he not do his work? (c) Where did he not go?

Past Continuous

Past Continuous में Affirmative एवं Interrogative sentences का structure निम्न होता है:

Subject + was/were + Verb (ing form) + Object. *Affirmative*
Was/Were + Subject + Verb (ing form) + Object ? *Interrogative*

Wh-words से शुरू होने वाले Interrogative sentences का structure निम्न होता है:

Wh-word + was/were + Subject + Verb (ing form) + ...?

(a) Why were you speaking so loudly?
(b) What was he doing?
(c) Where were they going?
(d) When were you leaving the hotel?
(e) What were you writing?

जब इस तरह के Interrogative sentences को Interrogative-negative में परिवर्तित किया जाता है तो Subject के बाद 'not' लगाया जाता है। Interrogative negative sentences का निम्न structure होता है:

Wh-word + was/were + subject + not + Verb (ing form) + ... ?

(a) Why were you not writing ?
(b) What was he not doing?
(c) Why was he not speaking?

Past Perfect

Past Perfect tense में Affirmative एवं Interrogative sentences का structure निम्न होता है:

Subject + had + V-III + Object. *Affirmative*
Had + Subject + V-III + Object ? *Interrogative*

Wh-words से शुरू होने वाले Interrogative sentences का structure निम्न होता है:

Wh-word + had + Subject + V-III + ... ?

(a) When had Ram reached Delhi ?
(b) Why had he gone to hospital ?
(c) What had he done before Ram came ?
(d) Where had he gone before Shyam arrived ?
(e) Why had she phoned to me ?

इस तरह के वाक्यों को negative में परिवर्तित करने पर sentences का structure निम्न होता है:

Wh-word + had + Subject + not + V-III + ...?

(a) Why had Ram not liked Shyam?
(b) Why had he not gone to hospital?
(c) Why had he not done the alloted work?

Past Perfect Continuous

Past Perfect Continuous में Affirmative एवं Interrogative sentences का structure निम्न होता है:

Subject + had been + Verb (ing form) + since/for + ... *Affirmative*
Had + subject + been + Verb (ing form) + since/for + ... *Interrogative*

Wh-words से शुरू होने वाले Interrogative वाक्यों का structure निम्न होता है:

Wh word + had + subject + been + Verb (ing form) + ...?

(a) Why had he been playing since morning ?
(b) Where had she been working ?
(c) What had they been doing for two hours ?
(d) Why had Nisha been crying for two hours ?
(e) How had you been passing your time since then?

इस तरह के वाक्यों को negative में परिवर्तित करने पर वाक्यों का structure निम्न होता है:

Wh-word + had + subject + not + been + V (ing form) + ...?

(a) Why had she not been working since last night ?
(b) What had they not been doing ?
(c) Why had Nisha not been saying anything for two hours ?

Future Indefinite

Future Indefinite Tense में Affirmative एवं Interrogative sentences का structure निम्न होता है:

Subject + shall / will + V-I + object *Affirmative*
Shall/Will + subject + V-I +object + ? *Interrogative*

Wh-word से शुरू होने वाले Interrogative sentence का structure निम्न होता है:

Wh-word + shall/will + subject + V- I + object + ?

(a) Why will he go to Jaipur?
(b) What shall I say to her ?
(c) Where will they meet us?
(d) When will you go to Meerut ?
(e) How will you treat him?

इस तरह के वाक्यों को negative में परिवर्तित करने पर Interrogative-negative sentences का Structure निम्न होता है:

Wh-word + will/shall + Subject + not + V-I + ... ?

(a) Where will he not go ?
(b) Why will she not work here ?
(c) What will he not do for me ?
(d) Why will Ram not cooperate you ?
(e) When will you not telephone me ?

Future Continuous

Future Continuous में Affirmative एवं Interrogative sentences का structure निम्न होता है:

Subject + will/ shall + be + V (ing form) + Object. *Affirmative*
Will/shall + subject +be + V (ing form) + Object ? *Interrogative*

Wh-words से शुरू होने वाले Interrogative sentences का structure निम्न होता है :

Wh-word + will/shall + Subject + be + V (ing form) + Object ?

इस structure में Wh-word को साधारण Interrogative sentence के पहले लगाया जाता है। जैसे :

(a) Where will he be going now?
(b) What will you be doing next month?
(c) Why will he be waiting for you?
(d) How Will he be enjoying his time?
(e) What will she be reading now?

इस तरह के Interrogative sentences को जब negative में परिवर्तित किया जाता है, तो Interrogative-negative sentences का structure निम्न होता है:

Wh-word + will/shall + Subject + not + be + V (ing form) + ...?

(a) Why will you not be doing anything ?
(b) Why will she not be flying the kites?
(c) Where will he not be staying now ?

Future Perfect

Future Perfect में Affirmative एवं Interrogative sentences का structure निम्न होता है:

Subject + will/shall have + V-III + Object +.......... . *Affirmative*

Will/Shall + Subject + have + V-III + Object + ...? *Interrogative*

Wh-words से शुरू होने वाले Interrogative sentences का structure निम्न होता है:

Wh-word + will/shall + Subject + have + V-III + Object ?

(a) Where will he have gone before she reaches here.
(b) Why will he have left before the train arrives.
(c) What will he have done, before his wife comes.

इस तरह के Interrogative sentences को जब negative में परिवर्तित किया जाता है, तो Interrogative-negative sentences का structure निम्न होता है:

Wh-word + will/shall + subject + not + have + V-III + object + ?

(a) Where will he not have gone before I reach there?
(b) Why will he not have left before the teacher comes?

Future Perfect Continuous

Future Perfect Continuous में Affirmative एवं Interrogative sentences का Structure निम्न होता है:

Subject + will/shall + have been + V (ing form) + since/for + ... *Affirmative*

Will/Shall + Subject + have been + V (ing form) + since/for + ... *Interrogative*

Wh-words से शुरू होने वाले Interrogative sentences का structure निम्न होता है:

Wh-word + will/shall + Subject + have been + V (ing form) +.... ?

(a) What will he have been doing since yesterday?
(b) Why shall they have been making a noise for so long?
(c) Where will you have been playing for two hours?

इस तरह के वाक्यों को negative में परिवर्तित करते समय 'not' को subject के बाद में लगाया जाता है एवं Interrogative-negative sentences का structure निम्न होता है:

Wh-words + will/shall + Subject + not + have been + V (ing form) + ... ?

(a) Why will they not have been playing for two hours ?
(b) What will you not have been doing since morning ?

Some Important Points about Questions with Wh-Words

(1) जब who, whose, which, what का प्रयोग subject रूप में होता है, तो इनके तुरन्त बाद main verb का प्रयोग निम्न प्रकार किया जाता है:

(a) Who pay the fees ?
(b) Who took my pen ?
(c) Whose horse won ?
(d) Whose vehicle broke down ?
(e) Which horse won ?
(f) Which animal arrived first ?
(g) What happened ?
(h) What caused this noise ?

(2) Whom, whose, which, what का प्रयोग verb के object के रूप में निम्न प्रकार किया जाता है:

(a) Whom did the society appoint ?
(b) Whose vehicle broke down ?
(c) Whose clothes did you borrow ?
(d) Which hand do you use?
(e) Which of these dates would you be available?
(f) What magazine do you subscribe?
(g) What did they eat?

यहाँ whom, whose, which एवं what का प्रयोग verb के object के रूप में हुआ है।

(3) प्रश्न के रूप में who, whom, which एवं what के साथ preposition का प्रयोग निम्न प्रकार किया जाता है:

Preposition + Whom :

(a) With whom did you go?
(b) To whom were you speaking?

आजकल whom की जगह who का प्रयोग प्रचलित है। who का प्रयोग निम्न प्रकार किया जाता है:

(a) Who did you go with?
(b) Who were you speaking to?

इसी तरह which/what के साथ preposition का प्रयोग निम्न structure में किया जा सकता है:

(a) In which class do you read?
(b) On what do you base your arguments?

इन वाक्यों को निम्न प्रकार भी लिखा जा सकता है:

(c) Which class do you read in?
(d) What do you base your arguments on ?

(4) Use of what : What का प्रयोग question हेतु कई अर्थ में होता है। जैसे:

(a) What bird is that? — यह कौन-सा पक्षी है?
(b) What makes that noise? — यह शोर कौन मचा रहा है?
(c) What country do you come from? — आप किस देश से आए हैं?
(d) What do you say? — आप क्या कहते हैं?
(e) What do you do that for?/ Why do you do that? — आप वह क्यों/किसके लिए करते हैं?
(f) What was the examination like? — परीक्षा कैसी थी?
(Ans : It was very difficult.)
(g) What was the weather like? — मौसम कैसा था?
(Ans : It was very hot.)
(h) What does she look like? — वह कैसी दिखाई देती है?
(Ans : She is tall and glamorous. She looks like a film heroine.)
(i) What is he? What is his profession? — वह क्या है? अर्थात् उसका व्यवसाय क्या है?
(j) What is his father? — उसके पिताजी का व्यवसाय क्या है?
(k) What age are you? — तुम्हारी कितनी उम्र है?
(l) What is your age? — तुम्हारी उम्र क्या है?
(m) What height is she? — वह कितनी ऊँचाई की है?
(n) What is her height? — उसकी ऊँचाई (लम्बाई) कितनी है?

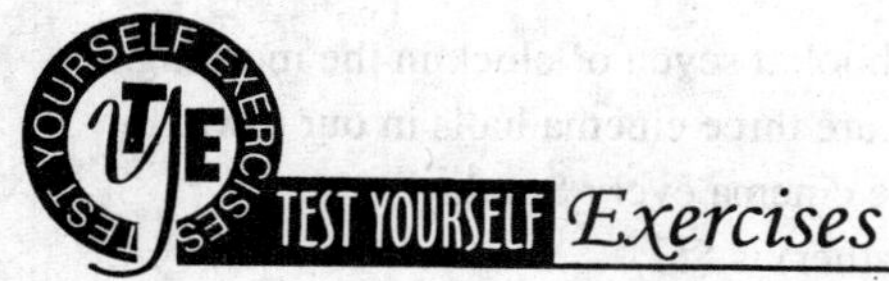

01

Frame a question to get the following answers :

Q. 1. ....? **Ans.** Yes, I play football.
Q. 2. When ....? **Ans.** He will go to Delhi next week.
Q. 3. How many ....? **Ans.** She has two sons and a daughter.
Q. 4. Where ....? **Ans.** He keeps his money in a nationalised bank.
Q. 5. How many ....? **Ans.** There are 366 days in the leap year.
Q. 6. How much ....? **Ans.** Our cow gives twenty kilo milk in a day.
Q. 7. Whose ....? **Ans.** It (car) is mine.
Q. 8. How old ....? **Ans.** He (his son) is ten years old.
Q. 9. ....? **Ans.** Yes, I have paid my tuition fees.
Q. 10. Who ....? **Ans.** Mr. Sharma teaches us Physics.

02

Frame a question to get the following answers :

Q. 1. Why ....? **Ans.** He has gone to the railway station to see off his cousin.
Q. 2. Who ....? **Ans.** It is my friend Rajendra (at the gate).
Q. 3. How many ....? **Ans.** I got three prizes.
Q. 4. How far ....? **Ans.** It (My village) is forty kilometers from here.
Q. 5. How much ....? **Ans.** We buy two kg. milk of cow daily.
Q. 6. What ....? **Ans.** My hobbies are reading novels and making friends.
Q. 7. Which ....? **Ans.** I play football and cricket.
Q. 8. ....? **Ans.** No, she could not catch the train.
Q. 9. What ....? **Ans.** He (my brother) is an engineer.
Q. 10. ....? **Ans.** Yes, we have tea in the morning.

03

Frame a question to get the following answers :

Q. 1. How far .... ? **Ans.** It (Delhi) is 160 kilometers from here.
Q. 2. What ....? **Ans.** I am writing a letter.
Q. 3. How ....? **Ans.** She was welcomed warmly by her friends.
Q. 4. Where ....? **Ans.** You can find it on the table.
Q. 5. Why ....? **Ans.** We eat to live.
Q. 6. ....? **Ans.** Yes , I'm afraid of ghosts.
Q. 7. How many ....? **Ans.** I made 58 runs yesterday.
Q. 8. Who ....? **Ans.** My friend has invited me.
Q. 9. How long ....? **Ans.** We have been living in this country for three years only.

Q. 10. When ....? Ans. I go to school at seven o' clock in the morning.
Q. 11. Is there...? Ans. Yes, there are three cinema halls in our town.
Q. 12. How often ....? Ans. I go to the cinema every Sunday.
Q. 13. How ....? Ans. He (my father) is 55.
Q. 14. Who ....? Ans. Mr. S.K. Jain is my class teacher.
Q. 15. When ....? Ans. I reached home at 9 p.m.

Solution TYE 01

(1) Do you play football?
(2) When will he go to Delhi?
(3) How many children has she?
(4) Where does he keep his money?
(5) How many days are there in the leap year?
(6) How much milk does your cow give in a day?
(7) Whose car is it?
(8) How old is your son?
(9) Have you paid your tuition fees?
(10) Who teaches you Physics?

Solution TYE 02

(1) Why has he gone to the railway station?
(2) Who is at the gate?
(3) How many prizes did you get?
(4) How far is your village from here?
(5) How much milk of cow do you buy daily?
(6) What are your hobbies?
(7) Which games do you play?
(8) Could she catch the train?
(9) What is your brother?
(10) Do you have tea in the morning?

Solution TYE 03

(1) How far is Delhi from here?
(2) What are you doing?
(3) How was she welcomed by her friends?
(4) Where can I find it?
(5) Why do we eat?
(6) Are you afraid of ghosts?
(7) How many runs did you make yesterday?
(8) Who has invited you on this occasion?
(9) How long have you been living in this country?
(10) When do you go to school?
(11) Is there any cinema hall in your town?
(12) How often do you go to the cinema?
(13) How old is your father?
(14) Who is your class teacher?
(15) When did you reach home?

CHAPTER

24

QUESTION TAG

जैसा पूर्व में बताया गया है। Question tag एक पूर्ण प्रश्न नहीं है, बल्कि यह एक कथन के पीछे लगा पुछल्ला प्रश्न है। Question tag का प्रयोग आपसी वार्तालाप में किया जाता है। इसका उद्देश्य, श्रोता का ध्यान वक्ता के कथन की ओर आकर्षित करना या अपने कथन की पुष्टि चाहना होता है।

Rules of Framing Question Tag

***Rule* 1** **Question tag बनाने के लिए Helping verbs जिन्हें Anomalous finites भी कहते हैं (Total 24) का प्रयोग subject के साथ किया जाता है। यदि Question tag, Negative है, तो Anomalous verb का प्रयोग संक्षिप्त रूप (abbreviated form) में किया जाता है। जैसे : Isn't he ?, Aren't I ?, Won't they? etc. इन Anomalous finites की 'not' के साथ Abbreviated form निम्न होती है :**

do + not	=	don't	will + not	=	won't
does + not	=	doesn't	can + not	=	can't
did + not	=	didn't	should + not	=	shouldn't
am I not...	=	aren't I	would + not	=	wouldn't
is + not	=	isn't	could + not	=	couldn't
are + not	=	aren't	may + not	=	mayn't
has + not	=	hasn't	might + not	=	mightn't
have + not	=	haven't	ought + not	=	oughtn't
had + not	=	hadn't	must + not	=	mustn't
was + not	=	wasn't	used + not	=	usedn't
were + not	=	weren't	need + not	=	needn't
shall + not	=	shan't	dare + not	=	daren't

***Rule* 2** **Question tag का structure निम्न होता है :**

Helping Verb + Subject ? *Positive*
Helping Verb + n't + Subject? *Negative*

यदि वक्ता का कथन Positive हो, तो Question tag, Negative होता है। यदि कथन Negative हो तो Question tag, Positive होता है।
वक्ता के कथन (statement) के बाद comma लगाकर, Question tag लिखा जाता है।

Question tag, Capital letter से शुरू नहीं किया जाता है।

***Rule* 3** **Question tag के साथ noun नहीं लगता है, pronoun का प्रयोग होता है। जैसे :**

(a) Ram is going to Jaipur, isn't he? (b) Sita is not cooking, is she?

***Rule* 4** **यदि कथन में कोई Helping verb नहीं हो तो Question tag में do/does/did को काम में लेते हैं। जैसे :**

(a) He goes to office, doesn't he ? (b) They play football, don't they?

***Rule* 5** **यदि वक्ता के कथन का subject, एक Personal pronoun है तो Question tag में वही personal pronoun प्रयुक्त होता है, लेकिन यदि कथन में subject कोई noun (किसी का नाम) है, तो Question tag में जो pronoun प्रयुक्त होगा, वह कथन के subject के Gender (male or female) तथा Number (singular or plural) के अनुसार होगा, अर्थात् यदि वक्ता के कथन में subject, male एवं singular है, तो Question tag में pronoun 'he' का प्रयोग होगा। जैसेः**

(a) It is not correct, is it? (b) It is true, isn't it ?
(c) They play, don't they? (d) He is watching TV, isn't he?
(e) You know it, don't you? (f) Ram and Sita are swimming, aren't they?
(g) She is very beautiful, isn't she? (h) We played a match, didn't we?

***Rule* 6** **यदि वक्ता के कथन में there, this, that, those, these आदि subject रूप में हो, तो Question tag में subject निम्न प्रकार लगता है :**

कथन का Subject	Question Tag में Subject
There	There
One	One
This	It
That	It
These	They
Those	They

Read the following examples :

(a) There is a cow, isn't there? (b) One can hold it, can't one?
(c) This is his pen, isn't it? (d) That is his house, isn't it ?
(e) These are animals, aren't they? (f) Those are birds, are't they?

***Rule* 7** **यदि one, this, that, these, those का प्रयोग कथन में एक adjective की तरह हुआ है अर्थात् यदि इनके साथ कोई noun आया है तो Question tag का subject, noun के gender एवं person के अनुसार लगता है। जैसे :**

(a) One man can pull it, can't he? (b) This girl was present there, wasn't she?
(c) This book is very useful, isn't it? (d) That boy has no manners, has he?
(e) This boy won the race, didn't he? (f) Those books are mine, aren't they?

***Rule* 8** **यदि वक्ता के कथन का Subject, no one, none, anyone, someone, everyone, everybody, somebody या nobody है, तो Question tag का subject they होगा। जैसे :**

(a) None can say so, can they? (b) No one voted against the bill, did they?
(c) Someone invited me, didn't they? (d) Somebody will be there, won't they?
(e) Anyone can attend the function, can't they?
(f) Nobody has praised the move, have they?

***Rule* 9** **यदि वक्ता के कथन का Subject, nothing, anything, something या everything हो, तो ध्यान रखें, Question tag का subject-it होगा। जैसे**

(a) Everything is arranged, isn't it? (b) Something is missing, isn't it?
(c) Anything can be arranged, can't it? (d) Nothing can be seen, can it?

***Rule* 10** **यदि वक्ता के कथन का Subject निम्न में से कोई होता है, तो Question tag का subject-we होता है।**

All of us, Some of us, Any of us, None of us, Most of us, Everyone of us, Either of us, Neither of us etc.

लेकिन यदि us की जगह you या they का प्रयोग किया गया हो, तो Question tag का subject you या they/them होता है। जैसे :

(a) All of us are invited, aren't we? (b) All of you are invited, aren't you?
(c) All of them are invited, aren't they? (d) Either of you can join, can't you?
(e) Neither of you can do it, can you? (f) None of us was present there, were we?

Rule 11 **जब कथन में I am का प्रयोग होता है एवं Question tag नकारात्मक में बनाना है, तो Amn't I कभी भी न लिखें। इस हेतु Aren't I लिखा जाएगा। लेकिन Affirmative में Question tag बनाना हो तो Am I लिखना सही है। जैसे :**

(a) I am going to meet her, aren't I? (b) I am not going there, am I?
(c) I am your friend, aren't I? (d) I am not your friend, am I?

Rule 12 **Dare/need को semi modal auxiliary माना जाता है, इनका प्रयोग Main verb के रूप में भी किया जाता है। जब Dare/need का प्रयोग modal auxiliary की तरह किया गया हो, तो Question tag में dare/need का प्रयोग किया जाता है। जैसे :**

(a) He dare not speak so, dare he? (b) She need not come here, need she?

(यहाँ dare not एवं need not का प्रयोग auxiliary की तरह हुआ है।)

लेकिन यदि dare/need का प्रयोग मुख्य verb की तरह हुआ हो, तो Question tag में किसी Auxiliary verb का प्रयोग पूर्व में बताए गए नियमानुसार किया जाता है। जैसे :

(a) He dares to speak like this, doesn't he? (b) They dare to meet the chairman, don't they?
(c) He needs your help, doesn't he? (d) They need my assistance, don't they?

(यहाँ dare, need का प्रयोग मुख्य Verb की तरह हुआ है।)

Rule 13 **यदि वक्ता के कथन में used to का प्रयोग हुआ हो, तो Question tag में usedn't या didn't का प्रयोग किया जा सकता है। यदि Question tag Affirmative में बनाना हो, तो used या did का प्रयोग किया जाता है। जैसे :**

(a) She used to go to temple, usedn't she? *or* didn't she?
(b) He used to smoke, usedn't he? *or* didn't he?
(c) He usedn't smoke, used he? *or* did he?
(d) He usedn't go to temple, used they? *or* did they?

Some Important Points

(1) कई बार वक्ता के कथन में 'not' का प्रयोग तो नहीं होता है, लेकिन ऐसे शब्दों का प्रयोन होता है जिससे वाक्य का अर्थ नकारात्मक (negative) हो जाता है। जैसे : Few, little, neither, none, no one, nothing, hardly, rarely, seldom, scarcely, never etc.

ऐसे कथन के साथ Question tag, Positive में बनता है। जैसे :

(a) None was present there, were they? (b) No one can solve this question, can they?
(c) Nobody believe it, do they? (d) They said nothing about it, did they?
(e) I know little about U.S.A, do I? (f) She rarely comes here, does she?
(g) Neither of them was available there, were they?
(h) Few people can live in such circumstances, can they?

(2) यदि कथन एक सकारात्मक (positive) Imperative sentence (जिसमें प्रार्थना, आदेश का भाव होता है) हो, तो Question tag, will या won't किसी से भी बन सकता है, लेकिन Negative imperative sentence का Question tag हमेशा positive बनता है। जैसे :

(a) Open the gate, will you? (b) Open the gate, won't you?
(c) Don't open the gate, will you? (d) Go there, will you? or won't you?
(e) Consult a doctor, won't you? (f) Don't pluck the flowers, will you?
(g) Please come here, will you? (h) Please come here, won't you?

इस तरह के Imperative sentence में बात को अधिक प्रभावशाली बनाने के लिए नकारात्मक (negative) Question tag का प्रयोग किया जाता है।

(3) यदि Imperative sentence से कोई नाराजगी जाहिर की जाती है या नाराजगी व्यक्त करते हुए कोई कथन किया जाता है, तो can't you, Question tag लगाना उचित रहता है। जैसे :

(a) Use your own vehicle, can't you ? (b) Keep shut, can't you?
(c) Use your own stationary, can't you? (d) Mind your own business, can't you?

(4) Let's (Let us) से शुरू हुए वक्ता के कथन के साथ Question tag, 'shall we?' लगता है एवं Let him/let you/let them से शुरू वक्ता के कथन के साथ Question tag 'will you' लगेगा, जैसे :

(a) Let's play, shall we? (b) Let us sing, shall we?
(c) Let's go, shall we? (d) Let them play, will you?
(e) Let him work, will you? (f) Let her cook, will you?

TEST YOURSELF Exercises

01

Complete the following sentences by using the correct Question tags :

(1) Everybody was watching the cricket match on TV,.........?
(2) He is a very wise man, ...? (3) Mrs. Meena is a good teacher, ...?
(4) We saw a rainbow in the sky yesterday, ...?
(5) Sita is a beautiful girl,.........? (6) You should not smoke, ...?
(7) Miss Neha does not play tennis, ...? (8) I am older than you, ...?
(9) You always have your lunch at 1 o'clock,.........?
(10) I can do it for you, ...? (11) She doesn't want to go to college today, ...?
(12) Let's pray to Almighty, ...? (13) He had met you before, ...?
(14) We couldn't enjoy the picnic,.........?

02

Write the letter a, b, c or d as the correct answer in the brackets :

(1) Do as I say, ...?
(a) didn't you (b) won't you (c) needn't you (d) shan't you ( )

(2) Now you can make question tags, ...?
(a) can you (b) won't you (c) can't you (d) will you ( )

(3) You fell on your back, ...?
(a) didn't you (b) weren't you (c) have you (d) did you ( )

(4) Few people know that you are an artist, ...?
(a) do they (b) don't they (c) aren't they (d) haven't they ( )

(5) Tomorrow we will attend our college, ...?
(a) shall we (b) will we (c) won't we (d) shouldn't you ( )

(6) The Bishnois of Rajasthan protect trees and animals, ...?
(a) have they (b) weren't they (c) do they (d) don't they ( )

(7) Everyone wanted a ticket, ...?
(a) didn't they (b) didn't he (c) didn't she (d) haven't they ( )

(8) Let's take a little rest before we start again, ...?
(a) will we (b) should we (c) shall we (d) needn't we ( )

(9) Anjali dances very well, ...?
(a) does she (b) doesn't she (c) aren't she (d) isn't she ( )

(10) Both Ram and Shyam are engineers, ...?
(a) isn't he (b) isn't she (c) are they (d) aren't they ( )

(11) He knows nobody in the colony, ...?
(a) does he (b) did he (c) doesn't he (d) didn't he ( )

(12) Jehangir was a great judge, ...?
(a) doesn't he (b) didn't he (c) wasn't he (d) weren't he ( )

(13) I am looking after the garden, ...?
(a) amn't I (b) aren't I (c) isn't I (d) don't I ( )

(14) It is quite hot outside today, ...?
(a) is it (b) isn't it (c) doesn't it (d) aren't it ( )

03

Write the letter a, b, c or d as the correct answer in the brackets :

(1) Nisha dances very well, ...?
(a) doesn't she (b) does she (c) aren't she (d) isn't she ( )

(2) We have not met before, ...?
(a) did we (b) didn't we (c) haven't she (d) have we ( )

(3) I am senior to you, ...?
(a) do I (b) don't I (c) aren't I (d) amn't I ( )

(4) You are a bit late today, ...?
(a) aren't you (b) don't you (c) are you (d) do you ( )

(5) I do not now live in this colony , ...?
(a) did I (b) aren't I (c) don't I (d) do I ( )

(6) We are learning English Grammar, ...?
(a) are we (b) shall we (c) aren't we (d) shan't we ( )

(7) She is too old, ...?
(a) doesn't she (b) isn't she (c) aren't she (d) is she ( )

(8) You will come tomorrow, ...?
(a) will you (b) shouldn't you (c) won't you (d) needn't you ( )

(9) The house needs immediate repairing, ...?
(a) does it (b) isn't it (c) is it (d) doesn't it ( )

(10) You don't like sugar in your coffee, ...?
(a) didn't you (b) do you (c) will you (d) don't you ( )

(11) Open the window, ...?
(a) don't you (b) aren't you (c) will you (d) should you ( )

(12) I have already taken tea, ...?
(a) didn't I (b) haven't I (c) did I (d) have I ( )

(13) I am working hard on this book, ...?
(a) don't I (b) won't I (c) aren't I (d) can't I ( )

(14) He was asleep, ...?
(a) was he (b) wasn't he (c) didn't he (d) did he ( )

(15) Let us start now, ...?
(a) shall we (b) should we (c) could we (d) would we ( )

04

Complete the following sentences by using the correct Question tags :

(1) Delhi is not very far from Meerut ....?
(2) Shalini is very young ....?
(3) You are always punctual, ...?
(4) Students are learning swimming ....?
(5) They don't like to bathe in winter, ...?
(6) You should not drink wine, ...?
(7) Miss Minu does not play chess, ...?
(8) I am elder to you, ...?
(9) You always have your lunch at 12 O'clock, ...?
(10) I can do it for you, ...?

05

Complete the following sentences by using the correct Question tags :

(1) He doesn't want to go to college today, ...?
(2) Let's pray to God, ...?
(3) You had met me before, ...?
(4) We couldn't enjoy the picnic, ...?
(5) He is a rude man, ...?
(6) Everybody was watching the TV, ...?
(7) Mrs. Saxena is a good lady, ...?
(8) Something must be done for us, ...?
(9) Someone might come, ...?
(10) He needs money, ...?
(11) I needn't write, ...?
(12) Nisha need not go there, ...?

SOLUTIONS TYE TEST YOURSELF *Exercises*

Solution TYE 01

(1) weren't they, (2) isn' the, (3) isn't she, (4) didn't we, (5) isn't she,
(6) should you, (7) does she, (8) aren't I, (9) don't you, (10) can't I,
(11) does she, (12) shall we, (13) hadn't he, (14) could we.

Solution TYE 02

(1) b, (2) c, (3) a, (4) a, (5) c, (6) d,
(7) a, (8) c, (9) b, (10) d, (11) a, (12) c,
(13) B, (14) B.

Solution TYE 03

(1) a, (2) d, (3) c, (4) a, (5) d, (6) c,
(7) b, (8) c, (9) d, (10) b, (11) c, (12) b,
(13) c, (14) b, (15) a.

Solution TYE 04

(1) is it, (2) isn't she, (3) aren't you, (4) aren't they, (5) do they,
(6) should you, (7) does she, (8) aren't I, (9) haven't you, (10) can't I.

Solution TYE 05

(1) does he, (2) shall we, (3) hadn't you, (4) could we, (5) isn't he,
(6) weren't they, (7) isn't she, (8) mustn't it, (9) mightn't they, (10) doesn't he,
(11) need I, (12) need she.

CHAPTER 25

USE OF CAPITAL LETTERS AND PUNCTUATION

Alphabet : अंग्रेजी भाषा 26 अक्षरों से बनी है, जिन्हें Alphabet कहते हैं।

A B C D E F G H I J K L M N O P Q R S T U V W X Y Z.

उपर्युक्त दर्शाए सभी Capital Letters हैं, जबकि Small Letters को निम्न प्रकार लिखा जाता है :

a b c d e f g h i j k l m n o p q r s t u v w x y z.

Capital letters एवं Small letters की आकृति भिन्न होती है लेकिन उच्चारण समान होता है

English भाषा में 5 स्वर अर्थात् Vowels (A E I O U) तथा 21 व्यंजन अर्थात् Consonants होते हैं। हिन्दी भाषा में 52 अक्षर (16 स्वर एवं 36 व्यंजन) होते हैं। हिन्दी भाषा में Capital letter या Small letter जैसा कोई अक्षर भेद नहीं होता है।

English में एक शब्द, कई प्रकार की ध्वनि हेतु प्रयुक्त होता है। जिन अक्षरों को स्वर (A E I O U) माना गया है उनका प्रयोग बहुत बार व्यंजन की तरह होता है अर्थात् उनसे बनने वाले शब्द का उच्चारण व्यंजन की तरह होता है। अत: अंग्रेजी भाषा में शब्दों के सही उच्चारण का बहुत महत्त्व है।

अंग्रेजी भाषा में Alphabet में Capital letter, Small letter में अन्तर किया गया है। अत: यह भी ध्यान रखना आवश्यक है कि कहाँ, किस word में Capital letter का प्रयोग होता है। सही अंग्रेजी लिखने हेतु Capital letters के सही प्रयोग का ज्ञान होना परम आवश्यक है।

Use of Capital Letters

Rules

निम्न स्थितियों में Capital letter के प्रयोग का *ध्यान रखें* :

(1) First letter of a sentence : हर वाक्य हमेशा Capital letter से शुरू होता है। जैसे :

(a) He is a good boy.

(b) They came to meet me.

(2) Proper noun एवं Proper adjective का पहला अक्षर Capital होता है। अर्थात् किसी व्यक्ति, शहर, देश, राज्य, समुद्र, नदी, दिन, माह, ग्रन्थ, भवन, जाति, त्यौहार तथा भाषा के नाम का पहला अक्षर Capital होता है जैसे :

Ram, Delhi, India, Rajasthan, Indians, The Himalayas, The Ramayan, Sunday, December, The Rajputs, Diwali, English, Hindi, The Tajmahal.

(3) ईश्वर (God) या उसके लिए प्रयुक्त समस्त nouns एवं pronouns; जैसे :
My God, Thou art merciful, The Lord, The Almighty, God is Omnipresent.

(4) पद का नाम, डिग्रियों के नाम का पहला अक्षर Capital letter में होता है। जैसे :
Prime Minister, M.A, B.A

(5) Pronoun 'I' एवं Interjection 'O' जब किसी वाक्य में अकेले आएँ, तो हमेशा Capital letter में लिखे जाते हैं। जैसे :
(a) He is taller than I. (b) O, my God !

(6) English Poem (कविता) में प्रत्येक लाइन का प्रथम अक्षर Capital letter होता है। जैसे :
Twenty days has September, April , June and November.

(7) Inverted commas (" ") के अन्दर के वाक्य का पहला अक्षर Capital letter होता है। जैसे :
He said, "She will go to market."

(8) Initials एवं abbreviations के लिए प्रयुक्त अक्षर Capital letter होता है। जैसे :
Sh. M.K. Gandhi, S.D.O., G.M., R.M.P.

(9) उपाधियों के नाम, राजनीतिक दलों के नाम, समाचार-पत्रों के नाम, मुख्य ऐतिहासिक घटनाओं के नाम, सार्वजनिक संस्थानों के नाम, किताब के नाम, Title या Heading के नाम का पहला अक्षर Capital letter होता है। जैसे :
Padma Bhushan, Congress, Bhartiya Janata Party, The Hindustan Times, The First World War, The Battle of Panipat, The Nirmal Shiksha Kendra, The General English Book, A Clever Monkey, A Visit to Water Park.

(10) अंग्रेजी में लिखे जाने वाले First, Middle एवं Last name का पहला अक्षर Capital होता है। जैसे :
Dipesh Jain, Suresh Chandra Gupta, Veer Pratap Rao, Man Mohan Singh.

(11) व्यक्ति के नाम से पहले लगने वाले Title का पहला अक्षर Capital letter में लिखा जाता है। जैसे :
Mr, Mrs, Miss, Sir, Madam, Dr., Lt., Prof.

(12) जब वाक्य में Father/Uncle/Mother/Aunt etc. का प्रयोग Proper noun की तरह होता है, तो इनके पूर्व my, his, her, your, the etc. का प्रयोग नहीं होता है और इनका पहला अक्षर Capital letter में लिखा जाता है। यदि इनके पहले my, his, her the, your etc. का प्रयोग होता है, तो इनका पहला अक्षर small letter ही होगा जैसे :
(a) Father was happy but Mother was sad. (b) I am waiting for Father.
(c) I dare not face Mother and Aunt. (d) My father is a businessman.
(e) Where is your uncle?

वाक्य (a), (b), (c) में Father/Mother/Aunt एक Proper noun की तरह प्रयुक्त हुए हैं।

Words

Alphabets को आपस में मिलाकर लिखने से जब उसका कोई अर्थ (meaning) निकलता है, तो उसे शब्द (word) कहते हैं। एक शब्द बनाने के लिए कम-से-कम एक स्वर एवं एक व्यंजन का होना आवश्यक होता है। यदि स्वर न हो तो उसकी ध्वनि वाला व्यंजन होना चाहिए। जैसे Sky, Try. यहाँ y स्वर का काम करता है, लेकिन A, I, O जैसे शब्द, जिनमें एक ही Alphabet है इसका अपवाद है। A = एक I = मैं, O = ओ।

यदि Alphabets को मिलाकर लिखने से उनका कोई अर्थ (meaning) नहीं निकलता है तो उसे शब्द नहीं कहा जाता है। जैसे : etahr, elhdi, yrt.

Punctuation

अधिकांश छात्रों को Punctuation का बहुत कम ज्ञान होता है। स्कूल, कॉलेज में भी इसे नितान्त महत्त्वहीन विषय समझकर, ढंग से नहीं पढ़ाया जाता है। शुद्ध अंग्रेजी लिखने हेतु तथा वाक्य का सही अर्थ व्यक्त करने हेतु Punctuation के नियमों का ज्ञान होना आवश्यक है।

Definition: The right use of putting in marks or stops in writing is called Punctuation. अर्थात् लिखते समय marks or stops या points का सही रूप में प्रयोग करना Punctuation कहलाता है।

यदि Punctuation marks गलत स्थान पर लगाए जाएँ तो वाक्य का अर्थ ही बदल सकता है। जैसे :

''The cat'', said the owner, ''is very faithful.''

The cat said, ''The owner is very faithful.''

Punctuation Marks

अंग्रेजी भाषा में मुख्य Punctuation marks निम्न हैं :

1. Full stop (.)
2. Ellipsis (...)
3. Question mark (?)
4. Mark of Exclamation (!)
5. Comma (,)
6. Semi colon (;)
7. Colon (:)
8. Dash (—)
9. Hyphen (-)
10. Inverted Commas (“ ”)

(1) Full stop [पूर्ण विराम (.)] :

(1) Interrogative एवं Exclamatory sentences के अतिरिक्त सभी प्रकार के sentences के अन्त में Full stop लगता है। चाहे वह वाक्य सामान्य statement हो अथवा command हो या sentence के मध्य में कोई प्रश्न (indirect question) हो। जैसे :

He is a good boy.	(Statement)
Do not open the gate	(Command)
He asked me where I was.	(Indirect question)

(2) Initials एवं Abbreviations के बाद Full stop का प्रयोग होता है। जैसे :

R.K. Sharma	P.K. Jain	M.L.A.	M.P.	U.K.
F.I.R.	M.Sc.	M.A.	A.M.	U.S.A.

(a) आजकल Mr, Mrs, Dr, Ltd. जैसे कई Abbreviations के बाद में Full stop नहीं लगाया जाता है।

(b) यदि कोई वाक्य Abbreviations से ही समाप्त हो तो वाक्य के अन्त में एक ही Full stop आता है।

He is an M.L.A.

(2) Ellipsis (... or ....) : जब वाक्य में से कुछ शब्द या शब्दों का लोप (omit) किया गया हो, तो Ellipsis का प्रयोग किया जाता है।

(1) यदि किसी वाक्य में शुरू के या बीच के शब्दों का लोप (omission) किया गया हो, तो Ellipsis में तीन full stop का प्रयोग किया जाता है। जैसे :

a beautiful girl she ... with her sister.

(2) यदि किसी वाक्य के अन्तिम शब्दों का लोप (omission) किया गया हो, Ellipsis में चार full stop (....) का प्रयोग किया जाता है। जैसे :

(a) Rahul went to Jaipur with ....

(b) Ramesh is the man who ....

(3) Question mark [प्रश्नवाचक चिह्न (?)] :

(1) Interrogative sentence के अन्त में तथा एक sentence में question पूछने वाले word (Question tag), clause या phrase के बाद भी Question mark लगाया जाता है। जैसे :

(a) Who invited you to dinner?
(b) Where does she live?
(c) "Is everything ok?", Ram asked.
(d) Open the window, will you?
(e) Whom shall we elect? Rahul? Meenakshi?

(2) जब वाक्य में किसी प्रकार की अनिश्चितता या शंकात्मक प्रश्न जैसा भाव हो तो Question mark लगाया जाता है। जैसे :

Gandhiji died in 1948?

उपरोक्त वाक्य 1948 के लिए uncertainty का भाव प्रदर्शित करता है।

(4) Mark of Exclamation [विस्मयादिबोधक चिह्न (!)] : ऐसे sentences, clause, phrase या single word जो अति आश्चर्य, अति दु:ख अति प्रसन्नता, प्रशंसा या कामना का भाव प्रकट करते हैं; के बाद Mark of exclamation (!) का प्रयोग किया जाता है। जैसे :

(a) Hurrah! we have won the match.
(b) What a beautiful bird it is!
(c) Alas! I have ruined!
(d) Wow! you are great.

(5) Comma [अल्प या अर्द्ध विराम (,)] :

(1) यदि किसी वाक्य में एक ही part of speech के तीन या अधिक (more than two) शब्द आते हैं, तो इन शब्दों को एक-दूसरे से पृथक् करने के लिए comma (,) का प्रयोग किया जाता है। अन्तिम शब्द से पहले यदि and का प्रयोग हुआ हो, तो वहाँ पर Comma नहीं लगाया जाता है। जैसे :

(a) She purchased an eraser, a pen, and some copies.
(b) She is a dedicated, sincere and honest lady.

उपरोक्त वाक्यों में and से पूर्व comma नहीं लगाया गया है लेकिन कई ऐसे वाक्य भी होते हैं जिनमें and से पूर्व comma लगाना आवश्यक होता है। जैसे :

Their equipments included airplanes, helicopters, artillery, amphibious, vehicles and tanks.

यदि and से पूर्व comma हटा दिया जाए तो यह समझा जा सकता है कि tanks भी amphibious है।

(amphibious means can be used in land and water both).

(2) वाक्य के शुरू में आने वाले adjective, adverb, participle या participle phrase के बाद भी comma का प्रयोग किया जाता है। जैसे :

(a) Technically, the scheme is quite feasible.
(b) Pleased with the result, she called a press conference.

(3) Words of address, interjection जो वाक्य को शुरू करने में प्रयुक्त होते हैं। जैसे : Oh, Yes, No, However, Nevertheless, Still, Anyway, Well, Why, Frankly, Really, Moreover, Incidentally etc. के बाद Comma का प्रयोग किया जाता है। जैसे :

(a) Ramesh, where have you gone?
(b) Oh, she is here!
(c) Why, you can't say so?
(d) Still, he must realise that he is my guest.
(e) Fine, we will organise a party.
(f) No, I can't solve it.

(4) Direct speech में Reporting verb को Reported speech से अलग करने के लिए comma का प्रयोग किया जाता है।

He said to me, "I will come on Monday."

(5) Compound sentence में छोटी-छोटी Coordinating clause को स्पष्ट रूप से पृथक्-पृथक् करने के लिए comma का प्रयोग किया जाता है।

(a) He sold his house, sold his furniture, rented his computer, and left the city.

(b) We went to hill station, made some purchasing, visited the temple, and returned home at 12 p.m.

(6) वाक्य में pair of words को पृथक् करने के लिए (He is intelligent and trustworthy, devoted and dedicated, sincere and honest.) comma का प्रयोग किया जाता है तथा Principal clause से Noun clause, Adjective clause तथा Adverbial clause को अलग करने के लिए comma का प्रयोग किया जाता है। जैसे :

(a) Since he says so, she should obey him. (b) How he passed, is a point of controversy.

(c) If he does not go there, he will loose.

(7) वाक्य के मध्य आने वाले words, phrases या clauses के दोनों तरफ उन्हें स्पष्ट रूप से पृथक्-पृथक् दिखाने हेतु comma लगाया जाता है। जैसे :

(a) The treaty, as everybody knows, may be signed today.

(b) She, as per my calculations, is not capable enough to carry out this work.

(c) Her way of cooking is as good as, or better than, yours.

(8) किसी शब्द को महत्त्वपूर्ण बनाने के लिए उसे बार-बार प्रयुक्त किया जाता है, जो उनके बीच comma लगाया जाता है। जैसे :

(a) Come, come ; don't delay. (b) Try, try and try again.

(9) वाक्य को सुन्दर बनाने हेतु कई बार शब्दों को omit कर दिया जाता है। इन शब्दों के लिए comma लगाकर इन शब्दों की पूर्ति की जाती है। जैसे :

(a) Rakhi is seventeen; Sarita, ten. (is-omitted)

(b) Rahul is twenty; Suraj, eighteen. (is-omitted)

(10) किसी Noun या Appositive या Phrase in apposition को अलग एवं स्पष्ट दिखाने के लिए उसके पहले एवं बाद में दोनों तरफ comma लगाते हैं। जैसे :

(a) Akbar, the great king, was a great religious scholar also.

(b) Ramesh, the son of a millionaire, was sent to jail.

(11) Letter में Salutation या Subscription के बाद comma अवश्य लगाया जाता है। जैसे :

My dear father, My dear friend, Yours faithfully, Yours sincerely.

(12) जब दो Independent clause आपस में and, but, or, yet, for, nor जैसे Coordinating conjunction से जुड़े हों, तो इनके पहले comma लगाया जाता है। जैसे :

(a) She can't talk, nor can she walk. (b) He is not only rich, but he is generous also.

(c) He is poor, yet he is honest.

(13) Address लिखते समय House no, street या अन्य सन्दर्भ को अलग स्पष्ट करने हेतु comma लगाया जाता है। जैसे :

(a) 129, South West Block. (b) 329, Kala Kuan, Near Jain Temple, Alwar

यदि Adjectives एक-दूसरे से closely सम्बद्ध हों, तो comma का प्रयोग नहीं करते हैं। इसके लिए यह देखना चाहिए कि comma की जगह 'and' का प्रयाग करने पर यदि वाक्य अधिक स्पष्ट एवं सुन्दर लगता है तो and लगाएँ अन्यथा comma लगाना चाहिए। जैसे :

(a) Three happy little children, (b) A dozen colourful oranges, (c) Beautiful tall European girls.

(6) Semi Colon (;) : Comma का प्रयोग वहाँ किया जाता है जहाँ full stop से कम रुकने/ठहरने की आवश्यकता होती है, जबकि Semi colon का प्रयोग वहाँ पर किया जाता है जहाँ comma से कुछ अधिक लेकिन full stop से कुछ कम रुकने/ठहरने की आवश्यकता है। Semi colon वास्तव में comma एवं full stop के बीच की स्थिति (ठहरने की) में प्रयुक्त किया जाता है। Semi colon का प्रयोग निम्न स्थिति में किया जाता है :

(1) जब विभिन्न प्रकार के नाम व पदनाम एक series में, एक ही वाक्य में एक-दूसरे के साथ आएँ तो इन्हें अलग एवं स्पष्ट रूप से व्यक्त/प्रदर्शित करने के लिए Semi colon का प्रयोग किया जाता है। जैसे :

The nominated members are S. Krishnan, Chairman; K. Krishnan Vice Chairman; L. Krishnan, Secretary and M. Krishnan, Joint Secretary.

(2) जब दो Independent clauses के मध्य कोई conjunction नहीं आया होता है, तो उनके बीच में Semi colon का प्रयोग किया जाता है। जैसे :

(a) The hotel burnt down; it was the biggest hotel in the city.

(b) The efforts must continue; war can be fruitless.

(3) दो Independent clauses के मध्य therefore, hence, henceforth, however जैसे conjunction प्रयुक्त हुए हों, तो इन conjunctions के पहले Semi colon लगाया जाता है। जैसे :

(a) He was not well; so, he could not attend the meeting.

(b) Registrations exceed all expectations; however, there is shortage of good teachers.

(4) जब कोई Phrase या कुछ शब्द, एक वाक्य में Introductory word या Explanatory word की तरह आते हैं तो उस Phrase या उन words से पूर्व Semi colon लगाया जाता है। जैसे :

(a) She completes her work in time; she never wastes her time in taking tea, in gossiping or in making useless calls.

(b) On the advice of a friend, he chose to invest in shares of some industries; i.e. steel, I.T, and Petro products.

(7) Colon (:) :

(1) Colon का प्रयोग किसी उदाहरण या सूची को शुरू करने हेतु किया जाता है। जैसे :

(a) The three committees are as follows : Finance, Administration and Sports.

(b) He nominated five members : Rahul, Sarla, Rajani, Girish and Janardhan.

(2) वाक्य में लम्बे quotation, statement या question से पूर्व colon का प्रयोग किया जाता है। जैसे :

(a) This is the point : Can an officer insult a clerk for no material reason.

(b) Ramesh replied : "You are absolutely correct. A fight requires atleast two persons."

(c) This I believe : Sincerity pays, if not today, after some time, but it pays.

(3) किसी शब्द या Noun के बाद उसकी definition या उसका description दिया जाता है। इसके बाद Colon का प्रयोग किया जाता है। जैसे :

Noun : Name of any person or a thing.

Peacock : A large beautiful bird with blue neck and colourful feathers.

(4) एक नाटक (play) में speaker के नाम के बाद Colon का प्रयोग होता है। जैसे :

(a) Ram : I shall forgive Ravana for his misdeeds.

(b) Laxman : I shall kill Ravana.

(5) समय लिखते समय Hours एवं minutes के बीच Colon का प्रयोग किया जाता है जैसे :
10 : 30 a.m.
3 : 45 p.m.

(6) Colon का प्रयोग वाक्य में 'For example' या 'Namely' के substitute के रूप में भी किया जाता है। जैसे :
It is a city renowned for beautiful parks : Every lane is clean, parks were full of beautiful flowers, trees are planted at the road side and so many other such things.

(7) Proportion या अनुपात बताने के लिए Colon का प्रयोग किया जाता है जैसे :
15 : 3 : : 5 : 1
4 : 3 : 7

(8) Dash (—) : Dash का प्रयोग निम्न स्थितियों में किया जाता है :

(1) यदि किसी वाक्य में, विचारों में या grammatical construction में abrupt change हो, तो Dash का प्रयोग किया जाता है। जैसे :
(a) He lost the game – but I am to go to hospital.
(b) He was passed in interview – but his father is ill.

(2) वाक्य में किसी प्रकार की रुकावट को प्रदर्शित करने हेतु भी Dash का प्रयोग किया जाता है। जैसे :
(a) "Rahul, don't go now – you are too late."

(3) वाक्य में हिचकिचाहट को प्रदर्शित करने के लिए भी Dash का प्रयोग किया जाता है। जैसे :
(a) "Well", he said, "You—you can't speak like this."

(4) अपनी कही बात को स्पष्ट करने के लिए brackets की जगह भी Dash का प्रयोग किया जा सकता है। जैसे :
(a) The other man – Mukul – didn't know me.

(5) Long pause को प्रदर्शित करने के लिए, किसी चीज को महत्त्वपूर्ण बनाने के लिए भी Dash प्रयुक्त करते हैं। जैसे:
(a) That agreement was signed differently – it must be taken into account.

(6) कभी-कभी colon की जगह भी Dash का प्रयोग किया जाता है। जैसे :
I have demanded following things:
(1) One eraser. (2) One pen. (3) One pencil.

(7) Dash का प्रयोग बीच में संख्याओं Page number etc. को Omit करने के लिए भी किया जाता है। जैसे :
1985—91 Page 24—48 Chapter V—IX

(9) Hypen (-) :

(1) वाक्य का अन्तिम शब्द पहली पंक्ति में यदि पूरा नहीं आ पाता है एवं दूसरी पंक्ति में पूरा किया जाए तो पहली पंक्ति में अपूर्ण शब्द के बाद Hyphen लगाया जाता है। जैसे :
(a) Ram was not pre-
sent yesterday in his shop.
(b) Sita is indeed an intelli-
gent girl.

(2) Twenty-one से Ninety-nine तक के Compound numerals लिखते समय निम्न प्रकार से Hyphen लगाया जाता है। जैसे :
(a) Thirty-nine feet. (b) Thirty-seven miles.

(3) बहुत से compound एवं complex words के भागों को अलग-अलग सा दिखाया जाता है एवं उनके बीच Hyphen प्रयोग किया जाता है। जैसे :
Anti-government
Ex-wife
Ex-President
Pre-planned

A 10-days journey | Self-respect
H-Bomb | Door-to-door campaign
House-to-house service | Co-operation
Co-ordination | bell-like

(4) बोलने की तुतलाहट को प्रदर्शित करने के लिए भी Hyphen प्रयोग किया जाता है। जैसे :
P-p-p-please madam, R-r-r-Rahul don't beat me.

(10) Inverted commas (" ") : Inverted commas को Quotation marks भी कहा जाता है। ये Single ('....') भी प्रयोग में आते हैं एवं Double ("....") भी।

Inverted commas का प्रयोग निम्न स्थिति में किया जाता है :

(1) Inverted commas का प्रयोग Direct narration में Reported speech को बन्द करने के लिए निम्न प्रकार किया जाता है :
(a) He said, "Where do you live?"
(b) She said to me, "I am going to market."

(2) किसी के कथन (Quotation) को भी Inverted commas में बन्द किया जाता है। जैसे :
(a) Shakespeare say, "Sweet are the uses of adversity."
(b) Ram says, "Honesty is the best policy."

(3) किसी पुस्तक, समाचार-पत्र, कविता, लेख, कहानी के नाम को भी Inverted commas से बन्द करके, उनको पृथक् रूप में दिखाया जाता है। जैसे :
(a) I haven't read 'Hamlet' so far?
(b) 'An Arrogant Hare' is a good story.
(c) 'Leap Year' is a famous poem.
(d) I read 'The Economic Times' daily.

(4) कई बार वाक्य में प्रयुक्त कुछ Phrases या Words को Inverted commas द्वारा बन्द किया जाता है, जिसका उद्देश्य ऐसे Words या Phrases को अलग से दिखाना या उन पर विशेष ध्यान देना होता है। जैसे :
(a) The word 'Nature' is also used to mean the aptitude of a person.
(b) Many persons were jailed under 'POTA' in Tamil Nadu.

(5) यदि किसी quotation के अन्दर भी कोई quotation हो या Direct narration के मध्य कोई quotation आए, तो उसे भी Inverted commas के मध्य रखा जाता है। इस सन्दर्भ में यह ध्यान रखें कि ये दोनों Inverted commas अलग-अलग प्रकार के होंगे। अन्दर वाला Inverted comma सामान्यतया Single होता है। जैसे :
(a) She said to me, "Have you read 'Godan' of Prem Chand ?"
(b) Ram said to me, "Haven't you seen 'The Spiderman' so far?"

Important

(a) Avoid using exclamation mark!
Someone once said using exclamation mark in your writting is like laughing at your own jokes!!
Never use exclamation mark in your formal writting!!!
(b) Never leave a space between the last word of the sentence and the punctuation mark.

01. *Punctuate the following sentences using capital letters where necessary :*

(1) if you don't understand it tell him.
(2) he said to me what is his name.
(3) try try and try again.
(4) ram and Shyam went to punjab.
(5) ram not shyam is responsible.
(6) do what you were told.
(7) oh you are here.
(8) o lord help me.
(9) gandhiji the father of the nation loved the poor.
(10) the answer she said is this.

02. *Punctuate the following sentences using capital letters where necessary :*

(1) hands up said the dy sp.
(2) oh dear where have you been.
(3) follow me ordered the jailer.
(4) she is after all an orphan.
(5) yes please he said.
(6) she said I cant do it.
(7) when you are ready tell me.
(8) where have you been.
(9) you must you can you shall do it .
(10) if you try you will pass.

03. *Punctuate the following sentences using capital letters where necessary :*

(1) I like reading he likes playing
(2) ppp please try again he said
(3) please move fast it is getting late
(4) I want the following items pencil rubber and a pen
(5) he said I can't agree with your policy divide and rule at this moment
(6) raju do you follow me. sudha yes I do
(7) the other girl gayatri sharma refused to accept the gift
(8) no I don't remember it
(9) ram is a hindu ashraf is a muslim
(10) I saw the note welcome

04. *Insert the correct punctuation mark in the gaps. Remember not to leave any spaces before or after the punctuation marks :*

(1) Alas, poor Bill ..
(2) Do you recall in the last grammar exercise, how he fell from his horse ..
(3) You may remember that he cracked his skull as he landed on the rocky ground ..
(4) Shall we resume the story ..
(5) I seized Bill's lifeless wrist and felt for a pulse ..
(6) Nothing ..
(7) How could he have died so easily, by merely falling from a horse ..
(8) What was I going to do ..
(9) It was such a God-forsaken place ..
(10) Help was at least a day's ride away ..
(11) Suddenly I became aware of the large, icy drops of rain on the wind ..
(12) There was nothing else I could do ..
(13) I would have to make camp for the night ..
(14) And what a very long and very cold night it was going to be.

Solution TYE 01

(1) If you don't understand it, tell him.
(2) He said to me, "What is his name?"
(3) Try, try and try again.
(4) Ram and Shyam went to Punjab.
(5) Ram, not Shyam is responsible.
(6) Do, what you were told.
(7) Oh! you are here.
(8) O, Lord, help me.
(9) Gandhiji, the father of the Nation, loved the poor.
(10) "The answer", she said, "is this."

Solution TYE 02

(1) "Hands up!", said the Dy. SP.
(2) "Oh dear! where have you been.''
(3) "Follow me!", ordered the jailer.
(4) She is, after all, an orphan.
(5) "Yes please", he said.
(6) She said, "I can't do it."
(7) When you are ready, tell me.
(8) Where have you been?
(9) You must, you can, you shall do it.
(10) If you try, you will pass.

Solution TYE 03

(1) I like reading; he likes playing.
(2) "P-p-p-please try again", he said.
(3) Please move fast; it is getting late.
(4) I want the following items : pencil, rubber and a pen.
(5) He said, "I can't agree with your policy 'Divide and Rule'at this moment."
(6) Raju : Do you follow me?
Sudha : Yes, I do.
(7) The other girl—Gayatri Sharma—refused to accept the gift.
(8) No, I don't remember it.
(9) Ram is a Hindu ; Ashraf is a Muslim.
(10) I saw the note Welcome.

Solution TYE 04

(1) Alas, poor Bill!
(2) Do you recall in the last grammar exercise, how he fell from his horse?
(3) You may remember that he cracked his skull as he landed on the rocky ground.
(4) Shall we resume the story?
(5) I seized Bill's lifeless wrist and felt for a pulse.
(6) Nothing!
(7) Could he be dead already, merely from falling off a horse?
(8) What was I going to do?
(9) It was such a God-forsaken place!
(10) Help was at least a day's ride away.
(11) Suddenly I became aware of the large, icy drops of rain on the wind.
(12) There was nothing else I could do.
(13) I would have to make camp for the night.
(14) And what a very long and very cold night it was going to be!

CHAPTER 26

FORMATION OF WORDS

'Word' के Base रूप से नए word का निर्माण करना Word Formation कहलाता है। Word Formation कई प्रकार से किया जा सकता है।

(1) Prefix द्वारा: Base word के पहले एक Syllable लगाकर नया Word बनाया जा सकता है। Prefix एक syllable है, जो मूल शब्द के पहले लगता है। जैसे:

Un + lucky	Unlucky
In + dependent	Independent
Im + polite	Impolite

(2) Suffix द्वारा: Base word के बाद एक syllable लगाकर भी नया शब्द बनाया जा सकता है। Suffix एक syllable है, जो मूल शब्द के बाद लगता है। जैसे:

Great + ness	Greatness
Social + ism	Socialism
Leak + age	Leakage

(3) Compounding द्वारा: दो या दो से अधिक शब्दों को मिलाकर भी नए शब्द का निर्माण किया जाता है। जैसे:

Drawing + room	Drawing room
Tax + paid	Taxpaid
Pre + paid	Prepaid

(4) Merging द्वारा: दो शब्दों को आपस में merge करने पर भी नया शब्द बन जाता है। जैसे:

Breakfast and lunch	Brunch
Hotel for motorist	Motel

(5) Cutting or clipping द्वारा: इसके द्वारा शब्दों के कुछ भाग को cut करके भी नया शब्द बनाया जा सकता है। जैसे:

Telephone	Phone
Teenagers	Teens
Picture with movement	Movie

Prefix द्वारा नए शब्द का निर्माण

मूल शब्द से पहले im, in, ir, il, re, em, en, de, un, dis, mis, pre, non, mini, semi, vice इत्यादि कुछ syllable लगाकर नए शब्द का निर्माण किया जा सकता है। इस तरह के बहुत से Prefix हैं, जिनसे नए शब्द का निर्माण होता है।

जैसे:

*im*polite	*im*potent	*im*pure
*im*material	*in*discipline	*in*competent
*ir*regular	*ir*relevant	*im*moral
*il*logical	*il*legal	*il*literate
*re*cast	*re*fund	*re*claim
*em*power	*em*body	*em*bark
*en*courage	*en*rich	*en*list
*de*form	*de*fame	*de*moralise
*un*fortunate	*un*tie	*un*expected
*dis*appear	*dis*like	*dis*courage
*mis*carriage	*mis*trust	*mis*manage
*pre*mature	*pre*paid	*pre*fix
non-cooperation	*non*-refundable	*non*sense
mini computer	*mini*-car	*mini*skirt
semi modal	*semi*circle	*semi*colon
vice captain	*vice* chairman	*vice*-president

Suffix द्वारा नए शब्द का निर्माण

मूल शब्द के बाद में ed, ist, ing, en, ish, ful, ly, ship, ness, less इत्यादि लगाकर नए शब्द का निर्माण किया जा सकता है।

gift*ed*	ruin*ed*	talent*ed*
social*ist*	art*ist*	right*ist*
paint*ing*	garden*ing*	water*ing*
bold*en*	hidd*en*	maid*en*
self*ish*	boy*ish*	woman*ish*
joy*ful*	truth*ful*	fear*ful*
colour*ful*	power*ful*	cheer*ful*
grace*ful*	god*ly*	man*ly*
sudden*ly*	friend*ship*	member*ship*
hard*ship*	kind*ness*	fast*ness*
good*ness*	art*less*	taste*less*

Conversion of Words

Noun को Verb या Adverb में बदलना या Verb को Noun या Adjective अथवा Adverb में बदलना। इसके लिए कई बार Suffix एवं कई बार Prefix का प्रयोग किया जाता है। नीचे दिए उदाहरणों को देखें। कई परीक्षाओं में परीक्षार्थियों से इस तरह के प्रश्न पूछे जाते हैं।

(A) Changing Noun into Adjective

Noun	**Adjective**	**Noun**	**Adjective**
Angle	Angular	Brass	Brazen
Adam	Adamic	Body	Physical
Ancestor	Ancestral	Beast	Bestial
Authority	Authoritative	Contempt	Contemptuous

Noun	Adjective	Noun	Adjective
Advice	Advisable	Coward	Cowardly
Brother	Fraternal	Cat	Feline
Blue	Bluish	City	Urban
Beginning	Initial	Calamity	Calamitous
Bounty	Bounteous	Circle	Circular
Brute	Brutal	College	Collegiate
Conscience	Conscientious	Nose	Nasal
Circumstance	Circumstantial	Ocean	Oceanic
Dog	Canine	Offence	Offensive
Emperor	Imperial	Omen	Ominous
Expectation	Expectant	People	Popular
Example	Exemplary	Population	Populous
Enemy	Inimical	Professor	Professorial
Earth	Earthen	Patriot	Patriotic
Essence	Essential	Pathos	Pathetic
Elephant	Elephantine	Picture	Picturesque
Explanation	Explanatory	Prejudice	Prejudicial
Egg	Oval	Problem	Problematic
Eye	Optical	Punishment	Penal
Famine	Famished	Sentence	Sententious
Fraud	Fraudulent	Place	Local
Foot	Pedal	Palace	Palatial
Flower	Floral	Ruin	Ruinous
Fear	Timorous	Sedition	Seditious
Fable	Fabulous	Service	Serviceable
Fever	Feverish	Secretary	Secretarial
Fate	Fatal	Study	Studious
Flesh	Carnal	Paradise	Paradisiacal
Grief	Grievous	Series	Series
Grass	Grassy	Salt	Saline
Hand	Manual	Serpent	Serpentine
Hypocrite	Hypocritical	Superstition	Superstitious
Island	Insular	Ship	Naval
Industry	Industrious (Industrial)	Sky	Etherial
Spring	Vernal	Joy	Joyous
Sun	Solar	Joke	Jocular
Star	Starry	Judge	Judicial (Judicious)
Tooth	Dental	Tribe	Tribal
Licence	Licentious	Town	Urban
Lustre	Lustrous	Talk	Talkative
Love	Amorous	Table	Tabular
Money	Monetary	Youth	Juvenile
Moon	Lunar	Vice	Vicious
Merchant	Mercantile	Voice	Vocal

Noun	Adjective	Noun	Adjective
Metal	Metallic	Village	Rural
Medicine	Medicinal	War	Martial
Myth	Mythical	Title	Titular
Minister	Ministerial	Worth	Worthy
Muscle	Muscular	Watch	Vigilant
Merit	Meritorious	Wood	Sylvan
Night	Nocturnal	Year	Annual
Neighbour	Neighbourly	Zodiac	Zodiacal
Nihil	Nihilistic	Zenith	Zenithal

(B) Changing Noun into Verb

Noun	Verb	Noun	Verb
Authority	Authorize	Hard	Harden
Assertion	Assert	Harmony	Harmonize
Apology	Apologize	Haste	Hasten
Allusion	Allude	Height	Heighten
Blood	Bleed	Idol	Idolize
Beauty	Beautify	Justice	Justify
Black	Blacken	Knee	Kneel
Brass	Braze	Loss	Lose
Bed	Embed	List	Enlist
Body	Embody	Monopoly	Monopolize
Circle	Encircle	Magnet	Magnetize
Centre	Centralize	Memory	Memorize
Cipher	Decipher	Nature	Naturalize
Class	Classify	Notice	Notify
Certainty	Ascertain	Necessity	Necessitate
Colony	Colonize	Night	Be Night
Collision	Collide	Origin	Originate
Company	Accompany	Office	Officiate
Conception	Conceive	Perception	Perceive
Custom	Accustom	Patron	Patronize
Character	Characterise	Peace	Pacify
Danger	Endanger	Person	Personify
Drop	Drip	Prison	Imprison
Enthusiasm	Enthuse	Power	Empower
Excellence	Excel	Relief	Relieve
Economy	Economize	Robe	Enrobe
Electricity	Electrify	Society	Associate
Furniture	Furnish	Sermon	Sermonize
Frost	Freeze	Spark	Sparkle
Food	Feed	Shrine	Enshrine
Force	Enforce	Slave	Enslave
Friend	Befriend	Title	Entitle
Fraud	Defraud	Tomb	Entomb

Grass	Graze	Utility	Utilize
Glory	Glorify	Vapour	Evaporate
Gold	Gild	Verse	Versify
Habit	Habituate	Vacancy	Vacate
Hand	Handle	Vice	Vitiate

(C) Changing Noun into Abstract Noun

Noun	Abstract Noun	Noun	Abstract Noun
Beggar	Beggary	Machine	Mechanism
Coin	Coinage	Priest	Priesthood
Coward	Cowardice	Person	Personage
Cunning	Cunningness	Royal	Royalty
Creature	Creation	Regent	Regency
Elector	Electorate	Servant	Service
Hero	Heroism	Witch	Witchery

(D) Changing Adjective into Verb

Adjective	Verb	Adjective	Verb
Abundant	Abound	Large	Enlarge
Able	Enable	Lamp	Lamp
Abusive	Abuse	Dramatic	Dramatize
Bitter	Embitter	Little	Belittle
Brief	Abbreviate	Long	Prolong
Brutal	Brutalize	Liquid	Liquidize
Base	Debase	Mad	Madden
Clear	Clarify	Moist	Moisten
Civil	Civilize	Noble	Ennoble
Clean	Cleanse	Public	Publish
Dense	Condense	Popular	Popularize
Different	Differentiate	Poor	Impoverish
Double	Duplicate	Perpetual	Perpetuate
Dramatic	Dramatize	Pure	Purify
Equal	Equalize	Real	Realize
Fat	Fatten	Rich	Enrich
Fertile	Fertilize	Safe	Save
Firm	Confirm	Stupid	Stupidity
Fresh	Refresh	Sweet	Sweeten
Feeble	Enfeeble	Solid	Solidity

(E) Changing Adjective into Noun

Adjective	Noun	Adjective	Noun
Adequate	Adequacy	Intense	Intensity
Acid	Acidity	Just	Justice
Bankrupt	Bankruptcy	Merry	Merriment
Brief	Brevity	Magnificent	Magnificence

Busy	Business	Notorious	Notoriety
Chaste	Chastity	Obedient	Obedience
Civil	Civility	Pious	Piety
Compulsory	Compulsion	Public	Publicity
Dense	Density	Rival	Rivalry
Gay	Gaiety	Solitary	Solitude
Double	Duplicate	Perpetual	Perpetuate
Grand	Grandeur	Splendid	Splendour
Hot	Heat	Vain	Vanity
Humble	Humility	Wide	Width
Local	Locality	Worthy	Worth

(F) Changing Verb into Noun

Verb	Noun	Verb	Noun
Acquit	Acquittal	Conceive	Conception
Bathe	Bath	Commit	Committal
Betray	Betrayal	Compare	Comparison
Deceive	Deception	Precise	Precision
Defy	Defiance	Predict	Prediction
Deny	Denial	Precede	Precedence
Do	Deed	Pursue	Pursuit
Prohibit	Prohibition	Yean	Yeanling
Heal	Health	Recede	Recess
Know	Knowledge	Rely	Reliance
Lend	Loan	Respond	Response
Give	Gift	Redeem	Redemption
Narrate	Narration	Steal	Stealth
Oblige	Obligation	Urge	Urgency
Move	Motion	Seize	Seizure
Please	Pleasure	Weave	Web
Persuade	Persuasion	Vary	Variety

इस तरह से आपने देखा कि नए शब्द का निर्माण किस तरह से किया जा सकता है। नए शब्द-निर्माण की विधि एवं शब्द को विभिन्न Part of Speech में बदलना, English Vocabulary की वृद्धि में काफी सहायक है।

Exercises

01.

Write the Adjective form of the following Nouns:

(1) Calamity, (2) Coward, (3) City, (4) Blue, (5) Emperor,
(6) Brute, (7) Cat, (8) Beast, (9) Body, (10) Brass.

02.

Write the Noun form of the following words:

(1) Floral, (2) Fatal, (3) Populous, (4) Inimical, (5) Penal,
(6) Saline, (7) Naval, (8) Solar, (9) Dental, (10) Jocular.

03.

Change the following Nouns into Verbs:

(1) Hard, (2) Loss, (3) Magnet, (4) Centre, (5) Bed,
(6) Circle, (7) Food, (8) Grass, (9) Collisicn, (10) Nature,
(11) Origin, (12) Office.

04.

Change the following Verbs into Noun:

(1) Bathe, (2) Predict, (3) Defy, (4) Please, (5) Lend,
(6) Move, (7) Pursue, (8) Steal, (9) Oblige, (10) Respond,
(11) Yean, (12) Do.

05.

Form the words as directed from the following words: **[Inspectors of Income-tax]**

(1) a noun from *err* (verb).
(2) A noun from *flow* (verb).
(3) a noun from *precise* (adjective).
(4) an abstract noun from *witch* (noun).
(5) a verb from *office* (noun).
(6) Adjectives from *coast, home.*
(7) Abstract noun from *fool, poor, laugh.*

06.

Use each of the following words as a noun and as a verb in your own sentences: **[IAS]**

(1) quarrel (2) book (3) hand (4) lock (5) water
(6) stand (7) field (8) chair (9) notes (10) sacrifice
(11) train (12) work (13) present (14) record

07.

Fill in the blanks with the appropriate word in the second sentence in the following pairs of sentences: **[Inspectors of Income-tax]**

(1) The corrupt politician is about to be exposed.
The corrupt politician faces ....
(2) Most of the cups broke in transit.
Most of the cups suffered .... in transit.
(3) The passengers were annoyed at the delay.
The passengers expressed their .... at the delay.
(4) The Court ordered the building to be demolished.
The Court ordered .... of the building.
(5) The strange word is repeated in all his poems.
All his poems shows .... of the strange word.
(6) He told me not to be in such haste.
He told me not to .... so much.
(7) My grandfather fell down.
My grandfather had a ....
(8) The visitor frightened the child.
The visitor gave the child a .... look.

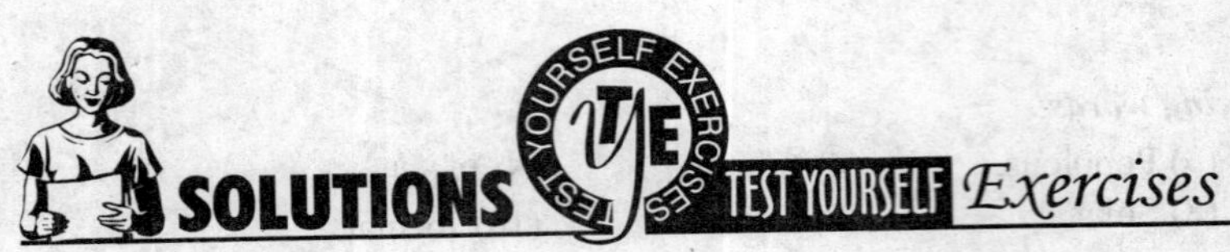

Solution TYE 01

(1) Calamitous, (2) Cowardly, (3) Urban (4) Bluish, (5) Imperial, (6) Brutal (7) Feline, (8) Bestial, (9) Physical (10) Brazen.

Solution TYE 02

(1) Flower, (2) Fate, (3) Population (4) Enemy, (5) Punishment, (6) Salt (7) Ship, (8) Sun, (9) Tooth (10) Joke.

Solution TYE 03

(1) Harden, (2) Lose, (3) Magnetize (4) Centralize, (5) Embed, (6) Encircle (7) Feed, (8) Graze, (9) Collide (10) Naturalize, (11) Originate, (12) Officiate.

Solution TYE 04

(1) Bath, (2) Prediction, (3) Defiance (4) Pleasure, (5) Loan, (6) Motion, (7) Pursuit, (8) Stealth, (9) Obligation (10) Response, (11) Yeanling, (12) Deed.

Solution TYE 05

(1) error, (2) flow, (3) precision (4) witchery, (5) officiating (6) coastal, homely, (7) folly, poverty, laughter.

Solution TYE 06

Use as a Noun:

(1) *Quarrels* take place over the property.
(2) The *books* written by Mr. S.C. Gupta are very useful.
(3) The *hands* of Mafia are many.
(4) The *locks* of Aligarh are durable.
(5) *Water* is necessary for life.
(6) You should have taken a tough *stand.*
(7) The *field* of Red Corner, China is plane.
(8) This is a comfortable *chair*.
(9) She has taken my *notes*.
(10) The *sacrifice* made by Subhash Chandra Bose is indeed great.
(11) The *train* is a good mode of travel.
(12) Complete your *work* today positively.
(13) This is a good *present* for her.
(14) Sachin has made several *records*.

Use as a Verb:

(1) You should not *quarrel* with your brother.
(2) The scooter was *booked* for Alwar.
(3) A representation was *handed* over to the Chairman.
(4) *Lock* the house properly while going out.
(5) He is *watering* the plants.
(6) The inflation rate now *stands* at 4% only.
(7) Sachin *fields* the ball very quickly.
(8) The Home Minister *chaired* the meeting of M.Ps.
(9) Please *note* down my telephone number.
(10) Subhash Chandra Bose *sacrificed* his service and fought for independence.
(11) Pakistan is *training* militants.
(12) He *works* in this office.
(13) She *presented* a wrong information.
(14) Please *record* my dissent in this matter.

Solution TYE 07

(1) exposure, (2) breakage, (3) annoyance (4) demolition, (5) repetition, (6) hurry (7) fall, (8) frightening.

CHAPTER

27

SPELLING RULES

सही अंग्रेजी लिखने हेतु न केवल व्याकरणिक नियमों का ज्ञान आवश्यक है बल्कि सही Spelling लिखना भी अनिवार्य है। गलत Spelling, न केवल आपकी अज्ञानता, लापरवाही एवं असावधानी को व्यक्त करती है, बल्कि परीक्षक पर भी बहुत नकारात्मक प्रभाव डालती है।

सही Spelling लिखने हेतु निरन्तर प्रयास की आवश्यकता है। सही Spelling लिखने हेतु निम्न बिन्दुओं पर अमल करें

(1) लिखते समय, जिस किसी शब्द की Spelling के गलत/सही होने का सन्देह हो, उसे तुरन्त Dictionary में देखकर Spelling सुनिश्चित कर लें।

(2) कुछ शब्दों की Spellings अन्य शब्दों से हटकर होती है, उन्हें अलग से लिखकर बार-बार Revise करने पर गलतियों से बचा जा सकता है।

(3) Formation of words में Suffix, Prefix लगाने के नियमों का भी ध्यान रखें।

(4) शब्दों का सही उच्चारण भी सही Spelling लिखने में सहायक होता है।

(5) कुछ शब्दों का उच्चारण एक जैसा लगता है अत: वाक्यों के अर्थ का ध्यान रखकर ही शब्द को लिखें।

(6) निम्न Spelling Rules का ध्यान रखें एवं बताए गए 'अपवाद' (Exceptions) को अच्छी तरह Revise कर लें।

Spelling Rules

***Rule* 1** **कुछ words, एक syllable के होते हैं, जिनके अन्त में एक consonant आता है एवं उससे पहले एक vowel (a, e, i, o, u) आता है। यदि इस प्रकार के word में consonant के बाद किसी vowel letter के साथ Suffix लगता है तो इस consonant को double कर दिया जाता है। जैसे:**

run	running	get	getting
rob	robbed	plan	planning
put	putting	war	warring

***Rule* 2** **एक से अधिक syllable वाले शब्द जो single vowel + single consonant में समाप्त होते हैं। इनमें अन्तिम consonant, double हो जाता है। जैसे:**

begin	beginning	refer	referring
permit	permitted	transfer	transferring
occur	occurred	control	controller

Exceptions are :

suffer	suffered	offer	offered
benefit	benefited	differ	differed

***Rule* 3** **बहुत से words के अन्त में l आता है तो वह 'l' double हो जाता है। जैसे:**

quarrel	quarrelled	equal	equalled
distil	distilled	travel	travelled
jewel	jeweller	expel	expelled

Exceptions are:

parallel	paralleled	peril	perilous

Rule 4 **(a) कुछ words के अन्त में e आता है। ऐसे words के साथ vowel से शुरू होने वाला Suffix लगाने पर e हट जाता है। जैसे:**

live	living	bite	biting
fame	famous	make	making
move	moving	blame	blaming
value	valuable	love	loving
note	notable	issue	issuing

(b) लेकिन e से समाप्त होने वाले शब्दों के साथ consonant से शुरू होने वाला Suffix लगाने पर e भी लगा रहता है। जैसे:

hope	hopeful	excite	excitement
engage	engagement	nice	nicely

Exceptions are:

true	truly	awe	awful
whole	wholly	argue	argument
due	duly	simple	simply

Rule 5 **जो words-ce या -ge से समाप्त होते हैं इनके साथ a, o, u से शुरू होने वाला Suffix लगाने पर e लगा रहता है। जैसे:**

replace	replaceable	manage	manageable
change	changeable	marriage	marriageable
courage	courageous	service	serviceable

Rule 6 **जब कोई word, y से समाप्त होता है एवं पहले कोई consonant आता है तो Suffix (except-ing) लगाने पर y, i में बदल जाता है। जैसे:**

cry	cried	pity	pitiful
mercy	merciful	carry	carried

Exceptions are:

shy	shyly	dry	dryly
sly	slyly		

Rule 7 **यदि कोई word, ll से समाप्त होता है तो उसके साथ 'full' Suffix लगाने पर word एवं Suffix दो में एक-एक l ही रह जाता है। जैसे:**

skill + full	skilful	will + full	wilful
full + fill	fulfil		

लेकिन यदि y के पहले कोई vowel आता है तो y वैसा ही रहता है।

pray	*prayed*	*buy*	*buyer*
play	*played*	*pay*	*payable*
enjoy	*enjoyment*	*stay*	*stayed*

Exceptions are:

say	*said*	*pay*	*paid*
lay	*laid*	*day*	*daily*

Rule 8 अगर किसी word का ie से अन्त हो और उसमें 'ing' Suffix लगाया जाए तो ie बदलकर 'y' हो जाता है। जैसे:

die	dying	lie	lying
tie	tying	vie	vying

Difference between American and British Spelling

(1) कुछ words के अन्त में American English में or रहता है, किन्तु British English में our रहता है। जैसे:

American English — labor, color, rumor, humor, neighbor etc.
British English — labour, colour, rumour, humour, neighbour etc.

(2) American English में कुछ शब्दों के अन्त में og रहता है, किन्तु British English में ogue आता है। जैसे:

American English — catalog, dialog
British English — catalogue, dialogue

(3) American English में word के अन्तिम शब्द l को double नहीं किया जाता है, किन्तु British English में यह double हो जाता है। जैसे:

American English — Traveler, leveling
British English Traveller, levelling

(4) बहुत से verbs के अन्त में American English में ize रहता है, किन्तु British English में -ise या -ize दोनों लगते हैं। जैसे:

American English — Realize, analyze
British English — Realise, realize, analyse

(5) American English में कुछ शब्दों के अन्त में ter रहता है, किन्तु British English में tre आता है। जैसे:

American English — Theater, meter, center
British English — Theatre, metre, centre

अनेक शब्दों में American English एवं British English में spelling सम्बन्धी अन्तर है। जैसे:

American English	**British English**
tire	tyre (on a vehicle)
program	programme
jail	gaol, jail
aluminum	aluminium
defense	defence
jewelry	jewellery

India में British English प्रचलित है। अत: हमें British English की spellings को ही ध्यान में रखना चाहिए।

List of Commonly Mis-spelt Words

Autumn	Conscience	Irresistible	Phenomenon
Accommodate	Cigarette	Irrelevant	Physique
Accustom	Colloquial	Irreparable	Psychology
Agility	Commemorate	Indefatigable	Potato
Athlete	Competition	Indigenous	Pharmaceutical

Accommodate
Acquaintance
Assailant
Aggregate
Acquiesce
Abbreviate
Ascetic
Annihilate
Appropriate
Aerodrum
Architecture
Alcohol
Adherent
Abhorrence
Accessible
Acknowledgement
Acquittal
Apparatus
Amateur
Appetite
Acclamation
Affectionate
Aesthetic
Alienate
Ambassador
Ambition
Assassin
Bankruptcy
Beneficent
Behaviour
Bequeath
Besiege
Bureaucracy
Budget
Buffoon
Circumstance
Commitment
Committee
Condescend
Connoisseur
Correspondence
Counterfeit
Catalogue
Convalesce
Convenient
Conceive
Condemn
Curriculum
Deceive
Discernible
Deficiency
Dialogue
Descendant
Division
Dilemma
Deteriorate
Dysentery
Ecclesiastical
Etiquette
Erroneous
Exaggeration
Ecstasy
Equilibrium
Exchequer
Extravagance
Efficiency
Efficacious
Embarrass
Fallacious
Fascinate
Facilitate
Felicitate
Freight
Favourable
Fourth
Genuine
Guarantee
Gorgeous
Grievance
Grotesque
Geometry
Grammar
Gazette
Harassment
Heinous
Heterogenous
Hygiene
Inflammable
Incarcerate
Incorrigible
Juggler
Jealousy
Jubilee
Juvenile
Knave
Kitchen
Knee
Knight
Kneeled
Knives
Leniency
Leisure
Laurel
Luxurious
Lieutenant
Manageable
Magnificent
Martyr
Manoeuvre
Misdemeanor
Meagre
Moustache
Mosquito
Missionary
Millionaire
Massacre
Museum
Mischievous
Musician
Noticeable
Nuisance
Neighbour
Necessary
Necessitate
Occurrence
Omitted
Oscillate
Ominous
Parallel
Pneumonia
Proletariat
Perceive
Proprietor
Perspicuous
Pursue
Quarrel
Queue
Quinine
Rogue
Routine
Regrettable
Restaurant
Repetition
Referee
Rehearsal
Rupee
Sceptre
Scissors
Schedule
Strategy
Simultaneous
Symmetrical
Soliloquy
Sovereign
Stomach
Technique
Transience
Tenacious
Transgressor
Utterance
Vacation
Vaccination
Vicissitude
Vocabulary
Vicious
Villainous
Wednesday
Weigh
Woolen
Written
Writing
Xenomania
Xylography
Yawning
Yeoman
Zodiac
Zealous
Zootomy
Zythepsary

Spelling सम्बन्धी गलती आपकी लापरवाही (negligency) एवं अधूरे ज्ञान को उजागर करती है, अतः आप इन्हें अच्छी तरह याद करें। इन शब्दों को बार-बार पढ़कर, लिखकर निरन्तर अभ्यास करें। इनको लिखते समय अधिकांश छात्र गलती करते हैं।

01

Insert 'ance' or 'ence' into the following words:

(a) exist .... (b) attend .... (c) correspond .... (d) magnific .... (e) occurr ....
(f) persist .... (g) entr .... (h) emin .... (i) prud .... (j) vigil ....
(k) compli .... (l) hindr .... (m) acquaint .... (n) assure .... (o) repent ....
(p) differ .... (q) refer ....

02

Insert 'ant' or 'ent' into the following words:

(a) attend .... (a) cog .... (c) immigr .... (d) complim .... (e) disinfect ....
(f) immin .... (g) serp .... (h) inhabit .... (i) serv .... (j) brilli ....
(k) monum .... (l) pertin .... (m) fragr .... (n) promin .... (o) perman ....
(p) vali .... (q) adjac .... (r) restaur .... (s) resist .... (t) suffici ...
(u) excell .... (v) benefic ....

03

Add 'tion', or 'sion' to complete the spelling of the following words:

(a) applica .... (b) discus .... (c) deci .... (d) colli .... (e) posses ....
(f) profes .... (g) combina .... (h) explo .... (i) confu .... (j) permis ....
(k) sugges .... (l) atten .... (m) ambi .... (n) ammuni .... (o) associa ....
(p) determina .... (q) divi .... (r) exclu .... (s) compul .... (t) conclu ....:
(u) commis .... (v) direc .... (w) administra .... (x) resolu .... (y) reputa ....
(z) ses ....

04

Insert 'ary', 'ery', 'ory' or 'ry' into the following words:

(a) brav .... (b) bound .... (c) contra .... (d) sal .... (e) slav ....
(f) jewell .... (g) gallant .... (h) second .... (i) prim .... (j) secret ....
(k) cook .... (l) coroll .... (m) dai .... (n) geomet .... (o) laborat ....
(p) liter .... (q) mercen .... (r) milit .... (s) mission .... (t) monast ....
(u) myst .... (v) necess .... (w) satisfact .... (x) machin .... (y) fact ....
(z) begg ....

05

Insert 'cial' or 'tial' in the following words:

(a) pala .... (b) residen .... (c) superfi.... (d) ra .... (e) par ....
(f) spe .... (g) influen .... (h) pruden .... (i) provin .... (j) sacrifi
(k) finan .... (l) judi .... (m) cru .... (n) nup .... (o) prejudi ....
(p) presiden .... (q) preferen .... (r) essen ....

06

Insert 'eous' or 'ious' into the spelling of the following words:

(a) nutrit .... (b) courag .... (c) court .... (d) notor .... (e) erron ....
(f) meritor .... (g) superstit .... (h) bount .... (i) industr .... (j) licent ....
(k) prec .... (l) prodig .... (m) cur .... (n) feroc .... (o) grac ....
(p) conscient .... (q) luxur ....

07

Add the suffix 'able' or 'ible' with the following words:

(a) agree .... (b) love .... (c) resist .... (d) blame .... (e) move ....
(f) access .... (g) value .... (h) eat .... (i) change .... (j) reduce ....
(k) contempt .... (l) force .... (m) pay .... (n) profit .... (o) discern ....

08

Fill in 'age', 'dge' or 'ege' in the following words:

(a) pill .... (b) coll .... (c) carri .... (d) mess .... (e) man ....
(f) line .... (g) ple .... (h) dam .... (i) bu .... (j) bri ....
(k) he .... (l) pres .... (m) pack .... (n) mortg .... (o) post i
(p) vill .... (q) suffr .... (r) lo .... (s) pass .... (t) cartri ....

09

Insert 'cious' or 'tious' into the following words:

(a) Mali .... (b) fero .... (c) supersti .... (d) conscien .... (e) ostenta ....
(f) ambi .... (g) vi .... (h) ficti .... (i) deli .... (j) perni ....
(k) atro .... (l) vora .... (m) sedi .... (n) infec .... (o) saga ....
(p) avari ....

10

Insert 'ei' or 'ie' into the following words:

(a) Perc..ve (b) hyg ..ne (c) bel..f (d) ach..ve (e) ch..f
(f) dec..ve (g) rel..f (h) conc..t (i) th..f (j) v..l
(k) n..gh (l) y..ld (m) br..f (n) n..ce (o) forf..t
(p) I..ge (q) surf..t (r) f..gn (s) retr..ve (t) rec..pt
(u) gr..ve (v) pr..st

11

Tick mark the word with correct spellings: **[Railway Apprentice]**

(1) (a) temperature (b) temprature (c) tempareter
(2) (a) definate (b) definite (c) difinite
(3) (a) expirience (b) exparience (c) experience
(4) (a) incident (b) insident (c) insidant
(5) (a) extasy (b) ecstacy (c) acstasy

12

Find out the wrongly spelt word:

(1) (a) pompous (b) populous (c) prejudiced (d) pretentous
(2) (a) exempleary (b) embarrass (c) envious (d) excellence
(3) (a) dispose (b) dipose (c) demote (d) denote
(4) (a) casual (b) candid (c) convercant (d) catastrophe
(5) (a) procession (b) passion (c) posession (d) profession

13

Find out the wrongly spelt word:

(1) (a) rein (b) neigh (c) neither (d) neice
(2) (a) efficient (b) reticent (c) magnificient (d) deficient
(3) (a) vocal (b) focal (c) mystical (d) vehical
(4) (a) altogether (b) alrigt (c) almighty (d) allottee
(5) (a) pretence (b) offence (c) dence (d) deference

SOLUTIONS TEST YOURSELF *Exercises*

Solution TYE 01

(a) existence, (b) attendance, (c) correspondence, (d) magnificence,
(e) occurrence, (f) persistance, (g) entrance, (h) eminence,
(i) prudence, (j) vigilance, (k) compliance, (l) hindrance,
(m) acquaintance, (n) assurance, (o) repentance, (p) difference,
(q) reference.

Solution TYE 02

(a) attendant, (b) cogent, (c) immigrant, (d) compliment,
(e) disinfectant, (f) imminent, (g) serpent, (h) inhabitant,
(i) servant, (j) brilliant, (k) monument, (l) pertinent,
(m) fragrant, (n) prominent, (o) permanent, (p) valiant,
(q) adjacent, (r) restaurant, (s) resistant, (t) sufficient,
(u) excellent, (v) beneficent.

Solution TYE 03

(a) application, (b) discussion, (c) decision, (d) collision,
(e) possession, (f) profession, (g) combination, (h) explosion,
(i) confusion, (j) permission, (k) suggestion, (l) attention,
(m) ambition, (n) ammunition, (o) association, (p) determination,
(q) division, (r) exclusion, (s) compulsion, (t) conclusion,
(u) commission, (v) direction, (w) administration, (x) resolution,
(y) reputation, (z) session.

Solution TYE 04

(a) bravery, (b) boundary, (c) contrary, (d) salary,
(e) slavery, (f) jewellery, (g) gallantry, (h) secondary,
(i) primary, (j) secretary, (k) cookery, (l) corollary,
(m) dairy, (n) geometry, (o) laboratory, (p) literary,
(q) mercenary, (r) military, (s) missionary, (t) monastery,
(u) mystery, (v) necessary, (w) satisfactory, (x) machinery,
(y) factory, (z) beggary.

Solution TYE 05

(a) palatial, (b) residential, (c) superficial, (d) racial,
(e) partial, (f) special, (g) influential, (h) prudential,
(i) provincial, (j) sacrificial, (k) financial, (l) judicial,
(m) crucial, (n) nuptial, (o) prejudicial, (p) presidential,
(q) preferential, (r) essential.

Solution TYE 06

(a) nutritious, (b) courageous, (c) courteous, (d) notorious,
(e) erroneous, (f) meritorious, (g) superstitious, (h) bounteous,
(i) industrious, (j) licentious, (k) precious, (l) prodigious,
(m) curious, (n) ferocious, (o) gracious, (p) conscientious,
(q) luxurious.

Solution TYE 07

(a) agreeable, (b) lovable, (c) resistible, (d) blamable,
(e) movable, (f) accessible, (g) valuable, (h) eatable,
(i) changeable, (j) reducible, (k) contemptible, (l) forcible,
(m) payable, (n) profitable, (o) discernible.

Solution TYE 08

(a) pillage, (b) college, (c) carriage, (d) message,
(d) manage, (e) lineage, (f) pledge, (h) damage,
(i) budge, (j) bridge, (k) hedge, (l) presage,
(m) package, (n) mortgage, (o) postage, (p) village,
(q) suffrage, (r) lodge, (s) passage, (t) cartridge.

Solution TYE 09

(a) malicious, (b) ferocious, (c) superstitious, (d) conscientious,
(e) ostentatious, (f) ambitious, (g) vicious, (h) fictitious,
(i) delicious, (j) pernicious, (k) atrocious, (l) voracious,
(m) seditious, (n) infectious, (o) sagacious, (p) avaricious.

Solution TYE 10

(a) perceive, (b) hygiene, (c) belief, (d) achieve,
(e) chief, (f) deceive, (g) relief, (h) conceit,
(i) thief, (j) veil, (k) neigh, (l) yield,
(m) brief, (n) niece, (o) forfeit, (p) liege,
(q) surfeit, (r) feign, (s) retrieve, (t) receipt,
(u) grieve, (v) priest.

Solution TYE 11

(1) (a), (2) (b), (3) (c), (4) (a), (5) (b).

Solution TYE 12

(1) (d), (2) (a), (3) (b), (4) (c), (5) (c).

Solution TYE 13

(1) (d), (2) (c), (3) (d), (4) (b), (5) (c).

CHAPTER

28

SENTENCE STRUCTURE AND ANALYSIS

Sentence क्या है ?

दो या दो से अधिक शब्दों को एक क्रम में लिखने से बनने वाले सार्थक शब्द-समूह को वाक्य (sentence) कहा जाता है। He goes to market एक वाक्य है।

क्योंकि, इस शब्द-समूह का अर्थ निकलता है। लेकिन To he market goes यद्यपि शब्द-समूह तो है लेकिन इस शब्द-समूह का कोई अर्थ नहीं निकलता है अर्थात् निरर्थक है। अत: यह एक वाक्य नहीं है।

Sentence के निम्नलिखित दो भाग होते हैं :

(1) Subject (2) Predicate

1. **Subject :** जो कार्य को करने वाला है या जिसके बारे में वाक्य में कुछ व्यक्त किया गया है Subject है।
2. **Predicate :** Subject द्वारा किए जाने वाले कार्य या Subject के बारे में जो कुछ वाक्य में कहा गया है, उसे Predicate कहते हैं। वाक्य में Subject के अतिरिक्त जो कुछ भी होता है, वह Predicate कहलाता है।

Subject	Predicate	Subject	Predicate
(a) Ram	is a good man.	(c) She	went to market.
(b) Rahim	plays football.	(d) He	is writing a letter.

Sentence structure के अनुसार sentences को निम्नलिखित चार भागों में वर्गीकृत किया गया है :

(1) Simple sentence (2) Compound sentence
(3) Complex sentence (4) Mixed sentence

Analysis : इसका अर्थ है वाक्य में विद्यमान clauses की पहचान करना एवं वाक्य किस प्रकार का है, इसकी जाँच करना अर्थात् वाक्य में Principal, Coordinate, Subordinate clause कौन-सी है, यह जानना, फिर यह जानना कि वाक्य किस प्रकार का; simple/compound /complex/mixed; है?

Clause क्या होती है ?

Clause is such a group of words that forms part of a sentence and contains a subject and a finite verb.

अर्थात् clause, एक sentence का भाग है, (ध्यान रखें, clause स्वयं एक वाक्य नहीं है) जिसमें एक subject एवं एक finite verb अवश्य होती है। Finite verb वह verb होती है, जो subject के number (singular/plural) एवं person (first /second /third person) के अनुसार बदलती है।

Kinds of Clause

Clause निम्नलिखित तीन प्रकार की होती हैं :

(1) Principal Clause (2) Subordinate Clause
(3) Coordinate Clause

(1) Principal clause : इसे Main या Independent clause भी कहा जाता है। Principal clause वह है जिसका स्वयं का पूर्ण अर्थ निकलता है, जो अपने अर्थ के लिए किसी अन्य clause पर आश्रित नहीं होती है। जैसे

(a) This is the fan, which I bought yesterday. (b) I will help her, as far as I can do.

उक्त वाक्यों में underlined clause, Principal clause है, जिसका अपना अर्थ निकलता है।

(2) Subordinate clause : इसे Dependent clause भी कहा जाता है, जो अपने पूर्ण अर्थ के लिए Principal clause या अन्य clause पर निर्भर है। वाक्य में Principal clause तथा Subordinate clause को पहचानने का सरल तरीका यह है कि Subordinate clause हमेशा Subordinating conjunctions से प्रारम्भ होती है। अत: यदि वाक्य में कोई clause निम्न Subordinating conjunction से शुरू होती है तो वह Subordinate clause है। शेष Clauses, Principal clause हैं।
When, where, which, what, how, who, whom, whose, whether, if, provided, provided that, notwithstanding, as, as if, as though, as much as, as far as, as soon as, as long as, so long as, according as, after, before, because, since, until, unless, for, in that, than that, now that, though, so that, in order that, so much, so that.

Important

Principal clause beginning with who/which/where/when.

कई वाक्यों में who/which/where/when का प्रयोग निम्न प्रकार के structure में होता है :

Noun +, (comma) + who/which/ where/when + ...

तो ऐसी स्थिति में who/which/where/ when से शुरू होने वाली clause, Principal clause होती है। उस स्थिति में who/which/where/ when एक दूसरे अर्थ में, continuous sense प्रयुक्त होते हैं।

Look at the following sentences :

(a) I worked there for three days, when I received a telegram.
यहाँ रेखांकित clause एक Principal clause है तथा when का अर्थ 'and then' है।

(b) I went to London, where I got a job.
यहाँ रेखांकित clause एक Principal clause है तथा when का अर्थ 'and there' है।

(c) The mirror, which was broken, is now changed.
यहाँ रेखांकित clause एक Principal clause है।

(d) The girl, who was there, is very beautiful.
यहाँ रेखांकित clause एक Principal clause है।

इस तरह के वाक्यों में noun के बाद comma अवश्य लगाया जाता है।

(3) Coordinate clause : यह एक वाक्य का भाग होते हुए भी अपने अर्थ के लिए किसी clause पर आश्रित नहीं होती है।
"A coordinate clause is not a component part of any other clause but forms a complete grammatical whole by itself." **—Nesfield**

Coordinate clause एक equal rank की clause होती है इसलिए Principal एवं Subordinate clause के भी Coordinate clause हो सकते हैं।

दो या अधिक Principal clauses या Subordinate clauses, Coordinating conjunctions; जैसे : and, both and, as well as, but, Not only.... but also, or, either ......or, neither......nor, इत्यादि; द्वारा coordinate किए जा सकते हैं।

Look at the following sentences :

(a) He as well as she is very wise.
(b) He went to hospital and saw her.
(c) He is poor but very honest.
(d) He met her and talked to her.

उपरोक्त वाक्यों में दोनों ही clause, Principal clause हैं। पहले भाग को Principal clause एवं दूसरे भाग को Coordinate to principal clause कहा जाता है।

इसी तरह Subordinate clauses भी Coordinating conjunction द्वारा coordinate की जा सकती हैं। जैसे :

(a) I don't know when she came and what she did.
(b) I can't say what he will do or what are his plans.

इन वाक्यों में दो Subordinate clauses, and/or, Coordinating conjunctions द्वारा coordinate की गई हैं।

Kinds of Subordinate Clause

Subordinate clause को वाक्य में इनके द्वारा किए कार्य के अनुसार *निम्नलिखित तीन भागों में वर्गीकृत किया गया है*

(1) Noun clause (b) Adjective clause (3) Adverb clause

(1) Noun Clause

जो Subordinate clause वाक्य में Noun का कार्य करती है, वह Noun clause कहलाती है। Noun clause को पहचानने हेतु, Main Verb से 'क्या' प्रश्न करने पर जो उत्तर आता है वह Noun clause है। Noun clause को शुरू करने वाले conjunction का अर्थ 'कि' होता है।

(a) She asked me where I was going. She asked me . . . . . . what?
Ans. Where I was going. **(Subordinate noun clause)**

(b) I know that you are an intelligent student. I know . . . what?
Ans. That you are an intelligent student. **(Subordinate noun clause)**

इस तरह noun clause की पहचान की जा सकती है।

Noun clause वाक्य में निम्न कार्य करती है:

Functions

(A) As subject of the verb : Noun clause, वाक्य में verb के subject का कार्य करती है। जैसे :

(a) What he does is not known to me.
यहाँ what he does, verb 'is' का subject है।

(b) What I will do is uncertain.
यहाँ what I will do, verb 'is' का subject है।

(c) That you abused him, surprised me.
That you abused him, verb 'surprised' का subject है।

(B) As object of the verb : Noun clause, वाक्य में verb के object के रुप में भी प्रयुक्त होती है। जैसे :

(a) I asked him where he was going.
रेखांकित clause, verb 'asked' का object है।

(b) I can't say what does he do.
रेखांकित clause, verb 'say' का object है।

(c) She told me that she would resign.
रेखांकित clause, verb 'told' का object है।

(C) As object of the preposition : Noun clause वाक्य में preposition के object के रुप में भी प्रयुक्त होती है। जैसे :

(a) Please listen to what he says.

रेखांकित Noun clause, preposition 'to' का object है।

(b) I have no problem, except that you should behave properly.

रेखांकित Noun clause, preposition 'except' का object है।

(c) I find no sense in what you spoke to her.

रेखांकित Noun clause, preposition 'in' का object है।

(D) As complement to a verb : Noun clause वाक्य में verb के complement की तरह भी प्रयुक्त होती है। जैसे :

(a) This is what I said.

What I said, एक noun clause है जो verb 'is' का complement है।

(b) Life is how we enjoy it.

रेखांकित Noun clause, verb 'is' का complement है।

(c) It is what I mean.

रेखांकित Noun clause, verb 'is' का complement है।

(E) As case in apposition to the noun or pronoun : यदि किसी वाक्य में कोई clause, noun या pronoun के अर्थ को स्पष्ट करती है, तो उसे apposition to the noun or pronoun कहते हैं। जैसे :

(a) The news that Rajeev Gandhi was killed shocked everyone.

यहाँ The news shocked everyone Principal clause है तथा that Rajeev Gandhi was killed -Subordinate noun clause, noun, news के साथ case in apposition की तरह प्रयुक्त है।

(b) The information that Osama bin Laden is killed is wrong.

यहाँ रेखांकित clause, noun information के साथ case in apposition है।

(c) His wish that he may become an MLA is unreasonable.

रेखांकित clause noun-wish के साथ case in apposition में प्रयुक्त है।

(F) As object to a participle : Noun clause वाक्य में participle के object के रूप में function करती है। जैसे :

(a) I reached there hoping that she would be there.

(b) He came to me, hoping that I would give him some money.

(c) She came to me thinking that I should help her.

उपरोक्त वाक्यों में रेखांकित clause, participle (hoping, thinking) के object के रुप में भी प्रयुक्त होती है। जैसे :

(G) Object to an Infinitive : वाक्य में Noun clause, infinitive के object के रुप में प्रयुक्त हुई है। जैसे :

(a) I want to know what he thinks. (b) I want to see how does he live.

(c) He wants to enquire where does he live.

उक्त वाक्यों में रेखांकित Noun clauses, Infinitives (to know, to see, to enquire) के object के रूप में भी प्रयुक्त हुई है।

(2) Adjective Clause

Subordinate clause वाक्य में adjective का कार्य करती है। यह वाक्य में noun/pronoun की विशेषता बताती है। जैसे :

(a) She is the girl who secured first position. (b) This is the house where I lived.

(c) That is the girl whom I love.

उपरोक्त वाक्यों में रेखांकित clause, एक adjective का कार्य करती है एव वाक्यों में प्रयुक्त noun (Girl, house, girl) की विशेषता को व्यक्त करती है।

यहाँ Noun एवं Adjective clause के मध्य comma नहीं लगता है।

(3) Adverb Clause

Subordinate clause वाक्य में एक adverb का कार्य भी करती है। Adverb के प्रकार (kind) के अनुसार ही Adverb clause के विभिन्न रुप भी हैं।

(A) Adverb clause of time : यह कार्य के होने का समय व्यक्त करती है। जैसे :

(a) I get up before the sun rises. (b) She cooked after her husband went to market.

रेखांकित clauses वाक्य में adverb का कार्य कर रही है एवं कार्य होने के समय को व्यक्त कर रही है।

(B) Adverb clause of place : कार्य के होने का स्थान व्यक्त करती है। जैसे

(a) This is the room, where I lived in. (b) This is the hotel where she was murdered .

रेखांकित Adverb clause, कार्य के होने का स्थान व्यक्त कर रही है।

(C) Adverb clause of manner : यह कार्य के सम्पन्न होने के ढंग को व्यक्त करती है। जैसे

(a) She behaved as if she is known to me. (b) He cried as though he was ruined.

रेखांकित clause, कार्य के होने का manner (ढंग या तरीका) व्यक्त करती है।

(D) Adverb clause of reason : यह कार्य के होने के कारण (reason) को व्यक्त करती है जैसे :

(a) I am happy because my son passed in IAS. (b) He is sad as he failed in the examination.

उपरोक्त रेखांकित clause, कार्य के reason को व्यक्त करती है। जैसे :

(E) Adverb clause of purpose : ये clauses कार्य के उद्देश्य को व्यक्त करती हैं। जैसे :

(a) He worked hard so that he could succeed. (b) Run fast lest you should miss the train.

रेखांकित clause कार्य के उद्देश्य (purpose) को व्यक्त करती है।

(F) Adverb clause of condition : ये clauses कार्य के पूर्ण होने की शर्त को व्यक्त करती हैं। जैसे:

(a) I will go if he comes. (b) You can't pass unless you study sincerely.

रेखांकित Adverb clauses, कार्य के पूर्ण होने की शर्त को व्यक्त करती है।

(G) Adverb clause of contrast or concession : ये clauses, वाक्य में विरोधाभास को व्यक्त करती हैं। यह clause, Principal clause में व्यक्त तथ्यों के विपरीत तथ्यों को व्यक्त करती है। जैसे :

(a) Though he is poor, he is reliable. (b) He didn't work hard, however he passed.

रेखांकित clause, वाक्य में contrast (विरोधाभास) को व्यक्त करती है।

(H) Adverb clause of comparison : यह वाक्य में तुलना हेतु प्रयुक्त होती है। जैसे:

(a) He is not so strong as his brother. (b) She is as beautiful as her elder sister.

Clause वाक्य में तुलना हेतु प्रयुक्त होती है।

(I) Adverb clause of result (consequence) : यह clause, कार्य के परिणाम को व्यक्त करती है। जैसे :

(a) He is so poor that he cannot buy a pen.

(b) She speaks so slowly that I cannot hear her.

उक्त वाक्यों में रेखांकित clause, Adverb clause of result है जो कार्य के परिणाम को व्यक्त करती है। इस तरह की clause सामान्यतया that से शुरू होती है।

आप clauses के विभिन्न के विभिन्न प्रकारों, उनकी विशेषताओं और उनके function के बारे में जान चुके हैं। अब sentence की पहचान करने व इसे बनाने के लिए अग्रांकित बिन्दुओं पर ध्यान दें :

Simple/Compound/Complex/Mixed Sentences

(1) Simple sentence : One Principal clause only (One finite verb only.)

ऐसे वाक्य जिनमें एक finite verb होती है। जैसे :

(a) I play football. (Finite verb 'play')
(b) She goes to market. (Finite verb 'goes')
(c) They make a noise. (Finite verb 'make')
(d) We swim in the river. (Finite verb 'swim')

उक्त सभी Simple sentence हैं। इनमें एक ही Principal clause होती है। एक ही Finite verb हैं, Finite verb ऐसी होती है जो subject के number एवं person के अनुसार संशोधित होती है।

(2) Compound sentence : At least two Principal clauses.

Principal clauses एक-दूसरे से Coordinating conjunction द्वारा जुड़ी रहती हैं। जैसे :

(a) He came (a) and he wrote a letter. (b)
(b) He is poor (a) but he is honest. (b)
(c) He is intelligent (a) so he passed. (b)
(d) He is not well (a) so he will not go there. (b)

उक्त सभी वाक्यों में (a) एवं (b) Principal clauses हैं, जो Coordinating conjunction द्वारा जुड़ी हुई हैं। यदि दो Simple sentences को Coordinating conjunction द्वारा जोड़ दिया जाए तो वह Compound sentence बन जाता है।

(3) Complex sentence : One Principal clause + at least one Subordinate clause
(Simple sentence + at least one subordinate clause)

Complex sentence में एक Principal clause एवं कम-से-कम एक Subordinate clause का होना आवश्यक है। Subordinate clause, Principal clause के साथ Subordinate conjunction द्वारा जुड़ी रहती है। जैसे :

Principal Clause	Subordinate Clause
(a) She is the girl	who stole my purse.
(b) He is the man	who was arrested by the police.
(c) I think	that she threw the gifts which I gave her.
(d) Ram is happy	because he passed the examination.

ध्यान रखें Subordinate clause अपने पूर्ण अर्थ के लिए Principal clause पर निर्भर (depend) रहती है।

(4) Mixed sentence : At least two principal clause + at least one Subordinate clause
(Compound sentence + At least one Subordinate clause)

ऐसे वाक्य, जिनमें कम-से-कम दो Principal clause एवं कम-से-कम एक Subordinate clause होती है, Mixed sentence कहलाते हैं। Compound sentence में यदि एक Subordinate clause और जुड़ी रहे तो वह Mixed sentence है। जो sentence, अन्य किसी sentence की definition में नहीं आता, वह Mixed sentence होता है। जैसे :

I met a girl, who informed me that my purse had been stolen by a thief.

I met a girl,	*Principal clause*
who informed me	*Principal clause*
that my purse had been stolen by a thief.	*Subordinate clause*

यह एक Mixed sentence है।

When to Use Which Sentence ?

Simple : The Simple sentence is ideal when what you have to say is a single thought. Without unrelated and unnecessary words and thoughts confusing the issue, your meaning will be much easier for readers to grasp.

Compound : Use a Compound sentence when you want to show that two ideas, are related, and of equal significance.

Complex : Use a Complex sentence when you want to show a relationship between two or more ideas, one of which is more important than the others are. Most of the sentences you write will probably be complex. It is up to you as a writer to decide what thoughts you wish to stress.

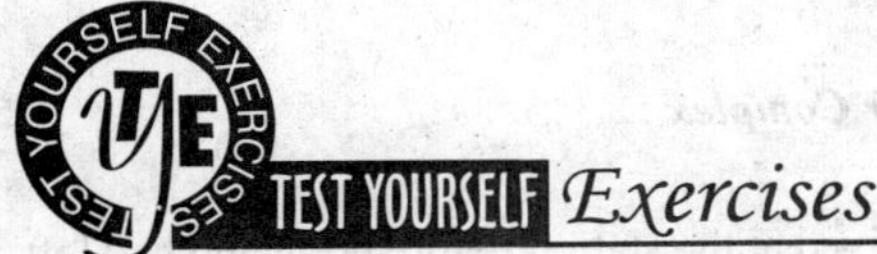

Exercises

01

Pick out the Principal clause and the Subordinate clause from the following sentences :

(1) He runs as fast as possible.
(2) Your shirt is better than mine.
(3) She as well as I went there.
(4) All that glitters is not gold.
(5) He drew the revolver, took aim and fired.

02

Pick out Relative clause from the following sentences :

(1) This is the pen, that Ram bought yesterday.
(2) He, who helps the poor, is helped by Almighty.
(3) I have found the purse, which I lost yesterday.
(4) The dog that barks does not bite.
(5) He, who serves the helpless, is always happy.

03

Pick out the Adverb clause from the following sentences :

(1) We eat that we may live.
(2) The more she gets, the more she demands.
(3) The tree is so tall that an old can't climb it up.
(4) However hard she may work, she will not succeed.
(5) Even if he doesn't cooperate me, I will fight alone.

04

Find out the Noun clause from the following sentences :

(1) Where he lives is not known to me.
(2) She told me that she would not support me.
(3) Please ask him, what he wants.
(4) I can't say what he does.
(5) It is useless to discuss, what he utters.

05

Pick out the Adjective clause from the following sentences :

(1) I know the place, where she is hidden.
(2) This is the place, where the murder was committed.
(3) The idea why she spoke so is now clear.
(4) This is the hotel, that my friend built.
(5) One who lives in glass house, should refrain from throwing stone at others.

06

State which of the following sentences are Simple, Compound or Complex :

(1) Take whatever you like.
(2) I am certain that she has gone mad.
(3) I am very tired for I have been walking all the morning.
(4) Honesty is the best policy.
(5) He acted according to my advice.
(6) God made the country and man made the town.
(7) She wrote a letter and posted it through her brother.
(8) Write as fast as you can.
(9) She as well as her sister is guilty.
(10) He is the leader whom we all respect.
(11) I gave her the bag because she needed it.
(12) He is sure of his success.
(13) I like you no less than him.
(14) I don't know the month of my birth.
(15) She told me that she would come on Monday.

07

State which of the following sentences are Simple, Compound or Complex :

(1) Joe waited for the train, but the train was late.
(2) I looked for Mary and Samantha at the bus station, but they arrived at the station before noon and had left on the bus before I arrived.
(3) Mary and Samantha arrived at the bus station before noon and they had left on the bus before I arrived.
(4) Mary and Samantha had left on the bus before I arrived, so I did not see them at the bus station.
(5) Because Mary and Samantha arrived at the bus station before noon, I did not see them at the station.
(6) While he waited at the train station, Joe realized that the train was late.
(7) After they left on the bus, Mary and Samantha realized that Joe was waiting at the train station.
(8) Joe waited for the train.
(9) The train was late.
(10) Mary and Samantha took the bus.
(11) I looked for Mary and Samantha at the bus station.

08

State about the following sentences, whether Simple/Compound/Complex/Mixed, and explain your answer :

(1) I do not own a Porche.
(2) When the train arrives and if Ms Langlois is on it, she will be served with a subpoena.
(3) Suzanne wanted to be here, but she cannot come because her car is in the shop.
(4) The football game was cancelled because of the rain.
(5) The football game was cancelled because it was raining.
(6) Unless my girlfriend postpones her visit from Calgary, I will not have time to study for my exam.
(7) I ate the sushi and left the restaurant.
(8) Call your father as soon as you arrive in Antigonish.
(9) Democracy is a noble goal; it is important, however, to protect the minority from the tyranny of the majority.
(10) Ottawa is the capital of Canada, but Toronto is the capital of Ontario.

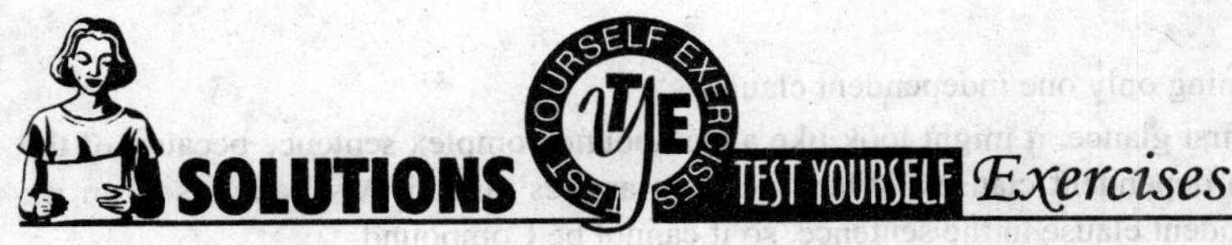

Solution TYE 01

Clause	Type
(1) He runs	*Principal clause*
as fast as possible	*Subordinate clause*
(2) Your shirt is better	*Principal clause*
than mine	*Subordinate clause*
(3) She went there	*Principal clause*
as well as I went there	*Subordinate clause*
(4) All is not gold	*Principal clause*
that glitters	*Subordinate clause*
(5) He drew the revolver	*Principal clause*
He took aim	*Principal clause*
He fired	*Principal clause*

Solution TYE 02

(1) that Ram bought yesterday.
(2) who helps the poor.
(3) which I lost yesterday.
(4) that barks.
(5) who serves the helpless.

Solution TYE 03

(1) that we may live.
(2) the more she gets.
(3) that an old can't climb it up.
(4) However hard she may work.
(5) Even if he doesn't cooperate me.

Solution TYE 04

(1) Where he lives.
(2) that she would not support me.
(3) what he wants?
(4) what he does?
(5) what he utters?

Solution TYE 05

(1) where she is hidden.
(2) where the murder was committed.
(3) why she spoke?
(4) that my friend built.
(5) Who lives in glass house?

Solution TYE 06

(1) Complex, (2) Complex, (3) Compound, (4) Simple, (5) Simple,
(6) Compound, (7) Compound, (8) Compound, (9) Compound, (10) Complex,
(11) Complex, (12) Simple (13) Complex, (14) Simple, (15) Complex.

Solution TYE 07

(1) Compound, (2) Compound, (3) Compound, (4) Compound, (5) Complex,
(6) Complex, (7) Complex, (8) Simple, (9) Simple, (10) Simple,
(11) Simple.

Solution TYE 08

(1) This is a Simple sentence, containing only one independent clause.

(2) This is a Complex sentence. At first glance, it might look like a Compound complex sentence because of the conjunction 'and' joining the two dependent clauses 'When the train arrives' and 'if Ms Langlois is on it'; however, there is only one independent clause in the sentence, so it cannot be Compound.

(3) This is a Mixed (Compound-complex) sentence. First, it contains two independent clauses 'Suzanne wanted to be here' and 'she cannot come because her car is in the shop' joined by the Co-ordinating conjunction 'but'; the second independent clause, however, contains the dependent clause 'because her car is in the shop', making the sentence Complex as well as Compound.

(4) This is a Simple sentence: since it does not have a predicate, 'because of the rain' is a phrase rather than a clause.

(5) This is a Complex sentence since it contains the dependent clause 'because it was raining.'

(6) This is a Complex sentence, containing the independent clause 'I will not have time to study for my exam' and the dependent clause 'Unless my girlfriend postpones her visit from Calgary.' Note the Subordinating conjunction 'unless' at the beginning of the dependent clause.

(7) This is a Simple sentence. It is easy to see, however, why someone might think that this is a Compound sentence, since it contains the Co-ordinating conjunction 'and'; however, the conjunction actually joins two predicates : 'ate the sushi' and 'left the restaurant' -- within a single clause. The clue that you are dealing with.

(8) This is a Complex sentence because it contains the dependent clause 'as soon as you arrive in Antigonish.' If that information were in a phrase instead of a clause, however, the sentence would be a Simple sentence:
Call your father upon your arrival in Antigonish.

(9) This is a special type of Compound sentence, where the two independent clauses : 'Democracy is a noble goal' and 'it is important, however, to protect the minority ...' are joined by a semicolon instead of a Co-ordinating conjunction.

(10) This is a Compound sentence, because it contains two independent clauses joined by the Co-ordinating conjunction 'and'.

CHAPTER 29

SYNTHESIS OF SENTENCES

Synthesis एक ऐसी प्रक्रिया है जिसके द्वारा बहुत से वाक्यों को जोड़कर एक वाक्य बनाया जाता है अर्थात् दो या अधिक वाक्यों को संयुक्त कर, एक Simple, Compound, Complex या Mixed Sentence बनाने की प्रक्रिया को Synthesis of Sentence कहा जाता है।

Synthesis of a Simple Sentence

आपने पढ़ा है कि Simple sentence ऐसा sentence है, जिसमें एक ही Finite verb होती है। अत: दो या अधिक Simple Sentences को संयुक्त कर जो Simple Sentence बनेगा, उसमें एक ही Finite verb होनी चाहिए। यह निम्न प्रकार से किया जा सकता है :

(A) Using Participle

(a) Simple Sentences को जोड़ने हेतु Participle का प्रयोग सामान्यतया तब किया जाता है जब वाक्यों में एक ही कर्त्ता (subject) हो या एक वाक्य में It का प्रयोग हो।

(b) वाक्य इस तरह के हों, जिनसे यह ज्ञात हो कि एक कार्य दूसरे कार्य के बाद सम्पन्न हुआ है।

Rule 1

यदि एक वाक्य में is/am/are/was/were जैसी verb का प्रयोग हुआ है, तो इनकी जगह being का प्रयोग करके नया simple वाक्य बनाया जाता है। जैसे :

(1) (a) He is very weak. (b) He cannot go alone.
Being very weak he cannot go alone.

(2) (a) He is intelligent (b) He can solve this question.
Being intelligent he can solve this question.

(3) (a) It was Sunday. (b) The market was closed.
Being Sunday the market was closed.

Rule 2

यदि दूसरे वाक्य में Action में fastness व्यक्त हो तो पहले वाक्य की verb को participle की तरह प्रयुक्त करते हैं जो कार्य पहले हुआ है, उस वाक्य की verb को participle के तरह प्रयोग करके नया वाक्य बनाना चाहिए। जैसे :

(1) (a) He saw a lion. (b) He fled away.
Seeing a lion he fled away.

(2) (a) She heard a noise. (b) She ran out.
Hearing a noise she ran out.

(3) (a) He was late. (b) He ran to the station.
It being late he ran to the station.

Rule 3

यदि वाक्य में Action में fastness व्यक्त न हो तो having + V-III को प्रयोग किया जाता है। जैसे :

(1) (a) I took my lunch. (b) I went to office.
Having taken my lunch I went to office.

(2) (a) He wrote a letter. (b) He posted it.
Having written a letter he posted it.

(3) (a) He played a match. (b) He went to college.
Having played a match he went to college.

Rule 4

Past participle का adjective की तरह प्रयोग करके भी simple sentence बनाया जा सकता है जैसे :

(1) (a) He met a child. (b) The child was weeping.
He met a weeping child.

(2) (a) She found a dog. (b) The dog was black.
She found a black dog.

(3) (a) I saw a lion. (b) The lion was wounded.
I saw a wounded lion.

(B) By Using Conjunction 'And'

'And' conjunction द्वारा इस तरह के वाक्यों को जोड़ा जा सकता है,जिनमें predicate समान हो, subject अलग हों। ऐसे वाक्यों को and से जोड़कर नया Simple sentence बनाया जा सकता है। जैसे :

(1) (a) Harish played cricket. (b) Ramesh played cricket.
Harish and Ramesh played cricket.

(2) (a) Ram knows driving. (b) Shyam knows driving.
Ram and Shyam know driving.

(3) (a) Ram went to hospital. (b) Sita went to hospital.
Ram and Sita went to hospital.

जब predicate अलग हो एवं subject समान हो, तो वाक्यों को निम्न प्रकार जोड़ा जाता है :

(1) (a) Ram can write. (b) Ram can read.
Ram can write and read.

(2) (a) Sita can dance. (b) Sita can swim.
Sita can dance and swim.

(3) (a) He will play. (b) He will support us.
He will play and support us.

(C) By Using Nominative Absolute

जब वाक्यों में Subject अलग-अलग हो एवं वाक्यों में व्यक्त कार्यों के बीच कारण परिणाम का सम्बन्ध हो, अर्थात् एक कार्य के होने के बाद दूसरा कार्य उसका परिणाम हो, तो ऐसे वाक्यों को जोड़ने हेतु Nominative absolute का प्रयोग किया जाता है।

Nominative absolute उस कर्त्ता (nominative) को कहा जाता है जो वाक्य की क्रिया पर प्रभाव नहीं डालता है। जैसे :

(i) (a) The police arrived. (b) The thieves fled away.

यहाँ Police (Nominative absolute) है।

वाक्य The police arrived में police द्वारा कोई कार्य नहीं किया गया है। Verb arrived, police के द्वारा किया कोई कार्य नहीं है (The police arrested him. यहाँ arrested, police द्वारा किया कार्य है) इसका Norminative thieves है।

ऐसे वाक्यों को निम्न प्रकार एक Simple sentence में बदला जाता है।

The police having arrived the thieves fled away.

Rule

यदि वाक्य Active voice में है, तो having + V-III का प्रयोग किया जाता है एवं Passive voice में having been + V-III का प्रयोग किया जाता है।

See the following examples :

(1) (a) The sun rose. (b) The fog disappeared.
The sun having risen the fog disappeared.

(2) (a) The building caught fire. (b) All household articles were burnt to ashes.
The building having caught fire, all the household articles were burnt to ashes.

(3) (a) The job was completed. (b) He went on leave.
The job having been completed he went on leave.

(4) (a) The lion was caught in the net. (b) He struggled to get free.
Having been caught in the net the lion struggled to get free.

वाक्य (1) एवं (2) Active voice में हैं, अत: having + v-III का प्रयोग किया गया है, जबकि वाक्य (3) एवं (4) Passive voice में हैं, अत: having been + v-III का प्रयोग किया गया है।

(D) By Using Noun or Phrase in Apposition

Appositon का अर्थ होता है, 'side by side', जब वाक्य इस तरह के होते हैं कि पहले वाक्य में आए किसी noun के बारे में ही दूसरे वाक्य में कुछ details दी जाती हैं, तो ऐसे वाक्यों में noun के साथ ही उस detail को देखा (apposition) जाता है। जैसे :

(1) (a) I went to London. (b) London is the capital of Britain.
I went to London, the capital of Britain.

(2) (a) I like Sakshi.
(b) Sakshi is the most beautiful girl in this town.
I like Sakshi, the most beautiful girl in this town.

(3) (a) Gandhiji was a moralist. (b) He had once been a lawyer.
(c) He struggled hard to attain freedom.
Gandhiji, a moralist, once a lawyer, struggled hard to attain freedom.

(E) By Using Preposition with Noun or Gerund

ऐसे Simple sentences को जोड़ने हेतु Preposition का प्रयोग किया जाता है, जिनमें आपस में कोई कारण या अन्य प्रकार का सम्बन्ध होता है। जैसे :

(1) (a) He was rusticated. (b) He had broken the school window.
He was rusticated for breaking the school window.

(2) (a) He completed his work. (b) It struck seven.
He completed his work upto seven O'clock.

(3) (a) His wife died. (b) He heard the news.
(c) He lost consciousness.
On hearing the news of his wife's death, he lost consciousness.

(F) By Using Infinitive

Infinitive का प्रयोग ऐसे वाक्यों को जोड़ने हेतु किया जाता है, जिन वाक्यों में आपस में Inter dependence दृष्टिगोचर होती है। ऐसे वाक्यों में भी Infinitive का प्रयोग किया जाता है, जिनमें आपस में कारण-परिणाम का सम्बन्ध दिखाई देता है। (ध्यान रखें ऐसे वाक्यों को Nominative absolute द्वारा इसलिए नहीं जोड़ा जा सकता क्योंकि Nominative absolute के मामले में कर्त्ता भिन्न होते हैं तथा एक कार्य के बाद दूसरा कार्य होता है)। Infinitive द्वारा जोड़े गए वाक्यों में कार्य आगे-पीछे नहीं होता है बल्कि साथ-साथ होने का आपस में सम्बन्ध-सा होता है। जैसे :

(1) (a) I will go there. (b) I will settle the matter.
I will go there to settle the matter.

(2) (a) He came here. (b) He signed the agreement.
He came here to sign the agreement.

(3) (a) I have no money. (b) I cannot pay you now.
I have no money to pay you now.

(G) By Using Adjective or Adverb

जब दो वाक्य इस तरह के होते हैं कि एक में कार्य होने का कारण, दूसरा वाक्य होता है, तो ऐसे वाक्यों में enough का प्रयोग करके एक Simple sentence बनाया जाता है। जैसे :

(1) (a) He is intelligent. (b) He can solve this puzzle.
He is intelligent enough to solve this puzzle.

(2) (a) I have time. (b) I can go to hospital.
I have time enough to go to hospital.

(3) (a) He is rich. (b) He can buy this hotel.
He is rich enough to buy this hotel.

(H) By Using 'Too -to'

जब दो Simple sentences में किसी कार्य के न होने का कारण, पहले वाक्य में दिया गया हो, तो 'Too-to' का प्रयोग करके एक Simple sentence बनाया जाता है। जैसे :

(1) (a) He is very week. (b) He cannot walk.
He is too weak to walk.

(2) (a) He is very poor. (b) He cannot pay his fees.
He is too poor to pay his fees.

(3) (a) The tea is very hot. (b) I cannot drink it.
The tea is too hot to drink.

Synthesis of a Compound Sentence

Compound sentence में दो Principal clause होती हैं। उनमें कोई Subordinate clause नहीं होती है। Compound sentence को बनाने के लिए दो Simple sentences को एक Coordinating conjunction द्वारा जोड़ा जाता है, जो निम्नलिखित हैं :

And, both....and, also, too, as well as, not only....but also, either....or, neither....nor, for, otherwise, or, but, yet, however, so, therefore etc.

मुख्य बात यह है कि Compound sentence बनाते समय Subordinating conjunction का प्रयोग कदापि न करें। कौन-सा Coordinating conjunction प्रयोग किया जाएगा, यह वाक्यों के अर्थ से पता चलेगा। यदि वाक्यों में कोई choice है तो either....or यदि कोई विरोधाभास है, तो but, however, yet इत्यादि का प्रयोग किया जाता है।

(A) By using Cumulative Conjunction

दो Simple sentences को Cumulative conjunnction द्वारा जोड़कर, एक Compound sentence बनाया जाता है। मुख्य Cumulative conjunctions निम्नलिखित हैं:

And, both ...... and, as well as, not only ...... but also, not less than etc.

(a) Using 'And' :

(1) (a) I watched T.V. (b) He played football.
I watched T.V and he played football.

(2) (a) The police came. (b) The thief ran away.
The police came and the thief ran away.

(3) (a) She came. (b) She watched T.V.
She came and watched T.V.

(b) Using 'Both ...... and' :

(1) (a) He ate a biscuit. (b) He ate an orange.
He ate both a biscuit and an orange.

(2) (a) He is a student. (b) He is a painter.
He is both a student and a painter.

(3) (a) She purchased a pen. (b) She purchased a pencil.
She purchased both a pen and a pencil.

(c) Using 'As well as' :

(1) (a) Suresh is going to Jaipur. (b) Kukku is going to Jaipur.
Suresh as well as Kukku is going to Jaipur.

(2) (a) Saurav is playing cricket. (b) Sachin is playing cricket.
Saurav as well as Sachin is playing cricket.

(3) (a) He is intelligent. (b) He is smart.
He is intelligent as well as smart.

(d) Using 'Not only ...... but also' :

(1) (a) He is a painter. (b) He is a student.
He is not only a painter but also a student.

(2) (a) Ram will go to Jaipur. (b) Sita will go to Jaipur.
Not only Ram but also Sita will go to Jaipur.

(3) (a) Sita is intelligent. (b) Sita is beautiful.
Sita is not only intelligent but also beautiful.

(B) By Using Adversative Conjunction

But, still, yet, however, where, whereas, only, while इत्यादि Adversative conjunctions कहलाते हैं। इनका प्रयोग दो विरोधाभासी वाक्यों को जोड़ने हेतु किया जाता है। जैसे :

(a) Using 'But' :

(1) (a) He is smart. (b) He is not intelligent.
He is smart but he is not intelligent.

(2) (a) He worked hard. (b) He could not pass.
He worked hard but he could not pass.

(3) (a) He is rich. (b) He is miser.
He is rich but he is miser.

(b) Using 'Still or yet' :

(1) (a) I don't support her. (b) She respects me.
I do not support her still she respects me.

(2) (a) He is poor. (b) He is honest.
He is poor yet he is honest.

(3) (a) He worked hard. (b) He failed.
He worked hard yet he failed.

(c) Using 'However' :

(1) (a) She did not prepare well. (b) She succeeded.
She did not prepare well however she succeeded.

(2) (a) Your leaves are not due. (b) You may go.
Your leaves are not due however you may go.

(3) (a) I do not like this pen. (b) I may buy it for you.
I do not like this pen however I may buy it for you.

(d) Using 'Nevertheless' :

(1) (a) He is a miser. (b) He spent one lac in the marriage.
He is a miser nevertheless he spent one lac in the marriage.

(2) (a) He is a rich man. (b) He is not contented.
He is a rich man nevertheless he is not contented.

(3) (a) He is poor. (b) He is trustworthy.
He is poor nevertheless he is trustworthy.

(e) Using 'Or' :

(1) (a) Go away. (b) Come in.
Go away or come in.

(2) (a) Run fast. (b) You will miss the train.
Run fast or you will miss the train.

(3) (a) Work hard. (b) You will be failed.
Work hard or you will be failed.

(f) Using 'Only' :

(1) (a) He could solve it. (b) He became hopeless.
He could solve it only he became hopeless.

(2) (a) Go anywhere you like. (b) You inform me.
Go anywhere you like only inform me.

(3) (a) You can do whatever you like. (b) You don't make unnecessary telephones.
You can do whatever you like only you don't make unnecessary telephones.

(g) Using 'While/Whereas' :

(1) (a) He was playing. (b) She was watching TV.
He was playing while she was watching TV.

(2) (a) I was reading. (b) He was flying kites.
While I was reading, he was flying kites.

(3) (a) Ram won the game. (b) Shyam lost this chance.
Ram won the game whereas Shyam lost this chance.

(C) By Using Causative Conjunction

जब वाक्यों में कारण परिणाम का सम्बन्ध होता है, तो Causative conjunction का प्रयोग करके Compound sentence बनाया जाता है। मुख्य Causative conjunction हैं; therefore, so, for, hence etc.

(a) Using 'Therefore' :

(1) (a) He broke the glass. (b) He was punished.
He broke the glass therefore he was punished.

(2) (a) He is honest. (b) He was rewarded.
He is honest therefore he was rewarded.

(b) Using 'So' :

(1) (a) You are late. (b) You are fined.
You are late so you are fined.

(2) (a) We are late. (b) We should move fast.
We are late so we should move fast.

(c) Using 'For'

(1) (a) Everyone has to die one day. (b) Man is mortal.
Everyone has to die one day for man is mortal.

(2) (a) He forgave her. (b) She apologized publicly.
He forgave her for she apologized publicly.

(d) Using 'Hence' :

(1) (a) It is very cold. (b) We purchased some winter wears.
It is very cold hence we purchased some winter wears.

(2) (a) He is a sincere worker. (b) He was promoted.
He is a sincere worker hence he was promoted.

(D) By Using Who, When, Where, Which, In Continuative Sense

Who, which, where, when का प्रयोग Continuative sense में किया जाता है, तो ये Subordinating conjunction की तरह प्रयुक्त नहीं होते हैं एवं शुरू होने वाली clause भी Principal clause होती है। जैसे :

(1) (a) I went to London. (b) I got a job.
I went to London, where I got a job.

(2) (a) I worked there for three days. (b) I received a telegram.
I worked there for three days, where I received a telegram.

(3) (a) There is a girl. (b) She is very intelligent.
There is a girl, who is very intelligent.

(4) (a) I killed a rat. (b) It was a cruel act.
I killed a rat, which was a cruel act.

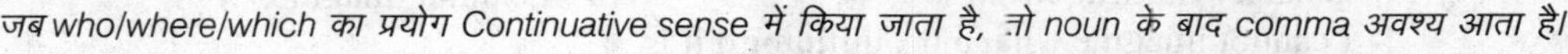

जब who/where/which का प्रयोग Continuative sense में किया जाता है, तो noun के बाद comma अवश्य आता है।

Synthesis of a Complex Sentence

Complex sentence में एक Principal clause होती है तथा एक या अधिक Subordinate clause होती है जो Subordinating conjunction द्वारा Principal clause से जुड़ी रहती है। अत: जब दो या अधिक Simple sentences को जोड़कर एक Complex sentence बनाना हो, तो एक sentence को Principal clause बनाएँ तथा अन्य को Subordinate clause बनाएँ।

Subordinate clause जैसा आपने analysis के अध्याय में पढ़ा है तीन प्रकार की होती हैं

(a) Noun clause (b) Adjective clause (c) Adverb clause

Subordinate clause को Principal clause के साथ Subordinating conjunction; जैसे : that, who, which, what because, since, so that, in order that, as, as if, as if, as soon as, though, before, after if, when, till untill etc., द्वारा जोड़ा जाता है।

कौन-सा Subordinating conjunction, प्रयुक्त होगा, यह वाक्यों के आशय या अर्थ पर निर्भर करता है।

(A) By Using Noun Clause

I. Use of conjunction (who/which/whom/whose/what/when/where/why/how/if/whether) : जब दो Simple sentences में एक तो Assertive/Imperative/Interrogative वाक्य होता है एवं दूसरा वाक्य Interrogative होता है, तो Complex वाक्य बनाते समय दूसरे Interrogative वाक्य को Assertive बनाते हुए पहले वाक्य से जोड़ा जाता है। यहाँ इन words से जो clause शुरू होती है वह Noun clause है। जैसे :

(1) (a) I do not know. (b) Who is he?
(Assertive + Interrogative)
I do not know who he is.

(2) (a) I cannot say. (b) Has he come?
(Assertive + Interrogative)
I cannot say whether he has come.

(3) (a) Tell me. (b) Where does she live ?
(Imperative + Interrogative)
Tell me where she lives.

(4) (a) Inform him. (b) When will she go ?
(Imperative + Interrogative)
Inform him when she will go.

(5) (a) Do you know? (b) What does he do ?
(Interrogative + Interrogative)
Do you know what he does ?

(6) (a) Can you inform me? (b) Where has she gone ?
(Interrogative + Interrogative)
Can you inform me where she has gone?

निम्न प्रकार के वाक्यों को भी Wh-word का प्रयोग करके (वाँक्यों के आशय के अनुसार) Complex sentence बनाया जा सकता है। Wh-words से शुरू होने वाली clause, Noun, clause है। जैसे :

(1) (a) Someone telephoned me. (b) I do not know who.
I do not know who telephoned me.

(2) (a) She will not come. (b) I do not know why.
I do not know why she will not come.

(3) (a) How had he performed ! (b) None could expect this.
None could expect how had he performed.

(4) (a) What a beautiful bird it is ! (b) I cannot imagine.
I cannot imagine what a beautiful bird it is.

II. Use of 'That' : यदि दो simple sentence इस तरह के हैं कि कथनों के स्वीकार या अस्वीकार का सम्बन्ध आपस में स्थापित किया जा सकता है, तो ऐसे वाक्यों का Complex sentence बनाने के लिए 'that' का प्रयोग निम्न प्रकार किया जाता है जैसे :

(1) (a) He is innocent. (b) I am confident of it.
I am confident that he is innocent.

(2) (a) He has committed a mistake. (b) I believe so.
I believe that he has committed a mistake.

(3) (a) She is an intelligent girl. (b) I do not doubt it.
I do not doubt that she is an intelligent girl.

III. इस तरह के वाक्यों को जोड़कर भी Complex sentence बनाया जा सकता है, जिनमें कोई इच्छा व्यक्त की गई हो। जैसे :

(1) (a) I wish to be a queen. (b) I am not a queen.
I wish I were a queen.

(2) (a) I wished to marry her. (b) I did not marry her.
I wished I had married her.

(B) By Using Adjective Clause

Adjective clause का प्रयोग उस स्थिति में करना उपयुक्त होता है जब एक वाक्य में किसी व्यक्ति/वस्तु के बारे में बताया गया है एवं अन्य वाक्यों में उसी noun के सम्बन्ध में कुछ कहा गया है, तो where/which/when/who/that etc. का प्रयोग करके एक या अधिक वाक्यों को Subordinate adjective clause बनाया जाता है एवं एक वाक्य को Principal clause बनाकर जोड़ा जाता है। जैसे :

(1) (a) This is the magazine. (b) I want to purchase.
This is the magazine that I want to purchase.

(2) (a) This is the hotel. (b) I lived here for three months.
This is the hotel where I lived for three months.

(3) (a) This is the girl. (b) She secured first position.
This is the girl who secured first position.

(C) By Using Adverb Clause

Adverb clause का प्रयोग तब किया जाता है, जब दो वाक्यों में किए गए कथनों में आपस में, विरोधाभास, तुलनात्मक, समय, स्थान, कारण या शर्त का सम्बन्ध व्यक्त हो। ध्यान रखें Adverb के functions के अनुसार जब दो वाक्यों में परस्पर सम्बन्ध हो, तो Adverb clause का प्रयोग करके, वाक्यों को जोड़कर Complex sentence बनाया जाता है। जैसे :

(1) (a) I wrote a letter. (b) I posted it.
I posted the letter after I had written it.

(2) (a) I watched T.V. (b) I went to market.
I went to market after I had watched T.V.

(3) (a) He is so poor. (b) He cannot buy his books.
He is so poor that he cannot buy his books.

(4) (a) He is intelligent. (b) His sister is equally intelligent .
He is as intelligent as his sister.

(5) (a) He finished his work. (b) Then he watched a movie.
He didn't watch a movie until he finished his work.

(6) (a) He is an intelligent student.
(b) No other student in the class is more intelligent.
No other student in the class is more intelligent than he.

Synthesis of a Mixed Sentence

Mixed sentence ऐसा वाक्य होता है जिसमें कम-से-कम दो Principal clauses होती हैं एवं कम-से-कम एक Subordinate clause होती है अर्थात् Mixed sentence एक Compound sentence में Subordinate clause जोड़कर बनाया जा सकता है या एक Simple sentence, जिसे Principal clause माना जाए, के साथ एक Complex sentence को संयुक्त कर एक Mixed sentence बनाया जा सकता है। इस हेतु Coordinating एवं Subordinating Conjunctions का प्रयोग किया जाता है, जिनके बारे में विस्तृत रूप से Synthesis of Simple/Compound/Complex sentences में बताया जा चुका है।

Exercises

01

Combine these Simple sentences into a simple sentences **:**

(1) (a) She heard a noise. (b) She woke up.
(2) (a) He saw a tiger. (b) He ran away.
(3) (a) He was tired of playing. (b) He went to take bath.
(4) (a) She sat on a chair. (b) She wrote a letter.
(5) (a) He has two kids. (b) He has to nourish them.
(6) (a) Turn to the right. (b) You will reach the railway station.
(7) (a) I will go to market. (b) I want to buy a box.
(8) (a) I received her message. (b) I was very happy.
(9) (a) My parents were much delighted. (b) They got the news of my promotion.
(10) (a) He was punished. (b) He had stolen my bag.

02

Combine these Simple sentences into a complex sentences **:**

(1) (a) He is a gangster. (b) Everybody knows it.
(2) (a) I informed you yesterday. (b) You should rely on it.
(3) (a) I met a girl. (b) She was very beautiful.
(4) (a) I met a woman. (b) Whose purse was snatched by some one.
(5) (a) Tell me the time. (b) You went there on Sunday.
(6) (a) I have seen the place. (b) The accident had taken place there.
(7) (a) The thief saw the constable. (b) He ran sway.
(8) (a) Ram is intelligent. (b) His brother Shyam is equally intelligent.
(9) (a) He fled somewhere. (b) The police could not trace him.
(10) (a) India is a powerful nation. (b) Pakistan is not so powerful.

03

Combine these Simple sentences into a compound sentences **:**

(1) (a) He is slow. (b) He is sincere.
(2) (a) He was annoyed. (b) He kept quite.
(3) (a) He is a hardworker. (b) He is an intelligent man.
(4) (a) I went to the market. (b) I purchased a pen.
(5) (a) Get in. (b) You may fall ill.
(6) (a) I shall try to help you. (b) I cannot make any promise.
(7) (a) Do not walk so quickly. (b) You may fall.

(8) (a) I went to the fair. (b) I bought a scenery.
(9) (a) You may have some cold. (b) You may have some coffee.
(10) (a) He got up. (b) He went to the college.

04

Convert these Compound sentences into Complex sentences :

(1) He is a poor man, but he is honest .
(2) My brother gave me a watch and I have lost it.
(3) She was very tired and so she didn't cook food.
(4) She is still in teens, but she has the wisdom of a matured woman.
(5) I have lost the purse, but I have found it now.
(6) She is very affable and so I love her.
(7) He is doing his best and I am sure of it.
(8) Be sincere and you will be respected by everyone.
(9) Send the money in advance or you will not get the magazine.
(10) You are a teetotaller and I know it.

05

Combine the following pairs of sentences :

(1) (a) Are you an editor? (b) Are you an author?
(2) (a) She is very weak. (b) She can't climb up the hill.
(3) (a) He will pass. (b) It is certain.
(4) (a) She is a thief. (b) She was sentenced to prison.
(5) (a) He heard the news. (b) He became sad.
(6) (a) It may rain. (b) We may cancel our programme.
(7) (a) He is a disabled. (b) He is self-confident of winning the race.
(8) (a) He did not attend the function. (b) He did not inform me.
(9) (a) He is a liar. (b) It is known to everybody.
(10) (a) The tea is very hot. (b) One cannot drink it.

06

Combine the following pairs of sentences :

(1) (a) He was absent. (b) He was ill.
(2) (a) He was cooking. (b) His wife arrived.
(3) (a) He was washing the clothes. (b) She was watching TV.
(4) (a) You must learn grammar. (b) You will not pass.
(5) (a) Hari cleaned the room. (b) Shyam washed the dishes.
(c) Ram cooked the food.
(6) (a) Jacob washed the clothes. (b) Jena ironed the clothes.
(c) Reena put the clothes in the cupboard.
(7) (a) Ram is my friend. (b) He is waiting for me.
(8) (a) He lost his purse. (b) He lost his bicycle.
(9) (a) Tell me. (b) How many times did you telephone her?
(10) (a) This is the office. (b) I work here.

SOLUTIONS TEST YOURSELF *Exercises*

Solution TYE : 01

(1) Hearning a noise she woke up.
(2) Seeing a tiger he ran away.
(3) Tired of playing he went to take bath.
(4) Sitting on a chair she wrote a letter.
(5) He has two kids to nourish.

(6) Turning to the right you will reach the railway station.
(7) I will go to market to buy a box.
(8) I was very happy to receive her message.
(9) My parents were much delighted to get the news of my promotion.
(10) He was punished for stealing my bag.

Solution TYE : 02

(1) Everybody knows that he is a gangster.
(2) You should rely on what I informed you yesterday.
(3) I met a girl who was very beautiful.
(4) I met a woman whose purse was snatched by someone.
(5) Tell me the time when you went there on Sunday.
(6) I have seen the place where the accident had taken place.
(7) As soon as the thief saw the constable he ran away.
(8) His brother Shyam is as intelligent as Ram.
(9) He fled where the police could not trace him.
(10) Pakistan is not so powerful as India.

Solution TYE : 03

(1) He is slow but he is sincere.
(2) He was annoyed but he kept quite.
(3) He is not only a hard worker but also an intelligent man.
(4) I went to the market and purchased a pen.
(5) Get in or you may fall ill.
(6) I shall try to help you but I can't make any promise.
(7) Do not walk so quickly, you may fall.
(8) I went to the fair and bought a scenery.
(9) You may have some cold or some coffee.
(10) He got up and went to the college.

Solution TYE : 04

(1) He is an honest man although he is poor.
(2) I have lost the watch which my brother gave me.
(3) As she was very tired, she didn't cook food.
(4) She has the wisdom of a matured woman, although she is still in teens.
(5) I have found the purse that I had lost.
(6) I love her because she is very affable.
(7) I am sure that he is doing his best.
(8) If you are sincere, you will be respected by everyone.
(9) You will not get the magazine unless you send the money in advance.
(10) I know that you are a teetotaller.

Solution TYE : 05

(1) Are you an editor or an author?
(2) She is too weak to climb up the hill.
(3) It is certain that he will pass.
(4) She is a thief so she was sentenced to prison.
(5) When he heard the news he became sad.
(6) If it rains, our programme may be cancelled.
(7) Though he is a disabled yet he is self-confident of winning the race.
(8) He neither attended the function nor informed me.
(9) That he is a liar is known to everybody.
(10) The tea is too hot to drink.

Solution TYE : 06

(1) He was absent because he was ill.
(2) When his wife arrived he was cooking.
(3) While he was washing the clothes, she was watching T.V.
(4) Unless you learn grammar you will not pass.
(5) Hari cleaned the room, Shyam washed the dishes and Ram cooked the food.
(6) Jacob washed, Jena ironed and Reena put the clothes in the cupboard.
(7) Ram, my friend, is waiting for me.
(8) He not only lost his purse but also his bicycle.
(9) Tell me how many times you telephoned her?
(10) This is the office where I work.

PHRASAL VERBS

Phrasal verbs are part of a group of verbs called 'multi-word verbs'. Multi-word verbs, including phrasal verbs, are very common, especially in spoken English. A multi-word verb is a verb like 'pick up', 'turn on' or 'get on with'. Generally people refer to all multi-word verbs as Phrasal verbs. These verbs consist of a basic verb + another word or words. The other word(s) can be preposition and/or adverb. The two or three words that make up multi-word verbs form a short 'phrase', which is why these verbs are often all called 'Phrasal verbs'.

The important thing to remember is that a multi-word verb is still a verb. 'Get' is a verb. 'Get up', is also a verb, a different verb. 'Get' and 'get up' are two different verbs. They do not have the same meaning.

There are three types of multi-word verbs :

(1) Prepositional Verbs (2) Phrasal Verbs (3) Phrasal-prepositional Verbs

Prepositional Verbs

Prepositional verbs are made of : Verb + Preposition

As a preposition always has an object, so all Prepositional verbs have direct objects. Here are some examples of Prepositional verbs:

Prepositional Verbs	Meaning	Examples	Direct Object
believe in	have faith in the existence of	We believe in	God.
look after	take care of	He is looking after the	dog.
talk about	discuss	Did you talk about	me?
wait for	await	She is waiting for	Mira.

Prepositional verbs cannot be separated. That means that we cannot put the direct object between the two parts. For example, we cannot say "look the baby after."

Phrasal Verbs

Phrasal verbs are made from a verb plus another word or words Many people refer to all multi-word verbs as Phrasal verbs.

Phrasal verbs are made of : **Verb + adverb**

Phrasal verbs can be : Transitive (direct object) or Intransitive (no direct object).

Here are some examples of Phrasal verbs :

Transitive phrasal verbs :

(a) put off (postpone) : We will have to put off *the meeting.* — *Direct Object*

(b) turn down (refuse) : They turned down *my offer.* — *Direct Object*

Intransitive phrasal verbs :

(a) get up (rise from bed) I don't like to get up.

(b) break down (cease to function) He was late because his car broke down.

When Phrasal verbs are transitive (that is, they have a direct object), we can usually separate the two parts.
For example, 'turn down' is a separable Phrasal verb.
We can say: "Turn down my offer" or "Turn my offer down."

However, if the direct object is a pronoun, we have no choice. We must separate the Phrasal verb and insert the *pronoun* between the two parts.

Look at this example with the separable Phrasal verb 'switch on' :

(a) John switched on the radio. (b) John switched the radio on.

(c) John switched it on.

We can write any of the above sentences, but we can't write the following :

John switchedless on it. *Incorrect*

Phrasal-prepositional Verbs

Phrasal-prepositional verbs are made of : Verb + Adverb + Preposition

Look at these examples of Phrasal-prepositional verbs :

(a) get on with (have a friendly relationship with) : He doesn't get on with *his wife.*

(b) put up with (tolerate) : I won't put up with *your attitude.*

(c) look forward (to anticipate with pleasure) : I look forward to *seeing you.*

(d) run out of (use up, exhaust) : We have run out of *eggs.*

Italic Words are Direct Objects

Because Phrasal-prepositional verbs end with a preposition, there is always a direct object. And, like Prepositional verbs, Phrasal-prepositional verbs cannot be separated. So, we can say that Phrasal-prepositional verbs are inseparable.

(a) We ran out of fuel. (b) We ran out of it.

Various Phrasal Verbs *and* Their Uses

Act up : [misbehave (for people); not work properly (for machines) :

(a) "The babysitter had a difficult time. The children *acted up* all evening."

(b) "I guess I'd better take my car to the garage. It's been *acting* up lately."

Act on : (produce effect) : In general, Acids *act on* metals.

Act upon : (in accordance with) : The captain *acting upon* the secret information caught the militants.

Act like : (behave in a way that's like ...) : "What's wrong with Bob? He's *acting like* an idiot."

Add up : (logically fit together.):

(a) "His theory is hard to believe, but his research *adds up*." *Note* : This Phrasal verb is often negative.

(b) "His theory seems, at first, to be plausible, but the facts in his research don't *add up*."

Add up : (find the total) : "What's the total of those bills? Could you *add* them *up* and see?"

Add up to : (to total) : "The bills *add up* to ₹ 8570/- only. That's more than I expected!"

Ask out : (ask for a date) : "Shalu has a new boy friend. Johny *asked* her *out* last night."

Back down : (not follow a threat) : "Tom was going to call the police when I told him I'd wrecked his car, but he *backed down* when I said I'd pay for the damages."

Back off : (Not follow a threat) : "Tom was ready to call the police when I told him I'd wrecked his car, but he *backed off* when I said I'd pay for the damages."

Back up : (Move backward; move in reverse) :

(a) "You missed the lines in the parking space. You'll have to *back up* and try again."

(b) "The people waiting in line are too close to the door. We won't be able to open it unless they *back up*."

Back up : [drive a vehicle backwards (in reverse)] :

(a) "You're too close! *Back* your car *up*, so I can open the garage door."

Back up : (confirm a story, facts or information) : "If you don't believe me, talk to Dev. He'll *back* me *up*."

Back up : (make a 'protection' copy to use if there are problems with the original) "When my computer crashed, I lost many of my files. It's a good thing *I backed* them *up*."

Beg off : (decline an invitation; ask to be excused from doing something) : "At first Lily said, she would be at the party. Later she *begged off*."

Blow up : (inflate) : "We needs lots of balloons for the party. Will you *blow* them *up*?"

Bear down : (to crush by force) : "She was successful in *bearing down* the opposition group."

Bear out : (verify or confirm) : "Your arguments do not *bear out* the facts."

Bear up : (to face hardships bravely) : "He must try to *bear up* against this temporary phase of economic slump."

Bear with : (endure to have patience) : "A good wife *bear with* the habits of her husband."

Beat down : (to crush) : "He *beat down* the opposition with a single trick."

Beat off : (to repulse, to drive back) : "Indian army successfully *beat off* the enemy forces."

Beat up : (to beat) : "Ramesh was *beaten up* by Suresh for no reason."

Blow up : (explode; destroy by exploding) :

(a) "That old building really came down quickly!"

(b) "That's because the construction company used dynamite to *blow* it *up*."

Blow up : (suddenly become very angry) : "When I told Jerry that I'd an accident with his car, he *blew up*."

Bone up on : (review/study thoroughly for a short time) : "If you're going to travel to the U.K., you'd better *bone up on* your English."

Break down : (separate something into component parts) : "We spent a lot of money at the supermarket. When we *broke* the total cost down, we spent more on cleaning supplies than food."

Break down : (stop working/functioning) : "Shalini will be late for work today. Her car *broke down* on the way."

Break in : [enter by using force : (and breaking a lock, window etc.)]:

(a) "John's apartment was burglarized last night. Someone *broke in* while John was at the movies."

(b) "Somebody broke in to John's apartment while she was at the movies."

Break in : (wear something new until it's/they're comfortable) : "These are nice shoes, but they're too stiff. I hope it doesn't take too long to *break* them *in*."

Break in : (train; get someone/something accustomed to a new routine) : "I hope I can learn my new job quickly. The manager hasn't scheduled much time for *breaking* me *in*."

Break up : (disperse; scatter) : "What time did the party *break up* last night?"

Break up : (end a personal relationship) :

(a) "Tom and Jassi aren't going steady any more. They got really angry with each other and *broke up*."

(b) "Have you heard the news? Jassi *broke up* with Tom!"

(c) "I'm sorry to hear that their marriage *broke up*. I'm sure the divorce will be difficult for the children."

Bring/take back : (return something) :

(a) "Yes, you can borrow my pen, don't forget to *bring* it *back* to me when you're finished."

(b) "This book is due tomorrow. I guess I should *take* it *back* to the library."

Bring off : (accomplish something difficult; accomplish something people had considered impossible or unlikely) : No one thought Raju could get an A in that course, but he *brought* it *off*."

Bring up : [mention (as a topic of discussion)] : "We planned to discuss overtime pay in the meeting. Why didn't someone *bring* that topic *up*?''

Bring up : (raise; rear) : "Shalu's parents died when she was a baby. Her grandparents *brought* her *up*."

Brush up : on (review/study thoroughly for a short time) : "If you're going to travel to the U.K., you'd better *brush up on* your English."

Burn down : (become destroyed/consumed by fire) : *Note*:. For upright things trees, buildings, etc. only ''Lightning struck Mr. Kallan's born last night. It burned down before the fire fighters arrived.''

Burn up : (become destroyed/consumed by fire) : *Note* : For people and non-upright things only. ''All of Mr. Kalhan's hay *burned up* when his *barn burned* down.''

Burn up : (cause someone to become very angry) : "Did you hear how rudely Golu talked to me? That really *burned* me *up*!"

Butt in : [impolitely interrupt (a conversation, an action)] : "Hey, you! Don't *butt in*! Wait for your turn!"

Butter up : (praise someone excessively with the hope of getting some benefit) : "I guess Mohan really wants to be promoted. He's been *buttering* his boss *up* all week."

Call off : (cancel something that has been scheduled) : "We don't have school today. The Collector *called* classes *off* because of the snow."

Call on : (ask someone for an answer in class) : "I don't know why the teacher never *calls on* you. You always know the answer."

Calm down : (become calm/less agitated or upset; help someone become calm/ less agitated or upset) :

(a) "Why are you so upset? Sheela didn't intend to spill orange juice on you. *Calm down*!"

(b) "I know Raju is upset, but can you *calm* him *down*? He's making so much noise that he's irritating everyone in the office."

Care for : (like; want) : *Note*: This Phrasal verb is usually negative though it may be used affirmatively in questions.

(a) "Would you *care for* something to drink? We have coffee, tea or orange juice."

(b) "Could I have water, please? I don't *care for* coffee, tea or juice."

Care for : (take care of; supply care to; attend/watch) : "Ann's father got out of the hospital last week. The family is *caring* for him at home."

Catch on : (develop understanding or knowledge of something) : "Bholu had never used a computer until he took this class, but he *caught on* very quickly and is now one of the best students."

Catch up (with) : (stop being behind) : "Toshu stopped to rest for a few minutes. He'll *catch up/catch up with* us later."

Check in (to) : (register for/at a hotel, conference, etc; let someone know officially that you have arrived) :

(a) "My plane will arrive around 5:00 p.m. I should be able to *check into* the hotel by 6:00 or 6:30 p.m."

(b) "When you arrive at the convention, be sure to *check in* at the registration desk."

Check off : (make a mark to indicate that something on a list has been completed) : "Here are the things you need to do. Please *check* each one *off* when you've finished it."

Check out (of) : (follow procedures for leaving a hotel etc.) : "Don't forget to take your room key to the front desk when you *check out* (when you check out of the hotel)."

Check out : [follow procedures for borrowing something (usually for a limited period of time)] : "I'm sorry, but you can't take that encyclopaedia home. The library won't allow you to *check* reference books *out*."

Cheer up : (help someone feel less worried/ depressed/sad) : "Shalu's brother was depressed about not getting a promotion, so she sent him a funny card to *cheer* him *up*."

Chew out : (scold someone severely; berate) : "Golu's father was really angry when Tom didn't come home until 3:00 a.m. He *chewed* Tom *out* and then said Tom had to stay at home for three weeks."

Chicken out : (lose the courage or confidence to do something-often at the last minute) : "Sahu said he was going to ask Tili for a date, but he *chickened out*."

Chip in : [contribute/donate (often money) to something done by a group] : "We're going to buy a birthday cake for our boss and I'm collecting donations. Do you want to *chip in*?"

Clam up : (suddenly become quiet/refuse to talk about something) : "Lila wouldn't talk about the accident. When I asked her what happened, she *clammed up*."

Come across : [find (unexpectedly)] : "I've lost my extra car keys. If you come across them while your're cleaning the room, please put them in a safe place."

Come down with : (become ill with _____) : "George won't be at the office today. He *came down with* the flu over the weekend."

Come to : (total) : "Your charges *come to* $124.38. Will you pay by check, in cash, or with a credit card?"

Come to : (regain consciousness) : "When I told Gita, that she'd won a million dollars, she fainted. When she *came to*, I told her it was a joke and she almost hit me!"

Count on : (depend on; trust that something will happen or that someone will do as expected) "I'm *counting on* you to wake me up tomorrow. I know I won't hear the alarm."

Cross out : (show that something written is wrong or unnecessary by making an X across it) : "We can't afford to buy everything on your shopping list, so I've *crossed* all the unnecessary things *out*."

Cut back : (on) (use less of something) :

(a) "You drink too much coffee. You should *cut back*."

(b) "You should *cut back* on the amount of coffee that you drink."

Do in : (cause to become very tired) : "Those three games of tennis yesterday afternoon really *did* me *in*. I slept for ten hours after I got home."

Do in : (to kill; to murder) : "The policeman said that the murdered man was done in between 10 and 11 o'clock last night."

Do over : (do something again) : "Oh, no! I forgot to save my report before I turned the computer off! Now I'll have to *do it* over!"

Drag on : (last much longer than expected or is necessary) : "I thought the meeting would be a short one, but it *dragged on* for more than three hours."

Draw up : (create a formal document) : "The Ajax and Tip-Top Banks have decided to merge. Their lawyers will *draw* all the official documents *up* sometime this month."

Drop off : [deliver something; deliver someone (by giving him/her a ride)] :

(a) "Yes, I can take those letters to the post office. I'll *drop* them *off* as I go home from work."

(b) "You don't have to take a taxi. You live fairly close to me, so I'll be happy to *drop* you *off*."

Drop in : (on) [visit informally (and usually without scheduling a specific time)] : "If you're in town next month, we'd love to see you. Please try to *drop in*./Please try to drop in on us."

Drop by : [visit informally (and usually without scheduling a specific time)] : "If you're in town next month, we'd love to see you. Please try to *drop by* the house."

Drop out : (of) (stop attending/ leave school or an organization) : "No, Parish isn't at the university. He *dropped out*./He *dropped out* of school."

Draw out : [prolong something (usually far beyond the normal limits)] : "I thought that speech would never end. The speaker could have said everything important in about five minutes, but he *drew* the speech *out* for over an hour!"

Eat out : [have a meal in a restaurant] : "I'm too tired to cook . Why don't we *eat out*?"

Egg on : [urge/encourage greatly toward doing something (usually something negative)] : "At first Boby and Kaku were just having a mild argument, but Boby's friends *egged* them on until they started fighting."

End up : (finally arrive at; arrive at an unexpected place) : "We got lost last night and *ended up* in the next town."

End up : (arrive somewhere as a result or consequence) : "You're working too hard. If you don't take it easy, you'll *end up* in the hospital!"

Face up to : (admit to; take responsibility for) : "You can't pretend that you're doing OK in this course, John. Sooner or later, you'll have to *face up* to the fact that you're failing it."

Fall through : [not happen (*Note* : Describes something that was planned but didn't happen.)] : "We had originally intended to go to Morocco for our vacation, but our trip *fell through* when I got sick."

Feel up to : (feel strong enough or comfortable enough to do something) : "I know the accident was a terrible shock. Do you *feel up* to talking about it?"

Figure out : (logically find the answer to a problem; solve a problem by thinking about it carefully) : "For a long time I couldn't understand the last problem, but I finally *figured* it out."

Figure out : (understand why someone behaves the way she/he does) : "I can't *figure* marry *out*. Sometimes she's very warm and friendly and sometimes she acts as if she doesn't know me."

Fill in : (add information to a form) : "The office needs to know your home address and phone number. Could you *fill* them *in* on this form?"

Fill in : (on) (supply information that someone doesn't know) : "I wasn't able to attend the meeting yesterday, but I understand that it was important. Could you *fill* me *in*?/Could you *fill* me *in on* what was discussed?"

Fill in for : (temporarily do someone else's work; temporarily substitute for another person) : "Professor Neeraj is in the hospital and won't be able to teach for the rest of the term. Do you know who's going to *fill in for* her?"

Fill out : (complete a form by adding required information) : "Of course I completed my application! I *filled* it *out* and mailed it over three weeks ago!"

Fill out : (become less thin; gain weight) : "Jerry used to be really skinny, but in the last year he's begun to *fill out*."

Find out : (about) [learn/get information (about)] : "I'm sorry that you didn't know the meeting had been cancelled. I didn't *find out* (Find out about it) myself until just a few minutes ago."

Get across : (make something understood; communicate something understandably) : "Alan is really intelligent, but sometimes he has problems *getting* his ideas *across*."

Get along : (with) [have a friendly relationship (with); be friendly (toward)] : "Why can't you and your sister get along? Everyone else *gets along* with her just fine!"

Get around : (avoid having to do something) : "Tisha *got around* the required math classes by doing well on a math proficiency test."

Get around : (move from place to place) : "She doesn't have a car. She *gets around* by bicycle, bus or taxi."

Get around to : (do something eventually) : "I really should wash the dishes, but I don't feel like it. May be I'll *get around to* them tomorrow morning."

Get by : (survive, financially, in a difficult situation) : "It's going to be hard to pay the rent now that you've lost your job, but somehow we'll *get by*."

Get in : (enter a small, closed vehicle) : "I don't know where Jasmine was going. She just *got in* her car and drove away."

Get in : (arrive) : "Do you know what time Ted's plane *gets in*?"

Get on : (enter a large, closed vehicle) : "I'm sorry, but you're too late to say goodbye to Anita. She *got on* the plane about 20 minutes ago."

Get off : (leave a large, closed vehicle) : "When you *get off* the bus, cross the street, turn right on Oak Street, and keep going until you're at the corner of Oak Hotel."

Get off : [be excused (for a period of time) from work, class or other regularly scheduled activities] "Some schools *got* President's Day *off*, but ours didn't. We had classes as usual."

Get off : (make it possible for someone to avoid punishment) : "Everyone knew he was guilty, but his lawyer was clever and *got* him *off*."

Get out of : (leave a small, closed vehicle) : "There's something wrong with the garage door opener. You'll have to *get out of* the car and open it by hand."

Get out of : (escape having to do something) : "Liz said, that she had a terrible headache and *got out* of giving her speech today."

Get over : [finish (*Note* : as for individual activities, not ones that happen again and again)] : "What time do your *classes get* over?"

Get over : (recover from an illness or painful experience) : "Kelly was really upset when she failed the test. She thought she would never *get over* feeling so stupid."

Get rid of : (dispose of; give away or throw away) : "That shirt is really ugly. Why don't you get rid of it?"

Get rid of : (dismiss someone; fire someone from a job; cause someone to leave) : "The treasurer of the ABC company was spending too much money, so the company president got rid of him."

Get up : (leave bed after sleeping and begin your daily activities) :

(a) "You'll have to *get up* much earlier than usual tomorrow. We have to leave by no later than 6:00 a.m."
(b) "I know I won't hear the alarm tomorrow morning. Can you *get me up* at 6:00 a.m.?"

Give up : [Stop doing something (usually a habit)] : "He knows smoking isn't good for his health, but he can't *give it up*."

Give up : [decide not to try (unsuccessfully) to solve a problem] :

(a) "What's black and white and red all over?" (b) "I give *up*. What?"
(c) "An embarrassed zebra!"

Go out with : (have a date with) : "You *went out* with Shalini last night, didn't you?"

Go with : [look pleasing together (*Note* : for clothes, furniture etc.)] : "You should buy that shirt. It will go well *with* your dark brown suit."

Go with : (date regularly and steadily) : "Is Hina *going with* Joe? I see them together all the time."

Goof off : (be lazy; do nothing in particular) :

(a) "Do you have any special plans for your vacation?"
(b) "No, I'm just going to stay home and *goof off*."

Grow up : (spend the years between being a child and being an adult) "Did you know that Kallu *grew up* in Malaysia?"

Grow up : (behave responsibly; behave as an adult, not a child) :

(a) "Lee really irritates me sometimes. He's really silly and childish."
(b) "I agree, I wish he would *grow up*."

Hand in : (submit homework, an assignment etc.) : "You'd better get started on your report. You know that you have to *hand* it *in* at 8:30 tomorrow morning!"

Hand out : (distribute) : "Why don't you have a course description and list of assignments? The teacher *handed* them *out* on the first day of class."

Hang up : (end a phone conversation by replacing the receiver) : "I'd like to talk longer, but I'd better *hang up*. My sister needs to make a call."

Have to do with : (be about) : "This class *has to do with* the behaviour of people in groups."

Hold up : (raise; lift to a higher-than-normal position) : "The winner of the race proudly *held* his trophy *up* for all to see."

Hold up : (delay) : "I'm sorry I'm late. There was an accident on the freeway and traffic *held* me *up*."

Hold up : (rob; threaten someone with harm unless he/she gives his/her money or other valuable things) : "Shalu is very upset. When she was walking home last night, two men *held* her *up* and took her purse and jewellery."

Iron out : (mutually reach an agreement; mutually resolve difficulties) : "Yes, I know we disagree on lots of things, Susan, but we can *iron* them *out*."

Jack up : (raise/life by using a jack) : "We'll have to *jack* the back of the car up before we can change the tyre."

Jack up : [raise (used for prices)] : "The car dealer bought my old Ford for ₹ one lack and *jacked* the price *up* to ₹ 150000.00, when they sold it."

Jump all over : [severely scold someone; berate someone] : "Amar is really upset. His boss *jumped all over* him because he's been late for work three times this week."

Keep on : (continue) : "I'm not ready to stop yet. I think I'll *keep on* working for a while."

Keep on : (someone) : [continue to remind someone to do something until he/she does it (even if this irritates her/him)] : "Jack's very forgetful. You'll have to *keep on* him or he'll never do all the things you want him to do."

Kick out : (expel; force someone to leave because of his/her poor performance or unacceptable behaviour) : "Jim's club *kicked* him *out* because he didn't pay his dues or come to beetings."

Knock out : (Make unconscious)

(a) "The boxing match ended when one boxer *knocked* the other one."
(b) "That medicine really *knocked* me *out*. I slept for 14 hours straight!"

Knock oneself out : (work much harder than normal or than what is expected) : "We completed the project on time because of Jack. He *knocked himself out* to be sure we didn't miss the deadline."

Lay off : (dismiss someone from a job because of lack of work or money (not because of poor performance) : "I feel really sorry Shalu's family. Her father was *laid off* yesterday."

Leave out : (forget; omit) : "Oh, no! When I made the list of those who attended the meeting, *I left* your name *out*!"

Let down : (disappoint) : "I know I *let* you *down* when I didn't do what I promised. I'm really sorry."

Let up : (become less intense or slower) : "It's been raining hard for a long time. Will it ever *let up*?"

Look back on : (remember; reflect on/consider something in the past) : "When they *looked back on* their many years together, they realized that their marriage had been a very happy one."

Look down on : (hold in contempt; regard as inferior) : "It's not surprising that Ted has few friends. He seems to *look down on* anyone who doesn't like the same things that he does."

Look forward to : (anticipate pleasantly; think about a pleasant thing before it happens) : "I'm really *looking forward to* vacation. I can't wait for it to begin!"

Look in on : (visit in order to check something's/ someone's condition) : "My father just came home from the hospital. I plan to *look in on* him today after I finish work."

Look into : (investigate/get more details about something) : "Someone said there was a meeting at 9:30, but I haven't heard anything about it. Shall I *look into it*?"

Look like : [resemble (in appearance)] : "Does he *look like* his father or his mother?"

Look over : [check; review] : "I think I may have some types in this report. Could you *look* it *over*?"

Look up : [find something in a reference work] : "I'm sorry, but I don't know what that word means. I'll have to *look* it *up*."

Look up : (find where someone lives or works and visit him/her) : "Thanks for giving me your brother's address. When I'm in Chicago next month, I'll be sure to *look* him *up*."

Look up to : (respect) : "Everyone *looks up to* John because he always makes time to help others."

Luck out : (be unexpectedly lucky) : "Gloria was worried because she wasn't prepared to give a report at the meeting, but she *lucked out* because the meeting was postponed."

Make fun of : [make jokes about (usually unkindly)] : "I agree that Bob looks ridiculous since he shaved his head, but don't *make fun of* him. You'll hurt his feelings."

Make up : [invent/create (Imaginary) information] : "Judy's story is hard to believe. I'm sure she *made it up*."

Make up : (compensate for something missed or not done by doing extra or equivalent work) : "I'm sorry I missed the test. May I *make* it *up*?"

Make up : (with) (re-establish a friendly relationship by admitting guilt) : "Jack and his girlfriend were very angry with each other, but last night they finally *made up*."

Make out : [see/hear something well enough to understand what it means (*Note* : often negative.)] :
(a) "Kath's writing is very small. I almost need a magnify glass to *make* it *out*."
(b) "What were the last two examples that he gave? I couldn't *make* them *out*."

Make for : (go to or toward) : "Her teen-aged children are always hungry. As soon as they arrive home from school, they *make for* the refrigerator."

Make for : (result in; cause) : "Many hands *make for* light work. (If many people work together, there's less work for everyone.)"

Mark up : [increase the price (for resale)] : "Mrs. Britt's import shop is profitable because she buys things inexpensively and then *marks* them *up*."

Mark down : [reduce the price (as an incentive to buy)] : "These shoes were really a bargain! The store *marked* them *down* by 40%!"

Mix up : (cause to become confused) : "I didn't complete the assignment because I didn't know how the directions *mixed* me *up*."

Nod off : [fall sleep (usually unintentionally)] : "The speech was so boring that several people in the audience *nodded off* before it was finished."

Pan out : [succeed; happen as expected (for plans)] : *Note* : almost always negative when in statements. "I'll be here next week after all. My trip to chicago didn't *pan out*"

Pass away : (die) : "I was very sorry to hear that your grandfather *passed away*."

Pass out : (faint; lose consciousness) : "When Kokila heard that she'd won a million dollars, she was so shocked that she *passed out*."

Pass out : (distribute) : "Everyone in the room needs one of these information sheets. Who will help me *pass* them *out*?"

Pick out : (choose; select) : "Kelly's grandmother especially liked her birthday card because Kelly had *picked it* out himself."

Pick up : (lift; take up) : "Those books don't belong on the floor. Will you help me *pick* them *up*?"

Pick up : (arrange to meet someone and give her/him a ride) : "Of course we can go there together. What time should I *pick* you *up*?"

Pick up : (get; buy) : "The children just drank the last of the milk. Could you *pick* some more *up* on your way home this evening?"

Pick up : (refresh; revitalize) : ''He was feeling a little tired, so he drank a glass of orange juice. *It picked* him *up* enough to finish his work."

Pick on : (bully; intentionally try to make someone upset) : "You should be ashamed of teasing your little brother, Tony! *Pick on* someone your own size!"

Pitch in : (help; join together to accomplish something) : "We'll be finished soon if everyone *pitches in*."

Pull over : (drive a vehicle to the side of the rode) : "When the policeman indicated that I should *pull over*, I knew he was going to give me a ticket."

Put away : (return something to the proper place) : "I just took these clothes out of the dryer. Will you help me *put* them *away*?"

Put off : (postpone; delay; avoid) :

(a) "I can't *put* this work off any longer. If I don't do it soon, it'll be impossible to finish it in time."

(b) "When will Mr. Jack agree to a meeting? I keep asking for an appointment, but he keeps putting me off."

Put on : (begin to wear; don) : "It's a little bit chilly outside. You'd better *put* a sweater *on*."

Put on : (try to make someone believe something that is ridiculous or untrue) : "Don't believe a word of what Jaru was saying. He was just *putting* us *on*."

Put (someone) **out** : (inconvenience someone) :"I hate to *put* you *out*, but I need a ride to the train station and hope you can take me."

Put up : (return something to the proper place) : "Your toys are all over the floor, Tinni. Please *put* them *up*."

Put up : (provide someone with a place to sleep) : "There's no need for you to check into a hotel. I'll be happy to *put* you *up*."

Put up with (tolerate) : "It's really important to come to work on time. The boss won't *put up with* tardiness."

Put back : (return something to the proper place) : "I've finished with these books. Do you want me to *put* them back on the shelves?"

Rip off : (cheat; take advantage of; charge too much) : "Don't even think about buying a car there. They'll *rip* you *off*."

Round off : (change from a fraction to the nearest whole number) : "*Round* all prices *off* to the closest whole rupee amount. For example round ₹ 83.71 off to ₹ 84.00."

Run into : (meet by chance) : "Yesterday at the super market, Jan *ran into* her former roommate. Before yesterday, they hadn't seen each other for nearly five years."

Run out of : (use the last of) : "On the way home from work, Art *ran out of* gas."

Set-up : (make arrangements for something) : "You'll see Mr. Kamas tomorrow. I've *set* a meeting *up* for 9:30 a.m."

Set back : (cause a delay in scheduling) : "We've had some problems with the project that have *set* us *back* at least two days. We'll give you a progress report tomorrow."

Set back : (cost) : "I wonder how much Am's new car *set* him *back*?"

Slip up : (make a mistake) : "You *slipped up* here. The amount should be ₹ 54,172.00, not ₹ 54127.00."

Stand out : (be noticeably better than other similar people or things) : "Good job, Ann! Your work really *stands out*!"

Stand up : (rise to a standing position) : "When the Chairperson entered the room, everyone *stood up*."

Stand up : (Make a date but not keep it) : "Angela was supposed to go to the dance with Fred, but she *stood* him *up* and went with Chuck instead."

Show up : (arrive; appear) :"The boss was very upset when you didn't *show up* for the meeting. What happened?"

Show up : [do a noticeably better job (often unexpectedly) : than someone else] : "Everyone thought Harsha would win, but Zean did. Actually, Zean really *showed* Harsha *up*."

Stand for : (represent) : "These letters seem to be an abbreviation. Do you know what they *stand for*?"

Stand for : [tolerate; permit (usually negative)] : "I'm not surprised that Mrs. John rejected your report. She won't *stand for* shoddy work."

Take after : (resemble; *Note* : used for people) : "Both my sister and I *take after* our father."

Take/bring back : (return) :

(a) "This book is due tomorrow. I guess I should *take it back* to the library."

(b) "Yes, you can borrow my pen, but don't forget to *bring* it *back* to me when you're finished."

Take care of : (provide care for; watch one's health) :

(a) "Louis has been *taking care* of her father since he returned home from the hospital."

(b) "You've been working too hard lately. You'd better *take care* of yourself !"

Take care of : [make arrangements (for something to happen): ; take responsibility for] "Will you *take care* of making reservations for our flight to London?"

Take off : [remove (Something you're wearing)] : "Please *take* your hat *off* when you go inside a building."

Take off : [leave; depart (often suddenly or quickly)] :

(a) "Was something wrong with Kelly? She *took off* without saying goodbye."

(b) "When does your plane *take off*?"

Take off : (make arrangements to be absent from work) : "Jusan isn't here today. She's *taking* today and tomorrow *off*."

Take up : [begin (a hobby or leisure-time activity)] :

(a) "Do you like to ski?"

(b) "I've never been skiing, but I think I'd like to *take* it *up*."

Tell (Someone) **off :** (speak to someone bluntly and negatively, saying exactly what she/ he did wrong) : "Julie was really angry at Bob; she *told* him *off* in front of all of us."

Tick off : (irritate someone; make someone upset or angry) : "It really *ticks* her *off* when someone is late for an appointment."

Tick off : [show that something has been completed by putting a tick (check) beside it] : "Here are the things you need to do. *Tick* each one *off* when you finish it."

Throw away : (discard; put in the garbage) : "You shouldn't *throw* those newspapers *away*; they're recyclable."

Throw out : (discard; put in the garbage) : "This food smells bad. You'd better *throw it out*."

Throw out : [forcibly make someone leave (usually because of bad behaviour)] : "Those people are drunk and making everyone uncomfortable. The manager should *throw* them *out*."

Throw up : (vomit) : "Rau was so nervous about his job interview that he *threw up* just before he left for it."

Try on : (wear something briefly to check its fit, how it looks etc.) : "I'm not sure that jacket is large enough. May I *try* it *on*?"

Try out : (use a machine briefly to determine how well it works) : "I really like the way this car looks. May *I try* it *on*?"

Try out : (for) (try to win a place on a team or other organization) :

(a) "I know you want to be on the football team. Are you going to *try out*?"

(b) "If you like to sing, you should *try out* for the choir."

Turn around : (move so that you are facing the opposite direction) : "Everyone *turned around* and stared when I entered the meeting late."

Turn around : (move so that someone/something is facing the opposite direction) : "I don't want this chair facing the window. Will you help me *turn* it *around*?"

Turn around : (make changes so that something that was unprofitable is profitable) : "The company was doing poorly until it hired a new president. He *turned* it *around* in about six months and now it's doing quite well."

Turn down : (decrease the volume) : "Your music is giving me a headache! Please *turn* it *down* or use your headphones!"
Turn down : (refuse) : "I thought I could borrow some money from Joe, but when I asked, he *turned* me *down*."
Turn in : (give/deliver/submit to someone) : "I've written my report, but I haven't *turned* it *in*."
Turn in : (go to bed) : "I'm pretty tired. I guess I'll *turn in*."
Turn in : (report or deliver wrongdoers to the authorities) : "Two days after the robbery, the thieves *turned* themselves *in*."
Turn off : (stop by turning a handle or switch) : "I'm cold. Do you mind if I *turn* the air conditioner *off*?"
Turn off : [bore; repel (very informal)] : "That music *turns* me *off*. Please play something else!"
Turn on : (start by turning a handle or switch) : "It's cold in here. I'm going to *turn* the heater *on*."
Turn on : [interest very much; excite (very informal)] : "What kind of music *turns* you *on*?"
Turn up : (increase the volume) : "I can barely hear the T.V. Can you *turn* it *up* a little?"
Turn up : (appear unexpectedly) : "We were all surprised when Rani *turned up* at the party. We didn't even know she was in town."
Wait on : [serve (usually customers in a restaurant, shop etc)] : "I want to make a complaint. The person who just *waited on* me was very impolite."
Wait for : (wait until someone/something arrives or is finished with something else) :
(a) "When will Jenny be finished with work? I've been *waiting for* him for almost an hour!"
(b) "I'm tired of *waiting for* the bus. I guess I'll take a taxi instead."
Wake up : (stop sleeping) : "I usually *wake up* around 6:00 a.m. each day."
Wake up : (rouse someone; cause someone to stop sleeping) : "I have an important meeting tomorrow and I'm afraid I won't hear my alarm. Will you *wake* me *up* at 6:00 a.m.?"
Watch out for : (be careful of; beware of) :
(a) "There's a school at the end of this block. *Watch out for* children crossing the street."
(b) "If you take that road, *watch out for* ice during the winter."
Wear out : (wear something/use something until it can no longer be worn/be used) :
(a) "I need a new pencil sharpener. I *wore* this one *out*."
(b) "I suppose I should get some new shoes. I've almost *worn* this pair *out*."
Wear out : (cause to become exhausted; cause to become very tired) :
(a) "I had four different meetings today. They *wore* me *out*."
(b) "I suppose I should get some new shoes. I've almost *worn* this pair *out*."
Work out : [exercise (usually in a gym etc.) to build muscles, body tone etc.] : "Instead of eating lunch on Monday, Wednesday, and Friday, Sheila goes to the recreation centre to *work out*."
Work out : [solve a problem/resolve a difficult situation (usually by working together)] : "I know we disagree on many points, but I believe we can *work* things *out*."
Wrap up : (wear enough clothes to keep warm) : "It's really cold today. Be sure you *wrap up* when you leave the house."
Wrap up : (finish something; bring something to a conclusion) : "We've been talking about the problem for nearly three hours. I hope we'll be able to *wrap* the discussion *up* soon."
Write down : (record something in writing) : "Could you tell me your e-mail address again? I want to *write* it *down*."
Write up : (record; report in writing) : "You'll need to make a report on your business meetings. Be sure you *write* them *up* as soon as possible after you return from your trip."
Zonk out : (fall asleep quickly because of exhaustion) : "I intended to go shopping after work, but I was so tired that I *zonked out* as soon as I got home."

01.

(1) Give the meaning of Phrasal verbs italicized in the following sentences and then use them in your own sentences : **[RAS 1989]**

(a) Don't worry. I shall try to ***bring*** him ***round***.
(b) You must ***make up*** your differences.
(c) He has promised to ***go into*** the matter.
(d) I shall ***stand*** by you through thick and thin.
(e) You will have to ***make good*** this loss.

(2) Make sentences by using any five of the Phrasal verbs given below : **[RAS 1992]**

(a) bear out (b) take off (c) look into (d) make for
(e) pick up (f) give in (g) come round

(3) Complete the Phrasal verb in each of the following sentences : **[RAS 1994]**

(a) If the business continues to lose money, I'm afraid we'll have to close ....
(b) You'd better ring her ...... and tell her you'll be late.
(c) I invited her to drop ..... any time she was passing, and have a cup of tea.
(d) He won't buy the car without trying it .... on the road first.
(e) If you can't afford it, you'll have to do .... it.

(4) Complete the Phrasal verbs in each of the following sentences : **[RAS 1996]**

(a) They left the bomb in the street. Many people died when it blew ....
(b) The dacoits refused to give .... even though they were surrounded by the troops.
(c) The Prime Minister pulled .... his partymen for their rude behaviour.
(d) Each time a new problem cropped ...., he rushed to his parents for advice.
(e) She broke ..... when she heard the news of her son's death.
(f) The chief guest gave .... the prizes.

(5) Make sentences by using any three of the following Phrasal verbs so as to bring out their meanings : **[RAS 1997]**

back up; look over; put out; put up; lay off; see back.

(6) Make sentences by using any four of the following Phrasal verbs so as to bring out their meanings :

hold up; lay off; call off; set back; calm down; bear with.

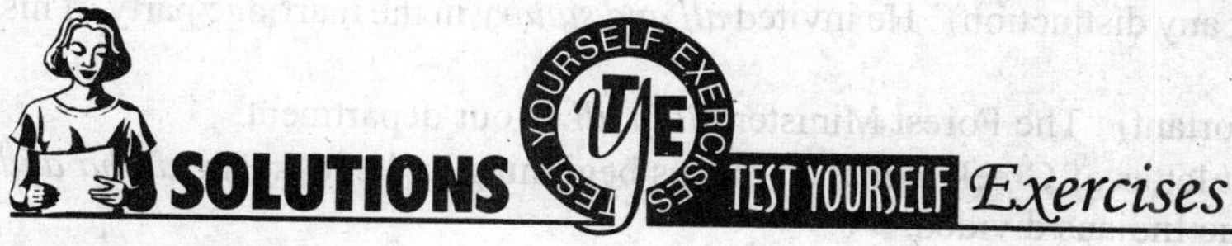

Solution TYE 01

(1) (a) persuade to accept something (b) finish a quarrel (c) investigate/go in detail
(d) support or help (e) compensate

(2) See the uses of Phrasal verbs.

(3) (a) down, (b) up, (c) in, (d) out, (e) without.

(4) (a) up, (b) in, (c) up, (d) up, (e) down, (f) away.

(5) See the uses of Phrasal verbs.

(6) See the uses of Phrasal verbs.

CHAPTER

31

IDIOMS AND PHRASES

दैनिक व्यवहार में प्रयुक्त होने वाले कुछ महत्त्वपूर्ण idioms एवं phrases को उनके वाक्य में प्रयोग करते हुए और सरल English में meaning समझाते हुए, नीचे दिया जा रहा है। छात्रों को इन idioms एवं phrases को ध्यानपूर्वक याद करना चाहिए। इनका प्रयोग, आपकी लेखन शैली को प्रभावी बनाता है। छात्रों द्वारा विभिन्न Competitive Examinations में लिखे जाने वाले Explanations, Essays आदि में इनका प्रयोग करने पर आपका लेख अधिक सशक्त, सुन्दर एवं प्रभावशाली बनेगा।

A gentleman at large (an unreliable person) : He is *a gentleman at large*, you must not trust him.

A man of straw (a weak person) : The assistant being *a man of straw*, his advice were often discarded by his colleagues.

A bull in a China shop (one who causes damage) : Many political leaders have proved *bulls in a China shop* in respect to the democratic fabric of the nation.

A damp squib (complete failure) : The visit of our Foreign Minister to USA proved a *damp squib* on terrorist issue.

A green horn (inexperienced) : Though *a green horn* in politics, he appears to win the election this time.

A stalking horse (pretence) : The demands of the trade union seem only *a stalking horse* to blackmail the management.

A mare's nest (a false invention) : The involvement of politicians in the developmental scheme proved to be a *mare's nest*.

A wolf in sheep's clothing (a dangerous person pretending harmless) : Charles Shobhraj is a *wolf in sheep's clothing* for general public.

ABC (very common knowledge) : He doesn't know *ABC* of Physics.

Above board (fair and honest) : He is a straight forward man. His financial dealings are *above board*.

Again and again (repeatedly) : One who tries *again and again* gets success positively.

All and sundry (without making any distinction) : He invited *all and sundry* in the marriage party of his younger brother.

All in all (whole-sole, most important) : The Forest Minister *all in all* of our department.

Alpha and omega (first and last letter of Greek alphabet, means beginning and end) : The *alpha and omega* of British policy was to keep the Indians divided.

An eye wash (a pretence) : He does nothing without self interest, all his excuses are, but *an eye wash*.

An iron hand (by force) : Indira Gandhi put down the opposition with *an iron hand*.

At odds (in dispute) : The two groups of the society are *at odds* over the selection procedure of peons.

At sixes and seven (persons who are having different opinions) : Economists are *at sixes and seven* on the policy of rationing.

Back and call (at the service) : Don't worry I am at your *back and call*.

Bag and baggage (with all goods): He returned his village *bag and baggage*.

Bated breath (in anxiety, expectancy) : Every Indian was waiting for the outcome of the cricket match with *bated breath*.

Bank on (depend on, count on) : You can *bank on* me in odd times.

Between Scylla and Charybdis (choice between two unpleasant alternatives) : Don't make haste, take care so that in avoiding *Scylla* you don't fall in *Charybdis*.

Between the cup and the lips (on the point of achievement) : Until I got the appointment letter in hand, I was not sure of the posting as there were many slips *between the cup and the lips*.

Black and white (in writing) : It is always better to get every thing in *black and white*.

Blow hot and cold (having no stand, shows favour at one time and unfavour at another) : He can't be relied upon as he *blows hot and cold* in this matter.

Body and soul (entirely) : She devoted *body and soul* to win the medal.

By fits and starts (irregularly) : Work done *by fits* and *starts* never completes in time.

By hook or by crook (by any means) : I want to get this licence *by hook or by crook*.

By leaps and bound (speedily) : The population is increasing *by leaps and bounds*.

By & By (gradually) : She is recovering *by and by* after long illness.

Call a spade a spade (straight talks) : He believes in *calling a spade a spade*.

Cats and dogs (heavy rain) : It has been raining *cats and dogs* for the last three hours.

Cock and bull story (untrue story) : All his excuses seems a *cock and bull story*.

Confusion worse confounded (be in further worse position) : Such demonstrations and communal speeches in present situation make *confusion worse confounded*.

Cut and dried (readymade form) : There is no *cut and dried* method of English speaking.

Curtain lecture (a reproof by wife to her husband) : My younger brother never pays any attention to his wife's *curtain lecture*.

Egg on (to urge somebody) : The Captain *egged* the players *on* to continue the struggle.

Ever and anon (now and then) : She goes to temple *ever and anon*.

Fair and square (honest) : He is *fair and square* in his dealings.

Fair field and no favour (equal opportunity to all) : All the staff want *fair field and no favour* in the matter of transfer.

Far and wide (everywhere) : Many tourists come to see the Taj from *far and wide*.

Fabian policy (policy of delaying decisions) : Mr. Narsimha Rao always followed a *Fabian policy* in all political issues.

Few and far between (very rare) : His visits to his parents are *few and far between* because of his busy schedule.

Fire and brimstone (fearful penalties) : The USA has threatened Iraq with *fire and brimstone*, if she refuses to follow the resolutions of UNO.

Fire and fury (extreme enthusiasm) : The speech of the leader was full of *fire and fury*.

First and foremost (highest priority) : To be sincere and devoted is the *first and foremost* requirement of a good employee.

Fishy (doubtful) : They seems to be something *fishy* going on.

Foot the bill (bear expenses) : Although, she hosted the feast, her father had to *foot the bill*.

Free and easy (natural and simple) : The principal found his arguments *free and easy*.

Flesh and blood (human nature) : I am only *flesh and blood* as anybody else.

Gall and wormwood (source of irritation) : Her remarks about his father were *gall and wormwood* to him.

Gird up the loin (to be ready) : We should *gird up the loin* to fight the poverty and menace of dowery.

Give in (surrender) : He is a brave man , he will not *give in* easily.

Goods and chattels (belongings of home) : On transfer he brought all *goods and chattels* by road.

Hand and gloves (very intimate friends) : Ram and Rahim are *hand and gloves* to each other.

Hard and fast (certain) : There are no *hard and fast* rules to sanction the loan in the banks.

Haughty and naughty (arrogant and naughty) : The *haughty and naughty* attitude of the president is not liked by any member of the society.

Heart and soul (with full devotion) : He threw himself *heart and soul* to pass the examination.

Head and shoulder (superior) : Shri Man Mohan Singh is *head and shoulder* above his counter parts.

Helter skelter (here and there) : On arrival of the police the strikers ran *helter skelter*.

Herculean task (a tedious job) : Getting selected in IAS is a *herculean task* for everybody.

Hit below the belt (contrary to principles of fairness) : By making his private secretes public he *hit* him *below the belt*.

Hither and thither (here and there) : He is in the habit of putting his goods *hither and thither*.

Hornet's nest (raise controversy) : The speaker of Lok Sabha stirred up *hornet's nest* by referring to impending changes in several rules.

Hole and corner policy (a secret policy for an evil purpose) : The officer adopted *hole and corner policy* to get his P.A. transferred.

Hue and cry (great noise) : A lot of *hue and cry* was raised in Parliament against this bill. I am ready to move heaven and Earth to bring him to justice.

Hush money (a bribe) : He managed to escape punishment by paying *hush money*.

Ins and outs (full detail) : Before starting any new business you must know all *ins and outs* of it.

Intents and purposes (practically) : My wife is the incharge of the house for all *intents and purposes*.

Ivory tower (imaginary world) : Those who talk of non-violence as a useful tool in tackling the militants live in *ivory tower*.

Kith and kin (blood relatives) : All *kith and kin* were invited in the marriage of his son.

Latin and Greek (unable to understand) : His speech in English was *Latin and Greek* to the rural folk.

Law and equity (legal and moral justice) : *Law and equity* demands that the reservation should be based on economic parameters.

Leave no stone unturned (make all possible efforts) : I shall *leave no stone unturned* to get the promotion.

Length and breadth (all over) : Anti English agitation spread through the *length and breadth* of the country.

Life and soul (main support) : Soniya Gandhi is the *life and soul* of congress(I).

Like a fish out of water (in every difficult and unsuitable situation) : Ram was given an unremunerative post. He is feeling *like a fish out of water*.

Live-wire (energetic) : India needs *live-wire* scientists who can put the country on the fast track of progress.

Loaves and fish (material interests) : Now-a-days Government servants are concerned with the *loaves and fish* of the office than to solve the problems of common public.

Lock and key (In safe place) : He keeps jewellery under *lock and key*.

Might and main (with all enthusiasm) : If you study with *might and main* you will positively secure the success.

Milk and water (weak) : The foreign policy of India is nothing more than a *milk and water* policy.

Neck and crop (completely) : The Pak army ruined the border village *neck and crop*.

Need of the hour (necessity of time) : Providing full security for the residents of border area is the *need of the hour*.

Nook and corner (everywhere) : I searched her in every *nook and corner.*

Not born yesterday (worldly wise) : You can't befool me as I was *not born yesterday.*

Now and then (occasionally) : I visit church *now and then.*

Null and void (of no use, without force of application) : The law passed by legislature was declared *null and void* by the Supreme Court.

Odds and ends (remaining goods) : Except *odds and ends*, all the items have since been arranged in order.

Odds and ends (scattered things) : The thief took away all the *odds and ends* lying in his bed room.

Often and often (frequently) : She visits her parents *often and often.*

Once and again (repeatedly) : I have told you *once and again* that I have no money to purchase the car at the moment.

One's Achilles'heel (a weak point) : Her involvement in sex scandal has been *her Achilles'heel.*

Open and above board (very clear, transparent) : He believes in *open and above board* discussion on every point before arriving at a conclusion.

Order of the day (in fashion) : Sending greetings on all occasions has beome a *order of the day.*

Out of gear (in disorder) : The strike of employees always put the government machinery *out of gear.*

Out and out (completely) : Mahatma Gandhi was a great leader *out and out.*

Over and above (besides) : I paid him rupees ten thousand *over and above* what he demanded.

Over head and ears (excessively) : He is *over head and ears* in debt.

Oily tongue (flattering words) : One should be aware of the persons with *oily tongue.*

Part and parcel (being an important part of) : Each employee should feel himself *part and parcel* of the business enterprises.

Pell mell (putting one upon the other, in confusion) : He was in such a hurry that he put all the articles *pell mell* and closed the room.

Pick and choose (to choose selectively as per wish) : The management adopted *pick and choose* policy in the promotions from clerical to assistant cadre.

Pins and needles (small items) : It is unwise to use swords and scissors where *pins and needles* can do.

Pin-money (allowance given to housewife for personal use) : My wife asked me to enhance her *pin-money.*

Pros and Cons (merits and demerits) : Before signing this agreement you must understand all *pros and cons* well.

Queer fish (strange person) : He is such a *queer fish* that we can't expect anything positive from him.

Rain or shine (favourable or unfavourable circumstances) : *Rain or shine*, I will speak oppose the proposal.

Rank and file (everyone without discrimination) : For the actual prosperity of the nation, the economic conditions of *rank and file* should be improved.

Rank and ruin (complete destructions) : The present drought has put the farmers at the verge of *rank and ruin.*

Rhyme or reason (rational cause) : He resigned from the service without any *rhyme or reason.*

Right and left (in all ways) : The robbers looted the village right and left and fled away.

Root and branch (complete) : Poverty among the public is the *root and branch* of all the crimes.

Safe and sound (quite well) : She reached their *safe and sound.*

Seamy side of life (immoral side of society) : The present day cinema depicts the *seamy side of life* in our society.

Speck and span (neat and smart) : Mr. J. L. Nehru was always *speck and span* in his dressing style.

Stuff and nonsense (worthless) : The judge found all his arguments *stuff and nonsense.*

Sum and substance (the actual theme) : The *sum and substance* of the paragraph must be reflected in a good precis.

Take bull by horns (to meet the danger boldly) : One should have courage to *take bull by horns* if one wants to succeed in life.

The die is cast (decided finally) : The *die is cast* there is not point of discussing over it now.

The last nail in the coffin (the last action which resulted in the complete end of something) : The reservation policy of V.P. Singh was *the last nail in the coffin* of Janta Party.

Thick and thin (in all circumstances) : I shall support you through *thick and thin.*

Through fire and water (in all sort of difficulties) : He can go *through fire and water* to achieve his goal.

Time and tide (course of time) : *Time and tide* waits for none.

To and fro (going and coming, backward and forward) : What are the *to and fro* taxi charges for Alwar to Delhi?

Toil and moil (hard labour) : It require too much of *toil and moil* to secure first position.

Tom Dick and Harry (everyone) : Every *Tom Dick* and *Harry* knows that Mohd. Kaif is the wonderful cricketer.

To lead up the garden path (to cheat) : The tricky traders try *to lead* the customers *up the garden path* by assuring them of warranty and good discount.

Tooth and nail (with all force) : Students of general caste opposed the reservation policy *tooth and nail*, but of no avail.

Ups and downs (prosperity and adversity) : There are *ups and downs* in every business.

Uphill task (difficult task) : Passing CAT examination is an *uphill task.*

Warp and woof (essential parts of a thing) : Blood and bones are *warp and woof* of human body.

Watch and ward (careful guard) : At least three guards are required to have perfect *watch and ward* of the building.

Weal and woe (prosperity and adversity) : I will abide by you in all *weal and woe.*

Whips and spur (with greatest hurry) : He completed the project *whips and spur.*

Why and wherefore (the basic roll season) : Please tell me the *why and wherefore* of your decision to take voluntary retirement.

Willy nilly (wish or not wish) : *Willy nilly* you are to obey the orders of your parents.

Yellow press (newspapers publishing sensational news) : These days newspapers with *yellow press* are earning like anything.

Idiomatic Expressions

अंग्रेजी भाषा में प्रयुक्त होने वाले कुछ Idiomatic expressions नीचे दिए जा रहे हैं। इनका प्रयोग आपकी लेखन शैली को प्रभावी बनाता है। छात्रों को इन Idiomatic expressions का प्रयोग करने का अभ्यास करना चाहिए। इनका प्रयोग करने पर आपका लेखन अधिक सशक्त, सुन्दर एवं प्रभावशाली बनेगा।

To add fuel to the flame or fire (to make matter worse or aggravated) : The arrest of the leader of agitators, the government only *added fuel to the flame.*

To assume airs (to pretend superiority) : He is in the habit of *assuming airs* in the presence of his inlaws.

To add a new feather in one's cap (Additional success) : His success in his ICFAI exams has *added a new feather in his cap.*

To be at sea (a person confused) : My wife is quite *at sea* in maths.

To be in fix (in a dilemma) : The police department was *in a fix* about the threatning calls sent by the militants.

To be in the good books (to be in favour with a person) : A good student is always *in the good books* of his teachers.

To be under a cloud (to be under suspicion) : His connections with the militants have brought him *under a cloud.*

To be at large (free) : The man who tried to kill her is still *at large.*

To be not worth one's salt (not deserving) : You should not help Ramesh, he is *not worth his salt.*

To be in tune (in agreement or mood) : The Principal asked the students, if they were *in tune* for organising the annual function.

To be out of sorts (to be unwell) : She had been *out of sorts* for several days and so could not do her office work.

To break the news (to give bad news) : He *broke the news* of her husband's death very cautiously in order to lessen the shock.

To burn the midnight oil (to work upto late hours) : I have *to burn the midnight oil* for several days in order to complete the work in time.

To be up to (to be familiar with) : He is not *up to* all the tricks of this new business.

To be born with a silver spoon in one's mouth (to be born in a rich family) : Indira Gandhi *born with a silver spoon in her mouth.*

To be worth its weight in gold (something extremely valuable) : For a hungry man a piece of bread is often *worth its weight in gold.*

To be lost in clouds (a person with confused or unclear thoughts) : Philosophers are *often lost in clouds.*

To be weak or vacant in the upper storey (a feeble minded person) : I can't assign such work to him, as he is *vacant in the upper storey.*

To be under a cloud (under suspicion): With the recovery of a revolver from his office has put him *under cloud.*

To be under one's thumb (to be under control) : She is no more *under the thumb* of her mother in law.

To be at daggers drawn (ready to fight) : Both the brothers are *at daggers drawn.*

To be at a loss (to be puzzled or confused) : In interview he found himself *at a loss*, couldn't answer even very simple questions.

To be at one's wit's end (unable to decide the right course of action) : Seeing the income tax officer at his shop he was *at his wit's end.*

To be at the helm of (enjoying the best position) : Until his father was a minister he was *at the helm* of affairs.

To be in a fix (unable to decide): The was in a fix when the inspector discovered many irregularities in the accouets book.

To be in the teens (between the age of twelve and twenty) : Two girls still *in their teens* caught taking alcoholic drinks.

To be on one's last legs (to be about to collapse) : It is wrong to say that caste system in India is *on its last legs.*

To be on the tenter hooks (to be in a state of distress) : When police caught him with stolen money, he was *on the tenter hooks.*

To be true to one's salt (to prove faithful) : The Rajput soldiers in Akbar's army were *true to their salt.*

To be at loggerheads (to quarrel) : The two brothers are now *at loggerheads.*

To bear the brunt of (to bear the main attack) : The secretary has *to bear the brunt of* minister's wrath.

To beard the lion in his own den (to attack a ferocious and powerful person in his own territory) : Only a person like Shivaji dared to *beard the lion in his own den.*

To bell the cat (doing anything at a great personal risk) : All can boast of their boldness, but none can *bell the cat.*

To blow one's own trumpet (to speak about self, boast about self) : You can't discuss with him, he is always *blowing his own trumpets.*

To break the ice (make a beginning): Everyone kept silence for sometime then Ramesh *broke the ice* by asking introductions.

To burn candle at both ends (to spend lavishly) : He will soon be a pauper as he is *burning the candle at both ends.*

To beat about the bush (to talk in an ambiguous manner) : Don't *beat about the bush*, come to the point.

To build castles in the air (to make visionary schemes) : He is in the habit of *building castles in the air* and so does not succeed in life.

To bring to book (to call to account) : The corrupt officer was *brought to book* for his neglect of duty.

To be at the bottom of (to be mainly responsible for) : It was found that Shanti was *at the bottom of* the whole family fuss.

To bury the hatchet (to make peace forgetting the past enemity) : Hindus and Muslims should *bury the hatchet* for the development and prosperity of the nation.

To burn one's boats (Point of no return) : Our country has *burnt the boats* by declaring that we will not talk to Pakistan.

To blaze the trail (to start a movement) : Bhagat Singh *blazed the trail* of Indian National Movement in Punjab youths.

To brow beat (to bully) : He always tries *to brow beat* his colleagues who are opposed to him.

To bite the dust (to be defeated) : Pakistan had *to bite the dust* in the war with India twice.

To breathe one's last (to die) : P. J. Nehru *breathed his last* in early sixties.

To be nipped in the bud (to destroy in the very beginning) : All kind of evils must be *nipped in the bud.*

To buy a pig in a poke (to purchase a thing without knowing its actual worth) : Please tell me full details of the company, so that I may think to purchase its shares otherwise I can't *buy a pig in a poke.*

To come home to (to understand) : It *came home to him* that he was not fit for the post of police inspector as his eye sight is very weak.

To check by jowl (very near to each other) : As the space was short, so he kept all the articles *check by jowl.*

To cool one's heels (to be kept waiting) : We had to *cool our heels* before we could meet the Prime Minister.

To cross one's mind (to occur to oneself) : In the examination hall, it *crossed my mind* that I had left my admit card in the canteen.

To change hands (passing from one hand to another) : That hotel has *changed hands* thrice within a short span of six months.

To cast a slur upon (to disrepute) : He assured not to do anything which might *cast a slur upon* the reputation of the family.

To cast pearls before swine (to offer to a person such valuable things, which he does not appreciate) : Presenting Shakespeare's book to an illiterate is *to cast pearls before swine.*

To catch a tartar (to catch a person who is more powerful than the catcher) : Aurangzeb soon found out that he had *caught a tartar* in Shivaji.

To clip one's wings (to deprive one of power) : The Prime Minister has *clipped the wings* of his minister by taking away the power of spending more than two lacs on a project.

To carry the day (to win a victory) : After initial setback, India *carried the day* in the hockey match against Pakistan.

To cut a sorry figure (to give a poor show) : The organiser *cut a sorry figure* in the meeting for not giving proper feedback to The Chief Guest.

To cry over spilt milk (to repent) : Careless students often have *to cry over spilt milk* during the examination days.

To come to a standstill (to come to a stop) : As the *car came to stand still* for want of petrol the thief ran away on foot.

To come off with flying colours (to come out from a conflict with brilliant success) : Everyone was trying for ticket of Congress party, but Ramesh *came off with flying colours.*

To count the chickens before they are hatched (to anticipate gain prematurely, before time) : You will feel unhappy, if you *count the chickens before they are hatched.*

To cross one's t's and dot one's i's (to make minor changes) : His book is almost ready, he has just to *cross his t's and dot its i's.*

To cry for the moon (to aspire for an impossible thing) : Your hope for marrying with Aishwarya is like a *cry for the moon.*

To curry favour (to win favour by gifts or flattery) : By giving present and visiting again and again you are trying *to curry* his *favour.*

To draw the long bow (exaggerate) : In calling her the best racer of the world, her admirers *draw the long bow.*

To dig the grave (to tarnish, to destroy) : By taking a side of the thief, he *dug the grave* of his honest image.

To end in smoke/fiasco (come to nothing) : He spoke a lot about his new book but it all *ended in smoke*, when the book was in the market.

To feather one's own nest (to provide first for one self) : Our leaders are busy *feathering their own nests* and have no concern for the general mass.

To flag a dead horse (to revive interest in old matters) : The rivals always *flag a dead horse* to insult their enemies.

To fall flat (to have no effect) : The Principal's speech *fell flat* on the students.

To get upper hand (to get the better position) : Between the two rivals, each is trying *to get upper hand* in the local politics.

To get into hot water (to be in a difficult situation) : The manager *got into hot water* participating in the union meeting.

To gild the pill (to cover an unpleasant thing by a pleasant one) : On one hand he was issued charge sheet and the officer *gild the pill* by verbally praising his sincere working.

To give the devil his dues (to give the credit to a bad man for his good work) : No doubt he is a haughty man, but *to give the devil his dues,* he is dedicated and hard working.

To give chapter and verse for a thing (to submit proof) : He can *give chapter and verse for* all the allegations he made against the minister.

To go on fool's errand (to go on an expedition where only a fool can go) : The key was in his pocket and he sent me *on a fool's errand* to search the same at the shopping complex.

To gain ground (to succeed slowly) : The belief in the abolition of Sati rites has *gained ground.*

To go with tail between the legs (to go as a defeated dog, behave cowardly) : The Minister was talking a lot about the values of honesty etc, but when Ramesh reminded him about the money paid to him for the work, he *went away with his tail between the legs.*

To get off scot free (to escape without punishment) : He *got off scot free* for lack of evidence.

To give one a long rope (to let someone commit mistakes) : He never *gives* his employees *a long rope* and so you will find his office neat and tidy.

To give currency (to make publicly known) : The Government refused *to give currency* to a number of secrets relating to national security.

To get down to brass tacks (deal with the matter straight) : Instead of wasting time in discussion, please *get down to brass tacks*.

To give a wide berth (to avoid) : I try my best to *give a wide berth* to such a selfish person.

To get oneself into a mess (to drift into trouble) : He seems to have *got himself into a mess* because of the involvement of his wife in a criminal case.

To go the dogs (to be ruined) : He *went to the dogs* because of his son's involvement in the murder of a girl.

To grease the palm (to bribe) : You cannot get this contract unless you *grease the palm* of the officials.

To have gift of the gab (art of speaking) : Ram is simply middle pass, but he has the *gift of the gab*.

To have an iron will (strong will) : A person *with iron will* can achieve anything.

To hold a candle to (match for, equal) : She is the daughter of a famous dancer, but she does not *hold a candle* to her mother.

To have brush with (to have encounter) : Our neighbours *had a brush with* one another over the matter of throwing the garbage.

To hang fire (remain unsolved) : The problem of poverty has been *hanging fire* for the last fifty five years.

To have feet of clay (full of faults) : The inquiry has revealed that most of the politicians *have feet of clay*.

To have thing at one's finger tips (to know a thing thoroughly) : He has all the statistics of employment *at his finger tips*.

To have an axe to grind (to have a personal interest) : I am sure he *has an axe to grind* in this proposal.

To have no backbone (to have no strength and support) : The movement against the reservation based on caste, *had no backbone* and to collapsed soon.

To harp on the same string (to repeat the same arguments) : Every new speaker had nothing new to say, everyone *harped on the same string* of his predecessor.

To keep abreast of (not to fall behind) : It is very important for the young persons, to *keep abreast of* all current events.

To keep one's fingers crossed (to wait expectantly) : We should *keep our fingers crossed* till the last ball is bowled.

To knit the brow (to frown) : My father always *knits the brow* at everything I do.

To kick the bucket (to die) : She had *kicked the bucket* after suffering from cancer for several years.

To keep someone at arm's length (to keep someone at a distance and not allow to get close) : She is not a good girl and must be *kept at arm's length*.

To keep body and soul together (to maintain life) : Because of the inflation it has become difficult *to keep body* and *soul together.*

To keep the wolf from the door (to avoid starvation) : In our country the poor have to struggle hard *to keep the wolf from the door.*

To lose ground (fail to keep position) : He has *lost ground* and so his opponent has won the election.

To leave no stone unturned (to make all possible efforts) : The Prime Minister has assured the country that he shall *leave no stone unturned* to uplift the condition of the countrymen.

To live in a fool's paradise (false hope) : It is wrong to *live in a fool's paradise* and do not put hard to achieve success.

To lie in the bed one has made (to reap the fruits of one's acts) : He has made his fortune so he must *lie in the bed he has made.*

To move heaven and earth (to make all possible efforts) : Prime Minister Man Mohan Singh is *move heaven and earth* to find the solution of Kashmir problem.

To make light of (not to care) : She is in the habit of *making light* of the advice of the doctors.

To make both ends meet (to live within one's earning) : Sudden increase in prices has made it difficult for the employees *to make both ends meet.*

To make much ado about nothing (to make a fuss over a small matter of no importance) : He is a quarrelsome man, he *makes much ado about nothing.*

To make hay while the sun shines (to seize the opportunity at the right time) : As the Congress party came into power, he became chairman of UTI. He rightly says *to make hay while the sunshines.*

To make the most of (to utilize time) : Students should *make the most of* their time, if they want to secure good marks.

To make sure (to ascertain) : I went to the college *to make sure* if our exams would commence from the next week.

To make neither head nor tail (not to understand) : The leader spoke so rapidly that the audience could *make neither head nor tail* of his lecture.

To nip in the bud (to destroy in the beginning) : The militancy must be *nipped in the bud.*

To play ducks and drakes (to waste money) : He is playing *ducks and drakes* with parental money.

To pass the buck (to blame each other) : Political parties *pass the buck* on to one another on all small or big matters.

To play the gallery (to gain popularity) : Every action of the political leaders aimed to *play the gallery.*

To pull a long face (to look sad) : My son *pulled a long face* when he was scolded by his mother.

To play truant (to be absent without permission) : It is a very bad habit of the students *to play truant* from class.

To put all eggs in one basket (to risk all money in one enterprise) : It is a wrong policy *to put all eggs in one basket.*

To pour oil on troubled water (to rectify the matter) : Both of them were fighting for the property, but the justified decision of their mother *poured oil on troubled water.*

To play fast and loose (repeatedly change one's attitude) : You should not trust her, she is used *to play fast and loose* with her friends.

To pay off old scores (to take revenge) : By suspending the clerk on frivolous grounds the officer *paid off old scores.*

To pay one back in the same coin (to return like for like) : I believe in the policy of *paying back in the same coin.*

To put the cart before the horse (being at the wrong side) : He made a contract with the publisher, without getting the book ready. He *put the cart before the horse* as such.

To put a spoke in one's wheel (to create hindrance) : Every competitor in the market is trying *to put a spoke in the wheel* of others.

To ripe up old sores (to revive forgotten quarrel) : Ramesh and his wife can't live in pleace; they are always *ripping up old sores.*

To rub one the wrong way (annoy) : If you *rub him the wrong way,* he will oppose the proposal.

To read between the lines (to understand the hidden meaning) : If you go through the book seriously, you will be able *to read between the lines.*

To rule the roost (to dominate) : Today the scheduled caste ministers *rule the roost* in the government.

To send about one's business (to dismiss) : His employer *sent him about his business* when he was caught involved in forgery.

To stand ones ground (remain firm) : He did not yield to pressure and *stood his ground* till he won the game.

To sail under false colours (hypocrite) : We should not believe the politicians because they *sail under false colours*.

To set Thames on fire (to achieve something impossible) : Qualifying Civil Services examination for you is like *setting Thames on fire*.

To say ditto to (to agree) : You are bound *to say ditto to* what your boss says.

To see a thing through coloured glasses (to Judge a thing with prejudiced mind) : A prejudiced man will *see the thing through coloured glasses*. He can't judge the things properly.

To show the white feather (to act as a cowardice) : He will *show the white feather* when the real time of action comes.

To stem the tide of (to put a check) : As a true social worker, first of all you *stem the tide of* poverty and unemployment.

To speak volumes for (to have abundant proof) : The sacrifice made by freedom fighters *speak volumes for* their true love for the country.

To steal a march (to get ahead secretly) : Shalini *stole a march* on her friend in marketing her products slowly and steadily.

To steer clear of (to avoid) : You should try *to steer clear* of such nasty girls.

To take people by storm (to surprise unexpectedly) : The refusal by Soniya to accept the Prime Ministership *took the nation by storm*.

To the backbone (thoroughly) : We need leaders who are honest *to the backbone*.

To take wind out of another's sails (to gain advantage by anticipation) : Intelligent Generals can gather a lot of important information by *taking wind out of enemy's sails*.

To take heart (feel bold) : You must *take heart* and face the failures boldly.

To take up arms (to fight) : We must not shy for *taking up arms* against the misdeeds of the public departments.

To turn the corner (to change the opinion) : He *turned the corner* by passing the examinations with good marks.

To take to one's heels (to run away) : On seeing the police, the thief *took to his heels*.

To take up the cudgels (to defend someone) : I *took up the cudgels* on behalf of my brother and proved him innocent.

To travel incognito (to travel under a false name) : The freedom fighters used *to travel incognito*.

To throw out of gear (not working properly) : Our small scale units have been *thrown out of gear* because of lack of infrastructure.

To throw cold water (to discourage) : He tried to *throw cold water* on my plans.

To win laurels (to win distinction) : Dr. Kalam *won laurels* in the world of Missiles.

To worship the rising sun (to respect a person who is becoming powerful) : Everyone *worships the rising sun*.

To wash hands of (to have nothing to do) : I have *washed hands of* this affair because he has no relations with me.

To wrangle over an ass' shadow (to quarrel over trifles) : Only foolish persons *wrangle over an ass' shadow*.

To wear the trousers (dominant) : It is Shalu who *wears the trousers* and her husband simply obeys her.

Frequently used Idioms *and* Phrases

Frequently used Idioms with verbs 'break, carry, cast, catch, come, cut, do, fall, get, give, go, have, hold, keep, lay, make, play, put, set, stand, take, throw, turn.

BREAK

To **break cover,** If you break cover, you leave a place where you have been hiding or sheltering from attack, usually in order to run to another place.
They began running again broke cover and dashed towards the road.

To **break a fall** is to lessen the force of a fall.

To **break ground** means to commence an undertaking.

To **break the heart** means to afflict grievously, to cause to suffer seriously from grief.

To **break the ice** means to start conversations. The phrase also means to get over the feeling of restraint which one may have in the presence of a new acquaintance.

To **break the news to a person** means to communicate news quite unexpectedly to him in such a way as to diminish the shock : He broke the news to his wife as gently as he could that he had lost all his money due to the failure of the bank.

To **break the back of a job** is to have disposed of the main part of the task assigned to him.

Broken health is impaired health or not in good health.

Broken sleep is interrupted sleep.

CARRY

To **carry one's point** is to achieve the desired goal; to overcome obstacles placed in the way; to defeat the opposition in a public debate : Most of the reformers find it very difficult to get people to give up a long prevailed custom, but they carry their point in the end.

To **carry everything** or all means to win the victory or to overcome the opposition fully. How is it that of these two persons engaged in the same business, one can scarcely get a living, while the other carries all before him?

To **carry away captive** means to take away into captivity, as prisoners of war.
In ancient times, many prisoners of war were led captive and forced to live as slaves.

To **carry a thing too far** means to continue it beyond what is logical or safe. How far will this gun carry? means, how far will a bullet shot from this gun go?

To **carry matters with a high hand** means to take strong measures, to exercise authority with full force. The principal of the college carried matters with a high hand and expelled two students for a trivial offence.

CAST

To **cast an eye upon** is to glance at : He cast a stern eye upon the two persons sitting against him, trying to tease the girl at the reception.

To **cast, or throw light upon** means to illuminate : After a long investigation, a woman came forward and stated some facts which cast fresh light upon the causes of suicide committed by the man.

To **cast into the shade** means to put into the shade; throw into the shade : A newspaper gives a thrilling account of Godhra carnage, next day's paper tells of more horrible things still; the latter account casts the other into the shade.

To **cast a slur upon one** means to cast a slight reproach upon him : Many a man brings a slur on his own reputation by stooping to some mean or hateful act.

To **cast in one's teeth** means to retort reproachfully, to make an insulting statement to one openly : She cast it in her husband's teeth that she had seem him drunk, whereas later on it turned out that she had mistaken another man for her husband.

CATCH

To **catch fire** is to become alight or ignited : The dry grass soon caught fire.

To **catch one's eye** means to attract one's notice by being seen, to came under one's notice or if I keep looking at a lady till her look meets mine, I am said to catch her eye : As I looked through the novel, printer's several errors caught my eye.

To **catch a train** means to arrive at the railway station in time to go by a train. If you want to catch the train, move at once.

To **catch it** means to get a scolding or a beating or some other unpleasant treatment.

To **catch at a straw.** There is a proverb 'A drowning man will catch at a straw': When a man is in difficulties, finding nothing substantial to lay hold of, grasps at something trifling he is said to catch at a straw.

To **catch a Tartar** is to seize or encounter an adversary who proves too strong for him. The story goes that in battle with the Turks an Irish soldier shouted to his comrade, 'I've caught a Tartar.' 'Then bring him with you', *i.e.* as a prisoner. 'But he won't came.' 'Then come along yourself.' 'But he won't let me.' The fact was that the Tartar had caught the Irishman. Hence, the general meaning of the phrase as given above.

COME

To **come to close quarters** means to tackle an enemy closely.

To **come to light** is to become known.

To **come to pass** is to happen, to occur.

To **come to grief** is said of a person who meets with disaster or of a scheme that proves abortive.

To **come to hand** is idiomatic for, to reach one : Her letter came to hand yesterday=it reached me yesterday.

To **come to be** means generally, to become important : He has come to be highly thought of means that he has so risen in people's esteem that they now think highly of him. His word has come to be considered of great value.

To **come amiss.** This means to come in an inconvenient or improper time or way. When it is said of a man that nothing comes amiss to him, the meaning is that he is a very capable man, able to do any work or meet any difficulty that presents itself to him. A legacy seldom comes amiss to anybody.

To **come home to a person** means to appeal successfully to his reason or his self-interest; to touch his feelings closely.

To **come to age** means to become adult.

To **come to a head** means to be ready to burst forth-said; e.g. of a conspiracy to make open. He allows his spiteful feelings to come to a head.

To **come to a standstill** means to bring to a standstill : When the steam was shut off, the engine soon came to a standstill.

To **come to his proper level** means to bring a man to his (proper) level. This expression means to bring a vain man down from his undue estimate of himself, and teach him to esteem himself at his true level.

To **come to know;** to get the knowledge or information : I came to know a thing, or a thing comes to my knowledge. It is the form of these idioms that needs to be noted.

To **come to no good** means to come to a bad end. It can be said of an idle young fellow, 'That youth will come to no good.'

To **come out of a business with clean hands** is sometimes said of a person who comes out perfectly innocent while others have done misdeeds. The phrase 'clean hands' is in this phrase synonymous with uprightness, innocence.

To **come, or fall, under one's notice or observation:** Such a worse case of small pox never fell under my notice earlier. If such conduct as you describe comes under my notice, I shall take serious notice of it.

To **come short of, or fall short of** means to be less than what is required or expected : When great deficiency is meant, the word 'far' is introduced into the phrase. And short of, which means 'less than', is sometimes used with other expressions. We have tried gold mining in India, but the results have come far short of or fallen far short of, our expectations.

To **come off with flying colours** means to emerge from a conflict with brilliant success. The idea involved is this : A regiment goes into battle with its banner or colours displayed; it engages in the fight and emerges with banner unscathed in the conflict, with colours fluttering in the breeze.
At the recent examinations, Rajani came off with flying colours.

To **come off second best** means to get the worst of it. These are similar in meaning. They mean to be defeated in a contest or in an argument or in a legal action.

CUT

To **cut short** means to shorten or abridge what is likely to lengthen out.
A man is said to have cut short his speech when he ceases speaking sooner than he was expected to. We also say of a person that his life was cut short meaning that he died prematurely.

To **cut, or sting, to the quick.** The quick is the sensitive flesh, that which is susceptible of keen feeling. The phrase means to cause acute pain.

Your scoldings cut him to the quick.

A reputated man is often stung to the quick by baseless imputations and slanders.

To **cut off in its prime** means to destroy a fair thing when in its prime. Cholera cut him off in his prime.

To **cut the Gordian knot** 'Gordian knot', a knot tied by Gordias, king of Phrygia, in the thong which connected the pole of his chariot to the yoke, and which was so very intricate that there was no finding where it began or ended. An oracle declared that he who should untie this knot should be master of Asia. Alexander the Great, fearing that his inability to untie it would prove an ill augury, cut it as under with his sword. Hence a Gordian knot is an inextricable difficulty; and to cut the Gordian knot is to remove a difficulty by bold or unusual measures. And the phrase is sometimes used when an unexpected turn of affairs opens a way out of a serious difficulty.

To **cut a figure; to cut a dash**: To cut a figure, is to perform a conspicuous part, to attract attention either in wonder or admiration.

To **cut a dash** means to make a flourish or to make a vain show. Both these expressions, especially the latter, are slightly contemptuous and rather old-fashioned.

To **cut and run** is to be off with all possible speed. The phrase was applied first to cutting a ship's cable and the ship sailing off immediately from her moorings.

DO

(1) It means to perform, to accomplish, to execute a work. Do your job. I cannot do more than indicate the line of thought which he pursued. Will you kindly show me how to do (=solve) this problem?

(2) Do also means to finish, to complete : Done is often used in the sense of completeness; so that to be done is often means to be used up, to be exhausted. For example If a tailor to say that his thread was done, we should understand him to mean that his supply of thread was used up and was exhausted. So, to have done, is to have finished. I have done writing means I have completed my writing work. To **have done with** is to have completed, to have no further concern with : I have now done with this dis-respectful business.

(3) **Do** sometimes means to bring about, to cause to happen : Have the heavy rains done your house any damage ?

(4) **Do** is sometimes intransitive and means behave or act : Be careful not to do such things again.

(5) **Do** has, in some particular context, the peculiar meaning of, to cook, to make ready a thing for eating. To do a mutton chop, is, to cook it and prepare it for eating. When it is done to a turn it is perfectly cooked.

It sometimes means cooked; so that expressions like, Are the cakes done? The rice is done, would mean Are the cakes exhausted ? or Are the cakes cooked? The rice is all used up or the rice is cooked. In such cases, all ambiguity is removed by the connection in which done stands in the sentence.

(6) **Do** is at times used in conversation for, to deceive, to play a trick upon, to outwit : He felt he had been done by designing man. Be careful as to the terms of your bargain, for that man will try to do you if he can.

(7) **Do,** again, sometimes means to fare, to thrive, to profit. How do you do? The first **do** is the auxiliary verb.

'**Do**' is also found with the meaning to answer an end, in such expressions as : 'That will do', meaning that will be enough to serve the purpose.
'It did very well', *i.e.* it suited very well, it was quite sufficient.

To **do good** means to act in a manner that others are benefitted : Do good in all the ways you can, to all the people you can .

He is doing well means succeeding in his new line of business.

The patient has been doing well means progressing favourably.

He is doing good by his lecturing means he is accomplishing good results.

He is doing well by his lecturing means he is making a good deal of money by his lecturing.

He is doing well in his lecturing means he is doing the work of a lecturer well.

To **do well out of something** means to derive profit from the activity.

Ramesh did well out of that investment.

To **do one's best** means to put forth one's best efforts.

To **be well to do** is to be in prosperous circumstances, to be well off.

Well-to-do is sometimes put before a noun as a Compound adjective, and is also used as a noun. He is a 'well to do man' means he is a prosperous man.

To **do one good** means to be of advantage or benefit to one.

These medicines did me good.

To **do one a favour** or **a kindness.** A formally polite expression.

Will you do me the favour of accepting this small gift ?

You will do me a kindness if you will append your name to the list of donors.

To **do a thing by fits and starts** means to do a thing impulsively and a small portion of it at a time.

To study by fits and starts is not the proper way to prepare oneself for the IAS examinations.

To **do a thing off-hand** means to do it at once without delay or hesitation;

To do it with ease and without preparation. I gave him a difficult problem in Algebra and he did it off-hand.

To **do a thing by hook or by crook** means to do it by any means fair or unfair, no matter by what means.

Now-a-days every one wants to make money by hook or by crook. It is said that a French admiral in a time of war once wanted to bring his warship into Waterford Bay, in the South of Ireland. At the entrance to the bay there are two headlands, one on each side, one called Hook Head, and the other Crook Head. The admiral declared that he would enter either 'by Hook or by Crook', meaning that he would pass in by keeping near to one or other of the headlands.

To **do wrong** means to make a blunder or to commit an error of judgement.

In my opinion you have chosen the right course and you would do wrong to make a change.

To **do honour to,** to **do reverence to** means to honour, to reverence.

To **do the honours** means to act as host or hostess at a party or function.

Do to death means to put to death. Byron uses the words, 'Done to death by sudden blow.'Jack done himself to death for his love lost.

To **do a city** or **do the sights** means to visit the city.

'done!' said in response to a proposal means I assent, I agree.

'No sooner said than done!' means that as soon as a thing is proposed to anyone, he immediately executes it, and utters this phrase as his response.

To **do a thing under the rose,** is to do it in a secret manner. In ancient times, the rose was taken as a symbol of secrecy and was hung up at entertainments, to indicate that nothing said there was to be divulged.

To **have to do with,** is to have business with, to deal with. She tried to clear herself of all blame, but she did have something to do with that immoral act.

FALL

To **fall foul of** means to come into collision with.

If this new manager continues his criticisms, he will soon fall foul of the Boss.

To **fall in love** means to fall into love.

The young couple quickly fell in love with each other.

To **fall out** means to quarrel. It is wrong to fall out for the ancestral property.

To **fall into abeyance** means to cease to be exerted or used.This law has been allowed to fall into abeyance.

To **fall out of use** means to cease to be used. We also say, drop out of use.

As a language grows, new words are coinsed and many words fall out of use.

To **fall to work** or **set to work** means to begin to do work. In these phrases work is a noun. We fell briskly to work and finished the job in two hours.

To **fall a prey to** means to be the victim of : When people plot against a man to ruin him and succeed in their malicious attempts, he is said to fall a prey to their designs.

Ramesh fell a prey to the ulterior designs of his colleagues and so he was not promoted.

To **fall to the ground** means to prove useless or to become ineffective.

The meeting was large, yet his motion found no support and therefore fell to the ground.

To **fall for** something means to yield to its charms : Mira fell for a pretty dress.

To **fall flat** means to collapse.

GET

To **get clear of** means to become free from difficulty or annoyance.

To **get drunk** means to become drunk : Where are you going to get drunk ?

To **get one's back up** to become irritated.

To **get on** means to advance; or to prosper : Let the men get on to the front.

He is a hard working man. He is sure to get on in the world.

To **get hold of** means to understand or to catch. I can't get hold of the meaning of this passage.With great difficulty the drowning man got hold of the rope.

To **get rid of;** to **be deprived of** means quitting of a thing or to get free from a thing : To be deprived of a thing means to have a thing taken from you which you wish to keep. Hence, we do not say that people are deprived of a tax, they get rid of a tax or are relieved of it, or are freed from it. A man may be deprived suddenly of his property.

To **get the upper hand;** to **get the better of.** These mean to get the superiority, to prevail over. Of two rival textile firms, one is richer and better managed than the other, and therefore soon gets the upper hand.

Trickery in trade may for a time being get the better of honesty, but soon lost its credibility.

To **get into hot water;** to **be in hot water.** To be in difficulty, irritating circumstances. The school master got into hot water with the Inspector for delivering a speech favouring a political party.

To **get into a mess** means to get into a muddle : His accounts seem to have got into a mess.

To **get into a scrape** means to find oneself in an awkward position.

The opposite is, to **get out of a scrape.**

It is easier to get into a scrape than to get out of one.

To **get wind of** means to hear a rumour of or to get the clue of : I got wind of the plot through hearing their conversation .

GIVE

To **give a person to understand** means to lead him to believe or to give him reason for believing a thing.

To **be given to understand** means to be led to believe.

The officer gave me to understand that there would soon be a vacancy for an assistant in his office.

To **give oneself to** means to devote oneself to it. This phrase express the habit. Give yourself to study and you will certainly secure good marks.

If a man give himself to bad habits, nothing good can be expected of him .

To **give oneself trouble about** or **over a thing** means to take pains about it : He gave himself great troubles over the problem of his younger brother.

To **give someone a bit** or a **piece of your mind** means to scold, to find fault with, to speak or write to :He has treated me very badly and I mean to write a letter and give him a bit of my mind.

To **give** or **show a person the cold shoulder** means to treat him coldly, to receive him in cold manner.

It is common to give a cold shoulder to one's poor friends.

To **give chase** means to pursue something that is running away.

The police gave chase to the thief, but he escaped.

To **give way** means to yield, to succumb.

Only once his faithful wife gave way to emotions.

His reason has given way means he has become insane.

To **give someone the slip** means to avoid someone who is looking for you.

The thief saw the policeman and took care to give him the slip.

To **gave** a thing a **wide berth** means to keep at a distance from it.

A sailor gives a rocky headland a wide berth, i.e. he keeps his ship at a safe distance from it.

To **gave good measure** means to give rather more than full, correct measure. When a draper selling cloth, measures off the stipulated number of yards and then gives freely a little piece more, he is said to give good measure. So a man rebuking or scolding another is sarcastically said to give good measure when the rebuke or the scolding is more severe than the justice of the case demands.

To **give chapter and verse for a thing** means to produce the proof of it. I can give you chapter and verse for every statement I am making.

To **give countenance** or **lend coutenance** to a project means to favour it, to give one's support to it. Some of the greatest benefactors of mankind have had few friends at first to give countenance to their inventions or discoveries.

To **give currency to** means to make publicly known. It is wicked to give currency to a dead scandal.

To **give place to** means to yield up one's place to. You give place to another when you allow him to take your place. The phrase is also used of inanimate things, customs etc. Carriages have given place to motor cars and sailing vessels to steamers.

A **give-and-take** policy means a policy involving mutual concessions : Now-a-days people believe in give and policy in maintaining their relations.

To **give a false colouring to** means to misrepresent : A man who is known to give a false colouring to any statement will not be believed even when he speaks the truth.

To **give loose rein to** means to give licence to, the leave without restraint. The idea is derived from leaving a mettlesome horse unchecked by the reins. A liberine is one who give loose rein to his lusts.

To **give rise to** means to be the cause of, to originate. The phrase is often applied to rumours or suspicions : What gave rise to this evil rumour? I don't know what gave rise to the idea that the capital of country was to be changed.

To **give vent to** means to allow to flow forth-usually said of one's own strong pent-up feeling, as anger, grief. I rushed out of the room to give vent to my feelings. He gave vent to his indignation in language more vigorous than polite.

To **give tone to** means to invigorate. In this phrase **tone** commonly means the healthy state of the organs of the body. The phrase is also used metaphorically of the character or faculties. The word **tonic** is derived from this use of tone.

The chairman's opening speech gave fine tone to the meeting.

The Swiss, living among mountains, are a hardy and thrifty people.

The very nature of their country gives tone to their character.

To **give** or **lend dignity** to an occasion means to bestow social importance. The attendance of the Queens gave dignity to the gathering.

GO

To **go mad** means to become mad. To **go crazy** is to become crazy.

My dog went mad and bit several other dogs.

To **go blind** means to become blind.

If you do not take care of your sight you will go blind.

To **go hand in hand.** When two or more persons cordially agree in pursuing the same course, they are said to go hand in hand.

In the matter of providing reservation to the scheduled castes and scheduled tribes most of the political parties go hand in hand.

To **go a long way** means to go far, to go to a great length : The newspapers went a long way in criticizing the Government.

To **go to law** means to litigate, to seek redressal through a court of law : Several people are too fond of going to law.

To **go halves; to (go) share and share alike** : When two persons agree to divide a thing equally between them, they are said to go halves or to (go) share and share alike. These phrases are commonly used of an enterprise, and the agreement to take equal shares—of say both risk and advantage—would be made before hand.

A party of ten students set out on a fortnight's tour and agreed to go share and share alike in the expenses.

To **go to great expense** means to be at great expense, both mean to expand much. The city has gone to great expense to give a suitable welcome to the President.

To **go out of one's way to do a thing** means to deviate from one's ordinary course of conduct in order to do something, generally a favour. You should be willing to go out of your way to oblige your friend.

To **go hard with** means to press heavily upon.

If Dengue breaks out again, it will go hard with the general mass.

To **go well with :** When a person prospers, it is often said that things go well with him, or that everyone goes well with him. Strictly speaking, to go well with means to agree with, to suit. I can't go well with such a quarrelsome girl. In harmonising colours, green goes well with red.

To **go on (sick) leave** When an official obtains leave of absence from ordinary duty, he is said to go on leave.

To **go on a fool's errand** means to go on an expedition such as a fool might go on, to go on an expedition which leads to a foolish end. There were many failed expeditions to Mount Everest : Can we say that those who took part in them were sent on a fool's errand?

To **go through fire and water for** a person or purpose means to ecounter any difficulty and undergo any risk, however great, for his sake. This man would go through fire and water to save his wife.

To **go to the wall** means to be hard pressed, to fail, to get the worst in a contest or in the struggle of life. When the struggle comes, the weakest goes to the wall.

To **go to the bad** means to become of depraved character, to associate with evil companions so to lose character. To **go to the dogs** is also used with the same meaning. He is sure to go to the bads because he has a company of such depraved people.

To **go to rack and ruin.** Here rack has the same meaning as ruin, the meaning being intensified by using both words. The phrase is used both with regard to one's outward circumstances and also with regard to character.

The house is going to rack and ruin for want of looking after.

HAVE

To **have one's hands** full **(Over busy)**: When a man is so busily engaged that he cannot attempt anything more, we say, he has his hands full. Do not expect him to help you; he has his hands full already.

To **have clean hands** means to be perfectly innocent, to be a person of honesty and integrity. The phrase is commonly used in speaking of business transactions. One who receives bribes or engages in any nefarious scheme has not clean hands.

To **have to do a thing** means to be forced to do it, either from necessity of circumstances or from the will of another person.

He had to cut down the tree to save his house.

I had to walk two hours before I could find any shelter.

To **have (cash) in hand** means to have cash in possession to pay.

To have a work **in hand** is to have undertaken it, to be busy in it.

To **have a hand,** or **a voice in a thing** means to have some part in doing it, to have a role in doing it. To **have a finger in the pie,** also means the same for the same.

I am glad to say I had no hand in getting him transferred from here.

You always like to have your finger in everyone's pie means you are always meddling with the affairs of other fellows.

To **have a thing at one's finger ends** means to be fully familiar with a thing or to be able to apply one's knowledge readily.
She has the history of the World Wars at her finger ends.

To **have a mind** to do a thing means to be willing to do it or to show willingness to do it.
She could tell you the secret of the Mahal if she had a mind.

To **have a way of one's own** means to have one's individual way of dealing with the thing. He has a way of his own in dealing with the subordinates.

To **have one's eye upon a thing; have an eye to a thing.** Either of these phrases may be used when a man has set a thing before him as the goal he desires or which he tries to achieve. The latter phrase also means to supervise or to watch so as to take care of.
The Headmaster of school has his eye upon the Principal's chair.
Please have an eye to the child and see that he does not go stray.

To **have the field before one** means to have full opportunity of showing what one can do, to be unopposed. **To have the field to oneself** means to be the sole worker in a particular field.

To **have a short memory** is to be unable to remember a thing even after a short time. The phrase is often applied to a person who says he forgets a thing while at the same time you suspect that he cannot have forgotten it.

To **have the face to do a thing** means to have the audacity to do it. Another slang expression is, to have the **cheek** to do it.

To **have a difference with a person** means to have mild quarrel (or difference of opinion) with him. When friendly relations are restored, the parties to the dispute, are said to have **made up their difference**.

To **have a bone to pick with one** means to have a difference with him which has not yet been expressed.

To **have a brush with** an opponent means to have a slight encounter : The President had a slight brush with one of the secretaries at the meeting.

To **have had its day;** to **have seen better days.** When an item which has been much used falls into disuse now, we say of it that it has had its day. When an article, *e.g.* a car, has become worn and shabby, we say that it has seen better days. The phrase would be use also of a *person* who, having been well off, had come down in the world.

Men drawn Palanquins used to carry the bride have had their day in India.

To **have too many irons in the fire.** If a blacksmith puts so many irons into the fire that he cannot attend to them all as they grow red hot, some will be wasted. The phrase means, to have so much work in hand that some part of it is left undone or is done very hastily.

He is sure to lose his health under the strain of overwork; he has too many irons in the fire.

To **have no backbone** (used for a vacilliating person or one easily disheartened) : At first there was a show of resistance to this new act passed by the Parliament, but the movement had no backbone and speedily collapsed.

To **have the true** or **right ring** means to be genuine. A perfect coin has a clear, metallic ring when let fall on something hard.
The speech of the Home Minister on Jammu and Kashmir had the right ring about it.

HOLD

To **hold one's tongue** means to be silent, not to speak.

The militants ordered the captives to hold their tongue or they will be punished.

To **hold oneself ready** or in **readiness** means to be ready, to be in a state of preparedness.The commander ordered the soldiers to hold themselves ready to attack.

To **hold in check** means to curb or restrain within limits. It is always better to hold the children in check so that they are not spoiled by the miscreants.

To **hold in play** means to keep a person's attention occupied in some other task while you are doing something which you do not wish him to know.

It is a right policy to hold the foe in play while accomplishing the actual task.

To **hold one's own** means to maintain one's own position against opposition candidates; to keep what advantage one already has. The same meaning is expressed by, to **hold one's ground,** or **keep one's ground,** or **maintain one's ground.**

In the present odd circumstances it is better to hold one's own position instead of making new advancement.

To **hold up one's head** means to be able to look every man in the face. The phrase implies pride of one's character or position. He has no reason to be ashamed of so he can hold up his head among the so called philantropists.

To **hold one's head high** means to bear oneself proudly.

To **hold true** means to regard as true, to continue to be true. The principles of Newton holds true even today.

KEEP

To **keep within bounds** means to keep within due limits.

To **keep happy** one should keep oneself within bounds. When his passion is roused, it is hard to keep him within bounds.

To **keep out of the way** means to absent oneself intentionally, to avoid being in the way.

She tried her best to keep herself out of the way of her paramour.

To **keep a thing to oneself; keep one's own counsel.** These are same and mean not to disclose the thing that one knows : She never shares her problems with any body. She keeps things to herself.

To **keep a thing dark** means to keep it hidden or concealed, not to disclose it or make it known to others: She never discusses anybody about her plans but keeps everything dark.

To **keep oneself to oneself** means to live apart, to shun society : He does not mixes with any of his friends. He keeps himself to himself.

To **keep company with** a person means to associate with him as a companion:

If you keep company with bad persons you will soon learn their ways.

To **keep to the house**, or **the room**, or **one's room** is said of a person who is ill or of one who is obliged from any cause to remain indoors: (a) She has had a severe illness, and still keeps to the house.

(b) A warrant is out for his arrest, and so Ramesh keeps to his rooms.

To **keep house** means to manage the business of a household. This phrase is used of a woman who acts as housekeeper.

To **keep open house** is to be ready to entertain all guests : She is a very nice lady and keeps her house open for all the friends.

To **keep a good table** means to entertain one's guests sumptuously and in the habit of providing food of excellent quality for one's own eating:

No one ever sees poor dinners at her house; I can tell you from long experience that she keeps a good table.

To **keep watch; keep watch and ward** means to be on the watch : We had better keep watch tonight against thieves.

To **keep a sharp look-out** means to maintain a keen watch : They keep a sharp look-out on boardship.

To **keep pace with** means to keep abreast of the development, to advance or progress equally fast with : (a) How can you expect that a child keeps pace with a full-grown man?

(b) You cannot keep pace with Renu in 'Logics'.

To **break the peace; to keep the peace.** These are contrary expressions:

(a) Two man quarrel and fight; they are said to break the peace.

(b) They were brought before a judge and were bound over to keep the peace, i.e., to refrain thenceforth from quarrelling.

To **keep one's eyes on another person** means to keep watch on him, to observe his movements and actions : The policeman tried to keep his eye on the thief so that he might catch him stealing.

To **keep someone at arm's length** means to keep someone at a distance and not allow him an opportunity of close contact : It is always better to keep the evil persons at arms length.

To **keep one's head above** means to avoid getting into debt or trouble so as to be overwhelmed by it : It is always prudent to keep one's head above water in order to be happy and free from lot of troubles.

To **get one's head above water** means to tide over difficulties successfully : He sold part of his property in order to get his head above water.

To **keep good hours** means to be habitually early in returning home at night : The opposite is, keep bad hours or late hours : He always comes late in the night, he does not keep good hours.

To **keep body and soul together** is to keep alive, to keep from starving.
She happily eats as much as would keep her body and soul together.

To **keep the wolf from the door** is to keep away extreme poverty, starvation, or death by hunger : In India thousands have a daily fight to keep the wolf from the door.

LAY

To **lay waste** means to make desolate : A few of the finest cities of Europe have been laid waste by bombing.

To **lay bare, lay open** means to disclose or reveal a secret thing.
He did not rest till he laid bare the whole conspiracy of his friend Pratham.

To lay someone under an obligation means to do a favour so that he feels indebted : You have laid me under a great obligation by helping me in my adversity.

To **lay oneself open** to means to expose oneself to: By spending a lot of money on trifle occasion, he lays himself open to the suspicion of tax authorities.

To **lie in wait for** means to await in concealment, to be waiting as if in ambush : The murderer lady lies in wait for her victim as the tigress, for its prey.

To **lay,** or **set, a trap** means to prepare a trap and place it in a position to catch prey. It also means to prepare a scheme to deceive another and draw him in : A hunter lays (or sets) a trap to catch elephants.

To **lay on the shelf** means to lay aside as no longer fit for use, just as books and magazines not in use are put on the shelves of the book case : A retired person is sometimes called as laid on the shelf. Also a question or scheme moved and set aside, is said to be laid on the shelf, or shelved.

To **lay down the law** means to speak in tones of authority.

To **lay up for a rainy day** means to make provision for an adverse time and difficulty.

To **lay their heads together** means to consult together or frame common opinion.

MAKE

To **make peace** means to reconcile, to agree on a peace proposal by the parties at variance : There had been feuds for ages between the rival groups, it was the effort of the great grand old man that finally made peace between them.

To **make room** means to open a space or passage, to remove obstruction.

Room here means open space, while **a room** is an apartment : There is enough room on this road for two cars to pass each other.

To **make way, make headway,** or to **make one's way** means to progress slowly and steadily under difficult circumstances. To **make way for** is to allow space or room for.

I've the guts to make my own way.

These students are studying Russian, but they do not seem to be making much headway.

The crowd made way for the 'Hero of the game' as he advanced.

To **make a hash** of anything means to spoil it : The secretary made a hash on the club accounts.

To **make haste** means to hasten, to hurry : Make haste or you will miss the train.

To **make friends** means to win or secure the friendship of others.

This man is so genial, he makes friends wherever he goes.

To **make a will** means to make a testamentary disposal of his property : He made a will and entrusted the same to his advocate.

To **make use of** means to use : She has so many sandals and shoes as she will not be able to make use of them in her life.

To **make love to** means to make love with a woman : It was in vain that the young boy tried to make love to Lady Diana.

He makes a good soldier means he possesses qualities of a good soldier.

She will make you a good wife means she possesses the qualities for becoming a good wife.

To **make answer** means to reply.

To **make sure** means to ascertain positively; also to make secure.

To **make sure of** means to consider as certain .

To **make terms** means to come to an agreement.

To **make short work of** means to bring to a sudden end, or to dispose of speedily : This lawyer will make short work of his adversary's arguments.

To **make amends for** means to compensate for damage, injury or insult : By helping her now, he is trying to make amends for his past misdeeds.

To **make an example of** a person means to treat (punish) him so that the result will be a deterrent (warning) to others : By suspending the subordinate for his misbehaviour the officer made an example of him to others.

To **make a point of** means doing a thing, to set it before you as a thing to be certainly done : Johni makes a point of writing ten English pages daily.

To **make a clean breast of something** means to disclose fully and without reserve : It is always better to make clean breast of the whole things before the lawyer.

To **make a living** means to earn a livelihood for oneself.

To **make (both) ends meet** means to be able to supply the necessities of life while keeping expenditure within income. The phrase implies that the pinch of poverty is felt : It is far better to struggle and make both ends meet than to get into the clutches of an evil person for making quick bucks.

To **make common cause with** means to co-operate with; to unite with and share the common risk, work, and reward : Now-a-days political parties with different ideologies make a common cause temporarily to win the elections.

To **make one's escape** means to escape by one's own efforts : He made his escape through water route.

To **make one's mark** means to do some noteworthy thing, which brings honour or distinction : He made his marks by writing a very good book for the children.

To **leave one's mark** means to leave behind the effect of one's work : He was not long at college before he made his mark.

Men like Jai Prakash Narain, and Lal Bahadur Shastri leave their mark on the history of our country.

To **make a mountain of a molehill** means, to give great importance to trifles A man through great timidity or sloth often exaggerates a small obstacle and makes a mountain out of a molehill.

To **make a virtue of necessity** means to do a very disagreeable thing as though from duty but really because you must do it : Knowing that the landlord would forcibly eject him from the house, he himself delivered the key, making a virtue of necessity.

To **make much ado about nothing** is to make a great fuss about a trifle : Mr Rehman made much ado about nothing when he again raised the matter of throwing waste papers in front of his house by someone.

To **make no bones about a thing** means to make no scruple about doing it. The phrase implies that the thing is disagreeable : You need not raise imaginary difficulties, but just go and do the work and make no bones about it.

To **make bold to do a thing** means to venture to do a thing even though it may seem bold to do it : He makes bold to say that Government should spend less on Highways and more on village roads.

To **make neither head nor tail** of a thing means not to understand it or any part of it; not to be able to see the thing clearly : She spoke so quickly and in such a confused manner that nobody could make neither head nor tail of her sayings.

To **take no account of** a thing means to disregard it through oversight or because it is not worth notice : Government take no account of such senseless agitation by the gays.

To **make a fool of oneself** means to act stupidly. To **make a fool of someone** is to dupe him : He went to meet the president without any pre appointment, so he was not allowd to enter. He made a fool of himself.

To **make little of, light of, nothing** of means to disparage, to treat as of no account.

To **make nothing of,** has a second meaning. If a person is too stupid to learn, we say the teacher **can make nothing of him** it means the teacher cannot succeed with him. If the phrase is used in reference to a passage in a book, if I say I can **make nothing of it**, it means I am unable to understand it.
When I talked about his health, he made **light of his illness.**
We can make nothing of what she says, *i.e.,* we cannot understand her.

To **make much of** means to value highly, to treat as of great importance.

To **make too much of** means to over-estimate. The phrase **'to make enough of '** is commonly used with a negative expression.

To **make the best** or **the most of** a thing means to reap the greatest advantage one can from it ; to reduce to the least possible inconvenience : The accident was very serious, but the surgeon made the best he could of the few appliances within his reach.

To **make the best of a bad bargain**. When a man buys a thing which does not turn out as well as he expected, that thing is often called a **bad bargain** Hence the phrase means to turn a disappointment to the best possible account.

To **make hay while the sun shines** Sunshiny weather is the most suitable for making hay. Hence the phrase metaphorically means to take advantage of a favourable opportunity before it lasts, to use the opportunity to advantage : When trade was brisk, he worked very hard, and made his fortune: he believes in making hay while the sun shines.

To **make a tool,** or **cats paw of** someone, is to use him as a means of attaining or accomplishing your object : The story goes that a monkey, seeing nuts roasting at a strong fire and wishing to have them, but not liking to burn his own paw, laid hold of the paw of the cat and by means of it pulled the nuts to himself.

To **make a man of someone** means to elevate him, to raise him from an inferior position into an independent and prosperous condition, so that he can act in a manly way : A rich friend of mine took up this poor lad and kept him at school for seven years, and his education has made a man of him.

To **make believe** means to pretend, to act under pretence : He made believe he was going off for a month, and then unexpectedly returned in a week and found his wife messed with a fellow.

To **make a shift** means to get along by some means, though with some difficulty : A miser will always make a shift to save money.

To **make faces** is to make grimaces : Most of the people make faces while looking into a mirror.

To **make merry** means to be happy and jovial; Hence, the word **merry-making.**

We spent our winter holidays in eating and drinking and merry-making.

To **make free** means to take a liberty to which one has no right: (a) No one should make free to open a letter addressed to someone else.

(b) I make free to say in this gentleman's presence, that his conduct has not been straightforward.

The phrase implies boldness or impertinence, whereas the phrase, **take the liberty of,** does not indicate anything disrespectful.

To **make free with** means to treat freely or without formality.

To **make oneself at home** means to act with as much freedom and with as little formality as if you were at home. The phrase is used of a person who is in another person's home so to make himself at home means to feel him at his ease in the house so that he will move and act as freely as though he were in his own house.

To **make one's mouth water.** If a hungry man smells food, the saliva gathers in his mouth, and he longs to taste the food, so the phrase means to excite a longing for. It is generally used when the thing desired cannot be achieved and enjoyed. In this phrase, **water** is as used as verb : The hungry man stood gazing at the baker's shop and it made his mouth's water to lump of fresh loaves.

PLAY

To **play,** is generally used in the sense of, to act, to operate on, e.g. the fire engine played (= poured water) on the burning house. In such phrases as, **call into play, bring into play,** the word **play** means active operation.

The guns of the fortress were called into play and the advancement of the enemy was checked.

To **play truant**, is to stay away, to loiter, to idle. The phrase is commonly used of a school-boy who when sent to school goes off to play. It also sometimes means to absent oneself from duty when one is supposed to be at his post : School boys playing truant should be punished.

To **play into the hands of another**, is so to act as to be of advantage to another.

Two contractors come to me with estimates for a work; they seem to be perfectly independent. One estimate is much higher than the other, and even the lower one seems high; so I accept neither. Afterwards I come to know that the contractors are friends, and that he, who gave the higher estimate, was only playing into the hands of the other; he meant by bringing his higher estimate to induce me to close at once with the other contractor.

To **play at cross purposes,** is said of two parties who oppose each other, or who have opposing plans but with the same end in view.

The Congress and the Communist parties have been at cross purposes for several months; yet in fact they are both working for the same object of keeping the BJP out of power.

To **play fast and loose with** means to disregard one's promises or engagements.

To **play second fiddle** the phrase means to take a subordinate part, like one who plays second to a leading performer on the violin. The phrase sometimes implies that he, who occupies the subordinate positon, is expected to further the designs of his superior. Sometimes the phrase is **to be second fiddle** the instrument being taken for the performer.

Mrs. Sonia is the president of the Congress party and Mr. Man Mohan Singh is content to be second fiddle.

To **play with edged tools**. There is a saying, 'Children and fools should not handle edged tools.' Hence, the phrase is applied to a man who has to do with a matter which requires delicate handling.

To interfere in a quarrel between Ram and his wife is like playing with edged tools.

To **play one false** means to be deceitful to him, to cheat him : I relied on her support and she played me false.

To **play a double game,** or **act a double part** These mean to do one thing openly and a different thing in secret. The thing done openly is done to deceive, whereas the thing done in secret is the real object aimed at.

(a) I do not believe in playing double game.

(b) Generals often play a double game in war, but this is regarded as part of the war tactics.

PUT

'Put' is also used in several idiomatic expressions as per following:

To **put in mind** means to remind.

To **put to the sword** means to slay with the sword.

To **put to trial** or to **put trial** means to try to check.

To **put a thing to the test** or **proof** means to try it to examine it sincerely.

To **put to shame** means to make ashamed to disgrace.

To **put a thing to the vote** means to take a vote upon a proposal.

To **put** (or **get**) **things ship-shape** means to settle them in an appropriate order.

To **put to sea** means to start on a voyage.

To **put one's oar in** means to interfere to meddle in something.

To **put to use** means to make use of it.

To **put one to silence** means to silence him.

To **put in order** means to array in orderly fashion.

A mother **puts** her children **to bed** means the children **go to bed.**

A commander **puts** his enemies **to flight** means the enemies **take to flight**.

A magistrate **puts** the law **in force** against a criminal means the magistrate dispense the justice.

To **put** or **set** one **at his ease** means to free him from restraint.

To **put one to it** means to press one hard, to press him to the utmost of his powers. It, in this phrase, is impersonal : I felt so exhausted that I was put to it not fall over.

To **put it to one** is to lay a matter before one for his consideration that he may form an opinion upon it. This phrase would be used by one who was trying to persuade others : I put it to you, Is it wise to remain indifferent while the Government is making great efforts to extend education?

To **put a case,** is to set it forward for consideration.

To **put down one's foot** is to make a decide stand, to resist further encroachments.

To **put one on his guard** is to warn him.

To **put one on his mettle** is to rouse him to do his best in trying circumstances : The cry of wolves behind put my horse on his mettle and he brought me in safety to the village.

To **put one's hand to a thing** is to undertake it to begin it.

To **put a thing well** is to express one's meaning clearly and forcibly in speech or writing.

To **put the screw on one.** This means to coerce him; particularly to restrain another in regard to expenditure or idling : He could put the screw upon his son George.

To **put the cart before the horse** is to begin at the wrong end to do a thing, to attempt a thing while neglecting to do first what ought to be done first.

You certainly do put the cart before the horse. You have actually brought the masons to build a house but have not yet got the bricks.

To **put one's shoulder to the wheel** is to make a great effort oneself instead of looking to others for help.

To **put a thing down in black and white** is to put it in writing, so that a record is available : You tell me a long story; but put down what you want in black and white; and I will weigh its merits.

To **put,** or **set, right,** or to **put to rights**. These mean to adjust, regulate, correct, put in correct order: The engineer soon put the damaged T.V. to rights.

To **put a good face,** or **the best construction, on a thing** means to regard it in the most favourable way. The phrases are applicable to conduct, and commonly to unseemly conduct : A lawyer generally tries to put the best face on the faults of his client.

To **put one out of countenance** means to make him appear ashamed.

To **put this and that together** is to infer from a conjunction of circumstances.

To **put forth,** or **throw out, a feeler:** When a person brings forward a proposal or makes an observation to elicit the opinions of others, he is said to put forth or throw out a feeler : In his statement about Pakistan in the Lok Sabha the Prime Minister threw out a feeler to test the opinion of Parliament.

To **put a spoke in one's wheel** means to obstruct progress, to prove a serious barrier or hindrance : Rahim was getting on well in business till Rehman opened a rival establishment, and that put a spoke in Rahim's wheel.

To **put something by for a rainy day** means to save money for the adverse circumstances.

To **put someone through it** means to wear him out, e.g. by long interrogation.

SET

To **set a scheme on foot** is to start it, to **set it going.**

To **set a thing on fire** is to apply fire to it and make it burn; also to inflame- said of the passions.

To **set** or **put** a thing **on the fire** means to place it upon the burning fire to heat or cook it.Use of 'THE' implies that fire was already there. You may set a kettle **on the fire** but you cannot set it **on fire**. The girl set the pot on the fire. He set the withered leaves on fire.

To **set store by** is to value highly.

To **set the Thames on fire** means to do something extraordinary or brilliant : Nisha is a steady worker but never likely to set the Thames on fire.

To **set one's face against** means resolutely to resist : Attempts were made to draw the prince into rebellion but he set his face against such intrigues.

To **set one's house in order** means to arrange one's affairs : When he joined the new office he found the affairs of the office in desperate confusion; it took several months to set the house in order.

To **set people by the ears** means to provoke them to quarrel or wrangle.

To **be well set up** means to have a good physique to have a strong and well-built body.

To **set one's teeth** is to determine to endure hardship.

STAND

To **stand in another man's shoes** means to occupy another man's place.

To **stand in need of** means to be in need of : The house stands in need of painting.

To **stand in terror of** means to be in terror of, to be afraid of : The old person stood in secret terror of his son.

To **stand in good stead** means to be of great advantage to one in a time of difficultly : The wolves were after the traveller but his horse stood him in good stead and the traveller was able to escape.

To **stand one's ground** means to maintain one's position : He tried hard to stand his ground against the veteran lawyer but he failed.

To **stand to one's guns** means to persevere when hardships press.

To **stand in one's own light** means to act in a way that is disadvantageous to oneself : He stood in his own light when he refused this posting.

To **stand to reason** means to be consistent with reason and propriety of action.

To **stand one's trial** means to be tried in a court of law.

He **cannot stand it** means He is not able to endure it.

To **stand on ceremony with** means to be over punctilious in etiquette.

To **stand on one's dignity** means to maintain a dignified and unbending attitude.

He was offended or insulted, now stands on his dignity and insists that an apology be made to him by the offenders.

TAKE

Many idioms using **take** are given in Chapter iii, Section 38.

To **take into account** means to regard, to consider : Before purchasing this house he has taken into account all the merits and demerits of the locality.

To **take to task, call to account** means to reprove and require explanation : Take him to task for his negligence and unauthorised absent.

To **take advantage of** means to use any benefit offered by; also, to get benefit by cunning means.

To **take a thing in hand** means to undertake to do it, to attempt, to accomplish it : Several persons have taken in hand to write the history of the country, but only a few have been successful.

To **take the law into one's own hands** means to punish a person supposed to be guilty without his being legally tried.

To **take notice of** a thing means to observe it : He listened to my logics, objections patiently, but took no notice of them in submitting his report.

To **take** a city **by storm** means to capture it through a fierce and surprised attack.

To **take** people **by storm** means to captivate them unexpectedly : His singing took the audience by storm.

To **take** one **by surprise** means to come upon him suddenly.

To **take upon oneself** means to assume or undertake some work : She takes all the reponsibility upon herself.

To **be taken aback** means to be taken by surprise, to be startled.

To **take part with** means to unite or join with.

To **take part in** is to unite or join in - said of things : Several good tennis players have consented to take part in this tournament.

To **take another person's part** means to side with him, to defend him.

To **take** (or **pay** or **give) heed to** means to attend to carefully : I will take heed to what my mother says.

To **take in good part** means to receive without resentment- said of a disagreeable thing, as a rebuke or admonition : I tried to give Johni some good advice, but instead of taking it in good part, he became unhappy.

To **take to one's heels** means to run away : Seeing the police, the thief took to his heels.

To **take to one's bed** means to be obliged to lie down in bed through illness.

To **take in tow** means to drag along in water by means of a cable or chain.

To **take a statement on trust** means to accept it as true without inquiry, to accept it as true believing that he who makes it is trustworthy : One should not take any statement on trust unless we have something to prove our contentions.

To **take it into one's head;** to **come into one's head** means to occur to one, to suggest itself to one. The expressions sometimes imply whimsicality : Jack took it into his head to wake up all the servants at midnight.

To **take pride in** means to delight in, to be proud of : She takes pride in doing her stitching very neatly.

To **take a leaf out of another's book** means to take a hint from another's mode of action, to adopt another person's plan in the hope of reaching a result like his : Ram took a leaf out of Shyam's book in the matter of dealing with the customers and got success.

To **take the bull by the horns** is to grapple courageously with a difficulty that lies in your way : If you have factious opposition to deal with, do not avoid it, but take the bull by the horns.

To **take a leap in the dark** means to do a hazardous thing without any idea of what it may result in : It is wrong to leap in the dark without knowing the results.

To **take things easy,** or **take it easy** means to pass through life without being worried by work or anxieties. The phrase to **have an easy time of it** means to be without worry or hard work. To have an easy time of it, is because of outward circumstances; to **take it easy** is because of inward disposition and way of living.

To **take a fancy** or **liking, to** a thing means to conceive an admiration for it or a desire to get it : She has taken quite a fancy to my car.

To **take**, or **let, one into a secret** means to make known the secret to him, he also being expected to regard it as a secret : Two persons plan a theft but are not able to accomplish their object without a third person; so they take a third into the secret and carry the nefarious business very cleverly.

To **take the lead;** to **get the start**. When of several competitors, one at starting gets ahead of the others, he is said to **get a start** . In a competition when one gets ahead and takes the leading place, he is said to **take the lead :** All the boats started together, but Ramesh's soon took the lead.

To **take one home** means to accompany one to his home.

To **take care of**, or **look after** means, to look carefully : You should take care of your old parents.

To **take the measure of a man** means to form after careful observation a due estimate of a man : I asked some irrelevant questions to her friend in order to take measure of him.

To **take the cake (or the biscuit)**. This is a slang expression meaning 'to take first prize'- usually in some absurdity.

To **take the bread out of another's mouth** means to deprive him of his means of living. He is said to have taken the bread out of his friend's mouth by getting his job.

THROW

To **throw cold water upon** a project means to discourage it, to disparage the project.

To **throw dust in one's eyes**. The phrase means to deceive one : He talked glibly to me about his schemes and tried to show me that if I would lend him two thousand dollars he would soon be able to repay me the double; but I felt that he was only trying to throw dust in my eyes.

To **throw off the mask** is said of one who, having acted a deceitful part for a time, suddenly declares his real intentions. His deceit was as a mask to conceal his intentions.
The tenant soon threw off his masks and openly tried to dictate his terms to vacate the house.

To **throw up the sponge** means to give up a contest, to surrender.

Don't expect him to throw up the sponge so easily.

TURN

To **turn one's back upon** means to abandon, to reject or refuse unceremoniously, to change to a directly opposite course : I am happy to note that he had turned his back upon his former vices.

To **turn one's coat** means to change sides, to change to the opposite party. One who does this is called a turncoat.

To **turn over a new leaf.** This means to change completely one's course of action particularly changing from bad conduct to better : After a long career of crime, the terrorist suddenly turned over a new leaf and became a model citizen.

To **turn** a matter **over in one's mind** means to consider it carefully and look at it from all sides :You have given a very important proposal to me; I will turn the thing over in my mind and tell you about my opinion tomorrow.

To **turn the scale**. When an item is being weighed with beam and scales, a little thing will finally make one scale or the other go down. And when a man's judgement is divided between two opinions and something arises which makes him decide to choose one rather than the other, that something is said **to turn the scale.**

To **turn one's hand to** is to engage oneself in : This handy fellow seems to be able to turn his hand to anything.

To **turn tail** means to retreat ignominiously. It is said when a person behaves like a coward.

To **turn the day against one; to turn the fortunes of the day**. These mean to reverse superiority or success : The fall of a king from his horse in a field of battle often turned the fortunes of the day.

To **turn the tables** on someone, is to reverse his success.

To **turn a thing to account** is to utilize it : She had kept the trinket in...... the hope of turning it to better account.—*Dickens*

To **turn one's nose at a thing** means to treat it with contemptuous dislike or disgust : He has been reduced almost to beggary, and yet he turns up his nose at any suggestion that he should work.

To **turn one's head** or **one's brain** means to confuse him that he seems to have lost his judgement; to make giddy or conceited, or wild or insane : The sudden good fortune has turned his head.

To **have a turn for** means to have capacity or fitness for : This boy has a turn for classical music; send him to a good school of Music.

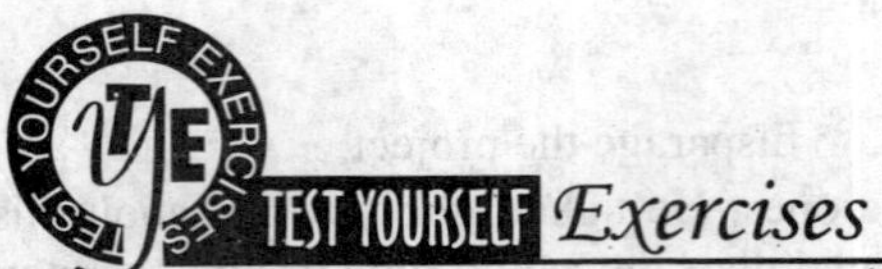

01

Directions (1-10): *Each of the following idiom is followed by four meanings. Indicate which one is correct:* **[RRB Ajmer, Bhopal]**

(1) To put two and two together
(a) to bear the brunt of
(b) to conclude from obvious fact
(c) to put off
(d) to put on a false appearance

(2) To wash dirty linen in public
(a) to quarrel openly
(b) to clean solid lines
(c) to understand the hidden meaning of the word
(d) to wash dirty clothes

(3) To read between the lines
(a) to suspect
(b) to read carefully
(c) to understand the hidden meaning of the word
(d) to do useless things

(4) To face the music
(a) to prepare to give a music performance
(b) to suffer evil consequences
(c) to suffer hardship
(d) to change the things

(5) To leave no stone unturned
(a) to keep clean and tidy
(b) to try utmost
(c) to work enthusiastically
(d) to change the things

(6) Between the devil and the deep sea
(a) a deep sea diver
(b) to be evil tempered
(c) in a dilemma
(d) a man who is drowning

(7) To flog a dead horse
(a) to revive interest in a subject which is out of date
(b) to beat a horse that is dead
(c) to do interesting things
(d) to try to take work from a weak horse

(8) To bait the hook to suit the fish
(a) to prepare a box to pack the fish
(b) to do things to please others
(c) to look at things from other person's point of view
(d) to catch fish by providing suitable food

02

Directions (1-10): *In the following, pick out the correct meanings of the following idioms:* **[RRB Bhopal, Mumbai]**

(1) Take exception to
(a) different
(b) to take with difficulty
(c) object to
(d) difficult

(2) Through thick and thin
(a) big and small
(b) large object
(c) under all conditions
(d) thin and fat

(3) Sitting on the fence
(a) unbalanced (b) uncomfortable
(c) coward (d) between two opinions

(4) An axe to grind
(a) difficult job (b) hard labour
(c) private ends to serve (d) punishment

(5) His wit's end
(a) finished (b) confused
(c) comedy (d) very intelligent

(6) To be born with a silver spoon in one's mouth
(a) to be born in a rich home (b) to be born in a jeweller's home
(c) to be fed milk with a silver spoon (d) to be a first born child

(7) A hard nut to crack
(a) difficult things require extra effort (b) a difficult problem to solve
(c) a difficult problem solved effortlessly (d) costly things need careful handling

(8) From hand to mouth
(a) something repeated often (b) consuming food
(c) to survive without saving (d) hitting someone by hand on the mouth

(9) To beat about the bush
(a) not to come to the point (b) vigorous search for the culprit
(c) easily achieved success without much effort (d) working hard to achieve the goal

(10) To burn one's fingers
(a) to get injured in an accident (b) to pay a heavy price
(c) to suffer from meddling in something (d) to get a burn injury on the hands

03

Directions (1-11) : *In the following questions, four alternatives are given for the idioms/phrases. Choose the one which best expresses the meaning of the given idiom/phrase:* **[RRB Ajmer, Kolkata, Patna]**

(1) To make mincemeat
(a) copy the appearance of somebody (b) take care of something
(c) refute utterly (d) have the same opinion

(2) To carry all before one
(a) finish quickly (b) make a promise
(c) be free from danger (d) be completely successful

(3) To run riot
(a) befool other (b) be violent in action
(c) criticise other (d) behave in an undisciplined way

(4) To carry the conviction
(a) be extremely fond of anything (b) bear the proof of the truth
(c) feel displeasure (d) make overtures of reconciliation

(5) To hold
(a) show unwillingness (b) keep at a distance
(c) stop by threats of violence (d) endure hardship or danger

(6) To come round
(a) to get well
(b) to reach a roundabout
(c) to succeed
(d) to reach and understanding

(7) A white elephant
(a) an elephant with white skin
(b) a costly thing
(c) a costly and useful thing
(d) a costly but useless thing

(8) To meet one's waterloo
(a) to meet a strong adversary
(b) to die fighting
(c) to meet one's final defeat
(d) to die an ignoble death

(9) To set the Thames of fire
(a) to wreak evil on something
(b) to destroy with fire
(c) to do a heroic deed
(d) to try to do the impossible

(10) To smell a rat
(a) to see hidden meaning
(b) to smell bad odour
(c) to misunderstand
(d) to suspect a trick or deceit

(11) To rise like a phoenix
(a) to resemble a phoenician
(b) to get up with a start
(c) to rise with a new life
(d) to rise with anger

04

Directions (1-10): *In the following questions, out of the given alternatives, choose the one which has meaning of sense of the idiom/phrase given at the question place:* **[RRB Bhopal, Income Tax Inspectors Exam]**

(1) On the spur of the moment
(a) at once or without any kind of deliberation
(b) in accordance with the prevailing style
(c) open to blame
(d) on the side of something undesirable

(2) To go hard with one
(a) to remain neutral
(b) to be busy over trifles
(c) to be unreliable
(d) to prove a serious matter

(3) To keep house
(a) to keep pace with
(b) to be silent about one's own purpose
(c) to waste time
(d) to manage the business of the household

(4) To talk over
(a) to consider
(b) to discuss
(c) to understand
(d) to think over

(5) To show one's white feather
(a) to show arrogance
(b) to show signs of cowardice
(c) seek peace
(d) to become polite

(6) To rule the roost
(a) to domineer
(b) to surrender
(c) to run away
(d) to fight

(7) To turn down
(a) give up
(b) reject
(c) follow
(d) throw

(8) He is *out and out* a liar
(a) surely
(b) consistently
(c) basically
(d) thoroughly

(9) She is a clever girl and she can *put two and two* together.
(a) make a formal statement (b) took very thoughtful
(c) draw a logical conclusion (d) count very well

05

Directions (1-9) : *In the following questions, out of the four alternatives, choose the correct meaning of the following idioms/phrases:* **[Income Tax Inspectors]**

(1) To cut one short
(a) to insult one (b) to criticise one
(c) to interrupt one (d) to love one

(2) To nail one's colours to the mast
(a) to understand the fact (b) to refuse to surrender
(c) to mishandle something (d) to accept the proposal

(3) Beside the mark
(a) out of assumptions (b) beyond the imagination
(c) beyond the reach (d) irrelevantly

(4) To put a good face on
(a) to smile graciously (b) to be lucky in a business
(c) to bear up courageously (d) to treat others politely

(5) A far cry
(a) a disadvantageous thing (b) an unfounded claim
(c) a long way off (d) a thing which is neglected by all

(6) I am *pissed off* with the behaviour of my employers.
(a) in a very delicate state (b) annoyed or bored
(c) to delay inordinately (d) very pleased or happy

(7) He is *really up in the creek* without his friends and family members
(a) in serious difficulties
(b) forced to do a very hard work
(c) in a situation of failure
(d) shy or modest

(8) He is a *silver tongued* doctor and patients listen to him.
(a) speaking in a helpful but authoritative language
(b) speaking in a way that make people angry
(c) speaking in a way that annoy or bore the people
(d) speaking in a way that charms persuade people

(9) Every piece of furniture in her house in an *apple-pie order.*
(a) very neatly arranged (b) painted in light colours
(c) kept in a disorganised way (d) very delicately arranged

06

Directions (1-10) : *Use the following idioms in your own sentences:* **[IAS]**

(1) To play with fire (2) To come across
(3) To burn one's boats (4) To read between the lines
(5) To live in an ivory tower (6) To differ with
(7) To carry the day (8) To skip over
(9) To get along (10) To fall out

07

Directions (1-12) : *Use the following idioms in your own sentences:* **[IAS, PCS, CDS]**

(1) To have an axe to grind
(2) To have many irons in the fire
(3) To burn one's boat
(4) To play second fiddle
(5) To burn the candle at both ends
(6) To laugh in one's sleeve
(7) To bury the hatchet
(8) To keep at an arm's length
(9) Through thick and thin
(10) Off and on
(11) The Alpha and Omega
(12) Tooth and nail

08

Directions (1-5) : *Given below are four alternatives for the idiom/phrase in italics in the sentence. Choose the one which best expresses the meaning of the idiom/phrase in italic:* **[Assistant Grade, Income Tax Inspectors]**

(1) We kept our fingers crossed till the final results were declared.
(a) kept praying
(b) waited anxiously
(c) felt sacred
(d) kept hopeful

(2) The smell from the kitchen *makes my mouth water.*
(a) makes me giddy
(b) makes me vomit
(c) stimulates my appetite
(d) makes me sick

(3) My friend *got the sack from* his first job.
(a) resigned
(b) got tired of
(c) was dismissed from
(d) was demoted from

(4) I stepped forward fully determined *to take the bull by the horns.*
(a) to act without any hesitation
(b) to be fully alive
(c) to meet the danger boldly
(d) to act without preparation

(5) He was unable *to account for the deficit* in the firm's bank balance.
(a) to give a satisfactory explanation
(b) speak the truth about
(c) maintain accounts properly
(d) give the accounts for

09

Directions (1-12) : *Make the correct meaning of the idioms from the alternatives given below:* **[SBI PO, CDS]**

(1) Will-o-the-wisp
(a) to cut in a childish way
(b) acting in a foollish way
(c) to have desires unbacked by effort
(d) anything which eludes or deceives
(e) yearning of the spirit

(2) A snake in the grass
(a) a hidden enemy
(b) unforeseen happening
(c) very ferocious enemy
(d) unrecognizable danger
(e) an reliable person

(3) To look down one's nose at
(a) to show anger
(b) to backbite
(c) to insult in the presence of other
(d) to regard with half-hidden displeasure or contempt
(e) None of the above

(4) Hobson's choice
(a) excellent choice
(b) no choice at all because their is only one thing to take or not
(c) choice to live or die
(d) big man's choice
(e) first choice

(5) To have a chip on one's shoulder
(a) to be boastful
(b) to be deserving of piece
(c) to have treated unfairly
(d) to have deep cut wound on the shoulder
(e) signs on the shoulder showing timidity

(6) To flog a dead horse
(a) to try to achieve an impossible thing
(b) to try to table work from a weak horse
(c) to beat a horse that is dead
(d) to revive interest in a subject which is out of date
(e) to act in a foolish way

(7) To be lost in the cloud
(a) to be concealed from the view
(b) to find oneself in a very uncomfortable position
(c) to be perplexed
(d) to fly deep in the clouds
(e) to meet with one's clouds

(8) To fish in troubled waters
(a) to indulge in evil conspiracies
(b) to aggravate the situation
(c) to be perplexed
(d) to catch fish in disturbed waters
(e) to make the most of a bad bargain

(9) To make the wind out of another's sails
(a) to defect the motives of another
(b) to cause harm to another
(c) to anticipate another and to gain advantage over him
(d) to manoeuvre to mislead another on the high seas
(e) None of the above

(10) To wrangle over an ass's shadow
(a) to do something funny
(b) to quarrel over the possession of an ass
(c) to waste time on pretty things
(d) to quarrel over trifles
(e) to act in a foolish way

(11) To fly off the handle
(a) to dislocate
(b) to be indifferent
(c) to lose one's temper
(d) to be airborne
(e) to act in a way unmindful of consequences

(12) To bring one's eggs to a bad market
(a) to fail in one's plans because one goes to the wrong people for help
(b) to bring one's commodities to a market where there is no demand for them
(c) to show one's talent before audience which is incapable of appreciating them
(d) to face a humiliating situation
(e) to act when the opportunity is lost

10

Directions (1-10) : *Frame sentences to bring out the meaning of the following:* **[PCS]**

(1) On the horns of a dilemma
(2) A wild goose chase
(3) Take a leaf out of somebody's book
(4) Play into someone's hands
(5) Jack of all trades
(6) To nip in the bud
(7) In accordance with
(8) To take to one's heels
(9) To bear up
(10) Through thick and thin

11

Directions (1-8) : *Frame sentences to bring out the meaning of the following:* **[PCS]**

(1) To curry favour
(2) To bury the hatchet
(3) To blow one's own trumpet
(4) A man of show
(5) Take to heels
(6) In the long run
(7) To be up and doing
(8) To make up one's mind

12

Directions (1-10) : *Frame sentences to bring out the meaning of the following:* **[IAS, PCS]**

(1) Hold out an olive branch
(2) Read between the lines
(3) To beat about the bush
(4) Off and on
(5) Win the rubber
(6) Out of the wood
(7) To make a clean breast of
(8) To be at loggerheads
(9) To lose heart
(10) Bury the hatchet

13

Directions (1-9) : *Frame sentences to bring out the meaning of the following:* **[IAS, PCS]**

(1) Ill at ease
(2) Man of letters
(3) Prime of life
(4) To fish in troubled waters
(5) A burning question
(6) To turn over a new leaf
(7) To laugh in one's sleeves
(8) Toe the line
(9) In full swing

14

Directions (1-9) : *Frame sentences to bring out the meaning of the following:* **[IAS, PCS]**

(1) At the eleventh hour
(2) Bag and baggage
(3) A red letter day
(4) To play the second fiddle
(5) To burn the candle at both ends
(6) Turn down
(7) To show the white feather
(8) An apple of discord
(8) The sword of Democles
(9) At sixes and sevens

15

Directions (1-12) : *Frame sentences to bring out the meaning of the following:* ***[PCS]***

(1) Null and void
(2) On the horns of a Dilemma
(3) Ad hoc
(4) Take your time
(5) A cold war
(6) Hot line
(7) A red letter day
(8) To mince words
(9) To have no axe to grind
(10) A bone of contention
(11) To have many irons in the fire
(12) A public secret

16

Directions (1-11) : *Frame sentences to bring out the meaning of the following:* **[IAS]**

(1) Break the ice
(2) Keep the wolf from the door
(3) Make hay while the sun shines
(4) A rainy day
(5) Cry over spilt milk
(6) Kill two birds with one stone
(7) A wet blanket
(8) Cold blood
(9) Blow one's own trumpet
(10) Fall upon
(11) Put the eggs in one basket

17

Directions (1-10) : *Choose the correct meanings of the following idioms from the alternatives given below:*

(1) To fight tooth and nail **[SBI PO]**

(a) making every possible effort to win
(b) to fight cowardly
(c) to fight heroically
(d) to fight a losing battle
(e) to lose every thing while engaged in fighting

(2) To let the grass grow under one's feet **[SBI PO]**

(a) to miss the opportunity
(b) to let things go on in their natural way
(c) to be indolent and let others take advantage of one's indolence
(d) to idle away the time; to delay and linger
(e) to move very cautiously in order to avoid harming anything

(3) Melting pot **[CDS]**

(a) an earthen vessel
(b) a cooking utensil
(c) an iron cauldron
(d) a witch's brewing pot
(e) circumstances in which things may changed greatly

(4) To be a good Samaritan **[CDS]**

(a) a religious person
(b) a genuinely charitable person
(c) to be obedient
(d) a citizen of Samaritan
(e) to be law abiding

(5) To fly off the handle **[CDS]**

(a) to dislocate
(b) to lose one's temper
(c) to take off
(d) to be airborne
(e) to be indifferent

(6) The Alpha and Omega **[CDS]**

(a) a Shakespearean play
(b) beginning and end
(c) a Greek song
(d) a Swiss watch
(e) a beautiful object

(7) Merry as a cricket **[CDS]**

(a) to enjoy a game of cricket
(b) to dance and sing
(c) to be carefree
(d) to be extremely cheerful
(e) to be good at sports

(8) To make one's pile **[CDS]**

(a) to construct one's house
(b) to make a successful career
(c) to make a fortune
(d) to keep up rubbish
(e) to hit one's target

(9) To blaze a trail **[CDS]**

(a) to set on fire
(b) to blow the trumpet
(c) to be annoyingly noise
(d) to initiate work
(e) to be vehemently opposed

(10) Gift of the gab **[CDS]**

(a) talent for speaking
(b) to win a prize
(c) to get something free
(d) to distribute gifts
(e) talent for dancing

Solution TYE 01

(1) (b), (2) (a) (3) (c), (4) (b), (5) (b), (6) (c), (7) (a), (8) (b),

Solution TYE 02

(1) (c), (2) (c), (3) (d), (4) (c), (5) (b), (6) (a), (7) (b), (8) (c), (9) (a), (10) (c).

Solution TYE 03

(1) (c), (2) (d), (3) (d), (4) (b), (5) (d), (6) (d), (7) (d), (8) (c), (9) (c), (10) (d), (11) (d),

Solution TYE 04

(1) (a), (2) (d), (3) (b), (4) (d), (5) (b), (6) (a), (7) (a), (8) (b),

Solution TYE 05

(1) (c), (2) (b), (3) (d), (4) (c), (5) (c), (6) (b), (7) (a), (8) (d), (9) (a),

Solution TYE 06

(1) USA is *playing with fire* by helping the government of Iraq.

(2) I *came across* that girl while I was going to USA.

(3) They have *burnt their boats* and taken the final plunge.

(4) If you *read between the lines,* you will find that he never meant to over rule your decision.

(5) If you describe someone as *living in an ivory tower,* you mean that they have no knowledge or experience of the practical problems of everyday life. They don't really, in their *ivory towers*, understand how pernicious drug crime is.

(6) The opposition *differed with* the government over the question of disinvestment.

(7) For the time being, the Congress seems to have *carried the day* (*To be winner*)

(8) She should *skip over* the past and should reinvented a new life.

(9) They seemed to be *getting along* fine.

(10) She *fell out* with her husband.

Solution TYE 07

(1) He suspects that your friend *has an axe to grind* in this proposal.

(2) He has too *many irons in the fire* means he is involved with many activities.

(3) The freedom fighter will not go back now from their decision. They *nor burnt their boats* and taken the final plunge.

(4) He hates the thought of *playing second fiddle* to Ramesh. *Playing second fiddle* to someone means to be treated as less important.

(5) He will soon come to road for he is *burning the candle at both ends.* (*To spend lavishly*)

(6) He *laughed in his sleeves* at the foolish behaviour of the wife of his close friend.

(7) India and Pakistan must *bury the hatchet* for the prosperity and progress of both the countries.

(8) Unloyal friends must be *kept at an arm's length.*

(9) I will abide by my wife *through thick and thin.*

(10) I have been visiting her *off and on* (occasionally).

(11) *The Alpha and Omega* of Mahatma Gandhi's life was to improve the pitiable condition of the untouchables.

(12) She opposed me *tooth and nail* but could not succeeded.

Solution TYE 08

(1) (b), (2) (c), (3) (c), (4) (c), (5) (a),

Solution TYE 09

(1) (d), (2) (d), (3) (d), (4) (b), (5) (c), (6) (a), (7) (c), (8) (e), (9) (c), (10) (d), (11) (c), (12) (a),

Solution TYE 10

(1) Mahatma Gandhi and other leaders were *on the horns of a dilemma* at the time of the division of the country in 1947.

(2) He wondered if his boss had deliberately sent him on *a wild goose chase*. (Searching for a thing that have no chance to be found.)

(3) The young generation must *take a leaf out of old generation's books* in the matter of observing moral values.

(4) The terrorists are playing *into our enemy's hands.*

(5) Ramesh is *jack of all trades,* but master of none.

(6) Unlawful activities must be *nipped in the bud.*

(7) The Assam accord was not *in accordance with* the expectations of the common mass.

(8) When he saw the police, he *took to his heels.*

(9) In present time of uncertainty, one must be ready *to bear up* against all disasters and misfortunes.

(10) Good friends abide with each other *through thick and thin.*

Solution TYE 11

(1) It seems that by presenting such a costly gift, he is trying *to curry favour* with her.

(2) It is believed that the Naxalites will *bury the hatchet*, once the accord is reached.

(3) One should not always *blow one's own trumpet.*

(4) He is merely a *man of show*, the real boss is his elder brother.

(5) As he saw her father, he *took to his heels.*

(6) Honesty and sincerity pay *in the long run.*

(7) One must be *up and doing* if one wish to achieve success in life.

(8) Mrs Soniya Gandhi has *made up her mind* to fight the BJP.

Solution TYE 12

(1) The Bush administration is *holding out an olive branch* in the matter of Iraq.

(2) He was unable to *read between the lines* to get the true meaning of the letter.

(3) It is of no use to *beat about the Bush* before the interview board.

(4) I visit my native place *off and on.*

(5) The Australians have *won the rubber.*

(6) Kashmir is still not *out of the wood.*

(7) This militant *made a clean breast* of the secrets before the Suprintendent of Police.

(8) USA and Iraq are *at loggerheads* now-a-days.

(9) We should never *lose hearts* in adverse circumstances.

(10) India and Pakistan must *bury the hatchet* for the peace and prosperity of both the nations.

Solution TYE 13

(1) The Finance Minister is *ill at ease* in his new office under the present financial crisis.

(2) Dr Abdul Kalam, the President of India, is a *man of letters.*

(3) He is a young man. He is in the *prime of life.*

(4) When two countries fight with each other, the other nations try *to fish in troubled waters.*

(5) The Kashmir problem is a *burning question.*

(6) The notorious terrorist Saudagar Lal *turned over a new leaf* of life by starting a new business.

(7) He *laughed in his sleeves* at the foolish behaviour for his boss' wife.

(8) India refused *to toe the line* of USA in the matter of Iraq.

(9) The trade fair is *in full swing* at Pragati Maidan.

Solution TYE 14

(1) The police party reached there at *the eleventh hour.*

(2) People are leaving Kashmir *bag and baggage.*

(3) 26th January is *a red letter day* in the history of India.

(4) I do not like *to play the second fiddle* in any matter.

(5) He will soon be in trouble for he is *burning the candle at both ends.*

(6) My request for leave has been *turned down* by the boss.

(7) When Ramesh asked him to argue in public he *showed the white feather*.

(8) Kashmir is *an apple of discord* between India and Pakistan.

(9) The fear of a war between India and Pakistan is hanging like a *sword of Democles* on the citizens of both the countries.

(10) A thief entered my quarter and left everything at *sixes and sevens*.

Solution TYE 15

(1) The recent Act for granting reservation based on religion was declared *null and void* by the court.

(2) The political parties were *on the horns of a dilemma* on the point of granting reservation to the upper class.

(3) She was given *ad hoc* posting.

(4) You must take *your own time to* take final decision in the matter.

(5) A *cold war* has been continuing between India and Pakistan since long.

(6) There is a *hot line* (telephone line) between India and Pakistan.

(7) August 15th, is a *red letter day* in the history of India.

(8) A sycophant always *minces words* of flattery before his boss.

(9) He has *no axe to grind* in this project, whatever is being done by him, is in the name of humanity.

(10) Kashmir has been *a bone of contention* between India and Pakistan since long.

(11) He is a man of multiple business. He has *many irons in the fire.*

(12) The murder of the college girl is *a public secret* now.

Solution TYE 16

(1) India and Pakistan have *broken the ice* by playing cricket matches after a long interval.

(2) The poor have to put a daily fight to *keep the wolf from the door.*

(3) He is a successful businessman. He believes in *making hay while the sun shines.*

(4) He is a prudent man. He believes in saving for *a rainy day.*

(5) It is useless to *cry over spilt milk* now.

(6) By asking the opposition to support the bill, P.M. slapped his critics.Thus he *killed two birds with one stone.*

(7) Ramesh is a *wet blanket,* do not include him in the list of picnic goers.

(8) *Cold blooded* murders have become very common now-a-days.

(9) Some leaders are in the habit of *blowing their own trumpet.*

(10) He will have to *fall upon* me for help.

(11) One must play safe and so must not *put all eggs in one basket.*

Solution TYE 17

(1) (a), (2) (d), (3) (e), (4) (b), (5) (b), (6) (b), (7) (d), (8) (b), (9) (d), (10) (a),

CHAPTER

32

A FEW PROVERBS

These are a variety of proverbs almost everyone is familiar with. Proverb is a short saying, which states a general truth or piece of advice. Some of the common proverbs are:

(1) A bad man is better than a bad name—बद अच्छा बदनाम बुरा।

(2) A bad workman quarrels with his tools—नाच न जाने आँगन टेढ़ा।

(3) A bird in hand is worth two in the bush—नौ नगद न तेरह उधार।

(4) A burnt child dreads the fire—दूध का जला छाछ या मट्ठा फूँककर पीता है।

(5) A drop in the ocean—ऊँट के मुँह में जीरा।

(6) A figure among cyphers—अन्धों में काना राजा।

(7) A fog cannot be dispelled by a fan—ओस चाटे प्यास नहीं बुझती।

(8) A honey tongue, a heart of gall—मुख में राम, बगल में छुरी।

(9) A little knowledge is a dangerous thing—नीम हकीम खतरा-ए-जान।

(10) All's well that ends well—अन्त भला तो सब भला।

(11) An empty vessel sounds much—थोथा चना बाजै घना।

(12) A nine day's wonder—चार दिन की चाँदनी फिर अँधेरी रात।

(13) A rotten apple injures its companions—एक सड़ी मछली सारे तालाब को गन्दा कर देती है।

(14) As the king so are the subjects—जैसा राजा वैसी प्रजा।

(15) As you sow, so you reap—जैसी करनी वैसी भरनी।

(16) Avarice is the root of all evils—लालच बुरी बला है।

(17) A wolf in lamb's clothing—मुख में राम, बगल में छुरी, इन्सान की शक्ल में शैतान।

(18) Barking dogs seldom bite—जो गरजते हैं सो बरसते नहीं।

(19) Beggars and borrowers could not be choosers—दान की बछिया के दाँत नहीं देखे जाते।

(20) Beneath the rose lies the serpent—विष रस भरा कनक घट जैसे।

(21) Better wear your shoes than your bed clothes—बैठे से बेगार भली।

(22) Between two stools we come to the ground—दुविधा में दोनों गए, माया मिली न राम।

(23) Birds of a feather flock together—चोर का साथी गिरह कट, चोर-चोर मौसेरे भाई।

(24) Black will take no other hue—सूरदास की काली कमरिया चढ़े न दूजो रंग।

(25) Cattle do not die from crow's cursing—बिल्ली के श्राप से छींका नहीं टूटता।

(26) Coming events cast their shadows before—होनहार बिरवान के होत चिकने पात।

(27) Contentment is happiness—सन्तोष परम सुखम्।

(28) Crows are never the whiter for washing—नीम न मीठी होय सींचो गुड़-घी से।
(29) Crying in wilderness—भैंस के आगे बीन बजाना।
(30) Cut your coat according to your cloth—तेते पाँव पसारिये जेती लाँबी सौर।
(31) Deep rivers move with silent majesty, shallow brooks are noisy—अधजल गगरी छलकत जाय। भरी गगरिया चुप्पे जाए।
(32) Diamond cut diamonds—लोहे को लोहा काटता है।
(33) Do evil and look for like—कर बुरा तो हो बुरा।
(34) Do good and cast it into the river—नेकी कर दरिया में डाल।
(35) Drowning man catches at straw—डूबते को तिनके का सहारा।
(36) Errors like straws upon the surface flow, one who is in search of truth must dive below—जिन खोजा तिन पाइयाँ गहरे पानी पैठ मैं बपुरी ढूँढन गई रही किनारे पैठ।
(37) Even death cannot be had for the asking—माँगे मुँह मौत भी नहीं मिलती।
(38) Every potter praises his pot—अपना पूत सब ही को प्यारा, अपनी दही को सभी मीठा कहते हैं।
(39) Everything looks yellow to a jaundiced eye—सावन के अन्धे को हरा ही हरा दिखाई पड़ता है।
(40) Evil gotten, evil spent—जैसा आया वैसे गया।
(41) Example is better than precept—उपदेश करने से स्वयं करना भला।
(42) Fool to others, to himself a sage—अपने मुँह मियाँ मिट्ठू।
(43) Forced labour is better than idleness—बेकार से बेगार भली।
(44) Fortune favours the brave—पुरुष सिंह जे उद्यमी ताकी चेरी, उद्यमी पुरुष की दासी लक्ष्मी भी होती है।
(45) Gather thistles and expect pickles—बोवे पेड़ बबूल का आम कहाँ से खाय।
(46) God's will be done—ईश्वरेच्छा बलीयसी।
(47) Good health is above wealth—तन्दरुस्ती हजार नियामत, शरीमाद्य खलु धर्मसाधनम्।
(48) Good marksman may miss—घोड़े का सवार भी गिरता है, बड़े-बड़े भी चूक जाते हैं।
(49) Good mind, good find—आप भला तो जग भला।
(50) Great cry little wool—ऊँची दूकान फीका पकवान।
(51) Guilty conscience is always suspicious—पापी का मन सदा शंकित रहता है, चोर की दाढ़ी में तिनका।
(52) Half a loaf is better than no bread—कुछ नहीं से थोड़ा भला, नाही मामा से काना मामा अच्छा।
(53) Hard nut to crack—लोहे का चना चबाना।
(54) He breaks his wife's head and then buys a plaster for it —चूहा मारकर गोबर सुँघाना।
(55) He jests at scars who never felt a wound—जाके पैर न फटी बेवाई, सो क्या जाने पीर पराई।
(56) He, that is warm, thinks all are so—आप सुखी तो जग सुखी।
(57) He who would catch fish must not mind getting wet—नाचने उठे तो घूँघट कैसा?
(58) He who would sow well, must reap well—अच्छा करो अच्छा पाओ, कर भला तो हो भला।
(59) High winds blow on high hills—बड़ों की बड़ी बात।
(60) His wits are gone a wool-gathering—उसकी अक्ल चरने गई है।
(61) If you want a thing well done, do it yourself—बिना अपने मरे स्वर्ग नहीं दिखाई पड़ता।
(62) Ill got, ill spent—पाप का धन प्रायश्चित में जाता है, सूम का धन शैतान खाता है।
(63) Ill gotten goods seldom prosper—चोरी का धन मोरी में जाता है।

(64) Innocent have nothing to fear—साँच को आँच नहीं।
(65) It is hard to live in Rome and to fight with the Pope—जल में रहकर मगर से बैर करना उचित नहीं।
(66) It is no use crying over spilt milk—बीती ताहि बिसार दे, आगे की सुधि लेय।
(67) It is too late to lock the stable-door when the steed is stolen—आग लगने पर कुआँ खोदना उचित नहीं, अब पछताए क्या होत है जब चिड़िया चुग गई खेत।
(68) It is work that makes a workman—काम को काम सिखलाता है।
(69) It takes two to make a quarrel—एक हाथ से ताली नहीं बजती।
(70) Killing two birds with one stone—एक पंथ दो काज, एक तीर से दो शिकार।
(71) Let bygones be bygones—बीती सो बीती, बीती ताहि बिसार दे, आगे की सुधि लेय।
(72) Let the past bury the dead—बीती को गाड़ो या भूल जाओ।
(73) Like cures like—विषस्य विषमौषधम।
(74) Like draws like—चोर-चोर मौसेरे भाई।
(75) Like father, like son—जस बाप, तस बेटा।
(76) Living from hand to mouth—रोज कुआँ खोदना रोज पानी पीना।
(77) Make hay while the sun shines—बहती गंगा में हाथ धोना।
(78) Man proposes, God disposes—मेरे मन में कुछ और है, कर्त्ता के कुछ और।
(79) Many a little makes a mickle—बूँद-बूँद करके घड़ा भरता है।
(80) Many a slip between the cup and the lip—कानी के ब्याह को नौ सौ जोखिम।
(81) Many men, many minds—जितने नर उतनी बुद्धि, नाना मुनि नाना मति।
(82) Measure for measure—हत्या के बदले फाँसी, जैसे को तैसा।
(83) Might is right—जिसकी लाठी उसकी भैंस।
(84) Misfortunes never come singly—मुफलिसी में आटा गीला, मुसीबत अकेले नहीं आती।
(85) Money begets money—धन से धन कमाया जाता है।
(86) Much cry and little wool—ऊँची दुकान फीका पकवान।
(87) No one knows the weight of another's burden—जाके पाँव न फटी बिवाई, सो का जाने पीर पराई।
(88) No pains, no gains—बिना सेवा मेवा मिलता नहीं, बिना कष्ट किए कृष्ण नहीं मिलते।
(89) One flower makes no garland—एक फूल से माला नहीं बनती।
(90) One nail drives out another—काँटे से काँटा निकलता है।
(91) One today is better than two tomorrows—नौ नगद न तेरह उधार।
(92) Out of the frying-pan into the fire—भाड़ से निकला मेंढ में पड़ा, आम से टपका, बबूल में अटका।
(93) Pennywise pound foolish—मोहर लुटा जाय कोयले पर छाप।
(94) Poverty breeds strife—दरिद्रता कलह की जड़ है, गरीबी झगड़े की जड़ है।
(95) Pure gold does not fear the flame—साँच को आँच नहीं।
(96) Quit not certainly for hope—आधी छोड़ सारी को धावै, आधी रहै न सारी पावै।
(97) Respect yourself and you will be respected—अपनी मर्यादा अपने हाथ।
(98) Riches have wings—लक्ष्मी चंचला होती है।
(99) Rome was not built in a day—हथेली पर दही नहीं जमता।
(100) Self praise is no recommendation—अपने मुँह मियाँ मिट्ठू बनने से काम नहीं चलता।
(101) Something is better than nothing—नहीं से कुछ भला, नाही मामा से काना मामा अच्छा।

(102) Steal a goose and give giblets in alms—निहाई की चोरी और सुई का दान।

(103) Strike the iron while it is hot—अवसर को कभी न गँवाओ, समय का उचित उपयोग करो।

(104) The innocent have nothing to fear—साँच को आँच नहीं।

(105) The wearer best knows where the shoe pinches—जिसका दुःख वही जानता है, जाके तन न फटी बिवाई, सो क्या जाने पीर पराई।

(106) Tit for tat—जैसे को तैसा, शठे शाठ्यम।

(107) To cast pearls before swine—बन्दर अदरक का स्वाद क्या जाने?

(108) To count one's chickens before they are hatched—घर घोड़ा नकास मोल।

(109) To kill two birds with one stone—एक पंथ दो काज।

(110) To make a mountain of a mole hill—राई का पर्वत बनाना, तिल से ताड़ बनाना।

(111) To lock the stable-door when the steed is stolen—का वर्षा जब कृषि सुखानी, समय चुकि पुनि का पछतानी।

(112) To make castles in the air—हवा में पुल बाँधना, हवाई किले बनाना।

(113) Too many cooks spoil the broth—बहुत से जोगी मठ उजाड़।

(114) Too much courtesy, too much craft—मधुर बानी, दगाबाजी की निशानी।

(115) To rob peter to pay Paul—गाय मारकर जूता दान।

(116) Union is strength—एकता ही बल है।

Conflicting Proverbs

Here are words of wisdom and taken by all with reverence, but some of these sayings look specious when weighed against each other.

Look at the following conflicting sayings:

(1) Actions speak louder than words—The pen is mightier than the sword.

(2) Knowledge is power—Ignorance is bliss.

(3) Look before you leap—He, who hesitates, is lost.

(4) A silent man is a wise one—A man without words is a man without thoughts.

(5) Beware of Greeks bearing gifts—Don't look a gift horse in the mouth.

(6) Clothes make the man—Don't judge a book by its cover.

(7) Nothing ventured, nothing gained—Better safe than sorry.

(8) Money talks—Talk is cheap.

(9) The only thing constant is change—The more things change, the more they stay the same.

(10) Two heads are better than one—If you want something done right, do it yourself.

(11) Many hands make light work—Too many cooks spoil the broth.

(12) The bigger, the better—The best things come in small packages.

(13) Absence makes the heart grow fonder—Out of sight, out of minc.

(14) What will be, will be—Life is what you make it.

(15) Cross your bridges when you come to them—Forewarned is forearmed.

(16) What's good for the goose is good for the gander—One man's meat is another man's poison.

(17) With age comes wisdom—Out of the mouths of babes and sucklings come all wise sayings.

(18) The more, the merrier—Two's company; three's a crowd.

CHAPTER 33

SPOTTING THE ERRORS

विभिन्न प्रतियोगी परीक्षाओं के अंग्रेजी के प्रश्न-पत्र में Spotting the Errors के लगभग 10-15 प्रश्नों का समावेश होता है। अधिकांश प्रश्न Grammatical Rules पर आधारित होते हैं। यद्यपि यह कहना बहुत मुश्किल है कि मुख्यतया किस तरह की errors वाले प्रश्न परीक्षा में पूछे जाते हैं, लेकिन Spotting the Errors में अधिकांश प्रश्न Verb, Noun, Pronoun, Article, Participle, Adjective, Adverb etc. के सही प्रयोग पर आधारित होते हैं। कई बार Unenglish expressions तथा Superfluous expressions से सम्बन्धित प्रश्न भी परीक्षा में पूछे जाते हैं। छात्रों को एक बात बहुत अच्छी तरह समझ लेनी चाहिए कि अंग्रेजी में बिना व्याकरण (Grammar) की अच्छी जानकारी हुए आपको अंग्रेजी के प्रश्न-पत्र को हल (Solve) करने में और अच्छे अंक प्राप्त करने में निश्चय ही परेशानी होगी।

इस पुस्तक में English Grammar के नियमों को बहुत सरल शब्दों में हिन्दी व अंग्रेजी में समझाया गया है। नियमों पर आधारित वाक्य दिए गए हैं। जिससे नियमों का Practical प्रयोग आसानी से समझ में आ जाता है। Grammar के हर Topic से सम्बन्धित बहुत-सी Solved exercises दी गई हैं। हर Exercise, हर Topic पर आधारित Spotting the Errors की Exercises दी गई है। उनका उत्तर Explanation/Justification सहित दिया गया है। जो छात्रों को इस तरह प्रश्नों को Solve करने में नियमों को याद करने में बहुत मददगार साबित होगा। छात्रों को इस पुस्तक में दिए गए Grammar के सभी Topics से सम्बन्धित Exercises स्वयं हल करनी चाहिए तथा दिए गए Explanation/Justification को समझते हुए, ऐसे नियमों (Rules) का पुन: अध्ययन करना चाहिए। Spotting the Errors प्रश्नों के सही हल हेतु आपको लगातार अभ्यास (Practice) करने की आवश्यकता है। नियम रटकर, अंग्रेजी के प्रश्नों को हल करना सम्भव नहीं।

Exercises

01

Directions (Q. 1-10): *Read the following sentences to find error. The error will be in one part of the sentence.*

(1) Her and the (a)/other members of the group (b)/spoke to the person (c)/after their final victory. (d)/No error (e)

(2) In early India (a)/there has been very little to read (b)/except for the books sent (c)/from Britain. (d)/No error (e)

(3) Still remaining in the ancient castle (a)/are the Duke's collection of early Dutch paintings (b)/which will be (c)/donated to a museum. (d)/No error (e)

(4) Most students preferred (a)/courses in the classical arts to (b)/courses in science unless (c)/they are science majors. (d)/No error (e)

(5) When she comes (a)/to see us (b)/she usually will bring (c)/some thing with her. (d)/No error (e)
(6) Why did you (a)/not told me (b)/that the meeting (c)/was postponed ? (d)/No error (e)
(7) I did not want (a)/him to have spent (b)/all the money at (c)/the fair yesterday. (d)/No error (e)
(8) The assistant (a)/is never found (b)/wherever the manager (c)/want him. (d)/No error (e)
(9) He picked up (a)/the books (b)/and put it (c)/on the table. (d)/No error (e)
(10) They decided (a)/to talk it over (b)/at dinner. (c)/No error (d)

02

Directions (Q. 1-10) *: Read the following sentences to find error. The error will be in one part of the sentence.*

(1) I am not hungry (a)/beside (b)/I do not like eggs. (c)/No error (d)
(2) Economics are (a)/now-a-days included as a subject (b)/in all colleges. (c)/No error (d)
(3) When he (a)/had got what (b)/he wanted (c)/he has gone home. (d)/No error (e)
(4) Of the two proposals (a)/we think (b)/the second is (c)/the most attractive. (d)/No error (e)
(5) If I wrote (a)/to my father now (b)/he will receive (c)/the letter tomorrow. (d)/No error (e)
(6) This road is (a)/worst than (b)/any other road (c)/of the city. (d)/No error (E)
(7) The driver as well as (a)/the conductor are (b)/responsible for this accident. (c)/No error (d)
(8) Some peoples (a)/feel that (b) no progress is possible (c)/without discipline. (d)/No error (e)
(9) She told (a)/her mother that (b)/she is busy. (c)/No error (d)
(10) After listening to (a)/little of songs (b)/she switched off (c)/the racio. (d)/No error (e)

03

Directions (Q. 1-10) *: Read the following sentences to find error. The error will be in one part of the sentence.*

(1) We erect monuments (a)/in the memory of great leaders (b)/lest their achievements (c)/might be forgotten. (d)/No error (e)
(2) He will not escape (a)/punishment unless (b)/he does not speak (c)/the truth. (d)
(3) Being a cold day (a)/neither my friend (b)/nor I was (c)/in a mood to go to market. (d)/No error (e)
(4) Such students (a)/who have not submitted (b)/their T.C. will not be allowed (c)/to appear in the examinations. (d)/No error (e)
(5) I went to the librarian and cashier (a)/and they gave me (b)/all facilities required (c)/to complete the project. (d)/No error (e)
(6) Milk is (a)/the most perfect (b)/food in the world. (c)/No error (d)
(7) What is there (a)/which is a secret (b)/between you and me. (c)/No error (d)
(8) By the death of Rajeev Gandhi (a)/a great statesman and politician (b)/were lost. (c)/No error (d)
(9) You had better (a)/to stop (b)/your work (c)/for some time. (d)/No error (e)
(10) A severe cold (a)/prevented the president (b)/being present (c)/at the function. (d)/No error (e)

04

Directions (Q. 1-10) *: Read the following sentences to find error. The error will be in one part of the sentence.*

(1) I dislike (a)/my child (b)/watching T.V. (c)/all the time. (d)/No error (e)
(2) These people (a)/get their bath water (b)/from the river (c)/and their drink water from a well. (d)
(3) It was evident (a)/to me that there (b)/was any mistake (c)/in that account. (d)/No error (e)
(4) He does not seem (a)/to be aware (b)/as to (c)/his merits. (d)/No error (e)
(5) He declared (a)/at the top of his (b)/voice that (c)/it was not possible. (d)/No error (e)

(6) Crossing the road (a)/a car knocked (b)/him down. (c)

(7) The captain (a)/with all his team (b)/were held responsible. (c)

(8) Bangladesh has come (a)/into existence (b)/thirty years ago. (c)

(9) No sooner did (a)/she saw me (b)/than she came up (c)/and spoke to me. (d)/No error (e)

(10) No monument in the world (a)/is so beautiful (b)/as the Taj Mahal. (c)/No error (d)

05

Directions (Q. 1-10) *: Read the following sentences to find error. The error will be in one part of the sentence.*

(1) Many a man (a)/have been (b)/working under me. (c)/No error (d)

(2) I told him (a)/the story (b)/in details (c)/to make him understand it fully. (d)/No error (e)

(3) Different authorities (a)/defines (b)/intelligence in different ways. (c)/No error (d)

(4) The old man (a)/told his sons (b)/that there was no such thing (c)/like luck. (d)/No error (e)

(5) Everyone knows (a)/that the tiger (b)/is faster (c)/of all animals. (d)/No error (e)

(6) Sakshi wrote an essay (a)/so well that (b)/her teacher was (c)/very pleased with her. (d)/No error (e)

(7) The conference was (a)/attended (b)/by more than one hundred delegates(c). No error (d)

(8) This is (a)/one of the most (b)/interesting book (c)/I have ever read. (d)/No error (e)

(9) Ram was happy (a)/that Rita and her sister was going (b)/by the same train (c)/the next day. (d) No error (e)

(10) The only criteria (a)/to judge (b)/a person (c)/is to observe his behaviour. (d)/No error (e)

06

Directions (Q. 1-10) : *Read each sentence to find out whether there is an error. The error, if any, will be in one part of the sentence. The number of that part is the answer. If there is no error, then the answer is E.*

[Bank PO]

(1) No country can long endure (a)/if its foundations (b)/were not laid deep (c)/in the material prosperity. (d)/No error (e)

(2) Mahatma Gandhi did not solve (a)/all the future problems (b)/but he did solve (c)/problems of his own age. (d)/No error (e)

(3) We now look forward for (a)/some great achievements (b)/which to some extent (c)/can restore the country's prestige once again. (d)/No error (e)

(4) While Mahendra was away (a)/on a long official tour (b)/his office receive an important letter (c)/which was marked 'Urgent'. (d)/No error (e)

(5) We will pack not only (a)/the material properly (b)/but will also deliver it (c)/to your valued customers. (d)/No error (e)

(6) We cannot handle (a)/this complicated case today (b)/unless full details are not given (c)/to us by now. (d)/No error (e)

(7) According to one survey (a)/only those forests which were (b)/not under village management (c)/succumbed from fires recently. (d)/No error (e)

(8) Our school is making (a)/every possible effort (b)/to provide best facilities (c)/and personal attention for each child. (d)/No error (e)

(9) We have done everything (a)/that could be done (b)/to avert the storm (c)/which is now coming on. (d)/No error (e)

(10) Jayesh loved his Guru immensely (a)/and gave him fullest loyalty, (b)/yet he had his own (c)/ independent way of thinking. (d)/No error (e)

07

Directions (Q. 1-10) : *Read each sentence to find out whether there is any error in it. The error, if any, will be in one part of the sentence. The number of that part is the answer. It there is no error, then the answer is E.*

[Bank PO, RRB Trivendrum]

(1) This laboratory of physicists is (a)/not only equipped with (b)/all state-of-the-art instruments (c)/but also with outstanding physicists. (d)/No error (e)

(2) No method of making other (a)/ people agree to (b)/your view point is (c)/as effective as this method. (d)/No error (e)

(3) I was pretty sure that (a)/he would support me (b)/for changing the age-old (c)/and static structure of our organization.(d)

(4) I did not like his (a)/comments on my paper (b)/but I had no alternative (c)/as I had agreed to keep quiet. (d)/No error (e)

(5) The report is candid in admitting (a)/that the investment by the government (b)/in health and family planning (c)/have eroded considerably. (d)/No error (e)

(6) He tried as he could (a)/,but Naveen did not (b)/succeed in getting (c)/his car to start up. (d)/No error (e)

(7) Foolishly Madhu threw (a)/some water on the electric heater (b)/when it catches fire and (c)/she got a shock. (d)/No error (e)

(8) Rajesh was expecting (a)/a telegram from his uncle (b)/which would inform (c)/him whether he went or not. (d)/No error (e)

(9) Either of the plans (a)/suits him and therefore (b)/he decided not to (c)/go out yesterday. (d)/No error (e)

(10) Inspite of the rumors (a) of an impending takeover (b)/by the government, (c)/Ramlal bought more shares of that company. (d)/No error (e)

08

Directions (Q. 1-10) *: Read each sentence to find out whether there is any grammatical or idiomatic error in it.*

[TC, RRB Kolkata]

(1) Our housing society comprises (a)/six block and thirty flats (b)/in an area of (c)/about thousand square meters. (d)/No error (e)

(2) They took to (a)/reading 'Times' (b)/for better knowledge (c)/of the facts. (d)/No error (e)

(3) As I was to reach early (a)/I preferred train (b)/instead of (c)/bus. (d)/No error (e)

(4) He did not go (a)/to the city on foot (b)/he went there (c)/by the train. (d)/No error (e)

(5) One of the most (a)/widely spread (b)/bad habit (c)/is the use of tobacco. (d)/No error (e)

(6) Myself and Ramanujam (a)/will take care of (b)/the function (c)/on Saturday. (d)/No error (e)

(7) All the doctors (a)/were puzzled on the (b)/strange symptoms (c)/reported by the patient. (d)/No error (e)

(8) India is in no way (a)/inferior than the USA (b)/in the fertility of soil (c)/and richness of resources. (d)/No error (e)

(9) The visitors (a)/complained at (b)/the poor accommodation (c)/they were given. (d)/No error (e)

(10) Amit's habit of (a)/delaying his work (b)/put his colleagues (c)/to a lot of trouble. (d)/No error (e)

09

Directions (Q. 1 -10) *: One part of following sentences has an error, point out the portion carrying error in the answer sheet. It case no error is there mention accordingly.* **[RRB Patna, Mumbai, ASM]**

(1) I have been to a few of his lectures (a)/but understood little of (b)/what he has said. (c)/No error (d)

(2) Not only the bandits robbed (a)/the traveller of his purse (b)/but also wounded him grievously. (c)/No error (d)

(3) The old woman has had the best medical facilities available (a)/but she will not be cured (b)/unless she does not have a strong desire to live. (c)/No error (d)

(4) Frozen foods are so popular today (a)/that many people wonder (b)/how they ever lived without them. (c)/No error (d)

(5) We should never be (a)/cent per cent sure of our success (b)/in any walk of our life. (c)/No error (d)

(6) Smith including (a)/all the members of his family (b)/goes to the church every Sunday. (c)/No error (d)

(7) The students of now-a-days (a)/hesitate to talk (b)/to their teachers. (c)/No error (d)

(8) If you would have (a)/practised regularly (b)/you would have won the match. (c)/No error (d)

(9) Kanchenjungha is one of the (a)/beautiful peak (b)/of the (c)/Himalayan range. (d)/No error (e)

(10) He is one of the (a)/most intelligent (b)/student (c)/I have ever taught. (d)/No error (e)

10

Directions (Q. 1-10) *: Read each sentence to find out whether there is any error in it. The error, if any, will be in one part of the sentence. The number of that part is the answer. If there is no error, then the answer is E.*

[RRB, Secunderabad, ASM/TC]

(1) Radha with (a)/her brothers (b)/and sisters (c)/are present here. (d)/No error (e)

(2) Men (a)/proposes (b)/but God (c)/disposes. (d)/No error (e)

(3) He gets (a)/up (b)/early at (c)/the morning. (d)/No error (e)

(4) The house (a)/is built (b)/in an (c)/attractive manner. (d)/No error (e)

(5) She worn (a)/a necklace (b)/studded (c)/with diamonds. (d)/No error (e)

(6) None (a)/of these (b)/students (c)/was there. (d)/No error (e)

(7) He (a)/was not (b)/blind (c)/from birth. (d)/No error (e)

(8) I said (a)/that a interesting (b)/face could (c)/also be pretty. (d)/No error (e)

(9) He love (a)/his father (b)/and his father (c)/also loved him. (d)/No error (e)

(10) Milking used (a)/to be a task (b)/or a duty cost (c)/on him. (d)/No error (e)

11

Directions (Q. 1-10) *: Read each sentence to find out whether there is any error in it. The error, if any, will be in one part of the sentence. The number of that part is the answer. If there is no error, then the answer is E.*

(1) The doctor (a)/did not (b)/ask Mohan (c)/the time. (d)/No error (e)

(2) How do (a)/Vinoba appeal (b)/to the (c)/landlords? (d)/No error (e)

(3) Bats are (a)/sometime seen (b)/ in our (c)/ houses. (d)/No error (e)

(4) I am glad (a)/Rex never saw (b)/a trained (c)/police dog jump. (d)/No error (e)

(5) His (a)/son met (b)/him (c)/on the door. (d)/No error (e)

(6) The plane (a)/was to (b)/take of (c)/at 6 a.m. (d)/No error (e)

(7) This is (a)/our attitudes (b)/towards (c)/Ahimsa and Truth. (d)/No error (e)

(8) I caught him (a)/from the hand (b)/and began (c)/to plead. (d)/No error (e)

(9) We ought (a)/not to (b)/speak ill (c)/for others. (d)/No error (e)

(10) Radha works (a)/harder than (b)/I did (c)/her age. (d)/No error (e)

12

Directions (Q. 1-10) *: Read each sentence to find out whether there is any error in it . The error, if any, will be in one part of the sentence. The number of that part is the answer. It there is no error, then the answer is E.*

(1) Krishna is (a)/the taller (b)/boy (c)/in the class. (d)/No error (e)

(2) Bhima was (a)/the man (b)/who all (c)/the Indians loved. (d)/No error (e)

(3) I can (a)/neither read (b)/or speak (c)/Hindi. (d)/No error (e)

(4) I have been (a)/suffering from (b)/fever since (c)/three days. (d)/No error (e)

(5) The committee (a)/is divided (b)/over (c)/this issue. (d)/No error (e)

(6) The Planning Commission expects (a)/the Gross Domestic Product to (b)/grow by a satisfactory (c)/rate during the year. (d)/No error (e)

(7) The language used for writing text books (a)/differs from other forms of writing (b)/in its preference on (c)/simplicity over style. (d)/No error (e)

(8) One of the basics of good writing (a)/is to have a (b)/clear understanding of the target audience (c)/and its requirements. (d)/No error (e)

(9) This is an (a)/excellent site for (b)/a stadium which we (c)/should like to acquire. (d)/No error (e)

(10) If you absent (a)/from college, your (b)/name is likely to be (c)/struck off the rolls. (d)/No error (e)

13

Directions (Q. 1-10) *: There is a mistake in each of the following sentences. Find out the part in which the mistake occurs.* **[RRB, Bhubaneshwar, ASM]**

(1) The man (a)/is (b)/a (c)/social animal. (d)

(2) Twenty five kilometers (a)/from Bhubaneshwar to Cuttack (b)/are (c)/a long distance. (d)

(3) The institute (a)/imparts training (b)/in (c)/the French. (d)

(4) Looking forward (a)/to meet (b)/you (c)/soon. (d)

(5) Pass on (a)/the salt, (b)/please, (c)/do you ? (d)

(6) He is (a)/a mason (b)/who (c)/built my house. (d)

(7) I cannot (a)/make from (b)/what you are saying (c)/about him. (d)

(8) What (a)/you will think (b)/if school boys (c)/make fun of you ? (d)

(9) The minister's speech (a)/has been reported (b)/to the newspaper. (c)/No error (d)

(10) No sooner (a)/we reached there (b)/than it started raining. (c)

14

Directions (Q. 1-10) *: The following sentences contain errors in grammer, usage, diction (choice of words) and idiom. Some sentences may be correct. No sentence has more than one error. Select the numbered part that according to you contains the error. Its number is the answer.* **[RRB, Mumbai]**

(1) Being a very cold day (a)/I would (b)/not go out for (c)/a morning walk. (d)

(2) Such an act of cruelty (a)/had never (b)/be commited (c)/before. (d)

(3) If you will/insist (a)upon (b)/challenging me, (c)/I will fight it out alone. (d)

(4) Fifty years (a)/have passed (b)/since (c)/Subhash Chandra Bose had died. (d)

(5) A good house (a)/and a good bank (b)/account is what (c)/he wants. (d)

(6) Of all the (a)/other teachers the (b)/students respected the history (c)/teacher the most. (d)

(7) He is one of those persons (a)/who listen (b)/to all advice but keep/his (c) own counsel. (d)

(8) No one but (a)/he knew (b)/who was (c)/setting the question paper. (d)/No error (e)

(9) A box (a)/of apples are (b)/in (c)/the car. (d)

(10) The principal threatened to (a)/inform to (b)/his father about (c)/his misdeeds. (d)

15

Directions (Q. 1-10) *: Read each sentence to find out whether there is any error in it . The error, if any , will be in one part of the sentence. The number of that part is the answer. If there is no error, the answer is E.*

[Stenographers Allahabad (U.P.)]

(1) Sharad was entrusted with (a)/the task of co-ordination yesterday (b)/but due to certain difficulties (c)/he does not do it. (d)/No error (e)

(2) One should make (a)/his best efforts if (b)/one wishes to achieve (c)/success in this organization. (d)/No error (e)

(3) Having deprived from their (a)/homes in the recent earthquake (b) they had no other option but (c)/to take shelter in a school. (d)/No error (e)

(4) The technician reminded (a)/them to have a (b)/throughly cleaning of the (c)/machine after use. (d)/No error (e)

(5) The villager told (a)/us where was the (b)/temple and even led (c)/us to the spot. (d)/No error (e)

(6) The person who (a)/they are referring (b)/to is none other (c)/than my close friend. (d)/No error (e)

(7) Mahesh was kind enough (a)/to inform us about the (b)/conspiracy but declined to (c)/name the person behind it. (d)/No error (e)

(8) He told the policeman (a)/that he would rather (b)/starve to stealing to get (c)/what he had been aspiring for. (d)/No error (e)

(9) In spite of the workload yesterday (a)/Nitin manages to play (b)/it cool and continued (c)/with his work as usual. (d)/No error (e)

(10) The demand of the workers' (a)/union that the dismissed (b)/employee to reinstated, has (c), been accepted by the management. (d)/No error (e)

16

Directions (Q. 1-10) : *(i) In this section a number of sentences are given. The sentences are divided in three separate parts and each one is labelled (A), (B), (C). Read each sentence to find out whether there is an error in any part. No sentence has more than one error. When you find an error in any one of the parts [(A), (B) or (C)] indicate your response. You may feel that there is no error in a sentence. In that case letter (D) will signify a 'No error' response. (ii)You are to indicate only one response for each item. (If you indicate more than one response, your answer will be considered wrong.) Error may be in grammar, word usage or idioms. There may be a word missing or there may be a word which should be removed. (iii) You are not required to correct the error. You are required only to indicate your response.*

[CDS 1998]

(1) Thinking that he has finally found (a)/someone with similar interests, (b)/the scholar tried to strike up a conversation. (c)/ No error (d)

(2) Earlier this year, (a)/Constantan had entered the news via a video-tapted interview (b)/telecasted by commercial television channel. (c)/No error (d)

(3) If you permit me to speak the truth, (a), I shall say without hesitation (b)/that you have done a mistake. (c)/No error (d)

(4) My friend is so rich that (a)/he is having six houses in Mumbai (b)/and four in Pune. (c)/No error (d)

(5) He asked me (a)/if I am ill (b)/and I answered that I was not. (c)/No error (d)

(6) He lost his new knife (a)/shortly after (b)/he bought it. (c)/No error (d)

(7) The ultimate problem of Physics (a)/is to reduce matter by analysis (b)/to its lowest condition or divisibility. (c)/No error (d)

(8) By the time (a)/she finished typing (b)/it was not hardly ten. (c)/No error (d)

(9) He like (a)/his companions (b) were deceived. (c)/No error (d)

(10) He told me that you had left the school (a)/a year ago (b)/and seeking for a job. (c)/No error (d)

17

Directions (Q. 1-10) : *(i) In this section, a number of sentences are given. The sentences are underlined in three separate parts and each one is labelled as (A), (B) and (C). Read each sentence to find out whether there is an error in any part. No sentence has more than one error. When you find an error in any one of the given parts 9 (A), (B) or (C)] indicate your response. You may feel that there is no error in a sentence. In that case letter (D) will signify a 'No error' response. (ii) You are to indicate only one response for each item. (If you indicate more than one response, your answer will be considered wrong.) Errors may be in grammar, word usage or idioms. There may be a word missing or there may be a word which should be removed. (iii) You are not required to correct the error. You are required only to indicate your response.*

(1) As I prefer coffee than tea (a)/my friends always take the trouble (b)/to get a cup of coffee, whenever I visit them. (c)/ No error (d)

(2) There has been (a)/little change in the patient's condition (b)/since he was moved to the special ward. (c)/No error. (d)

(3) The king was perturbed (a)/to found evidence (b)/against his own queen. (c)/No error (d)

(4) They begged her (a)/not to go but she was determined (b)/ and left the castle. (c) /No error (d)

(5) They cook meal, (a)/lay the table, (b)/clean the house and iron the clothes. (c)/No error (d)

(6) No sooner did (a)/the doctor enter the house (b)/then the patient died. (c)/No error (d)

(7) The drawing room was a mess (a)/with all the furnitures (b)/scattered in total disarray. (c)/No error (d)

(8) The gap between what he preaches (a)/and what he practises is too wide (b)/to be accepted by anyone. (c)/ No error (d)

(9) While flying over India (a)/we had glimpses of the two sources of her culture (b)/Ganges and Himalayas. (c)/No error (d)

(10) This picture (a)/is the best (b)/of the two. (c)/No error (d)

18

Directions (Q. 1-10) : *In this section, a number of sentences are given. These sentences are marked in three parts indicated by the letters (A), (B), and (C). Read each sentence to find out whether there is an error in any part of it. No sentence has more than one error. When you find an error in any one of the parts (A), (B) or (C), select that part as your answer. You may feel that there is no error in a sentence. In that case letter (D) will signify a 'No error' response. Errors may be in grammar, word usage or idioms. There may be a word missing or there may be a word which should be removed.*

(1) Finishing the work (a)/he was allowed rest (b)/for half an hour. (c)/ No error (d)

(2) The pirates, who had hidden the treasure on the island, (a)/went back again (b)/because they thought they can now remove it with safety. (c)/No error (d)

(3) In those early days (a)/the West paid lip-service (b)/to United Nations. (c)/ No error (d)

(4) Ten Shillings (a)/was charged (b)/by him for the service. (c)/No error (d)

(5) To an amusing degree (a)/he was addicted to read the jokes in punch aloud (b)/even when he was alone. (c)/No error (d)

(6) Why not stop the first man you meet next and ask, (a)/"could you tell me (b)/what the time is?" (c)/No error (d)

(7) The invention of the internal combustion engine (a)/is considered to be (b)/a most unique development. (c)/No error (d)

(8) Put off (a)/the fire (b)/quickly. (c)/No error (d)

(9) A fight (a)/took place (b)/on the board of the ship. (c)/No error (d)

(10) Hardly the rains started (a)/when a child in the corner (b)/sent out a piercing wail. (c)/No error (d)

19

Directions (Q. 1-10) : *(i) In this section, a number of sentences are given. The sentences are in three separate parts and each one is labelled (A), (B), (C). Read each sentence to find out whether there is an error in any of these part. No sentence has more than one error. When you find an error in any one of these parts choose that part as your response. You may feel that there is no error in a sentence, in that case choose (D) as your response. Errors may be in grammar, word usage of idioms. There may be a word missing or a word which should be removed.*

(1) Don't think you can say unpleasant things (a)/about someone behind his back (b)/and not found out. (c) /No error (d)

(2) The Americans speak (a)/different from us (b)/ though our grammar is the same. (c)/No error (d)

(3) This is an instance (a)/of the blind (b)/leading the blinds. (c)/No error (d)

(4) He took to drink (a)/to lessen (b)/his mental worries. (c)/No error (d)

(5) My father could lead (a)/a full and happy life (b)/ without spending lot of money. (c)/No error (d)

(6) All India Radio broadcasted (a)/a very good programme (b)/this morning. (c)/No error (d)

(7) There were so much cattle (a)/on the road that (b)/it was difficult to drive safely. (c)/No error (d)

(8) What, could have provoked him to behave (a)/in such a rude manner (b)/at dinner last night? (c)/No error (d)

(9) They were rich zamindars in the thirties (a)/but now they have fallen on the evil days (b)/and have lost much of their property. (c)/No error (d)

(10) The foreign ambassador was (a)/both noted for his charming manners (b)/as well as his wide knowledge of languages. (c)/No error. (d)

20

Directions (Q. 1-10) : *(i) In this section, a number of sentences are given. The sentences are divided in three separate parts and each one is labelled (A), (B), (C). Read each sentence to find out whether there is an error in any part. No sentence has more than one error. When you find an error in any one of the given parts [(A), (B) or (C)] indicate your response according. You may feel that there is no error in a sentence. In that case letter (D) will signify a 'No error' response. (ii) You are to indicate only one response for each item. (If you indicate more than one response, your answer will be considered wrong. Errors may be in grammar, word usage or idioms. There may be a word missing or there may be a word which should be removed. (iii) You are not required to correct the error. You are required only to indicate your response.*

(1) The news of the disturbance (a)/was braodcasted (b)/the same evening. (c)/ No error (d)

(2) Everyone visiting the house asked the young girl (a)/how could she kill the wolf (b)/single handed and without a weapon. (c)/No error (d).

(3) While walking slowly in the park (a)/on a quiet summer afternoon (b)/a mad dog suddenly attacked him from behind. (c)/No error (d)

(4) Since the attachment of air-conditioned sleeping cars to all important trains. (a)/travelling became very pleasant (b)/especially during the summer season. (c)/No error (d)

(5) It is the newspapers (a)/that exposes us to the widest range (b)/of human experiences and behaviour. (c)/No error (d)

(6) The method suggested in the lecture (a)/enables a student to learn more quickly (b)/and to have remembered for a longer period of time. (c)/No error (d)

(7) Last month we celebrated (a)/the wedding of our sister for whom (b)/we have been looking for suitable alliance for three years. (c)/No error (d)

(8) A leading textile manufacturer, one of the fastest growing in the industry. (a)/is looking for a marketing manager (b)/to look up the marketing network of the company. (c)/No error (d)

(9) There was very heavy rain last night. (a)/and the rivers have over flown their banks. (b)/ causing severe hardship to the people living by them. (c)/No error (d)

(10) The government warned the shopkeepers (a)/that if they persist in charging unfair prices (b)/ their licences would be cancelled. (c)/No error (d)

21

Directions (Q. 1-10) *: Read each sentence to find out whether there is any error in it. The error, if any will be in one part of the sentence. The number of that part is the answer. If there is no error, the answer is (E) (Ignore the errors of punctuation, if any.)*

(1) Kamlesh asked the dealer (a)/what was the price (b)/of that bicycle and whether (c)/it is really made in Germany ? (d)/No error (e)

(2) While luminaries of the dance world (a)/has no dearth of opportunities to display their art, (b)/upcoming dancers suffer from (c)/an unfortunate lack of exposure. (d)/No error (e)

(3) Scarcely had I (a)/finished washing the car (b)/than the master came (c)/and asked me to clean the floor of the house. (d)/No error (e)

(4) The job is much worse than I expected (a)/if I would have realised (b)/how awful it was going to be (C)/I would not have accepted it.(d)/No error (e)

(5) I am trying to finish (a)/this letter for the last one hour (b)/I wish you would (c)/go away or stop disturbing me. (d)/No error (e)

(6) I offered him part-time work (a)/ but he turned it over (b)/saying that he would (c)/rather wait for a full-time job. (d)/No error (e)

(7) He fixed a metal ladder (a)/for the wall below his window (b)/so as to be able to (c)/escape if there was a fire. (d)/No error (e)

(8) The foremost criteria of selection we adopted (a)/were the number of years of training (b)/a dancer had received (c)/under a particular guru. (d)/No error (e)

(9) He refused to disclose to his friends (a)/whether he will leave (b)/for England immediately (c)/after finishing his studies. (d)/No error (e)

(10) Despite for her protests (a)/I decided (b)/to buy the saree (c)/which she did not like. (d)/No error (e)

22

Directions (Q. 1-10) : *Read each sentence to find out whether there is any grammatical or idiomatic error in it . The error, if any, will be in one part of the sentence. The number of that part is the answer. If there is no error, the answer is (E). (Ignore the errors of punctuation, if any.)*

(1) The principle of equal justice (a)/for all is one of (b)/the corner stones of our (c)/democratic way of life. (d)/No error (e)

(2) The trust has succeeded (a)/admirably in raising (b)/money for (c)/future programmes. (d)/No error (E)

(3) Honesty, integrity and being intelligent (a)/are the qualities which (b)/we look for when (c)/ we interview applicants. (d)/No error (e)

(4) In order to save petrol, (a)/motorists must have to (b)/be very cautious (c)/while driving along the highways. (d)/No error (e)

(5) If the by-stander had not been (a)/familiar with first-aid techniques,(b)/the driver which had met (c)/with the accident would have died. (d)/No error (e)

(6) Not one of the children (a)/has ever sang (b)/on any occasion (c)/in public before. (d)/No error (e)

(7) Neither the earthquake (a)/nor the subsequent fire (b)/was able to dampen (c)/the spirit of the residents. (d)/No error (e)

(8) The customer scarcely had (a)/enough money to pay (b)/to the cashier (c)/at the cash counter. (d)/No error (e)

(9) The apparently obvious solutions (a)/to most of his problems (b)/were over look by (c)/many of his friends. (d)/No error (e)

(10) By arresting the local criminals (a)/and encouraging good people (b)/we can end (c)/hostilities of that area. (d)/No error (e)

23

Directions (Q. 1-10) : *In this section ten sentences are given. Each sentence has three parts, indicated by (A) ,(B) and (C). Read each sentence to find out whether there is an error. If you find an error in any one of the parts, [(A), (B) or (C)]. Indicate your response by blackening the letter related to that part in the answer sheet provided. If a sentence has no error, indicate this by blackening (D) , which stands for 'No error'. Errors may be in grammar, appropriate word usage or idioms.* **[NDA 1998]**

(1) The flicker of light from the gas lamps (a)/indicated that the night (b)/was barely passed. (c)/ No error (d)

(2) India was committed to keep maintaining peace (a)/and solving all outstanding problems (b)/ with her neighbours through dialogue. (c)/No error (d)

(3) Being the second Saturday of the month, (a)/he got up late and spent the whole day at home, (b)/doing his share of the household chores. (c)/No error (d)

(4) As economic restructuring in Central and Eastern Europe progresses, (a)/an estimated 15 million people may be out of work (b)/by the end of the year. (c)/No error (d)

(5) Such of those who have not paid the fees, (a)/the circular says, (b)/will not be permitted to attend classes. (c)/No error (d)

(6) There is a good British Library in the city (a)/and anyone interested in books (b)/can avail of the facility. (c)/No error (d)

(7) Those who are excessively careful (a)/for their health (b)/are not generally healthy. (c)/ No error (d)

(8) Once we have agreed on (a)/the fundamentals, there will hardly be (b)/anything left to discuss about. (c)/No error (d)

(9) I did ask him (a)/where you were (b)/but he didn't tell me. (c)/No error (d)

(10) I will wait for you (a)/at the office (b)/till you will finish your work. (c)/No error (d)

24

Directions (Q. 1-10) *: Read each sentence to find out whether there is any grammatical or idiomatic error in it. The error, if any, will be in one part of the sentence. The number of that part is the answer. If there is no error, then the ansser is E. (Ignore the errors of punctuation, if any.)*

(1) We had swam (a)/across the river (b)/before (c)/the sunsets. (d)/No error (e) **[SBI PO]**

(2) Madhuri is (a)/more prettier (b)/than her (c)/ younger sister. (d)/No error (e) **[SBI PO]**

(3) A cell (a)/is the smallest (b)/identifiable unit of life and cannot be (c)/seen with a naked eye. (d)/No error (e) **[IIT Kharagpur]**

(4) If a student needs advices about (a)/careers, (b)/he or she should consult (c)/the Career officer. (d)/No error (e) **[IIT Kharagpur]**

(5) Had they have been in (a)/my condition, (b)/they would have felt (c)/miserable and thought of committing suicide. (d)/No error (e) **[RRB, Kolkata]**

(6) The Secretary of the worker's union (a)/remarked that the present government is so selfish (b)/that it cared very little (c)/about solving anyone else's problem. (d)/No error (e) **[RRB, Kolkata]**

(7) He don't know (a)/the difference between (b)/a ship and a submarine. (c)/No error (d) **[SSC Clerical]**

(8) Yesterday I met an old friend (a)/when I am going (b)/to the market. (c)/No error (d) **[SSC Clerical]**

(9) Cattles (a)/were grazing (b)/in the meadows (c)/near our farm. (d)/No error (e) **[BSRB Clerical]**

(10) You are really (a)/senior than (b)/me (c)/in age. (d)/No error (e) **[BSRB Clerical]**

25

Directions (Q. 1-10) *: Read each sentence to find out whether there is any grammatical or idiomatic error in it . The error, if any, will be in one part of the sentence. The number of that part is the answer. It there is no error, then the ansser is E. (Ignore the errors of punctuation, if any.)*

(1) Make haste (a)/lest (b)/you should not miss (c)/the train. (d)/No error (e) **[BSRB Clerical]**

(2) Many of us (a)/do not know (b)/to swim (c)/at all. (d)/No error (e) **[BSRB Clerical]**

(3) His car is (a)/more bigger than (b)/that of any of us. (c)/No error (d) **[SSC Clerk Grade]**

(4) One of my uncles (a)/is a doctor / in America. (c)/No error (d) **[SSC Clerk Grade]**

(5) This machine looks (a)/good but is very (b)/badly designed (c)/and doesn't work good. (d)/No error (e) **[IIT Kharagpur]**

(6) He is well-known for both (a)/his kindness (b)/as well as (c)/his understanding. (d)/No error (e) **[IIT Kharagpur]**

(7) Ramu closely (a)/resembles to his father (b)/not only in physical features. (c)/but also in habits. (d)/No error (e) **[SBI PO]**

(8) After he had read the two first chapters (a)/of the novel (b)/he felt like reading (c)/the book at one sitting. (d)/No error (e) **[SBI PO]**

(9) India is (a)/one of the leading (b)/film producing country (c)/in the world. (d)/No error (e) **[CSRB Patna]**

(10) Hardly had (a)/I left the house (b)/then it began (c)/to rain. (d)/No error (e) **[CSRB Patna]**

26

Directions (Q. 1-10) *: Read each sentence to find out whether there is any grammatical or idiomatic error in it . The error, if any, will be in one part of the sentence. The number of that part is the answer. If there is no error, the answer is (E). (Ignore the errors of punctuation, if any)*

(1) He told me (a)/that he wrote a letter (b)/to his superior (c)/for a certain reason. (d)/No error (e) **[BSRB Clerical Bhopal]**

(2) The teacher told the boys (a)/that one (b)/ought to work hard (c)/to earn one living (d)/No error. (e) **[BSRB Clerical Bhopal]**

(3) The obstacles to which (a)/Gandhiji had to surmount (b)/were mostly (c) on the moral and spiritual grounds (d)/No error (e) **[BSRB Lucknow]**

(4) Unless you do not (a)/take care of your health (b)/you will continue (c)/to suffer (d)/No error (e) **[BSRB Lucknow]**

(5) After Ravi (a)/read the (b)/magazines, and newspapers and watched the TV programme, he decided (c)/to go out and meet some old friends. (d)/No error (e) **[RRB Kolkata]**

(6) Everyone agrees that (a)/the Ganga is the holiest (b)/of all other rivers (c)/of India (d)/No error (e) **[BSRB Bhopal Clerical]**

(7) The issues are (a)/complex and (b)/has been obscured (c)/by other factors. (d)/No error (e) **[CSRB Patna]**

(8) The bus was (a)/hired by (b)/the ladies (c)/for its picnic. (d)/No error (e) **[CSRB Patna]**

(9) If (a)/it snowed tomorrow (b)/we'll go (c)/skating. (d)/No error (e) **[SBI PO]**

(10) A quarrel arose between the five members (a)/and for a time (b)/it appeared as if the party (c)/had been heading for a split. (d)/No error (e) **[SBI PO]**

27

Directions (Q. 1-10) : *Read each sentence to find out whether there is any grammatical or idiomatic error in it . The error, if any, will be in one part of the sentence. The number of that part is the answer. If there is no error, the answer is (E). (Ignore the errors of punctuation, if any.)*

(1) We had swam (a)/across the river (b)/before (c)/the sun sets. (d)/No error (e) **[SBI PO]**

(2) Madhuri is (a)/more prettier (b)/than her (c)/younger sister. (d)/No error (e) **[SBI PO]**

(3) Everyone of (a)/the staff members present here (b)/has given a day's pay (c)/as their contribution to the fund. (d)/ No error (e) **[CSRB Patna]**

(4) Found guilty (a)/on murder (b)/the accused was (c)/sentenced to death. (d)/No error (e) **[CSRB Patna]**

(5) The criminal was (a)/sentenced to death (b)/and was hung for his crime. (c)/No error (d) **[SSC Clerical]**

(6) He said that (a)/he will help me (b)/to secure a decent job. (c)/No error (d) **[SSC Clerical]**

(7) The recent symposium on censorship (a)/indicated that to refrain with saying or writing (b)/something, others might object, (c)/to, is a form of self-censorship. (d)/No error (e) **[RRB Kolkata]**

(8) The Indian way (a)/of thinking is superior (b)/to most of the (c)/countries of the world. (d)/No error (e) **[RRB Kolkata]**

(9) I am certain that none (a)/of these two books (b)/is useful to the (c)/students of the 8th standard. (d)/No error (e) **[BSRB Lucknow]**

(10) The lawyer asked me (a)/where had I (b)/kept clothes (c)/before taking a dip in the river. (D)/No error (e) **[BSRB Lucknow]**

28

Directions (Q.1-10) : *Read each sentence to find out whether there is any grammatical or idiomatic error in it . The error, if any, will be in one part of the sentence. The number of that part is the answer. It there is no error, then the ansser is E. (Ignore the errors of punctuation, if any.)*

(1) Like most young (a)/women living at homes, I can't really (b)/talk about my ideas or what I really feel, to my parents. (c)/No error (d)

(2) The minister conferred /(a) with his colleagues (b)/and agreed that the new projects on education (c)/should be sanctioned immediately. (d)/No error (e) **[RRB Kolkata]**

(3) Sunil is (a)/a best student (b)/in our class (c)/at present. (d)/No error (e) **[CSRB Patna]**

(4) It is in 1929 (a)/that we first (b)/flew to (c)/the United States. (d)/No error (e) **[CSRB Patna]**

(5) Being a (a)/fine day we went out (b)/for picnic (c)/at Okhla. (d)/No error (e) **[BSRB Clerical]**

(6) Many a man (a)/have been (b)/working (c)/under me. (d)/No error (e) **[BSRB Clerical]**

(7) Please explain to me (a)/how is a digital computer (b)/different from (c)/an analog computer. (d)/No error (e) **[IIT Kharagpur]**

(8) I'll work for you (a)/as long as (b)/you'll pay (c)/well. (d)/No error (e) **[IIT Kharagpur]**

(9) Had you informed me earlier (a)/I would have (b)/certainly purchase (c)/the car for you. (d)/No error (e) **[BSRB Lucknow]**

(10) It was seven o'clock (a)/in the evening that (b)/the train steamed (c)/into the station. (d)/No error (e) **[CSRB Patna]**

29

Directions (Q. 1-10) : *Read each sentence to find out whether there is any grammatical or idiomatic error in it . The error, if any, will be in one part of the sentence. The number of that part is the answer. If there is no error, the answer is (E). (Ignore the errors of punctuation, if any.)*

(1) Even if he had been driving more slowly (a)/it will have been quite impossible (b)/to avoid the accident. (c)/No error (d) **[Investigators]**

(2) Would you please (a)/stop from smoking (b)/while the ceremony (c) is in progress. (d)/No error (e) **[Investigators]**

(3) When I offered him to help (a)/which he needed, (b)/he persisted in refusing it (c)/so I left him to his fate. (d)/No error (e) **[BSRB Clerical Bhopal]**

(4) He reminded me (a)/that he has (b)/often told me not to (c)/play with fire. (d)/No Error (e) **[BSRB Clerical Bhopal]**

(5) Our country need (a)/a number of (b)/self sacrificing and (c)/devoted political leaders. (d)/No error (e) **[CSRB Patna]**

(6) Instead of (a)/his busy and hard life (b)/he still retains (c)/freshness and robustness. (d)/No error (e) **[CSRB Patna]**

(7) The smuggler yielded (a)/for the tempatation (b)/and fell into (c)/the police trap. (d)/No error (e) **[CSRB Patna]**

(8) The girl said (a)/that she preferred (b)/the blue gown (c)/than the black one. (d)/No error (e) **[CSRB Patna]**

(9) Of the two principles (a)/he put forward, the last one (b)/was the more (c)/difficult to understand. (d)/No error (e) **[IIT Kharagpur]**

(10) All of us (a)/surprised (b)/to see an old man of (c)/sixty taking part in the Marathon held last month. (d)/No error (e) **[IIT Kharagpur]**

30

Directions (Q. 1-10) : *Read each sentence to find out whether there is any grammatical or idiomatic error in it . The error, if any, will be in one part of the sentence. The number of that part is the answer. It there is no error, then the answer is E. (Ignore the errors of punctuation, if any.)*

(1) The new railway line will greatly improve (a)/transport and communication (b)/in eastern part of the country (c)/No error (d) **[SSC Clerical]**

(2) The receptionist asked me (a)/who do I want (b)/to meet in the office. (c)/No error (d) **[SSC Clerical]**

(3) At last (a)/he was married (b)/with a poor girl (c)/No error (d) **[BSRB Clerical]**

(4) She said (a)/that she will help me (b)/whenever I was in difficulty. (c)/No error (d) **[BSRB Clerical]**

(5) Neither Rakesh (a)/nor I are leaving (b)/for Hyderabad. (c)/No error (d) **[SBI PO]**

(6) Death (a)/is preferable (b)/than life. (c)/No error (d) **[SBI PO]**

(7) We were still talking (a)/about what we should do (b)/when we heard (c)/the children shouting. (d)/No error (e) **[BSRB Clerical Bhopal]**

(8) As soon as the peon rings (a)/the first bell (b)/then all the students assemble (c)/on the playground for prayer. (d)/No error (e) **[BSRB Clerical Bhopal]**

(9) Have you (a)/turned detective (b)/that you keep your eye (c)/on me like this ? (d)/No error (e) **[BSRB Clerical Bhopal]**

(10) She asked him (a)/what it was that made him (b)/so much stronger and braver (c)/than any man. (d)/No error (e) **[BSRB Clerical Bhopal]**

31

Directions (Q. 1-9) *: Read each sentence to find out whether there is any grammatical or idiomatic error in it. The error, if any, will be in one part of the sentence. The number of that part is the answer. If there is no error, the answer is (E). (Ignore the errors of punctuation, if any.)*

(1) Being that he (a)/is interested in getting himself examined (b)/by a heart specialist (c)/we must try our best to take him to a reputed doctor. (d)/No error (e) **[RRB Kolkata]**

(2) The college is (a)/hoding special lectures for their students (b)/and teachers so that they (c)/may get enlightened about the economic problems (d)/No error (e) **[RRB Kolkata]**

(3) A cell (a)/is the smallest (b)/identifiable unit of life and cannot be (c)/seen with a naked eye. (d)/No error (e) **[IIT Kharagpur]**

(4) If a student needs advices about (a)/carreers, (b)/he or she should consult (c)/the Career officer. (d)/No error (e) **[IIT Kharagpur]**

(5) Many a man (a)/have been (b)/working (c)/ under me. (d)/No error (e) **[BSRB Clerical]**

(6) To our surprise (a)/we noticed that (b)/every soldier and every sailor (c)/was in his place (d)/No error (e) **[BSRB Lucknow]**

(7) Neither he nor I (a)/was able to (b)/finish the task within (c)/the time limit. (d)/No error (e) **[BSRB Lucknow]**

(8) No sooner we entered (a)/than he got up (b)/and left the room. (c)/No error (d) **[SSC Clerical]**

(9) The villagers fled away their houses (a)/when they saw (b)/the flood water rising. (c)/No error (d) **[SSC Clerical]**

32

Directions (Q. 1-10) *Read each sentence to find out whether there is any grammatical or idiomatic error in it. The error, if any, will be in one part of the sentence. The number of that part is the answer. If there is no error, the answer is (E). (Ignore the errors of punctuation, if any.)*

(1) I know (a)/he is having (b)/a lot of books (c)/on how to improve English. (d)/No error (e) **[IIT Kharagpur]**

(2) The theory of relativity is (a)/so complicated (b)/as we cannot describe (c)/it in a few sentences. (d)/No error (e) **[IIT Kharagpur]**

(3) After the brief appearence before the waiting crowds, (a)/he was taken (b)/to the Governor chamber (c)/for the swearing in ceremony. (d)/No error (e) **[RRB Kolkata]**

(4) Congress dissidents and (a)/a wide range among the (b)/opposition has mounted a (c)/campaign to have the President renominated. (d)/No error (e) **[RRB Kolkata]**

(5) If I would have (a)/worked regularly (b)/I would have passed (c)/the examination. (d)/No error (e) **[CSRB Patna]**

(6) The gentleman (a)/together with his (b)/wife and daughter (c)/were drowned. (d)/No error (e) **[CSRB Patna]**

(7) No man (a)/in our country (b)/is as rich (c)/as he is. (d)/No error (e) **[BSRB Clerical Bhopal]**

(8) The teacher remarked (a)/very angrily yesterday (b)/that the boys have (c)/all done it very badly. (d)/No error (e) **[BSRB Clerical Bhopal]**

(9) A letter of recommendation (a)/from the principal and (b)/the head of English department have helped him to (c)/get this lucrative job. (d)/No error (e)

(10) An Indian driver or carpenter has to work (a)/about two hours to buy kilogram of rice (b)/while his counterparts in Austria, the Netherlands and Switzerland (c)/need work only fifteen minutes for it. (d)/No error (e) **[Rly Rec Board Kolkata]**

33

Directions (Q. 1-10) *: Read each sentence to find out whether there is any grammatical or idiomatic error in it . The error, if any, will be in one part of the sentence. The number of that part is the answer. If there is no error, the answer is (E). (Ignore the errors of punctuation, if any.)*

(1) The vehicle which is stopped (a)/by the policeman (b)/contained a number (c)/of smuggled watches. (d)/No error (e) **[BSRB Lucknow]**

(2) One should look for his (a)/own faults first (b)/and then those (c)/of others (d)/No error (e) **[BSRB Lucknow]**

(3) Sitting under the shade (a)/of a tree for a while (b)/made us fresh (c)/for the further journey (d)/No error (e) **[BSRB Lucknow]**

(4) Although it is summer (a)/yet the weather at the (b)/hill station was (c)/quite pleasant (d)/No error (e) **[BSRB Lucknow]**

(5) The smuggler yielded (a)/for the tempatation (b)/and fell into (c)/the police trap. (d)/No error (e) **[CSRB Patna]**

(6) The girl said (a)/that she preferred (b)/the blue gown (c)/than the black one. (d)/No error (e) **[CSRB Patna]**

(7) Cattles (a)/were grazing (b)/in the meadows (c)/near our farm. (c)/No error (e) **[BSRB Clerical]**

(8) You are really (a)/senior than (b)/me (c)/in age. (d)/No error (e) **[BSRB Clerical]**

Solution TYE 01

(1) (a) 'Her' की जगह 'She' प्रयुक्त करें। Her एक Pronoun Object है, जो कि subject की तरह प्रयुक्त नहीं हो सकता है।

(2) (b) 'has been' की जगह 'was' का प्रयोग किया जाना चाहिए। जब वाक्य में Past tense (In early India) के बारे में चर्चा है, तो Present perfect tense के स्थान पर Past tense का प्रयोग होगा।

(3) (b) 'are' की जगह 'is' होगा subject, Duke's collection of early Dutch paintings है, जो Collective noun है और singular है अत: verb 'are' की जगह 'is' आएगी।

(4) (a) 'preferred' की जगह 'prefer' आएगा। (The sentence is in Present tense.)

(5) (c) 'Will bring' की जगह 'brings' आएगा। Subordinate clause का Tense, Principal clause के Tense के अनुसार ही होना चाहिए।

(6) (b) 'told' की जगह 'tell' आएगा। Past interrogative में जब did का प्रयोग होता है, तो verb की Ist form ही आती है।

(7) (b) 'to have spent' की जगह 'to spend' लिखना ही पर्याप्त है। have spent का प्रयोग अनावश्यक रूप से किया गया है।

(8) (d) 'want' की जगह 'wants' आएगा। manager, Singular number IIIrd person है, अत: wants आएगा।

(9) (c) Put it की जगह 'Put them' होगा, यहाँ them का प्रयोग books के लिए है, जो Plural है।

(10) (d) No error.

Solution TYE 02

(1) (b) 'beside' की जगह 'besides' प्रयुक्त करें।

(2) (a) Economics एक subject है, अत: इसके साथ 'is' का प्रयोग होगा।

(3) (d) 'has gone' की जगह 'went' प्रयुक्त करें। जब वाक्य में Past tense है, तो Present Perfect का प्रयोग करना अनुचित है।

(4) (d) 'the most' की जगह 'more' प्रयुक्त करें। more, comparison हेतु प्रयुक्त होता है, यहाँ दो proposals का comparison किया जा रहा है। 'most' Superlative degree है।

(5) (a) 'wrote' की जगह 'write' प्रयुक्त करें।

(6) (b) 'worst' की जगह 'worse' आएगा। comparison हेतु Comparative degree का ही प्रयोग होगा, Superlative degree का नहीं।

(7) (b) 'are' की जगह 'is' आएगा। जब वाक्य में as well as, besides, in addition आए, तो पहले noun के अनुसार verb आएगी। यहाँ पहला noun, 'driver' singular है अत: verb भी singular ही लगेगी।

(8) (a) 'peoples' की जगह 'people' आएगा। people का यहाँ अर्थ व्यक्ति विशेष (Individual) से है।

(9) (c) 'is' की जगह 'was' प्रयुक्त करें। Indirect narration में Reported speech का tense, Reporiting verb के अनुसार होगा।

(10) (b) 'little of' की जगह 'some of' का प्रयोग करें। 'little' का प्रयोग uncountables हेतु किया जाता है।

Solution TYE 03

(1) (d) 'might' की जगह should प्रयुक्त करें। 'lest' is always followed by 'should'.

(2) (c) 'does not speak' की जगह 'speaks' प्रयुक्त करें। जब वाक्य में unless प्रयोग हुआ है, जो स्वयं negative है, तो double negative को avoid करें।

(3) (a) 'Being' से पहले it लगाएँ। This is the problem of unrelated participle.

(4) (b) 'who' की जगह 'as' or 'that' आएगा। such के साथ 'as' या 'that' का प्रयोग होता है।

(5) (b) 'they' की जगह 'he' प्रयुक्त करें। यहाँ librarian एवं cashier एक ही व्यक्ति को refer कर रहे हैं।

(6) (b) 'most' को delete करें क्योंकि perfect स्वयं ही Superlative है।

(7) (b) 'which' की जगह 'that' प्रयुक्त करें। Interrogative sentences वाक्यों में सामान्यतया 'that' pronoun का प्रयोग किया जाता है। What is followed by 'that' instead of 'which'.

(8) (c) 'were' की जगह 'was' प्रयुक्त करें। statesman एवं politician एक ही व्यक्ति को refer कर रहे हैं।

(9) (b) 'to' को delete करें। यहाँ infinitive 'to' का प्रयोग गलत है।

(10) (c) 'being' से पहले 'from' लगाएँ। prevented is always followed by preposition 'from'.

Solution Tye 04

(1) (b) 'my child' की जगह 'child's होगा, noun के बाद में, जब gerund (यहाँ watching) का प्रयोग होता है तो noun, possessive होगा।

(2) (d) 'drink' की जगह drinking आएगा।

(3) (c) 'any' की जगह 'some' प्रयुक्त करें। some का प्रयोग Affirmative में तथा any का प्रयोग Interrogative एवं negative में होता है।

(4) (c) 'as to' की जगह 'of' प्रयुक्त करें। यहाँ aware के बाद preposition 'of' लगेगा।

(5) (e) No error.

(6) (a) 'Crossing the road' की जगह When he was crossing the road प्रयुक्त करें। This is the problem of unrelated paritciple.

(7) (c) 'were' की जगह 'was' आएगा। यहाँ subject of the verb, captain है, जो singular है।

(8) (a) जब वाक्य में past time adverbs 'ago, yesterday' etc. हों, तो Present Pefect का प्रयोग नहीं किया जाता है। change 'has come' to 'came.'

(9) (b) 'saw' की जगह 'see' प्रयुक्त करें। did के साथ verb की Ist form आएगी।

(10) (d) No error.

Solution TYE 05

(1) (b) 'have की जगह 'has' आएगा। 'Many a' is followed by singular verb.

(2) (c) 'details' की जगह 'detail' आएगा।

(3) (b) 'defines' की जगह 'define' प्रयुक्त करें। जब subject, 'authorities' plural है तो verb उसके अनुसार ही होगी।

(4) (d) 'like' की जगह 'as' प्रयुक्त करें। 'such' के साथ सामान्यतया 'as' का प्रयोग होता है।

(5) (d) 'of all animals' की जगह 'than any other animal' होना चाहिए।

(6) (a) 'an essay' की जगह 'the essay' होना चाहिए। यहाँ essay particular हो गया है।

(7) (d) No error.

(8) (c) Change 'book' to 'books'. 'one of' is always followed by plural noun.

(9) (b) change 'was' to 'were', as the subject 'Rita and her sister' is plural.

(10) (a) Change 'criteria' to criterion', criteria का singular criterion होता है।

Solution TYE 06

(1) (c) Change 'were not' to 'are not'.

(2) (b) Change 'all the future problems' to 'the problems of the future'.

(3) (a) Change 'forward for' to forward to'.

(4) (c) Change 'receive' to 'received'.

(5) (a) Change Part (A) to 'We will not only pack'.

(6) (c) Avoid using double negative. Part (C) should be 'unless full details are given'.

(7) (d) Change 'from' to 'to'. Part (D) should be 'succumbed to fires recently'.

(8) (d) Change 'for' to 'to'. Part (D) should be 'and personal attention to each child'.

(9) (e) No error.

(10) (d) Delete independent. Part (D) should be 'way of thinking'.

Solution TYE 07

(1) (d) The word 'physicists' is meaningless.

(2) (a) Change Part (A) to 'No other method of making'.

(3) (c) Change Part (C) to 'in changing the age-old'.

(4) (e) No error.

(5) (d) Change 'have' to 'has' the verb should agree with the subject 'investment'.

(6) (d) Change 'his car to start up' to 'his car start up'.

(7) (c) Change 'when it catches fire' to 'when it caught fire' क्योंकि वाक्य Past tense में है और इसमें प्रयुक्त संज्ञाओं का वाक्य के tense के साथ agreement होना आवश्यक है।

(8) (d) Change 'he went or not' to 'he had gone or not'.

(9) (b) Change suits him and therefore' to 'suited him therefore'. Superfluous use of and. Incorrect use of tense.

(10) (e) No error.

Solution TYE 08

(1) (b) वाक्य में प्रयुक्त six block and thirty flats के स्थान पर six blocks and thirty flats का प्रयोग होगा। six is plural so write blocks.

(2) (c) वाक्य में प्रयुक्त for better knowledge के स्थान पर for the better knowledge का प्रयोग होगा। 'knowledge' is particularised in the sentence.

(3) (c) Change 'instead of 'to'. Preposition to' is used with prefer, senior, junior etc.

(4) (d) वाक्य में प्रयुक्त by the train के स्थान पर by train का प्रयोग होगा। In phrases like by train, by water, by bus etc. we should not make any change.

(5) (c) वाक्य में प्रयुक्त 'bad habit' के स्थान पर 'bad habits' का प्रयोग होगा, क्योंकि one of के बाद noun या pronoun के plural form का प्रयोग होता है।

(6) (a) वाक्य में प्रयुक्त Myself and Ramanujam के स्थान पर Ramanujam and I का प्रयोग होगा।

(7) (b) Change puzzlud on' to puzzled over' Wrong use of preosition.

(8) (b) Change 'inferior than' to 'inferior to'. Wrong use of preposition, since, inferior, superior, senior, junior, prefer etc. take preposition 'to' instead of 'than.'

(9) (b) Change 'complanined at 'to' complained about'. Wrong use of preposition.

(10) (e) No error.

Solution TYE 09

(1) (c) Change 'what he has said' to 'what he said'. Wrong use of tense.

(2) (a) Change 'Not only the bandits robbed' to 'The bandits not only robbed'. Improper placement of conjunction.

(3) (c) Change 'unless she does not have a strong desire to live' to 'unless she has a strong desire to live'. Avoid double negative.

(4) (d) No error.

(5) (b) Change 'cent per cent' to 'hundred per cent'. Cent per cent is a wrong expression.

(6) (c) Delete 'the' before church. Wrong use of article 'the'. Public insitutions, जैसे church, temple, hospital, mosque, school, prison, college etc. के पहले 'the' उसी स्थिति में लगता है जब व्यक्ति इन स्थानों पर किसी अन्य उद्देश्य से visit किया करते हैं।

(7) (b) अगर वाक्य से hesitation, dislike तथा risk का बोध हो तो हमें verb infinitive के बदले gerund का प्रयोग करना चाहिए। अत: यहाँ talk के स्थान पर talking होना चाहिए।

(8) (a) Change 'would have' to 'had'. See the structure of Conditional sentence.

(9) (b) Change 'peak' to 'peaks'. After of noun is pluralised in such sentences.

(10) (c) Change 'student' to 'students'. After 'of' noun is pluralised in such sentences.

Solution TYE 10

(1) (d) Change 'are' to 'is'. When two nouns are joined by the conjunction; 'with', 'as well as', 'together with', 'besides' etc., the verb should agree with the Ist noun. इसी कारण वाक्य में 'are present here' के स्थान पर 'is present here'का प्रयोग होना चाहिए।

(2) (a) Change 'Men' to 'Man'.

(3) (c) Change 'early at' to 'early in'. Wrong use of preposition.

(4) (d) No error.

(5) (a) Change 'worn' to 'wore'. Wore is the past form of wear.

(6) (e) No error. None can be used as singular and as plural also.

(7) (d) Change 'from' to 'by'. Wrong use of preposition.
(8) (b) Change 'a' to 'an'. Wrong use of article.
(9) (a) Change 'love' to 'loved' or used to love'. Wrong use of verb tense.
(10) (c) Change 'a duty cost' to 'a duty cast'.

Solution TYE 11

(1) (d) Change 'the time' to 'about the time'. Wrong use of preposition.
(2) (a) Change 'How do' to 'How did'. Wrong use of tense verb .
(3) (b) Change 'sometime' to 'sometimes'. Wrong use of word.
(4) (d) Change 'police dog jump' to 'police dog jumping'.
(5) (d) Change 'on the door' to 'at the door'. Wrong use of preposition.
(6) (c) Change 'of ' to 'off '. Wrong use of phrase.
(7) (b) Change 'attitudes' to 'attitude'.
(8) (b) Change 'from the hand' to 'by the hand police'. Wrong use of verb phrase.
(9) (d) Change 'for' to 'of '. Wrong use of preposition.
(10) (d) Change 'her age' to 'at her age'.

Solution TYE 12

(1) (b) Change 'taller' to 'tallest'. Wrong use of degree of adjective.
(2) (c) Change 'who' to 'whom'. Wrong use of pronoun.
(3) (c) Change 'or' to 'nor'. Wrong use of conjunction.
(4) (c) Change 'since' to 'for'. For used for period of time.
(5) (b) Change 'is divided' to 'are divided'. Here, committee is not used as Collective noun as a unit.
(6) (e) No error.
(7) (c) Change 'in its preference on' to 'in its preference to'. Wrong use of preposition. Preference के पश्चात् Preposition के रूप में 'to' प्रयोग किया जाता है।
(8) (e) No error.
(9) (d) Change 'should like to acquire' to 'would like to acquire'.
(10) (a) Change 'If you absent' to 'If you absent yourself'. Absent be used reflexively.

Solution TYE 13

(1) (a) Delete 'The'.Wrong use of definite article 'The'.
(2) (c) Change 'are' to 'is'. Wrong use of verb. Here, twenty five kilometers is used as a unit, so singular verb is used.
(3) (d) Change 'the French' to 'French'. Do not use definite article 'the' before name of language.
(4) (b) Change 'to meet' to 'to meeting'. Wrong use of infinitive.
(5) (d) Change 'do you' to 'won't you'. It is a request.
(6) (b) Change 'a mason' to 'the mason'. Wrong use of article.
(7) (b) Change 'make from' to 'make out'. Wrong use of preposition or phrasal verb .
(8) (b) Change 'you will think' to 'will you think'. Proper use of Inversion is necesary in questions.
(9) (d) No error.
(10) (b) Change 'reached there' to 'did we reached there'. Wrong use of inversion.

Solution TYE 14

(1) (a) It should be 'It being a very cold day'. This is the problem of dangling participle.
(2) (c) Change 'be' to 'been'.
(3) (a) Change 'will insist' to 'insist'. Do not use will after if in such Conditional Type of sentences.
(4) (d) Delete had. It should be Subhash Chandra Bose died.
(5) (c) Change 'is' to 'are'. Wrong use of singular verb. When two nouns are joined with the conjunction 'and' use plural verb वाक्यों में 'is' के साथ पर 'are' का प्रयोग होना चाहिए।
(6) (d) Delete 'the' before most.Wrong use of article 'the'.
(7) (c) Change'keep his' to 'keep their'. Pronoun their refer to 'those persons' not 'he'.
(8) (e) No error.
(9) (b) Change 'are' to 'is'. Wrong use of plural verb with singular subject 'box'.
(10) (b) delete 'to' after inform.

Solution TYE 15

(1) (d) Change 'he does not do it' to 'he did not do it'. Wrong use of tense.
(2) (b) Change 'his best' to 'one's best'. Wrong use of pronoun. one का possessive one's होता है, न कि his.
(3) (a) Change 'deprived from' to 'deprived of'. Wrong use of preposition.
(4) (c) Change 'throughly' to 'through'. Unnecessary use of adverb.
(5) (b) Indirect speech में Interrogative word के बाद subject आता है और फिर verb. So it should be : The villager told us where the temple was and even led us to the spot.
(6) (d) Change 'than' to 'but'.
(7) (e) No error.
(8) (c) Change 'to' to 'than'. rather के बाद than का प्रयोग किया जाता है, न कि to का
(9) (b) Change 'manages to play' to 'managed to play'. Wrong use of tense verb. वाक्य Past tense structure पर आधारित है।
(10) (c) Change 'to reinstated' to 'be reinstated'.

Solution TYE 16

(1) (a) It should be 'Thinking that he had finally found'. The sentence is in Past tense so to use Present perfect is incorrect.
(2) (c) It should be 'telecast by a commercial television channel'. The Past of telecast is telecast.
(3) (c) It should be 'that you have made a mistake' or 'you have committed a mistake'.
(4) (b) It should be 'he has six houses in Mumbai'. Generally, the verb 'have' is not used in continuous form.
(5) (b) It should be 'if I was ill'. If the reporting verb is in Past , the tense of the reported speech be also Past.
(6) (c) It should be 'he had bought it'. For the action completed first, use Past perfect tense.
(7) (b) It should be 'is to reduce matter by an analysis'. Use article a/an before countables.
(8) (c) It should be 'it was hardly ten'. Hardly has negative meaning. Avoid using double negative .
(9) (c) It should be 'was deceived'. If two nouns are joined with; like , in addition to, together with, etc., the verb will be as per the Ist noun.
(10) (c) It should be 'and were seeking a job'. Use Past verb before seeking.

Solution TYE 17

(1) (a) Part (A) should be: 'As I prefer coffee to tea'. Prefer always take preposition 'to'.
(2) (d) No error.
(3) (b) Part (B) should be : ".....to find evidence....."
(4) (d) No error.
(5) (d) No error.
(6) (c) Change 'then' to 'than'. Than is used here in conjunctions.
(7) (b) Noun 'furniture' can't be pluralise as 'furnitures'. Part (b) should be : ".....with all the furniture'.
(8) (d) No error.
(9) (c) Insert definite article 'the' as. 'The Ganges and the Himalayas'.
(10) (b) Change to 'is the better.....'. For the comparison of two, use Comparative degree.

Solution TYE 18

(1) (a) Change the Part (A) to 'After he finished the work'.
(2) (c) Change 'can' to 'could' as. 'Because they thought that they could now remove it with safety'. The sentence is in Past tense.
(3) (c) Insert 'the' before United Nations.
(4) (b) Change 'was' to 'were'.
(5) (b) Part (B) should be, 'he was addicted to reading the jokes in punch aloud'. Gerund form is used in such sentence structure.
(6) (a) Use either first or next in the sentence. Part (B) should be, 'Why not stop the first man you meet and ask' Or 'Why not stop the man you meet next and ask'.
(7) (c) 'Unique' cannot be compared. Part (C) should be, 'a unique development'.
(8) (a) Put out means to extinguish. Part (A)should be, 'Put out.'
(9) (c) Part (C) should be, 'on the deck of the ship'.
(10) (a) Always use auxiliary had after hardly. Part (A) should be, 'Hardly had the rains started'.

Solution TYE 19

(1) (c) Change 'and not found out' to 'and are not found out'. Use of verb is necessary here.
(2) (b) Change 'different' to 'differently'. Incorrect use of verb in place of adverb.
(3) (c) Change 'leading the blinds' to 'leading the blind'. The blind means the blind people.
(4) (a) Change 'took to drink' to 'took to drinking'.
(5) (c) Change 'lot of money' to 'a lot of money'as 'A lot of' is a phrase.
(6) (a) Change 'broadcasted' to 'broadcast'. Broadcasted is the past of broadcast.
(7) (a) Change 'much' to 'many'. Much is used for uncountables.
(8) (a) Change 'What, could have provoked him' to 'What provoked him'. Incorrect use of Perfect tense.
(9) (a) Change 'They were rich zamindars in thirties'. to 'They had been rich zamindars in thirties'.
(10) (c) Change 'as well as' to 'and'. Incorrect use of conjunction as well as.

Solution TYE 20

(1) (b) Change 'broadcasted' to 'broadcast'.
(2) (b) Change 'how could she kill' to 'how she could kill'. Incorrect use of inversion in Indirect speech.
(3) (a) Change 'While walking slowly in the park'. to 'While he was walking slowly in the park'. This is a problem of unrelated participle.
(4) (b) Change 'travelling became very pleasant'. to 'travelling has become very pleasant'. Incorrect use of tense.

(5) (b) Change 'exposes' to 'expose'. Incorrect use of singular verb.
(6) (c) Change 'and to have remembered for' to 'and to remember for'. Incorrect use of Perfect tense.
(7) (c) Change 'we have been looking for' to 'we had been looking for'. Incorrect use of tense.
(8) (c) Change 'look up the marketing' to 'look after the marketing'. Incorrect use of Phrasal verb.
(9) (b) Change 'have overflown' to 'have overflowed'. Part (b) should be 'and the rivers have overflowed their banks'.
(10) (b) Change 'persist' to 'persisted'. The sentence structure is in Past.

Solution TYE 21

(1) (d) Change 'it is really made' to 'it was really made'. Incorrect use of tense in Indirect speech.
(2) (b) Change 'has no dearth of ' to 'have no dearth of '. Incorrect use of verb.
(3) (c) Change 'than' to 'when'. Incorrect use of than with 'scarcely'.
(4) (b) Change 'if I would have realised' to 'if I had realised'. See the structure of Conditional sentences.
(5) (a) Change 'I am trying' to 'I have been trying'. Incorrect use of tense.
(6) (b) Change 'but he turned it over' to 'but he turned it down'. Incorrect use of Phrasal verb.
(7) (b) Change 'for the wall below' to 'against the wall below'. Incorrect use of preposition.
(8) (a) Change 'criteria' to 'criterion'. Criteria is plural of criterion.
(9) (b) Change 'will' to 'would'. The sentence structure is in Past.
(10) (a) Delete 'for '. Incorrect use of preposition.

Solution TYE 22

(1) (a) Change 'principal' to 'principle'. Incorrect use of word.
(2) (d) Change 'future programmes' to 'its future programme'.
(3) (a) Change 'Honesty, integrity and being intelligent' to 'Honesty, integrity and intelligence'.
(4) (b) Change 'must have' to 'have to' or 'must'.
(5) (c) Change 'which' to 'who'.'who' is used for living persons.
(6) (b) Change 'sang' to 'sung'. Incorrect past participle of verb.
(7) (c) Change 'was able to dampen' to 'could dampen'.
(8) (b) Change 'enough money' to 'any money'.
(9) (c) Change 'were overlook' to 'were overlooked'. In passive structure IIIrd form of the verb is used.
(10) (d) Change 'hostilities of that area' to 'hostilities in that area'.

Solution TYE 23

(1) (c) Change 'was' to 'had'. Incorrect use of tense.
(2) (a) Change 'to keep maintaining' to 'to maintaining'.
(3) (a) Change 'Being the second' to 'It being the second'. It is a problem of unrelated participle.
(4) (d) No error.
(5) (a) Change 'Such of those who have not paid the fees' to 'They who have not paid the fees'.
(6) (c) Insert himself after avail. Avail is used reflexively.
(7) (b) Change 'for' to 'of ' ".... of their health..."
(8) (c) Omit 'about'. Part (C) should be : "....anything left to discuss."
(9) (b) Change pronoun 'you' to 'he'. Part (B) should be : "..... where he was."
(10) (c) Part (C) should be : "...... till you finish your work." In such type of sentences don't use will after; when, as soon as, till, after, as etc.

Solution TYE 24

(1) (a) 'swam की जगह 'swum' का प्रयोग होगा क्योंकि swim की IIIrd form swum होती है।

(2) (b) 'more' का प्रयोग नहीं होगा, क्योंकि Double comparative का प्रयोग वाक्य में नहीं किया जाता है। Avoid using double compartives in a sentence.

(3) (d) 'A' की जगह 'The' का प्रयोग होगा। 'with the naked eyes' is correct expression.

(4) (a) 'advices' की जगह 'advice' का प्रयोग होगा यहाँ 'advice' Uncountable noun है। We cannot pluralise advice as such (Advices).

(5) (b) 'they' के बाद 'have' का प्रयोग नहीं होगा। This is a conditional sentence with following structure. Had they invited me, I would have attended the function.

(6) (b) 'is' की जगह 'was' होगा, क्योंकि Indirect narration में है और चूँकि Reporting verb Past tense में हैं, अत: Reported speed में भी Past tense का प्रयोग होगा।

(7) (a) 'don't' के बदले 'doesn't' का प्रयोग होगा,

(8) (b) 'am' की जगह 'was' का प्रयोग होगा। The sentence structure is in Past.

(9) (a) 'Cattles' की जगह 'Cattle' का प्रयोग होगा क्योंकि 'cattle' स्वयं plural noun है।

(10) (b) 'than' की जगह 'to' का प्रयोग होगा। Superior, senior, junior, inferior, prior के साथ 'to' preposition लगता है।

Solution TYE 25

(1) (c) 'not' का प्रयोग नहीं होगा। Avoid double negative. Lest का अर्थ ही negative होता है।

(2) (c) 'to' के पहले 'how' का प्रयोग होगा। ध्यान दें इस तरह के वाक्यों में know के बाद how/when/where/what आदि में से अर्थ के अनुसार किसी एक का प्रयोग कर infinitive का प्रयोग करते हैं। जैसे :

(i) I do not know how to swim.
(ii) I don't know how to play carrom.
(iii) I do not know where to go.

(3) (b) 'more' का प्रयोग नहीं होगा, क्योंकि Double comparatives का प्रयोग वाक्य में नहीं किया जाता है। जैसे : He is stronger than you. (न कि more stronger)

(4) (d) No Error.

(5) (d) 'good' की जगह 'well' का प्रयोग होगा, क्योंकि यह 'work' (verb) की विशेषता बतलाता है, और यह काम एक Adverb ही कर सकता है, न कि Adjective. well एक Adverb है तथा good एक Adjective है। Adjective qualifies a noun.

(6) (c) 'as well as' के बदले 'and' का प्रयोग होगा। The structure of the sentence is Both...and.

(7) (b) 'resembles' के बाद 'to' का प्रयोग नहीं होगा। सदैव याद रखिए कि resemble एक Transitive verb है। अत: इसके बाद सीधा object का प्रयोग किया जाता है। इसके बाद prepositions का प्रयोग गलत है।

(8) (a) 'the two first' की जगह 'the first two', क्योंकि जब Ordinal number (जैसे first, second, third, last आदि) Cardinal number (जैसे one, two three, four आदि) का प्रयोग एक साथ करना हो, तो पहले Ordinal और तब Cardinal आता है।

(9) (c) 'country' की जगह 'countries' का प्रयोग होगा। 'one of, most of' के बाद आने वाला Noun Plural होता है।

(10) (c) 'then' की जगह 'when' का प्रयोग होगा। 'Hardly', 'Scarcely' के बाद conjunction 'when' का प्रयोग होगा। जैसे : Hardly/scarcely had she left the hotel when it began to rain.

Solution TYE 26

(1) (b) 'he wrote' की जगह 'he had written' का प्रयोग होता है। जब Direct Narration में Reporting Verb, Past Tense में हो तथा Reported speech में Simple past का प्रयोग हो तो Indirect narration में Reported speech को Past Perfect Tense में बदला जाता है।

(2) (d) 'one' पर' s (Apostrophe) का प्रयोग होता है। सही expression होगा one's living.

(3) (a) 'to' का प्रयोग Superfluous (अनावश्यक) है।

(4) (a) 'do not' का प्रयोग गलत है। Unless, until के साथ not का प्रयोग नहीं होगा। 'Unless' is itself negative.

(5) (b) 'read' के पहले 'had' का प्रयोग होगा, क्योंकि जब Past की दो घटनाओं का वर्णन हो, जिनमें से एक पहले तथा दूसरी बाद में घटी हो तो पहली घटना के लिए Past Perfect तथा दूसरी के लिए Past Indefinite का प्रयोग करते है; जैसे :
(i) After he had reached the station, the train arrived.
(ii) The patient had died before the doctor reached here.

(6) (c) 'other' का प्रयोग Superfluous (अनावश्यक) है।

(7) (c) 'has' की जगह 'have' का प्रयोग होगा। वाक्य का subject 'The issues' है, जो कि plural है।

(8) (d) 'its' की जगह 'a' का प्रयोग होना चाहिए। 'for a picnic' is correct phrase.

(9) (b) 'snowed' की जगह 'snows' का प्रयोग होगा, क्योंकि 'Tomorrow' future को सूचित करता है, जबकि snowed, Verb 'snow का Past रूप है जो कि Past tense में प्रयुक्त होता है। The use of future and past like this is an incorrect combination.

(10) (a) 'between' की जगह 'among' का प्रयोग होगा। 'between' is used for two and 'among' for more than two.

Solution TYE 27

(1) (a) 'swam' की जगह 'swum' का प्रयोग होगा क्योंकि swim की IIIrd form swum होती है।

(2) (b) 'more' का प्रयोग नहीं होगा, क्योंकि Double comparative का प्रयोग वाक्य में नहीं किया जाता है। Avoid using double compartives in a sentence.

(3) (d) 'their' की जगह 'his' का प्रयोग होगा। With 'everyone, everybody, anyone, anybody' always use singular possessive pronoun (his or her).

(4) (b) 'on' की जगह 'of ' Preposition का प्रयोग होगा।

(5) (c) 'hung' की जगह 'hanged' का प्रयोग होगा। Verb 'hang' has two forms and two meanings as per following:

Ist form	IInd form	IIIrd form
(i) Hang (लटकाना)	hung	hung
(ii) Hang (फाँसी देना)	hanged	hanged

यही कारण है कि 'hang' की V-I form और V-III form रूप में confusion होता है।

(6) (b) 'will' की जगह 'would' का प्रयोग होना चाहिए, क्योंकि वाक्य Past tense में है।

(7) (b) refrain के बाद 'with' के स्थान पर, 'from' का प्रयोग होगा, क्योंकि refrain, abstain, prohibit आदि के बाद 'from' का प्रयोग होता है।

(8) (c) 'to' के बाद 'that of ' का प्रयोग होगा, क्योंकि comparison 'The Indian way' तथा 'the way of most of the countries' के बीच है।

(9) (a) 'none' की जगह 'neither' का प्रयोग होगा। दो व्यक्तियों या वस्तुओं के लिए 'neither' का प्रयोग होता है, जबकि दो से अधिक के लिए 'none' का प्रयोग होता है।

(10) (b) 'where had I' की जगह 'where I had' का प्रयोग होगा। In 'Indirect narration' the sentence changes from Interrogative to Affirmative.

Solution TYE 28

(1) (b) 'homes' की जगह 'home' का प्रयोग होगा, क्योंकि 'at home' एक phrase है।
(2) (e) No error.
(3) (b) 'a' की जगह 'the' प्रयोग होगा। Superlative के Adjective से पहले 'the' का प्रयोग होता है।
(4) (a) 'is' की जगह 'was' का प्रयोग होगा, क्योंकि 'in 1929' से Past time का बोध होता है। The whole sentence reflects action in the Past.
(5) (a) 'Being' के पहले 'It' का प्रयोग होगा। This is the problem of urrelated participle.
(6) (b) 'have' की जगह 'has' का प्रयोग होगा। 'Many a' के बाद Singular noun and singular verb का प्रयोग होता है। जैसे:

(i) Many a <u>pen</u> is on the <u>stool</u>. (ii) Many a <u>person</u> comes here <u>daily</u>.

(7) (b) 'is' का प्रयोग 'a digital computer' के बाद होगा। This is an Assertive sentence, not an interrogative one.
See the following examples :

(i) I do not know where he lives (न कि where does he live?)
(ii) I know what he says (न कि What does he say?)

(8) (c) 'you'll pay' के बदले 'you pay' होगा। जब Principal clause में future Indefinite tense हो, तो subordinate clause में simple present का प्रयोग होता है।
(9) (c) 'purchase' की जगह 'purchased' का प्रयोग होगा। This is a conditional sentence with the following structure:
Had + Sub + V-III...+would have + V-III?
(10) (e) No error.

Solution TYE 29

(1) (b) 'will' की जगह 'would' का प्रयोग होगा। When the sentence reflects an action in the past it is incorrece to use will.
(2) (b) 'from' का प्रयोग Superfluous है।
(3) (a) 'help' के पहले 'to' का प्रयोग नहीं होगा।
(4) (b) 'has' की जगह 'had' का प्रयोग होगा। Reporting Verb में Past tense का प्रयोग है। अत: Indirect narration में Reported Speech में Present Perfect का प्रयोग नहीं होगा, Past Perfect का प्रयोग होगा।
(5) (a) 'need' की जगह 'needs' का प्रयोग होगा। वाक्य का Subject 'our' country' Singular number में है।
(6) (a) 'Instead of ' की जगह 'In spite of ' का प्रयोग होगा, क्योंकि 'Instead of ' का अर्थ है ' के बदले में ', किन्तु 'In spite of ' का अर्थ है 'के बावजूद'।
(7) (b) 'for' की जगह 'to' का प्रयोग होगा, क्योंकि yield के बाद 'to' preposition का प्रयोग होता है।
(8) (d) 'than' की जगह 'to' का प्रयोग होगा। Remember use 'to' after, 'senior, junior, prefer, prior' instead of 'than'.
(9) (b) 'last' की जगह latter का प्रयोग होगा, क्योंकि दो व्यक्तियों या वस्तुओं के क्रम को बताने के लिए 'latter' का प्रयोग किया जाता है, किन्तु दो से अधिक व्यक्तियों या वस्तुओं के क्रम को बताने के लिए 'last' का।
जैसे :

(i) Ramesh and Suresh are friends. The latter is an engineer.
(ii) Ramesh, Suresh and Medha are friends. The last is a banker.

(10) (b) 'surprised' के पहले were का प्रयोग होगा। This is a Passive structure.

Solution TYE 30

(1) (c) 'eastern' के पहले 'the' का प्रयोग होगा।

(2) (b) 'who do I want' के बदले 'whom I wanted' का प्रयोग होगा, चूँकि वाक्य में Reporting verb, Past tense में है। अत: Reported speech में भी Past tense का ही प्रयोग होगा। In Indirect narration the sentence changed to Affirmative.

(3) (c) 'with' की जगह 'to' का प्रयोग होगा।

(4) (b) 'will' की जगह 'would' का प्रयोग होगा, क्योंकि वाक्य में Reporting verb है, जिसकी Reporting verb 'She said' Past tense में है। The tense of the reported speech changes accordingly.

(5) (b) 'are' की जगह 'am' का प्रयोग होगा। जब दो-दो subjects Either....or, Neither....nor, Not only...but also से जुड़ते हैं, तो verb पास वाले subject के अनुसार प्रयुक्त होती है।

(6) (c) 'than' की जगह 'to' का प्रयोग होगा, क्योंकि perferable, senior, junior, superior, inferior, prior, anterior, posterior etc. के बाद 'to' का प्रयोग किया जाता है। जैसे :

(i) They are senior to me (न कि than me) (ii) I prefer tea to coffee.

(7) (e) No error.

(8) (c) 'then' का प्रयोग superfluous (अनावश्यक) है। As because, since, as soon as के बाद therefore, so, then आदि का प्रयोग नहीं किया जाता है।

(9) (e) No error.

(10) (d) 'any' के बाद 'other' का प्रयोग होगा।

Solution TYE 31

(1) (a) 'Being' की जगह 'That, Because, Since, As' आदि में से किसी का प्रयोग होगा। In this question Being is used in place of That or Because or Since or As.

(2) (b) 'their' की जगह 'its' का प्रयोग होगा, क्योंकि वाक्य का subject 'the college' IIIrd Person Singular number में है और इसके लिए यहाँ Pronoun its का प्रयोग किया जाएगा।

(3) (d) 'A' की जगह 'The' का प्रयोग होगा। 'with the naked eyes' is correct expression.

(4) (a) 'advices' की जगह advice का प्रयोग यहाँ 'advice' Uncountable noun है। We cannot pluralise advice as such (Advices).

(5) (b) 'have' की जगह 'has' का प्रयोग होगा। 'Many a' के बाद singular noun and singular verb का प्रयोग होता है। जैसे :

(i) Many a <u>pen</u> is on the <u>stool</u>.

(ii) Many a person comes here daily.

(6) (e) No error.

(7) (e) No error.

(8) (a) No sooner के बाद 'had' का प्रयोग होगा, क्योंकि No sooner के बाद Auxiliary verb लगाना आवश्यक है। This is the question of inversion.

(9) (a) 'fled' के बाद 'away' का प्रयोग Superfluous (अनावश्यक) है, क्योंकि 'fled' का अर्थ ही run away होता है। This is the question of superfluous expression.

Solution TYE 32

(1) (b) 'is having' की जगह 'has का प्रयोग होगा। Possession बताने वाले verbs (जैसे own, possess, have, belong आदि) का प्रयोग Continuous tense में नहीं होता है, बल्कि Simple Present में होता है।

(2) (c) 'as' की जगह का 'that' का प्रयोग होगा, क्योंकि वाक्य का structure 'so....that' पर आधारित है। देखें :

(i) He is so poor that he connot buy a pen.

(ii) She is so weak that she cannot climb up the staris.

(3) (c) 'Governor chamber' की जगह 'Governor's chamber' का प्रयोग होगा। This is the question of use of apostrophe.

(4) (c) 'has' की जगह 'have' का प्रयोग होगा, क्योंकि वाक्य का Subject 'Congress dissidents and a wide range' है, जो Plural number में है। If the subject is plural, verb is plural.

(5) (a) 'would have' की जगह 'had' का प्रयोग होगा। This is a Conditional sentence with specific structure: **IF + Subject + had + V-III + Would have + V-III.**

(6) (d) 'were' की जगह 'was' का प्रयोग होगा। जब दो Subjects with, as well as, along with, in addition to, besides, together with आदि से जुड़ते हैं, जो Verb इन Conjunction के पहले आने वाले Subject के Number और Person पर निर्भर करता है। If this subect is singular, verb is singular, If subject is plural, verb is plural.

(7) (a) 'No' के बाद 'other' का प्रयोग करना पड़ेगा। While making comparison the item (being compared) is required to be excluded. As:

No other girl of this class is so/as beautiful as Rani.

(8) (c) 'have' की जगह 'had' का प्रयोग होगा। Reporting verb Past tense में है।

(9) (c) 'have' की जगह 'has' का प्रयोग होगा, क्योंकि वाक्य का Subject 'A letter' Singular number में है।

(10) (b) 'kilogram' के पहले 'a' का प्रयोग होगा, क्योंकि kilogram एक Countable noun है।

Solution TYE 33

(1) (a) 'is' की जगह 'was' का प्रयोग होगा। The sentence reflects an action is the past.

(2) (a) 'his' की जगह one's का प्रयोग होगा, क्योंकि 'one' का Possessive 'one's' होता है।

(3) (a) 'under' की जगह 'in' preposition का प्रयोग नहीं होगा। Sit in the shade of a tree तथा Sit under a tree होता है।

(4) (c) 'was' की जगह 'is' का प्रयोग होगा, क्योंकि वाक्य Present tense (It is summer) में है।

(5) (b) 'for' की जगह 'to' का प्रयोग होगा, क्योंकि yield के बाद 'to' preposition का प्रयोग होता है।

(6) (d) 'than' की जगह 'to' का प्रयोग होगा। After, senior, junior, prefer, prior. etc., always use 'to' instead of 'than'.

(7) (a) 'cattles' की जगह 'cattle' का प्रयोग होगा, क्योंकि 'cattle' स्वयं plural noun है।

(8) (b) 'than' की जगह 'to' का प्रयोग होगा। Superior, senior, junior, inferior, prior के साथ 'to' preposition लगता है।

CHAPTER 34

CLOZE TEST/ CLOZE PASSAGE

विभिन्न Competitive examination में अंग्रेजी प्रश्न-पत्र में Cloze Test/Cloze Passage भी दिया गया होता है। Cloze Test का उद्देश्य छात्रों के अंग्रेजी ज्ञान को जाँचना होता है। इस प्रकार के प्रश्नों में एक Passage में खाली स्थान दिए गए होते हैं जिन्हें Passage के अन्त में दिए गए विकल्पों में से सही शब्द चुनकर भरना होता है। इस तरह के Passage में उपयुक्त शब्द का चुनाव आपके सम्पूर्ण अंग्रेजी ज्ञान की परीक्षा है। कई रिक्त स्थानों में Verb की सही form भरनी होती है, तो किसी खाली स्थान में सही Phrasal Verb या उपयुक्त Preposition को भरना होता है। किसी रिक्त स्थान में वाक्य के सन्दर्भ/आशय के अनुसार किसी उपयुक्त शब्द को भरना होता है। अत: Cloze Test/Passage हेतु न केवल अच्छी Grammatical knowledge की आवश्यकता है बल्कि अच्छी Vocabulary की भी आवश्यकता होती है।

How to Attempt a Cloze Passage?

इस तरह के Passage को छात्र को एक बार पूरा पढ़ना चाहिए। इससे छात्र को Passage का कुछ अर्थ/आशय/सन्दर्भ समझ में आ जाता है। कई बार Passages में शुरू के, खाली स्थानों की पूर्ति तथा सन्दर्भ मिल जाते हैं। अत: सर्वप्रथम छात्र को सारे Passage को पूरा पढ़कर, खाली स्थानों की पूर्ति करके शुरू करना चाहिए। ध्यान रखें यदि Passage के शुरू मे या मध्य में कुछ Confusing शब्द या कठिनाई आए तो बिना परेशान हुए, आगे के रिक्त स्थानों की पूर्ति करें। कई बार Passage में आए शुरू के तथ्यों का स्पष्टीकरण अन्त के वाक्य में होता है, जिससे शुरू के रिक्त स्थानों की पूर्ति अन्त के वाक्यों को पढ़ने पर ही सही रूप से हो सकती है। अत: छात्रों को सर्वप्रथम पूरा Passage पढ़कर ही रिक्त स्थानों की पूर्ति करना प्रारम्भ करना चाहिए।

***Cloze Passages** test not only your grammatical knowledge, but also your vocabulary and your common sense.*

Exercises

Solved Exercises

01

Directions (Q. 1-6) : *Fill up the blanks in the passage given below with the most appropriate word from the options given for each blank :*

"Between the year 1946 and the year 1955, I did not file any income tax returns." With that (1)...... statement, Ramesh embarked on an account of his encounter with the Income Tax Department. "I originally owed ₹ 20,000 in unpaid taxes. With (2)....... and (3)........ the 20,000 became 60,000. The Income Tax Department then went into action, and I learned first hand, just how much power the Tax Department wields. Royalties and trust funds can be (4)........ automobiles may be (5)........ and auctioned off. Nothing belongs to the (6)..... until the case is settled." **[CAT Nov 2004]**

(1) (a) devious (b) blunt (c) tactful (d) pretentious
(2) (a) interest (b) taxes (c) principal (d) returns
(3) (a) sanctions (b) refunds (c) feet (d) fines
(4) (a) closed (b) detached (c) attached (d) impounded
(5) (a) smashed (b) seized (c) dismantled (d) frozen
(6) (a) purchaser (b) victim (c) investor (d) offender

02

Directions *(1-4) : Fill up the blanks in the passage given below with the most appropriate word from the options given for each blank :*

At the time The White House was as serene as a resort hotel out of season. The corridors were (1)...... in the various offices. (2)...... gray men on waistcoats talked to one another in low-pitched voices. The only color or choler, curiously enough, was provided by President Eisenhower himself. Apparently, his (3)...... was easily set off; he scowled when he (4)...... the corridors. **[CAT Nov 2004]**

(1) (a) striking (b) hollow (c) empty (d) white
(2) (a) quiet (b) faded (c) loud (d) stentorian
(3) (a) laughter (b) curiosity (c) humour (d) temper
(4) (a) paced (b) strolled (c) stormed (d) prowled

03

Directions (Q. 1-10) : *Fill up the blanks in the passage below with the most appropriate word from the options given for each blank :*

Someone (1)........at the door. A lady opened it. A stranger was standing at the (2)........He said, "Madam, please excuse me for.......... (3) you. May I ask you something ? I (4)......by your house everyday on my (5).........to work, I have (6).........that every day you hit your son on (7).........head with a loaf of bread." The lady replied, "Yes, that's (8).......". The stranger asked, "This morning, I saw you (9)......him with a chocolate. Why (10)......? The lady replied, "Today is his birthday. Therefore I hit him with a sweet thing."

(1) (a) pointed (b) knocked (c) looked (d) moved (e) stood
(2) (a) fence (b) gate (c) compound (d) door (e) step
(3) (a) disturbing (b) harassing (c) asking (d) enquiring (e) worrying
(4) (a) wait (b) watch (c) stand (d) pass (e) connect
(5) (a) office (b) steps (c) legs (d) journey (e) way
(6) (a) decided (b) felt (c) noticed (d) remembered (e) surprised
(7) (a) your (b) his (c) my (d) our (e) fore
(8) (a) right (b) obvious (c) surprising (d) clear (e) funny
(9) (a) feeding (b) bestowing (c) giving (d) hitting (e) offering
(10) (a) bread (b) then (c) so (d) change (e) thus

04

Directions (Q. 1-15) : Fill up the blanks in the passage below with the most appropriate word from the options given for each blank :

Erosion in nature is a beneficent process without which the world would have died long ago. The same process (1).....by human mismanagement has become one of the most. (2).....and destructive forces that had ever been. (3).....by man.What is (4).....known as (5).....erosion or denudation is a universal (6).....which through thousands of years (7).....carved the earth (8).....its present shape. Denudation is an early and (9).....process (10).....soil formation where by the (11).....rock material is continuously broken

(12).....and sorted out by wind and water until it becomes (13).....for colonisation (14).....plants. Plants by the binding (15).....of their roots bring denudation almost to a standstill. **[CDS]**

(1) (a) started	(b) accelerated	(c) adopted
(2) (a) drastic	(b) degrading	(c) vicious
(3) (a) produced	(b) released	(c) caused
(4) (a) normally	(b) generally	(c) usually
(5) (a) geological	(b) ecological	(c) natural
(6) (a) aspect	(b) phenomena	(c) experience
(7) (a) has	(b) had	(c) have
(8) (a) to	(b) in	(c) into
(9) (a) inevitable	(b) important	(c) accurate
(10) (a) at	(b) in	(c) for
(11) (a) basic	(b) early	(c) original
(12) (a) up	(b) down	(c) off
(13) (a) natural	(b) necessary	(c) suitable
(14) (a) of	(b) by	(c) for
(15) (a) forces	(b) effect	(c) powers

05

Directions (Q. 1-10) : *Fill up the blanks in the passage below with the most appropriate word from the options given for each blank :*

The king of Rampur was not (1).....The following story proves that. Once he paid a (2)........to a town away from his capital.

The king's staff governing the town welcomed the king. As per the king's desire a (3)........of the renowned people of the town was called at night. The people (4)........the king and bestowed their praise on him and all sat down to listen to (5).......the king had to tell them.

Suddenly the lantern gave away. It became very dark. "Light the lantern !" ordered the king to his servants. Five minutes passed. The king shouted to know there was (6).......in lighting the lantern. "My Lord, I am (7).........to lay my hand on the match box. It is so dark!" replied the servant . "Fool !" screamed the king (8).......... . If that is the case, why (9)........you light the candle first? You can certainly (10)......the match box with the help of the candle.

(1) (a) kind	(b) cruel	(c) generous	(d) wise	(e) brave
(2) (a) homage	(b) visit	(c) donation	(d) fund	(e) contribution
(3) (a) meeting	(b) majority	(c) procession	(d) survey	(e) list
(4) (a) bowed	(b) surrendered	(c) greeted	(d) offered	(e) complained
(5) (a) carefully	(b) about	(c) which	(d) all	(e) what
(6) (a) difficulty	(b) time	(c) patience	(d) delay	(e) haste
(7) (a) unable	(b) looking	(c) confident	(d) ready	(e) trying
(8) (a) loudly	(b) angrily	(c) anxiously	(d) happily	(e) pertinently
(9) (a) must	(b) should	(c) don't	(d) did	(e) do
(10) (a) watch	(b) try	(c) touch	(d) light	(e) locate

06

Directions (Q. 1-10) : *Fill up the blanks, in the passage below with the most appropriate word from the options given for each blank :*

Tea prices in the domestic (1).....continue to rule high in the (2).....year despite the expectation of a (3).....production as compared to the previous year. According to a preliminary assessment (4).....on the weather (5).....in recent months. Tea output in1990 may reach 740 million kg as (6) .....700 million kg. last year. During the past three months, tea prices have generally shown an (7)..... . Unlike last year, when tea prices rose dramatically, this year, prices seem to have (8).....at a rather high level. In the subsequent four months, the (9).....average price showed a downtrend, but in September the prices have (10).....hardened to a considerable extent.

[Assistant Grade]

	(a)	(b)	(c)	(d)	(e)
(1)	sector	production	area	market	flour
(2)	last	first	second	current	general
(3)	higher	maximum	optimum	large	lower
(4)	conducted	based	shared	strategy	carried
(5)	outbursts	outbreak	conditions	forecast	pattern
(6)	above	per	to	compared	against
(7)	downtrend	increment	reduction	uptrend	upgrade
(8)	increased	surfaced	synchronised	moderated	stabilised
(9)	monthly	weekly	daily	annual	quarterly
(10)	then	never	again	since	now

07

Directions (Q. 1-10) : *Fill up the blanks in the passage below with the most appropriate word from the options given for each blank :*

Each species has its special place or habitat. An (1).....bird-watcher can look at (2).....forest, meadow, lake, swamp or field and (3).....almost exactly what birds he (4).....find there (5).....birds are found all over the world; other (6).....themselves to certain areas. Still (7).....migrate from one country to another in (8).....in search of warmth and (9).....and then return in spring (10).....the season is more favourable.

[SSC Stenographer Grade C]

	(a)	(b)	(c)	(d)
(1)	experience	expert	advanced	active
(2)	the	some	a	certain
(3)	predict	suggest	prophesy	calculate
(4)	should	must	might	will
(5)	more	some	most	all
(6)	keep	entrust	confine	involve
(7)	some	others	few	all
(8)	winter	summer	spring	autumn
(9)	seeds	crops	fruit	food
(10)	while	until	after	when

08

Directions (Q. 1-20) : Fill up the blanks, in the passage below with the most appropriate word from the options given for each blank :

I noticed George Ramsay at the restaurant. He was staring into space. He looked as though the burden of the whole world sat on his shoulders. I (1).....at once that his unfortunate brother (2).....trouble again. I suppose every family has a black.(3).....Tom had been a (4).....trial to his family (5).....twenty years. He had begun life decently enough he went (6).....business, married and had two children. The Ramsays were (7).....respectable people and there was every (8).....to suppose that Tom Ramsay would have a useful and (9).....carrier. But one day without warning, he (10).....that he did not like to work and that he was not suited (11).....marriage. He wanted to enjoy (12).....He would listen (13):....no advice. He left his wife and his (14)..... He had (15).....money and he spent two happy years in the various capitals of Europe. Rumours of his (16).....reached his relations from time to time and they were (17).....He certainly (18).....a very good time. They shook their heads and asked what (19).....when his money was spent. They soon found out that he was broke and wanted to (20).....home.

[MBA Entrance]

(1) (a) believed (b) suspected (c) agreed
(2) (a) had been causing (b) was causing (c) will case
(3) (a) goat (b) sheep (c) wolf
(4) (a) sore (b) bitter (c) sweet
(5) (a) since (b) for (c) in
(6) (a) into (b) for (c) to
(7) (a) utterly (b) perfectly (c) wholly
(8) (a) reason (b) cause (c) point
(9) (a) profitable (b) bad (c) honourable
(10) (a) said (b) announced (c) wrote
(11) (a) to (b) for (c) with
(12) (a) himself (b) idleness (c) others
(13) (a) to (b) in (c) with
(14) (a) job (b) house (c) relatives
(15) (a) a little (b) little (c) no
(16) (a) habits (b) doings (c) whereabouts
(17) (a) deeply (b) shocked (c) disappointed
(18) (a) has (b) had (c) will have
(19) (a) would happen (b) happened (c) will happen
(20) (a) come back (b) go (c) settle

09

Directions (Q. 1-10) : In the following passage there are blanks each of which has been numbered. These numbers are printed below the passage and against each five words are suggested one of which fits the blanks appropriately. Find out the appropriate word in each case :

Desire and action are often coordinated in that desire may the person to action or that desire may (1)....the person to action or that desire may be (2).....from action . If *P* is seen as trying to do *X*, it is often inferred that *P* desires *X*. However, desire and action are not (3).....coordinated. The person may desire X without (4).....in any action directed towards the attainment of *X*. This event happens when *X* appears (5).....or when the other effects resulting from the action (6).....to attain *X* are sufficiently undesirable as to (7).....the desire for *X*. Sometimes, of course, no action is necessary; the desire may or may not be (8).....quite independently of *P*'s action. Furthermore, a given desire may lead to different actions, depending upon the environmental requirements. Actions are (9).....not only by desire, but also by the way the person (10).....the causal structure of the environment. **[SBI PO]**

(1) (a) dampen (b) hinder (c) indulge (d) arouse (e) prohibit
(2) (a) expelled (b) ceased (c) abstained (d) refrained (e) inferred
(3) (a) invariably (b) hopefully (c) deliberately (d) purposely (e) negatively
(4) (a) wanting (b) associating (c) engaging (d) supporting (e) exhibiting
(5) (a) manageable (b) valuable (c) unattainable (d) reachable (e) approachable
(6) (a) hostile (b) necessary (c) incidental (d) insensible (e) detrimental
(7) (a) express (b) appreciate (c) reciprocate (d) damage (e) negate
(8) (a) realised (b) hypothesised (c) verbalised (d) criticised (e) actualised
(9) (a) projected (b) determined (c) controlled (d) galvanised (e) pronounced
(10) (a) downgrades (b) fabricates (c) develops (d) sees (e) enlarges

10

Directions (Q. 1-15) : *In the following passage there are blanks each of which has been numbered. These numbers are printed below the passage and against each three words are suggested one of which fits the blanks appropriately. Find out the appropriate word in each case :*

One day while I was discussing a new strategy to locate the wild dogs, a forgest guard at Sariska informed me that about 15-16 metres to the right of Pandupole road, a chital lay killed apparently by wild dogs. This was difficult to (1) ...... because wild dogs usually do not leave, (2) ...... any kill. They finish it, (3) ..... to the bone. Still an examination would, (4) .....interesting information and vital clues about the, (5) .....so I proceeded in the direction pointed, (6) ..... by the guard, Scanning the area I, (7) .....across the dead Chital. The, (8) ..... had been opened but not (9) ..... eaten. Its owner had, (10) ..... dressed the dinner ready for eating. I looked about for marks and (11) ..... I found them, the marks, (12) ..... indicated the presence of a canine. But, (13) Jackals or wild dogs? Since Jackals were active in Sariska independently, (14) ..... Chital-kills, the actual presence, (15) the wild dog still remained doubtful. **[CDS]**

(1) (a) presume	(b) believe	(c) know
(2) (a) behind	(b) away	(c) after
(3) (a) up	(b) over	(c) off
(4) (a) prove	(b) reveal	(c) involves
(5) (a) predator	(b) chital	(c) man-eater
(6) (a) out	(b) to	(c) at
(7) (a) found	(b) located	(c) came
(8) (a) body	(b) corpse	(c) carcass
(9) (a) now	(b) yet	(c) at all
(10) (a) probably	(b) surely	(c) really
(11) (a) when	(b) where	(c) which
(12) (a) frankly	(b) openly	(c) clearly
(13) (a) what	(b) which	(c) who
(14) (a) having	(b) hunting	(c) making
(15) (a) about	(b) of	(c) regarding

11

Directions (Q. 1-10) : *In the following sentences there are some blanks which are numbered. Below the sentences you are given a choice of three words (a), (b), (c), one of which is the most appropriate. Choose the best word as your answer :*

It is one of the tragic ironies of our age that the rocket which could have been symbol of humanity's aspirations for the stars, has become one of the weapons threatening to destroy civilisation. This state of affairs has (1).....a difficult moral problem to (2).....wishing to take an active (3).....in the development of astronautics, (4).....almost all research on rockets (5).....now carried out by military (6).....and is covered by various (7).....classifications. The technical problems involved (8).....designing long-range guided missiles are (9).....identical with those involved in the (10).....of reconnaissance rockets.

[UPSC Assistant Provident Fund]

(1) (a) produced	(b) caused	(c) presented
(2) (a) those	(b) others	(c) men
(3) (a) part	(b) position	(c) interest
(4) (a) when	(b) for	(c) where
(5) (a) was	(b) are	(c) is

(6) (a) establishments	(b) officers	(c) centres
(7) (a) secret	(b) security	(c) defence
(8) (a) in	(b) with	(c) for
(9) (a) hardly	(b) never	(c) practically
(10) (a) launching	(b) construction	(c) deployment

12

Directions (Q. 1-10) : In the following passage there are blanks each of which has been numbered. These numbers are printed below the passage and against each, five words are suggested, one of which fits the blank appropriately. Find out the appropriate words :

New industries supported by foreign interests (1).....offer (2).....salaries to their employees at all levels of responsibility than (3).....locally-owned industries. They need (4).....people and are (5).....to pay high wages to (6).....them. Local industries often (7).....the high salaries offered by foreign-supported industries, arguing that this will (8).....raise all wages to an excessive level. Workers in local industries, seeing the sharp (9)..... in job-pay will agitate for an improvement in their salaries. This eventually will drain the resources and (10).....their profitability.

[Bank PO Madras]

(1) (a) hardly	(b) reluctantly	(c) seldom	(d) never	(e) usually
(2) (a) disproportionate	(b) better	(c) proportionate	(d) comparable	(e) unreasonable
(3) (a) did	(b) could	(c) do	(d) their	(e) does
(4) (a) local	(b) several	(c) more	(d) talented	(e) less
(5) (a) willing	(b) bound	(c) forced	(d) reluctant	(e) authorised
(6) (a) entertain	(b) retain	(c) enrich	(d) hire	(e) bribe
(7) (a) uphold	(b) imitate	(c) protest	(d) pay	(e) accept
(8) (a) hardly	(b) considerably	(c) not	(d) unreasonably	(e) artificially
(9) (a) difference	(b) cut	(c) hike	(d) decrease	(e) injustice
(10) (a) augment	(b) fulfil	(c) enhance	(d) lower	(e) check

13

Directions (Q. 1-10) : *In the following passage there are blanks, each of which has been numbered. These numbers are printed below the passage and against each five words are suggested one of which fits the blank appropriately. Find out the appropriate words :*

Belief systems the framework upon which cultures and societies function. It is the bond that (1).....civilizations together, and it is the small voice (2).....each of us that urges us to be (3).....to what we have been taught. We cannot (4).....our spiritual teachings from our learning, nor can we separate our beliefs about who and what we are (5).....our values and our behaviours. We ask that educational systems (6).....our right to religious freedom and our right to live in harmony tribal beliefs vary, as does the (7).....to which a tribe embraces (8).....traditional cultural beliefs (9).....tribal group has distinct and unique beliefs that are basic to that tribe's culture. Most tribes cling to the old teachings because they know that once gone it means the (10).....of their culture.

[Bank PO]

(1) (a) compels	(b) holds	(c) makes	(d) breaks	(e)completes
(2) (a) outside	(b) around	(c) about	(d) inside	(e) near
(3) (a) true	(b) habitual	(c) accurate	(d) graceful	(e) upright
(4) (a) see	(b) separate	(c) upset	(d) distinguish	(e) search
(5) (a) near	(b) on	(c) from	(d) about	(e) across
(6) (a) recognise	(b) destroy	(c) diminish	(d) reach	(e) infer

(7) (a) capacity	(b) nearness	(c) practise	(d) extent	(e) principle
(8) (a) for	(b) their	(c) itself	(d) about	(e) its
(9) (a) many	(b) all	(c) one	(d) several	(e) each
(10) (a) mark	(b) regeneration	(c) death	(d) tradition	(e) mistake

14

Directions (Q. 1-10) : In the following passage there are blanks each of which has been numbered. These numbers are printed below the passage and against each five words are suggested, one of which fits the blank appropriately. Find out the appropriate words in each case :

Faced with an (1).....number and variety of products on the market, managers are finding it more difficult to (2).....demand and plan production and orders (3)..... As a result, (4).....forecasts are increasing and along with them, the costs of those errors.

Many managers today, (5).....speed is the (6).....have turned to one or an other popular production scheduling system. But these tools tackle only part of the problem. (7).....really needed is a way to (8).....forecasts and simultaneously redesign planning processes to (9).....the impact of (10).....forecasts.

(1) (a) equal	(b) exact	(c) optimum	(d) unanimous	(e) unprecedented
(2) (a) ignore	(b) meet	(c) predict	(d) accept	(e) register
(3) (a) immediately	(b) quickly	(c) accordingly	(d) positively	(e) spontaneously
(4) (a) inadequate	(b) buoyant	(c) frequent	(d) inaccurate	(e) exorbitant
(5) (a) consider	(b) neglecting	(c) visualising	(d) believing	(e) notwithstanding
(6) (a) problem	(b) answer	(c) source	(d) outcome	(e) lacuna
(7) (a) one	(b) that's	(c) what's	(d) managers	(e) companies
(8) (a) ignore	(b) obtain	(c) vitiate	(d) negate	(e) improve
(9) (a) rationalise	(b) substantiate	(c) minimise	(d) counter	(e) tolerate
(10) (a) dangerous	(b) absolute	(c) unpredicted	(d) erroneous	(e) popular

15

Directions (Q. 1-10) : *In the following passage at certain points, you are given a choice of three words marked (a), (b), (c). Choose the best word from these three and indicate your choice :*

From that moment his life became intolerable. He passed his days in apprehension of each succeeding night; and (1).....night the vision (2).....back again. As soon as he (3).....locked himself up in his room he (4).....to struggle; but in vain. An (5).....force lifted him up and pushed him (6).....the glass, as if to call the phantom and before long he saw it (7).....in the spot where the crime was (8).....lying with arms and legs outspread the way the body (9).....found. Then the dead girl (10).....and came toward him with little steps just as the child had done when she came out of the river.

(1) (a) all	(b) each	(c) every
(2) (a) comes	(b) come	(c) came
(3) (a) had been	(b) had	(c) was
(4) (a) strives	(b) strived	(c) strove
(5) (a) compelling	(b) irresistible	(c) overwhelming
(6) (a) upon	(b) towards	(c) against
(7) (a) laid	(b) lying	(c) laying
(8) (a) perpetrated	(b) done	(c) committed
(9) (a) has been	(b) had been	(c) was
(10) (a) stood up	(b) raised up	(c) rose up

16

Directions (Q. 1-10) : *In the following passage there are blanks each of which has been numbered. These numbers are printed below the passage and against each five words are suggested, one of which fits the blank appropriately. Find out the appropriate words in each case :*

Do women (1).....leadership differently from what men do ? And it so, will feminine leadership (2).....where (3).....leadership does not ? A recent study suggests somewhat paradoxically that female managers (4).....their male (5).....even when the personal characteristics of both are very (6).....of the two schools of thought, the structuralist theory argues that men and women do not receive the same treatment in the workplace and that stamping out (7).....bias would stamp out the observed (8)..... In contrast, the socialisation theory contends that men and women experience work differently because men seek work as more (9).....to their lives. These (10).....explanations, apart, today business appears to be undergoing a feminisation of leadership. **[PO]**

	(a)	(b)	(c)	(d)	(e)
(1)	exercise	undertake	authorise	empower	tolerate
(2)	affect	succeed	compete	progress	dominate
(3)	traditional	charismatic	masculine	benevolent	authoritarian
(4)	outlive	outcast	outwork	outstand	outdo
(5)	employees	subordinates	managers	counterparts	superiors
(6)	minimal	distinct	unique	similar	constant
(7)	employment	ulture	gender	class	category
(8)	variations	discriminations	resemblances	distortions	equalities
(9)	needy	desperate	preliminary	trivial	central
(10)	contradictory	corresponding	discriminating	analogical	identical

17

Directions (Q. 1-6) : *In the following sentences at certain points you are given a choice of three words one of which is most appropriate. Choose the best word out of the three words—one of which is most appropriate. Mark the letter, viz, (a), (b), (c) relating to this word :*

Smallpox, the most devastating and feared pestilence in human history, is making its last stand in two remote areas of Ethiopia, one in the desert and one in the mountains.

As of the end of August (1).....five villages had experienced cases (2).....the preceding eight weeks. More (3).....necessary, the oneset of the last (4).....case was on 9th August. (5).....man is the only known (6).....of the smallpox virus, the disease should be eliminated forever when the last infected person recovers. **[NDA]**

	(a)	(b)	(c)
(1)	rarely	the	only
(2)	in	about	of
(3)	necessary	important	urgent
(4)	found	remembered	known
(5)	because	when	while
(6)	culprit	reservoir	producer

18

Directions (Q. 1-10) : In the following passage there are blanks each of which has been numbered. The numbers are printed below the passage and against each five words are suggested one of which fits the blank appropriately. Find out the appropriate words :

The world economy is in recession, the deepest and the most widespread (1).....the 1930s. There are (2).....of (3).....in the industrial countries, but most serious economic (4).....anticipate the rates of growth and levels of economic activity will remain low.

In all that has been written about world (5).....the (6).....have been overwhelmingly and narrowly economic. Few have (7).....the human consequences in more than a superficial manner. Not a single international study has (8).....the recession's (9).....on the most vulnerable half of the world's population—the children.

The need for (10).....clearly the contrast between world economic conditions and child welfare has thus, become even more urgent in the last few years. The world scale of current child distress also makes it artificial to restrict the analysis of causes to the national level.

(1) (a) in (b) for (c) by (d) before (e) since
(2) (a) risks (b) glimmers (c) studies (d) tips (e) histories
(3) (a) development (b) downfall (c) recovery (d) slackness (e) impact
(4) (a) analysts (b) journalists (c) surveys (d) findings (e) students
(5) (a) development (b) economy (c) wars (d) recession (e) conflicts
(6) (a) emphasis (b) aims (c) glimpses (d) supposition (e) preoccupations
(7) (a) delved (b) taught (c) propagated (d) investigated (e) manifested
(8) (a) understood (b) analysed (c) highlighted (d) prepared (e) planned
(9) (a) analysis (b) undercurrents (c) impact (d) overtures (e) study
(10) (a) chalking out (b) curbing (c) bringing out (d) implementing (e) propagating

19

Directions (Q. 1-10) : In the following passage there are blanks each of which has been numbered . The numbers are printed below the passage and against each four words are suggested, one of which fits the blank appropriately. Find out the appropriate words :

Many parents greet their children's teenage years with needless dread. While teens (1)......assault us with heavy-metal music (2)......outlandish clothes and spend all (3)......time with friends, such behaviour (4)......adds up to full scale revolt. Teenage (5)......according to Psychologist Laurence Steinberg, has been (6)......exaggerated. Sociologist Sanford Dombusch agrees. "The (7)......that teenagers inevitably rebel is a (8)......that has the potential for great family (9)......"says Dornbusch. He believes the notion can (10)......communication during this critical time for parents to influence youngesters.

[Assistant Grade]

(1) (a) can (b) must (c) may (d) should
(2) (a) show (b) dress (c) put (d) flaunt
(3) (a) her (b) his (c) their (d) our
(4) (a) sporadically (b) always (c) infrequently (d) scarcely
(5) (a) rebellion (b) subversion (c) mania (d) revolution
(6) (a) always (b) never (c) greatly (d) hardly
(7) (a) complaint (b) surmise (c) accusation (d) idea
(8) (a) myth (b) story (c) fact (d) reality
(9) (a) ruin (b) downfall (c) harm (d) defeat
(10) (a) destroy (b) suffocate (c) damage (d) injure

20

Directions (Q. 1-5) : *In the following passage there are blanks each of which has been numbered. The numbers are printed below the passage and against each five words are suggested, one of which fits the blank appropriately. Find out the appropriate words :*

Nations which have (1)....programmes of economic development often run into unsuspected barriers which threaten and often (2)....the (3)....needed growth of the economy. Industrialisation (4)....productivity fails to respond and the nations goals of rising standard of living for its people are (5).... **[BPO]**

(1) (a) decided (b) progressed (c) insisted (d) embarked (e) initiated
(2) (a) activate (b) deteriorate (c) halt (d) cut (e) enlighten
(3) (a) positively (b) hopefully (c) alarmingly (d) deceptively (e) deseperately
(4) (a) falters (b) deviates (c) fluctuates (d) lowers (e) dissolves
(5) (a) postponed (b) frustrated (c) suspended (d) criticised (e) fulfilled

21

Directions (Q. 1-10) : In the following passage there are blanks each of which has been numbered. The numbers are printed below the passage and against each four words are suggested, one of which fits the blank appropriately. Find out the appropriate words :

For generations man has (1)......against the wilds to create a world where only he (2)......whether animals and plants survive or are (3)......out. Earlier we accepted as self-evident that any (4)......in our environment brought about by science and technology must be improvements (5)......the world of our (6)......However, many people all over the world have begun to feel that (7)......are going too far and that we should try to (8)......some of the world's original life before we find it (9)......too late. The same science which had led us away from nature is now (10)......the miracle of creation. **[Delhi Police]**

(1) (a) faced (b) stood (c) struggled (d) challenged
(2) (a) decides (b) thinks (c) advises (d) observes
(3) (a) taken (b) wiped (c) put (d) thrown
(4) (a) differences (b) increments (c) changes (d) replacements
(5) (a) in (b) at (c) over (d) for
(6) (a) aborigins (b) ancients (c) successors (d) ancestors
(7) (a) overselves (b) we (c) us (d) some
(8) (a) demolish (b) cherish (c) save (d) renovate
(9) (a) occurs (b) sounds (c) seems (d) gets
(10) (a) unfolding (b) discussing (c) arguing (d) narrating

22

Directions (Q. 1-10) : *In the following passage there are blanks each of which has been numbered. These numbers are also printed below the passages and against each five words are suggested, one of which fits the blanks appropriately find out the appropriate words in each case :*

The latest stage of the continuing (1)....between India and the United States on the nuclear issue is now punctuated with pleasing diplomatic observations. Our latest round of talks with the American Deputy Secretary of State is "positive and encouraging". The US Deputy Secretary of State remarked that none or us are pleased to have any clouds over the (2).... . We in India know that these clouds have (3)....towards the sub-continent from the West. The US can easily disperse the clouds if it wants. But the economic sanctions are still in place. The US is only (4)....trying to come to terms with the fact that the nuclear weapons are not the (5)....of the Permanent Members of the Security Council. If they do not recognise India as a nuclear power, then what is it that they are (6)....to ? India will not (7)....by their derecognising the nuclear tests both sides can happily close (8)....eyes and agree to (9)....what has happened . The fact that India is a sovereign nation entitled to take decision beneficial for its own security, has not been altered by the tests. The US has come round to (10)....that India has some say in this matter. **[Bank PO]**

(1) (a) adversaries (b) negotiations (c) strifes (d) strategies (e) disputes
(2) (a) relationship (b) struggle (c) matter (d) talks (e) countries
(3) (a) formed (b) eclipsed (c) ruined (d) covered (e) floated
(4) (a) spontaneously (b) generously (c) grudgingly (d) gracefully (e) willingly

(5) (a) threats	(b) creations	(c) properties	(d) monopoly	(e) possession
(6) (a) prepared	(b) objecting	(c) pointing	(d) clinging	(e) planning
(7) (a) gain	(b) differ	(c) flourish	(d) suffer	(e) develop
(8) (a) their	(b) our	(c) naked	(d) inward	(e) both
(9) (a) imitate	(b) undo	(c) cherish	(d) reiterate	(e) ignore
(10) (a) expecting	(b) suspecting	(c) accepting	(d) advocating	(e) rejecting

23

Directions (Q. 1-10) : *In the following passage there are blanks each of which has been numbered. These numbers are printed below the passages and against each five words are suggested, one of which fits the blanks appropriately find out the appropriate words :*

Although John Wisdom's writings in Philosophy show clearly the influence of Wittgenstein, they nevertheless also display a (1)....originality. Despite the (2)....and difficulty of his style, a careful reading of Wisdom is seldom (3)....He is unique kind of genius in Philosophy.

This essay is an excellent example of Wisdom's repeated attempts to (4)....the ultimate bases of philosophical perplexity. A great deal of the time Wisdom is (5)....interested in finding out why metaphysicians feel (6)....to utter such strange sentences e.g., "Time is unreal", "There are no material things", etc. According to Wisdom such sentences are both false (and perhaps meaningless) and year. (7).... Even more than Wittgenstein, Wisdom has stressed the 'The rapeutic conception of Philosophy, a view that comes out clearly in this essay where the emphasises that analogy between philosophical and neurotic distress (8)....them with other kinds of problems.

The reader who is interested in gaining a fuller (9)....with Wisdom's thought is referred to his famous article 'gods' in Philosophy and Psycho-analysis. Other Minds is Wisdom's most....(10).... discussion of a single topic and in many ways his finest work. **[Bank PO]**

(1) (a) concise	(b) virtual	(c) marked	(d) limited	(e) relative
(2) (a) individuality	(b) novelty	(c) originality	(d) complexity	(e) creativity
(3) (a) unprofitable	(b) useful	(c) advantageous	(d) unreliable	(e) durable
(4) (a) jettison	(b) delimit	(c) augment	(d) fortify	(e) explore
(5) (a) admirably	(b) primarily	(c) advertently	(d) reluctantly	(e) happily
(6) (a) depressed	(b) confined	(c) alluded	(d) compelled	(e) adapted
(7) (a) illuminating	(b) damaging	(c) confusing	(d) critical	(e) unreliable
(8) (a) compelling	(b) associating	(c) contrasting	(d) describing	(e) advocating
(9) (a) comparison	(b) analysis	(c) agreement	(d) elaboration	(e) acquaintance
(10) (a) projected	(b) sustained	(c) prolonged	(d) prolific	(e) attributed

24

Directions (Q. 1-6) : In the following sentences at certain points you are given a choice of three words one of which is most appropriate. Choose the best word out of the three . Mark the letter, viz, (a), (b) or (c) relating to this word on your answer sheet :

One summer a Brazilian farmer took his donkey, pele, with him to town (1)....the market place, a small boy began (2)....Pele with a, stick and the donkey struck (3)....injuring the boy with a kick on the head. The police chief (4)....the farmer arrested. The (5)....wept so profusely in the jail cell that the police chief changed his mind and locked up the (6)....instead. The charge against the animal was attempt to murder.

(1) (a) at	(b) on	(c) in
(2) (a) teaching	(b) tormenting	(c) playing

(3) (a) back (b) backward (c) forward
(4) (a) has (b) ordered (c) had
(5) (a) donkey (b) boy (c) farmer
(6) (a) donkey (b) boy (c) farmer

25

Directions *(Q. 1-15) : In the following passage at certain points, you are given a choice of three words marked (a), (b), (c) . Choose the best word from these three :*

The most attractive and unique feature of crossword puzzle is that it is a game one can play alone! There are several kinds of crossword puzzles. One kind is the prize competition in which the (1)....who finds the correct answers gets a big prize (2)....the answers are very hard to find, since several (3)....appear equally appropriate : bad, mad or sad for (4)....in the clue sentence, people are seldom popular. Such (5)....attract people who are fond of gambling because by (6)....a small entry fee, they can win big prizes. The (7)....type of crossword puzzle is one in which (8)....is only one possible answer to every clue. But (9)....answer is elusive and calls for some detective work (10)....our part. The clue gives only hints about the word A (11)....like 'Mate changes to flesh for food' (12)....elude you till you realise that any changing the (13)....of 'mate' you get 'meat'. Your comprehension and your (14)....knowledge are put to the test. The effort to (15)....such crossword is an intellectual exercise. **[CDS]**

(1) (a) person (b) actor (c) persons
(2) (a) though (b) although (c) but
(3) (a) letters (b) words (c) alphabets
(4) (a) assumption (b) illustration (c) example
(5) (a) competitions (b) puzzles (c) races
(6) (a) paying (b) buying (c) giving
(7) (a) another (b) second (c) two
(8) (a) this (b) their (c) there
(9) (a) am (b) this (c) any
(10) (a) on (b) in (c) upon
(11) (a) puzzle (b) word (c) clue
(12) (a) will (b) did (c) shall
(13) (a) lettering (b) words (c) spelling
(14) (a) general (b) overall (c) common sense
(15) (a) solve (b) dissolve (c) think of

26

Directions (Q. 1-15) : *In the following passage at certain points, you are given a choice of words marked as (a), (b), (c)and (d) . Choose the best word out of these four :*

Our scientific spirit must be shocked not only by the (1)......of fabulous (2)......and (3)......poverty, but also by those of intense holiness and (4)......superstition. In our relations with one another, we have (5)......to apply scientific and social wisdom. The failure is (6) large (7)......our society. Some social (8)......like untouchability are (9)......simply because the spirit in us is oppressed by the force of (10)......These are practised by (11)......kindly persons, who have ceased to feel and whose understanding is (12)......any tradition. There are millions in our country today who use scientific (13)......and yet (14)......superstition as mystical revelation and adhere to absured social customs..15..the name of tradition. **[Assistant Grade]**

(1) (a) phenomenon (b) contrasts (c) existence (d) comparison
(2) (a) property (b) prosperity (c) resources (d) wealth

(3) (a) common (b) rampant (c) grovelling (d) growing
(4) (a) religious (b) blind (c) popular (d) prevailing
(5) (a) attempted (b) refused (c) succeeded (d) failed
(6) (a) writ (b) written (c) wrought (d) wrapped
(7) (a) in (b) on (c) among (d) for
(8) (a) abuses (b) ceremonies (c) function (d) obligations
(9) (a) allowed (b) approved (c) tolerated (d) resisted
(10) (a) opinion (b) habit (c) society (d) custom
(11) (a) fairly (b) very (c) otherwise (d) somewhat
(12) (a) stupefied (b) sanctified (c) subsidized (d) substantiated
(13) (a) discoveries (b) devices (c) apparatus (d) machines
(14) (a) consider (b) decry (c) declare (d) revere
(15) (a) on (b) for (c) in (d) with

27

Directions (Q. 1-10) : *In the following passage at certain points, you are given a choice of words marked as (a), (b), (c)and (d). Choose the best word out of these four :*

There is an old story told (1)......a man who (2)......into a drunken sleep. His friend stayed by him as long as he (3)......but being compelled to go and fearing that he might be in want, the friend hid a (4) ......in the drunken man's garment. When the drunken man (5)......not knowing that his friend had (6)......jewel in his garment he wandered about in (7)......hungry. A long time afterwards the two men met again and the friend told the poor man about the jewel and advised him to look (8)......it. Like the drunken man of the story people (9)......about suffering in this life of birth and death (10)......of what is hidden away in their inner nature. Pure and untarnished, the price-less treasure of God. **[SSC Clerks]**

(1) (a) of (b) to (c) with (d) by (e) that
(2) (a) left (b) felt (c) fail (d) fell (e) gone
(3) (a) might (b) can (c) would (d) had (e) could
(4) (a) garment (b) drink (c) jewel (d) treasure (e) sleep
(5) (a) slept (b) recovered (c) covered (d) drinking (e) realised
(6) (a) taken (b) presented (c) substituted (d) replaced (e) hidden
(7) (a) vain (b) search (c) sleep (d) poverty (e) persuit
(8) (a) for (b) to (c) at (d) in (e) with
(9) (a) search (b) wonder (c) wander (d) trouble (e) unknown
(10) (a) conscious (b) unconscious (c) knowingly (d) expected (e) useless

28

Directions (Q. 1-10) : *In the following passage at certain points, you are given a choice of five words marked as (a), (b), (c), (d)and (e) . Choose the best word out of these five :*

The (1)......of a survey by the National institute of (2)......health give (3)......for (4)...... . According to the survey about 14 million people in Indian are affected (5)......mental (6)......at any point of time. In the case of mentally ill, it is (7)......enough difficult to (8)......them, let alone (9)......them. The most (10)......are those in the (11)......areas, for whatever (12)......for the mentally sick exist are concentrated around major urban centres.

(1) (a) verdicts (b) decisions (c) judgements (d) measures (e) findings
(2) (a) spiritual (b) psychical (c) social (d) physical (e) mental
(3) (a) food (b) cause (c) purpose (d) support (e) reinforcement
(4) (a) alarm (b) discontent (c) fear (d) dissatisfaction (e) vexation

(5) (a) dangerous (b) strong (c) serious (d) fatal (e) important
(6) (a) disorder (b) perturbation (c) dislocation (d) confusion (e) involvement
(7) (a) seldom (b) occasionally (c) often (d) hardly (e) never
(8) (a) cure (b) recognize (c) identify (d) select (e) rehabilitate
(9) (a) facilitate (b) guide (c) cure (d) advice (e) treat
(10) (a) indifferent (b) neglected (c) careless (d) abandoned (e) serious
(11) (a) urban (b) rural (c) forest (d) suburban (e) metropolitan
(12) (a) facilities (b) advantages (c) avenues (d) remedies (e) solicitations

Solution TYE 01

(1) (b), (2) (a), (3) (d), (4) (c), (5) (b), (6) (d).

Solution TYE 02

(1) (c), (2) (a), (3) (d), (4) (a).

Solution TYE 03

(1) (b), (2) (b), (3) (a), (4) (d), (5) (e), (6) (c), (7) (b), (8) (a), (9) (d), (10) (c).

Solution TYE 04

(1) (b), (2) (c), (3) (a), (4) (b), (5) (b), (6) (b), (7) (a), (8) (c), (9) (a), (10) (c), (11) (c), (12) (a), (13) (c), (14) (a), (15) (a).

Solution TYE 05

(1) (d), (2) (b), (3) (a), (4) (c), (5) (e), (6) (d), (7) (a), (8) (b), (9) (c), (10) (e).

Solution TYE 06

(1) (d), (2) (d), (3) (a), (4) (b), (5) (c), (6) (e), (7) (d), (8) (e), (9) (a), (10) (c).

Solution TYE 07

(1) (b), (2) (c), (3) (a), (4) (c), (5) (b), (6) (c), (7) (b), (8) (a), (9) (d), (10) (d).

Solution TYE 08

(1) (b), (2) (b), (3) (b), (4) (b), (5) (b), (6) (a), (7) (b), (8) (a), (9) (a), (10) (b), (11) (b), (12) (a), (13)(a), (14) (a), (15) (a), (16) (b), (17) (b), (18) (b), (19) (a), (20) (a).

Solution TYE 09

(1)(d), (2) (a), (3) (a), (4) (c), (5) (c), (6) (b), (7) (a), (8) (a), (9) (a), (10) (d).

Solution TYE 10

(1) (b), (2) (a), (3) (a), (4) (b), (5) (a), (6)(b), (7) (c), (8) (c), (9) (c), (10) (a), (11) (a), (12) (c). (13)(b), (14) (a), (15) (b).

Solution TYE 11

(1) (b), (2) (a), (3) (a), (4) (a), (5) (c), (6) (a), (7) (a), (8) (a), (9) (b), (10) (a).

Solution TYE 12

(1) (e), (2) (b), (3) (c), (4) (d), (5) (a), (6) (b), (7) (c), (8) (c), (9) (a), (10) (d).

Solution TYE 13

(1) (b), (2) (d), (3) (a), (4) (b), (5) (c), (6) (a), (7) (d), (8) (e), (9) (e), (10) (c).

Solution TYE 14

(1) (e), (2) (c), (3) (c) (4) (d), (5) (d), (6) (b), (7) (c), (8) (e), (9) (c), (10) (d).

Solution TYE 15

(1) (c), (2) (c), (3) (b), (4) (c), (5) (b), (6) (b), (7) (b), (8) (c), (9) (b), (10) (a).

Solution TYE 16

(1) (a), (2) (b), (3) (c), (4) (e), (5) (d), (6) (d), (7) (a), (8) (b), (9) (e), (10) (a).

Solution TYE 17

(1) (c), (2) (c), (3) (c), (4) (a), (5) (a), (6) (b).

Solution TYE 18

(1) (e), (2) (a), (3) (d), (4) (a), (5) (b), (6) (b), (7) (a), (8) (b), (9) (c), (10) (c).

Solution TYE 19

(1) (c), (2) (d), (3) (c), (4) (b), (5) (a), (6) (c), (7) (d), (8) (a), (9) (a), (10) (b).

Solution TYE 20

(1) (d), (2) (d), (3) (e), (4) (a), (5) (b).

Solution TYE 21

(1) (c), (2) (a), (3) (b), (4) (c), (5) (a), (6) (d), (7) (b), (8) (c), (9) (d), (10) (a).

Solution TYE 22

(1) (b), (2) (a), (3) (e), (4) (c), (5) (d), (6) (b), (7) (d), (8) (a), (9) (e) (10) (c).

Solution TYE 23

(1) (c), (2) (d), (3) (a), (4) (e), (5) (b), (6) (b), (7) (a), (8) (b), (9) (e), (10) (b).

Solution TYE 24

(1) (c), (2) (b), (3) (a), (4) (c), (5) (c), (6) (a).

Solution TYE 25

(1) (a), (2) (c), (3) (b), (4) (c), (5) (b), (6) (a), (7) (b), (8) (c), (9) (b), (10) (a), (11) (a), (12) (c), (13) (c), (14) (a), (15) (a),

Solution TYE 26

(1) (c), (2) (c), (3) (d), (4) (a), (5) (d), (6) (a), (7) (b), (8) (a), (9) (c), (10) (b), (11) (a), (12) (b), (13) (b), (14) (a), (15) (c).

Solution TYE 27

(1) (a) (2) (d) (3) (e) (4) (c) (5) (b) (6) (e) (7) (a) (8) (a) (9) (c) (10) (b)

Solution TYE 28

(1) (e), (2) (e), (3) (b), (4) (a), (5) (c), (6) (a), (7) (c), (8) (c), (9) (c), (10) (b), (11) (b), (12) (a).

CHAPTER 35

PHRASE SUBSTITUTION OR SENTENCE IMPROVEMENT

विभिन्न Competitive examinations में अंग्रेजी के प्रश्न-पत्र में Phrase substitution or Sentence improvement के 5 या 10 प्रश्नों का समावेश होता है। इस तरह के प्रश्नों में एक sentence दिया होता है जिसमें एक Phrase (कुछ शब्दों) को Bold या Italic किया होता है। इस Phrase में कुछ अशुद्धि होती है। उत्तर में 4 या 5 विकल्प देकर इन विकल्पों में से सही विकल्प (इस Phrase का Substitution) चुनना होता है।

इस तरह के प्रश्न में Phrase verb का गलत प्रयोग या Conditional verb का गलत प्रयोग या Adverb, Preposition का गलत प्रयोग या अन्य किसी तरह की गलती पाई जाती है। वास्तविकता यह है कि जब तक छात्र को Grammar के Rules का पूर्ण ज्ञान नहीं होता है, वह इस तरह के प्रश्नों को हल करने में स्वयं को अक्षम पाता है। छात्रों को सर्वप्रथम Grammar का अच्छी तरह अध्ययन करना चाहिए और इसके पश्चात् Book में दी गई समस्त Exercises को Solve करना चाहिए।

इस तरह के प्रश्न बहुत आसान होते हैं। यदि आप थोड़ा-सा प्रयास करते हैं तो आप इन प्रश्नों को निश्चित ही सही रूप से हल कर लेंगे।

अंग्रेजी के किसी भी प्रकार के प्रश्नों को हल करने का कोई Shortcut method नहीं है। बार-बार Grammatical rules को पढ़ने, नियमों पर आधारित Sentences को पढ़ने एवं Unsolved exercises को Solve करने से आपको इस तरह के प्रश्नों को Solve करने में बहुत सुविधा होगी।

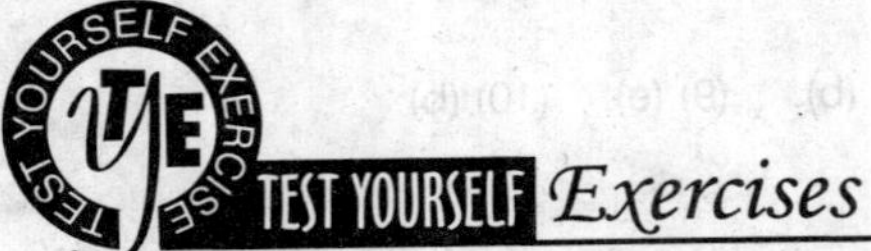

Exercises

01

Directions (Q. 1-5) *Which of the phrases (a) , (b) , (c) and (d) given below each sentence should replace the phrase that care **bold** to make the sentence grammatically correct ? If the sentence is correct as it is, mark (e) as your answer.*

(1) My doctor knew that I would eventually recover and do the kind of work I **would be doing before.**

(a) would have been doing
(b) would have done
(c) had been done
(d) had been doing
(e) No correction required

(2) If you are thinking about investing overseas **isn't make** sense to find an experienced guide ?

(a) is it not makinge
(b) doesn't it make
(c) does it make
(d) is it making
(e) No correction required

(3) In addition **to enhanced their reputation** through strategic use of philanthropy, companies are sponsoring social initiatives to open new markets.
(a) of enhancing their reputations
(b) to having enhance their reputation
(c) to enhancing their reputation
(d) to have their reputation enhancing
(e) No correction required

(4) Technology **must use to feed** the forces of change.
(a) must be used to feed
(b) must have been using to feed
(c) must use having fed
(d) must be using to feed
(e) No correction required

(5) The **crime has growth rapidly** in Russia since the disintegration of the communist system.
(a) rapid crime has grown
(b) crime has grown rapidly
(c) crimes grow rapidly
(d) crimes have been rapidly grown
(e) No correction required

02

Directions (Q. 1-5) *In the following questions, each sentence has an* **bold** *word or phrase followed by four alternatives. You are to choose the one that best keeps the meaning of the original sentence, if it is substituted for the* **bold** *word or phrases.*

(1) Veterinarians usually give dogs an anesthetic so that they don't **cry out in pain.**
(a) gulp *(b)* flip *(c)* yelp *(d)* purr

(2) City taxes are based on an **estimate of the value** of one's property.
(a) appraisal *(b)* forecast *(c)* diagnosis *(d)* outline

(3) Although buses are **scheduled** to depart at a certain hour, they are often late.
(a) listed *(b)* requested *(c)* obligated *(d)* loaded

(4) Because light travels faster than sound, lightning appears to **go before** thunder.
(a) prolong *(b)* traverse *(c)* repel *(d)* precede

(5) When students do not have time to read a novel before class, they read **an outline of the plot instead.**
(a) an article *(b)* a synopsis *(c)* a critique *(d)* an essay

03

Directions (Q. 1-5) *Which of the phrases (a), (b), (c) and (d) given below each sentence should replace the phrase that are* **bold** *to make the sentence grammatically correct? If the sentence is correct as it is, mark (e) as the answer.*

(1) The performance of our players was rather **worst than I had expected.**
(a) bad as I had expected
(b) worse than I had expected
(c) worse than expectation
(d) worst than was expected
(e) No correction required

(2) It is always better to make people realise the importance of discipline **than to impose them on them on it.**
(a) impose it with them
(b) impose them with it
(c) imposing them on it
(d) impose it on them
(e) No correction required

(3) The crops are dying **it must not had rained.**
(a) must had not
(b) must not be
(c) must not have
(d) must not have been
(e) No correction required

(4) They **were all shocked at** his failure in the competition.
(a) were shocked at all
(b) had all shocked at
(c) had all shocked by
(d) had been all shocked on
(e) No correction required

(5) He is too impatient **for tolerating** any delay.
(a) to tolerate
(b) to tolerating
(c) at tolerating
(d) with tolerating
(e) No correction required

04

Directions (Q. 1-10) *Look at the **bold** part of each sentence. Below each sentence are given three possible substitutions for the **bold** part. If one of them (a), (b) or (c) is better than the **bold** part, select that part as your response. If none of the substitution improve the sentence, choose (d) as your response. Thus, a 'No improvement' response will be signified by the letter (d).*

(1) Just before the commencement of the examination, the invigilator advised us **from** copying or indulging in any other malpractices.
(a) against
(b) upon
(c) about
(d) No improvement

(2) The whole country is disappointed **over** the defeat of the cricket team.
(a) on
(b) above
(c) by
(d) No improvement

(3) If he joins the coaching class so late, I am afraid it will be hard for him to **catch up** with the others.
(a) speed up
(b) join up
(c) get in line
(d) No improvement

(4) If a definite care for cancer is discovered **in few years** it is unlikely that it will be a simpler or safer affair than that of diabetes.
(a) in some few years
(b) in the next few years
(c) after few years
(d) No improvement

(5) The tourists insured their luggage because they assumed it **must be** stolen.
(a) will be
(b) was going to be
(c) might be
(d) No improvement

(6) By the end of May each year the agricultural produce comprising wheat and gram goes **to the market**.
(a) to markets
(b) to market
(c) into a market
(d) No improvement

(7) The old man looked **with caution before** he crossed the busy street.
(a) cautiously before
(b) at cautiously when
(c) cautiously when
(d) No improvement

(8) Make haste lest **you should not be** caught in the storm.
(a) that you should not be
(b) you can be
(c) you should be
(d) No improvement

(9) The contesting candidates agreed to **seek** a common platform while canvassing for votes.
(a) have
(b) share
(c) find
(d) No improvement

(10) The new bank clerk kicked **off a** row with a colleague.
(a) out a
(b) on to a
(c) up a
(d) No improvement

05

Directions (Q. 1-10) *Look at the* **bold** *part of each sentence. Below each sentence are given three possible substitutions for the* **bold** *part. If one of the alternatives (a), (b) or (c) is better than the* **bold** *part, indicate your response accordingly against the corresponding letter (a) , (b) or (c). If none of the substitution improve the sentence, indicate (d) as your response. Thus, a 'No improvement' response will be signified by the letter (d).*

(1) Other countries **have eradicated** this disease ten years ago.
(*a*) eradicated (*b*) had eradicated
(*c*) did eradicate (*d*) No improvement

(2) We were **not** the wiser for all his effort to explain the case to us.
(*a*) none (*b*) neither
(*c*) nevertheless (*d*) No improvement

(3) If I stood alone in defence of truth and the whole would world **is banded** against me and against truth, I would fight them all.
(*a*) will be banded (*b*) were banded
(*c*) banded (*d*) No improvement

(4) During his long discourse, he did not **touch** that point.
(*a*) touch upon (*b*) touch on
(*c*) touch of (*d*) No improvement

(5) He died **in the year 1960 at 11 pm on 14 July.**
(*a*) on 14th July in the year 1960 at 11 p.m. (*b*) in the year 1960 on 14th July at 11 p.m.
(*c*) at 11 p.m. on 14 July in the year 1960 (*d*) No improvement

(6) For all our powers of reason and understanding we know **a little about life's secrets.**
(*a*) a little of life's secrets (*b*) little about life's secrets
(*c*) nothing about life's secrets (*d*) No improvement

(7) You have come here with a view **to insult me.**
(*a*) to insulting me (*b*) of insulting me
(*c*) for insulting me (*d*) No improvement

(8) This matter **admits** of no excuse.
(*a*) admits to (*b*) admits for (*c*) admits (*d*) No improvement

(9) He **has not and can never be** in the good books of his employer because he lacks honesty.
(*a*) has not and cannot be (*b*) has not and can never been
(*c*) has not been and can never be (*d*) No improvement

(10) The logic of the Berlin Wall **already had been undermined**, but when the news came through that the wall itself had been opened I jumped into a car.
(*a*) had been undermined already (*b*) had already been undermined
(*c*) had been already undermined (*d*) No improvement

06

Directions (Q. 1-7) *In each of these questions some part of the sentence or the whole sentence is* **bold**. *Five choices numbered (a) , (b) , (c) , (d) and (e) rephrasing the* **bold** *part follow each sentence. If the original part itself seems better than the alternatives and 'no change' is desired, choose answer (a) and if not, choose one of the other. For each sentence, consider the requirement of standard written English. Your choice should be correct and effective expression, not awkward or ambiguous. If a choice changes the meaning of the original sentence, do not select it.*

(1) If the present trend continues the cost of a good personal computer system **even can be as low as ` 15,000 soon.**

(1) If the present trend continues the cost of a good personal computer system **even can be as low as ` 15,000 soon.**
(a) No change.
(b) even soon can be as low as ₹15,000
(c) can soon be as low as ₹15,000
(d) as low as even ₹ 15,000 soon can be
(e) as low can soon be even ₹ 15,000

(2) As the message of the freedom struggle could not be spread over the government controlled radio, it **effectively was carried to the masses by the press.**
(a) No change.
(b) it was effectively carried to the masses by the press
(c) by the effective press it was carried to the masses
(d) it was carried to the effective masses by the press
(e) to the effective masses it was carried by the press.

(3) From a study of University enrolment figures over the past decade, **evidence is that women are increasingly opting for professional courses.**
(a) No change
(b) the increasingly opting for professional courses by women is evidence
(c) evidently it is increasing the enrolment of women in professional courses
(d) it is evident that women are increasingly opting for provisional courses
(e) women are increasingly opting for professional courses, that is evident

(4) The new draft legislation seeks to ensure that some of the profits form the commercialisation of biodiversity **goes to the know how actually possessed by local communities.**
(a) No change
(b) goes to the actual communities who possess the local know how
(c) actually goes to the communities that possess the know how locally
(d) to the local communities that possess the know how actually
(e) goes to the local communities that actually possess the know how

(5) The rapid fall in birthrate achieved by China over the 1980s is **placing a retiring strain on many old workers who must retire now from the workforce.**
(a) No change
(b) places a strain on the old workers as they retire from the workforce
(c) is placing a strain on the workforce now as many old workers retire
(d) is placing many old workers on a strain as they must retire from the workforce
(e) is placing many old workers who must retire as a strain on the workforce

(6) A recently carried out mega-analysis of two decades of published research **does not suggest that there should be an association between coffee drinking and coronary ailments**.
(a) No change
(b) suggests that there is no association between coffee drinking and coronary ailments
(c) suggests for no association between coffee drinking and coronary ailments
(d) any association between coffee drinking and coronary ailments is not suggests
(e) shows that coffee drinking should not be suggested to have an association with coronary ailments

(7) In relation to the forthcoming parliamentary election the EC clarified that as no legislation had been formulated, there was **no question of raising the official ceiling on election expenses of candidates.**

(a) No change

(b) raising the ceiling on official election expenses of candidates could not be questioned

(c) no question had been raised regarding the official ceiling on election expenses of candidates

(d) the official ceiling on election expenses of candidates should be raised, there is no question

(e) there was no need to question the official ceiling on election expenses of candidates

07

Directions (Q. 1-10) Which of the following phrases (a), (b), (c) and (d) given below each sentence should replace the phrase that are ***bold*** to make the sentence grammatically correct ? If the sentence is correct as it is, mark (e) as the answer.

[Bank PO]

(1) It is true that there **has been a considerable decline** in rural poverty.

(a) has been considerably declining *(b)* was considerably a decline
(c) have been considered decline *(d)* has a considerable decline
(e) No correction required

(2) They **have been attending** classes since the term began.

(a) would attend *(b)* had attended
(c) would be attending *(d)* should attend
(e) No correction required

(3) He considers the new assignment as more challenging than **much of the other** assignments.

(a) none for the other's *(b)* most of the other
(c) more of the other *(d)* rest of the other
(e) No correction required

(4) Resolutions must **be introducingquickly to repeal** the outdated laws.

(a) be introducing to quick repeal *(b)* have to be introduced to quick repealing
(c) be quickly introduced to repeal *(d)* be quick introducing to repeal
(e) No correction required

(5) The driver **didn't accede at the demand** of the people as he was aware of the risk involved in it.

(a) was not accede at the demand *(b)* didn't accede at demanding
(c) was not acceded by the demand *(d)* didn't accede to the demand
(e) No correction required

(6) Though his actions **were severe criticisum** he didn't lose his temper.

(a) were severely criticised *(b)* had severely criticised
(c) were at severely criticising *(d)* had severe criticised
(e) No correction required

(7) Yogic exercises and meditation **seems to be a help** modern men and women deal effectively with anxiety.

(a) seem to help *(b)* seems to be helping
(c) seem to have help *(d)* seems to help
(e) No correction required

(8) Despite all the complaints against him, we must admit that his behaviour with other **has always courteous.**

(a) had always courteous *(b)* have always courteous
(c) has always been courteous *(d)* has always been courteously
(e) No correction required

(9) **Whom did you intend to** to offer the job besides the two young boys?
(a) Who are you intending to
(b) Whom do you intended to
(a) Who do you intend for
(d) Whom had you been intended for
(e) No correction required

(10) She always behaves **as if she has not** care at all about my feelings.
(a) as though she will not
(b) as if she doesn't
(c) as far as she doesn't
(d) like if she does not
(e) No correction required

08

Directions (Q. 1-15) *Look at the **bold** part of each sentence. Below each sentence are given three possible substitutions for the **bold** part. If one of them (a) , (b) or (c) is better than the **bold** part, indicate your response against the corresponding letter (a) , (b) or (c) . If none of the substitutions improves the sentence, indicate (d) as your response. Thus, (a) 'No improvement' response will be signified by the letter (d).*

[CDS 1998]

(1) Being given to understand that there is a vacancy of an assistant in the firm, **an application was submitted by me.**
(a) an application has been submitted by myself
(b) an application by me was submitted
(c) I submitted an application
(d) No improvement

(2) She drives her car at eighty miles **each hour.**
(a) an hour
(b) every hour
(c) hourly
(d) No improvement

(3) I hope it will not rain when **they have started their journey.**
(a) they will have started their journey
(b) they will start their journey
(c) they start their journey
(d) No improvement

(4) After a six-hour marathon session, the two political parties are **united together.**
(a) joined
(b) together
(c) united
(d) No improvement

(5) I gave my niece a **children's very colourfully illustrated encyclopedia.**
(a) a very colourfully illustrated children's encyclopedia.
(b) a child's very colourfully illustrated encyclopedia.
(c) an illustrated child's very colourful encyclopedia.
(d) No improvement

(6) **Nearly everyone** suffers when unemployment rises.
(a) Everyone nearly *(b)* Nearly all *(c)* Nearly each one *(d)* No improvement

(7) If you **wrote** to me earlier, I would have easily solved your problem.
(a) were writing *(b)* had written *(c)* have written *(d)* No improvement

(8) Can't you **never understand** what has been said ?
(a) ever understand *(b)* rather understand *(c)* at all understand *(d)* No improvement

(9) The limestone formations suggest that in the distant past, the area was a vast sea filled with creatures that **absorb** calcium compounds from the water.
(a) absorbs *(b)* absorbed *(c)* had absorbed *(d)* No improvement

(10) He asked me where **was my book.**
(a) my book was *(b)* my book is *(c)* is my book *(d)* No improvement

(11) Suddenly she became conscious **regarding** the presence of a stranger in the room.
(a) about *(b)* of *(c)* over *(d)* No improvement

(12) This is the first time in my memory that the river **has overflown** the banks.
(a) overflew *(b)* has overflowed
(c) overflowed *(d)* No improvement

(13) What I learned is that freedom is really the result of how **you will remove** obstacles.
(a) you would remove *(b)* you can remove
(c) you remove *(d)* No improvement

(14) The workers **are waiting** for their pay packet since morning.
(a) would be waiting *(b)* were waiting
(c) have been waiting *(d)* No improvement

(15) Ensure to **contact with** as many teachers as possible.
(a) contact *(b)* contact on *(c)* contact to *(d)* No improvement

09

Directions (Q. 1-6) *Look at the **bold** part of each sentence. Below each sentence are given in three possible substitutions for the **bold** part. If one of them (a), (b) or (c) is better than the bold part, indicate your response on the Answer Sheet against the corresponding letter (a), (b) or (c). If none of the substitutions improves the sentence, indicate (d) as your response on the answer Sheet. Thus, a 'No improvement' response will be signified by the letter (d).* **[NDA]**

(1) I can't tackle this problem which with all its complications **have** confused me.
(a) has *(b)* had *(c)* will have *(d)* No improvement

(2) My friend **would have missed** the train if he had not hurried.
(a) had missed *(b)* has missed *(c)* missed *(d)* No improvement

(3) We have plenty of time **isn't it**?
(a) haven't we *(b)* have we *(c)* is it *(d)* No improvement

(4) The criminal as well as his accomplice **was** arrested.
(a) were *(b)* are being *(c)* have been *(d)* No improvement

(5) The world's population will continue to grow **when** the birthrate exceeds the death-rate.
(a) as long as *(b)* unless *(c)* until after *(d)* No improvement

(6) Until he **does not ask for** an apology, I am not going to reinstate him.
(a) does ask for *(b)* asked for *(c)* asks for *(d)* No improvement

10

Directions (Q. 1-10) *Which of the following phrases (a), (b), (c) and (d) given below each sentence should replace the phrase that are **bold** to make the sentence grammatically correct? If the sentence is correct as it is, mark (e) as the answer.* **[Bank PO]**

(1) All the members of the club **were assembled to celebrate** the 50th anniversary of the club.
(a) had assembled to celebrate *(b)* were assembling to celebrate
(c) had been assembled for celebrating *(d)* assembled to celebration
(e) No correction required

(2) **Increased productivity necessary** reflects greater efforts made by the employees.
(a) Increase in productivity necessary *(b)* Increased productivity is necessary
(c) Increase of productivity necessary *(d)* Increased productivity necessarily
(e) No correction required

(3) The earnest appeal by the staff members that the salaries be subjected to **up ward revision were rejected** by the industrialist.
(a) upwardly revision was rejected
(b) upward revision was rejected
(c) upward revising were rejectable
(d) upwardly revision was rejectable
(e) No correction required

(4) Speculations and **hypothesising are** the most essential and well known aspects of inventions.
(a) hypothesis has been
(b) hypothesising needs
(c) hypothesis makes
(d) hypothesising confronts
(e) No correction required

(5) The **alarming report** of the building collapse made everyone spell bound.
(a) alarmed report
(b) alarmed reporting
(c) reporting alarm
(d) reported alarm
(e) No correction required

(6) Your good gestures **will highly appreciate.**
(a) will be highly appreciate
(b) will be high appreciative
(c) will be highly appreciated
(d) would be high appreciation
(e) No correction required

(7) Yogic exercise **seems to be help** urban population deal effectively with stress.
(a) seems to be helpful
(b) seems to be helped
(c) seems to help
(d) seemed to be of helping
(e) No correction required

(8) They **fell very proudly** that their team had won the match.
(a) feel very proudly
(b) felt very pride
(c) feel very pride
(d) felt very proud
(e) No correction required

(9) The pedestrians **must to be** very cautious while crossing the road.
(a) should have to
(b) must be
(c) should have
(d) are required to be
(e) No correction required

(10) I am sure that he has recovered from his illness **and he will accompany** us to the picnic spot.
(a) and that he will accompany
(b) and that he will be accompanied
(c) but he will accompany
(d) although he will accompany
(e) No correction required

11

Directions (Q. 1-10) *In these questions, which of the phrases (a), (b), (c) and (d) given below should replace the phrase **bold** in the following sentence to make the sentence grammatically meaningful and correct. If the sentence is correct as it is and no correction is required, mark (e) as the answer.* **[Indian Bank PO]**

(1) He will be greatly surprised if he **was felicitated** by his staff members
(a) if he will have felicitated
(b) unless he was felicitated
(c) if he is felicitated
(d) if he would have felicitated
(e) No correction required

(2) Did you know when **shall he be leaving** for higher studies to the USA?
(a) should he be left
(b) he would be leaving
(c) he would be left
(d) would he have left
(e) No correction required

(3) The labour contractors reported that they **had finished** the work of building the stone wall.
(a) had been finished
(b) was finished
(c) could be finished
(d) has finished
(e) No correction required

(4) For want of financial resources, he was **unable to continue** his studies.
(a) unabled to continue
(b) unable to be continued
(c) unable to have continued
(d) unable to continuing
(e) No correction required

(5) He complained of **being unjustily treatment.**
(a) of being unjustly treated.
(b) for being injustice in treatment.
(c) that unjust treatment being given
(d) for being unjustly treatment.
(e) No correction required

(6) The donation amount was **such that as I was expected** him to donate.
(a) so that as I expected
(b) such that I expected of
(c) such as that I expect
(d) exactly as I had expected
(e) No correction required

(7) It is pity that no one in the family **disapproves by his getting up** late.
(a) disapproved by his getting up
(b) disapproves of his getting up
(c) disapproved that he is getting up
(d) disapproved why he got up
(e) No correction required

(8) He is less likely to win **unless he practised** rigorously and regularly.
(a) until he practised
(b) unless he practise
(c) unless he practises
(d) unless he does not practise
(e) No correction required

(9) Because it was a stormy night, **be dare not to go** out in the dark.
(a) dared not to go
(b) dare not went
(c) dared not to have gone
(d) dare not goes
(e) No correction required

(10) **Just when they reach** the station, the train had departed.
(a) Just before they reach
(b) After they just reach
(c) Just when they had reached
(d) Just before they reached
(e) No correction required

12

Sentence Improvement

Directions (Q. 1-15) *In these questions look at the* **bold** *part of each sentence. Below the sentence are given three possible substitutions for the* **bold** *part. If any one of substitutions (a), (b) or (c) is better than the* **bold** *part, choose that substitution as your response. If none of the substitutions improves the sentence, choose (d) as your response. Thus, a 'No improvement' response will be signified by the letter (d).* **[CDS]**

(1) The sun was shining **such** brightly that Leela had to put on her sun-glasses.
(a) very *(b)* too *(c)* so *(d)* No improvement

(2) If I **were** you, I would report the matter at once.
(a) be *(b)* am *(c)* was *(d)* No improvement

(3) The document is **concerning** your health and that of your family.
(a) concerns with *(b)* is concerned with *(c)* concerns *(d)* No improvement

(4) The lady **laid** out a special dinner for her husband on his birthday.
(a) laid *(b)* laid up *(c)* laid by *(d)* No improvement

(5) Epidemics are likely to **break off** in the areas from where flood-water has receded.
(a) break out *(b)* break up *(c)* break in *(d)* No improvement

(6) There is no objection **to him** joining the party.
(a) on him *(b)* to his *(c)* upon his *(d)* No improvement

(7) You are **too big** to go out alone.
(a) big enough *(b)* so big *(c)* very big *(d)* No improvement

(8) One of my old friends has invited me **for tea** in the evening.
(a) To take tea *(b)* to tea *(c)* on tea *(d)* No improvement

(9) Hardly had he saddled the horse **than** the mare broke loose and galloped down the hill.
(a) that *(b)* when *(c)* than *(d)* No improvement

(10) The speaker tried to work **up** the emotions of his audience.
(a) round *(b)* off *(c)* in *(d)* No improvement

(11) **Until** the sky is overcast, I take my raincoat with me.
(a) When *(b)* Even if *(c)* Whenever *(d)* No improvement

(12) His discourse **about** the meteorology was very stimulating.
(a) on *(b)* of *(c)* concerning *(d)* No improvement

(13) Mira **told** her brother that she had made a mistake.
(a) said to *(b)* pleaded to *(c)* admitted to *(d)* No improvement

(14) You don't want a beggar to look happy **isn't it** ?
(a) aren't you ? *(b)* do you ? *(c)* don't you ? *(d)* No improvement

(15) The instructor told the student to hold the club lightly to keep his eye on the ball **but should not** use too much force.
(a) and not *(b)* and not to *(c)* still not to *(d)* No improvement

13

Directions (Q. 1-11) *In these questions look at the **bold** part of each sentence. Below the sentence are given three possible substitutions for the **bold** part. If any one of substitutions (a) , (b) or (c) is better than the **bold** part, choose that substitution as your response. If none of the substitutions improves the sentence, choose (d) as your response. Thus, a 'No improvement' response will be signified by the letter (d).*

(1) It is **no good to cry over** spilt milk. **[NDA]**
(a) It is no good crying *(b)* It is of no good to cry *(c)* It is of no good crying
(d) No improvement

(2) He has been working **off** and on **for** several years to compile a dictionary. **[SBI PO]**
(a) on or off *(b)* on and off *(c)* regularly *(d)* No improvement

(3) Rohit assured Sunita that he **would look** at her work while she was on leave. **[BSRB]**
(a) would overlook *(b)* would look after *(c)* will look *(d)* No improvement

(4) Newton wanted to **know why did the apple fall** to the ground. **[CBJ]**
(a) know that why did the apple fall *(b)* know why the apple fell
(c) know that why the apple fell *(d)* No improvement

(5) He was extremely unhappy because of **the inordinately delay**. **[Bank PO]**
(a) the inordinate delaying *(b)* the inordinate delay
(c) the inordinately delaying *(d)* No improvement

(6) **There is no more room** for you in this compartment. **[Section Officer]**

(a) There is no more accommodation (b) There is no more space
(c) There is no more seat (d) No improvement

(7) When he arrived to attend the wedding of his brother, he **had been dressed** in dark suit. **[NDA]**

(a) dressed (b) was dressed (c) had dressed (d) No improvement

(8) I can always **count on him** in times of difficulty. **[BSRB Patna]**

(a) count at him (b) count on he (c) count him on (d) No improvement

(9) Sunita told me that she would not mind to **stand and eating** the lunch. **[Income Tax]**

(a) to stand and eat (b) standing and eating
(c) standing and eat (d) No improvement

(10) Modern industrialised communities have lost touch with the soil and do not experience that joy which nature gives and the rich glow of health **that which comes from contact** with mother earth. **[CBI]**

(a) which comes from contact with. (b) which comes out from contact with
(c) which flows how from contact with (d) No improvement

(11) He has been receiving no other message than an urgent telegram **asking him to rush his village** immediately. **[Bank PO]**

(a) asking him rushing at his village (b) asked him to rush his village.
(c) asking him to rush to his village (d) No improvement

14

Directions (Q. 1-7) *In these questions look at the **bold** part of each sentence. Below the sentence are given three possible substitutions for the **bold** part. If any one of substitutions (a) , (b) or (c) is better than the **bold** part, choose that substitution as your response. If none of the substitutions improves the sentence, choose (d) as your response. Thus, a 'No' 'improvement' response will be signified by the letter (d).*

(1) Each of our **students pay their** tuition fee at the beginning of the month. **[Asstt Grade]**

(a) student pay their (b) students pays their (c) students pays his (d) No improvement

(2) I told him clearly that he **hadn't ought to do** that to me. **[Bank PO]**

(a) ought not to have done (b) ought not done
(c) ought not has done (d) No improvement

(3) The fast train **come a halt to before** crossing the bridge. **[BSRB]**

(a) came before to a halt (b) came to a halt before
(c) came to halts before a (d) No improvement

(4) I took the cycle **which he has bought** yesterday. **[Stenographers]**

(a) that he bought yesterday (b) that he had bought yesterday
(c) that which he had bought yesterday (d) No improvement

(5) The practical importance of the role of the industrialist in the establishment of the new order is greater than the **economist and the politician.** **[Railways]**

(a) of the economist and politicians (b) that of the economists and the politicians
(c) that of the economist and the politician (d) No improvement

(6) The poor villagers **have waited** in the bitter coller more than four hours now. **[IES]**

(a) has been waiting (b) had waited
(c) have been waiting (d) No improvement

(7) They succeeded **without hardly** making any effort. **[CBI]**

(a) hardly without making (b) with hardly making
(c) without making (d) No improvement

15

Directions (Q. 1-6) *In these questions look at the **bold** part of each sentence. Below the sentence are given three possible substitutions for the **bold** part. If any one of substitutions (a), (b) or (c) is better than the **bold** part, choose that substitution as your response. If none of the substitutions improves the sentence, choose (d) as your response. Thus, a 'No improvement' response will be signified by the letter (d).*

(1) He was urgently in need to **get his eye** operation. **[CBI]**
(a) of an eye operation *(b)* for operation on eye
(c) for eye to be operated *(d)* No improvement

(2) **By definition, make a map** is to select certain features as relevant and ignore others. **[RBI]**
(a) To make a map by definition *(b)* In making a map, the definition
(c) Map making is defined as *(d)* No improvement

(3) We demonstrated to them how we **were prepared** the artistic patterns. **[SBI PO]**
(a) are prepared *(b)* have prepared
(c) had prepared *(d)* No improvement

(4) Asking me **why was I absent, I was punished by the Headmaster.** **[CBI]**
(a) why was I absent, was I punished by the Headmaster.
(b) why I was absent, was I punished by the Headmaster.
(c) why I was absent, the Headmaster punished me.
(d) No improvement

(5) Do you **remember to meet her at** my house last year ? **[UDC]**
(a) remember of meeting her *(b)* remember about meeting her
(c) remember having met her *(d)* No improvement

(6) If you had attended the meeting, *you would have benefitted* a great deal. **[Stenogarphers]**
(a) would benefit *(b)* could benefit *(c)* benefited *(d)* No improvement

16

Directions (Q. 1-8) *In these questions look at the **bold** part of each sentence. Below the sentence are given three possible substitutions for the **bold** part. If any one of substitutions (a), (b) or (c) is better than the **bold** part, choose that substitution as your response. If none of the substitutions improves the sentence, choose (d) as your response. Thus, a 'No improvement' response will be signified by the letter (d).*

(1) **Although partially destroyed, the experts were able to infer** from what remained that the treasure was buried in the cave.
(a) Although partially destroyed, the experts had inferred
(b) Destroyed partially, the experts were able to infer
(c) Although it had been partially destroyed, the experts were able to infer
(d) No improvement **[RBI]**

(2) The Principal lamented that though a detailed report was submitted to the management a month ago, **no action is being taken so far.** **[Bank PO]**
(a) no action had taken *(b)* no action has been taken
(c) any action had been taken *(d)* No improvement

(3) May I know **who did accompany you** to the bus station ? **[BSRB]**
(a) who accompanied you *(b)* must be
(c) whom did you accompany *(d)* No improvement

(4) **Leaving aside little room** for misinterpretation, the senior politician offered clarification about his role in the past elections. **[Bank PO]**
(a) Leaving less room for
(b) Leaving little room for
(c) Having left less room for
(d) No improvement

(5) We should take up the first item, **let us begin this song.** **[UDC]**
(a) this song begin us
(b) us begin with this song
(c) this song begin us
(d) No improvement

(6) **Any able bodied man** is eligible for the job. **[NDA]**
(a) Any able bodied men are
(b) Each able bodied man is
(c) Any able bodied men have been
(d) No improvement

(7) **I, your brother and you will** be partners in the business. **[NDA]**
(a) I, you and your brother
(b) You, your brother and I
(c) You, I and your brother
(d) No improvement

(8) While we would like **that all Indian children** to go to school, we need to ponder why they do not.
(a) all Indian children
(b) that all the Indian children
(c) if all the children of India
(d) No improvement **[CDS]**

17

Directions (Q. 1-5) *In these questions look at the **bold** part of each sentence. Below the sentence are given three possible substitutions for the **bold** part. If any one of substitutions (a), (b) or (c) is better than the **bold** part, choose that substitution as your response. If none of the substitutions improves the sentence, choose (d) as your response. Thus, a 'No improvement' response will be signified by the letter (d).*

(1) **I think in my opinion that** all those who claim to be honest are not really so.
(a) In my opinion
(b) It seems to me
(c) It is my believing
(d) No improvement **[CBI]**

(2) Will you **lend me few** rupees in this hour of need. **[Section Officers]**
(a) borrow me a few rupees
(b) lend my any rupees
(c) lend me a few rupees
(d) No improvement

(3) Hold **hands of your child** while crossing the road.
(a) your child's hands
(b) your child's hand
(c) hand of your child
(d) No improvement **[CBI]**

(4) Have **you not reached** in time, we would have lost our lives? **[Bank PO]**
(a) Had you not reach
(b) If you have not reached
(c) Had you not reached
(d) No improvement

(5) You must **accustom yourself** with new ideas.
(a) accustomed with
(b) accustom to
(c) accustom yourself to
(d) No improvement **[NDA]**

18

Directions (Q. 1-10) *In these questions look at the **bold** part of each sentence. Below the sentence are given three possible substitutions for the **bold** part. If any one of substitutions (a), (b) or (c) is better than the **bold** part, choose that substitution as your response. If none of the substitutions improves the sentence, choose (d) as your response. Thus, a 'No improvement' response will be signified by the letter (d).* **[CDS]**

(1) The climate of Delhi is somewhat **like Jaipur**.
(a) like Jaipur's
(b) as Jaipur's
(c) as Jaipur
(d) No improvement

(2) His brother **never has** and never will be dependable.
(a) never had *(b)* never has been *(c)* was never being *(d)* No improvement

(3) If you would **have remembered** to bring the map, we would not have lost our way.
(a) had remembered *(b)* were remembering *(c)* remembered *(d)* No improvement

(4) You must **carry on my** order.
(a) carry off *(b)* carry out *(c)* carry of *(d)* No improvement

(5) The boat **was drowned**.
(a) was drown *(b)* was drowned *(c)* was sunk *(d)* No improvement

(6) Now I must **beg leave of you**.
(a) beg your leave *(b)* beg of your leave *(c)* beg off your leave *(d)* No improvement

(7) **When describing** the accident he was in tears.
(a) In describing *(b)* When he was describing *(c)* As describing *(d)* No improvement

(8) The two thieves distributed the loot **between themselves.**
(a) among themselves. *(b)* amongst themselves *(c)* with themselves. *(d)* No improvement

(9) **The preservation of peace** is necessary.
(a) maintenance of peace *(b)* establishment of peace *(c)* persuasion of peace *(d)* No improvement

(10) The spirit of democracy had *sped into* our way of thinking.
(a) leaked into *(b)* permeated *(c)* soaked into *(d)* No improvement

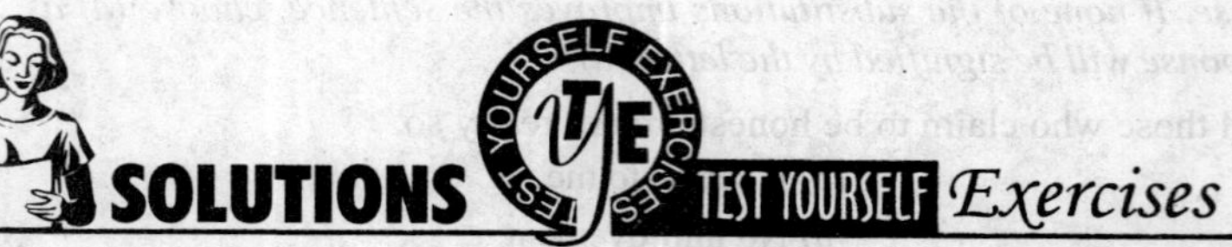

Solution TYE 01

(1) (d), (2) (b), (3) (c), (4) (a), (5) (b).

Solution TYE 02

(1) (c), (2) (a), (3) (a), (4) (d), (5) (b).

Solution TYE 03

(1) (b), (2) (d), (3) (c), (4) (e), (5) (a).

Solution TYE 04

(1) (a), (2) (c), (3) (d), (4) (b), (5) (c),
(6) (a), (7) (a), (8) (c), (9) (b), (10) (d).

Solution TYE 05

(1) (a), (2) (a), (3) (b), (4) (a), (5) (c),
(6) (b), (7) (a), (8) (d), (9) (c), (10) (b).

Solution TYE 06

(1) (c), (2) (b), (3) (d), (4) (e), (5) (c),
(6) (b), (7) (a).

Solution TYE 07

(1) (e), (2) (e), (3) (b), (4) (c), (5) (d),
(6) (a), (7) (a), (8) (c), (9) (e), (10) (b).

Solution TYE 08

(1) (c), (2) (a), (3) (c), (4) (c), (5) (a),
(6) (d), (7) (b), (8) (a), (9) (b), (10) (a),
(11) (b), (12) (d), (13) (c), (14) (c), (15) (a).

Solution TYE 09

(1) (a), (2) (d), (3) (a), (4) (d), (5) (a),
(6) (c).

Solution TYE 10

(1) (a), (2) (d), (3) (b), (4) (e), (5) (e),
(6) (c), (7) (c), (8) (d), (9) (b), (10) (a).

Solution TYE 11

(1) (c), (2) (b), (3) (e), (4) (e), (5) (a),
(6) (b), (7) (b), (8) (c), (9) (a), (10) (d).

Solution TYE 12

(1) (c), (2) (d), (3) (b), (4) (a), (5) (a),
(6) (b), (7) (d), (8) (b), (9) (b), (10) (d),
(11) (c), (12) (a), (13) (d), (14) (b), (15) (b).

Solution TYE 13

(1) (a), (2) (d), (3) (b), (4) (b), (5) (b),
(6) (c), (7) (b), (8) (d), (9) (b), (10) (a),
(11) (c).

Solution TYE 14

(1) (c), (2) (a), (3) (b), (4) (d), (5) (c),
(6) (c), (7) (c).

Solution TYE 15

(1) (a), (2) (c), (3) (c), (4) (c), (5) (c),
(6) (d).

Solution TYE 16

(1) (c), (2) (b), (3) (a), (4) (b), (5) (b),
(6) (d), (7) (b), (8) (a).

Solution TYE 1

(1) (a), (2) (c), (3) (b), (4) (c), (5) (c),

Solution TYE 18

(1) (a), (2) (b), (3) (a), (4) (b), (5) (c),
(6) (d), (7) (b), (8) (d), (9) (a), (10) (b).

CHAPTER

36

ORDERING OF SENTENCES

आजकल विभिन्न Competitive Examinations में English Question Paper में 'Ordering of Sentences' के पाँच या दस प्रश्नों का समावेश होता है। इस तरह के प्रश्नों में पहला एवं अन्तिम Sentence दिया जाता है एवं मध्य के चार sentences को सही क्रम में Set करना होता है। इस तरह के वाक्य एक Paragraph के भाग होते हैं। इस Paragraph में से बीच के चार वाक्यों को असम्बद्ध क्रम में प्रश्न के रूप में दिया गया होता है। इस तरह के प्रश्नों द्वारा छात्र की Composition की योग्यता तथा तथ्यों को समझने एवं सही Order में Set करने की योग्यता का आंकलन किया जाता है। इस तरह के प्रश्नों को हल करने हेतु छात्रों को सर्वप्रथम, प्रथम एवं अन्तिम वाक्य को पढ़ना चाहिए तत्पश्चात् शेष चारों वाक्यों को धैर्यपूर्वक पढ़ना चाहिए। सभी वाक्यों को पढ़ने से Paragraph का आशय समझ में आ जाता है। फिर चारों वाक्यों को उचित क्रम के अनुसार लिखना चाहिए। इस तरह प्रश्नों को सही ढंग से हल करने के लिए छात्र की न केवल Vocabulary अच्छी होनी आवश्यक है, बल्कि उसे English Grammar के Rules की भी अच्छी Knowledge होनी चाहिए। कई बार इस तरह के प्रश्न हल करते समय एक-दो वाक्यों के क्रम में कुछ Confusion हो सकता है। ऐसी स्थिति में Answer में दिए गए विकल्पों का सहारा लेकर, सही उत्तर लिखा जा सकता है। छात्रों को Competitive Examinations में समय का विशेष ध्यान रखना चाहिए। यदि किसी भी प्रश्न में समय अधिक लग रहा है या आपको वह प्रश्न समझ नहीं आ रहा है या कठिन लग रहा है तो आप उस प्रश्न को छोड़कर अगले प्रश्न को हल करने का प्रयास करें। Competitive Examinations में 'Time Management' अर्थात् दिए गए समय का पूर्ण एवं उचित प्रयोग करना बहुत महत्त्वपूर्ण है।

Exercises

01

Directions (Q. 1-2) : *The sentences given in each question, when properly sequenced; form a coherent paragraph. Each sentence is labelled with a letter. Choose the most logical order of sentences from among the given choices to construct a coherent paragraph :*

[CAT November, 2004]

(1) (A) But this does not mean that death was the Egyptians' only preoccupation.
(B) Even papyri come mainly from pyramid temples.
(C) Most of our traditional sources of information about the Old Kingdom are monuments of the rich like pyramids and tombs.
(D) Houses, in which ordinary Egyptians lived have not been preserved, and when most people died they were buried in simple graves.
(E) We know infinitely more about the wealthy people of Egypt than we do about the ordinary people, as most monuments were for the rich.

(a) CDBEA (b) ECDAB (c) EDCBA (d) DECAB

(2) (A) Experts such as Larry Burns, head of research at GM, reckon that only such a full hearted leap will allow the world to cope with the mass mootorisation that will one day come to China or India.

(B) But once hydrogen is being produced from biomass or extracted from underground coal or made from water, using nuclear or renewable electricity, the way will be open for a huge reduction in carbon emissions from the whole system.

(C) In theory, once all the bugs have been sorted out, fuel cells should deliver better total fuel economy than any existing engines.

(D) That is twice as good as the internal combustion engine, but only five percentage points better than a Diesel hybrid.

(E) Allowing for the resources needed to extract hydrogen from hydrocarbon, oil, coal or gas, the fuel cell has an efficiency of 30%.

(a) CEDBA (b) CEBDA
(c) AEDBC (d) ACEBD

02

Directions (Q. 1-3) : *The sentences given in each question, when properly sequenced, form a coherent paragraph. Each sentence is labelled with a letter. Choose the most logical order of sentences from among the given choices to construct a coherent paragraph :* **[CAT November, 2004]**

(1) (A) He felt justified in by passing Congress altogether on a variety of moves.

(B) At time he was fighting the entire Congress.

(C) Bush felt he had a mission to restore power to the presidency.

(D) Bush was not fighting just the democrats.

(E) Representative democracy is a messy business and a CEO of the White House does not like a legislature of second guessers and time wasters.

(a) CAEDB (b) DBAEC
(c) CEADB (d) ECDBA

(2) (A) The two neighbours never fought each other.

(B) Fights involving three male fiddler crabs have been recorded, but the status of the participants was unknown.

(C) They pushed or grappled only with the intruder.

(D) We recorded 17 cases, in which a resident that was fighting an intruder was joined by an immediate neighbour, an ally.

(E) We, therefore, tracked 268 intruder males until we saw them fighting a resident male.

(a) BEDAC (b) DEBAC
(c) BDCAE (d) BCEDA

(3) (A) In the west, Allied Forces had fought their way through Southern Italy as far as Rome.

(B) In June 1944, Germany's military position in II World War appeared hopeless.

(C) In Britain, the task of amassing the men and materials for the liberation of Northern Europe had been completed.

(D) The Red Army was poised to drive the Nazis back through Poland.

(E) The situation on the Eastern front was catastrophic.

(a) EDACB (b) BEDAC
(c) BDECA (d) CEDAB

03

Directions (Q. 1-5) : *In these questions, each passage consists of six sentences. The first and the sixth sentences are given in the beginning. The middle four sentences in each have been removed and jumbled up. These are labelled P,Q,R and S. You are required to find out the proper sequence of the four sentences from the given alternatives (a), (b), (c) and (d) :* **[CDS]**

(1) S_1 : In 1945, America faced two powerful enemies in the World War.
S_6 : This was the weapon that ended the second World War.
P : America found conventional weapons insufficient to crush them.
Q : These were Germany and Japan who posed strong opposition to America.
R : The result of this was the production of the Atom bomb.
S : The government ordered scientists to conduct research and produce a new, deadly weapon.
The proper sequence should be :
(a) Q P S R (b) P Q R S (c) Q P R S (d) P Q S R

(2) S_1 : Advertising is also advantageous to the consumer in that if it increases the sale of goods, industry prospers and prices may be reduced.
S_6 : Advertising of this particular kind is planned to stimulate new wants or to induce buyers to change their habits.
P : There is no obvious connection, for example between a picture of a smiling girl and a certain brand sweets.
Q : The advertiser's assumption is that by looking at such pictures, the consumer would be influenced to buy his products.
R : On the other hand, much of the canvassing of which the consumer is the object does not convey information but endeavours merely to draw the public attention to certain products.
S : But most people like looking at pictures of pretty girls.
The proper sequence should be :
(a) R Q S P (b) S P R Q (c) R P S Q (d) S Q R P

(3) S_1 : We are living in an age in which technology has suddenly 'annihilated distance.'
S_6 : In that event, we should be dooming ourselves to wipe each other out.
P : We have never been so conscious of our variety as we are now that we have come to such close quarters.
Q : Physically we are now all neighbours, but psychologically we are still strangers to each other.
R : Are we going to let this consciousness of our variety make us fear and hate each other ?
S : How are we going to react ?
The proper sequence should be :
(a) Q P S R (b) Q P R S (c) P R Q S (d) S R P Q

(4) S_1 : Mom was pleased to receive your wishes on her birthday.
S_6 : Your Mom has forgotten all the bitterness and sends her blessings to you.
P : Girl ! wishes are more powerful than any things in the world.
Q : Both of us had forgotten the day.
R : Your letter holds a proof of it.
S : It was your letter and the card which reminded us of it.
The proper sequence should be :
(a) P S Q R (b) Q R S P (c) R Q S P (d) Q S P R

(5) S_1 : A century ago, the cinema was just a mechanical toy.
S_6 : Finally, it has evolved as the century's most potent and versatile art form.
P : Thus, it gained respectability and acceptance.

Q : It gradually came to be considered as an art form of the new era.
R : By the 1920s, even its worst critics had to take it seriously.
S : Later it was viewed as an extension of photography.

The proper sequence should be :

(a) P Q R S (b) S Q R P (c) S P Q R (d) Q R S P

04

Directions (Q. 1-5) : *Rearrange the following four sentences (A), (B) (C) and (D) in the proper sequence to form a meaningful paragraph then mark the correct sequence as your answer :*

[Agriculture Officers' Conducted by BSRB]

(1) (A) It also gives rise to a feeling of antimosity among the different sections of society.
(B) In a democratic system, frequent use of power is never desirable, it on the part of government or the people.
(C) Therefore, citizens should never resort to violent ways and means in democracy, though they have the right to oppose the government.
(D) It destroys the stability and security in public life.

(a) DBAC (b) BDAC (c) BDCA (d) DACB
(e) DCBA

(2) (A) He was so busy with them that he did not get time to eat.
(B) Thousands of people came to him and asked different types of questions.
(C) No one cared to see that he had his food or rest that night.
(D) Swami Vivekanand once stayed in a small village.

(a) BCDA (b) CBAD (c) DBAC (d) DBCA
(e) ABCD

(3) (A) The facts speak for themselves so they need exposition only, not demonstration.
(B) At the present moment, it is widely recognised that India holds the balance in the world-wide competition between rival ideologies.
(C) It is not, of course, only in geographical sense that India is in a key position.
(D) India's key position simply needs pointing out.

(a) DACB (b) CDAB (c) BCDA (d) BDAC
(e) DABC

(4) (A) This feeling of an extensive group gives rise to a fellow feeling, a feeling of brotherhood among the citizens.
(B) This feeling takes up beyond the bounds of family, caste, religion and region and helps us develop a broad perspective that we all of us together constitute an extensive group called the nation.
(C) National integration is the feeling among all the citizens of a country that they are all a part of one nation .
(D) We do not then limit our thinking to our own caste or religion, but think about all our fellow citizens.

(a) CDAB (b) CABD (c) CDBA (d) CBDA
(e) CBAD

(5) (A) The peasant, the shoemaker, the sweeper and such other lower classes of India have much greater capacity for work and self-reliance than you.
(B) Remember that the nation lives in the cottage.
(C) They are producing the entire wealth of the land without a word of complaint.
(D) This process of production is going through long ages.

(a) BDAC (b) BDCA (c) DCBA (d) BACD
(e) ADCB

05

Directions (Q. 1-5) : *In questions 1 to 5, there are six sentences marked S_1, S_6, P,Q,R,S. The positions of S_1 and S_6 are fixed as the first and last sentence of the passage. You are required to choose one of the four alternatives given below every passage which would be most logical sequence of the sentences in the passage* : **[NDA]**

(1) S_1 : His wrist watch had gone out of order.
S_6 : His estimate appeared reasonable.
P : He took it to a watch repairer.
Q : He gave an idea of the likely cost of the replacement based on the examination of the watch.
R : He found that some parts needed replacement.
S : The repairer opened the outer case and checked the parts.
The proper sequence should be :
(a) P Q S R (b) R Q S P (c) P S R Q (d) R P S Q

(2) S_1 : Now-a-days, soap is going almost out of use as a washing agent.
S_6 : There are better washing agents than soap,but scientists are not yet sure if their use is harmless to man.
P : They produce lather due to the presence of calcium salts in water.
Q : Its place has been occupied by a new range of chemicals, called detergents.
R : So, they are called soapless soap.
S : Detergents are not soap because they are not sodium or potassium derivatives of fatty acids, as normal soap is.
The proper sequence should be :
(a) S Q R P (b) Q S R P (c) S Q P R (d) Q P R S

(3) S_1 : Our house is high up on the Yorkshire coast, and close to the sea.
S_6 : Between the two, shifting backwards and forwards at certain seasons of the year, lies the most horrible quicksand on the shores of Yorkshire.
P : One is called the North spit and one the South.
Q : The sand hills here run down to the sea and end in two stretches of rock, sticking out opposite each other.
R : This one leads through a dark plantation of fir-trees, and brings you out between low cliffs to the loneliest and ugliest little bay on all our coast.
S : There are beautiful walls all around us in every direction except one.
The proper sequence should be :
(a) S Q R P (b) Q S P R (c) Q P S R (d) S R Q P

(4) S_1 : Unhappiness and discontent spring not only from poverty.
S_6 : We suffer from sickness of spirit and hence we should discover our roots in the eternal.
P : Man is a strange creature fundamentally different from other animals.
Q : If they are undeveloped and unsatisfied, he may have all the comforts of the wealth, but will still feel that life is not worthwhile.
R : He has far horizons invariable hopes, spiritual powers.
S : What is missing in our age is the soul, there is nothing wrong with the body.
The proper sequence should be :
(a) P R Q S *(b)* S P R Q
(c) S P Q R *(d)* P R S Q

(5) S_1 : Before we left Bareilly jail, a little incident took place which moved me then and is yet resh in my memory.
S_6 : This spontaneous act of courtesy and the kindly thought that prompted, it touched me and I felt very grateful to him.

P : He told me the packet contained old German illustrated magazines.

Q : The superintendent of Police of Bareilly, an Englishman, was present there and as I got into the car, he handed to me rather shyly a packet.

R : I had never met him before, nor have I seen him since and I do not even know his name.

S : He said that he had heard that I was learning German and so he had bought these magazines for me.

The proper sequence should be :

(a) R Q P S (b) Q P S R (c) Q P R S (d) R Q S P

06

Directions (Q. 1-5) : *Each passage consists of six sentences. The first and the sixth sentences are given in the beginning. The middle four sentences in each have been removed and jumbled up. These are labelled P, Q, R and S. You are required to find out the proper order for the four sentences :*

[Engineering Service]

(1) S_1 : Our ancestors thought that anything which moved itself was alive.

S_6 : Therefore, some scientists think that life is just a very complicated mechanism.

P : This philosopher Descartes thought that both men and animals were machines.

Q : But a machine such as a motorcar or a steamship moves itself, and as soon as machines which moved themselves had been made, people asked, "Is man a machine ?"

R : And before the days of machinery that was a good definition.

S : He also thought that the human machine was partly controlled by the soul action on a certain part of the brain,while animals had no souls.

The proper sequence should be :

(a) P R S Q (b) R P Q S (c) P S Q R (d) R Q P S

(2) S_1 : On vacation in Tangier, Morocco, my friend and I sat down at a street cafe.

S_6 : Finally, a man walked over to me and whispered, "Hey buddy ... this guy's your waiter and he wants your order.

P : At one point, he bent over with a big smile, showing me a single gold tooth and a dingy fez.

Q : Soon I felt the presence of someone standing alongside me.

R : But this one wouldn't budge.

S : We had been cautioned about beggars and were told to ignore them.

The proper sequence should be :

(a) S Q R P (b) S Q P R
(c) Q S R P (d) Q S P R

(3) S_1 : The heart of the pump of life.

S_6 : All this was made possible by the invention of the heart lung machine.

P : They have even succeeded in heart transplants.

Q : Now-a-days surgeons are able to stop a patient's heart and carry out complicated operations.

R : A few years ago it was impossible to operate on a patient whose heart was not working properly.

S : If the heart stops we die in about five minutes.

The proper sequence should be :

(a) S R Q P (b) S P R Q
(c) S Q P R (d) S R P Q

(4) S_1 : In 1934, William Holding published a small volume of poems.

S_6 : But Lord of the flies which came out in 1954 was welcomed as "a most absorbing and instructive tale''.

P : During the World War II (1939-45) he joined the Royal Navy and was present at the sinking of the Bismarck.

Q : He returned to teaching in 1945 and gave it up in 1962 and is now a full-time writer.

R : In 1939, he married and started teaching at Bishop Wordsworth's School in Salisbury.
S : At first his novels were not accepted.

The proper sequence should be :

(a) R P Q S (b) R P S Q (c) S R P Q (d) S Q P R

5. S_1 : Sunbirds are among the smallest of India birds.
S_6 : Our common sunbirds are the purple sunbird, the glossy black species, and purple rumped sunbird, the yellow and maroon species.
P : Though, they are functionally similar to the humming birds of the New World, they are totally unrelated.
Q : They do eat small insects too.
R : They are also some of the most brilliantly-coloured birds.
S : Sunbirds feed on nectar mostly and help in pollination.

The proper sequence should be :

(a) S Q P R (b) R P S Q (c) Q P R S (d) P S R Q

07

Directions (Q. 1-5) : *In questions 1 to 5 each passage consists of six sentences. The first and the sixth sentences are given in the beginning. The middle four sentences in each have been removed and jumbled up. These are labelled P, Q, R and S. You are required to find out the proper order for the four sentences :*

[CDS]

(1) S_1 : There are numerous kinds of superstitions in different parts of the country.
S_6 : A dog's howling predicts death— this is a typical superstition.
P : But people go on respecting it through force of blind custom.
Q : Most of them have a bearing on ''luck''—good or bad.
R : Superstitions, usually have their origin in fear and ignorance.
S : Nobody remembers now how a superstition first started in remote ages.

The proper sequence should be :

(a) Q P R S *(b)* R S P Q *(c)* R S Q P *(d)* Q S P R

(2) S_1 : Society in every country shapes itself out of it own initiative.
S_6 : And our Indian women are as capable of doing it as any in the world.
P : No one can or ought to do this for them.
Q : Our part of duty lies in imparting true education to all men and women in society.
R : Woman must be put in a position to solve their own problems in their own way.
S : It will not be then necessary to pull down or set us anything in society by coercion.

The proper sequence should be :

(a) S R Q P (b) Q R S P (c) Q S R P (d) S R P Q

(3) S_1 : Many people believe that it is cruel to make use of animals for laboratory studies.
S_6 : It is in view of these facts that the Government of India has banned the export of monkeys to America.
P : They point out that animals too have nervous systems like us and can feel pain.
Q : These people, who have formed the Anti-vivisection Society, have been pleading for a more humane treatment of animals by scientists.
R : Monkey, rabbits, mice and other mammals are used in large numbers by scientists and many of them are made to suffer diseases artificially produced in them.
S : We can avoid such cruelty to animals if we use alternative methods such as tissue culture, gas chromatography and chemical techniques.

The proper sequence should be :

(a) Q P R S (b) P R Q S (c) Q R S P (d) P S Q R

(4) S_1 : A spider's web, after a shower of rain, is a very beautiful thing.
S_6 : They are also feared because their bites may have unpleasant effects like a rash on the skin.
P : This explains partly why spiders are thoroughly disliked.
Q : But no poet has ever sung of the beauty of the spiders, for most spiders are not beautiful.
R : On the contrary, most of them are rather unattractive, if not ugly !
S : Poets have sung about the beauty of the spider's webs, comparing the water drops on them to ropes of pearls.

The proper sequence should be :

(a) S P Q R (b) Q S R P (c) Q R S P (d) S Q R P

(5) S_1 : We are what our thoughts have made us.
S_6 : If good impressions prevail, the character becomes good, if bad it become bad.
P : And so take care of what you think.
Q : Every man's character is determined by the sum total or these impressions.
R : Every work we do, every thought that we think, leaves an impression on the mind-stuff.
S : Thought live, they travel far.

The proper sequence should be :

(a) S P R Q (b) R Q S P (c) P R S Q (d) R Q P S

08

Directions (Q. 1-8) : *In each of the questions below four sentences are given which are denoted by (A), (B), (C) and (D). By using all the four sentences you have to frame a meaningful para. The correct order of the sentences is your answer. Choose from the five alternatives the one having the correct order of sentences and mark it as your answer :* **[SBI Probationary Officers']**

(1) (A) Now under liberated economy they are learning to compete domestically and globally.
(B) In India corporations until recently achieved success by avoiding competition, using protected and regulated domestic markets.
(C) The trend is irreversible.
(D) Business leaders are preparing themselves to meet competitive challenges, and to avoid being swept away.

(a) ABDC (b) BDCA (c) BDAC (d) CDBA
(e) BADC

(2) (A) Recovery was given inadequate attention and consequently some bank branches regularly incurred heavy losses and their parent bodies had to bale them out.
(B) As a result, banks indulged in extensive lending to borrowers who had little or no potential to make repayments.
(C) To fulfil the social objectives laid down by the masters of nationalisation, banks were asked to lend to identified priority sectors.
(D) 1992-93 results showed that the loss making branches of public sector banks increased from 10000 to 13000 and the quantum of losses showed at ₹ 3,369 crores.

(a) BACD (b) DABC (c) CBAD (d) BCAD
(e) CDBA

(3) (A) However, different rulers and governments dealt with the different groups in a compartmentalised manner.
(B) Various situational and political changes have taken place over the past three and half centuries.
(C) This tendency resulted in deeply embedded fragmented South American Society which became even more prominent in the period 1948 until the commencement of the new constitution on May 19, 1994.
(D) South Africa is a racially divided society since the first European settlers arrived in 1652.

(a) BDAC (b) DBAC (c) CABD (d) ACDB
(e) BACD

(4) (A) Such a system will help identify and groom executives for positions of strategists.
(B) Evaluation of performance is more often than not done for the purpose of reward or punishment for past performance.
(C) They must become an integral part of the executive evaluation system.
(D) Even where the evaluation system is for one's promotion to assume higher responsibilities it rarely includes items that are a key for playing the role of strategists effectively, *e.g.,* the skills for playing the role of change agent and creative problem solving.
(a) DBAC (b) DCBA (c) ABCD (d) BDCA
(e) CDBA

(5) (A) Finally, the bureaucratic organisation took over from the pioneering enterprise.
(B) The nineteenth century was the age of entrepreneur, the self-made man.
(C) Thoughtful business administration took over from action centred business entrepreneurship.
(D) In the twentieth century the rational executive took command.
(a) DBAC (b) CABD (c) BDCA (d) BCDA
(e) DBAC

(6) (A) But categorisation schemes are not always helpful in determining what one can do with or about organisational culture.
(B) Much of the literature on organisational cultures is focused on categorising types of cultures.
(C) It has taken the understanding of corporate culture far beyond what used to be called the informal organisation.
(D) This literature is both interesting and informative.
(a) BDAC (b) BADC (c) BCDA (d) DABC
(e) DBAC

(7) (A) Much of the argument that goes on around the alternative solution occurs because people hold different perceptions of the problem.
(B) One of the reasons that Japanese managers are perceived as making superior decisions compared to Western managers is that they spend a great deal of effort and time determining that the problem is correctly defined.
(C) Unfortunately, too often in the West, managers assume that the initial definition of the situation is correct.
(D) Up to half the time in meetings is spent in asking "Is this the real problem ?"
(a) BDCA (b) BCDA (c) CBDA (d) ACDB
(e) ABCD

(8) (A) Participation involves more than the formal sharing of decisions.
(B) Through anticipation, individuals or organisations considers trends and make plans, shielding institutions from trauma of learning by shock.
(C) Innovative learning involves both anticipation and participation.
(D) It is an attitude characterised by cooperation, dialogue and empathy.
(a) BCAD (b) ABCD (c) DACB (d) CBAD
(e) ACBD

09

Directions (Q. 1-5) : *Rearrange the following five sentences (A), (B), (C), (D) and (E) in the proper sequence so as to form a meaningful paragraph and then answer the questions given below them :* **[Bank PO]**

(A) A study to this effect suggests that the average white-collar worker demonstrates only about twenty five percent listening efficiency.
(B) However, for trained and good listeners it is not unusual to use all the three approaches during a setting, thus, improving listening efficiency.

(C) There are three approaches to listening; listening for comprehension, listening for empathy and listening for evaluation.
(D) Although, we spend nearly half of each communication interaction listening, we do not listen well.
(E) Each approach has a particular emphasis that may help us to receive and process information in different settings.

(1) Which sentence should come SECOND in the paragraph ?
(a) A (b) B (c) C (d) D (e) E

(2) Which sentence should come FIFTH in the paragraph ?
(a) A (b) B (c) C (d) D (e) E

(3) Which sentence should come FOURTH in the paragraph ?
(a) A (b) B (c) C (d) D (e) E

(4) Which sentence should come FIRST in the paragraph ?
(a) A (b) B (c) C (d) D (e) E

(5) Which sentence should come THIRD in the paragraph?
(a) A (b) B (c) C (d) D (e) E

10

Directions (Q. 1-5) : *Rearrange the following five sentences (A), (B), (C), (D) and (E) in the proper sequence to form a meaningful paragraph, then answer the questions given below them :* **[PO]**

(A) The history of mankind is full of such fightings between communities, nation and people.
(B) From the primitive weapons of warfare, man has advanced to the modern nuclear weapons.
(C) Ever since the dawn of civilisation, man has been fighting with man.
(D) A modern war is scientific in character, but the effect is the same, wiping human existence out of this earth.
(E) The only difference now seems to be in the efficiency of the instruments used for killing each other.

(1) Which of the following should be the FIRST sentence ?
(a) A (b) B (c) C (d) D (e) E

(2) Which of the following should be the SECOND sentence ?
(a) A (b) B (c) C (d) D (e) E

(3) Which of the following should be the THIRD sentence ?
(a) A (b) B (c) C (d) D (e) E

(4) Which of the following should be the FOURTH sentence ?
(a) A (b) B (c) C (d) D (e) E

(5) Which of the following should be the FIFTH (last) sentence ?
(a) A (b) B (c) C (d) D (e) E

11

Directions *(Q. 1-7) : In each of the following questions, the first and the last parts of the passage are numbered S_1 and S_6. The rest of the passage is split into four parts and named P, Q, R and S. These four parts are not given in their proper order. Read the sentences and find out which of the four combinations is correct. Then find the correct answer :* **[SSC Clerks]**

(1) S_1 : "As matter of fact", said the boy modestly, "I'm a spaceman."
P : "You can't see it from here."
Q : "From another planet."
R : "I'm a spaceman", he said again.

S : George and Cathy stared at the boy.

S_6 : Cathy gasped, George gave a shout of laughter.

(a) PSRQ (b) QPSR (c) RQPS (d) SRQP

(2) S_1 : I suddenly it began to climb swiftly and the next I knew it was speeding eastward again till it became a speak in the blue morning.

P : I didn't know what force they could command, but I was certain it would be sufficient.

Q : My enemies had located me, and the next thing would be a cordon round me.

R : This made me do some savage thinking.

S : The aeroplane had seen my bicycle, and would conclude that I would try to escape by the road.

S_6 : In that case there might be a chance on the moors to the right or left.

(a) RQPS (b) QPSR (c) PSRQ (d) SRQP

(3) S_1 : His penance grew harder, he abjured even fruit.

P : Then the water, too, that the girl offered him in leaf-cups lay untouched

Q : Birds pecked at them as they lay rotting at his feet.

R : She gathered wild blossoms and laid them humbly before him.

S : The girl mused in sorrow: 'Is there nothing left for me to do'.

S_6 : The ascetic took no notice.

(a) RQPS (b) SRQP (c) QPSR (d) PSRQ

(4) S_1 : In other words, grammar grows and changes and there is no such things as correct use of English for the past, the present, and the future.

P : "The door is broke."

Q : Yet this would have been correct in Shakespeare's time !

R : Today, only an uneducated person would say, "My arm is broke."

S : For example, in Shakespeare's play Hamlet, there is the line.

S6 : All the words that man has invented are divided into eight classes which are called parts of speech.

(a) PSQR (b) SPRQ (c) QPSR (d) RSPQ

(5) S_1 : There is no transportation system in any city that can compare in efficiency with the circulatory system of the body.

P : The larger one goes from the heart to the various parts of the body.

Q : If you will imagine two systems of pipes, one large and one small, both meeting at a central pumping station, you'll have an idea of the Circulatory system.

R : These pipes are called arteries, veins and capillaries.

S : The smaller system of pipes goes from the heart to the lungs and back.

S_6 : Arteries are blood vessels, in which blood is going away from the heart.

(a) QSPR (b) PQSR (c) RSQP (d) SPRQ

(6) S_1 : Gandhiji's first political fast was made soon after his return from Africa.

P : He had also received help from their man's sister.

Q : This was when the poor labourers of the cotton mills of Ahmedabad were on strike.

R : He was a friend of the largest mill-owner.

S : Gandhi had made the strikers promise to remain on strike until the owners agreed to accept the decision of an arbitrator.

S_6 : He did not fast against the mill-owners, but in order to strengthen the determination of the strikers.

(a) SRPQ (b) QSRP (c) RPQS (d) PQSR

(7) S_1: A certain young man was entrusted to the care of a teacher.
P : 'This dullard will come to grief, if i send him away without a single lesson', thought the teacher.
Q : He was so dull of the mind that he could not, even in three months' time, learn as much as a single lesson.
R : The young man came to ask the teacher's permission to go home.
S : "It's my business to provide a good education to my pupils to get on in life."
S_6 : The teacher asked him to wait.
(a) QPSR (b) PSRQ (c) SRQP (d) RQPS

12

Directions (Q. 1-7) : *In each of the following questions, the first and the last part of the sentence are numbered S_1 to S_6 respectively. The rest of the sentence is split into four parts and named P, Q, R and S. These four parts are not given in their proper order. Read the sentence and find out which of the four combinations is correct. Then find the correct answer and indicate on the Answer-Sheet.*

(1) S_1: A study
P : success increases
Q : concludes that
R : and chances for
S : commitment to future tasks
S_6 : future success.
(a) RQPS (b) SRQP (c) QPSR (d) PSRQ

(2) S_1 : Putting it another way
P : what we see as our
Q : our goals throughout our lives
R : we are constantly resetting
S : in response to
S_6 : wins and losses.
(a) RQSP (b) QPRS (c) PRSQ (d) RSQP

(3) S_1: Studies of Nobel laureates show that.
P : or encounter professional
Q : and have strained relationship with friends and colleagues
R : they often publish less frequently
S : after winning the prize
S_6 : envy and rivalry
(a) SRQP (b) RQPS (c) QPSR (d) PSRQ

(4) S_1 : There is
P : no such thing
Q : from one nation
R : as the gift
S : of independence
S_6 : to another.
(a) SPQR (b) PRSQ (c) QPRS (d) RSPQ

(5) S_1 : People who
P : are terrible
Q : no way of taking
R : there is
S : have no weaknesses.
S_6 : advantage of them.
(a) PSQR (b) RSPQ (c) SPRQ (d) QSRP

(6) S_1 There are
P any other kind of
Q more ants
R land animal
S than
S_6 in the world.
(a) PSQR (b) RSPQ (c) SPRQ (d) QSPR

(7) S1 : For sometime
P : it was commonly assumed
Q : after the treaty of Versailles
R : that Germany had caused World War I by her aggressive acts
S : by scholars and laymen alike
S6 : and by encouraging Italy in her aggression.
(a) PRQS (b) SPQR (c) QPRS (d) QPSR

13

Directions (Q. 1-6) : *Put the given sentences in each of the following questions in proper order :*

(1) (A) His mother was dead.
(B) They had not sent him the sad information.
(C) Probably they knew his deep love for her.
(D) When Gandhi returned to India his son Hiralal was four.
(a) DCAB (b) DABC (c) DBAC (d) DCAB

(2) (A) It results from a carefully revised plan.
(B) Men work together for a cause or purpose.
(C) Team work does not just happen.
(D) It must be clearly known to them.
(a) BCAD (b) CBDA (c) BCDA (d) CABD

(3) (A) I will give you a copy of it.
(B) The book was published in New York.
(C) It is a very interesting book.
(D) It deals with mankind's political future.
(a) DCBA (b) CBDA (c) BDCA (d) DBCA

(4) (A) He had inherited that money from an uncle.
(B) Mr Maini was an innocent man.
(C) It was regarding investing ten thousands rupees in my firm.
(D) He agreed to my proposal.
(a) DCAB (b) BADC (c) CDAB (d) BDCA

(5) (A) His elbow was bleeding.
(B) He had a few bruises on his left hand.
(C) I went into the crowd and was relieved to see that he wasn't very badly injured.
(D) A crowd gathered around my brother before he could stand up.
(a) BCDA (b) DABC (c) BADC (d) DCBA

(6) (A) They were generally fed in the afternoon.
(B) But father said that it was most interesting to see them being fed.
(C) Gopal wanted to see the tigers and the lions first.
(D). When we entered the gate it was difficult to decide which way to go first.
(a) ACDB (b) DCBA (c) BCDA (d) CBAD

14

Directions (Q. 1-5) : *Rearrange in each of the following five sentences A, B, C, D and E in the proper sequence so as to form a meaningful paragraph; then answer the questions given below them :*

(1) (A) She said that she was a school teacher and a social worker.
(B) Then for sometime we discussed her plans for schooling of the children living in slums.
(C) Our conversation now took another direction.
(D) She also said that social work was her hobby only and not the job.
(E) I asked Meena about her occupation.

(i) Which of the following should be the Second sentence?
(a) B (b) D (c) C (d) E (e) A

(ii) Which of the following should be the Fourth sentence?
(a) E (b) A (c) B (d) C (e) D

(iii) Which of the following should be the First sentence?
(a) A (b) C (c) D (d) E (e) None of these

(iv) Which of the following should be the Last sentence ?
(a) C (b) D (c) B (d) E (e) None of these

(v) Which of the following should be the Third sentence ?
(a) A (b) B (c) C (d) D (e) E

(2) (A) But he added that there was a good deal to be said in favour or it.
(B) Govind asked what it was.
(C) Gopal told Govind that India would not progress until the caste system was abolished.
(D) Govind expressed hits surprise on hearing that there was a good deal to be said in favour of it.
(E) Gopal observed that there was truth in what he said.

(i) Which of the following should be the Last sentence?
(a) A (b) B (c) C (d) D (e) E

(ii) Which of the following should be the First sentence?
(a) A (b) B (c) C (d) D (e) E

(iii) Which of the following should be the Second sentence?
(a) A (b) B (c) C (d) D (e) E

(iv) Which of the following should be the Fourth sentence?
(a) A (b) B (c) C (d) D (e) E

(v) Which of the following should be the Third sentence?
(a) A (b) B (c) C (d) D (e) E

(3) (A) Seema's parents died in her early childhood.
(B) Her uncle who had been kind to her was dead.
(C) She spent most of her first ten years with her unkind aunt.
(D) She always treated her wickedly and not as a loving niece.
(E) Her three cousin sister also treated her as servant.
(F) Despite such ill treatments, she grew up as sensitive and self-reliant lady.

(i) Which of the following should be the Second sentence?
(a) A (b) B (c) C (d) D (e) F

(ii) Which of the following should be the Last sentence?
(a) A (b) B (c) C (d) D (e) E

(iii) Which of the following should be the First sentence?
(a) B (b) C (c) D (d) E (e) F

(iv) Which of the following should be the Fifth sentence?
(a) A (b) B (c) D (d) E (e) F

(v) Which of the following should be the Fourth sentence?
(a) B (b) C (c) D (d) E (e) F

(4) (A) It is fixed on Tuesday.
(B) We have, therefore, called him for interview.
(C) Due to his illness he lost that job.
(D) Ramesh was working in a factory.
(E) Hence, he has applied for a job in my office.

(i) Which of the following should be the First sentence?
(a) A (b) B (c) C (d) D (e) E

(ii) Which of the following should be the Second sentence?
(a) A (b) B (c) C (d) D (e) E

(iii) Which of the following should be the Third sentence?
(a) A (b) B (c) C (d) D (e) E

(iv) Which of the following should be the Fourth sentence?
(a) A (b) B (c) C (d) D (e) E

(5) (A) Some of the world's highest peaks are in the Himallayas.
(B) The Himalayas are beautiful mountains to the north of India.
(C) Therefore, we call them the Himalayas of the 'abodes of snow'.
(D) The highest peak is Mount Everest.
(E) Thy stretch for two thousand miles from Kashmir to Assom.
(F) The top of the mountains are covered with snow.

(i) Which of the following should be the First sentence?
(a) B (b) E (c) C (d) A (e) D

(ii) Which of the following should be the Second sentence?
(a) B (b) C (c) E (d) D (e) A

(iii) Which of the following should be the Third sentence?
(a) B (b) D (c) A (d) E (e) C

(iv) Which of the following should be the Fifth sentence?
(a) A (b) F (c) B (d) A (e) C

(v) Which of the following should be the Last sentence?
(a) D (b) A (c) E (d) C (e) B

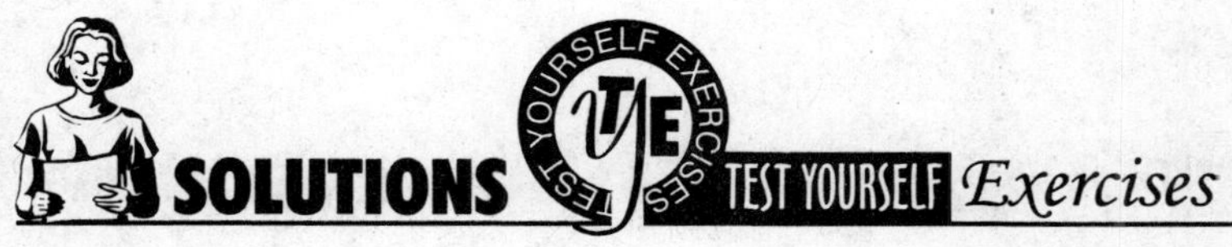

Solution TYE 01

(1) (c), (2) (a).

Solution TYE 02

(1) (d), (2) (a), (3) (b).

Solution TYE 03

(1) (a), (2) (c), (3) (b), (4) (d), (5) (d).

Solution TYE 04

(1) (b), (2) (c), (3) (c), (4) (e), (5) (d).

Solution TYE 05

(1) (c), (2) (d), (3) (d), (4) (b), (5) (c).

Solution TYE 06

(1) (c), (2) (c), (3) (a), (4) (a), (5) (a).

Solution TYE 07

(1) (d), (2) (c), (3) (a), (4) (d), (5) (a).

Solution TYE 08

(1) (e), (2) (c), (3) (b), (4) (d), (5) (c), (6) (a),
(7) (b), (8) (d).

Solution TYE 09

(1) (e), (2) (a), (3) (d), (4) (c), (5) (b).

Solution TYE 10

(1) (c), (2) (a), (3) (b), (4) (d), (5) (e).

Solution TYPE 11

(1) (c), (2) (d), (3) (d), (4) (b), (5) (a), (6) (b),
(7) (a).

Solution TYE 12

(1) (c), (2) (a), (3) (a), (4) (b), (5) (c), (6) (d),
(7) (d).

Solution TYE 13

(1) (b), (2) (d), (3) (c), (4) (a), (5) (d), (6) (b).

Solution TYE 14

(1) (i) (e), (ii) (d) (iii) (d), (iv) (c), (v) (d).
(2) (i) (b), (ii) (c), (iii) (a), (iv) (e), (v) (d).
(3) (i) (a), (ii) (d), (iii) (b), (iv) (b), (v) (d).
(4) (i) (d), (ii) (c), (iii) (e), (iv) (b).
(5) (i) (b), (ii) (c), (iii) (c), (iv) (b), (v) (d).

CHAPTER

37

DOUBLE BLANKS IN A SENTENCE

विभिन्न Competitive Examinations में English Question Paper में एक वाक्य में दो Blank Spaces देकर 4-5 विकल्पों में से एक विकल्प का चुनाव करने सम्बन्धित 5-10 प्रश्नों का समावेश होता है।

इन दो Blank Spaces में दिए गए विकल्पों (Pairs of Words) में से एक उचित विकल्प (Pair of Words) को भरने से वाक्य का समुचित अर्थ निकलता है। इन दो रिक्त स्थानों में भरा जाने वाला उपयुक्त Pair of Words मुख्यतया वाक्य के सारांश एवं अर्थ पर निर्भर करता है। यदि छात्र वाक्य के अर्थ को समझने में सक्षम हो तो वह इस तरह के प्रश्नों को सही तरीके से हल कर सकता है। इस तरह के प्रश्नों को हल करने हेतु छात्र की Vocabulary अच्छी होनी आवश्यक है, क्योंकि दिए गए विकल्पों का बिना सही अर्थ जाने छात्र कुछ नहीं कर सकते हैं। छात्र को इस Book में दिया Word Power का पूरा Section अच्छी तरह पढ़ना चाहिए, यह आपको इस तरह के प्रश्नों को हल करने में बहुत सहायक साबित होगा।

01

Directions (Q. 1-5) *: In each of the following sentences there are two blank spaces in the given sentences. Below each sentence there are five pair of words denoted by numbers (a), (b), (c), (d) and (e). Find out which pair of words can be filled up in the blanks in the sentence in the same sequence to make the sentence meaningfully complete :*

(1) Our latest battle plan ...... some projects .... at saving the earth's biological diversity.
(a) finishes, stirring
(b) covers, aimed
(c) finances, looking
(d) encloses, looked
(e) excludes, arriving

(2) Unless the authorities adopt the principle .... the strategies cannot become.......... .
(a) whole-heartedly, successful
(b) fully, defunct
(c) finally, obsolete
(d) legitimately, noteworthy
(e) ligically, trivial

(3) Trying to .... a team without a good and simple system is like trying to drive a car without a steering wheel ....
(a) form, working
(b) place, exploratory
(c) organise, empowering
(d) make, guidance
(e) achieve, developmental

(4) .... members of a group often .... influence the outcome of a consensus forecast.
(a) Fixed, exert
(b) Majority, rightly
(c) Oral, legitimately
(d) Minority, Inadvertently
(e) Dominant, unduly

(5) Transforming .... bureaucracies into dynamic, this task of customer-driven organisations is .... under prevailing circumstances.
(a) ideal, important
(b) lazy, undesirable
(c) inefficient, challenging
(d) civilised, ineffective
(e) lethargic, insurmountable.

02

Directions (Q. 1-10) : *In each of the following sentences there are two blank spaces in the given sentences. Below each sentence there are five pair of words denoted by numbers (a), (b), (c), (d) and (e). Find out which pair of words can be filled up in the blanks in the sentence in the same sequence to make the sentence meaningfully complete :*

(1) The Deputy Manager........to resign because all his proposals were......down by his superiors. **[Bank PO]**
(a) planned, thrown
(b) gave, held
(c) began, kept
(d) willing, knocked
(e) threatened,turned

(2) The counter clerk was very busy and.........not pay.......to Sameer's request. **[Bank PO]**
(a) can, help
(b) could, cooperation
(c) had, cash
(d) did, attention
(e) certainly,acceptance

(3) He was initially.............at the suggestion but was soon..........it himself. **[SBI PO]**
(a) anger, rejecting
(b) shocked, advocating
(c) impressed, negating
(d) thrilled, propagating
(e) suspicious, trusting

(4) Shalini was not..........by the criticism and paid no...........even when her best friend talked against her. **[SBI PO]**
(a) bothered, attention
(b) troubled, brained
(c) threatened, warning
(d) deterred, heed
(e) shaken, indication

(5) She was..........because all her plan had gone............ . **[Asstt Grade]**
(a) happy, selected
(b) dejected, splendidly
(c) distraught, awry
(d) frustrated, magnificently

(6) He preaches liberal views but in practice, he is not..............and is.........narrow minded than almost any other person. **[Bank PO]**
(a) tough, openly
(b) tolerant, more
(c) ambitious, hardly
(d) acceptable, genuinely
(e) approachable, less

(7) Ravi.........a bit........he was not invited by his friend to attend the party. **[Bank PO]**
(a) annoyed, before (b) angered, since
(c) expressed, than (d) grumbled, when
(e) surprised,about

(8) He is...........to...........any kind of work with due sincerity. **[BSRB Clerk]**
(a) fond, perform (b) reluctant, entrust
(c) determined, undertake (d) eager, avoid
(e) willing, ignore

(9) Children are more........than adults, it is........their quickness in learning a new language. **[Indian Bank PO]**
(a) intelligent, disproved by (b) adaptable, reflected in
(c) conservative, seen in (d) susceptible, demonstrated in
(e) resourceful, proportionate to

(10) ......of crops was due to continuous............. .
(a) Loss, draught (b) Ruin, draft
(c) Failure, drought (d) Depreciation, drift
(e) None of these

03

Directions (Q. 1-9) *: In each of the following sentences there are two blank spaces in the given sentences. Below each sentence there are five pair of words denoted by numbers (a), (b), (c), (d) and (e). Find out which pair of words can be filled up in the blanks in the sentence in the same sequence to make the sentence meaningfully complete :*

(1) Prabha's.........in athletics yielded rich......as she got a scholarship. **[SBI PO]**
(a) performance, money (b) defeat, results
(c) behaviour, appreciation (d) excellence, dividends
(e) failure, disappointment

(2) The police........any attempt of arson by.....at the trouble spot quite in time. **[SBI PO]**
(a) squashed, surrounding (b) made, encircling
(c) predisposed, visiting (d) thwarted, presenting
(e) pre-empted, arriving

(3) The......imposed for non-payment was too......for it to bring in improvement in collection. **[SBI PO]**
(a) fine, severe (b) toll, simple (c) penalty, low (d) damage, cruel
(e) punishment, harsh

(4) Somesh......me coming to his table, he smiled and.......me a chair. **[Bank of Mah PO]**
(a) found, signalled (b) met, sat (c) looked, gave (d) saw, offered
(e) welcomed, took

(5) The leaders were.....needed by those to.....they addressed. **[Bank PO]**
(a) angrily, who (b) readily, which (c) scarcely, whom (d) rarely, where
(e) joyfully, when

(6) I am not.....to sell you my house unless you offer a more.......price. **[Asstt Grade]**
(a) agree, better (b) prepared, realistic (c) ready, correct (d) having, actual
(e) None of these

(7) Due to.......rainf All this year, there will be........cut in water supply. **[BSRB Clerk]**
(a) scanty, substantial (b) meagre, least (c) sufficient, no (d) surplus, abundant
(e) abundant, considerable

(8) In a changing and........unstructured business environment, creativity and innovation are being .... demanded of executives. **[MBA Entrance]**

(a) excessively, rapidly
(b) highly, extremely
(c) increasingly, moderately
(d) progressively, increasingly
(e) highly, speedily

(9) We are......to have him.....here to make this function a great success. **[Bank PO]**

(a) happy, have
(b) unhappy, arrive
(c) sure, come
(d) pleased, over
(e) wonderful, again

04

Directions (Q. 1-18) *: In each of the following sentences there are two blank spaces in the given sentences. Below each sentence there are five pair of words denoted by numbers (a), (b), (c), (d) and (e). Find out which pair of words can be filled up in the blanks in the sentence in the same sequence to make the sentence meaningfully complete :*

(1) To......yourself from.....wear warm clothes. **[BSRB Officers]**

(a) prohibit, heat
(b) protect, cold
(c) save, heat
(d) suffer, cold
(e) prevent, ice

(2) We.........him with many promises, but nothing would.....him. **[N Bank PO]**

(a) tempted, influence
(b) provoked, desicate
(c) attracted, fascinate
(d) gave, deprive
(e) negotiated, please

(3) In his......., he followed the.....course. **[SBI PO]**

(a) agony, funny
(b) ignorance, wrong
(c) hurry, diversified
(d) predicament, proper
(e) bewilderment, appropriate

(4) The construction of the hall has been.......because of the.......cement in the market. **[Bank PO]**

(a) held, non-availability
(b) denied, restrictions
(c) hampered, shortage
(d) prevented, supply
(e) completed, disappearance

(5) Only when..........failed, the police resorted to..... **[Bank PO]**

(a) efforts, power
(b) arrests, imprisonment
(c) persuasions, force
(d) power, punishment
(e) manipulations, arrests

(6) The partners broke off as they found each other......of......breach of promise.

(a) faulty, severe
(b) responsible, serious
(c) guilty, flagranst
(d) accused, rigid
(e) None of these

(7) They wanted to....all these books, but they could not find.....time to do so. **[BSRB Clerk]**

(a) cover, almost
(b) pursue, necessary
(c) dispose, some
(d) read, sufficient
(e) buy, some

(8) Though he is reputed for his technical...., his books were sadly........of the work of others as he lacked originality. **[Bank PO]**

(a) advice, unconscious
(b) skill, independent
(c) knowledge, ignorant
(d) expertise, derivative
(e) dependence, indicative

(9) He had managed to........several times, but was finally........by the police.
(a) deceive, cheated (b) defend, acquitted
(c) escape, arrested (d) cheat, robbed
(e) abscond, kidnapped

(10) The candidate's ....at the polls was.....as he won with a striking margin. **[SBI PO]**
(a) claim, unrealistic (b) victory, overwhelming
(c) image, real (d) strategy, unsuccessful
(e) candidature, inappropriate

(11) In......of International matters, there is always an element of risk in.....one might do. **[Bank PO]**
(a) view, whichever (b) many, doing
(c) defence, wrong (d) case, whatever
(e) spite, whatever

(12) We must prevent endangered wild animal species from becoming.....in order that our future generation may.....the great diversity of animal life. **[Bank PO]**
(a) rare, escape (b) outdated, know
(c) volatile, notice (d) powerful, protect
(e) extinct, enjoy

(13) We cannot....such a/an.....act of violence. **[SBI PO]**
(a) tolerate, insipid (b) consider, important
(c) commit, magnificent (d) pardon, egregious
(e) neglect, insignificant

(14) The secretary.........the society's funds,.....he was dismissed. **[Asstt Grade]**
(a) misplaced, soon (b) rolled, thus
(c) pirated, therefore (d) misappropriated, so
(e) None of these

(15) The.......words of the mother comforted the........child. **[SBI PO]**
(a) harsh, naughty (b) sweet, happy
(c) soft, energetic (d) melodious, playful
(e) None of the above

(16) Santosh looked very happy and.........when he heard that his proposed scheme was.......by the committee. **[SBI PO]**
(a) energetic, rejected (b) elated, accepted
(c) satisfied, stalled (d) disconsolate, approved
(e) overwhelming, received

(17) It is indeed........that fifty years after independence, we have failed to.......a suitable education or examination system.
(a) bed, produce (b) improper, create
(c) sad, evolve (d) objectionable, present
(e) None of these

(18) The bandit...........the traveller of his purse, gold and........him grievously. **[BSRB Clerk]**
(a) snatched, hurt (b) stole, injured
(c) demanded, beat (d) robbed, wounded
(e) None of these

05

Directions (Q. 1-17) *: In each of the following sentences there are two blank spaces in the given sentences. Below each sentence there are five pair of words denoted by numbers (a), (b), (c), (d) and (e). Find out which pair of words can be filled up in the blanks in the sentence in the same sequence to make the sentence meaningfully complete:*

(1) It is.......for every tax payer to.....the tax returns to the Income Tax Department. **[RBI]**
(a) necessary, lodge (b) binding, pay (c) obligatory, submit (d) possible, remit
(e) worthwhile, evade

(2) The.....of glory lead but to the...... .
(a) ways, happiness (b) acts, prosperity
(c) paths, grave (d) achievements, suffering
(e) None of these

(3) If we do not take........care in our industry, we will have to........a grave problem. **[Bank PO]**
(a) normal, experience (b) proper, face
(c) adequate, catch (d) intensive, aggravate
(e) preventive, solve

(4) He shifted to his late parent's house not because of the.....it provided but for purely.........reasons.
(a) convenience, sentimental (b) satisfaction, aesthetic
(c) reasons, monetary (d) comforts, personal
(e) benefit, extraneous

(5) The increasing revival of dramatic classics is to one critic,.......; it seems to him a sign of ....of the modern theatre. **[MBA Entrance]**
(a) auspicious, resurgence (b) tragic, anaemia
(c) incomprehensible, paradox (d) astounding, liveline
(e) None of these

(6) The activities of the association have.........from the.........objectives set for it in the initial years. **[SBI PO]**
(a) grown, simple (b) deviated, original
(c) details, grand (d) emerged, total
(e) increased, perverse

(7) Those suffering from glaucoma find that their.......vision is.......and that they can no longer see objects not directly in front of them. **[MBA]**
(a) optical, distorted (b) peripheral, impaired
(c) prephrastic, demurred (d) peripatetic, diminished

(8) ....the broker had warned him that the stock was a..........investment, he insisted on buying a thousand shares. **[SBI PO]**
(a) because, prudent (b) since, negligible (c) because, speculative (d) as, vulnerable
(e) although, precarious

(9) Due to......rainfall this year, they had to.....cut in water supply. **[BSRB]**
(a) scantly, lift (b) heavy, regulate (c) regular, clamp (d) sufficient, enforce
(e) inadequate, impose

(10) He is so.....that everyone is always......to help in his work. **[RBI]**
(a) helpful, reluctant (b) aloof, cooperative
(c) adamant, enthusiastic (d) miserly, ignorant
(e) magnanimous, eager

(11) Instead of.........prove your worth by......something. **[Bank PO]**
(a) begging, demanding (b) talking, doing (c) worrying, paying (d) writing, reading
(e) donating, demanding

(12) The great scientist........himself with ability and modernation all......the conference. **[Bank PO]**
(a) felt, about (b) displayed, in (c) disclosed, besides (d) conducted, through
(e) presented, though

(13) The speech........with subtle threats has resulted in........tension in the sensitive areas of the city. **[Bank PO]**
(a) started, reduced (b) replete, increased (c) full, escalating (d) forced, dissolving
(e) followed, continuous

(14) The minister felt that the........made by the committee was.....even though similar schemes had worked earlier.
(a) decision, gainful (b) choice, profitable (c) acceptance, approved (d) election, acceptable
(e) recommendation, infeasible

(15) We can.......to travel by air, but we........train journey. **[SBI PO]**
(a) spend, enjoy (b) desire, commute (c) afford, prefer (d) decide, undertook
(e) become, accept

(16) He was convinced that people were driven by........motives that he believed there was no such thing as a purely........act. **[SBI PO]**
(a) personal, vengeful (b) personal, eternal
(c) altruistic, praiseworthy (d) ulterior, selfless
(e) sentimental, divine

(17) I don't.........I shall be.......to go. **[Bank PO]**
(a) know, able (b) consider, desirous
(c) think, able (d) believe, liking
(e) feel, available

06

Directions (Q. 1-10) *: Each sentence below has one or two blanks, each blank indicates that something has been omitted. Beneath the sentence there are four alternatives. Choose the alternative that best fits the meaning of the sentence as a whole :*

(1) The .... tactics of the party drove the community .... and all hell broke loose.
(a) dilatory, berserk (b) timely, crazy (c) opportune, wild (d) apposite, excited

(2) The female members of the group later.......... and went on to become divas.
(a) joined (b) distended (c) distorted (d) disbanded

(3) The chief........ him of his administrative powers and .... him to the Bahamas.
(a) invested, shipped (b) augmented, deported
(c) incremented, sent (d) divested, deported

(4) The valley was winding with the faint camp-fires of the scattered.......... .
(a) twigs (b) schools (c) coteries (d) contingents

(5) The Republicans thought Adams a far-seeing statesman and a/an.........politician.
(a) bacchanalian (b) neurotic (c) aphasic (d) astute

(6) They feared that they might....... develop the.........raiding activity of the tribe into regular operation.
(a) abruptly, spontaneous (b) incidentally, resplendent
(c) knowingly, spurious (d) inadvertently, spurious

(7) Her sister, of whose..........and delicacy she was sure her opinion could never be shaken, was the talk of the town now.
(a) turpitude (b) rectitude (c) loose morals (d) wickedness

(8) She denounced the fiendish pronouncements of the General as the........schemes of ....and power-crazy radical.
(a) spurious, lenient (b) radical, beguiled (c) loose, morals (d) beneficial, high-strung

(9) Already............tensions between the ethnic group and the refugees were..........last week after fresh riots broke out.
(a) reducing, toned down (b) low, sparked off
(c) attenuated, driven away (d) escalating, aggravated

(10) The spirit of the New year Eve's celebrations was..........by the downpour of rains, much to their............. .
(a) aggravated, delight (b) fired up, joy (c) dampened, chagrin (d) blown out, valour

07

Directions (Q. 1-10) : *Each sentence in the questions has one or two blanks, each blank indicates that something has been omitted. Beneath the sentence are four lettered words or sets of words. Choose the word or set of words for each blank that best fits into the meaning of the sentence as a whole :*

(1) She stoically revealed that armed robbers had ransacked the home and .... added that her grandparents could not survive.
(a) euphemistically (b) gravely (c) soberly (d) miserably

(2) Ronnie was shocked to see his score in mathematics, getting one mark short was nothing short of a ....
(a) parody (b) heresy (c) travesty (d) carrion

(3) He cleverly drew upon the.......... motives of his colleagues and made them contribute to the .... fund.
(a) miserly, sincere (b) insular, relief (c) craven, justice (d) altruistic, dubious

(4) The world is ...., its suffering.......... .
(a) perfect, sincere (b) just, scarce (c) diverse, sparse (d) imperfect, random

(5) There were two baskets kept for the garbage's disposal, one was marked ....and one was marked ....to simplify matters.
(a) low, high (b) upward, downgraded
(c) parasitic, renewable (d) biodegradable, recyclable

(6) The task of the special committee was to put a .... to the accelerating spread of the highly contagious disease across the .... states.
(a) spur, far-flung (b) hold , warring
(c) brake, contiguous (d) downclamp, factions

(7) Aimed at putting a check on .... disruptions to the WTO proceedings, the Riot Guards made it clear that they can match the protestors' efforts stone by stone, ...
(a) rational, bridge by bridge (b) justified, day by day
(c) putrid, hour by hour (d) irrational, brick by brick.

(8) Our initial days at Rockford were ...., quite surprising, the head boy was the biggest ...., and we earned the nickname of the 'Peevish Batch'.
(a) calm, mediator (b) tempestuous, dissenter
(c) turbid, arbiter (d) sane, leader

(9) The poet .... the beauty of the courtesan with his lyrical melodies.
(a) condemned (b) disparaged
(c) scorned (d) extolled

(10) To the dismay of her friends, her father .... shouted at the authorities and hurled .... abuses at them.
(a) vociferously, vituperative
(b) gently, decibel
(c) malignantly, carnal
(d) cowardly, harsh

08

Directions (Q. 1-10) : *Each sentence in the questions has one or two blanks, each blank indicates that something has been omitted. Beneath the sentence are four lettered words or sets of words. Choose the word or set of words for each blank that best fits into the meaning of the sentence as a whole :*

(1) A .... is a.................... .
(a) norm, standard
(b) knowledge, mistake
(c) student, school
(d) doctrine, follower
(e) thesis, superstition

(2) A .... shade of distinction is a ....
(a) beautiful, vindication
(b) complete, profanity
(c) subtle, nuance
(d) thorough, prejudice
(e) entire, paradox

(3) .... flattery is known as ....
(a) regular, maturity
(b) indiscriminate, encomium
(c) servile, adulation
(d) unasked for, gratitude
(e) cowardly, temerity

(4) At some private schools pupils are under the .... of a ....
(a) guidance, palladium
(b) tutelage, preceptor
(c) coaching, verity
(d) assiduity, palladium
(e) consensus, mentor

(5) A large .... centre is a/an ....
(a) district, affliction
(b) transport, automobile
(c) civic, utarchy
(d) shopping, emporium
(e) educational, indignity

(6) .... persons are inclined to ....
(a) obese, corpulence
(b) generous, leanness
(c) domineering, temperance
(d) vacillating, determination
(e) cowering, effrontery

(7) A .... is a temporary ....
(a) deviation, rest
(b) shambles, journey
(c) respite, relief
(d) paradox, enchantment
(e) feint, spell

(8) .... language may also be termed ....
(a) eloquent, exiguous
(b) frenzied, placid
(c) abusive, scurrilous
(d) contumelious, flattering
(e) denunciatory, peripatetic

(9) A .... of small stones is called a ....
(a) design, numismatist
(b) collar, tiara
(c) seller, connoisseur
(d) mound, lithograph
(e) pattern, mosaic

(10) Suzerainty is .... control over a .... state.
(a) full, democratic
(b) domestic, backward
(c) central, unified
(d) political, dependent
(e) economic, federate

09

Directions (Q. 1-12) *: Each sentence in the questions has one or two blanks, each blank indicates that something has been omitted. Beneath the sentence are four lettered words or sets of words. Choose the word or set of words for each blank that best fits into the meaning of the sentence as a whole :*

(1) To encourage colonial peoples in their aspirations to attain independence before it is .... proved that a .... state will evolve instead of anarchy is unforgivable.
(a) unchanged, formidable
(b) certainty, sympathetic
(c) succinctly, redoubtable
(d) incontrovertibly, viable
(e) unequivocally, mobile

(2) Human memory is not .... especially on ancienty happenings that smack of the ....
(a) infallible, mythological
(b) dependable, simple
(c) confidant, fanciful
(d) reliable, inventive
(e) noteworthy, fanciful

(3) Athletes have so perfected their techniques in track and field events that the .... becomes .... before record books can be published.
(a) announcement, public
(b) meet, official
(c) time, authentic
(d) fantastic , commonplace
(e) result, universal

(4) Like the .... part of an iceberg, much of what is really interesting in the capital is not...... .
(a) inner, known
(b) submerged, visible
(c) greater, dangerous
(d) upper, viable
(e) lower, penetrable

(5) Hence the word sophistry has an unfavourable .... and means arguing deceitfully, attempting to turn a poor case into a good one by means of clever but .... reasoning.
(a) denotation, ingenuous
(b) meaning, ingenious
(c) connotation, specious
(d) significance, vague
(e) impact, cogent

(6) He warned the workers against supporting these antisocial policies, which he declared would .... rather than .... the plight of the common people.
(a) rescue, destroy
(b) encourage, defy
(c) aggravate, alleviate
(d) empower, improve
(e) protract, inhibit

(7) The defense proposes to show that the incident that the prosecution so .... rejects as did indeed take place, is indeed historical fact.
(a) blithely, undesirable
(b) cavalierly, apocryphal
(c) cautiously, factual
(d) persuasively, ignorance
(e) positively, inevitable

(8) We have criticized our university students for preferring the security of political silence and the safety of .... to the excitement of social .... and humanitarian action.
(a) acquiescence, dissent
(b) college, adventure
(c) concealment, revolution
(d) tolerance, antagonism
(e) security, insecurity

(9) The practice of painting slogans on rock faces, once a thriving industry in Britain, has fallen into .... but there has recently been a/an .... in Country Antrim.
(a) oblivion, demand
(b) misuse, artisan
(c) disfavor, puheaval
(d) mediocrity, surfeit
(e) disuse, recrudescence

(10) Curiously enough the very passages which set out to clarify only ....; the details are served up in .... three-page paragraphs which stupefy the reader.
(a) adumbrate, excessive
(b) obscure, succinct
(c) mystify, stimulating
(d) disturb, compact
(e) obfuscate, monolithic

(11) Oddly enough .... the prestige of the United States in such countries as Britain, France and Italy is considered important here, Congress has been .... about supplying funds to the U.S. Information Agency in these countries.
(a) in as much as, chary
(b) since, delaying
(c) while, generous
(d) whereas, wasteful
(e) although, niggardly

(12) The increasing revival of dramatic classics is, to one critic, ... ; it seems to him a sign of the .... of the modern theatre.
(a) Inconceivable, revival
(b) deplorable, anemia
(c) suspicious, resurgence
(d) astounding, uselessness
(e) incomprehensible, fatuousness

10

Directions (Q. 1-11) : *Each sentence in the questions has one or two blanks, each blank indicates that something has been omitted. Beneath the sentence are four lettered words or sets of words. Choose the word or set of words for each blank that best fits into the meaning of the sentence as a whole*

(1) It is a well-known .... that the lover of the sea craves for dry land- the age- old....... to be where we are not.
(a) belief, antipathy (b) anomaly, demiurge (c) credo, inspiration (d) contention, duplicity
(e) paradox, yearning

(2) Why should a university .... the values which are supposedly basic to its functioning and give an honourary doctorate to one who has not distinguished himself in a/an .... manner?
(a) deflate, scholarly (b) foretell, worldly (c) vilify, collegiate (d) abuse, doctrinaire
(e) debase, academic

(3) Such stalling tactics are .... to all fens and cannot be ....
(a) repugnant, condoned
(b) anathema, ascertained
(c) injurious, explained
(d) unfair, superseded
(e) understandable, countenanced

(4) The .... of democratic freedom is dialogue and the .... interchange of diverse ideas.
(a) deterioration, untrammeled
(b) height, restrained
(c) essence, unhampered
(d) alienation, compulsory
(e) epitome, discriminating

(5) Although there were .... circumstances in this particular violation of the law, the judge ruled that there had to be strict .... or there would be no law at all.
(a) extraordinary, complaisance
(b) specific, obedience
(c) tantalizing, adherence
(d) extenuating, compliance
(e) questionable, observation

(6) In spite of all .... , in spite of penalties for examinees when cheaters were caught, there is evidence of the ..... of the rigid rules of external help on civil service tests.
(a) threats, encompassment
(b) surveillance, vulnerability
(c) temptation, flouting
(d) precautions, circumvention
(e) discouragement, acceptance

(7) Hungarians may grumble about the difficulty of acquiring cars, but they point quickly to a compensation: the .... look of their tree-lined avenues and the absence of .... exhaust fumes.
(a) calm, superfluous
(b) otiose, poisonous
(c) tranquil, copious
(d) anomalous, fetid
(e) uncluttered, noxious

(8) In architecture, much more than in any of the other fine arts, there is a marked time lag between the .... of ideas and their .... in the shape of completed building.
(a) settlement, fruition
(b) creation, welcoming
(c) tradition, modernization
(d) dawn, practicability
(e) emergence, appliction

(9) In analyzing the .... teen age population, Madison Avenue has decided that it is eminently receptive to the .... of advertising.
(a) proliferating, buncombe
(b) ubiquitous, mystique
(c) diminishing, fantasy
(d) burgeoning, blandishments
(e) viable, syndrome

(10) No matter how .... the Russians are of wish to appear, they, as well as we, know that to survive it is necessary to reach agreements which may .... mutual sacrifices.
(a) fatuous, necessitate
(b) bellicose, evade
(c) refractory, obliterate
(d) indifferent, subsume
(e) intransigent, entail

(11) Into the limited space given him a headline writer must compress the .... of the news and he must do it without ....
(a) synopsis, reservations
(b) gist, ambiguity
(c) magnitude, distortion
(d) totality, hedging
(e) bias, apology

11

Directions (Q. 1-12) *Each sentence in the questions has one or two blanks, each blank indicates that something has been omitted. Beneath the sentence are four lettered words or sets of words. Choose the word or set of words for each blank that best fits into the meaning of the sentence as a whole.*

(1) For some years past, French governments had been .... and divided, and French parliaments had been incoherent and............
(a) inarticulate, responsive
(b) untable, domineering
(c) weak, inchoate
(d) many, few
(e) vacillating, irresponsible

(2) Scientific imagination is a specific intellectual power that is .... in every population that has learned to be .... about the mechanisms governing the physical world.
(a) encouraged, wary
(b) evoked, self-deprecatory
(c) latent, curious
(d) growing, self-possessed
(e) language, diffident

(3) In diplomatic .... the .... sought by on government from another to the name of a proposed ambassador is known as an "agreement."
(a) dealing, understandings
(b) parlance, assent
(c) circles, permission
(d) channels, condition
(e) language, interpretation

(4) Camille Pissarro, eldest of France's great impressionist .... that included Monet, Manet, Rennoir, and Degas, was both the movement's .... and its saint.
(a) cabal, doyen
(b) sodality, gadfly
(c) entity, defector
(d) hierarchy, patriarch
(e) brotherhood, demon

(5) The westerlies normally cross the United States at altitudes from 10,000 to 50,000 feet along the Canadian border, acting as a .... to Arctic winds and giving the Middle Atlantic States relatively .... winters.
(a) counterpart, unsettled
(b) propellant, mild
(c) counterpart, unsettled
(d) buffer, temperate
(e) deterrent, cold

(6) But even Mr. Moses, one of the most .... public servants of our time, is at a loss to convey in words the size, the imaginative engineering............ that built this contribution to the welfare of family and industry.
(a) tongue-tied, miracle
(b) dedicated, appositeness
(c) unappreciated, technique
(d) public-spirited, skill
(e) articulate, ingenuity

(7) Among the younger people there are complaints that the sight of ex-Nazis flourishing recommends .... to youth, that it instills, instead of needed moral values, the dubious precept that .... is the best policy.
(a) precepts, intolerance
(b) desperation, dishonesty
(c) emulation, honesty
(d) cynicism, expediency

(8) Even as .... machines free men from drudgery, they .... displace men from jobs.
(a) automated, simultaneously
(b) robotlike, unwillingly
(c) animated, ineluctably
(d) accelerated, seemingly
(e) antiquate, understandably

(9) To cross the Rubicon means to take a final .... step which may have dangerous ....
(a) hazardous, precedent
(b) unwarranted, potentialities
(c) inconsequential, concomitants
(d) well-considered, implications
(e) irrevocable, consequences

(10) Though the Oxford English Dictionary is undoubtedly the greatest dictionary ever ...., it is designed for scholars and research workers rather than for the .... dictionary user.
(a) assembled, assiduous
(b) demonstrated, amateur
(c) projected, omniscient
(d) published, professional
(e) compiled, casual

(11) For nearly a century the .... travellers chech has been the nearest thing to an internationals currency yet devised by man, and has guided generations of Americans and other tourists through the ...... of foreign exchange.
(a) useful, excesses
(b) surreptitious, complexities
(c) plausible, maze
(d) sacrosanct, fluctuations
(e) ubiquitous, labyrinth

(12) If it were true that enduring lesson are learned from .... errors, Broadway would be the repository of............. theatrical wisdom.
(a) accidental, occult
(b) egregius, sublime
(c) dubious, profound
(d) dramatic, lasting
(e) stupid, attennuated

SOLUTIONS TEST YOURSELF *Exercises*

Solution TYE 01

(1) (b), (2) (a), (3). (a), (4) (e), (5) (c).

Solution TYE 02

(1) (e), (2) (d), (3) (b), (4) (a), (5) (c),
(6) (b), (7) (d), (8) (c), (9) (b), (10) (c).

Solution TYE 03

(1) (d), (2) (e), (3) (c), (4) (d), (5) (c),
(6) (b), (7) (a), (8) (d), (9) (d).

Solution TYE 04

(1) (b), (2) (a), (3) (b), (4) (c), (5) (c),
(6) (c), (7) (d), (8) (d), (9) (c), (10) (b),
(11) (d), (12) (e), (13) (d), (14) (d), (15) (d),
(16) (b), (17) (c), (18) (d).

Solution TYE 05

(1) (c), (2) (c), (3) (b), (4) (a), (5) (a),
(6) (b), (7) (b), (8) (e), (9) (e), (10) (e),
(11) (b), (12) (d), (13) (b), (14) (e), (15) (c),
(16) (d), (17) (c).

Solution TYE 06

(1) (a), (2) (d), (3) (d), (4) (d), (5) (d),
(6) (d), (7) (b), (8) (b), (9) (d), (10) (c).

Solution TYE 07

(1) (a), (2) (c), (3) (d), (4) (d), (5) (d),
(6) (c), (7) (d), (8) (c), (9). (d), (10) (a).

Solution TYE 08

(1) (a), (2) (c), (3) (c), (4) (b), (5) (d),
(6) (a), (7) (c), (8) (c), (9) (e), (10) (d).

Solution TYE 09

(1) (d), (2) (a), (3) (d), (4) (b), (5) (c),
(6) (c), (7) (b), (8) (a), (9) (e), (10) (e),
(11) (e), (12) (b).

Solution TYE 10

(1) (e), (2) (e), (3) (a), (4) (c), (5) (d),
(6) (d), (7) (e), (8) (e), (9) (d), (10) (e),
(11) (b).

Solution TYE 11

(1) (e), (2) (c), (3) (b), (4) (d), (5) (d),
(6) (e), (7) (d), (8) (a), (9) (e), (10) (e)
(11) (e), (12) (b).

CHAPTER 38

MISCELLANEOUS EXERCISE
(CORRECT THE SENTENCES)

TEST YOURSELF *Exercises*

01

Correct the following sentences:

(1) His father gave him many advices.
(2) The boys went to the college directly.
(3) I am much pleased to see you both.
(4) He has just returned back from London.
(5) Because he does not work hard, therefore he will fail.
(6) He does not know wrong from right.
(7) The English is difficult to speak.
(8) What to speak of food, even water was not available there.
(9) Bible is a sacred book of Christians.
(10) I am much thankful to you for this act of kindness.

02

Correct the following sentences:

(1) This book gives us many informations about Prithvi Raj.
(2) The furnitures of office house are very costly.
(3) He is one of the best poet the world has ever produced.
(4) He asked from me that I had gone there or no.
(5) Where you spent your last summer vacations?
(6) The hen has lain two eggs.
(7) He enjoys very bad health.
(8) He never said anything of the kind.
(9) I should be glad if you will come in the evening.
(10) I am the one who am to blame.

03

Correct the following sentences:

(1) At his sight I trembled with fear.
(2) We should pray God everyday.
(3) Open your book on Page 78.
(4) He was born in nineteen hundreds ten.
(5) The subject to her essay is about Politeness.
(6) As I am ill, so I will not be able to attend office today.
(7) I do not know who are you.
(8) So quickly we walked that we reached the station in time.
(9) I neither met Gopal or his sister.
(10) English is not only difficult to read, but also to write.

04

Correct the following sentences:

(1) It is half past six in my watch.
(2) He is true to his words.
(3) The magistrate passed order for his an acquittal.
(4) His family members have gone to Kashmir.
(5) The examinations begins from Monday.
(6) He hesitated in complying with my request.
(7) He was displeased at Mira going to the theatre last night.
(8) He was angry at me not complying with his request.
(9) Health is more preferable than riches.
(10) His claim in prior than yours.

05

Correct the following sentences:

(1) He is the most happiest man living on this Earth.
(2) The elephant is larger than any animal.
(3) Akbar was wiser than any king.
(4) No girl in the class is so intelligent as Kanika.
(5) This book is as good or even better than yours.
(6) He is the worthiest and sympathetic man in the town.
(7) He has been suffering from fever from Tuesday last.
(8) He has been ill since ten days.
(9) I have not seen him since a long time.
(10) His brother died since a fortnight.

06

Correct the following sentences:

(1) We shall not be here before two months.
(2) You must finish this work before two hours.
(3) I except a letter from her in a week.
(4) I received his letter long before.

(5) The train will arrive just now.
(6) Character and not riches, win us respect.
(7) Every flower and every leaf proclaim the glory of God.
(8) The sum and substance of her speech are as follow.
(9) Fifty rupees are not a large sum for that painting.
(10) Aesop's Fables are book everybody should read.

07

Correct the following sentences:

(1) The majority was present at the meeting.
(2) The committee was divided in its opinions.
(3) None but those having a teaching experience needs apply.
(4) It were the girl that defied their teacher's orders.
(5) Everyone should be careful of one's health.
(6) Neither the students nor the Principal was there.
(7) Walking along the Mall Road, his head dashed against a lamp-post.
(8) Being a fine day, they went to the river to enjoy a picnic.
(9) Failing in the first attempt, no second attempt was made.
(10) He has an urgent business at home.

08

Correct the following sentences:

(1) Ramesh has many businesses today.
(2) There was not any temple there but I visited.
(3) He as well as I am wrong.
(4) We have come here to take your leave.
(5) I cannot endure her separation.
(6) Do you know who are you referring to?
(7) You should follow their advice who are superior to you in intellect.
(8) He dares not to speak against me.
(9) I was greatly wondered at what met my eyes.
(10) I admitted my brother to the D.A.V. College.

09

Correct the following sentences:

(1) He took admission in to the DAV High School.
(2) She did nothing but sang.
(3) I am feeling feverish.
(4) I intend to inform his misbehaviour to his father.
(5) Please excuse me for giving you this trouble.
(6) He told these news to his mother.
(7) Her arguments hold no water.
(8) Many kinds of fruits grow in Kashmir, such as apples, plums, pears, cherries etc.
(9) With regard my conduct, I beg to submit as follows.

10

Correct the following sentences:

(1) He packed his luggages.
(2) He provided the blinds with food and clothes.
(3) Scouts wear half pants.
(4) There is no place in this compartment.
(5) Give my B.C's to all.
(6) He hit an over-boundary.
(7) He saw a joker at the circus.
(8) We had a good play of hockey.
(9) I saw a theatre last night.
(10) Won't you like to take part in drama?

11

Correct the following sentences:

(1) He is a tall gentleman.
(2) These females have come here to take your advice.
(3) He got a bad companionship.
(4) Here is my cup; please fill.
(5) I asked for my book, but he did not give me.
(6) The boy who stand first he will get a prize.
(7) I with some friend went for a walk.
(8) The master tested the boy if he could speak English.
(9) He is elder than me.
(10) He will spend his remaining life here.

12

Correct the following sentences:

(1) This is a worth seeing building.
(2) He got nearly centper cent marks.
(3) He got an employment in a Nationalised Bank.
(4) You should not make noise.
(5) What a fun!
(6) I do not care for you.
(7) He does not care for his money.
(8) He got angry before I said a word.
(9) If I would have worked hard, I would have passed.
(10) I left playing.

13

Correct the following sentences:

(1) I take my food.
(2) I want that I should get leave.
(3) I like to play football.
(4) He is troubling me.
(5) He gave a speech.
(6) He would not hear me.
(7) I cannot pull on with my work.
(8) He has ordered for a new requite.
(9) He has disposed off his bicycle.
(10) I put up with him.

14

Correct the following sentences:

(1) Keep this on the table.
(2) I had a mind to play.
(3) He cannot maintain his livelihood.
(4) I struck a blow on his face.
(5) He is reading at the High School.
(6) He won his opponents.
(7) They made a goal.
(8) I hope she must come.
(9) The committee is consisted of fifteen members.
(10) Always fair out a written exercise.

15

Correct the following sentences:

(1) Open the light.
(2) Shut the light.
(3) His hand has been operated.
(4) It is written in this letter.
(5) He was very kind enough to comply with my request.
(6) He did it anyhow.
(7) To tell in brief.
(8) He told the story in details.
(9) This book is much interesting.
(10) He behaved cowardly.

16

Correct the following sentences:

(1) He lives miserly.
(2) Never I had seen such a sight.
(3) Though he is old, still he can run fast.
(4) As he is old so he walks slowly.
(5) If he works hard then he will pass.
(6) Because he is clever therefore he gets good marks.
(7) He did not attend the meeting because he was ill.
(8) Until he does not apologies, he must not be allowed to sit in the class.
(9) No sooner I had reached the station, than the train started.
(10) Not only he will go, but also he will stay there.

17

Correct the following sentences:

(1) Neither she comes nor she writes.
(2) I am fond of all game as for an example tennis.
(3) I want to know as to why I have not been allowed to sit in the examination.
(4) He called her as a fool.
(5) Supposing if he fails, what will he do?
(6) He is ill since three months.
(7) He wrote me a long letter.
(8) I shall explain him this.
(9) Send this letter on my address.
(10) He suggested me this.

18.

Correct the following sentences:

(1) He goes in the school.
(2) He goes on his work.
(3) He was favourite to his friends.
(4) I did not ask any question to him.
(5) From our class he did best.
(6) The term begins from June 1st.
(7) He will be cured from his fever.
(8) There are many advantages from this.
(9) He wasted much time in trifles.
(10) There is a saying in Hindus.

19.

Correct the following sentences:

(1) There is no harm to go there.
(2) Write with ink.
(3) He rides on a car.
(4) This is a comfortable house to live.
(5) This is the road to go.
(6) I gave her a chair to sit.
(7) He is called with different names.
(8) He went away for doing some business.
(9) We discussed about the matter.
(10) When this was searched it was found.

20

Correct the following sentences:

(1) Due to illness, I can not go to school.
(2) He walked all the way by foot.
(3) The bank will compensate the loss of the cheque.
(4) I must go; there is no help.
(5) There was a match between Delhi against Jaipur.
(6) No mention.
(7) He is running thirty.
(8) In my opinion I think it is right.
(9) In the way I met a woman.
(10) It has its origin from a story in Ramayana.
(11) We sat under the shade of a mango tree.
(12) Tears streamed on her cheeks.
(13) The match starts from 4 o'clock.
(14) The holidays will commence from June the 20th.

Solution TYE : 01

(1) His father gave him many pieces of advice.
(2) The boys went to the college direct.
(3) I am very pleased to see both of you.
(4) He has just returned from London.
(5) He does not work hard, therefore he will fail.

Or

Because he does not work hard, he will fail.

(6) He does not know right from wrong.
(7) English is difficult to speak.
(8) Not to speak of food, even water was not available there.
(9) The Bible is a sacred book of the Christians.
(10) I am very thankful to you for this act of kindness.

Solution TYE : 02

(1) This book gives us much information about Prithvi Raj.
(2) The furniture of this office is very costly.
(3) He is one of the best poets the world has ever produced.
(4) He asked me whether I had gone there or not.
(5) Where did you spend you last summer vacations?
(6) The hen has laid two eggs.
(7) He has very bad health.
(8) He said nothing of the kind.
(9) I should be glad if you would come in the evening.
(10) I am the one who is to blame.

Solution TYE : 03

(1) At the sight of him I trembled with fear.
(2) We should pray to God everyday.
(3) Open your book at page 78.
(4) He was born in nineteen hundered and ten.
(5) The subject of her essay is 'Politeness'.
(6) As I am ill, I will not be able to attend office today.
(7) I do not know who you are?
(8) So quickly did we walk that we reached the station in time.
(9) I met neither Gopal nor his sister.
(10) English is difficult not only to read, but also to write.

Solution TYE : 04

(1) It is half past six by my watch.
(2) He is true to his word.
(3) The magistrate passed orders for his acquittal.
(4) The members of his family have gone to Kashmir.
(5) The examination begins on Monday.
(6) He hesitated to comply with my request.
(7) He was displeased at Mira's going to the theatre last night.
(8) He was angry at my not complying with his request.
(9) Health is preferable to riches.
(10) His claim is prior to yours.

Solution TYE : 05

(1) He is the happiest man living on this earth.
(2) The elephant is larger than any other animal.
(3) Akbar was wiser than any other king.
(4) No other girl in the class is so intelligent as Kanika.
(5) This book is as good as or even better than yours.
(6) He is the worthiest and most sympathetic man in the town.
(7) He has been suffering from fever since Tuesday last.
(8) He has been ill for ten days.
(9) I have not seen him for a long time.
(10) His brother died a fortnight since.

Solution TYE : 06

(1) We shall not be here for two months.
(2) You must finish this work within two hours.
(3) I expect a letter for her in a week
(4) I received his letter long ago.
(5) The train will arrive soon.
(6) Character and not riches, wins us respect.
(7) Every flower and every leaf proclaims the glory of God.
(8) The sum and substance of her speech is as follows.
(9) Fifty rupees is not a large sum for that painting.
(10) Aesop's Fables is a book everybody should read.

Solution TYE : 07

(1) The majority were present at the meeting.
(2) The committee were divided in their opinions.
(3) None but those having teaching experience need apply.
(4) It was the girl that defied their teacher's orders.
(5) Everyone should be careful of his heath.
(6) Neither the Principal nor the students were there.
(7) As he was walking along the Mall Road, his head dashed against the lamp-post.
(8) It being a fine day, they went to the river to enjoy a picnic.
(9) Failing in the first attempt, he made no second attempt.
(10) He has an urgent piece of business at home.

Solution TYE : 08

(1) Ramesh has much business today.
(2) There was no temple there that I did not visit.
(3) He is wrong as well as I.
(4) We have come here to take leave of you.
(5) I cannot endure separation from her.
(6) Do you know whom you are referring to?
(7) You should follow the advice of those who are superior to you in intellect.
(8) He dares not speak against me.
(9) I was greatly astonished at what met my eyes.

Or

I wondered greatly at what met my eyes.
(10) I got my brother admitted to the DAV College.

Solution TYE : 09

(1) He was admitted to the D.A.V. High School.
(2) She did nothing but sing.
(3) I feel feverish.
(4) I intend to inform his father of his misbehaviour.
(5) Please excuse me for the trouble I am giving you.
(6) He told his mother this news.
(7) Her arguments will not hold water.
(8) Many kinds of fruit, such as apples, pears, plums and cherries, grow in Kashmir.

Or

Many kinds of fruit-apples, pears, plums, cherries, etc grow in Kashmir.
(9) With regard to my conduct I beg to submit as follows.

Solution TYE : 10

(1) He packed his luggage.
(2) He provided the blind with food and clothes.
(3) Scouts wear shorts.
(4) There is no room in this compartment.
(5) Give my (kind) regards to all.
(6) He hit a six.
(7) We saw a clown at the circus.
(8) We had a good game of hockey.
(9) I saw a play last night.
(10) Won't you like to act ?

Solution TYE : 11

(1) He is a tall man.
(2) These women have come here to take your advice.
(3) He got into bad company.
(4) Here is my cup; please fill it.
(5) I asked for my book, but he did not give it to me.
(6) The boy who stands first will get a prize.
(7) I went for a walk with some friends.
(8) The master tested if the boy could speak English.
(9) He is elder to me.
(10) He will spent the rest of his life here.

Solution TYE : 12

(1) This is a building worth seeing.
(2) He got nearly full marks.
(3) He got employment in a Nationalised Bank.
(4) You should not make a noise.
(5) What fun !
(6) I do not care what you do.
(7) He does not take care of his money.
(8) He got angry before I had said a word.
(9) If I had worked hard, I would have passed.
(10) I stopped playing.

Solution TYE : 13

(1) I have my food.
(2) I want to get leave.
(3) I want to play football.
(4) He is giving me trouble.
(5) He made a speech.
(6) He would not listen to me.
(7) I cannot manage my work.
(8) He has ordered a new requite.
(9) He has disposed of his bicycle.
(10) I stayed with him.

Solution TYE : 14

(1) Put this on the table.
(2) I intended to play.
(3) He cannot earn a living.
(4) I gave him a blow on the face.

Or

I struck him in the face.

(5) He is at the High School.
(6) He beat his opponents.
(7) They scored a goal.
(8) I hope she will come.

Or

She must come.

(9) The committee consists of fifteen members.
(10) Always make a fair copy of a written exercise.

Solution TYE : 15

(1) Turn on the light.
(2) Turn off the light
(3) His hand has been operated upon.
(4) This letter says that...
(5) He was kind enough to comply with my request.
(6) He managed to do it somehow.
(7) In short.
(8) He told the story in detail.
(9) This book is very interesting.
(10) He behaved in a cowardly manner.

Or

He behaved like a coward.

Solution TYE : 16

(1) He lives in a miserly way.
(2) Never had I seen such a sight.
(3) Though he is old, yet he can run fast.
(4) As he is old, he walks slowly.
(5) If he works hard, he will pass.
(6) Because he is clever, he gets high marks.
(7) He did not attend the meeting because he was ill.
(8) He must not be allowed to sit in the class until he apologizes.
(9) No sooner had I reached the station than the train started.
(10) He will not only go but also stay there.

Solution TYE : 17

(1) Neither does she come nor does she write.
(2) I am fond of all games, for example tennis.
(3) I want to know why I have not been allowed to take the examination.
(4) He called her a fool.
(5) Supposing he fails, what will he do?

Or

If he fails, what will he do?
(6) He has been ill for three months.
(7) He wrote a long letter to me.
(8) I shall explain this to him.
(9) Send this letter at my address.
(10) He suggested this to me.

Solution TYE : 18

(1) He goes to school.
(2) He goes to his work.
(3) He was a a favorite with his friends.
(4) I did not ask him any question.
(5) He did best in our class.
(6) The term begins on June 1st.
(7) He will be cured of his fever.
(8) The advantages of this are many.
(9) He wasted much time on trifles.
(10) There is a saying among the Hindus.

Solution TYE : 19

(1) There is no harm in going there.
(2) Write in ink.
(3) He rides in a car.
(4) This is a comfortable house to live in.
(5) This is the road to go by.
(6) I gave her a chair to sit on.
(7) He is called by different names.
(8) He went away on business.
(9) We discussed the matter.
(10) When this was searched for it was found.

Solution TYE : 20

(1) Because of illness, I cannot go to school.
(2) He walked all the way on foot.
(3) The Bank will compensate for the loss of the cheque.
(4) I must go; there is no help for it.
(5) There was a match between Delhi and Jaipur.
(6) Please do not mention it.
(7) He is in his thirtieth year *or* He is thirty.
(8) In my opinion it is right *or* I think it is right.
(9) On the way I met a woman.
(10) It has its origin in a story in the Ramayan.
(11) We sat in the shade of a mango tree.
(12) Tears streamed down her cheeks.
(13) The match starts at four 0' clock.
(14) The holidays will commence on June 20th.

CHAPTER

39

WORD POWER

"One can neither write correctly, nor speak fluently without knowledge of appropriate words to cloth one's thoughts and imaginations."

शुद्ध लेखन एवं शुद्ध बोलचाल हेतु 'Good Vocabulary' or 'Word Power' एक आवश्यक शर्त है। Grammar के rules के ज्ञान के बाद विभिन्न प्रकार के वाक्य बनाने हेतु अपने विचारों को अंग्रेजी में (लिखित एवं बोलचाल में) व्यक्त करने हेतु उचित शब्दों का ज्ञान होना आवश्यक है। आपने Vocabulary बढ़ाने हेतु स्कूल या कॉलेज के दिनों में या Competitions की तैयारी करने हेतु, कई बार शब्दों एवं उनके Meanings को रटा होगा। कुछ शब्दों के Meanings अभी भी याद होंगे, कुछ भूल गए होंगे। जो Words एवं Meanings आपको याद नहीं होंगे उनमें से अधिकांश का प्रयोग, आप अपने वाक्यों में करने में स्वयं को असक्षम पाते होंगे।

यह स्थिति अधिकांश छात्रों की है जब तक आप शब्दों (Words) का प्रयोग अपने वाक्यों में करने में सक्षम नहीं हैं तब तक आप उस शब्द का सही अर्थ नहीं जान सकते हैं। मात्र किसी Word का हिन्दी अर्थ जानना पर्याप्त नहीं है। Vocabulary को Improve करने हेतु थोड़ी-सी मेहनत एवं थोड़े दिन लगातार प्रयास की आवश्यकता है।

आइए हम आपको कुछ ऐसे तरीकों से परिचित करवाते हैं जो आपकी Vocabulary में न केवल उल्लेखनीय वृद्धि करेंगे बल्कि आप शब्दों का उचित प्रयोग भी करने में सक्षम होंगे।

Learn Three Steps to Improve Your Word Power
(A Self-Experimented Technique)

Step one:

सर्वप्रथम निश्चय करें कि आप प्रतिदिन किसी Newspaper, Magazine, Standard Book अथवा Course Book में से 20-30 या 50 कठिन शब्द लिखेंगे। जब आप Daily Newspaper, Magazine, Course Book या कोई Standard Book का अध्ययन करते हैं तो आपको जो भी शब्द कठिन (Difficult word) लगें, उन्हें एक कॉपी या रजिस्टर में लिखें। किसी अच्छी Dictionary में देखकर इन शब्दों का हिन्दी एवं अंग्रेजी में अर्थ लिख लें। शब्दों के कई-कई अर्थ (Meanings) लिखे रहते हैं, प्रयास करें कि सभी अर्थ या जो भी अर्थ आपको महत्त्वपूर्ण प्रतीत हो, वे सभी लिख लें। इसके बाद उस शब्द का जिस Sentence में प्रयोग हुआ है, उस पूरे Sentence को भी सामने लिख लें। याद रखें, Sentence अपने मन से बनाकर न लिखें, बल्कि वही sentence लिखें जो आपने पढ़ा है। Word के Meanings के साथ पूरे Sentence को लिखना आवश्यक है, इसमें आलस्य नहीं करना।

Step two

आपने प्रथम दिन जितने भी Words, उनके Meanings एवं Sentences लिखे हैं, इन शब्दों को रटना नहीं है। मात्र Revise करना है। इन शब्दों को याद करने में, रटने में समय नष्ट नहीं करना है बल्कि इन शब्दों को, इनके Meanings को एवं उन सभी Sentences को जिनमें इन शब्दों का प्रयोग हुआ है, मात्र तीन बार धैर्य सहित, ध्यानपूर्वक Revise करना है।

जैसा Step one में बताया गया है, आपको प्रतिदिन 20-30 या 50 शब्द लिखने हैं। आपको दूसरे, तीसरे,....हर दिन इस तरह से शब्दों को लिखना है, उनके हिन्दी एवं अंग्रेजी में Meanings लिखने हैं, उन Sentences, को लिखना है, जिनमें इन शब्दों का प्रयोग किया गया है। याद रखें, ये Words आपको किसी Standard Book या अपनी Course Book से ही लिखने हैं।

दूसरे दिन शब्द लिखना शुरू करने से पूर्व पहले दिन लिखे सभी Words, उनके Meanings एवं Sentences को Revise करना है तथा उस दिन लिखे हुए सभी Words सहित सभी Sentences को भी तीन बार Revise करना है। न केवल शब्दों को बल्कि, उनके हिन्दी, अंग्रेजी Meanings , एवं सभी Sentences को भी धैर्य सहित, ध्यानपूर्वक Revise करें। याद रखें, इन कठिन शब्दों को रटना नहीं है, केवल Revise करना है।

तीसरे दिन, पूर्व में दो दिन लिखे गए सभी शब्दों को उनके Meanings एवं Sentences सहित निश्चित रूप से तीन बार Revise कर लें। इस तरह तीसरे दिन आप पहले दिन लिखे सभी Words एवं उनके Meanings एवं Sentences को Nine Times Revise कर लेंगे तथा दूसरे दिन लिखे समस्त Words को 6 बार Revise कर लेंगे। इसी तरह आप Fourth, fifth दिन भी करें। याद रखें, आपको शब्द लिखने एवं Revise करने का कार्य धैर्य सहित, ध्यानपूर्वक एवं पूर्ण ईमानदारी से करना है अर्थात् बिना जल्दी किए शब्द के हिन्दी एवं अंग्रेजी Meanings एवं Sentences लिखने हैं उनको ध्यानपूर्वक Revise करना है। Sentences का भी Revision अवश्य करना है। पूर्ण ईमानदारी का अर्थ है कि Sentence भी लिखते हैं एवं Sentence को Revise भी करना है एवं प्रतिदिन पिछले दिनों में लिखे सभी Word एवं Sentences का Revision पूरा करना है। मात्र 30 दिन तक यदि आप ऐसा करते हैं तो आपकी Word power (Vocabulary) में उल्लेखनीय वृद्धि होगी। आप Words का उचित एवं शुद्ध प्रयोग करने में निश्चित ही सफल होंगे।

Step three : Welcome New Words

मात्र 30 दिन उक्त Step one एवं Step two का पालन करने पर आप स्वयं में एक आत्मविश्वास का अनुभव करेंगे। आपको अब जहाँ भी कोई नया Difficult word दिखाई देगा, आप उसका अर्थ तुरन्त जानना चाहेंगे, यही है Step three : Welcome New Words। नए Words के Avoid न करें बल्कि उनका स्वागत करें। उनका सही अर्थ जानें एवं अपनी Vocabulary Powerful करें। Dictionary में किसी भी Word का Meaning देखते समय, आप इधर-उधर अन्य Words पर भी नजर दौड़ाएँ, अन्य कोई अच्छा शब्द मिले तो उसे तथा उसका Meaning भी Note कर लें। बहुत से Words ऐसे होते हैं जो as a verb तथा as a noun प्रयोग किए जाते हैं। इन शब्दों का अध्ययन ध्यानपूर्वक करके अपने वाक्यों में उनका प्रयोग करना सीखें। धीरे-धीरे आपकी Vocabulary, Word Power बहुत Powerful हो जायेगी। Welcome new words. Make them your frinds.

"Perseverance and Dedication are the keys to Success".
"Excellence is an ever approaching Target."

CHAPTER

40

SYNONYMS

Frequently Used Words

Abase	Degrade, Disgrace, Humiliate, Demean, Dishonour, Stigmatise
Abandon	Desert, Forsake, Leave, Relinquish
Abhor	Hate, Detest, Loathe, Abominate
Abut	Adjoin, Border, Verge on, Join
Abstain	Refuse, Renounce, Avoid, Shun
Abbreviate	Curtail, Abridge, Compress, Shorten, Truncate
Aberration	Deviation, Wandering, Errant, Irregular, Weird, Abnormal
Abet	Aid, Assist, Condone, Favour, Support, Promote
Absurd	Ridiculous, Silly, Foolish, Preposterous
Abstruse	Recondite, Hidden, Difficult
Assiduous	Painstaking, Diligent, Industrious, Laborious, Meticulous
Abundant	Ample, Copious, Plentiful, Bountiful, Existing in large quantities
Adequate	Enough, Sufficient, Proportionate
Accommodate	Adapt, Adjust, Reconcile
Acme	Summit, Apex, Zenith, Peak
Acclaim	Applaud, Cheer, Celebrate, Extol
Acquiesce (in)	Assent, Rest, Accede, Comply, Concur, Consent, Submit
Admiration	Esteem, Praise, Respect, Approval, Approbation, Awe, Regard
Adherent	Sticking to, Follower, Partisan, Devotee
Affliction	Distress, Ordeal, Suffering, Sorrow
Adversity	Misfortune, Calamity, Catastrophe, Hostility
Ameliorate	Make better, Improve, Amend
Ally	Colleague, Helper, Partner, Accomplice
Audacious	Bold, Brazen, Impudent, Daring
Astonish	Amaze, Surprise, Astound, Flabbergast
Assistance	Help, Aid, Succor, Collaboration, Sustenance
Aphorism	Maxim, Apothegm, Axiom, Proverb, Motto, Adage
Apprehend	Seize, Know, Fear, Arrest, Understand
Appraise	Evaluate, Estimate
Antithesis	Contrasting, Reverse
Alms	Dole, Gratuity, Money, clothes and food that are given to poor people
Beg	Implore, Solicit, Supplicate, Beseech, Request, Plead
Behaviour	Conduct, Demeanour, Deportment, Manner
Base	Ignoble, Mean, Low, Foundation
Bad	Evil, Wicked, Devilish, Naughty, Worthless
Blame	Censure, Reprove, Condemn, Reproach

Blessing	Benediction, God's help or protection
Banish	Exile, Ostracise, Deport, To order somebody to leave a place
Barbaric	Savage, Uncivilised, Primitive Align
Bait	Snare, Trap, Decoy
Brittle	Frail, Fragile, Hard but easily broken
Bizarre	Unusual, Grotesque, Fantastic
Bewilder	Confound, Perplex, Befuddle, Befog, Baffle, Daze, Stun
Belligerent	Warlike, Pugnacious, Hostile
Bedlam	Pandemonium, Chaos, Mayhem, Clamour, Confusion
Bravo	Fearless, Intrepid, Dauntless, Valiant, Bold
Burlesque	Mock, Imitate, Tease, Satirise, Ridicule, Jeer, Deride
Browbeat	Intimidate, Bully, Frighten, Threaten
Backlash	Repercussion, Reaction, Recoil
Banal	Dull, Trite, Hackneyed, Prosaic
Bigoted	Biased, Prejudiced, Dogmatic, Opinionated
Calm	Quiet, Tranquil, Peaceful, Sedate, Composed, Placid, Tranquil
Cajole	Persuade, Flatter, Wheedle, Coax
Captious	Censorious, Hypercritical, Faultfinding
Care	Solicitude, Anxiety, Misgiving, Foreboding
Charlatan	Impostor, Mountebank, Quack, Chicane, Trickster
Choleric	Irascible, Petulant, Bad-tempered
Conceit	Pride, Vanity, Ego, Arrogance
Colossal	Gigantic, Huge, Enormous, Mammoth, Vast
Cynical	Misanthropic, Moody, Eccentric, Sardonic, Sarcastic
Conversant (with)	Familiar, Well Versed, Acquainted
Condign	Due, Merited, Well deserved, Due, Suitable
Condone	Pardon, Forgive, Excuse, Overlook
Confess	Admit, Apologise, Own, Acknowledge
Contingent (on)	Liable, Possible, Uncertain
Constant	Eternal, Perpetual, Incessant, Continuous
Cross	Crusty, Fretful, Ill-humoured
Cursory	Hasty, Superficial, Careless
Concise	Short, Brief, Abridged, Compact
Crafty	Cunning, Artful, Sly, Calculating
Cruelty	Tyranny, Persecution, Brutality, Oppression, Ferocity
Damage	Loss, Harm, Injury, Detriment
Decay	Wither, Fade, Corrode, Decline
Destitute	Needy, Forsaken, Orphan
Didactic	Teaching, Instructive, Perfecting
Denounce	Accuse, Condemn, Arraign, Decry, Censure
Divine	Heavenly, Celestial, Graceful, Godlike
Dangerous	Perilous, Risky, Hazardous, Precarious
Dear	Expensive, Costly, Loved by or important to somebody
Definitive	Limiting, Final, Positive
Desultory	Discontinuous, Irregular, Rambling
Diffident	Modest, Bashful, Shy
Discourse	Lecture, Sermon, Exhortation, Dissertation

Dissipate	Scatter, Waste
Economy	Management, Frugality, Thrifty, Judicious expenditure
Effete	Exhausted, Old, Worn out, Tired
Elicit	Draw out, Discover
Elude	Baffle, Avoid, Cheat, Fool
Emancipate	Free, Liberate, Release, Deliver, Uplift
Emulate	Imitate, Rival
Entice	Lure, Persuade, Allure, Entrap
Extravagant	Prodigal, Wasteful
Exquisite	Elegant, Fine, Matchless, Exclusive
Exceptional	Anomalous, Unique, Extraordinary
Extricate	Disentangle, Untangle
Ephemeral	Transient, Short-lived
Exterminate	Uproot, Eradicate, Eliminate, Destroy, Annihilate
Exacerbate	Magnify, Heighten, Enlarge, Overstate, Amplify
Exculpate	Absolve, Vindicate
Exigency	Emergency, Distress
Fascinate	Charm, Enchant, Mesmerize, Bewitch
Fastidious	Dainty, Squeamish, Hard to please
Fate	Lot, Destiny, End
Fatuous	Silly, Purposeless
Fight	Battle, Contention, Combat, Struggle, Conflict, Strife
Fury	Anger, Rage, Wrath, Ire
Fecund	Prolific, Fertile, Fruitful, Luxuriant, Productive
Ferocious	Savage, Barbaric, Fierce, Wild, Uncivilized
Fictitious	False, Imaginative, Illusionary, Fabricated, Fanciful
Flagrant	Notorious, Outrageous, Disgraceful
Fortuitous	Chance, Accidental
Forerunner	Precursor, Herald, Harbinger
Forbid	Prohibit, Preclude, Inhibit, Debar
Flippant	Pert, Frivolous, Impudent, Saucy
Flamboyant	Bombastic, Ostentatious, Ornate
Fatal	Deadly, Mortal, Lethal, Virulent
Fallacy	Imperfection, Ambiguity, Quirk, Error
Fallible	Imperfect, Erring, Wrong
Furbish	Polish, Spruce, Renovate
Fortitude	Strength, Firmness, Valour, Determination
Guile	Fraud, Trickery, Cunning
Gratification	Satisfaction, Enjoyment
Garrulous	Talkative, Loquacious
Humane	Kind, Generous, Benevolent, Compassionate
Haughty	Arrogant, Proud, Egoist, Obstinate
Humility	Politeness, Meekness, Modesty
Hamper	Hinder, Block, Impede, Prevent
Illiterate	Unlearned, Ignorant, Uneducated
Impotent	Powerless, Disabled, Inadequate, Incapable
Immaterial	Unimportant, Insignificant, Useless, Irrelevant
Imminent	Threatening, Impending, Approaching

Irresolute	Undecided, Wavering, Vacillating, Unsettled
Indignant	Angry, Furious, Irate, Exasperated, Outraged
Inanimate	Lifeless, Dead, Dormant, Stagnant, Extinct
Ingenuous	Artless, Sincere, Naive, Innocent
Insidious	Cunning, Clever, Inventive, Deceitful, Sly
Intimate	Close, Confidant, Inform, Cherished
Inexorable	Relentless, Merciless, Apathetic, Harsh
Impertinent	Irrelevant, Impudent, Insolent, Saucy
Jolly	Jovial, Merry, Cheerful, Affable
Jubilant	Elated, Triumphant
Joy	Delight, Pleasure, Ecstasy, Elation
Knave	Fraud, Cheat, Scoundrel, Rogue
Lament	Sorrow, Mourn, Grieve
Liberal	Generous, Kind, Tolerant, Permissive
Lenient	Forbearing, Forgiving, Compassionate, Mild
Lethargy	Laziness, Stupor, Sluggishness, Idleness
Likeness	Similarity, Resemblance, Affinity
Lively	Active, Enthusiastic, Agile, Brisk
Loyal	Devoted, Faithful, Trustworthy, Honest
Meagre	Small, Tiny, Inadequate, Scanty
Mean	Low, Petty, Abject, Selfish
Misery	Sorrow, Distress, Affliction, Grief
Morbid	Unhealthy, Diseased, Ghastly, Horrid
Mournful	Sad, Sorrow, Gloomy, Dejected
Mighty	Powerful, Massive, Strong, Almighty
Malice	Bitterness, Spite, Ill-will, Rancour, Malevolence
Melancholy	Gloomy, Sadness, Sorrow, Dejected
Magnificent	Splendid, Grand, Good, Glorious
Notorious	Infamous, Dishonourable, Flagrant, Blatant
Notable	Memorable, Remarkable, Renowned, Eminent
Obscene	Filthy, Indecent, Awful, Bawdy, Vulgar, Gross, Crude
Obsolete	Antiquated, Old-fashioned, Extinct, Outworn
Obtrude	Thrust, Pressure, Importunate, Interfere
Obliterate	Destroy, Efface, Demolish, Erase
Opportune	Timely, Convenient, Appropriate, Well-chosen
Pensive	Thoughtful, Rational, Contemplative, Reflective
Pathetic	Moving, Touching, Distressing, Lamentable
Pious	Religious, Holy, Devout, God-fearing
Perennial	Perpetual, Permanent, Long lasting, Constant
Portray	Delineate, Depict, Draw, Sketch
Possess	Have, Own, Acquire, Occupy, Seize
Prate	Chatter, Babble, Tattle, Talkative
Prodigal	Extravagant, Wasteful, Spendthrift, Squander
Precocious	Premature, Forward, Advanced, Developed
Philanthropist	Altruist, Charitable, Benevolent, Kind
Patronize	Condescend, Stoop, Snub
Penalize	Castigate, Chastise, Punish
Picturesque	Charming, Pictorial, Scenic, Sylvan

Prerogative	Privilege, Advantage, Exemption, Right
Prohibit	Forbid, Interdict, Prevent, Ban
Pillage	Plunder, Loot, Rob, Destroy, Steal
Poignant	Touching, Moving, Heart-rending
Quaint	Queer, Odd, Singular, Whimsical
Quirk	Whim, Caprice, Fancy, Peculiarity
Quip	Retort, Repartee, Remark, Jest
Quarantined	Separated, Isolated, Restrained
Qualm	Scruple, Doubt, Uncertainty, Suspicion
Queer	Strange, Odd, Indifferent, Weird
Questionable	Doubtful, Disputable, Accountable, Objectionable
Quest	Search, Pursuit, Inquisitive, Crusade
Quick	Alive, Swift, Keen, Fast
Radiant	Brilliant, Bright, Intelligent, Beaming
Refined	Elegant, Polished, Cultured, Sophisticated
Rebellion	Mutiny, Revolt, Struggle, Fight
Reiterate	Repeat, Do it again, Rewrite, Emphasis
Remorse	Repentance, Regret, Anguish, Grief
Renown	Reputation, Fame, Famous, Distinguished
Rejoice	Exult, Delight, Happy, Glad
Relevant	Execute, Applicable, Pertinent, Implement
Resistance	Opposition, Hindrance, Combat, Struggle
Ruin	Destruction, Downfall, Wreckage, Devastation
Rigid	Stiff, Unyielding, Stern
Rash	Impetuous, Hasty, Foolhardy, Impulsive, Heedless, Brash
Refute	Disprove, Answer, Deny
Ricochet	Rebound, Reflect, Bounce, Carom
Rut	Groove, Hollow, Furrow, Habit, Course, Routine, Practice
Rural	Suburban, Rustic, Agrarian, Country
Radical	Fundamental, Native, Original, Extreme, Progressive, Rebellious
Rimy	Frosty, Hazy, Blurred
Remote	Far, Distant, Interior place, Aloof
Ridiculous	Absurd, Silly, Comical, Ludicrous
Sane	Wise, Sensible, Sound, Balanced
Satiate	Satisfy, Surfeit, Glut, Happy
Sacred	Holy, Consecrated, Blessed, Divine
Scanty	Meagre, Slender, Insufficient, Limited
Scold	Chide, Rebuke, Rail, Complain
Scrutinise	Examine, View, Study, Analyse, Inspect
Scorching	Sweltering, Searing, Burning, Fiery
Spry	Nimble, Agile, Animated, Brisk, Lively, Quick
Statute	Law, Decree, Ordinance, Edict, Rule, Act, Bill
Stipulation	Prerequisite, Condition, Qualification, Requirement, Clause
Subterfuge	Ploy, Scheme, Stratagem, Deceit, Deception
Substantiate	Authenticate, Validate, Confirm, Verify, Corroborate, Attest
Succinct	Brief, Concise, Terse, Abbreviated
Sensual	Carnal, Fleshy, Voluptuous, Attractive
Servile	Slavish, Docile, Timid, Mean

Shrewd Astute, Perspicacious, Canny, Calculative
Shy Bashful, Coy, Diffident, Hesitant
Solitary Single, Hermetic, Isolated, Desolate
Sordid Ugly, Dirty, Squalid, Debauched
Specimen Prototype, Model, Sample, Dummy
Static Firm, Adamant, Fixed
Spurious Fake, Counterfeit, Artificial, False
Sterile Unproductive, Barren, Impotent, Disinfected
Sublime Exalted, Elevated, Improved, Magnified
Superficial Shallow, Illusion, Dream, Outward
Synonymous Identical, Equivalent, Alike, Similar
Taboo Forbidden, Banned, Prohibited
Tenacious Resolute, Persistent, Obstinate
Tenet Belief, Conviction, Dogma, Doctrine, Creed, Theology
Therapeutics Curative, Restorative, Recuperative, Remedial
Temperate Moderate, Balanced, Controlled, Sensible
Thrive Flourish, Succeed, Grow
Temporal Worldly, Materialistic, Impermanent, Ephemeral
Tirade Outburst, Denunciation, Harangue, Speech, Diatribe
Thankful Grateful, Obliged, Indebted, Appreciative
Tentative Temporary, Transitory, Brief
Tyrant Autocrat, Despot, Dictator, Oppressor
Tyro Amateur, Novice, Apprentice, Neophyte
Ulterior Concealed, Shrouded, Obscured
Urchin Waif, Stray, Foundling, Orphan
Urbane Sophisticated, Suave, Polite, Refined, Polished
Unique Unparalleled, Single, Peerless, Unusual, Exceptional, Matchless
Urge Incite, Press, Implore, Instigate, Drive, Impel, Goad, Stimulate
Utopian Idealistic, Perfect, Visionary
Vigilance Watchfulness, Alertness, Attentiveness, Caution
Vindictive Revengeful, Malicious, Resentful, Spiteful
Vehemence Force, Passion, Emphasis, Obsession
Veracity Truth, Honesty, Accuracy, Exactness, Correctness
Veto Reject, Discard, Void, Nullify, Invalidate, Dismiss
Vilify Malign, Slur, Defame, Slander
Vivacious Sprightly, Spirited, Energetic
Weary Exhausted, Tired, Devitalised, Drained
Wreck Destroy, Devastate, Ruin, Demolish
Wistful Melancholic, Sentimental, Plaintive, Nostalgic
Wile Trickery, Artifice, Ruse
Winsome Beautiful, Captivating, Comely, Delightful, Charming
Waive Forgo, Relinquish, Defer, Renounce
Yield Surrender, Submit, Admit, Agree
Yearn Crave, Desire, Aspire, Urge
Zeal Zest, Passion, Enthusiasm, Fervour, Tempo
Zenith Peak, Apex, Summit, Acme

CHAPTER 41

ANTONYMS

Words	Antonyms	Words	Antonyms
Accustomed	Unusual	Confession	Denial
Acquittal	Conviction	Credit	Cash, Discredit
Active	Inert	Continuity	Discontinuity
Alert	Careless	Conceited	Modest
Ample	Scanty or Meagre	Courage	Timidity
Arrival	Departure	Complication	Simplification
Arrogant	Humble	Converge	Diverge
Attract	Repeal	Civilized	Savage
Aches	Ecstasy	Creation	Destruction
Activity	Passivity	Cause	Effect
Barbarism	Civilization	Christian	Pagan
Blunt	Sharp	Celebrated	Obscure
Bravery	Cowardice	Decrease	Increase
Belief	Disbelief	Deep	Independent
Beauty	Ugliness	Destroy	Create
Beneficial	Injurious	Discouragement	Encouragement
Barren	Fertile	Economical	Extravagant
Bride	Bridegroom	Elevation	Depression
Bless	Curse	Ease	Difficulty
Blustering	Gentle	Enthrone	Dethrone
Boon	Bane	Expedite	Impede
Care	Neglect	Entrance	Exit
Cheerfulness	Gravity	Earning	Spending
Comparison	Contrast	Enjoy	Suffer
Classicism	Romanticism	Enmity	Friendship
Confidence	Diffidence	Fame	Infamy
Consent	Dissent	Faith	Doubt
Concord	Discord	Faithful	Treacherous

Words	Antonyms	Words	Antonyms
Fail	Succeed	Persuade	Dissuade
Frankness	Reserve	Plaintiff	Defendant
Fresh	Stale	Pride	Humanity
Friendly	Hostile	Prohibition	Permission
Full	Empty	Pure	Adulterated
Firm	Infirm	Polite	Impolite
Fortune	Misfortune	Poverty	Affluence
Fatigue	Refresh	Pursuit	Avoidance
Flexible	Rigid	Renounce	Denounce
Front	Rear	Ruthless	Humane
Fine	Coarse	Salubrious	Unhealthy
Favour	Frown	Tragedy	Comedy
Foreign	Native	Town	Country
Genuine	Spurious	Top	Bottom
Gain	Lose	Uniform	Varied
General	Particular	Uncle	Nephew
Genuine	Spurious	Virtue	Vice
Guest	Host	Violent	Gentle
Gaiety	Gravity	Vivacious	Languid
Giant	Dwarf	Voluntary	Compulsory
Lady	Lass	Victor	Vanquished
Legal	Illegal	Venturesome	Timid
Optimist	Pessimist	Vague	Definite
Obscure	Clear	Wild	Domestic
Principal	Subordinate	Worry	Comfort
Prodigality	Parsimony	Wrap	Open
Philanthropist	Misanthropist	Written	Verbal
Patriot	Traitor	Wrong	Right
Peace	War	Yesteryear	Modern
Plenty	Scarce	Yuppie	Approve

CHAPTER 42

HINDI WORDS

Names of Parts of the Body

S. No.	Words	Pronunciation	Hindi Meaning
1.	Abdomen	अब्डोमन	पेट
2.	Ankle	एंकल	टखना
3.	Anus	ऐनस	गुदा
4.	Arm	आर्म	भुजा, बाँह
5.	Arm pit	आर्म-पिट	काख
6.	Artery	आर्टरी	धमकनी
7.	Back	बैक	पीठ
8.	Backbone	बैक-बोन	रीढ़ की हड्डी
9.	Beard	बियर्ड	दाढ़ी
10.	Beak	बीक	चोंच
11.	Belly	बैली	उदर
12.	Bile	बाइल	पित्त
13.	Bladder	ब्लैडर	मूत्राशय
14.	Blood	ब्लड	खून
15.	Bone	बोन	हड्डी
16.	Brain	ब्रेन	मस्तिष्क
17.	Breast	ब्रेस्ट	छाती
18.	Buttock	बुटक	नितम्ब
19.	Breath	ब्रीद	साँस
20.	Calf	काफ	पिण्डली
21.	Cartilage	कार्टिलेज	उपास्थि
22.	Cheeks	चीक्स	गाल
23.	Claw	क्लॉ	पंजा
24.	Chest	चैस्ट	पुरुष की छाती
25.	Chin	चिन	ठोड़ी
26.	Collar-bone	कॉलर-बोन	हंसली की हड्डी
27.	Ear	ईयर	कान
28.	Ear-drum	ईयर-ड्रम	कर्ण पटल
29.	Elbow	एल्बो	कोहनी
30.	Embryo	एम्ब्रिओ	भ्रूण
31.	Eye	आई	आँख
32.	Eye-ball	आइ-बॉल	आँख की पुतली
33.	Eye-brow	आई-ब्रो	भौंह
34.	Eye-lid	आई-लिड	पलक
35.	Eye-lash	आई-लैश	बरौनी
36.	Face	फेस	चेहरा
37.	Feather	फीदर	पर
38.	Finger	फिंगर	अंगूली
39.	Fist	फिस्ट	मुट्ठी
40.	Fin	फिन	मछली का पर
41.	Foot	फुट	पैर, पाँव
42.	Forehead	फोर-हैड	माथा, ललाट
43.	Fang	फैंग	सर्प का विषाक्त दन्त
44.	Flesh	फ्लैश	मांस
45.	Gum	गम	मसूढ़ा
46.	Groin	ग्राइन	पेट और जाँघ के बीच का अंग
47.	Hair	हेयर	बाल
48.	Hand	हैण्ड	हाथ
49.	Head	हैड	सिर
50.	Hood	हूड	फन
51.	Heart	हार्ट	दिल, हृदय
52.	Hoof	हूफ	खुर
53.	Heel	हील	एड़ी
54.	Horn	हॉर्न	सींग
55.	Index-finger	इन्डेक्स-फिंगर	तर्जनी
56.	Intestine	इन्टेस्टाइन	आंत
57.	Jaw	जॉ	जबड़ा
58.	Joint	ज्वाइण्ट	जोड़
59.	Kidney	किडनी	गुर्दा
60.	Knee	नी	घुटना
61.	Lap	लेप	गोद
62.	Leg	लैग	टाँग
63.	Loin	लायन	कमर
64.	Lip	लिप	होंठ, अधर
65.	Little Finger	लिटिल फिंगर	छोटी अंगूली
66.	Liver	लीवर	जिगर

S. No.	Words	Pronunciation	Hindi Meaning
67.	Lung	लंग	फेफड़ा
68.	Marrow	मैरो	मज्जा
69.	Middle Finger	मिडिल फिंगर	मध्यमा
70.	Mole	मोल	मस्सा
71.	Molar teeth	मोलर टीथ	दाढ़
72.	Moustache	मुश्टॉश	मूँछ
73.	Mouth	माउथ	मुँह
74.	Muscle	मसल	मांस-पेशी
75.	Nail	नेल	नाखून
76.	Navel	नेवल	नाभि
77.	Neck	नेक	गर्दन
78.	Nerve	नर्व	रग
79.	Nipple	निप्पल	चुचुक
80.	Nose	नोज	नाक
81.	Nostril	नॉस्ट्रिल	नासिका छिद्र
82.	Orbit	ऑरबिट	आँख का गड्ढा
83.	Palate	पैलेट	तालू
84.	Palm	पाम	हथेली
85.	Plume	प्लूम	पंख
86.	Penis	पेनिस	शिशन
87.	Phalange	फैलेंज	अँगुली का पोर
88.	Pores	पोर्स	रोमकूप
89.	Phlegm	फ्लेम	कफ
90.	Pulse	पल्स	नाड़ी
91.	Pupil	प्यूपिल	आँख की पुतली
92.	Pus	पस	पीप
93.	Rib	रिब	पसली
94.	Ring Finger	रिंग फिंगर	अनामिका
95.	Rump	रम्प	चूतड़
96.	Saliva	सलाइवा	लार
97.	Wrist	रिस्ट	कलाई
98.	Shoulder	शोल्डर	कंधा
99.	Skin	स्किन	त्वचा
100.	Skull	स्कल	खोपड़ी
101.	Snout	स्नाउट	थूथनी
102.	Sole	सोल	पैर का तलवा
103.	Soul	सोल	आत्मा
104.	Spleen	स्पलीन	तिल्ली
105.	Sting	स्टिंग	डंक
106.	Stomach	स्टॉमक	पेट
107.	Spittle	स्पिटल	थूक
108.	Slough	स्लाउ	सर्प की केंचुली
109.	Stool	स्टूल	मल
110.	Sweat	स्वैट	पसीना
111.	Teat	टीट	स्तन
112.	Temple	टैम्पल	कनपटी
113.	Tail	टेल	पूँछ
114.	Thigh	थाइ	जाँघ
115.	Throat	थ्रोट	गला, कण्ठ
116.	Thumb	थम्ब	अँगूठा
117.	Toe	टो	पाँव का पंजा
118.	Tongue	टंग	जीभ
119.	Tooth	टूथ	दाँत
120.	Trachea	ट्रकि	श्वास नली
121.	Trunk	ट्रंक	धड़
122.	Tears	टीयर्स	आँसू
123.	Tonsil	टॉन्सिल	गले की घाटी
124.	Testicles	टेस्टिकल्स	अण्डकोश
125.	Udders	अडर्स	पशु के स्तन
126.	Womb	वूम्ब	गर्भाशय
127.	Uterus	यूट्रस	गर्भाशय
128.	Waist	वेस्ट	कमर
129.	Uvula	यूव्युला	काग
130.	Urine	यूरीन	मूत्र
131.	Vagina	वेजिना	योनि
132.	Vein	वेन्	नस

Names of Relations

S. No.	Words	Pronunciation	Hindi Meaning
1.	Adopted daughter	एडॉप्टिड डॉटर	दत्तक पुत्री
2.	Adopted son	एडॉप्टिड सन	दत्तक पुत्र
3.	Ancestors	ऐनसेस्टर्स	पूर्वज
4.	Aunt	आण्ट	मौसी, चाची
5.	Bride	ब्राइड	दुल्हन
6.	Bridegroom	ब्राइडग्रूम	दूल्हा
7.	Brother	ब्रदर	सगा-भाई
8.	Brethren	ब्रदरन	भाई-बन्धु
9.	Brother-in-law	ब्रदर-इन-ला	देवर, जेठ
10.	Concubine	कॉन्क्यूबिन	रखैल
11.	Class-fellow	क्लास-फेलो	सहपाठी
12.	Co-wife	को-वाइफ	उप-पत्नी
13.	Student	स्टूडेण्ट	विद्यार्थी
14.	Client	क्लाइण्ट	मुवक्किल
15.	Customer	कस्टमर	ग्राहक
16.	Daughter	डॉटर	पुत्री
17.	Daughter-in-law	डॉटर-इन-लॉ	पुत्र-वधू
18.	Disciple	डिस्सीपल	शिष्य

S. No.	Words	Pronunciation	Hindi Meaning
19.	Father	फादर	पिता
20.	Fellow	फेलो	संगी, साथी
21.	Father-in-law	फादर-इन-लॉ	ससुर
22.	Foe	फो	शत्रु
23.	Friend	फ्रैन्ड	मित्र
24.	Granddaughter	ग्राण्ड-डॉटर	पोती
25.	Grandfather	ग्राण्ड-फादर	दादा
26.	Grandmother	ग्राण्ड-मदर	दादी
27.	Grandson	ग्रान्ड-सन	पोता
28.	Guest	गेस्ट	अतिथि
29.	Heir	हेअर	वारिस
30.	Husband	हसबैण्ड	पति
31.	Lover	लवर	प्रेमी
32.	Maternal aunt	मैटर्नल आण्ट	मामी
33.	Maternal uncle	मैटर्नल अंकल	मामा
34.	Teacher	टीचर	अध्यापक
35.	Uncle	अंकल	चाचा, मौसा
36.	Maternal sister	मैटर्नल सिस्टर	मौसी
37.	Mamma	मम्मा	अम्मा
38.	Mother	मदर	माँ
39.	Mother-in-law	मदर-इन-लॉ	सास
40.	Master	मास्टर	स्वामी
41.	Maid-servant	मेड-सर्वेण्ट	नौकरानी
42.	Nephew	नेफ्यू	भांजा, भतीजा
43.	Neighbour	नेबर	पड़ोसी
44.	Niece	नीस	भांजी, भतीजी
45.	Parents	पैरेण्ट्स	माता-पिता
46.	Posterity	पॉसटेरिटी	वंशज
47.	Paramour	पैरामर	यार
48.	Relative	रिलेटिव	नाती-सम्बन्धी
49.	Step-brother	स्टेप-ब्रदर	सौतेला भाई
50.	Step-daughter	स्टेप-डॉटर	सौतेली बहन
51.	Step-father	स्टेप-फादर	सौतेला पिता
52.	Step-mother	स्टेप-मदर	सौतेली माँ
53.	Step-son	स्टेप-सन	सौतेला पुत्र
54.	Servant	सर्वेण्ट	नौकर
55.	Sister	सिस्टर	बहन
56.	Sister-in-law	सिस्टर-इन-लॉ	भाभी,ननद
57.	Son	सन	बेटा
58.	Son-in-law	सन-इन-लॉ	दामाद, जामाता
59.	Wife	वाइफ	पत्नी
60.	Cousin	कजिन	चचेरा भाई/बहन
61.	Maternal grandmother	मैटर्नल ग्राण्डमदर	नानी
62.	Maternal grandfather	मैटर्नल ग्राण्ड फादर	नाना

Names of Ornaments and Jewels

S. No	Words	Pronunciation	Hindi Meaning
1.	Anklet	ऐंकलैट	पाजेब
2.	Armlet	आर्मलैट	बाजूबन्द
3.	Bangle	बैंगल	कड़ा
4.	Belt	बैल्ट	पेटी
5.	Bracelet	ब्रेसलेट	कंगन
6.	Brooch	ब्रोच	साड़ी का काँटा
7.	Cat' s eye	कैट्स आई	लहसुनिया
8.	Chain	चेन	जंजीर, कड़ी
9.	Coral	कोरल	मूँगा
10.	Diamond	डायमण्ड	हीरा
11.	Ear stud	इयर स्टड	कान का छल्ला
12.	Emerald	एमरल्ड	पन्ना
13.	Ear-ring	इयर रिंग	कान की बाली
14.	Garland	गार्लैण्ड	हार, माला
15.	Girdle	गर्डल	कमरबन्द
16.	Gem	जेम	रत्न
17.	Hair Pin	हेयर पिन	बालों की चिमटी
18.	Head Locket	हैड लॉकेट	टीका
19.	Locket	लॉकेट	लटकन
20.	Medal	मैडल	तमगा
21.	Mother of Pearl	मदर ऑफ पर्ल	मोती की सीप
22.	Necklace	नैकलेस	हार
23.	Nose-pin	नोज पिन	लौंग
24.	Nose ring	नोज रिंग	नथ, नथुनी
25.	Opal	ओपल	दूधिया पत्थर
26.	Pearl	पर्ल	मोती
27.	Quartz	क्वाट्र्ज	बिल्लौर
28.	Ring	रिंग	छल्ला, अँगूठी
29.	Ruby	रूबी	माणिक
30.	Sapphire	सफायर	नीलम
31.	Tiara	टियारा	ताज, मुकुट
32.	Tops	टोप्स	टोप्स
33.	Topaz	टोपाज	पुखराज
34.	Turquoise	टरक्वाइज	फिरोजा
35.	Wreath	रीथ	माला
36.	Wristlet	रिस्टलेट	कंगन

Names of Animals

S.no	Words	Pronunciation	Hindi Meaning
1.	Ant eater	ऐन्ट ईटर	चींटीखोर
2.	Antelope	ऐण्टीलोप	मृग
3.	Ape	एप	लंगूर, बन्दर
4.	Ass	ऐस	गधा, गर्दभ
5.	Bear	बीअर	भालू, रीछ
6.	Bitch	बिच	कुतिया
7.	Boar	बोर	जंगली सूअर
8.	Buffalo	बफैलो	भैंस
9.	Bull	बुल	सांड, बैल
10.	Beast	बीस्ट	जंगली पशु
11.	Calf	काफ	बछड़ा
12.	Camel	कैमल	ऊँट
13.	Cat	कैट	बिल्ली
14.	Charmois	शैमॉय	पहाड़ी हिरण
15.	Colt	कोल्ट	बछेरा
16.	Cow	काऊ	गाय
17.	Chimpanzee	चिम्पांजी	वनमानुष
18.	Deer	डियर	हिरण
19.	Dog	डॉग	कुत्ता
20.	Donkey	डंकी	गधा
21.	Elephant	एलीफैंट	हाथी
22.	Ewe	यू	मेंढ़ी
23.	Fawn	फौन	हिरण का बच्चा
24.	Fox	फॉक्स	लोमड़ी
25.	Giraffe	जिराफ	जिराफ
26.	Goat	गोट	बकरी
27.	Hare	हेअर	खरगोश
28.	Hind	हाइण्ड	हिरणी
29.	Hippopotamus	हिप्पोपोटेमस	दरियाई घोड़ा
30.	Horse	हॉर्स	घोड़ा
31.	Hound	हाउण्ड्	शिकारी कुत्ता
32.	Hyena	हयोना	लकड़बग्घा
33.	Hog	हॉग	सूअर
34.	Jackal	जैकाल	सियार
35.	Kangaroo	केंगरू	कंगारू
36.	Kid	किड	बकरी का बच्चा
37.	Kitten	किटन	बिल्ली का बच्चा
38	Lamb	लैम्ब	भेड़ का बच्चा
39.	Leopard	लिओपर्ड	तेंदुआ
40.	Lion	लायन	शेर
41.	Mare	मेयर	घोड़ी
42.	Mole	मोल	छछूँदर
43.	Mongoose	मंगूज	नेवला
44.	Monkey	मंकी	बन्दर
45.	Mouse	माऊस	चूहा
46.	Mule	म्यूल	खच्चर
47.	Musk-rat	मस्क रैट	छछूँदर
48.	Musk-deer	मस्क-डियर	कस्तूरी मृग
49.	Ox	ऑक्स	बैल
50.	Panther	पेंथर	चीता
51.	Pig	पिग	सूअर
52.	Pony	पोनी	टट्टू
53.	Porcupine	पॉर्क्यूपाइन	साही
54.	Puppy	पप्पी	पिल्ला
55.	Rabbit	रैबिट	खरगोश
56.	Ram	रैम	मेंढा
57.	Rat	रैट	चूहा
58.	Reindeer	रेंडियर	हिरण
59.	Rhinoceros	राइनसेरोज	गैंडा
60.	She-calf	शी-कल्फ	बछड़ी
61.	Sheep	शीप	भेड़
62.	She-goat	शी-गोट	बकरी
63.	Sire	सायर	प्रजनक सांड
64.	Spaniel	स्पेनियल	झबरा कुत्ता
65.	Squirrel	स्क्वीरल	गिलहरी
66.	Steer	स्टीयर	बधिया पशु
67.	Stag	स्टैग	बारहसिंगा
68.	Sow	साउ	सूअरी
69.	Swine	स्वाइन	शूकरी
70.	Tiger	टाइगर	बाघ, चीता
71.	Wolf	वुल्फ	भेड़िया
72.	Yak	याक	पर्वतीय बैल
73.	Zebra	जेबरा	गोर खर
74.	Zebu	जेबू	सांड

Names of Birds

S. No	Words	Pronunciation	Hindi Meaning
1.	Adjutant	एड्जुटेण्ट	सारस
2.	Bat	बैट	चमगादड़
3.	Bittern	बिटर्न	तितलौया
4.	Chicken	चिकन	चूजा
5.	Cock	कॉक	मुर्गा
6.	Crane	क्रेन	सारस
7.	Crow	क्रो	कौआ
8.	Cuckoo	कुक्कू	पिक, कोयल
9.	Cygnet	सिगनैट	हंस शावक
10.	Cocatoo	कॉकाटू	काकातुआ

S. No	Words	Pronunciation	Hindi Meaning
11.	Dove	डॉव	पेड़ुकी
12.	Duck	डक	बत्तख (मादा)
13.	Duckling	डकलिंग	बत्तख का बच्चा
14.	Drake	ड्रेक	बत्तख (नर)
15.	Eagle	ईगल	चील
16.	Falcon	फाल्कन	बाज
17.	Fowl	फाऊल	मुर्ग
18.	Goose	गूज	बत्तख
19.	Hawk	हॉक	बाज
20.	Hen	हैन	मुर्गी
21.	Heron	हैरन	बगुला
22.	Jay	जे	नीलकण्ठ
23.	Kite	काइट	चील
24.	Lark	लार्क	लवा
25.	Magpie	मैग्पाई	नीलकण्ठ
26.	Macaw	मैका	मनकावी तोता
27.	Nightingale	नाइटिंगेल	बुलबुल

S. No	Words	Pronunciation	Hindi Meaning
28.	Ostrich	ओस्ट्रिच	शतुरमुर्ग
29.	Owl	आऊल	उल्लू
30.	Parrot	पैरट	तोता
31.	Partridge	पार्टरिज	चकोर, तीतर
32.	Peacock	पीकॉक	मोर
33.	Peahen	पीहैन	मोरनी
34.	Pigeon	पिजन	कबूतर
35.	Pheasant	फीजैण्ट	तीतर
36.	Quail	क्वेल	बटेर
37.	Rook	रूक	डोम कौआ
38.	Raven	रेवन	पहाड़ी कौआ
39.	Sparrow	स्पैरो	गौरैया
40.	Stork	स्टार्क	सारस
41.	Swallow	स्वालो	अबाबील चिड़िया
42.	Swan	स्वैन	हंस
43.	Vulture	वल्चर	गिद्ध
44.	Weaver-bird	वीवर-बर्ड	बया
45.	Wood pecker	वुडपैकर	कठफोड़ा

Names of Some Reptiles, Water-living Creatures, Worms and Insects

S. No.	Words	Pronunciation	Hindi Meaning
1.	Adder	एड्डर	गेहुँआ सांप
2.	Alligator	एलीगेटर	घड़ियाल
3.	Ant	ऐंट	चींटी
4.	Beetle	बीटेल	गुबरैला
5.	Bee	बी	मधुमक्खी मादा
6.	Boa	बोआ	अजगर
7.	Body-licer	बोडी-लाइसर	चीलर
8.	Bug	बग	खटमल
9.	Wasp	वास्प	ततैया, भिड़
10.	Butterfly	बटरफ्लाई	तितली
11.	Centipede	सेण्टीपेड	गोजर कनखजूरा
12.	Chameleon	शैमीलियन	गिरगिट
13.	Cobra	कोबरा	काला सांप
14.	Cocoon	कोकून	रेशम का कीड़ा
15.	Cod-fish	कॉड-फिश	कॉड मछली
16.	Conch	कोंच	शंख
17.	Cowire	कौरी	कोड़ी
18.	Crab	क्रैब	केकड़ा
19.	Cricket	क्रिकेट	झींगुर
20.	Crocodile	क्रोकोडाइल	मगरमच्छ
21.	Drone	ड्रोन	मधुमक्खी (नर)
22.	Earthworm	अर्थवोर्म	केंचुआ
23.	Eel	ईल	सर्प मछली
24.	Fire-fly	फायर-फ्लाई	जुगनू
25.	Fish	फिश	मछली
26.	Flea	फ्ली	पिस्सू

S. No.	Words	Pronunciation	Hindi Meaning
27.	Fly	फ्लाई	मक्खी
28.	Frog	फ्रॉग	मेढक
29.	Gad-fly	गैडफ्लाई	गोमक्खी
30.	Grass-hopper	ग्रास हपर	टिड्डा
31.	Hippopotamus	हिप्पोपोटेमस	दरियाई घोड़ा
32.	Honey-bee	हनी-बी	मधुमक्खी
33.	Hood	हुड	फन
34.	Hornet	हॉर्नेट	भिड़, बर्र
35.	Leech	लीच	जोंक
36.	Lizard	लिजार्ड	छिपकली
37.	Lobster	लॉबस्टर	एक प्रकार का केकड़ा
38.	Locust	लोकस्ट	टिड्डी
39.	Louse	लाउस	जूँ
40.	Mosquito	मॉस्कीटो	मच्छर
41.	Nit	निट	लीख
42.	Oyster	आयस्टर	सीप
43.	Poison	पॉइजन	विष
44.	Rat flea	रेटफ्ली	पिस्सू, मूषक
45.	Scorpion	स्कॉरपिअन	बिच्छू
46.	Serpent	सर्पेण्ट	सर्प
47.	Shark	शार्क	शार्क मछली
48.	Silk-worm	सिल्क-वर्म	रेशम का कीड़ा
49.	Snail	स्नेल	घोंघा
50.	Snake	स्नेक	सांप
51.	Spider	स्पाइडर	मकड़ी

S. No.	Words	Pronunciation	Hindi Meaning
52.	Tadpole	टेडपोल	मेढक का बच्चा
53.	Termite	टरमाइट	दीमक
54.	Toad	टॉड	भेक, टोड
55.	Tortoise	टॉर्टाइज	कछुआ
56.	Turtle	टर्टल	कछुआ
57.	Walrus	वालरस	दरियाई घोड़ा

Names of Domestic Articles

S. No	Words	Pronunciation	Hindi Meaning
1.	Almirah	अलमिरा	अलमारी
2.	Anvil	एनविल	निहाई
3.	Ash	ऐश	राख
4.	Ash-Tray	ऐशट्रे	राख का पात्र
5.	Attache Case	अटैचीकेस	अटैची
6.	Auger	ऑगर	पेंचदार बरमा
7.	Axe	ऐक्स	कुल्हाड़ी
8.	Balance	बैलेन्स	तराजू
9.	Basket	बास्केट	टोकरी
10.	Bed	बैड	बिस्तर
11.	Bed-stead	बैड-स्टैड	पलंग
12.	Bed-sheet	बैड-शीट	चादर
13.	Bench	बैंच	बैंच
14.	Blanket	ब्लैंकिट	कम्बल
15.	Bobbin	बॉबिन	अन्टा
16.	Bolster	बोल्स्टर	गोल तकिया
17.	Bottle	बॉटल	बोतल
18.	Box	बॉक्स	सन्दूक
19.	Bowl	बाउल	कटोरा
20.	Broom	ब्रूम	झाड़ू
21.	Brush	ब्रुश	ब्रुश
22.	Bucket	बकेट	बाल्टी
23.	Bulb	बल्ब	बल्ब
24.	Button	बटन	बटन
25.	Candle	कैण्डिल	मोमबत्ती
26.	Candle-stand	कैण्डिल-स्टैण्ड	शमादान
27.	Cabinet	कैबिनेट	अलमारी
28.	Carpet	कारपैट	गलीचा
29.	Canister	कानिस्टर	कनस्तर
30.	Cauldron	काल्ड्रन	कड़ाही
31.	Censor	सैनसर	धूपदानी
32.	Chair	चेयर	कुर्सी
33.	Chest	चैस्ट	पेटी
34.	Chimmey	चिमनी	चिमनी
35.	Cotton	कॉटन	रूई
36.	Chandelier	शैन्डीलियर	झाड़फानूस
37.	Chisel	चीजल	छैनी
38.	Churn	चर्न	मथानी
39.	Comb	कॉम्ब	कंघी
40.	Cooking gas	कुकिंग गैस	भोजन पकाने की गैस
41.	Cup	कप	प्याला
42.	Curtain	कर्टेन	पर्दा
43.	Cushion	कुशन	गद्दा
44.	Chinese-ware	चाइनीज वेअर	चीनी-मिट्टी के बर्तन
45.	Couch	काउच	सेज
46.	Clock	क्लॉक	घड़ी
47.	Cream	क्रीम	क्रीम
48.	Cot	कॉट	चारपाई
49.	Cinders	सिन्डर्स	अंगारे
50.	Cup-board	कप-बोर्ड	अलमारी
51.	Desk	डेस्क	डेस्क
52.	Dish	डिश	रकाबी
53.	Door-mat	डोर-मैट	पायदान
54.	Drawers	ड्राअर्स	दराज
55.	Drill	ड्रिल	बरमा
56.	Electricity	इलेक्ट्रिसिटी	बिजली
57.	Fan	फैन	पंखा
58.	File	फाइल	रेती
59.	Fire	फायर	आग
60.	Fire place	फायर प्लेस	अँगीठी
61.	Flower-vase	फ्लावर वेस	फूलदान
62.	Fork	फोर्क	काँटा
63.	Frying pan	फ्राईंग पैन	कड़ाही
64.	Fuel	फ्यूल	ईंधन
65.	Funnel	फनल	कीप
66.	Flagon	फ्लेगॉन	सुराही
67.	Fire pan	फायर पैन	अँगीठी
68.	Grate	ग्रेट	चूल्हा
69.	Gramophone	ग्रामोफोन	ग्रामोफोन
70.	Hammer	हैमर	हथौड़ा
71.	Hand-pump	हैण्ड पम्प	बर्मा
72.	Hearth	हार्थ	अँगीठी
73.	Hatchet	हैचेट	फावड़ा
74.	Iron	आयरन	इस्तरी
75.	Ice-box	आइस-बॉक्स	बर्फ पेटी
76.	Iron plate	आयरन-प्लेट	तवा
77.	Iron-chest	आयरन-चेस्ट	लोहे की सन्दूक
78.	Iron-safe	आयरन सेफ	लोहे की अलमारी
79.	Jar	जार	मर्तबान
80.	Jug	जग	जग

S. No	Words	Pronunciation	Hindi Meaning
81.	Kerosene oil	कैरोसिन ऑयल	मिट्टी का तेल
82.	Kettle	कैटल	केतली
83.	Key	की	चाबी
84.	Knife	नाईफ	चाकू
85.	Kiln	किल्न	भट्टी
86.	Lancet	लांसेट	छुरिका
87.	Lamp	लैम्प	दीया
88.	Lid	लिड	ढक्कन
89.	Lock	लॉक	ताला
90.	Lantern	लैण्टर्न	लालटेन
91.	Loom	लूम	करघा
92.	Ladle	लैडल	कड़छी
93.	Looking glass	लुकिंग ग्लास	दर्पण
94.	Mackintosh	माकिन्टोश	मोमजामा
95.	Mat	मैट	चटाई
96.	Match-Box	मैच-बॉक्स	माचिस
97.	Mallet	मैलट	हथौड़ा
98.	Mattress	मैट्रैस	गद्दा
99.	Mirror	मिरर	दर्पण
100.	Mortar	मोरटर	ओखली
101.	Needle	नीडल	सूई
102.	Nut-cracker	नट-क्रैकर	सरौंता
103.	Newspaper	न्यूज पेपर	अखबार
104.	Oil	ऑयल	तेल
105.	Oven	ओवन	तन्दूर
106.	Palanquin	प्लैनकिन	पालकी
107.	Pastry-board	पेस्ट्री बोर्ड	चकला
108.	Pastry-roller	पेस्ट्री रोलर	बेलन
109.	Paper	पेपर	कागज
110.	Picture	पिक्चर	तस्वीर
111.	Pan	पेन	कड़ाही
112.	Pen	पैन	कलम
113.	Pestle	पैसल	मूसली
114.	Phial	फियल	शीशी
115.	Pillow	पिलो	तकिया
116.	Pillow-case	पिलो केस	गिलाफ
117.	Pincers	पिंसर्स	संडासी
118.	Pitcher	पिचर	घड़ा
119.	Pot	पॉट	मटका
120.	Probe	प्रोब	सलाई
121.	Plate	प्लेट	थाली
122.	Plough	प्लो	हल
123.	Plane	प्लेन	रन्दा
124.	Pad-lock	पैड-लॉक	बड़ा-ताला
125.	Powder	पाउडर	बुकनी
126.	Quilt	क्विल्ट	रजाई

S. No	Words	Pronunciation	Hindi Meaning
127.	Rope	रोप	रस्सी
128.	Radio	रेडियो	रेडियो
129.	Razor	रेजर	उस्तरा
130.	Sack	सैक	बोरी
131.	Safe	सेफ	तिजोरी
132.	Saucer	सॉसर	छोटी तश्तरी
133.	Sieve	सिव	चलनी
134.	Soap	सोप	साबुन
135.	Soap-case	सोप-केस	साबुनदानी
136.	Spoon	स्पून	चम्मच
137.	Spittoon	स्पिटन	पीकदान
138.	Stick	स्टिक	छड़ी
139.	Stove	स्टोव	दम चूल्हा
140.	Swing	स्विंग	झूला
141.	Screw-driver	स्क्रू-ड्राइवर	पेचकस
142.	Sickle	सिकल	दरांती
143.	Shovel	शावेल	खुरपी
144.	Spade	स्पेड	फावड़ा
145.	Saw	सॉ	आरा
146.	Spear	स्पीयर	भाला
147.	Sword	स्वोर्ड	तलवार
148.	Stool	स्टूल	तिपाई
149.	Sofa	सोफा	सोफा
150.	Shelf	शैल्फ	खुली अलमारी
151.	String	स्ट्रिंग	रस्सी
152.	Switch	स्विच	खटका
153.	Scissors	सीजर्स	कैंची
154.	Sewing machine	स्यूइंग मशीन	सिलाई मशीन
155.	Table	टेबल	मेज
156.	Tap	टैप	टोंटी (नल)
157.	Tumbler	टम्बलर	गिलास
158.	Thimble	थिम्बल	अंगुश्ताना
159.	Tongs	टोंग्ज	चिमटा
160.	Tooth brush	टूथब्रुश	ब्रुश
161.	Tooth powder	टूथ पाउडर	दन्त मन्जन
162.	Tray	ट्रे	थाली
163.	Twine	ट्वाईन	रस्सी
164.	Table fan	टेबल फैन	मेज पंखा
165.	Table lamp	टेबल लैम्प	मेज का लैम्प
166.	Telephone	टेलीफोन	दूरभाष
167.	Umbrella	अम्ब्रेला	छाता
168.	Wick	विक	बत्ती
169.	Wardrobe	वार्डरोब	अलमारी
170.	Wire	वायर	तार

Names of Homes and Abodes

Alodes	Hindi Meaning	Homes	Hindi Meaning	Alodes	Hindi Meaning	Homes	Hindi Meaning
Babies	शिशु	live in a nursery	नर्सरी	Monks	भिक्षु	live in a monastery	मठ
Bees	मधु-मक्खियाँ	live in a beehive	शहद का छत्ता	Nuns	भिक्षुणी	live in a convent	विहार
Birds	पक्षी	live in nest	घोंसले	Invalids	दुर्बल व्यक्ति	live in a sanatorium	स्वास्थ्यालय
Convicts	अपराधी	live in prison	कारावास	Pigs	सूअर	live in a sty	सूअरबाड़ा
Cows	गायें	live in shed	गोशाला	Officers	ऑफिसर	live in quraters	क्वार्टर
Dogs	कुत्ते	live in kennels	घर	Parson	पादरी	live in a parsonage	पादरीघर
Foxes	लोमड़ी	live in forests	वन	Peasants	किसान	live in cottages	झोपड़ी
Kings	राजा	live in palaces	महल	Prisoners	कैदी	live in cell	कोठरी
Horses	घोड़े	live in stables	अस्तबल	Sheep	भेड़	live in a pen or fold	बाड़ा
Lions	शेर	live in dens	मांद	Soldiers	सैनिक	live in barracks	सैनिक क्वार्टर
Lunatics	पागल	live in asylums	पागलखाना	Spiders	मकड़ियाँ	live in webs	जाला
Men	आदमी	live in house	घर	Owls	उल्लू	live in trees	वृक्ष
Mice	चूहे	live in a holes	बिल	Tigers	चीते	live in lairs	मांद

Names of Musical Instruments

S. No	Words	Pronunciation	Hindi Meaning	S. No	Words	Pronunciation	Hindi Meaning
1.	Bell	बेल	घंटी	17.	Harp	हार्प	वीणा
2.	Bugle	बिगुल	शहनाई	18.	Horn	हार्न	सिंगा (भोंपा)
3.	Bag pipe	बैग पाइप	मशकबाजा	19.	Haut boy	हॉटबॉय	शहनाई
4.	Banjo	बैंजो	बैंजो	20.	Jew's Harp' lute	ज्यूज हार्प ल्यूट	मरचंग
5.	Bassoon	बसून	अलगोजा	21.	Kettle-drum	केटलड्रम	नगाड़ा
6.	Clarion	क्लैरियन	बाँसुरी, तुरही	22.	Mandolin	मैनडोलिन	एक वाद्य यन्त्र
7.	Clarionet	क्लैरियोनेट	क्लैरियोनेट	23.	Mouth Organ	माउथ आर्गन	बीन-बाजा
8.	Cymbal	सिम्बल	झाँझ	24.	Piano	पियानो	पियानो
9.	Conch	कौंच	शंख	25.	Sarod	सरोद	सरोद
10.	Drum	ड्रम	ढोलक, नगाड़ा	26.	Sitar	सितार	सितार
11.	Drumnet	ड्रमेट	डुगडुगी	27.	Tabor	टैबर	तबला
12.	Flute	फ्लूट	बाँसुरी	28.	Tomtom	टमटम	ढोलक
13.	Guitar	गिटार	सितार	29.	Tambourine	टैम्बूरीन	डफ
14.	Gong	गांग	घंटा	30.	Trombone	ट्रम्बोन	तुरही
15.	Gourd flute	गोर्ड फ्लूट	बीन	31.	Violin	वायलिन	वायलिन
16.	Harmonium	हारमोनियम	हारमोनियम	32.	Whistle	व्हिसल	सीटी

Names of Minerals

S. No	Words	Pronunciation	Hindi Meaning	S. No	Words	Pronunciation	Hindi Meaning
1.	Antimony	एण्टीमॉनी	सुरमा	7.	Bell-metal	बेल-मेटल	कांसा
2.	Arsenic	आर्सेनिक	संखिया	8.	Bluevitrio	ब्लूविट्रियो	तूतिया
3.	Alum	ऐलम	फिटकरी	9.	Chalk	चाक	खड़िया
4.	Bitumen	बिटुमन	शिलाजीत	10.	Cinnabar	सिन्नेबार	सिन्दूर
5.	Bronze	ब्रोन्ज	कसकुट	11.	Charcoal	चारकोल	लकड़ी का कोयला
6.	Brass	ब्रास	पीतल	12.	Coal	कोल	कोयला

S. No	Words	Pronunciation	Hindi Meaning
13.	Copper	कॉपर	ताँबा
14.	Cornelian	कोर्नेलियन	अकीक
15.	Copper sulphate	कॉपर सल्फेट	तूतिहा
16.	Diamond	डायमण्ड	हीरा
17.	Emerald	एमरल्ड	पन्ना
18.	Flint	फ्लिंट	चकमक पत्थर
19.	Fuller's Earth	फुलर्स-अर्थ	मुल्तानी मिट्टी
20.	Grey copper	ग्रे कॉपर	भूरा ताँबा
21.	Grey Tin	ग्रेटिन	धूसर राँगा
22.	Gold	गोल्ड	सोना
23.	Greenvitriol	ग्रीनविट्रियल	कसीह
24.	Iron	आयरन	लोहा
25.	Iron Ore	आयरन ओर	खनिज लोहा
26.	Kerosene	कैरोसिन	मिट्टी का तेल
27.	Lead	लेड	सीसा
28.	Marble	मार्बल	संगमरमर
29.	Mercury	मर्करी	पारा
30.	Metal	मेटल	धातु
31.	Mica	माइका	अभ्रक
32.	Natron	नैट्रॉन	सज्जीखार

S. No	Words	Pronunciation	Hindi Meaning
33.	Orpiment	आर्पिमैण्ट	हरताल
34.	Ochre	ओकर	गेरू
35.	Plastic Clay	प्लास्टिक क्ले	सुघट्य मिट्टी
36.	Red ochre	रेड ओकर	गेरू
37.	Ruby	रूबी	लाल
38.	Rock oil	रॉक आयल	शैल तेल
39.	Saltpetre	साल्टपीटर	शीरा
40.	Shale	शेल	स्लेटी पत्थर
41.	Silver	सिल्वर	चाँदी
42.	Soapstone	सोपस्टोन	सेलखड़ी
43.	Steatite	स्टीटाइट	सेलखड़ी
44.	Steel	स्टील	फौलाद
45.	Sulphur	सल्फर	गन्धक
46.	Tin	टिन	राँगा
47.	Touch-stone	टच-स्टोन	कसौटी
48.	Vermilion	वर्मिलियन	सिन्दूर
49.	White lead	व्हाइट लेड	सफेदा
50.	Yellow ochre	येलो ओकर	राजरज
51.	Zinc	जिंक	जस्ता

Names of Professions and Occupations

S. No	Words	Pronunciation	Hindi Meaning
1.	Actor	ऐक्टर	नाटक का पात्र
2.	Accountant	अकाउन्टैण्ट	मुनीम
3.	Advocate	एडवोकेट	वकील
4.	Agent	एजेण्ट	प्रतिनिधि
5.	Agriculturist	एग्रीकल्चरिस्ट	कृषक
6.	Architect	आर्किटेक्ट	शिल्पकार
7.	Artist	आर्टिस्ट	कलाकार
8.	Artisan	आर्टीसन	कारीगर
9.	Astrologer	एस्ट्रोलोजर	ज्योतिष
10.	Astronomer	अस्ट्रोनॉमर	खगोलशास्त्री
11.	Auditor	ऑडीटर	हिसाब निरीक्षक
12.	Auctioneer	आक्शनीयर	नीलामी करने वाला
13.	Author	ऑथर	लेखक, ग्रन्थकार
14.	Baker	बेकर	नानबाई
15.	Banker	बैंकर	साहूकार
16.	Bankrupt	बैंकरप्ट	दिवालिया
17.	Beggar	बैगर	भिखारी
18.	Blacksmith	ब्लैकस्मिथ	लोहार
19.	Book-binder	बुक-बाइण्डर	जिल्दसाज
20.	Book-seller	बुक सेलर	पुस्तक विक्रेता
21.	Boatman	बोट-मेन	नाविक
22.	Brasier	ब्रेजियर	ठठेरा
23.	Bursar	बर्सर	कोषाधिकारी
24.	Butler	बटलर	भण्डारी

S. No	Words	Pronunciation	Hindi Meaning
25.	Butcher	बुचर	कसाई
26.	Barrister	बैरिस्टर	बैरिस्टर
27.	Betel-seller	बीटेल सेलर	पनवाड़ी
28.	Broker	ब्रोकर	दलाल
29.	Carder	कार्डर	धुनिया
30.	Carpenter	कारपेण्टर	बढ़ई
31.	Carrier	कैरियर	माल ढोने वाला
32.	Cashier	कैशियर	रोकड़िया
33.	Chauffeur	शौफर	कार चालक
34.	Cultivator	कल्टिवेटर	कृषक
35.	Chemist	कैमिस्ट	दवाई विक्रेता
36.	Clerk	क्लर्क	मुंशी, लिपिक
37.	Cobbler	कॉबलर	मोची
38.	Coachman	कोचमेन	कोचवान
39.	Cleaner	क्लीनर	सफाई करने वाला
40.	Contractor	कॉण्ट्रेक्टर	ठेकेदार
41.	Constable	कांस्टेबल	सिपाही
42.	Conductor	कण्डक्टर	संवाहक
43.	Confectioner	कन्फैक्शनर	हलवाई
44.	Cook	कुक	रसोइया
45.	Compounder	कम्पाउण्डर	औषधि बनाने वाला
46.	Coolie	कुली	कुली
47.	Compositor	कम्पोजिटर	प्रेस में अक्षर लगाने वाला

S. No	Words	Pronunciation	Hindi Meaning
48.	Cloth-merchant	क्लाथ मर्चेण्ट	बजाज
49.	Carter	कार्टर	गाड़ीवान
50.	Clergyman	क्लर्जीमेन	पुरोहित
51.	Dancer	डांसर	नर्तक/नर्तकी
52.	Darner	डार्नर	रफूगर
53.	Dentist	डैण्टिस्ट	दन्त चिकित्सक
54.	Doctor	डॉक्टर	डॉक्टर
55.	Draper	ड्रैपर	बजाज
56.	Draughtsman	ड्राफ्ट्समैन	नक्शानवीस
57.	Dramatist	ड्रामाटिस्ट	नाटककार
58.	Druggist	ड्रगिस्ट	औषधि-विक्रेता
59.	Dyer	डायर	रंगसाज
60.	Driver	ड्राइवर	यान चालक
61.	Drummer	ड्रमर	ढोलकी
62.	Editor	एडिटर	सम्पादक
63.	Enameller	इनेमलर	मीनाकार
64.	Engineer	इंजीनियर	अभियन्ता
65.	Examiner	एग्जामिनर	परीक्षक
66.	Farmer	फार्मर	किसान
67.	Fisherman	फिशरमैन	मछेरा
68.	Florist	फ्लोरिस्ट	फूल बेचने वाला
69.	Gardener	गार्डनर	माली
70.	Gatekeeper	गेटकीपर	दरबान
71.	Glazier	ग्लेजिअर	जड़ने वाला
72.	Goldsmith	गोल्डस्मिथ	सुनार
73.	Grocer	ग्रोसर	पंसारी
74.	Groom	ग्रूम	सईस
75.	Green-grocer	ग्रीन ग्रोसर	कुंजड़ा
76.	Gleaner	ग्लीनर	सिल्ला बटोरने वाला
77.	Haberdash	हेबरडेश	बिसाती
78.	Hawker	हॉकर	फेरीवाला
79.	Inkman	इंकमेन	रोशनाई वाला
80.	Inspector	इंस्पैक्टर	निरीक्षक
81.	Jeweller	ज्वैलर	जौहरी
82.	Juggler	जगलर	मदारी
83.	Landlord	लैण्डलॉर्ड	जागीरदार
84.	Lawyer	लायर	वकील
85.	Maid-servant	मैड-सर्वेण्ट	नौकरानी
86.	Magician	मैजिशियन	जादूगर
87.	Manager	मैनेजर	प्रबन्धक
88.	Mason	मेसन	राज, राजगीर
89.	Merchant	मर्चेण्ट	सौदागर
90.	Messenger	मैसेंजर	दूत
91.	Mechanic	मैकेनिक	मिस्त्री
92.	Midwife	मिडवाईफ	दाई
93.	Milkman	मिल्कमैन	ग्वाला
94.	Milkmaid	मिल्कमेड	ग्वालन
95.	Musician	म्यूजिशियन	संगीतकार

S. No	Words	Pronunciation	Hindi Meaning
96.	Miner	माइनर	खान खोदने वाला
97.	News-agent	न्यूज-एजेण्ट	समाचार-पत्र विक्रेता
98.	News-monger	न्यूज-मांगर	खबर फैलाने वाला
99.	Novelist	नॉवलिस्ट	उपन्यासकार
100.	Nurse	नर्स	दाई, आया
101.	Oilman	ऑयलमैन	तेली
102.	Operator	ऑपरेटर	मशीन चालक
103.	Painter	पेण्टर	रंगसाज
104.	Palmist	पामिस्ट	हाथ देखने वाला
105.	Peon	पीअन	चपरासी
106.	Perfumer	पर्फ्यूमर	गन्धी
107.	Photographer	फोटोग्राफर	फोटोग्राफर
108.	Physician	फिजीशियन	वैद्य, चिकित्सक
109.	Pilgrim	पिल्ग्रिम	तीर्थ-यात्री
110.	Poet	पोयट	कवि
111.	Potter	पॉटर	कुम्हार
112.	Postman	पोस्टमैन	डाकिया
113.	Printer	प्रिण्टर	मुद्रक
114.	Priest	प्रीस्ट	पुरोहित, पुजारी
115.	Politician	पॉलीटिशियन	राजनीतिज्ञ
116	Porter	पोर्टर	कुली, दरबान
117.	Proprietor	प्रोप्राइटर	मालिक
118.	Pedlar	पैडलर	फेरीवाला
119.	Pilot	पाइलट	वायुयान-चालक
120.	Pleader	प्लीडर	वकील
121.	Publisher	पब्लिशर	प्रकाशक
122.	Principal	प्रिन्सिपल	प्रधानाचार्य
123.	Parcher	पार्चर	भड़भूजा
124.	Procurer	प्रोक्योरर	प्रापक, दलाल
125.	Proctor	प्रोक्टर	अनुशासनाधिकारी
126.	Professor	प्रोफेसर	प्राध्यापक
127.	Procurator	प्रोक्युरेटर	कोषाधिकारी
128.	Quack	क्वेक	नीमहकीम
129.	Quaestor	केस्टॉर	दण्डनायक
130.	Quizzer	क्विजर	परीक्षाकर्ता
131.	Retailer	रिटेलर	खुदरा व्यापारी
132.	Repairer	रिपेयर	मरम्मत वाला
133.	Sailor	सेलर	नाविक
134.	Sanitary Inspector	सैनिटरी-इंस्पैक्टर	सफाई दरोगा
135.	Sculptor	स्कल्पटर	पत्थर काटने वाला
136.	Seedsman	सीड्समैन	बीज-विक्रेता
137.	Shepherd	शैफर्ड	गडरिया
138.	Shoemaker	शू-मेकर	मोची
139.	Shopkeeper	शॉपकीपर	दुकानदार
140.	Stamp Vendor	स्टाम्प वेण्डर	टिकट विक्रेता
141.	Surgeon	सर्जन	शल्य-चिकित्सक
142.	Sweeper	स्वीपर	भंगी

S. No	Words	Pronunciation	Hindi Meaning
143.	Stationer	स्टेशनर	कागज-कलम विक्रेता
144.	Sorcerer	सोर्सेरर	तान्त्रिक
145.	Tailor	टेलर	दर्जी
146.	Tanner	टेनर	चमड़ा रंगने वाला
147.	Teacher	टीचर	अध्यापक
148.	Treasurer	ट्रेजरर	कोषाध्यक्ष
149.	Turner	टर्नर	खरादिया
150.	Tutor	ट्यूटर	ट्यूशन पढ़ाने वाला
151.	Trader	ट्रेडर	व्यापारी
152.	Tinman	टिनमैन	कलई करने वाला
153.	T.T.E	टी०टी०ई	टिकट निरीक्षक
154.	Usurer	यूजरर	सूदखोर
155.	Washerman	वाँशरमैन	धोबी
156.	Watchman	वॉचमैन	चौकीदार
157.	Water Carrier	वाटर कैरियर	महरा
158.	Weaver	वीवर	जुलाहा
159.	Writer	राइटर	लेखक
160.	Watchmaker	वाचमेकर	घड़ीसाज

Names of Importants Tools

S.No	Words	Pronunciation	Hindi Meaning
1.	Anchor	एन्कर	लंगर
2.	Anvil	एन्विल	निहाई
3.	Auger	ऑगर	बरमा
4.	Awl	ऑल	टंकुआ
5.	Axe	ऐक्स	गेंती, कुल्हाड़ी
6.	Bagging-hook	बैगिंग हुक	दराँती
7.	Balance	बैलेन्स	तराजू
8.	Bar share	बार-शेअर	कस्सी, फाली
9.	Bead-plane	बीड-प्लेन	गोल रन्दा
10.	Bellows	बिलौज	धौकनी
11.	Blow-pipe	ब्लो-पाइप	फूँकनी
12.	Clamp	क्लैम्प	काँटा
13.	Cleat	क्लीट	फन्नी
14.	Chisel	चिजेल	छैनी
15.	Colter	कोल्टर	हल की फाल
16.	Compass	कम्पास	कुतुबनुमा
17.	Cone	कोन	शंकु
18.	Dagger	डैगर	छुरा, खंजर
19.	Dibble	डिब्बल	खन्ती
20.	Divider	डिवाइडर	परकार
21.	Drill	ड्रिल	बरमी
22.	Fast	फास्ट	मोची का फरमा
23.	File	फाइल	रेती
24.	Fishing rod	फिशिंग रॉड	मछली पकड़ने की डोरी
25.	Gauge	गेज	नापने का यन्त्र
26.	Hammer	हैमर	हथौड़ा
27.	Hand saw	हैण्ड सॉ	आरी
28.	Hand vice	हैण्ड वाइस	हाथ बांक
29.	Jack plane	जैक प्लेन	बड़ा रन्दा
30.	Last	लॉस्ट	जूता बनाने का फरमा
31.	Lancet	लांसेट	नश्तर की छुरी
32.	Lever	लीवर	उत्तोलक
33.	Loom	लूम	करघा
34.	Lathe	लेथ	खराद
35.	Mallet	मैलेट	मुँगरी
36.	Needle point	नीडल प्वाइण्ट	विरंजी
37.	Oar	ओर	डाण्डा, चप्पू
38.	Oil-mill	ऑयल मिल	कोल्हू
39.	Plough	प्लो	हल
40.	Plough share	प्लो शेयर	हल की फार
41.	Plumb line	प्लम्ब लाइन	साहुल
42.	Pruning shear	प्रूनिंग शीअर	दस्ती कैंची
43.	Rasp	रास्प	मोटी रेती
44.	Razor	रेजर	उस्तरा
45.	Rebate Plane	रिबेट प्लेन	पतामारन्दा
46.	Rudder	रड्डर	पतवार
47.	Saw	सॉ	आरी
48.	Screw	स्क्रू	पेच, ढिबरी
49.	Screw driver	स्क्रू ड्राइवर	पेचकस
50.	Scissors	सीजर्स	कैंची
51.	Sickle	सिक्कल	दराँती
52.	Spade	स्पेड	कुदाल, फावड़ा
53.	Spanner	स्पैनर	ढिबरी कसने की चाबी
54.	Stone chisel	स्टोन चिजल	छैनी
55.	Smoothing plane	स्मूथिंग प्लेन	बारीक रन्दा
56.	Still	स्टिल	अर्क खींचने का डेग
57.	Stock and dies	स्टॉक एण्ड डायस	वादिया
58.	Tooling plane	टूलिंग प्लेन	धारी रन्दा
59.	Trying plane	ट्राइंग प्लेन	छोटा रन्दा
60.	Try square	ट्राइ स्कवेअर	गुनिया
61.	Trowel	ट्रावल	करनी
62.	Trying angle	ट्राइंग एंगल	गुनिया

Terminologies of War-fare

S.No	Words	Pronunciation	Hindi Meaning
1.	Aggression	अग्रैसन	आक्रमण
2.	Anti-aircraft gun	ऐण्टी एअरक्राफ्ट गन	वायुयान तोप
3.	Army	आर्मी	सेना
4.	Arms	आर्म्स	हथियार
5.	Armaments	आर्मामैण्ट्स	युद्ध के शस्त्र
6.	Ammunition	एम्युनिशन	गोला-बारूद
7.	Armour	आर्मर	कवच
8.	Atom bomb	एटम बम	अणुबम
9.	Atomic Warfare	एटॉमिक वारफेअर	परमाणु युद्ध
10.	Attack	अटैक	आक्रमण
11.	Auxillary force	आग्जिलियरी फोर्स	सहायक सेना
12.	Battle	बैटल	युद्ध
13.	Battle field	बैटलफील्ड	युद्ध क्षेत्र
14.	Belligerent Nation	बैलिजैरेंट नेशन	लड़ने वाला राष्ट्र
15.	Battle-ship	बैटल-शिप	युद्धपोत
16.	Blockade	ब्लाकेड	नाकाबन्दी
17.	Bombardment	बम्बार्डमेण्ट	बमबारी
18.	Bloodshed	ब्लडशैड	बमबारी
19.	Bomb	बॉम्ब	बम
20.	Brute force	ब्रूट फोर्स	पाशविक शक्ति
21.	Bullet	बुलेट	गोली
22.	Bunker	बंकर	मोर्चा
23.	Campaign	कैम्पेन	युद्ध-प्रवृत्ति
24.	Cannon	कैनन	तोप
25.	Cannon Ball	कैनन बाल	तोप के गोले
26.	Cartridge	कारट्रेज	कारतूस
27.	Cavalry	कैवलरी	घुड़सवारी सेना
28.	Ceasefire	सीजफायर	युद्धविराम
29.	Civil war	सिविल वार	गृह युद्ध
30.	Combatants	कम्बैटेण्ट्स	योद्धा
31.	Commander-in-chief	कमाण्डर-इन -चीफ	सेनापति
32.	Conscription	कान्सक्रिप्शन	अनिवार्य भर्ती
33.	Defence	डिफेन्स	सुरक्षा
34.	Defence Ministry	डिफेन्स मिनिस्ट्री	रक्षा मन्त्रालय
35.	Defence Service	डिफेन्स सर्विस	फौजी नौकरी
36.	Demobilization	डिमोबिलाइजेशन	सेनाभंग
37.	Destroyer	डेस्ट्रायर	विध्वंसक
38.	Enemy	एनिमी	शत्रु
39.	Expedition	एक्सपेडीशन	अभियान
40.	Explosive bomb	एक्सप्लोसिव बॉम्ब	विस्फोटक बम
41.	Field Marshal	फील्ड मार्शल	सेना अधिकारी
42.	Fighter plane	फाइटर प्लेन	लड़ाकू जहाज
43.	Fortification	फोर्टीफिकेशन	किलाबन्दी
44.	Gas-mask	गैस-मास्क	गैस नकाब
45.	Guerilla	गुरिल्ला	गुरेला
46.	Gun Powder	गन पाउडर	बारूद
47.	Land-force	लैण्ड-फोर्स	स्थल सेना
48.	Machine-gun	मशीनगन	तोप
49.	Magazine-gun	मैगजीन गन	कारतूस वाली बन्दूक
50.	Magazine	मैगजीन	बारूद खाना
51.	Mutiny	म्यूटिनी	बगावत, विद्रोह
52.	Navy	नेवी	जल सेना
53.	Operation	ऑपरेशन	सेना की गति
54.	Prisoners of war	प्रिजनर्स ऑफ वार	युद्ध बन्दी
55.	Provisions	प्रोविजन्स	रसद, सामग्री
56.	Recruitment	रिक्रूटमेण्ट	सेना-प्रवेश
57.	Siege	सीज	घेरा
58.	Strategy	स्ट्रेटजी	युद्ध कौशल
59.	Sub-marine	सबमेरीन	पनडुब्बी
60.	Treaty	ट्रीटी	सन्धि
61.	Trench	ट्रेंच	खाई
62.	Troops	ट्रूप्स	सेना की टुकड़ी
63.	Torpedo-boat	टॉरपीडो बोट	गोला वाली नौका
64.	War	वार	युद्ध
65.	War Minister	वार मिनिस्टर	युद्ध मन्त्री

Names of Flowers

S. No	Words	Pronunciation	Hindi Meaning
1.	Bud	बड	कली, कोपल
2.	Balsam	बालसम	गुल मेंहदी
3.	Chrysenthemum	क्रिसेंथेमम	गुल दाउदी
4.	Colera-flower	कोलरा-फ्लावर	नागभिका
5.	Creeper	क्रीपर	लता, बेल
6.	Daisy	डेजी	गुलबहार
7.	Erythrinia	एरीथ्रिनिया	पारिजात
8.	Fir	फर	सनीवर
9.	Hiptage	हिप्टेज	माध्वी पुष्प
10.	Jasmine	जैसमीन	चमेली
11.	Knop	नोप	कली
12.	Lily	लिली	कुमुदिनी
13.	Lotus	लोटस	कमल
14.	Magnolia	मेग्नोलिया	चम्पा
15.	Marigold	मेरीगोल्ड	गेंदा
16.	Mushroom	मशरूम	कुकुरमुत्ता

S. No	Words	Pronunciation	Hindi Meaning
17.	Motia	मोतिया	मोतिया
18.	Murraya	मरैया	कामिनी
19.	Narcissus	नार्सिसस	नरगिस
20.	Oleander	ओलीण्डर	करबीर, कनेर
21.	Pandanus	पैण्डेनस	केतकी
22.	Poppy	पोपी	पोस्ता का फूल

S. No	Words	Pronunciation	Hindi Meaning
23.	Prickly pear	प्रिकली पियर	नागफनी
24.	Rose	रोज	गुलाब
25.	Stramonium	स्ट्रामोनियम	धतूरा
26.	Sun flower	सनफ्लावर	सूरजमुखी
27.	Touch-me-not	टच-मी-नॉट	छुई-मुई

Names of Vegetables

S. No.	Words	Pronunciation	Hindi Meaning
1.	Amaranthus	एमरान्थस	चौलाई
2.	Arum	ऐरम	अरबी
3.	Bean	बीन	सेम
4.	Bitter gourd	बिटर गार्ड	करेला
5.	Brinjal	ब्रिंजल	बैंगन
6.	Cabbage	कैबेज	बन्दगोभी
7.	Carrot	कैरेट	गाजर
8.	Cauliflower	कॉलिफ्लावर	फूलगोभी
9.	Charantis	चारनटिस	करेला
10.	Chilli	चिली	लाल मिर्च
11.	Citron	सिट्रान	गलगल
12.	Clocasia	क्लोकासिया	कचालू
13.	Coriander	कोरिअण्डर	धनिया
14.	Cow-pea	काऊ-पी	लोबिया
15.	Cucumber	क्यूकुम्बर	ककड़ी
16.	Fenugreek	फेनुग्रीक	मैथी
17.	Garlic	गार्लिक	लहसुन
18.	Ginger	जिंजर	अदरक
19.	Gourd	गर्ड	घीया, कद्दू
20.	Greens	ग्रीन्स	साग

S. No.	Words	Pronunciation	Hindi Meaning
21.	Jack-fruit	जैकफ्रूट	कटहल
22.	Lady finger	लेडी फिंगर	भिण्डी
23.	Lettuce	लेट्यूस	सलाद
24.	Lime	लाइम	खट्टा
25.	Luffa	लुफा	घीया तोरी
26.	Mint	मिंट	पौदीना
27.	Mushrom	मशरूम	कुकुरमुत्ता
28.	Onion	ऑनियन	प्याज
29.	Pea	पी	मटर
30.	Potato	पोटैटो	आलू
31.	Pumpkin	पम्पकिन	लोकी
32.	Radish	रेडिश	मूली
33.	Red Pumpkin	रैड पम्पकिन	सीताफल, पेठा
34.	Snake Gourd	स्नेक गार्ड	चिचड़ा
35.	Spinach	स्पइनक	पालक
36.	Sweet Potato	स्वींट पोटैटो	शकरकन्दी
37.	Tamarind	टैमारिण्ड	इमली
38.	Tomato	टोमैटो	टमाटर
39.	Turnip	टर्निप	शलजम
40.	Yam	याम	कचालू

Names of Dry Fruits and Fruits

S.No	Words	Pronunciation	Hindi Meaning
1.	Almond	एलमण्ड	बादाम
2.	Apple	एप्पल	सेब
3.	Apricot	एप्रीकोट	खुमानी
4.	Banana	बनाना	केला
5.	Betel-nut	बीटल नट	सुपारी
6.	Beet-root	बीट-रूट	चुकन्दर
7.	Berry	बेरी	बेर
8.	Black-berry	ब्लैक-बेरी	जामुन
9.	Carambola	कैरमबोला	कमरख
10.	Cashewnut	कैश्युनट	काजू
11.	Cherry	चेरी	चेरी
12.	Chestnut	चेस्टनट	अखरोट

S.No	Words	Pronunciation	Hindi Meaning
13.	Coconut	कोकोनट	नारियल
14.	Currant	करेण्ट	किशमिश
15.	Citron	सिट्रॉन	चकोतरा
16.	Custard apple	कस्टर्ड एप्पल	शरीफा
17.	Date	डेट	खजूर
18.	Fig	फिग	अंजीर
19.	Grape	ग्रेप	अंगूर
20.	Grapefuit	ग्रेपफूट	मौसमी
21.	Gravia Asiatica	ग्रेविया एसियाटिका	फालसा
22.	Ground-nut	ग्राउण्ड-नट	मूँगफली
23.	Guava	गुआवा	अमरूद
24.	Lychee	लीची	लीची

S.No	Words	Pronunciation	Hindi Meaning
25.	Lilac	लिलैक	बिकाइन
26.	Loquat	लोकाट	लोकाट
27.	Malta	माल्टा	माल्टा
28.	Mango	मैंगो	आम
29.	Melon	मैलन	खरबूजा
30.	Mosambi	मौसम्बी	मौसमी
31.	Musk-melon	मस्क मेलन	खरबूजा
32.	Mulberry	मलबेरी	शहतूत
33.	Okra	ओक्रा	एक फल
34.	Olive	ऑलाइव	जैतून
35.	Orange	औरेंज	सन्तरा
36.	Palm	पाम	ताड़ का फल
37.	Peach	पीच	आड़ू
38.	Pear	पीयर	नाशपाती
39.	Papaya	पपाया	पपीता
40.	Pineapple	पाइनएप्पल	अनानास
41.	Pistachio	पिस्टैशियो	पिस्ता
42.	Plum	प्लम	आलूचा
43.	Pomegranate	पोमग्रेनेट	अनार
44.	Pyrus malus	पाइरस मैलस	बब्बूगोशा
45.	Plantain	प्लैन्टेन	केला
46.	Raisin	रेजन	किशमिश
47.	Sapodilla	सेपोडिला	चीकू
48.	Sole	सोल	आलू बुखारा
49.	Sour Cherry	सोर चेरी	खट्टी चेरी
50.	Sugarcane	सुगरकेन	गन्ना
51.	Watermelon	वाटरमैलन	तरबूज
52.	Waternut	वाटरनट	सिंघाड़ा

Names of Trees and Plants

S. No	Words	Pronunciation	Hindi Meaning
1.	Acacia	अकेशिया	बबूल
2.	Apple Tree	एप्पल ट्री	सेब का पेड़
3.	Abbizzia Labbek	अबिजिया लैबेक	सिरस
4.	Bamboo	बम्बू	बाँस
5.	Banyan	बैन्यिन	बरगद
6.	Betelnut tree	बीटल-नट ट्री	सुपारी का पेड़
7.	Birch	बर्च	भोजपत्र
8.	Teak	टीक	सागवान
9.	Cactus	कैक्टस	थूहर
10.	Cane	केन	बेंत
11.	Cedar	सीडर	देवदार
12.	Cypress	साइप्रेस	सरु
13.	Coco	कोको	नारियल का पेड़
14.	Creeper	क्रीपर	लता, बेल
15.	Conifer	कॉनिफर	झाऊ वृक्ष
16.	Date-palm	डेट-पाम	खजूर का पेड़
17.	Ebony	एबॉनी	आबनूस
18.	Eleocarpus	एलियोकारपस	रुद्राक्ष
19.	Fig	फिग	अंजीर
20.	Fir	फर	देवदार, सनोवर
21.	Flax	फ्लेक्स	सन
22.	Grass	ग्रास	घास
23.	Guava	गुआवा	अमरूद
24.	Grape Vine	ग्रेप-वाइन	अंगूर की बेल
25.	Indigo	इन्डिगो	नील
26.	Jack tree	जैक ट्री	कटहल का पेड़
27.	Jute	जूट	पट्सन
28.	Mahogany	महोगेनी	महोगनी
29.	Mango tree	मैंगो ट्री	आम का पेड़
30.	Oak	ओक	वलूत का पेड़
31.	Peepal	पीपल	पीपल का पेड़
32.	Palm Tree	पाम ट्री	ताड़ का पेड़
33.	Paddy	पैडी	धान का पौधा
34.	Pine	पाइन	चीड़ का पेड़
35.	Polyalthia	पोलयाल्थिया	अशोक
36.	Sandal	सन्दल	चन्दन
37.	Sal tree	साल ट्री	साल का पेड़
38.	Shrub	श्रब	झाड़ी
39.	Silk Cotton	सिल्क कोटन	सेमल
40.	Stamen	स्टेमेन	जीरा
41.	Sugarcane	सुगरकेन	गन्ना
42.	Shishman	शीशम	शीशम

Names of Parts of Trees and Plants

S.No	Words	Pronunciation	Hindi Meaning
1.	Bark	बार्क	छाल
2.	Branch	ब्रांच	टहनी, शाखा
3.	Bud	बड	कली
4.	Bulb	बल्ब	कन्द
5.	Bush	बुश	झाड़ी
6.	Bubil	ब्यूबिल	पत्रकन्द
7.	Coir	कॉइर	जटा
8.	Conifer	कॉनिफर	झाऊ
9.	Fibre	फाइबर	रेशा
10.	Flower	फ्लावर	फूल

S.No	Words	Pronunciation	Hindi Meaning
11.	Fruit	फ्रूट	फल
12.	Graft	ग्राफ्ट	कलम
13.	Germ	जर्म	बीज (अंकुर)
14.	Gum	गम	गोंद
15.	Juice	जूस	रस
16.	Leaf	लीफ	पत्ता
17.	Pistil	पिस्टिल	गर्म केसर
18.	Pollen grain	पोलेन ग्रेन	परागकेसर
19.	Pollen tube	पोलेन ट्यूब	पराग नलिका
20.	Pulp	पल्प	पुमंग

S.No	Words	Pronunciation	Hindi Meaning
21.	Root	रूट	जड़
22.	Root stalk	रूट स्टॉक	प्रकन्द
23.	Seed	सीड	बीज
24.	Skin	स्किन	छिलका
25.	Sprout	स्प्राउट	कोंपल
26.	Stamen	स्टेमैन	पुमंग
27.	Stem	स्टैम	धड़
28.	Thorn	थॉर्न	काँटा
29.	Trunk	ट्रंक	तना
30.	Wood	वुड	लकड़ी

Names of Cereals/Grains

S.No	Words	Pronunciation	Hindi Meaning
1.	Barley	बार्ले	जौ
2.	Beaten Paddy	बीटन पैडी	चिवड़ा
3.	Bran	ब्रान	चोकर
4.	Buck Wheat	बक व्हीट	मेथी
5.	Cluster bean	क्लस्टर बीन	ग्वार
6.	Corn	कॉर्न	अनाज, दाना
7.	Castor seed	कास्टर-सीड	अरण्डी
8.	Flour	फ्लोर	आटा
9.	Fine flour	फाईन फ्लोर	मैदा
10.	Field pea	फील्ड पी	गोल मटर
11.	Grain	ग्रेन	अनाज
12.	Gram	ग्राम	चना
13.	Great millet	ग्रेट मिलेट	ज्वार
14.	Kidney bean	किडनी बीन	मूँग
15.	Lentil	लैण्टिल	मसूर
16.	Linseed	लिनसीड	अलसी
17.	Maize	मैज	मकई

S.No	Words	Pronunciation	Hindi Meaning
18.	Millet	मिलैट	बाजरा, ज्वार
19.	Mustard	मस्टर्ड	सरसो, राई
20.	Oat	ओट	जई
21.	Paddy	पैडी	धान
22.	Pea	पी	मटर
23.	Pigeon pea	पिजन पी	अरहर
24.	Phaseolies mungo	फैसियोलीज मंगो	उड़द
25.	Pearl Millet	पर्ल मिलैट	बाजरा
26.	Poppy seed	पापी सीड	पोस्त
27.	Pulse	पल्स	दाल
28.	Rice	राईस	चावल
29.	Sago	सागो	साबूदाना
30.	Sesamum	सीसेमम	तिल
31.	Semolina	सैमोलीना	सूजी
32.	Wheat	व्हीट	गेहूँ

Names of Some Eatables and Potables

S. No	Words	Pronunciation	Hindi Meaning
1.	Arrow-root	ऐरोरूट	अरारोट
2.	Bacon	बैकन	सूअर का मांस
3.	Beef	बीफ	गाय का मांस
4.	Breakfast	ब्रेकफास्ट	क्लेवा, नाश्ता
5.	Biscuit	बिस्किट	बिस्कुट
6.	Broth	ब्राथ	शोरबा, रस
7.	Butter	बटर	मक्खन
8.	Bread	ब्रैड	रोटी
9.	Boiled rice	बॉयल्ड राइस	भात
10.	Butter milk	बटर मिल्क	छाछ
11.	Brandy	ब्रैण्डी	शराब

S. No	Words	Pronunciation	Hindi Meaning
12.	Betel	बीटेल	पान
13.	Cake	केक	केक
14.	Cheese	चीज	पनीर
15.	Clarified butter	क्लैरीफाइड बटर	घी
16.	Coffee	कॉफी	कहवा
17.	Comfit	कॉम्फिट	इलायचीदाना
18.	Cream	क्रीम	मलाई
19.	Cocoa	कोको	कोको
20.	Cigar	सिगार	चुरट
21.	Cigarette	सिगरेट	सिगरेट

S. No	Words	Pronunciation	Hindi Meaning
22.	Curd	कर्ड	दही
23.	Curry	करी	कढ़ी
24.	Chapati	चपाती	रोटी
25.	Condensed Milk	कन्डैण्स्ड मिल्क	खोया
26.	Corn-ear	कॉर्न ईयर	भुट्टा
27.	Dinner	डिनर	रात का भोजन
28.	Frumenty	फ्रमेण्टी	खीर, दलिया
29.	Feast	फीस्ट	दावत
30.	Field pea	फील्ड पी	गोल मटर
31.	Flesh	फ्लेश	कच्चा मांस
32.	Flour	फ्लोर	आटा
33.	Food	फूड	भोजन
34.	Gruel	ग्रूएल	दलिया
35.	Honey	हनी	शहद
36.	Ice	आइस	बर्फ
37.	Ice-cream	आइसक्रीम	कुल्फी
38.	Jam	जैम	मुरब्बा
39.	Loaf	लोफ	पाव रोटी
40.	Lemon Juice	लेमन ज्यूस	नींबू का रस
41.	Loaf Sugar	लोफ शुगर	शक्कर
42.	Meat	मीट	मांस
43.	Mid-day meal	मिड-डे-मील	दोपहर का भोजन
44.	Milk	मिल्क	दूध
45.	Minced meat	मिन्स्ड मीट	कीमा
46.	Mutton	मटन	बकरे का मांस
47.	Meal	मील	भोजन

S. No	Words	Pronunciation	Hindi Meaning
48.	Molasses	मोलेसैज	शीरा, राब
49.	Oil	ऑयल	तेल
50.	Opium	ओपियम	अफीम
51.	Puffed rice	पफ्ड राईस	मुरमुरा
52.	Pickle	पिकल	अचार
53.	Poppy	पोपी	पोस्त
54.	Porridge	पोरिज	दलिया
55.	Pork	पोर्क	सूअर का मांस
56.	Pudding	पुडिंग	दलिया
57.	Parched rice	पार्च्ड राइस	लावा
58.	Sago	सागो	साबूदाना
59.	Snacks	स्नेक्स	जलपान
60.	Sauce	सॉस	चटनी
61.	Soup	सूप	शोरबा
62.	Sugar candy	शुगर कैण्डी	मिश्री
63.	Supper	सपर	दिन का अन्तिम भोजन
64.	Sweet-meat	स्वीट मीट	लड्डू
65.	Syrup	सिरप	शर्बत
66.	Surti	सुर्टी	सुर्टी
67.	Smoking	स्मोकिंग	धूम्रपान
68.	Tea	टी	चाय
69.	Tiffin	टिफिन	जलपान
70.	Treacle	ट्रीकल	राव, खाण्ड
71.	Whey	व्हे	मट्ठा
72.	Vinegar	विनेगर	सिरका
73.	Wine	वाइन	मदिरा

Names of Spices and Grocery Items

S. No	Words	Pronunciation	Hindi Meaning
1.	Aconite	ऐकोनाइट	कुंचला
2.	Aloe	अलो	अगरू
3.	Alum	ऐलम	सौंफ
4.	Arsenic	ऑर्सेनिक	संखिया
5.	Aniseed	एनीसीड	फिटकरी
6.	Asafoetida	आसफोटिडा	हींग
7.	Aflatoon	अफलाटून	गूगल
8.	Alkali	अलकली	सज्जीखार
9.	Acid	एसिड	अम्ल
10.	Basil	बेसिल	तुलसी
11.	Barilla	बरिल्ला	सब्जखार
12.	Belladona	बैलाडोना	धतूरा
13.	Betel-nut	बीटल-नट	सुपारी
14.	Black-pepper	ब्लेक पेपर	काली मिर्च
15.	Bitumen	बिटूमेन	शिलाजीत
16.	Borax	बोरेक्स	सुहागा

S. No	Words	Pronunciation	Hindi Meaning
17.	Bonezin	बोनजीन	लोबान
18.	Bamboo camphor	बेम्बू-कैम्फर	वंश लोचन
19.	Caraway	कैरावे	अजवायन
20.	Camphor	केम्फर	कपूर
21.	Cassia	केसिया	तेजपात
22.	Catechu	कैटचू	कत्था
23.	Cinnamon	सिनामोन	दालचीनी
24.	Chirata	चिराता	चिरायता
25.	Clove	क्लोव	लौंग
26.	Cocaine	कोकेन	कोकीन
27.	Coriander seed	कोरिएण्डर सीड	धनिया
28.	Cardamom	कार्डेमम	इलायची
29.	Cumin seed	क्यूमिन सीड	जीरा
30.	Carbonate of soda	कार्बोनेट ऑफ सोडा	पापड़ खार

S. No	Words	Pronunciation	Hindi Meaning
31.	Cubeb	क्यूबेब	कबाब चीनी
32.	Chilli	चिली	लाल मिर्च
33.	Dry ginger	ड्राई जिंजर	सौंठ
34.	Gall-nut	गॉल नट	माजूफल
35.	Garlic	गार्लिक	लहसुन
36.	Ginger	जिंजर	अदरख
37.	Indian madder	इण्डियन मैडर	मजीठ
38.	Hemp	हेम्प	भाँग
39.	Hog plums	हॉग प्लम्स	आँवला
40.	Linseed	लिनसीड	अलसी
41.	Liquorice	लिकोराइस	मुलेठी
42.	Litharge	लिथार्ज	सफेदा
43.	Long pepper	लॉग पेपर	पीपल
44.	Mace	मेस	जावित्री
45.	Mangosteen	मैंगोस्टीन	अमचूर
46.	Menthol	मेंथॉल	पोदीने का सत
47.	Musk	मस्क	कस्तूरी
48.	Mustard	मस्टर्ड	सरसों
49.	Myrobalan	माइरोबालान	हर्र, हरड़
50.	Nigella	नाइजेला	कलौंजी
51.	Nux Vomica	नक्स वोमिका	कुचला
52.	Nutmeg	नटमेग	जायफल
53.	Nitre	नाइटर	सुरिया खार
54.	Niger	नाइगर	तिल्ली का तेल
55.	Oat	ओट	जई
56.	Origanum	ओरिगैनम	शिकाकाई
57.	Pellitory	पेलिटोरी	अकरकरा
58.	Pepper	पेपर	मिर्च
59.	Pepper root	पेपर रूट	पीपल मूल
60.	Parsley	पारस्ले	अजवायन
61.	Pistil	पिस्टिल	गर्म केसर
62.	Poppy seed	पोपी सीड	खसखस
63.	Phyllanthus embbica	फिलेंथस एम्बलीका	आँवला
64.	Red Pepper	रेड पेपर	लाल मिर्च
65.	Rock salt	रॉक साल्ट	सेंधा नमक
66.	Red powder	रेड पाउडर	अबीर
67.	Ruddle	रडल	गेरू
68.	Saffron	सैफ्रॉन	केसर
69.	Salt	साल्ट	नमक
70.	Salammoniac	साल-अमोनिआक	नौसादर
71.	Saltpetre	साल्टपीटर	शोरा
72.	Sandal	सन्दल	चन्दन
73.	Senna	सैना	सनाय
74.	Soap-nut	सोप नट	रीठा
75.	Sago	सागो	साबूदाना
76.	Stamen	स्टेमन	जीरा
77.	Tamarind	टैमेरिण्ड	हल्दी
78.	Turmeric	टरमैरिक	हल्दी
79.	Vinegar	विनेगर	सिरका
80.	Vitriol	विट्रिऑल	कसीस
81.	Yeast	यीस्ट	खमीर

Names of Conditions of the Body and Diseases

S. No	Words	Pronunciation	Hindi Meaning
1.	Abortion	अबॉर्शन	गर्भपात
2.	Acne	एक्ने	मुहाँसों का रोग
3.	Acidity	एसिडिटी	अम्लपित्त
4.	Anaemia	एनेमिया	खून की कमी
5.	Asthma	अस्थमा	दमा
6.	Asphyxy	ऑसफिक्सी	दम घुटना
7.	Amnesia	एम्नीसिया	स्मृति विभ्रम
8.	Antiseptic	एण्टिसेप्टिक	संक्रमण-प्रतिरोधी
9.	Anorexia	अनोरिक्सीया	अरुचि
10.	Bald	बाल्ड	गंजा
11.	Belching	बेल्चिंग	डकार
12.	Blind	ब्लाइण्ड	अंधा
13.	Boil	बॉयल	फोड़ा
14.	Breath	ब्रीथ	साँस
15.	Bronchitis	ब्रोंकाइटिस	कास
16.	Bubu	ब्यूबो	गिल्टी
17.	Blood-flux	ब्लड-फ्लक्स	रक्तातिसार
18.	Conjunctivitis	कन्जक्टाइविटीज	नेत्र पीड़ा
19.	Cataract	कैटारेक्ट	मोतियाबिन्द
20.	Carries	कैरीज	दाँत में गड्ढा
21.	Catarrah	कैटर	जुकाम
22.	Chill	चिल	शीतल
23.	Cold	कोल्ड	ठण्डक
24.	Cough	कफ	खाँसी
25.	Consumption	कन्सम्पशन	क्षय रोग
26.	Colic pain	कालिक पेन	उदरशूल
27.	Constipation	कान्स्टिपेशन	कब्ज
28.	Cholera	कॉलरा	हैजा
29.	Corns	कॉर्न्स	बिवाई फटना
30.	Carbuncle	कार्बन्कल	जहरबाद
31.	Canker	कैंकर	कीड़े पड़ना
32.	Coryza	कोरीजा	जुकाम, नजला

S. No	Words	Pronunciation	Hindi Meaning
33.	Deaf	डीफ	बहरा
34.	Dengue	डेंगू	लँगड़ा बुखार
35.	Diabetes	डाइबिटीज	मधुमेह
36.	Diarrhoea	डायरिया	अतिसार
37.	Dropsy	ड्रॉप्सी	जलोदर
38.	Dumb	डम्ब	गूँगा
39.	Dysentery	डिसेन्टरी	पेचिस, आंव
40.	Dwarf	ड्वार्फ	बौना
41.	Debility	डेबिलिटी	कमजोरी
42.	Diptheria	डिफ्थीरिया	कंठरोहिणी
43.	Dyspepisa	डिसपेप्सिया	अजीर्ण
44.	Eczema	एक्जीमा	उकवत, छाजन
45.	Epilepsy	ऐपिलेप्सी	मिरगी
46.	Eunuch	यूनक	नपुंसक
47.	Eyesore	आईसोर	आँखों का दुखना
48.	Epistaxes	एपिसटेक्सिस	रक्तपित्त
49.	Emissions	इमिशन्स	स्वप्नदोष
50.	Eschal	एस्चाल	फफोले
51.	Elephantiasis	ऐलिफैण्टियासिस	फीलपांव
52.	Fever	फीवर	बुखार, ज्वर
53.	Fistula	फिस्टुला	भगन्दर
54.	Fainting	फेन्टिंग	बेहोशी
55.	Giddiness	गिडिनेस	चक्कर आना
56.	Gland	ग्लैण्ड	गिल्टी
57.	Griping	ग्राइपिंग	पेट की ऐंठन
58.	Goitre	गॉइटर	गलगण्ड
59.	Gonorrhoea	गनोरिया	सुजाक
60.	Gout	गाउट	गाँठ पड़ना
61.	Hunch-backed	हंच-बैक्ड	कुबड़ा
62.	Headache	हेडएक	सिर दर्द
63.	Hiccup	हिकप	हिचकी
64.	Hiccough	हिकफ	हिचकी
65.	Hoarseness	होर्सनैस	गला बैठना
66.	Hysteria	हिस्टीरिया	मूर्च्छा रोग
67.	Hernia	हर्निया	आंत
68.	Hydrocele	हाइड्रोसील	अण्डकोश वृद्धि
69.	Haemorrhage	हेमोरेज	लहू बहना
70.	Hypermetropia	हापरमेट्रोपिया	दृष्टि का रोग
71.	Hurt	हर्ट	चोट
72.	Insomnia	इन्सोमनिया	नींद न आना
73.	Influenza	इन्फ्लूऐंजा	मोतिझरा
74.	Indigestion	इण्डाइजेशन	अपच
75.	Itch	इच	खुजली
76.	Insanity	इनसैनिटी	पागलपन

S. No	Words	Pronunciation	Hindi Meaning
77.	Iritis	आइराइटिस	बिलनी
78.	Jaundice	जॉण्डिश	पीलिया
79.	Lame	लेम	लँगड़ा
80.	Lock-jaw	लॉक-जॉ	दाँत बैठना
81.	Lumbago	लुम्बेगो	कमर दर्द
82.	Leucorrhoea	लूकोरिया	श्वेत प्रदर
83.	Leprosy	लेप्रोसी	कुष्ठ रोग
84.	Leucoderma	ल्यूकोडर्मा	श्वेत कुष्ठ
85.	Lunacy	लूनेसी	पागलपन
86.	Madness	मेडनेस	पागलपन
87.	Measles	मीजल्स	खसरा
88.	Myopia	मायोपिया	दृष्टि का रोग
89.	Malaria	मलेरिया	मलेरिया ज्वर
90.	Melena	मेलिना	खूनी दस्त
91.	Mole	मोल	मस्सा
92.	Mumps	मम्प्स	कनफेड़ा
93.	Night blindness	नाइट-ब्लाइण्डनेस	रतौंधी
94.	Nausea	नासिया	जी मिचलाना
95.	Narcolepsy	नार्कोलेप्सी	निद्रा रोग
96.	Obesity	ओबेसिटी	मोटापन
97.	One-eyed	वन आईड	काना
98.	Ortitis	आरटिटस	कर्ण रोग
99.	Pain	पेन	दर्द
100.	Palpitation	पाल्पीटेशन	धड़कन
101.	Piles	पाइल्स	बवासीर
102.	Pimple	पिम्पल	फुंसी
103.	Plague	प्लेग	प्लेग, महामारी
104.	Phlegm	फ्लेज्म	बलगम
105.	Paralysis	पौरालिसिस	लकवा
106.	Pus	पस	पीप
107.	Pneumonia	न्यूमोनिया	आंत्र ज्वर
108.	Phycosus	फाइकोसस	दुस्साध्य उन्माद
109.	Phthisis	पाइथिसिस	राज्यक्ष्मा रोग
110.	Rheumatism	रुमाटिज्म	गठिया
111.	Ring worm	रिंग वर्म	दाद
112.	Saliva	सलाइवा	लार
113.	Scabies	स्केबीज	खाज
114.	Short sightedness	शोर्ट-साइटेडनेस	अल्प/मन्द दृष्टि
115.	Sneezing	स्नीजिंग	छींक
116.	Sore	सोर	व्रण
117.	Sun stroke	सन स्ट्रोक	लू लगना
118.	Small pox	स्माल पॉक्स	शीतला

S. No	Words	Pronunciation	Hindi Meaning
119.	Spittle	स्पिटल	थूक
120.	Sprain	स्प्रेन	मोच
121.	Stool	स्टूल	विष्टा
122.	Swelling	स्वेलिंग	सूजन
123.	Sweat	स्वैट	पसीना
124.	Syphilis	सिफिलिस	आंतराक, गर्मी
125.	Squint-eyed	स्किवंट-आईड	ऐंचा
126.	Scrofula	स्क्रॉफुला	कंठमाला
127.	Stone	स्टोन	पथरी
128.	Semen	सिमेन	वीर्य
129.	Stammer	स्टैमर	हकलाना
130.	Sprue	स्प्रू	संग्रहणी
131.	Spesis	स्पेसिस	विषाक्त खून होना
132.	Sinus	साइनस	नासूर
133.	Tonsil	टॉन्सिल	गलसुआ
134.	Tomour	ट्यूमर	गांठ, गिलटी
135.	Typhoid	टॉयफायड	मोतीझरा
136.	Typhus	टॉयफस	काला ज्वर
137.	Tuberculosis	ट्यूबरक्यूलसिस	टी० बी०
138.	Urine	यूरीन	मूत्र
139.	Ulcer	अलसर	नासूर
140.	Vomit	वोमिट	कै/उल्टी करना
141.	Vertigo	वर्टिगो	आंख चौंधियाना
142.	Yawn	यॉन	जंभाई
143.	Worm	वर्म	कृमि
144.	Wound	वूंड	घाव

Names of Building Parts and Some Buildings

S. No	Words	Pronunciation	Hindi Meaning
1.	Arch	आर्च	वृककखण्ड
2.	Attic	अटिक	अटारी
3.	Aviary	एवियर्री	चिड़ियाखाना
4.	Bar	बॉर	दड़
5.	Barrack	बैरेक	सेना निवास
6.	Bathroom	बाथरूम	स्नानगृह
7.	Battlement	बैटमेंट	मुंडेर
8.	Bedroom	बैडरूम	शयनागार
9.	Booking office	बुकिंग-ऑफिस	टिकटघर
10.	Bracket	ब्रैकिट	कोनिया
11.	Bungalow	बंगलो	बंगला
12.	Building	बिल्डिंग	इमारत
13.	Balcongy	बालकनी	बरामदा
14.	Brick	ब्रिक	ईंट
15.	Bolt	वोल्ट	चटखनी
16.	Church	चर्च	गिरजाघर
17.	College	कॉलेज	महाविद्यालय
18.	Cement	सिमेंट	सीमेंट
19.	Courtyard	कोर्टयार्ड	सहन (आंगन)
20.	Cell	सेल	तहखाना
21.	Cornice	कॉर्निस	कॉर्निस
22.	Ceiling	सीलिंग	छत
23.	Cottage	कॉटेज	झोंपड़ी
24.	Chimney	चिमनी	धुंआकश
25.	Cloister	क्यॉयस्टर	मठ
26.	Dais	डायस	मचान
27.	Dome	डॉम	गुम्बद
28.	Door	डोर	दरवाजा
29.	Door Frame	डोर फ्रेम	चौखट
30.	Door still	डोर स्टिल	देहली
31.	Drain	ड्रेन	नावदान, नाली
32.	Factory	फैक्ट्री	कारखाना
33.	Floor	फ्लोर	फर्श
34.	Fort	फोर्ट	किला
35.	Foundation	फाऊण्डेशन	नींव, बुनियाद
36.	Fountain	फाऊटेन	फव्वारा
37.	Gate	गेट	दरवाजा
38.	Fort	ग्रेटिंग	जाली
39.	Girder	गर्डर	गाटर
40.	Gutter	गटर	परनाला
41.	Granary	ग्रेनरी	खलिहान
42.	Gymnasium	जिम्नेजियम	जिमशाला
43.	House	हाऊस	मकान
44.	Hamlet	हेमलेट	गांव
45.	Hermitage	हर्मिटेज	साधु कुटी
46.	Hospital	हॉस्पिटल	अस्पताल
47.	Hotel	होटल	होटल
48.	Hinge	हिंज	कब्जा
49.	Hall	हाल	बड़ा कमरा
50.	Hook	हुक	हुक
51.	Hearth	हर्थ	अंगीठी
52.	Inn	इन	सराय
53.	Kitchen	किचन	रसोई
54.	Latch	लैच	चटखनी
55.	Laboratory	लेबोरेट्री	प्रयोगशाला
56.	Latrine	लेट्रीन	शौचालय
57.	Lattice	लेटिस	जाली
58.	Lunatic Asylum	ल्यूनेटिक एसीलम	पागलखाना
59.	Library	लायब्रेरी	पुस्तकालय
60.	Lime	लाइम	चूना
61.	Ladder	लेडर	सीढ़ी
62.	Mosque	मॉस्क	मस्जिद
64.	Minaret	मिनारेट	मस्जिद की मीनार
63.	Mud	मड	कीचड़
65.	Niche	निचे	आला
66.	Nail	नेल	कील

CHAPTER

43

ANTONYMS/SYNONYMS

अधिकांश Competitive Examinations में English Question Paper में Antonym (Opposites) or Synonyms (Similar Meanings) से सम्बन्धित पाँच या दस प्रश्न पूछे जाते हैं। इस तरह के प्रश्न दो प्रकार से पूछे जाते हैं। एक तो सीधे-सीधे एक Word दे दिया जाता हैं एवं उसके Antonym/Synonym हेतु पाँच विकल्प दिए जाते हैं, उनमें से एक Word, दिए गए शब्द का उचित Synonym होता है। दूसरे प्रकार में एक Sentence दिया गया होता है एवं उस Sentence में एक Word को Bold or Italic करके, उसका Antonym/Synonym पूछा जाता है।

विकल्प के रूप में 4-5 शब्द दिए जाते हैं। उनमें से एक उचित शब्द को चुनना होता हैं। Antonym/Synonym के प्रश्नों को हल करने हेतु छात्र की Word Power अच्छी होनी चाहिए। Word Power Improve करने हेतु इस book में बताए गए 'Learn Three Steps to Improve Your Word Power' पढ़ें। यह लेखक की Self Experimented Technique है। English Question Paper के अधिकांश प्रश्न किसी न किसी रूप में Word Power से सम्बन्धित होते हैं। अत: छात्रों को Word Power को Improve करने हेतु पूरा ध्यान देना चाहिए।

इस तरह के प्रश्नों को हल करने के दो तरीके हैं। एक तो आप सीधे ही सही Answer का चुनाव करे लें। कई बार हमें दिए गए किसी Word का सही Meaning ध्यान नहीं रहता हैं तो आप Answers में दिए गए विकल्पों में से एक-एक Word को Exclude करके अपना सही Answer चुनने का प्रयास करें। Antonym/Synonym हेतु इस book में काफी Exercises दी गई हैं। छात्रों को इन Exercises को Solve करना चाहिए एवं Answers में विकल्प के रूप दिए गए सभी शब्दों का भी Meaning याद करना हैं। इस Book का Word Power का Section बहुत महत्त्वपूर्ण हैं।

Improving Word Power is not an easy task, but it is not either so difficult, that one can't improve it. Moreover... 'If, something is difficult doesn't mean that one should not try. It means one should try HARDER'.

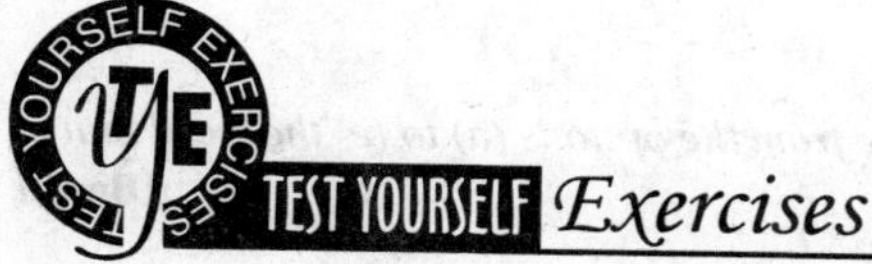

Exercises

01

Directions (Q. 1-5) *: Choose the word which is most nearly the same in meaning as the word given in capital letters :*

[Bank of Maharashtra Specialist Officers]

(1) **OSTENTATION**
(a) Calmness (b) Equianimity (c) Deception (d) Declaration
(e) Pageantry

(2) **PENITENT**
(a) Eccentric (b) Profound (c) Remorseful (d) Observant
(e) Blameless

(3) **SATIATE**
(a) Direct (b) Gratify (c) Manage (d) Defeat
(e) Expose

(4) **MUSE**
(a) Ponder (b) Infect (c) Appease (d) Taint
(e) Hold

(5) **PROFANE**
(a) Assert (b) Benefit (c) Lengthen (d) Desecrate
(e) Advance

02

Directions (Q. 1-5) *: Choose the word which is most nearly the same in meaning as the word given in capital letters :*

[All India Management Trainees]

(1) **INTERPOLATE**
(a) Clarify (b) Investigate (c) Reverse (d) Insert

(2) **CAULDRON**
(a) Computer term (b) Pot for boiling (c) Static electricity (d) Laser fusion

(3) **INSOLVENT**
(a) Flourishing (b) Bankrupt (c) Soluble (d) Opprobrious

(4) **OFFICIOUS**
(a) Pushing (b) Modest (c) Stubborn (d) Mystic

(5) **VERACITY**
(a) Mendacity (b) Truth (c) Imperfection (d) Judgement

03

Directions (Q. 1-3) *: Choose the word which is most nearly the same in meaning as the word given in capital letters :*

[IITM]

(1) **VIA MEDIA**
(a) By the way (b) Through communication (c) A middle course (d) The reverse order

(2) **IN TOTO**
(a) In the heart (b) In peace (c) Within the walls (d) Entirely

(3) **RESUME**
(a) A summary (b) To carry on after interaction
(c) A report of the work done (d) A review

04

Directions (Q. 1-10) **:** *Read the list of word given below and choose from the options (a) to (e) the word that is similar in meaning to the word given in capital letters :* **[Bank]**

(1) **EXIGUOUS**
(a) Tall (b) Large (c) Wide (d) Scanty
(e) Broad

(2) **RECREANCY**
(a) Recreation (b) Recuperation (c) Bravery (d) Cowardice
(e) Obstinate

(3) **PROSCRIBE**
(a) To nominate (b) To be supportive of (c) To give early warning signals
(d) Outlaw (e) None of these

(4) **INGEST**
(a) Enrage (b) Invigorate (c) To absorb (d) Burn up completely
(e) To stir up

(5) **MONTICULE**
(a) A small river (b) A small hut (c) A lane (d) A small hill
(e) A small plane

(6) **COMPENDIOUS**
(a) Comprehensive (b) Illustrative (c) Unbearable (d) Elaborate
(e) None of these

(7) **NADIR**
(a) Asylum (b) Heaven (c) Depth (d) Nebulous
(e) None of these

(8) **SOMNAMBULISTIC**
(a) Sleep walking (b) Ghost dancing (c) Women's group activity
(d) Colourful scenario (e) Over-eating

(9) **PRIMORDIAL**
(a) Feeling of elation (b) Original (c) Elementary (d) Daunting
(e) None of these

(10) **SOMBRE**
(a) Causing sleep (b) Squalid (c) Gloomy (d) Complacent
(e) Malicious

05

Directions (Q. 1-10) **:** *In this section, you find a number of sentences, parts of which are underlined. You may also find only a group of words which is underlined. For each underlined part, four words/phrases are listed below. Choose the word/phrase nearest in meaning to the underlined part :* **[CDS]**

(1) We were taken aback at the <u>fulsome</u> praise heaped upon his former enemy.
(a) elaborated (b) extravagant (c) excessive (d) exorbitant

(2) You may think at first that it is <u>queer to</u> talk of having too much paper money and that money is so nice and useful that you cannot have too much of it.
(a) ridiculous (b) absurd (c) anomalous (d) odd

(3) The Government is under no obligation to offer contracts to companies which choose to <u>flout</u> guidelines.
(a) condemn (b) ignore (c) defy (d) neglect

(4) Soon he felt uncomfortable, for the coach was now moving over a rugged road.
(a) rough (b) narrow (c) dusty (d) sturdy

(5) Indians exhibited a remarkable solidarity at the time of war.
(a) coalition (b) cooperation (c) unification (d) unity

(6) A great statesman is actuated by love of his country.
(a) compelled (b) induced (c) impelled (d) persuaded

(7) The cutting curved sharply and in the darkness the black entrance to the tunnel loomed up menacingly.
(a) harmfully (b) imminently (c) dangerously (d) threateningly

(8) Had he delivered his speech without a long and winding preamble, people would have understood him better.
(a) digression (b) introduction (c) explanation (d) background

(9) His impeccable style caught the attention of all critics.
(a) faultless (b) inoffensive (c) upright (d) harmless

(10) We should not look down on people who are not educated.
(a) dislike (b) despise (c) disown (d) denounce

06

Directions (Q. 1-5) *: In the following questions, out of the four alternatives choose the one which best expresses the meaning of the word given in capital letters and mark it on the Answer Sheet :*

[SSC Stenographer]

(1) **OBJECT**
(a) Disapprove (b) Challenge (c) Deny (d) Disobey

(2) **UNTIE**
(a) Unfold (b) Unchain (c) Undo (d) Unhinge

(3) **ALERT**
(a) Energetic (b) Observant (c) Intelligent (d) Watchful

(4) **MOVING**
(a) Taking (b) Toying (c) Shifting (d) Turning

(5) **RECKLESS**
(a) Courageous (b) Rash (c) Bold (d) Daring

07

Directions (Q. 1-3) *: Choose the word which is most nearly the same in meaning as the word or group of words given in capital letters :*

[Bank PO]

(1) **LAUNCH**
(a) Review (b) Begin (c) Propel (d) Push
(e) Force

(2) **RELIED**
(a) Emphasised (b) Depended (c) Convinced (d) Followed
(e) Referred

(3) **OBTAINED**
(a) Combined (b) Procured (c) Acquired (d) Conquered
(e) Attained

08

Directions (Q. 1-10) *In this section, you find a number of sentences, part of which is underlined. You may also find only a group of words which is underlined. For each underlined part, four words/phrase are listed below. Choose the word nearest in meaning to the underlined part :* **[Indian Bank PO]**

(1) In spite his best efforts the officer could not redeem his prestige.
(a) recover (b) raise (c) extend (d) fulfil

(2) There is abundant supply of water for the crops.
(a) considerable (b) plentiful (c) adequate (d) sufficient

(3) All his attempts to win the favour of his boss proved infructuous.
(a) meaningless (b) unnecessary (c) redundant (d) fruitless

(4) As she had never been in such a situation before, her apprehension was understandable.
(a) eagerness (b) fear (c) hesitation (d) excitement

(5) You should not get paranoid about what others think of you.
(a) flattered by (b) influenced by (c) obsessed with (d) upset by

(6) I wonder if his intervention in the dispute will be of any help.
(a) interception (b) interruption (c) mediation (d) meddling

(7) A strange mental aberration often made her forget her own name.
(a) eccentricity (b) insanity (c) disorder (d) illusion

(8) He treats with disdain anyone who goes to him for help.
(a) contempt (b) disgust (c) insolence (d) displeasure

(9) He spoke impromptu on the occasion.
(a) eloquently (b) without preparation (c) without enthusiasm (d) with great force

(10) The perpetual noise made it impossible for them to concentrate on the problems.
(a) irritating (b) constant (c) unlimited (d) recurrent

09

Directions (Q. 1-5) *: In this section, you find a number of sentences, part of which is underlined. You may also find only a group of words which is underlined. For each underlined part, four words/phrase are listed below. Choose the word nearest in meaning to the underlined part :*

[UPSC Assistant Provident Fund Commissioners March 1998]

(1) It is possible for a writer to be copious in his words, and at the same time, to give the reality of a natural form.
(a) scanty (b) plentiful
(c) repetitive (d) arrogant

(2) The security arrangements made for the visiting dignitary were impeccable.
(a) flawless (b) elaborate
(c) grand (d) tight

(3) Even today many people are guided by abstruse moral values.
(a) dangerous (b) impracticable
(c) obscure (d) irrational

(4) The workers tried their best to thwart the plans of the management.
(a) embarrass (b) embitter
(c) frustrate (d) hasten

(5) The prisoners of war signed the document under coercion.
(a) compulsion (b) confusion
(c) supervision (d) security

10

Directions (Q. 1-5) **:** *In this section, you find a number of sentences, part of which is underlined. You may also find only a group of words which is underlined. For each underlined part, four words/phrase are listed below. Choose the word nearest of the opposite of the underlined word or phrase :*

[UPSC Assistant Provident Fund Commissioners March 1998]

(1) The proposal was denounced by one and all .
(a) announced (b) pronounced (c) appraised (d) commended

(2) Where ignorance is sometimes bliss, illiteracy is always considered a curse.
(a) erudition (b) experience (c) education (d) information

(3) The news brought by the maidservants authentic.
(a) authoritative (b) baseless (c) ridiculous (d) vacuous

(4) The doctor said that there is no improvement in the condition of the patient.
(a) depression (b) deterioration (c) change (d) degradation

(5) He plunged into the turbid waters of the stream.
(a) deep (b) muddy (c) clear (d) fresh

11

Directions (Q. 1-10) **:** *In this section, you find a number of sentences, part of which is underlined. You may also find only a group of words which is underlined. For each underlined part, four words/phrase are listed below. Choose the word nearest opposite in meaning of the underlined part :* **[CDS]**

(1) His repulsive behaviour could not be ignored by the members of the jury.
(a) lovely (b) mild (c) admirable (d) attractive

(2) He is an amateur photographer.
(a) average (b) experienced (c) professional (d) skilled

(3) The witness affirmed on oath that he was an eyewitness to the crime under study.
(a) contradicted (b) opposed (c) disputed (d) denied

(4) On the hillside, he could see the vague shapes of sheep coming through he mist.
(a) clear (b) transparent (c) plain (d) apparent

(5) His casual remarks were taken note of by all members of the board.
(a) careful (b) sincere (c) precise (d) flawless

(6) If you pamper the child you will regret it.
(a) scold (b) scorn (c) discourage (d) neglect

(7) These rules are meant to prevent further appointments .
(a) facilitate (b) accelerate (c) expedite (d) aggravate

(8) The artist led a very austere life.
(a) luxurious (b) boisterous (c) exciting (d) eventful

(9) The new boss is well-known for his rigid approach to all problems.
(a) swift (b) logical (c) sympathetic (d) flexible

(10) Adversity is the source of numerous vices.
(a) Wealth (b) Prosperity (c) Luxury (d) Money

12

Directions (Q. 1-3) **:** *Choose the word which is opposite in meaning to the word given in capital letters :* **[PO]**

(1) **CHRONIC**
(a) Acute (b) Fleeting (c) Irregular (d) Temporary
(e) Recurring

(2) **LETTING**
(a) Demanding (b) Permitting (c) Disallowing (d) Refusing
(e) Rejecting

(3) **INTEGRATE**
(a) Isolate (b) Analyse (c) Distinguish (d) Mark
(e) Distribute

13

Directions (Q. 1-5) **:** *Choose the word which is most opposite in meaning to word given in capital letters:* **[SSC Stenographers]**

(1) **CONFESS**
(a) Refuse (b) Deny (c) Contest (d) Contend

(2) **ABSOLUTE**
(a) Deficient (b) Faulty (c) Limited (d) Scarce

(3) **VALUABLE**
(a) Invaluable (b) Worthless (c) Inferior (d) Lowly

(4) **HINDRANCE**
(a) Aid (b) Persuasion (c) Cooperation (d) Agreement

(5) **ALIEN**
(a) Native (b) Domiciled (c) Natural (d) Resident

14

Directions (Q. 1-5) **:** *Each question below consists of a word in capital letters followed by four alternatives. Choose the alternative that is most nearly opposite in meaning to the word given in capital letters :* **[Tourism Management Entrance June 1998]**

(1) **GARBLE**
(a) Enjoy (b) Rinse (c) Clarify (d) Accept

(2) **FORTITUDE**
(a) Timidity (b) Laxity (c) Placidity (d) Ambition

(3) **PERNICIOUS**
(a) Precious (b) Healing (c) Swerving (d) Conservative

(4) **ANATHEMA**
(a) Appreciation (b) Blessing (c) Protection (d) Obstacle

(5) **CONCUR**
(a) Pertain (b) Reveal (c) Oppose (d) Delay

15

Directions (Q. 1-10) **:** *In this section, each item consists of a word or a phrase which is underlined in the sentence given. It is followed by four words or phrase. Select the word or phrase which is closest to the opposite in meaning of the underlined word or phrase :* **[CDS]**

(1) My brother is very sensitive about hurting animals.
(a) callous (b) senseless (c) indifferent (d) inconcerned

(2) He did it purposely.
(a) half-heartedly (b) timidly (c) unintentionally (d) hesitatingly

(3) After a week-long strike, the workers took to the path of collision when the chairman intervened.
(a) retaliation (b) atonement (c) reconciliation (d) expiation

(4) He yielded to temptation.
(a) succumbed (b) rescinded (c) skirted (d) resisted

(5) The dishevelled appearance of the two men on the street made everyone take notice of them.
(a) composed (b) tidy (c) confident (d) complacent

(6) He has penchant for writing satirical poems.
(a) dislike (b) bias (c) repulsion (d) hatred

(7) The lawyer was convinced that his client had made a/an authentic statement.
(a) absurd (b) false (c) unreasonable (d) ridiculous

(8) He was on pins and needless while his wife was undergoing an operation.
(a) unexcited (b) at rest (c) undisturbed (d) relaxed

(9) The coach was too lax about the training of the team.
(a) stern (b) strict (c) firm (d) steadfast

(10) The rebels held out in the face of stiff odds.
(a) gave in (b) deserted (c) fled away (d) betrayed

16

Directions (Q. 1-5) *: To answer the following questions, choose the alternative that is nearly opposite in meaning to the word given in capital letters :* **[All India Management Trainees]**

(1) **LACONIC**
(a) Terse (b) Loquacious (c) Curt (d) Sagacious

(2) **RENEGADE**
(a) Traitor (b) Heretic (c) Loyalist (d) Fugitive

(3) **ADIPOSE**
(a) Corpulent (b) Glutinous (c) Thin (d) Oleaginous

(4) **PUTRID**
(a) Fresh (b) Rancid (c) Recondite (d) Choleric

(5) **VULGAR**
(a) Plebeian (b) Aristocratic (c) Impervious (d) Licentious

17

Directions (Q. 1-10) *: To answer the following questions, choose the alternative that is nearly opposite in meaning to the word given in capital letters :* **[MAT]**

(1) **SANCTIMONIOUS**
(a) Holy (b) Realistic (c) Humble (d) Callous
(e) Pessimistic

(2) **MUNIFICENT**
(a) Miserly (b) Faulty (c) Perplexing (d) Rudimentary
(e) Grandiose

(3). **OPAQUE**
(a) Vague (b) Firm (c) Transparent (d) Poor
(e) None of these

(4) **RESTIVE**
(a) Unrestrained (b) Communicate (c) Peaceful (d) Quarrel
(e) Disturbing

(5) **CATAPULT**
(a) Reach great heights (b) Downfall (c) Caterpillar (d) Gaining
(e) Losing

(6) **ENIGMATIC**
(a) Industrious (b) Mysterious (c) Enthusiastic (d) Straightforward
(e) Sincere

(7) **TRAIPSE**
(a) Walk (b) Stroll (c) Crawl (d) Run
(e) None of these

(8) **PIQUANT**
(a) Jovial (b) Merry (c) Blunt (d) Rigorous
(e) Shocking

(9) **BIGOTED**
(a) Dignified (b) Tolerant (c) Wide (d) Contrite
(e) Sincere

(10) **OBLIQUITY**
(a) Thin (b) Frank (c) Self-righteous (d) Depreciation
(e) Conformity

18

Directions (Q. 1-8) *: To answer the following questions, choose the alternative that is nearly opposite in meaning to the word given in capital letters :* **[Bank PO]**

(1) **DENOUNCE**
(a) Accept (b) Accuse (c) Condemn (d) Faith

(2) **DIPSOMANIAC**
(a) Alcoholic (b) Teetotaler (c) Sick (d) Lunatic

(3) **PRECIPITOUS**
(a) Rash (b) Steep (c) Thoughtful (d) Rain

(4) **MAGNANIMOUS**
(a) Generous (b) Giving (c) Stingy (d) Greedy

(5) **INCOMMODE**
(a) Cause trouble (b) Comfortable (c) Inconvenience (d) Small

(6) **EXPLICIT**
(a) Clear (b) Straight forward (c) Hidden (d) Closed

(7) **CHURLISH**
(a) Ill-mannered (b) Rude (c) Pleasant (d) Decent

(8) **ASTATIC**
(a) Dynamic (b) Unstable (c) Stable (d) Directionless

19

Directions (Q. 1-5) *: To answer the following questions, choose the alternative that is nearly opposite in meaning to the word given in capital letters :*

(1) **MOTLEY**
(a) Homogeneous (b) Deadly (c) Gloomy (d) Concise
(e) Dreary

(2) **BELITTLE**
(a) Allure (b) Disturb (c) Entangle (d) Ascend
(e) Magnify

(3) **PREMEDITATION**
(a) Compression (b) Impromptu (c) Audacity (d) Succession
(e) Terminal

(4) **PEEVISH**
(a) Dreamy (b) Acquisitive (c) Genial (d) Decorous
(e) Conscious

(5) **FORBID**
(a) Appeal (b) Dispose (c) Examine (d) Permit
(e) Obtain

20

Directions (Q. 1-5) *: In the following questions choose the alternative which is almost the same in meaning to the word given in capital letters :* **[RRB Bhopal Non-Tech 1998]**

(1) **INCLEMENT**
(a) Pleasant (b) Stormy (c) Feeble (d) Dignified

(2) **AFFECTATION**
(a) Hypocrisy (b) Simplicity (c) Antipathy (d) Harmony

(3) **LATENT**
(a) Apparent (b) Dormant (c) Ample (d) Illegal

(4) **VANITY**
(a) Humility (b) Pride (c) Ostentation (d) Pity

(5) **LAUD**
(a) Lord (b) Eulogy (c) Praise (d) Extolled

21

Directions (Q. 1-5) *: Rewrite the following sentences, selecting the most appropriate word from the ones given in the brackets :* **[IFS]**

(1) The story of his escape was very (excitable/exciting/excited).
(2) The (scene/scenery) around here is very beautiful.
(3) I have been studying English (since/for) ten years.
(4) The old man asked if we had any articles of (cloth/clothes/clothing).
(5) If you annoy the God it is (apt/liable/likely) to bite you.

22

Directions (Q. 1-10) *: Choose the word which is most nearly the same in meaning :* **[RRB Kolkata]**

(1) **COMMEMORATE**
(a) Boast (b) Harmonise (c) Manipulate (d) Remember

(2) **CONNOISSEUR**
(a) Lover of art (b) Interpreter (c) Delinquent (d) Ignorant

(3) **LETHAL**
(a) Unlawful (b) Sluggish (c) Deadly (d) Smooth

(4) **NEBULOUS**
(a) Tiny (b) Vague (c) Insignificant (d) Dead

(5) **ELICIT**
(a) Induce (b) Divulge (c) Insignificant (d) Dead

(6) **PROLIFIC**
(a) Plenty (b) Competent (c) Predominant (d) Fertile

(7) **EXORBITANT**
(a) Odd (b) Excessive (c) Ridiculous (d) Threatening

(8) **DILIGENT**
(a) Industrious (b) Energetic (c) Modest (d) Intelligent

(9) **ADMONISH**
(a) Support (b) Praise (c) Appeal (d) Reprove

(10) **BOUNTY**
(a) Gift (b) Donation (c) Pleasure (d) Reward

23

Directions (Q. 1-2) *: From the given words, choose a word which means the same as the word given in capital letters :* **[RRB Bhopal]**

(1) **UNCOUTH**
(a) Ungraceful (b) Rough (c) Slovenly (d) Dirty

(2) **LYNCH**
(a) Hang (b) Madden (c) Killed (d) Shoot

24

Directions (Q. 1-2) *: Choose the nearest similar meaning of the words/phrase :* **[RRB Kolkata, ADM]**

(1) To come round
(a) To get well (b) To reach a roundabout (c) To succeed (d) To complete a circle

(2) A white elephant
(a) An elephant with white skin (b) A costly thing
(c) A costly and useful thing (d) A costly but useless thing

25

Directions (Q. 1-4) *Choose one word which is similar in meaning to the key-word given in capital letters.* **[RRB Tech Trivendrum]**

(1) **BLITZ**
(a) Concentrated attack (b) News (c) Happiness (d) Fall

(2) **DROOP**
(a) Straight (b) Curved (c) Hanging down (d) Line

(3) **FALLACY**
(a) False opinion (b) Deep fall (c) Dream (d) Death

(4) **INFER**
(a) To conceive (b) To deduce (c) To attack (d) To take away

26

Directions (Q. 1-5) *: In the following questions, choose the word similar in meaning to given words given in capital letters :* **[RRB Ajmer]**

(1) **WORTH**
(a) Merit (b) Fright (c) Anger (d) Pity

(2) **TOUCHSTONE**
(a) Kill (b) Criterion (c) Precious (d) Roll

(3) **TRADUCE**
(a) Trade (b) Defame (c) Dance (d) Dunce

(4) **TRAIL**
(a) Drag (b) Defame (c) Dance (d) Die

(5) **SWATH**
(a) Envelop (b) Gallant (c) Blanket (d) Wholesale

27

Directions (Q. 1-5) *: Choose the word of words which is most nearly the same in meaning given in capital letters :* **[RRB Guhati]**

(1) **ESTABLISH**
(a) Prove (b) Hold on (c) Removed (d) Set up

(2) **CONFERRED**
(a) Offered (b) Divulged (c) Damaged (d) Advised

(3) **COMMAND**
(a) Consolation (b) Order (c) Amendment (d) Assignment

(4) **POWER**
(a) Training (b) Electricity (c) Authority (d) Drive

(5) **ELEMENT**
(a) Prime (b) Component (c) Particle (d) Persons

28

Directions (Q.1-5) *: In following questions, choose from the alternatives a word which is similar in meaning to the word given in capital letters :* **[RRB Trivendrum]**

(1) **IMPROMPTU**
(a) Offhand (b) Unimportant (c) Unreal (d) Effective

(2) **RABBLE**
(a) Mob (b) Noise (c) Roar (d) Rubbish

(3) **TROUPE**
(a) Fast (b) Group (c) Medium (d) Energetic

(4) **MAYHEM**
(a) Jubilation (b) Havoc (c) Excitement (d) Defeat

(5) **TEPID**
(a) Hot (b) Warm (c) Cold (d) Boiling

29

Directions (Q. 1-5) *: To answer the following questions choose the alternative that is nearly opposite in meaning to the word given in capital letters :* **[MBA Entrance]**

(1) **LACONIC**
(a) Terse (b) Loquacious (c) Curt (d) Sagacious

(2) **RENEGADE**
(a) Traitor (b) Heretic (c) Loyalist (d) Fugitive

(3) **ADIPOSE**
(a) Corpulent (b) Glutinous (c) Thin (d) Oleaginous

(4) **PUTRID**
(a) Fresh (b) Rancid (c) Recondite (d) Choleric

(5) **VULGAR**
(a) Plebeian (b) Aristocratic (c) Impervious (d) Licentious

30

Directions (Q.1-15) *: Choose from the alternatives, provide a same in meaning for each of the following words given in capital letters :* **[RRB Secundrabad]**

(1) **BUSY**
(a) Active (b) Quiet (c) Secure (d) Bold

(2) **DENY**
(a) Negate (b) Differ (c) Disagree (d) Vary

(3) **GRIEF**
(a) Cheerful (b) Happy (c) Sorrow (d) Injury

(4) **FAITH**
(a) Cordial (b) Woe (c) Noble (d) Belief

(5) **CLEVER**
(a) Novel (b) Talented (c) Insane (d) Useful

(6) **GENEROUS**
(a) Friendly (b) Liberal (c) Cordial (d) Graceful

(7) **REGARD**
(a) Civil (b) Grateful (c) True (d) Respect

(8) **QUARREL**
(a) Rough (b) Secure (c) Dispute (d) Grief

(9) **SHELTER**
(a) Cover (b) Secure (c) Repose (d) Pity

(10) **WORSHIP**
(a) Yield (b) Retain (c) Adoration (d) Differ

(11) **UNHAPPY**
(a) Timid (b) Dispute (c) Agreeable (d) Sad

(12) **SUITABLE**
(a) Strong (b) Brief (c) Benefit (d) Fit

(13) **FAME**
(a) Reputation (b) Modesty (c) Right (d) Majestic

(14) **ABOLISH**
(a) Desert (b) Forsake (c) Eradicate (d) Perform

(15) **AFRAID**
(a) Rage (b) Frightened (c) Mean (d) Accuse

31

Directions (Q. 1-3) *: In each of the following questions four words are given below the numbered word. Choose the word/phrase which is most nearly similar in meaning to the numbered word given in capital letters :* **[RRB Mujaffarpur]**

(1) **INTEGRITY**
(a) Edifice (b) Honesty (c) Essence (d) Embodiment

(2) **MONUMENTAL**
(a) Upright (b) Indefinite (c) Confusing (d) Memorable

(3) **PLOY**
(a) Entrance (b) Composure (c) Device (d) Investigation

32

Directions (Q. 1-4) *: Choose the word which is most opposite in meaning of the word given in capital letters.* **[BPO]**

(1) **FOLLY**
(a) Right (b) Exact (c) Mistake (d) Action
(e) Wisdom

(2) **HEIGHTEN**
(a) Widen (b) Decrease (c) Strengthen (d) Dissolve
(e) Disappear

(3) **LETHARGIC**
(a) Immobile (b) Indolent (c) Unpleasant (d) Irresponsible
(e) Hyperactive

(4) **DRAWS**
(a) Pushes (b) Extracts (c) Spends (d) Replenishes
(e) Recharges

33

Directions (Q. 1-5) *: In the following questions choose the word or words which is closest in meaning to the keyword or words given in capital letters :* **[RRB Clerk Bhopal]**

(1) **CONSOLE**
(a) Comfort (b) Control (c) Sole of a container (d) Sole of self

(2) **PERSONNEL**
(a) Belonging to oneself (b) Belonging to one person
(c) Group of persons (d) Staff employed in an institution

(3) **ON PURPOSE**
(a) Deliberate (b) Selfish (c) For one's self (d) Biting one's aim

(4) **HUE AND CRY**
(a) Desperate (b) With discovered (c) Sad (d) Public outcry

(5) **INVINCIBLE**
(a) Unseen (b) Undiscovered (c) Defeated (d) Unconquerable

34

Directions (Q. 1-5) *: Select the word which is most nearly the same in meaning to the word given in capital letters :* **[RRB Mumbai]**

(1) **DEMISE**
(a) Result (b) Default (c) Death (d) Apprehension

(2) **DISPARITY**
(a) Distaste (b) Dissimilarity (c) Criticism (d) Distinction

(3) **FORUM**
(a) An Assembly (b) Place Of Public Discussion
(c) An Application (d) Rss

(4) **DISMANTLE**
(a) Take Apart (b) Destroy (c) Shatter (d) Upset

(5) **CURTAIL**
(a) Decorate (b) Celebrate (c) Cut Short (d) Deprive

35

Directions (Q. 1-5) : *Choose the correct antonym of the words given in capital words, out of the four choices given in capital letters :* **[RRB Chandigarh]**

(1) **ADAGE**
(a) Motto (b) Harangue (c) Proverb (d) Heresy

(2) **COMPLIANCE**
(a) Condone (b) Clamour (c) Resistance (d) Condense

(3) **EXHILARATE**
(a) Depress (b) Elate (c) Ambiguous (d) Serene

(4) **GRUESOME**
(a) Disgusting (b) Attractive (c) Grisly (d) Stern

(5) **MACABRE**
(a) Gruesome (b) Attractive (c) Splendour (d) Trash

36

Directions (Q. 1-4) : *In the following questions choose the alternative which is opposite in meaning to the word given in capital letters :* **[RRB Non-Tech Bhopal]**

(1) **INCLEMENT**
(a) Pleasant (b) Stormy (c) Feeble (d) Dignified

(2) **AFFECTATION**
(a) Hypocrisy (b) Simplicity (c) Antipathy (d) Harmony

(3) **LATENT**
(a) Apparent (b) Dormant (c) Ample (d) Illegal

(4) **VANITY**
(a) Humility (b) Pride (c) Ostentation (d) Pity

37

Directions (Q. 1-10) : *Choose the word which is opposite in meaning to the word given in capital letters:* **[RRB Calcutta]**

(1) **VENERATE**
(a) Accuse (b) Abuse (c) Criticise (d) Defame

(2) **CAPACIOUS**
(a) Changeable (b) Limited (c) Caring (d) Foolish

(3) **DOUR**
(a) Cheerful (b) Active (c) Young (d) Radical

(4) **WRATH**
(a) Solace (b) Delight (c) Peace (d) Cheer

(5) **DEFIANCE**
(a) Obedience (b) Suspicion (c) Dismay (d) Anxiety

(6) **VAGUE**
(a) Known (b) Published (c) Popular (d) Definite

(7) **CROWDED**
(a) Empty (b) Lonely (c) Deserted (d) Barren

(8) **CONVENE**
(a) Adjourn (b) Contact (c) Dissolve (d) Postpone

(9) **DORMANT**
(a) Ancient (b) Modern (c) Permanent (d) Active

(10) **SHAME**
(a) Exaltation (b) Glory (c) Dignity (d) Enshrine

38

Directions (Q. 1-2) *: Choose the word which is most opposite in meaning to the word given in capital letters :* **[RRB Telecom Bhopal]**

(1) **VISIONARY**
(a) Pragmatic (b) Practical (c) Realist (d) Pragmatist

(2) **INFALLIBLE**
(a) Unreliable (b) Dubious (c) Untrustworthy (d) Erring

39

Directions (Q. 1-2) *: In questions 1 and 2 choose the correct antonym of the words given in capital letters :* **[RRB Chandigarh]**

(1) **ANONYMOUS**
(a) Desperate (b) Expert (c) Known (d) Written

(2) **CURTAIL**
(a) Lengthen (b) Shorten (c) Entail (d) Close

40

Directions (Q. 1-2) *: Choose the correct antonym of the key word from the four alternative to the word given in capital letters :* **[RRB Tech Trivendrum]**

(1) **VICE**
(a) False (b) Fool (c) Wrong (d) Virtue

(2) **PRIDE**
(a) Jealously (b) Prestige (c) Humility (d) Pride

41

Directions (Q. 1-5) *: In the following questions, choose the word or phrase which is opposite in meaning to given word in capital letters :* **[RRB Ajmer]**

(1) **CRYPTIC**
(a) Tomblike (b) Secret (c) Famous (d) Candid

(2) **CLOUDY**
(a) Shadowy (b) Murky (c) Ominous (d) Illuminating

(3) **CURB**
(a) Encourage (b) Discourage (c) Repress (d) Restrain

(4) **CURTAIL**
(a) Shortened (b) Enlarged (c) Robust (d) Active

(5) **CONFESS**
(a) Grant (b) Conceal (c) Concede (d) Acknowledge

42

Directions (Q. 1-6) *In this section each item consists of a word or a phrase which is underlined in the sentence given. It is followed by four words or phrases. Select the word or phrase which is closest to the opposite in meaning or the underlined word or phrase :* **[CDS]**

(1) An obscure traveller was found dead on the road.
(a) A decent (b) An affluent (c) A famous (d) A respectable

(2) We have carefully studied your explanation and it sounds plausible.
(a) incoherent (b) unconvincing (c) undesirable (d) impertinent

(3) Only a pragmatic approach to these problems can solve them.
(a) practical (b) diplomatic (c) theoretical (d) idealistic

(4) In the olden days the prisoners were kept in dark and dank cells.
(a) small (b) old (c) dry (d) dingy

(5) My father is a very stern man.
(a) liberal (b) emotional (c) indulgent (d) lenient

(6) The pleasures of life are eternal.
(a) brief (b) transient (c) occasional (d) periodical

43

Directions (Q. 1-5) *: In the following questions, choose the word opposite in meaning to the word given in capital letters :* **[RRB Trivendrum]**

(1) **EQUANIMITY**
(a) Resentment (b) Dubiousness (c) Duplicity (d) Excitement

(2) **DENSITY**
(a) Rarity (b) Intelligence (c) Clarity (d) Brightness

(3) **DEFIANCE**
(a) Anxiety (b) Obedience (c) Suspicion (d) Dismay

(4) **BASE**
(a) Climax (b) Height (c) Top (d) Roof

(5) **PATCHY**
(a) Attractive (b) Uniform (c) Simple (d) Clear

44

Directions (Q. 1-4) *: Choose the word which is most nearly opposite in meaning to the word given in capital letters :* **[RRB (ASM) Patna]**

(1) **CLANDESTINE**
(a) Dim (b) Clear (c) Open (d) Congested

(2) **ONEROUS**
(a) Light (b) Tough (c) Heavy (d) Dark

(3) **LACKADAISICAL**
(a) Dull (b) Sensible (c) Hopeful (d) Enthusiastic

(4) **TURGID**
(a) Fair (b) Rough (c) Tall (d) Smooth

45

Directions (Q. 1-10) Choose from the alternatives provided an antonym (opposite in meaning) for each of the words given in capital letters : **[RRB Secundrabad]**

(1) **ABOVE**
(a) Retreat (b) Shallow (c) Deep (d) Below

(2) **ATTRACT**
(a) Differ (b) Deny (c) Repel (d) Exit

(3) **RISE**
(a) Rash (b) Smooth (c) Pride (d) Fall

(4) **INFERIOR**
(a) Shame (b) Superior (c) Senior (d) Narrow

(5) **PERMIT**
(a) Prohibit (b) Partly (c) Profane (d) Polite

(6) **SAINT**
(a) Complex (b) Polite (c) Sinner (d) Rough

(7) **MISER**
(a) Spiritual (b) Foreign (c) Villain (d) Spendthrift

(8) **FLOAT**
(a) Loose (b) Sink (c) Empty (d) Follow

(9) **CHEAP**
(a) Dull (b) Fair (c) Dear (d) False

(10) **COMMON**
(a) Rare (b) Light (c) Easy (d) Ugly

46

Directions (Q. 1-2) *: In each of the following sentences, four words phrases are given below the numbered word. Choose the word which is most nearly opposite in meaning to the numbered word given in capital letters :* **[RRB (ASM) Mujjafarpur]**

(1) **MOLEST**
(a) Evade (b) Abolish (c) Mislead (d) Inspire

(2) **PLENARY**
(a) Restricted (b) Confidential (c) Mysterious (d) Basic

47

Directions (Q. 1-5) *: Choose the word opposite in meaning to the word given in capital letters :* **[Stenographers Allahabad]**

(1) **ENMITY**
(a) Friendship (b) Agreement (c) Amity (d) Cooperation

(2) **FRUGAL**
(a) Charitable (b) Extravagant (c) Generous (d) Gaudy

(3) **PERILOUS**
(a) Innocuous (b) Healthy (c) Safe (d) Fine

(4) **VIVACIOUS**
(a) Languid (b) Open (c) Strong (d) Bright

(5) **OBVIOUS**
(a) Isolated (b) Celebration (c) Ancient (d) Illusion

48

Directions (Q. 1-5) *: Each of the following items contains a word given below, followed by four words or phrases. Select the word/ phrase most nearly opposite in meaning the the mumbled word given in capital letters :* **[RRB (ASM) Bhuvneshwar]**

(1) **ADAPTABLE**
(a) Adoptable (b) Flexible (c) Yielding (d) Rigid

(2) **BUSY**
(a) Occupied (b) Engrossed (c) Relaxed (d) Engaged

(3) **FLIMSY**
(a) Frail (b) Filthy (c) Firm (d) Flippant

(4) **RELINQUISH**
(a) Abdicate (b) Renounce (c) Possess (d) Deny

(5) **MOUNTAIN**
(a) Plain (b) Plateau (c) Precipice (d) Valley

49

Directions (Q. 1-5) : *Select the word which is most nearly opposite in meaning to the word given in capital letters :* **[RRB Mumbai]**

(1) **CONCISE**
(a) Wrong (b) Smooth (c) Precise (d) Wordy

(2) **LETHARGIC**
(a) Alert (b) Careless (c) Prudent (d) Promising

(3) **DISINTERESTED**
(a) Avid (b) Related (c) Opposed (d) Partial

(4) **ACQUIT**
(a) Disclose (b) Convict (c) Adjudge (d) Sentence

(5) **SCARE**
(a) Sacred (b) Transpire (c) Abundant (d) Excellent

50

Directions (Q. 1-4) *: Choose the word which is most nearly the same in meaning as the word given in capital letters :* **[Bank PO]**

(1) **VEXED**
(a) Annoying (b) Recurring (c) Unresolvable (d) Complex
(e) Dangerous

(2) **EVOLVE**
(a) Introduce (b) Start (c) Develop (d) Abandon
(e) Establish

(3) **REINFORCED**
(a) Strengthened (b) Re-examined (c) Replaced (d) Reconstructed
(e) Restructured

(4) **UNABATED**
(a) Unsympathetic (b) Unaltered (c) Unparalleled (d) Uncompromising
(e) Unexpected

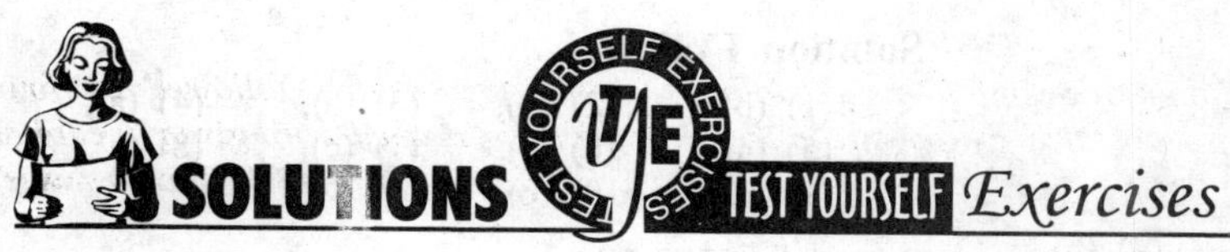

Solution TYE 1.

(1) (e), (2) (c), (3) (b), (4) (a),
(5) (d).

Solution TYE 2.

(1) (d), (2) (d), (3) (b), (4) (a),
(5) (b).

Solution TYE 3.

(1) (c), (2) (d), (3) (a).

Solution TYE 4.

(1) (d), (2) (d), (3) (e), (4) (c),
(5) (d), (6) (a), (7) (c), (8) (a),
(9) (c), (10) (c).

Solution TYE 5.

(1) (c), (2) (d), (3) (c), (4) (a),
(5) (d), (6) (c), (7) (d), (8) (b),
(9) (a), (10) (b).

Solution TYE 6.

(1) (b), (2) (b), (3) (d), (4) (c),
(5) (b).

Solution TYE 7.

(1) (b), (2) (b), (3) (e).

Solution TYE 8.

(1) (d), (2) (a), (3) (a), (4) (b),
(5) (c), (6) (a) (7) (c), (8) (b),
(9) (a), (10) (d).

Solution TYE 9.

(1) (b), (2) (a), (3) (c), (4) (c),
(5) (a).

Solution TYE 10.

(1) (d), (2) (a), (3) (b), (4) (b),
(5) (c).

Solution TYE 11.

(1) (d), (2) (a), (3) (a), (4) (b),
(5) (b). (6) (c), (7) (c), (8) (d),
(9) (a), (10) (d).

Solution TYE 12.

(1) (d), (2) (c), (3) (a).

Solution TYE 13.

(1) (b), (2) (c). (3) (b), (4) (a),
(5) (a).

Solution TYE 14.

(1) (c), (2) (a), (3) (b), (4) (b),
(5) (c).

Solution TYE 15.

(1) (a), (2) (c), (3) (c), (4) (d),
(5) (b), (6) (c), (7) (b) (8) (d),
(9) (d), (10) (a)

Solution TYE 16.

(1) (b), (2) (c), (3) (c), (4) (a),
(5) (b).

Solution TYE 17.

(1) (d), (2) (a), (3) (c), (4) (c),
(5) (b), (6) (d), (7) (c), (8) (a),
(9) (a), (10) (e).

Solution TYE 18.

(1) (a), (2) (b), (3) (c), (4) (c),
(5) (b), (6) (c), (7) (d), (8) (c).

Solution TYE 19.

(1) (a), (2) (e), (3) (b), (4) (c),
(5) (d).

Solution TYE 20.

(1) (a), (2) (b), (3) (a), (4) (a),
(5) (c).

Solution TYE 21.

(1) exciting, (2) scene, (3) for, (4) clothes,
(5) likely.

Solution TYE 22.

(1) (d), (2) (a), (3) (c), (4) (b),
(5) (b), (6) (d), (7) (b) (8) (a),
(9) (d), (10) (a).

Solution TYE 23.

(1) (b), (2) (c).

Solution TYE 24.

(1) (d), (2) (d).

Solution TYE 25.

(1) (a), (2) (c), (3) (a), (4) (b).

Solution TYE 26.

(1) (a), (2) (b), (3) (b), (4) (a),
(5) (a).

Solution TYE 27.

(1) (d), (2) (a), (3) (b), (4) (c),
(5) (b).

Solution TYE 28.

(1) (a), (2) (a), (3) (b), (4) (b),
(5) (b)

Solution TYE 29.

(1) (b), (2) (c), (3) (c), (4) (a),
(5) (b).

Solution TYE 30.

(1) (a), (2) (a), (3) (c), (4) (d),
(5) (b), (6) (b), (7) (d), (8) (c),
(9) (a), (10) (c), (11) (d), (12) (d),
(13) (a), (14) (c), (15) (b).

Solution TYE 31.

(1) (b), (2) (d), (3) (c).

Solution TYE 32.

(1) (e), (2) (b), (3) (e), (4) (d).

Solution TYE 33.

(1) (a), (2) (d), (3) (a), (4) (d),
(5) (d).

Solution TYE 34.

(1) (c), (2) (b), (3) (b), (4) (b),
(5) (c).

Solution TYE 35.

(1) (d), (2) (c), (3) (a), (4) (b),
(5) (b).

Solution TYE 36.

1. (a), 2. (b), 3. (a), 4. (a).

Solution TYE 37.

(1) (b), (2) (b), (3) (a), (4) (a),
(5) (a) (6) (a), (7) (c), (8) (a),
(9) (d), (10) (c).

Solution TYE 38.

(1) (a), (2) (d).

Solution TYE 39.

(1) (c), (2) (a).

Solution TYE 40.

(1) (d), (2) (c).

Solution TYE 41.

(1) (d), (2) (d), (3) (a), (4) (b),
(5) (b).

Solution TYE 42.

(1) (c), (2) (b), (3) (c), (4) (c),
(5) (d),
(6) (b).

Solution TYE 43.

(1) (d), (2) (a), (3) (b), (4) (c),
(5) (b).

Solution TYE 44.

(1) (c), (2) (a), (3) (d), (4) (d).

Solution TYE 45.

(1) (d), (2) (c), (3) (d), (4) (b),
(5) (a), (6) (c), (7) (d), (8) (b),
(9) (c), (10) (a).

Solution TYE 46.

(1) (d), (2) (a).

Solution TYE 47.

(1) (a), (2) (b), (3) (c), (4) (a),
(5) (d).

Solution TYE 48.

(1) (d), (2) (c), (3) (c), (4) (c),
(5) (d).

Solution TYE 49.

(1) (d), (2) (a), (3) (d), (4) (b),
(5) (c).

Solution TYE 50.

(1) (a), (2) (b), (3) (c), (4) (d).

CHAPTER 44

HOMONYMS

Definition : Word similar in sound or pronunciation, but different in meaning, are called Homonyms.

English में ऐसे बहुत से शब्द हैं जिनका उच्चारण लगभग एक जैसा होता है, लेकिन उनके अर्थ में अन्तर होता है, ऐसे शब्दों को Homonyms or Homophones कहा जाता है। जैसे : Access, Excess, Affect, Effect इन शब्दों का उचित ज्ञान न होने पर एक की जगह पर दूसरे शब्द को लिखने से सब कुछ गलत हो जाता है अत: छात्रों को ऐसे शब्दों का बहुत ध्यानपूर्वक अध्ययन करना आवश्यक है। नीचे इस तरह के बहुत से शब्दों के बारे में बताया गया है।

(1) **Affect** (*to act upon, to pretend* प्रभाव डालना) She affects too much innocence.
The drought affected a large part of the district.
Effect (*Result*–प्रभाव) Internet produces a bad effect on the young generation.

(2) **Adapt** (*accomodate*-व्यवहार) One should adapt oneself to the new circumstances.
Adept (*expert*-निपुण) He is an adept in Folk dance.
Adopt (*take up*-गृहण करना) One should not adopt unfair means to secure good marks.

(3) **Addition** (*putting more*–जोड़ना) I am to buy two more copies in addition to this one.
Edition (*printing books*) The first edition of this book has sold like hot cakes.

(4) **Accede** (*Agree*–स्वीकार करना) He will not accede to your request.
Exceed (*to be greater*–बढ़ना, बढ़ाना) Write an essay not exceeding three hundred words.

(5) **Access** (*approach,* reach–पहुँच) Now-a-days, every person has an easy access to the temples irrespective to his caste.
Excess (*more than enough*–अधिकता) Excess of everything is bad.

(6) **Accept** (*to take*–स्वीकार करना) He cannot accept this gift.
Except (*leaving out*–बजाय) Except Nisha everyone was present in the party.

(7) **Alter** (*change*–बदलना) You cannot alter my opinion about her.
Altar (*place of offering*—वेदी) (a) S.C. Bose sacrificed everything at the altar of freedom.
(b) In India incense is burnt at the altar in temples.

(8) **Antic** (*odd, strange*–अपरिचित) His behaviour on yesterday was antic.
Antique (*ancient*–प्राचीन) I am fond of collecting antique items.

(9) **Assay** (*attempt*–प्रयास, *testing the purity of metals*–धातुओं की शुद्धता की जाँच)
(1) He assayed hard to secure top position.
(2) He assayed the gold ornaments.
Essay (*a piece of composition*–निबन्ध) Write a brief essay on 'Indian Films'.

(10) **All ready** (*all are ready*–सभी तैयार) They were all ready to welcome the groom.
Already (*earlier*–पूर्व में) I have already informed him.

(11) **Allusions** (*indirect reference*– अप्रत्यक्ष संकेत) The poem is full of allusions.
Illusion (*a deceptive show*–मृगतृष्णा) Indian mythology regards the material world as an illusion.

(12) **Apposite** (*proper*–योग्य) His arguments were not apposite to the subject.
Opposite (*contrary*–विपरीत, *in front of*) His house is opposite to the college.

(13) **Assent** (*agreement*–स्वीकारोक्ति)He gave his assent to the new proposal.
Ascent (*going up*–ऊपर चढ़ना) He pushed the button and the elevator began its slow ascent.

(14) **Arc** (*part of circle*–चाप) If a straight line is drawn in a circle it will divide it into two arcs.
Ark (*covered floating vessel*–ढका हुआ जहाज) He crossed the Black Sea with his family in an ark.

(15) **Aloud** (*high volume*–ऊँचा स्वर) I can't hear you well, please speak aloud.
Allowed (*permitted*–इजाजत दी) He was allowed to enter.

(16) **Angle** (*an angle of degree* कोण) This is a ninety degree angle.
Angels (*a divine messenger*–फरिश्ता) Angels reside in heaven while men reside on Earth.

(17) **Advice** (*noun*–सलाह) I need your expert advice in this matter.
Advise (*verb*–सलाह देना) Please advise me in this matter.

(18) **Amiable** (*lovable*–प्यार योग्य) She is not only a beautiful but also an amiable girl.
Amicable (*friendly*–मित्रवत्) Finally they came to an amicable settlement.

(19) **Ail** (*to be ill*–बीमार होना) What ails the Industry is to be sorted out?
Ale (*a drink*–शराब) He has gone to the ale-house.

(20) **All together** (*in a body*–साथ-साथ) Let us move there all together.
Altogether (*completely*–पूर्णतया) It seems altogether impossible to cross the river in the night.

(21) **Ad** (*short form of advertisement*) He has given an ad in the newspaper.
Add (*short for addition*) Add two to three.
Aid (*to assist*–सहायता करना) He has given aid of ₹ 5000/- to the poor family.
Aide (*an assistant*) He is a close aide to the Prime Minister.

(22) **Aerie** (*eagle's nest*–घोंसला) There is an aerie on this tree.
Airy (*breezy*–हवादार) The house is quite airy.

(23) **Aisle** (*walkway*–रास्ता)

(a) An aisle is a long narrow gap that people can walk along between rows of seats in a public building such as a church or between rows of shelves in a super market.

(b) The aisle is also used in expressions such as walking down the aisle to refer to the activity of getting married.

I am in no hurry to walk down the aisle.

Isle (*island*–द्वीप) I have seen many isles, but this is the best isle.

(24) **All** (*everything*–सब) He has donated all his property.
Awl (*a small pointed tool for pricking or piercing holes, esp. such a tool used by shoemakers*– औजार)

(25) **Ate** (*past tense of eat*–खाया) He ate two apples.
Eight (*the number base of octal, seven, eight, nine*-आठ) I have eight pens.

(26) **Auger** [(*a drill (tool*–औजार)] I need an auger to make a hole.
Augur (*foretell*–भविष्य कहना) The recent communal riots do not augur well for the smooth running of government.

(27) **Aural** (*of hearing*–सुनने सम्बन्धित) He became famous as an inventor of astonishing visual and aural effects)
Oral (*of the mouth*–मौखिक) He presented his ideas in a nice way orally.

(28) **Auricle** (*External part of the ear*–कान का बाहरी हिस्सा)
Oracle (*seer*–श्रेष्ठ) He regards himself as an oracle on architecture.

(29) **Away** (*distant*–दूर) Do not go far away from the house.
Aweigh (*just clear of the bottom*)

(30) **Awed** (*in a state of wonder*–चकित) Awedly she was unable to recall his name.
Odd (*not usual*) Find the odd word from the following passage.

(31) **Aye** (*Aye means yes*–हाँ) used in some dialects of British English.
Do you remember your first day at school?' 'Oh aye. Yeah.'
Eye (*ocular organ*–आँख) Her eyes are very beautiful.

(32) **Bale** (*package*–गाँठ) I received thirty bales of cotton last month.
Bail (*security*–जमानत) The magistrate didn't grant him bail in theft case.

(33) **Berth** (*sleeping place in train*–ट्रेन में बर्थ) I have booked two berths in Shatabadi Express.
Birth (*coming to life*–जन्म)This is not the birth place of Buddha.

(34) **Bare** (*uncovered*–नंगा, बिना ढका) He came here bare footed.
Bear (*to tolerate*–सहन करना) I cannot bear your insulting remarks.
(*an animal*–रीछ) There are three bears in that circus.
Beer (*a kind of wine*–बीयर) I prefer to take beer.

(35) **Blow** (*to whistle*–बजाना) A cool wind is blowing. Don't blow the whistle.
Below (*underneath*–नीचे) Hitting below the belt is not allowed.

(36) **Born** (*to take birth*–जन्म) My wife was born in 1960.
Borne (*supported*–सहन किया) He is suffering from water borne disease.

(37) **Bad** (*not good*–बुरा) He is a bad man.
Bed (*sleeping place*–बिस्तर) I go to bed at 11 P.M.

(38) **By** (*assistance*–द्वारा) A snake was killed by Ram with a stick.
Buy (*purchase*–खरीदना) I want to buy a car.

(39) **Beet** (*a vegetable*–चुकन्दर) I prefer mango to beet.
Beat (*to thrash*–पीटना) It is wrong to beat the students with a stick.

(40) **Borrow** (*to take loan*–उधार लेना) I have borrowed some money from Bank.
Burrow (*a hole in earth*–छेद) A mouse lives in this burrow.

(41) **Cell** (*a small cottage*–छोटी कोठरी) There are more than twenty cells in that prison.
Sell (*to dispose off*–बेचना) He sells fruits and vegetables.
Sale (*noun-act of selling*–बिक्री) I have purchased this dress from that shop.

(42) **Beach** (*shore*–किनारा) Many people like to walk along the sea beach.
Beech (*a kind of tree*–पेड़) There are many beech trees near the railway station.

(43) **Brake** (*lever*–ब्रेक) I am going to get the brake wire changed.
Break (*to make a part*–तोड़ना) Can you break this stick with your hands?

(44) **Bow** (*bend*–झुकना) Let us bow to our motherland India.
Bough (*a branch of tree*–टहनी) Many birds are sitting on the bough of the tree.

(45) **Bridal** (*pertaining to marriage*–शादी से सम्बन्धित) She is looking beautiful in her bridal dress.
Bridle (*reins*–लगाम) It is not easy to bridle a vicious horse.

(46) **Baron** (*a landlord*–जमींदार) There was a time when all powers rested in the hands of rich barons.
Barren (*not fertile*–अनुपजाऊ) In barren land you can't cultivate any thing.

(47) **Blue** (*a colour*–नीला) I like blue colour.
Blew (*whistled*–बजाई) The refree blew the whistle again and again.

(48) **Bait** (*food placed on a hook or in a trap to entice fish*) Let your bait falls gently upon the water.
Bate (*to lessen*–कम करना) We listened with bated breath the stories of grandmother's travel.

(49) **Bald** (*hairless*–गंजा) She is bald headed.
Balled (*carnal knowledge*) He picked up the sheets of paper and balled them tightly in his fists.
Bawled (*cried aloud*–जोर से पुकारना) Someone in the audience bawled out 'Once More'.

(50) **Band** (*a group*–समूह) A band is a group of musician.
Banned (*forbidden*–प्रतिबन्धित) Drinking is banned in Gujarat.

(51) **Bard** (*a poet*–कवि) People sometimes refer to William Shakespeare as the Bard.
Barred (*enclosed by poles*–घेरना) The windows were closed and shuttered and the door was barred.

(52) **Basal** (*forming the base*–आधार बनाना) The basal layer of the skin was also torn.
Basil (*an herb*–तुलसी) Basil is used in cooking also.

(53) **Base** (*the bottom support for anything*—आधार) The base of the bottle is very narrow.
Bass (*the lowest musical pitch or range*–धीमी आवाज)
A bass is also a man with deep singing voice.

(54) **Bask** (*to warm oneself pleasantly*–गर्म करना) Crocodiles bask on the small sandy beaches.
Basque (*tight fitting bodice or tunic*–कसे हुए कपड़े) She was advised to wear basque.

(55) **Baud** (*bits per second*) A unit of data transmission speed equal to one information unit per second.
Bawd (*brothel manager*–करनी) She is the bawd of that brothel.

(56) **Beau** (*male friend*–मर्द मित्र) A woman's beau is her boy friend or lover.
Bow (*a curve or bend*–मुड़ा हुआ) He bowed slightly for taking her bag.

(57) **Bell** (*ding ding*–घंटी) Don't try to bell the cat.
Belle (*beautiful woman*–सुन्दर स्त्री) She was the belle in last night party.

(58) **Besot** (*to get drunk*–नशे में होना) He became so besotted with her that even he forgot his children.
Besought (*past tense of beseech*) She besought him to cut his drinking and reduce his smoking.

(59) **Better** (*superior*–अच्छा) It is always better to drive carefully.
Bettor (*one who bets*–जुंआरी) The person who bets is called a bettor.

(60) **Bight** (*the loop of a rope*–रस्सा) is called bight.
Bite (*a mouthful*–गुस्सा) You can have a bite of chocolates.
Byte (*eight bits*–बइट) Byte is a unit of storage in computers.

(61) **Bloc** (*an alliance*–मित्रगण) A bloc is a group of countries which have similar aims and interest and that generally act together over some issue.
Block (*a block in a town is an area of land with streets on all its sides*–घरों की पंक्ति) She walked four blocks down High Street.

(62) **Boar** (*wild pig*–जंगली सुअर) We can find wild boars in the valleys .
Boer (*a South African of Dutch descent*) He is a boer.
Boor (*tasteless buffoon*–स्वादरहित) If we refer someone as a boor, we think his behaviour and attitude rough and rude.
Bore (*not interesting*–अरुचिकर) He bored me all through the meal with stories of the army life.

(63) **Bode** (*an omen*) She says the way bill was passed bodes ill for the democracy.
Bowed (*curved*–मुड़ा हुआ) He has bowed legs bold brave.

(64) **Bole** (*trunk*–पेड़ का धड़) He was standing behind the bole of a tree.
Bowl (*dish*–बर्तन) Put all the soup in a large bowl.

(65) **Boos** (*disparaging sounds from audience*–आवाज) Demonstrators booed and jeered him.
Booze (*whisky*–ह्विस्की) I have five empty bottles of booze.

(66) **Bough** (*tree branch*–पेड़ की टहनी) I rested my fishing rod against a pine bough.
Bow (*front of a ship; respectful bend*–जहाज का उगता भाग) I gave a theatrical bow and waved.

(67) **Bra** (*brassiere*–पहनने की ब्रा) She wears beautiful coloured bra.
Braw (*well-groomed*–तैयार करना) He always keeps himself in braw shape.

(68) **Braid** (*A narrow piece of twisted thread or cloth used to decorate clothes*)
He was wearing a coloured uniform with lots of gold braid.
Brayed (*a donkey cried*–गधे की आवाज) The donkey brayed and tried to bolt.

(69) **Braise** (*cook with oil and water*–पकाना) I like braised cabbage.
Brays (*loud, harsh cry of donkey*–गधे की आवाज) A donkey is braying.

(70) **Bread** (*a loaf*–रोटी) Bread is necessary for the living.
Bred (*past tense of breed*–नस्ल का भूतकाल) He is an ill bred fellow.

(71) **Brewed** (*fermented*–शराब बनाना) I like nicely brewed beer.
Brood (*family*–परिवार, सोचना) A brood is a group of baby birds that were born at the same time to the same mother.
If someone broods over something they think about it a lot seriously.

(72) **Bruise** (*an injury*–चोट) How did you get that bruise on your cheek?
Brews (*making beer*–बीयर बनाना) I brew my own beer.

(73) **Broach** (*to raise a subject*–शास्त्रार्थ करना) At last I broached the subject of her early life.
Brooch (*an ornament fastened to clothes which has a pin at the back*)
I have five brooches.

(74) **Brows** (*multiple foreheads*–भौंहें) Your brows on your forehead.
Browse (*grazing*–चरना) Three red deer were browsing near my lodge.

(75) **Burger** (*meat sandwich*–बर्गर) I do not like eating burger.
Burgher (*merchant*–व्यवसायी) The burghers of a town are the people who live there especially the richer or more respectable people.

(76) **But** (*excepting*–लेकिन) He is but a good man.
Butt (*the thick end*–मोटा सिरा) A number of cigarette butts are lying there.

(77) **Buyer** (*one who purchases*–खरीदार) Only a prospective buyer can purchase this house.
Byre (*a cow barn*–गौशाला) A byre is a cowshed.

(78) **Check** (*to verify, to stop*–जाँचना) He checked my passport. He checked me from leaving the function.
Cheque (*bank document*–चेक) I issued a cheque favouring P.N.B.

(79) **Calendar** (*chart showing dates etc*–कलैण्डर) I have only one calendar in my office.
Calender (*to press paper, cloth etc.*–प्रेस करना) Please calender my dress.

(80) **Cannon** (*big gun*–तोप) A cannon of ancient time is placed near the railway station.
Canon (*rule*–सिद्धान्त) He believes in canons of justice.

(81) **Canvas** (*a kind of rough cloth*–तिरपाल) My shoes are made of canvas.
Canvass (*to solicit votes*–वोट माँगना) Now-a-days students are busy in canvassing for their friends.

(82) **Casual** (*accidental, occasional*–आकस्मिक) I was granted only one day casual leave.
Causal (*showing cause*–कारण बनाने वाला) There is a causal link between balanced diet and sound mind.

(83) **Corpse** (*dead body*–लाश) The corpse was covered with a white bedsheet.
Corps (*a body of troops*–सेना की टुकडी) I want to join National Cadet Corps.

(84) **Coma** (*state of senselessness*–बेहोशी) The patient has been in coma since Monday.
Comma (*mark of punctuation*–कोमा) One should be careful about proper use of comma.

(85) **Cession** (*to yield*–छोड़ना) India should not have made a cession of an inch of its land for the establishment of Pakistan.
Session (*sitting of assembly or court*–सत्र) The winter session of Parliament will be over tomorrow.

(86) **Censer** (*a pot in which incense is burnt*–यज्ञ की वेदी) Place some incense into the censer.
Censor (*an official* examination–सेंसर) The Censor Board has awarded 'U' certificate to this film.
Censure (*criticize adversely*–निन्दा) His conduct was censured by the Parliament.

(87) **Chord** (*a string of musical instrument*–तार) He is playing with the chords of the violin.
Cord (*a thin rope*–रस्सी) I need a fifteen fit cord for packing the luggage.

(88) **Cease** (*discontinue*–छोड़ना) He resigned and thus, ceased to be the Chairman of our society.
Seize (*to catch*–पकड़ना) Heroin worth 2 lacks rupees was seized from his office.
Siege (*surrounded*–घेरना) Akbar's army sieged the castle of Chittorgarh.

(89) **Career** (*profession*–व्यवसाय) For better career opportunities, join computer courses.
Carrier (*one who carries*–ले जाने वाला) Mosquitoes are carriers of virus.

(90) **Coarse** (*rough*–खुरदरा) Do not use a coarse cloth to clean the glasses.
Course (*line of action*–कार्य की दिशा) A disciplined course of action is required to achieve success.

(91) **Collision** (*clashing*–टकराना) In a collision between train and bus, three persons died on the spot.
Collusion (*secret agreement for an evil plan*–षड्यन्त्र) He planned to execute a robbery in collusion with the clerk.

(92) **Cloth** (*unstitched cloth*–बिना सिले कपड़े) I want to purchase cloth for a shirt and a trousers.
Clothe (*stitched cloth*–सिले हुए कपड़े) I have given my clothes to washerman for drycleaning.

(93) **Capital** (*centre of administration*–राजधानी) Delhi is the capital of India.
Capitol (*roman temple of Jupiter, US Congress House*–एक बिल्डिंग का नाम)
A meeting of US Congress be held in capitol tomorrow.

(94) **Defy** (*challenge*–चुनौती) One should not defy the orders of one's superiors.
Deify (*worship a God*–ईश्वर की तरह पूजना) Mr. M.K. Gandhi is defied by all Indians.

(95) **Complacent** (*self satisfied*–सन्तुष्ट)He seems complacent with his job and earning.
Complaisant (*polite*–नम्र) He is a man of very complaisant nature.

(96) **Complement** (*which completes*–पूरक) Husband and wife are complementary to each other.
Compliment (*regards*–अभिनन्दन) Please convey my best compliments to your parents.

(97) **Cautious** (*aware*–जागरूक) I am quite cautious of his activities.
Conscientious (*careful, scrupulous*–धार्मिक आस्था) My mother is very hard working, sincere and conscientious lady.

(98) **Council** (*assembly*–सदन) He was nominated to the Council of State .
Counsel (*advice*–सलाह) He counsels in a right way.

(99) **Credible** (*believable*–विश्वास योग्य) He is not a credible person.
Creditable (*worthy of praise*–प्रशंसनीय) His achievements are indeed creditable.

(100) **Cymbal** (*a musical instrument*–मंजीरा) I like the melodious sound of the Cymbal.
Symbol (*sign*–चिन्ह) What is the symbol of 2004 Olympic Games?

(101) **Current** (*present*–वर्तमान, ताजा) What is the current news?
Currant (*dried grapes*–किशमिश) I am fond of currants.

(102) **Cite** (*speak*–कहना) He cited the example of bravery of Maharana Pratap.
Site (*location*–स्थान) In my opinion this site for the departmental store is commercially viable.
Sight (*view*–दृश्य) (*vision*–दृष्टि) It was a pitiable sight.
Get your eyesight checked at the earliest.

(103) **Caste** (*Community*–जाति) He belongs to schedule caste.
Cast (*to give*–देना) Please cast your votes in favour of me.

(104) **Cattle** (*animal*–पशु) Cattle were grazing in the field.

Kettle (*vessel*–पतीली) Put the kettle on the gas burner.

(105) **Corporal** (*pertaining to body*–शारीरिक) Corporal punishment are banned now-a-days in all schools and colleges.

Corporeal (*bodily*–शरीर सम्बन्धित) God has no corporeal existence.

(106) **Cache** (*hidden storage*–कोई वस्तु या चीज छिपाना) A huge arms cache was discovered by police.

Cash (*legal tender*–नकद) I do not accept cash, but cheque.

(107) **Canter** (*a moderate gallop*–कदम चाल) When a horse canters, it moves at a speed that is slower than a gallop but faster than a trot.

Cantor (*singer*–गायक) An official who sings liturgical music and leads prayer in a synagogue is called cantor.

(108) **Carat** (*unit of weight for precious stones, equal to 200 milligrams*)

Caret (*proofreader's insertion mark*–छुटा हुआ शब्द दिखाने का चिन्ह)

Carrot (*edible orange root*–गाजर) Carrot contains aburdent iron.

Karat (*one-24th part of otherwise pure gold*–24वाँ भाग या पूर्ण सोना)

(109) **Carol** (*christmas song*–गाना) Carols are Christian religious songs that are sung at Christmas day.

Carrel (*study enclosure*–अध्ययन कक्ष) A small enclosure or study in a cloister.

(110) **Cause** (*generative force*–कारण) Smoking is the biggest preventive cause of death.

Caws (*sounds of crows* कौओं की आवाज) When a crow caws it makes a loud sound.

(111) **Cent** (*one hundredth of a dollar*–डॉलर का सौवाँ हिस्सा)

Scent (*an aroma*–सुगन्ध) I like the aroma of freshly baked bread .

Sent (*dispatched*–भेजा) I have sent you a packet of wool.

(112) **Cents** (*hundredths of a dollar*–डॉलर का सौवाँ हिस्सा) A dollar has hundred cents.

Scents (*many things to smell*–सुगन्ध) Flowers are chosen for their scent as well as their look.

Sense (*physical abilities of sight, smell, hearing, touch and taste*–चेतना)

She has a good sense of humour.

(113) **Cere** (*waxy fleshy covering at the base of the upper beak in some birds*–पक्षियों में चोंच का निचला हिस्सा)

Sear (*to sear something means to burn its surface with a sudden intense heat*–झुलसाना)

Grass fires have seared the land near the farming village .

Seer (*a prophet*–महान) A seer is a person, who foretells about the future.

(114) **Chalk** (*calcareous earthy substance*–चाक) He writes on the board with a chalk.

Chock (*wedge to keep wheels from rolling*–रोक) The small roads are chock a block with traffic.

(115) **Chard** (*spinach-like vegetable*–सब्जी) She is fond of chard.

Charred (*burnt*–जलकर खाक हो जाना) In the fire broke out yesterday seven persons were charred to ash.

(116) **Chased** (*quickly followed*–पीछा करना) I chased the thief for 100 yards.

Chaste (*virginal*–पवित्र) If you describe a person or their behaviour as chaste, you mean that they do not have sex with anyone or they only have sex with their husband or wife.

(117) **Chews** (*masticating*–चबाना) Chew your food well and eat slowly.

Choose (*to select*–चुनना) They will be able to choose their own leader through election.

(118) **Chile** (*a South American country*–एक देश) Keshav is living in Chile.
Chilli (*dried pod of red pepper*–मिर्ची) Chillies are used in cooking.
Chilly (*uncomfortably cool*–अत्यधिक ठण्डा) It was a chilly night.

(119) **Choir** (*church singers*–गायक) A choir is a group of people who sing together for example *in a church or school.*
Quire (*the twentieth part of a ream of paper*–कागज की रीम का बीसवाँ हिस्सा)

(120) **Collar** (*around your neck*–कॉलर) The collar of this shirt has worn out.
Choral (*music sung by a choir*–गीत) His collection of choral music is very large and wonderful.
Coral (*a hard substance formed from the bones of very small sea animals*–मूँगा)
Corral (*a space surrounded by a fence where cattle or horses are kept*–तबेला)

(121) **Clack** (*a chattering sound*–आवाज) The windshield wipers clacked back and forth.
Claque (*a group hired to applaud, sycophants*–प्रशंसक) Whenever our team scored a goal the claque made a superb clappings which further boosted the spirit of the team.

(122) **Claus** (*fat, jolly guy with presents*–सांताक्लॉज) Santa Claus comes to town on every Christmas.
Clause (*clause is a group of words*–शब्द समूह) Containing a verb, contractual unit.
Claws (*big fingernails*–पंजा) The cat tried to cling to the edge by its claws.

(123) **Click** (*ticking noise*–क्लिक करना) You can check your e-mail with a click of your mouse.
Clique (*exclusive group*–अलग समूह) Clique is a group of people that spend a lot of time together and seem unfriendly towards people who are not in the group.

(124) **Climb** (*ascending*–चढ़ना) He climbed up the stairs.
Clime (*climate*–वातावरण) She left Britain for the sunnier climes of Southern France.

(125) **Coal** (*black mineral*–कोयला) A number of families even today use the coal for cooking.
Cold (*opposite to warm*–ठण्डा) I like tea neither too hot nor too cold.

(126) **Coax** (*persuade*–बहलाना) The government coaxed them to give up their strike by promising them some temporary benefits.
Cokes (*more than one soft drink*–रूपये पदार्थ) Several kinds of cokes were available in the party.
Cocks (*more than one male bird*–मुर्गे) I have two beautiful cocks.
Cox (नाव में अधिकारी) In a rowing boat, the cox is the person, who gives instructions to the rowers.

(127) **Coddling** (*tenderly treating*–स्नेहपूर्ण व्यवहार) She coddled her younger daughter madly.
Codling (*small, unripe apple*–छोटे सेब) is also called codling.

(128) **Conch** (*shellvish*–शंख) A conch is a shellfish with a large shell.
Conk (*blow to the head*–जोर की ध्वनि) The dynamo conked out so we have no electricity.

(129) **Coo** (*a soft murmuring sound*–धीमी आवाज) 'Isn't she beautiful?' he cooed.
Coup (*a successful stroke*–सच्चा आघात) He was sentenced to death for his part in the coup.
Copes (*gets along with adversity*–मुकाबला करना) It was amazing how my mother coped with bringing up three children on less than ₹ one thousand a month.
Copse (*a stand of trees*–पेड़ों की पंक्ति) A copse is a small group of trees growing very close to each other.
Cops (*police officers*–पुलिस अधिकारी) I do not like the cops standing near my house.

(130) **Creak** (*a short high pitched sound*–तेज ध्वनि) The door creaked open by the storm.

Creek (*small stream*–जल की धारा) If someone is up the creek , he is in a difficult situation.

(131) **Desert** (*a waste track of land* –रेगिस्तान *noun, to forsked; verb* त्यागना) Churu is a desert area in Rajasthan. He has deserted his wife.

Dessert (*fruit served after dinner*–भोजन के बाद फल आहार) The dessert course after dinner was liked by all.

(132) **Decry** (*to cry down*–निन्दा करना) The Iraq policy of US Government is decried by Indian Government.

Descry (*to see dimly*–दूर से देखना) Across the river you can descry a hut near the palm tree.

(133) **Dye** (*a verb-to colour*-रँगना) Dye my shirt in sky blue .

Die (*expire*–मरना) He died from cholera.

(134) **Dose** (*quantity of medicine*–दवा की खुराक) I have already taken four doses of this medicine by now.

Doze (*sleep*–ऊँघना) You were dozing in the class yesterday.

(135) **Draught** (*a quantity of liquid*–तरल की मात्रा) The patient was given a draught of medicine.

Drought (*want of rain*–सूखा) Due to scanty rain whole of the district is in the grip of drought.

(136) **Dam** (*surrounding area to stop flow of water*–बाँध) A dam is being built up here to storage the rainy water.

Damn (*condemn*–निन्दा) His behaviour is damned by all the members of the society.

(137) **Dear** (*loving*–प्रिय) He is my very dear friend.

Deer (*an animal*–हरिण) I saw many deer in that forest.

(138) **Deduce** (*draw conclusion*–नतीजा निकालना) You can't deduce such a conclusion of the discussion.

Deduct (*to take something*–कम करना) Deduct cash discount 3% and make the payment by tomorrow.

(139) **Deference** (*respect*–आदर) I treat my elders with due deference.

Difference (*dissimilarity*–अन्तर) There was a difference of opinion on this point.

(140) **Decent** (*good*–बढ़िया) Because of his decent behaviour he was promoted to the post of General Manager.

Descent (*coming down*–नीचे उतरना) That hill has a steep descent to the south.

Dissent (*to differ*–मतभेद) He recorded his dissent on this proposal.

(141) **Device** (*noun-plan*–योजना) He used all devices to popularise the game.

Devise (*verb—to plan*–योजना बनाना) You are to devise a plan to increase the turn over.

(142) **Duel** (*a fight between two*–दो के बीच युद्ध) There was a duel between Dara Singh and Kingkong.

Dual (*double*–दोहरा) Dual system of governance is a bad governance.

(143) **Disease** (*illness*–रोग) Malaria is a curable disease.

Decease (*death*–मृत्यु) The sudden decease of his father forced him to abandon his studies.

(144) **Dam** (*holds back water*–बाँध) Government is building a dam on this river.

Damn (*a curse*–शाप देना) Don't be flippant , damn it! This is serious.

(145) **Darn** (*to mend*–रफ़ू करना) She is darning the old socks to wear in winter.

Darne (*a fish steak*) He had a darne with his lunch.

(146) **Dine** (*to eat*–खाना) He dines alone most nights.

Dyne (*unit of energy*–ऊर्जा मापने की इकाई) Three dyne energy is needed to pull this pump.

(147) **Dire** (*desperate*–भयानक) He was in dire need of hospital treatment.
Dyer (*one who dyes*–रँगने वाला) Ram is working in the firm of drycleaners as dyer.

(148) **Do** (*an auxiliary in grammar*–करना) They do not know me. Do come tomorrow again.
Doe (*a female deer*–मादा हरिण) There are several does in the forest.
Dough (*uncooked bread*–साना हुआ) Roll out the dough into one large circle.
Dos (*part of computer operating system*) He is learning DOS now-a-days.

(149) **Done** (*completed*–पूर्ण करना) I have done my job.
Dun (*something that is dun is a dull grey-brown colour.*)

(150) **Eruption** (*bursting out*–फूटना) There was an eruption of Volcano near Gujarat border.
Irruption (*invasion*–आक्रमण) The irruption of Mughals destroyed the glory of Rajput empire.

(151) **Emerge** (*to come out*–बाहर आना) He emerged successfully out of the miserable circumstances.
Immerge (*to plunge into*–डूबना) He is immerged in mythological thoughts.

(152) **Eminent** (*distinguish*–विशिष्ट) Indira Gandhi was an eminent politician.
Imminent (*impending*–तुरन्त) Indian army is ready to face any imminent attack of Pakistan.

(153) **Eligible** (*fit to be chosen*–योग्य) He is eligible for the post.
Illegible (*that which cannot be read*–अपठनीय) His writing is illegible.

(154) **Earn** (*to come to deserve*–कमाना) Companies must earn a reputation for honesty.
Urn (*a jar*–बर्तन) An urn is a container, in which a dead person's ashes are kept.
An urn is a metal container used for making a large quantity of tea or coffee and keeping it hot.

(155) **Elude** (*to escape from*–बचाना) He eluded the police for ten years.
Allude (*refer*–इशारा करना) She also alluded to her rival's post marital troubles.

(156) **Epic** (*a narrative poem or story*–काव्य) Like 'Gone with the wind' it's an unashamed epic romance.
Spoch (*a noteworthy period in history*–ऐतिहासिक काल) The birth of Christ was the beginning of a major epoch of world history.

(157) **Eunuchs** (*a castrated male person*–हीजड़ा) In India eunuchs are turning to politics.
Unix (*operating system*–ऑपरेटिंग सिस्टम) Unix is a operating system in computers.

(158) **Ewe** (*female sheep*–मादा भेड़) A ewe is an adult female sheep.
Yew (*a type of tree*–पेड़) is a evergreen tree which has sharp leaves.
You (*the second person*–तुम) Where are you going?

(159) **Eyelet** (*small hole for laces*–छोटे छिद्र) My shoes have eight eyelets.
Islet (*small island*–छोटा द्वीप) An islet is a small island.

(160) **Ere** (*before*) Take the water ere the clock strikes four.
Err (*to make a mistake*) If you make a threat be sure to carry it out if he errs again.
Heir (*one who will inherit*) The younger prince was declared heir to the throne.

(161) **Facility** (*ease,* opportunity–सुविधा) Facility of STD is also available in this hotel.
Felicity (*happiness*–प्रसन्नता) True felicity can't be enjoyed by a dishonest man.

(162) **Foul** (*unfair*–अनुचित) One can't achieve true success through foul means.
Fowl (*a bird*–पक्षी) He is fond of fowl's meat.

(163) **Find** (*to get*–पाना) Go there you will find a tree near the river.
Fined (*to charge*–जुर्माना) The court fined him ₹ 20000 for the offence.

(164) **Floor** (*surface*–फर्श) Clean the floor with dettol and water.
Flour (*wheat meal*–आटा) He has a flour mill.

(165) **Forth** (*onward*–आगे आना) He alone came forth to assist that poor lady .
Fourth (*third-fourth*–चौथा) April is the fourth month of the year.

(166) **Farther** (*more distant*–दूर) Delhi is farther from Alwar in comparison to Jaipur.
Further (*next*-आगे) Please settle the case without any further delay.

(167) **Faint** (*to swoon*–बेहोश होना) She fainted after taking wine yesterday .
Feint (*pretension*–दिखावा) She made a feint of reading the books.

(168) **Fain** (*gladly*–खुशी से) She would fain on seeing me.
Feign (*pretend*–दिखावा) When his boss scolded him, he feigned as a deaf.

(169) **Fair** (*pure, a show*–पवित्र, मेला) I believe in using fair means to achieve the target.
Let us go to the fair.
Fare (*passage money*–किराया) A strike was called by the truckers demanding hike in minimum fare.

(170) **Feat** (*an exploit*–साहसिक कार्य) A racing car is an extraordinary feat of engineering.
Feet (*plural of foot*–पाँव) Do not put your feet on the table.

(171) **Forego** (*go before*–पहले जाना) We have already discussed this point in foregoing lessons.
Forgo (*to let go*–त्याग देना) I cannot forgo my rights.

(172) **Fairy** (*imaginary magic person*–जादूगर) Fairies are often represented as small people with wings.
Ferry (*river-crossing boat*–छोटी नाव) They crossed the river by ferry.

(173) **Fey** (*whimsical*–सनकी) If you describe someone as fey, you mean that they behave in a shy, childish or unpredictable way and you are often suggesting that this is unnatural or insincere. Her fey charm and eccentric ways were legendary.
Fays (*more than one fairy*–एक से अधिक जीव)

(174) **Faze** (*to stun*–आश्चर्य) He was fazed to see such a big hall.
Phase (*a part of the sequence*–कला) The crisis is entering a crucial phase.

(175) **Ferrate** (*a salt containing iron and oxygen*)
Ferret (*a domesticated polecat*–छोटी बिल्ली) A ferret is a small fierce animal which is used for hunting rabbits and rats.

(176) **Feted** (*celebrated*–कार्य करने वाला) If someone is feted , they are celebrated, welcomed or admired by the public.
Fetid (*stinking*–बदबूदार) Fetid water or air has a very unplesant smell.

(177) **Few** (*not many*–थोड़ा) I gave a dinner party for a few close friends.
Phew (*expression of relief*) Phew, what a relief, I am feeling now!

(178) **File** (*a folder for holding papers*–फाइल) Please put this paper in a file.
Phial (*a small glass bottle*–छोटी बोतल) A phial is a small tube shaped glass bottle used to hold medicine.

(179) **Finish** (*to complete*–समाप्त) I will finish my work by tomorrow.
Finnish (*from Finland*–फिनलैण्ड के निवासी) Finnish is the language spoken in Finland.

(180) **Flair** (*verve, talent*–प्रवृत्ति) If you have a flair for a particular thing , you have a natural ability to do it well.
Flare (*to spread*–बढ़ाना) Camp fire flares like beacons in the dark.

(181) **Flea** (*parasitic insect*–मक्खी) A flea feeds on the blood of humans or animals.
Flee (*to run away*–भाग जाना) He tried to flee from the sight, but he was caught.

(182) **Flecks** (*many tiny specks*–छोटा धब्बा जैसा) His hair is dark grey with flecks of ginger.
Flex (*to bend*–मोड़) He slowly flexed his muscles and tried to stand.

(183) **Flew** (*past tense of fly*–उड़ायी) He flew many kites yesterday.
Flu (*short for influenza*–बुखार) I got flu day before yesterday.
Flue (*chimney pipe*–चिमनी पाइप) The flue of the chimney required to be changed.

(184) **Floe** (*sheet of floating ice*–तैरती बर्फ की परत) Ice floe is a large area of ice floating in the sea.
Flow (*to glide along*–बहाना) A stream flowed gently down into the valley.

(185) **For** (*in place of*–के लिए) It is enough for me.
Fore (*in front*–सामने) There is no direct damage in the fore part of the ship.
Four (*number after three*–चार) I have four pens.

(186) **Frees** (*releasing*–छोड़ना) He frees the bird from the cage.
Freeze (*very cold*–ठण्डा) The trees are damaged by a freeze in December.
We want the government to freeze the prices.
Frieze (*a wall decoration*–दीवार सजाने की वस्तु) A frieze is a decoration high up on the walls of a room or just under the roof of a building. It consists of a long panel of carving or a long strip of paper with a picture or pattern on it.

(187) **Friar** (*a monk*–तपस्वी) He is a friar.
Fryer (*a utensil*–बर्तन) A fryer is a type of deep pan which is used to fry food in hot oil.

(188) **Gild** (*thin coating of metal*–धातु का पत्तर चढ़ाना) Gilded ornaments look more beautiful than the original.
Guild (*group of same profession*–संघ) Now-a-days all the workers have organised themselves into guilds.

(189) **Gage** (*security*–जमानत) I do not lend without sufficient gage.
Gaze (*to look attentively*–एकटक देखना) She stood gazing at herself in the mirror.

(190) **Gait** (*manner of walk*–चाल) That model girl has a graceful and sexy gait.
Gate (*large door*–दरवाजा) You should not enter through the main gate.

(191) **Goal** (*aim*–उद्देश्य) To achieve this goal you are to work hard.
Gaol (*jail*–जेल) He has been to gaol earlier also.

(192) **Gaff** (*a barbed spear*–भाला) A gaff is a pole with a point or hook at one end, which is used for catching large fish.
Gaffe (*a stupid mistake*–मूर्खतापूर्ण गलती) He made an embarrassing gaffe at the convention last weekend.

(193) **Galley** (*ship's kitchen*–जहाज की रसोई) The galley of this ship is well maintained and full of eatables.
Gally (*to frighten or terrify*–डराना) He tried to gally the child with a mask of demon.

(194) **Gilt** (*gold-plated*–धातु की परत चढ़ा हुआ) This is a gilt ornament.
Guilt (*culpable*–दोषी) You aren't convinced of Mr. Charles guilt.

(195) **Gnawed** (*chewed*–चबाना) He gnawed his long fingernail .
Nod (*head tilting*–सिर हिलाना) "Are you fine?" I asked. She nodded and smiled.

(196) **Gnu** (*african deer*–अफ्रीकन हरिण) I saw a Gnu in the zoo.
Knew (*past tense of know*–जाना) He knew me well.
New (*not old*–नया) What is new in the market ?

(197) **Gored** (*pierced by an animal's horns*) He was gored to death in front of his family.
Gourd (fleshy fruit with hard skin–फल) I like gourd very much.

(198) **Gorilla** (*large ape*–गोरिल्ला) Gorilla has long arm, black fur and a black face.
Guerrilla (*irregular soldier*–अनियमित सिपाही) The guerrillas threatened to kill their hostages.

(199) **Grade** (श्रेणी) What grade are you going to get?
Grayed (turned gray–ग्रे रंग) I like grayed colour walls.

(200) **Graft** (*to attach*–जोड़ना) The top layer of skin has to be grafted onto the burns.
Gaphed (*plotted*–ग्राफ बनाना) You can see a graphed diagram of the progress made by the country in population control.

(201) **Grate** (*a lattice*–जाली) A grate is a framework of metal bars in a fireplace, which holds the coal or wood. A wood fire burned in the grate.
Great (*extremely good*–बड़ा, महान्) Gandhi was a great man.

(202) **Grill** (*to sear cook*–पकाना) A grill is a flat frame of metal bars on which food can be cooked over fire. Place the omellete under agentle grill.
Grille (*an iron frame work*–लोहे की जाली) The door has no grille.

(203) **Groan** (*a long low sound uttered in pain* –कराहना) He opened his eyes and he began to groan with pain.
Grown (*has gotten larger*–बड़ा, बढ़ना) Dad, I am a grown woman. I know what I am doing.

(204) **Guise** (*appearance*–दिखना) She presented her dance in the guise of a rabbit.
Guys (*man*–व्यक्ति) Hi, guys! How are you doing?

(205) **Hail** (*frozen rain*–ओले) It is hailing. It hailed yesterday.
Hale (*healthy*–स्वस्थ) May God keep you hale and healthy!

(206) **Horde** (*a gang*–समूह) A horde of mischievous students attacked the shop keepers.
Hoard (to store–एकत्र करना) Hoarding of sugar beyond the prescribed limit is an offence.

(207) **Hair** (बाल) She has black hair.
Heir (*successor*–उत्तराधिकारी) He is an heir apparent to the throne.

(208) **Hurt** (*injury*–चोट) Your comments can hurt her feelings.
Hart (*a male deer*–हिरण) I have a beautiful pair of harts.
Heart (*an organ in the body*–दिल) He is suffering from heart disease.

(209) **Humane** (*kind*–दयालु) UNO has advised the member countries to meet out humane treatment to Prisoners of war.
Human (*pertaining to mankind*–मनुष्य से सम्बन्धित) You will find almost the same human nature everywhere.

(210) **Heel** (*part of shoe*–जूते की एड़ी) The heels of my shoe are pinching.
Heal (*to cure*–अच्छा होना) This medicine will help you in quick healing.

(211) **Hole** (*a burrow*–छेद) A serpent lives in this hole.
Whole (*complete*–सम्पूर्ण) He ate whole of the breakfast.

(212) **Hall** (*a large room*–बड़ा कमरा) He has hired a hall for the concert.
Haul (*a*–उठाना) If you haul something which is heavy or difficult to move, you move it using a lot of effort. A crane had to be used to haul the car out of the stream...(b) If someone is hauled before a court or someone in authority, they are made to appear before them because they are accused of having done something wrong.
He was hauled before the managing director and fired.

(213) **Hammock** (*rope bed*–रस्सी वाली खाट) A hammock is a piece of strong cloth or netting which is hung between two supports and used as a bed.
Hummock (*low, rounded hill*–छोटी पहाड़ी) A hummock is a small raised area of ground, like a very small hill.

(214) **Hangar** (*garage for airplanes*–हवाई जहाज रखने का स्थान) Some repairing is going on in the hangar of the airport.
Hanger (*from which things hang*–लटकाने वाला) I want to purchase a coat hanger.

(215) **Ho** (*an expression of admiration or surprise*–हो-हो) Ho ! you are here.
Hoe (*a garden tool*–औजार) Today he is hoeing in the vineyard.

(216) **He'll** (*contraction of 'he will'*) He'll come tomorrow.
Hill (*smaller than a mountain*–छोटी पहाड़ी) There is a temple on that hill.

(217) **Hear** (*to listen*) I hear his voice.
Here (*at this location*–यहाँ) Come here.

(218) **Heard** (*listened to*–सुनना) I heard a strange sound yesterday in the night.
Herd (*a group of animals*–भीड़) They are individuals. They will not follow the herd.

(219) **Hi** (*greetings*–हाय) "Hi Luis", she said.
High (*way up*–ऊँचा) I looked down from the high window.

(220) **Heroin** (*narcotic*–अफीम) Heroin is a powder drug.
Heroine (*female hero*–एक्ट्रेस) My favourite heroine is Ash.

(221) **Hew** (*to chop*–काटना) He fell, peeled and hewed his own timber.
Hue (a colour–रंग) The same hue will look different in different light.

(222) **Higher** (*farther up*–अपेक्षाकृत ऊँचा) He has gone to USA for higher studies.
Hire (*to employ*–किराए पर लेना) Cars are available for hire.

(223) **Him** (*pronoun*–उसका) I know him.
Hymn (*religious song*–धार्मिक गीत) I like singing hymns.

(224) **Hoard** (*store*–एकत्र करना) They have begun to hoard food and sugar .
Horde (*a great many people*–भीड़-भाड़) This attracted hordes of tourists to Las Vegas.

(225) **Hoarse** (*rough voice*–कर्कश ध्वनि) His voice is hoarse.
Horse (*equine*–घोड़ा) He has a black horse.

(226) **Hold** (*to grip*–पकड़ना) Hold the bucket please.
Holed (*full of holes*–छिद्रदार) The wall seems to be holed by a drill.

(227) **Holy** (*with religious significance*–पवित्र) Ayodhya is a holy place for the Hindus.
Wholly (*completely*–पूर्णतया) This approach for the urban area is wholly inadequate.

(228) **Hostel** (*inexpensive lodging for travelers*–छात्रावास) He is living in the college hostel.
Hostile (*unfriendly*—दुश्मनी) Pakistan has not yet changed its hostile attitude towards India.

(229) **Idle** (*indolent*–निकम्मा) An idle man can't make any progress.
Ideal (*visionary*–आदर्श) My teacher, Mr. Shrivastava, is an ideal for me.
Idol (*an image of a deity*–मूर्ति) A section of the Hindus believe in idol worship.

(230) **Ingenious** (*clever*–चतुर) He is an ingenious engineer.
Ingenuous (*simple*–सीधा) His ingenuous attitude is liked by all .

(231) **Incite** (*to provoke*–उत्तेजित करना) His arrogant behaviour incited me a lot.
Insight (*a clear vision*–स्पष्ट देखना) Do you know the insight story of this murder?

(232) **Indite** (*to compose*–रचना) Though he indited the letter carefully, yet it was not liked by the chairman.
Indict (*to accuse*–दोषारोपण करना) He was indicted for theft and murder.

(233) **In** (*expressing inclusion*–में) He is in the room.
Inn (*hotel*–होटल) This is a well maintained inn.

(234) **Inc.** (*short for incorporated*) Inc. is an abbreviation for 'Incorporated' when it is used after a company's name.
Ink (*writing fluid*–स्याही) I have an ink pen.

(235) **It's** (*contraction of 'it is'*) It's a large hotel.
Its (*possessive pronoun*) I know its true position.

(236) **Jealous** (*envious*–ईर्ष्या) He is not liked by anybody because of his jealous nature.
Zealous (*enthusiastic*–उत्साही) She is very zealous about her new book.

(237) **Jewel** (*precious stone*–जवाहरात) This watch contains many jewels.
Joule (*unit of energy measure*–ऊर्जा की इकाई) In Physics joule is a unit of energy or work.

(238) **Juggler** (*one who juggles*–जादूगर) He is a good juggler.
Jugular (*artery to head*–सर की नस)
(a) A jugular or jugular vein is one of the three important veins in your neck that carry blood from your head back to your heart.
(b) If you say that someone went for the jugular, you mean that they strongly attacked another person's weakest points in order to harm him.

(239) **Naughty** (*mischievous*–शैतान) She is a naughty girl.
Knotty (*difficult*–कठिन) This was indeed a knotty problem.

(240) **Knap** (*crest of a hill; break with a hammer*–तोड़ना) We unfurled the flag at the knap of the hill at 6.30 P.M. He knapped the glass box to uncountable pieces.
Nap (*a short sleep*–झपकी) You should use your lunch hour to have a nap in your chair.

(241) **Knead** (*working bread dough*–गुंदना) He kneaded the mixture on a floured surface.
She felt him knead the aching muscles.
Need (*must have*–आवश्यकता) He needs your help.

(242) **Knight** (*chivalrous man*–बहादुर) He was knighted on the queen's birthday.
Night (*darkness*–रात) Night comes after day.

(243) **Knit** (*interlocking loops of yarn*–बुनना) She has already started knitting baby sweators.
Nit (*louse egg*–जूं के अण्डे)
(a) Nits are the eggs of insects called lice which live in people's hair.
(b) If you refer to someone as a nit, you think they are stupid or silly. You'd rather leave the business than work with such a nit.

(244) **Knob** (*handle*–हैंडल का सिरा) He turned the knob and pushed against the door.
Nob (*rich person*–धनी व्यक्ति) The nobs, who live in that big house are very generous.

(245) **Knock** (*to rap*–ठोकना) Someone had knocked him unconscious. I heard a knock at the front door.
Nock (*a notch in an arrow*–तीर का सिरा जैसा) A V shape cut or indentation in an edge or across a surface.

(246) **Knot** (*fastening in cord*–गाँठ) He tied a knot at the end of the lace.
Naught (*or nought is zero*–शून्य) Sales rose by naught point four percent last month.
Not (*negation*–नहीं) He was not present in the party.

(247) **Know** (*to possess knowledge*–जानना) I know him.
No (*negation*–नहीं) I have no pen.

(248) **Knows** (*only the shadow knows*–जानना) Everyone knows about Mahatma Gandhi.
Nose (*plain as the nose on your face*–नाक) Clean your nose daily.

(249) **Lightening** (*make lighter*–हल्का करना) We had appealed to the court for lightening the punishment, but of no avail.
Lightning (*electric discharge in clouds*–बिजली चमकना) There was occasional lightning in the sky last night.

(250) **Loath** (*unwilling*–इच्छा के विरुद्ध) Nothing loath he did, as he was saying.
Loathe (*to dislike greatly*–घृणा करना) I loathe her dressing pattern and arrogant way of talking.

(251) **Latter** (*antonym of former*–बाद में आने वाला) Between Ram and Shyam, the latter (Shyam) is a diligent student.
Later (*comparative of late*–देरी से आने वाला) He came later than his friend.

(252) **Lose** (*to part with*–खोना) Where did you lose your briefcase?
Loose (*to slack*–ढीला करना) He was wearing a loose cotton shirt.

(253) **Lesson** (*chapter*–पाठ) Learn your lesson well.
Lessen (*to make less*–कम करना) Even this medicine has not lessen my pain.

(254) **Last** (*antonym to first*–अन्तिम) Bahadur Shah was the last emperor of India.
Latest (*superlative of late*–ताजा) She always prefers latest design clothes.

(255) **Lacks** (*does not have*–नहीं होना) He lacks the judgement and political acumen for the post of General Manager.
Lax (*loose discipline*–अनुशासन में कमी) One of the point of contention is the lax security for the airport personnel.

(256) **Lain** (*past tense of lay or lie*–लेटना) He has lain there for sometime.
Lane (*narrow road*–गली) Shyam lives at the end of the lane.

(257) **Lam** (*headlong flight*–भागना) If someone is on the lam or if they go on the lam, they are trying to escape or hide from someone such as the police or an enemy.
He was on the lam for seven years.
Lamb (*baby sheep*–भेड़ का बच्चा) A lamb is a young sheep.

(258) **Lay** (*to recline*–समपंण) Lay a sheet of paper on the floor.

Lei (*a flower necklace*–फूलों का हार) A garland made of flowers, feathers, shells etc, often given as a symbol of affection.

(259) **Lea** (*a meadow*–सूत की लम्बाई) They live in a hut constructed in the lea.

Lee (*a sheltered position*–सुरक्षित स्थिति) The lee of a place is the shelter that it gives from the wind or bad weather.

Lease (*rented*-किराए पर) She leased out her bungalow at a good rent.

(260) **Leach** (*a dish consisting of sliced meat, eggs, fruits and spices in jelly etc* खाने की डिश)

Leech (*sucking parasite*–छोटा जन्तु)

(a) A leech is a small animal which looks like a worm and lives in water. Leeches feed by attaching themselves to other animals and sucking their blood.

(b) If you describe someone as a leech, you disapprove of them because they deliberately depend on other people, often making money out of them.
They're just a bunch of leeches cadging off others .

(261) **Leak** (*accidental escape of liquid*–रिसना) The roof is leaking.

Leek (*variety of onion*–प्याज) I like leek vegetables.

(262) **Lean** (*angle of repose*–झुकना) They stopped to lean over the gate.

Lien (*a claim on property*–अधिकार) Please mark my lien over the property.

(263) **Liar** (*tells falsehoods*–झूठा) He is a liar and a cheat.

Lyre (*stringed instrument*–यन्त्र) A lyre is a stringed instrument that looks like a harp.

(264) **Lichen** (*a fungus*–एक प्रकार का पौधा) Lichen is a group of tiny plants like moss and grows on the surface of things such as rocks, trees and walls.

Liken (*to compare*–तुलना करना) If you liken one thing or person to another thing or person , you say that they are similar. The pain is often likened to being drilled through the side of the head.

(265) **Lie** (*an untruth*–झूठ) He is telling a lie.

Lieu (*instead*–बजाय) He gave his T.V. to the landlord in lieu of rent.

(266) **Loo** (*british toilet*–ब्रिटिश टायलेट) I asked if I could go to the loo.

Lou (*short for Louis*) Where has Lou gone so early.

Low (*not high*–नीचा) He put it down on the low table.

(267) **Limb** (*tree branch*–पेड़ की शाखा) The entire structure was hanging from the limb of an enormous leafy tree. She would be able to stretch out her cramped limbs for some time.

Limn (*illuminate*–चमकना) His face was limned in the dim glow from the match.

(268) **Links** (*pieces of chain*–चैन के टुकड़े) I have no links with that man.

Lynx (*a lynx is a wild animal similar to a large cat*–बड़ी बिल्ली जैसा)

(269) **Literal** (*taking words in their primary sense*–वास्तविक) He was saying no more than the literal truth.

Littoral (*having to do with the shore*–किनारा) In Geography the littoral means the coastal.

(270) **Load** (*cargo*–सामान) I have just loaded my truck up.

Lowed (*a cow mooed*–रम्भाना) The cow lowed in agony.

(271) **Loan** (*allow to borrow*–ऋण) She has taken loan from a bank.

Lone (*by itself*–अकेला) He was shot by a lone gunmen.

(272) **Loch** (*a lake*–नहर) A loch is a large area of water that is almost surrounded by land.
Lock (*a security device*–ताला) I need a good lock .

(273) **Loot** (*ill-gotten gains*–लूटना) The troule began when the students began the looting of shops.
Lute (*stringed instrument*–यन्त्र) A lute is a stringed instrument with a rounded body that is quite like a guitar and is played with the help of fingers.

(274) **Lumbar** (*lower part of back*–पीठ का नीचे का हिस्सा) Lumbar support is very important if you are driving along way.
Lumber (*dimensional wood*–लकड़ी) Noun: It was made of soft lumber. Verb : He turned and lumbered back to his chair.

(275) **Meat** (*flesh*–मांस) I don't like eating meat.
Meet (*to assemble*–मिलना) She came here only to meet me.

(276) **Mead** (*meadow*–चरागाह) I met a beautiful girl in the meads yesterday.
Meed (*reward*–प्रतिफल) Kalidas has got a universal meed of praise.

(277) **Metal** (*iron, brass etc.*–धातु) Silver is a white metal.
Mettle (*spirit, courage*–साहस) Our leaders have no mettle to fight against corruption.

(278) **Metre** (*poetic rhythm*–छन्द) Can you tell me in what metre Shelley's 'Skylark' is written?
Meter (*a measuring instrument =100 cm.*, –मीटर) One meter is equal to hundred centimetres.

(279) **Minor** (*underage*–छोटा) Minors are not allowed to open current account in Banks.
Miner (*one who works in mine*–खान पर काम करने वाला) He is a miner, works in a coal mine.

(280) **Moat** (*a ditch surrounding a castle*–खाई) There is a bridge over the moat near main gate.
Mote (*a particle of dust*–धूल का कण) You cannot see small mote by naked eyes.

(281) **Monetary** (*pertaining to money*–मुद्रा सम्बन्धित) Have you any book on monetary theory?
Monitory (*giving advice*–सलाह देना) He acted against the monitory advise of his friends and so failed.

(282) **Male** (*opposite to female*–पुरुष) A male candidate can't be posted against the post reserved for a woman.
Mail (*post*–डाक) Have you received my mail ?

(283) **Mite** (*small thing*–अल्प मात्रा) He contributed his mite for the service of mankind.
Might (*strength*–शक्ति Your might will be tested in battle against the foreign power.
Might (*past of may*–सकना) He told me that he might come to attend the function.

(284) **Marry** (*to get married*–विवाह करना) I want to marry your sister.
Merry (*joyous*–आनन्द करना) Don't lose heart and be merry.

(285) **Main** (*chief*–मुख्य) Ramesh is the main culprit in the bank robbery case.
Mane (*long hair of an animal's neck*–गर्दन के बाल) His horse had a fine mane.

(286) **Marshal** (*a military officer*–मार्शल) He is a marshal of the court.
Martial (*war like*–युद्ध जैसा) He has martial spirit and courage to fight in odd circumstances.

(287) **Maize** (*corn*–मक्का) I like to eat maize cake.
Maze (labyrinth–घुमाव) This castle has many hidden mazes.

(288) **Mach** (speed of sound–ध्वनि की गति) Mach is used as a unit of measurement in stating the speed of a moving object in relation to the speed of sound. for example, if an aircraft is travelling at Mach 1, it is travelling at exactly the speed of sound.
Mock (parody–व्यंग्य) I thought you were mocking me.

(289) **Made** (*accomplished*–बनाया) The table is made of wood.
Maid (*young woman*–नौकरानी) She is our maid-servant.

(290) **Mall** (*a large shopping area*–शापिंग की जगह)
Maul (*savage*–क्रूर) He had been mauled by a tiger.
Moll (*gangster's girlfriend*–लड़की मित्र) She is the moll of the don.

(291) **Manner** (*method*–तरीका) I am a professional and I have to conduct myself in a professional manner. She smiled in a friendly manner.
Manor (*lord's house or a large private house*–बड़ा व्यैक्तिक घराना) The thieves broke into the manor at night.

(292) **Marc** (*coarse brandy*–ब्रांडी) I don't like the taste of marc.
Mark (*a sign*–निशान) He made some peculiar marks with a pen.

(293) **Marquee** (*a rooflike projection over a theatre entrance*–बड़ा टैंट)
(a) A marquee is a large tent which is used at a fair, garden party or other outdoor event, usually for eating and drinking in.
(b) A marquee is a cover over the entrance of a building, *for example* a hotel or a theatre.
Marquis a nobleman ranking between a duke and a count.

(294) **Marshal** (*to organise*–संयोजक) He was marshalling the teachers and other officials, showing them where to go.
Martial (*warlike*–पुत्र समान स्थिति) The newspapers were banned during martial regime.

(295) **Massed** (*grouped together*–समूह) He could not escape the massed ranks of newsmen.
Mast (*sail pole*–जहाज का मस्तूल) The mast of a boat are the tall upright poles that support its sails.

(296) **Mews** (*stables*–अस्तबल) The house is in a secluded mews.
Muse (*creative inspiration*–प्रेरणा)
(a) Noun : Once she was a nude model and muse to French artist Henri.
(b) Verb : (Think) Many scholars muse on the role of President in Indian polity.

(297) **Mince** (*chop finely*–टुकड़े करना) I'll buy lean meat and mince it myself.
Mints (*aromatic candies*–सुगन्धित खाद्य) Mint is a herb with fresh tasting leaves.

(298) **Mind** (*thinking unit*–मस्तिष्क) Mind your business, please.
Mined (*looked for ore*–खनिज कार्य) The pit was shut down because it hadn't enough that could be mined economically.

(299) **Missal** (*hymn book*– किताब) A book containing the service of the Mass for the whole year; loosely a Roman Catholic book of prayers.
Missile (*projectile*–मिसाइल) The football supporters began throwing missiles one of which it the captain of the rival team.

(300) **Mist** (*fog*–कोहरा) The mist made the flying impossible.
Missed (*not hit*–चूकना) He scored four of the goals but missed a penalty.

(301) **Moan** (*to groan*–कराहना) She gave a low choking moan and began to tremble.
Mown (*the lawn is freshly cut*–घास काटी) He has mown the lawn today itself.

(302) **Mood** (*emotional state*–मानसिक स्थिति) She is in a jolly mood today.
Mooed (*what the loquacious cow* did–गाय का रंभाना) When cattle especially cows moo, they make a long low sound that cattle typically make.

(303) **Moor** (*swampy coastland; to anchor*–रुकना, बाधन) I decided to moor near some tourist boats.
More (*additional*–अधिक) I need some more rice.

(304) **Moose** (*a large elk*–बड़ा हिरण) Moose are large type of deer have big flat horns.
Mousse (*dessert of whipped cream and eggs*) Mousse is a sweet light food made from eggs and cream.

(305) **Morning** (A.M.–प्रात:) I get up early in the morning.
Mourning (*remembering the dead*–मृतक हेतु मातम) On the death of Rajeev Gandhi, the whole of India was in the mourning.

(306) **Muscle** (*fibrous, contracting tissue*–मांसपेशी) He is doing a lot of exercises to keep his muscles strong.
Mussel (*mussels are a kind of shellfish that you can eat from their shells*–एक प्रकार की मछली)

(307) **Mussed** (*made messy*–गड़बड़ी) His clothes are all mussed up.
Must (*required*–आवश्यक) You must go there to get his support.

(308) **Mustard** (*spicy yellow sauce*–सरसों) This is fried in mustard oil.
Mustered (*assembled for roll call*–एकत्र होना) He travelled through out India to muster support for his movement.

(309) **Nice** (*good*–अच्छा) She is a nice and beautiful girl.
Niece (*daughter of brother*–भतीजी) I am going to attend the marriage of my niece positively.

(310) **Naval** (*pertaining to ships and the sea*–जहाज से सम्बन्धित) He is captain in naval forces.
Navel (*pertaining to the belly button*–नाभिक) There is a black mole near her navel.

(311) **Nay** (*no*–नहीं) The Rajya Sabha can merely say yea or nay to such a bill.
Neigh (*a horse's cry*–हिनहिनाना) The horse gave a loud neigh.

(312) **Our** (*plural of 'my'*–हमारा) This is our house.
Hour (*a period of time*–घण्टा) I have been waiting for you for half an hour.

(313) **Oar** (*used for rowing a boat*–नाव का डण्डा Life without aim is like a boat without an oar.
Ore (*mineral from which metal can be extracted*–खनिज) Iron is extracted from its ore by melting.

(314) **Ordinance** (*A rule*–अध्यादेश) The President has promulgated an ordinance for administering the minority community.
Ordnance (*Gun*–युद्ध सामग्री) There is an ordnance factory in Jamshedpur Bihar.

(315) **Oohs** (*informal*–ऊह) People say 'ooh' when they are surprised, looking forward to something or find something pleasant or unpleasant.
'Ooh dear me, that's a bit of a racist comment isn't it.'... 'Red? Ooh how nice.'
Ooze (बहना, निकलना) When a thick or sticky liqued oozes from something owhen something oozes the liquid flows slowly and in small quantities.
The lava will just ooze gently out of the crater...
The wounds may heal cleanly or they may ooze a clear liquid.

(316) **Overdo** (*carried to excess*–अधिक) It is important never to overdo new exercises.
Overdue (*past time for payment or some action*–देर) The meeting is long overdue.

(317) **Pray** (*entreat*–प्रार्थना) I pray to God everyday.
Prey (*hunt*–शिकार) Do not prey upon the innocent animals.

(318) **Principal** (*head of school or college–प्राचार्य*) Sh. R.C. Jha is the new Principal of our college.
Principle (*rule–सिद्धान्त*) Do you understand anything about the principles of justice?

(319) **Prophecy** (*noun-foretold–भविष्यवाणी*) It is his prophecy that America will not attack Iraq.
Prophesy (*verb—to foretell–भविष्यवाणी करना*) He prophesied that Iraq would attack Kuwait.

(320) **Proffer** (*offer–प्रस्ताव*) Many lucrative proposals were proffered to him for acceptance.
Prefer (*like–पसन्द*) I prefer coffee to tea.

(321) **Practice** (*noun–अभ्यास*) Practice makes a man perfect.
Practise (*verb—to practise*) Don't preach but practise.

(322) **Plain** (*easy, simple–साधारण*) One should try to write his thoughts in plain language.
Plane (*to smoothen, level–चमकदार करना*) I use cream to plane my hair.

(323) **Peel** (*to remove the skin–छीलना*) You cannot eat a banana without peeling it.
Peal (*sound of thunder or Bells–घंटियों की ध्वनि*) I am hearing peals of trumpets.

(324) **Pare** (*to trim–टुकड़े करना*) Pare your nails and then polish them.
Pair (*two–जोड़ी*) I have only three pair of shoes.

(325) **Peace** (*tranquility–शान्ति*) Peace of mind is more precious than the materialistic richness.
Piece (*fragment–टुकड़ा*) The dog found a piece of meat .

(326) **Price** (*value–कीमत*) What is the price of this shirt?
Prize (*reward–ईनाम*) She could not win any prize this time.

(327) **Persecute** (*to harass–परेशान करना*) Pakistani soldiers persecuted the Hindus in a cruel manner.
Prosecute (*to bring before a court–अभियोग चलाना*) He was prosecuted for murdering his wife.

(328) **Physic** (*medicine–दवा*) No physic can cure him of cancer.
Physique (*bodily fitness–शारीरिक बनावट*) He possesses an attractive physique.

(329) **Prescribe** (*to direct–निर्देश देना*) The doctor has prescribed three doses of medicine after four hours daily.
Proscribe (to banish–देश निकाला देना) The minister was proscribed by the king.

(330) **Patrol** (*going round–गश्त लगाना*) A chowkidar was patrolling at the main gate.
Petrol (*oil–पकठ–पेट्रोल*) Petrol is required to run vehicles.

(331) **Popular** (*Familiar–लोकप्रिय*) Rajeev Gandhi was a very popular leader.
Populous (*Thickly inhabited–आबादी वाला*) Delhi is a highly populous city.
Pail (*Bucket–बाल्टी*) I have two pails full of water.
Pale (*Yellowish appearance–पीला*) On seeing a lion , his face turned pale.

(332) **Paced** (*Measured by footsteps–कदम*) This excellent thriller is fast paced and in unbelievable.
Paste (*Thick glue–चिपकाना*) I need a tooth paste.

(333) **Pain** (*It hurts–दर्द*) I felt a sharp pain in my lower back.
Pane (*A single panel of glass–पैनल*) The left pane of this window required change.

(334) **Pair** (*A set of two–जोड़ा*) I need a new pair of socks.
Pare (*Cutting down–काटना*) Local authorities were instructed to pare their budget.
Pear (*Bottom-heavy fruit–नाशपाती*) I am fond of red pears.

(335) **Palate** (मुँह से ऊपर का भाग) The top part of the inside of your mouth is called palate.

Pallet (छोटा, कठोर, बिस्तर) A pallet is a narrow mattress filled with straw which is put on the floor for someone to sleep on.(b) A pallet is a hard, narrow bed.

He was given only a wooden pallet with a blanket. (c) A pallet is a flat wooden or metal platform on which goods are stored so that they can be lifted and moved using a forklift truck. The warehouse will hold more than 90,000 pallets storing 30 million Easter eggs.

(336) **Pall** (*to become wearisome*–अरुचिकर) Already the allure of meals in hotels and restaurants begun to pall.

Pawl (*locks a ratchet*–रोक) A pivoted, usually curved, bar or lever whose free end engages with the teeth of a cog-wheel or ratchet so that it can only turn or move one way.

(337) **Pause** (*to hesitate*–रुकना) He talked for three hours regularly without pausing for a minute.

Paws (*cat transportation*–पंजा) The cat has white front paws.

(338) **Pea** (*round, green* legume–मटर) I like peas vegetable.

Pee (*piss*–पेशाब करना) The driver was probably having a pee. He needed to pee.

(339) **Peak** (*mountain top*–पहाड़ की चोटी) He climbed up to the peak of the mountain.

Peek (*secret look*–चोरी से देखना) On one occasion she had peeked at him through a hole in the door.

Pique (नाराज होना)

(a) Pique is the feeling of annoyance you have when you think someone has not treated you properly. Simi had gotten over her pique at Rue's refusal to accept the job.

(b) If something piques your interest or curiosity, it makes you interested or curious. This phenomenon piqued Dr. Mohit's interest.

(c) If someone does something in a fit of pique, they do it suddenly because they are annoyed at being not treated properly. Lally , in a fit of pique, left the Army and took up a career in the town.

(340) **Pearl** (*round, luminescent gem from an oyster*–मोती) She wore a string of pearls at her throat.

Purl (धातु का तारा) Thread or cord of twisted gold or silver wire, used esp. for edging; edging etc made from this.

(341) **Pedal** (*foot control*–पैडल) I am too tired to pedal again.

Peddle (*to sell*–बेचना) He attempted to peddle his paintings around the city .

(342) **Peer** (महान् व्यक्ति)

(a) If you peer at something, you look at it very hard, usually because it is difficult to see clearly. I had been peering at a computer print-out that made no sense at all.

(b) In Britain, a peer is a member of the nobility who has or had the right to vote in the House of Lords) Lord Swan was made a life peer in 1981.

(c) Your peers are the people who are the same age as you or who have the same status as you. His engaging personality made him popular with his peers.

Pier (प्लेटफार्म) A pier is a platform sticking out into water, usually the sea, which people walk along or use when getting onto or off boats.

(343) **Pi** (*3.1416*–पाई) Pi is a number, approximately 3.1416, which is equal to hedistance round a circle divided by its width. It is usually represented by the Greek letter p.

Pie (*good eating*–स्वादिष्ट खाने की वस्तु) A pie consists of meat, vegetables or fruit baked in pastry. Well known the truth once. The police have piead all the facts together.

(344) **Pieced** (*assembled from pieces*–टुकड़े) Do you want another piece ?

Piste (*a ski run of compacted snow*–बर्फ) A track of firm snow for skiing on.

(345) **Pincer** (*claw-like gripping action*–पंजे से पकड़ना) The pincers of an animal such as a crab or a loberster are its front claws.

Pincher (*one who pinches*–परेशान करने वाला) None like a pincher.

(346) **Pistil** (डोडी) Seed-bearing organ of a flower.

Pistol (*hand gun*–पिस्तौल) He was caught with a pistol.

(347) **Place** (*a location*–स्थान) This is a good place to live at.

Plaice (एक प्रकार की मछली) Plaice are a type of flat sea fish.

(348) **Plait** (*braid*–तह बनाना) She parted her hair and then began to plait it into two thick braids.

Plate (*a dish*–थाली) She pushed her plate away. She had eaten nothing.

(349) **Plum** (*purple fruit*–बेर) A plum is a small , sweet fruit with a smooth red or yellow skin and a stone in the middle.

Plumb (*straight up and down*–पाइप कार्य) He knows how to plumb the pipe well.

(350) **Pole** (*a person from Poland*–पोलैण्ड के निवासी) He is a Pole.

Pole (*big stick*–बड़ी लकड़ी) I need a pole to climb up that house.

Poll (*a voting*–चुनाव कार्य) More than 60 percent of those polled said that they approved of his record as Chairman.

(351) **Poor** (*no money*–निर्धन) A poor man can't afford a car.

Pore (*careful study; microscopic hole*–ध्यान में लीन, छोटा छिद्र) We spent hours poring over the visa rules.

Pour (*to flow freely*–बहना)

He poured himself another drink.

(352) **Precedence** (*priority*–प्राथमिकता) Enjoy fully but don't let it take precedence over work.

Precedents (*established course of action*–परिपाटी) This case can set an important precedent for dealing with such cases in future.

Presidents (*the chief*–प्रधान) The President is all in all of this society.

(353) **Presence** (*the state of being present*–उपस्थिति) The meeting took place in the presence of the Judge.

Presents (*gifts*–उपहार) He gave a nice present to his friend on his wedding anniversary.

(354) **Pride** (*ego*–गर्व) We take pride in offering you the best services.

Pried (*opened*–खोला) I pried the top off a can of chilli.

(355) **Profit** (*money earned*–लाभ) The company has earned good profit in this quarter.

Prophet (*seer*–महान् व्यक्ति) He did it as per the instructions of the prophet.

(356) **Pros** (*benefits*–फायदा) Motherhood has both its pros and cons.

Prose (*ordinary language*–गद्य) Shute's prose is stark and chillingly unsentimental.

(357) **Quite** (*altogether*–पूरी तरह से) I am quite well now.

Quiet (*silent*–शान्त) Please keep quiet.

(358) **Rein** (*bridle*–लगाम) Keep the rein tight, otherwise you may be thrown out by the horse.

Reign (*rule*–शासन करना) The reign of Akbar is known for communal harmony.

(359) **Rite** (*ceremony*–रस्म) Only a few rites were performed in his wedding.
Write (*compose*–लिखना) I am to write a letter immediately.
Right (*antonym of left*–दायाँ) This is my right leg.
Right (*antonym to wrong*–सही) You have taken a right decision.
Wright (*a worker*–बनाने वाला) He is a wonderful play wright.

(360) **Raise** (*to life*–ऊँचा उठाना) I will raise this issue in Parliament.
Raze (to destroy–नष्ट करना) The storm razed many buildings tc the ground.

(361) **Route** (*course*–रास्ता) By which route you came here.
Rout (*flight*–भगाना) The Pakistan armies were put to rout.

(362) **Rap** (*a sharp blow*–थप्पड़) He rapped her on the cheek.
Rape (*to ravish*–बलात्कार) He raped a college girl.
Wrap (*to enclose*–बन्द करना) The book was wrapped in a piece of white paper.

(363) **Reclaim** (*to win back*–सुधारना) He was reclaimed from his bad habits by his devoted wife.
Re-claim (*to claim again*–पुन: दावा करना) He is thinking to re-claim the property on some other ground.

(364) **Recover** (*regain*–ठीक होना) He has now recovered a lot from the weakness.
Re-cover (*to cover again*–पुन: ढकना) Re-cover the sweets with some clean cloth.

(365) **Road** (*way*–रास्ता) The road has recently been repaired.
Rode (*past of ride*–सवारी की) He rode on the horse yesterday.

(366) **Ring** (*an ornament for fingers*–अँगूठी) This ring is made of gold.
Wring (*to twist, to squeeze*–ऐठना निचोड़ना) Wring the clothes well and put them on the ground.

(367) **Rest** (*respite*–आराम) I want some rest before starting the next assignment.
Wrest (*snatch by force*–छीनना) Ram wrested a bag from Shyam.

(368) **Roll** (*to run overly* – नामावली, लोटपोट होना) He rolled over the log to the right side of river.
Role (*part*–भाग लेना) I am playing the role of Ravana in this serial.

(369) **Raise** (*elevate*–उठाना) He raised is hand in support of the resolution.
Rays (*thin beams of light*–किरण) The sun rays can penetrate water up to ten feet.
Raze (*to tear down completely*–नष्ट करना) Many of villages have been razed.

(370) **Read** (*having knowledge from reading*–पढ़ना) I have read this novel.
Red (*a primary colour*–लाल रंग) I like red colour shirt.

(371) **Rede** (*advice*–सलाह) It is always fruitful to listen to the rede of your elders.
Reed (*tall, thin water plant*–पेड़) He has a beautiful reed plant.

(372) **Real** (*authentic*–वास्तविक) Yes it is a real story.
Reel (*wavering move*–चक्कर) He lost is balance and reeled back.

(373) **Recede** (*to move backward*–पीछे जाना) As he receded she waved goodbye.
Reseed (*to plant again*–पुन: बीजारोपण) He is trying to reseed the rose plant.

(374) **Reek** (*smells bad*–गंदी बदबू) Your breah reeks of stale cigar smoke.
Wreak (*to inflict*–बदला लेना) She threatened to wreak vengeance on the men who toppled him some years ago.

(375) **Retch** (*heave*–वमन करना) If you retch, your stomach moves as if you are vomiting. The smell made me retch.

Wretch (*wicked*–नीच व्यक्ति) Oh, what have you done , you wretch!

(376) **Review** (*a general survey or assessment*–विचार करना*)* The P.M. reviewed the situation with his cabinet.

Revue (*a series of theatrical sketches or songs*) A revue is a theatrical performance consisting of songs, dances, and jokes about recent events.

(377) **Rheum** (*watery discharge of mucous*–नाक बहना) A mucous discharge caused by infection with a cold.

Room (*partitioned space*–कमरा) I need a three room set.

(378) **Rho** (*seventeenth letter of Greek alphabet*–ग्रीक भाषा का 17वाँ शब्द*)*

Roe (*fish eggs*–मछली के अण्डे) He is fond of cod's roe .

Row (*aisle; pull an oar*–पंक्ति) They were standing in rows.

(379) **Rigger** (*one who rigs*–छल करने वाला) A person who works with lifting-tackle; a person who erects and maintains scaffolding.

Rigour (*discipline*–अनुशासित) He found the rigours of the tour too demanding.

(380) **Rise** (*to stand up*–उठना) The sun rises in the east.

Ryes (*varieties of grain*–राई) I am fond of cheese on rye.

(381) **Roam** (*to wander*–घूमना) Barefoot children roamed the streets.

Rome *(italian capital*–रोम) Rome was not built in a day.

(382) **Roil** (*to make turbid*–अशान्त) If water roils, it is rough and disturbed.

The water roiled to his left as he climbed carefully at the edge of the waterfall.(b) Something that roils a state or situation makes it disturbed and confused.

Times of national turmoil generally roil a country's financial markets.

Royal (*worthy of a king or* queen–शाही) He belongs to a royal family.

(383) **Rood** (*a cross*–क्रॉस चिन्ह) A cross as an instrument of execution; The Cross on which Jesus suffered; the cross as the symbol of the Christian faith. We wears a graden rood.

Rude (*coarse*–असभ्य) He is rude to her friends and obsessively jealous.

(384) **Rot** (*decay*– सरण) Sugary canned drinks can rot your teeth.

Wrought (*made*–बना हुआ) The recent results of presidential elections in USA wrought a change in US policy towards India.

Rote (*by memory*) I am very sceptical about the value of rote learning.

(385) **Rough** (*coarse*–कठोर) His hands are rough.

Ruff (*pleated collar*–कॉलर) A ruff is a stiff strip of cloth or other material with many small folds in it, which some people wore round their neck in former times.

(386) **Rude** (*impolite*–असभ्य) I am unable to understand as to why she behaved so rudely.

Rued (*regretted*–पश्चाताप) If you rue something that you have done, you are sorry that you did it, because it has had unpleasant results.(b) If you rue the day that you did something, you are sorry that you did it, because it has had unpleasant results.You'll live to rue the day you said that to me, my girl.

(387) **Rye** (*grain*–राई) Rye is a kind of grain.

Wry (*twisted*–मुड़ा हुआ)

(a) If someone has a wry expression, it shows that they find a bad situation or a change in a situation slightly amusing. He allowed himself a wry smile.

(b) A wry remark or piece of writing refers to a bad situation or a change in a situation in an amusing way.

There is a wry sense of humour in his work.

(388) **Sooth** (*truth* सच) Sooth to speak, he is not a good boy.

Soothe (*to calm*–शान्त करना) You can't soothe his anger with lame excuses.

(389) **Spacious** (*enough space*–खुला) His office is quite spacious and well decorated.

Specious (*attractive*–आकर्षक) With your specious look, you can't be foot her.

(390) **Stationary** (*Fixed*–स्थिर) Earth is not stationary, it moves round the sun.

Stationery (*Writing material*–स्टेशनरी) I am going to market to purchase several stationery items for the office.

(391) **Straight** (*opposed to curved*–सीधा) I believe in straight talks.

Strait (*narrow*–तंग) The lane is too strait to pass through for an elephant.

(392) **Sore** (*painful*–दर्दकारक) I can't sing as my throat is sore.

Soar (*to fly high*–ऊँचा उड़ना) Birds soar in sky.

Sour (*not sweet*–खट्टा) The grapes were sour.

(393) **Suit** (*an action in court*–दावा) Bank has filed a civil suit against you for recovery.

Suite (*a set of room*–कमरों का सेट) I have reserved a suite for you in Ashoka Hotel.

(394) **Story** (*a tale*–कहानी) My grandmother told me a story of an oldman.

Storey (*floor of a building*–मंजिल) I have taken a room at first storey.

(395) **Serge** (*a kind of cloth*––एक प्रकार का कपड़ा) This suit is made of serge.

Surge (*move like waves* –तरंगों की तरह) The waves of ocean surge violently in night.

(396) **Shear** (*to c*lip the wool–ऊन कतरना) The sheep are being shorn.

Sheer (*downright*–एकमात्र) He achieved success by the sheer force of his hard labour.

(397) **Sun** (सूर्य) The sun is a far.

Son (*a person's male child*–पुत्र) He is my son.

(398) **Sole** (*lower surface of shoe*–जूते का तला एकमात्र) The sole of the right shoe requires repairing. The sole aim of my life is to earn reputation in the society.

Soul (*immaterial part*–आत्मा) You can't see soul. Soul is immortal.

(399) **Stair** (*step*–सीढ़ी) Let us go up stairs.

Stare (*gaze*–घूरना) It is wrong to stare at girls.

(400) **Sing** (*melodious sound*–गाना) She will sing a sweet song.

Swing (*to oscillate*–झूलना) She has gone to enjoy swing ride.

(401) **Sale** (*to exchange for money*–बिक्री) This is not for sale.

Sail (*to travel in water*–तैरना) Ships can sail in deep sea only.

(402) **Sachet** (*a small bag containing perfumed powder*–छोटा पैकेट) I found twenty sachet of coffee.

Sashay (*to strut or flounce*–चलना) The models sashay down the catwalk.

(403) **Sacks** *(bags–थैला)* I found twenty sacks for potatoes.

Sax short for saxophone

(404) **Sane (*mentally normal*–मानसिक रूप से स्वस्थ)** He is perfectly sane.

Seine (fishing net–मछली पकड़ने का जाल) A large fishing net having floats at the top and weights at the bottom so as to hang vertically in the water, the ends being drawn together to enclose the fish and the net usu, hauled ashore.

(405) **Saver** (*one who saves*–बचाने वाला) Low interest rates are bad news for savers.

Savor (*to relish a taste*–स्वादिष्ट) People come here to savor the exquisite food provided by the owner.

(406) **Sawed** (*cut timber*–लकड़ी काटना) He sawed the timber very quickly.

Sod (*to express anger*–गुस्सा व्यक्त करना) If someone uses an expression such as 'sod it', 'sod you' or 'sod that', they are expressing anger or showing that they do not care about something.

(407) **Scull** (*rowing motion*–नाव चलाना) Scull are small oars which are held by one person and used to move a boat through water.

Skull (*head bone*–खोपड़ी) He was treated for a fractured skull.

(408) **Seal** (*to close*–बन्द करना) He sealed the envelope and put on a stamp.

Seel (*to close someone's eyes*–आँखे बन्द करना) Close the eyes of (a hawk etc.) by stitching up the eyelids·

(409) **Seam** (*row of stitches*–सिलाई)

(a) A seam is a line of stitches which joins two pieces of cloth together.

(b) If something is coming apart at the seams or is falling apart at the seams, it is no longer working properly and may soon stop working completely.

Britain's university system is in danger of falling apart at the seams.

(c) If a place is very full, you can say that it is bursting at the seams.

The hotels of New Delhi were bursting at the seams during Asia 1996 Trade Fair.

Seem (*appears*–दिखना) Everyone seems very busy here.

(410) **Seamen** (*sailors*–नाविक) He emigrated to work as seamen.

Semen (*male discharge*–वीर्य) He is being treated for some semen problem.

(411) **Sear** (*scorched*–मुरझाया या सूखा) To sear something means to burn its surface with a sudden intense heat. Grass fires have seared the land near the farming villages of Haryana seer (a person who sees). A seer is a person, who tells what will happen in the future.

(412) **Serf** (*slave*–दास) In former times, serfs were a class of people, who had to work on a particular person's land and could not leave without that person's permission.

Surf (लहर) Surf is the mass of white bubbles that is formed by waves as they fall upon the shore.

(a) If you surf, you ride on big waves in the sea on a special board.

I'm going to buy a surfboard and learn to surf...

I'm going to be surfing bigger waves when I get to Australia!

(b) If you surf the Internet, you spend time finding and looking at things on the Internet. (COMPUTING)

No one knows how many people currently surf the Net.

(413) **Sewer** (मल मार्ग) A sewer is a large underground channel that carries waste matter and rain water away, usually to a place where it is treated and made harmless.

Sower (*one who sows*–बोने वाला)

Suer (*one who sues* –दावा करने वाला)

(414) **Shell** The shell of a nut or egg is the hard covering which surround it.

They cracked the nuts and removed their shell.

She'll (*contraction of 'she will'*)

She'll cooperate you positively.

Shill (*a decoy*–प्रलोभन) A decoy, an accomplice, esp. one posing as an enthusiastic or successful customer to encourage buyers, gamblers·

(415) **Shear** (*to cut or wrench*–कतराना) He shears his shhep twice in a year.

Sheer (*pure*–शुद्ध)

(a) You can use sheer to emphasize that a state or situation is complete and does not involve or is not mixed with anything else.His music is sheer delight...Sheer chance quite often plays an important part in making career.

(b) A sheer cliff or drop is extremely steep or completely vertical. There was a sheer drop just outside my window.

(c) Shees material is very thin, light and delicete... sheer black tights.

(416) **Sic** (इस प्रकार से) You write sic in brackets after a word or expression when you want to indicate to the reader that although the word looks odd or wrong, you intended to write it like that or the original writer wrote it like that.

The latest school jobs page advertises a 'wide range (sic) of 6th form courses.'

Sick (*ill*–बीमार) He is very sick . He needs medical treatment.

Six (*whole number*–छः) I have six pencils.

(417) **Side** (*lateral*–बगल) There is a park on the left side of the road.

Sighed (*breathed sorrowfully*–आह भरना) He sighed wearily.

(418) **Sign** (*displayed board bearing information*–निशान) Equations are generally written with a two bar equals sign.

Sine (*reciprocal of the cosecant*) Find the sine value of this angle.

(419) **Sink** (*to submerge*–डूबना) A fresh egg will sink and an old egg will float.

Synch (*together in time*–साथ-साथ) If two things are out of synch, they do not match or do not happen together as they should. If two things are in synch, they match or happen together as they should. Normally, when demand and supply are out of sync, you either increase the supply, or you adjust the price mechanism.

(420) **Slay** (*kill*–मारना) He slew a man with a sword.

Sleigh (*snow carriage*–बर्फ की गाड़ी) A sleigh is a vehicle which can slide over snow. Sleighs are usually pulled by horses.

(421) **Slew** (*past tense of slay*–हत्या की)

Slough (*shed*–झुकना) When a plant sloughs its leaves, or an animal such as a snake sloughs its skin, the leaves or skin come off naturally.

All reptiles have to slough their skin to grow.

Sloe (*blackthorn berries*–जंगली बेर) A sloe is a small, sour fruit that has a dark purple skin. It is often used to flavour gin.

Slow (*not fast*–धीमा) The traffic is heavy and slow....

(422) **Solace** (*comfort*–आराम) I found soalce in writting when my friend died three months ago.

Soulless (*lacking a soul*–मृत) If you describe a thing or person as soulless, you mean that they lack human qualities and the ability to feel or produce deep feelings.

He is a soulless person.

(423) **Some** (*a few*–कुछ) Please give me some money.

Sum (*result of addition*–फेड़) The sum of all the angles of a triangle is 180 degree.

(424) **Soot** (*black residue of burning*–काजल) Soot is black powder which rises in the smoke from a fire and collects on the inside of chimneys.

This wall is blackened by soot.

Suit (*clothes*–पहनने का सूट) I have a blue suit.

Suite (*a set of rooms*–कमरों का समूह) We enjoyed our time during the week in a suite at London.

(425) **Spade** (*shovel*–फावड़ा) He used a spade for digging this pit.

Spayed (*to sterilise a female animal*–बधिया करना) When a female animal is spayed, it has its ovaries removed so that it cannot become pregnant.

All bitches should be spayed unless being used for breeding.

(426) **Spoor** (*trail of an animal*–गन्ध से पशु की खोज करना) The spoor of an animal is the marks or substances that it leaves behind as it moves along, which hunters can follow.

Spore (*single cell reproductive body*–जीवाणु) Spores are cells produced by bacteria and fungi which can develop into new bacteria or fungi.

(427) **Staid** (*reserved*–गम्भीर) If you say that someone or something is staid, you mean that they are serious, dull and rather old-fashioned.

Stayed (*remained*–ठहरना) In the old days the woman stayed at home and the man earned the livelihood.

(428) **Stake** (दाव)

(a) If something is at stake, it is being risked and might be lost or damaged if you are not successful. The tension was naturally high for that game with so much at stake.

(b) If you stake something such as your money or your reputation on the result of something, you risk your money or reputation on it.
He has staked his political future on this election victory...

(c) If you have a stake in something such as a business, it matters to you, *for example,* because you own part of it or because its success or failure will affect you.
He was eager to return to a more entrepreneurial role in which he had a big financial stake in his own efforts...

(d) A stake is a pointed wooden post which is pushed into the ground, *for example* in order to support a young tree.

(e) If you stake a claim, you say that something is yours or that you have a right to it. Jasmine is determined to stake her claim as an actress...

Steak (*slice of meat*–माँस का टुकड़ा) He hates eating steak.

(429) **Step** (*a measure taken*–कदम) The next step is to put the theory into practice.

Steppe (*a level, grassy, unforested plain*–बिना जोता हुआ) Steppes are large areas of flat grassy land where there are no trees, especially the area that stretches from Eastern Europe across the south of the former Soviet Union to Siberia.

(430) **Stile** (*narrow passage*–संकरा रास्ता) A stile is an entrance to a field or path consisting of a step on either side of a fence or wall to help people climb over it.

Style (*mode*–तरीका) She had not lost her grace and style.

(431) **Stoop** (झुकना)

(a) If you stoop, you stand or walk with your shoulders bent forwards.
She was taller than he was and stooped slightly.

(b) If you stoop, you bend your body forwards and downwards.
He stooped to pick up the carrier bag of groceries.

(c) If you say that a person stoops to doing something, you are criticizing him because be do something wrong or immoral that he would not normally does.
He had not, until recently, stooped to personal abuse...
How could anyone stoop so low?

(d) A stoop is a small platform at the door of a building, with steps leading up to it.
They stood together on the stoop and rang the bell.

Stoup (*A drinking cup*–कप) She served wine in beautiful stoups.

(432) **Succour** (*relief, assist*–आराम) Helicopters fly in appaling weather to succour ship wrecked mariners.

Sucker (*one who sucks*–चूसने वाला) If you call someone a sucker , you mean that it is easy to cheat him.

(433) **Suede** (*split leather*–एक प्रकार का चमड़ा) He wore asuede jacket and jeans.

Swayed (प्रकृत करना)

(a) When people or things sway, they lean or swing slowly from one side to the other. The people swayed back and forth with arms linked....
The whole boat swayed and tipped.

(b) If you are swayed by someone or something, you are influenced by them.
Don't ever be swayed by fashion.

(c) If someone or something holds sway, they have great power or influence over a particular place or activity.
South of the Usk, a completely different approach seems to hold sway.

(d) If you are under the sway of someone or something, they have great influence over you.
How mothers keep daughters under their sway is the subject of the next five sections.

(434) **Sundae** (आईसक्रीम) A sundae is a tall glass of ice cream with whipped cream and nuts or fruit on top.

Sunday (*the first day of the week*–रविवार) Today is Sunday.

(435) **Team** (*a group of players*–टीम) Our college team has won the trophy.

Teem (*to be full of*–बहुतायात) Rajasthan is a state teeming with natural resources.

(436) **Toe** (*a part of foot*–पैर का अँगूठा) She hurt her left toe in an accident.

Tow (*to draw by a rope*–बाँधना) The boat was towed with a tree near the shore.

(437) **Tail** (*part of body*–पूँछ) Cow has a long tail.

Tale (*story*–कहानी) My grandmother told me an interesting tale.

(438) **Their** (*belong to they*–उनका) They have learnt their lessons.

There (*at that place*–वहाँ) I am to go there now.

(439) **Throne** (*royal seat*–सिंहासन) All the brothers are fighting for the throne.

Thrown (*third form of throw*–फेंक दिया) She has thrown her certificates into the river.

Thorn (*impediment*–काँटा) You need a needle to get the thorn out.

(440) **Tenor** (*purpose*–ितात्पर्य) The tenor of his speech was important from religious point of view.

Tenure (*right of holding an estate*–भूमि नियमन) The Zamindari Abolition Act has finished the big problem of land tenure system in our country.

(441) **Tare** (*the seed of a vetch used in refence to its small size*–एक प्रकार की घास) When the harvest is gleaned the evil tares will be separated from the good wheat.

Tear (*salty drops from eyes*–आँसू) Her eyes are filled with tears.

Tier (*a horizontal row*–पंक्ति) I have booked your seats in two tier compartment.

(442) **Taught** (*past tense of teach*–पढ़ाया) Who taught you English?

Taut (*stretched tight*–तना हुआ) The clothes line is pulled taut and secured.

(443) **Tea** (*herbal infusion*–चाय) I am fond of tea.

Tee (*golfball prop*–गोल्फ से सम्बन्धित) The tee was broken accidentally.

(444) **Tenner** (*english slang for a ten pound note*–दस का) I have only a tenner in my pocket.

Tenor (*tendency*–तात्पर्य) The whole tenor of discussion has changed.

(445) **Tern** (*a shorebird*–एक चिड़िया) A tern is a small black and white seabird with long wings and a forked tail.

Terne (*alloy of lead and tin*–मिश्रित धातु) This plate is made of terne.

Turn (*rotate*–घुमाव) He turned left and went away.

(446) **The** (*denoting persons already mentioned*–आर्टिकल) The is the definite article.

Thee (*objective case of thou*–तुझे) I missed thee , beloved mother.

(447) **Through** (*from end to end*–बीच से) Go straight through that door under the 'exit' word.

Throe (*a spasm of pain*–दर्द) A violent physical spasm or pang, esp. in the pain and struggle of childbirth or death. Also, a spasm of feeling; mental agony; anguish.

Throw (*to discharge through the air*–फेंकना) The crowd began throwing stones.

(448) **Thyme** (*herb*–एक प्रकार का पौधा) Thyme is a type of herb used in cooking.

Time (*natures way of keeping everything from happening at once*–समय) What is the time by your watch?

(449) **Tic** (*twitch*–ऐंठना) If someone has a tic, a part of their face or body keeps making a small uncontrollable movement, *for example,* because they are tired or have a nervous illness.

Tick (*small noise; parasitic bug*–टिक-टिक) He sat listening to the tick of the clock.

(450) **Tighten** (*to make tighter*–जोर से बाँधना) I use my nail to tighten the screw on my torch.

Titan (*a giant*–बहुत बड़ा) He is the richest business titan of our country.

(451) **Timber** (*wood for building*–लकड़ी) In Japan timber is used for construction of house.

Timbre (*musical quality*–ध्वनि) The timbre of someone's voice or of a musical instrument is the particular quality of sound that it has. (FORMAL)

His voice had a deep timbre... The timbre of the violin is far richer than that of the mouth organ.

(452) **Toad** (*frog*–मेढक) A toad is a creature similar to frog.
Toed (*to conform a policy*–अनुसरण) He tried to persuade the rivals to toe the line of his party.
Towed (*pulled ahead*–ले जाना) The policeman threatened to tow away my car.

(453) **Told** (*what was spoken*–बोला) He told me how to do it.
Tolled (*a bell was rung*–घण्टी बजाना) The pilgrims tolled the bell.

(454) **Track** (*narrow path or road*–संकरा रास्ता) We set of once more , over a rough mountain track.
Tract (*a plot of land*–भूमि) A vast tract of land is available for stadium.

(455) **Tray** (*a platter*–ट्रे) I need a tray for six cups of tea.
Trey (*three*–तीन) The side of a die marked with three pips or spots; a throw which turns up this side.

(456) **Troop** (*a company of soldiers*–सिपाहियों का समूह) Twenty thousands troops were deployed on the border.
Troup (*a company of actors*–एक्टर्स का समूह) She belongs to an acrobatic performing troup.

(457) **Trussed** (*tied up*–बाँधना) She trussed him quickly with a rope and gagged his mouth.
Trust (*faith*–विश्वास) I trust you completely.

(458) **Umpire** (*a referee*–अम्पायर) You must not disobey the umpire.
Empire (*dominion*–राज्य) The king was unable to manage his empire properly.

(459) **Vein** (*a blood vessel*–शिरा) Veins take the blood to all parts of body.
Vane (*weather cock*–मुर्गा) There is a vane at the top of the temple.

(460) **Vale** (*valley*–घाटी) The beautiful vale of Manali is worthseeing.
Veil (*a cover*–पर्दा) Muslim ladies generally put a veil on her face.
Wail (*to lament*–विलाप) Don't wail please, he is safe and sound.

(461) **Wave** (*unevenness*–लहर) The waves of ocean are rising higher and higher.
Wave (*movement*–हिलाना) She waved her hand as the bus started.
Waive (*relinquish*–छोड़ना) I request the officer to waive the punishment.

(462) **Waste** (*useless*–व्यर्थ करना) Don't waste your precious time.
Waist (*part of body*–कमर) The boy had a chain round his waist.

(463) **Weather** (*atmosphere*–मौसम) It is cold weather today .
Whether (*which of two*–यदि) I asked her whether she would come .

(464) **Vain** (*useless*–व्यर्थ) I made several request to our Principal but all in vain .
Wane (*to decrease*–कम होना) I see the moon waning these nights.

(465) **Vary** (*to change*–बदलना) Your actions vary from the promise you made.
Very (*more*–बहुत) She is a very beautiful girl.
Wary (*cautious*–सतर्क) Because of his wary nature, he was saved.

(466) **Vacations** (*holidays*–छुट्टियाँ) We are going to Delhi in summer vacations.
Vocation (*occupation*–पेशा) What vocation do you intend to join after graduation?

(467) **Verses** (*paragraphs*–गद्य) This verse describes three reasons of his failure.
Versus (*against*–विपरीत) India versus Pakistan is a greatly contesting cricket match.

(468) **Vial** (*narrow glass container*–छोटा, शीशे का पात्र) A vial is a very small bottle which is used to hold something such as perfume or medicine. Please give me a vial of rose perfume.

Vile (*despicable, unpleasant*–अरुचिकर) She was in too vile a mood to work.

Viol (*stringed instrument*–यन्त्र) Viols are a family of musical instruments that are made of wood and have six strings. You play the viol with a bow while sitting down.

(469) **Vice** (*bad habit*–गलत आदत) She described that those responsible for offences are connected with vice, like drugs or gaming.

Vise (*bench-mounted clamp*–क्लैंप) I need a good vise while I repair the furniture.

(470) **Weigh** (*to ascertain the weight*–तौलना) I am to purchase one weighing machine.

Way (*passage*–रास्ता) This way leads to hospital.

(471) **Weight** (*weight*–वजन) He gained ten kg. of weight within a month.

Wait (*to attend*–इन्तजार) Don't wait for me, I will go myself.

(472) **Week** (*period of seven days*–सप्ताह) Monday is the first day of a week.

Weak (*feeble*–कमजोर) Ram is too weak to walk.

(473) **Ware** (*article*–समान) He has sold all his cook wares.

Wear (*to put on*–पहनना) I like to wear silk sarees.

Wear (*to diminish*–घिसना) My shirt has worn out.

(474) **Wine** (*drink*–शराब) Drinking wine is harmful for lever.

Vine (*creeper*–बेल) The hut is covered with grapevines.

(475) **Wax** (*candle stuff*–मोम) Candles had spread pools of wax on the furniture.

Whacks (*several blows*-धमाका) He has the donkey a whack across the back with a stick. Someone whacked him on the head.

(476) **Wade** (*talk in shallow water*–पानी में हलचल) Rescuers had to wade across a river to reach them.

Weighed (*weight was measured*–वजन मापना) He weighed approximately 270 kilos.

(477) **Wain** (*a wagon*–छकड़ा गाड़ी) He has hired a wain for transporting his household goods.

Wane (*decrease, fad*-कम होना) His interest in sports began to wane, a passion for golf developed.

(478) **Want** (*desire*–इच्छा) I want to become a surgeon.

Wont *(inclined*–जरूरत)

(a) If someone is wont to do something, they often or regularly do it. Both have committed their indiscretions, as human beings are wont to do.

(b) (accustomed) If someone does a particular thing as is their wont, they do that thing often or regularly. Ram woke up early, as was his wont.

(479) **War** (*large scale armed conflict*-युद्ध) A war like situation is prevailed between India and Pakistan.

Wore (*past tense of wear*-पहना) She wore a silken saree last night.

Ware (*merchandise*–सामान) The box seems to contain glass wares.

(480) **Warship** (*naval implement of destruction*–युद्धपोत) Warships played a decisive role in the victory of our forces.

Worship (*revere in a religious manner*–पूजा) I enjoyed worshipping God.

(481) **Wary** (*cautious*-सावधानी) People do not teach their wards to be wary of strangers.

Wherry (छोटी नाव) A light rowing boat used chiefly on rivers and in harbours for carrying passengers.

(482) **We** (हम) We are going to market.

Wee (छोटा साइज)

(a) Wee means small in size or extent. He just needs to calm down a wee bit.

(b) To wee means to urinate. Wee is an informal word used especially by children. He said that he wanted to wee.

(c) Wee is also a noun.The baby has done a wee in his potty.

(483) **We'd** (*contraction of 'we would'*) We'd meet you there positively.

Weed (*wild plants*–जंगली पौधा) If you don't care the garden it will be soon full of weeds.

(484) **We're** (*contraction of 'we are'*) We're friends.

Weir (*a low dam or a fence in a river for catching fish*–रोकथाम) A weir is a low barrier which is built across a river in order to control or direct the flow of water. (b) A weir is a wooden fence which is built across a stream in order to create a pool for catching fish.

Were (*past tense plural of 'to be'*) Where were you playing?

Whir or whirr (prolonged swish or buzz) When something such as a machine or an insect's wing whirrs, it makes a series of low sounds so quickly that they seem like one continuous sound. The camera whirred and clicked.

(485) **We've** (*Contraction of 'we have'*) We've twenty pencils only.

Weave (*to make cloth*–कपड़े बुनना) They were busy in weaving cotton fabrics.

(486) **Wheeled** (*having wheels*–पहियों पर) We wheeled her out on the stretcher.

Wield (*to apply or use*–काम में लाना)

(a) If you wield a weapon tool, or piece of equipment, you carry and use it.The assistant was wielding a kitchen knife.

(b) If someone wields power, they have it and are able to use it.
He remains president, but wields little power at the company.

(487) **Weld** (*to join metal by melting its edges*-वेल्डिंग) Where did you learn to weld?

Welled (*pouring forth*-अधिक होना) Her love for him welled stronger than ever.

(488) **Wet** (*watery*-गीला) She towelled her wet hair.

Whet (*prime*–भूख बढ़ाने या जगाने वाली वस्तु) If someone or something whets your appetite for a particular thing, they increase your desire to have it or know about it, especially by giving you an idea of what it is like.

A really good catalogue can also whet customers' appetites for merchandise.

(489) **Which** (*selection*-किसका) Which dress do you like most ?

Witch (जादूगरनी) In fairy stories, a witch is a woman, usually an old woman, who has evil magic powers. Witches often wear a pointed black, hat and have a pet black cat.

(490) **While** (*during*–जबकि) He was reading while she was cooking.

Wile (*a crafty, cunning or deceitful trick*; *a stratagem, a ruse*–चालाक धोखेबाज)
She used all her wiles to earn his favour.

(491) **Whine** (*annoying cry*–दर्द भरी आवाज) I can hear my dog whining in the courtyard.

Wine (*fermented grape juice*–दारू) This is a nice wine.

(492) **Whit** (*insignificant amount*–बहुत थोड़ी राशि) He cared not a whit for the social, political or religious aspects of literature.

Wit (*cleverness; sense of humour*–चतुराई) He was at his wit's end.

(493) **Whither** (*to which place, point, condition, etc? –*कौनसा स्थान) They knew not whither they went.
Wither (*shrivel up–*मुरझाना) The flowers withered away within three hours.

(494) **Whoa** (*whoa is a command that you give to a horse to slow down or stop–*वाह)
You can say whoa to someone who is talking to you, to indicate that you think they are talking too fast or assuming things that may not be true.
Woe (*despair–*दु:ख, निराशा) She listened to my tale of woe very patiently.

(495) **Yearn** (*to long–*इच्छा करना) I am anxiously yearning to meet my wife.
Yarn (*thread–*धागा) I have purchased three bundles of yarn.

(496) **Yoke** (*slavery–*दास बनाना) He is under the yoke of his master.
Yolk (*yellow portion of an egg–*अण्डे की पीली जर्दी) Some people eat only the yolk of an egg.

(497) **Yore** (*the past-*भूतकाल) Yore is used to refer to a period of time in the past.
The images provoked strong surges of nostalgia for the days of yore.
You're (*contraction of 'you are'*) You're a great writer.
Your (*belonging to you-*तुम्हारा) Which is your house?

(498) **You'll** (*contraction of 'you will'*) You'll be asked to explain your conduct.
Yule (*christmas-*क्रिसमस) Everyone makes enjoyment in his own way during yule time.

01

Fill in the blanks choosing the correct words given in the brackets :

(1) This remarks about the dominance of casteism in elections are quite..........to the present position. (apposite/opposite)
(2) The.........to this mountain is not an easy task. (ascent/assent)
(3) Yesterday his behaviour with the guests was .... (antic/antique)
(4) The boat man ....the boat with a chain. (tow/toe)
(5) Bihar is a State..........with coal mines. (teeming/teaming)
(6) She achieved this distinction by the....... force of hard work. (sheer/shear)
(7) The reading of cheap books produce a bad.........on the minds of youth. (affect/effect)
(8) You cannot...........my opinion about her. (altar/alter)
(9) This rhyme is full of.......... . (allusions/illusions)
(10) He says that the word to nothing but an...... . (allusion/illusion)

02

Fill in the blanks choosing the correct words given in the brackets :

(1) He was kind enough to.........to my request. (accede/exceed)
(2) Everybody should be given.......to this temple. (access/excess)
(3) He refused to...........the gift. (accept/except)

(4) She ......hard to secured first position in the college. (assayed/essayed)
(5) She is ....with malaria. (ailing/aleing)
(6) Please keep........... . (quiet/quite)
(7) What is the name of the....of this college? (principal/principle)
(8) This house is near the...........of India. (border/boarder)
(9) This world is nothing but an .... (allusion/illusion)
(10) The property of the ....was confiscated by the government. (deceased/diseased)

03

Fill in the blanks choosing the correct words given in the brackets **:**

(1) India is now free from the....... of British empire. (yoek/yoke)
(2) At last she left the house of her parents, knowing not........... . (whither/wither)
(3) All the flowers have now........away. (wither/whither)
(4) It is wrong to conclude that all...........him are corrupt. (except/accept)
(5) She is ....in the art of painting. (adapt/adept)
(6) The drought........a large part of the state. (attected/effected)
(7) This office is situated at the second.......... . (storey/story)
(8) This hotel has twenty A. C......... (suites/suits)
(9) I am going to purchase........ items for the office. (stationery/stationary)
(10) The earth is not ....,it revolves. (stationary/stationery)

04

Fill in the blanks choosing the correct words given in the brackets **:**

(1) Please.........my clothes. (calendar/calender)
(2) He is on.........leave. (casual/causal)
(3) The policeman........the thief by collar. (seized/seiqed)
(4) We heard ....of trumpets. (peal/peel)
(5) Through process of melting, iron is extracted from.......... . (oar/ore)
(6) He has some.........benefits in this project. (monetary/monitory)
(7) You can show your ....by fighting against injustice. (metal/mettle)
(8) This wife came........than him. (latter/later)
(9) An.......................man always plans in a clever manner. (ingenious/ingenuous)
(10) I have already clarified this point in..........paragraphs. (forgo/forego)

05

Fill in the blanks choosing the correct words given in the brackets **:**

(1) A good fellow will not ....a friend in need. (desert/dessert)
(2) This house was ......by earthquake. (wreck/wreak)
(3) A good writes always uses..........at appropriate places. (comma/coma)
(4) What he says is hardly.......... . (creditable/credible)
(5) He built his.............by hard work. (career/carrier)
(6) The ....was covered with white sheet. (corpse/corps)

(7) This bill has already been passed by legislative.......... . (council/counsel)
(8) Pay my best ....to your parents. (compliments/complement)
(9) He has................ to be the chairman of society. (cease/seize)
(10) True........cannot be enjoyed by a man of jealous nature. (felicity/facility)

06

Fill in the blanks choosing the correct words given in the brackets :

(1) ....makes a man perfect. (Practice/Practise)
(2) The ....of many pundits about destruction of the word didn't come true.(prophecy/prophesy)
(3) He can..........many cases to prove his arguments. (Site/Cite)
(4) Can you........this stick? (Break/Brake)
(5) He defeated the earlier champion in........ . (Dual/Duel)
(6) We should not adopt.........means to achieve success. (fowl/foul)
(7) She is a woman of ....nature. (jealous/zealous)
(8) It is raining and ....in the sky. (lightning/lightening)
(9) New Delhi is the ....of India. (capitol/capital)

Solution TYE 01

(1) apposite, (2) ascent, (3) antic, (4) tow, (5) teeming,
(6) sheer, (7) effect, (8) alter, (9) allusion, (10) illusions.

Solution TYE 02

(1) accede, (2) access, (3) accept, (4) assayed, (5) ailing,
(6) quiet, (7) principal, (8) border, (9) illusion, (10) deceased.

Solution TYE 03

(1) yoke, (2) whither, (3) wither, (4) except, (5) adept,
(6) affected, (7) storey, (8) suites, (9) stationery, (10) stationary.

Solution TYE 04

(1) calender, (2) casual, (3) seized, (4) peal, (5) ore,
(6) monetary, (7) mettle, (8) later, (9) ingenious, (10) foregone.

Solution TYE 05

(1) desert, (2) wrecked, (3) comma, (4) credible, (5) career,
(6) corpse, (7) council, (8) compliment, (9) ceased, (10) felicity.

Solution TYE 6

(1) Practice, (2) prophecy, (3) cite, (4) break, (5) duel,
(6) foul, (7) jealous, (8) lightning, (9) capital.

CONTRONYMS

Contronyms, ऐसे words हैं जिनके synonyms एक–दूसरे के Antonyms होते हैं अर्थात् ऐसे शब्द जिसके दो meanings एक–दूसरे के विपरित अर्थ देते हैं। नीचे contronyms की list दी जा रही है इसके (A) एवं (B) दो meanings, एक दूसरे antonym हैं। Contronyms भी एक प्रकार के Homographs (ऐसे शब्द जिसके दो अलग–अलग अर्थ हैं) ही हैं।

The word contronym (Also the synonym antagonym) is used to refer to words that by some freak of language evolution, are their own antonyms. Both contronym and antagonym are relatively recent neologisms.

Contronyms are special cases of homographs (two words with the same spellings).

Some Examples :

(1)	**Anabasis**	(A) Military advance	(B) Military retreat
(2)	**Aught**	(A) All	(B) Nothing
(3)	**Bolt**	(A) Secure	(B) Run away
(4)	**Buckle**	(A) Fasten	(B) Fall apart
(5)	**By**	(A) Multiplication (e.g., a three by five matrix)	(B) Division (e.g., Dividing eight by four)
(6)	**Chuffed**	(A) Pleased	(B) Annoyed
(7)	**Cleave**	(A) Separate	(B) Adhere
(8)	**Clip**	(A) Fasten	(B) Detach
(9)	**Consult**	(A) Ask for advice	(B) Give advice
(10)	**Copemate**	(A) Partner	(B) Antagonist
(11)	**Custom**	(A) Usual	(B) Special
(12)	**Deceptively Smart**	(A) Smarter than one appears	(B) Dumber than one appears
(13)	**Dike**	(A) Wall	(B) Ditch
(14)	**Discursive**	(A) Proceeding coherently from topic to topic	(B) Moving aimlessly from topic to topic
(15)	**Dollop**	(A) A large amount	(B) A small amount
(16)	**Dust**	(A) Add fine particles	(B) Remove fine particles
(17)	**Enjoin**	(A) Prescribe	(B) Prohibit
(18)	**Fast**	(A) Quick	(B) Unmoving
(19)	**First Degree**	(A) Most severe (e.g., Murder)	(B) Least severe (e.g., Burn)
(20)	**Fix**	(A) Restore	(B) Castrate

(21)	**Flog**	(A) Criticize harshly	(B) Promote aggressively
(22)	**Garnish**	(A) Enhance (*e.g.*, Food)	(B) Curtail (e.g., Wages)
(23)	**Give out**	(A) Produce	(B) Stop production
(24)	**Grade**	(A) Incline	(B) Level
(25)	**Handicap**	(A) Advantage	(B) Disadvantage
(26)	**Help**	(A) Assist	(B) Prevent (e.g., ''I Can't help it if...'')
(27)	**Left**	(A) Remaining	(B) Departed from
(28)	**Liege**	(A) Sovereign lord	(B) Loyal subject
(29)	**Mean**	(A) Average	(B) Excellent (e.g., 'Plays a mean game')
(30)	**Off**	(A) Off	(B) On (e.g., 'The alarm went off')
(31)	**Out**	(A) Visible (*e.g.,* Stars)	(B) Invisible (e.g., Lights)
(32)	**Out of**	(A) Outside	(B) Inside (e.g., 'Work out of one's home')
(33)	**Oversight**	(A) Error	(B) Care
(34)	**Put out**	(A) Extinguish	(B) Generate (e.g., Something putting out light)
(35)	**Quiddity**	(A) Essence	(B) Trifling point
(36)	**Quite**	(A) Rather	(B) Completely
(37)	**Rent**	(A) Buy use of	(B) Sell use of
(38).	**Rinky-dink**	(A) Insignificant	(B) One who frequents rinkworks
(39)	**Sanction**	(A) Approve	(B) Boycott
(40)	**Sanguine**	(A) Hopeful	(B) Murderous (Obsolete synonym for 'Sanguinary')
(41)	**Screen**	(A) Show	(B) Hide
(42)	**Seed**	(A) Add Seeds (e.g., 'To seed a field')	(B) Remove seeds (e.g., 'To seed a tomato')
(43)	**Strike**	(A) Hit	(B) Miss (In Baseball)
(44)	**Table**	(A) Propose (In the United Kingdom)	(B) Set aside (In the United States)
(45)	**Transparent**	(A) Invisible	(B) Obvious
(46)	**Unbending**	(A) Rigid	(B) Relaxing
(47)	**Variety**	(A) One type (e.g., 'This variety')	(B) Many types (e.g., 'A variety')
(48)	**Wear**	(A) Endure through use	(B) Decay through use
(49)	**Weather**	(A) Withstand	(B) Wear away
(50)	**Wind up**	(A) End	(B) Start up (e.g., A Watch)
(51)	**With**	(A) Alongside	(B) Against

CHAPTER 46

HETERONYMS

Heteronyms ऐसे शब्द (Words) हैं जिनके एक से अधिक अर्थ होते हैं एवं अलग-अलग अर्थ में उनका उच्चारण भी अलग होता है। [A] एवं [B] अलग-अलग अर्थ हैं एवं [A] एवं [B] के उच्चारण भी अलग-अलग होते हैं। शब्द के अर्थ के साथ उसका अलग-अलग उच्चारण भी बताया गया है।

Heteronyms are also a type of Homograph. They are words that are spelled the same but differ in meaning and pronunciation. All heteronyms are also homographs, but all homographs are not heteronyms. Many heteronyms are similar in meaning (especially a related noun and verb are spelled the same, but pronounced differently) while others are wholly unrelated.

ऐसे शब्दों (Heteronyms) की list नीचे दी जा रही हैं :

(1) **Affect** [A] (ah-fect) to change;
[B] (af-fect) feeling or emotion

(2) **Alternate** [A] (alt-er-nit) another choice;
[B] (alt-er-nait) switch back and forth

(3) **Appropriate** [A] (ap-prope-ri-ate) to take possession of;
[B] (ap-prope-ri-it) suitable

(4) **Are** [A] (air) 100 square meters (a hundredth of a hectare);
[B] (ahr) plural present tense of 'to be'

(5) **Arithmetic** [A] (a-rith-me-tic) a branch of mathematics;
[B] (air-ith-met-ic) characteristic of arithmetic

(6) **Attribute** [A] (at-trib-ute) to ascribe;
[B] (at-trib-ute) characteristic

(7) **Axes** [A] (ax-ez) plural of axe;
[B] (ax-eez) plural of axis

(8) **Bass** [A] (base) a stringed instrument;
[B] (bass) a fish

(9) **Bow** [A] (rhymes with 'how') to incline the head in greeting;
[B] (rhymes with 'tow') weapon that is used for shooting arrows;
[C] front of a ship

(10) **Bowed** [A] (rhymes with 'how'd') inclined the head in greeting;
[B] (rhymes with 'towed') bent

(11) **Buffet** [A] (buf-fet) to hit;
[B] (buf-fay, boof-fay) a meal at which guests serve themselves from dishes on display

(12) **Close** [A] (cloze) to shut;
[B] (clohss) nearby

(13) **Combine** [A] (com-bine) threshing machine;
[B] (com-bine) put together

(14) **Conduct** [A] (con-duct) behaviour;
[B] (con-duct) to direct or manage

(15) **Conflict** [A] (con-flict) disagreement or fight;
[B] (con-flict) to be in opposition

(16) **Console** [A] (con-sole) upright case; also, computer terminal;
[B] (con-sole) to comfort

(17) **Consort** [A] (con-sort) companion or partner;
[B] (con-sort) to keep company

(18) **Construct** [A] (con-struct) something constructed;
[B] (con-struct) to assemble

(19) **Content** [A] (con-tent) substantive part;
[B] (con-tent) satisfied

(20) **Contest** [A] (con-test) competition;
[B] (con-test) to dispute

(21) **Contract** [A] (con-tract) agreement;
[B] (con-tract) to shrink or to agree on a project

(22) **Convert** [A] (con-vert) one whose belief was changed;
[B] (con-vert) to change one's belief

(23) **Converse** [A] (con-verse) opposite;
[B] (con-verse) to talk

(24) **Convict** [A] (con-vict) prisoner;
[B] (con-vict) to find guilty

(25) **Crooked** [A] (crookd) bended;
[B] (crook-ed) bent

(26) **Deliberate** [A] (de-lib-er-ate) carefully considered;
[B] (de-lib-er-ate) to consider

(27) **Desert** [A] (des-ert) arid region;
[B] (de-sert) to leave; also, something deserved

(28) **Digest** [A] (die-jest) collection of published material;
[B] (die-jest) absorb nutrients

(29) **Do** [A] (doo) to accomplish;
[B] (doe) musical note

(30) **Does** [A] (duz) performs;
[B] (doze) multiple one female deer

(31) **Dove** [A] (rhymes with ''love'') a bird;
[B] (rhymes with ''hove'') jumped off

(32) **Drawer** [A] (door) compartment that is opened by pulling out;
[B] (draw-er) one who draws

(33) **Ellipses** [A] (ee-lip-sez) plural of ellipse;
[B] (ee-lip-seez) plural of ellipsis

(34) **Entrance** [A] (en-trance) entry way;
[B] (en-trance) to captivate

(35) **Evening** [A] (eve-ning) the time of day between afternoon and night;
[B] (eve-en-ing) making even

(36) **Excuse** [A] (ex-cuze) to let someone off;
[B] (ex-kyewss) justifying explanation

(37) **House** [A] (howss) building that serves as living quarters;
[B] (howz) to provide with living quarters

(38) **Incense** [A] (in-cense) substance that produces a pleasant aroma when burned;
[B] (in-cense) to anger

(39) **Intern**	[A]	(in-tern) a worker in training;
	[B]	(in-tern) confine to a prescribed area
(40) **Invalid**	[A]	(in-val-id) someone who is sick or disabled;
	[B]	(in-val-id) not valid
(41) **Laminate**	[A]	(lam-in-it) a layered construct;
	[B]	(lam-in-ate) to construct by layering
(42) **Lather**	[A]	(hard 'th') foam or suds;
	[B]	(soft 'th') one who installs lath (lattice)
(43) **Lead**	[A]	(leed) to guide;
	[B]	(led) a metallic element
(44) **Minute**	[A]	(min-it) sixty seconds;
	[B]	(my-noot) tiny
(45) **Moderate**	[A]	(mod-er-it) not excessive or extreme;
	[B]	(mod-er-ate) to preside over
(46) **Mow**	[A]	(rhymes with 'cow') pile of hay stored in a barn;
	[B]	(rhymes with 'tow') to cut grass
(47) **Multiply**	[A]	(mult-i-ply) to perform the mathematical operation of multiplication;
	[B]	(mult-i-plee) in a multiple manner
(48) **Number**	[A]	(num-ber) a discrete value or quantity;
	[B]	(num-mer) more numb
(49) **Nun**	[A]	(nun) woman in a religious order;
	[B]	(noon) the fourteenth letter of the hebrew alphabet
(50) **Object**	[A]	(ob-ject) thing;
	[B]	(ob-ject) to protest
(51) **Overhead**	[A]	(ove-er-head) operating expenses; also, an overhead projector;
	[B]	(ov-er-head) high; above the level of the head
(52) **Pasty**	[A]	(pay-stee) like glue;
	[B]	(pass-tee) meat pie
(53) **Pate**	[A]	(pate) top of the head;
	[B]	(pat) porcelain paste; (pa-tay) a minced food
(54) **Perfect**	[A]	(per-fect) flawless;
	[B]	(per-fect) to make flawless
(55) **Periodic**	[A]	(peer-ee-odd-ic) occasional;
	[B]	(pure-eye-odd-ic) an iodine compound
(56) **Permit**	[A]	(per-mit) document giving permission;
	[B]	(per-mit) to allow
(57) **Present**	[A]	(prez-ent) gift;
	[B]	(pre-zent) to introduce
(58) **Primer**	[A]	(prihm-er) elementary book;
		(pry-mer) undercoat of paint
(59) **Produce**	[B]	(pro-duce) vegetables;
		(pro-duce) bring forth
(60) **Project**	[A]	(pro-ject) task;
	[B]	(pro-ject) to forecast; also, to show a movie
(61) **Protest**	[A]	(pro-test) an objection;
	[B]	(pro-test) to object
(62) **Pussy**	[A]	(puhs-ee) having pus;
	[B]	(pooh-see) kitten
(63) **Raven**	[A]	(ray-ven) a black bird;
	[B]	(rav-en) hungry
(64) **Rebel**	[A]	(reb-el) one who refuses allegiance or opposes;

[B] (re-bel) to refuse allegiance or oppose

(65) **Record** [A] (rec-ord) a documented account;
[B] (re-cord) to set down to preserve

(66) **Recreation** [A] (rec-ree-a-shun) entertaining or relaxing pastime;
[B] (ree-cree-a-shun) something that is remade, recreated

(67) **Refuse** [A] (ref-yoos) garbage;
[B] (ref-yooz) to deny

(68) **Relay** [A] (ree-lay) a race in which members of a team take turns racing;
[B] (ree-lay) to lay again;
[C] (rih-lay) to pass along

(69) **Repeat** [A] (re-peat) repeated television show;
[B] (re-peat) to perform again

(70) **Rerun** [A] (re-run) repeated television show;
[B] (re-run) to run again

(71) **Resign** [A] (re-zine) to quit;
[B] (re-sign) to sign again

(72) **Resume** [A] (ree-zoom) to restart;
[B] (reh-zoom-ay) document of professional experience

(73) **Row** [A] (rhymes with ''cow'') a fight;
[B] (rhymes with ''tow'') a series of objects; also, to propel a boat with oars

(74) **Sake** [A] (sake) purpose;
[B] (sah-kee) alcoholic drink

(75) **Secreted** [A] (see-cret-ed) placed out of sight;
[B] (see-creet-ed) emitted

(76) **Separate** [A] (sep-ar-ate) to set apart;
[B] (sep-ret) not joined together

(77) **Sewer** [A] (soe-wer) one who sews;
[B] (soo-wer) channel for human waste

(78) **Slough** [A] (rhymes with ''tough'') outer layer or covering that is shed;
[B] (rhymes with ''cow'') a hole filled with deep mud or mire;
[C] (rhymes with ''through'') a marsh

(79) **Sow** [A] (rhymes with ''cow'') a pig;
[B] (rhymes with ''tow'') to plant seed

(80) **Subject** [A] (sub-ject) the theme; also, one ruled by another;
[B] (sub-ject) to force upon

(81) **Suspect** [A] (sus-pect) one suspected of a crime;
[B] (sus-pect) to have suspicion

(82) **Tear** [A] (tare) to rip;
[B] (teer) a drop of the clear liquid emitted by the eye

(83) **Unionized** [A] (yoon-yon-ized) belonging to a union;
[B] (un-i-on-ized) not converted into ions

(84) **Wind** [A] (rhymes with ''find'') to coil up;
[B] (winned) moving air

(85) **Wound** [A] (woond) to injure;
[B] (wound) coiled up

Some Heteronymic Sentences :

(a) When the brush fire was **close**, the authorities had to **close** the road.
(b) I **subject** my friends to pain when I discuss the **subject** of my operation.
(c) The **bass** swam around the **bass** drum on the ocean floor.
(d) She wished she could **desert** him in the **desert**.

CHAPTER 47

PALINDROMES

A palindrome is a word or sentence that reads the same forward as it does backward. The words 'A' and 'I' are perhaps the simplest palindromes. The word 'Refer' and the name 'Malayalam' are more interesting and illustrative palindromes.

Palindromes are a type of palingram called letter palingrams. A palingram is a sentence in which the letters, syllables, or words read the same backward as they do forward. The sentence, ''I was, was I ?'' is a word palingram, because the words can be placed in reverse order and still read the same. The sentence, ''I did, did I ?'' is not only a word palingram, but a letter palingram (Or palindrome) as well.

A number of interesting palindromes are given below for your amusement. Can you make up your own?

Words

Aibohphobia, Alula, Cammac, Civic Deified
Deleveled, Detartrated, Devoved, Dewed
Evitative, Hannah, Kayak, Kinnikinnik
Lemel, Level, Madam, Malayalam
Minim, Murdrum, Peeweep, Racecar
Radar, Redder, Refer, Reifier
Repaper, Reviver, Rotator, Rotavator
Rotor, Sagas, Solos, Sexes
Stats, Tenet, Terret, Testset

Phrases and Sentences

(1) A tin mug for a jar of gum, Nita.
(2) A Toyota. Race fast, safe car. A Toyota.
(3) Able was I ere I saw Elba.
(4) Anne, I vote more cars race Rome to Vienna.
(5) As I pee, sir, I see Pisa!
(6) Cigar? Toss it in a can. It is so tragic.
(7) Dammit, I'm mad!
(8) Ten animals I slam in a net.
(9) Too bad I hid a boot.
(10) Was it a car or a cat I saw ?
(11) Won't lovers revolt now ?

PANGRAMS

A pangram is a sentence that contains all letters of the alphabet. Such sentences are also called holalphabetic sentences. Constructing a sentence that includes the fewest repeat letters possible is a challenging task.

By far the most well-known pangram is, *"The quick brown fox jumps over a little lazy dog."* This sentence is generally used to test out new typewriters, presumably because it includes every letter of the alphabet.

A number of pangrams are given below :

Examples

(a) No kidding —Lorenzo called off his trip to visit Mexico City just because they told him the conquistadores were extinct. (99 letters)

(b) Six javelins thrown by the quick savages whizzed forty paces beyond the mark. (64 letters)

(c) The public was amazed to view the quickness and dexterity of the juggler. (60 letters)

(d) We quickly seized the black axle and just saved it from going past him. (57 letters)

(e) Six big juicy steaks sizzled in a pan as five workmen left the quarry. (56 letters)

(f) A mad boxer shot a quick, gloved jab to the jaw of his dizzy opponent. (54 letters)

(g) A quart jar of oil mixed with zinc oxide makes a very bright paint. (53 letters)

(h) Crazy Fredericka bought many very exquisite opal jewels. (48 letters)

(i) Sixty zippers were quickly picked from the woven jute bag. (48 letters)

(j) Heavy boxes perform quick waltzes and jigs. (36 letters)

(k) The quick brown fox jumps over a little lazy dog. (33 letters)

(l) Pack my box with five dozen liquor jugs. (32 letters)

(m) The five boxing wizards jump quickly. (31 letters)

(n) How quickly daft jumping zebras vex. (30 letters)

(o) Jackdaws love my big sphinx of quartz. (31 letters)

CHAPTER 49

UNUSUAL WORD FORMS

A very peculiar thing about English is that for almost all rules, we find exceptions to them. Both the beauty and the bane of English is find in the exceptions to everything. Pluralizing words isn't always a simple matter of adding an on the end, and switching a word from masculine form to feminine form isn't always a matter of adding ess.

Plurals-Peculiarity :

(a) The words alms, amends, cattle, clothes, doldrums, ides, pants, pliers, scissors, shorts, smithereens, and trousers are all plural, but have no singular form.

(b) Many words, such as deer, moose, and sheep, are spelled and pronounced the same way in both their singular and plural forms. More interesting words with this property are congeries, kudos, premises, shambles, series, and species. Fish can be both singular and plural, yet fishes is also a correct pluralization of the word.

(c) The words bourgeois, chassis, corps, faux pas, gardebras, précis, pince-nez, and rendezvous all have plurals spelled the same way but pronounced differently.

(d) Kine, an obsolete plural form of cow, shares no letters with its singular form.

(e) The plural of man is men. The plural of woman is women. The plural of human is humans.

(f) The plural of foot is feet. The plural of goosefoot is goosefoots.

(g) The plural of moose is moose. The plural of goose is geese. The plural of mongoose is mongooses.

(h) The plural of mouse, the rodent, is mice. The plural of mouse, the computer hardware device, is mouses.

Other Unusually Pluralized Words :

Other unusually pluralized words are brother which may be pluralized to brothers, but also brethren; cherub, which is pluralized to cherubim; die, which is pluralized to dice, formula, which may be pluralized to formulas but also formulae; landsman, which is pluralized to landsleit; libretto, which is pluralized to libretti; ox, which is pluralized to oxen; paries, which is pluralized to parietes; person, which is pluralized to people; rubai, which is pluralized to rubaiyat; schema, which is pluralized to schemata; seraph, which is pluralized to seraphim; tempo, which is pluralized to tempi. Most of these words were taken from other languages—like Hebrew, Greek, German, and Italian—with the foreign pluralization rules retained.

The singular form of braces, when used in the orthodontic sense, is bracket. One bracket per tooth is attached when someone gets braces.

Hair is a singular word that suggests more than its plural, hairs.

The plural words abbes, abys, adventures, bas, bos, bras, bulgines, cares, chapes, cites, cosines, deadlines, esquires, fras, gamines, gaus, glassines, gues, hos, kavas, kas, larges, las, los, lownes, marques, mas, millionaires, mis, moras, mos, multimillionaires, nervines, ogres, pas, pis, pos, posses, prelates, princes, pros, sagenes, saltines, shines, sightlines, squires, tartines, timelines, tyrranes, and usures all become different singular words if you add another onto the end of each. Many of them switch from masculine plural form to feminine singular form.

Gender—Peculiarity :

Widower is the only word in the English language whose masculine form is longer than its feminine form, which is widow. Demirep is the only word in the English language which is made feminine by applying a prefix, rather than a suffix to the masculine form which is rep.

CHAPTER 50

HOMOGRAPHS

A homograph is a "word of the same written form as another but of a different origin and meaning." (buck—buck). Following list tells you the use of homographs in sentence (A) and, (B) depicting different meanings.

Homograph ऐसा शब्द हैं जिसके एक से अधिक अलग-अलग अर्थ होते हैं। Same Spelling but different meanings (Homograph) वाले शब्दों का उच्चारण कई बार अलग होता हैं, एवं कई बार समान होता हैं। Homographs के विभिन्न अर्थों का ज्ञान छात्र की अच्छी vocabulary हेतु आवश्यक हैं। छात्रों को इनका अध्ययन ध्यानपूर्वक करना चाहिए।

(1) **Act** (A) Jack will act in a play. (B) He's in the second act of the play.

(2) **Arms** (A) My arms and legs hurt. (B) The soldiers laid down their arms.

(3) **Block** (A) The puppy ran around the block. (B) The chairs will block the door.

(4) **Buck** (A) It costs one buck to get in. (B) The horse will buck you off.

(5) **Blue** (A) I feel very blue today. (B) She wore a blue dress.

(6) **Box** (A) Put your things in a box. (B) The fighters will box tonight.

(7) **Brand** (A) They put a brand on the horse. (B) What brand is your computer?

(8) **Base** (A) The base of the statue broke. (B) The player ran to third base.

(9) **Back** (A) My back hurts. (B) The dog came back home.

(10) **Bank** (A) The river overflowed its bank. (B) I have a $1000 in the Bank.

(11) **Bear** (A) The grizzly bear is dangerous. (B) I cannot bear to be alone.

(12) **Bark** (A) The dog has a loud bark. (B) The bark peeled off the tree.

(13) **Bit** (A) The tiger bit the giraffe. (B) My finger hurts a little bit.

(14) **Ball** (A) My wife went to a ball. (B) The ball bounced off my head.

(15) **Bright** (A) The light is bright in my room. (B) Some students are very bright.

(16) **Blow** (A) They will blow up the bridge. (B) He received a blow to the head.

(17) **Bangs** (A) The shots were like loud bangs. (B) She wears her hair in bangs.

(18) **Bat** (A) The baseball bat was broken. (B) A bat flew out of the cave.

(19) **Bow** (A) Bow to the audience before playing. (B) The bow of the ship was breaking.

(20) **Bluff** (A) You can bluff when playing poker. (B) The man stood on the bluff.

(21) **Bill** (A) We have received a large bill. (B) The ducks bill is orange.
(C) He wants change for a $5 bill.

(22) **Bulb** (A) We planted a daffodil bulb. (B) The light bulb is burned out.

(23) **Bed** (A) My bed is warm and soft. (B) We planted a bed of flowers.

(24) **Coat** (A) She is wearing a new coat. (B) There is a coat of dust on the car.
(25) **Court** (A) The criminal was tried in a court. (B) The man wanted to court the lady.
(26) **Chest** (A) He found a pirate's chest of gold. (B) He pounded his chest in rage.
(27) **Change** (A) I need fifty cents in change. (B) Can I change my class time?
(28) **Can** (A) A tin can of food will solve hunger. (B) Can you try to come this evening?
(29) **Check** (A) I received a check from my bank. (B) We need to check on the date.
(30) **Charge** (A) You can charge your purchase. (B) What is the charge for lessons? (C) Elephants can charge at any time.
(31) **Cast** (A) The cast of the play went home. (B) He had a cast on his broken arm. (C) He cast the money into the sea.
(32) **Calf** (A) A calf is a baby cow. (B) The calf of my leg hurts.
(33) **Corn** (A) We ate corn at dinner. (B) I have a corn on my foot.
(34) **Crow** (A) A big black crow ate the corn. (B) Most roosters crow in the morning.
(35) **Date** (A) I ate a date with my lunch. (B) I have a date with my wife.
(36) **Dart** (A) She sewed a dart in her dress. (B) He threw a dart at the dartboard. (C) Don't dart into the street.
(37) **Dull** (A) The knife is too dull to cut. (B) The movie was dull and stupid.
(38) **Deck** (A) The captain stood on the deck. (B) I need a deck of cards.
(39) **Draw** (A) If you draw a gun, then shoot. (B) I cannot easily draw pictures. (C) They were down in the draw.
(40) **Down** (A) A duck has down on its back. (B) Walk down the stairs carefully.
(41) **Duck** (A) Duck when walking in a cave. (B) A small duck swam with its mother.
(42) **Ear** (A) I cannot hear in one ear. (B) She ate an ear of corn.
(43) **Fly** (A) A fly landed on his nose. (B) We shall fly to Paris today.
(44) **Fall** (A) The Fall weather is cool. (B) Be careful that you don't fall.
(45) **Fine** (A) If you speed, you will pay a fine. (B) I feel fine today.
(46) **Float** (A) Astronauts can float in space. (B) There was a float in the parade.
(47) **Fair** (A) The State Fair is in October. (B) Today was fair and warm.
(48) **Fast** (A) Some cars can go very fast. (B) Some people keep fast at Easter.
(49) **Firm** (A) I work in a law firm. (B) I sleep on a firm mattress. (C) They made us a firm offer.
(50) **Foot** (A) The stick is one foot long. (B) My foot won't fit my shoe.
(51) **Faint** (A) Did you ever faint from hunger? (B) He heard a faint noise.
(52) **Fool** (A) They tried to fool me. (B) The fool did tricks for the king.
(53) **Fit** (A) She had a fit over the job. (B) The pants will not fit me.
(54) **Face** (A) Your face is red. (B) You must face the audience. (C) He will lose face.
(55) **Felt** (A) The dress was made from felt. (B) She felt sorry for the victim.
(56) **Fleet** (A) He owns a fleet of taxis. (B) She is fleet of foot.

(57) **File** (A) You must file the papers. (B) You must file your fingernails.
(C) He used a file to escape.
(58) **Ground** (A) The snow covered the ground. (B) We ground up the meat for dinner.
(59) **Gobble** (A) A pig will gobble his food fast. (B) A turkey will gobble for attention.
(60) **Game** (A) I enjoy the game of football. (B) We went hunting game to eat.
(61) **Hand** (A) He had a glove on his hand. (B) We gave the singer a hand.
(62) **Hide** (A) Did you hide the money? (B) The hide of a cow is very useful.
(63) **Hit** (A) The movie was a big hit. (B) I hit the ball for a home run.
(64) **Hang** (A) Hang your coat on a hook. (B) We will hang around for an hour.
(65) **Head** (A) He is the head of our company. (B) A book fell on my head.
(66) **Hold** (A) Hold onto your money. (B) Put the cargo into the ship's hold.
(C) They put us on hold.
(67) **Hard** (A) It was a hard test. (B) The cement will get hard soon.
(68) **Iron** (A) We seldom iron clothes. (B) The chair was made of iron.
(C) We must iron out our problems.
(69) **Ice** (A) We will ice the cake before eating. (B) Make sure you don't slip on the ice.
(70) **Jumper** (A) She wore a cotton jumper. (B) She is a good high jumper.
(71) **Jam** (A) I like berry jam on toast. (B) The traffic jam made me late.
(72) **Jar** (A) Put the sugar into the jar. (B) Don't jar the doctor's hand.
(73) **Joker** (A) She is a practical joker. (B) A deck of cards has two jokers.
(74) **Kid** (A) There is a new kid in my class. (B) A kid is a baby goat.
(C) He loves to kid people.
(75) **Kind** (A) You should be kind to animals. (B) It is the wrong kind of cloth.
(76) **Lean** (A) I only eat lean meat. (B) You can lean on the desk.
(77) **Letter** (A) I got a letter in the mail. (B) What is the first letter in China?
(78) **Light** (A) Is that chair light or heavy? (B) Please turn on the light.
(79) **Like** (A) Do you like to watch TV? (B) She looks like her mother.
(80) **Log** (A) I keep a log of my flying hours. (B) Put another log on the fire.
(81) **Land** (A) We shall land in Paris at noon. (B) Farmers need land to grow crops.
(82) **Lap** (A) Cats lap milk with their tongue. (B) She sat in my lap eating candy.
(83) **Leaves** (A) In Fall leaves drop to the ground. (B) She leaves for London today.
(84) **Left** (A) I can only write with my left hand. (B) There are two cookies left.
(C) She left the house an hour ago.
(85) **Line** (A) She was first in the line of workers. (B) He drew a long line on the paper.
(86) **Loaf** (A) A fresh loaf of bread smells good. (B) Some people loaf all day.
(87) **Lie** (A) A lie can get you into trouble. (B) Cats often lie down to sleep.
(88) **Last** (A) It did not last very long. (B) She came in last in the race.
(89) **Long** (A) I long to see my home again. (B) It is a long time until winter.
(90) **Mine** (A) He worked in an iron mine. (B) That book is mine.
(91) **Match** (A) She is no match for him. (B) Light a match for my stove.

(92) **Miss** (A) Do you miss your home? (B) Your arrow may miss the target. (C) Did Miss Brown meet her?

(93) **Mean** (A) What did she mean by that? (B) He is a mean teacher. (C) The mean temperature is low.

(94) **Mold** (A) The bread has mold on it. (B) Pour wax into the mold.

(95) **Might** (A) We might hire her for the job. (B) Might does not make it right.

(96) **Note** (A) He knows not a note of music. (B) Send her a note of apology.

(97) **Nap** (A) We often take a nap at noon. (B) The blanket has a lot of nap.

(98) **Nail** (A) She painted her nails. (B) He used a nail to fasten the shelf.

(99) **Perch** (A) Birds often perch on trees. (B) Many perch live in the ocean.

(100) **Pen** (A) The pigs are in the pen. (B) My pen needs some ink.

(101) **Pupil** (A) She is the best pupil in class. (B) The pupil in her eye is blue.

(102) **Point** (A) You should not point at people. (B) My knife has a sharp point. (C) You missed the point of the story.

(103) **Pitcher** (A) She is the pitcher on our team. (B) She poured a pitcher of juice.

(104) **Pound** (A) I bought a pound of chocolates. (B) We bought a dog at the pound. (C) Don't pound on the table.

(105) **Pit** (A) A peach has a large pit inside. (B) We will pit her against him. (C) Some snakes were in the deep pit.

(106) **Plane** (A) A plane flew them to Paris. (B) We use a plane to smooth wood.

(107) **Play** (A) He is an actor in a play. (B) We play basketball each day.

(108) **Park** (A) We had a picnic in the park. (B) I park my car near my office.

(109) **Pop** (A) Do you drink soda pop? (B) Don't pop the balloon.

(110) **Pipe** (A) My dad smokes a pipe. (B) The water pipe broke.

(111) **Palm** (A) There is a palm tree there. (B) He hurt the palm of his hand.

(112) **Part** (A) I part my hair on the right. (B) I need a part to fix my car.

(113) **Pass** (A) She will pass the test easily. (B) He threw a pass to his friend. (C) He went through the narrow pass.

(114) **Pool** (A) She has a pool table at her house. (B) We swam in the swimming pool.

(115) **Pet** (A) A cat can make a nice pet. (B) You can pet my horse.

(116) **Peep** (A) A tiny chick can peep very loud. (B) They can peep through the window.

(117) **Page** (A) It is at the top of the page. (B) The page knelt before the king.

(118) **Punch** (A) We will drink orange punch. (B) He punched the man on his chin.

(119) **Pick** (A) Pick out the one you like. (B) A miner uses a pick and shovel.

(120) **Quack** (A) A duck will quack when it sees you. (B) The doctor was a quack.

(121) **Rare** (A) I don't like my steak rare. (B) Diamonds are rare jewels.

(122) **Ruler** (A) The king is the ruler of the nation. (B) Measure it with the ruler.

(123) **Record** (A) She bought a new record album. (B) He set the record in the high jump.

(124) **Racket** (A) She bought a new tennis racket. (B) The kids made a racket at dinner. (C) His racket made him money.

(125)	**Range**	(A) The cattle are feeding on the range. (C) They range in age from 20 to 30.	(B) She cooked on her new range.
(126)	**Roll**	(A) The ball will roll into the road.	(B) We ate a roll for dinner.
(127)	**Rock**	(A) She will often rock in her chair.	(B) The rock went through my window.
(128)	**Run**	(A) She will run five miles a day.	(B) She had a run in her stocking.
(129)	**Right**	(A) I have a ring on my right hand.	(B) She got all the answers right.
(130)	**Race**	(A) He ran the school race.	(B) He is a member of the human race.
(131)	**Round**	(A) Her watch is round.	(B) He was injured in the fifth round.
(132)	**Rest**	(A) We will rest until dinner.	(B) The rest will arrive after dinner.
(133)	**Rose**	(A) The rose is a pretty flower.	(B) The crowd rose to greet her.
(134)	**Rung**	(A) He has rung the bell twice.	(B) A rung on the ladder is missing.
(135)	**Rear**	(A) The horse will rear if frightened.	(B) We sat at the rear of the room.
(136)	**Scales**	(A) Fish have many scales.	(B) We weighed on the scales.
(137)	**Strike**	(A) Did you strike her on the arm?	(B) The workers are on strike.
(138)	**Stand**	(A)They sold fruit at the stand.	(B) Stand up if he comes into the room.
(139)	**Shine**	(A) Shine your shoes everyday.	(B) Shine your flashlight over here.
(140)	**Shock**	(A) She got a shock from the wire.	(B) That movie will shock my mom.
(141)	**Swallow**	(A) The swallow flew up into the tree.	(B) My throat hurts when I swallow.
(142)	**Stick**	(A) Stick the stamp on the letter.	(B) He broke the stick in two pieces.
(143)	**Sink**	(A) The kitchen sink is full of dishes.	(B) The boat will sink if over loaded.
(144)	**Stump**	(A) She sat on the tree stump.	(B) That question will stump everyone.
(145)	**Spoke**	(A) The bike has a broken spoke.	(B) She often spoke to me about that.
(146)	**Sock**	(A) He lost his sock in the park.	(B) She got a sock on her chin.
(147)	**Skip**	(A) Children often skip when happy.	(B) Skip any question you don't know.
(148)	**Sheet**	(A) She put a new sheet on the bed.	(B) I need a sheet of paper.
(149)	**Stall**	(A) The horse is eating in its stall.	(B) My car will stall at times.
(150)	**Spray**	(A) We need to spray the apple trees.	(B) The spray of flowers is pretty.
(151)	**Spring**	(A) Spring is a good time of the year.	(B) The car has a broken spring.
(152)	**Speaker**	(A) She was a speaker in our class.	(B) My stereo has a new speaker.
(153)	**Steer**	(A) You must steer your car carefully.	(B) The steers were out in the field.
(154)	**Space**	(A) The rocket flew into space.	(B) Put your name in that space.
(155)	**Set**	(A) Our T.V. set is broken.	(B) Please set the table for dinner.
(156)	**Screen**	(A) Please set-up the movie screen. (C) Screen them for infections.	(B) The screen door slammed.
(157)	**Story**	(A) We live on the sixth story.	(B) She told a story to the children.
(158)	**Shift**	(A) I worked on the night shift.	(B) Shift gears when you go uphill.
(159)	**Soil**	(A) Plant the flower in good soil.	(B) Do not soil your dress.
(160)	**Shed**	(A) Cats will shed their fur.	(B) The cow is eating in the shed.
(161)	**Seal**	(A) The seal swam in the ocean. (C) He put a seal on the document.	(B) Seal the envelope before mailing.

(162)	**Squash**	(A) I like to eat squash.	(B) You'll squash it if you step on it.
(163)	**Train**	(A) We will train all students.	(B) We rode the train home.
(164)	**Trip**	(A) We will take a long trip this year.	(B) Don't trip over the rug.
(165)	**Top**	(A) The top was spinning fast.	(B) It is on the top of the desk.
(166)	**Tip**	(A) He left a tip for the waiter.	(B) He cut the tip of his finger.
(167)	**Tablet**	(A) Take a tablet after dinner.	(B) I need a new tablet of paper.
(168)	**Tag**	(A) We played tag with the children.	(B) Put an ID tag on each suitcase.
(169)	**Well**	(A) She can play the piano well.	(B) The water comes from a well.
(170)	**Wave**	(A) A large wave knocked her down.	(B) Wave good-bye to your mother.
(171)	**Watch**	(A) She had a new gold watch.	(B) Watch your children at all times.

Exercise : For Fun

(1) Tracey didn't feel **well** after falling into the **well**. (in good health)
(2) Jim hunts, but he **does** not shoot **does**. (female deer)
(3) There was a big **row** in the first **row** of the theatre. (fight)
(4) Let's **wind** up the kite string, before the **wind** gets too wild. (moving air)
(5) If the judges are **fair**, our rabbit will win a ribbon at the **fair**. (just)
(6) That creaking **sound** makes me wonder if this building is **sound**. (in good condition)
(7) The oil well is yours and the gold **mine** is **mine**. (belonging to me)
(8) The **dove dove** to the ground to eat the peanut. (dived)
(9) I **found** it hard to believe that he planned to **found** a new church. (establish, or start)
(10) The **rose** bushes **rose** out of the fertile ground. (a kind of flower)
(11) I won't shed a **tear** if you **tear** my old shirt into shreds. (rip)
(12) The dog was happy when you dropped the **ground** beef onto the **ground**. (past form of grind)

The meaning of the bold word (printed in dark type) is given in the brackets.

CHAPTER 51

PARONYMS

In English we find several words which are derived from the same root word.These words differ slightly in form, but in many cases the meaning differ a lot. Such words are also called Paronyms.

Paronyms ऐसे शब्दों को कहते हैं जो एक ही parent word से बनते हैं। दिखने में काफी मिलते-जुलते लगते है एवं कई बार इनका अर्थ काफी भिन्न होता है। नीचे ऐसे ही शब्दों को दिया गया है। छात्रों को ऐसे शब्दों का अध्ययन काफी ध्यानपूर्वक करना चाहिए।

	Word	Example
(1)	**Alternate** (*By turn*)	He comes here on alternate days.
	Alternative (*Choice between two things*)	There were alternative methods of travel available.
(2)	**Acceptance** (*Accepting a thing*)	I am happy to learn that she has given her consent for the attending the court.
	Acceptation (*Interpretation*)	There are several acceptations of the word 'Nature'.
(3)	**Access** (*Approach*)	I was not allowed access to a lawyer.
	Accession (*Becoming sovereign*)	Today is the 50th anniversary of the queen's accession to the throne.
(4)	**Act** (*To do*)	I shall act as per the wishes of my parents.
	Action (*Doing things*)	His timely action saved him from the loss.
(5)	**Admission** (*Being admitted*)	He has taken admission in evening college.
	Admittance (*To let in*)	He was denied admittance in the hall.
(6)	**Artist** (*Performer of fine art*)	A poet is no less an artist than a sculpture.
	Artiste (*Performer in singing, dacing etc.*)	The group of five consists of several artistes.
(7)	**Artistic** (*Having aesthetic values*)	This painting is indeed very artistic.
	Artful (*Cunning, clever*)	He wants to achieve success by artful means.
	Artificial (*Antonym of natural*)	City life is becoming more artificial day by day.
	Artisan (*Well versed in hardicrafts*)	The artisans of Nepal are very hardworking and efficient.
(8)	**Appropriation** (*To take possession of*)	He was charged for appropriation of Bank's fund.
	Appropriateness (*Suitability*)	The work of Harivansh Rai Bachchan is renowned for its appropriateness in style.
(9)	**Affecting** (*Touching, pathetic*)	The movie has many affecting scenes and situations.
	Affectation (*False pretense*)	Political leaders speak with affectation and artfulness.
(10)	**Besides** (*In addition*)	Besides paying my debt he also gave me money for the medicines.
	Beside (*By the side*)	In Republic Day function none was sitting beside President.
(11)	**Barbaric** (*Simple, used in good sense*)	I like her barbaric simplicity.
	Barbarian (*Primitive*)	'Johar'and 'Sati' are the barbarian customs.
	Barbarous (*Cruel used in bad sense*)	War is indeed a barbarous act.
(12)	**Barbarism** (*Uncivilised condition*)	In some part of Bihar, absolute arbarism prevailed even now-a-days.
	Barbarity (*Cruelty*)	Aurangzeb was notorious for his barbarity.
(13)	**Confident** (*Certain*)	I am confident that she will come.

Word	Example
Confidant (*Reliable*)	He is a cheat, don't make him your confident.
(14) **Completion** (*End*)	After completion of this work you are to go to Kolkata.
Completeness (*Perfection*)	None can claim completeness of knowledge in any field.
(15) **Ceremonious** (*Overdone formalities*)	His greetings and salutations are too ceremonious.
Ceremonial (*Pertaining to ceremony*)	Diwali is a ceremonial occasion for Hindus.
(16) **Comprehensive** (*Involves all aspects*)	This book gives us comprehensive knowledge of English.
Comprehensible (*Understandable*)	His views on this subject are not only clear, but comprehensible also.
(17) **Considerable** (*Much*)	I have spent a considerable time in solving this problem.
Considerate (*Thoughtful*)	He being a considerate man can't refuse to sign this proposal.
(18) **Continuous** (*Uninterrupted*)	He has been continuously working on computer for the last three hours.
Continual (*Occasional breaks*)	There has been continual raining since yesterday.
(19) **Child-like** (*In good sense act like a child*)	Her child-like face attracts everybody.
Childish (*In bad sense-silly act*)	His childish habits annoyed everybody.
(20) **Complacent** (*Pleasing look*)	Indian farmer are complacent in their look.
Complaisant (*Polite*)	She is a complaisant and intelligent girl.
(21) **Dependent** (*To rely on*)	I am not dependent on anybody for my livelihood.
Dependant (*Depend on others*)	My younger brother is dependant on me.
(22) **Disinterested** (*Without self interest*)	Mother Teresa rendered disinterested service to downtrodden.
Uninterested (*Indifferent*)	Amitabh is uninterested in politics.
(23) **Divers** (*Who swim under the water*)	Divers are trying to reach the top.
Diverse (*Dissimilar-different*)	Diverse opinions were given by the members on this proposal.
(24) **Decided** (*Past form of decide*)	He decided to go to Europe the next week.
Decisive (*That which decides some thing important*)	The battle of Plassey was a decisive one.
(25) **Destination** (*The place to reach*)	The last destination of this train is Puri.
Destiny (*Fate*)	One can make his destiny with hard labour.
(26) **Envious** (*Feeling envy*)	You should not be envious of your friend's progress.
Enviable (*A rousing envy*)	His enviable posting made many jealous of him.
(27) **Effectual** (*Creating desired effects*)	He adopted the effectual means and so got the contract.
Efficacious (*Sufficient to have desired result*)	Quinine now-a-days is not efficacious in malaria.
(28) **Egotist** (*Self conceited*)	I cannot discuss anything with an egotist like you.
Egoist (*Selfishness, self interested*)	He is an egoist, he believes that self interest is the base of all actions.
(29) **Especially** (*Pertaining to exceptional degree*)	Her mother was especially invited on the occasion.
Special (*For the purpose*)	I came specially to attend the function.
(30) **Exceptional** (*Unusual*)	JL Nehru was a man of exceptional qualities.
Exceptionable (*Objectionable*)	His speech was full of exceptionable remarks.
(31) **Exposition** (*Description*)	Tennin's exposition of Ramayan is incomparable.
Exposure (*Open air, cold etc*)	Protect yourself from exposure otherwise you may catch cold.
(32) **Economic** (*Relating to economy*)	The economic condition of our country is not so good.
Economical (*Thrifty*)	He is very economical in spending the money .
(33) **Funeral** (*Ceremony after death*)	More than ten thousand persons attended the funeral of his father.
Funereal (*Gloomy*)	He came to the office with a funereal countenance.
(34) **Fatal** (*Deadly*)	He received a fatal wound in his chest.
Fatalist (*Believes in fate*)	I am not a fatalist.

Word	Example
Fateful (*Lucky, important*)	Fifteen August is a fateful day in Indian History.
(35) **Forceful** (*Commanding force*)	He enjoys a forceful personality.
Forcible (*Under compulsion*)	Police made a forcible entry in his house.
(36) **Godly** (*Pious*)	Mahatma Gandhi led a godly life.
God-like (*Like God*)	Mahatma Gandhi was a God-like man.
(37) **Graceful** (*Handsome-smart*)	She has a graceful appearance.
Gracious (*Kind*)	God is gracious.
(38) **Honorary** (*Without any remuneration*)	He was nominated 'Honorary' Chairman of the society.
Honourable (*Deserve honour, respected*)	I request the honourable Principal to come on the dais.
(39) **Imaginary** (*Not real*)	Equator is an imaginary line.
Imaginative (*Pertaining to imagination*)	A good writer must have imaginative ideas.
(40) **Industrious** (*Laborious*)	Nothing is impossible for an industrious and sincere student.
Industrial (*Relating to industry*)	Bhiwani is an industrial town.
(41) **Intelligent** (*Wise*)	He is an intelligent guy.
Intelligible (*Understandable*)	He delivered an intelligible speech on educational necessities of rural area.
(42) **Judicial** (*Pertaining to legal system or Judge*)	Government has ordered a judicial enquiry in the matter.
Judicious (*Prudent , wise*)	Going for a war is not a judicious decision.
(43) **Loudly** (*High volume*)	Please do not speak so loudly in library room.
Aloud (*Audible voice*)	He spoke aloud so that all could hear him.
(44) **Luxuriant** (*Refer more growth*)	There is a luxuriant growth of vegetable in our kitchen garden.
Luxurious (*Luxury*)	He is leading a luxurious life after the death of his father.
(45) **Lovable** (*Worthy of love*)	He is a lovable person.
Lovely (*Charming*)	What a lovely girl she is !
(46) **Limit** (*Boundary*)	Keep yourself within the limits, otherwise you have to face the music.
Limitation (*Restrictions*)	Being a girl, I have many limitations.
(47) **Memorial** (*Statue, building to commemorate*)	You can find many memorials at Rajpath New Delhi.
Memorable (*Rememberable*)	26th January is a memorable day in Indian History.
(48) **Momentary** (*For a moment*)	His anger is momentary, soon things will be okay.
Momentous (*Important*)	The battle of Plassey was a momentous event in the history of India.
(49) **Negligible** (*Unimportant*)	There is a negligible difference between this shirt and the shirt we saw in that shop.
Negligent (*Careless*)	She is generally negligent about her health.
Neglectful (*Careless about a thing*)	She is so neglectful that she does not care even for her career.
(50) **Officious** (*Over kind*)	His officious attitude towards her creates doubts.
Official (*Relating to office*)	As a responsible official of a company you must behave properly.
(51) **Practical** (*Antonym of theoritical*)	He failed in practical examination. He is a practical businessman.
Practicable (*Capable of being carried out*)	This is not a practicable plan.
(52) **Political** (*Relating to politics*)	We should not trust the political statements of leaders.
Politic (*Sagacious, prudent*)	It is not politic to argue with an intoxicated person.
(53) **Pitiable** (*Relating to pity*)	His condition is indeed pitiable.
Pitiful (*Feeling pity*)	Seeing her pitiable condition everyone became pitiful.
(54) **Prophecy** (*Noun-forecast*)	He made a prophecy that whole of the world would be destroyed in 2202.

Word	Example
Prophesy (*To forecast*)	I can prophesy that within five years India will be a very powerful country.
(55) **Respective** (*Particular thing or person*)	After prayer, students should join their respective teams.
Respectful (*Full of respect*)	One should be respectful to one's teachers, elders.
(56) **Righteous** (*Just*)	Her anger was righteous as no girl could tolerate such insult.
Rightful (*Just claim*)	I am the rightful owner of this car.
(57) **Regrettable** (*Causing regret*)	It is quite regrettable that you are not taking care of your father.
Regretful (*Full of regret*)	I am not at all regretful for my actions.
(58) **Servility** (*Flattery*)	I can't adopt an attitude of servility to get promotion.
Servitude (*Slavery*)	Try to come out of this state of servitude.
(59) **Sociable** (*Fond of getting social*)	She has a sociable, nature.
Social (*Relates to society*)	She is not only social but also very cooperative.
(60) **Sensuous** (*Used in good sense for appreciation of beauty*)	Keats was a sensuous poet.
Sensual (*Used in bad sense means voluptuous*)	He was jailed for his sensual advancement towards his college friend.
(61) **Sensitive** (*Touchy*)	Cow slaughter is a sensitive matter for Hindus.
Sensational (*Exciting*)	There are many sensational stories of murder in this magazine.
(62) **Spirituous** (*Alcoholic*)	Gujarat has banned the use of spirituous drinks in restaurants.
Spiritual (*Pertaining to soul*)	She is a spiritual lady.
(63) **Tolerant** (*Refer to a person, who respects different opinion also*)	Akbar was regarded as a tolerant king.
Tolerable (*Bearable*)	Because of his tolerable nature, he didn't lodge FIR against you.
(64) **Temperament** (*Disposition*)	Because of his violent temperament, he gets into trouble.
Temperance (*Sobriety*)	He should observe temperance in drinking and dancing.
(65) **Temporal** (*Antonym to spiritual*)	Now-a-days people are ready to do anything for temporal gains.
Temporary (*A short time*)	I offered her a temporary job.
(66) **Transitory** (*Short lived*)	The life is not eternal, but transitory.
Transient (*Of short duration*)	The world is transient.
(67) **Union** (*To be united*)	Union is strength.
Unity (*Oneness*)	There is no unity among different classes of the society.
Unison (*Harmony*)	There was a good unison of Tabla and Violin in the cultural programme.
(68) **Virtual** (*In effect*)	Sanjay Gandhi was the virtual head of Congress Party.
Virtuous (*Of good moral values*)	Sita was a virtuous lady.
(69) **Wilful** (*Knowingly*)	He was charged for wilful negligence.
Willing (*Ready*)	I am willing to help her.
(70) **Womanly** (*Used in good sense, affectionately*)	My wife posseses all womanly qualities.
Womanish (*Used in bad sense, means cowardly and weak like woman*)	Everyone likes to dominate a man of womanish temperament.
(71) **Wait** (*Generally used intransitively*)	Please wait for me .
Await (*Lie in wait*)	A surprise awaited them at their home.
(72) **Weary** (*Tired*)	You look pale and weary.
Wearisome (*tiring*)	The journey was wearisome.
(73) **Yield** (*Return*)	What is the annual yield from the fields?
Yielding (*Submissive*)	He is a man of yielding nature.

CHAPTER

52

ONE WORD SUBSTITUTIONS

(1) **Abdication**	Voluntaily renouncing throne.
(2) **Aborigines**	Original inhabitants of a country.
(3) **Ablaut**	A vowel change that accompanies a change in grammatical function. Same as 'gradation.' *Sing, sang,* and *sung.*
(4) **Accismus**	Pretended refusal of something desired.
(5) **Acrolect**	A variety of language that is closest to a standard main language, especially in an area where a creole is also spoken. *Standard Jamaican English,* where Jamaican Creole is also spoken.
(6) **Adianoeta**	An expression that carries both an obvious meaning and a second, subtler meaning.
(7) **Adynaton**	A declaration of impossibility, usually expressed as an exaggerated comparison with a more obvious impossibility. *"I will sooner have a beard grow in the palm of my hand than he shall get one of his cheek."* — William Shakespeare
(8) **Alexia**	Inability to read, usually caused by brain lesions; word blindness.
(9) **Alliteration**	Repetition of the same sound beginning several words placed close together, usually adjacent.
(10) **Alphabetism**	The expression of spoken sounds by an alphabet.
(11) **Ambigram**	A word, phrase, or sentence written in such a way that it reads the same way upside down as right.
(12) **Anadiplosis**	Rhetorical repetition of one or more words, particularly a word at the end of a clause. "*Men in great place are thrice servants: servants of the sovereign or state; servants of fame; and servants of business.*" — Francis Bacon
(13) **Anagram**	A rearrangement of a group of letters, especially a word that can be formed by rearranging the letters in another word.
(14) **Accessible**	Which can be approached.
(15) **Acclimatize**	To accustom oneself in new climate.
(16) **Aggressor**	One who attacks first.
(17) **Alimony**	Allowance paid to wife on legal separation.
(18) **Altruist**	One who loves others.
(19) **Amateur**	Who does thing for pleasure and not for money.
(20) **Ambassador**	Person representing a State in a foreign country.

(21) **Ambidextrous** One who can use either hand without any problem.
(22) **Ambiguous** That can be interpreted in any way.
(23) **Amnesia** Loss of memory.
(24) **Amphibia** Animals live both on land and sea.
(25) **Anarchy** Absence of rule or law and order.
(26) **Annual** Which happens once a year.
(27) **Anomaly** Deviation from common rule.
(28) **Anonymous** Which does not bear the name of writer.
(29) **Antiseptic** Medicine used to save plant and animals from being rotten or decaying.
(30) **Anaphora** Repetition of a word or phrase at the beginning of successive phrases, clauses or sentences.
(31) **Antonym** Words which are opposite in meaning.
(32) **Aphasia** Loss of speech.
(33) **Aquarium** Vessel in which fish and water plants are kept.
(34) **Aquatic** Animals live in water.
(35) **Archeology** Study of Antiquities.
(36) **Aristocracy** Government by the rich/aristocrats.
(37) **Ascetic** One who tortures himself for the good of soul.
(38) **Atheist** One who does not believe in existence of God.
(39) **Audible** Sound which can be heard.
(40) **Auditor** One who audits the accounts.
(41) **Aurist** A specialist with regard to the ear.
(42) **Autobiography** Life history written by oneself.
(43) **Autocracy** Government by one man.
(44) **Autograph** Getting signature of some important person in his handwriting.
(45) **Bachelorhood** State of being unmarried.
(46) **Bankrupt** One who can't pay the debts.
(47) **Bellicose** One who is fond of fighting .
(48) **Belligerents** Nations engaged in war.
(49) **Billingsgate** Coarsely abusive language.
(50) **Bibliophile** One who loves and collects books.
(51) **Biennial** Happening every second year.
(52) **Bigamy** Have two husband or two wives at a time.
(53) **Biography** Life history of a person.
(54) **Biped** Animal having two feet.
(55) **Blasphemy** Speaking disrespectfully about sacred or religious things.
(56) **Bookworm** One who devotes full time in studying course books.
(57) **Botany** Study of plants.
(58) **Brigand** A bandit or robber, esp. one of a band living by pillage and ransom.
(59) **Brittle** Which can be easily broken.
(60) **Bullion** Gold or silver before using for manufacturing ornaments.
(61) **Bureaucracy** Government run by officials.
(62) **Caducity** The infirmity of old age, senility.
(63) **Calligraphy** The art of beautiful handwriting; elegant penmanship.

(64) **Cannibal** One who eats human flesh.
(65) **Centrifugal** Anything tending to move away from centre.
(66) **Centripetal** Anything tending to move towards centre.
(67) **Century** One hundred years.
(68) **Chrestomathy** A collection of choice literary passages, especially to help in learning a language.
(69) **Coprolalia** Uncontrolled, excessive use of obscene or scatological language, sometimes accompanying certain mental disorders.
(70) **Cruciverbalist** A constructor of crossword puzzles; also, an enthusiast of word games, especially crossword puzzles.
(71) **Colleagues** Persons working in the same office.
(72) **Compatriot** Belonging to same country.
(73) **Congenital** Belongs to a person by birth.
(74) **Contemporaries** Persons living at the same time.
(75) **Convalescence** Period of gradual recovery after illness.
(76) **Cosmopolitan** A citizen of the world.
(77) **Credulous** Who easily believes others.
(78) **Cryptography** Study of secret writing and coded words.
(79) **Curable** Which can be cured.
(80) **Cytology** Study of cell.
(81) **Dead letter** An unclaimed letter.
(82) **Deaf** One who cannot hear.
(83) **Democracy** Government of the people, for the people, by the people.
(84) **Dermatology** Study of skin.
(85) **Digestible** That which can be digested.
(86) **Dilogy** An ambiguous speech.
(87) **Dittograph** A letter or word repeated unintentionally in writing or copying.
(88) **Dittology** Two distinct interpretations of the same text.
(89) **Dipsomania** A strong desire to take liquor.
(90) **Divisible** That which can be divided.
(91) **Dotage** Extreme old age when one behaves like a child.
(92) **Drawn** A game in which no party wins.
(93) **Dumb** One who can't speak.
(94) **Dysgraphia** Impairment of the ability to write, usually caused by brain dysfunction or disease.
(95) **Dyslexia** A learning disorder distinguished by impaired ability to recognize and comprehend written words.
(96) **Edible** A thing fit to eat.
(97) **Effeminate** Womanish in habits.
(98) **Eligible** One who is fit for the post.
(99) **Elision** The omission of a letter or syllable. "*Don't*" instead of "do not."
(100) **Emigrant** One who goes to live in a foreign country.
(101) **Employee** One who is employed.
(102) **Employer** One who employs.
(103) **Endemic** A disease prevailing in a locality.

(104) **Entomology** Study of insects.
(105) **Endophoric** Characteristic of a reference to something outside the speech or text in which the reference occurs. See also: exophoric.
(106) **Epic** A long narrative poem.
(107) **Epanorthosis** Immediate rephrasing for emphasis, intensification or justification. "You, young lad, are most brave! Brave, did I say? No, heroic!"
(108) **Epistrophe** Repetition of the same word or phrase at the end of successive phrases, clauses, or sentences.
(109) **Epicure** One who is fond of sensuous enjoyment.
(110) **Epilogue** A speech given after conclusion of drama.
(111) **Epitaph** Words inscribed on the tomb of the dead.
(112) **Etymology** Science deals with formation of words.
(113) **Eucrasia** A good or normal state of health.
(114) **Etymon** An earlier form of a word in the same language or an ancestor language.
(115) **Examinee** One who is taking examination.
(116) **Examiner** One who examines the copies of examinees.
(117) **Exonym** A name by which one people or social group refers to another, but which is not used by said group to refer to themselves.
(118) **Expatriate** To send out of native country.
(119) **Expurgate** To remove all objectionable matter.
(120) **Extempore** A speech without previous preparations.
(121) **Extradite** To send back the criminal to the country of his origin.
(122) **Fanatic (Bigot)** Unreasonably enthusiastic about religion.
(123) **Fastidious** Having very selective taste. Hard to please.
(124) **Fatalist** One who believe in fate.
(125) **Feminist** One devoted to the welfare of women.
(126) **Foster child** Child brought by persons, who are not his parents.
(127) **Franchise** Constitutional right to cast vote.
(128) **Fratricide** Murder of brother.
(129) **Garage** A shed for motor car.
(130) **Geology** Study of Earth.
(131) **Germicide** Which destroy germs.
(132) **Glossolalia** Fabricated, nonmeaningful speech, especially such speech associated with a trance state or some schizophrenic syndromes.
(133) **Glottochronology** The determination of how long ago different languages evolved from a common source language.
(134) **Glutton** Fond of eating too much.
(135) **Gratis** Without any payment, free.
(136) **Gregarious** Animals live in flocks.
(137) **Harangue** A noisy and loud speech before a large gathering.
(138) **Haplology** The process by which a word is formed by removing one of two identical or similar adjacent syllables in an earlier word.
(139) **Hearse** Vehicle to carry dead bodies.
(140) **Herbivorous** Animals live on herbs.
(141) **Hendiadys** The use of a conjunction rather than the subordination of one word to another.

(142) **Heterography** A method of spelling in which the same letters represent different sounds in different words, as in ordinary English orthography.
(143) **Heterophemy** The unconscious saying, in speech or in writing, of some thing that one does not intend to say, especially when what is said is the reverse of what was intended.
(144) **Heterogeneous** Things of different nature.
(145) **Histology** Study of tissue.
(146) **Hobson-jobson** An Anglicized word or phrase corrupted from one or more words of an Asian language.
(147) **Holonym** A concept that has another concept as a part.
(148) **Homicide** Murder of a human being.
(149) **Homogeneous** Things of same nature.
(150) **Honeymoon** The first night of newly married couple.
(151) **Honorary** A post without any remuneration.
(152) **Hydra** A serpent with many heads.
(153) **Hydrophobia** A fear from water.
(154) **Hygienist** Who cares fully of his health.
(155) **Hypothesis** A tentative assumption, made to drive a logical conclusion.
(156) **Hypallage** Interchange of two elements in a phrase or clause from the order, in which they would normally appear. "A mind is a terrible thing to waste," instead of "To waste a mind is a terrible thing."
(157) **Hypercorrect** Characteristic of an incorrect linguistic construction, in which the error is produced from a mistaken effort to be correct. "Between you and I," which should be 'between you and me.'
(158) **Hyponym** A word that is more specific than a given word.
(159) **Iconoclast** Breaker of art and literature.
(160) **Idiosyncrasy** Peculiar temper of an individual.
(161) **Idolatry** Worshipping of idols.
(162) **Ignorant** Person have no knowledge of any happening.
(163) **Illegal** Unlawful.
(164) **Illegible** Which cannot be read.
(165) **Illiterate** One who can neither read nor write.
(166) **Illeism** The practice of referring to oneself in the third person.
(167) **Imitable** Which can be imitated.
(168) **Immigrant** A person from another country comes to our country to settle.
(169) **Immovable** Which can't be moved, fixed.
(170) **Imposter** One who assumes name or title of someone else for deceiving others.
(171) **Impregnable** A fort which can't be entered into.
(172) **Incorrigible** Cannot be corrected.
(173) **Ingressive** Characteristic of a speech sound produced with an inhalation of breath.
(174) **Incredible** Which can't be believed.
(175) **Inevitable** That cannot be avoided.
(176) **Infallible** One who cannot make a mistake.
(177) **Infanticide** Murder of an infant.
(178) **Infections** A disease spread by contact.
(179) **Inimitable** Cannot be imitated.

(180) **Insomnia** Loss of sleep.
(181) **Interpolate** Inserting new matter in a book.
(182) **Intervein** Anything pushed inside veins.
(183) **Invisible** That which cannot be seen.
(184) **Invulnerable** Cannot be wounded.
(185) **Irreparable** That can't be repaired.
(186) **Irrevocable** A decision that can't be revoked.
(187) **Isocolon** A sequence of parallel structures, having the same number of words and sometimes the same number of syllables.
"*What else can one do when he is alone in a jail cell, other than write long letters, think long thoughts, and pray long prayers*?" ***Martin Luther King***
(188) **Itinerant** One who travels from place to place.
(189) **Kindergarten** A school for small children.
(190) **Kleptomania** An abnormal desire to steal.
(191) **Linguist** One who knows many languages.
(192) **Ligature** A character that combines two or more letters, such as e.
(193) **Lipogram** Writing composed of words lacking a certain specific letter or letters.
(194) **Litotes** Understatement by negating the opposite; a type of meiosis. "*I was not disappointed with the news.*"
(195) **Loquacious** A continuous talker.
(196) **Lunar** Eclipse of Moon.
(197) **Maiden speech** Speech made for the first time.
(198) **Mammals** Animals which give milk.
(199) **Manuscript** Book written by hand.
(200) **Masochism** The condition or state of deriving (esp. sexual) gratification from one's own pain or humiliation.
(201) **Materialistic** One for whom money is the most important thing.
(202) **Matins** Morning prayer in church.
(203) **Matricide** Murder of own mother.
(204) **Matrimony** State of being married.
(205) **Maxim** An established principle.
(206) **Meadow** A low level tract of uncultivated grassland.
(207) **Meditation** The action or practice of profound spiritual or religious reflection or mental contemplation.
(208) **Melodrama** A sensational dramatic piece with crude appeals to the emotions and usually a happy ending.
(209) **Mercenary** One who fights for the sake of money.
(210) **Mesomorph** A person whose build is powerful, compact, and muscular.
(211) **Meteorology** Study of climate or weather.
(212) **Meticulous** Very particular even about small details.
(213) **Migratory** That moves from one place to another.
(214) **Misogamist** One who hates the custom of marriage.
(215) **Misogynist** Hater of women.
(216) **Misologist** One who hates learning.
(217) **Mobocracy** Rule by mob.

(218) **Metonymy**	Substitution of a word or phrase with another which it suggests. *"The pen is mightier than the sword,"* in which both "pen" and "sword" are substituted for "written prose" and "military."
(219) **Morphology**	The study of structure and form of words in language including inflection, derivation and formation of compounds.
(220) **Monogamy**	Marrying one at a time.
(221) **Morphology**	Study of animal and plant structure.
(222) **Narcotic**	Medicine which induces sleep.
(223) **Neologism**	New word coined by an author.
(224) **Neology**	Study of formation of new words.
(225) **Notorious**	A man with bad reputation.
(226) **Nosism**	The practice of referring to oneself as "we"; a type of enallage.
(227) **Numismatics**	Study of Coins.
(228) **Obsolete**	No longer in practice.
(229) **Oceanography**	Study of ocean.
(230) **Odontology**	Study of teeth.
(231) **Oligarchy**	Government by a few.
(232) **Omnipotent**	One who is all powerful.
(233) **Omniscient**	One who knows everything.
(234) **Omnivorous**	Who eats everything.
(235) **Opaque**	That which can't be seen through.
(236) **Ophthalmology**	Study of eye.
(237) **Optics**	Study of light.
(238) **Optimist**	One who sees bright side of things.
(239) **Orthography**	The study of correct spelling according to established usage.
(240) **Ornithology**	Study of birds.
(241) **Orography**	Study of mountain.
(242) **Orphan**	A child whose parents are dead.
(243) **Orthodox**	One who believes in traditional values.
(244) **Orthography**	Study of correct spelling of words.
(245) **Ostracize**	To expel from society.
(246) **Pacifist**	One who believes in total abolition of war.
(247) **Paleontology**	Study of fossils.
(248) **Panacea**	A remedy for all ills.
(249) **Pantisocracy**	Government by all.
(250) **Pantomime**	A dumb show.
(251) **Palilogy**	The repetition of a word or phrase in immediate succession, for emphasis.
(252) **Palindrome**	A word, phrase, clause or sentence that reads the same regularly as it does when its letters are reversed; a type of palingram.
(253) **Palingram**	A word, phrase, clause or sentence that reads the same backwards after rearranging segments. "*Workmate did teamwork.*"
(254) **Pangram**	A sentence that uses all the letters of the alphabet; a holalphabetic sentence.
(255) **Paragoge**	The process by which a new word is formed by adding a letter or syllable to the end of another word. Same as "proparalepsis." "*Climature*," derived from "climate."

(256) **Paraprosdokian**	Unexpected ending of a phrase or series.
(257) **Parasite**	One who depends on others.
(258) **Parasol**	A lady's umbrella.
(259) **Pathology**	Study of Disease.
(260) **Patricide**	Murder of one's own father.
(261) **Patrimony**	Properties inherited from one's father.
(262) **Patriot**	One who loves own country.
(263) **Pedagogy**	Study of art of teaching.
(264) **Pedantic**	A style in which author displays his knowledge.
(265) **Perpilocutionist**	One who expounds on a subject of which he has little knowledge.
(266) **Polyptoton**	Repetition of a word in different forms, cases, or with different inflection, in the sentence.
(267) **Purr word**	A word with positive connotations and therefore desirable to use in building and sustaining good public relations.
(268) **Pedestrian**	One who travels on foot.
(269) **Pessimist**	One who sees dark side of things.
(270) **Philanderer**	One who enjoys by love making.
(271) **Philanthropist**	A lover of mankind.
(272) **Philately**	Study of stamp collection.
(273) **Philistine**	Who does not care for art or literature.
(274) **Philogynist**	Lover of womankind.
(275) **Philology**	Study of words and their roots.
(276) **Phonetics**	Acoustics study of sound.
(277) **Phrenology**	Study of skull with regard to human character.
(278) **Physiology**	Study of structure of human body.
(279) **Pioneer**	One who leads others.
(280) **Plagiarism**	Literary theft. Using ideas and words of another person presenting them as own.
(281) **Platitudes**	Common place remarks.
(282) **Plutocracy**	Government by rich.
(283) **Polyandry**	Marrying more than one husband at a time.
(284) **Polygamy**	Marrying more than one wife at a time.
(285) **Post mortem**	An examination of body after death.
(286) **Primogeniture**	Right of succession belonging to the first born.
(287) **Pseudonym**	An imaginary name of author assumed to disguise himself.
(288) **Pugnacity**	Tendency to quarrel.
(289) **Purist**	One who is particular about the purity of one's language.
(290) **Quadruped**	Animal having four foot.
(291) **Rebel**	One who take up arms against Government.
(292) **Redtapism**	Too much official formalities.
(293) **Regicide**	Murder of a king.
(294) **Reticule**	A lady's purse.
(295) **Retrospective**	Which takes effect from some earlier date.
(296) **Sacrilege**	Violating sanctity of some religious place.

(297) **Sadist**	A person who derives (esp. sexual) pleasure from inflicting pain, suffering, humiliation.
(298) **Shrew**	A woman with peevish nature.
(299) **Simultaneous**	Happening at the same time.
(300) **Smuggle**	Importing goods illegally without paying custom duties.
(301) **Solar**	Eclipse of Sun, relating to Sun.
(302) **Soliloquy**	Speaking himself when alone.
(303) **Somnambulism**	Walking in sleep.
(304) **Somniloquism**	Talking in sleep.
(305) **Spokesman**	One who speaks on behalf of other.
(306) **Stoic**	One who is indifferent to pleasure and pain.
(307) **Suicide**	Killing of self.
(308) **Snarl word**	A word with negative connotations and therefore not desirable to use lest good public relations be undermined.
(309) **Superordinate**	A word that is more generic than a given word.
(310) **Syllogism**	Deductive reasoning in which a conclusion is derived from two premises. "*All human beings are mortal. I am a human being. Therefore, I am mortal.*"
(311) **Synesis**	Agreement of words to logic rather than grammatical form. '*The wages of sin is death.*' **Romans 6:23**
(312) **Synchronize**	Occurring two or more events at a time.
(313) **Teetotaller**	One who does not take alcoholic drinks.
(314) **Telltale**	One who enjoys talking about others private affairs.
(315) **Thearchy**	Government by the God.
(316) **Theist**	One who believes in the existence of God.
(317) **Theomania**	A belief that one is God.
(318) **Transmigration**	Passing of soul from one body to another after death.
(319) **Transparent**	That which can be seen through.
(320) **Truant**	A student left school or class without permission.
(321) **Truism**	An often repeated truth.
(322) **Twins**	Two child born together.
(323) **Usurer**	One who lends money at higher rate of interest.
(324) **Utopia**	A state of highest perfection.
(325) **Uxoricide**	Murder of wife.
(326) **Valetudinarian**	One who always think that he is ill.
(327) **Venial**	An excusable fault.
(328) **Verbatim**	Repetition word by word.
(329) **Verbicide**	The destruction of the sense or value of a word.
(330) **Verbose**	Style full of words.
(331) **Vesper**	Evening prayer in a church.
(332) **Veteran**	A well and long experienced person in a particular occupation.
(333) **Wardrobe**	An almirah where clothes are kept.
(334) **Widow**	A woman whose husband has died.
(335) **Widower**	A man whose wife has died.
(336) **Xenoepist**	One with a foreign accent.
(337) **Zoology**	Study of animals.

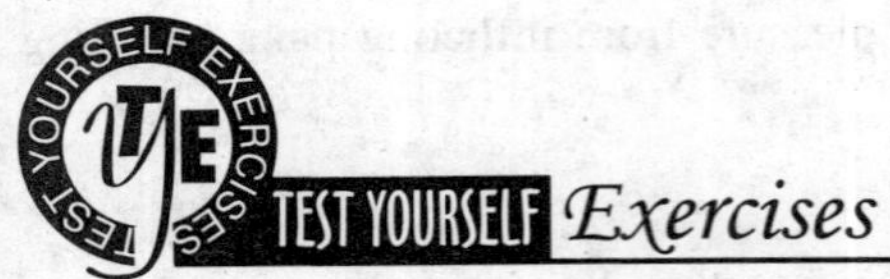

Exercises

01

Directions (Q. 1-10) : *Give one word for each of the following expressions choosing from those given below each such expression* **[Income Tax Inspectors]**

(1) Life history of a man written by himself.
(a) Biography (b) Autobiography (c) Calligraphy (d) Bibliography

(2) A statement that can have a double meaning.
(a) Verbose (b) Ambivalent (c) Epigraph (d) Ambiguous

(3) Work inscribed on the tomb.
(a) Eulogy (b) Epitaph (c) Epigraph (d) Eloquence

(4) The intelligent and educated class.
(a) Literate (b) Aristocrat (c) Educated (d) Intelligentsia

(5) Science of plants.
(a) Zoology (b) Geology (c) Anthropology (d) Botany

(6) List of headings of the business to be transacted at a meeting.
(a) Minutes (b) Agenda (c) Excerpts (d) Proceedings

(7) One filled with excessive and mistaken enthusiasm in a cause.
(a) Pedant (b) Patriot (c) Fanatic (d) Martyr

(8) Regard for others as a principle of action.
(a) Altruism (b) Philanthropy (c) Nepotism (d) Cynicism

(9) One who promotes the idea of absence of government of any kind, when every man should be a law unto himself.
(a) Agnostic (b) Iconoclast (c) Belligerent (d) Anarchist

(10) Study of mankind.
(a) Pathology (b) Philology (c) Physiology (d) Anthropology

02

Directions (Q. 1-10) *Give one word for each of the following expressions choosing from those given below each such expression :* **[RRB ASM, Excise Inspector]**

(1) An office with no work, but high pay.
(a) Honorary (b) Sinecure (c) Ex-officio (d) Reticent

(2) One who deserts his religion.
(a) Deserter (b) Apostate (c) Opportunist (d) Turn coat

(3) The act of looking back upon past events.
(a) Introspection (b) Retrospection (c) Extrospection (d) Circumspection

(4) Very vigilant and cautious.
(a) Meticulous (b) Fastidious (c) Anxious (d) Alert

(5) Matter written by hand.
(a) Handwritten (b) Manuscript (c) Amnesty (d) Proof

(6) A small shop that sells fashionable clothes, cosmetics, etc.
(a) Store (b) Dtall (c) Boutique (d) Both

(7) One who is honourably discharged from service.
(a) Retired (b) Emeritus (c) Relieved (d) Emancipated

(8) One who cannot be corrected.
(a) Incurable (b) Incorrigible (c) Hardened (d) Invulnerable

(9) One who is incharge of a museum.
(a) Curator (b) Supervisor (c) Caretaker (d) Warden

(10) The study of ancient societies.
(a) Anthropology (b) Archaeology (c) History (d) Ethnology

03

Directions (Q. 1-5) *: Give one word for each of the following expressions choosing from those given below each such expression :* **[SBI PO]**

(1) Responsible according to law.
(a) Eligible (b) Legitimate (c) Legalised (d) Liable
(e) Offensive

(2) Constant effort to achieve something.
(a) Patience (b) Vigour (c) Enthusiasm (d) Attempt
(e) Perseverance

(3) Opposed to great or sudden change.
(a) Conservative (b) Revolutionary (c) Evolutionary (d) Static
(e) Unalterable

(4) Anything written in a letter after it is signed.
(a) Corrigendum (b) Manuscript (c) Postscript (d) Post diction
(e) Posterity

(5) That which cannot be done without.
(a) Impracticable (b) Indispensable (c) Impossible (d) Unmanageable
(e) Irrevocable

04

Directions (Q. 1-5) *Give one word for each of the following expressions choosing from those given below each such expression :* **[Bank PO]**

(1) He could not give a good explanation for his extraordinary behaviour.
(a) Be satisfied with (b) Account for
(c) Provide evidence for (d) Count for
(e) Readily dispense

(2) Those who pass through this gate without permission be prosecuted.
(a) Bypassers (b) Absconders
(c) Thoroughfares (d) Trespassers
(e) Culprits

(3) A careful preservation and protection of wildlife is the need of the hour.
(a) Management (b) Embarkment
(c) Enhancement (d) Promotion
(e) Conservation

(4) I could achieve success through conscious efforts.
(a) Tremendous efforts (b) Efforts made with critical awareness
(c) Efforts done after gaining consciousness (d) Efforts done after being awakened
(e) Efforts done without any desire

(5) We are looking forward to a good monsoon this year.
(a) Getting
(b) Predicting
(c) Hoping
(d) Visualising
(e) Encouraging

05

Directions (Q. 1-13) : *Substitute one word for each of the following sentences :* **[IAS]**

(1) A person incharge of a museum.
(2) One who does not believe in the existence of God.
(3) One who collects postage stamps.
(4) One who goes on a journey to holy place.
(5) One who abstains from alcoholic drinks.
(6) That which can be understood.
(7) One who studies the stars and sky.
(8) A plant that draws sustenance from another.
(9) A child whose parents are dead.
(10) A dead body of a human being.
(11) A child born after the death of his father.
(12) Descending from parent to child.
(13) The story of one's own life.

06

Directions (Q. 1-10) : *Substitute one word for each of the following sentences :*

(1) The science of words and language is known as :
(a) philology
(b) paleontology
(c) bibliography
(d) entomology

(2) One of the time-tested ways of remembering a series of items is known as a/an :
(a) recollection
(b) schematizing
(c) mnemonic
(d) ingenuity

(3) Nations that do not trust each other look upon each other :
(a) calmly
(b) hopefully
(c) askance
(d) retrospectively

(4) If a person cannot be easily handled or dealt with, he will not be complimented for his :
(a) domesticity
(b) knowledge
(c) tractability
(d) eulogy

(5) A person who constantly thinks, he is sick is a :
(a) hypochondriac
(b) misogynist
(c) misanthrope
(d) hyperpituitary

(6) But a person who is really sickly and is unduly solicitous about his health is a :
(a) valedictorian
(b) vegetarian
(c) valetudinarian
(d) dialectician

(7) The order to stay in one's own bailiwick means that a person should remain in his own :
(a) room
(b) district
(c) country
(d) bed

(8) Because the orator's speech was high-flown and pretentious, the reporters termed it :
(a) bombastic
(b) austere
(c) untruthful
(d) vituperative

(9) When the courtier had advanced to the highest positon attainable, he was said to have reached the :
(a) vigil
(b) precipice
(c) threshold
(d) pinnacle

(10) Accepting his fate with calmness, the camel driver said, "It is...." :
(a) growing late
(b) kismet
(c) kiosk
(d) suttee

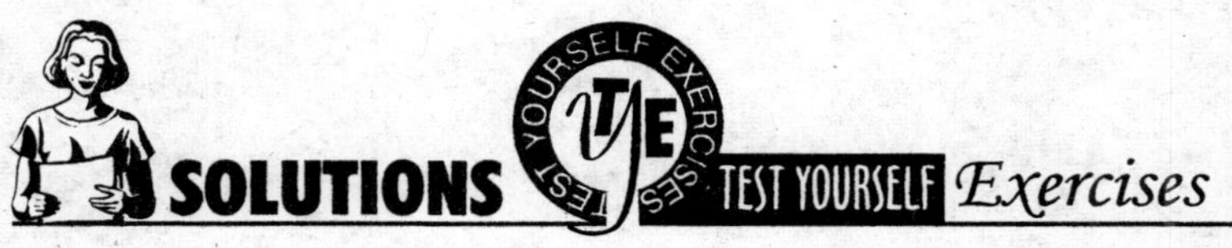

Solution TYE 01

(1) (b), (2) (d), (3) (b), (4) (d), (5) (d), (6) (b),
(7) (c), (8) (a), (9) (d), (10) (d).

Solution TYE 02

(1) (b), (2) (b), (3) (b), (4) (a), (5) (b), (6) (c),
(7) (b), (8) (b), (9) (a), (10) (a).

Solution TYE 03

(1) (d), (2) (e), (3) (a), (4) (c), (5) (b).

Solution TYE 04

(1) (b), (2) (d), (3) (e), (4) (b), (5) (d).

Solution TYE 05

(1) Curator, (2) Atheist, (3) Philatelist, (4) Pilgrim, (5) Teetotaller,
(6) Intelligible, (7) Astronomer, (8) Parasite, (9) Orphan, (10) Corpse,
(11) Posthumous, (12) Hereditary, (13) Autobiography.

Solution TYE 06

(1) (a), (2) (c), (3) (c), (4) (c), (5) (a), (6) (c),
(7) (b), (8) (a), (9) (d), (10) (b).

CHAPTER

53

FOREIGN WORDS

We are giving below a number of foreign words used in newspapers, standard books and magazines. Students are advised to learn these words. These words are often seen in competitive examinations papers.

A

Ab aeterno (L.), from eternity.	अनादि काल से।
Ab ante (L.), from before.	पूर्व काल से।
Ab antiquo (L.), from olden time.	प्राचीन काल से।
Ab initio (L.), from the beginning.	आरम्भ से।
Ab intra (L.), from within	भीतर से।
Ab irato (L.), in a fit of passion.	उद्वेग से, क्रोध से।
Abonnement (Fr.) subscription.	शुल्क, चन्दा।
Ab origine (L.), from the beginning.	आरम्भ से, आदि से।
Ad arbitrium (L.) at pleasure.	इच्छानुसार।
Ad extra (L.), outward.	बाहर की ओर।
Ad finem (L.), to the end.	अन्त तक।
Ad infinitum (L.) up to infinity.	अनन्त तक, अन्तिम सीमा तक।
Ad interim (L.), for the meantime.	बीच के समय के लिए, अन्तरिम।
A' discretion (Fr.), without restriction.	बिना किसी रुकावट के, अबाध।
Ad modum (L.), After the method of .	रीति से, रीति के अनुसार।
Ad valorem (L.), according to value.	मूल्य के अनुसार।
Ad verbum (L.), word for word.	शाब्दिक रूप में, अविकल।
Advivum (L.), to the life.	जीवनपर्यन्त या तक।
Aequanimiter (L.) calmly.	शान्तिपूर्वक।
A' fond (Fr.), thoroughly.	पूर्ण रूप से।
A' gauche (Fr.), to the left.	बाईं ओर।
Age quod agis (L.), do with all your power what you do.	जो कुछ करो अपनी शक्ति लगाकर करो।
Alinude (L.), from another place.	दूसरे स्थान से।
Allons ! (Fr.), come along, let us go!	आओ हम लोग चलें।
Alter ego (L.), one's second self, intimate friend.	द्वितीय आत्मा, परम मित्र।

Alter ipse amicus (L.), a friend is another self. मित्र दूसरी आत्मा है।

A' maximis ad minima (L.), from the greatest to the smallest. सबसे बड़े से छोटे तक।

Amicus curiae (L.), a friend of the law-court. अदालत का मित्र।

Amicus humani generis (L.), a friend of humanity. मनुष्य जाति का मित्र।

Anglice (L.), in English. अंग्रेजी में।

Anima mundi (L.), the soul of the world संसार की आत्मा।

Animo et Jide (L.), by courage and faith. साहस और विश्वास से।

Annus mirabilis (L.), year of wonders. अद्भुत घटनाओं का वर्ष।

Ante bellum (L.), before the war. युद्ध के पहले।

Ante mer idiem (L.), before noon. मध्यान्ह (दोपहर) से पहले।

Antiquarium (L.), collection of antiquities. प्राचीन पदार्थों का संग्रह।

A posteriori (L.), from the effect to the cause. परिणाम से कारण तक।

A' propos (Fr.), to the point. आशय तक।

Arbitrium (L.), power of decision. निर्णय का अधिकार।

Arcana imperii (L.), state secrets. राज्य के गुप्त भेद।

B

Bella, horrida bella (L.), wars, horrible wars. युद्ध, भयंकर युद्ध।

Bellum lethale (L.), deadly war. भयंकर युद्ध, भीषण संग्राम।

Biennium (L.), period of two years. दो वर्ष का काल या समय।

Bona fides (L.), good faith. सच्चा हृदय य विश्वास।

Bona mobilia (L.), movable goods. चल सम्पत्ति।

C

Cadeau (Fr.), a present , a gift. उपहार, ईनाम।

Caeca est invidia (L.), envy is blind. ईर्ष्या अन्धी होती है।

Casus belli (L.), whatever involves a war. युद्ध का (आदि) कारण।

Caveat actor (L.), let the doer beware. करने वाला, सचेत या होशियार रहो।

Centum (L.), a hundred. शत, सौ।

Cito (L.), quickly. शीघ्रता से।

Compos mentis (L.), of sound mind, sane. स्थिर चित्त वाला।

Consilio et animis (L.), by wisdom and courage. बुद्धि या साहस द्वारा।

Con spirito (It.), with spirit. उत्साह से।

Contra bonos mores (L.), **against good manners or morals.** सदाचार या नैतिकता के विरूद्ध।

Coram populo (L.), in the presence of the public. जनता की उपस्थिति में।

Coup de hasard (Fr.), a lucky chance. सौभाग्य।

Crimen falsi (L.), crime of perjury. विश्वासघात।

Culpa levis (L.), a slight fault. छोटा-सा अपराध।

Currente calamo (L.), with a running pen. घसोट लिखावट में।

D

Data et accepta (L.), expenses and receipts. आय-व्यय।

De bon augure (Fr.), of good omen. अच्छे शकुन का।

De die in diem (L.), form day to day. दिन-दिन, प्रतिदिन।

De facto (L.), really, in fact, actual. वस्तुत: सचमुच, यथार्थ में।

Dei gratia (L.), by the grace of God. ईश्वर की दया से।

De integro (L.), afresh, anew. नया, ताजा।

De jure (L.), by right, in law. अधिकार से, कानून।

Deo favente (L.), with God's favour. ईश्वर की कृपा से।

Deo gratias (L.), thanks to God. ईश्वर को धन्यवाद।

Deus avertat ! (L.), God forbid ! ईश्वर न करे।

Deus det (L.), God grant ! ईश्वर करे।

Dictum de dicto (L.), hearsay, report. जनश्रुति अफवाह।

Domine, dirige nos ! (L.), God, direct us ! ईश्वर हमें मार्ग दिखलाये।

Dum spiro, spero (L.), while I breathe, I hope. जब तक मैं जीवित हूँ मुझे आशा है, जब तक साँस तब तक आशा।

E

Editio princeps (L.), original edition (of a book). किसी पुस्तक की मूल प्रतिलिपि।

Eo nomine (L.), by that name. इस नाम का।

Erenata (L.), according to the exigencies of the case. मामले की आवश्यकता के अनुसार।

Et hoc genus omne, et id grnus ome (L.), and everything of this or that sort. और इस या उस प्रकार का प्रत्येक पदार्थ।

Et, tu, Brute (L.), and you too Brutus. और ब्रूट्स तुम भी।

Ex curia (L.), out of court. अदालत से बाहर।

Ex delicto (L.), owing to crime. अपराध के कारण।

Ex dono (L.), as a gift. उपहार के रूप में।

Ex officio (L.), by virtue of his office. पदाधिकारेण।

Ex parte (L.), on one side only. एक ओर से, एकतरफा।

Expressis verbis (L.), in express terms. स्पष्ट शब्दों में।

Ex tacito (L.), silently. चुपचाप।

Ex utraque parte (L.), on either side. दोनों ओर।

Ex voto (L.), according to one's prayer. प्रार्थना के अनुसार।

F

Faber est quisque fortunae suae (L.), everyone fashions his own fortune. हर मनुष्य अपना भाग्य स्वयं बनाता है।

Facta non verba (L.), deeds not words. काम होना चाहिए, केवल शब्द नहीं।

Factum est (L.), it is done. कार्य हो गया।

Fadaise (Fr.), a silly talk. मुर्खता की बात।
Fait accompli (Fr.), a thing already done. पहले से किया हुआ काम।
Fata obstant (L.), the Fate opposes it. भाग्य इसके विरुद्ध है।
Fecit (L.), made or executed. बनाया हुआ।
Fiat justitia, ruat clelum (L.), let justice be done, though the heavens should fall. न्याय करो चाहे आकाश ही क्यों न गिर पड़े।
Fide et amore (L.), by faith and love. श्रद्धा और प्रेम से।
Fidus et audax (L.), faithful and bold. विश्वासी तथा साहसी।
Fillius nullius (L.), a bastard. दोगला।

G

Gaillard (Fr.), lively. आनन्दपूर्ण, प्रसन्न।
Garcon (Fr.), a boy, bachelor. लड़का, छोकरा, कुंआरा।
Gloria in excelsis (L.), Glory to God is the highest. सबसे वड़ी महिमा ईश्वर की है।

Hoc age (L.), attend to what you do. जो करो उस पर ध्यान दो।
Hoc anno (L.), in this year. इस वर्ष।
Hoc loco (L.), in this place. इस स्थान में।
Hoc tempore (L.), at this time. इस समय।
Hominis est errare (L.), to err is human. दोष मनुष्य से होता है।

I

Impromptu (L.), without study. बिना अध्ययन का।
In abstracto (L.), in the abstract. भाव रूप में।
In camera (L.), in the private room. कमरे के भीतर, गुप्त स्थान में।
In curia (L.), in court. न्यायाल्य में।
In equilibris (L.), in equilibrium. बराबरी में, सन्तुलन में।
In esse (L.), infact. स्थिति में, वस्तुतः।
In extenso (L.), at full length. पूरी तरह से।
Infra dignitatem (L.), below one's dignity. मर्यादा के विरुद्ध।
In pace (L.), in peace. शान्ति में।
In statu quo (L.), in the former state. पहले की अवस्था में।
Inter alia (L.), among other things. दूसरी वस्तुओं के बीच में।
In terrorem (L.), as a warning. चेतावनो के रूप में।
Inter se (L.), amongst themselves. परस्पर, आपस में।
In toto (L.), in the whole, entirely. पूर्ण रूप से, निपट।
Ipso facto (L.), really. सत्यता में, वास्तविक रूप में।

Jure divino (L.), by divine law. देवी नियम से।

Jure humano (L.), by human law. मनुष्य के बनाए नियम पर।

Labor ipsev oluptas (L.), labour itself is pleasure. परिश्रम ही आनन्द है।

Lapsus calami (L.), a slip of the pen. लेखनी की भूल।

Lapsus linguae (L.), a slip of the tongue. बोलने की चूक या भूल।

Lapsus memoriae (L.), a slip of the memory. स्मरण शक्ति की भूल।

Lese majeste (Fr.), high treason. राजद्रोह।

Lingua Franca (It.), a mixed language spoken by the Europeans. मिश्रित भाषा जिसको यूरोप के लोग बोलते हैं।

Locus standi (L.), place for standing, right of interferring. खड़ा होने का स्थान, हस्तक्षेप करने का अधिकार।

Lucri causa (L.), for the sake of gain. लाभ के लिए।

Lusus naturae (L.), a freak of nature. प्रकृति की विषमता।

Magnum bonuni (L.), a great good. बड़ा उपकार या लाभ।

Magnum opus (L.), a great work. बड़ा कार्य।

Mala fide (L.), faithlessly, treacherously. विश्वासघात से।

Memento mori (L.), remember that thou shalt die. याद रख कि तू मरेगा।

Mirabile dictu (L.), wonderful to tell. कहने में विलक्षण।

Mirabile visu (L.), wonderful to see. देखने में विलक्षण।

Nolens volens (L.), willing or not willing, whether he will or not. उसकी इच्छा हो अथवा न हो।

Noli me tangere (L.), do not touch me. मुझे स्पर्श मत करो।

Nota bene (L.), abbr. N.B take notice, mark well. भली-भाँति ध्यान दो।

Nulli secundus (L.), unparalleled, second to none. अद्वितीय।

Nunc est bibendum (L.), now is the time for drinking. अब (मदिरा) पीने का समय है।

O

Omnia bona bonis (L.), all things are good to the good. भले के लिए सब भला होता है।

Onus probandi (L.), the burden of proof. सिद्ध करने का आधार।

P

Pari passu (L.), with equal pace, together.	बराबरी की गति से, एक साथ।
Particeps criminis (L.), an accomplice.	अपराध करने में सहायक।
Per annum (L.), per year.	प्रतिवर्त्र।
Per centum (L.), by the hundred.	प्रति सैकड़ा।
Per diem (L.), per day, daily.	प्रतिदिन।
Per se (L.), by itself.	स्वयं।
Populus vult decipi (L.), the people wish to be fooled.	लोग मूर्ख बनना चाहते हैं।
Post mortem (L.), after death.	मृत्यु के उपरान्त।
Post obitum (L.), after death.	मृत्यु के बाद।
Prima facie (L.), on the first view.	पहली दृष्टि में।
Primo (L.), in the first place.	पहिले पहल।
Pro rata (L.), in proportion.	अनुपात में, यथोचित।
Pro tempore (L.), for the time being temporarily.	इस वर्तमान समय के लिए, अस्थायी रूप में।

Q

Quid pro quo (L.), something given or taken as equivalent to another.	दूसरी वस्तु के समान दी या ली गई कोई वस्तु।
Qui tacet consentit (L.), he who keeps silence consents.	चुप रहने से स्वीकृति का अनुमान होता है, मौनं सम्मतिलक्षणम्।

R

Res gestae (L.), exploits.	साहस के कार्य।
Resume (Fr.), a summary or abstract.	संक्षेप, सारांश, तत्त्व।

Sine die (L.), without a definite day, of a meeting adjourned for an indefinite period.	बिना निश्चित दिन के, अनिश्चित काल के लिए स्थगित।
Sine odium (L.), without hatred.	बिना घृणा के।
Sine qua non (L.), without which not, an indispensable condition.	जिसके बिना न (हो सके) आवश्यक या अनिवार्य स्थिति।
Sponte sua (L.), of one's own accord.	अपनी इच्छा से, अपने आप।
Status quo (L.), the state or condition in which a thing is existing.	जिस स्थिति या अवस्था में कोई वस्तु हो, वर्तमान स्थिति।
Sub judice (L.), under consideration.	विचाराधीन।
Suus cuique mos (L.), everyone has peculiar habits.	प्रत्येक्न मनुष्य का अलग-अलग स्वभाव होता है।

T

Terra incognita (L.), an unknown country. अज्ञात देश।
Tu quoque Brute ! (L.) and thou too Brutus ! और ब्रुट्स तू भी।

U

Ultima thule (L.), the utmost limit. अन्तिम सीमा।
Ultra vires (L.), beyond one's powers. किसी की शक्ति सामर्थ्य के बाहर।

V

Vale (L.), farewell. विदाई।
Veni, vidi, vici (L.), I came, I saw, I conquered. मैं आया, मैंने देखा, मैंने जीता।
Versus (L.), (abbreviation V.), against. विरुद्ध।
Vice (L.), in place of. बदले में, वास्ते।
Vice versa (L.), the order being reversed, the terms being exchanged. क्रम बदल दिया गया, शब्द का उल्टा हुआ।
Vis-a-vis (Fr.), opposite, facing. आमने-सामने।
Volente Deo (L.), God willing. यदि ईश्वर की इच्छा हो।
Vox populi,vox Dei (L.), the voice of the people is the voice of God. पंचों का कथन ईश्वर का वाक्य है।

X

Xystum (L.), a shaded walk in a garden. बगीचे का वृक्षों से आच्छादित मार्ग।

Z

Zonam perdidit (L.), he has lost his wealth, he is in need of money. उसका धन चला गया, उसे धन की आवश्यकता है।

CHAPTER 54

GROUP TERMS

A stack of wood.
A stack of arms.
A pair of shoes.
A herd of swine.
A herd of deer.
A shoal of fish.
A flock of geese.
A stack of corn.
A tribe of Arabs.
A flight of birds.
A shower of rain.
A suit of clothes.
A flock of sheep.
A flight of steps.
A bunch of keys.

A swarm of flies.
A sheaf of wheat.
A pack of wolves.
A pack of hounds.
A series of events.
A bundle of hay.
A sheaf of grain.
A bundle of sticks.
A group of islands.
A hoard of gold.
A horde of savages.
A leash of hounds.
A host of men.
A litter of puppies.
A gang of labourers.
A regiment of soldiers.
A bunch of plantains.
A box of cigars.

A heap or mass of ruins.
A heap of stones or sand.
A fall of snow or rain.
A clump or grove of trees.
A convoy of partridges.
A chain of mountains.
A nest or swarm of ants.
A hive or swarm of bees.
A sheaf of arrows.
A flight or swarm of locusts.
A brood or flock of chickens.
A gang of thieves or robbers.
A herd of cattle (*i.e.,* cattle pasturing).
A drove of cattle. (*i.e.,* cattle being driven).
A crowd, or throng, or concourse, or A bunch of grapes. Multitude of people.
A cluster or galaxy of stars.
A bunch or boucuet of flowers.
A range of hills or mountains.
A group of figures in a painting.
A collection of relics or curiosities.
A brace of pigeons.
A bevy of ladies.
A crew of sailors.
A fell of hair.
A council of advisers.
A gallery of pictures.
A library of books.
A nosegay of flowers.
A division of troops.
A string of camels.
A band of musicians.
A brace of pistols.
A panel of jury.

A brew of beer.
A pile of arms.
A muster of peacocks.
A nursery of plants.
A posy of flowers.
A stud of horses.
A team of players.
A yoke of oxen.
A board of directors.
A brood of hens.
A flock of birds.
A team of oxen.
A staff of officials.
A basket of fruits.
A fight of stairs.
A galaxy of beauties.
A kennel of dogs.
A museum of art.
A muster of soldiers.
A cellar of wine.
A faggot of sticks.
A family of sardines.
A packet of cigarettes.
A clique of people.
A clutch of eggs.
A colony of people.
A squad of soldiers.
A posse of arrows.
A quiver of arrows.
A flotilla of boats.
A squadron of cavalry.
A suite of rooms.
A bench of magistrates.
A parade of soldiers.
A throng of people.
A troupe of actors.
A battery of guns.
A company of actors.
A gathering of people.
A shrubbery of shrubs.
A party of people.
A detachment of soldiers.
A conference of delegates.
A constellation of delegates.
An outfit of clothes.
An orchard of fruit trees.
A fleet of cars or ships.
A syndicate of merchants.
A commission of enquiry.
An assembly of people.
A genus of animals or plants.
A jamboree of boy scouts.
A congregation of worshippers.
A tuz of hair.

RELATED PAIRS OF WORDS

कुछ Competitive Examinations में 'Related Pairs of Words' के 5-10 प्रश्नों का समावेश English Question Paper में रहता है। इस तरह के प्रश्नों में एक Pair of Words दिया गया होता है। जिसमें दिए गए दोनों Words में आपस में एक प्रकार का सम्बन्ध होता है। उत्तर में चार अन्य Pairs of Words दिए गए होते है। छात्र को Question में दिए गए Words में जो Relation है उसी Relation के अनुसार उत्तर में दिए गए Pair को चुनना होता है। जैसे निम्न प्रश्न को देखो:

Trailer		**Picture**
(a) Truck	:	Cargo
(b) Theatre	:	Play
(c) Synopsis	:	Thesis
(d) Commercial	:	Product

यहाँ दिए गए Pair में Trailer एवं Picture में जो आपस में सम्बन्ध है, इसी तरह का सम्बन्ध वाला Pair दिए गए विकल्पों में से चुनना होता है। अत: यहाँ उत्तर (c) है : Synopsis : Thesis जिस तरह Trailer एक Picture की Brief व्यक्त करता है, उसी तरह Synopsis भी Thesis को Briefly व्यक्त करती है।

इस तरह के प्रश्नों को हल करने हेतु छात्र को न केवल अपनी Vocabulary को Strong करना चाहिए बल्कि Words के आपस के सम्बन्धों को भी Common sense से सही तुलना करते हुए विकल्प चुनना चाहिए। इस तरह के प्रश्न न केवल छात्र की Word Power की जाँच करते हैं बल्कि उसकी Analytical Power को भी जाँचने में सहायक होते हैं।

Some Related Pair of Words

As bald as a badger.
As black as a coal.
As black as ink.
As black as pitch.
As blind as a beetle.
As blithe as a bee.
As blithe as a lark.
As brave as a lion.
As bright as the light.
As brittle as glass.
As busy as a bee.

As black as a gall.
As black as a crow.
As black as midnight.
As blind as a bat.
As blind as a mole.
As blithe as a butterfly.
As bold as a lion.
As bright as the day.
As bright as the silver.
As brown as a berry.
As changeable as the moon.

As changeable as a weather cock
As clear as crystal.
As cold as ice.
As cold as a cucumber.
As cunning as a fox.
As dark as pitch.
As dead as a herring.
As drunk as a lord.
As dry as a bone.
As free as the air.
As fresh as a rose.
As gaudy as a butterfly
As gentle as a lamb.
As graceful as a swan.
As greedy as a dog.
As happy as a king.
As hard as a stone.
As heavy as lead, sand.
As round as a ball or a globe.
As silent as the dead.
As silent as the stars.
As silly as a sheep.
As slender as a thread.
As smooth as velvet.
To follow as a shadow.
As hot as fire.
As innocent as a dove.
As loud as thunder.
As merry as a cricket.
As mute as a fish.
As obstinate as a mule.
As pale as a ghost.
As playful as a butterfly.
As plentiful as blackberries.
As proud as a peacock.
As quiet as thought.
As rapid as lightning.
As red as a cherry.
As red as rose.
As regular as clockwork.
As rich as a Jew.
As fair as a rose.
As fast as a hare.
As fierce as a tiger.
As flat as a board.
As soft as butter wax.
As steady as a rock.

As cheerful as a lark.
As clear as day, noon day.
As cold as marble.
As cold as a stone.
As dark as midnight.
As dead as a door-nail.
As deep as a well.
As drunk as a fiddler.
As dry as dust.
As fresh as a daisy.
As gay as a lark.
As gaudy as a peacock.
As good as gold.
As grave as a judge.
As green as grass.
As hard as fling, marble.
As harmless as a dove.
As hoarse as a crow, a raven.
As sharp as a needle, a razor.
As silent as the grave.
As silly as a goose.
As slender as a gossamer.
As smooth as a glass.
To spread like wild fire.
To shake, trembl, or quiver like an aspen leaf.
As hungry as a horse.
As light as a feather.
As mad as a hatter
As merry as a lark.
As nimble as a bee.
As old as the hills.
As patient as an ox.
As playful as a squirrel or a kitten.
As poor as lazarus.
As quick as lightning.
As quiet as a lamb.
As red as blood.
As red as crimson.
As red as scarlet.
As rich as Croesus.
As dumb as a statue.
As false as a Scot.
As fat as Big Ben.
As firm as a rock.
As fleet as a deer.
As sound as a bell.
As still as death.

As strong as the grave.
As strong as a lion.
As sure as death.
As swift as an arrow.
As tall as a maypole.
As tame as a hare.
As tricky as a monkey.
As vain as a peacock.
As weak as a baby.
As white as wool.
As wise as a serpent.
As yellow as saffron.
She wept a flood of tears.
He knows no more than a child how to do this.

As stupid as a statue.
As stupid as a donkey.
As sweet as honey, sugar.
As swift as lightning.
As tall as a steeple.
As timid as a hare.
As ugly as a scarecrow, a toad.
As warm as wool.
As white as a sheet.
As white as snow.
As wise as Solomon.
As yielding as wax.
As merry as the day is long.

Exercises

01

Directions (Q. 1-10) *: Choose the correct alternative given below to show close relation with the words given in capital words:*

(1) WE : OUR ::
(a) Him : His (b) It : Its (c) You : You're (d) They : There
(e) Who : Whose

(2) SLEEK : GLOSSY ::
(a) Contrite : Unrepentant (b) Rapid : Tepid (c) Vapid : Complete (d) Dejected : Jubilant
(e) Credible : Believable

(3) ASTRONOMY : ASTROLOGY ::
(a) Symbolism : Superstition (b) Geology : Geometry (c) Magic : Science (d) Chemistry : Alchemy
(e) Folklore : Fable

(4) DOUGH : BREAD ::
(a) Words : Speech (b) Paper : Writing (c) Cold : Ice (d) Ink : Pen
(e) Sugar : Cake

(5) ENGINEER : CAB ::
(a) Shepherd : Flock (b) Passenger : Taxi (c) Sailor : Cabin (d) Driver : Wheel
(e) Aviator : Cockpit

(6) STRINGS : VIOLIN ::
(a) Wind : Leaves (b) Air : Flute (c) Pedal : Organ (d) Membrane : Drum
(e) Plectrum : Mandolin

(7) SCALP : HAIR ::
(a) Shoe : Foot (b) Cloth : Table (c) House : Root (d) Curtain : Window
(e) Earth : Grass

(8) ISTHMUS : LAND ::
(a) Wire : Pole
(b) Strait : Body of water
(c) Neck : Head
(d) Bar : Trapeze
(e) Opening : Tunnel

(9) MEMORANDUM : MEMORANDA ::
(a) Insignia : Insigne
(b) Strata : Stratum
(c) Alumna : Alumni
(d) Automata : Automata
(e) Bacillus : Bacilli

(10) PRONE : SUPINE ::
(a) Likely : Unlikely
(b) Asiant : Akimbo
(c) Recumbent : Prostrate
(b) Face down : Face up
(e) Backward : Forward

02

Directions (Q. 1-10) *: Choose the correct alternative given below to show close relation with the words given in capital words.*

(1) MULE : BURDEN ::
(a) Scholar : books (b) Animal : Oppression (c) Ship : Cargo (d) Musician : Cello
(e) House : Tenants

(2) ALTHOUGH : NEVERTHELESS ::
(a) Albeit : However (b) Because : Therefore (c) Since : Yet (d) Notwithstanding : If
(e) When : Simultaneously

(3) ZENITH : NADIR ::
(a) High : Higher (b) Zero : Cipher (c) Perfection : Baseness (d) Slough : Despair
(e) Pinnacle : Bottom

(4) SPATE : TRICKLE ::
(a) Much : Little (b) Much : More (c) Copious : Abundant (d) Much : Many
(e) Small : Less

(5) RAM : EWE ::
(a) Doe : Hart (b) Swan : Cygnet (c) Marquis : Marquee (d) Stallion : Colt
(e) Testator : Testatrix

(6) FACADE : BUILDING ::
(a) Drawer : Desk (b) Dial : Watch (c) Page : Book (d) Fence : Garden
(e) Cork : Bottle

(7) PULSATE : THROB ::
(a) Condone : Condemn (b) Abate : Increase (c) Disperse : Gather (d) Expropriate : Deprive
(e) Accede : Disagree

(8) MORASS : SWAMP ::
(a) Peak : Mountain (b) Desert : Oasis (c) Sea : Gulf (d) Forest : Tree
(e) Prairie : Plain

(9) ISLANDS : ARCHIPELAGO ::
(a) Stamps : Philately (b) Stars : Constellation (c) Nickels : Follar bill (d) Hors d'oeuvre : Banquet
(e) Birds : Apiary

(10) SERRATED : SAW ::
(a) Mountain : Jagged (b) Sharpness : Knife (c) Dappled : Horse (d) Pronged : Fork
(e) Incisor : Tooth

03

Directions (Q. 1-10) : *Choose the correct alternative given below to show close relation with the words given in capital letters :*

(1) FRIGHT : STAMPEDE ::
(a) Flow of water : Erosion
(b) Clouds : Tornado
(c) Rain : Snow
(d) Haste : Crowds
(e) Wildness : Cattle

(2) GUTTURAL : THROAT ::
(a) Venal : Wine
(b) Mantle : Cloak
(c) Hair : Hirsute
(d) Palmar : Wrist
(e) Brachial : Arm

(3) LOBSTER : CRUSTACEAN ::
(a) Eagle : Sparrow
(b) Reason : Man
(c) Tiger : Cat
(d) Dolphin : Whale
(e) Lion : Man

(4) ABOMINATE : MAGNATE ::
(a) Noun : Noun
(b) Adjective : Noun
(c) Noun : Adjective
(d) Verb : Verb
(e) Verb : Nouns

(5) PREDATORY : HAWK ::
(a) Contortion : Grimace
(b) Voracious : Glutton
(c) Tawny : Lion
(d) Speedy : Cruiser
(e) Ugly : Vulture

(6) MINARET : MOSQUE ::
(a) Cross : Basilica
(b) Muezzin : Prayer
(c) Have : Cathedral
(d) Belfry : Steeple
(e) Campanile : Church

(7) INCONGRUOUS : HARMONIOUS ::
(a) Tall : Short
(b) Fickle : Rebellious
(c) Wearisome : Tedious
(d) Laughable : Ludicrous
(e) Nonplussed : Distracted

(8) COGENT : CONVINCING ::
(a) Dubious : Certain
(b) Nonchalant : Disturbed
(c) Banal : Unoriginal
(d) Cunning : Disingenuous
(e) Insular : Continental

(9) DECANTER : CARAFE ::
(a) Salver : Tray
(b) Bottle : Barrel
(c) Cruet : Kettle
(d) Cup : Plate
(e) Crystal : Glass

(10) INTERMITTENTLY : INCESSANTLY ::
(a) Interminably : Wearily
(b) Slowly : Rapidly
(c) Strongly : Weakly
(d) Vicariously : Frequently
(e) Occasionally : Continuously

04

Directions (Q. 1-10) *Choose the correct alternative given below to show close relation with the words given in capital letters :*

(1) MERCURY : CADUCEUS ::
(a) Vulcan : Forge
(b) Pegasus : Muses
(c) Palladium : Athena
(d) Jupiter : Thunderbolt
(e) Neptune : Trident

(2) ENERVATE : STRENGTHEN ::
(a) Aver : Attribute
(b) Divert : Turn
(c) Apprise : Appraise
(d) Stultify : Enliven
(e) Invigorate : Brighten

(3) DOLT : DOUR ::
(a) Bolt : Door
(b) Escape : Subterfuge
(c) Reticent : Silence
(d) Numbskull : Sullen
(e) Infant : Cry

(4) EXORDIUM : PERORATION ::
(a) Epilogue : Prologue
(b) Incipient : Inchoate
(c) Certain : Uncertain
(d) Alpha : Omega
(e) Exhortation : Denunciation

(5) MENDACITY : DISTRUST ::
(a) Begging : Charity
(b) Stupidity : Failure
(c) Truth : Falsehood
(d) Untruth : Doubtful
(e) Integrity : Confidence

(6) CARELESSNESS : JEOPARDIZE ::
(a) Penalty : Chastise
(b) Failure : Discouragement
(c) Carefulness : Security
(d) Neglect : Endanger
(e) Crowding : Discomfort

(7) PERMEATE : RUEFUL ::
(a) Truculent : Merciful
(b) Sadden : Pitiful
(c) Evaporate : Mournful
(d) Penetrate : Sorrowful
(e) Frighten : Lamentable

(8) FLAMBOYANT : ROCOCO ::
(a) Ornate : Baroque
(b) Inflammable : Phlegmatic
(c) Counterfeit : Invaluable
(d) Flagrant : Flagitious
(e) Florid : Fragrant

(9) HYPERTENSION : HYPOTENSION ::
(a) High : Low
(b) Excessive : Deficient
(c) Super : Minimal
(d) Abnormal : Normal
(e) Iso : Sub

(10) OAF : FRESHET ::
(a) Lout : Novice
(b) Stupidity : Impertinence
(c) Fool : Flood
(d) Silly : Brash
(e) Gaucherie : Elan

05

Directions (Q. 1-10) *: Choose the correct alternative given below to show close relation with the words given in capital letters :*

(1) IMPLICATE : COMPLICATE ::
(a) Vitality : Inevitable
(b) Empathy : Sympathy
(c) Importune : Construct
(d) Imply : Simplify
(e) Belligerent : Embellish

(2) CUPID : PSYCHE ::
(a) Zeus : Aphrodite
(b) Damon : Pythias
(c) Hero : Leander
(d) Apollo : Cassandra
(e) Venus : Adonis

(3) PRECEDENT : JUSTIFICATION ::
(a) Kindness : Obedience
(b) Authority : Sanction
(c) Usage : Submission
(d) Tradition : Novelty
(e) Orthodoxy : Heresy

(4) RACHITIC : RICKETS ::
(a) Adulatory : Adoration
(b) Oxford : Oxonian
(c) Scorbutic : Scurvy
(d) Deification : Deify
(e) Therapy : Therapeutic

(5) LAUREL : VICTOR ::
(a) Chevrons : Army
(b) Oscar : Movie star
(c) Power : Glory
(d) Blue ribbon : Cooking
(e) Rabbit's foot : Fuck

(6) CORVINE : CROW ::
(a) Elephantine : Dinosaur
(b) Lioness : Lion
(c) Viceregal : Viceroy
(d) Corvette : Automobile
(e) Urbane : Urban

(7) ZEALOT : FANATICISM ::
(a) Impostor : Sham
(b) Orator : Frenzy
(c) Umpire : Game
(d) Vagabond : Vagrant
(e) Parasite : Food

(8) PAIN : ANODYNE ::
(a) Savagery : Music
(b) Grief : Solace
(c) Harshness : Softness
(d) Trifle : Enormity
(e) Accident : Insurance

(9) FORGERY : SIGNATURE ::
(a) Faked : Genuine
(b) Proxy : Delegate
(c) Carbon copy : Original
(d) Embezzlement : Blank check
(e) Multigraph : Duplicate

(10) PHILOLOGIST : LANGUAGE ::
(a) Numismatist : Stamps
(b) Herbalist : Tropical flowers
(c) Philatelist : Charms
(d) Fish : Ichthyologist
(e) Conchologist : Shells

06

Directions (Q. 1-10) *: Choose the correct alternative given below to show close relation with the words given in capital letters :*

(1) DONKEY : BRAYS :: WOLF : ?
(a) Bellows (b) Howls (c) Whimpers (d) Roars
(e) Whines

(2) ANXIETY : ALLAY :: GRIEF : ?
(a) Banish (b) Condole (c) Heighten (d) Assuage
(e) Display

(3) MOSAICS :: WORDS : SENTENCES : ?
(a) Colours (b) Small stones (c) Straw (d) Papyrus
(e) Bricks

(4) MINOTAUR : BULL :: CHIMERA : ?
(a) Heifer (b) Lion (c) Goddess (d) Tiger
(e) Dog

(5) BLANDISH : COAX :: ASSEVERATE : ?
(a) Affirm (b) Cut (c) Repeat (d) Complain
(e) Twist

(6) SYLVAN : WOODS :: TERRESTRIAL : ?
(a) Urban (b) Fear (c) Earth (d) Planets
(e) Stars

(7) ASTRONAUTS : SPACE :: ARGONAUTS : ?
(a) Fire (b) Ship (c) Birds (d) Treasure
(e) Sea

(8) SCION : PROGENITOR :: DESCENDANT : ?
(a) Children (b) Brother (c) Ancestor (d) Progeny
(e) Guardian

(9) PEDIATRICIAN : HAIR : : DEMATOLOGIST : ?
(a) Children (b) Feet (c) Plants (d) Philosophy
(e) Skin

(10) SLEAZY : FLIMSY :: SHODDY :
(a) Tenable (b) Despicable (c) Queasy (d) Tenuous
(e) Detrimental

07

Directions (Q. 1-10) *Choose the correct alternative given below to show close relation with the words given in capital letters :*

(1) GENUINE : SIMULATED :: UNAFFECTED : ?
(a) Elevated (b) Bombastic (c) Dynamic (d) Destructive
(e) Emulated

(2) ACTOR : STAGE :: ? : ROSTRUM : ?
(a) Pilot (b) Acrobat (c) Soldier (d) Rider
(e) Orator

(3) ANSWER : TEST :: DENOUEMENT : ?
(a) Symphony. (b) Horse race (c) Mystery story (d) Circus
(e) Complete understanding

(4) ? : SULLIVAN :: HAMMERSTEIN : ROGERS : ?
(a) Lerner (b) Bellini (c) Gilbert (d) Mozart
(e) Purcell

(5) RECONDITE : ABSTRUSE :: BANTER : ?
(a) Delay (b) Tease (c) Bargain (d) Exchange
(e) Deceive

(6) BASILICA : CHURCH :: DORMER : ?
(a) Movie (b) Chapel (c) Room (d) Window
(e) Servant

(7) CICERONE : GUIDE :: DRAGOMAN : ?
(a) Cavalry officer (b) Interpreter (c) Hauler (d) Turnkey
(e) Mythological monster

(8) VILIFICATION : DEFAMATION ::? : TRAVESTY : ?
(a) Parody (b) Garment (c) Stripping (d) Deterioration
(e) Journey

(9) SUPPOSITITIOUS : FALSE :: SPURIOUS :?
(a) Inciting (b) Duplicate (c) Exhilarating (d) Not authentic
(e) Not technical

(10) MULCT : DEFRAUD :: RATIOCINATION : ?
(a) Reasoning (b) Bilk (c) Detective (d) Proportion
(e) Self-defenses

08

Directions (Q. 1-10) *: Choose the correct alternative given below to show close relation with the words given in capital letters :*

(1) INVEIGLE : CAJOLE :: MALIGN :
(a) Slander (b) Enlighten (c) Acclaim (d) Eulogize
(e) Compile

(2) CYGNET : SWAN :: ? : HORSE
(a) Bridle (b) Hoof (c) Mule (d) Colt
(e) Stallion

(3) SNAKE : REPTILIAN :: LION : ?
(a) Leotard (b) Vulpine (c) Lemurine (d) Tiger

(4) HERCULES : ? :: CUPID : ARROW
(a) Trident (b) Spear (c) Club (d) Soisoned bow
(e) Hydra

(5) SINECURE : CARE :: INTREPIDITY : ?
(a) Hesitation (b) Entanglement (c) Fear (d) Support
(e) Forethought

(6) SANCHO PANZA : DON QUIXOTE :: ? : SHERLOCK HOLMES
(a) Perry Mason (b) Don Ameche (c) Maigret (d) John H Watson
(e) Nero Wolfe

(7) OGLE : EYES :: MANEUVER : ?
(a) Fingers (b) Human beings (c) Minds (d) Machines
(e) Hands

(8) PURLOIN : STEAL :: NEBULOUS : ?
(a) Frustrating (b) Scanty (c) Dishonest (d) Stormy
(e) Vague

(9) RUBESCENT : RED :: CERULEAN : ?
(a) Sky (b) Brilliant (c) Pale (d) Seagreen
(e) Blue

(10) CLAPTRAP :: PITHY : MAXIM : ?
(a) Sincere (b) Simple (c) Pretentious (d) Thoughtless
(e) Accidental

SOLUTIONS TEST YOURSELF *Exercises*

Solution TYE 01

(1) (e), (2) (e), (3) (d), (4) (a), (5) (e),
(6) (d), (7) (e), (8) (b), (9) (e), (10) (d).

Solution TYE 02

(1) (c), (2) (a), (3) (e), (4) (a), (5) (e),
(6) (b), (7) (d), (8) (e), (9) (b), (10) (d).

Solution TYE 03

(1) (a), (2) (e), (3) (c), (4) (e), (5) (b),
(6) (e), (7) (a), (8) (c), (9) (a), (10) (e).

Solution TYE 04

(1) (e), (2) (d), (3) (d), (4) (d), (5) (e),
(6) (d), (7) (d), (8) (a), (9) (b), (10) (c).

Solution TYE 05

(1) (b), (2) (d), (3) (b), (4) (c), (5) (b),
(6) (c), (7) (a), (8) (b), (9) (a) (10) (e).

Solution TYE 06

(1) (b), (2) (d), (3) (b), (4) (b), (5) (a),
(6) (c), (7) (e), (8) (c), (9) (a), (10) (d),

Solution TYE 07

(1) (b), (2) (e), (3) (c), (4) (c), (5) (b),
(6) (d), (7) (b), (8) (a), (9) (d), (10) (a).

Solution TYE 08

(1) (a), (2) (d), (3) (e), (4) (e), (5) (c),
(6) (d), (7) (e), (8) (e), (9) (e), (10) (c).

CHAPTER

56

CHOOSING APPROPRIATE WORDS

कुछ Competitive examinations में इस तरह के प्रश्न पूछे जाते हैं जिनमें एक वाक्य देकर उसमें एक शब्द या स्थान रिक्त छोड़ा गया होता है तथा चार-पाँच विकल्पों में से एक उपयुक्त शब्द को choose करना होता है जो उस रिक्त स्थान हेतु उपयुक्त हो। इस तरह के प्रश्न में सामान्यतया लगभग समानार्थक शब्दों में से एक उपयुक्त शब्द (Appropriate word) को चुनना होता है या वाक्य के सारांश के अनुसार दिए गए विकल्पों में से एक उपयुक्त शब्द का चुनाव करना होता है।

इस तरह के प्रश्नों को हल करने हेतु आपकी Vocabulary powerful होनी चाहिए। दिए गए विकल्पों में से उपयुक्त शब्द का चुनाव आपकी शब्द की समझ, उसके उचित प्रयोग की जानकारी पर निर्भर होता है। ऐसे प्रश्नों में कई बार एक जैसे उच्चारण वाले शब्द देकर, उनमें से उपयुक्त शब्द का चयन करना होता है। इस Book में इस तरह के बहुत सारे शब्दों का उनके अर्थ एवं प्रयोग सहित समावेश किया गया है। छात्रों को इन शब्दों में अन्तर को बहुत अच्छी तरह समझना चाहिए तथा Specific use of words के Chapter को अच्छी तरह पढ़ना चाहिए। ये Chapters इस तरह के प्रश्नों को Solve करने मे बहुत सहायक साबित होंगे। Vocabulary को powerful बनाने हेतु इस Book में दिए ***'Learn three steps to improve your word power'*** का ध्यानपूर्वक अध्ययन करें एवं इन steps का पालन करें। न केवल आपकी vocabulary strong हो जाएगी बल्कि आपको शब्दों का सही एवं उचित प्रयोग करना भी बहुत अच्छी तरह आ जाएगा।

Exercises

01

Directions (Q. 1-8) *Fill in the blanks choosing appropriate word from the options given below.*

(1) My mother upset the kettle of boiling water and......her right hand badly. **[SSC Clerks]**
(a) scorched (b) burn (c) woulded (d) scalded

(2) Please do not .... an offer made by the Chairman. **[Income Tax]**
(a) refuse (b) deny (c) refrain (d) refuge

(3) The government is confident that the standard of living will begin to .... again soon. **[Income Tax]**
(a) rise (b) lift (c) flourish (d) revive

(4) On second reading, his poems strike us as singularly .... of sublime emotions. **[CDS]**
(a) attributive (b) significative (c) symptomatic (d) evocative

(5) Health is too important to be .... **[Asstt Grade]**
(a) neglected (b) discarded (c) dispised (d) detested

(6) Even a .... glance will reveal the mystery. **[Hotel Management Entrance]**
(a) crude (b) cursory (c) critical (d) curious

(7) Like any other country, India has its .... share of superstitions. **[Central Bureau]**
(a) abundant (b) fair (c) proper (d) peculiar

(8) Hindus believe that .... from the cycle of birth and rebirth can be attained only by good deeds. **[CDS]**
(a) bondage (b) deliverance (c) delivery (d) retirement

02

Directions (Q. 1-10) *Each of the following sentences has a blank space and four words given after the sentence. Select whichever word you consider most appropriate for the blank space and indicate your choice on the answer sheet.*

(1) An employment advertisement should .... the number of vacancies. **[CDS]**
(a) provide (b) declare (c) contain (d) specify

(2) The family gave father a gold watch on the .... of his fiftieth birthday.
(a) time (b) event (c) occasion (d) celebration

(3) The passengers were afraid but the captain .... them that there was no danger.
(a) promised (b) advised (c) assured (d) counselled

(4) It's very kind of you to .... to speak at the meeting.
(a) comply (b) agree (c) accept (d) concur

(5) I haven't seen you...........a week.
(a) within (b) since (c) for (d) from

(6) Do you know...........?
(a) where she comes from
(b) where does she come from
(c) where from she comes
(d) from where does she come

(7) The battalion operating from the mountain was able to .... three enemy divisions.
(a) tie up (b) tie down (c) tie on (d) tie with

(8) She .... a brief appearance at the end of the party.
(a) put on (b) put in (c) put across (d) put up

(9) Once he has signed the agreement, he won't be able to ....
(a) back up (b) back in (c) back at (d) back out

(10) .... of old paintings is a job for the experts.
(a) Resurrection (b) Retrieval (c) Restoration (d) Resumption

03

Directions (Q. 1-5) *From among the four alternatives given under each questions, find the one that fits into the blank space most appropriately.*

(1) The terrorists made a vain attempt to .... the bridge. **[Tourism Management]**
(a) blow down (b) blow up (c) blow over (d) blow out

(2) The Finance Minister may ...... new proposals in his budget speech.
(a) bring out (b) bring forward (c) bring round (d) bring forth

(3) The main suspect in the Rajiv Gandhi assassination are still ....
(a) under a cloud (b) at daggers drawn (c) at large (d) at sea

(4) The building was so old and dilapidated that it was not ....
(a) habitation (b) habitat (c) habitant (d) habitable

(5) Polyster shirts are more .... than the cotton ones.
(a) durably (b) duration (c) durability (d) durable

04

Directions (Q. 1-7) *Pick out the most effective word from the given words to fill in the blank to make the complete meaningful sentence.*

(1) Leadership define what the future should like and .... people with that vision. **[SBI PO]**
(a) encourages (b) develops (c) trains (d) aligns
(e) transforms

(2) We upset ourselves by responding in an .... manner to someone else's actions.
(a) invalid (b) irrational (c) arduous (d) arguable
(e) unabashed

(3) All the people involved in that issue feel a great .... to his suggestion.
(a) contradiction (b) adherence (c) indifference (d) objection
(e) erepugnance

(4) The election will be remembered as much for its anti-incumbency mood as for its .... mandate.
(a) invincible (b) rational (c) unprecedented (d) deliberate
(e) pervasive

(5) How do you expect us to stay in such a .... building even if it can be hired on a nominal rent?
(a) scruffy (b) desperate (c) fragmented (d) robust
(e) damaging

(6) .... efforts from all concerned are required to raise the social and economic condition of our countrymen.
(a) Perpetual (b) Dynamic (c) Massive (d) Exploring
(e) Penetrative

(7) Many companies see technology as a .... for a whole host of business problems.
(a) consideration (b) preference (c) linking (c) craving
(e) panacea

05

Directions (Q. 1-15) *In the following questions, sentences are given with blanks to be filled in with an appropriate word. Four alternatives are suggested for each question. Choose the correct alternative out of the four and indicate on the answer sheet.*

(1) He admired precision in everything, but it never hampered his quick .... **[Stenographer Grade]**
(a) decision (b) action (c) dealing (d) finalisation

(2) .... you meet my son in the market, ask him to come home at once.
(a) Should (b) Would (c) While (d) Will

(3) The proud king turned a deaf ear to the .... of wise counselors.
(a) advices (b) advises (c) advise (d) advice

(4) I shall not desert him .... all the world.
(a) for (b) by (c) from (d) with

(5) The judge acquitted the prisoner .... the charge of murder.
(a) from (b) about (c) with (d) of

(6) More than twenty years have now passed .... I had my first flight.
(a) when (b) since (c) while (d) as

(7) .... being hard-working, he is thoroughly honest.
(a) Along with (b) Betimes (c) Over and above (d) Although

(8) Through perseverance and hard work we can keep the .... of liberty burning even during dark and trying times.
(a) light (b) goal (c) lamp (d) flame

(9) He became the Governor of a province ....
(a) by and large (b) in course of time (c) at times (d) little by little

(10) You're coming to the movie, ... ?
(a) isn't it (b) won't you (c) aren't you (d) can't you

(11) While strolling on Janpath, I chanced to meet .... European.
(a) one (b) the (c) an (d) a

(12) Because of the heavy rain, the match was ....
(a)set aside (b) called off (c) fallen off (d) broken off

(13) Usually the ascent of mountain face is much easier than the ....
(a) fall (b) decent (c) descent (d) descend

(14) This is a .... translation of the speech.
(a) literal (b) literary (c) verbal (d) verbatim

(15) I spend much of my time .... writing letters and memos.
(a) in (b) to (c) on (d) at

06

Directions (Q. 1-10) *Each of the following sentences has a blank space and four words given after the sentence. Select whichever word you consider most appropriate for the blank space.*

[CDS]

(1) The .... effect of suitably chosen firms on children's minds cannot be overestimated.
(a) educative (b) debilitating (c) baneful (d) educational

(2) A number of scientists in the country think that they are on the .... of a major breakthrough.
(a) frontier (b) threshold (c) gateway (d) periphery

(3) .... from the campaigns have been used to buy medical supplies, food and educational materials.
(a) Revenue (b) Profit (c) Proceed (d) Proceeds

(4) When I joined the flying club, my instructor gave me the first lecture on the .... of flying.
(a) foundations (b) basics (c) need (d) theory

(5) You must .... your house in order before you venture to offer advice to others.
(a) arrange (b) bring (c) get (d) organise

(6) Fact is often stranger than ....
(a) fancy (b) fiction (c) imagination (d) dream

(7) It is becoming increasingly difficult for a housewife to pick up a genuine article from the crowd of the .... ones in a store.
(a) fake (b) duplicate (c) counterfeit (d) spurious

(8) His rustic and robust humour was an embarrassment to the .... sensibility of the young ladies.
(a) fragile (b) delicate (c) soft (d) sober

(9) His teacher said that his comments on his performance was not demoralise him but to .... him to do still better.
(a) encourage (b) persuade (c) instruct (d) goad

(10) Diseases are .... through contact with infected animals.
(a) transmited (b) transported (c) transferred (d) transplanted

07

Directions (Q. 1-5) *Fill in the blanks in the following sentences with the most appropriate word from among those given in brackets after each sentence.* **[IFS]**

(1) Our charming hostess was very .... to all her guests. (graceful, gracious, grateful)
(2) There was nothing unusual about the man .... he smiled, but that happened only rarely. (except, except for, except that)
(3) The doctor .... the woman that her son would recover. (ensured, assured, insured)
(4) I like .... music. (classic, classical, classics)
(5) I don't think I dare ask for a .... at the moment. (raise, rise, arise)

08

Directions *(Q. 1-5) Fill in the blanks in the following sentences with the most appropriate word from among those given in brackets after each sentence.* **[CDS, 1986]**

(1) An .... man is sure to be successful.
(a) industrus (b) indistrious (c) industrious (d) indestrious

(2) Students will go on an ....
(a) excusion (b) excurtion (c) ascursion (d) excursion

(3) You cannot leave without ....
(a) permision (b) premission (c) purmission (d) permission

(4) It is difficult to cross the ....
(a) barier (b) berrier (c) borier (d) barrier

(5) Ravi was .... from the school.
(a) expeled (b) espelled (c) expilled (d) expelled

09

Directions (Q. 1-8) *Fill in the blanks in the following sentences with the most appropriate word from among those given in brackets after each sentence.*

(1) After a recent mild paralytic attack his movements are........restricted, otherwise he is still very active. **[Banking Service Recruitment Board]**
(a) frequently (b) not (c) nowhere (d) slightly
(e) entirely

(2) The prisoner was released on.......for good behaviour. **[RRB Ajmer]**
(a) parole (b) bail (c) probation (d) guarantee
(e) surity

(3) Rajeev is too.......as far as his food habits are concerned. **[Bank PO]**
(a) enjoyable (b) fastidious (c) curious (d) interesting
(e) involved

(4) My father keeps all his.......papers in a lock and key. **[Banking Service Recruitment Board]**
(a) required (b) necessary (c) useful (d) confidential

(5) The brilliant students will be .... scholarships. **[RRB]**
(a) honoured (b) rewarded (c) awarded (d) forwarded

(6) Several of our players were injured so our losing the match was almost .... **[Central Bureau]**
(a) necessary (b) indispensable (c) inevitable (d) inexcusable

(7) My friend says that he drinks tea because it is the best.........in the world. **[Asstt Grade]**
(a) fluid (b) drink (c) beverage (d) liquid

(8) Life is to death as pleasure is to .... **[CDS]**
(a) suffering (b) pain (c) poverty (d) anguish

10

Directions (Q. 1-5) *Fill in the blanks in the following sentences with the most appropriate word from among those given in brackets after each sentence.* **[Bank PO]**

(1) These essays are intellectually........and represent various levels of complexity.
(a) modern (b) revealing (c) superior (d) demanding
(e) persistant

(2) The soldiers were instructed to.....restraint and handle the situation peacefully.
(a) control (b) exercise (c) prevent (d) enforce
(e) remain

(3) Since one cannot read every book, one should be content with making a ...... selection.
(a) normal (b) standard (c) moderate (d) judicious
(e) imposed

(4) He is too........to be deceived easily.
(a) strong (b) modern (c) intelligent (d) kind
(e) honest

(5) There has been a..........lack of efficiency in all the crucial areas of the working of Public Sector Undertakings.
(a) positive (b) surprising (c) conspicuous (d) stimulative
(e) insignificant

11

Directions (Q. 1-9) *Fill in the blanks in the following sentences with the most appropriate word from among those given in brackets after each sentence.*

(1) I write a letter to you tentatively........the dates of the programme. **[Banking Service Recruitment Board]**
(a) involving (b) indicating (c) guiding (d) urging
(e) propagating

(2) Contemporary economic development differs ....from the Industrial Revolution of the 19th century. **[Bank PO]**

(a) naturally (b) markedly (c) literally (d) usually

(3) Ravi had to drop his plan of going to picnic as he had certain .... to meet during that period. **[SBI PO]**

(a) preparations (b) observations (c) urgencies (d) commitments
(e) transactions

(4) It was.....hot that day and the cable suffered the brunt of the heat. **[SBI PO]**

(a) treacherously (b) acceptably (c) unfailingly (d) unbelievably
(e) uncompromisingly

(5) ....eye-witness, the news reporter gave a graphic description of how fire broke out. **[Indian Bank PO]**

(a) Reporting (b) Observing (c) Seeing (d) Quoting
(e) Examining

(6) His life consists of........of drinking punctuated by periods of drunken sleep. **[Central Excise]**

(a) barrels (b) bouts (c) bowls (d) pints

(7) When the morning......the murder was discovered. **[Asstt Grade]**

(a) occured (b) came (c) arrived (d) happened

(8) He lives in the world of .... **[Hotel Management]**

(a) allusions (b) illusions (c) conclusions (d) delusions

(9) There was a serious .... between the two brothers. **[Hotel Management]**

(a) altieration (b) alteration (c) altercation (d) aberration

12

Directions (Q. 1-15) *Fill in the blanks in the following sentences with the most appropriate word from among those given in brackets after each sentence.*

(1) The primary purpose of modern weapons is .... to prevent a particular course of action by a specific threat.

(a) deterrent (b) prognostic (c) minatory (d) hegemony

(2) As for the free world, trade with Cuba as been taking place on a modest scale despite the............ opposition of the United States.

(a) casual (b) independent (c) clandestine (d) overt

(3) The basic structure of the living cell is a problem whose .... can be judged by reference to the difficult exploration of the structure of the atom.

(a) importance (b) universality (c) complexity (d) antiquity

(4) The endless battle to modernize the .... structure of work rules on the nation's railroads appears destined to reach the showdown stage with a strike at one minute after midnight tonight.

(a) anemic (b) impracticable (c) archaic (d) streamlined

(5) Cyprus is still not economically viable, and though.............. important, it is militarily weak in its own right.

(a) necessarily (b) strategically (c) scarcely (d) independently

(6) He' s gone through a .... He is not at all the man be was when he was a combat officer.

(a) metamorphosis (b) crisis (c) frustration (d) surveillance

(7) It was Jacob Grimm, who transformed philology from an .... study into an exact science.

(a) abstruse (b) alleged (c) esoteric (d) errant

(8) As the waves rose and the ship tossed, many of the passengers felt........... .
(a) lethargic (b) subdued (c) tremulous (d) queasy

(9) Although advertising men often complain that their industry is hemmed in by government regulations, the fact remains that a/an .... attitude toward Madison Avenue continues to exist in this country.
(a) laissez faire (b) savoir faire (c) bete noire (d) idee fixe

(10) The knockout wallop travelled only seven or eight inches and, admittedly, did not look like much. But boxing experts, and .... scientists, will attest that punches that travel more than a foot lose much of their initial force.
(a) nuclear (b) biological (c) electronic (d) kinetic

(11) Are not the youngsters, viewing such war films, hypnotized by .... thrills and the oldsters, especially the veterans, deluded into identifying themselves with the hero breed?
(a) sensational (b) specious (c) auspicious (d) vicarious

(12) It is fascinating to note how many travelers return from their gastronomic tours of Europe with a .... of la grande cuisine and a haunting hunger for the simplicity of local dishes.
(a) memory (b) suspicion (c) surfeit (d) superfluity

(13) To avoid any outside influences, the judge has wisely decided to .... the jury.
(a) admonish (b) preclude (c) sequester (d) dismiss

(14) The remarkable thing about Spoon River Anthology is the way its .... little autobiographies merge into a unity.
(a) desparate (b) undeveloped (c) superficial (d) concatenated

(15) The general scientific assumption is that any amount of radiation, however small, will cause genetic damage that will appear as .... in the future.
(a) mutations (b) disabilities (c) diseases (d) handicaps

13

Directions (Q. 1-15) *In the following, sentences are given with blanks to be filled in with an propriate word. Four alternatives are suggested for each question. Choose the correct alternative.*

(1) The problems that India's economic development faces are ....
(a) enormous (b) great (c) myopic (d) morbid

(2) She refused to wear the new dress as she felt it to be ....
(a) odd (b) uncouth (c) outmoded (d) unfashioned

(3) Leah Robin saw him .... his tranformation from warrior to peacemaker.
(a) off (b) through (c) about (d) up

(4) Few countries can .... India in variety, colour and the richness of dance forms.
(a) rival (b) depict (c) prevail (d) perform

(5) The magistrate sent a ....of 50 policemen to the village where disturbances had occurred.
(a) team (b) force (c) battalion (d) cover

(6) Take possession of the records immediately so that they are not ....with.
(a) destroyed (b) manhandled (c) tampered (d) mishandled

(7) Having lived a .... life for 40 years, he is not able to take any independent decision.
(a) happy (b) successful (c) safe (d) cloistered

(8) I like listening to the radio, but I am not always impressed .... the quality of the programmes.
(a) with (b) at (c) about (d) on

(9) I saw a man .... the wire and walking away.
(a) picked (b) having picked (c) picking (d) picking up

(10) Sometimes truth is stronger than ....
(a) falsehood (b) lies (c) fiction (d) history

(11) It is felt that India, even with limited .... and funds, could still become a reckoning force in the art world.
(a) resources (b) sources (c) wealths (d) enthusiasm

(12) According to the recent, ... made by the Government of India, the target of foodgrains production for this year is 190 million tonnes.
(a) inferences (b) statistics (c) accounts (d) estimates

(13) Gopal Krishna Gokhale's patriotic speeches .... people to dedicate their lives for the nation.
(a) forced (b) inspired (c) inflamed (d) prompted

(14) There have been quite a large number of .... in the Himalayas now and some of them have been extremely successful.
(a) attempts (b) journies (c) expeditions (d) attractions

(15) We though that the Sadhu had miraculous powers, but we soon found out that we were ....
(a) wronged (b) mistaken (c) befooled (d) deceived

14

Directions (Q. 1-10) *In the following you find a number of sentences, parts of which are printed in bold type. You may also find only a group of words, which is printed in bold type. For each part printed in bold type, four words/phrases are listed below. Choose the word nearest in meaning to the part printed in bold type.*

(1) He displayed a distinct tendency to **long winded** speeches when asked how he was.
(a) boring (b) repetitive (c) circumlocutory (d) hyperbolic

(2) The data is **misleading.**
(a) illusory (b) deceptive (c) misplaced (d) misinfomative

(3) This library was built with donations from the **munificent** citizens of this city.
(a) well-to-do (b) generous (c) respectable (d) learned

(4) Some satirists are known for their **trenchant** style.
(a) sharp (b) critical (c) aggressive (d) incisive

(5) Many educationists think that the class-room instruction should be made more **vigorous.**
(a) serious (b) brisk (c) lively (d) active

(6) Medical science is yet to come out with a **panacea** for cancer.
(a) remedy (b) medicine (c) treatment (d) drug

(7) The navy gave **tactical** support to the marines.
(a) sensitive (b) strategic (c) expedient (d) expert

(8) Businessmen who lack **acumen** cannot be expected to be very successful.
(a) cleverness (b) sharpness (c) keenness (d) smartness

(9) In modern hospitals, computers **check** the patients before they see the doctor.
(a) screen (b) protect (c) cover (d) stop

(10) A genius tends to **deviate** from the routine way of thinking.
(a) dispute (b) disagree (c) differ (d) distinguish

15

Directions (Q. 1-5) *In the following you find a number of sentences, parts of which are printed in bold. You may also find only a group of words which is printed in bold. For each bold part, four words/phrases are listed below. Choose the word/phrase nearest in meaning to the part and choose the corresponding space on the Answer Sheet.*

[NDA, 1998]

(1) The teacher **reiterated** the importance of steady and hard work for getting through the examinations.
(a) emphasised (b) stressed (c) repeated (d) furthered

(2) There is **affectation** in the way he talks.
(a) beauty (b) sincerity (c) artificiality (d) sadness

(3) He is in the habit of using **obsolete** words.
(a) difficult (b) outdated (c) wrong (d) simple

(4) He talked on a passage from Hamlet; the **explication** was lucid.
(a) discussion (b) explanation (c) argument (d) description

(5) The books supplied by the shop were not only rare, they were also **invaluable.**
(a) valueless (b) priceless (c) useless (d) cheap

16

Directions (Q. 1-10) *The most appropriate word/phrase to fill in the blank in each of the following sentences is given as one of the four alternatives under it. That is your answer. Mark it on the Answer Sheet.*

[Hotel Management Entrance]

(1) He is very keen...........going abroad for higher studies.
(a) for (b) at (c) over (d) on

(2) You are not justified...........laying the blame...........my door.
(a) in, over (b) in, at (c) at, at (d) over, at

(3) What you have done...........no excuse.
(a) admits (b) admits to (c) admits about (d) admits of

(4) Timid by nature the doctor, who was alone in his house was frightened ....
(a) out of wits (b) out at his wits (c) at his wits end (d) out of his wits

(5) His approach to work is so...........that none of his colleagues considers him dependable.
(a) uninteresting (b) low (c) casual (d) common

(6) He has full facts...........but is deliberately hiding them.
(a) up his sleeves (b) in his sleeves (c) under his sleeves (d) upon his sleeves

(7) Their faults are...........by their masters.
(a) winked after (b) winked at (c) winked out (d) winked

(8) Having had........crops for the last two years, the government is falling short of storing space.
(a) bloated (b) bumper (c) booming (d) blooming

(9) Having been set...........he is now free to go anywhere he likes.
(a) at freedom (b) freedom (c) at liberty (d) liberty

(10) .... come to my rescue, I would have been killed by the bandits.
(a) If he had not (b) If he did not (c) Having not (d) He having not

17

Directions (Q. 1-10) *The most appropriate word/phrase to fill in the blank in each of the following sentences is given as one of the four alternatives under it. That is your answer. Mark it on the Answer Sheet.*

[Hotel Management Entrance]

(1) The child kept on crying while it............ .
(a) is bathed (b) is being bathed (c) was bathed (d) was being bathed

(2) He has such good manners that he can easily............a gentleman.
(a) pass out (b) pass on (c) pass in (d) pass for

(3) Shivaji............a plan to escape from jail.
(a) hit upon (b) hit out (c) hit about (d) hit against

(4) We chose to............our views in the light of the new information made available to us.
(a) disclose (b) revive (c) diagnose (d) revise

(5) Although, the Rajput Army was out numbered, the brave general refused to............ .
(a) give away (b) give over (c) give in (d) give out

(6) Having earned a lot of money in business, Mr. Sharma............his poor cousins.
(a) looks down upon (b) hits upon (c) shows off (d) looks upon

(7) The price of gold as well as silver............risen.
(a) are (b) have (c) has (d) is

(8) The building was so old and dilapidated that it was not............ .
(a) habitable (b) habitat (c) habitability (d) habituating

(9) Your son had promised to call you to USA,............ ?
(a) didn't he (b) did he (c) hadn't he (d) had he

(10) A large majority of students............absent from the college yesterday.
(a) was (b) were (c) has been (d) had been

18

Directions (Q. 1-10) *In the following, sentences are given with blanks to be filled in with an appropriate word Four alternatives are suggested for each question. Choose the correct alternative.*

(1) Dowry is no longer permitted by law even in ....marriages.
(a) natural (b) love (c) conventional (d) polygamous

(2) Family planning is essential for curbing the rapid ....in population.
(a) spurt (b) augmentation (c) spread (d) growth

(3) The transfer to territories could not take place because one State............the findings of the Commission.
(a) disputed (b) rejected (c) questioned (d) objected

(4) Kings have few things to desire and many things to............ .
(a) crave (b) long (c) fear (d) apprehend

(5) Vikram shouted............her at the top of his voice, but she did not hear and went on.
(a) at (b) to (c) against (d) for

(6) The winding road was no doubt a .... climb and, though at every steep turn the car groaned, we finally reached the top.
(a) tortuous (b) easy (c) fast (d) slow

(7) A light breeze...........the forest fire and made it more dangerous.
(a) blew (b) ignited (c) fanned (d) lit

(8) Take care of the...........and the hours will take care of themselves.
(a) days (b) years (c) seconds (d) minutes

(9) The way Dara kept knocking over things, he was more like a bull in a............ .
(a) English (b) China (c) cattle (d) grocery

(10) Though he took a leap in the ....when he invested all his savings in Reliance shares, he later on found that it was well worth the risk.
(a) abyss (b) dark (c) light (d) hole

19

Directions (Q. 1-9) *Fill in the blanks in the following sentences with the most appropriate word from among those given in brackets after each sentence.*

(1) The committee's appeal to the people for money.......little response. **[CDS]**
(a) provoked (b) evoked (c) gained (d) provided

(2) Colgate has also got an ambitious aim of.......an eight percent value share of the tooth paste market by the end of the first year. **[MBA Entrance]**
(a) keeping (b) distributing (c) cornering (d) soliciting

(3) He is very..........on meeting foreigners and befriending them. **[SSC Clerk]**
(a) anxious (b) find (c) insistent (d) keen

(4) If a speech is full of prompous words, it is...... . **[MBA Entrance]**
(a) verbose (b) bombastie (c) grandiose (d) grandiloquent

(5) We don't know what.........him to commit this crime. **[SSC Clerk]**
(a) excited (b) roused (c) prompted (d) attracted

(6) He is like a body without a soul, an eye without light or flower without ... . **[Insurance]**
(a) smell (b) fragrance (c) petal (d) colour

(7) It is difficult to believe what he tells us because his account of any event is always full of ...... of all sorts. **[CDS]**
(a) discretions (b) differences (c) discrepancies (d) distinction

(8) The country needs a.........government to tackle the challenges it faces today. **[SSC Clerk Grade]**
(a) sustained (b) stable (c) stationary (d) stagnant

(9) .... an accident the train will arrive in time. **[SSC Clerk Grade]**
(a) Despite (b) Accepting (c) Besides (d) Barring

20

Directions (Q. 1-10) *In the following, sentences are given with blanks to be filled in with an appropriate word. Four alternatives are suggested for each question. Choose the correct alternative.*

(1) The rank and...........of the party had turned against the leader.
(a) file (b) class (c) officers (d) people

(2) After being caught in the act, Rajneesh knew that he was in...........trouble.
(a) intense (b) dreaded (c) terrible (d) dire

(3) Zairian health officials said that 93 people have died...........the Ebola virus so far.
(a) of (b) for (c) from (d) on

(4) Owing to their unruly behaviour, some members of the cricket team were............ .
(a) excluded (b) exempted (c) banned (d) outlawed

(5) It is not the right............to ask for my help; I am far too busy even to listen to you.
(a) opportunity (b) situation (c) circumstance (d) moment

(6) The Government has agreed to pay compensation............damaged crops, land and cattle.
(a) to (b) through (c) for (d) of

(7) As the driver swerved violently at the turning, the wheel came off, as it was already.............
(a) lose (b) loose (c) loss (d) lost

(8) The interior of the concert hall is a............feast to the eye.
(a) veritable (b) hopeless (c) delicious (d) visual

(9) If you have already paid your dues, please do not take............of the letter.
(a) note (b) notice (c) care (d) consideration

(10) The writer, like a spider............a web; the creatures caught in the web have no substance, no reality.
(a) writes (b) catches (c) spins (d) compiles

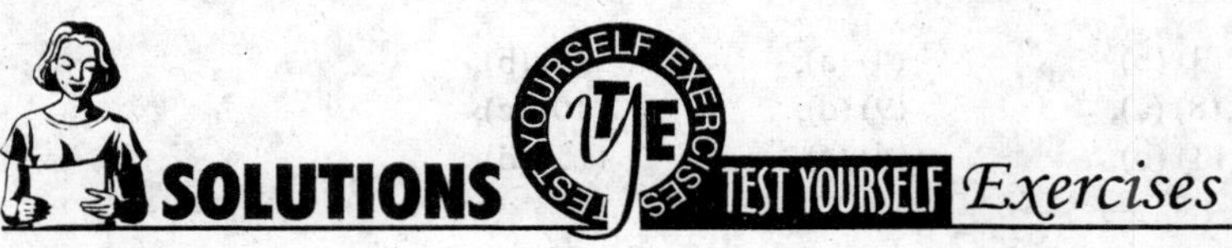

Solution TYE : 01

(1) (d), (2) (a), (3) (a), (4) (d), (5) (a),
(6) (b), (7) (b), (8) (b).

Solution TYE : 02

(1) (d), (2) (c), (3) (c), (4) (b), (5) (c),
(6) (a), (7) (b), (8) (b), (9) (d), (10) (c).

Solution TYE : 03

(1) (b), (2) (b), (3) (c), (4) (d), (5) (d).

Solution TYE : 04

(1) (d), (2) (e), (3) (e), (4) (c), (5) (a),
(6) (a), (7) (e).

Solution TYE : 05

(1) (b), (2) (a), (3) (d), (4) (a), (5) (d),
(6) (d), (7) (a), (8) (d), (9) (b), (10) (c),
(11) (b), (12) (b), (13) (c), (14. (a), (15) (a).

Solution TYE : 06

(1) (a), (2) (b), (3) (d), (4) (b), (5) (c),
(6) (a), (7) (b), (8) (b), (9) (c), (10) (a).

Solution TYE : 07

(1) grateful, (2) except that, (3) assured, (4) classical, (5) rise.

Solution TYE : 08

(1) (c), (2) (d), (3) (d), (4) (d), (5) (d).

Solution TYE : 09

(1) (d), (2) (a), (3) (b), (4) (d), (5) (c),
(6) (c), (7) (c), (8) (b).

Solution TYE : 10

(1) (b), (2) (b), (3) (d), (4) (c), (5) (c).

Solution TYE : 11

(1) (b), (2) (b), (3) (d), (4) (d), (5) (d),
(6) (b), (7) (c), (8) (b), (9) (c).

Solution TYE : 12

(1) (a), (2) (d), (3) (c), (4) (c), (5) (b),
(6) (a), (7) (c), (8) (d), (9) (a), (10) (d),
(11) (d), (12) (c), (13) (c), (14) (a), (15) (a).

Solution TYE : 13

(1) (a), (2) (c), (3) (b), (4) (a), (5) (b),
(6) (c), (7) (d), (8) (a), (9) (d), (10) (c),
(11) (a), (12) (d), (13) (b), (14) (c), (15) (d).

Solution TYE : 14

(1) (d), (2) (b), (3) (b), (4) (d), (5) (d),
(6) (a), (7) (b), (8) (a), (9) (a), (10) (c).

Solution TYE : 15

(1) (c), (2) (c), (3) (b), (4) (b), (5) (b).

Solution TYE : 16

(1) (d), (2) (b), (3) (d), (4) (d), (5) (c),
(6) (a), (7) (b), (8) (b), (9) (c), (10) (a).

Solution TYE : 17

(1) (d), (2) (d), (3) (a), (4) (d), (5) (c),
(6) (a), (7) (c), (8) (a), (9) (b), (10) (a).

Solution TYE : 18

(1) (c), (2) (d), (3) (a), (4) (c), (5) (b),
(6) (a), (7) (c), (8) (d), (9) (b), (10) (b).

Solution TYE : 19

(1) (b), (2) (c), (3) (d), (4) (d), (5) (c),
(6) (b), (7) (c), (8) (b), (9) (a).

Solution TYE : 20

(1) (a), (2) (d), (3) (c), (4) (a), (5) (d),
(6) (c), (7) (b), (8) (a), (9) (b), (10) (c).

SPECIFIC USE OF WORDS
(Similar Meaning)

(1) **Abstain** *(from a thing)*– One should abstain from sex without condom.
Refrain *(from doing)*– One should refrain from making unwarranted comments.

(2) **Revenge** *(to return injury for injury)*– She revenged herself upon Ramesh, her former lover.
Avenged *(to punish the evil doers)*– He has devoted the past three years to avenging his daughter's death.

(3) **Allow** *(giving permission for otherwise unreasonable thing)*– The girls were allowed to talk in the class by the Principal.
Permit *(to give a positive assent)*– I was permitted to appear in the M.A. examination.

(4) **Anger** *(a sudden feeling of unhappiness)*– The people showed great anger at the news.
Resentment *(more lasting feeling of unhappiness)*– My words could not lessen her resentment.

(5) **Atain** *(to get by labour)*– We attained a high degree of success through quality management.
Acquire *(to have something permanently)*– The students of this section have acquired a thorough knowledge of Naturopathy.

(6) **Ancient** *(opposite to modern)*– We can learn a lot by the events of ancient history of India.
Old *(opposed to new and to young)*– The old dressing pattern is liked by the people even today. Old people prefer simplicity to show.

(7) **Astonishment** (extreme surprise with some perplexity or confusion)– I was astonished to see him driving a two wheeler.
Surprise (arising on the occurence of something unexfrcted)– for failure in the examination has surprised everyone.

(8) **Admit** *(to acknowledge as true)*– He didn't admit that he was present in the house.
Confess *(to acknowledge responsibility or guilt)*– He confessed that he had stolen the bike.

(9) **Anger** *(sudden feeling)*– He showed great anger on his sudden departure from the party.
Resentment *(more lasting feeling)*– Your assurances cannot lessen his resentment.

(10) **Reply** *(to a letter)*– He always replies in time.
Answer *(to a question)*– Answer only five questions.

(11) **Ability** *(Intellectual quality)*– He is promoted on the basis of his ability to perform in a better way.
Capacity *(capable to hold or achieve)*– His capacity to work, regularly is praiseworthy.

(12) **Surprise** *(when something unexpected happens)*– He was surprised to see the result.
Astonishment *(extreme surprise)*– I was astonished to see my ex-peon maintaining a car.
Wonder *(surprise with admiration)*– I wondered at his securing first position at all India level.

(13) **Bravery** *(in the blood)* The bravery of Rajputs is well known.
Courage *(in mind)*– He has the courage to speak the truth.
Valour *(a quality more than bravery or courage)*– The black commandoes are known for their deeds of valour.

Daring *(rashn)*– He is daring, but not prudent.

Boldness *(a shortlived quality)*– He showed his boldness in catching the robber single handed.

(14) **Battle** *(a contest between two opposing armies)*– The third battle of Panipat was the last nail in the coffin of the Mughal Empire.

War *(a series of contests continued for a long time)*– The World War I and II saw the pinnacle of inhumane face of the weapons made by the men.

(15) **Begin** *(used on all occasions)*– The sooner you begin the better it is.

Commence *(used only in official and formal language)*– The examinations will commence on the 25th of May.

(16) **Beautiful** *(used for girls)*– She is a beautiful girl.

Handsome *(used for man)*– He is a handsome boy.

(17) **Custom** *(relates to community or society)*– Wearing kumkum after marriage is a custom among the Hindus.

Habit *(relates to individual)*– Smoking is a bad habit.

(18) **Crime** *(against law of the state)*– Theft is a crime.

Vice *(offence against morals)*– Drinking is a vice.

Sin *(against law of religion or society)*– Abusing elders is a sin.

(19) **Ceiling** *(inner portion of roof)*– I want to purchase one ceiling fan.

Roof *(upper covering of house)*– They are playing at the roof of their house.

(20) **Cite** *(is used for things or persons)*– He cited the authority of the Supreme Court Judgement.

Quote *(is used for things only)*– He quoted passage after passage from Geeta.

(21) **Compulsion** *(is physical, what is generally against our wishes)*– He was compelled by the court to be present on the next date of hearing.

Obligation *(is moral; what is imposed on us as a duty)* – We are obliged to maintain those who depend on us.

(22) **Confer** *(conferring is an act of authority)*– The government confers titles like Bharat Ratna, Padma Bhushan etc. on eminent persons.

Bestow *(an act of generosity/charity)*– Many presents were bestowed on the refugees.

(23) **Character** *(mental or moral nature)*– A man of character overcomes all temptations.

Conduct *(one's actions)*– None can blame you if your conduct is good.

(24) **Contentment** *(inner satisfaction when nothing more is required)*– Actual happiness consists in contentment.

Satisfaction *(fulfillment of one's desire)*– She completed the preparations to my entire satisfaction.

(25) **Contagious** *(disease spread by contact)*– Small pox is a contagious disease.

Infectious *(disease spread through air or mosquitoes)*– Malaria is an infectious disease.

(26) **Cool** *(pleasant feeling)*– A cool wind is blowing.

Cold *(unpleasant feeling)*– Weather is very cold today.

(27) **Defend** *(against an attack)*– Indian army is capable to defend the nation against any attack.

Protect *(relates to an approaching injury)*– Woollen clothes protect us from cold.

(28) **Deny** *(relates to a past a action)*– He denied his involvement in the murder.

Refuse *(relates to a future action)*– He refused to lend me any money.

(29) **Doubt** *(a negative feeling)*– I doubt his loyalty *(I think that he is not loyal.)*

Suspect *(a positive feeling)*– I suspect his involvement in the crime. *(I am thinking that he was not involvement.)*

(30) **Discover** *(relates to thing already in existence)*– A new star was discovered by him.

Invent *(a new thing is created)*– Who invented telephone?

(31) **Drown** *(relates to living beings)*– Many persons drowned in this river last year.
Sink *(relates to things)*– A ship dashed against this rock and sank last year.

(32) **Wish** *(used in reference to a remote thing)*– I wish, I were a king!
Desire *(used in reference to achievable things)*– I desire to have a beautiful house and a name in the society.

(33) **Want** *(relates to a thing, which is absent)*– I want to buy a car.
Need *(relates to necessary things)*– I need a pen to write with.
Require *(to demand)*– You are required to attend the meeting.

(34) **Envy** *(bad feeling)*– He is envious of his friend's prosperity.
Jealousy *(positive feeling of possessing something)*– I am jealous of our ancestral heritage.

(35) **Sufficient** *(necessary for)*– Two persons are sufficient for this job.
Enough *(more than necessary)*– I have enough money for the education of my children.

(36) **Accident** *(an unexpected happening)*– Train accidents have become common now-a-days.
Incident *(an ordinary occurrence)*– Our newspapers are full of daily incidents.
Event *(an important happening)*– The third battle of Panipat was an important event in the history of India.

(37) **Notorious** *(in bad sense)*– He is a notorious cheat.
Famous *(in good sense)*– NewYork is famous for multi-storeyed buildings.
Renowned *(high reputation)*– Shakespeare was a renowned dramatist.

(38) **Excuse** *(courteously used for trifle matters)*– Please excuse me for troubling you at this time.
Forgive *(used for comparatively big offences)*– Please forgive me for my speaking ill about your friend.
Pardon *(generally used for asking repetition of something)*– I beg your pardon (Please repeat, I was unable to understand earlier.

(39) **Freedom** *(implies absence of restraint)*– We enjoy several kinds of freedom.
Liberty *(implies previous restraint)*– The prisoners were set at liberty.

(40) **Falsehood** *(something said or done with wrong intentions)*– He was guilty of falsehood when he spoke against the character of the Chairman.
Lie *(speak untrue words)*– Never tell a lie.

(41) **House** *(refer to a dwelling unit)*– I am going to purchase a new house.
Home *(place to live with family association)*– Men make houses, women make homes.

(42) **Listen** *(to hear attentively)*– The teacher asked the students to listen.
Hear *(to get through ears)*– I am hearing your voice.

(43) **Hope** *(is used when what we anticipate is welcome)*– I hope to get selected this time.
Expect *(is used when what we anticipate is certain whether welcome or not)*– Every student is expected to carry out the instructions given in the notes.

(44) **Hardly** *(refers to degree)*– You can hardly imagine how much I suffered because of her allegation.
Scarcely *(refers to quantity)*– Don't ask me for milk, I have scarcely enough for my own use.

(45) **Idle** *(having nothing to do, due to circumstances)*– He has been sitting idle due to great slump in the market.
Lazy *(habit of not doing things in active manner)*– He is too lazy to reply letters.

(46) **Sick** *(mental feeling)*– He is a sick man.
Ill *(out of health)*– She is ill now-a-days.

(47) **Libel** *(written)*– His statement in the press release amounts to libel.
Slander *(spoken)*– His public speech was taken note of and an action for slander is being initiated.

(48) **Oral** *(spoken words)*– He was failed in oral examination.
Verbal *(written words)*– Teachers were abused verbally and assaulted physically.

(49) **Presume** *(pre decision of a thing)*– I presume he is responsible for the loss in business.
Assume *(assuming anything true)*– I assume he will help you in case of need.

(50) **Place** *(to put)*– Place the keys on the chair.
Keep *(o put at some defined place)*– Keep the books on the table.

(51) **Possible** *(can be done)*– It is not possible to reach there by car.
Probable *(likely to happen)*– It is probable that she may agree with our proposal.

(52) **Blunder** *(a gross mistake)*– Disclosing business secrets to the rivals is a blunder on your part.
Mistake *(small act)*– It is a mistake to go on leave without taking prior permission.
Error *(doing things against the recognise norms)*– Your essay is full of grammatical errors.

(53) **Praise** *(for actions)*– His actions are praiseworthy.
Admire *(for qualities)*– Everybody admires him for his benevolent nature.

(54) **Prohibit** *(has force of law)*– The government has prohibited the cow slaughter.
Forbid *(relating to personal life)*– Forbidden fruits are more sweet.

(55) **Recollect** *(remember after some efforts)*– Can you recollect what exact words did he use?
Remember *(having in memory)*– I remember his words well.

(56) **Regret** *(for a thing done or left undone)*– I felt regret for not completing the job in time.
Sorrow *(for big harm or evil)*– Her husband's death caused her deep sorrow.

(57) **Redress** *(to correct something wrong)*– A victim looks to the court for redress.
Relief *(feeling happiness because something wrong did not happen)*– I breathed a sigh of relief.

(58) **Rob** *(to take away by force)*– He was robbed of his money and jewellery.
Steal *(to take away secretly)*– The thieves stole away all the goods of my house last Sunday.

(59) **Talk** *(speaking with others)*– I want to talk to him in this matter.
Tell *(to inform)*– He tells me to wear neat dress.
Speak *(to say in ordinary way)*– He speaks loudly.
Say *(to assert)*– How did you say so ?

(60) **Seem** *(something assumed by our mind)*– The moon seems moving very fast.
Appear *(impression of objects on us)*– The statue appears to be of ancient time.

(61) **See** *(in an ordinary way)*– I can see that house.
Look *(see with some attention)*– Look at that house.
Watch *(to observe closely)*– Keep a watch on that house.

(62) **Scenery** *(a view of landscape)*– The scenery of Manali is indeed beautiful.
Scene *(a place of any happening, a landscape)*– He captured many beautiful scenes in his camera.

(63) **Treaty** *(a written or formal arrangement)*– India and the USA have signed a treaty .
Truce *(a temporary suspension of conflict)*– On new year eve there was a truce between the fighting militant groups.

(64) **Trifling** *('no importance' matter,)*– She never neglects even a trifling matter.
Trivial *('a small matter, no seriousness)*– Do not waste your time on trivial details.

(65) **Trade** *(small or large scale buying selling; it can be within or out of the country)*– India has a long history of trade with USA.
Commerce *(on a large scale; generally with foreign countries)*– They have made their fortune from industry and commerce.

(66) **Empty** *(having nothing in it)*– The briefcase is empty.
Vacant *(having some occupancy)*– Only one berth is vacant in this compartment.

WORDS NEVER USED IN GOOD SENSE

Certain words and phrases are never used in good sense. To use these words where a good sense is meant will be ridiculous. It would be ridiculous to say ; 'He is a notorious scientist', or 'He concocted a good plan for the welfare of the poor'. Some of such words in common use are given here under. Students should learn these words well and try to understand the difference. Mere Hindi meanings of these words will not suffice to use these words properly.

Accident	They met with an accident.
Accomplice	Partner in some crime. He was an accomplice in the theft.
Addicted	To some bad habit, drinking, gambling etc.
Adversary	An opponent : one who can cause harm.
Airs	He should not give himself airs (Conceited = airs).
Apprehensive	Of some danger, loss or injury.
Artisan	Who practises some art of inferior nature.
Blunder	A very serious mistake.
Catastrophe	A disastrous happening.
Coalition	Of men of divergent or opposite views : It refers a kind of partnership which is not homogeneous.
Commit	To do something wrong : as to commit a suicide.
Concoct	To make a plan for an evil purpose. He concocted a false story to deceive her.
Counterfeit	To imitate for a unlawful purpose. Counterfeit notes.
Concubine	A woman having sexual relations with many persons.
Cunning	Doing things cleverly but in a deceiving manner.
Credulity	A simpleton readiness to believe easily.
Dictator	A despot ruler , uses brutal force.
Despot	A tyrannical kind of ruler.
Demagogue	An unprincipled leader or a ring leader.
Effeminate	Womanly ('Feminine' and 'womanly are used in good sense.).
Fabricate	To invent with a bad motive. He fabricated a false story
Fancy	Imaginations which are not guided by reason.
Fine figure	He cuts a fine figure (disgraceful or ridiculous figure) (The phrase 'fine figure' is ironical.)
Fulsome	Full or excessive, so as to produce disgust, hatred.

Glaring	Conspicuous or something evil, as glaring error.
Hasty	Quick to fault; rash, easily excited; patience less.
Inveterate	Used for something bad, as 'an inveterate liar,' 'an inveterate enemy'.
Loiter	To linger at a time when greater haste is required.
Lonely	Depressed or sad from being alone.
Minion	An unworthy favourite.
Notorious	Evil reputation.
Perpetrate	Used only for crimes or offences.
Plight	A sad or painful condition. "She is in a sad plight."
Pocket	To put into one's pocket fraudulently, as "He pocketed the money fraudulently." Or to submit patiently to an insult, as "He pocketed the insult patiently."
Prone	To some vice or weakness, as "He is prone to fever".
Sheer	Used as ' sheer nonsense', 'sheer folly'. We never say 'sheer virtue,' but perfect or pure virtue.'
Shrewd	Clever, but often in a sense implying some dishonesty or cunningness.
To a degree	"He is insolent or dishonest to a degree (That is of high degree). This phrase is usually applied to some bad quality.
Totally	Always used for something bad; as 'totally incompetent,' 'totally blind'.
Trivial	Things of little importance. A trivial or common place subject.
Utter	An utter fool, an utter failure, always used for something bad.

Words Used in a Good Sense

Some words and phrases are used in a good sense only , so students should learn the proper use of these words and nouns. Mere knowledge of Hindi meanings of these words will not suffice to use them in proper manner. Students must learn the proper use of these words.

Age	She is of age (= grown up). She is under age (= a minor).
Breed	He is a man of (high) breed (= a well-breed man).
Bosom	He is my bosom (fast friend) friend.
Family	He is a man of (high) family.
Feeling	He is a man of (tender and good) feeling.
Famous	He is a famous artist.
Form	The boatman pulled together in form (= in good form or style).
Order	Everything is in (proper) order.
Place	Everything was in place (= in its right place).
Position	He is a man of (good) position.
Principle	He is a man of (high) principles.
Quality	He is a person of (good or high) quality.
Renowned	Shakespeare was a renowned dramatist.
Rank	Man of (high) rank.
Taste	His remark was not in taste (= in good taste).
Temper	He is out of temper (= ordinary or good temper). (But in 'temper' or in a temper' means in bad temper; as, " She said all that in a temper = in a rage").
Time	He arrived in time (= at the proper or right time).

CHAPTER 59

WORDS USED AS DIFFERENT PARTS OF SPEECH

The grammatical character of a word can be determined by its use in a sentence. It is difficult to say whether a particular word is a noun or a verb. Only by study the use and position of the word in a sentence we can say that it is used as noun or pronoun or as verb or as an adjective or an adverb. We are giving below some of the important words which are used as different parts of speech in the sentences. A careful study of the use of these words will help the students in increasing their grammatical knowledge of words and their uses.

All	Noun	All is well that ends well.
	Adjective	All men are mortal.
	Adverb	They are now alright.
	Pronoun	All were in favour of the motion.
Any	Pronoun	Do any of you know anything about her temperament ?
	Adjective	Take any magazine that you like.
	Adverb	We must take lunch before doing any other work.
As	Pronoun	He is not such a good man as looks.
	Adverb	She wrote as fast as she could.
	Conjunction	As he was poor so I helped him.
About	Adverb	She wandered about in inner garments.
	Preposition	There is nothing pleasing about her gait.
Above	Noun	The blessings came from above.
	Adverb	The Gods live above in heaven.
	Preposition	The sun was above our head at that time.
After	Adverb	She arrived soon after.
	Conjunction	She went away after her husband had left.
	Preposition	He looks after his mother.
	Noun	Age is more important than the physical fitness.
	Verb	He is aging, my dear.
Arm	Noun	He received a serious wound in his right arm.
	Verb	Border people were asked to arm themselves with weapons.
Before	Adverb	I have not met you before.
	Conjunction	She went away before he came.
Better	Noun	Give place to your betters.
	Adjective	I think yours is a better pen.
	Verb	Let us first better our financial position.
	Adverb	You are working better today.

Word	Part of Speech	Example
Both	Pronoun	Both of them have gone.
	Adjective	You cannot make it both ways.
	Conjunction	Both the cashier and the clerk are on tour.
But	Pronoun	There is no one, but praise her.
	Adverb	It is, but a natural consequence.
	Conjunction	He tried hard, but failed.
Back	Noun	She carried the load on his back.
	Verb	Do not back false friends.
Book	Noun	He is writing a book.
	Verb	Please book a cycle for Kota through this train.
Bare	Adjective	He has bare feet.
	Adverb	He walked bare feet.
	Verb	Bare your arm.
By	Adverb	Time passes by.
	Preposition	He was much loved by his wife.
Close	Noun	The meeting came to a close at 5 p.m.
	Adjective	They are very close friends.
	Verb	The school will close tomorrow.
	Adverb	Both walked close to each other.
Calm	Noun	The calm of mind, is in fact required.
	Adjective	Today the weather is very calm and quiet.
	Verb	First calm yourself and then write your report.
Cold	Noun	Wear the woollen clothes lest you should catch cold.
	Adjective	It is very cold today.
Court	Noun	Ramesh was summoned to the court of law.
	Verb	He courted her all the week.
Cane	Noun	This is a beautiful cane.
	Verb	He was caned publicly by the teacher.
Cut	Noun	I do not like the cut of your hair.
	Verb	Cut the paper in desired sizes.
Cover	Noun	Put a cover on your copy.
	Verb	Cover your head lest you should catch cold.
Down	Noun	He has seen the ups and downs of life.
	Adjective	The man was thrown from the down train.
	Verb	Down with dowry.
	Preposition	The engine came rushing down the hill very fast.
Deep	Noun	She fell down into the deep.
	Adjective	It is a very deep river.
	Adverb	My pen fell deep into the tank.
Drive	Noun	My brother has gone out for a drive.
	Verb	You are driving very fast.
Date	Noun	His date of birth is 26th April.
	Verb	The Vikram era dates from 57 B.C.
Either	Pronoun	Ask either of them to bring a pen.
	Adjective	Either pen is good enough.
	Conjunction	He must either work or take rest.
Enough	Adjective	There is enough time to go there.
	Adverb	He knows well enough what she mean to say.

Even	Adjective	The chances of winning the game are even.
	Verb	Let them even the field first.
	Adverb	He cannot even see me.
Else	Adjective	He brought something else for her.
	Adverb	We should look anywhere else.
	Conjunction	Walk fast, else you should miss the bus.
Eye	Noun	He has one eye only.
	Verb	The policeman eyed him with suspicion.
Elder	Noun	We must show respect to our elders.
	Adjective	He is my elder brother.
For	Conjunction	We should help him because he is very poor.
	Preposition	I was looking for her.
Fast	Noun	He keeps fast on Tuesday.
	Adjective	He is a very fast today.
	Verb	He fasted for a week.
	Adverb	He ran so fast to win the race.
Free	Adjective	We are citizens of a free country.
	Verb	Let us free ourselves from social bondage .
Fix	Noun	He was in a terrible fix .
	Verb	Fix some other date for our marriage.
Face	Noun	There are red pimples on her face
	Verb	He faced the situation with courage.
Fool	Noun	He is a fool to behave like that.
	Verb	He cannot fool me now.
Fish	Noun	Whale is a kind of large fish.
	Verb	Do not try to fish in troubled water.
Half	Noun	One half of this task is completed.
	Adjective	Half hearted man do not succeed.
	Adverb	She was half dead with fear.
Help	Noun	His timely help saved him.
	Verb	God help those who help themselves.
Hand	Noun	A bird in hand is better than two in the bush.
	Verb	The postman handed him two parcels.
Head	Noun	She was wearing a large and beautiful hat .
	Verb	He headed the list of successful students.
Less	Noun	She won't be happy with less.
	Adjective	He paid less attention to sports and more to studies.
	Adverb	The soil of her garden is less fertile than that of yours.
Like	Noun	You cannot see her like again.
	Adjective	They are man of like physic and stature.
	Verb	I like to take some fruit after dinner.
Light	Noun	There is no light in the room.
	Adjective	It is not a light matter.
	Verb	Light the candle, please.
Love	Noun	I have great love for her.
	Adjective	She does not like love stories.
	Verb	I love you.
Laugh	Noun	She raised many a laugh at his cost.
	Verb	Do not laugh at the poor .

Much	Adjective	He has wasted much time.
	Adverb	I am much annoyed with you.
More	Adjective	He wants more workers like you.
	Adverb	You must talk less and work more.
Meek	Noun	God helps the meek and gentle.
	Adjective	She is quite meek.
Master	Noun	She was my master in all matters.
	Adjective	He conceived a master plan.
	Verb	She has mastered this book.
Move	Noun	This army is on the move.
	Verb	Let us move to some other hotel.
Make	Noun	What is the make of your T.V. ?
	Verb	Do not make a noise.
Near	Adjective	He is my near relative.
	Verb	We are nearing the end of the project.
	Adverb	Come near and listen to me.
	Preposition	His house is near the temple.
Needs	Noun	My needs are few.
	Verb	It needs great care.
Neither	Pronoun	Neither of them can be relied.
	Adjective	Neither charge is true.
	Conjunction	Neither he nor his brother was present there.
No	Noun	His answer was a perfect no.
	Adjective	It is no joke.
	Verb	She is no more with me.
Next	Adjective	I shall see you next Monday.
	Adverb	What next ?
	Preposition	He was sitting next to her.
Number	Noun	Put it on the tenth number.
	Verb	His days are now numbered.
Once	Noun	Let me see her for once.
	Adverb	I was young once.
	Conjunction	Once you hesitate, you are dead.
One	Noun	The little one cried for joy.
	Pronoun	One would think he was mad.
	Adjective	One day, I met her in a function.
Only	Adjective	It was his only chance.
	Adverb	He was only foolish.
Over	Noun	In first over, he took three wickets.
	Adverb	Read it over carefully.
	Preposition	Last year, a chance came over to him again.
Off	Adjective	Ramesh picked the horse's off nail.
	Adverb	He is falling off.
	Preposition	The rider fell off the bike.
Open	Adjective	This is an open letter.
	Verb	Please open the door.
Poor	Noun	The rich should help the poor.
	Adjective	He is a poor man.

Pocket	Noun	I have two rupees in my pocket.
	Verb	He pocketed the insult patiently.
Right	Noun	I asked him favour as a right.
	Adjective	He is the right man for the job.
	Verb	This is a fault that will right itself.
	Adverb	She stood right in my gate.
Round	Noun	That night was a round of pleasures.
	Adjective	It is a round hole.
	Verb	You cannot round it by pen.
	Adverb	He brought her round to my point of view.
	Preposition	The earth revolves round the sun.
Reach	Noun	The bunch of grapes was not within his reach.
	Verb	I shall reach there in time.
Refuse	Noun	The refuse of hospital is put into public drains.
	Verb	She refused to help her.
Since	Adverb	I have not seen him since.
	Conjunction	Since there is no way, let us kiss and part.
	Preposition	Since Monday, I have not seen her.
Some	Pronoun	Some say one thing and other say another.
	Adjective	We must find some way out of this problem.
	Adverb	Some thirty people were present in the party.
Still	Noun	I could hear her cry in the still of night.
	Adjective	Still waters run deep.
	Verb	With his name the mother still their babes.
	Adverb	They are still sleeping.
Such	Pronoun	Such was not his meaning.
	Adjective	Don't move in such a hurry.
So	Adverb	I am so tired that I cannot go.
	Conjunction	He was poor, so they helped him.
Slow	Adjective	He is a very slow writer.
	Verb	The car slowed down as it reached the hotel.
	Adverb	How slow she works ?
Sound	Noun	Hearing the sound of the trumpets the people woke up.
	Adjective	His arguments were not sound and acceptable.
	Verb	Sound the horn, please.
Spring	Noun	It was a spring of fresh water, spring has set off.
	Adjective	We use spring water for bathing.
	Verb	See how the dog springs upon the cat.
Stone	Noun	The house is made of stone.
	Adjective	That house has stone walls.
	Verb	He was stoned to death.
Stand	Noun	Everybody praised him for his stand against the injustice.
	Verb	Stand in a queue.
Stay	Noun	He has to cut short the period of my stay at Alwar.
	Verb	She will stay with me for a few days.
Second	Adjective	He is second to none.
	Verb	No one seconded her candidature.
School	Noun	There is no school in our colony.
	Verb	He was not schooled properly .

Silence	Noun	There was perfect silence in the hall.
	Verb	He soon silenced her with his arguments and the evidences.
That	Pronoun	That is what I want.
	Adjective	What is that noise ?
	Adverb	You have done that much only.
	Conjunction	He says that he wants to leave.
Till	Conjunction	Do not start till I say.
	Preposition	He put off this work till tomorrow .
Than	Conjunction	He likes this more than that.
	Preposition	He was fond of any drink other than milk.
Time	Noun	What is the time by your watch ?
	Verb	The train is timed to come at 10 p.m.
Touch	Noun	Midas loved the Golden touch.
	Verb	She will not touch this point.
Turn	Noun	There is a turn after five kilometeres.
	Verb	He turned to be a thief.
Up	Adjective	She will come by the next up train.
	Adverb	These days prices are up.
	Preposition	Can you climb up this tree ?
Well	Noun	There are only two wells in the village.
	Adjective	I hope you are now well.
	Adverb	Well begun is half done.
While	Noun	Sit down and rest a while.
	Verb	They while away their days with books and watching T.V.
	Conjunction	He was reading while his friends were playing.
Why	Noun	You should not be worried about why and wherefore of it ?
	Adverb	I know why she did it.
Wrong	Noun	The minister did no wrong.
	Adjective	It is a wrong policy.
	Verb	He was wronged by the leader of his party.
	Adverb	I think that my son is going wrong.
Watch	Noun	I have lost my watch.
	Adjective	I require a watch-man.
	Verb	Let us watch her movements.
Water	Noun	Bring me some cold water.
	Adjective	There are water snakes and land snakes.
	Verb	He is watering in the garden.
Walk	Noun	They go for a walk in the evening.
	Verb	She was so weak that she could not walk.
Which	Pronoun	Which of these two pens you like more ?
	Adjective	Which coaching you have joined ?
Want	Noun	Owing to the want of rains, there occurred a drought.
	Verb	I want to purchase a good new T.V. sets.
Whose	Pronoun	He is the man whose brother met me yesterday.
	Adjective	Whose book is this ?
Yet	Adverb	There is more evidence yet to be given.
	Conjunction	Though he worked hard, yet he failed

SOME PECULIAR EXPRESSIONS

In certain phrases the use of some word is restricted to a certain connection, and where no other word can be substituted for it. See the following phrases :

Bevy of ladies	We never say "a bevy of gentlemen."
Bosom friend	We never speak of "bosom enemy."
Broad daylight	We do not speak of "broad moonlight," but "bright moonlight."
Burning question	We should not say "burning problem."
Drawn battle	We never say "a drawn fight." But we can say "a drawn match."
Fast friend	We do not speak of "a fast enemy"or "a fast foe."
Foregone conclusion	We never speak of "a foregone result"or "a foregone consequence."
Forlorn hope	We never say "forlorn success" or "forlorn expectations."
Golden age	We do not speak of "the golden time or period."
Gratuitous insult	We do not speak of "gratuitous abuse."
Honest penny	We do not speak of " an honest six pence."
Implicit confidence, faith or reliance	We do not say, "implicit love or hatred."
Leading question	We should not say "a leading inquiry."
Livelong day or night	We cannot say "a livelong hour, or week, or year."
Maiden speech	We cannot say "a maiden song"or "a maiden attempt."
Market rate or market value	We cannot say "trade rate"or "trade value."
Moot point	We cannot say "a moot question."
Open question	We cannot speak of "an open point."
Open secret	We cannot say "an open point."
Out of doors	We never say "out of door" or "out of gates."
Retrench expenditure	We cannot say "retrench trade of business."

Sinews of war	We cannot say "the muscles of war."
Snail's pace	We cannot say "snail's movement."
Spin in yarn or yarns	We never say "spin a thread."
Standing army	We never say "standing navy or regiment."
Standing joke	We never say "a standing jest."
Standing nuisance	We never say, "a standing trouble." We may say "a constant trouble."
Standing water	We can never say "standing need."
Standing rule	We can never say "standing practice or custom or habit."
Standing orders	Generally we do not say "standing instructions." (In some offices we use "Standing instruction.")
Stubborn fact	We can never say "an obstinate fact" or "a stubborn truth."
Sworn friends	We can never say, "a sworn enemy." We may say "an avowed enemy."
Stone's throw	We never say "pebble's throw" or "brick's throw."
Tall talk	We never speak of "lofty talk."
Vials of wrath	We cannot say "vials of anger or fury."
Whirligig of time	We cannot say "whirligig of period."
White lie	We do not say "white falsehood" or "black lie."
Willing slave	We do not speak of "willing servant."
Watery grave	We do not say " a watery tomb" or "watery burial."

CHAPTER

61

ANIMALS, MALES, FEMALES, YOUNGS AND GROUP TERMS

Animal	Male	Female	Young	As a group
Antelope	Bull	Cow	Calf	Herd
Bear	Boar	Sow	Cub	Sloth
Cat	Tom	Queen	Kitten	Clowder
Cattle	Bull	Cow	Calf	Herd/Drove
Chicken	Cock/Rooster	Hen	Chick	Flock
Deer	Buck/Hart/Stag	Doe/Hind	Fawn	Herd
Dog	Dog	Bitch	Pup	Kennel
Donkey	Jackass	Jeneet/Jenny	Foal/Colt	Pace
Elephant	Bull	Cow	Calf	Herd
Fox	Dog	Vixen	Cub	Skulk
Giraffe	Bull	Cow	Calf	Herd
Goat	Billy/Buck	Nanny/Doe	Kid	Herd
Goose	Gander	Goose	Gosling	Flock/Gaggle
Horse	Stallion	Mare	Foalt/Colt (Male)	Herd/Filly (Female)
Kangaroo	Buck/Boomer	Doe/flier	Joey	Herd/Troop/mob
Lion	Lion	Lioness	Cub	Pride
Ostrich	Cock	Hen	Chick	Flock/Troop
Pig	Boar	Sow	Shoat/Farrow/Piglet	Herd/Drove
Rabbit	Buck	Doe	Kindle/kitten	Warren
Seal	Bull	Cow	Pup/whelp	Rookery/Trip
Sheep	Ram	Ewe	Lamb	Flock
Swan	Cob	Pen	Cygnet	Flock
Turkey	Cock/Gob	Bler/Tom	Hen	Poult dule
Whale	Bull	Cow	Calf	School/Pod
Zebra	Stallion	Mare	Foal	Herd

COLLECTIVE NAMES OF ANIMALS

A herd of antelope
A colony or an army of ants
A shrewdness of apes
A herd or pace of asses
A culture of bacteria
A cete of badgers
A shoal of bass
A sleuth or sloth of bears
A colony of beavers
A swarm, grist or hive of bees
A flock, flight, congregation or volery of birds
A sedge or siege of bitterns
A sounder of boars
A herd of buffalo
A brace or clash of bucks
An army of caterpillars
A clowder or clutter of cats
A herd or drove of cattle
A brood or peep of chickens
A clutch or chattering of chicks
A bed of clams
A quiver of cobras
A rag of colts
A cover of coots
A kine of cows (Twelve cows are a flink)
A band of coyote
A sedge or siege of cranes
A float of crocodiles
A murder of crows
A pod of elephant seals
A weaner pod is yearling elephant seals
A gang of elks
A mob of emus
A business or fesnyng of ferrets
A charm of finches
A school, shoal, run, haul, catch or draught of fish
A swarm of flies
A skulk or leash of foxes
An army or colony of frogs
A flock, gaggle or skein (In flight) of geese
A cloud or horde of gnats
A herd, tribe or trip goats
A charm of goldfinches
A band of gorillas
A leash of greyhounds
A down or husk of hares
A cast or kettle of hawks
A brood of hens
A hedge of herons
A drift, or parcel of hogs
A team, pair or harras of horses
A pack, mute or cry of hounds
A smack of jellyfish
A troop or mob of kangaroos
A kindle or litter of kittens
An ascension or exaultation of larks
A leap (Leep) of leopards
A pride of lions

A litter of cubs
A herd of curlews
A cowardice of curs
A herd of deer
A pack of dogs
A dule of doves
A brace, paddling or team of ducks
A clutch of eggs
A herd of elephants
A yoke, drove, team or herd of oxen
A bed of oysters
A company of parrots
A covey of partridges
A muster or ostentation of peacocks
A litter of peeps
A nest, nide (nye) or bouquet of pheasants
A flock or flight of pigeons
A litter of pigs
A wing or congregation of plovers
A string of ponies
A pod of porpoises
A covey or bevy of quail
A nest of rabbits
A pack or swarm of rats
A rhumba of rattlesnakes
An unkindness of ravens
A crash or herd of rhinos
A bevy of roebucks
A building or clamour of rooks
A herd or pod of seals
A drove or flock of sheep
A plague of locusts
A tiding of magpies
A sord of mallards
A stud of mares
A richness of martens
A labour of moles
A troop of monkeys
A barren or span of mules
A parliament of owls
A nest of snakes
A walk or wisp of snipe
A host of sparrows
A dray of squirrels
A murmuration of starlings
A mustering of storks
A flight of swallows
A bevy, herd, lamentation or wedge of swans
A flock of swifts
A sounder or drift of swine
A spring of teal
A knot of toads
A hover of trout
A rafter of turkeys
A pitying or dule of turtledoves
A bale of turtles
A pod of walrus
A school, gam or pod of whales
A nest of vipers
A pack or route of wolves
A fall of woodcocks
A descent of woodpeckers

YOUNG ONES OF ANIMALS

Animals	Young One	Animals	Young One
Antelope	Calf	Hen	Pullet
Bear	Cub	Hippo	Calf
Beasts of Prey	Whelp	Horse	Foal, Yearling, Or Colt (Male), Filly (Female)
Beaver	Kit	Kangaroo	Joey
Birds	Fledgling, Nestling	Lion	Cub
Cat	Kitten	Owl	Owlet
Codfish	Codling, Sprat	Partridge	Cheeper
Cow	Calf	Pig	Piglet, Shoat, Farrow, Suckling
Deer	Fawn, Yearling	Pigeon	Squab, Squeaker
Dog	Pup, Puppy	Rat	Pup
Duck	Duckling	Rhino	Calf
Eagle	Eaglet	Rooster	Cockerel
Eel	Elver	Salmon	Parr, Smolt, Grilse
Elephant	Calf	Seal	Pup
Elephant Seal	Weaner	Shark	Cub
Fish	Fry	Sheep	Lamb, Lambkins
Fowl	Chick, Chicken	Swan	Cygnet
Fox	Cub, Pup	Tiger	Cub, Whelp
Frog	Polliwog, Tadpole	Turkey	Poult
Goat	Kid	Whale	Calf
Goose	Gosling	Zebra	Foal
Grouse	Cheeper	Quail	Cheeper
Guinea Fowl	Keet	Rabbit	Bunny, Kit
Hawk	Eyas		

WORDS USED IN THE CONSTITUTION

नीचे लिखे शब्द भारतीय गणतंत्र के संविधान में प्रयुक्त हुए हैं। इन शब्दों के हिन्दी में समानार्थक शब्द व पद दिए जा रहे हैं।

A

Abandonment — परित्यजन, परित्याग
Abridgement — न्यून
Abrogation — निराकरण
Access — प्रवेश, पहुँच
Account — लेखा गणना
Accrual — प्रापण, प्रोद्भवन
Accured — प्राप्त, प्रोद्भूत, उपार्जित
Accusation — अभियोग
Accused — अभियुक्त
Acquisition — अर्जन
Act — अधिनियम
Acting — कार्यकारी
Actionable — अभियोज्य दोष
Adaptation — अनुकूलन सम्बोधन
Addressed — सम्बोधित
Adherence — अनुषिक्ति
Adhoc — तदर्थ
Adjournment — स्थगन, अवधिदान, कालदान
Administer — प्रशासन करना
Administered — प्रशासित
Administration — प्रशासन
Administrative — प्रशासकीय
Administrative Function — प्रशासकीय कृत्य
Administrator General — महाप्रशासक
Admiralty — नौकाधिकरण, नावाधिकरण
Additional Judge — अपर न्यायाधीश
Admissible — ग्राह्य
Adoption — दत्तक ग्रहण, दत्तक स्वीकरण
Adulteration — अपमिश्रण
Adult Suffrage — वयस्क मताधिकार
Advance — अग्रिम धन, पेशगी
Advice — मंत्रणा, उपदेश, सलाह
Advise — मंत्रणा देना
Advisory Council — मंत्रणा परिषद्
Advocate — अधिवक्ता
Advocate General — महाधिवक्ता
Affect Prejudicially — प्रतिकूल प्रभाव डालना
Affirmation — प्रतिज्ञान
Agency — अभिकरण
Agent — अभिकर्ता
Agreement — करार
Air Force — विमान बल, वायुसेना
Air Navigation — विमान परिवहन
Air Traffic — विमान यातायात
Air Ways — वायु पथ
Alien — अन्य विदेशी
Alienate — अन्य संक्रमण करना
Alienation — अन्य संक्रमण, परकीयकरण
Allegation — अभिकथन, आरोप
Allegiance — निष्ठा
Allocation — बँटवारा
Allot — बाँट लगाना
Allotment — बाँट
Amensty — सर्वक्षमता

Amount — राशि
Annuall — वार्षिक
Annual Financial Statement — वार्षिक वित्त विवरण
Annuity — वार्षिक
Annulment — रद्दीकरण
Appeal — अपील, पुनर्विचार, प्रार्थना
Appear — उपस्थित होना
Appended — संलग्न
Application — प्रयुक्ति, आवेदन पत्र
Appointment — नियुक्ति
Appropriation — विनियोग
Appropriation Bill — विनियोग विधेयक
Approval — अनुमोदन
Approve — अनुमोदन करना
Arbitral Tribunal — मध्यस्थ न्यायाधिकरण
Arbitration — मध्यस्थ निर्णय
Arbitrator — मध्यस्थ
Area — क्षेत्र
Armed Forces — सशस्त्र सेना
Arrest — बंदी करना, बंदीकरण
Article — अनुच्छेद
Assemble — जमा होना, समवेत होना
Assembly — सभा
Assent — अनुमति
Assessment — कर निर्धारण
Assignment — समर्पण
Association — संस्था संघ
Assurance of Property — सम्पत्ति हस्तान्तरण
As the case may be — यथास्थिति, यथा प्रसंग
Attachment — कुर्की, टाँच
Attorney General — महान्यायवादी
Audit — लेखा परीक्षा, गणना परीक्षा
Auditor General — महालेखा परीक्षक
Authentication — प्रमाणीकरण
Authority — प्राधिकारी
Authorise — प्राधिकृत करना
Autonomous — स्वायत्त
Autonomy — स्वायत्तता, स्वायत्त शासन
Auxiliary — सहायक
Award — पंचाज्ञा

B

Bail — प्रतिभूति, जमानत
Ballot — शलाका, शलाका पद्धति, गूढ़पत्र
Bank — बैंक, अधिकोष
Banking — महाजनी, अधिकोषण
Bankruptcy — दिवाला
Bar — रुकावट
Benefit — हित
Betting — पण लगाना, पण क्रिया
Bicameral — दोघर, द्विगृही
Bill — विधेयक, बिल
Bill of Exchange — विनिमय पत्र
Bill of Indemnity — परिहान विधेयक
Bill of Lading — वहन पत्र
Board — मंडली, बोर्ड, परिषद
Body — निकाय
Bona Vacancia — स्वामिहीनत्व
Borrowing — उधार ग्रहण
Boundary — सीमा
Broadcasting — प्रसारण
Business — कारोबार
Bye-election — उपनिर्वाचन
Bye-law — उपविधि

C

Calling — अजीविका
Camp — शिविर
Candidate — अभ्यर्थी, उम्मीदवार
Cantonment — कटक, छावनी
Capacity — सामर्थ्य
Capital — मूलधन, पूँजी
Capital Value — मूलधन मूल्य
Capitation Tax — प्रति व्यक्ति कर
Carriage — परिवहन
Casting Vote — निर्णायक मत
Cattle Pound — पशु अवरोध
Cause — वाद
Cause of Action — वाद मूल
Central Intelligence Bureau — केन्द्रीय गुप्त वार्ता विभाग

Certificate — प्रमाणपत्र
Certiorari — उत्प्रेरण लेख
Cess — उपकर
Chairman — सभापति, अध्यक्ष
Charge — दोषारोपण, अभियुक्ति
Charge — भार, भारित करना
Charitable and Religious Endowments — दातव्य तथा धार्मिक धर्मस्व
Charitable Institution — दातव्य संस्था
Charity — पूर्त दातव्य
Casting vote — निर्णायक मत
Cheque — चेक, धनादेश
Chief — मुख्य, प्रधान
Chief Commissioner — मुख्य आयुक्त
Chief Election Commissioner — मुख्य निर्वाचन आयुक्त
Chief Judge — मुख्य न्यायाधीश
Chief Justice — मुख्य न्यायाधिपति
Chief Minister — मुख्यमंत्री
Citizenship — नागरिकता, पोरत्व
Civil — व्यवहारिक, असैनिक
Civil Court — व्यवहार न्यायालय, व्यय हारालय, दीवानी या व्यवहार, असैनिक शक्ति
Civil Power — व्यवहार शक्ति, असैनिक
Civil Wrong — व्यवहार विषयक अपकृत्य
Civil Suit — व्यवहार वाद
Civil Court — व्यवहार न्यायालय
Claim — दावा
Clarification — स्पष्टीकरण
Clause — धारा
Code — संहिता
Coinage — टंकण
Colonization — उपनिवेशन
Commerce — वाणिज्य
Commercial — वाणिज्य सम्बन्धी
Commission — आयोग
Commissioner — आयुक्त
Committee — समिति
Court of Record — अभिलेख न्यायालय
Corporate Body — निगम निकाय
Common Good — सार्वजनिक कल्याण, कल्याण
Common Seal — सामान्य मुद्रा, सामान्य मुहर
Communicate — संचार करना
Means of Communication — संचार साधन
Community — लोकसमाज, समुदाय
Commutation — लघुकरण
Company — समवाय, कम्पनी
Compensation — प्रतिकर क्षतिपूर्ति
Competent — सक्षम
Complaint — फरियाद
Comptroller and Auditor General — नियंत्रक तथा महालेखा परीक्षक
Computation — संगणना
Concurrence — सहमति
Concurrent list — समवर्ती सूची
Condition — शर्त
Conditions of Service — सेवा की शर्तें
Conference want of — विश्वास का अभाव
Conscience — अंत:करण
Consent — सम्मति
Consequential — आनुषंगिक
Consideration — विचार
Consolidated Fund — संचित निधि
Constituency — निर्वाचन क्षेत्र
Constituent Assembly — संविधान सभा
Constitution — संविधान
Construe — अर्थ करना
Consul — वाणिज्य दूत
Consultation — परामर्श
Consumption — उपभोग
Contact — सम्पर्क
Contagious — सांसर्गिक
Contempt — अवमान
Contempt of Court — न्यायालय का अवमान
Contex — सन्दर्भ, प्रसंग
Contingency Fund — आकस्मिकता निधि
Contract — संविदा
Contravention — प्रतिकूलता उल्लंघन
Contribution — अर्थदान

Control — नियंत्रण
Controversy — प्रतिवाद
Convention — अभिसमय, प्रथा, रूढ़ि, परम्परा
Conveyance — सम्पत्ति हस्तान्तरण
Convicted — सिद्धिदोष, अभिशस्त दोष प्रमाणित
Conviction — दोष सिद्धि, अभिशस्त
Co-operative Society — सहकारी संस्था या सम्पत्ति
Copy — प्रतिलिपि, प्रतिकृति
Copyright — प्रकाशनाधिकार, कृति स्वाम्य
Corporation — निगम
Corporation Sole — एकल निगम
Corporation-tax — निगम कर
Corresponding — तत्स्थानी
Corrupt — भ्रष्ट
Cost — परिव्यय खर्च, लागत
Council — परिषद्
Council of States — राज्यपरिषद्
Council Tribal — जनजाति परिषद्
Countervailing Duty — प्रतिशुल्क
Court — न्यायालय
Court Criminal — दण्ड न्यायालय
Court District — जिला न्यायालय
Court Federal — संघ न्यायालय
Court, High — उच्च न्यायालय
Court, Magistrate — दण्डाधिकारी न्यायालय
Court Matrial — सेना न्यायालय
Court of Appeal — पुनर्विचार न्यायालय
Court of Wards — प्रतिपालक अधिकरण
Court of Revenue — राजस्व न्यायालय
Court Session — सत्र न्यायालय
Concurrent List — समवर्ती सूची
Credit — प्रत्यय साख, पत्र, आकलन
Crime — अपराध
Criminal — अपराधी, आपराधिक, दण्ड सम्बन्धी
Criminal Law — दण्ड विधि
Currency — चल अर्थ, मुद्रा प्रचलन
Custody — अभिरक्षा, निरोध, कावल
Custom — रूढ़ि, आचार
Custom Duty — बहिः सीमा शुल्क

D

Dealings — व्यवहार लेन-देन
Debate — वाद-विवाद
Debenture — ऋण-पत्र
Debit — विकलन
Debt — ऋण
Decision — विनिश्चय
Decree — घोषणा
Dedication — आज्ञप्ति, डिग्री
Deed — विलेख
Defamation — मानहानि
Defence — प्रतिरक्षा
Deliberation — पर्यालोचन, विचार-विमर्श
Delimitation — परिसीमन
Demand — माँग अभियाचना
Demarcation — सीमांकन
Demobilisation — सैन्य वियोजन
Deprive — वंचित करना
Deputy Chairman — उपसभापति
Deputy Commissioner — उपायुक्त, मण्डलायुक्त
Deputy President — उपराष्ट्रपति
Deputy Speaker — उपाध्यक्ष
Derogation — अप्रतिष्ठा, अपमान
Descent — उद्भव
Design — रूपांकरण तक्ष
Detrimental — अहितकारी
Death Duty — मरण शुल्क, मृत्यु कर
Diplomacy — राजनय, कूटनीति
Direction — निर्देश
Disability — निर्योग्यता
Discharge — निर्वहन
Disciplinary — अनुशासन सम्बन्धी

Discipline — अनुशासन
Discovery — आविष्कार
Discretion — स्वविवेक
Discrimination — विभेद
Discussion — चर्चा, बहस
Dismiss — पदच्युत करना
Disperse — विसर्जन करना
Dispute — विवाद
Disqualification — अनर्हता
Disqualify — अनर्ह या अयोग्य ठहराना
Dissent — विमति
Dissolution — विघटन
Distribution — वितरण, विभाजन
District — जिला
District Board — जिला परिषद्
District Council — जिला सभा
District Fund — जिला निधि
Dividend — लाभांश
Divorce — विवाह विच्छेद, तलाक
Document — लेख्य, दस्तावेज
Domicile — अधिवास
Domiciled — अधिवासी
Dullness — मतिमान्य
During Good Behaviour — सदाचार पर्यन्त
During the Pleasure of President — राष्ट्रपति प्रसाद पर्यन्त
Duty — शुल्क कर्त्तव्य
Duty Stamp — मुद्रांक शुल्क
Duty Succession — उत्तराधिकार शुल्क

E

Economic — आर्थिक
Education — शिक्षा
Efficiency of Administration — प्रशासन कार्यक्षमता
Elect — निर्वाचित करना
Elected — निर्वाचित, चुने हुए
Election — निर्वाचन
Election Commissioner — निर्वाचन आयुक्त
Election Tribunal — निर्वाचन अधिकरण
Electrol Roll — निर्वाचन नामावली
Electorate — निर्वाचन गण, निर्वाचन क्षेत्र
Eligibility — पात्रता, योग्यता
Eligible — योग्य
Emergency — आपात
Emergent — आपाती
Emigration — उत्प्रवास
Emoluments — उपलब्धियाँ
Employer's Liability — नियोजक दातव्य, नियोजक उत्तरवादिता
Enactment — अधिनियम
Encumbered Estate — भारग्रस्त सम्पदा
Endorse — पृष्ठांकन करना, समर्थन करना
Endorsed — पृष्ठांकित, अंकित
Endowment — धर्मस्व
Engagement — वचनबद्ध
Engineering — यंत्र शास्त्र
Enterprise — उद्यम
Entitled — अधिकारी, हकदार
Entrust — न्यस्त करना, सौंपना
Entry — प्रविष्टि, दाखिला
Equality — समता
Equal Protection of Laws — विधियों का समान संरक्षण
Escheat — राजगामी धन
Establishment — स्थापना, संस्थापन कर्मचारी वर्ग
Estate Duty — सम्पत्ति शुल्क
Estate — सम्पदा
Estimate — आकाप्राक्कलन, आगणन, अनुमान
Evidence — साक्ष्य
Excess Profit — अतिरिक्त लाभ
Exclude — अपवर्जन करना
Excise Duty — उत्पादन शुल्क
Export Duty — निर्यात शुल्क
Exclusion — अपवर्जन
Exclusive Jurisdiction — अनन्य क्षेत्राधिकार
Executive — कार्यपालिका
Executive Power — कार्यपालिका शक्ति या अधिकार
Exempt — मुक्त

Exercise — प्रयोग, अनुष्ठान
Ex-officio — पदेन
Expenditure — व्यय
Explanation — व्याख्या, स्पष्टीकरण
Explosives — विस्फोटक
Export — निर्यात
Extend — विस्तार करना, फैलाना
External Affairs — वैदेशिक कार्य
Extradition — प्रत्यर्पण
Extra Territorial Operation — राज्य क्षेत्रातीत प्रवर्तन
Extra Judge — अतिरिक्त न्यायाधीश

F

Factory — कारखाना
Faith — धर्म भावना, श्रद्धा
Fare — भाड़ा, किराया, खाद्य भोजन
Federal Court — संघ न्यायालय
Fee — देय शुल्क
Finance — वित्त
Finance Bill — वित्त विधेयक
Finance Commission — वित्तायोग
Financial — वित्तीय
Financial Obligation — वित्तीय भार
First Reading — प्रथम पठन
Finance Statement — वित्तीय वितरण
Fine — अर्थ दण्ड
Fishery — मीन क्षेत्र, मीन पण्य
Forbid — निषेध करना
Forbidden — निषिद्ध
Forces — बल सेना
Foreign Affairs — विदेशीय कार्य
Foreign Exchanges — विदेशीय विनिमय
Form — रूप, प्रपत्र, फॉरम
Formula — सूत्र
Formulated — सूत्रीय
For the Time Being — तत्समय, उपस्थित समय के लिए
Freedom — स्वतंत्रता, स्वातंत्र्य आजादी
Freedom of Speech — वाक्स्वातंत्र्य
Freight — वस्तु भाड़ा
Frontiers — सीमान्त
Function — कृत्य
Function Administrative — प्रशासकीय कृत्य
Fund — निधि
Fund Sinking — निक्षेप निधि
Future Market — वायदा बाजार

G

Gambling — द्यूत, जुआ
Gazzette — सूचना पत्र, राजपत्र
General Election — साधारण निर्वाचन
Govern — शासन करना
Governance — शासन
Government — सरकार शासन
Government of State — राज्य की सरकार
Government of India — भारत सरकार
Governor — राज्यपाल
Governing Body — शासी निकाय
Grant — अनुदान
Grant in aid — सहायक अनुदान
Gratuity — उपदान
Guarantee — प्रत्याभूति
Guardian — संरक्षक
Guidance — मार्गदर्शन

H

Habeas Corpus — बंदी प्रत्यक्षीकरण
Handicrafts — हस्तशिल्प दस्तकारी
Hazardous — संकटमय
Headman — मुखिया
High Court — उच्च न्यायालय
Honorarium — मानदेय
House — सदन
House of People — लोकसभा

I

Illegal — अवैध
Illegal Practice — अवैधाचरण
Immuned — उन्मुक्त
Immunity — उन्मुक्त
Impeachment — महाभियोग
Implementing — परिपालन

Impose — दोषारोपण या कर लगाना
Imprisonment — कारावास, कैद
Improvement Trust — सुधार प्रन्यास
Inport Duty — आयात शुल्क
Incapacity — असमर्थता
Incidental — प्रासंगिक
Incompetency — अक्षमता
Incompetent — अक्षम
Incorporation — निगमन
Incumbent of an Office — पदधारी
Indebtedness — ऋणग्रस्तता
Industry — उद्योग
Ineligible — अपात्र
Infants — शिशु
Infectious — संक्रामिक
Influence — प्रभाव
Influence Undue — अयुक्त प्रभाव
Inheritance — दाय उत्तराधिकार
Initiate — उपक्रमण करना, दीक्षा देना
Injury — क्षति
Inland Waterways — अन्तर्देशीय जलपथ
Inoperative — अप्रवृत्त
Inquiry — परिपत्र जाँच
Insolvency — दिवाला
Inspection — पर्यवेक्षण निरीक्षण
Institution — संस्था
Instruction — शिक्षा अनुदेश, हिदायत
Instrument — लिखित, संविदा, विलेख दलील, उपकरण, साधन
Insurance — बीमा
Intercourse — समागम
Interest — ब्याज
Indirect Election — परोक्ष निर्वाचन
International — अन्तर्राष्ट्रीय
Interpretation — निर्वचन, व्याख्या
Intestacy — इच्छापत्र, हीनत्व, निर्वसीयता
Intestate — इच्छा, पत्रहीन निर्वसीयत
Introduce — पुरस्थापना करना
Introduction — पुरस्थापना
Invalid — अमान्य, असमर्थ
Invalidity Pensions — असमर्थता निवृत्ति वेतन
Investigation — अनुसंधान
Involve — अन्तर्ग्रस्त करना
Involved — अन्तर्ग्रस्त
Irregularity — अनियमितता
Issue — वाद पद

J

Joining time — योग काल
Joint Family — अविभक्त या संयुक्त कुटुम्ब या परिवार
Judge — न्यायाधीश
Judgement — निर्णय
Judicial Power — न्यायिक शक्ति या अधिकार
Judicial Proceeding — न्यायिक कार्यवाही, न्यायिक कार्यरीति
Judicial Stamp — न्यायिक मुद्रांक
Judiciary — न्यायपालिका
Jurisdiction — क्षेत्राधिकार

L

Labour — श्रम
Labour Union — श्रमिक संघ
Land Records — भू-अभिलेख
Land Revenue — भू-राजस्व
Land Tenures — भू-धृति
Law — विधि
Law of Nations — राष्ट्र की विधि
Legal — विधि सम्बन्धी
Legislation — विधान
Legislative Power — विधायिका शक्ति
Legislative Assembly — विधान सभा
Legislative Council — विधान परिषद्
Legislature — विधान मण्डल
Letters of Credit — प्रत्यय पत्र
Levy — आरोपण, उद्ग्रहण, उगाहना
Legal Tender — विधि मान्य
Liability — दायित्व
Libel — अपमान लेख
Liberty — स्वाधीनता
License — अनुज्ञप्ति, लाइसेंस
Lieutenant Governor — उपराज्यपाल

Limitation — परिसीमा
List — सूची
Livelihood — जीविका
Living Wage — निर्वाह मजदूरी
Loans — उधार ऋण
Local Area — स्थानीय क्षेत्र
Local Authorities — स्थानीय प्राधिकारी
Local Board — स्थानीय मण्डली
Local Body — स्थानीय निकाय
Local Government — स्थानीय शासन
Local Self Government — स्थानीय स्वशासन
Lockup — बंदीखाना
Lower House — प्रथम सदन
Lunacy — उन्माद
Lunatic — उन्मत्त

M

Maintain — पोषण करना, बनाये रखना
Maintenance — पोषण
Major — वयस्क
Majority — बहुमत
Mandamus — परमादेश
Manufacture — निर्माण
Maritime Shipping — समुद्र नौवहन
Maternity Relief — प्रसूति सहायता, साहाम्य
Member — सदस्य
Memo — ज्ञाप, स्मृतिपत्र
Memorandum — ज्ञापन
Memorial — स्मारक
Mental Deficiency — मनोवैकल्य
Mental Weakness — मनोदौर्बल्य
Merchandise Marks — पण्य चिन्ह
Merchandise Marine — वणिक पोत
Migration — प्रवर्जन
Mind Unsound — विकृत चित्त
Mineral — खनिज
Mineral Resources — खनिज सम्पत्ति
Mining Settlement — खनिज वसति
Minor — अवयस्क, अल्पवयस्क नाबालिग
Minority — अल्पसंख्यक वर्ग
Misbehaviour — कदाचार
Modification — रूपभेद सुधार
Money Bill — धन विधेयक
Morality — सदाचार
Motion of Confidence — विश्वास प्रस्ताव
Motion of No-Confidence — अविश्वास प्रस्ताव
Municipal Area — नगर क्षेत्र
Municipal Committee — नगर समिति
Municipal Corporation — नगर निगम
Municipal Tramways — नगर रथ्यायान, नगर ट्राम वे

N

Nation Highways — राष्ट्रीय राजपथ
Naturalization — देशीयकरण
Naval — नौसेना सम्बन्धी
Navigation — नौ परिवहन
Newspaper — समाचान-पत्र
Nomination — नाम निर्देशन मनोनयन
Notice in Writing — लिखित सूचना
Notification — अधिसूचना

O

Obligation — आभार
Occupation — उपजीविका, धंधा
Officer — पदाधिकारी
Official Residence — पदावास
Opinion — अभिप्राय राय
Order in Council — परिषद् आदेश
Order Standing — स्थायी आदेश
Ordinance — अध्यादेश
Organization — संगठन
Owner — स्वामी

P

Parliament — संसद
Partnership — भागिता
Pass — पारण आदेश या परिचय पत्र
Passed — पारित
Passport — पारपत्र
Patent — एकस्व
Pecuniary Jurisdiction — आर्थिक क्षेत्राधिकार
Penalty — शास्ति दण्ड
Pending — लम्बित लम्बमान
Pension — निवृत्ति वेतन
Permission — अनुज्ञा
Perpetual succession — शाश्वत उत्तराधिकारी
Perquisite — परिलब्धि
Personal Law — स्वीय विधि
Piracy — जल दस्युता
Plead — वकालत करना
Police — आरक्षक
Police Force — आरक्षक दल
Policy of Insurance — बीमा पत्र
Port-quarantine — पत्तन निरोधा
Possession — स्ववश अधिकार, कब्जा
Preamble — प्रस्तावना
Perference — अधिमान
Prejudice — प्रतिकूल प्रभाव, पक्षपात की भावना
Preside — पीठासीन होना, सभापतित्व करना
Previous Consent — पूर्व सम्मति
Previous Sanction — पूर्व स्वीकृति
President — राष्ट्रपति
Presiding Officer — अधिष्ठाता
Preventive Detention — निवारक
Prisoner — काराबंदी, कैदी
Privileges — विशेषाधिकार
Process — आदेशिका विधि
Proclamation — उद्घोषणा
Proclamation of Emergency — आपात काल की उद्घोषणा
Prohibited — प्रतिषिद्ध, निषिद्ध
Prohibition — प्रतिषेध, निषेध
Proportional Representation — अनुपाती, प्रतिनिधित्व
Proposal — प्रस्थापना
Prorogue — सत्रावसान
Provided — परन्तु, बशर्ते कि
Proxy — प्रतिमात्री
Publication — प्रकाशन
Public Debt — राष्ट्र ऋण
Public Demand — सार्वजनिक अभियाचना
Public Health — लोक स्वास्थ्य
Public Notification — सार्वजनिक अधिसूचना, लोक अधिसूचना
Public Order — सार्वजनिक व्यवस्था
Public Service Commission — लोक सेवा आयोग
Public Service — लोक सेवा

Q

Qualification — अर्हता
Quarantine — निरोधा
Question of Law — विधि प्रश्न
Quorum — गणपूर्ति
Quo Warranto — अधिकार पृच्छा

R

Ratification — अनुसमर्थन
Receipt Paper — पावती रसीद
Recommend — सिफारिश या संस्तुति करना
Recommendation — संतुति या सिफारिश
Record of Right — अधिकाराभिलेख
Recruitment — भर्ती
Recurring — आवर्तक
Redemption Charges — विमोचन भार
Reference — निदेश
Reformatory — सुधारालय
Refundable to — लौटाई जाने योग्य
Regional Commissioner — प्रादेशिक आयुक्त
Regional Council — प्रादेशिक परिषद्

Regional Fund — प्रादेशिक निधि
Registered — पंजीबद्ध निबद्ध
Registration — पंजीयन बंधन, निर्बंधन
Regulation — विनिमय
Relevancy — सुसंगति
Relevant — सुसंगत
Remission — परिहार
Remuneration — पारिश्रमिक
Repeal — निरसन
Representation — प्रतिनिधित्व
Representative — प्रतिनिधि
Reprieve — प्रविलम्बन करना
Repugnancy — विरोध
Repugnant — विरुद्ध
Requisition — अधिग्रहण
Reserved Forest — रक्षित वन
Respite — विराम
Restriction — निर्बंधन
Retire — निवृत्त होना
Retirement — निवृत्ति
Review — पुनरावलोकन
Revoke — प्रतिसंहार करना
Reward — पारितोषिक
Rule of the Road — पथ नियम
Ruler — शासक

S

Safeguard — रक्षा, संरक्षण
Sale — विक्रय
Savings — बचतवृत्ति
Standing Committee — स्थायी समिति
Select Committee — प्रवर समिति
Security — प्रतिभूति जमानत
Sentence — दंडादेश
Service Charges — सेवाभार
Session — सत्र
Single Transferable Vote — एकल संक्रमणीय मत
Sinking Fund — निक्षेप निधि
Slander — अपमान वचन
Social Custom — सामाजिक रूढ़ि
Social Insurance — सामाजिक बीमा
Social Service — सामाजिक सेवा
Sovereign — प्रभु
Sovereign Democratic Republic — सम्पूर्ण प्रभुत्व सम्पन्न लोकतंत्रात्मक गणतंत्र
Speaker — अध्यक्ष
Staff — कर्मचारी वृन्द
Stamp Duties — मुद्रांक शुल्क
Standing Orders — स्थायी आदेश
State Funds — राज्य निधि
State List — राज्य सूची
Stock Exchange — श्रेष्ठि चत्वर
Subject Matter — श्रेष्ठि चत्वरवाद विषय
Subordinate Officer — अधीन अधिकारी
Succession — उत्तराधिकार
Successor — उत्तराधिकारी
Sue — वाद करना
Suffrage — मताधिकार
Summon — आह्वान
Superintendent — अधीक्षक
Supplementary Grant — अनुपूरक अनुदान
Supreme Command — सर्वोच्च समादेश
Suspend — निलम्बित करना
Subordinate Court — अधीन न्यायालय
Supreme Court — उच्चतम न्यायालय

T

Tax Calling — आजीविका कर
Tax Capitation — प्रतिव्यक्ति कर
Tax Corporation — निगम कर
Tax Employment — नौकरी कर
Tax Entertainment — प्रमोद कर
Tax Export — निर्यात कर
Tax Profession — वृत्ति कर
Tax Income — आयकर
Tax Sales — विक्रय कर

Tax Terminal — सीमा कर
Tax Trades — व्यापार कर
Technical Training — शिल्पी प्रशिक्षण
Tenant — कृषक किसान आसानी
Tenure — पदावधि
Term — निबंध अवधि
Territorial Charges — प्रादेशिक भार
Territorial Jurisdiction — प्रादेशिक क्षेत्राधिकार
Territorial Waters — जल प्रांगण
Territory — राज्य क्षेत्र
Territorial Constituency — प्रादेशिक निर्वाचन क्षेत्र
Tidal Water — वेला जल, ज्वार जल
Tolls — पथ कर
Trade Marks — व्यापार चिन्ह
Trade Union — कार्मिक या व्यापार संघ
Traffic Human — मानव पणन
Training — प्रशिक्षण
Tramcar — रथ्यायान
Transfer — स्थानान्तरण, हस्तान्तरण
Transition — संक्रमण
Transport — परिवहन
Transportation — निर्वासन
Treasure Troves — निखात निधि
Treaty — सन्धि
Tribal Area — जनजाति क्षेत्र
Tribe — जनजाति
Tribunal — न्यायाधिकरण
Triennial — त्रैवार्षिक, तिसाला
Trust — न्यास

U

Undischarged — अनुन्मुक्त
Unemployment — बेकारी
Union — संघ
Union hist — संघ सूची
Unity — एकता
Unsoundness of Mind — चित्त विकृत

V

Vacancy — रिक्ति, रिक्तता
Vagrancy — आहिडन, आवारागर्दी
Validity — मान्यता
Vice-President — उपराष्ट्रपति
Village Council — संग्राम परिषद्
Violation — अतिक्रमण
Visas — द्रष्टांक, बीसाद्रष्टांक
Vocation — व्यवसाय
Voter — मतदाता
Votes on Account — लेखानुदान, गणनानुदान
Votes of Crecit — प्रत्ययानुदान

W

Wage — मजदूरी
Warrant — अधिपत्र
Will — समापन
Writ — लेख आदेश

PARAGRAPH WRITING

अनेक Competitive परीक्षाओं में दिए गए कई Topics में से एक या दो पर Paragraph लिखने को कहा जाता है। इस तरह से Paragraph लिखवाने का उद्देश्य, छात्र की Topic को समझने और उसे Analyse करके Expand करने की क्षमता एवं उसकी Writing Power (Descriptive writing) का आंकलन करना होता है।

What is a Paragraph?

A Paragraph is a collection of related sentences dealing with a single topic or we can say that a Paragraph is a unit of thoughts with one idea developed adequately. A Paragraph should contain each of the following : Unity, Coherence, A topic Sentence and Adequate Development. All of these traits overlap so using and adapting them to our specific purpose will help us to construct effective paragraphs.

(1) Unity : The entire paragraph should concern itself with a single focus. If it begins with one focus or major point of discussion, it should not end with another or wander within different ideas.

(2) Coherence : Coherence is the trait that makes the paragraph easily understandable to a reader. Coherence can be created or maintained in your paragraphs by carrying over the same idea from sentence to sentence. These sentences are related to the main idea and give more information about the main idea. These sentences include, facts, details explanations, reasons, examples, including, illustrations.

(3) A topic sentence : (Main idea sentence) A topic sentence is a sentence that indicates in a general way what idea or theme the paragraph is going to deal with. Although not all paragraphs have clear-cut topic or main idea sentences, and despite the fact that topic sentences can occur anywhere in the paragraph (as the first sentence, the last sentence, or somewhere in the middle), an easy way to make sure your reader understands the topic of the paragraph is to put your topic sentence near the beginning of the paragraph.

A main idea sentence (Topic sentence) answer the following questions :
What is the paragraph about?
What is the main point I want to make?
What do I want to say?

(4) Adequate development : The topic (Which is introduced by the topic sentence) should be discussed fully and adequately. Again, this varies from paragraph to paragraph, but it solely depends on the purpose of writing and demand of the examination.

Some points to make sure your paragraph is well developed **:**

(a) Use examples and illustrations
(b) Cite data (facts, statistics, evidence, details, and others)
(c) Examine testimony (what other people say such as quotes and paraphrases)
(d) Use an anecdote or story
(e) Define terms in the paragraph
(f) Compare and contrast
(g) Evaluate causes and reasons
(h) Examine effects and consequences
(i) Analyse the topic
(j) Describe the topic
(k) Offer a chronology of an event (time segments) if need be.

Solved Examples

(1) Familiarity Breeds Contempt

[PCS]

Familiarity means closeness, means lack of formalities, means knowing all the ins and outs of others, means lot of expectations that all results in arising of causes of dispute and breeding reasons for quarrel or contempt, as expectations can't be calculated and very difficult to be fulfilled in this world where everyone is busy in his own affairs. On the other hand in formal acquaintances we know little about others and take more formal care and pay more formal respect so there is little cause of quarrel or contempt. A reasonable distance in relations so is necessary to avoid quarrel and contempt. Rightly said, "A hedge between keeps the friendship green and familiarity breeds contempt."

(2) Romance Is The Magic of Distance

[PCS]

One likes to acquire what is not within one's ambit. Any rare thing once possessed, lost charm of having it but a thing of whatever quality till not acquired is a rare thing and so has its importance. There is a saying : 'Distant bells are charming.' The future is always more charming because that is far from the present.

A man generally pines for distant objects and moments in the hope of getting imaginative pleasure. We often discover an element of magic in the distant objects. Romance vanishes as soon as the object of Romance is achieved or acquired by us. The fact is that the element of distance casts some magical spell on us. All human faces, and distant objects look romantic till they are at a distance. Keats has so rightly said, "Heard melodies are sweet, but those unheard are sweeter."

(3) God Helps Those Who Help Themselves

[Asstt Grade]

God has gifted the man with such wonderful and tremendous powers that he can achieve anything. A person who is sincere and dedicated to his task gets success. In time of distress, when one aspires some divinely help to get one free from the period of distress, the divine help comes only to those who help themselves. God only helps those who do not lose heart and fight tooth and nails to get success. One who is hard working, sincere and devoted honestly to one's work is certain to achieve his goal and get success and to such fellows God is there to come to their aid and rescue. So one must not keep oneself idle and waste one's time in the hope of any divine help as *God helps those who help themselves.* Everyone pushes the moving cart but none lifts the bogged down one.

(4) They Also Serve Who Only Stand And Wait

[Asstt Grade]

This is one of the crucial line from Milton's sonnet '*On His Blindness*'. This is a concluding and proverbial sentence of the poem means that God does not require any active service from his creatures. What He requires from man is obedience and His commandments. Those who only stand and wait at His service also serve Him as do His trusted angels. It means those who surrender themselves to His will and act as per the wishes of the Almighty are also doing a service. The persons who are though not putting any active service but always at the call of Him are not lesser devotees.

(5) Man Is A Social Animal

[Asstt Grade]

The functions of Man and other animals are to a great extent similar. Man has a developed brain while other animals do not have such a developed brain. So man is also an animal. The natural impulses like hunger, thirst, sex and pugnacity are found in all animals alike. Because of the gift of brain possessed by the man, he is superior and created a world of its own, developed families, societies, towns, cities, countries. Man acts and live for the welfare of his family, society. All the actions of the man are oriented for the good causes and for the welfare of the human being, while other animals live only for themselves. Therefore, man is called a social animal.

(6) The Fruits Of Labour Are Sweeter Than The Gifts Of Fortune

What is received in gift or what is inherited from the parents is never as charming or important as the things achieved by us by our own efforts, by our own labour. The sweet acquired through 'sweat' will be much sweeter than the sweet given to us by someone. Nothing tastes so sweet as that is earned by hard labour. 'By the sweat of thy brow thou shalt earn thy bread', was the divine wish. The things achieved by hard work shall be more permanent, more delicious, more lovable, more enjoying and render us real happiness.

Anything acquired by the grace of God or by luck will not give us the real enjoyment and real respect, because this fortune does not have anything your own. The history remembers those who changes the path of adversity by their hard labour. The world adores those who make their own fortune and create$ examples for others. Abraham Lincoln, Dhiru Bhai Ambani etc., are several example who achieved the success by their sheer hard work and so they are adored today. 'Honest labour bears a beautiful face.'

(7) Fame Is The Last Infirmity Of A Noble Mind

Fame does not make a man noble, nobility makes a man famous. If a noble mind becomes sensitive to the fame, he is no more noble. Noble means doing everything without any ambition. Nobility does not require or aspire any reward. A noble mind works with selfless, detached spirit and considers work to be its own reward.

Milton, the author of this quotation, has well said that a noble soul may conquer all weaknesses but he cannot override the desire to acquire fame. But whatever said or done by anybody it is undoubtedly true that the day the noble mind gets influenced by the lust of fame, his nobility diminishes upto the degree the lust is there. It is right that desire of getting famous is a great desire which an ordinary man cannot override but for a noble man nothing is more important than the nobility in real terms.

(8) Character Is Destiny

[Asstt Grade]

A fatalist believes in destiny. According to him fate is a pre-written thing, can't be changed or make by the human being. Such people believe that a man's fate is preordained by God, and man has no power over his fate. To such people, destiny is character. While many persons believe that man is the maker of his own destiny and fate. A man who wins, is the man, who thinks he can.

A man can change his fate, creates his fortune, who believes in himself, has positive attitude, strong will, firm determination and zeal to achieve the goals. Character is nothing, but these qualities, which shapes the conduct of a person. So character is the real destiny and it is wrong to think that destiny is somewhat a prewritten thing. God also helps those who help themselves.

(9) Attack Is The Best Form Of Defence

[Asstt Grade]

Defence is necessary for a happy living. The imperialistic persons try to grab the neighbour's territory and so attack him. Under such circumstances it is better to make first attack instead of waiting for the attack and then defend. All the planning be made in advance considering the imminent attack by the enemy. It also does not mean that one should not resort to the peaceful means to avoid war. but after exhausting all the solutions of maintaining peace, if the war seems definite then it is always better to attack than to wait for attack and defend. *Attack is the best defence in such circumstances.*

(10) To Thine Owns Self Be True

Most of the persons find faults with others and blames other for all the wrongs and troubles of the present day. We never judge ourselves, we don't analyse our actions, but always find solace in searching faults or mistake of others. We ignore our inner voice when we do something wrong. This is the reason why everybody is unhappy and suffering from one or other infirmity. If we want to live in peace with real happiness, we should try to perform our duties. Society consists of individuals and if each individual takes care for his conduct most of our troubles will cease to exist. The above quotation from Shakespeare's 'Hamlet' is a maxim which should be followed by all. One must be true to his own conduct.

(11) Poverty Is The Mother Of All Crimes

[IAS]

A hungry man can commit any sin or crime. He knows no morality no ethics. How can we expect from a hungry man to think of good or bad, reasonable or unreasonable action when his own existence is at stake. Right to life is the paramount right. Rightly said that poverty is the mother of all crimes. A poor person can commit any crime to save his family from the clutches of illness, hunger etc. When a person finds that his wife and children are starving to death, he can resort to any measure to save his wife and his children. Crimes like theft, robbery, dacoity, pick-pocketing are generally committed by those whose means of living are very meagre. The poor parents cannot afford to educate their children. They fail to teach them what is right and what is wrong. A poor man, in fact, has no idea of ethics. It also does not mean that all the crimes are committed by the poor. Now-a-days the abductions—murders, kidnapping, rapes, high-jacking and all other heinous crimes are being committed by the rich, who have never seen the face of poverty. They commit such crime not for the sake of hunger of stomach but hunger of power, hunger of more and more money. In the present world, the above saying should be amended to some extent to mean that *the poverty is not alone a cause of crime.*

(12) Spare The Rod And Spoil The Child

What is good and what is bad can't be understood by a child. He tries to do what he feels good and enjoyful. Sometimes he puts unreasonable demands and presses upon it to get it fulfilled by all the means he knows. If we fulfil such demands it means we are not sincere to our child in real terms and spoiling his habits, making him peevish and obstinate. To make a child disciplined and hard working we have to put a check on the wrong demands, wrong actions of the child. Even if we are to use some force we must not hesitate because if we spare the rod we spoil the child. Unjustified and wrong demands must be nipper in the bud.

(13) Time And Tide Wait For None

Time and tide have their own course, in their routine as per nature's rule. They do not wait for anyone. They come and go their own ways. A wise man makes the best use of his time. The time once gone never comes back. Those who do not make a proper use of opportunity often repent later on. One should siege the opportunity whenever it is within one's reach. If you loose, other fellow will grab it and then you will be blaming your luck or anything else for your losing such a good opportunity. Time and tide wait for none and they will not wait for us also.

(14) All That Glitters Is Not Gold

Guided by the appearance can be disastrous. In this world of deception and deceit, what is seen outwardly, is not the reality. Often the glittering appearance, hide the foulness of wickedness. When advertisements display, showiness, have all become the day of life and the judgement of the reality have become very difficult. The good looking innocent people are the perfect cheat of the day. The only way to save ourselves from such hypocrites is to be very attentive and careful in life with good observance.

What is exhibited and displayed outwardly should not be taken, as creditworthy. Visual appearances are commonly deceptive. The quality of a thing can only be judged by its use only. In many cases, a thing appears to be very durable and cheap may turn out a duplicate. Duplicates or imitations commonly have more shining or glittering than the original one.

A person can be judged by his deeds, attitude and aptitude towards show off others. A coarse man may be more helpful and co-operative than a person of pleasant countenance. A well dressed, gentlemanly looking person is apt to deceive you by his outwards looks. What he intend to show, may not be his actual intention. Appearance may be delusory and misleading. Try to ascertain his motives, and analyse his actions. Keep a close vigil.What appears to be gold, may turn out a yellow metal, a polish of Gold on iron, a fake colour of gold on brass. So beware of the appearance, judge the things from its original contents, *'All that glitters is not Gold'*.

(15) As You Sow So Shall You Reap

In other words, you shall harvest what you plant, spiritual or natural, as God said that if you sow the flesh, you shall reap corruption, but if you sow the spirit of love for all, you shall reap life everlasting. God is the great paymaster, we are under his workmanship. We are the clay and he is the potter, so do something for the God, who made you and he will not forget the things that you do but you shall receive your pay, good or bad.

The theory of *Karma* is spoken about in many of the sacred texts of all the religions in the world and is implied in the Golden Rule : *Do unto others as you would have them do unto you.* The implication: as you treat others, so you will be treated.

Every tragedy we live through is the result of some terrible wrongs we did in our past life. A child who dies of an illness at an early age, *for example* might simply have chosen to experience the birth and young adult stages of life before deciding what he wanted to do with his life as an adult in his next incarnation.

Karma is inescapable. Your actions do return to you. It may not be in this lifetime, but it certainly will return in some way. 'As you sow, so shall you reap', has relevance in today's competitive market place as well as in the timeless arena of human relationships. At every juncture, in all times, this theory of *karma (As you sow so shall you reap)* is well respected and well observed.

(16) Delayed Justice No Justice

Many Chief Justices, Judges of the Supreme Court, the High Courts, the Law Ministers, the Law Commission, the media, the great writers and thinkers have all lamented over the delay in the dispensation of justice. The inordinate delay in the provision of relief amounts to the virtual denial of any relief found in number of cases. The litany of woes caused by delay in the administration of justice is disastrous. A layman does not want and understand that he has the right to get the justice and that is too within reasonable time. An aggrieved, if doesn't get the justice within reasonable time, then all his sufferings and hardships because of such delay, is like a punishment inflicted on him for no fault of his own.

Delayed justice is the biggest cause of prevalent corruption in the country. Many political leaders are enjoying the chairs of Ministers while a number of cases are pending against them. Are our courts not their accomplice? It is unimaginable that how much loss our nation be suffering from ethical and moral point of view at least, because of the delay in disposing of the cases.

Innocent person is the worst effected unfortunate, who has to take shelter of the courts for getting justice, which he can never calculate as to when that so called justice be finally arrive. None can compute his worries and the frustrations. Such sufferings and hardships made him to conclude that *Delayed Justice is no Justice.*

(17) Diligence Is The Mother Of Success

There can't be any short cut to success. The toil of years, the sweat of your brow, struggle you make, everything counts in achieving the goal. Looking at the biographies of greatmen we find that the most of the successful persons whether inventors, artists, scientists, technocrats, sculptures, thinkers, leaders and workers of any kind, owe their success to their indefatigable hard work and dedication. They were the men who achieved their successes with dedication, devotion and true hard work. This really holds that the secret of success consisted in being master of our subject. Such mastery is attainable through continuous application and study.

Those who work diligently not only achieve their goals and get success, but also remain happy, cheerful and active, which is itself a great reward even if the work does not bring success. Idleness or laziness is worse as it brings jealousy, gloom, frustration, depression which are more degrading than the failure itself.

No doubt diligence is very necessary for the success, but intelligent decision is again an important factor that can't be ignored. We know so many daily wage earners toiling hard day and night to earn their livelihood, can't be termed as successful, but a person putting little labour and managing the things properly, earning handsomely is a successful man. *Thus, not only diligence but intelligentsia is also necessary for the success in life.*

(18) Educating A Girl Child Means Educating A Family

Today's girl child will be the mother of tomorrow. As a mother she can give her child a sound nursing and capable upbringing. A woman has the maximum impact on the social, economical decisions made in the family generally. At micro level, educated woman help in making the whole family including the older family members, understand the values and importance of education, and at macro level, educated women add to the social and economical development of the nation.Girl's education is like sowing the seed which gives rise to green, cheerful and full grown family plant. In ancient time girl's education had a significant place in the society. *Gargi* and *Maitreyi* played very encouraging role in spreading the education to a great extent.

The educated girl can shoulder any kind of responsibility. See the example of Indira Gandhi, Kalpna Chawla, Kiran Bedi, Sonia Gandhi, Sushma Swaraj, Uma Bharati, and so....., everyone has earned a name in the society in our country. Education for the girls is more important as she not only builds the home but all routine responsibilities are taken care of by her. An educated woman not only helps in nourishing the family in a better way but can also help in earning. *"One could judge the degree of civilization of a country by the social and political position of its women."*

—Charles Fourier.

Education for a girl child means making the next generation well educated, full of virtues, free from the useless superstitions, confident and capable to do something good for the family, for the society and for the country as a whole. The present day girl is the mother of tomorrow.

"Give me good mothers and I will give you a great nation."

— Napolean

(19) Failures Are The Pillars Of Success

Every successful man fails at some time. Failure tells you about your weaknesses, shortcomings, lack of preparations, lack of efforts so if you can manage to learn from failures, you will definitely reach where you started out to go. Making a mistake is not a crime, the ability to learn from it contribute to lasting success. Extract the lesson to be learnt from failure and try again with redoubled vigour. Facing failure make one strong, more wise and more resolute, spur them on to greatest efforts. There is no failure in truth save from within; unless we are beaten there, we are bound to succeed.

'Failures' means lack of preparation, lack of competitiveness, lack of analysing the things properly. Failures not only tell us that we couldn't prepare ourselves upto the level of success and reveal our shortcomings, but also give us encouragement to try again with more preparations, with more labour and with more hard work. Failures are the stepping stones to achieve success. Every successful man failed, not once but several times in their life, but they analysed the things in real perspective and tried again with more vigour and zeal and got success. Failures should not allowed to create frustration, desperateness or disappointment, instead failure should be taken as a boon which give you strength to fight back with fierce fortitude and invincible zeal.

"Failure is not fatal, it can be the stepping stone to success, if you can make 'the failure' to work for you."

"Failures are our best teachers, they are the mirrors who show us our real face."

(20) Fate And Coincidence

Many people believe that there is something bigger than us. There is a reason for everything. Some believe that everything is a coincidence. Some believe that coincidence is real and not fate. However, none of this can ever be truly proven. Coincidence is a seemingly planned sequence of accidentally occurring events. One might think the collision of events was fated to occur, but one is mistaken. It signified nothing. But searching like we all do for an explanation and a sense of importance, one creates his fate by spelling out meaning from a jumble of coincidences.

We've all had it happen to us. We think about someone who we haven't seen in a while, and later that same day, we bump into them. We have an ominous feeling that something bad is going to happen and it does. We have a dream that predicts our future. We look back at events in our lives and we see them fitting together like a puzzle. If one thinks to oneself, "If I hadn't been in that exact place, at that exact moment, my life would have gone in a totally different direction. I wouldn't have met this or that person. I wouldn't have done this thing or that thing. I would have taken that job instead of this one. I would have married that boy instead of my husband." Is it all connected somehow? Or Is it just a coincidence?

To many, fate only occurs on a personal level. Chain reactions exist, certainly, where one person's behaviour results in a massively far-reaching effect, but they are not ruled by fate. Incidents and chain reactions with a broader range of impact, such as the butterfly effect, have no intended purpose. It is fate that can play the triggering role within the intimate confines of a single person's life. Sometimes, there are certain events in our lives that are just meant to be happened. Those events happen for some reason in some person's lifetime meant to influence only the person they happen to.

No doubt coincidences happen too. Not every occurrence in a person's life is fated.

So what exactly is the difference between fate and coincidence? Rather, what evidence is there that fate exists in a world of randomness? That's where personal faith comes in.

(21) Habit : Good Servant But A Bad Master

A habit is like a tree grown crouched. One cannot go to orchard and take hold of a tree grown such and straighten it and say now get straight and make it obey him. When one is young, he can acquire good or bad habits. One starts doing certain act for the sake of pleasure, for the sake of fun and if he is doing that things, that particular act at regular or irregular intervals, he starts enjoying it and starts feeling the necessity of doing it again at that particular time and it gradually takes a form of a habit.

Every chain smoker or a habitual drunkard never starts smoking or drinking as a habit. He simply begins with such act for the sake of company for the curiosity of taste, or for the sake of fun in the company of his friends or otherwise and he starts smoking or drinking alcohol, now and then and afterwards, he consumes it often, these now become his necessity and then the habit is formed. Habit is cultivated slowly and gradually. Habit is nothing but a slow and gradual intake of something, performing of some act, slowly and gradually, when becomes a necessity, is called a habit.

People enjoy smoking, people enjoy drinking, but habit of smoking or drinking when becomes our master, we feel uneasy or wearisome, without smoking or drinking, it is felt bad. So rightly said, *"Habit is a good servant but a bad master."*

"Don't let the habits control you, conquer you, keep them your 'servants' and enjoy their company", is the secret of enjoying the life to the fullest extent.

(22) Ideas Rule The World

Ideas rule the world and thoughts decide the way of life. It is the mind which sculptures one's destiny. If one thinks positively, if one thinks in right direction, one achieves the goal, what one aspires for.

Life consists in what a man is thinking of all day. Ideas are nothing, but an outcome of one's detailed thinking. They shape and determine the destiny of human being, and contribute to the growth and well beings of the civilisation. Every great achievement whether in the field of religion, science, medicine, space technology, information and communication sector or in any field, was at the first stage an idea. The most scintillating success, the astonishing scientific discovery, the splendid technological feats like splitting the atom, heart transplantation, cloning of sheep, unravelling the secrets of Mars, walking on the surface of Moon, have all the results of an idea in the beginning.

Have we ever think of the present revolution in Information Technology two decades back? It was the vision of Azim Hashm Premji, N. R. Narayan Murthy, as also the late Dewang Mehta who catapulted India among the super powers in IT sector, making the first two Mr. Premji and Narayan Murthy, enter the elite Billionaire Club. Ideas with knowledge lead to action and success comes to you with hugging hands. Knowledge is power, when one applies his knowledge and understands the problems, analyses the prevailing situation with hard work and perseverance, the solution is not far to reach, and when one knows the answer, the success is yours.

The flash of new idea strikes to those who have worked hard and given full thoughts to the problem. See the historical examples of Archimedes jumping out of his bathtub screaming 'Eureka' finding out the solution, the idea of a razor with a cheap disposable blade came to Gillette while he was shaving himself. It was the noble idea of Alfred Nobel inventor of Dynamite, to use his fortune for the establishment of annual awards to people, who contributed outstandingly in the field of Physics, Chemistry, Medicine, Literature, Economics and Peace. An idea just in mind or on paper without implementation is no idea. we are talking about. How to handle and implement the new idea is the most important thing to realise the goal.

"Ideas are like rabbits, you get a couple, learn how to handle them and pretty soon you have a dozen."

— John Steinbeck

In brief, it is the idea that verify rule the world and also the minds of people. Idea and determination to translate it in practice can do wonders.

(23) Knowledge Is Power

Knowledge means knowing the things in an appropriate and better way. A man of knowledge can understand the circumstances more wisely, so can decide the things favourably. Knowledge inspires confidence, courage, to act at a right time. A man of knowledge possesses immense influence in society. He has the capacity to lead the society, mould the society in a positive direction, keep away the society from the many social evils. A man of knowledge can turn the sleeping people into a thundering force.

Time has gone, when power of sword rule the world. Even during that period, the power of sword alone never ruled, but the knowledge about enemy, knowledge about own strength and knowledge of the right time attack always had played a crucial role in grabbing the power. In other words, knowing what to do at what time—in what direction and how, are the various parameters that leads to sure success. Knowing the timings well, knowing our goals well, knowing our strengths and weaknesses well and shape them in right direction, we can achieve what we aspire to achieve. Knowledge gives power to mobilise the things in right direction and so it is said that knowledge is power.

If one ventures to establish any business, wishes to achieve any goal, he must acquire full knowledge of all the things including his own limitations and weaknesses. Knowledge gives one capacity and capabilities to know the result of his actions, probability of success and failure, propriety of his venture and so knowledge is said to be a power.

For a country knowledge about its friends and foes, knowledge about the capabilities of its enemies is very important. In the present world, scenario many satellites and spy aircrafts are deployed for the purpose of gaining maximum knowledge of activities going on in other countries. A country having the maximum and accurate knowledge of other countries can use them for its advantage, it is the 'Knowledge' that rules the world. Knowledge gives one immense power, so rightly said, *'Knowledge is Power.'*

(24) Money Is A Good Servant, But A Bad Master

No doubt, Money is an essential, almost indispensable article in the present day world. It is the '.money' through which we can purchase all the necessary comforts and amenities of life. If you have money, you can obtain what seems impossible to others. It is the money which gives confidence, credit worthiness, credentials, capacity, capabilities and courage to a man. In present materialistic world, money has become very powerful. In the present day corruption, cut throat competition, callous degradation of moral and ethical values, are for the sake of grabbing and accumulating more and more money. The prestige, respect, social status, commanded by a person is calculated as per his monetary status.

Money is regarded as omnipotent by a few people, particularly by the poor. As whatever one does not possess, one aspires it badly, and it becomes mono aim of achievement. For the rich that owe lots of money still craving to earn more and more by hook or by crook with fair or foul means without caring even for their own health, own family. They are the servants of money, earning money not for the sake of themselves but for the sake of money and a time comes they find themselves unable to use the money for their happiness. They are unable to eat, unable to taste the most delicious dish, unable to move, walk or enjoy because they suffer from many diseases which are the result of their undue craving for wealth at the cost of health.

Those who earn money simply to a have more money, more balance in their accounts are no better than the proverbial miser king 'Midas'. Excessive love for money makes a man slave of money. Those who use money for fulfilling their necessities, acquiring reasonable comforts and for the welfare of a common good, are the masters of money. But those, who earn money just for the sake of increasing its volume and number, are slaves of the money. They are the most unfortunate creatures of God who know well that whatever money they are earning, can't be carried along an iota of that when they die even they are minting more and more money. What a paradox ! Money has become their master and they are just slaves, having no peace of mind, no moral and ethical values, no inner satisfaction.

So it is rightly said that *money is a good servant but a bad master.* Let us earn the money for our comfort, not for the sake of money, minting more and more money.

(25) Preparedness For War For Preserving Peace

Very strange and paradoxical it seems that preparedness for war is essential for preserving peace. But the saying, appears to be true for if a country be well equipped with all the modern war gadgets and weapons, other nations will have to think twice before entering into any conflict with it. On the other hand, a weak nation becomes prey to the whims and aggressions of powerful neighbours. Balance of Power is must for preserving the peace.

Peace means freedom from war, but how can one preserve it unless or until you are well equipped you can't preserve your peace. A peace loving nation may not have the intention to enlarge its empire but who can guarantee the dictates of other neighbour countries. What happened with our country when China attacked in

1962 ? We, being a fully peace loving country, never felt necessity till then to equip ourself with modern war gadgets and weapons. China, took the opportunity and attacked us, made encroachment on our land. What did UNO do? What other Super power could have done ? In the present world, your power decides your relation with neighbours.

Nothing but power, your preparations to face any eventualities, your preparations to face any imperialistic whims, can guarantee you the peace. So it is the right conclusion that *preparedness for war is necessary for preserving peace.*

(26) The Child Is The Father Of Man

This line which has since taken the shape of a proverb, really occurs in the famous poem 'My Heart Leaps when I behold' of Wordsworth, the great poet. It implies that the qualities and characteristics shown by a child often indicate, what the child is going to be as a grown up man. The childhood is the reflection of future personality. The habits, traits and qualities of a man are usually the development of the habits, traits, qualities he had as a child. A careful study of the characteristic and qualities in a child can help us to foretell his future prospectus.

'The Child is the Father of Man', is proved true in many cases. See the example of Shivaji who during his childhood, loved so much to hear the stories of famous heroes of *Ramayana and Mahabharat,* became later a great warrior himself. Michael, the famous sculptor and painter, during his childhood used to make drawings on the pots, easels, stools and other things belonging to an old painter. The old painter said, " One day this boy will beat me." A Young Italian lad, Titian, was very fond of painting pictures, but had no paints to colour with. He was so genius, he made his own paints. Nelson, the daring Naval Commander of British Navy, showed his traits of courage and fearlessness during his childhood.

Many more example like that of Florence Nightingale, Macaulay, can be quoted to prove the veracity of the proverb that 'The Child is the Father of Man', but we can find hundreds and thousands other example where childhood of a man did not reflect anything about the grown up personality of the man. Sonia Gandhi, never thought to entangle in the political arena. In her childhood, none could imagine that one day she would be in a position to become the Prime Minister of India, the world's largest democracy.Though she did not accept the position of Prime Minister.

Lal Bahadur Shastri never showed any such trait in his childhood. He was an average student from a poor and simple family. George Bernard Shaw was known as a hopeless dullard. Mahatma Gandhi was inclined to become a rich Barrister. Shelley, the great poet and writer never showed such traits during his childhood. Amitabh Bachchan, the great Super Star of Bollywood today, didn't show such traits and qualities in his childhood.

Inspite of apparent exceptions, it is generally observed that the characteristics and qualities during childhood are developed in the grown up personality of a man. Circumstances can change the life of a person. Fate and coincidence play a great role in developing qualities of a person. The childhood ordinarily reflects the calibre of a person, but in changed circumstances, with several coincidences and the destiny, which is called predetermined can change everything. An average child can reach the highest position and a brilliant may have to survive in rectitude. An old proverb, "As the twig is bent, so the tree will grow", endorses the saying *"The Child is the Father of Man."*

(27) Think Positive Win Positively

Positive thinking leads a man to success. One, who thinks that he can achieve the things will put his best to achieve, will not fetter by the problems in the path of success and one day he will win positively. Self-confidence, determination, perseverance, and hard work are the key factors of success. Every small or big, easy or complex problem have its solution. There is a way out of every labyrinth, there is an answer to every enigma. The only requirements are the confidence, hard work and determination and you get the answer.

Dedication, devotion to the task and positive thinking with determination have been the important factors of success of every successful celebrity. Take the recent example of Mrs. Sonia Gandhi, the widow of former Prime Minister Rajeev Gandhi, participated and campaigned in the latest Lok Sabha elections of 2004, undaunted by the criticisms, personal attacks and all kinds of perversities she went alone, campaigning alone without having any other 'Star' campaigner, covered almost whole of the country against the BJP and showed the world that Congress (I) got the majority.

A winner never quits and a quitter never wins shows that one who constantly tries to achieve something, one who endeavours hard incessantly to achieve something, he is the winner, later or sooner, but a quitter could never be a winner.

Your biggest assets are your enthusiasm that enriches with your positive thinking. Never lose hope, keep cheerful, put the best possible efforts with your total involvement, have confidence in you and you are the winner. Through positive thinking one can overcome the mountains. One who always thinks positively, even in adverse circumstances, wins. *'Positive thinking always pays'*. Life belongs to the ambitions.

(28) Where There Is A Will There Is A Way

'Will' means not the ordinary desire but an unflinching, undaunting wish to achieve something. If you have a will to achieve your goal, you will positively overcome the difficulties that come in your way. Every problem has its solution. Whatever inventions are seen today were a problem one day, but the will and hard work of the inventor found their solution. Impossible is possible for the persons of strong will. Path of success runs through many labyrinth of failures. One who has a will to achieve the success, never gets frustrated by the odds and failures of the path. Every successful man failed many times but with his unshaken faith and strong will, he becomes successful one day. Think high, try your best, without being daunted by the odds of the path, success is yours.

One can certainly win and achieve one's goal, if one firmly believes in self and makes up one's mind to lead and succeed. The secret of success lies in the determination, dedication, perseverance of a man. A man who strides majestically with firm steps and unshaken faith, no matter what the odds and obstacle, is the man who actually finds his way and achieve success.

It is the unwavering faith and self-confidence that makes the man a winner. Faith brings miracle. It looks beyond all boundaries, transcends all limitations, conquer all obstacles and carries one to one's goal. Therefore, whosoever has resolution, indefatigable 'will' unfettered confidence and faith in himself will march ahead, onward, upward till he achieves his goal. One step at a time and that well placed will take you to the grandest height. One seed at a time and the forest grows, one stone at a time and the palace rises, one drop at a time and the river flows, one word at a time and the great book is written. The only thing is to start with firm determination strong and unfettered 'will' and the way is yours. So rightly said, *"Where there is a will there is a way."*

(29) Your Enemies Are Your Best Friends **[IIT Year]**

Our enemies could be treated as friends, as they disclose our weaknesses and try to get benefit of our drawbacks.They teach us to remove our weaknesses and take care of our drawbacks. In this way, we are bound to improve ourselves and thus, the fear of enemy results in the overall improvements in ourselves and thus, they really help us to get improved, so they are our friends.

If we don't have any enemy we shall not take care of our misdeeds and our shortcomings, as such we shall be losing. We will ignore our weaknesses as friends do not care to take benefit of our weaknesses. An enemy is, therefore, sometimes better than a friend. Moreover, it is because of enemies that we are cautious otherwise they may have the upper hand. We are forced to apply your best to give a strong reply to the enemy. Moreover competition and rivalry infuse enthusiasm and jest for better and greater work. So in this way too our enemies are our friends as they help us to improve and excel in the world.

(30) Better To Rule In Hell Than To Serve In Heaven

[IIT]

King is always King even if the empire is small and far better than a servant of a large empire. This famous line is taken from the Milton's *'Paradise Lost'*. Satan is the king of Hell. He prefers supremacy in hell to subordination in heaven. The sovereignty is very important. Freedom of will is one of the most sought after things in man's life. Man is by nature does not like subordination to others.

Our Constitution guarantees equality to all .The Charter of UN also have the provisions of freedom from the dominance of the rich and developed over the poor and the under developed. Full sovereignty is guaranteed to all the nations. Why anyone would be slave to others ? It is because even poor and undeveloped nations cannot tolerate interference from other rich and developed countries. Such nations prefer policies of their own in spite of their limited resources. The same thing applies both to individuals and the nations. Even the luxuries of heaven are of no use if one is not independent there. The most important thing is that one must be free from any dominance so that one can feel free and enjoy life in one's own way.

(31) The Man, Who Makes No Mistakes, Does Not Usually Make Anything

[Income Tax Inspectors]

If one does something, one may or may not commit mistakes but a person who does not do any thing will not at all commit any mistake. Committing mistakes is not a bad thing because a mistake today will lead us to do correct things tomorrow. It is natural that human beings commit mistakes. Errors and mistakes lead us to success. We should learn from the mistakes we make. Repeated errors compel us to do that particular work again and again resulting in ultimate success.

But a person, who for fear of committing mistake does not do any thing, never succeed. It is always better to travel hopefully than to arrive. We shall have to take the initiatives otherwise laziness and idleness will overcome us and we shall be suffering from the indolence. Our friends will march ahead of us. It is better to make mistakes and lose than never to try at all. Failures are the stepping stones to success.

(32) Work is Worship

[B 1998, Asstt Grade 1997]

We do worship because we want something from the Almighty. In fact it is work, which gives us everything we aspire for. Idleness or laziness could not bring us anything. Unless we work hard with dedication and devotion we can't achieve anything. Self-confidence, determination, perseverance, and hard work are the key factors of success.

Whatever inventions are seen today are the result of hard work. The will and hard work of the inventor found their solution. Impossible is possible for the persons having strong will. Path of success runs through many labyrinth of failures. So it is nothing but hard work that gives us all the things we aspire for or we desire or we think of. So, *'Work is worship'*.

(33) Man Is Ruled By Nature

[Asstt Grade]

A fatalist thinks that a man's destiny is determined by the stars and everything is ordained by God, which for practical purposes, means the natural forces over which man has no control. Some people with logical and scientific temperament believe that the man is the master of his own efforts. According to them one can make one's destiny by the sheer force his labour, energy, and determination, and there is no anything like fate or destiny.

Nature also plays an important role in making the things happen, in shaping the things. Sometimes the role of nature is so predominant in determining the course of events that the people who do not believe in the dominance of nature are bound to accept the role of nature in determining the fate of man. It is a very controversial issue and no conclusion can be drawn whether man is ruled by nature or whether man himself rule.

(34) If winter Comes, Can Spring Be Far Behind ?

[Income Tax Insp, PCS, Asstt Grade]

Day is followed by night and night is followed by day. Fortune and misfortune are part of life. Period of misfortunes is not a permanent one. Sooner or later the days of misfortunes and miseries will be over and the bright rays of hope and joy spread over. Man gets perturbed and disappointed when misfortune loom large on him, and feels totally dejected. One must realize the basic truth of life that after every patch of sorrow there comes a period of happiness and hope. Winter is a kind of misfortune, treated as gloomy days when everything is pale and in gloomy shape, is also followed by spring which brings days of hope and happiness with all the bright colours and new leaves blooming. This is what the nature also tells us that don't be panicky during the bad days and pass this period with patience. The good days are ahead as spring follows the winter. Rightly said *if winter comes, can spring be far behind.*

(35) Love Knows No Barriers

[Asstt Grade]

Barriers of caste, creed, status and religion are generally imposed by the parents and the society on the lovers. But the history has witnessed that the true lovers do not accept any such barriers. The stories of Shiri-Farhad, Laila-Majanu, Sohni-Mahiwal are the best example to support the above saying. But all this does not mean that others who sacrificed their love for the sake of parents or the society, were not true lovers. Love does not mean the love of lovers only. The point is that love is not started with a planning, so it does not accept any barrier as lovers are unable to know as to when they are entangled in love. Love is a great phenomenon, love is a bundle of emotions, love is unconditional. So we can say *'that love knows no barriers'*.

(36) The Old Order Changeth Yielding Place To New

[Asstt Grade PCS]

Change is inevitable, it is the law of nature. Nothing in this world is perfectly stable, constant and permanent. Man is also mortal, the world itself is mortal. The civilization of today will finish one day and new civilisation will take place. The present will become past and future will become present. This is the rule of nature. The old order changes and gives way to a new order. Old fashions, old customs, old traditions and old ways undergo natural and virtual change in the course of time. Ancient kingdoms and empires, old culture and civilisation, ancient beliefs and superstitions give way to new kingdoms, new thoughts and new ideologies. Time is the great remedy of all changes, whatever seems inevitable once extinct, the world does not stop and runs with the same pace and people forget him after some days. A new system takes place as the older one changes.

(37) Only The Wearer Knows Where The Shoe Pinches

[Asstt Grade]

It is very difficult to calculate the sufferings or problems of others without putting oneself entirely in others place. Looking from the outside a man of power like a king or a minister seems enjoying all the luxuries of life, but his problems and pains can't be understood by the people. The pains and the difficulties and responsibilities of enjoying position of authority are so immense that can't be realised until we are in the same position. Crown carries with it not only the power but also the liabilities and the responsibilities. So it is rightly said that *Only the wearer knows where the shoe pinches.*

(38) Charity Begins At Home

[Asstt Grade PCS]

If we like to improve our society, bring some good changes in the society. We must first bring such improvements and changes in our own home itself. If you preach value of cleanliness to your neighbours and keep your own home dirty, it will not do to make others to follow you or to make others to accept your changes, it is always better to follow them first in your own life. *Charity begins at home* means that start all the good things from your home, so that others can follow you in letter and spirit.

(39) There Is Nothing Good Or Bad, But The Thinking Makes It So

[Asstt Grade PCS]

Good or bad lies in the eyes not in the things itself. Every thing has two sides good or bad. It is in your eyes what you see. An artist will see art in a naked picture, while an ordinary man will find sex in it. A painter will find a beautiful object in such a picture, while a critic will see indecency in the nakedness. Every decision taken by the government is favoured by the ruling party MPs, while for the opposition every action is a point for criticism especially in India.

The opposition do not find anything good in any decision of the government, while the government pro MPs find nothing wrong in that decision. Nothing is either good or bad. How is our approach, positive or negative, our thinking and our opinion will automatically framed accordingly. For an optimist a glass with half water is half filled glass, while for a pessimist it is half unfilled (blank) glass. The glass is same but how do we look upon it is important. So it is right that *There is nothing good or bad, but the thinking makes it so.*

(40) Politeness Costs Nothing, Gains Everything **[Asstt Grade]**

Anger defeats itself is a well known proverb. History is evident of the fact that more works are done by politeness than by anger. We can't get anything with anger. Anger gets you nowhere. Instead of getting the favour we get disfavour. While with politeness we can win even our enemies. Politeness gets you favour and happiness while anger gets you disfavour and sorrow. Politeness does not mean cowardice, but it means maturity, it means your highness. It is wrongly believed that strong man rules the world, but to rule the hearts you have to be polite and generous. Any problem can be well solved with politeness, but nothing can be solved with hatred and anger. Politeness is the most important trait in the personality of a human being. It costs us nothing but it could gain us upto any extent.

(41) Virtue Is Its Own Reward **[PCS]**

Virtues and evils are what every being possesses. Evils generate miseries while virtues bring happiness in life. A man with virtues is contented, satisfied and really rich. Virtues are such good habits that bring peace in life, that bring happiness in life, that keep you happy, healthy and prosperous. The practice of virtue in the manner gives a peculiar spiritual satisfaction and saves man from disappointment and frustration. Whatever is needed by a man in life is achieved by him because of the virtues he possesses, and so it is more than correct to say that virtue is its own reward.

(42) United We Stand And Divided We Fall **[PCS]**

None but we Indians can well understand the value of Unity and the saying 'United we stand and divided we fall.' India was ruled by the British, who came to India as traders and because of the fractions and infighting here they became the ruler. A closed fist may be valued in lacs of rupees, but open hands are valueless. We can break a stick one by one but we can't break the bundle of these sticks whatever power we may enjoy. The unity of a nation depends not on the number of individuals but because these individuals have a natural feeling of sincerity and loyalty towards the nation. History is a witness to the fact that we were defeated by foreigners only when we were divided. So it is very correct to say that *United we stand and divided we fall.*

(43) Rome Was Not Built In A Day

[PCS]

Hard toil for years is necessary to achieve anything great or everlasting. The city of Rome which ultimately became the wonder of the civilized world was not built in a day, it took many years to get it in this shape. Nothing important or great can be attained by a mere thought of attaining it, a serious planning, hard labour, dedication and positive thinking and a regular perseverance is required to get it. To reach the Moon, to reach the Saturn it took many many years of research and hard work.

We must remember that there is no royal road to anything and that the true success can be attained only by hard work. We must not yield to discouragement because our efforts are not crowned with success. Failures are the pillars of success. Nothing but hard work, dedication and perseverance is necessary to achieve the goal. Slow progress must not make us impatient and difficulties must not discourage us. We must remember that *Rome was not built in a day.*

(44) Look Before You Leap

[PCS]

Check your pocket before you enter a hotel. Haste makes waste. Rash decisions are always dangerous. This is what the saying "Look before you leap" means. You must see the pros and cons of your decision before you act according to it. It is always better to find the merits and demerits of any venture, before entering into it. See where are you going to leap, it is always better to know the risk involved in it. History is full of such *e.g.*, when the rashness costs a lot.

Napolean decided to attack Russia without taken into consideration the fierce winter of that country. As a result of this rashness and miscalculation, his armies were trapped in the snows and thus, lost the iron guard, the main strength of the army. One must have patience, must plan well, must see the risk involve and then act, he will positively get success. So it is true to say that *look before you leap.*

(45) Example Is Better Than Precept

[IFS, PCS]

If you actually wish others to follow what you say, it is necessary that you yourself follow what you want others to follow. Mere words of advice, laying down rules of action and the like are of no use. People do not believe in the preaching or if some believe the strength is very meagre. Living example which the persons for whom they are meant can see before his eyes, can make better impression and have the desired end, being something concrete: but precepts, which are things only in abstract, do not make good impressions upon the mind or even if they make any impression at all, it lasts only for a short time.

Mahatma Gandhi always believed in the saying that *example is better than precept* and so he had lacs of followers. He never did what he asked other not to do. He was an apostle of creating examples in real terms.

(46) Forgiveness Is The Noblest Revenge

[PCS Asstt Grade 1996, IFS]

If you want to destroy your enemy, forgive him, he will not be your enemy any more and so the enmity is destroyed and a friend takes birth. And in this way to destroy the enemy, forgiveness is the biggest tool. Revenge is an ordinary tool, does not destroy the enmity, it can cause some harm, physical or financial to the enemy but the enemy becomes more determined to avenge it. While the forgiveness not only makes him feel sorry and finishes the enmity but also makes you safe for ever and the enemy now becomes your friend. So to destroy the enemy *forgiveness is the noblest revenge.*

(47) Handsome Is That Handsome Does [PCS]

Outward looks or beautiful face does not makes a man really good or handsome. The inner virtues, and the good actions are the real beauty of a person. A person is considered to be handsome, if he has physical outwardly bright eyes, pointed nose, rosy cheeks, pearly teeth, curly hair and strong body. In reality, handsome is he whose deeds are handsome. The greatness lies neither in wealth nor in rank and nor in physical beauty but in our actions and our deeds. We can find number of beautiful prostitutes, but the deeds of these pimps are not worthful. The noble laureate Mother Teressa was not a handsome lady but her deeds made her so great. So if we want to make our life noble, dignified and handsome, we must do noble deeds.

Mahatma Gandhi, the father of the nation, was not good-looking but still he is regarded as the finest specimen of humanity because of his noble deeds.We must not judge a person from his outward looks but we must judge him from his character, thoughts and the most important his deeds.

(48) Capital Punishment

The punishment of criminals has always been a problem for society. Citizens have had to decide whether offenders such as first-degree murderers should be killed in a gas chamber, imprisoned for life, or rehabilitated and given a second chance in society. Many citizens argue that serious criminals should be executed. They believe that killing criminals will set an example for others and also get rid society of a cumbersome burden. Other citizens say that no one has the right to take a life and that capital punishment is not a deterrent to crime. They believe that society as well as the criminal is responsible for the crimes and that killing the criminal does not solve the problems of either society or the criminal.

(49) He Is Strong Who Conquers Others; He Who Conquers Himself Is Mighty

It is very easy to direct others to do this or that. It is also easy to use force to make others to obey you. It is also easy to use brutal force to subjudicate others, you may be a winner, but if you are asked to change your life style or to give up your habits or give up any kind of lust you are having, you will find it the most difficult task or impossible to do so. The sacrifices to be made to win over ownself is really tremendous. For an ordinary man relinquishing the empire is not possible, but Gautam Buddha did it. Though Nadir Shah defeated a number of kings with his brute force, but he can't be equated with Gautam Buddha. Samrat Ashoka became great only when he renounced the throne, but not on defeating the Kalinga. Rightly said that the man who could conquer himself is indeed great and mighty and who conquers others is simply more powerful or strong.

(50) Slow And Steady Wins The Race

The story of the fast runner hare who was defeated by the slow running tortoise is a well known story. The saying teaches us three things- Firstly, one should not believe in shortcuts and secondly, one should not rest until one achieves one's goal and thirdly, one should not underestimate the rivals. In this competitive world, we must be totally vigilant and put hard work and make all our efforts or better efforts in order to excel others. *'Slow and steady wins the race'* is not so relevant in this competitive world. In my opinion 'Fast but perfect wins the race', slow remains far behind now a days.

(51) A Little Knowledge Is A Dangerous Thing [PCS, IFS, Asstt Grade]

Superficial and shallow knowledge always leads to dangerous consequences. An incompetent doctor or surgeon may play with the lives of his patients; a teacher with shallow knowledge of his subjects will misguide his students; a lawyer without a thorough knowledge of law will ruin his clients; similarly an inefficient engineer will build bridges and buildings that could cause major accidents. These people expose the lives of others to serious risks. They are so conceited that they never realise their shortcomings and hence make no progress. We can find such people in every walk of life whether art, science or literature or economics or medicines and these are hazards for the common people. One must, therefore, never rely on persons who are not thorough in their profession or vocation and be cautious to deal with such fellows.

(52) The Pen Is Mightier Than The Sword

[Engg Services, PCS]

It has been a point of contention since long that what is more powerful, physical force or the intellectuality or who rules the world sword or the pen. During the primitive age, the Sword ruled the world and the maxim 'Might is Right' was accepted by all. In the civilized world of today, the pen is surely mightier and Sword is worked for the Pen. In today's world where every rule and law are coded and democratic values are being accepted the pen becomes more powerful.

The President of USA, who is regarded as the most powerful man of the world, is because of his power of pen, means the intellectuality prevails over the physical force. In the jungle, where the animals rule prevails, only there the physical force is more important. An empire created by the physical force is of temporary nature, soon will crumbled to dust within some years, but the empire of literature is immortal. So in this civilised world *the pen is mightier than the sword.*

(53) Laugh And The World Laughs With You : Weep And You Weep Alone

In general, man does not like to share his sorrow with others, as sorrow is otherwise a private or personal affair. Happiness is a matter to be shared with all the relatives and friends, as happiness increases when you share it. Laughter is essentially a wonderful virtue and a great medicine for the depressed also. One never laughs alone, there are always friends and companions to share and increase your laughter.

It does not mean that the world is altogether indifferent to the sorrow. When we weep there are certain friends and relatives who share our sorrow. But a common man does not ready to share your sorrow, he can only laugh with you.

(54) Our Sweetest Songs Are Those That Tell Of Saddest Thought

Man's character and conduct are often largely governed by his environment and circumstances. The mixed threads of good and evil embedded in his nature are drawn out by the circumstances through which he has to pass. Experience shows that in times of prosperity, ease and luxury, man's base nature gets the upperhand whereas in adverse circumstances, the best in him comes to the surface. Nations which gave themselves up to a life of pleasure and indolence rapidly declined, whereas those which had to face ordeal after ordeal emerged harder and more powerful than before.

It is in times of difficulty that a man exerts himself utmost, reaches unsuspected heights of endurance and perseverance, whereas in easy times the sturdier part of his nature remains dormant and begins to deteriorate. A rich man with plenty of money often gives himself up to sensual pleasures, but a poor man leads a blameless and straightforward life so that he may keep his body and soul together.

(55) It Is Always Better To Light One Little Candle Than To Curse The Darkness

Man is by nature a critic. He always tries to take the excuses for his failure instead of trying to solve the things. It is no use to blame the circumstances or the lacking of something for not getting anything done. Everybody knows there cannot be perfection anywhere, so to criticise the shortcomings is of no use. The right approach should be to find the solution instead of criticising.

A winner always finds his way among the adverse circumstances. He does not blame the shortage or lack of infrastructure or any other thing for not getting the desired results but he actually finds the solution in the given circumstances. We should remember where there is a will there is a way. *So it is always better to light a little candle than of cursing the darkness.*

(56) A Thing Of Beauty Is A Joy Forever [PCS]

If the beauty means simply the physical beauty of a thing or person, it is of very temporary nature. A beauty with aesthetic value is of permanent nature. But whatever kind of beauty it may be, it is very unreasonable to conclude that it will be the source of joy forever. Nothing in this world is so beautiful which can always give us happiness and joy.

The pretty face of a most beautiful woman of the world, the innocence smile of a child, any kind of beautiful scene of nature, the sculpture of Leonardo da Vinci, the paintings of Raphael, the music of Beethoven, the plays of Shakespeare, the verses of Kalidas, the epics of Homer and Milton, the poetry of Keats or Tagore or anything else is so beautiful as to give joy forever.

Even the loveliest of objects lose some of their charm with the period of time. Variety is necessary even in preserving the charm and appeal of beautiful objects. As such it is not true to say that a *thing of beauty is a joy forever*.

(57) Where Ignorance Is Bliss It Is Folly To Be Wise

It means that in cases happiness lies on the side of ignorance, it would be folly to be wise. Every ignorance is not bliss. Ignorance could be a cause of great loss, ignorance could be a cause of failure, ignorance could be resulted in the defeat of empire and so many very drastic and dangerous consequences may be the result of the ignorance.

But when knowing any thing may result in unhappiness, or result in a something drastic, then it is wrong to put efforts in knowing that thing.

Adam tasted the forbidden fruit of the Tree of Knowledge and was so expelled from the Garden of Eden. "He that increaseth knowledge increaseth sorrow" was the verdict of Solomon; and the experience of ages has confirmed the truth of the verdict.

(58) Do Unto Others As You Would Have Them Do Unto You

The theory of *Karma* is spoken about in many of the sacred texts of all the religions in the world and is implied in the Golden Rule 'Do unto others as you would have them do unto you.' The implication: 'as you treat others, so you will be treated.'

Karma is inescapable. Your actions do return to you. It may not be in this lifetime, but it certainly will return in some way. How you deal with the return of this karmic energy determines whether or not you bring your soul further into balance or create more karmic energy that must be dealt with at a later stage. If you seek to learn from the seeming injustices in your life, chances are that you will be balancing your karmic books rather than increasing your karmic debt.

It is helpful to look at *Karma* as a sort of credit card. Each time we do something in our lives motivated by love, we are 'paying off' some of the karmic debts we have built up over our many lifetimes. Each time we act in selfish interest, we are charging something else to our credit card.

(59) The Heights By Great Men Reached And Kept Were Not Attained By Sudden Flight, But They, While Their Companions Slept, Were Toiling Upward in The Night

There can't be any short cut to success. The toil of years, the sweat of your brow, struggle you make, everything counts in achieving the goal. Looking at the biographies of greatmen, we find that the most of the successful persons whether inventors, artists, scientists, technocrats, sculptures, thinkers, leaders and workers of any kind, owe their success to their indefatigable hard work and dedication. They were the men who achieved their success with dedication, devotion and true hard work. This really holds that the secret of success consisted in being master of our subject. Such mastery is attainable through continuous application and study.

Those, who work diligently, not only achieve their goals and get success, but also remain happy, cheerful and active, which is itself a great reward even if the work does not bring success. Enthusiasm is the best asset of a person, self-determination and hard work, could achieve anything.

(60) Failure is Not Fatal, It Can be The Stepping Stone to Success

Every successful man fails at some time. Failures are natural happenings, every successful man faced failures of many kinds but they worked with more enthusiasm, more determined zeal, analysed their shortcomings and tried again and got success. If you can manage to learn from failures, you will definitely reach where you started out to go. Making a mistake is not a crime, the ability to learn from it contribute to lasting success. Extract the lesson to be learnt from failure and try again with redoubled vigour. Facing failure makes one strong, more wise and more resolute, spur them on to greatest efforts. There is no failure in truth save from within; unless we are beaten there, we are bound to succeed.

One who tries, is always the better than the one who dare not to try, only a person who dares to try can have a chance of success. Blessed are those, who once failed, is a saying worth to follow. It means that the failures make us capable to evaluate our shortcomings and purge us to reach the higher ideals, higher planks.

Abraham Lincoln failed many times in his life, but never got frustrated and fought with more determination, with full devotion and became the President of America. Indian freedom fighters including Mahatma Gandhi, Jawahar Lal Nehru, Vallabhbhai Patel, saw face of failures not once but several times, but never daunted or became desperate, they all had fought to attain the sacred goal of attaining freedom and as a result, they attained it. Failures should not allowed to create frustration, desperateness or disappointment, instead failure should be taken as a boon which gives you strength to fight back with fierce fortitude and invincible zeal.

(61) "A Man Who Wins, Is The Man Who Thinks, He Can"

Confidence is the most important key to success. It boosts the morale and creates determination to attain a goal. The loss of confidence makes a man pessimist, coward or a dead man. A winner never quits and a quitter never wins, shows that one who constantly tries to achieve something, one who endeavours hard incessantly to achieve something, he is the winner, later or sooner, but a quitter could never be a winner.

When Vallabhbhai Patel told that 'Swaraj is my birth right' so many people find it mere a slogan, but the incessant struggle put by all the freedom fighters supported the claim of Patel and we could win the freedom.

Organising the efforts properly, in right direction, striking at the opportune time, are essential for achieving a target. Optimism, determination, undaunted will power makes every impossible task possible. Your biggest assets are your enthusiasm that enriches with your positive thinking. Never lose hope, keep cheerful, put the best possible efforts with your total involvement, have confidence in you and you are the winner.

Through positive thinking one can overcome the mountains. One who always think positively even in adverse circumstances wins. Positive thinking always pays. Life belongs to the ambitions.

LETTER WRITING

How *to* Write a Good Letter?

पत्र लेखन एक कला है। एक अच्छा लिखा हुआ पत्र, पढ़ने वाले व्यक्ति पर, लेखक के व्यक्तिगत एवं वैचारिक सामंजस्य की छाप छोड़ता है। पत्र की शैली, सुन्दर एवं सुपाठ्य होनी चाहिए। पत्र एक ऐसा लिखित संदेश है जो लेखक दूर स्थित किसी व्यक्ति को प्रेषित करता है। पत्र दो दूर बैठे व्यक्तियों के मध्य व्यक्तिगत वार्तालाप का साधन है। अच्छा लिखा पत्र प्राप्त करने वाले को शान्ति प्रदान करता है। जबकि खराब लिखा पत्र, लेखक की अदूरदर्शिता, लापरवाही या असामाजिकता को व्यक्त कर सकता है।

पत्रों को मुख्य रूप से निम्न चार भागों में वर्गीकृत किया जा सकता है:

(1) Personal Letters (व्यक्तिगत पत्र): मित्र, पिता, माता, भाई इत्यादि को लिखे पत्र।

(2) Business Letters (व्यापारिक पत्र): एक व्यापारी द्वारा अन्य व्यापारी को, व्यापारी द्वारा अपने किसी ग्राहक को, व्यापारी द्वारा अपने व्यापार के सम्बन्ध में किसी को भी लिखा गया पत्र।

(3) Official Letters (Applications and Complaints): किसी सरकारी या गैर-सरकारी कार्यालय में एक व्यक्ति या समूह द्वारा किसी सरकारी या किसी तरह की जानकारी या सुविधा प्राप्ति हेतु लिखे पत्र, नौकरी हेतु किया आवेदन या किसी अधिकारी को किसी भी सम्बन्ध में की गई शिकायत।

(4) Social (Invitational) Letters (सामाजिक पत्र): इस तरह के पत्रों में शादी, Parties या भोज (dinner, lunch) इत्यादि के लिए निमन्त्रण-पत्रों को शामिल किया जाता है। इस तरह के पत्रों को लिखने हेतु एक निश्चित प्रकार का Format सामान्यतया प्रयोग किया जाता है। आजकल, निमन्त्रण-पत्रों के Formats मे बहुत विविधता एवं नूतनता दिखाई पड़ती है।

Parts of a Letter :

एक सम्पूर्ण पत्र को छः भागों में विभाजित किया जा सकता है:

(1) The Heading (Address and date)
(2) The Salutation or Greeting (Opening words)
(3) Body of the letter (Soul of the letter)
(4) Closing line
(5) Subscription and Signature
(6) The Address

(1) The Heading : एक पत्र मे Heading सामान्यतया दायीं तरफ लिखा जाता है जिसमें लेखक का Address एवं पत्र को लिखने की दिनांक लिखी जाती है। यदि पत्र letter head पर लिखा गया है तो Letter Head में Address ऊपर ही लिखा होता है या Letter Head में नीचे पट्टी में लिखा होता है। ऐसी स्थिति में दायीं तरफ मात्र Date ही लिखी जाती है। यदि पत्र Personal Letter के अतिरिक्त कोई पत्र है एवं letter head पर लिखा जा रहा है तो इसमें Reference भी लिखा जाता है जो बायीं तरफ लिखा जाता है।

2/53, Aravali Vihar
Near Jain Tample,
Alwar (Raj.) 301001,
16-12-20xx

Heading में Address लिखते समय यदि मकान नं. या Plot No. लिखा गया है तो उसके आगे Comma अवश्य लगायें। यदि किसी गली, near वगैरहा का उल्लेख भी है तो उसके पहले के Address के बाद भी Comma लगाना आवश्यक है। City के बाद Pin Code लिखना भी उचित रहता है।

Data को कई तरह से लिखा जा सकता है; जैसे:

16-12-20xx,
Dec. 16, 20xx,
16th December, 20xx

(2) The Salutation: पत्र लेखक, पत्र पाने वाले के साथ अपने सम्बन्धों की घनिष्ठता के आधार पर अभिवादन स्वरूप जो शब्द लिखता है, उसे Salutation कहते हैं जैसे:

My dear Father, My dear Friend, Dear Sir, etc. Hi Rani, Hello Ashish, इसमे My dear या Dear के बाद सम्बोधन शब्द Capital letter से शुरू होता है एवं उसके बाद comma लगाया जाता है। Salutation को पत्र में Left hand side को लिखा जाता है।

Personal letter में सम्बोधन का बहुत महत्त्व है। यदि आप मित्र को पत्र लिख रहे हैं जिनका नाम Prem Prakash **है और आप उसे बातचीत में PP बोलते हैं तो सम्बोधन में My Dear PP लिखना ज्यादा अच्छा लगेगा। इसी तरह यदि आप अपनी Mother** को **Mom कहकर पुकारते हैं तो Mother को पत्र लिखते समय My dear Mom, लिखना अधिक उपयुक्त, हृदयपूर्ण एवं मन से लिखा प्रतीत होगा।**

Business या Official letters मे Dear Sir, Sir, Dear Sh–, लिखा जाता है।

यदि पत्र किसी Lady को official capacity में लिखा जा रहा है तो **Respected Madam, Madam, लिखने से भी काम चल जाता है।**

(3) Body of the Letter (Soul of the letter) : Salutation के बाद next line से कुछ space छोड़कर पत्र प्रारम्भ किया जाता है। पत्र का मजमून सरल भाषा में, स्पष्ट भाषा में तथा छोटे-छोटे Paragraph में सुन्दर तरीके से लिखा जाना चाहिए। **पत्र का मजमून लेखक के व्यक्तिव एवं वैचारिक सुदृढ़ता को स्पष्ट करता है।**

(a) Personal Letters: X व्यक्तिगत पत्रों में शुरूआत कैसे की जाये इसको नियमों में नहीं बाँधा जा सकता है, क्योंकि व्यक्तिगत पत्र, एक-दूसरे के साथ सम्बन्धों में घनिष्ठता या अन्य कई व्यक्तिगत बातों पर निर्भर करता है। जैसे : यदि परिवार में सर्वप्रथम अभिवादन Jai Sri Krishna से होता है तो Salutation के बाद Jai Sri Krishna लिखकर ही पत्र शुरू किया जाता है।

साधारणतया Personal Letters को हम निम्न प्रकार शुरू कर सकते हैं:

(1) I am in receipt of your letter... (2) I got you letter day before yesterday...
(3) I haven't heard from you since long... (4) I couldn't reply your letter dated...
(5) Hope this letter finds you happy, healthy and enjoying the life.

Personal Letters के सम्बन्ध में भी कई Books में ऐसा लिखा गया है कि पत्र में उक्त वाक्य को लिखने में समय व्यर्थ नहीं करना चाहिए बल्कि सीधे ही शुरू कर देना चाहिए। हमारा मानना यह है कि Personal Letters से आत्मीयता एवं अंतरंगता झलकनी चाहिए। पत्र पाने वाले को ऐसा महसूस होना चाहिए कि पत्र लेखक सामने ही बैठा है। अत: उक्त प्रकार के वाक्यों से ही पत्र शुरू कराना अच्छा लगता है।

(b) Business Letters : Business letters की शुरूआत के लिए उक्त वाक्यों का प्रयोग करने की आवश्यकता नहीं है, लेकिन यदि किसी पत्र के जवाब में कोई पत्र लिखा जा रहा है तो हमें निम्न प्रकार से पत्र को शुरू करना चाहिए।

We are in receipt or your letter of 4th instant.....

लेकिन यदि हम सीधे ही पत्र लिख रहे हैं तो

We beg to say ......
or

We beg to inform you ......
or
In response to your advertisement published in the local newspaper dated......

- **Actually, business / official letters में किसी भी भूमिका की आवश्यकता नहीं होती है, पत्र सीधे-सीधे मुख्य बात से शुरू किये जाते हैं।**
- **Business letters में यदि पत्र व्यक्तिगत नाम से नहीं लिखा जा रहा है तो I का प्रयोग नहीं करके We का प्रयोग करते हैं।**

Official Letters, Applications and Complaints

इस तरह के पत्र प्रार्थना पत्र या शिकायत पत्रों में कोई भूमिका बनाने की सामान्यतया आवश्यकता नहीं होती है। पत्र की शुरूआत सीधे ही निम्न प्रकार से की जा सकती है:

(1) We like to draw your kind attention.....
(2) In reference to your advertisement published in local newspaper dated.....
(3) I came to know......
(4) With due respect, I beg to say.
(5) In response to your requirement....

Applications and Complaints: यदि कोई Application एक समूह के रूप में प्रेषित की जा रही है तो हमें I की जगह We का प्रयोग करना चाहिए। व्यक्तिगत मामलों में ही I का प्रयोग करना होता है।

Body of the Letter (Soul of the Letter): पत्र की body सरल भाषा में एवं स्पष्ट होनी चाहिए। छोटे-छोटे paragraphs में विभाजित पत्र अच्छा लगता है। पत्र की शैली प्रभावशाली एवं सुन्दर होनी चाहिए। पत्र की body ही पत्र की आत्मा होती है। यह लेखक के व्यक्तित्व एवं वैचारिक गम्भीरता को स्पष्ट करती है।

(4) Closing line : Body of the letter की समाप्ति निम्न प्रकार करनी चाहिए

(a) Personal Letters में:
(i) With due regards.
(ii) With love and best wishes.
(iii) Convey my best regards to....
(iv) Wishing you better health.

(b) Business/Official Letters में:
(i) Thanking you.
(ii) Thanking you in anticipation.
(iii) We are at your service.

(c) Applications में:
(i) Thanking you.
(ii) Thanking you in anticipation.

(d) Complaints में
(i) In anticipation of your earliest reply.
(ii) In anticipation of the earliest redressal of the problem.
(iii) Thanking you.

(5) Subscription and Signature: पत्र के अन्त में Next line में दायीं तरफ को subscription लिखा जाता है। इसका पहला अक्षर Capital होता है, अंत में comma लगाया जाता है।

(1) Personal Letters में :
Yours affectionately,
Yours loving son/daughter,

अपने से बड़ों को लिखा जाये तो :

Yours affectionately,

मित्रो :

Yours sincerely,

Yours truly,

(2) Business/Official letters में :

Yours faithfully,

यदि Demi official letter लिखा जाये तो :

Yours sincerely,

Principal को लिखा जाये तो :

Yours obediently,

(3) Application या complaint में :

Yours faithfully,

लिखना चाहिए।

Signature हमेशा Subscription के नीचे किये जाते हैं। जैसे:

Yours faithfully,

P.K. Singh

हमें यदि अपना नाम देना हो तो Signature के नीचे Bracket ( ) लगाकर नाम देते हैं।

Yours faithfully,

P.K. Singh

(P.K. Singh)

यदि Letter official capacity में लिखा गया है तो Signature के नीचे Designation लिखना होता है।

Yours faithfully,

P.K. Singh

Manager

or

Director

or

Partner

पत्र यदि Letter head पर लिखा जाये तो Stamp लगाने की आवश्यकता नहीं होती है अन्यथा Official letter में Stamp लगानी चाहिए।

(6) Address: Address, लिफाफे पर बाहर, स्पष्ट एवं सुन्दर अक्षरों में लिखा जाना चाहिए। जैसे:

To

Mr. P.K. SHARMA,
109, Lake Colony,
Udaipur (Raj.)
Pin Code–234500

Address में Pin Code अवश्य लिखा जाना चाहिए। पत्र यदि Registered भेजा जाना है तो लिफाफे पर ऊपर Registered लिखा जायेगा एवं पत्र पाने वाले का पूरा पता लिखा जाता है।

Registered

To,

Sh. N.K. Gupta
A-552, Talwandi, Kota (Rajasthan)
Pin Code–307 245

From:
P.K. Jain
105, S.W.B
ALWAR (RAJ.)

प्रेषक का पता लिफाफे के पीछे भी लिखा जा सकता है। Official Letters में फर्म या Office का Address लिखा जाता है।

Punctuating Letters

Don't forget to Punctuate the letters as per following norms

Commas

(a) Use commas after the salutation (Also called the greeting) in a personal letter and after the complimentary closing in all letters.

(i) Salutation:
Dear Ram,
My dearest Hina,

(ii) Closing:
Sincerely,
Truly yours,

Colons in Special Cases

There are half a dozen special uses for the colon.

(1) Numerical expressions of time.

Example: 5 : 31 P.M.

The colon goes between the hour and minute. If seconds are noted, a colon goes between the minute and second.

Example: He ran the marathon in 2:14:33.2.

(Two hours, fourteen minutes and thirty-three point two seconds.)

Example: He ran the mile in 4:12. (Four minutes and twelve seconds)

(2) Periodical references in a bibliography or formal reference.

This may vary slightly depending on the form followed. Most frequently the reference is Volume : Issue Number or Volume : Page Number.

(3) Bible references, Chapter:Verse.

Example: John 3:16 ("The book of John, chapter 3, verse 16.")

(4) Subtitles for books, periodicals and articles are preceded by a colon.

Example: Ben-Hur : A Tale of the Christ

(5) We can also use 'colon' with salutations in business letters as per following:

Dear Sir:
Dear Ms Hathaway:

(6) Colons follow labels that identify important ideas meant to get attention.

Warning: To be opened by authorised personnel only.

Notice: Do not use before October 15.

Capital Letters

There are two additional rules for capitalising when writing letters.

(1) Capitalize the first word and all nouns in the salutation (or greeting).

Correct:

Dear Sir,
My dearest Aunt,
Greetings!

(2) Capitalize the first word in the complimentary closing.

Correct:

Sincerely,
Truly yours,
With best wishes,

Personal Letters

Q. 1. Write a letter from a father giving advice to his son who has taken admission in a college.

Ans.

1/42, Aravali Vihar
Rajgarh (Alwar)
July 14, 20xx

My dear Son,

This is the first letter I am writing to you after you left home for higher studies at the college. You have been a very sincere and hard working student so far. You are at the threshold of making and shaping your future career. If you would be sincere to your studies, you could get what you desire. These four years of sincerity and devotion to the studies are very important in shaping the career of a student. You are venturing into a new life where you find everything to decide yourself. There is none to tell you to study or play or watch T.V. You are to manage all your time yourself.

I know that you will not disappointment me with respect to your studies, but you are in your youth and know little of the temptations and allurement with which youth is beset now-a-days. The bad habits and evils which might catch during this period can spoil not only your own career but also destroy the aspirations of the parents .

Companions influence one's character greatly : good companions make good one's character and bad companions make one's career. Choose the friends who are sincere, honest and industrious. Education plays very important role in the formation of character. Morals are of greater importance in life than the subjective knowledge.

Indolence is the worst habit a student can form. Remember that doing nothing may do you even more harm. You may find plenty of books in your college library. Read history and biography, both for instruction and amusement and if you feel inclined for something lighter.

I don't want to say anything more.You are also a wise boy. Remember :

Heights by the great men reached and kept,,
Were not attained by sudden flight,
But while their companions were slept,
They were toiling upwards in the night.

Write to me regularly and unreservedly. Always look upon me as your best friend, hiding nothing, not even your mistakes or faults.

Your mother conveys you her fondest love.

Your affectionate father,
S.C. Gupta

Q. 2. Write a letter to your friend congratulating him on his success in the RAS examination.

Ans.

32/31,West Patel Nagar,
Jaisalmer,
July 23, 20xx

My dear Pramod,

I am glad to see your result in the *Rajasthan Patrika* of today that you have been successful in the RAS examination and secured good rank. I conveyed this happy news to my father who was sitting beside me. He too was overjoyed.

I thank God for his kindness and wish you a bright future. I know well that you have been intelligent and diligent in your school and college days. Certainly your success is due to God's grace as well as your hard work and also timely guidance of your respected parents.

Please convey my respectful compliments to your parents. Again congratulations to you.

Yours sincerely,
Raj Kumar

Q. 3. Write a letter to your friend Who has recently lost his mother.

Ans.

10, Barkat Nagar,
Jaipur
May 4, 20xx

My dear Mahesh,

It is really a very sad news that you have lost your mother. I knew your mother was ill but the illness was not so serious. The news of your mother's death came to me as a shock. I know you will feel it deeply for you always thought so much of your mother and loved her very much. I also feel it as a personal loss to myself. She was always very kind and loving to me. I can't forget her love and affection for me and her motherly care and worries for me. She was such a good and noble woman.

In such sorrow we are always alone. Words, I know can't soothe your wounds. May God give you strength to bear this uncompensationable loss.

Yours sincerely,
Kailash Jaiman

Q. 4. Write a letter of apology to a friend for not keeping an appointment.

Ans.

29, Janta Colony
Jaipur,
June 19, 20xx

My dear Pradeep,

I am sorry I could not join you at dinner last night. You must have waited for me and cursed me as well for not keeping the appointment. But this lapse on my part was due to the fact that I met with an accident while coming over to your place.

Near Ghat Gate a motor cycle came from the opposite direction. It was without lights. It hit my scooter. I fell off the scooter and lay on the road. My left arm was badly injured. Some people took me to hospital. I was allowed to leave the hospital only after midnight. My arm was plastered. I hope you will excuse my absence.

Yours sincerely,
Ashok

Q. 5. Write a letter to your younger brother advising him to take part in evening games.

Ans.

12, South West Block,
Alwar
February 15, 20xx

My dear Taspan,

I met your class teacher yesterday. He told me that you stood first in the class. I was glad to hear it. But he also told me that you have become a bookworm. You do not take part in any kind of games. It is not good. It will affect your health.

I suggest you to take part in evening games. Do not study at the cost of your health. Play hockey or football. Play any game at least for an hour. It will refresh your mind and keep you physically fit. This will help you in your studies. Do study hard, but do play a while. Always remember the saying *'Work while you work and play while you play; that is the way to be happy and gay'*.

With love,

Yours affectionately,
Prakash Gupta

Q. 6. Write a letter to your elder brother from the town in which you have just joined a new appointment describing the important features of the town, of the people with whom you are associated.

Ans.

13, Mayur Colony,
Bhilwara
April 25, 20xx

My dear Brother,

I am glad to receive your loving letter and happy to learn that everyone is fine at home. You have asked me to give you a brief description of this town. I like this town and the people here am sure that the description as follows will make you like the place and fill you with a longing to see it.

It is a big trade centre. There are two cloth mills here which supply cloth to the whole of the country. There is a large cloth market where you can buy cloth of all qualities and designs . There are four Boys Colleges and eight Senior Secondary Schools.There are two Girls' College also. There are three Government Hospitals, one for male, other for female and child and several private nursing homes.

Besides these, there is a charitable eye hospital also. It is a Railway junction . Three beautiful Picture Halls are also situated in the town. There is one Engineering and one Dental College too in the town, located in the Industrial Area about 8 km far from the town. The most interesting feature of the town is its magnificent temples where hymns are sung and cymbals are clashed daily in the morning and evening.

People are nice, honest, straight forward, hardworking and trustworthy. They are not addicted to any vices as drinking and gambling. My colleagues are also very cooperative and of helping nature. The General Manager of my company is a through gentleman and takes keen interest in the welfare of the staff. He is very kind and sympathetic to all the employees.

I am fine here. Everything is going on here nicely as per scheduled routine. Regards to Daddy and Mom.

Yours affectionately,
Maneesh

Q. 7. Write a letter from a student to his friend, telling him about the first impression of the college.

Ans.

215, Aravali Vihar,
Near Jain Temple,
Alwar (Raj.) 301001

Dear Shankar,

As you know, I got admission in Rajasthali Commerce College, Alwar Rajasthan this year. You have asked me to tell you about my new college.

The atmosphere and the environment of the college is entirely different from that of our schools. The discipline in the college is not as strict as in our school. No bindings of wearing any uniform. The professors treat us in very friendly way. There is no terror of the teachers as in school . Professors just come in the class, deliver the lectures and generally do not bother to ask any question from the students. They are not worried whether any student follow them or not. All kinds of facilities like library, sports, games and canteen are available in this college.

Students enjoy the freedom of college life. Everyone is at liberty to go wherever he likes, do whatever he likes and speaks what he has in his mind within some limits. There is none to check the students. They can spoil or they can make their lives.

I can't afford to waste my time in useless things and have started making notes, consulting the library books for the last one week.

I have to do a lot of hard work to achieve good marks.Tell me about you.

Convey my regards to your parents.

Yours sincerely,
Dinesh

Q. 8. Write a letter to your elder brother writing him the reasons of your failure in Public Service Commission Examination.

Ans.

304, Shastri Nagar,
Jodhpur (Raj.) ,
Jan.16, 20xx

My dear Brother,

I am in receipt of your letter. You have asked me the reasons of my failure in Public Service Commission Examination. I do not like to take any excuse but believe in narrating the facts of my failure as per my imaginations. As you also know, this was not an easy exam. I made full preparations for all the four papers, but the time table of my exams was very cumbersome. I had to take three papers continuously. The Economics paper was on 12th January from 3 P.M. to 6 P.M. and the paper of Statistics-I was scheduled on 13th January from 10 A.M. to 1 P.M. and after that I had to take the paper of Statistics-II from 3 P.M. on the 13th January itself. This all caused a lot of tension to my mind. I couldn't sleep even for a minute on the night of 12th January and so when I went to the examination hall on 13th January I could take the paper of Statistics-I satisfactorily, but I could not take the paper of Statistics-II properly and so in this paper I got only 31 marks out of 100 marks and that spoiled my percentage.

I did very good preparations for all papers, but to whom can I blame, it is my hard luck or say I was unfortunate as the time table was so uneasy and tedious. This is the first time when all the students who opted Economics and Statistics have suffered a lot because of such time schedule. I am myself not happy with the result but nothing can be done now. I am determined to take this examination again with more hard work. I remember your words *"A man who wins, is the man who thinks, he can."*

Convey my regards to Papa and Mummy.

Yours loving brother,
Prakash

Q. 9. Write a letter to your uncle thanking him for the birthday gift you have received from him.

Ans.

105, Mangal Vihar,
Alwar,
February 28, 20xx

My dear Uncle,

Yesterday was my birthday. I received many gifts, but your gift was the best. You have sent me a beautiful wrist watch. Everybody liked it. I thank you very much for such a lovely gift.

Your gift is very precious to me. I was often late for school. Now I shall be punctual. This watch will help me during my examination days also.The watch is a token of your love for me. I shall always keep it with me. Once again I thank you.

Convey my regards to Aunty.

Yours lovingly, Harsh

Q. 10. Write a letter to your father asking for some money.

Ans.

415, Lajpat Nagar,
Alwar (Rajasthan)
February 23, 20xx

My dear Father,

I hope this letter will find everybody at home in the best of health and happiness. I am well here. You might have received my progress report from the school. You will be glad to know that I secured first position in my terminal examination. I assure you that I will maintain this position in the Annual Examination also. As you know my dues for the next quarter are due, kindly send me ₹ 1100/- by draft at the earliest.

Please pay my respects to dear mother and convey my love and affection to Puppy and Raju.

Yours loving son,
Raman

Q. 11. You are Putin. Your sister, Ragini, has just completed X standard and has sought your advice in the matter of opting Science or Commerce group. Write a letter advising her to select the group in XI standard.

Ans.

KH-3, South West Block
Near Eid Gah, Alwar (Raj.).
18th March, 20xx

Dear Ragini,

I am in receipt of your letter dated 15th March. You have sought my advice in the matter of opting Science or Commerce group in your XI standard.

First of all, I like to tell you very frankly that whatever stream you opt, you are to put hard to achieve success. In the present competitive world, poor show in any stream is of no use. In Science group, you can opt either Engineering or Medical. If we compare Engineering and Medical profession, the medical profession is more suitable, particularly for female candidates. On the other hand, through Commerce stream, you can become a Chartered Accountant, ICWA, Company Secretary and can also go for MBA. Along with Commerce stream, you are required to take computer training also, because now-a-days all business is being carried through the computer. As such commerce also opens new vistas of career opportunities to you.

So if you are interested in becoming an Engineer or a Doctor, you should opt for the Science stream and if you are interested in the work of accounting nature, the commerce stream is more suitable to you. Any way, choice is yours.

Whatever may be your decision, please convey me positively. I also like to tell you that you should also improve your English alongwith your academic achievements. English is very important for acquiring higher qualifications.

Everything is normal at my end. Do write for any work.

Convey my regards to Mummy and Papa.

Yours loving brother, Putin

Q. 12. You are Sweta living in the hostel of PQR School, New Delhi. Write a letter to your sister, Rashmi, describing your hostel life.

Ans.

Indira Hostel,
PQR School,
New Delhi
25th March, 20xx

My dear Rashmi,

I received your loving letter three days ago, but because of my preoccupation in making preparations for the annual function of our hostel, I could not spare time to reply you.

I feel pleasure in informing you that I stood first in the quiz competition and our team stood second in folk dance competition held during the annual function programmes. As I am staying in the hostel, I am devoting more than two hours daily in improving my General Knowledge and General Awareness in addition to course studies. Ours is a very good hostel. Most of the students are well disciplined and sincere. Our hostel warden Mrs. Savita Vermani is a very strict lady. She keeps close watch on every student. All the students are required to attend the morning and evening prayers daily and both the time attendance is marked.

The quality of food being served is very good, consisting of two vegetables curd and salad, with Tawa chapatis and a sweet dish. Breakfast is served at 8 A.M., after that I go to school and take lunch at 12 P.M. and dinner is served from 7 P.M. to 9 P.M. In the evening we play games like badminton, hockey, cricket in the hostel playground from 4 P.M. to 7 P.M. As such I find this hostel a well maintained one, with everything of good quality and caring.

What about you ? How are your studies going on ? Do write to me for any help or work.

Convey my regards to mummy and love to Sunny.

Yours loving sister,
Sweta

Q. 13. You are Sarwesh living at 1215, Qutab Enclave, New Delhi. Write a letter to your father telling him of your plan to go to a village with a group of students to teach illiterate villagers.

Ans.

1215, Qutab Enclave,
New Delhi,
22nd April, 20xx

Respected Daddy,

I received your affectionate letter three days ago, but I was busy in my examinations so I could not reply earlier. I am very happy to note that Sonu has been selected in IIT with very good rank. Please congratulate him on my behalf . He deserves the kudos.

As I informed you earlier that my annual examination will be over on 29th April. On 30th April I along with a team of ten students are planning to go to a nearby village Hatina to educate the illiterate villagers. The team will be headed by our professor Dr Pannikaran. We will teach them how to read and write our mother tongue Hindi. We will also train them to write their signatures.

Illiteracy is a curse in our society. Many problems and hardships are faced by the poor villagers because of the illiteracy. Our tour will not only help the villagers but it will also be beneficial for us to get the first hand knowledge of rural problems. I will write you about our detailed programme later on. Every other thing is fine at my end. I am preparing well for my annual examinations.

Convey my deep regards to Mom and heartily congratulations to Sonu.

Yours loving son,
Sarvesh

Q. 14. You are Girish living in a hostel of BTR School, New Delhi. Write a letter to your friend Mohan, telling him about an interesting weekend that you spent at your friend house recently.

Ans.

Subhash Hostel,
BTR School,
New Delhi
30th March, 20xx

Dear friend Mohan,

I have been thinking to write to you for the last several days about my short, but enjoyful stay at my friends. As you are aware that I am well settled in the hostel now. I have got some very good friends here. I wrote you earlier about my friend Pankaj who belongs to Kolkata. The school was closed for winter vacations. Pankaj took me with him to Kolkata. His father is an Executive Engineer in PHED. He owns a big house and a small farm house. Kolkata is a large metropolitan city. We visited National Library, Victoria Palace and New A.C. market. We also travelled in tram, a small train with two coaches. It was really thrilling to visit zoo and Birla Planetarium there. I also visited Bara Bazar, a commercial market. I purchased two shirts and a wrist watch from the Madaan Market at very economical prices.

I really enjoyed my short stay with Pankaj. His parents are very generous and amiable. Every family member gave me love and affection. Their love and affection will always be fresh in my mind.

What about you ? When are you going to London ? Please write me your exact programme, so that I may plan to visit you accordingly.

Yours truly,
Girish

Q. 15. You are Anubhuti. Write a letter to your friend Reena about the futility of exploding crackers on Deepawali.

Ans.

1876, Mount Villa,
Mount Abu.
24th May, 20xx

Dear friend Reena,

Hope this letter finds you happy and enjoying the leisure after examinations. You know that the festival of Diwali is approaching fast. I like to inform you that in our town, I along with my four friends decided to make the people aware of futility of using crackers on Diwali.

I do not find any reason for wasting so much money on firing and exploding crackers which not only pollutes the atmosphere but also causes outbreak of fire on many occasions. Many times the fire caused by the crackers endangers human lives and destroys huge properties. On the one side people are wasting money in exploding crackers and on the other side people are not having sufficient food to eat and clothes to cover their bodies. We have decided to collect rupees fifty from every house to distribute sweets and clothes to the poor. I think by this way we will be celebrating this festival in real sense. Tell me what you think about our plan of celebrating Diwali as in such manner.

Convey my regards to your parents

Yours friend,
Anubhuti

Q. 16. You are Prakash. Write a letter to your friend Ramesh asking him about his studies for competitive examinations.

Ans.

103, Narpat Colony,
Near Ahimsa Circle,
Jaipur (Raj.) 302015.
15th March, 20xx

Dearest Ramesh,

I haven't heard from you since long. It seems that you are very busy in preparing for the State Service Commission Examinations or something else ? Anyway, tell me about your preparations. I think you should have completed all the optional papers so far. I like to tell you only one thing that whenever you start revising your papers, try to prepare short notes, so that you can revise the same again during examination period. This will help you in making several revisions and you will be able to secure good marks. A good percentage in theory papers means your selection is almost confirm.

I know you must be putting all your strength and wisdom as you are a very hard working and devoted guy. I wish to see you among the first fifty candidates.

I am doing my job well. My good wishes for the exams..

Do write for any deserving service.

Yours truly, Prakash

Q. 17. Write a letter to your father explaining him the reasons of your not securing good marks in English paper.

Ans.

24, Subhash Hostel,
WXT College, Jaipur
March 26, 20xx

Respected Papa,

I received your letter today in the morning. You have asked me the reasons of my securing poor marks in English paper.

First of all I like to tell you that I put very hard labour in English. As you are aware that I am not good at Grammar, so I couldn't attend the Grammar portion so well. I need tuition for English Grammar. I have talked with our Grammar teacher who has consented to give me tuitions for two months only. Without good command over English Grammar, it is not possible to secure good marks in English. Please allow me to take English tuition so that the problem of English is solved for ever.

You can see that in other subjects I have secured more than 85 % marks, but in English I could not manage to secure more than 40% .

Convey my regards to Mom and Grandmom.

Yours loving son,
Jaipal

Q.18. Write a letter to your elder brother telling him about the discomforts of a railway journey without reservation.

Ans.

214, Nehru Nagar, Ambala.
3rd March, 20xx

Dear brother.

As I informed you telephonically also I reached here safe and sound yesterday.

I like to tell you about the discomfort I suffered because I had no reservation. As you know I could not get the reservation so I had to travel in second class general compartment. The journey was very tiring and cumbersome. First of all the train was late by two hours. As soon as the train arrived I managed to push myself into the general compartment. It was overcrowded, but after one hour I got half a seat, just managed to sit on the corner of a seat. Six persons were sitting on a seat for three, but it was comparatively comfortable. It was not possible to take rest or sleep the whole night, but I had no option .

However, the night passed and the train reached Ambala at 5 A.M. I found myself safe and sound but extremely tired. I took a lesson to plan the journey in such a way that either get a reservation or if not better travel by bus. How the things are going at your end. Convey my regards to Mom and love to Tini.

Yours younger brother,
Pulkit

Business Letters

Q. 19. Write a letter from M/s V.K. Gupta and Sons Jaipur to M/s Arihant Prakashan, Karol Bagh New Delhi, requesting them to supply the books.

M/s V.K. Gupta & Sons
University Road Jaipur

Ref:Un/ Date 08/3/20xx

M/s Arihant Prakashan
106, Karol Bagh
New Delhi 110013.

Ans. ***Sub :*** *Supply of books.*

Dear Sir,

We are sending herewith draft No. 1478952 dated 25/01/05, drawn on Punjab National Bank, favouring yourselves payable at New Delhi for ₹ 15000/- in advance against the supply of the following books

1. 60 Days Grammar	By S.C. Gupta	200 copies
2. Objective Physics	By Sharma and Gupta	150 copies

Please send the above books through Jaipur Golden Transport Company, duly packed with polythene. Please send the bill after allowing discount as usual.

Thanking you.

Yours faithfully,
V.K. Gupta,
Partner
V.K. Gupta & Sons

Q. 20. Write a letter to the retailer from whom you purchased a TV but its picture tube is not functioning well. Write him to get it changed.

Ans.

15, Ganesh Colony
Alwar (Raj)
Aug 25, 20xx

M/s Preeti Electronics
Jayanti Market,
Jaipur.

Sub : *Replacement of T.V.*

Dear Sir,

I have purchased a T.V. make BPL-21FSTW from you vide bill No. 2581 dated 1/7/20xx for ₹ 11300/-.

The picture tube of the T.V. is not functioning properly. You have sent the mechanic twice to check the same, but of no avail.

As the T.V. is under one year guarantee period, so you are requested to get the T.V. changed immediately. I think you will not make any excuse in the matter and the T.V. be replaced without any delay.

Thanking you.

Yours faithfully,
Vikas Sharma

Q. 21. Write a letter to M/s Jaipur Publications returning the book wrongly supplied by him and asking him to supply the proper books.

Ans.

R.K. Book Depot

155, Nangali Circle, Alwar

Dated 16/3/20xx

Ref:Po/

M/s Jaipur Publications
Chaura Rasta,
Jaipur

Sub : *Supply of Proper Books.*

Dear Sir,

Today we have received the parcel of books sent by you. We are surprised to find that you have sent all the twenty books of English Grammar written by some Mr. Sarraff, while we have ordered for the English Grammar written by Mr. Gupta and Gupta.

We are returning the books. You are requested to supply the books of English Grammar written by Mr. Gupta and Gupta. Please be kind enough to supply the proper books immediately. The parcel be packed properly with polythene.

Thanking you.

Yours faithfully,
R.K. Jain
Partner

Q. 22. As Principal of a college, place an order for supplying some sports items to M/s Sports and Sports Ludhiana.

Ans.

Subhash Gandhi College

Lucknow (U.P.)

Ref Ord/sport

Dated 18/4/20xx

M/s Sports & Sports,
Lal Bazar, Ludhiana

Sub**:** *Supply of Sports items.*

Dear Sir,

You are requested to supply the following sports goods at the rates mentioned by you in your quotation dated 10/3/20xx

Name of items	Quantity
(1) Cricket Bats	12 Pieces
(2) Volley Balls	12 Pieces
(3) Badminton rackets	12 Pieces

Please dispatch the above items duly packed to avoid any damage in transit.

Thanking you.

Yours faithfully,
R.P. Ojha

Q. 23. You are Anil Shah, General Manager of M/s Cement Associates, Karol Nagar, Nimbahera. Mr. R.K. and Sons has placed with you an order for two thousand bags of cement. Please write a letter asking them to send 50% amount in advance by draft and also to submit you two references as this is the first dealing.

Ans.

M/s Cement Associates
Karol Nagar, Nimbahera.

Ref Adv/ Dated 27/8/20xx

Mr. R.K. & Sons
Akbar Nagar
Shri Ganganagar (Rajasthan).

Sub: Supply of 2000 bags of cement.

Dear Sir,

We thankfully acknowledge your order No. 1841 dated 21/8/20xx for supplying of two thousand bags of cement.

Please be informed that this is our first dealing and as per our business policy, yours being a new firm, need to send 50 % advance payment by draft and also two references for all future dealings.

For your ready reference, we are attaching herewith list of firms in Rajasthan who are registered with us.

We hope you will get these formalities fulfilled at the earliest.

Thanking you.

Yours faithfully,
Anil Shah
General Manager

Q. 24. You are the dealer of Pakija Biscuits for the State. Due to strike of Transport operators, your supply of biscuits has been disrupted. One of your distributors has asked you to arrange the supply of biscuits at whatever cost. Draft a letter to your distributer telling him regarding increase in the supply rates.

Ans.

Bengal Bakeries Ltd.
Registered Office,181, Nanitalla Lane
Kolkata—700023

Dated 17/4/20xx

Ref : Supply/ad/

M/s Priya Distributers
Asansol (W.B.)

Sub : Supply of Pakija Biscuits

Dear Sir,

We are in receipt of your urgent call for supplying the biscuits at whatever cost.

As you are aware due to strike of transport operators it has become impossible to supply the biscuits by trucks. We are sending you biscuits with our sales executive Mr. P.V. Vardhan by passenger train as per your requirements.

You are requested to pay him ₹ 350 /- extra, as excess charges borne by us in supplying the biscuits through train.

Thanking you.

Yours faithfully,
Kamal Bose
Marketing Executive

Official Letters, Applications and Complaints

Q. 25. Write a letter to the Postmaster complaining that your sister at Ambala has not received the parcel sent by you last month.

Ans.

129, South Block
Alwar (Raj.)
26/4/20xx

The Postmaster,
Head Post Office,
Alwar

Sub: *Non-receipt of parcel sent on 25/03/20*xx

Dear Sir,

I had sent a Registered Parcel to my sister Jaya at House No. 16, Sector 5, Ambala on dated 25/3/20xx vide your receipt No. 1479. The parcel has not so far been received by her. More than two months have since passed. It appears either the parcel is delivered to somebody else or it has been lost in transit.

You are requested to enquire into the matter and apprise us the factual position without any further delay.Your early action is highly appreciated.

Thanking you.

Yours faithfully,
S.K. Gupta

Q. 26. Draft a First Information Report regarding theft of your Scooter.

Ans.

15, Kalindi Market,
Near University
Jaipur
28/5/20xx

The S.H.O.
University Road Thana
Jaipur.

Sub: *FIR regarding theft of scooter.*

Dear Sir,

I have to lodge an FIR for the theft of my scooter from the University Road. It was about 1 P.M. I went to the market to make some purchasing. I locked my scooter as usual and parked it outside the shop of M/s K.K. and Sons, University Road, Kalindi Market. After about half an hour I came out of the shop and was shocked to find that my scooter was missing. I made enquiries from the nearby shopkeepers but of no avail. The Scooter was of 2003 model, Priya, blue coloured 100 cc, self start bearing Registration No. RJ 02, C 2879.

I request you to lodge the FIR and arrange to trace the scooter at the earliest. Your immediate action in the matter is solicited.

Yours faithfully,
Pramod Jhalani

Letters to/from Bank

Q. 27. You are Rajesh. You have deposited a cheque for collection in your current account. Even after passing more than one month, the amount of cheque has not been credited in your account so far. Write a letter to the Manager of the Bank, to get the amount of cheque deposited in your account and make a demand for payment of interest for the delayed period.

Ans.

The Manager,
Quick Bank,
New Delhi

Ref : *Non-crediting the proceeds of cheque.*

Dear Sir,

I had deposited a cheque bearing No. 175896 dated 25/03/20xx for ₹ 56200 /- drawn on State Bank of India, Alwar for collecting the proceeds in my Current Account No. 7816 with your branch.

I regret to note that even after passing of more than a month, the amount of cheque has not been credited in my account so far.

You are requested to look into the matter and arrange to get the amount of cheque credited in my current account immediately along with the interest for the delay as per norms.

Thanking you.

Date 27.4.20xx

Yours faithfully,
Rajesh
Current A/c No. 7816
12/ 7, Vikas Nagar
New Delhi

Q. 28. As manager of a Bank, write a letter to a customer that his cheque has been dishonoured.

Ans.

Quick Bank Ltd.

Ram Nagar Jaipur

Ref. Com/05/ Dated 29th April, 20xx

Mr. Rajesh Sharma
12/ 7, Vikas Nagar
Jaipur

Sub : *Dishonour of your cheque No. 175896 dated 25/03/20xx for ₹ 56200 /- drawn on SBI Alwar.*

Dear Sir,

In reference to your letter dated 27.4..., we beg to inform you that your above cheque was received back by us for the following reason:

1. Funds Insufficient.

The cheque has since been sent to you by Registered Post on dated 29.04.20xx at your residential address.

We are always at the service of our clients.

Thanking you.

Yours faithfully,
T.K. Bose
Sr Manager

Q. 29. There is an advertisement in the local newspaper for the post of Office Assistant. Make an application and write your biodata.

Ans.

The General Manager,
Tilak Associates,
Faluja Road,
New Delhi.

Sub : *Application for the post of Office Assistant.*

Dear Sir,

With reference to your advertisement in the Indian Express dated................. for the post of 'Office Assistant' I am sending my biodata with this application. My biodata contains all the details regarding my qualifications and experience.

I like to assure you that if I am given a chance to serve in your esteemed organisation, you will positively feel satisfied with my attitude and working.

Bio-Data

(1) **Name** R.K. Sharma
(2) **Father's Name** Mr P.K. Sharma
(3) **Address** 4/47, Shah Nagar Near Nai Mandi, New Delhi—110007
(4) **Telephone No.** 011—22094521 (R)
(5) **E-mail** rksharma_147@yahoo.com.
(6) **Date of Birth** 25th April, 1984
(7) **Qualifications**

Degree	**University**	**% Marks**	**Year of Passing**
BA(Maths)	University of Delhi	78 %	2001
MA (Economics)	University of Delhi	75 %	2003

(8) **Experience** One year at M/s Sandeep Associates as cashier-cum-Accountant (Experience certificate enclosed).
(9) **Hobbies** Playing cricket, Reading Newspapers, Watching T.V. serials.
(10) **Extra**
(1) English Typing speed on computers 60 wpm.
(2) Hindi Typing speed on computers 40 wpm.
(3) Well versed in Tally 5.4 and 6.3 versions
(4) Have good knowledge of MS Word, MS Excel.

I hope you will find my bio-data as per your requirements.

Your faithfully,
R.K. Sharma

Q. 30. Write an application to the Principal of your college/school requesting him to grant you fee concession.

Ans. The Principal
....
....

Sub: *Concession is Fee.*

Sir,

Most humbly I beg to state that I am a student of class BCom II Year B of your college. My father is a retired clerk. He is getting a pension of ₹ 1800 /- P.M. I have two younger brothers. They are also studying in this college. There is no other source of income. My father is unable to pay my fee. Last year too, your goodness granted me 100 % concession in my fee. This year too I request you to grant me 100 % concession in my college fee, so that I shall be able to continue my studies. I like to apprise you that I secured 83 % marks in B.Com I Year.

Please be kind enough to grant me full fee concession.

Thanking you.

Dated 24/ 03 /20xx

Yours obediently, Saurabh

Q. 31. Send a reply to the following advertisement in a newspaper. Indicate to which post you are applying for. Include your Bio-Data. Suppose you are Satish Pradhan from New Delhi.

Ans.

Advertisement

Wanted male/female Marketing Executives, Accountants, well qualified, experienced. Salary no constraint for the right candidate. Apply to General Manager, XYZ, Company, New Delhi within seven days.

The General Manager,
XYZ Company,
New Delhi.

Sir,

With reference to your advertisement published in the Hindustan Times,dated January 28, 20xx, for the posts of Marketing Executives, Accountants etc. I offer myself as a candidate for the post of Accountant. As far as my academic and other qualifications are concerned, these are indicated in the bio-data attached herewith

Bio-Data

(1) Name Satish Pradhan
(2) Father's Name Shiv Kumar Pradhan
(3) Date of Birth 11.7.82
(4) Educational Qualifications M.Com
(5) Nationality Indian
(6) Marital Status Unmarried
(7) Experience One year experience of working in a private company
(8) Reference (a) Mr. P.K. Mishra (Bank Manager)
142,Nehru Nagar, New Delhi-18
Tel. 011-25761081
(b) Sh S.R. Sharma, MBBS (Councillor)
145, Patel Nagar, New Delhi-11

(9) Extra: Apart from the above mentioned Bio-Data, I have an additional record of extra- curricular activities. I participated in debates, dramas and sports and had won many prizes from time to time.

In light of the above mentioned facts, I request you to consider my application favourably I like to assure you, that you will never feel disappointed with my work and attitude. I believe in working with full dedication and positive attitude.

Date 30/01/20xx

Yours faithfully, Satish Pradhan

Q. 32. Write a letter to the District Education Officer, Jaipur, applying for the post of a temporary teacher.

Ans.

231, Arya Nagar, Alwar,
February 14, 20xx

The District Education Officer,
Jaipur District, Jaipur.

Sir,

I have come to know through some reliable sources that the post of a teacher of English is lying vacant in one of the schools under your control. I beg to apply for the same. As regards my qualifications and experience, I submit as follows

I passed the Matriculation Examination from the D.S. High School, Jaipur in the year 1994, securing 87% marks and stood first in the school. I passed the B.A Examination from D.S. College, Jaipur in 1998 with 76% marks. I took my M.A. Degree in English from University of Rajasthan, Jaipur with first division securing 61% marks in 2000 and stood first in the University in the B.Ed Examination in 2002. I have seven months experience of teaching English in a Higher Secondary School. The experience certificate is enclosed here with for your kind perusal.

I like to assure you that if I am selected, I shall do my best for the students and everybody concerned shall feel satisfied with my conduct and devotion.

Yours faithfully,
Vijay Kumar

Q. 33. You have read an advertisement in 'The Hindustan Times' about the application of appointment of teachers. Write an application to the Director of Education, Rajasthan, Jaipur asking for a job as a teacher in an educational institution.

Ans. The Director of Education,
Rajasthan
Jaipur.

Sir,

With reference to your advertisement published in 'The Hindustan Times' dated 15th January for the post of teachers, I beg to offer my services as a candidate for one of them.

Relevant particulars of my career are given below

Name Bahadur Khan
Age 27 years (Date of Birth 1.1. 1978)

Examinations Passed	Division	Year
High School	2nd	1990
Intermediate	2nd	1992
B.A.	2nd	1995
B.Ed.	2nd	1996

Experience: Working as a temporary of teacher of English in a private college since July, 2002. I am enclosing photocopies of my qualifications and the experience certificate for your kind perusal. A favourable decision will oblige me.

My address:
Bahadur Khan,
S/o Mr. Rashid Khan,
20, Nai Basti,
Jaipur (Rajasthan)
April 25, 20xx

Yours faithfully,
Bahadur Khan

Complaints and Letters to the Editor

Q. 34. Write a letter to the editor of Newspaper, complaining against the increasing nuisance of beggars in the city.

Ans

S.K. Joshi,
17, Mahabir Colony,
Asansol (W.B.)
Jan. 23, 20xx

The Editor,
The Times of India,
New Delhi.

Dear Sir,

Through, the columns of your esteemed newspaper, I like to draw the attention of local authorities towards the increasing nuisance of beggars in our city.

Now-a-days, the population of beggars has abruptly increased in the city. Everywhere in the city, whether market, park or outside a restaurant or even in every street and on Red Light stoppage, you will find such obstinate beggars who can't be easily put off. The pity is that most of them are physically fit. Begging is their well thought of profession.

Some of them must be involved in other crimes also. Some of the beggars also suffer from highly infectious diseases such as leprosy and TB etc. and while begging they come in contact with general public. It is necessary that such cases be taken care of and be treated in General Hospital and other able bodied beggars be taken to the task. Either they be given jobs or they must not be allowed to make the begging their profession.

I am sure the authorities will positively take care of this increasing nuisance of beggars at the earliest.

Thanking you.

Yours faithfully,
S.K. Joshi

Q. 35 Write a letter to the Editor of a newspaper about very irregular and short water supply in your locality.

Ans. The Editor,
The Times of India,
New Delhi

Dear Sir,

I crave the hospitality of the 'HELP LINE' columns of your esteemed newspaper to draw the attention of local authorities, particularly the authorities of "Water Works Department".

For the last one month the water supply in our colony has become very irregular and scanty. Out of the seven days, the supply was given for three days only and that too for one hour to 90 minutes.

On yesterday and day before yesterday, the water was supplied only for 35 minutes. When contacted the Assistant Engineer in the matter, he replied that due to some electric problem the water supply had become irregular. His reply was very evasive. I was not satisfied with the reply. It appears that the concerned AEn is not taking the problem seriously.

In the summer season, water is of utmost necessity. I hope you will be kind enough to publish this letter in your daily, so that the higher authorities take notice and solve this acute problem immediately and warn those who are responsible for it.

Dated
28/4/20xx

Yours faithfully,
Ram Chand
21/7, Janakpuri Road,
New Delhi 1100031

Q. 36. Write a letter to the District Collector drawing his attention to the nuisance caused by loudspeakers in the city during examinations days.

Ans. The District Collector
Hoshiyarpur (Punjab)

Sub: *Nuisance caused by the loudspeakers during examination days.*

Dear Sir,

I beg to draw your kind attention to the problem of nuisance being caused by the loudspeakers in the city.

Now-a-days students are preparing for their examinations. The loud noise of loudspeakers is causing a lot of problems to the students . Every year, a prohibitive order is issued by your office banning the use of loudspeakers during the days of examination, but this year no such action has been taken so far.

I request you to ban the use of loudspeakers totally for the period of two months so that the students can prepare well for the ensuing examinations and not suffered due to the unwarranted noise of loudspeakers.

Hope to get your immediate attention.

Thanking you.

Yours faithfully,
P.K. Mehra
Student of B.E. (Computers) III Year
17, Janta Colony
Hoshiyarpur (Punjab)

Date: 15th March, 20xx

Q. 37. Write a letter, in not more than 200 words, to a national daily about the neglect of priceless Historical Monuments in and around your city. Suggest ways and means to preserve them.

Ans. The Editor,
The Hindustan Times,
New Delhi.

Sir,

Through the esteemed columns of your prestigious newspaper I like to draw the attention of the general public on the neglectful and miserable conditions of Historical Monuments which are the evidential witnesses of our past glory and grandeur. They are the proven records of our past history, but have fallen victims to the criminal neglect of the officials. I had earlier tried to bring it to the notice of the department of Archaeological Survey of India, Government of India, but there was no response. This callous indifference on the part of concerned authorities has compelled me to approach you through this letter.

Sir, if you personally visit some of the monuments like the Humayun Tomb, Tughlak Kila, Qutab Minar, etc you will realise that they are gradually losing their shape and are getting dilapidated day by day in the flames of times. Their walls are mouldering, their roofs are getting cracked, their bricks and stone pieces are losing plaster and the top corner of walls have already crumbled. All this is due to the lack of proper maintenance and criminal neglect by the government servants. These monuments are the heritage of the glorious period of our past history. We must realise that even the present will be past one day. I was shocked to witness the sight of these worn and torn monuments.

I request you to publish this letter in your esteemed paper so that the concerned authorities are awakened in time and the priceless Historical Monuments are saved and preserved.

Thanking you.

Yours trulyX,
XYZX

Q. 38. Write a letter in about 200 words to the Municipal Corporation of you city describing the miserable condition of roads in your locality, also suggest some remedies for improvement.

Ans. The Commissioner
Municipal Corporation,
New Delhi x

Sir,

I would like to attract your kind attention to the miserable conditions of roads in my locality, Nehru Nagar, Near Subzi Mandi, Delhi. The roads are broken at many places.One can't drive the vehicle for ten minutes regularly without making adjustments with the broken roads. The buses, trucks, cars, three-wheelers and two-wheelers, all have to halt at every five to seven minutes just to adjust with the road breaks and pits. It has been repeatedly brought to the notice of P.W.D. but all in vain. There is always a traffic problem on the roads. The first showers of monsoon will put the things in its worst shape. The residents are in deep distress on this account and they have repeatedly expressed their resentment through Press as well as through written complaints but nothing has so far been done. People have also staged demonstrations last month and the authorities have assured to take necessary action in the matter but so far all the assurances are proved only the assurances for the sake of assurances.

I request you to get the roads constructed without any further delay lest the anger of the public should explode. I hope to get immediate attention of you.

Date: 25th Aug. 20xx

Yours sincerely,
Secretary (S.R.K. Tyagi)
Nehru Nagar Residents Society,
Near Subzi Mandi
Delhi

Q. 39. You are a resident of Indira Nagar a posh colony of DDA. There are no street lights on the main road leading to this colony. The road gets so dark after seven in the evening that the possibility of some major accident cannot be ruled out. Write a letter to the Editor of a Daily, drawing attention of the authorities to this serious problem. (in not more than 200 words).

Ans. The Editor,
The Hindustan Times,
New Delhi

Sub : *Provision for street lights on the main road.*

Sir,

Through the columns of your esteemed newspaper I want to draw the attention of the authorities concerned towards the provision of street lights on the main road leading to Indira Nagar. I like to apprise that Indira Nagar is a posh colony of DDA and inhabited by more than 3500 flats on both the sides of the road. The electricity board has installed poles on either side of the road to supply light to the residents, but they are just poles without the electricity. The civic authority is lacking in providing basic amenities to the residents.

During these days of winter, after seven there is pitch dark. There is every possibility of accurance of some major accident because of the heavy traffic passes over this road round the clock. The necessity of electrification requires no emphasis. In addition to accidents, cases of thefts and robbery can also not be denied. Darkness may lead to any kind of mishappening. It may also be stated that many residents go on pouring into their flats even after late hours in the night.The residents pay house tax to the Municipality regularly but facility of street lights are denied to the residents. The matter has been taken up with the authorities again and again, every time mere assurances were given but problem stid persists in the same way.

I hope, if the letter is published in your esteemed newspaper, the authorities shall be awakened from the slumber and the problem will be finally solved.

Thanking you.

Yours faithfully, XYZ
(A Resident of Indira Nagar)

27th Oct. 200X

152, Indira Nagar.
New Delhi,

Q. 40. You are a resident of the 'Aparna Apartments', Mayur Vihar, Delhi. There is no bus-stop within the radius of 2 km. from the apartments, causing a lot of inconvenience to the residents. Write a letter to the Editor of The Hindustan Times drawing attention of the government to this problem.

Ans.

271, Aparna Apartments,
Mayur Vihar, New Delhi
23rd Jan, 20xx

The Editor,
The Indian Express
New Delhi.

Sub : *Providing nearby Bus-stops*

Sir,

Through the columns of your esteemed newspaper I like to attract the attention non availability of the concerned Government officials and the leaders representing the public, towards the problem of bus stop surrounding area near Mayur Vihar Aparna Apartments. These apartment are spread within the radius of at least 4 km and are situated on the main road of Mayur Vihar.One can notice the running of buses on the main road in all the directions of Delhi after every five minutes.

But it is very strange to note that the Government has not provided enough bus stops to cover all the apartments and colonies on the road. The residents have to run more than 2 km. to catch a local bus. Hiring of a rickshaw or three-wheeler is very costly for all of us in order to reach the bus stand. The chilly or the hot rough weather often puts the passengers in a great dolldrum. This also wastes time, energy, stamina and strength of a traveller.

For lady passengers it is all the more awesome from the safety point of view. No investment or no financial burden be passed on to the government in making more bus stops keeping in view the necessities and the convenience of the residents. It being fully residential area, it is need of the hour to provide bus stops at the most near points in this area instead of having a bus stop at a distance of more that 2 km.

I hope the government would definitely consider our difficulty and provide enough bus stops for the convenience of the passengers. It will provide relief to all of us as moving to a long distance of 2 km. in winter and hot Summer is very troublesome and tiresome.

Hoping for doing the needful.

Yours faithfully,
XYZ
A resident of Aparna Apartments,
Mayur Vihar,
New Delhi

Q. 41. You are resident of Mangal Vihar Colony, Alwar. Write a letter to the Editor, Rajasthan Patrika, about the misuse and poor maintenance of the public park in your area.

Ans.

118-A, Mangal Vihar Colony, Alwar
December 15, 20xx

The Editor,
Rajasthan Patrika
Alwar.

Sub: *Poor maintenance of Public Park.*

Sir,

Through the columns of your esteemed daily, I want to draw the attention of the authorities concerned towards the poor maintenance of the public park in our area.

Public Parks are the lungs of the locality where residents come and refresh their tired and fatigue minds. But in our colony, the park is not well maintained or say not at all maintained. The park suffers from the utter neglect of the authorities. The residents of a nearby basti are using the area as public convenience. Some rowdies create disturbance and abstract in proper up keeping of the park. The park has become the favourite halting place of stray cattle, dogs and pigs. Miscreants sit and gamble here in the broad daylight. They create disturbance and affect the normal health and hygiene of the common man. In reality, the park has become a safety heaven for all types of evil characters. If no immediate actions are taken, the park will turn into a devil's den and a cause of nuisance for the colony.

I hope the authorities concerned will take immediate steps in the matter.

Yours faithfully,
XYZ

Q. 42. You are a resident of South West Block, Alwar. Write a letter to the Superintendent of Police about the unauthorised construction of a block of three shops adjacent to the public park.

Ans.

329-South West Block,
Alwar
15th Dec, 20xx

The Superintendent of Police
Alwar (Rajasthan)

Sub: *Unauthorised construction adjacent to the public park.*

Sir,

May I lodge a complaint against Sh Ram Nath who has constructed a block of three shops adjacent to the Nehru Park in our colony. The construction was completed in the late hours of night when there was none to oppose. In the morning, a block of shops was found disfiguring the park area. This has created a good example for others to occupy the government land, in any way one likes. There is complete "Goonda Raj" in this area. Powerful men are usurping the property of the Government for their own benefits. It is not out of place to mention 'Might is Right'. In the morning some residents opposed but instead of listening to their voice, he threatened them to shoot. There is complete chaos and an atmosphere of fear prevails in the area.

It looks he has got good relations with high ups. If this remains the state of affair, a day will come when others will also occupy the available land. This is the only main park where children can play and rest in the morning and evening.

Please take action and protect the park from the misercants spoiling its use and beauty.

Yours faithfully,
XYZ

Q.43. You are Pralay Kumar of 125, Jahangir Road, New Delhi.Write a letter to the Police Commissioner (Traffic) about inadequate parking facility in the Connaught Place area of New Delhi.

Ans.

125, Jahangir Road,
New Delhi.,
20th Aug, 20xx

The Police Commissioner (Traffic)
Connaught Place, New Delhi.

Sub: *Inadequate parking facility at Connaught Place .*

Sir,

Connaught Place is the heart and soul of our capital. It is the most busiest and cleanest site of the capital. It attracts a large number of businessmen, foreigners and tourists daily. Being the centre of trade, there is great hustle and bustle in the market. During the peak hours one cannot park his car at a safe place here because the parking facilities are very much inadequate. If one has to park his vehicle, he has to look here and there for safety of vehicles and availability of a parking place. If a suitable site is available by chance, it becomes difficult to get one's vehicle back because of the shortage of sufficient space. Under these circumstances it is imperative on the part of the authorities to make sufficient spots available for parking the vehicles.

I hope you will definitely realise the inconvenience caused to all as above. Please take suitable steps to solve this genuine problem.

Thanking you.

Yours faithfully,
Pralay Kumar

Q. 44. You are Tek Chand of 115, Subhash Nagar, Jaipur. Write a letter to The Postmaster complaining about the irregular delivery of letters and parcels etc.

Ans.

115, Subhash Nagar,
Jaipur,
25th August, 20xx

The Postmaster
General Post Office,
Jaipur (Rajasthan)

Sub : *Irregular Delivery of Letters.*

Sir,

I want to draw your kind attention towards the negligent working style of Mr. P.K.Verma, the postman of this area. He is very irregular and negligent in his work. He does not deliver the letters and delivery parcels on daily basis. He never comes in time. He often throws the letters either in the "Ganda Nala" or gives them to the small children playing in the streets. Many times the letters are lost and the business is also hampered due to irregular and late delivery of letters. This is a matter of great concern and can cause a great loss. On many occasions he has been warned to mend his ways but he paid a deaf ear to the requests of the residents.

Kindly take necessary action in this matter and Mr Verma be immediately transferred to some other area, lest he should take revengeful action against some of the residents.

Thanking you.

Yours faithfully,
Tek Chand

Q. 45. You have visited the general hospital by chance. You find the condition of the hospital very pathetic.Write a complaint letter to the CMHO, Jaipur Hospital in this matter.

Ans.

12, Gurunanakpura,
Adarsh Nagar,
Jaipur
24th September, 20xx

The CMHO,
General Hospital ,
Jaipur (Rajasthan)

Sub : *Uncleanliness and negligency of the staff in the General Hospital.*

Sir,

May I lodge a simple but very important complaint to draw your attention towards the poor facilities available in the General Hospital and the neglectful attitude of the medical staff. The nurses hardly attend to their duties and generally busy in gossiping. Even the low priced tablets and medicines remain out of stock in the hospital. The toilets are never found clean, always emit a very foul smell. Yesterday an attendant took her mother to toilet, the nauseating smell made her nervous and she fainted. A complaint was also lodged with the staff nurse on duty, she took no care of the complaint.

The electric wiring is lying uncovered and tubes don't emit proper lights. The sweepers even leave the rubbish in the small corners. Everywhere a smell, uncleanliness, dust and negligence prevails. I don't know how the staff is so indifferent and working in such unhygienic conditions.

I hope you will take steps to improve the conditions and proper arrangements to keep the hospital clean be made immediately.

Thanking you.,

Yours faithfully,
XYZ

Q. 46. You are Dipti Sharma of 110, Raja Park, Jaipur. Write a letter to the General Manager, Rajasthan Roadways, Jaipur, complaining about rude and irresponsible behaviour of the drivers and the conductors.

Ans.

110, Raja Park,
Jaipur
25th June, 20xx

The General Manager,
Rajasthan Roadways
Jaipur (Rajasthan)

Sub : *Complaining about rude and irresponsible behaviour of the drivers and the conductors.*

Sir,

I want to draw your kind attention towards the rude and irresponsible behaviour of both the drivers and the bus conductors with the commuters. They look towards the passengers with indifference and behave with them in a very strange and absurd way. They lack etiquettes and use filthy language.

Generally the bus drivers do not stop the bus at the fixed stops, they rather disdain the travellers and stop before or after the stop so the passengers have to run after the bus. The passengers hardly approach the bus when it starts. In this way many commuters fall and feel lot of irritation and insult.

No less irresponsible is the behaviour of conductors. They never bother whether the passengers have got into the bus or not but they are bent on blowing the whistle. The bus moves while passengers have only one foot on the foot board. This leads to the falling of the poor passengers and sustaining injuries by them several times.

They have forgotten the elementary duties of a good driver and conductor and behave indecently. They show no courtesy and sympathy fowards the senior citizens and the ladies.

It is my humble suggestion that at the time of their recruitment and during the initial training they must be taught how to deal with the passengers. Regular training in this matter may help them to understand the problems of the commuters. Presently, they must be instructed and advised suitably to mend their ways and a surprise checking in this respect also be done.

Thanking you

Your faithfully,
Dipti Sharma

Q. 47. Write a suitable letter in reply to the following advertisement signing yourself as "Somebody".

Found a Suitcase
A suit case is found in Jammu Mail on 28/02/20xx, the owner should contact thekeâ Station Master, Delhi Cantt. with proof of belongings.

Ans.

B-423, Man Singh Park
New Delhi, April 27, 20xx

The Station Master,
Delhi Cantt.

Sub: *Missing suitcase*

Dear Sir,

Please refer to your advertisement published in the 'Times of India' on dated 23.3.20xx, regarding the suitcase found in the Jammu Mail on 28.2.20xx, I want to bring to your kind notice that the suitcase belongs to me.

It is a VIP Suitcase-22 inches, of grey colour. My name 'ABC' is pasted on it. It contains three white shirts, two trousers, one blue-coloured pant, one towel, a comb and one ball pen and some coins also. It also contains my original certificate (Matric and MA Economics) with attested copies, one issue of 'Akhand Jyoti ' monthly, as well as a newspaper of that day. I had returned on that day after from Kanpur an attending interview.

I shall feel obliged if the same is returned to me. Please let me know the date and the time, convenient to you, when I may collect my suitcase.

Yours faithfully,
Somebody

Social Letters (Invitations)

Formal Invitations:

Invitations are of two kinds—Formal and Informal Invitations. A formal invitation is generally written to third person and contains no heading, no salutation and no complimentary. The writer's name should appear in the body of the invitation. The address of the writer and the date should be written to the left, below the communication.

Formal Invitations
Smt and Shri Chawla
request the pleasure of Shri SK Mathew's company
at dinner
on Monday, the 24th of July at 8 P.M.
at
Jai Palace, Jaipur.

20th July, 20xx

Informal Invitations:

Informal invitations are like ordinary letters, though using more formal language. They are addressed to the recipient by name and the formal close is generally any of the following

Sincerely Yours, Yours Sincerely, Yours affectionately, etc.

Informal Invitations

My dear Shri Verma,

Will you please give me the pleasure of your company at dinner on Monday, the 18th July, 20xx at 8.30 P.M. at my residence.

Yours very sincerely,
Prakash Jha
12, Alka Puri, Alwar,
15th July, 20xx

Examples of Invitations

Q. 48. As Mrs. and Mr. Ramesh Dutt invite Mrs. and Mr. C.R. Pathak on the occasion of their daughter, Anu's marriage with Uttam at 8 P.M. on Monday, 4th Oct., 20xx

Ans.

Mrs. and Mr. Ramesh Dutt
request the pleasure of the company of
Mrs. and Mr. C.R. Pathak
on the occasion of the marriage of their daughter
ANU
with
UTTAM
S/o Mrs. and Mr. Vivek Dutt
at 8 P.M. on Monday, 4th Oct. 2003
AT THEIR RESIDENCE.

RSVP
49, Manu Marg
Alwar

Q. 49. As the Principal of Bal Bharati School which is holding its Annual Day Function at 6.00 P.M. on 12th November 20xx in the school auditorium. Design an invitation card to be sent to the parents and other invitees. The Chief Minister of Delhi has agreed to be the Chief Guest on this occasion. Do not exceed 50 words.

Ans.

BAL BHARATI SCHOOL, ALWAR
CELEBRATES ITS
Annual Day Function
on
12th November, 20xx
at
6.00 P.M. in the
SCHOOL AUDITORIUM
CHIEF GUEST: The Hon'ble Chief Minister of Delhi

The Honourable Chief Minister will give away the prizes to all the meritorious students. You are cordially invited to grace the occasion with your besign presence.

Principal

Q. 50. Write a formal letter of invitation to a friend of your son inviting him to your son's birthday party.

Ans.

MRS. AND MR. GAURAV NAGPAL
request the pleasure of the company of
MR. HITESH SHARMA
on the occasion of the 20th birthday of their son
RAHUL
at 7.00 pm on 12th August, 20xx

6-C, Model Town
Delhi–110007
Phone : 011-2334329

RSVP
With Compliments
Friends & Relatives

Q. 51. Write a formal letter of invitation to your friend inviting him to your son's birthday party.

Ans.

Mrs. and Mr. P. K. Sharma
request the pleasure of the company of
Mrs and Mr. S. C. Gupta
on the auspicious occassion of the 18th birthday of their son
GAURAV
at 6.00 P.M. on 5th January, 20xx
132/13 Panchsheel Colony, Udaipur.

Phones No : 4312342, 4769790

RSVP
XYZ

Q. 52. Draft an invitation for a formal dinner at Home.

Ans.

Mrs. and Mr S. C. Gupta
invite
Mrs. and Mr P. K. Sharma
to
THE BIRTHDAY PARTY
of their son
HEMANT
On Tuesday, the 1st Oct., 20xx, at 6.00 P.M.
at their residence, M-3 Satywadi Colony, Purjan Vihar, Jaipur.
Please grace the occasion with your presence.

RSVP

Q. 53. Write a formal reply to your neighbour accepting the invitation to his brother's birthday party. Invent names, date, time and place etc.

Ans.

Mrs. and Mr. G.K. Kapoor
of Kota City
Thank
Mrs. and Mr. K. L. Arora
for their invitation
on
the auspicious occasion
of
the birthday of

Mr. S. L. Arora
(Younger brother of Mr. K.L. Arora)
and
accept the same and promise to be there
on Tuesday 5th October, 20xx at 6.30 P.M.
at their residence at
M-43 , Purjan Vihar Udaipur.

Q. 54. You are R. Kumar S/O Shri K. Kumar of 31 Janta Colony, Jaipur. Prepare a draft for an invitation card to be sent on behalf of your parents on the occasion of the wedding of your sister.

Ans. **Smt. and Shri K. Kumar**
request the pleasure of your company of
on the auspicious occasion of the marriage
of their daughter
REENA
with
MAYANK
(Son of Shri KL Gupta of Rohtak)
on Friday, 4th December, 20xx at 8.00 P.M.
at their residence 31, Janta Colony, Jaipur
as per the following programmes

Reception of Barat	7.00 P.M.
Dinner	9.30 P.M.,

5th December, 20xx
5.00 A.M.

RSVP Doli
M/s R. K. Garments
20, Park Square Bangalore
Phone–653434

With Best Compliments from
All Relatives
&
Friends

Q. 55. You are Miss Komal Mittal of 134/32, Panchsheel Colony, Udaipur. You are celebrating your 20th birthday next week. Draft a formal invitation to a tea party. (Do not mention the invitee's name).

Ans. **MISS KOMAL MITTAL**
requests the pleasure of your company
at a
TEA PARTY
on the occasion of her 20th birthday
at 5.30 P.M. on Sunday, August 12th, 20xx
at her residence 134/32, Panchsheel Colony, Udaipur.

RSVP
Mittal Refractories
Udaipur, (Rajasthan)
0294 2512103

Q. 56. You have set up a cooperative store in your colony, Nayabas, Alwar. You have decided to invite one member from each family settled their to its inaugural ceremony. Prepare a draft of the invitation letter for the purpose.

Ans.

M/S G. N. Nagpal and Sons
announces the opening of their new establishment
NAGPAL COOPERATIVE STORE
Nayabas Alwar
INAUGURATION
on Sunday, the 2nd October, 20xx at 9.00 P.M.
by Dr. Gaurav Mittal
One member from each family settled in Nayabas Alwar
is cordially invited.
Visit for all kinds of domestic items Readymade Garments
Cosmetics, Medicines and Electrical items.
AVAIL INAUGURAL DISCOUNT OF 10% ON ALL GOODS.

RSVP
Nagpal Cooperative Store
Phone : 2334329.

Office Circulars

Q. 57. As the Head of your office, draft a circular for the staff outlining the need and value of punctuality in keeping office hours and quick disposal of writs and other work. (RAS 97)

Office of Dy. Commissioner Commercial Taxation
Hasan Khan Mewat Nagar Alwar
Circular

Ref.No.KB/14/15/20xx Date: 27th Sept, 20xx

For All the members of the staff including the Officers

All the members of the staff including the officers are instructed to adhere to the punctuality in coming to the office and leaving the office. Hence, attendance in the office is desired upto 10.00 am positively. It has been noticed that some of the employees including the officers are habituated of coming late and leaving the office before time that is before 5 P.M. This causes great inconvenience to the public. Lack of punctuality and leaving the office before time is an act of indiscipline and it leads to delay in disposing of the files and hinders smooth working. Intentional delay and keeping the work pending must be stopped forthwith. All the officers are instructed to dispose off all the pendency within a week and apprise the undersigned in the matter positively on next Monday.

Noncompliance on the part of any staff including the officers shall be viewed by the undersigned seriously.

XYZ
Dy. Commissioner (Administration)

Q. 58. Draft a circular from the Government of Rajasthan, Department of Civil Supplies, addressed to all District Supply Officers advising the steps to be taken for proper distribution of essential commodities from fair price shops.

Government of Rajasthan
Secretary Department Civil Supplies, Jaipur

Circular Ref: Civil Sup /26/20xx Date : 15th July, 20xx

Subject : *Distribution of essential commodities through Fair-price shops.*

For: All District Supply Officers

It has come to the notice of the Government that some fair-price shop dealers are not making the proper distribution of the essential commodities, instead they are selling the commodities in open market. Some fair price shops are not being opened on regular basis. In rural areas specially the shops remain either closed or the commodities are not distributed to all the people, which frustrates the aim and objective of opening these fair price shops. People are facing great problems in getting the commodities from these shops and the dealers are getting undue advantages by selling the commodities in open market. The matter was discussed in a meeting presided over the Minister for Civil Supplies and a very serious view was taken of the situation.

I therefore, advise you to make all our efforts to make the supply regular in a proper manner.You are also being advised to implement the following measures agreed upon in the meeting :

(1) The enforcement Inspectors should visit personally all the fair price shops and should also meet the Panch or the Sarpanch of the villages. Not only this, reports and views of the general should also be taken and noted in their daily diary to ascertain the factual position.

(2) The DSOs should also make a point to visit at least 15 fair price shops in a month and verify the daily diary of the enforcement Inspectors invariably. Out of the 15 fair price shops 10 must locate in rural areas.

(3) Action including the suspensions and termination of licence of the dealer of the fair price shop should be resorted to, in the first instance. In second chance the dealership of the fair price shop must be terminated and legal action should also be initiated as per the advice of the legal cell.

(4) Periodical inspection report and the visit reports are be submitted to my office on the monthly basis.

Intimate the compliance to the undersigned within seven days.

S.K. Mahajan

Secretary Civil Supplies

Q. 59. Draft a Circular to all Commissioners and District Collectors working as District Election Officers to make adequate arrangements for the free and fair General Assembly Election.

Office of The Election Commissioner

Government of Rajasthan, Jaipur

Circular Ref: EC/3/05

Date : 21/9/ 20xx

Phone : 23334512

Fax:2334511

Sub : *Election Urgent*

For : All Commissioners / Dist.Collectors

As per instructions and guidelines received from the office of the Chief Election Commissioner Government of India, New Delhi vide Cir .No CEC/GE/2/03dated 15/9/0...... and in compliance of the same, you are hereby instructed to make proper arrangements, planning and preparations for conducting the free and fair Assembly Elections.

Please get all the voterlists updated and printed timely. Ensure to get the Photo-identity card issued to all voters. Get the Ballot boxes checked if required get the same repaired and new ones ordered. Marking and mapping of polling stations and polling booths are also to be done. Sensitive areas be marked and requisition for additional Police Force be sent in advance.

Lists of Zonal Magistrates, Presiding officers, Polling Officers and employees for election duty be chalked out in advance. In all circumstances the elections must be conducted in free and fair atmosphere. Compliance be made under intimation to the undersigned. This should be treated as most urgent.

XYZ
Election Commissioner

Q. 60. Draft a circular from the Finance Secretary, Government of Rajasthan, to all Departments, District Officers and Commissioners requesting them to adopt measures of further economy.

Government of Rajasthan

Office of the Secretary Finance, Jaipur

Circular No.F 348/26/20035 Date: 28.8.20xx

Subject: *Economy Drive*

For: All Head of Deptts., Commissioners and District Collectors.

To review the drought and famine conditions prevailed in the State, a High Power Committee has instituted under the Chairmanship of Chief Minister. The Committee has decided in its last meeting held on 23rd August to adopt some thrift measures as per following

(1) An overall cut of 20% in all non-plan expenditure with immediate effect.
(2) All unnecessary and avoidable TA bills be reduced by 25% with immediate effect.
(3) Expenses on Office purchase be stopped forthwith. No expenditure will be made on office purchase without the permission of the Deputy Secretary of the respective Ministry.
(4) All the Medical Bills be thoroughly checked before making the payments.

All the concerned Departments under your jurisdiction be informed of the instructions immediately.

Compliance of the order be submitted to the undersigned within three days.

KK Jha,
Finance Secretary

Memorandums

Q. 61. As Deputy General Manager of a Private Limited Company, write a memo to the General Manager informing him about the damage caused by fire in the factory.

Kotsons Mills Pvt. Ltd.

Mall Road, Mumbai

Ref. No GM/26/0..... 23rd Aug. 20xx

Memorandum

From: Dy General Manager
To: The General Manager

Subject: *Damage caused by Fire.*

It was on 22nd August 20xx a fire broke out in the Mills Showroom at about 3 O'clock in the night. It seems to be caused by short circuit and the entire Showroom was in full blazes within minutes. It took nearly four hours by the two fire brigades to control the fire. The total damage estimated is not less than ₹ One crore, as some goods lying in the adjacent godown also caught fire, lot of the goods was saved by the timely arrival of the fire brigades. The Insurance Company has since been informed and a requisite claim for the damage will be submitted within three days.

I am trying to chalk out the plans and the measures to be taken to prevent such happenings in future. A detail report will be submitted to you at the earliest.

Sd/-
Dy. General Manager

Q. 62. As Deputy Secretary in the Ministry of Home Affairs, Central Government, New Delhi, write a memorandum to be sent to all the State Home Ministers, expressing the Government's concern about police excesses in the States .

Government of India

Ministry of Home Affairs, New Delhi

Ref No.HM /SHM/5/0....... 18th July, 20xx

Memorandum

Subject: *Police Excesses in States.*

Undersigned has been directed to apprise all the State Home Ministers that the entire Lok Sabha has expressed its sincere concern and taken a serious view of the excesses committed by the police more or less throughout the country. The department of Police comes under the State List, so it is the sacred responsibility of all the States to check the recurrences of any such cases. Cases of deaths in police custody, indiscreet firing, cases of violence and rape against the women and similar other cases of indecent and torture, have been reported frequently by the Press. Human Rights violation is a crime even committed by a government deptt. The honourable Home Minister has expressed great concern over the situation and he has earnestly desired that the police ought to be sensitise and police officials be trained to deal with common mass politetly and should exercise the powers within their limits. Strong and strict action must also be initiated against the criminals irrespective of their status in the society.

Therefore it is urgently required that a meeting of all the Superintendents of Police of the States be called to discuss the ways and means to check this social evil. A report be sent to the Ministry at the earliest.

Ram Dhari Dinkar
Deputy Secretary

Copy to:

All the Home Ministers of All States.

CHAPTER

67

PRECIS WRITING

How to Write a Good Precis?

(Brevity is the Soul of a Good Precis)

Definition: Precis शब्द का उद्भव लैटिन शब्द praecisum से हुआ है, जिसका अर्थ है : to cut short. Precis शब्द का English में अर्थ precise, exact, concise से लिया जाता है।

What is a Precis?

It is a short summary of the essential ideas of a longer composition; the basic thought of a passage is reproduced in miniature, retaining the mood and tone of the original. It must possess clear, emphatic diction and effective sentence construction. Its unity and coherence should be emphasised through smooth, unobtrusive transitions.

Precis denotes a brief, concise and clear, well connected abstract, summary or gist of a given passage. As per the Oxford Dictionary it means a concise or abridged statement of a summary. To make precis of a given passage, we should extract its main points, and then express them clearly in as few words as possible. Precis is a summary or a condensed composition of bare facts.

Essentials of a Good Precis

(1) Completeness (पूर्णता): किसी भी Passage की Precis करते समय यह ध्यान रखना आवश्यक है कि Precis में कोई महत्त्वपूर्ण बिन्दु न छूट जाए। Passage के पूर्ण तथ्य, विचार और उद्देश्य Precis में दृष्टिगोर होने चाहिए।

(2) Compactness or Well connected (दृढ़ता या निरन्तरता): Precis के sentences परस्पर आबद्ध (well connected) होने चाहिए। Precis को पढ़ने पर ऐसा प्रतीत नहीं होना चाहिए कि उसमें निरन्तरता (Continuity) नहीं है। Compactness, Continuity तथा तथ्यों का परस्पर आबद्ध (Well connected) होना, एक अच्छी Precis की विशेषता है।

(3) Brevity (संक्षिप्ता): Precis लेखन के सन्दर्भ में कहा जा सकता है कि *'Brevity is the soul of a good precis'*.सामान्यतया Precis हेतु शब्द-सीमा दी जाती है। यदि शब्द-सीमा न दी गई हो तो Precis, दिए गये passage की 1/3 होनी चाहिए। Brevity के लिए ध्यान रखने योग्य मुख्य बात यह है कि Passage में दी गई superfluous, unnecessary और irrelevant details हटा देनी चाहिए। Passage में दिए गए Comparison, Illustration या anecdote इत्यादि को Precis लिखते समय हटा देना चाहिए। Precis लिखते समय Important एवं Unimportant को अच्छी तरह छाँट लेना चाहिए एवं unimportant को हटा देना चाहिए।

संक्षिप्तता (Brevity) के लिए अच्छी vocabulary एवं One word substitution का भी पर्याप्त ज्ञान होना चाहिये, लेकिन brevity के लिए हमें Clarity, Compactness एवं Completeness का त्याग नहीं करना है। जहाँ तक सम्भव हो Precis में स्वयं के बनाए हुए वाक्य ही प्रयुक्त करने चाहिए। Passage में दिए गए sentences को जैसे का तैसा (as it is) उतार लेना नहीं है।

(4) Precis को Indirect speech में Third person एवं Past tense में नियमानुसार लिखा जाता है।

(5) Precis लिखते समय अपने Views या Opinion नहीं दिए जाने चाहिए।
(6) Precis की भाषा Simple तथा grammatically correct होनी चाहिए।
(7) Precis का Heading, Passage की theme के अनुरूप ऐसा होना चाहिए जो एक शब्द में पूरे Passage के बारे में बताए। Heading सामान्यतया Passage के शुरू में या अन्त में मिल जाता है जो पूरे Passage के Idea या theme को बताता है।

How to Write a Good Precis?

उपरोक्त आवश्यक तत्वों को ध्यान में रखते हुए जिस Passage की Precis लिखनी है उस Passage को दो बार पढ़िए। उसमें से Important बिन्दुओं को Underline कर लीजिए या अलग से उतार लीजिए। फिर उन्हें और भी संक्षिप्त करने हेतु ऐसे sentences में से भी Decorative words, Comparison आदि हटाकर इन्हें आपस में जोड़ दीजिए/ध्यान रखिए Precis की completeness, compactness तथा clarity बनी रहे।

Do's and Don'ts of Precis Writing:

(a) Start your precis by stating the main idea of the Passage.
(b) Do not use the words 'in this article'. Use the style 'Jackob argues that the most significant contribution of the Iraqies was.'
(c) When writing about history, use the Past tense.
(d) Do not use abbreviations or contractions.
(e) Avoid words like big, good, bad, little, and a lot. Also do not use the phrase 'throughout history'. This is cliche.
(f) Titles of texts should be put in italics or underlined.

Precis Writing : Examples

Q1. Make a precis of each of the following passages. The precis should be as far as possible in your own words. Suggest a suitable title also for your precis.

When our childhood has fallen behind us and taken on some of the glamour of distance we often ransack our memories in order to call up to our mind's eye the picture of the children we were. Then we are surprised to discover how little we remember of our earliest days; they have gone for ever and seemingly have left nothing behind them. All is lost in haze, and no definite image rewards our efforts to recapture the incidents of infancy.

Some, however, can recall more than others; one may remember something that happened when he was only a child of two, while another may find his memory blank–a clean sheet of paper as far as anything is concerned which befell him before he was five. Yet, perhaps as regards things generally, the memory of the latter may be stronger than that of the former, it is only in regard to his early childhood that the first man's memory is stronger.

To account for these variations is not easy : there are so many factors to be taken into account. Nature and circumstances have to be considered. One may be markedly introspective, unconsciously looking into himself from his earliest days : another may have had an accident which could not fail to impress itself on his memory. Again, one man may remember earlier events because his memory is a visual one, while another looks not so far back because his memory is more of the mind and a child's mind is of slower development than his sight.

Some Tips : Memory of Childhood

Main points of the passage are to be noted down :

(1) We remember little of our earlier days.
(2) The memory of some extends farther back than that of others.
(3) Variations in the memory of childhood are due to a person's nature and early circumstances.

Use above points to write a precis leaving aside unimportant and superfluous items :

Precis : Memory of Childhood

After some years, if we look back to our earliest days of childhood, we would find that we remember very little. The memories of some however can go back farther than that of others. It is not necessarily the stronger memory that does it. It is the nature of a man and his circumstances that determine the extent of his memory. A man with visual memory may have better memory than others.

Q2. Make a precis of following passage. The precis should be as far as possible in your own words. Suggest a suitable title also for your precis.

It is possible to score goals and lose the game. It is possible to win battles and lose the campaign. It is possible to make money and miss a fortune. The short-sighted man suffers, no matter where he is found; he may see some things with excessive clarity, but he fails to get the true perspective which will enable him to arrive at wise conclusions. He gains one thing, but he loses something better.

This is a very common error. The student makes it when he forgets the life-goal in thinking of the medal or the scholarship. The saint forgets it when he thinks of today and forgets the greater tomorrow. The businessman misses his way when he choses a present gain and forfeits ten times as much in the future. The youth makes such a mistake when he marries a girl of good look, and forgets the character which will be necessary to command his respect for forty years to come.

Man was made to think and unless he uses his brain he will stumble into no end of unseen morasses.There is a future, and it cannot be evaded; and when it is reached it cannot be changed, for we are just deciding what it shall be.We are our own destiny-makers. It is well to face the future with care and caution.

How to make the precis ? Learn through the following example :

Disadvantages of Short-sightedness

Main points of the passage are to be noted down :

(1) Winning and losing game and money are possible in life of everybody. A man who suffers from short-sightedness sees only the immediate gain with clarity, but loses something better and greater in the future.

(2) The students who cares more for the medal than for the goal of life, the saint who thinks of the present and not of the glorious future, the businessman who for an immediate gain forgoes greater future gain, and the youth who marries a girl of good looks rather than of character, all are the victims of this grave error.

(3) Our future lies in our own hands. We are our own destiny-makers. We should face the future with care and caution.

Use above points to write a precis leaving aside unimportant and superfluous items :

Precis : Disadvantages of Short-sightedness

Wining and losing game or money are part of life. A short-sighted person loses the greater future gain for an immediate small gain. The student misses his life-goal for the medal or scholarship, the saint ignoring future bliss for the present achievement, the businessman forgoing a larger future fortune for the present trifle gain and the youth marrying a good looking girl rather than one of character, all are short-sightedness of the respective fellows. We are the architect of our future, and therefore, of our destiny; we should face it warily and carefully.

Q3. Make a precis of each of the following passages. The precis should be as far as possible in your own words. Suggest a suitable title also for your precis.

How many apparent defeats, Enthusiasm has transformed into victories ? It is one of the most vital elements in all successes, but in the sphere of religious activity its value cannot be overestimated. Nevertheless it must be admitted that enthusiasm is not something that can always be had merely for the asking.

In the first place, to be effective, enthusiasm must be genuine. Simulated enthusiasm is a weak, vapid thing that soon dies. People do not become enthusiastic merely by wanting to be. It is not something that can be thrust upon others at will. Nothing could be more ridiculous than for someone to rise before a large gathering and say, " I move them all and they became enthusiastic ! " Enthusiasm is not necessarily a noise or shouting or even feverish activity. These may be, and sometimes are, manifestations of its presence, but not necessarily so. Often, indeed, such symptoms are merely spurious imitations, and as far from the genuine articles as the counterfeit money from the real money.

All genuine, lasting enthusiasm must be built upon knowledge. This is the true fountain from which it bubbles up, and nothing will take its place. People cannot be lastingly enthusiastic about that of which they know nothing.

Learn to make Precis through the following example :

The Power of Enthusiasm

Main points of the passage are to be noted down :

(1) Enthusiasm has transformed many apparent defeats into victories.

(2) It is the most vital element in all successes. But enthusiasm cannot be had for the asking.

(3) Genuine enthusiasm is effective. Simulated enthusiasm is a dull and temporary thing. Enthusiasm cannot be forced upon others.

(4) Genuine enthusiasm can be built upon knowledge alone. One cannot be enthusiastic about a thing for long unless one has complete knowledge of it.

Use above points to write a precis, leaving aside unimportant and superfluous items :

Precis : The Power of Enthusiasm

Enthusiasm is one of the most important elements to achieve successes and has turned many sure tumbling into victories. But in order to be effective and lasting, it must be genuine. Simulated enthusiasm dies soon. We should distinguish real from false enthusiasm which consists in noise, shouting or feverish activity. Genuine enthusiasm can be built upon knowledge alone. To be lastingly enthusiastic about a thing, the people should have complete knowledge of it.

Q4. Make a precis of each of the following passages. The precis should be as far as possible in your own words. Suggest a suitable title also for your precis.

When in the course of human events it becomes necessary for one people to dissolve the political bonds which have connected one another and to assume among the powers of the earth a separate and equal station, a decent respect for the opinions of mankind requires that they should declare the causes which impel them to separation.

We hold truth to be self evident that all men are created equal; that they are endowed by their creator with certain inalienable rights; that among these are life, liberty and the pursuit of happiness; that to secure these rights, governments are liberty and the pursuit of happiness; that to secure these rights, governments are instituted deriving their just powers from the consent of the governed; that whenever any form of government becomes destructive of these ends, it is the right of the people to abolish it and to institute a new government, laying its foundation on such principles and organising its power in such form, as to them shall seem most likely to effect their safety and happiness.

Prudence will dictate that governments, long established should not be changed for light and transient causes and accordingly all experience hath shown that mankind are more disposed to suffer while evils are sufferable than to right themselves by abolishing the forms to which they are accustomed. But when a long train of abuses and usurpations, pursuing invariably the same object, evinces a design to reduce them under absolute despotism. It is their duty to throw off such government, and to provide new guards for their future security.

Precis : The People and the Government

Whenever one people forces to break the political bonds with another and assumes an independent status as a separate nation, they should declare the causes of such a separation.

All men are created equal and they possess certain inalienable rights : life, liberty and the pursuit of happiness. Governments are created by the people to protect these rights. If a government fails to secure these, the people have a right to change that government. Prudence requires that long-established governments should not be changed for trivial causes. Only when constant abuses and usurpations threaten to bring them under despotism, then such a government should be thrown off to secure the future well beings.

Q5. Make a precis of each of the following passages. The precis should be as far as possible in your own words. Suggest a suitable title also for your precis.

Trading is a social activity. Whoever undertakes to sell any kinds of goods to the public, does what affects the interest of other persons and of society in general. Thus, his conduct, in principle, comes within the jurisdiction of society. Accordingly, it was once held to be the duty of governments, in all cases which were considered of importance, to fix prices, and regulate the process of manufacture. But it is now recognized, though not till after a long struggle, that both the cheapness and the good quality of commodities; are most effectively provided for by leaving the producers and sellers perfectly free, under the sole check of equal freedom to the buyers for supplying themselves from elsewhere.

This is the so-called doctrine of Free Trade, which rests on grounds different from, though equally solid with, the principle of individual liberty. Restrictions on trade or on production for purposes of trade are indeed restraints; and all the restraints, as the restraint, is evil. But the restraints in question affect only that part of conduct which society is competent to restrain and those are wrong solely because they do not really produce the results which are desired to be produced by them. As the principle of individual liberty is not involved in the doctrine of Free Trade, so neither is in most of the questions which arise respecting the limits of the doctrine : as, for example, what amount of public control is admissible for the prevention of fraud by adulteration; how far sanitary precautions or arrangements to protect work-people employed in dangerous occupations, should be enforced on players. Such question involves considerations of liberty, only in so far as leaving people to themselves is always better than controlling them.

Precis : Control over Trade

Trade affects the society. Governments in the past, as a duty, fixed the prices and regulated the manufacturing processes. Things of cheap and good quality can be available only when the buyers and sellers are free to deal with each other and with anybody else. This is called a Free Trade which may or may not have personal freedom. Restraints for the sake of restraints of trade are unjustified. Restraints imposed by the society itself are improper because the result is not as desired. Enforcement of control to prevent adulteration and to protect people from health hazards again involves the point of liberty. So it is always better to left the people free and let them control themselves.

Q6. Make a precis of each of the following passages. The precis should be as far as possible in your own words. Suggest a suitable title also for your precis.

One has to function in line with the highest ideals of the age one live in. It had been classified under two heads : humanism and the scientific spirit. Between these two there has been an apparent conflict, but the great upheaval of thought today, with its questioning of all values, is removing the old boundaries between the external world of science and the internal world of introspection. There is a growing synthesis between humanism and the scientific spirit, resulting in a kind of scientific humanism. Science also, while holding on to fact, is on the verge of the other domains or at any rate has ceased to deny them contemptuously. Our five senses and what they can perceive obviously, do not exhaust the universe.

During the past seventy-five years or so there has been a profound change in the scientists picture of the physical world. Science used to look at nature, as something almost apart from man. But now, Sir James Jeans tells us that the essence of science is that man no longer sees nature as something distinct from 'himself'. And then the old question arises which troubled the thinkers of the *Upanishads* : How can the knower be known?

How can the eyes that can see external objects see themselves? Science has begun to touch it still, the earnest scientist of today is what the philosopher and the man of religion were in earlier ages. 'In this materialistic age of ours', says Professor Albert Einstein, 'the serious scientific workers are the only profoundly religious people. In all this there appears to be a firm belief in science and yet an apprehension the purely factual and purposeless science is not enough. Was science providing so much of life's furniture, ignoring life's significance?

There is an attempt to find a harmony between the world of fact and the world of spirit, for it was becoming increasingly obvious that the over emphasis on the former was crushing the spirit of man. The question that troubled the philosopher of old has come up again in a different form and context : How to reconcile the life of the world with the inner spiritual life of the individual ? The physicians have discovered that it is not enough to treat the body of the individual or of society as a whole.

Precis : Scientific Humanism

One has to act according to the age one lives in. Humanism and Scientific spirit have been treated as the two conflicting and different thoughts in the past, but now the two are being synthesized and being called Scientific Humanism. Science relates to factual analysis of the things, but it has been realised by the scientists also that pure factual science is not serving the purpose of humane. Earlier scientist thought that the nature and man are different and have no relation with each other, but now the perceptions have changed. It resulted into the happy blending of science and religion. The need of harmony between the facts of the science and the spirituality is felt necessary, as both are essential for an individual. Taking care of both the physical and the spiritual aspects are necessary to keep a man fit.

Q7. Make a precis of each of the following passages. The precis should be as far as possible in your own words. Suggest a suitable title also for your precis.

Although our age far surpasses all previous ages in knowledge yet there has been no correlative increase in wisdom. The agreement between the two ceases as soon as we attempt to define 'wisdom' and consider means of promoting it. I want to ask first what wisdom is and then what can be done to teach it.

There are, I think, several factors that contribute to wisdom. Of these, I should put first a sense of proportion the capacity to take account of all the important factors in a problem and attach to each its due weight. This has become more difficult than it used to be owing to the extent and complexity of the specialized knowledge required of various kinds of techniques.

Suppose, for example that you are engaged in research in scientific medicine. The work is difficult and is likely to absorb the whole of your intellectual energy. You have no time to consider the effect which your discoveries or inventions may have outside the field of medicine. You succeed (let us say) as modern medicine has succeeded, in enormously lowering the infant death-rate, not only in Europe and America but also in Asia and Africa. This has the entirely unintended result of making the food supply inadequate and lowering the standard of life in the most populous parts of the world.

To take an even more spectacular example, which is in everybody's mind at the present time : You study the composition of the atom from a disinterested desire for knowledge and incidentally place in the hands of powerful lunatics the means of destroying the human race. In such ways the pursuit of knowledge may become harmful unless it is combined with wisdom and wisdom in the sense of comprehensive vision is not necessarily present in specialist in the pursuit of knowledge.

Comprehensiveness alone, however, is not enough to constitute wisdom. There must be also, a certain awareness of the ends of human life. This may be illustrated by the study of history. Many eminent historians have done more harm than good because they viewed facts through the distorting medium of their own passions. Hegel had a philosophy of history which did not suffer from and lack of comprehensiveness, since it started from the earliest time and continued into an indefinite future. But the chief lesson of history which he sought to inculcate was that from the AD 400 down to his own time Germany had been the most important nation and the standard-bearer of progress in the world.

Perhaps, one could stretch the comprehensiveness that constitutes wisdom to include not only intellect but also feeling. It is by no means uncommon to find men whose knowledge is wide but whose feelings are narrow. Such men lack what I am calling wisdom.

Precis : Knowledge vs Wisdom

Our age is far ahead of previous ages in the matter of knowledge, but not so in case of wisdom. Wisdom means a sense of proportion. It further means to analyse a problem in the light of all the related factors. Comprehensiveness itself does not mean the 'wisdom'. Technical knowledge about medicines and atomic energy does not bother about the far-reaching consequences of its use. So, there should be wisdom to control and guide the use of knowledge. Besides comprehensiveness, wisdom includes the awareness about the ends of our lives. The study of history well threw light on this point. Some historians distorted the facts of history because of their personal passion and interest. Indifferently pursuing for acquiring the knowledge may result in its misuse , if used by a man having no wisdom. A man with wide knowledge but no feelings is a man without wisdom.

Q8. Make a precis of each of the following passages. The precis should be as far as possible in your own words. Suggest a suitable title also for your precis.

What is a perfectly free person ? Evidently a person who can do what he like, when he like and where he like, or do nothing at all if he prefers it. Well, there is no such person, and there never can be any such person. Whether we like it or not we must all sleep for one-third of our lifetime; wash and dress and undress; we must spend a couple of hours eating and drinking; we must spend nearly as much time in getting about from place to place. For half the day we are slaves to necessities which we cannot shirk, whether we are monarchs with a thousand servants or humble labourers with no servants. And the wives must undertake the additional heavy slavery of child-bearing if the world is still to be full of people.

These natural jobs cannot be shirked. But they involve other jobs which can. As we must eat we must first provide food; as we must sleep, we must have beds and beddings in houses with fireplaces and cool; as we must walk through the streets, we must have clothes to cover ourselves. Now, food, houses and clothes can be produced by human labour. But when they are produced they can be stolen. If you like honey you can let bees produce it by their labour, and then steal it from them. What you can do to a bee you can also do to a man or a woman or a child if you can get the upper hand of them by force or fraud or trickery of any sort, or even by teaching them that it is their religious duty to sacrifice their freedom for yours.

So, beware if you allow any person, or class of persons, to get the upper hand of you, they will shift all that part of their slavery to Nature that can be shifted on to your shoulders; and you will find yourself working from eight to fourteen hours a day when, if you had only yourself and your family to provided for, you could do it quite comfortably in half the time or less. The object of all honest governments should be to prevent your being imposed on in this way. But the object of most governments is exactly the opposite. They enforce your slavery and call it freedom. But they also regulate your slavery, keeping the greed of your master within certain bounds. They promise that in future you shall govern the country for yourself. They redeem this promise by giving you a vote, and having a general election every five years or so.

At the election, two of their rich friends ask for your vote : and you are free to choose which of them you will vote for to spite the other....a choice which leaves you no freer than you were before, as it does not reduce your hours of labour by a single minute. But the newspapers assure you that your vote has decided the election, and that this constitutes you a free citizen in a democratic country. The amazing thing about it is that you are foolish enough to believe them.

Precis : Perfect Freedom

Perfect Freedom is an illusory thing. None can be perfectly free. Neither the Kings nor the labourers are perfectly free. They also have to obey the natural calls of sleeping, eating, clothing, drinking etc. For fulfilling these calls, we need food, beddings, which is produced by human labour, but which can be stolen also, just as man steals honey from bee hives. In the same way, man exploits other weak people through force or fraud. Strong are the slaves of nature. They in turn, enslave the weak by forcing them to work from eight to fourteen hours a day. This exploitation should have been stopped by the governments, but instead of stopping this, they perpetuate slavery in the name of freedom.

By extending a right to vote, they hoodwink the people with the idea of self governance by choosing their rulers themselves. But the choice is limited because the poor have to choose one rich man everytime who does not bother to give any relief to the poor. The newspapers also make the people feel that they have chosen their leaders and they are befooled to believe that they are the free citizens of a democratic country.

Exercises

Make a precis of each the following passages. As far as possible the precis should be in your own words. Suggest a suitable title for the precis.

(1) Disarmament assumes a very special importance for us, overriding all other issues. For many years past, there have been talks on disarmament and some progress has undoubtedly been made in so far as the plans and proposals are concerned. Still we find that the race for armaments continues, as also the efforts to invent ever more powerful engines of destruction. If even a small part of these efforts was directed to the search for peace, probably the problem of disarmament would have been solved by this time. Apart from the moral imperative of peace, every practical consideration leads us to that conclusion. The choice today in this nuclear age is one of utter annihilation and destruction of civilization or of some way to have peaceful coexistence between nations. There is no middle way.

If war is an abomination and an ultimate crime which has to be avoided, we must fashion our minds and policies accordingly. In order to achieve peace we have to develop a climate of peace and tolerance and to avoid speech and action which tend to increase fear and hatred. It may not be possible to reach full disarmament in one step, though every step should be conditioned to that end. Much ground has already been covered in the discussion on disarmament. But the sands of time run out, and we dare not play about with this issue or delay its consideration. This, indeed, is the main duty of the United Nations today and if it fails in this, the United Nations fails in its main purpose.

(2) If the rule of reason, in the region of thought, is the aim of science, the rule of equality, in the region of behaviour, is the aim of democracy. Democracy is not a political arrangement or a form of government. It is a pattern of life, an active conviction which informs and inspires every thought, word and deed. Our present constitution of society induces in its more fortunate members far too great readiness to accept privilege as though it were inherent in the social order as though it were normal and even proper and just.

If we are sincere in our professing of democracy, we should not shut our eyes to the most obvious defects of the present social order. A system which does not offer security and decent employment to multitudes of trained young men suffers from fundamental vice. Society is in danger of splitting to pieces if the few who have the benefits of civilization are not willing to share them with the rest. No state is stable unless it procures for all its members the essentials of a good life.

We acknowledge that health is better than disease, sufficiently better than poverty, shelter better than cold and exposure, ease of mind better than racking anxiety. It is our duty tc obtain these essentials of civilized life or the mass of the population to work for basic economic justice for all, if necessary; by the imposition of higher taxes on incomes, land , property and inheritance. Riches were created by the maker for being spent on social purposes. It was Blackstone, not Lenin, who wrote, " The law not only regard life and protects every man in enjoyment of it, but also furnishes him with everything necessary for its support. For there is no man so indecent or wretched, but that he may demand a supply sufficient for all the necessities of life from the more opulent part of the community."

(3) We talk so much about democracy, without going into ancient records. Parliamentary democracy, roughly speaking, is something of the growth of the last 150 or 200 years. We might remember that, say in England and in other countries too, this parliamentary democracy and the system of giving the franchise to the people was very strictly limited. Till quite recently, some 20 to 30 years ago relatively small number of people had the vote. Even now in quite advanced countries, half the population consisting of women do not have the vote. Therefore, democracy in those countries is presumably thought of in terms of 'male democracy' not female.

When we talk about democracy in the nineteenth century it was a democracy which was limited very strictly to certain classes and gradually after great struggles it widened out; the franchise went wider and wider. Then again after a good deal of trouble, the actual representatives, who were chosen, also spread out from certain limited classes to other. It is a relatively slow process, therefore, it is only in the last, I believe, thirty years or so, that adult franchise has come into being in a number of countries.

That clearly is long enough, I suppose, and yet it is not long enough really to tell us what the ultimate effects of this are likely to be in solving problems etc., because the ultimate test, of course, is how far a system of government solves the problems which the country had a face and the people have to face. Any broadly theoretical approach to this question, good as it may be, does not take you very far if the best of these fails to solve the problems that the country. Of course, the problems are solved not merely by good machines, the structure of government, but by many other things, by the quality of human beings, by their training, by their education, by their character and any number of other things. All that the machine can do is to make it easier for these qualities to develop and remove any element of suppression and actually encourage them to grow.

Now, we talk about democracy again. Democracy has been spoken of chiefly, in the past, as political democracy, roughly represented by every person having a vote. This is a substantial idea, but it becomes obvious that a vote by itself does not represent very much to a person who is down and out, to a person, let us say, who is starving or hungry or has no other resources. He is much more interested in getting food to eat than a vote apart from some few individuals who might be.

Therefore, political democracy, by itself, is not enough except that it may be used to obtain a gradually increasing measure of economic democracy, equality and the spread of the good things of life to other and removal of gross inequalities. That process has, no doubt, continued for some time in countries where there is political democracy and brought about a lessening of these differences, and because of the growth in other ways it has lessened internal tensions,though not completely.

(4) Conversation is indeed the most easily teachable of all arts.All you need to do in order to become a good conversationalist is to find a subject that interests you and your listeners. There are, for example numberless hobbies to talk about. But the important thing is that you must talk about the other fellow's hobby rather than your own. Therein lies the secret of your popularity. Talk to your friends about the things that interest them, and you will get a reputation for good fellowship, charming with, and a brilliant mind. There is nothing that pleases people so much as your interest in their interests.

It is just as important to know what subjects to avoid and what subjects to select for good conversation. If you don't want to be set down as a wet blanket or a bore, be careful to avoid certain unpleasant topics. Avoid talking about yourself, unless you are asked to do so. People are interested in their own problems, not in yours. Sickness or death bores everybody. The only one who willingly listens to such talk is the doctor, but he gets paid for it.

To be a good conversationalist, you must know not only what to say, but how to say it. Be civil and modest. Don't over emphasize your own importance. Be mentally quick and witty. But don't hurt others with your wit. Finally, try to avoid mannerism in your conversation. Don't bite your lips or click your tongue or roll your eyes or use your hands excessively as you speak. Don't be like the Frenchman who said, "How can I talk if you hold my hands?"

(5) Then there is the newspaper press that huge engine for keeping discussion on low level and making the politics test final. To take off the taxes on knowledge was to place a heavy tax on broad and independent opinion. The multiplication of journals "delivering brawing judgements on all things all day long" has done much to deaden the small stock of individuality in public verdicts. It has done much to make vulgar ways of looking at things and vulgar ways speaking them stronger and stronger, by formulation and repeating and stereotyping them incessantly from morning until afternoon and from year's end to year's end. For a newspaper must live, and to live it must please, and its conductors suppose, perhaps not altogether rightly, that it can only please by being very cheerful towards prejudices, very chilly to general theories, loftily disdainful to the man of principle.

Their one cry to an advocate of improvement is some sagacious silliness about recognising the limits of the practicable in politics and seeing the necessity of adapting theories to facts. As if the fact taking a broader and wise view than the common crowd disqualifies a man from knowing what the view of the common crowd happens to be, and from estimating it at the proper value for practical purposes. Why are the men who despair of improvement to be the only person endowed with the gift of deserving the practicable ? It is, however only too easy to understand how a journal existing for a day, should limit its view to the possibilities of the day, and how being most closely affected by the particular, it should coldly turn its back upon all that is general, and it is easy too to understand the reaction of this intellectual timorousness upon the minds of ordinary readers who have too little natural force and too little cultivation to be able to resist the narrowing and deadly effect of the daily iteration of shortsighted common places.

(6) When people who are tolerable fortunate in their outward lot do not find in life sufficient enjoyment to make it valuable to them, the cause generally is caring for nobody, but themselves. To those who have neither public nor private affections, the excitements of life are much curtailed, and in any case dwindle in value as the time approaches when all selfish interests must be terminated by death : while those who leave after them objects of personal affection and specially those who have also cultivated a fellow—feeling with the collective interests of mankind, retain as lively an interest in life on the eve of death as in the vigour of youth and health.

Next to selfishness, the principal cause which the fountains of knowledge have been opened, and which has been taught, in any tolerable degree, to exercise its faculties—finds sources of inexhaustible interest in all that surrounds it : in the objects of nature, the achievements of art, the imaginations of poetry, the incidents of history, the ways of mankind past and present, and their prospects in the future. It is possible, indeed, to become indifferent to all that and that too without having exhausted a thousands part of it; but only when one has had from the beginning no moral of human interests in these things, and has sought in them only the gratification of curiosity.

(7) The problem of unemployment, I venture to submit, so far as the educated classes are concerned, cannot be solved without reorganising our entire system of education so as to produce not merely men of culture but also practical-minded men who can become useful economic units of the nation. Side by side with this and as an indispensable accompaniment of educational reform we have actually to provide more careers for our educated young men to establish modern lines of cottage industries, to absorb those possessing technical, scientific and practical knowledge in large-scale industries to open other avenues of work.

While I realise the growing importance of vocational education and industrial training. I also feel that such education and such training themselves cannot solve the problem unless each province assumes responsibility for developing those wealth producing activities which alone can find employment for our young men.

If I may be permitted to quote from the report with which I was associated, "There cannot be one single remedy which can solve the question of unemployment, nor can it be solved immediately, but I think that if it is attacked systematically on a well conceived plan with the resources available to Government, great deal of relief can be given to the unemployed among the educated.

While, if Governments are prepared to spend more money on the development of the resources of the country, reorganising the entire system of education and on encouraging and fostering the true spirit of industrialization, a great deal more may be done." I think the time has come when our Provincial Governments, who under the new constitution will be concerned with unemployment should definitely recognise the importance and the urgency of the problem and also the danger of postponing the solution or the danger of proceeding at a leisurely pace. Such steps as have hitherto been taken by governments only touch the fringe of the problem and at times I feel as if there is not that keen and close appreciation of it, which in these days, we are entitled to expect and demand from Governments.

I agree with the point of view that the success or failure of the new Governments, which are to come into being in the provinces within the next few months, will be measured by their ability or inability to face and cope with our economic problems. I do not forget that we have got to work in the midst of imperfect conditions and with such tolls as we can command.

I do not however, believing she paralysing doctrine that we can do nothing to relieve unemployment or economic distress generally until the dream of a new order of society has been realised. It is pleasant to think of "the church of the future, the commonwealth of the future and the society of the future", but the essential and the immediate problem of consideration should be how harmonise this tempting idea with the actual condition of human life in our country.

I may, therefore, hope that whatever may divide your future legislators, the will all be united in taking this very practical problem in a practical spirit. I think the problem is big enough in all its ramification to engage the attention of a whole time Minister and in any case I sincerely hope that it will not be relegated to a subordinate position in the departmental work of the Government.

(8) The essential qualities for a man of business are of a moral nature; these are to be cultivated first. He must learn besides to love truth. That same love of truth will be found a potent charm to bear him safely through the world's entanglement—I mean safely in the worldly sense. Besides, the love of truth not only makes a man act with more simplicity, and therefore, with less chance of error, but it conduces to the highest intellectual development. The following passage in the *Statesman* gives the reason : "The correspondence of wisdom and goodness are manifold, and that they will accompany each other is to be inferred; not only because men's wisdom makes them good, but also because their goodness makes them wise.

Questions of right and wrong are a perpetual exercise of the faculties of those who are solicitous as to the right and wrong of what they do and see; and a deeper interest of the heart in those questions carries with it a deeper cultivation of the understanding that can be easily affected by any other excitement to intellectual activity." What has just been said of the love of truth applies also to other moral qualities. Thus, charity enlightens the understanding quite as much as it purifies heart. And indeed knowledge is not more girt about with power than goodness is with wisdom.

The next thing in the training of one who is to become a man of business will be for him to form principles; for without these, when thrown on the sea of action, he will be without rudder and compass. They are the best results of study. Whether it is history or political economy, or ethics that he is studying, these principles are to be the reward of his labour.

A principle resembles a law in the physical world; though it can seldom have the same certainty as the facts which it had to explain and embrace do not admit of beings weighed and umbered with the same exactness as material things. The principles which our student adopts may be unsound, may be insufficient, but he must not neglect to form some : and must only nourish a love of truth that will not allow him to hold any, the moment that he finds them erroneous.

Much depends upon the temperament of a man of business. It should be hopeful, that it may bear him against the faintheartedness, the folly, the falsehood, and the numberless discouragements which even a prosperous man will have to endure. He should also be calm : for else he may be driven wild by any great pressure of business, and lose his time, and his head, in rushing from one unfinished thing, to begin something else. Now this wished for conjunction of the calm and the hopeful is very rare. It is, however, in every man's power to study well his own temperaments, and to provide against the defects in it.

(9) Culture is an abstract word, the thing is an abstraction and all abstraction tend to become dopes and a dope habit is bad. Let us make it easier by translating it into concrete terms :

"Culture is the training or discipline by which man's moral and intellectual nature is refined and enlightened."

Culture is the product of cultivation. Culture pertains to people and things. You cannot have cultivation an abstraction. You must have something or some person who is cultivated. But people and things differ in their nature. They differ both as objects of observation and as objects of speculation. They are different in shapes and sizes; they are different in their ends or purposes.

The culture of human beings is their cultivation according to their nature, *i.e.*, their purpose, both immediate and ultimate. There is, therefore, no cultivation of men in general except religious cultivation. Religious cultivation is the cultivation of the whole race of men with a view of eternal beatitude or temporal happiness. It is the quality of being cultivated according to the character of your particular purpose religious in relation to your 'last end', secular in relation to your means of earning as living.

Culture, then, that it to say, the cultivation of men means the quality of men who are trained, cultivated according to their common ends of attaining eternal beatitude, but as all men differ from one another and therefore, live and earn their living in different manners, the qualities and kinds of culture will differ.

Such is the nature of culture as I understand it. It is not something added like sugar on a pill. It is the quality of being cultivated according to your way and purpose of living. A peasant culture is the product of peasants cultivated according to the nature of peasant life. A town culture is the product of townsmen cultivated according to the nature of town life. There is no such thing as culture apart from purpose. And human culture is the product of what men do for a living.

(10) The importance of education in forming character and opinion is very great and well recognized by all. The genuine beliefs, though not usually unconsciously acquired by most children; and even if they depart from these beliefs in later life, something of them remains deeply implanted, ready to emerge in a time of stress of crisis.

Education is, as a rule, the strongest force on the side of what exists and again fundamental change : threatened institutions while they are still powerful, process themselves of the education machine, and instil a respect for their own excellence into the malleable minds of the young. Reformers retort by trying to dust their opponents from position of vantage.

The children themselves are not considered by either party; they are merely so much material, to be recruited into one army or the other. If the children themselves, were considered, education would not aim at making them belong to this party or that, but at enabling them to choose intelligently between the parties; it would aim at making them able to think, not at making them think what their teachers think.

Education as a political weapon, could not exist if we respected the rights of children. If we respected the rights of children, we should educated them so as to give them the knowledge and the mental habits required for forming independent opinions; but education as a political institution endeavours to form habits and to circumscribe knowledge in such a way as to make one set of opinions inevitable.

(11) People confound literature and article dealing because the plan in both cases is similar, but no two things can be more distinct. Neither the question of money nor that of friend or foe can enter into literature proper. Here, right feeling, or good taste, if this expression be preferred-is alone considered. If a bonafide writer thinks a thing want saying he will say it as tersely, clearly and elegantly as he can. The question whether it will do him personally good or harm, or it will affect this or that friend never enters his head, or if it does, it is instantly ordered out again. The only personal gratifications allowed to him (apart, of course, from such as are conceded to everyone, writer or not) are those of keeping his good name spotless among those whose opinion is along worth having and of maintaining the highest tradition of a noble calling. If a man lives in fear and trembling lest he should fail in these respects, if he finds these consideration alone weigh with him, if he never writes without thinking how he shall best serve good causes and damage bad ones, then he is a genuine man of letters. If in addition to this he succeeds in making his manner attractive, he will become a classic. He knows, although the Greeks in their mythology forgot to say so, that conceit was saved to mankind as well as Hope when Pandora clapped the lid on to the box. With the article-dealer, on the other hand, money is and ought to be the first consideration. Literature is an art : article writing, when a man is paid for it, is a trade and genuine pictures another.

People have, indeed, been paid for some of the most genuine pictures ever painted, and so with music and with literature itself—hard and fast lines ever cut the fingers of those who draw them–but, as a general rule, most lasting art has been poorly paid so far as money goes till the artist was near the end of his time, and whether money passed or not, we may be sure that it was not thought of. Such work is done as bird sings for the love of the thing; it is preserved as long as body and soul can be kept together, whether be pay or no, and perhaps better if there be no pay.

(12) There are more literate people in India today then ever before. But there are also more illiterates than ever before. More children go to school than at any time in the past. But more children today are out of school than any time in the past. But it is not enough to blame the high birth-rate for this state of affairs. Indeed, it can be reasonably argued that continued mass illiteracy is not the result, but the cause of the high birth-rate. Consequently spread of literacy can be a potent weapon of socio-economic development.

Unfortunately official thought and planning in this regard has betrayed a failure of perception. The problem of illiteracy is related to but not the same as that of education. And while it is a colossal task to provide proper and full academic education to all children and youth in the country, the eradicating illiteracy calls for a different and less leisurely blueprint. The following measures will be in the right direction; more primary schools, new part-time educational centres for those who cannot attend regular schools, and functional literacy centres for adults, especially in semi-urban and rural areas.

(13) Democracy always needs a kind of public honesty which expresses itself in there being a permanent supply of people who are prepared to question the popular, the accepted and the convenient and to suggest alternatives. Some systems using the name of democracy deny this. They maintain that certain things have been, as it were, revealed to be true and cannot be questioned; certain alternatives are held not to be only desirable, but even indiscussible. This cannot be democracy.

We live in an age of slogans. Slogans are very necessary to make big issue understandable to simple people. One of the most memorable phrases in world history in such a slogan, the French Revolutionaries slogan of 'liberty, equality, fraternity.

But very often sloganology is the art of making an unclear idea appear to be clear when it is no such thing. A functioning democracy must, therefore, be very careful to explain, as far as possible to its citizens what it is talking about, what its terms mean and not simply to speak in resounding formulae.

(1) Heading: Importance of Disarmament

Precis: Disarmament has acquired a special significance today. Inspite of talks, plans and proposals to stop it, mad race for armaments and search for more destructive weapons still continue. In this Nuclear Age we are to choose either total destruction or an atmosphere of peaceful coexistence. To create a peaceful environment we must avoid speeches and talks mounting tensions, fear and hatred. Total disarmament is not possible in one step, but gradual move towards this goal can be fruitful. In order to prove its utility the U.N.O must endeavour to achieve this goal.

(2) Heading: Essentials of Democracy

Precis: The aim of democracy is to establish the rule of equality in the behavioural conduct of society. Democracy is not simply a form of government, but a way of life, an important mode of conduct. In the prevailing order of our society a few classes flourish but masses suffer.

Unless the inequality is removed and the States provide security, employment, health, shelter, peace of mind, basic economic justice and other essentials of civilized life to all the citizens, it cannot be said to be truly democratic. A few affluent can't be safe, if the masses are wretched. For its own existence, it is the first duty of the State to protect the basic rights of the poor and to provide economic justice to all.

(3) Heading: Parliamentary Democracy

Precis: Parliamentary democracy is a product of gradual growth of 150 to 200 years. In the past, franchise was limited in many countries to a few people. Even now there are countries where women do not have any franchise. It was after a long drawn struggle that the right of voting was extended to others. But the ultimate effect of this change has to be seen not simply in the kind of government that it promises to introduce, but in the way it helps the people in solving their economic and other problems. A vote by itself has no value for a starving person. For true political democracy it is necessary that it leads to economic equality, equal distribution of wealth among the people, and to the lessening of their social and economic differences and for all round gradual growth with little internal tensions.

(4) Heading: Art of Conversation

Precis: Art of conversation is a most easily teachable art. A good conversationalist finds a subject of common interest that make him popular among his friends. Unpleasant topics and mannerism should be avoided. One must know what to say and how to say it. One must not only be civil and courteous in his talks but also be mentally quick and witty. Biting lips, clicking tongue, rolling eyes or using hands in excess must be avoided during conversations.

(5) Heading: The Effect of the Press on Public Mind

Precis: By providing own public opinion on all subjects, the newspaper press discourages broad, independent and individual opinions. In fact, the increase in journals has kept the discussion on a low level and destroyed the individuality of judgement. Every hour and every day publication of cheap mass opinion has vulgarly effected the outlook of general public. The presumption of the edition that they can make the newspapers or journals interesting only by feeding to the common passion and prejudices of the general public. They are mainly concern only to the things of temporary and practical interest and disregard the general good and the ideal things. The effect of this press-tendency is very serious on the minds of the common readers who are not capable to resist the force of the common place.

(6) Heading: Happiness in Life

Precis: Persons who fail to enjoy happiness in life in spite of their fairly good means are themselves responsible for this. Only those who are philanthropic and who believe in collective good and have fellow feeling enjoy the life up to the last. For a self-centred man who has no respect for others, finds no enjoyment in life. Further to it is the need of a well cultivated mind for the achievement of true happiness. A disciplined and enlightened man with a curious mind finds interest, in nature, art, poetry and history and every thing. For such a man, the whole world is a consistent source of affection and happiness.

(7) Heading: Unemployment among the Educated Youth

Precis: The problem of unemployment among the educated youth can't be solved by a single remedy. Not only the entire system of education is required to be reconstituted, but also job opportunities for the technically trained and educated youth is required to be created. Each province should encourage and create its employment generating economic activities by having thrust upon the modern cottage and Industrial units. The problem is required to be dealt with patiently and systematically. The steps that our newly formed Provincial Governments have taken so far are not adequate. These Governments should now realise that their success or failure in future depends upon the extent of solving the economic problems of the society particularly this problem of unemployment. The time is very difficult, whatever may be the other differences but this problem is to be tackled unitedly and with all sincerity.

(8) Heading: The Qualities of a Businessman

Precis: The essential qualities of a man of business are not only the wisdom, but also the love of truth. Truthfulness keeps one free from many entanglements and contributes in his intellectual development charity, honesty and other moral values exercise a whole some influence on him. A businessman should also form principles of action. The study of history and ethics would help a businessman enormously and provide ready cut solutions for the actions in case of need. He should at once rectify those principles which prove to be erroneous when put into practice. Temperament also plays an important role in the life of a successful businessman. A patient and cool temperamental businessman can take prudent and wise decisions in difficult circumstances. So one should analyse his temperament well and take care of the shortcomings.

(9) Heading: Cultivation of Culture

Precis Culture is the result of cultivation, it is a kind of training which refines and enlightens the man's moral and intellectual nature. It belongs to both men and things. For men, their cultivation is according to their present or last ends and purposes in life. The form of cultivation may be religious or secular as the purpose of man to attain eternal beauties or to find temporal happiness. As men differ in their ways and means of achieving their purpose, so there are different kinds of culture.

Thus, there is a peasant culture which is the product of peasant life, a town culture is the product of town life. Similarly, human culture is the product of what men do for achieving the purpose of their life. Culture is not at all apart or different from the purpose of life and it is cultivated accordingly.

(10) Heading: The True Aim of Education

Precis: Education plays an important role information of the character and opinion of children. The lessons learned by the children from their parents and teachers last throughout their life. And so the reformers and politicians try to keep education under their control and use education as a tool to frame one - sided opinion for their own advantage. If the rights of children be given due weightage then, we should educate them to think critically and judge independently. Education to be true to its salt, must be kept free from all kinds of social and political influences and prejudices.

(11) Heading: A True Literary Artist

Precis: Literature and article writing are entirely different things. For an article writer money is primary, but a true literary artist does not care for money or for the good opinion of his friends. He writes clearly and elegantly whatever he believes is right. If he has any personal consideration, it is his desire to keep his name respectable among those whose opinion is really worth having. One who writes without fearing the bad opinion of people and without the object of supporting or rejecting any particular cause is a true literary artist. It is true that some artists, have been paid for their work, but a true artist did it, never for money's sake, but for the love of the thing itself and preserved to the last.

(12) Heading: Illiteracy

Precis: High birth-rate is not the cause but the result of wide-spread illiteracy. However, official thought and planning have failed to perceive that spread of literacy can lower birth-rate and bring about socio-economic development. The problem of literacy, is concerned with the education, but its solution is different. Opening primary schools, part time educational centres and literacy centres for adults particularly in semi-urban and rural area can be helpful in tackling the problem of illiteracy.

(13) Heading: Functioning of Democracy

Precis: Democracy needs public honesty, means freedom to the people to question the popular and accepted ideas and to suggest alternatives. In some systems, though named democratic, deny this right are indeed undemocratic. Slogans help in understanding the big issues, but for the proper functioning of democracy the sloganology must not be used to make an unclear thing appear clear, instead things must be made crystal clear to the public .

Directions *Four alternative summaries are given below each text. Choose the option that best captures the essence of the text.* **[CAT 2004]**

(A) You seemed at first to take no notice of your school-fellows, or rather to set yourself against them because they were strangers to you. They knew as little of you did of them: this would have been the reason for their keeping aloof from you as well, which would have felt as a hardship. Learn never to conceive a prejudice against others because you know nothing of them. It is bad reasoning, and makes enemies of half the world. Do not think ill of them till they behave ill to you; and them strive to avoid the faults which you see in them. This will disarm their hostility sooner than pique or resentment or complaint.

(1) The discomfort you felt with your school fellows was because both sides knew little of each other. You should not complain unless you find others prejudiced against you and have attempted to carefully analyse the faults you have observed in them.

(2) The discomfort you felt with your school fellows was because both sides knew little of each other. Avoid prejudice and negative thoughts till you encounter bad behaviour from others, and then win them over by shunning the faults you have observed.

(3) You encountered hardship amongst your school fellows because you did not know them well. You should learn to not make enemies because of your prejudices irrespective of their behaviour towards you.

(4) You encountered hardship amongst your school fellows because you did not know them well. You should learn to not make enemies because of your prejudices unless they behave badly with you.

(B) Thẹ human race is spread all over the world, from the polar regions to the tropics. The people of whom it is made up eat different kinds of food. Partly according to the climate, in which they live, and partly according to the kind of food which their country produces. In hot climates, meat and fat are not much needed; but in the Arctic regions they seem to be very necessary for keeping up the heat of the body. Thus, in India, people live chiefly on different kinds of grains, eggs, milk, or sometimes fish and meat. In Europe, people eat more meat and less grain. In the Arctic regions, where no grains and fruits are produced, the Eskimo and other races live almost entirely on meat and fish.

(1) Food eaten by people in different regions of the world depends on the climate and produce of the region, and varies from meat and fish in the Arctic to predominantly grains in the tropics.

(2) Hot climates require people to eat grains while cold regions require people to eat meat and fish.

(3) In hot countries people eat mainly grains while in the Arctic they eat meat and fish because they cannot grow grains.

(4) While people in Arctic regions like meat and fish and those in hot regions like India prefer mainly grains, they have to change what they eat depending on the local climate and the local produce.

Solutions : **A.** (1) **B.** (2)

REPORT WRITING

What is a Report?

A report is a factual description of some incident taken place or a consolidated statements of some plan or scheme either existing or being implemented based upon some logics collected verbally or in writing.

How to Write a Good Report ?

रिपोर्ट एक औपचारिक सूचना है जो तथ्यों के आधार पर एक विशेष उद्देश्य को ध्यान में रखकर तैयार की जाती है। रिपोर्ट एक घटना से सम्बन्धित हो सकती है, किसी विशेष स्थान या किसी विशेष प्रोजेक्ट को लागू करने से पूर्व या किसी विशेष प्रोजेक्ट या योजना को सफलता-असफलता के सन्दर्भ में या किसी आकस्मिक समस्या के सन्दर्भ में तैयार की जाती है। मुख्य बात है रिपोर्ट तैयार करने हेतु तथ्यों का संकलन। रिपोर्ट में तथ्य **Eye witness** की भाँति या सरकारी-गैर सरकारी आँकड़ों के आधार या सम्बन्धित व्यक्तियों, संस्थाओं से मौखिक वार्तालाप, साक्षात्कार या अन्य आँकड़ों के आधार पर संकलित किए जाते हैं। एक अच्छी रिपोर्ट में समस्त आवश्यक तथ्यों को संकलित कर, उनका समुचित तरीकों से विश्लेषण कर, सम्बन्धित उद्देश्यों हेतु प्रस्तुत करना होता है

रिपोर्ट को निम्न भागों में वर्गीकृत किया जा सकता है:

(1) Report to a Newspaper by a reporter: Newspaper के संवाददताओं द्वारा किसी घटना के सम्बन्ध में प्रकाशन हेतु प्रेषित रिपोर्ट सामान्य रूप से स्वयं घटनास्थल का अवलोकन कर मौखिक जानकारी करने के पश्चात् भेजी जाती है। इस तरह की रिपोर्ट का Heading, Eye Catching होता है।

(2) Report for a Specific Purpose: कई बार Newspaper के columnist एवं correspondents द्वारा एक विशेष समस्या, एक विशेष प्रोजेक्ट, किसी सरकारी-गैर सरकारी योजना या संस्था के सम्बन्ध में रिपोर्ट तैयार की जाती है जो तथ्यों के वास्तविक संकलन एवं उचित विश्लेषण पर आधारित होती है।

(3) Official Report: आधिकारिक रिपोर्ट, सामान्यतया, एक अधिकारी या समिति द्वारा किसी उच्च अधिकारी को, सार्वजनिक महत्त्व की किसी समस्या के सन्दर्भ में प्रेषित की जाती है। इस तरह की रिपोर्ट किसी एक अधिकारी द्वारा या एक समिति द्वारा उपलब्ध सरकारी-गैर सरकारी आँकड़ों, वर्तमान परिस्थितियो एवं दूरगामी परिस्थितियों एवं परिणामों को ध्यान में रखकर, रिपोर्ट के उद्देश्यों के सन्दर्भ में तैयार की जाती है। कई बार इस तरह की रिपोर्ट, किसी सरकारी योजना की सफलता, असफलता के सन्दर्भ में तथा कई बार इस तरह की रिपोर्ट, वर्तमान समस्या या आने वाली समस्या के समाधान हेतु लिए जाने वाले निर्णय के लिए उपलब्ध आँकड़ों का तथ्यात्मक विश्लेषण करके, संस्तुतियों सहित तैयार की जाती है।

(4) Technical/Research Report: तकनीकी ज्ञान रखने वाले अधिकारी द्वारा या समिति द्वारा इस तरह की रिपोर्ट, किसी विशेष प्रोजेक्ट, योजना के सम्बन्ध में तैयार की जाती है। इसमें आँकड़ों का जटिल विश्लेषण कर तथ्यात्मक टिप्पणी की जाती है। यह महत्त्वपूर्ण रिपोर्ट होती है, जिसके आधार पर बड़े-बड़े वित्तीय निर्णय लिए जाते हैं।

What is a Good Report?

एक अच्छी रिपोर्ट में निम्न विशेषताएँ होती हैं:

(1) Factual Description: रिपोर्ट तथ्यों के उचित संकलन एवं समुचित विश्लेषण के आधार पर तैयार की जानी चाहिए। Report कर्ता के व्यक्तिगत दुराभाव से प्रभावित नहीं होनी चाहिए।
Report must be factual and free from personal prejudices.

(2) Clear, Compact and Concise: रिपोर्ट, स्पष्ट तथ्यात्मक होनी चाहिए तथा अनावश्यक रूप से लम्बी-चौड़ी नहीं होनी चाहिए। यदि आँकड़ों की अधिकता के कारण रिपोर्ट विस्तृत हो गई है तो अन्त में उसे Summarise करना, अच्छी रिपोर्ट की आवश्यकता होती है।

(3) Purpose: रिपोर्ट का उद्देश्य, बहुत महत्त्वपूर्ण है। जिस उद्देश्य से रिपोर्ट तैयार की जानी है, उससे असम्बद्ध चित्रों तथा तथ्यों (Irrelevant figures and facts) का संकलन एवं विश्लेषण, रिपोर्ट को अनावश्यक रूप से जटिल बना देता है।

A Good Report must contain relevant points as per the purpose of the Report.

मुख्य बात यह है कि एक रिपोर्ट, तथ्यों के आधार पर निष्पक्ष (Impartial) रिपोर्टर द्वारा स्पष्टता एवं संक्षिप्तार (Brevity) को ध्यान में रखकर उद्देश्य के अनुकूल आँकड़ों के संकलन एवं उचित विश्लेषण के आधार पर तैयार की जानी चाहिए।

Examples of Reports

(1) ***You are Ankit, working as the news correspondent for the Times of India, Mumbai. You are invited by the organisers to cover the programme of the National Film Festival Awards. Write a report giving necessary details in not more than 100 words.***

Sanjay, Manisha Won the Best Awards

Mumbai: 15th April, 200.... (From our news correspondent Mr. Ankit)

The much awaited 9th Film Festival Award 20...., was organised at the famous Buddha Auditorium. The auditorium was fabulously decorated with dazzling light and an electronical effect was given to the stage, to welcome the film stars. The Chief Minister of Maharashtra graced the occasion as Chief Guest. A large gathering cheered the respected leader and the film stars. The awards were given for the best film in Hindi and other regional languages. The best film actor and actress award was conferred on Sanjay Dutt and Manisha Koirala. Other awards included for the best director, character actor, movie director and the best singer. When the function was closed, people crowded the stars to get their autographs. The function was a grand success.

(2) ***As a staff reporter of the Hindustan Times, who witnessed a multiple collision of a Maruti car, a scooter and a tourist bus in a road accident, write a report in not more than 100 words.***

Two Dead, Six Injured in Road Accident

New Delhi, 10th May, 20.... (From our staff reporter)

It was perhaps the most unfortunate and saddest day of many people who witnessed a multiple collision of a Maruti car, a scooter and a tourist bus near ITO, New Delhi. A tourist bus of U.P. Roadways, full of passengers, was on a picnic to India Gate. When it reached near ITO, it hit a Maruti car from the left side and a scooter from the back. The two young boys in their teens, on the scooter were thrown on the road and died at the spot. The dead bodies were lying on the road in a pool of blood. The scooterists were not wearing helmets so they succumbed to the head injury caused in the accident. Even the driver of the Maruti car lost his sense, hit a wall, but didn't get hurt. Passengers in the bus got a sudden jerk. Six passengers seriously injured. All were crying for help. There was a loud hue and cry. The injured were taken to the hospital for immediate medical aid. The whole traffic came to a standstill. The police arrived in no time and registered a case for negligent driving and homicide against the bus driver.

(3) ***You are Mohan, a staff reporter at Times of India. You have witnessed a severe road accident involving a Truck and a Maruti car. Write a report including details about number of people injured and extent of damage caused to the colliding vehicles in not more than 100 words.***

Truck Hits Maruti, One Dead

New Delhi, 16th September, 20.... (From our staff reporter Mohan)

A serious accident took place near Naraina, in which a truck bearing Registration No. DLI 023, D 4573 suddenly jumped the red light and turned to right. It was about to collide with a Maruti car Registration No. DLJ 012, J 1572, but the driver was very smart and careful. He saw the impending danger and took a turn to the left, but could not escape fully. The Truck hit the Maruti and lost its balance and hit the wall in the right. The truck was overturned causing serious injuries to the passengers sitting in the cabin. The driver was thrown out and his head struck against the wall and died on the spot. The three passengers sitting in the cabin of the truck were badly injured, two suffered minor injuries. The Maruti driver got minor injuries. The traffic came to a standstill. The injured were removed to the hospital. Police rushed to the spot and a case was lodged against the truck driver.

(4) ***You are Nisha working as a newspaper reporter for the Hindustan Times. Yesterday, you were invited to attend a press conference convened by the Union Minister for Parliamentary Affairs on the proposed changes in the Constitution of India. Write a report for publication in the newspaper in not more than 150 words.***

Constitutional Amendments Necessary for Stability : Minister

New Delhi, 24th March, 20.... (By Miss Nisha, staff reporter from HT New Delhi)

The Union Minister for Parliamentary Affairs convened a press conference at his residence on the proposed changes in the Constitution of India in order to provide a stable government to the country. Here, in India, Members of the Parliament are elected to run the government. In case any political party fails to get a clear majority to form the government, it has to get the support of other political parties to form a government. Thus, a coalition the government takes place. At present we are having a coalition government, but its success is neither certain nor admirable, as the allies parties in general forced its motives and decisions on the government. This creates great hurdles in the smooth functioning of the government. Sometimes the coalition partners start working against the Government. In order to put a check over such practice, certain changes in the Constitution are under process. The majority party shall be allowed to form a government. In the first instance no candidate should be allowed to change a party after winning the election. On the issues of national interest all parties have to give their consensus. There should be only four political parties which have secured at least 20% votes in the last three elections. Once accepted as coalition partner that party shall not be allowed to withdraw the support. Once a government is formed, that cannot be thrown out unless a majority of two-third of the total membership put a demand in writing to the President and a no-confidence motion is passed by the same majority. When asked about the feasibility of such a move the Minister replied that it is well in the interest of the nation and for the peace and progress stability is must.

(5) ***Paresh Tonk, a correspondent from Statesman, was asked to submit a report on Environment Pollution. Write a report on Environmental Pollution in 80-100 words.***

Environmental Pollution

New Delhi, 25th Oct., 20.... (From our special correspondent Mr. Paresh Tonk)

Environmental Pollution has assumed alarming proportion resulting in a serious health hazard now-a-days. Not only air, but also water has become dangerously polluted. Smoke pollutes the air, sewage pollutes the water and solid wastes (garbage and junk etc) pollute the land. Population explosion, urbanization and industrialization are the biggest causes of the present pollution. Industrial units throw their wastes and chemicalized water in the rivers. Sewage of big cities is being dumped into rivers. This has resulted into spreading of harmful chemicals in the environment which are harmful for the living creatures.

Plants, animals and human beings are suffering from many known and unknown diseases because of this pollution.The polluted water causes cancerous diseases like cholera, jaundice and diarrhoea etc.

The smoke coming out of the chimneys of the factories and vehicles causes serious health problems. We regularly breathe the polluted air and as a result headache, nausea and many diseases of lung and heart take place. This is a serious health hazard to all of us. The public be made aware to the harms and the problems caused due to environmental pollution. Public be advised to use anti-pollutant instruments in their vehicles and regular tuning and pollution check to be made compulsory. Industrial units be forced to take anti-pollution measures. A proper arrangement for dumping of Industrial and sewage wastes be made. Use of Polythene bags be banned. A mass awareness programme be launched by the Governmental and Non-governmental agencies. To save the younger generation from the side-effects of the environmental pollution it is necessary to take immediate and proper action.

(6) ***You are Mr. Ashok Jain. You have seen a student demonstration near Moti Nagar, New Delhi. Write your report in about 80-100 words for the newspaper.***

Students Demonstrated Against Fees Hike

New Delhi, 29th August 20…. (From our special correspondent Mr. Ashok Jain)

The students of Senior Classes of Government School, Moti Nagar walked out of their classes and held massive demonstration against the hike in board fees. They were raising slogans against the government decision for increasing Board fees and abolishing the compartment examinations altogether. They were having hand bills and many posters. They were shouting slogans for restoring the compartment examination and maintaining the status quo in the matter of Board fees. This peaceful procession proceeded towards the office of Education Minister. Approximately 20,000 students gathered at the office of the Education Minister from all corners of Delhi. The police tried to disperse the students, but they did not budge even a single inch. There was complete chaos and the traffic was jammed. The Minister arrived on the spot and had discussion with the student leaders. After discussion, he assured the students for prompt and positive action. The situation was thus controlled and then the students left the place winningly and peacefully.

(7) ***You are Sarla. You visited the Industrial Exhibition at Pragati Maidan. Your teacher has asked you to write a report for the school magazine. Write your report in about 100 words.***

A Report on Exhibition

Delhi, 25th Dec, 20…. (Report by Miss Sarla, a staff correspondent)

A national level exhibition commenced at Pragati Maidan today, inaugurated by the Home Minister. On the inaguration the Home Minister said, "Exhibitions are the reflections of a country's progress into and this exhibition is unique, in which all the States and the Union Territories are participating." Every year many exhibitions and trade fairs are organised by the Governmental and Non- governmental Agencies. This year a specific industrial exhibition was held in Pragati Maidan. All the States participated in this exhibition. It attracted a throng of visitors from all over the country. It reflects that India has made an exemplary progress in the field of Industry. People could be seen in long queues before the different pavilions.

At the machinery section, one could not find a place to keep foot on. Agricultural implements of Punjab were in great demand. Hand made Galichas and dresses of Kashmir also attracted a lot of visitors. The pavilion of Rajasthan was also very interesting as it had very cheap and beautiful items of clay and mud. Some of the stall-keepers distributed hand-bills to the visitors. People were walking here and there in an enthusiastic mood. Small children were enjoying the merry-go-rounds, horse and camel rides. The refreshment corner was also full of hustle and bustle.

(8) *You are Bhawani Dev, a correspondent from Indian Express. You were an eye witness to an Electioneering campaign in Ahmedabad. Write a report for the newspaper in about 100 words.*

Elections Held Peacefully

Ahmedabad, 25th Nov, 200.... (Report by Bhawani Dev, a correspond from Indian Express)

India being the largest democracy of the world a great emphasis is laid on the free and fair elections. In Gujrat, the election commission declared elections and the schedule of filing and withdrawing nominations as well as the date of election was also announced. This time the Electronics Voting Machines will be used in the elections. All preparations were made in advance. More than thirty candidates filed their nomination papers for Ahmedabad (North) assembly seat. After date of withdrawal there were ten candidates in the fray. Accordingly different symbols were allotted to the contesting candidates. The candidates arranged meetings and put forth their charter of manifesto. Every candidate was trying to tempt and woo the voters through his oily and sweet slogans and speeches. Posters and slogans were decorating the walls.

Several meetings of many high profile leaders and Film stars were organised during the campaign. Hand bills were being circulated among the residents. The candidates were holding corner meetings under a certain code of conduct. The election campaign came to a standstill 48 hours before the date of polling. On the polling day tight security arrangements were made. The voters came in great number and there were long queues in the beginning. The voting started at 7.00 P.M. and continued till 5.00 pm. The counting was scheduled after three days. It was started in the presence of the candidates and their agents as per the scheduled programme. The returning officer declared the result then. The elections were held peacefully and in a congenial atmosphere.

(9) *Imagine you are posted as SDM in a district, prepare a report on the Pulse Polio Programme carried out in the district.*

From:

Sub Divisional Magistrate
District ....

To,

The Chief Secretary,
Government of ....

Sub: *Pulse Polio Programme*

Sir,

Under National Programme of Polio Eradication, we have carried out the Pulse Polio Campaign on 15th August in the district. A good advance publicity campaign was launched to make the general public aware of the Programme and about the date 15th August, the day of vaccination. A wide publicity was made not only in the city area, but in the remote rural areas also.

Forty teams of doctors and nurses, fifteen for the city area and twenty five for the rural areas deployed on the vaccination day to provide polio drops to every child. Male and Female nurses were deployed to visit door to door and give the drops to the children wherever possible. More than twenty thousand children were given the polio drops on that day.

We are planning to repeat this campaign in the month of October again. This time we shall be covering only the rural areas of the district. Our target for the district is 90,000 children. We have already covered twenty thousand plus forty thousand (in earlier camps) total sixty thousand children so far. We hope not only to achieve our target but also to exceed the same. Every child will be given the drops positively. We are determined to make the Polio Eradication programme a grand success positively.

R.K. Purohit 23rd Aug, 20….
S.D.M

(10) ***You are posted as District Family Planning Officer in the district. Submit a report to the Director, Medical and Health of the State in respect to the Family Planning Campaign launched in your district.***

From:

District Family Planning Officer

District ....

To,

The Director,

Medical and Health Department

....

....

Sub *Family Planning Campaign in the district of ...*

Sir,

As per the instructions received from your office vide letter No. RJ/FP/103/200.... dated 25th December. We launched the Family Planning Campaign on 20th January, 2006.

All the staff of our department was deployed for the purpose. Various voluntary organisations including Panch, Sarpanch and the respected persons of each village were motivated to make the campaign a grand success. In city area the public is well aware to the advantages of adopting family planning measures, but in rural area, more awareness is required to be created.

During this campaign, 315 operations were done and 3,000 packets of condoms were distributed.

To make this programme a regular feature, I like to suggest that at least two Mobile Operation van be made available for the district to cover the rural areas.We want to fix a day for every village, on which the pending cases and the interested cases may be operated on a regular basis.

However we will be achieving our targets positively.

PK Sharma 22nd Jan, 20….

D F P O

Ahmedabad, 25th Nov. 20….

(11) ***You are posted as Assistant Collector in a district. Flood has caused a lot of damage in the district, submit a factual report to Chief Secretary of the State, stating therein the measures taken by you to control the situation and your recommendations to assist the flood affected people.***

From:

Assistant Collector

District ....

To,

The Chief Secretary,

....

....

Sub: *Flood in the district of ....*

Sir,

I have personally visited the area affected by the recent flood. The villages lying in the path of river 'Sone' are the worst affected. As there had been little rain during the last three-four years so the people started settling nearby the river. The sudden rains have overflooded the river and all the huts and houses within approximately one km range of the river were completely washed away and destroyed. Flood water entered the houses. People have taken shelter in hills. A huge damage to properties have been done. Two persons died in Takupaka village. An acute shortage of eatables, drinking water and dry fire wood, is being faced.

We have taken all measures to help the flood victims. Packets of food, bottles of drinking water, wheat flour, kerosene etc, are being supplied to the people, with the assistance of the generous people and the NGOs and other voluntary organizations and selfless clubs. To check the spread of any epidemic diseases CMHO was called to take necessary measures immediately. A team of doctors was dispatched to every affected village to take care of spreading of any water borne or any other kind of diseases.

We are taking all possible measures to assist the flood affected people. But looking at the heavy damage caused by the flood, more funds are required immediately. You are requested to arrange at least five crore rupees urgently, so that the relief work can be carried out effectively.

JC Bhagat 19th Sept, 20....

Assistant Collector

(12) ***Suppose you are Collector of a district. Submit a report to the Chief Secretary of the State in respect to the drought situation in the district. Inform the remedial measures taken by you and what further measures required to control the situation.***

From:

Collector
District ....

To,

The Chief Secretary,
Government of ....
....

Sub : *Havoc caused by the drought in the district of ...*

Sir,

Our district has been suffering from the shortage of rains regularly for the last four years. Due to scanty rainfall, the water level in whole of the district has gone down tremendously. Without water in the wells and no rainfall, all the crops have dried up thus causing huge loss to every farmer. Our agriculture depends mainly on rainfalls. The dams and ponds are also fully dried up. An acute shortage of water is being faced. Cattle are either sold by the farmers or left to die for the shortage of water and fodder. The cost of fodder has increased tremendously. This drought has so far claimed 120 lives of cattle and affected more than 600 villages of the district with a population of 78 lacs.

'No rains' and 'shortage of water' have created famine like conditions. The drought has rendered lacs of villagers jobless. The dead bodies of animals are stinking in the fields and creating a health hazard. The danger of spreading an epidemic is immense.

I have visited almost all the affected villages. I found the situation very alarming. We are arranging fodder from the nearby state. Water is being supplied in tanks from the city area. Loans are being arranged for the farmers for deepening of wells and electrification of wells. The CMHO is instructed to check the spreading any disease. Free dry wood is made available for the cremation of dead animals.

We have also taken assistance of voluntary organisations, NGOs and other generous people to help the affected people. The situation is under control, yet lot of fund is needed to help the affected people. We need at least 150 crores rupees to start relief work in a proper manner.

Please arrange the necessary funds, so that the situation caused due to the drought may be checked effectively.

Piyush Dixit 28th Aug, 20....

District Collector

(13) ***As a newspaper correspondent of a national daily, write a report for your paper on the destruction caused by flood and the relief measures have been taken by the administration.***

The Editor,
Indian Express,
Bahadur Shah Zafar Marg,
New Delhi–110002

Sir,

I hereby submit to you a report on the flood situation in district Ropar of Haryana. Floods have become a common feature in our country during rainy season. This time it has affected many areas of Haryana, but the situation in district Ropar is the worst. Thousands of people have been rendered homeless. At least twenty-two persons are reported to have been drowned. Thousands of people have been marooned owing to heavy rainfall. One railway track is badly damaged and many roads are under knee-deep water. Property worth crores of rupees has been washed away huts/houses destroyed.

The people of the area are facing the calamity bravely. The Haryana Government is handling the situation on a war footing. The rescue and relief operations are going on in full swing. The medicines, clothes and other necessary articles are being supplied to the flood-stricken people by the Government and voluntary organizations. Many boats have been pressed into service to rescue the marooned people. The Chief Minister of Haryana is personally supervising the relief operations and he has announced an outlay of ₹ 250 crores to rehabilitate the affected people. Many voluntary organizations from neighbouring States Punjab, Rajasthan and Delhi have sent men and materials to assist the relief work. The Government has exempted the farmers from payment of land revenue and postponed the repayment of loans. The situation now appears to be quite under control though most of the areas in the district are still submerged in water. An active team of policemen and two battalion of military soldiers have been keeping round the clock vigil on strategic points. Due to active role played by the political leaders and vigilance of the Government machinery a lot of sufferings of the affected people have since mitigated. It is hoped that, in a week or so, there will be a remarkable improvement in the situation.

XYZ
Correspondent

(14) ***Imagine that you have conducted a survey of teenagers in your city and the television programmes they watch. Write a report for a newspaper about the survey, your findings and your critical remarks.***

The Editor,
The Indian Express,
New Delhi

Sir,

I have conducted a survey of TV watching teenagers about their preferences. A peculiar similarity was observed in the likings of the present teens. A few important points which are universally applicable to all the children who fall between the age of thirteen and nineteen are being discussed here under.

A few special traits and tendencies govern their minds. The teenagers generally select those T.V. programmes, which are action oriented or have love triangle. They prefer adventurous stories, serials involving love, romance and separation, detective episodes, comedy serials and some other programmes like cartoon films etc. They do not relish things of lofty and sublime nature. They enjoy funny, imaginative, romantic and tragedy items, which can make them jump and in themselves one of the heros of the serials. Some serials which show conflict with the society in the matter of love and marriage are also liked by the teenagers very much. They do not need things of intellectual nature.

I think such type of tendencies are not good for their real development. They are living in imaginations and dreams. They are being carried away by the imaginatives of the serials and unable to understand the reality of the life, of the world. They should be inspired to watch different programmes connected with political, social, religious and economic subjects. It is must for the healthy development of the teenagers. The parents should check the children and try to discuss with them and quench their querries. Something radical should be done to raise the level of teenagers thinking. Infact the parents can play a vital role in this matter.

I request you to publish this survey report in one of the columns of your leading daily and oblige.

Yours faithfully,
Rajesh Prassanna
A free lancer.

(15) ***Imagine that you have travelled by train and as a result of derailment of the train all the passengers were delayed and faced many kinds of problems. Write a report for newspaper describing the problem the passengers faced. Narrate the accidents as eye witness.***

The Editor,
The Hindustan Times,
New Delhi

Sub: *A report on Train Accident.*

Sir,

Hardly had the Meerut Shuttle travelled about 20 Kms, when suddenly its three bogies and the engine derailed about 7.15 P.M. on Saturday, the 20th December, 20.... Nine passengers were reportedly died on the spot and 85 injured, some of them were serious.

The Ghaziabad-Meerut Administration of U.P. Government started rescue and relief operations immediately. The nearby local residents helped in the rescue work. The policemen and military jawans have rushed to the place of accident. The injured were taken to Ghaziabad and Meerut hospitals where they are being given treatment. Senior Police Officers and the District Magistrate have already reached the accident site. They are personally supervising the relief work. But still the accident victims are facing a number of problems. Some dead bodies are still lying in the wreckage.The arrangement of power crane could not be made for five hours. In the hospital some patients are complaining against the lack of up-to-date facilities and prompt attention. The relatives of the seriously injured are not able to meet them. Proper arrangements of food, medicines etc, are not being made. However, the Chief Minister of U.P. is in constant touch with the local administration. He has announced a compensation of ₹ 5 lacs to next of kin of the dead and ₹ Fifty thousand for the injured. I hope that the situation will come back to normalcy within two or three days. Further developments will be communicated to you in the next despatch.

Yours sincerely
XYZ.

(16) ***You participated in an inter-college debate competition as a conteztant, organized by the Lions Club of your area, in which you spoke in favour of the motion and stood first. The topic for the debate was, "In the opinion of the house, free education upto secondary level should be the fundamental right of every Indian Child." Write a report in not more than 120 words for publication in your college magazine.***

Jaipur, 15th Aug, 20.... (From Rajdeep TDC IInd Yr. Sc.)

Yesterday an inter-college debate competition was organized by Lions Club in our college. Total twelve participants spoke in favour of the topic that free education upto the secondary level should be the fundamental right of every Indian child. Simultaneously twelve contestants spoke against the motion. Many college lecturers, students and parents were there to listen to the different ideas. I was also one of the contestants. I pleaded that without education a man is just like a devil who can disrupt the life of a nation. It is the education that ennobles our souls and remove darkness from our minds. Education is a window that opens channels to achieve the highest learning. It joins us with the master minds of other nations, whose achievements can be made use of, in the best possible way. Getting education upto secondary level should be a Fundamental Right of every child of India. The government should see that every school going child must attend the school. It is the education that provides wisdom, wealth, prosperity and what not. The audience clapped time and again when I cited many examples supporting my contentions. When the result was declared, I was adjudged as the best contestant. The function was a grand success. Chief Guest, the District Collector, exhorted the president of the Lions Club to organise such type of competitions on regular basis, as such debate opens the minds of the students and make them a good citizen.

(17) ***You are a reporter from the Times of India News service. Being an eye witness to AN-52 aircraft, which crashed near Delhi airport. Draft a report of the crash in about 150 words.***

New Delhi, 21st Sept, 20.... (By a staff reporter)

An Indian Air Force transport aircraft crashed near the upcoming Dwarka township in South-West Delhi on 21st Sept., killing 22 persons including all the 17 IAF officials and the pilot on board and injuring seven. The UK built AN-52 first hit electric wires strung across two poles, with one of its wheels breaking off after hitting a concrete structure. It burst into flames after hitting a ten-feet high boundary wall and finally crashed into an under construction DDA water tank. As per one eye witness the pilot saved the residential area by slightly changing the direction of the plane, otherwise a huge loss to the lives and the property could have taken place. The accident took place at about 7:20 A.M. Besides the IAF Men, a 60 years old mason, two children of another mason and two passerby were also killed due to the burning fuselage of the aircraft. The aircrafts' fuselage lay embedded in the water-tank with parts of its engine, wings, scattered on top of the structure. Broken wings of metal and the debris of the aircraft were spread over an area of around 500 meters around large stretches of vacant land. IAF sources said a court of inquiry has been constituted.The Government of Delhi has also ordered a judicial enquiry into the cause accident.

(18) ***You are working for Times of India as reporter. Last week, you attended a seminar on 'Pleasures of Eye-Donation', organized by the Medical Association of your district. Write a report of this seminar is not more than 120 words for publication in the Newspaper.***

New Delhi, 29th April, 20.... (By a staff reporter of Times of India)

Last week, a seminar on *'Pleasures of Eye Donation'* was organized by the Medical Association of out district at the Andrew's Community Centre on 27th April. A large number of residents attended the seminar. The President of the Association Mr J.H. Jha, stressed the need for protection of our eyes and emphasised the pleasures of Eye donation, *"We can provide eyes to the blind and the others who need eyes."* People can mention in their will that their eyes can be taken for the benefit of others after their death. It will be a great source of pleasure for the departing soul. They will provide light to the needy people. Much of our generation fail to get proper light and become prematurely blind. It is our duty to help them. Stressing the need of the eye donation the Chief guest of the function Sh. Vijay Dutta said, "*By donating eyes we can give support and light to others.*" It is said, "*Eyes are the greatest Blessings on Earth. We can help others even after our death.*" More than thousand rose to register their names for eye donation after their death. Such functions can solve the problems of blinds to a great extent.

(19) ***You are a reporter of the Hindustan Times. One day you happened to attend a seminar on 'Case for Reducing the Retirement Age in the Public Sector from 60 to 55', organised by the 'Society of Public Sector Employees'. Write a report on this seminar in not more than 100 words for publication in the Newspaper.***

New Delhi, 25th June, 20…. (From our staff reporter)

A very exhilarating seminar on reducing the retirement age in Public Sector from 60 to 55 was organizesd at Sapru House yesterday by the 'Society of Public Sector Employees'. Eminent jurists and legal experts participated in the seminar and spoke vehemently against the reduction of the retirement age and they compared the employees with the politicians who have no age limit for their retirement. They advocated that they can work with more zeal and zest,with more responsibility and sincerity than the modern youth and the politicians. On the other side government advocated that by reducing the retirement age, they will be opening avenues for unemployed youths.

The employment among the youth rather posed a greater threatening to the nation. They can never be compared with politicians as after retirement they can too join politics. It was also pleaded that this will be less costly for the exchequer to recruit new men in the Public Sector. After a heating debate, a consensus was arrived at to fix the retirement age in Public Sector to 58. The recommendations will be sent to the Government for being looked into. The society also asserts that if the Government does not agree to the consensus arrived at, the association of the public sector employees can go to the court and resort to the strikes and other direct actions in the matter.

(20) ***On International Women's Day, different women activists organized functions, seminars etc, in the capital. Being a reporter from Indian Express News Service you attended one of the programmes. Draft a report in about 150 words.***

New Delhi, 9th March, 20…. (By a staff reporter, Indian Express)

From workshops to burning of effigies of politicians and seminars to puppet shows, women activists organized a wide range of programmes in the capital to mark '*International Women's Day*' on Monday. The 'Joint Action Forum for Women' organized a seminar on 'Necessity of Women's Empowerment for the Development of the Nation', in which Union Human Resource Development Minister was the Chief Guest. Several other political leaders also graced the occasion with their presence. Most of the speakers asserted the need of passing the bill on providing Women's reservation in Parliament and State Assemblies. The minister informed that the bill on reservation had already been introduced in this budget session of Parliament and the government is trying to get the bill passed with support of the opposition.

He also informed that some political parties are opposing the bill just for the sake of opposition. The member activists exemplify the role of women in the freedom struggle and in the development of the nation. The president of the forum Mrs. Kidwai told that by giving 33 Percent reservation for women, no political party is doing any favour to the women. Women constitute 50% of the total population. A demand for free education for women upto graduation, making judiciary more quick in disposing the cases of crimes against the women was also made. Though participants expressed jubilation at the progress women have made in several fields, but the crude statistics of crime against women and low literacy among women bothered many. Many politicians stressed the need that the women and the girls should avoid invitational and inciting fashions, which resulted in the increase in the crimes against the women and girls. The necessity of moral and ethicals values was also emphasised in the education of the young generations. The seminar was a grand success.

(21) ***Pollution has become a problem for all. Write an article on Environmental Pollution in Metropolitan cities. Suppose you are a correspondent of a local newspaper.***

Environmental Pollution in Big Cities

New Delhi, 15th Feb, 20…. (By a correspondent)

Preservation of environment is one of the most alarming problem of today. Most of the big cities are suffering from the problem of conservation and preservation of purity of environment. Our atmosphere is being polluted by various factors like smoke, noise, dirt, dust, chemicals and gases. Even water has become polluted. We need a safer and healthy environment for our survival and for the survival of the young generation. Water, air and food are the basic necessities of life that all are becoming polluted day-by-day. The rapid industrializsation has made everything polluted, no care has been placed for the safe drainage of the chemical wastes, safe exhaling of the gases. The nature has provided a very balanced and correct system for our survival. For example we inhale oxygen and exhale carbon-di-oxide. This carbon gas is absorbed by plants. Still we need care to preserve our environment.

The recent decisions and directions of the Supreme Court that the vehicles run by the CNG should replace the vehicles run by the petrol and diesels is very important in keeping the air pure and inhalable in big cities. We as a member of the civic society should also not spoil it by spreading unhygienic items, *e.g.*, garbage and rubbish that produce foul smell. We can save our atmosphere by applying and paying careful attention for their proper disposal. It will help us in stopping the spread of dangerous diseases and pollution of the atmosphere. So, it is sacred duty of all to preserve our environment for our survival. We should also adopt the motto. '*Keep clean and Remain clean.*'

(22) ***English is a link language and opens a gateway to knowledge. Write a case on 'Importance of English in Education'. Write your description in about 100 words.***

Importance of English in Education

Meerut, 26th Jan, 20…. (From special correspondent)

India became free 15 August, 1947. The Britishers ruled over India, they left their imprint on us. Since, then English forms an important part of our educational system. All the technical, medical and professional courses are taught in English. The literature of these subjects are available in great abundance written in English. Without English our education seems to remain incomplete. It has opened a way to see the world in its entirety. It has become a universal language. In every country, we find people speaking, talking and understanding English. In reality, English has become a link language and we cannot do without it. It paves our way to understand the culture, customs and other activities of different nations. In this period of globalization it is, but necessary to learn writing and speaking good and correct English.

(23) ***'Drug Addiction' has become great menace against the society. Write an article for your college magazine on Drug Addiction in about 100 words.***

Drug Addiction

Mumbai, 15th March, 20…. (By Kapil Nagar)

The word 'addiction' implies to be habitual to something and it is generally applicable in bad sense. Of course, addiction to anything is bad, but drug addiction is the worst of all. The modern scientific research has proved the harmful effects of regular use of a particular drug. It not only damages our digestive system, but also spoils our nervous system. In reality it is a breeder and an invitation to death. It is a slow poison, degrades one to the lowest level. All our energy and vitality is sucked like a bacteria sucks our blood. The user becomes hollow just like a coconut. The addict person loses his moral values and to get the drug he can commit any crime like theft, dacoity, even the murder. He cannot do any thing properly, can't work, can't rest, can't play, even can't sleep without taking drugs. Addiction to smoking, wine, smack, hashish and heroine distort the mental ability, agility, confidence, propriety of any decision of a drug addict. We should avoid use of such narcotics.

(24) ***As the correspondent of a local daily, write a report for the paper on need of vocational education in India.***

Vocational Education

Hisar, 30th April, 20…. (From Local Correspondent)

The Britishers provided us a very outdated and defective system of education. That system produces clerks and white collar job-seekers. India is facing a great problem of educated unemployment because of this educational system. After Independence many changes have taken place in our educational system.

The Kothari and Chattopadhaya Commissions have strongly recommended for the vocationalization of education. Many vocational schools or colleges find place in our society. Vocational Education helps us in controlling unemployment. Above all, vocational education gives us a sense of dignity of labour. We can stand on our foot without feeling any work ignoble. It is a high time that Government and our society should come forward to open more and more such vocational institutions, so that the youth do not feel frustrated after completion their studies and get employment or can start their own ventures.

(25) ***You are correspondent of a local daily, you find very unhealthy craze among the students for the foreign goods. Write an article for a newspaper in about 100 words.***

Craze for Foreign Goods

Chandigarh, 12th May, 20….

(From Local Correspondent)

A general tendency is now-a-days seen among the students that they are attracted by foreign goods, whether good or bad, but whatever they purchase should be originated from a foreign country. This idea never enters into our brains that Indian goods are not in any way inferior. We have advanced to such an extent that many items are being exported by us. Our goods are of the superb quality. Still we have a sensation to buy a foreign make. We are admired in construction, utility and acclaim its worth. In some of the cases, even our manufactured items are labelled as made in foreign, *e.g.*, Japan, England and Germany etc. We never try to examine its worth, utility and consumption. Gone are the days when even from the smallest needle to the highest implement was imported from England or USA. This led to a habit of liking for the foreign goods. It is also a worth mentioning fact that foreigners do not like to purchase foreign goods. They believe in purchasing their own national goods. Let us come forward and initiate steps to buy own *Swadeshi* goods. Consuming goods made in our own country saves very precious foreign exchange.

Look at the following Original Reports taken from a Newspaper :

Economic Times, dated 4th Jan, 20….

Sensex Rise Makes MF Investors Junk Debt

Mumbai, 4th January

Financial Correspondent

Equity culture is making deeper inroads due to the rising sensex. Mutual fund investors who have been traditional debt schemes takers are opting for the riskier equity oriented schemes to crash into the sensex party, Puja Mehra reports from New Delhi. Historically, MF investors in India have had a huge debt bias. Total share of assets under management in equities, however, has grown gradually, but steadily, over the past few months. As per latest data, the share of assets deployed in equities has risen to 21.6% against 16.0% in 03. Significantly, the jump in the equity share has come despite the blow of net outflows from existing equity schemes. These schemes suffered heavy redemption pressures from investors booking profits. Investor preference for equities, however, is most visible in subscriptions to new equity schemes launched by domestic funds.

Economic Times, dated 04-01-20….

SC Notice to Government on Soft Drink PIL

Our Delhi Bureau

New Delhi, 3rd January

The Supreme Court today stepped up pressure on the government to review the contents of soft drinks marketed in the country. The court issued a notice to the Centre on a petition seeking a thorough examination of the contents of soft drinks on the ground that they pose 'health hazards'. This follows the court's observation earlier last month when it dismissed petition filed by soft drink makers Pepsi and Cocacola, challenging a Rajasthan High Court order asking them to print on containers, the extent of pesticide residues in their products.

In its latest salvo, a Bench comprising Chief justice R.C. Lahoti and justice G.P. Mathur issued the notice on a petition by the Centre for Public Interest Litigation (CPIL) alleging that the government, which has a duty to protect the life of citizens, has not taken any initiative in this regard despite several researches finding soft drink contents to be harmful, especially for children. The petitioner requested the court to direct the Centre to constitute an expert technical committee to evaluate the harmful effects of soft drinks on human health, particularly children and put in place a regulatory regime to control and check the contents of particular chemical additives in foods and soft drinks. It also requested the court to make it mandatory for soft drink manufacturers to disclose the contents and the quality of their products including appropriate warning about ingredients and their harmful effects.

Economic Times, 31st Dec 20….

Fresh Tsunami Fear Causes Alert

Chennai, 30th December

Fresh panic swept the Tsunami ravaged coasts of southern India as the government today issued a high alert against more titanic waves a possible quake near Australia could generate. The warning issued after an emergency meeting of the home ministry's crisis management team, triggered fresh fears as the already traumatised people along the southern and south-eastern coastline scurried for safe ground. The warning was flashed through television, whereby the administration asked the people to vacate their homes in the more vulnerable villages.

In some areas, loudspeakers were also used to relay the alert. But, despite the warnings, Prime Minister Manmohan Singh's aides said he was not cutting short his tour of the affected areas. All coastal states and union territories, especially the worst hit Tamil Nadu and the Andaman and Nicobar Islands, were asked be on the highest alert for the next 48 hours for tidal waves hitting Indian coasts. This is barely four days after Sunday's giant waves generated by a huge undersea quake off Sumatra ravaged seven South and South-East Asian nations including India and swallowed up large tracts of coast claiming at least 60,000 lives. Amid experts fears of an ominous tectonic sea bed shift around Australia, heightened sea turbulence was being reported from the 1,000 km.

East Coast of Tamil Nadu and people were being warned to keep off the shore. Choppy conditions and sea incursions of upto 10 metres have been reported Thursday morning from the Thiruvanmiyur Beach in South Chennai and rough sea has been reported also at Chennai's Marina beach. Large ripples were said to be hitting the Kalpakkam and Cuddalore coast once again besides the Kanyakumari coast. Based on inputs from experts and weather-men, the home ministry directed immediate evacuation of people to safer places and all shorelines to be made in accessible to the public.

Economic Times, 30 Dec, 20….

NC Leader among 9 Killed in Valley

Masood Hussain

Srinagar, 29th December

In a sudden escalation in violence, militants killed a National Conference (NC) leader in old city. Another incidents claimed eight lives including that of a soldier in other areas of the Stsgate. Police said they have busted a number of hideouts in border Poonch-Rajouri region where a few militants were also killed. Police said unidentified militants shot dead Farooq Ahmad Zargar, provincial president of the Youth NC in old city's Kawdara locality around noon. Massive protests were reported from South Kashmir Tral township after reports of soldiers raining bullets on a passenger bus spread like wild fire. Residents resorted to brick-bating and damaged many government buildings and vehicles. Details revealed that when Rashtriya Rifles-42 stopped a Srinagar bound passenger bus in Lalgam village in Tral, a militant alighted from the bus and shot at one of the soldiers.

This led to an encounter, in which three passengers and the militant were killed. Four other commuters received serious bullet injuries and they were admitted to hospitals. Some of them are stated to be critical. Police said the slain militant Abdul Rashid Bhat was a Hizb-ul Mujahideen cadre who was set free after two years detention in October last. Defence spokesman Lt. Col. V.K. Batra said, the soldiers were attacked by the militant who was killed in retaliatory fire. Asked about civilian casualties, the spokesman said it was actually a BSF party that was passing througsh and opened fire on the bus.

However, a BSF spokesman said their party reached around 30 minutes after the incident had taken place. A fierce gun battle was killed and a soldier was wounded. In Sopore, militants shot dead a BSF man Anuraj Kumar near the local bus stand and fled with his rifle. A hitherto unknown outfit Al-Khandak has staked the claim for the attack. Reports from Jammu said police recovered the corpse of civilian Ali Mohammed whom militants had kidnapped a day earlier from Sarwara belt in Rajouri. In neighbouring Darhal belt, soldiers killed a militant whose identity was not immediately known.

Economic Times, 30th Dec, 20….

More Hooch Victims Pour in Hospitals

Our Political Bureau

Mumbai, 29th December

Municipal hospitals across Mumbai continue to register more casualties in the Hooch tragedy. The toll from the spurious liquor tragedy in suburban Vikroli along has mounted to 65 with seven more persons succumbing to the lethal drink. The condition of a majority of the over 80 people undergoing treatment is reported to be serious. Of the 174 affected individuals admitted to the Rajawadi hospital in Ghatkopar, 49 succumbed to internal haemorrhage caused by the spurious liquor. "Ten persons were brought dead", said hospital dean Dr. V.B. Shukla. In Sion hospital, six of the 34 persons admitted died, hospital sources said. Over 80 people are still under going treatment in the hospitals, while some have been discharged.

Taking stern action against the erring officials the State Government on Tuesday suspended 27 officials including five from the excise department and 22 policemen. The Police also arrested 24 persons in neighbouring Thane and Nhava Sheva for their alleged involvement in the illicit liquor trade. Taking a serious note of the tragedy, the Maharashtra Government today decided to hand over the probe into the spurious liquor tragedy, to the CID,

"The CID will conduct a thorough probe into the illicit liquor tragedy, once the present probe being handled by an officer of the rank of Additional Police Commissioner is completed", State Deputy Chief Minister R.R. Patil, who also holds the home portfolio. Following the twin Hooch tragedy, massive raids have been conducted over the last two days at various places in Navi Mumbai, Raigad and Thane said the deputy CM. He said, that a large stock of illegal liquor had been destroyed. He attributed the tragedy to the small number of licenced liquor shops and availability of cheaper illegal liquor.

Interestingly, the proposal to legalise bootleggers, by offering them country liquor licences was raised during the winter session in Nagpur. However, it is believed that the political parties were divided on this front, which is why the subject was not brought up for discussion at the cabinet meeting today. The Deputy CM also gave a clean chit to city police chief A.N. Roy, whose transfer was sought by opposition leader Narayan Rane holding him responsible for the incidents. "The Police Commissioner had directed police officials to take precautionary measures", said Patil.

CHAPTER

69

COMPREHENSION

What is a Comprehension?

Comprehension का अर्थ है Ability of understanding, समझने की योग्यता या समझ। Comprehension का उद्देश्य न केवल छात्र को Passage समझने की योग्यता का आंकलन करना होता है बल्कि उसकी Vocabulary एवं passage को समझकर दिए गए प्रश्नों का सही, सटीक उत्तर देने की योग्यता को भी जाँचना होता है।

विभिन्न Competitive Examinations के प्रश्न-पत्र में Comprehension का समावेश होता है। Comprehension (Passage) में प्रयुक्त शब्दों के आधार पर हम Comprehension को (i) Lengthy Passage (ii) Short Passage में विभक्त कर सकते हैं।

Lengthy Passage में लगभग 2000 Words होते हैं। जबकि Short Passage में 200 से 400 Words होते हैं।

Comprehension से सम्बन्धित प्रश्नों मे Descriptive एवं Objective दोनों प्रकार के प्रश्न पूछे जाते हैं। कुछ Competitive examinations में पूछे गए Descriptive प्रश्नों का उत्तर Comprehension में से ही उसे ध्यानपूर्वक पढ़कर देना होता है। Objective प्रश्नों में, प्रश्न में ही दिए गए चार-पाँच उत्तरों में से, एक को चुनना होता है। Comprehension में Vocabulary से सम्बन्धित प्रश्न जैसे: Synonym or Antonym भी आते हैं। कई बार Comprehension में प्रयुक्त Idioms, Verbal Phrases का भी अर्थ पूछा जाता है। वस्तु : Comprehension का उद्देश्य छात्र की अंग्रेजी भाषा को न केवल पढ़ने/समझने की योग्यता/क्षमता का आंकलन करना है बल्कि छात्र की Idioms, Vocabulary, Phrasal verbs इत्यादि की Knowledge की जाँच करना भी है।

How to Attempt the Comprehension?

बहुत से महत्त्वपूर्ण Competitive Examinations जैसे: CAT, GMAT, Management Courses, Bank Probationary Officers इत्यादि के प्रश्न-पत्रों में 3 से 5 Passages का समावेश होता है। इस तरह की परीक्षा में समय का अभाव होता है एवं छात्रों द्वारा बहुत Speed से प्रश्न हल करने के बावजूद भी वे प्रश्न-पत्र को पूरा हल नहीं कर पाते हैं।

Some Tips to Score Maximum Marks

(A) सर्वप्रथम Passage से सम्बन्धित प्रश्नों को Speedily पढ़ें, फिर Passage को Speedily पढ़ना शुरू करें। जैसे ही किसी प्रश्न का उत्तर दिखाई दे, उस भाग को पुन: पढ़कर प्रश्न का उत्तर देना चाहिए। यह **Technique उस स्थिति में अपनानी चाहिए जब आपके पास समय का अभाव है, एवं कम समय में अधिकांश प्रश्नों के उत्तर देना है।** इस तरह अच्छे अंक प्राप्त करने हेतु छात्र की Passage पढ़ने की अच्छी Speed एवं अच्छी Vocabulary एवं अच्छी Analytical Power की आवश्यकता होती है।

(B) यदि छात्र के पास **comprehension को पढ़ने का पर्याप्त समय है तो बिन्दु (A) में बताई गई Technique उपयुक्त नहीं है।** ऐसी स्थिति में निम्न Technique छात्र को अच्छे marks प्राप्त करने में सहायक होगी :

(1) सर्वप्रथम छात्र को एक बार पूरे Passage को पढ़ना चाहिए, साथ ही पूछे गए प्रश्नों को भी पढ़ लेना चाहिए। पुन: छात्र को इस Passage को पढ़ना चाहिए एवं पूछे गए प्रश्नों के अनुसार Passage में जहाँ-जहाँ प्रश्नों के उत्तर हैं वहाँ numbering कर लेनी चाहिए।

(2) दो बार पढ़ने से Passage की theme, idea का पता लग जाता है। यदि दो बार में भी Passage समझ में नहीं आता तो तीसरी बार पुन: पढ़ें।

(3) अब प्रश्नों का उत्तर देना शुरू करें। आपने Questions के आधार पर Passage में Numbering कर ली है। इस portion को पुन: पढ़कर अपना answer जहाँ तक सम्भव हो, अपने शब्दों में लिखने का प्रयास करें। यदि answer देने हेतु कोई शब्द सीमा दी गई है तो उसका ध्यान रखना चाहिए।

(4) Answer कभी भी Because या Therefore से शुरू नहीं करना चाहिए। Answer बहुत लम्बा भी नहीं लिखा जाना चाहिए, irrelevant बातों को avoid करें।

(5) ध्यान रखें प्रश्न का उत्तर Passage से ही देना है अपने ideas, opinion नहीं देनी चाहिए।

(6) Answer grammatically correct तथा to the point होना चाहिए।

(7) कई बार Comprehension में Verbal phrases या words दिए जाते हैं उसे explain करने को कहा जाता है या meaning पूछा जाता है। ध्यान रखें इसके लिए न केवल अच्छी Vocabulary की आवश्यकता है बल्कि आपकी Expression power भी अच्छी होनी चाहिए। ऐसे प्रश्नों का उत्तर, Simple भाषा में न बहुत लम्बा न बहुत छोटा दिया जाता है। Answers में Grammatical errors न हो, इसका ख्याल रखें यदि Phrase को explain करना कठिन महसूस हो तो आप अन्य उदाहरण देकर अपने उत्तर को स्पष्ट कर सकते हैं।

Short Passages

कई Competitive examinations में Short Passage करीब 200-400 Words के आते हैं। इन Passages द्वारा छात्र की अंग्रेजी समझने की योग्यता, power of analysing the things properly एवं Passage को पढ़कर, पूछे गए प्रश्नों का सही एवं सटीक उत्तर देने की योग्यता का मूल्यांकन किया जाता है। इस तरह के Passage में प्रयुक्त Phrases, Idioms का अर्थ भी कई बार पूछा जाता है तथा कई बार Passage का Title या Theme of the passage भी पूछा जाता है। Descriptive प्रश्नों का उत्तर Passage के आधार पर लिखना चाहिए तथा Objective प्रश्नों का उत्तर, प्रश्नों में दिए गए Alternative Answers में से चुनना होता है।

"Comprehension judges your capability and ability of understanding the passage, your power of analysing the problem in proper perspective and your ability of presenting your answers systematically".

Examples

Directions for Questions : *Each of the passages given below is followed by a set of questions choose the best answer to each question.* **[CAT November 2014]**

Passage I

The painter is now free to paint anything he chooses. There are scarcely any forbidden subjects and today everybody is prepared to admit that a painting of some fruit can be as important as painting of a hero. The impressionists did as much as anybody to win this previously unheard of freedom for the artist. Yet, by the next generation, painters began to abandon the subject altogether, and began to paint abstract pictures. Today, the majority of pictures painted are abstract.

Is there a connection between these two developments? Has art gone abstract because the artist is embarrassed by his freedom. Is it that, because he is free to paint anything, he doesn't know what to paint? Apologists for abstract art often talk of it as the art of maximum freedom . But could this be the freedom of the desert island? It would take too long to answer these questions properly. I believe, there is a connection. Many things have encouraged the development of abstract art. Among them has been the artists' wish to avoid the difficulties of finding subjects when all subjects are equally possible.

I raise the matter now because I want to draw attention to the fact that the painter's choice of a subject is a far more complicated question than it would at first seem. A subject does not start with what is put in front of the easel or with something which the painter happens to remember. A subject starts with the painter deciding he would like to paint such-and-such because for some reason or other he finds it meaningful. A subject begins when the artist selects something for special mention. (What makes it special or meaningful may seem to the artist to be purely visual its colours or its form.) When the subject has been selected, the function of the painting itself is to communicate and justify the significance of that selection.

It is often said today that subject matter is unimportant. But this is only a reaction against the excessively literary and moralistic interpretation of subject matter in the 19th century. In truth, the subject is literally the beginning and end of a painting. The painting begins with a selection (I will paint this and not everything else in the world); it is finished when that selection is justified (now you can see all that I saw and felt in this and how it is more than merely itself).

Thus, for a painting to succeed it is essential that the painter and his public agree to succ~ed it is essential that the painter and his public agree about what is significant. The subject may have a personal meaning for the painter or individual spectator, but there must also be the possibility of their agreement on its general meaning. It is at this point that the culture of the society and period in question precedes the artist and his art. Renaissance art would have meant nothing to the Aztecs and vice-versa. If, to some extent, a few intellectuals can appreciate them both today it is because their culture is an historical one: its inspiration is history and therefore it can include within itself, in principle if not in every particular, all known development to date.

When a culture is secure and certain of its values, it presents its artists with subjects. The general agreement about what is significant is so well established that the significance of particular subject accrues and becomes traditional. This is true, for instance of reeds and water in China, of the nude body in Renaissance, of the animal in Africa. Furthermore, in such cultures the artist is unlikely to be a free agent he will be employed, for the sake of particular subjects and problem, as we have just described it will not occur to him.

When a culture is in a state of disintegration or transition the freedom of the artist increases, but the question of subject matter becomes problematic for him has to choose for society. This was the basic of all the increasing crises in European art during the 19th century. It is often forgotten how many of the art scandals of the time were provoked by the choice of subject (Gericault, Courbet, Daumier, Degas, Lautrec, Van Gogh, etc).

By the end of the 19th century, there were roughly speaking two ways, in which the painter could meet this challenge of deciding what to paint and so choosing for society. Either the identified himself with the people and so allowed their lives to dictate his subjects to him; or he had to find his subjects within himself as painter. By people I mean everybody except the bourgeoisie. Many painter did, of course, work for the bourgeoisie according to their copy-book of approved subjects, but all of them filling the Salon and the Royal Academy year after year and now forgotten, buried the hypocrisy of those they served so sincerely.

(1) *In the sentence, 'I believe there is a connection'(second paragraph), what two developments is the author referring of?*

(a) Painters using dying hero and using a fruit as a subject of painting

(b) Growing success of painters and an increase in abstract forms

(c) Artists gaining freedom to choose subjects and abandoning subjects altogether

(d) Rise of impressionists and an increase in abstract forms

(2) *When a culture is insecure, the painter chooses his subject on the basis of* :
(a) the prevalent style in the society of his time (b) it is meaningfulness to the painter
(c) what is put no front of the easel (d) past experience and memory of the painter

(3) *In the context of the passage, which of the following statements would not be true?*
(a) Painters decided subjects based on what they remembered from their own lives
(b) Painters of reeds and water in China faced on serious problem of choosing a subject
(c) The choice of subject was a source of scandals in 19th century European art
(d) Agreement on the general meaning of a painting is influenced by culture and historical context

(4) *Which of the following views is taken by the author?*
(a) The more insecure a culture, the greater the freedom of the artist
(b) The more secure a culture, the greater the freedom of the artist
(c) The more secure a culture, more difficult the choice of subject
(d) The more insecure a culture, the less significant the choice of the subject

(5) *Which of the following is not necessarily among the attributes needed for a painter to succeed?*
(a) The painter and his public agree on what is significant
(b) The painting is able to communicate and justify the significance of its subjects selection
(c) The subject has a personal meaning for the painter
(d) The painting of subjects is inspired by historical developments

Answers : **1.** (a), **2.** (c), **3.** (c), **4.** (a), **5.** (a).

Passage II

Recently I spent several hours sitting under a tree in my garden with the social anthropologist William Ury, a Harward University professor who specialises in the art of negotiation and wrote the best selling book, *Getting to Yes*. He captivated me with his theory that tribalism protects people from their fear of rapid change. He explained that the pillars of tribalism that humans rely on for security would always counter any significant cultural or social change.

In this way, he said, change is never allowed to happen too fast. Technology, for example is a pillar of society. Ury believes that every time technology moves in a new or radical direction another pillar such as religion or nationalism will grow stronger-in effect, the traditional and familiar will assume greater importance to compensate for the new and untested. In this manner, human tribes avoid rapid change that leaves people insecure and frightened.

But we have all heard that nothing is as permanent as change. Nothing is guaranteed. Pithy expressions, to be sure, but no more than cliches. As Ury says, "people don't live that way from day-to-day. On the contrary, they actively seek certainty and stability. They want to know they will be safe. "

Even so we scare ourselves constantly with the idea of change. An IBMCEO once said "We only restructure for a good reason, and if we haven't restructured in a while, that's a good reason. We are scared that competitors technology, and the consumer will put us out of business so we have to change all the time just to stay alive. But if we asked our fathers and grandfathers, would they have said that they lived in a period of little change? Structure may not have changed much. It may just be the speed with which we do things. "

Change is over-rated, anyway, consider the automobile. It's an especially valuable example, because the auto industry has spent tens of billions of dollars on research and product development in the last 100 years. Henry Ford's first car had a metal chassis with an internal combustion, gasoline-powered engine, four wheels with rubber tyres, a foot operated clutch assembly and brake system, a steering wheel and four seats and it could safely do 18 miles per hour.

A hundred years and tens of thousands of research hours later we drive cars with a metal chassis with an internal combustion gasoline-powered engine, four wheels with rubber tyres, a foot operated clutch assembly and brake system, a steering wheel, four seats and the average speed in London in 2001 was 17. 5 miles per hour !

That's not a hell of a lot of return for the money. Ford evidently doesn't have much to teach us about change. The fact that they're still manufacturing cars is not proof that Ford Motor Co. is a sound organization, just proof that it takes very large companies to make cars in great quantities—making for an almost impregnable entry barrier. Fifty years after the development of the jet engine, planes are also little changed. They've grown bigger, wider and can carry more people. But those are incremental, largely cosmetic changes.

Taken together, this lack of real change has come to mean that in travel—whether driving or flying—time and technology have not combined to make things much better. The safety and design have, of course, accompanied the times and the new volume of cars and flights, but nothing of any significance has changed in the basic assumptions of the final product.

At the same time, moving around in cars or aeroplanes becomes less and less efficient all the time. Not only has there been no great change but also both forms of transport have deteriorated as more people clamour to use them. The same is true for telephones, which took over hundred years to become mobile or photographic film which also required an entire century to change.

The only explanation for this is anthropological, once established in calcified organizations humans do two things: sabotage changes that might render people dispensable and ensure industry-wide emulation. In the 1960s, German auto companies developed plans to scrap the entire combustion engine for an electrical design. (The same existed in the 1970s in Japan and in the 1980s in France) So for 40 years we might have been free of the wasteful and ludicrous dependence on fossil fuels. Why didn't it go anywhere? Because auto executives understood pistons and carburettors, and would be loath to cannibalise their expertise, alongwith most of their factories.

(1) *Which of the following views does the author fully support in the passage?*
(a) Nothing is as permanent as change
(b) Change is always rapid
(c) More money spent on innovation leads to more rapid change
(d) Over decades structural change has been incremental

(2) *According to the passage, which of the following statements is true?*
(a) Executives of automobile companies are inefficient and ludicrous
(b) The speed at which an automobile is driven in a city has not changed much in a century
(c) Anthropological factors have fostered innovation in automobiles by promoting use of new technologies
(d) Further innovation in jet engines has been more than incremental

(3) *Which of the following best describes one of the main ideas discussed in the passage?*
(a) Rapid change is usually welcomed in society
(b) Industry is not as innovative as it is made out to be
(c) We should have less change than what we have now
(d) Competition spurs companies into radical innovation

(4) *According to the passage, the reason why we continued to be dependent on fossil fuels is that* :
(a) auto executives did not wish to change
(b) no alternative fuels were discovered
(c) change in technology was not easily possible
(d) German, Japanese and French companies could not come up with new technologies

Answers : **(1)** (b), **(2)** (d), **(3)** (b), **(4)** (a).

Passage III

Fifty feet away three male lions lay by the road. They didn't appear to have a hair on their heads. Nothing the colour of their noses (leonine noses darken as they age, from pink to black), Craig estimated that they were six years old-young adults. "This is wonderful!" he said, after staring at them for several moments. "This is what we came to see. They really are maneless." Craig, a professor at the University of Minnesota, is arguably the leading expert on the majestic Serengeti lion, whose head is mantled in long, thick hair. He and Peyton West, a doctoral student who has been working with him in Tanzania, had never seen the Tsavo lions that live some 200 miles East of the Serengeti. The scientists had partly suspected that the maneless males were adolescents mistaken for adults by amateur observes. Now they knew better.

The Tasvo research expedition was mostly Peyton's was mostly Peyton's show. She had spent several years in Tanzania compiling the data she needed to answer a question that ought to have been answered long ago: why do lions have manes? It's the only cat, wild or domestic, that displays such ornamentation. In Tsavo she was attacking the riddle from the opposite angle. Why do its lions not have manes? (Some ''maneless'' lions in Tsavo East do have partial manes but they rarely attain the real glory of the Serengeti lions'.) Does environmental adaptation account for the trait? Are the lions of Tsavo, as some people believe, a distinct subspecies of their Serengeti cousins?

The Serengeti lions have been under continuous observation for more than 35 years, beginning with George Schaller's pioneering work in the 1960s. But the lions in Tsavo, Kenya's oldest and largest protected ecosystem have hardly been studied. Consequently legends have grown up around them. Not only do they took different; according to the myths, they behave differently, displaying greater cunning and aggressiveness. "Remember too," Kenya: The Rough Guide warns, "Tsavo's lions have a reputation of ferocity." Their fearsome image became well-known in 1898, when to males stalled construction of what is now Kenya Railways by allegedly killing and eating 135 Indian and African labourers. A British Army officer incharge of building a railroad bridge over the Tasavo River, Lt. Col. J. H. Peterson, spent nine months pursuing the pair before he brought them to bay and killed them. Stuffed and mounted, they now glare at visitors to the Field Museum in Chicago. Petterson's account of the leonine reign of terror, the Man-Eaters of Tsavo, was an international best-seller when published in 1907. Still in print the book has made Tsavo's lions notorious. That annoys some scientists.

"People don't want to give up on mythology. "Dennis King me one day.'' The zoologist has been working in Tasvo off and on for four years. "I am so sick of this man-eater business. Petterson made a helluva lot of money off that story, but Tsavo's lions are no more likely to turn man-eater than lions from elsewhere."

But tales of their savagery and wiliness don't all come from sensationalist authors looking to make a buck. Tsavo lions are generally larger than lions elsewhere, enabling them to take down the predominant prey animal in Tsavo, the Cape buffalo one of the strongest, most aggressive animals of Earth. The buffalo don't give up easily: They often kill or severely injure an attacking lion, and a wounded lion might be more likely to turn to cattle and humans for food. And other prey is less abundant in Tsavo than in other traditional lion haunts. A hungry lion is more likely to attack humans. Safari guides and Kenya Wildlife Service rangers tell of lions attacking Land Rovers, raiding camps, stalking tourists. Tsavo is a tough neighbourhood, they say and it breeds tougher lions.

But are they really tougher? And if so, is there any connection between their manelessness and their ferocity? An intriguing hypothesis was advanced two years ago by Gnoske and Peterhans. Tsavo lions may be similar to the unmaned cave lions of the Pleistocene. The Serengeti variety is among the most evolved of the species—the latest model, so to speak—while certain morphological differences in Tsavo lions (bigger bodies, smaller skills and may be even lack of a mane) suggest that they are closer to primitive ancestor of all lions. Craig and Peyton had serious doubts about this idea, but admitted that Tsavo lions pose a mystery to science.

(1) *The sentence which concludes the first paragraph. ''Now they knew better'', implies that :*

(a) the two scientists were struck by wonder on seeing maneless lions for the first time
(b) though Craig was an expert on the Serengeti lion, now he also new about the Tsavo lions
(c) earlier, Craig and West thought that amateur observers had been mistaken
(d) Craig was now able to confirm that darkening of the noses as lionsaged applied to Tsavo lions as well

(2) *The book 'Man-Eaters' of Tsavo annoys some scientists because :*

(a) it revealed that Tsavo lions are ferocious
(b) Petterson made a helluva lot of money from the book by sensationalism
(c) it perpetuated the bad name Tsavo lions had
(d) it narrated how to male Tsavo lion were killed

(3) *Which of the following, if true, would weaken the hypothesis advanced by Gnosake and Peterhans most?*

(a) Craig and Peyton develop even more serious doubts about the idea that Tsavo lions are primitive
(b) The maneless Tsavo East lions are shown to be closer to the cavelions
(c) Pleistocene cave lions are shown to be far less violent than believed
(d) The morphological variations in body and skull size between the cave and Tsavo lions are found to be insignificant

(4) *According to the passage, which of the following has not contributed to the popular image of Tsavo lions as savage creatures?*

(a) Tsavo lions have been observed to bring down one of the strongest and most aggressive animals-the Cape buffalo
(b) In contrast to the situation in traditional lion haunts, scarcity of non-buffalo prey in the Tsavo makes the Tsavo lions more aggressive
(c) The Tsavo lion is considered to be less evolved than the Serengeti variety
(d) Tsavo lions have been observed to attack vehicles as well as humans

Answers : **1.** (a), **2.** (c), **3.** (d), **4.** (d).

Passage IV

Throughout human history the leading causes of death have been infection and trauma. Modern medicine has scored significant victories against both, and the major causes of ill health and death are now the chronic degenerative diseases, such as coronary artery disease, arthritis, osteoporosis, Alzheimer's, muscular degeneration, cataract and cancer. These have a long latency period before symptoms appear and a diagnosis is made. It follows that the majority of apparently healthy people are pre-ill.

But are these conditions inevitably degenerative? A truly preventive medicine that focused on the pre-ill, analysing the metabolic errors which lead to clinical illness, might be able to correct them before the first symptom. Genetic risk factors are known for all the chronic degenerative diseases, and are important to the individuals who possess them. At the population level, however, migration studies confirm that these illness are linked for the most part to lifestyle factors—exercise, smoking and nutrition. Nutrition is the easiest of these to change, and the most versatile tool for affecting the metabolic changes needed to till the balance away from disease.

Many national surveys reveal that malnutrition is common in developed countries. This is not the calorie and/or micronutrient deficiency associated with developing nations (Type A malnutrition): but multiple micronutrient depletion, usually combined with calorific balance or excess (Type B malnutrition) . The incidence and severity of Type B malnutrition will be shown to be worse if never micronutrient groups such as the essential fatty acids, xanthophylls and flavonoids are included in the surveys. Commonly ingested levels of these micronutrients seem to be far too low in many developed countries.

There is now considerable evidence that Type B malnutrition is a major cause of chronic degenerative diseases. If this is the case, then it is logical to treat such diseases not with drugs but with multiple micronutrient repletion, or pharmaco-nutrition'. This can take the form of pills and capsules—'nutraceuticals', or food formats known as functional foods'.

This approach has been neglected hitherto because it is relatively unprofitable for drug companies—the products are hard to patent—and it is a strategy which does not sit easily with modern medical interventionism. Over the last 100 years, the drug industry has invested huge sums in developing a range of subtle and powerful drugs to treat the many diseases we are subject to Medical training is couched in pharmaceutical terms and this approach has provided us with an exceptional range of therapeutic tools in the treatment of disease and in acute medical emergencies.

However, the pharmaceutical model has also created an unhealthy dependency culture, in which relatively few of us accept responsibility for maintaining our own health. Instead, we have handed over this responsibility to health professionals who know very little about health maintenance or disease prevention.

One problem for supporters of this argument is lack of the right kind of hard evidence. We have a wealth of epidemiological data linking dietary factors to health profiles/disease risks, and a great deal of information on mechanism: how food factors interact with our biochemistry. But almost all intervention studies with micronutrients, with the notable exception of the omega 3 fatty acids, have so far produced conflicting or negative results. In other words, our science appears to have no predictive value. Does this invalidate the science? Or are we simply asking the wrong questions?

Based on pharmaceutical thinking, most intervention studies have attempted to measure the impact of a single micronutrient on the incidence of disease. The classical approach says that if you give a compound formula to test subjects and obtain positive results, you cannot know which ingredient is exerting the benefit, so you must test each ingredient individually. But in the field of nutrition, this does not work. Each intervention on its own will hardly make enough difference to be measured. The best therapeutic response must, therefore, combine micronutrients to normalise our internal physiology.

So do we need to analyse each individual's nutritional status and then tailor a formula specifically for him or her? While we do not have the resources to analyse millions of individual cases, there is no need to do so. The vast majority of people are consuming suboptimal amounts of most micronutrients, and most of the micronutrients concerned are very safe. Accordingly, a comprehensive and universal program of micronutrient support is probably the most cost-effective and safest way of improving the general health of the nation. **[CAT November 2004]**

(1) *Tailoring micronutrient-based treatment plans to suit individual deficiency profiles is not necessary because* :

(a) it very likely to give inconsistent or negative results
(b) it is a classic pharmaceutical approach not suited to micronutrients
(c) most people are consuming suboptimal amounts of safe-to-consume micronutrients
(d) it is not cost effective to do so

(2) *The author recommends micronutrient-repletion for large-scale treatment of chronic degenerative diseases because* :

(a) it is relatively easy to manage
(b) micronutrient deficiency is the cause of these diseases
(c) it can overcome genetic risk factors
(d) it can compensate for other lifestyle factors

(3) *Why are large number of apparently healthy people deemed pre-ill?*
(a) They may have chronic degenerative diseases
(b) They do not know their own genetic risk factors which predispose them to diseases
(c) They suffer from Type-B malnutrition
(d) There is a lengthy latency period associated with chronically degenerative diseases

(4) *Type-B malnutrition is a serious concern in developed countries because :*
(a) developing countries mainly suffer from Type-A malnutrition
(b) it is major contributor to illness and death
(c) pharmaceutical companies are not producing drugs to treat this condition
(d) national surveys on malnutrition do not include newer micronutrient groups

Answers : **1.** (c), **2.** (c), **3.** (c), **4.** (c).

Passage V

The viability of the multinational corporate system depends upon the degree to which people will tolerate the unevenness it creates. It is well to remember that the 'New Imperialism' which began after 1870 in a spirit of Capitalism Triumphant, soon became seriously troubled and after 1914 was characterised by war, depression, breakdown of the international economic system and war again rather than Free Trade, Pax Britannica and Material Improvement. A major reason was Britain's inability to cope with the by-products of its own rapid accumulation of capital; *i.e.,* a class-conscious labour force at home; a middle class in the hinterland, and rival centres of capital on the Continent and in America. Britain's policy tended to be atavistic and defensive rather than progressive—more concerned with warding off new threats than creating new areas of expansion. Ironically, Edwardian England revived the paraphernalia of the landed aristocracy it had just destroyed. Instead of embarking on a 'big push' to develop the vast hinterland of the Empire, colonial administrators often adopted policies to arrest the development of either a native capitalist class or a native proletariat which could overthrow them.

As time went on, the centre had to devote an increasing share of government activity to military and other unproductive expenditures; they had to rely on alliances with an inefficient class of landlords, officials and soldiers in the hinterland to maintain stability at the cost of development. A great part of the surplus extracted from the population was thus wested locally.

The new Mercantilism (as the Multinational Corporate System of special alliances and privileges, aid and tariff concessions is sometimes called) faces similar problems of internal and external division. The centre is troubled: excluded groups revolt and even some of the affluent are dissatisfied with the roles. Nationalistic rivalry between major capitalist countries remains an important divisive factor. Finally, there is the threat presented by the middle classes and the excluded groups of the underdeveloped countries.

The national middle classes in the underdeveloped countries came to power when the centre wakened but could not, their policy of import substitution manufacturing, establish a viable basis for sustained growth. They now face a foreign exchange crisis and an unemployment (or population) crisis—the first indicating their inability to function in the international economy and the second indicating their alienation from the people they are supposed to lead. In the immediate future, these national middle classes will gain a new lease of life as they take advantage of the spaces created by the rivalry between America and non-American-oligopolists striving to establish global market positions.

The native capitalists will again become the champions of national independence as they bargain with multinational corporations. But the conflict at this level is more apparent than real, for in the end the fervent nationalism of the middle class asks only for promotion within the corporate structure and not for a break with that structure. In the last analysis their power derives from the metropolis and they cannot easily afford to challenge the international system. They do not command the loyalty of their own population and cannot really compete with the large, powerful, aggregate capitals from the centre. They are prisoners of the taste patterns and consumption standards set at the centre.

The main threat comes from the excluded groups. It is not unusual in underdeveloped countries for the top 5 percent to obtain between 30 and 40 percent of the total national income, and for the top one-third to obtain anywhere from 60 to 70 percent. At most one-third of the population can be said to benefit in some sense from the dualistic growth that characterises development in the hinterland. The remaining two-thirds, who together get only one-third of the income, are outsiders, not because they do not contribute to the economy, but because they do not share in the benefits. They provide a source of cheap labour which helps keep exports to the developed world at a low price and which has financed the urban-biased growth of recent years. In fact, it is difficult to see how the system in most underdeveloped countries could survive without cheap labour since removing it (*e.g.* diverting it to public works projects as is done in socialist countries) would raise consumption costs to capitalists and professional elites.

(1) *According to the author, the British policy the 'New Imperialism' period tended to be defensive because*
(a) it was unable to deal with the fallouts of a sharp increase in capital
(b) its cumulative capital had undesirable side-effects
(c) its policies favoured developing the vast hinterland
(d) it prevented the growth of a set-up which could have been capital istic in nature

(2) *In the sentence. "They are prisoners of the taste patterns and consumption standards set at the centre." (fourth paragraph), what is the meaning of 'centre'?*
(a) National government (b) Native capitalists
(c) New capitalists (d) None of these

(3) *The author is in a position to draw parallels between New Imperialism and New Mercantilism because*
(a) both originated in the developed Western capitalist countries
(b) New Mercantilism was a logical sequel to New Imperialism
(c) they create the same set of outputs—a labour force, middle classes and rival centres of capital
(d) both have comparable uneven and divisive effects

(4) *Under New Mercantilism, the fervent nationalism of the native middle classes does not create conflict with the multinational corporations because they (the middle classes)*
(a) negotiate with the multinational corporations
(b) are dependent on the international system for their continued prosperity
(c) are not in a position to challenge the status quo
(d) do not enjoy popular support

Answers : **1.** (b), **2.** (c), **3.** (b), **4.** (a).

Passage VI

Directions (Q. 1 to 15) *Read the following passage carefully and answer the questions given below. If certain words are printed in bold to help you to locate them while answering some of the questions.*

[Indian Bank PO August 2004]

Can India make it to a leadership position in the new millennium or will it retain the 'fast train-going-show' image of the last 50 odd years? Most people believe that the potential for our country to succeed is huge. They are also disappointed at the inability to convert the natural advantages we possess into tangible benefits. The recent success of our infotech industry globally has reinforced the belief that when we put our mind to it we can and do succeed. Now, the expectation is that this success will be replicated in other areas.

There is not doubt that India's further will be driven by the intellectual capital of its people. Even though many of the billion Indian people are and will continue for the foreseeable further to live in a third-world setting, there are many Indians with the skills, ability and aspiration to prosper and flourish in a first-world environment. It is, therefore, likely that India will, at the same time, belong to both the first and third worlds.

That first-world environment will be powered increasingly by knowledge workers and brainware India clearly has the numbers. It needs to invest in training and skill-building and also encourage entrepreneurship and risk-taking.

I have no magic recipe to convert India's people power into a competitive advantage on global basis. Also, I am nowhere near qualified to address macro issues like universal education and school curriculam. Therefore, I have to shrink the issue into a familiar **framework** of 'growing our people. '

It is imperative that Indian business pay more than lip service to the empowerment of their employees. We have to break the 'do-as-you are told' mentality which inhibits creativity and promotes the culture of servitude long after our 'foreign masters' are gone. Together with empowerment, there has to be a culture of personal accountability so that everyone realises the necessity of valuing commitment.

In all areas of activity, seniority and hierarchies (if any) must be based purely on merit. **Seniority, like respect, must be earned** and not 'termed,' *i.e.,* based on the length of service. Future organisations will be based on communities and interaction between individuals and teams both within and outside the organisation. The work environment both with respect to physical space as well as culture, must be barrierless/boundryless, allowing the **impromptu** and regular and regular interaction across workgroups/teams.

Organisations must accept that empowerment and personal accountability should go hand in hand with a degree of tolerance for mistakes and failures. Mistakes and failures are good learning opportunities for our people and should be regarded as such unless repeated. Tolerance would also provide a safety net for those prepared to take risks, a quality rarely seen among Indian executives today but crucial to succeed in the new economy.

Organisations must be as transparent as possible with their employees. Both good and bad news must be shared. Often organisations and their leadership wrongly believe that the employees aren't interested in certain information or more arrogantly, decide that information is best withheld as it is beyond the comprehension of their employees. Knowledge sharing must be pushed at all levels through a carrot-and-stick approach. Those who continuously hoard knowledge must be weeded out. Everyone must come to work thinking that they will learn and add to their skills.

Performance management must be institutionalised to give everyone a clear understanding of organisational goals, team goals, the individual's role or goals within a team, rewards which follow from meeting goals and career opportunities in the organisation. Encourage a sense of commitment to the community among your employees. Apart from making them feel good about themselves it also affords opportunities for them to work as teams in a non-work environment. Above all, make work fun. If people, however talented, show up at work because it is a job', then they are unlikely to realise their full potential.

The above is not an exhaustive list for each organisation to get the best out of its people. But if each organisation addresses some of these issues then people will grow individually and collectively. Thus, is bound to have a beneficial effect on harnessing and driving their intellectual capital.

(1) *The author attributes success of India in infotech industry to* :

(a) do-as-you are told mentality
(b) lazy and intolerant attitude of Indians
(c) growing global economy
(d) realising the latent intellectual capital
(e) None of these

(2) *Which of the following is the best way for organisations to be transparent?*
(a) Share both good and bad news at all levels
(b) Share only that information which employees can understand
(c) Share only good news and withhold bad news
(d) Only relevant information should be shared
(e) None of the above

(3) *The carrot-and-stick method will realise which of the following objectives?*
(a) The accountability of the employees will improve
(b) The confidential information will remain as guarded secret
(c) There will be improvement in the skill of employees
(d) The free flow of knowledge and information will improve
(e) None of the above

(4) *Which of the following measures, if adopted, according to the passage will make employees value commitment?*
1. Stresngthening the skills
2. Giving necessary instructions
3. Fixing accountability
(a) All of these
(b) 2 and 3
(c) 1 and 3
(d) Either 1, 2 and 3
(e) None of these

(5) *What does the word impromptu communicate in the passage?*
(a) The communication should be unprovoked
(b) Employees interaction should be spontaneous and natural
(c) The work groups should be prompted to talk less, work more
(d) Work groups and teams should interact only if it is necessary
(e) None of the above

(6) *The phrase fast-train-going-slow in the passage refers to* :
1. Following the old policies of governance
2. Not realising the inbuilt potential
(a) Only 1
(b) Only 2
(c) Either 1 and 2
(d) Neither 1 and 2
(e) Both 1 and 2

(7) *According to author, which of the following factors inhibits creatvity?*
(a) Giving more emphasis on seniority
(b) Less emphasis on team work
(c) Asking employees to follow directions only
(d) Liability of organisation to address macro issues
(e) None of these

(8) *According to the passage which of the following is predicament of Indian business?*
(a) The core issues of universal education are not addressed
(b) The Government policies are not favourable
(c) While strengthening employees potential the policies are more talked implemented
(d) The field of competition is uneven
(e) None of the above

(9) *To realise the full potential of the talent, what are recommendations of the passage?*
(a) Making the working place as funny as possible
(b) Love your job even if you hate to work
(c) Make clear difference between job and work
(d) Make your work as interesting as if it is fun
(e) None of the above

(10) *Which of the following provides good learning opportunities?*
(a) High level of tolerance for failure
(b) Repeating the mistakes till learning takes place
(c) Overlooking the mistakes of the employees
(d) Making efforts not to do the same mistake again
(e) None of these

(11) *The phrase 'seniority, like respect, must be earned'. . . . . . . refers to :*
1. the seniority must reflect the expertise and knowledge
2. the earning of seniority should be related to length of services.
3. merit should decide seniority.
(a) 1 and 3 (b) 1 and 2 (c) 2 and 3 (d) All of these
(e) None of these

(12) *What is the expectation of the author from the Indians?*
(a) They will realise their potential in areas other than Information Technology
(b) Despite being slow they will think fast
(c) They will stop working oif forced to work like 'do as you are told'
(d) Indian will turn natural disadvantage to advantage
(e) None of the above

(13) *Which of the following is not true in the context of the passage?*
(a) India has huge potential to succeed
(b) To empower its employees Indian business pay more for the services of the employees
(c) The seniority should not be based on age
(d) India should encourage the risk taking behaviour
(e) Business bodies of future will have more knowledge workers

(14) *Which of the following best describes the word framework as used in the passage?*
(a) Working within frame
(b) Fixing frame for the assigned work
(c) The basic premise
(d) Divising a defined work culture
(e) None of these

(15) How does sense of commitment to community among employees help people?
(a) It develops competition feeling in them.
(b) People learn risk-taking even in non-work situation
(c) It encourages accountability in them
(d) People start perceiving opportunities for them to work as teams in non-work situation also
(e) None of the above

Answers **1.** (d), **2.** (a), **3.** (c), **4.** (c), **5.** (b), **6.** (b) **7.** (c) **8.** (c) **9.** (d), **10.** (a), **11.** (a), **12.** (a), **13.** (b), **14.** (c) **15.** (d)

Passage VII

Directions (Q. 16 to 25) *Read the following passgae carefully and answer the questions given below it. Certain words are printed in bold to help you to locate them while answering some of the questions*

[Inddian Bank PO August 2014]

Many people believe that science and religion are contrary to each other. But this notion is wrong as a matter of fact, both are complementary to each other. The aim of both these institutions is to explain different aspects of life, universe and human existence. There is no doubt that the methods of science and religion are different. The method of science is observation, experimentation and experience. Science takes its recourse to progressive march towards perfection the rules of religion are faith, intuition and spoken word of the **enlightened**, in general, while science is inclined towards reason and rationality, spiritualism is the essence of religion.

In earlier times when man appeared on Earth, he was over-awed at the sight of violent and powerful aspects of nature. In certain cases, the usefulness of different natural objects of nature overwhelmed man. Thus began the worship of forces of nature—fire, the Sun, the rivers, the rocks, the trees, the snakes, etc. The holy scriptures were written by those who had developed harmony between external nature and their inner self. Their object was to ennoble, elevate and liberate the human spirit and mind. But the priestly class took upon itself the monopoly of scriptural knowledge and interpretation to its own advantage.

Thus, the entire human race was in chains. Truth was **flouted** and progressive, liberal and truthful ideas or ideas expressing doubt and skepticism were suppressed and their holders punished. It was in these trying circumstances the science emerged as a saviour of mankind but its path was not smooth and safe. The scientists and free thinkers were tortured. This was the fate of Copernicus, Galileo, Bruno and others but, by and by science gained ground.

(16) *Why does man worship the force of nature?*
(a) The holy scriptures advocate the worship of forces of nature
(b) The worship elevates and liberates the human spirit and mind
(c) The worship makes man believe in faith and intuition
(d) Forces of nature reach us spiritualism
(e) None of the above

(17) *Which of the following statements is true in the context of the passage?*
(a) Science and religion are antagonistic to each other
(b) Science encourages worshipping of nature
(c) Religion is essential for external peace and harmony
(d) Regimental religion was replaced by scientific principles
(e) Science is essential for inner peace of mind.

(18) *According to the passage science and religion both* :
(a) rely on the spoken word of the enlightened
(b) emerged out of the fear of man
(c) emerged from the desire of man to worship the forces of nature
(d) employ different methods of enquiry
(e) work at the cross-purpose of each other

(19) *Why is it said in the passage that, "science emerged as a saviour of mankind"?*
(a) Many great thinkers contributed to the progress of science
(b) Science takes recourse to progressive march towards perfection
(c) Science is inclined towards reason and rationality
(d) Man was bound in chains by religious orthodoxy
(e) The free thinkers and enlightened men were tortured

(20) *Which of the following statements is not true in the context of the passage?*
(a) Man worships the forces of nature
(b) Methods of science and religion are different
(c) Regimental religion got degenerated into orthodoxy
(d) Galileo and Bruno were disciples of Copernicus
(e) The holy scriptures were written by people who had tremendous inner strength

(21) *Choose the word which is most nearly the same in meaning as the word "flouted" as used in the passage:*
(a) mocked (b) nourished (c) expressed (d) deflated
(e) concealed

(22) *According to the passage science and religion* :
(a) are contrary to each other
(b) have the same origin
(c) are supportive to each other
(d) have the same aim of controlling universe
(e) do not allow any deviation from their rules

(23) *According to the passage, at the present juncture, there is a need to* :
(a) encourage spiritualism as much as possible
(b) teach people to worship the forces of nature.
(c) free man from all sorts of bondages
(d) explain to the people different aspects of life and universe
(e) judiciously mix the principles of science and true spirit of religion

(24) *What was the object of the authors of the holy scriptures?*
(a) To teach man the methods of worshipping nature
(b) To advocate the progressive and liberal ideas
(c) To educate and raise the human spirit and mind
(d) To develop harmony between external nature and their inner self
(e) None of the above

(25) *Choose the words which is most opposite in meaning of the word ''enlightened'' as used in the passage.*
(a) uninformed
(b) derogatory
(c) downtrodden
(d) educated
(e) authority

Answers : **16.** (b), **17.** (d), **18.** (d), **19.** (d), **20.** (d), **21.** (a), **22.** (c), **23.** (e), **24.** (c), **25.** (a).

Passage VIII

Directions (Q. 1 to 15) *Read the following passage carefully and answer the questions given below it. Certain words /phrases are printed in bold to help you to locate them while answering some of the questions*

[Bank PO]

In modern time Abraham Lincoln stands as the model of a compassionate statesman. He showed this quality not only in striving for the emancipation of the American blacks but in the dignity with which he conducted the American Civil War.

Lincoln did not fancy himself as a liberator. He thought it would be better for all if emancipation was a gradual process spread over many years. He proposed compensation for slave—owners in US bonds and grants for the rehabilitation of blacks— 'colonisation' as the called it. But fate was to deem otherwise. The haste with which the South wanted to break away from the Union with the North, compelled him to move faster than he expected, perhaps more than most men of his time he had thought through the issue of slavery. 'We must free the slaves', he said, 'or be ourselves subdued. 'Before reading he first draft of the proclamation of Emancipation, he told his colleagues. 'In giving freedom to the slaves, we assure freedom to the free'.

On September 22nd, 1862. Lincoln set his hand on the Proclamation of Emancipation declaring that on the first day of January 1863, all persons held as slaves within any state 'shall the then and forever free. '

Lincoln's revulsion for slavery left him without any moral indignation or passion against the slave-owners. The guilt of the slave-owners, he felt , should be shared by the whole country the North and the South, for it seemed to him that everyone in the nation was an accomplice in perpetuating that system. To have whipped up any hatred against slave-owners would, to him, have been an act of malice.

"I shall do nothing in malice", he wrote, 'what I deal with is too vast for malicious dealing". As the Civil War was coming to a successful conclusion, a Northerner demanded of Lincoln, "Mr President, how are you going to treat the Southerners when the war is over?" Lincoln replied, "As if they never went to war?"

When the news came of the Victory of the Northern against the Confederate forces, someone suggested that the head of the Confederation Administration, Jefferson Davies, really ought to be hanged. "Judge not, that ye be not judged", Lincoln replied, as to the demand for the prosecution of rebels, Lincoln replied , "We must extinguish our resentments if we expect harmony and union". This was his last recorded utterance.

(1) *The sentence : 'In giving freedom . . . . to the free'(last sentence of para 2) means* :
(a) by freeing slaves, we are honouring the concept of freedom
(b) by freeing slaves, we are safeguarding our own interests
(c) if we give freedom to the slaves, they will serve us better
(d) if we do not give freedom to the slaves, they will free themselves
(e) None of the above

(2) *What came in Lincoln's way of carrying out emancipation as a gradual process?*
(a) The haste of the South to break away from the Union with the North
(b) The inadequate compensation given to slave-owners
(c) His own over-enthusiasm to complete the process fast
(d) His proposition to give grant for the rehabilitation of slaves
(e) None of the above

(3) *Which of the following makes Abraham Lincoln a compassionate statesman?*
(a) His hesitation in striving for emancipation of American blacks
(b) His indifference in conducting the American Civil War
(c) His efforts to force the American blacks from slavery
(d) His efforts to conclude the American Civil War without dignity
(e) None of the above

(4) *The term 'colonisation' as used in passage means* :
(a) making separate dwelling arrangements for slave-owners
(b) rehabilitation arrangements made for slave-owners
(c) efforts made by American blacks to free themselves
(d) handing over slaves to the slave-owners
(e) None of the above

(5) *The incidents in the passage prove that Lincoln was* :
(a) not a firm administrator
(b) afraid of the majority of slaves
(c) unduly concerned for the safety of the rebels
(d) sympathetic and kind-hearted statesman.
(e) unreasonably in favour of slaves.

(6) *The author of the passage seems to be*
(a) a staunch and biased critic of Abraham Lincoln :
(b) an advocate of the system of slavery
(c) an opponent of the system of slavery
(d) indifferent to Lincoln's remarkable achievements
(e) impressed with Lincoln's good qualities

(7) *According to Lincoln, the culprits of the system of slavery were* :
(a) the slaver-owners alone
(b) the slaves alone
(c) both the slaves and the slave-owners
(d) all the people in the country
(e) None of these

(8) *Which of the following statements is true in the context of the passage?*
(a) Lincoln hated the demand of hanging Jefferson Davies
(b) Lincoln turned down the demand of the prosecution of rebels
(c) Lincoln wondered how mere compassion cold lead to harmony
(d) The Civil War was fought by the Northerners and Southerners against the enemies
(e) None of the above

(9) *Lincoln didn't have any hatred for the slave-owners because* :
(a) they were in a vast majority
(b) they all belonged to upper caste
(c) they would have treated him with malice
(d) they were not guilty at all
(e) None of the above

(10) Lincoln's reply to the Northerner's question regarding the treatment to Southerners proves that :
(a) the Southerners were wicked in their dealings
(b) Lincoln did not have revengeful attitude towards the Southerners
(c) the Northerners were in favour of the Southerners
(d) Lincoln did not like the Southerner's act of breaking away from the union with the North
(e) Lincoln could control his anguish against the Southerners while expressing himself

Answers : **1.** (a), **2.** (a), **3.** (e), **4.** (e), **5.** (d), **6.** (e), **7.** (d), **8.** (b), **9.** (e), **10.** (b).

Short Passages

Passage 1

Directions (Q. 1-5) *Read the following passage and answer the questions based on it.*
[CDS January 2002]

At low tide he walked over the sands to the headland and round the corner to the little bay facing the open sea. It was inaccessible by boat, because seams of rock jutted out and currents swirled round them treacherously. But you could walk there if you chose one of the lowest ebb tides that receded a very long way. You could not linger on the expedition, for once the tide was on the turn, it came in rapidly. For this reason very few people cared to explore the little bay and the cave at the back of it.

But the unknown always drew this man like a magnet. He found the bay fresh and unlittered, as it was completely covered by the sea at high tide. The cave looked mysteriously dark, cool and inviting and he penetrated to the farthest corner where he discovered a wide crack, rather like a chimney. He peered up and thought he could see a patch of daylight.

(1) *According to the writer, the bay could not be reached by boat, because* :
(a) it had numerous layers of rock
(b) there were too many eddies
(c) it was facing the open sea
(d) there were seams of rock and treacherously swirling currents

(2) *One could visit the bay*
(a) at any time one chose
(b) on certain specified occasions
(c) when there was a low tide
(d) during the evening walk

(3) *It was not possible to 'linger on the expedition' because* :
(a) the water rose rapidly
(b) the tide turned quickly
(c) the tide turned sprightly
(d) the water rushed in with a great force

(4) *He found the bay "fresh and unlittered" because* :

(a) the sea water had receded
(b) he was the first visitor there
(c) the high tide had just washed the litter away
(d) it was not frequented by people who would pollute it

(5) *While passing through the cave, the writer discovered a* :

(a) cool and secluded corner
(b) large opening
(c) chimney-shaped rock
(d) big crack through which light came in

Answers : **(1)** (d), **(2)** (c), **(3)** (c), **(4)** (c), **(5)** (d).

Passage 2

Directions (Q. 6-10) *Read the following passage and answer the questions based on it.*

[CDS January 2002]

Regular physical activity provides numerous health benefits—from leaner bodies and lower blood pressure to improved mental health and cognitive functioning. As the school physical education programme promotes physical activity and can teach skills as well as from or change behaviour, it holds an important key to influencing health and well-being across the life span. To improve the fitness of students, we need to rethink the design and delivery of school-based physical education programme.

Adults in the United States think that information about health was more important for students to learn the content in language arts, mathematics, science, history or any other subject. Deposite this high ranking, most schools devote minimal curriculum time to teaching students how to lead healthy lives. Our first step might be to consider ways to increase curriculum time devoted to physical education. In addition, schools need to thoughtfully analyse the design and delivery of school physical education programme to ensure that they are engaging, developmentally appropriate, inclusive and instructionally powerful.

(6) *According to this passage, regular physical activity is needed to* :

(a) control one's blood pressure
(b) lose one's weight
(c) improve one's cognitive skills
(d) improve one's physical as well as mental health

(7) *In order to tone up the physical education programme* :

(a) it should be made compulsory at school
(b) as assessment of the existing programme should be made
(c) a committee should be set up in every school
(d) the programme should be reoriented and implemented

(8) *According the Americans, health education is more important than teaching* :

(a) social sciences
(b) liberal arts
(c) any subject
(d) natural sciences

(9) *The author wants the reoriented physical education programme to be* :

(a) given minimal curriculum time
(b) very comprehensive
(c) relevant to the modern society.
(d) thoughtful

(10) *In order to improve the physical education programme, we should, first of all* :

(a) allot more time to the teaching and learning of physical activity
(b) decide on the number of activities to be taught
(c) employ qualified instructors
(d) increase the teaching load of instructors

Answers : **(6)** (d), **(7)** (d), **(8)** (c), **(9)** (d), **(10)** (d).

Passage 3

Directions (Q. 11-15) *Read the following passage and answer the questions based on it.*
[CDS January 2002]

The highbrows reverse the numerical argument and imply that, because they are so few, they must therefore be right but where they chiefly offend is in their excessive self-congratulation and contempt for others. In the past, the highbrows were alone in expressing a feeling of superiority; the lowbrows humbly accepted the position assigned to them. Recently, however, there has been a change and the lowbrows now adopt towards the highbrows exactly the same attitude as the highbrows adopted towards them.

(11) *The reversal of the numerical argument in the context of the passage means that the highbrows* :
(a) have no regard for the majority
(b) respect the majority
(c) are indifferent to numbers
(d) have regard for the minority

(12) *A highbrow is* :
(a) a liberal minded person
(b) a believer in conservative values
(c) a self-opinionated intellectual
(d) a democrat

(13) *The phrase 'self-congratulation' can best be replaced by* :
(a) self-effacement
(b) self-admiration
(c) self-negation
(d) self-criticism

(14) *The attitude of the lowbrows towards the highbrows in the past was one of* :
(a) violent rejection
(b) resentful acceptance
(c) open rebelliousness
(d) unprotesting submission

(15) *The recent change in the attitude of the lowbrows towards the highbrows suggests that* :
(a) the lowbrows have rejected the superiority of the highbrows
(b) the lowbrows have become highbrows
(c) the lowbrows have become indifferent to the highbrows
(d) the highbrows have become meek and humble

Answers : **(11)** (c), **(12)** (c), **(13)** (b), **(14)** (d), **(15)** (a).

Passage 4

Directions (Q. 16-20) *Read the following passage and answer the questions based on it.*

Crude mineral oil comes out of the earth as a thick brown or black liquid with a strong smell. It is a complex mixture of many different substances, each with its own individual qualities. Most of them are combinations of hydrogen and carbon in varying proportions. Such hydrocarbons are also found in other forms such as bitumen, asphalt and natural gas. Mineral oil originates from the carcasses of tiny animals and from plants that live in the sea.

Over millions of years, these dead creatures form large deposits under sea-bed and ocean currents cover them with a blanket of sand and slit. As this material hardens, it becomes sedimentary rock and effectively shuts out the oxygen, so preventing the complete decomposition of the marine deposits underneath. The layers of sedimentary rock become thicker and heavier. Their pressure produces heat, which transforms the tiny carcasses into crude oil in a process that is still going on today.

[CDS January 2002]

(16) *Marine deposits under the sea do not get decomposed because they* :
(a) become rock and prevent oxygen from entering them
(b) are covered by the sand and slit brought by the current
(c) contain a mixture of hydrogen and carbon
(d) are constantly washed by the ocean current

(d) are constantly washed by the ocean current

(17) *Sedimentary rock leads to the formation of oil deposits because* :
(a) it becomes hard and forms into rocks which produce oil
(b) its pressure produces heat and turns the deposits of animal carcasses and plants into oil
(c) it turns heavy and shuts out the oxygen
(d) it becomes heavy and hard and applies pressure to squeeze oil

(18) *In order to have mineral oil, hydrogen and carbon are combined in* :
(a) equal proportions (b) fixed proportions
(c) varying proportions (d) the proportion of two and one

(19) *The time it takes for the marine deposits to harden into rocks is* :
(a) a few years (b) thousands of years
(c) hundreds of years (d) million of years

(20) *The most apt title for the passage is*
(a) crude mineral oil (b) how sedimentary rock is formed?
(c) how mineral oil is formed? (d) marine deposits under the sea

Answers : **(16)** (b), **(17)** (b) **(18)** (c), **(19)** (d), **(20)** (c).

Passage 5

Directions (Q. 21-25) *Read the following passage and answer the questions based on it.*
[CDS January 2002]

To avoid the various foolish opinions to which mankind is prone, no superhuman brain is required. A few simple rules will keep you free, not from all errors, but from silly errors. If the matter is one that can be settled by observation, make the observation yourself. Aristotle could have avoid the mistake of thinking that women have fewer teeth than man, by the simple device of asking Mrs. Aristotle to keep her mouth open while he counted. Thinking that you know when in fact you do not is a bad mistake, to which we are all prone. I believe myself that hedgehogs eat black beetles, because I have been told that they do; but if I was writing a book on the habits of hedgehogs, I should not commit myself until I had been one enjoying this diet. Aristotle, however, was less cautious. Ancient and medieval writers know all about unicorns and salamanders; not one of them thought it necessary to avoid dogmatic statements about them because he had never seen one of them.

(21) *The author portrays mankind as* :
(a) very intelligent (b) having superhuman qualities
(c) nervous and weak (d) by and large, lazy and ignorant

(22) *The author is in favour of drawing conclusions on the basis of*
(a) reasoning (b) study of eminent thinkers
(c) empirical evidence (d) discussion and consultation

(23) *According to the author, unicorns and salamanders* :
(a) existed in the past but now have become extinct
(b) are invisible (c) never really existed
(d) have caused strange stories to be written about them

(24) *The author implies that* :
(a) hedgehogs eat black beetles (b) hedgehogs do not really eat black beetles
(c) he is writing a book about hedge-hogs (d) he is never seen a hedgehog eating beetles

(25) *The attitude of the author is* :
(a) philosophical (b) scientific
(c) cultural (d) commonsensical

Answers : **(21)** (d), **(22)** (c), **(23)** (c), **(24)** (d), **(25)** (b).

Passage 6

Directions (Q. 26-30) *Read the following passage and answer the questions based on it.* **[CDS January]**

Long ago Emperson wrote: ''A man's task is his life-preserver''. This seems to be remarkably correct in our modern life. The man without task is like a ship without a ballast and anchor, he is all too often merely a drifter. Few men seem to have initiative enough to choose a task for themselves if they do not need to work. When the inevitable disappointments come, as they assuredly will, they are completely overwhelmed. But the man who has his task has no time for vain regret, he escapes the disastrous fate which overtakes his less fortunate brother. Work is one of the greatest safety-valves which was ever invented, and youth especially needs it.

(26) *It seems to be remarkably correct in modern life that* :

(a) a man has enough leisure (b) youth needs less work and more rest
(c) the correct choice of the task preserves one's life
(d) men fail to choose a task for themselves

(27) *The expression 'safety-valve' means* :

(a) something which blows up safety (b) an outlet for rent-up energy
(c) something which guarantees safety (d) a leaf of a folding door

(28) *A ship without ballast and anchor* :

(a) is in great danger (b) merely drifts (c) is very safe (d) may not go in the right direction

(29) *A man who suffers from vain regrets must have* :

(a) chosen his life's work rather carelessly (b) met with disastrous fate
(c) been a victim of adverse circumstances to do

(30) *A person who has chosen the right task has no time to regret because he*

(a) is engrossed in his work (b) has too much to do
(c) has succeeded in life (d) has a safe and secured life

Answers : **(26)** (c), **(27)** (c), **(28)** (d), **(29)** (a) **(30)** (b).

Passage 7

Directions (Q. 1-5) *Read the following passage and answer the questions based on it.* **[SSC Stenographers]**

Mountaineering is now looked upon as the king of sports. But men have lived amongst the mountains since prehistoric times and in some parts of the world, as in the Andes and Himalayas, difficult mountain journeys have inevitably been part of their everyday life. However, some of the peaks there were easily accessible from most of the cities of Europe. It is quite interesting that while modern mountaineers prefer difficult routes for the greater enjoyment of sport, the early climbers looked for the easiest ones, for the summit was the prize they all set their eyes on. Popular interest in mountaineering increased considerably after the ascent of the Alpine peak of Matterhorn in 1865 and Edward Whymper's dramatic account of the climb and fatal accident which occurred during the descent.

In the risky sport of mountaineering the element of competition between either individuals or teams is totally absent. Rather one can say that the competition is between the team and the peaks themselves. The individuals making up a party must climb together as a team, for they depend upon one another for their safety. Mountaineering can be dangerous unless reasonable precautions are taken. However, the majority of fatal accidents happen to parties which are inexperienced or not properly equipped. Since many accidents are caused due to bad weather, the safe climber is the man who knows when it is time to turn back, however, tempting it may be to press on and try to reach the summit.

(1) *Mountaineering is different from other sports because* :
(a) it is risky and dangerous
(b) it can be fatal
(c) it is most thrilling and exciting, there is no competition between individuals

(2) *People living in the Andes and the Himalayas made mountain journeys because* :
(a) it was a kind of sport
(b) they had to undertake them in their day-to-day life
(c) they lived in pre-historic time
(d) of the challenge offered by the difficult journey

(3) *Mountaineers climb as a team because* :
(a) the height is too much for one individual
(b) the competition is between the team and the peak
(c) they have to rely on each other for safety
(d) there is no competition among them

(4) *". . . . . the summit was the prize they all set their eyes on". In the context of the passage, this means* :
(a) reaching the top was their exclusive concern
(b) they kept their eyes steadily on reaching the summit
(c) they cared for nothing but the prize of reaching the summit
(d) they chose a route from which they could see the summit clearly

(5) *"to press" in the last sentence of the passage means* :
(a) to struggle in a forceful manner
(b) to force upon others
(c) to work fearlessly
(d) to continue in a determined manner

Answers : **(1)** (c), **(2)** (b), **(3)** (c), **(4)** (a), **(5)** (d).

Passage 8

Directions (Q.6-10) *Read the following passage and answer the questions based on it.*

[SSC Stenographer]

On the morning of 31st August, 1573, 3000 horsemen of the imperial Mughal army paused at the banks of the Sabarmati. The rebels, they were after, lay just beyond the swollen river but the soldiers were exhausted: they had traversed 960 kilometers of difficult terrain in nine days, riding almost continuously. Suddenly a warrior on a chestnut charger plunged into the raging torrent. As man and horse struggled on to the opposite bank, a thrill ran through the army. It was the emperor, Jalaluddin Akbar ! with a roar, the soldiers followed him across and within two days, they had put down the rebellion so thoroughly that Gujrat remained in Mughal hands for the next 185 years.

(6) *The rebels were camped* :
(a) across the Sabarmati river
(b) on the banks of Sabarmati river
(c) in Gujrat
(d) in imperial Mughal courts

(7) *The expression 'swollen river' means* :
(a) a river in flood
(b) a calm and serene river
(c) a deep river
(d) a shallow river

(8) *The Mughal soldiers didn't cross the river because*
(a) they were cowards
(b) they had joined hands with the rebels
(c) they were waiting for the king to arrive
(d) they were tired after a difficult journey

(9) *The sudden arrival of King Akbar* :
(a) surprised the soldiers
(b) angered the soldiers
(c) dismayed the soldiers
(d) enthused the soldiers

(10) *The attack on the rebels turned out to be* :
(a) a dismal failure
(b) a grand success
(c) of no particular significance
(d) an ordinary affair

Answers : **(6)** (b), **(7)** (a), **(8)** (d), **(9)** (d), **(10)** (b).

Passage 9

Directions (Q. 11-15) *Read the following passage and answer the questions based on it.*
[SSC Stenographer]

He saw nothing he had no knife or sharp instrument, the grating of the window was of iron and he had too often assured himself of its solidity. His furniture consisted of a bed, a chair, a table, a pail and a jug. The bed had iron clamps, but they were screwed to the wall and it would have required a screwdriver to take them off.

Dantes had but one resource which was to break the jug and with one of the sharp fragments attack the wall. He let the jug fall on the floor and it broke in pieces. He concealed two or three of the sharpest fragments in his bed, leaving the rest on the floor.

The breaking of the jug was too natural an accident to excite suspicion and next morning the gaoler went grumblingly to fetch another, without giving himself the trouble to remove the fragments. Dantes heard joyfully the key grate in the lock as the guard departed.

(11) *Dantes was in* :
(a) a hostel (b) a dining room
(c) an army barracks (d) a prison

(12) *Dantes' was planning to* :
(a) carve his name (b) make his escape
(c) tease the guard (d) call for breakfast

(13) *The guard left the fragments because he*
(a) didn't notice them (b) wished to punish dantes
(c) was too lazy to bother (d) wanted Dantes to clear up

(14) *Dantes probably broke the jug* :
(a) in the morning (b) during the night
(c) after breakfast (d) at exactly 3 P.M.

(15) *Dantes heard the key grate in the lock when the*
(a) cell door was shut (b) cell door was opened
(c) storeroom was opened (d) storeroom was shut

Answers : **(11)** (d), **(12)** (b), **(13)** (c), **(14)** (b), **(15)** (a).

Passage 10

Directions (Q. 16-20) *Read the following passage and answer the questions based on it.*
[SSC Stenographer]

Wild peacocks live together in large flocks in the forests of Central Africa. They scratch about in the ground during the day for seeds to eat and at nightfall they fly up to the trees where they perch and sleep. Every peacock has several wives, known as peahens. The female birds build their nests on the ground and lay from four to six whitish, sometimes spotted eggs. During the mating season the male utters a harsh raucous cry.

(16) *Why do peacocks live in flocks?*
(a) They are frightened of wild animals. (b) They cannot fly very well
(c) They can get more food (d) The passage does not tell us

(17) *'Perch' in the passage means* :
(a) rest (b) nest (c) climb (d) fly

(18) *Peacock eggs are* :
(a) pure white (b) whitish (c) spotted (d) Both 'a' and 'c'

(19) *"Harsh raucous cry' in the passage means* :
(a) loud cry (b) deep cry (c) roaring cry (d) loud and hoarse cry

(20) *A suitable title for the passage could be* :
(a) Peacock Eggs (b) The Habitat of the Peacock
(c) Wild Peacocks (d) Wild Birds of Africa

Answers : (16) (d), **(17)** (a), **(18)** (d), **(19)** (d), **(20)** (b).

Passage 11

Directions (Q. 1-9) *Read the following passage carefully and answer the questions given below it. Certain words/ phrases are given in bold to help you to locate them while answering the questions.*

[Reserve Bank of India, Grade 'B' Officers]

Alleviation of rural poverty has been one of the primary objectives of planned development in India. Ever since the inception of planning, the polices and the programmes have been designed and redesigned with this aim. The problem of rural poverty was brought into a sharper focus during the Sixth Plan. The Seventh Plan too emphasised growth with social justice. It was realised that a sustainable strategy of poverty alleviation has to be based on increasing the productive employment opportunities in the process of growth itself.

However, to the extent the process of growth bypasses some sections of population, it is necessary to formulate specific poverty alleviation programmes for generation of a certain minimum level of income for the rural poor. Rural development implies both the economic betterment of people as well as greater social transformation. Increased participation of people in the rural development process, decentralisation of planning, better enforcement of land reforms and greater access to credit and inputs go a long way in prospects for economic development improvements in health, education drinking water, energy supply sanitation and housing coupled with attitudinal changes also facilitate their social development.

Rural poverty is inextricably linked with low rural productivity and unemployment, including underemployment. Hence, it is imperative to improve productivity and increase employment in rural areas. Moreover, more employment needs to be generated at higher levels of productivity in order to generate higher output. Employment at miserably low levels of productivity and incomes is already a problem of far greater magnitude than unemployment as such. It is estimated that in 1987-88 the rate of unemployment was only 3% and inclusive of the underemployed, it was around 5%.

As per the currently used methodology in the Planning Commission, poverty for the same year was estimated to be 30%. This demonstrates that even though a large proportion of the rural population was working' it was difficult for them to eke out a living even at subsistence levels from it. It is true that there has been a considerable decline in the incidence of rural poverty over time. In terms of absolute numbers of poor, the decline has been much less. While this can be attributed to the demographic factor, the fact remains that after 40 years of planned development about 200 million are still poor in rural India.

(1) *According to the passage, rural poverty is associated with which of the following one or more factors?*
(1) Want of effectiveness of productive efforts. (2) Dearth of employment opportunities.
(3) Better sanitation and housing facilities.
(a) Only 1 (b) Only 2 (c) Only 3 (d) 1 and 2
(e) 2 and 3

(2) *Which of the following statements is/are true in the context of the passage?*
1. There has been a significant increase in the number of the rural poor.
2. Before the Sixth Plan, the policies regarding alleviation of rural poverty were almost nonexistent.
3. Social change coupled with financial upliftment is implied in rural development.
(a) Only 1 (b) Only 2 (c) Only 3 (d) 1 and 2
(e) 1 and 3

(3) *Under which of the following circumstances is employment a greater problem than unemployment?*
(a) There cannot be such circumstances
(b) In rural areas where employment opportunities are less
(c) In urban areas where sanitary conditions are subnormal
(d) In areas where magnitude of unemployment is more serious
(e) None of the above

(4) *Which of the following is not mentioned in the passage as an important factor for rural development?*
(a) Better enforcement of land reforms
(b) Greater access of credit and inputs
(c) Transferring planning from central to local authorities
(d) Involvement of rural folk in the development process
(e) Enhancing production in the various new industries in rural areas

(5) *The passage deals mainly with. . . . .*
(a) the shortcomings in the implementation of poverty alleviation
(b) improvement in industrial growth strategies
(c) alleviation of rural poverty
(d) methodology of Planning Commission
(e) the growth rate of unemployment

(6) *Which of the following necessitates formulation of specific poverty alleviation programmes?*
(a) Certain sections are not covered in the process of growth
(b) The sharper focus given in the Sixth Plan
(c) Extension of social justice to rural areas
(d) To keep the rural population outside the periphery of growth
(e) None of the above

(7) *Which of the following inferences can be drawn from the passage?*
(a) The number of the rural poor people in India is quite substantial
(b) The development activities during the past 40 years had all been futile
(c) Alleviation of rural poverty needs a strong political will
(d) The unemployment situation in the country has been worsening year after year
(e) None of the above

(8) *What is the desired probable impact of formulation of specific poverty alleviation programmes?*
(a) Provision of good sanitation and housing for the rural poor
(b) Ensuring certain minium income for the rural poor
(c) Change in attitude of the rural masses
(d) Increased involvement of the rural people in developmental activities
(e) None of the above

(9) *Which one or more of the following statements show/shows a striking paradox?*
1. In 1987-88, the rate of unemployment was only 3% and inclusive of underemployment it was 5%.
2. Unemployment together with underemployment was 5 % whereas the poverty was 30%.
3. More employment needs to be generated at higher levels of productivity in order to generate higher output.

(a) Only 1
(b) Only 2
(c) Only 3
(d) 1 and 2
(e) 2 and 3

Answers : **(1)** (a), **(2)** (c), **(3)** (d), **(4)** (a), **(5)** (b), **(6)** (b), **(7)** (c), **(8)** (b), **(9)** (c).

Passage 12

Directions (Q. 1-9) *Read the following passage carefully and answer the questions given below it. Certain words/phrases in the passage are given in bold to help you to locate them while answering the questions.* **[Bank PO conducted by BSRB Delhi]**

Globalisation, liberalisation and free market are some of the most significant modern trends in economy. **Most economists** in our country seem **captivated** by the spell of the free market. Consequently, nothing seems good or normal that does not accord with the requirements of the free market.

A price that is determined by the seller or for the matter, established by anyone other than the aggregate of consumers seems **pernicious.** Accordingly, it requires a major act of will to think of price-fixing as both normal and having a valuable economic function, In fact, price fixing is normal in all industrialised societies because the industrial system itself provides, as an effortless consequence of its own development, the price-fixing that it requires.

Modern industrial planning requires and rewards great size. Hence, a comparatively small number of large firms will be competing for the same group of consumers that each large firm will act with consideration of its own needs and thus avoid selling products for more than its competitors charge is commonly recognised by **advocates** of free-market economic theories.

But each large firm will also act with full consideration of the needs that it has in common with the other large firms competing for the same customers. Each large firm will thus avoid significant price cutting, because price-cutting will be prejudicial to the common interest in a **stable** demand for products. Most economists do not see price-fixing when it occurs because they expect it to be brought about by a number of **explicit** agreements among large firms; it is not.

Moreover, those economists who argue that allowing the free-market to operate without interference is the most efficient method of establishing prices have not considered the economics of non-socialist countries. Most of these economies employ intentional price-fixing, usually in an **overt** fashion. Formal price-fixing by cartel and informal price-fixing by agreements covering the members of an industry are common place.

Were there something peculiarly efficient about the free market and inefficient about price-fixing, the countries that have avoided the first and used the second would have suffered drastically in their economic development. There is no indication that they have.

Socialist industry also works within a framework of controlled prices. In the early 1970's the Soviet Union began to give firms and industries some flexibility in adjusting prices that a more informal evolution has accorded the capitalist system. Economists in the USA have hailed the change as a return to the free-market.

But the then Soviet firms were not in favour of the prices established by a free-market over which they exercised little influence; rather, Soviet firms acquired some power to fix prices.

(1) *The author's primary objective of writing the passage seems to* :
(a) belie the popular belief that the free market helps enhance development of industrial societies
(b) advocate that price-fixing is unavoidable and it is beneficial to the economy of any industrialised society
(c) explain the methodology of fixing price to stabilise free-market
(d) prove that price-fixing and free market are compatible and mutually beneficial to industrialised societies
(e) create awareness among the general public regarding combating price-fixing by large firms

(2) *Which of the following statements (1), (2) and/or (3) is/are true in the context of the information given in the passage?*
The information in the passage is helpful to :
(1) know some of the ways in which prices can be fixed
(2) identify the products for which price-fixing can be more beneficial
(3) differentiate between the economies of various countries
(a) Only 1 (b) Only 2 (c) Only 3 (d) 1 and 2
(e) None of these

(3) *Considering the literal meaning and connotations of the words used in the passage, the author's attitude towards 'most economists' can best be described as :*
(a) derogatory and antagonistic (b) impartial and unbiased
(c) spiteful and envious (d) critical and condescending
(e) indifferent

(4) *The author feels that price fixed by seller seems pernicious because :*
(a) people don't have faith in large firms
(b) people don't want the Government to fix prices
(c) most economists believer that consumers should determine prices
(d) most economists believe that no one group should determine prices
(e) people do not want to decide prices

(5) *Which of the following statements is definitely true in the context of the passage? Price fixing is :*
(a) a profitable result of economic development
(b) an inevitable result of the industrial system
(c) the joint result of a number of carefully organised decisions
(d) a phenomenon uncommon to industrialised societies
(e) a result of joint venture of the Government and industry

(6) *According to the passage, price fixing in non-socialistic is generally :*
(a) intentional and widespread (b) illegitimate but beneficial
(c) conservative and inflexible (d) legitimate and innovative
(e) conservative and scarce

(7) *What was the result of the then Soviet Union's change in economic policy in the 1970's?*
(a) They showed greater profits (b) They had less control over the free-market
(c) They were able to adjust to techno advancement
(d) They acquired some authority to fix prices
(e) They became more responsive to free market

(8) *The author's primary concern seems to*
(a) summarise conflicting viewpoints (b) make people aware of recent discoveries
(c) criticise a point of view (d) predict the probable results of a practice
(e) prepare a research proposal

(9) *Which of the following statements about the socialist industry is/are false?*
(1) It works under certain price restrictions (2) It has no authority to determine price
(3) It hails the strategy of price fixing, as a major deviation
(a) Only 1 is false (b) Only 2 is false
(c) Only 3 is false (d) 1 and 2 are false
(e) 2 and 3 are false

Answers : **(1)** (b), **(2)** (a), **(3)** (b), **(4)** (c), **(5)** (b), **(6)** (a), **(7)** (e), **(8)** (a), **(9)** (c).

Passage 13

Directions (Q. 1-5) *Read the following passage carefully and then answer these questions based on what is stated or implied therein.*

[Management Aptitude 2001]

Are the 1980s and 1990s the era of colour? According to some people, they are. Now you can buy radios and electric fans in lavender and pink. Restaurants have an emphasis on flowers and colourful plates. Cars are coming out in pink and aqua.

Even bathroom fixtures are being made in 'honeydew' and 'blond'. Part of the importance of the colour of an object is that the colour affects the way one feels about it. You want a vacuum cleaner to look light and easy, which is why it may be coloured in pastels and light colours. But gardening equipment and athletic equipment you want to look powerful.

You would never find a lawn mower in pink, but red would be fine. Not very long ago, sheets were always white and refrigerators commonly came in colours like 'old gold' 'avocado green' and 'coppertone'. Now those are thought of as old-fashioned, popular colours change because fashion influences everything.

In fact, new colours often spring from the fashion industry. It's a lot cheaper to make a blouse or skirt than a sofa. After people get used to seeing new colours on clothing or towels, they are ready to accept those colours in carpeting, refrigerators or cars. Colour- analysis consultants have been very successful in recent years. People want to choose the most flattering colours for make up and clothing.

Some car designers are even saying that people may begin buying cars of the colour that goes with their skin colouring. This sounds too extreme. It's hard to believe that people are that impressionable.

(1) *The main subject of the passage is* :

(a) popular colours today
(b) colour consultants
(c) the influence of colour
(d) colours that flatter people

(2) *The word 'era' in line I could best be replaced by which of the following words?*

(a) Season
(b) Age
(c) Epic
(d) Generation

(3) *According to the author which of the following is not popular now?*

(a) Coppertone
(b) Colourful cars
(c) Pastels
(d) Colourful bathroom fixtures

(4) *According to the author, why would red be a good colour for a lawn mower?*

(a) Because it is strong
(b) Because it is cheap
(c) Because it is light
(d) Because it is pastel

(5) *In this passage, which of the following are not used names for colours?*

(a) Fruit
(b) Hair colour
(c) Minerals
(d) Drinks

Answers : **(1)** (c), **(2)** (b), **(3)** (a), **(4)** (a), **(5)** (a).

Passage 14

Directions (Q. 1-5) *Read the following passage carefully and then answer these questions based on what is stated or implied therein.* **[Management Aptitude 2001]**

If life exists on Mars, it is most likely to be in the form bacteria buried deep in the planet's permafrost or lichens growing within rocks, say scientists from NASA. There might even be fossilised Martian algae locked up in ancient lake beds, waiting to be found. Christopher Mckay of NASA's Ames Research Centre in California told the AAAS that exobiologists, who look for life on other planets, should look for clues among the life forms of the Earth's ultra-cold regions, where conditions are similar to those on Mars. "Lichens, for example are found within some Antarctic rocks, just beneath the surface where sunlight can still reach them. The rock protects the lichen from cold and absorbs water providing enough for the lichen's need", said Mckay.

Bacteria have also been found in 3-million-year-old permafrost dug up from Siberia. If there are any bacteria alive on Mars today, they would have had to have survived from the time before the planet cooled more than 3 billion years ago. Nevertheless, McKay is optimistic, "It may be possible that bacteria frozen into the permafrost at the Martian South Pole may be viable. "

McKay said, "Algae are found in Antarctic lakes with permanently frozen surfaces. Although no lakes are thought to exist on Mars, they might have existed long ago. If so, the dried-out Martian lake beds may contain the fossilised remains of algae. " " On Earth, masses of microscopic algae form large, layered structures known as stromatolites, which survive as fossils on lake beds and the putative", Martian said, Jack Farmer, one of McKay's colleagues. The researchers are compiling a list of promising Martian lake beds to be photographed from spacecraft" said farmer. Those photographs could help to select sites for landers that would search for signs of life, past or present. " "If we find algae on Mars, I would say the Universe is lousy with algae, "McKay said. "Intelligence would be another question. "

(1) *The passage is primarily concerned with*
(a) the possibility of life on Mars
(b) selecting sites for landers on Mars
(c) research on Mars
(d) Findings of Christopher McKay on Mars

(2, *Lichens survive in the extreme cold conditions of Antarctica on Earth for all the following reasons, except* :
(a) some Antarctic rocks protect lichens beneath their surface
(b) bacteria in the Antarctic frost protect lichen from the residual cold after the rock absorbs water
(c) sunlight penetrates the surface of the Antarctic rock where lichen grows
(d) the Antarctic rocks protect the lichen from cold by absorbing water and leaving enough for the lichen's needs

(3) *Which of the following statements is not true?*
(a) If any bacteria are alive today on Mars, they must have survived from the time before the planet cooled
(b) Space photographs of Martian craters should reveal to the explorers signs of life there
(c) Bacteria frozen into permafrost at the Martian South Pole may be viable
(d) On digging up, more than 3 million years old Siberian permafrost has revealed bacteria

(4) *The most primitive forms of life likely to exist on Mars are all the following except*
(a) villus and spare
(b) bacteria
(c) algae
(d) lichen

(5) *Exobiologists might find on Mars algae similar to stromatolites on earth because :*
(a) on our planet stromatolites are formed by microscopic algae
(b) martian lake beds may contain fossilised remains of algae similar to stromatolites on earth
(c) there is evidence that photosynthesis which takes place in Earth's algae can be found in Martian algae on be found in Martian algae too
(d) All of the above

Answers : **(1)** (a), **(2)** (b), **(3)** (b), **(4)** (a), **(5)** (d).

Passage 15

Directions (Q. 1-5) *Read the following passage carefully and then answer these questions based on what is stated or implied in the passage.* **[Management Aptitude May 2001]**

A jolly musicologist by the entirely unobjectionable name of Henry Pleasants has written a book called *'The Agony of Modern Music'*. That word 'Agony' is right. Much of it is just not written down but improvised. Much of what passes for music of these times is raucous noise and the excuse for persisting with it is that every common youngster understands and likes it.

The pleasant fellow concedes that 'serious' music is virtually dead. This may be dismissed as yet another pleasantry which the undirected young indulge in. Paul Hindesmith, possibly one the last of the classical giants. Once said that some composers tended to develop an oversublimated technique "which produces images of emotions that are far removed from any emotional experience a relatively normal human being ever has."

That is just the point. High art can never be totally democratised. There is a barrier between the egghead and the hoipolloi and it would be lazy idealism to ignore this. When Bach played and beethoven roared, who was then the gentleman?

The pity of it is that while talking music to the masses, all known rules are broken and improvisation becomes king. That, roughly speaking is how jazz was born; by dropping discipline, inspiration, deep personal emotions and every element of creative art and adopting improvisation as its main rationale. Why, they even tried to smuggle bits of jazz into serious music so that the composer could somehow survive.

Now they are going one step further : learn it by ear, don't write down the stuff, make it up as you go along and hope, by these shoddy techniques, that everyone present will applaud and thus, provide the composer and the performers with their daily bread.

(1) *The author uses the word 'improvisation' to suggest* :
(a) making the original more sublime (b) tampering with the original
(c) rendering the original more popular (d) simplifying the original

(2) *According to the author high art cannot be democratised because* :
(a) high art is oversublimated
(b) people differ in their emotional experience
(c) masses cannot be expected to appreciate what only the few intelligent can
(d) democratising necessarily involves improvisation

(3) *They tried to introduce bits of jazz in serious music so that* :
(a) music might survive
(b) the masses could take to serious music
(c) the new composers might survive
(d) music is democratised

(4) *Which of the following words can best replace the word raucous in the paragraph?*
(a) shrill (b) soothing
(c) pleasant (d) popular

(5) *Speaking of the techniques of some composers Paul Hindesmith said that they evoked image of emotions:*
(a) not experienced by normal people (b) felt only by subnormal people
(c) never felt by masses (d) not experienced by eggheads

Answers : **(1)** (b), **(2)** (b), **(3)** (c), **(4)** (a), **(5)** (a).

Passage 16

Directions (Q. 1-5) *Read the passage given below carefully and then answer these questions based on what is stated or implied in the passage.* **[Management Aptitude 2001]**

One simple concept lies behind the formation of the stars : gravitational instability. The concept is not new. Newton first perceived it late in the 17th Century. Imagine a uniform, static cloud of gas in space. Imagine then that the gas is somehow disturbed so that one small spherical region becomes a little denser than the gas around it so that the small region's gravitational field becomes slightly stronger. It now attracts more matter to it and its gravity increases further, causing it to begin to contract. As it contracts its density increases, which increases its gravity even more, so that it picks up even more matter and contracts even further. The process continues until the small region of gas finally forms a gravitationally bound object.

(1) *The primary purpose of the passage is to* :
(a) describe a static condition (b) support a theory considered outmoded
(c) depict the successive stages of a phenomenon (d) demonstrate the evolution of the meaning of a term

(2) *It can be inferred from this passage that the author views the information contained within it as* :
(a) lacking in elaboration (b) original but obscure
(c) speculative and unprofitable (d) uncomplicated and traditional

(3) *With which of the following words can you replace the word uni 'form' as given in this passage?*
(a) uniting (b) varying (c) gaseous (d) unvarying

(4) *What does the underlined word 'it' stands for in the passage?*
(a) gravitational instability (b) cloud of gas
(c) small spherical denser region (d) matter

(5) *The author provides information that answers which of following questions?*
(1) What causes the disturbances that changes the cloud from its original static condition?
(2) How does this small region's increasing density affect its gravitational field?
(3) hat is the end result of the gradually increasing concentration of the small region of gas?
(a) Only 1 (b) Only 2 (c) 2 and 3 (d) 1, 2 and 3

Answers : (1) (c), (2) (d), (3) (d), (4) (c), (5) (c).

Passage 17

Directions (Q. 1-4) *Read the passage given below carefully and then answer these questions based on what is stated or implied in the passage.* **[UPSC Assistant Provident Fund Commissioners]**

A great deal of the world's work is neither producing material things nor altering the things that Nature produces, but doing services of one sort or another. Thoughtless people are apt to think a brickmaker more of a producer than a clergyman. When a village carpenter makes a gate to keep cattle out of a field of wheat, he has something solid in his hand which he can claim for his own until the farmer pays him for it. But when a village boy makes as noise to keep the birds off he has nothings to show, though the noise is just as necessary as the gate.

The postman does not make anything—the policeman does not make anything—the doctor makes pills sometimes; but that is not his real business, which is to tell you when you ought to take pills and what pills to take, unless indeed he has the good sense to tell you not take them at all and you have the good sense to believe him, when he is giving you good advice instead of bad. The lawyer does not make anything substantial—they are all in service.

(1) *Thoughtless people think a brickmaker more of a producer than a clergyman because more of a producer than a clergyman because :*

(a) a clergyman is an idler
(b) a brickmaker produces something solid which he can keep with him till he gets its price
(c) a brickmaker, being physically stronger than a clergyman, can naturally produce more
(d) he cannot understand the philosophical lectures of the clergyman

(2) *According to the author of the passage, a large number of persons :*
(a) are producing material things
(b) are altering the things that nature produces
(c) are doing nothing in particular
(d) offer services

(3) *The writer thinks that :*
(a) both the doctor and the patient are sensible when one makes pills and the other buys them
(b) the doctor is sensible and the patient is insensible
(c) the doctor is insensible and the patient is insensible.
(d) both the doctor and the patient make sense when one offers and the other receives a service.

(4) *The writer's description of the doctor's business :*
(a) strengthens the main argument of the passage because the doctor's business is to make pills
(b) is irrelevant to the main argument of the passage
(c) weakens the main argument of the passage
(d) illustrates the difference between producing something and offering a service

Answers : (1) (b), **(2)** (d), **(3)** (d), **(4)** (d).

Passage 18

Directions (Q. 1-6) : *Read the passage carefully, then answer the questions which are based on what is stated or implied in the passage.*

[Management Aptitude]

Since the world has become industrialised, there has been an increase in the number of animal species that have either become extinct or have neared extinction. Bengal tiger, for instance, which once roamed the jungle in vast numbers, now number only 2300 and by the year 2025 their population is estimated to be down to zero. What is **alarming** about the case of Bengal tiger is that this extinction will have been caused almost entirely by poachers who according to some sources, are not interested in material gain but in personal gratification. This is an example of the callousness that is part of what is causing the problem of extinction. Animals like the Bengal tiger, as well as other endangered species, are a valuable part of the world's ecosystem. International laws protecting these animals must be enacted to ensure their survival and the survival of our planet.

Countries around the world have begun to deal with the problem in various ways. Some countries, in order to circumvent the problem, have allocated large amount of land to animal reserves. They then charge admission to help defray the costs of maintaining the parks and they often must also depend on world organisations for support. With the money get, they can invest in equipment and patrols to protect the animals. Another solution that is an attempt to **stem the tide**, of animal extinction is an international boycott of products made from endangered species. This seems fairly effective, but it will not, by itself, prevent animals from being hunted and killed.

(1) *What is the author's main concern in this passage?*
(a) Problems of industrialisation
(b) The Bengal tiger
(c) Endangered species
(d) Callousness of man

(2) *According to the passage, poachers kill for :*
(a) material gain
(b) personal satisfaction
(c) Both 'a' and 'b'
(d) None of these

(3) *Which of the following words is closest in meaning to the underlined word 'alarming'?*
(a) Serious
(b) Dangerous
(c) Distressing
(d) Frightening

(4) *Certain species are becoming extinct because of*:
(a) industrialisation (b) poaching
(c) love of products made from them (d) all of these

(5) *The Phrase 'Stem the tide' means*
(a) save (b) stop (c) touch (d) spare

(6) *Which of the following best describes the author's attitude?*
(a) Concerned (b) Vindictive (c) Surprised (d) Generous

Answers : **(1)** (c), **(2)** (b), **(3)** (d) **(4)** (d), **(5)** (b), **(6)** (a).

Passage 19

Directions (Q. 1-6) *Read the passage carefully and then choose the best answer for each question.*

[Management Aptitude]

The conservative is not an extreme individualist. He may be willing to concede numerous arguments of the unqualified individualists, for his own respect for the dignity of the individual is not surpassed by that of any man. Yet he cannot agree to the full implications of individualism, which is based so he thinks on an incorrect appraisal of man, society, history and government. In his own way, the individualist is as much a perfectionist as the Socialist and with perfectionism the conservative can have no **truck.**

In particular, the conservative refuses to go all the way with economic individualism. His distrust of unfettered man, his recognition to groups, his sense of the complexity of the social process, his recognition of the real services that government can perform all these sentiments make it impossible for him to subscribe to the dogmas and shibboleths of economic individualism : laissez-faire, the negative state, enlightened self-interest, the law of supply and demand, the profit motive.

The conservative may occasionally have kind word for each of these notions, but he is careful to qualify his support by stating other, more important social truths. For example he does not for a moment deny the prominence of the profit motive, but he insists that it be recognised for the selfish thing it is and be kept within reasonable, socially imposed limits.

(1) *The conservative is* :
(a) a perfectionist (b) an economist (c) a socialist (d) None of these

(2) *The conservative is against economic individualism for all the following reasons except* :
(a) he does not trust free men (b) he believes in the authority of the government
(c)he believes in groups (d) he feels that social processes are important

(3) *The author mentions all the following catchwords of economic individualism except* :
(a) free trade (b) the profit motive (c) balance of trade (d) the negative state

(4) *Which of the following words can replace the underlined word 'truck'?*
(a) Dealing (b) Bargain (c) Debate (d) Transport

(5) *Which of the following statements is true?*
(a) The socialist and the individualist tend to be broadly similar in their views
(b) The conservative believes that profit motive originates in selfishness
(c) The conservative is also an extreme individualist
(d) None of the above

(6) *Which of the following could be an appropriate title for the passage?*
(a) Anarchy and freedom (b) Progress and The conservating
(c) A conservative Apology (d) The conservative stand

Answers : **(1)** (d), **(2)** (d), **(3)** (a), **(4)** (a), **(5)** (b), **(6)** (d).